JUDIKA ILLES

The Element Encyclopedia of 5000 Spells

Dedication

For Herta and Zoltan Illes, and Rachel and Jordan Nagengast,
without whose love, patience, and support this book could never have been written.

HarperElement
An Imprint of HarperCollins*Publishers*
77–85 Fulham Palace Road,
Hammersmith, London W6 8JB

The website address is: www.thorsonselement.com

and *HarperElement* are trademarks of
HarperCollins*Publishers* Ltd

First published by HarperElement 2004

7 9 10 8

Author website: www.judikailles.com

A catalogue record of this book is
available from the British Library

ISBN 0 00 716465 3

Printed and bound in Germany by
Bercker Graphischer Betrieb, Kevelaer

 Contents

WARNING!

The Element Encyclopedia of 5000 Spells contains an overview of magical spells and practices from a multitude of eras, traditions, and places. It is intended as an inclusive encyclopedia and reference book. Many of the spells contained within these pages are not to be used and should not be reproduced. Some involve dangerous, potentially harmful, and deadly poisonous botanicals. The author and the publisher strongly advise against using any spells containing noxious substances or poisonous botanicals, or spells containing blood (the use of which could result in the transmission of blood-borne diseases which may be fatal). These spells are only reproduced here to provide a historical context.

Any reader uses the spells entirely at their own risk and the author and publisher accept no liability if the spells do not have the desired effect or if adverse affects are caused.

THIS BOOK IS NOT SUITABLE FOR CHILDREN.

✪ Acknowledgements

Many people contributed greatly to these pages. First and foremost, Greg Brandenburgh first envisioned and then developed the initial concept for this book; although it sounds a cliché, *The Element Encyclopedia of 5000 Spells* truly would not have been written without him. I thank him for his vision, good humor, knowing when and when not to push, and most especially for his patience. (Although Greg, when I tell you not to read a manuscript before buying a bottle, you should know me well enough by now to believe me.)

In London, Charlotte Ridings, Kate Latham, Nicole Linhardt, Graham Holmes, and Jo Ridgeway labored many, many, *many* long hours painstakingly stitching this book together, section by section, page by page, spell by spell, with grace, good cheer, sharp insight, dependable judgment and yet even more of that elusive quality, patience, that this book demanded.

Thanks and love to family, friends, and compatriots: the Asch family, Irma Illes, Clara Fisher, Susan Gross, Mary Bauer, Marianne Carroll, Aris Dervis of Serving Spirits, the Katz family in Sydney, Sandi Liss, Morgana of Morgana's Chamber in New York City, Dorothy Morrison, the Salpeter Family, Andy and Morse Taylor, and Raya Zion. My thanks to Leor Warner for throwing me all those life-lines over the years, not least the assurance that this book would be finished even before I began to have doubts, to Jason Wilkinson of Moon Phase Design Company for keeping me up and running, and to the Girlgang for initiating me into the mysteries of Saint Rita.

My thanks to Lisa Goldstein for generously allowing me to take her wonderful novel, *The Alchemist's Door*, in what were perhaps unexpected directions, to Nora Elgammal of Kyphi Inc. who fueled my test kitchens with her beautiful essential oils, and to the librarians of the Teaneck Public Library who cheerfully and, yes, patiently located many, many long-out-of-print books.

Clara Fisher provided translations from the Czech and Slovak; Rebecca Asch and Mike Peto provided translations from the Spanish and Portuguese respectively, while Raya and Lea Zion researched and translated some very obscure, archaic Arabic and Hebrew terms for me. Rose Jimenez provided translations from the Spanish and very generously shared her extensive botanical knowledge. I thank them all.

Carole Murray introduced me to the joys of condition oils many years ago, for which I am eternally grateful. She is my authority on the saints; I cannot count how many times I've called her at odd hours with questions like, *"Quick! What color candle would you offer Saint Dymphna?"* She has never once failed me.

Thankfully Theresa Mannino shares my proclivity for keeping vampire's hours and was my partner in many phone calls during those wee, wee hours, discussing magic, metaphysics and spells.

Inside every spell is a kernel of hope for a happier future, so a gift of a spell is a gift of love. Heartfelt thanks to Sandi Liss of Soul Journey, Butler, New Jersey, Theresa Mannino, and Carole Murray who generously and without hesitation opened up their own personal grimoires. My gratitude goes to one and all.

For every single traditional spell that remains, who knows how many more have been lost? This book could never have been written without those who preserved and shared occult knowledge, often at tremendous, unspeakable, personal risk and sacrifice. Thanks, respect, and appreciation to those countless hoodoo doctors and Pow-Wow artists, power doctors, *feuilles-doktes* and fairy doctors, root men and women, conjurors, readers, witches, workers, *ba'al-shems*, reverend mothers, and mothers and fathers of the saints.

Preface

The image is so familiar as to qualify as an archetype. It appears in countless movies, television shows, and theatrical productions. If you're of a literary bent, you'll find it in countless novels, too. Although there may be variations on the theme, the core image remains consistent: someone, usually but not always a witch or wizard, faced with a serious dilemma, reaches for a massive book of magic spells.

The contents of this book are rarely displayed. (An exception occurs on the television series, *Sabrina the Teenage Witch*. As befitting a twenty-first-century witch, Sabrina's edition is interactive.) Oversized, well-worn, and clearly *used*, this book is obviously no coffee-table book but a familiar companion—in every sense of the word familiar. Sabrina's book makes almost as many appearances as her black cat, and consistently proves more reliable.

The book's very presence transmits subliminal messages. If there were previously any doubts regarding someone's identity, then the act of reaching for the book, mere possession of this book in fact, is usually sufficient to establish occult credentials. Consider depictions of Merlin or Morgan le Fay: their big books of spells are as much a part and parcel of their magical trappings as any animal familiar, crystal ball, or wizard's robes. Millions of kitschy statues feature an elderly gray-bearded man clutching a massive book. He may or may not be wearing his peaked wizard's hat but his identity is clear. How do we know he's a wizard? By the book that he holds.

This book thus signals that its reader is a metaphysician or is striving to be one. If the reader handles the book with comfort and ease, the implication is that he or she is a person of power. The book, however, can also compensate for the reader's very lack of experience and knowledge. One frequent variation on the theme depicts a complete novice discovering sophisticated magical solutions within the book's pages. Typically the novice is in way over his head in disaster. The very appearance of the book signals that salvation is at hand: the secrets of salvation are contained within the book's pages, if only the novice will follow its directions. (Conversely, Mickey Mouse's inability to use such a book for anything other than a flotation device in *The Sorcerer's Apprentice* only underscores his magical ineptitude and general incompetence.)

This massive spell book thus possesses enormous transformative powers. It can transform anyone (well, Mickey excepted) into a magical adept. Its aged, well-worn appearance also indicates that this book is timeless: it never outlives its usefulness.

The appearance of this book within this scenario also underscores that the situation at hand is genuinely an emergency. Subliminally, it is understood that no matter how extensive the library, this is the *real deal* book, the authentic article brought out when there is no time to lose. In the image, the hand that reaches for the book never wavers. The gesture is always sure. Regardless how many books are crammed onto the bookshelf, the hand reaches for one and only one book. An extension of the core image often shows the seeker desperately turning pages to no avail. The book is thrust down in despair; the seeker is left to either yield to bitter fate or else to creatively conjure his or her own solutions. There is no suggestion that perhaps another book holds the key. If it's not in the big book of spells, there's no point looking elsewhere.

This archetypal book is based on both fact and fantasy.

Collections of spells rank among Earth's earliest written documents. Not only are magical texts among the oldest surviving pieces of literature, but many scholars and anthropologists suggest that it was the need to record spells and divination results that stimulated the very birth of writing. Magic, as we will see, is the true mother of invention. In ancient Egypt, the lunar god Thoth is credited as the inventor of both magic and writing. He is the patron of scribes and magicians. It was rumored that in addition to inventing the systems of spelling and writing, Thoth created the very first book, authoring no less than a sacred revelation of Earth's most powerful secret spells and rituals. The legendary

Book of Thoth was believed to hold the key to all the secrets of the universe. To possess a copy of the book enabled one to command and control destiny itself.

The ancient Egyptians loved stories featuring books of power. Several of their legends remain to us, including the original version of Walt Disney's *The Sorcerer's Apprentice*. Egypt, at the time, was a theocracy: religion and government were one. The reigning pharaoh was simultaneously the child of the god, the living embodiment of the god, and the god's foremost high priest, and vast temple complexes, financed by the state, contained literary annexes known as *Houses of Life*.

These combination scriptoria/emergency clinics housed wizard priests, on the government payroll. For a fee, these professional magicians would consult their extensive library of magic texts to provide clientele with enchanted solutions to life's many dilemmas. Perhaps, legend had it, the *Book of Thoth* was hidden in the depths of one of these magic libraries. Perhaps it was stashed in some priest or pharaoh's tomb. Or perhaps it was eventually deemed so dangerous that, too powerful to destroy, the book had been locked into a chained, weighted iron box and thrown into the depths of the sea.

Access to occult knowledge bestowed power and prestige. The magical texts were hoarded and kept secret. Many were written in code, to prevent profane eyes from understanding what was read.

A few centuries before the dawning of the Common Era, the independent Egyptian nation was defeated, first by the Persians, then by the Greeks and Romans. Indigenous Egyptian religion and political structure degenerated. The *Houses of Life* were abandoned; the lucrative, respected profession of government-employed wizard-priest no longer existed. It was the last time in history that working with magic was a secure, respectable profession.

Although the profession ceased to exist, the big spell books survived, at least in fragments. It's difficult for modern readers, so accustomed to printed, standardized texts, to recall that until the invention of the printing press, every book was hand-written and frequently unbound. Copies of copies of copies were made, each perhaps slightly different than the next. In the chaos that ensued as Egypt was successively conquered, individual pages were either smuggled out of the now unguarded temple libraries as personal treasures or auctioned off, page-by-page, papyrus by papyrus for personal profit. When Alexandria's famed library, which boasted a copy of every book then in existence (the city stole them from arriving ships), was burned to the ground, the value of the few surviving manuscripts increased.

With the rise of Christianity, magic, together with its texts and professionals, was vilified. Spell books were burned en masse. Yet some were saved, if not whole books, then individual pages and pieces. We know this to be true, because some still remain, their spells reproduced in many books including this one, preserved at great personal risk throughout the ages, during eras where possession of magical texts warranted the death penalty.

These treasured pages survived, secretly passed between adepts and initiates, as did legends of mysterious books of power just waiting to be recovered. The *Book of Thoth* is one but there were others: *The Book of Raziel* is a rival with Thoth's book for the title of first book ever. Another book of spells and rituals, *The Book of Raziel* was allegedly written by a sympathetic angel and given to Adam to compensate for his exile from Eden. Rumors regarding the existence of magical manuscripts attributed to Israel's wizard king, Solomon, were first recorded, at least as far as we know, during the time of Josephus, the first-century chronicler of the Roman conquest of Judea. Fragments of Solomon's pages were allegedly discovered and exist today. Treasure hunters searched desperately for these manuscripts, just like Sidney Greenstreet looking for the Maltese falcon.

In the fourteenth century, a large group of nomadic people arrived in Europe from parts unknown. Although the Romany people derive originally from India, another land steeped in magical and spiritual legend, they may or may not also have spent considerable time in Egypt. (According to some Romany legends, their ancestor was the sole survivor of Pharaoh's army, drowned in the Red Sea.) The association with Egypt was powerful enough and appealing enough that Europeans called the Romany *Egyptians*, the name eventually being corrupted into *Gypsies*.

At the same time as the arrival of the Romany, a deck of mysterious cards began to circulate through Europe. Rumors spread that these tarot cards were what was left of the *Book of Thoth*. Readers scoured them searching for spiritual secrets and clues for obtaining personal power.

With the advent of the printing press came publication and standardization of spell books. Enough were published to warrant their own literary category, the *grimoire*. The word, "grimoire," defined as a book of spells, is related to grammar. The grimoire is basically another type of grammar book, just teaching different spelling skills. The classic grimoires were published in the midst of anti-magic, anti-witchcraft persecutions and, like alchemists' texts, they are often heavily coded to protect authors, compilers, and publishers, and also to maintain secrecy and control over their precious information, reserving true comprehension for a private club of initiated adepts.

On the whole, grimoires are not books of practical magic. The novice cannot pick one up and instantly begin casting life-saving spells. Instead they are largely oriented towards an educated male reader so devoted to his spiritual path that he has largely withdrawn from everyday life, like Dr. Faust, and can thus spend weeks in complex, tortuous preparation for summoning angels and demons.

Other books of magic circulated through Europe. These were still hand-written rather than printed editions. *Books of Shadows* meticulously recorded an individual witch's personal spells and knowledge. These books were intended to be passed from person to person, but as a means of saving persecuted traditions from complete eradication. Few of these books remain. When a witch was caught, convicted, and killed, her Book of Shadows was inevitably destroyed with her. Modern Wicca has, however, revived the tradition of beautiful, lovingly preserved personal spell and ritual books.

Neither the Books of Shadows, nor the classic grimoires fulfill the Hollywood fantasy of that large, accessible book packed with every spell you might possibly need. One mustn't mock that vision: we long for magical solutions to insoluble situations. We crave the inherent promise of the hidden *Book of Thoth*. We long to discover that one word of power strong enough to stop the sun in its tracks if we utter it, potent enough to vanquish our enemies, fill our bank accounts, and deliver our true love.

Perhaps somewhere, someday, in some archaeological dig, that *Book of Thoth* will be found.

Until then, here is *The Element Encyclopedia of 5000 Spells*: five thousand spells drawn from all over Earth, from ancient to modern Egypt, old Mesopotamia to today's African Diaspora. There are spells from every continent, from Celtic, Italian, Jewish, and Romany traditions. There's practical magic, high ritual magic, spells requiring virtually no preparation, and spells that should perhaps never be performed. No secret code has been applied; instead there are explanations so that you understand how and why the spells should work.

Be forewarned: in these pages you will discover methods of communicating with the dead, taming an errant lover, summoning spirits, handcrafting magic tools, and tips for creating magic mirrors and rings—including the one that allegedly gave Helen of Troy her seductive power. I will tell you up-front, however, this book does *not* contain that sole word of power, guaranteed to stop the sun and fulfill your every desire.

Perhaps one day you will find the volume that contains that one word, although the ancient Egyptians warned that in order to attain it you might have to break into a pyramid and wager with its guardian mummy, or else make the sea roll back in order to find the manuscript locked in the iron box and guarded by an army of many-headed venomous sea snakes. In the meantime, enjoy *The Element Encyclopedia of 5000 Spells*.

Magic ... is the ancient
and absolute science of nature
and her laws

A. L. CONSTANT, *THE HISTORY OF MAGIC*, LONDON, 1922

✪ Introduction

Five thousand spells. Is any of it *real?*

What is magic anyway?

What a question. Rational people know how to define magic—magic is illusion, sleight of hand, at best the fine art of tricks, at worst fraudulence—or so goes the definition usually taught to school-children. Another interpretation dismisses magic as supernatural fantasy and wishful thinking—the stuff of fairy tales, Mother Goose, and mythology; tales for children and hence of little value; its only purpose entertainment; its only possible truth metaphoric. A third interpretation is more malev-olent, with occult masters—the proverbial evil wizards and wicked sorceresses—attempting to maintain control over gullible and innocent plain folk, their tools fear and superstition, not *true* magic, which, of course, rationalists argue, doesn't exist anyway. Yet another explanation suggests that magic works solely by psychological means, a sort of self-hypnosis. According to this theory, usually offered by old-school anthropologists and psychologists, the poor benighted native's very belief in something, such as a death curse or a tra-ditional healing, is what causes it to come true. Magic happens because you believe in the system not because the system works or even exists, although explanations for why, if their powers of belief are so all-powerful, the natives remain poor and benighted, and forced to tolerate outside observers, are rarely offered.

Occult is a word commonly misinterpreted. It doesn't mean evil or satanic. It has no moral con-notations whatsoever. Occult really means *"secret"* or *"hidden."* Secrets may be kept hidden for a host of valid reasons. In many cultures and at many times, the definition of real true working magic wasn't a hidden secret, subject to false interpreta-tion, but a normal fact of life. In other cultures and at different times, however, real true working mag-ical practitioners have been subject to torture, per-secution, and oppression. Magic's very survival has often depended upon secrecy and a willingness to tolerate patronizing, false definitions.

True magical practitioners, of whom there remain many, would reject the definitions of magic given above, although there are vestiges of truths in all of them. Real magical practitioners consider themselves guardians, preservers, and (some-times) revivers of Earth's forgotten, besieged, and suppressed occult truths and traditions.

Magic, at its most basic, is the science of Earth's hidden powers. For the true practitioner, there's nothing *supernatural* about magic. *Natural* is just a lot more complex than conventional modern wisdom allows.

Although there are many ways to practice magic, many schools, philosophies, methods, and traditions, the bottom-line definition of what actually constitutes real magic, and why and how it works, is amazingly consistent throughout the world.

According to general worldwide metaphysical wisdom, common to all magical understanding and tradition, there is an inherent energy radiating from Earth and all living things. Analytical traditions and cultures have studied this energy in depth; others simply accept its existence and work with it. Many languages have specific names for this energy. English does not. This increases the confusion when discussing magic—an already vast and confusing topic. In the same manner that English, a language so rich in descriptive adjectives, has but one word for *snow*, while Inuit has many, one word for *love*, while Sanskrit has many, so English has but one word, *magic*, to define its various aspects. Harry Houdini, Harry Potter, Helena Blavatsky, Aleister Crowley, and countless anonymous village wise-women are all lumped together as masters of magic, as if it were a monolithic art.

English also lacks a specific word to name that power that radiates from all life.

The ancient Egyptians called it *heka*; on the other side of Africa, the Yoruba, parent culture of myriad spiritual and magical traditions, call it *ashé*. The most familiar word may be the Polynesian *mana*. In Morocco, this radiant energy is known as *baraka*. For lack of a better word, let's just call it *magic power*.

This magic power, this capacity for magic, radiates from all living beings to a greater or lesser extent. In fact, it is the existence of this power that defines what, in magical terms, is considered "*alive*," a very different criterion than that required by a coroner's report. (In magical terms, death is not the absence of life. Absence of power equals absence of life. A corpse, although no one denies the person is dead in the conventional sense, is still very much alive, as is the pine box and, most especially, the iron coffin nails. The average plastic bottle, however, lacks life. Confused? More about this crucial concept later.)

This magical life-power is formless: you can't see it, hear it or touch it. So how do you know it exists? How is it quantified and measured? By its effects upon you.

Baraka, the Moroccan term for this power, contains significant implications. The root word can be recognized in another Semitic language, Hebrew, where it translates as "*blessing*." To be in the presence of this power is to receive blessings. Although people have learned to manipulate magic powers for malevolent purposes and ill intent, it is intrinsically a positive, benevolent, and sacred energy. According to an Egyptian legend, having contemplated creation, the Creator foresaw that all would *not* be good and felt pangs of remorse. He therefore imbued Earth with *heka* as a gift to people, so that they might use it to ward off the harsh blows of fate. Magic is the system that attempts to harness this energy.

The closest comparison one might make is to radioactive energy. That, too, is formless, cannot be seen, touched, or smelled. Yet its impact is profound and cannot be denied. Because nuclear radiation has had such a devastating impact on our world, it's difficult to recall how recent a discovery it truly is. Marie and Pierre Curie, and the other early scholars of radioactive energy, were visionaries. They recognized the existence of something that others did not. Not everyone *believed* in their theories, including many very educated people, in much the same way that people say they don't *believe* in magic. Many thought the Curies deluded, crazy or just incorrect, at least until the power they sought had been unleashed with too much force to ever be denied.

If one tells the story of Marie Curie's quest in simple terms, it resembles a modern-day fairy tale. Marie, laboring obsessively in her laboratory/shack resembles the quintessential alchemist feverishly attempting to extract and develop the philosopher's stone, that legendary substance reputed to bestow eternal youth, health, and life.

In a sense, Marie Curie extracted the *anti-*philosopher's stone. Modern fairy tales are sanitized for children; today's adults are uncomfortable transmitting the truths contained in them. Real fairy tales—the original versions—don't always have happy endings, just like the tale of Marie Curie doesn't. Marie's quest ultimately led her to death; many of her surviving books, materials, and tools are so packed with the deadly power into which she tapped that even today they remain too radioactive to handle.

The goal of magic is to tap into a different energy, an energy so powerful and benevolent that all aspects of life improve. The most potent magical books, tools and materials (just like those books and papers of Marie Curie) hold, retain and radiate their power and energy infinitely.

How do you measure exposure to nuclear radiation? While scientific tools of measurement have been developed, ultimate, undeniable proof comes in its effects on the body. Similar scientific tools to quantify, measure, and identify magic power have not been invented, yet (to the magical practitioner) its effect upon the individual is equally clear. The term, *a person of power*, is meant literally. People who possess magical power in substantial quantities, who live in close proximity to it, are magnetic and charismatic personalities. They radiate personal power. Other people find merely being in their presence invigorating and empowering. Although into every life some rain must fall, for the person with strong reserves of magic power, the world exists as a place of possibility. If, on the other hand, you feel consistently drained or frustrated, if your libido and life-force are chronically diminished, if you foresee nothing ahead of you but monotony or gloom, if life lacks joy, if your goals seem so out of reach that it's pointless to try, and it's hard to muster enthusiasm for anything, then it's very likely that you suffer from a serious deficiency of this life-power. Most of us fall somewhere in the middle, although these power reserves are continually shifting. Like a gas tank, magical life-power needs to be replenished as you use it, and acquired if you lack it.

This power is contagious. It can be transferred, transmitted, increased, decreased, or lost. These power-exchanges occur continuously, with or without human participation. The power is contained within a botanical plant or crystal, for instance, whether or not a human taps into it. You can ignore this power and these energy transactions, although their effects upon you continue and remain, for good or ill. You can also attempt to harness this power for your own benefit and the benefit of your loved ones.

Perhaps magic may best be understood by considering one of its branches: the school of magical arrangement, *feng shui*. Once obscure outside China, the art of feng shui is now discussed and debated worldwide; it has even grown sufficiently commonplace to merit, for a time, a newspaper column in the *Sunday Los Angeles Times'* real estate section! (Although apparently there were enough complaints about the intrusion of magic into real life for the column to eventually disappear.)

Feng shui's literal translation, *"wind and water,"* implies that this is a natural art, not a manufactured one. According to feng shui, objects are manipulated to create good fortune, minimize hardship, and (hopefully) eliminate disaster. Likewise, one must pay attention to natural earth formations (mountains, valleys, waterways) in order to harmonize one's own energies and desires with them for your maximum benefit. This conscious manipulation and harmonizing of energies and forces is the basis of all magic. By manipulating various magical powers, goals are achieved, success attained, and misfortune prevented. For instance, the presence of lavender theoretically empowers any other spell or materials. Powdered vinca, the sorcerer's violet, transforms any bouquet of flowers into a tool of seduction, although some flowers (roses, orchids, tuberoses) are powerful enough not to require any assistance.

Of course, rationalists refute all of this as nonsense. It can't be proven scientifically—therefore it doesn't exist. Magical practitioners are either gullible idiots or outright charlatans.

The magical practitioners' response to this criticism is that rationalists have invented and are clinging to a very limited notion of a world that really doesn't exist. Practitioners would say that scientific method, as well as so-called logic, are unrealistic, artificial human-created constructs designed to deny and place limits on Earth's true mystery and grandeur. According to magical theory, some sacred mysteries cannot be explained, defined or controlled, although one can attempt to use them for one's benefit. Ultimately, one could say, magic is another way of looking at and understanding the world. If you are not yet initiated into this magical world, then be prepared: once you've learned some real magic and successfully cast some spells, you will see the world in a different way than you did before. Will you trust your own experiences and insights? Or will you be among the many who say, "*I can't believe what just happened to me?*"

Although modern science is the child of the magical arts, most especially alchemy, its world vision and goals are diametrically opposed to its parents'. To enter into the magical world is to be a willing, conscious participant in a dream landscape. One accesses power by surrendering control over boundaries. The magical world is a huge, unruly, fluid, dream-like place filled with invisible powers, psychic debris, positive *and* negative forces, guardian spirits, and radiant beings existing on all sorts of planes of energy that defy human definition, domination, and control. Everything pulsates with vibrant, potentially powerful life, including you.

Magic is a partnership between powers, human and otherwise. The question of whether magic is used for good or ill depends upon the practitioner's intentions, not the inherent nature of the system. Every interaction is an energy transaction of some kind, although, obviously, some are more significant than others.

Scientific method demands consistent, predictable replication of results. Magic revels in the unique, the unusual, the individual, and the exception. Magic refutes the entire concept of coincidence. Anything that appears coincidental possesses some magical significance; the more unusual and freakish the coincidence, the more worthy of attention and analysis. Anything too easily replicated is either a very basic natural law (stick your finger into fire and it will hurt) or else lacks power and is thus magically worthless (that lifeless plastic bottle).

Confusion derives from a limited word pool, as we have seen. Identical words are used to indicate different meanings. Magic defies boundaries: life doesn't terminate with death. Death is not the end, nor is it the opposite of life; it's merely another mysterious stop on the spectrum of existence. *Dead* as in "Uncle Joe is dead," may be meant literally, but *life, living,* or *alive* usually refers to something very different in magic-speak. *Life* in magical parlance is a quality, a capacity for power: someone or something has it, in varying quantities, or they don't. If something is unique, not entirely predictable or reproducible, and also possesses potential for power, it's *alive.*

Everything that exists naturally on Earth or is constructed from naturally occurring parts possesses the capacity for power, including you. This

★ By magical definition, anything occurring naturally on Earth, whether plant, animal, element, stone, or metal, is alive

★ Anything radiating any degree of magical power whatsoever is perceived to be alive, although the manner in which different beings are alive is not identical. A stone may be alive but even the most hard-core practitioner won't look for a pulse

★ If something can be recreated so that there are identical, indistinguishable specimens, and if that something is completely predictable and controllable, it lacks life. Lacking life, it contains no power, no innate magic, and is of little value to the magical practitioner

magic power, this *baraka*, is what ultimately fuels Earth. Fans of Philip Pullman's *His Dark Materials* trilogy may recognize parallels to those novels' controversial power, *dust*. Without it, existence is drained, *lifeless*, frustrating, joyless, and bereft.

This holistic power expresses itself on all planes simultaneously: physical, spiritual, mental, sexual, and emotional. This power is not generic. Every plant, every stone, every species of living creature radiates a specific type of power, although the most powerful are incredibly versatile. Roses seduce, but they also heal, comfort, and summon benevolent spirits. Individual members of a species radiate these powers to varying degrees, depending upon circumstances and personal power.

That's a lot of powers to remember. Luckily practitioners have been contributing to the magical repertoire of materials, the *materia magica*, since that old, proverbial time immemorial and continue to do so. It's not necessary to re-invent the wheel, although experimentation can be fun. A font of established information exists for you to draw upon. *The Element Encyclopedia of 5000 Spells* merely scratches the surface of world magic.

What is Magic?

Magic is an individual action, undertaken because the cosmos is not believed to be benevolent by nature, or, at least, not benevolent enough to that person.
Maya Deren, Divine Horsemen: The Living Gods of Haiti, *London, 1953*

Magic spells stem from the observation and consideration of an Earthly paradox.

Earth is beautiful, full of power and promise. Yet despite all that potential for fulfillment and happiness, individual existence is too often harsh,

★ Magic is the manipulation of Earth's naturally occurring powers in an attempt to provide the spell-caster with the success and happiness she or he desires

★ Magic spells are deliberate, specific attempts to harness and manipulate this energy, following some sort of formula or direction

★ Magic power is inherent on Earth; people didn't create it, imagine it or make it up. By various means, they learned how to use it: magic spells are the result

★ Every magic spell was created by at least one person and probably refined and improved by thousands more

hungry, painful, limited, bitter, dangerous, and just plain miserable. Yes, life holds promise, but will *your* promise be fulfilled? Can you depend upon benevolent forces of the universe to provide your needs and desires for you, or is further action required? It is significant that Adam didn't need a book of magic spells until he was forced to leave the paradise of Eden.

Magic is a realistic art, not an idealistic one, although it is a game for optimists. The *one* thing magic requires is a belief that things *could* get better.

Not every promise is fulfilled, not every power is realized. Life is not fair. Some are born with looks, brains, talent, vibrant health, all their limbs, and a loving family, while others are not. Some have a head start towards success that others lack, even within the realm of metaphysics. Some come from families immersed in magic traditions, eager to transmit secrets and techniques. Others do not.

Occult knowledge, however, is egalitarian. All you have to do is acquire it. In theory it's not even necessary to understand it in order to tailor your destiny more to your liking, fulfill your dreams

and aspirations and, perhaps most crucially, ward off life's harsh blows, just like the ancient Egyptians said you could.

Magic levels the playing field.

Magic encourages creativity and inventiveness. It rewards persistence and curiosity. People have discovered thousands of ways to exploit Earth's natural magic power. There is basically no technique, no material, providing it possesses some life (and, once upon a time, prior to mass industry, there was virtually nothing on Earth that didn't possess life), that can't be used for a magical purpose. Magic accesses a huge repository—rock, paper, scissors, you name it, somewhere it has been used in a spell.

Wealth and status are not necessary for acquiring magical power; the crucial requirements are desire, will, curiosity, awareness, knowledge, and education. That is the secret message hidden within the Celtic tale of Taliesin. A poor, beaten, oppressed orphan child is forced to labor endlessly for the great witch-goddess Cerridwen, stirring the fuming, boiling cauldron where she brews a potion capable of transmitting all Earth's wisdom. By accident the child tastes the brew intended for Cerridwen's own son. Those mere few drops of wisdom immediately transform a miserable, ignorant child into a shape-shifting master shaman, a pre-eminent wizard, and his ultimate rebirth as a true child of the goddess, a child Cerridwen cannot deny. Who cares about transforming pumpkins into coaches or pulling rabbits from hats? Real magic holds the key to self-transformation.

Although rare, precious materials, gemstones, and fragrant tree resins are packed with power; there's also tremendous magic in blades of grass, handfuls of dirt, moonbeams, and ocean water. Plenty of the most powerful magic is free, available and abundant for all.

Is Magic Evil? A (Very Abridged) Secret History of Magic

Another issue must be addressed, as it is the rationale most frequently offered for centuries of concerted efforts to eliminate magic and persecute practitioners, and because it is an issue that prevents some from accessing their personal power. You think you'd like to cast a spell, but you're afraid. Is practicing magic evil?

According to general worldwide metaphysical wisdom, magic is a source of power. Power may be used benevolently or selfishly, with varying degrees of mal intent. Thus it isn't the abstract practice of magic that is either good or bad; it's what each practitioner chooses to do with it. Responsibility for one's actions and the consequences that stem from them rest securely on the individual practitioner's shoulders. Have evil people ever abused magic power? Sure. Just take a look at some of the hexes in this book. Is magic the

only power capable of being abused? Of course not. How about financial power, political power, brute strength, nuclear power, and so on and so forth? In the sweep of history abuse of magic power is far less responsible for the accumulated sufferings of the world than many other forms of abuse.

There is a general rule, accepted across the board, that magicians reap what they sow. Cast an evil spell—ultimately receive evil back. Negative efforts attract negative returns, at a return rate of three-, seven-, or nine-fold. The standard rule of witchcraft is do what thou will, but harm none. Many modern witches are absolutely terrified of transgressing that rule.

So then, why magic's bad reputation?

Yes, there are legends of wicked sorcerers using their skills to hold others in thrall. However, if one examines those legends closely, it's usually revealed that the magical aspect is but a smoke screen for more reliable, conventional methods of coercion, like brute force and access to greater wealth, although I suppose one could argue that magical prowess enabled their acquisition. Suffice it to say that any position of power, in any profession, is vulnerable to corruption and temptation. Let's talk about the average working magical practitioner.

Magic is concerned with the immediate needs and desires of the practitioner in the here and now, or at least in the immediately foreseeable future. It is not about "pie in the sky." The average magician doesn't want to wait for the possible rewards of the sweet hereafter. Magic is not for the passive; if you're willing to passively accede to your fate, the destiny others decide for you, whatever it is, why waste time, effort or money casting a spell?

Magic recognizes that Earth is full of gifts and the practitioner wants his or her share *now*. Magic is not the same as religion, although many religions have historically incorporated magic into their practice, and still do. To put it mildly, magic is not an inherently reverential system. Magic demands that *my* will be done, not necessarily *thine*, or at least, let's find a compromise. It is not a humble art. Magic possesses an intensely powerful independent, egalitarian streak.

An infinite quantity of magic power exists in the world, enough for everyone. It's not like a scarce commodity, where if I have it, you don't. Magic power is constantly being generated, although various modern practices, especially those that affect the natural environment, have diminished present quantities drastically. Similar to Pullman's *His Dark Materials'* dust, the energy that each individual generates enters the universe where it affects and may be drawn upon by others. It is to everyone's benefit (except perhaps for that elite few already achieving their heaven on Earth at the expense of others) that every individual, creature or thing, maximizes its potential for power.

Furthermore, not all powers on Earth are positive: intense extended misery, suffering and oppression generate a negative energy that ultimately affects everyone badly, diminishes *baraka*, obstructs magic power and limits everyone's access to it. In addition, the extinction of Earth's life forms—the loss of plant and animal species—eliminates every practitioner's potential access to their unique powers. Thus general oppression and certain policies affecting the environment, beyond any ethical considerations of right or wrong, hamper the magician's ability to maximize personal power and the power of their spells.

There is an inherent tension between the individual practitioner seeking power, and authority of all kinds, most especially religious authority, which seeks to maintain its authority by retaining and controlling access to the divine, as well as to tools, theology and ritual. Religion frequently seeks to establish rules and boundaries about who has direct access to the divine, and who bestows that access and the proper channels. Correct methods of worship and spiritual communication are prescribed, including what is permitted and what is not.

If something has power, magicians usually want to try it out, regardless of whose tradition or faith it comes from, regardless of whether some authority says use is forbidden. Although magic is a conservative force in ways, harking back to humanity's most primal arts, it also evolves endlessly, adapting new materials, new traditions and new methods as they appear. It is fluid and defiant and resists control.

Fundamentalists of all kinds are inevitably opposed to magic, but this tension exists even among liberal faiths that prize their magical traditions—so-called magical religions. Here, inevitably, religious tradition stipulates a right way to practice magic. Knowledge may be reserved for the few, with methods reserved for those going through the proper, authorized channels. Tension will exist between the officially initiated and independent practitioners.

That tension between authority and magical practitioner is, I suspect, the real reason why secular rulers and religious authorities (frequently in conjunction with each other) attempt to brand magic and its practitioners as evil influences, a cancer among the submissive. Lack of obedience rather than lack of morality is what really draws down the wrath of authority.

It is no accident that the Bible records that Israel's diviners, shamans and necromancers were "*put away*" during the reign of its very first king, Saul. When the prophet Samuel warned the children of Israel that choosing a king would mean losing sons, daughters, land and livestock, he neglected to mention that they would also lose their previous access to professional magical advice. Or perhaps he didn't bother to mention it because he was aware, as apparently was the king, that those magical services are so crucial that they are never entirely suppressed. In fact, King Saul himself is very soon shown, in his hour of need, searching out one of those prescribed, forbidden bone-conjurers for a private consultation.

Because the Bible has so often been used as an excuse to persecute and exterminate witches, it's significant to note how the Bible depicts the Witch of Endor actually accomplishing her task. She's not painted as a stranger with strange talents, or as a foreigner, but as a member of the community. Neither is she shown to be a fraud; she capably fulfills her royal client's request. Nor is she depicted as malevolent or evil, but as a good hearted woman: having accomplished the unhappy task that every fortune-teller dreads, of delivering *really* bad news, she comforts and feeds the distraught king, providing his last meal on Earth, at personal sacrifice (she kills a calf to feed him) considering that he is responsible for her loss of profession and presumably income.

Fortune-tellers, readers and diviners hold an especially tense relationship with political authority. Historically, rulers, particularly the all-powerful, very much like to have the future revealed. They also typically wish to retain exclusive control over this information. Because others may use a diviner's skill to plot rebellion, historically diviners have been imprisoned, or one is imprisoned for the ruler's private's use, while others are killed. To make matters worse, rulers usually desire to hear only the future as they envision it; a diviner can only read what entrails, shoulder blades, or other tools reveal. You see the need sometimes to keep one's power secret. Although it frustrates us today, there's a very good reason Nostradamus recorded his prophesies in code.

Wherever efforts have been made either to subjugate or convert another country or people, among the first acts traditionally taken is the attempted subversion or elimination of native shamans and traditional magical practices and practitioners. This is inevitably perceived as necessary for the pacification of the masses. This is not purely paranoia on the part of those seeking to assert and retain authority.

Traditional shamans and magical practitioners are consistently in the forefront of resistance to oppressive authority. (Because winners write history, the conventional historical explanation for this phenomenon is that shamans attempt to impede the *"path of progress."*) In the British West Indies, historical records show that Obeah men and women (the local shamans) led slave revolts or attempted to do so. The Haitian revolution, which ended slavery in that French colony and established the first independent black republic in the Western Hemisphere, was inaugurated at a Vodoun ceremony dedicated to the Spirit of Iron, the material, with the sole exception of menstrual blood, singularly most charged with magical power—although as soon as native dictators proceeded to seize and consolidate power, not surprisingly, they too attempted to restrict or eliminate Vodoun.

This, not evil, power-hungry sorcerers, is the hidden history of magic. In the United States, the prominent Voodooists Marie Laveau and Mary Ellen Pleasant rescued and redeemed slaves, with Pleasant providing funding for John Brown's raid on Harper's Ferry. (Their male counterpart, Dr John Montanet, was himself a freed slave, as was Pleasant.) Lest you think that this association between magic and social justice is limited to African influence, Native American shamans were (and remain) in the forefront of resistance to white encroachment, and traditional practitioners led desperate resistance to Christian domination of Europe. Who knows what attempts to defy limitations on women's magical and spiritual traditions were destroyed in the flames of the craze of medieval witch-burning? Virtually all the records that remain are filtered through the eyes of the torturers.

Although men suffer too, societies that suppress the magical arts will, as a rule, also limit women's voices and power, often with terrible brutality. Significantly King Saul, in need of a necromancer, requested that his minions find him a conjuring *woman*. Although it's since taken many twists and turns, magic ultimately derives from women's mysteries and the mysteries of creation, and the history of magic's suppression cannot be separated from the history of women's oppression.

Is magic evil? Well, if your perception is that sex is inherently evil, Creation inherently tainted with sin, and that women constitute Earth's weakest link, then I guess you'd better lump magic in there with the rest of these moral dilemmas.

If magic cannot be entirely divorced from religion, even less can it be separated from herbalism, the root of all traditional medicinal systems, systems that for millennia have investigated botanical impact on health and (above all) on reproduction. Magic is the primordial human art and science. It stems from awe inspired by all Earthly creation, but especially the mysteries of human creation. Every new human life is the ultimate act of magic. Conscious attempts at conception probably constitute the first magic spells, especially if you consider that our remote ancestors didn't understand pregnancy in the detached, technical manner that we do today. Primordial religions venerated the divine in the form of human genitalia with joy, awe and respect, not prurience, recognizing their capacity for sacred generation and creation.

Although these symbols still survive in isolated pockets of official religion, magic remains suffused with sexual imagery, in ways that may surprise us today, in efforts to maximize the blessings inherent in the powers of anatomy, both male and female. However, magic stems from fascination, on the part of both women and men, with women's mysteries: the capacity to produce life where it didn't exist before, magic blood that flows on schedule from no wound and then is mysteriously retained, the links between that blood, fertility, women, the moon, and the sea. These were and remain conduits to the sacred for primordial magic and spirituality alike.

Where Do Magic Spells Come From?

According to the author, folklorist and scholar of magic, Zora Neale Hurston, *"magic is older than writing. So nobody knows how it started."* Very true, but what we do know is that magic comes from all over the globe. There is not a people or culture on Earth that did not at one time possess a magical tradition, whether they recall it today or whether or not they still use it. Some cultures and religions revel in their magical traditions. Others are ashamed of them or deny that the traditions ever existed. Some ethnic groups like to point the finger and suggest that magic comes from other people, not them, oh no, never—any practices of their own are only isolated bad habits picked up from disreputable magical wanderers or neighbors.

When a large cache of papyri from Alexandria in Egypt was found to be largely devoted to magic spells, anthropologists, Egyptologists and other scholars exulted. Not because they were necessarily so interested in magic, although some were, but because magic spells reveal a tremendous amount about a culture and its circumstances. Read between the lines of a spell and you will discover important details about people's expectations of life and death, their daily problems, the materials that they cherish, their spiritual outlook. For example, recently published books intended for the urban magical practitioner attempt to minimize or even eliminate the need for botanicals. Beyond their value to their intended audience, these books also transmit a crucial message to all of us regarding the state of our environment. As another example, only cultures that possess a belief in the possibility of legal justice, however remote, produce court case spells. Love spells reveal cultural sexual dynamics. So you see, magic spells have tremendous value as history, anthropology, and sociology way beyond their practical value to the spell-caster.

Translations of these Alexandrian papyri, now known as the Magical Papyri, were eagerly awaited. Stemming mainly from the second century BCE to the fifth century CE, they span a crucial, fascinating period of history: the times of Cleopatra, Jesus, the rise of Rome, the fall of Jerusalem, and the emergence of Christianity as a cohesive faith and world power.

Alexandria, although it became Egypt's capital, is not an ancient pharaonic city. It was founded by the Macedonian conqueror, Alexander the Great, one of several cities he named in his own honor. Its orientation is the Mediterranean, not the Nile, like other older Egyptian cities. At various periods, indigenous Egyptians were not even permitted to live within Alexandria's boundaries. It was a Greek outpost in Egypt, with Greeks as the elite citizenry. Cleopatra, descendant of one of Alexander the Great's generals and the last of her dynasty, was the only one of her lineage who troubled to learn the Egyptian language.

The city achieved a reputation as a world-capital of magic. Alexandria supported a sizeable population of magic practitioners of all kinds— diviners, dream interpreters, professional spell-casters—all presumably serving the needs of their specific communities rather than Alexandria as a whole, because Alexandria was a rigidly divided city. Although Alexandria, like many cities of its time, was divided into quarters, true divisions, like many a modern city, were cast along ethnic lines. Two of Alexandria's quarters were Greek; one was Egyptian (the only area in which they were permitted to reside), and the fourth housed a sizeable Jewish community.

Divisions between the quarters were distinct, reflecting hostility between these communities, which periodically bubbled over into rioting and violence. It was a turbulent, volatile city, demonstrating ethnic tensions only too familiar today. This may be ancient history but it's a familiar landscape to many contemporary urban dwellers or anyone who reads a current newspaper. It was precisely the city's divisions and its multi-ethnic population and varied religious and spiritual traditions (Alexandria was also the birthplace of Gnosticism) that so excited the archeologists and scholars—it provided the potential for something like historical "control groups."

Expectation was that the orientation of the papyri would be largely Greek. In Athens, there was a tendency to associate magic with out-of-towners—Thracians or Thessalians. Would this practice continue? Would there be completely Greek magic, or would the Alexandrians transfer the outsider role to the native Egyptians? Would the Greeks, traditionally impressed by Egyptian mysticism (Pythagoras studied in Egypt) adopt some of their host country's practices? Would it be possible to clearly trace the emergence of Gnosticism as well as Pagan reactions to Christianity? Answers to these crucial questions were anticipated with baited breath as translation of the papyri progressed.

What was uncovered is a mess. The spells, on the whole, are neither clearly nor even mostly Greek, or Egyptian, or that third ethnic group, Judaic, but a scrambled jumble of all three, with a healthy dose of Pagan *and* Christian Gnosticism, together with a sprinkling of influences from other parts of the Greek and Roman empires. Any individual spell may incorporate the God of Israel, assorted angels, Egyptian gods, Mesopotamian gods, Greek gods, Nubian gods, Jesus Christ and Christian spirituality, botanical magic, divination, names of mysterious things we have no way of presently identifying, some or all of the above, and definitely not necessarily in that order.

What was a poor scholar to do? How to interpret and sort this material, determine who wrote it, and to whom it truly belongs and applies?

None of the information in the papyri is mundane everyday material that you might say any individual on the street was bound to know. The spells and incantations are the height of occult knowledge. The Magical Papyri are the descendants of highly guarded spiritual secrets, the ancestors of high ritual magic. Alexandria was an intensely urban community. These spells don't reflect the knowledge common to any village wise-woman or cunning man but are highly detailed and specialized, occult in every sense, the stuff of initiates and adepts. Who wrote them? The information contained in them defies all attempts to pigeonhole these spells.

They derive from over centuries and so can't be attributed to one person, not even the legendary Hermes Trismegistus. Nothing in Alexandria's history indicates a mingling of cultures that would provide a general intercultural exchange like this—quite the opposite. Furthermore, although Greek was Alexandria's *lingua franca* and many Jews, for instance, spoke that language rather than their own, spiritual secrets were still recorded in each community's distinct tongue. Sacred, secret, spiritual texts in each possible tradition were maintained in the most obscure version possible specifically so that profane eyes could not access them. Egyptian, Greek, and Hebrew aren't even written with the same alphabets. Who had access to all this vast information? How was it transmitted?

Intense debate ensued regarding who compiled these spells and who actually cast them. Were they Greeks, as had originally been anticipated, or were they Egyptians? Were they Greeks gone native? Controlled attempts had been made to combine aspects of Greek and Egyptian religion, culminating in the cult of Serapis. But then, why the Jewish references? Were they Egyptians striving to Hell-enize? But then, why the Christian references? Maybe the spells were compiled by unemployed wizard-priests trying to find a new professional niche market, but then why don't they hew more faithfully to centuries of conservative Egyptian tradition? They couldn't be Jews, because, of course, Jews are monotheistic and don't participate in this kind of thing, but then, if not, how did the spell-casters learn all those obscure Hebrew names of power, names extremely difficult to access even within the Jewish community? But if they were Jews, what were they doing invoking Hecate, Hathor and Hermes? They couldn't be Christians because Christians forbade magic in general, because Alexandria was home to a particularly militant branch of Christianity and because the rift between Christians and Pagans was especially violent and bitter in Alexandria. But if they were not Christians, why all the references to Jesus Christ? These mysteries were not the ones that scholars had so eagerly anticipated investigating and debating.

Translation of the Magical Papyri occurred only recently. Perhaps more information will be uncovered. Volume one of *The Greek Magical Papyri in Translation Including the Demotic Spells* was first published in 1986. Egyptologists, anthropologists, historians, linguists, and other scholars continue to discuss their origin and broad scope. The only experts, I suspect, who have not been consulted are contemporary urban magical practitioners, for whom the entangled ethnic and spiritual roots of the Magical Papyri's spells would come as no surprise.

When historians counted Alexandria's four quarters, they neglected a fifth community, who quite obviously rejected, transcended, and ignored those boundaries: Alexandria's vast community of magical practitioners, a quarter unto themselves. Where other residents of Alexandria found divisions, these magical practitioners discovered a crossroads. Magic thrives where roads meet.

What the Magical Papyri manifest is the birth of modern magic.

If you were an up-and-coming metaphysical seeker or magical practitioner back then, Alexandria was the place to go. Why? Not just to make money; you'd retain more of a monopoly by staying home as a big fish in a small pond. No, you'd go to Alexandria to meet other practitioners, learn what they had to teach and share some secrets of your own. The spells of the Magical Papyri demonstrate what happens at those crossroads.

Where others obeyed the rules and kept to their own kind, magical practitioners went wandering, with magic as the *lingua franca*, the common tongue, exploring each other's secrets, deconstructing them and putting them back together in whole new confabulations. This mixing is not necessarily about improvement; spells that hew faithfully to one tradition work just as powerfully as blended spells. Instead it's about experimentation and the desire (common to all practitioners), to adapt something of power to one's own needs. (This process is not always a happy one. One person's *sharing* is another person's *appropriation*. The Egyptians, for example, were appalled when they learned that Greeks had discovered aphrodisiac properties in their sacred temple incense, *kyphi*.)

Alexandria presaged the modern city, filled with immigrants from Earth's different corners. Previously, opportunities to meet other practitioners were limited. Nearby practitioners probably came from your own family; everyone shared the same knowledge and repertoire of tools and materials. Sure, there was the occasional wandering stranger, but nothing like the vast landscape of Alexandria, where practitioners from so many traditions could sit and share secrets. Magic, back then as it does today, transcends and defies boundaries of language, ethnicity, race, gender or religion to form its own community.

When I first read the Magical Papyri my immediate reaction was recognition: all those mixed-up, boundary-jumping spells resembled, in nature if not in specific detail, the culturally diverse magic that I learned in my own hometown, that crossroads of the modern world, New York City. New York, like Alexandria, has had its moments of tense ethnic division, but you wouldn't know it from the metaphysical community. Fearing the law, fearing ridicule, people may hold themselves aloof, at least until genuine magical credentials, knowledge, respect and curiosity are demonstrated, but then the walls come down.

One thing magical practitioners have in common all around the world is curiosity, the quest for knowledge. We are the original enquiring minds who wish to know. Obstacles to knowledge are bitterly resented and are persistently undermined. Magicians always wish to expand their power and increase their knowledge and repertoire. There is a reason that so many of the earliest books printed were grimoires, or books of magic—the same reason that Lord Thoth is patron both of scribes and magicians. Providing that a society is at all literate, magical practitioners, on the whole, are great readers, from ancient Egypt's *Houses of Life* to the Voodoo queens of New Orleans.

There is only one thing better than learning from a book and that's learning from each other. Magical practitioners are, in general, an open-minded bunch. Put a few in a room together and fairly quickly tools will be compared, secrets shared, and demands for knowledge made.

Spells are constantly evolving to suit changing needs. This is particularly true where cultures live closely alongside each other. Nothing crosses borders faster than a magic spell. For instance it can be almost impossible to separate totally the intermingled strands of various European magical traditions. Because certain methods, materials and styles are more popular and prevalent in one area than another doesn't necessarily mean that they originated there or, at least, not in isolation. Even the most sedentary, isolated communities received periodic magical cross-pollination from Jews, Romany, tinkers, and assorted wanderers.

These entwined traditions become even more complex in the magical and spiritual traditions of America and the Western Hemisphere.

During the height of the African slave trade, people were kidnapped from all over Africa. What were originally distinct cultures, each with specific spiritual and magical traditions, found themselves thrown together in dire circumstances, the type of circumstances in which many reach for magic. In Haiti, the traditions of the Fon people of Dahomey were dominant and evolved into Vodoun, although not in isolation. These traditions evolved, adding components of indigenous Taino magic, diverse other African traditions, French, and Spanish magic, thus also transmitting Basque, Jewish, Moorish, and Romany influences and, last but not least, Freemasonry. You think this is beginning to make Alexandria look simple? Just wait.

Following later political turbulence, many Haitian refugees fled to New Orleans, where Vodoun evolved once more, retaining its frame but picking up new influences, this time from the local black population, whose own magic derived from Congolese sources rather than Fon, and also British, Italian and Native American magical traditions. New Orleans, the Crescent City, became known as the capital of American magic. Its traditions would soon be incorporated into what might be called mainstream magic, that magic most accessible to the population at large. This magic would eventually be transmitted to Europe where, who knows? Maybe it's now been picked up by African emigrants to evolve and transform once more.

After extended contact, New Orleans Voodoo can be hard to distinguish from Hoodoo. Hoodoo's basic framework also derives from Africa, mainly from Congolese traditions, but again not in isolation. Deprived of the botanicals with which they had been familiar in Africa, their *materia magica*, enslaved African magical practitioners consulted with Native Americans and acquired a whole new botanical tradition, sharing magical and spiritual secrets as well. These Hoodoo doctors typify the proverbial questing, intellectually curious magician. In addition to Native American, West and Central African roots, their tradition soon incorporated European folk magic, the Egyptian mysteries, Freemasonry and Kabbalah. The great grimoires became available to all. Transmission was cross-cultural. With the exception of a very few isolated mountain pockets, American magic in general demonstrates tremendous African influence.

Further north, Pow-Wow is the magic of German immigrants to Pennsylvania, the Pennsylvania Dutch (a corruption of *Deutsch*). The basic framework is, of course, the German magic the migrants carried with them, both high ritual and folk magic, which incorporated a healthy dose of Jewish and Romany influence as well as those of neighboring European people. In America, strong further influence (and the tradition's name) came from Native Americans, especially the Iroquois, and from the Chikkeners, the so-called *Black Dutch*: Romany (Zigeuners) forcibly deported from Europe who, separated from clan and family, found discreet safety among the Pow-Wow artists.

In 1819 or 1820, dates vary, Pow-Wow artist and *hexenmeister*, John George Hohman compiled a canon of Pow-Wow wisdom and published it under the title *The Book of Pow-Wows: The Long Lost Friend*. This book, still in print, traveled to the cities of the South, carried largely by Jewish merchants, who sold it to Voodoo and Hoodoo practitioners, who incorporated it into their already multi-cultural blend of magic and, no doubt, sent some equally valuable information up North with the returning merchants, who were learning from everybody and spreading the news.

There is an important exception to this magic melting pot, of course. Very isolated areas, places where people have historically had little or no contact with others, maintain extremely pristine, ancient magical traditions. Like the unique creatures of the Galapagos Islands, their traditions developed in isolation and thus may have very unique, easily identifiable characteristics. It's much easier to clearly identify a spell from Papua New Guinea, for instance, than it is to distinguish between French, German, or Swiss spells. Because these traditions are so unique and because one *can* identify the spell's origins, it's very tempting to constantly point out which spell came from which isolated culture. The danger is that this creates a lopsided effect, akin to those old-school anthropologists who were so quick to note the curious habits of the "Natives" while failing to remark on similar practices, parallels and traditions back home.

I can't emphasize more that every distinct people, every culture, every nation, every religion and spiritual tradition has, at one time or another, incorporated, developed, and created magic spells. Each one of us has a magical history somewhere along the line. Loss and abandonment of these traditions tends to accompany loss of cultural or religious autonomy. These spells, therefore, are our shared human heritage, not isolated odd things engaged in only by strange *other* people, very different from us.

In some cases, in this book, I have pointed out where spells come from and which traditions they represent, especially if there's some interesting factoid associated with it or if that knowledge may help you cast the spell, or sometimes just to give credit where credit is due for a particularly beautiful spell. However, I have not done so in every case. Sometimes I did not wish to keep emphasizing one culture, as if they were Earth's only magical ones, especially those cultures whose vast magical repertoire has stimulated others to vilify, stereotype and persecute them. In other cases, the roots were too tangled to identify their origins honestly.

Although many of the spells in this book are meant for use, others are included purely for

historic value and perspective, so that we may remember and learn from them.

Magic Today

These are both the best and the worst of times for magic.

On one hand, there is currently less persecution of magical practitioners in more parts of the world than at any time since the rise of Christianity. This very book that you hold in your hands would once upon a time have earned reader, writer, publisher, and bookseller alike a slow and painful death.

Materials, once rare, craved, hoarded and often forbidden are available and affordable to more people than ever before. Think about that the next time you sip some mugwort tea, an herb that might have branded you a witch just a few centuries ago. Frankincense and myrrh, once the most precious expensive commodities on Earth, may now be purchased in any well-stocked health food store. Salt, packed with magic power, once extracted from Earth and sea with terrible human effort, once very expensive and precious, is now so cheap and common that every fast-food vendor gives away free packets by the handful.

Although fewer people have private gardens, there is greater access than ever before to the botanical material that constitutes the foundation of magic. Some spells in this book refer to what may seem to be very obscure items and plants: virtually nothing is unattainable, however. Once upon a time, a practitioner was limited to local botanicals. Now you can import living as well as dried plants from virtually anywhere on the globe for your private use. Do you want to access the power of Peruvian shamanic plants? Go on the Internet; you'll be able to buy some. Where botanical material isn't practical, modern essential oils and flower essence remedies reproduce alchemical methods to bring you the power of even more flowers, available in a simple, easy to store, user-friendly, inexpensive form.

Practitioners are unafraid to teach and to share information. I remember when booksellers didn't generally stock spell-books. Now you can buy them everywhere. Classes are advertised in newspapers. You don't have to be a member of an inner circle to discover metaphysical companions. There's little need to hide in back rooms, fearing arrest or worse, as in previous days. In industrialized nations there is new-found appreciation for magical wisdom and traditions.

Yet it's also the worst of times in other areas— ironically, in those isolated communities where magical knowledge was preserved in such purity for so long. Many of Earth's surviving magical traditions are vanishing as quickly as the rainforest, coral reefs or any other endangered species.

While some re-embrace a magical heritage rejected for so long, traditional practitioners who've maintained those spiritual traditions for millennia, lack similar privileges and protection. Like those vulnerable creatures of the Galapagos, having never before met attempts at suppression, they may never have developed the skills of subterfuge developed over generations amongst other more frequently oppressed people.

As rainforests are cut down, as ancestral lands are annexed, traditional practitioners and shamans have less access to the botanicals they depend upon than ever before. Instead of open-minded, questing fellow magical practitioners, eager to learn and share knowledge, the only outsiders these traditional practitioners are likely to meet are those who undermine their magical traditions and pressure them to abandon their own faiths and convert to others.

Every day, somewhere on Earth, a traditional practitioner is pressured to abandon shamanism, divination, or some variant of the magical arts. Sometimes suppression is violent. Tools are destroyed, modes of transmission suppressed.

Shamans and leaders of magic are isolated from their communities, or as the Bible so eloquently says, "*put away.*" The stimulus to reject old magical traditions may also come from within, from a culture's desire for modernity, to appear *civilized* and *rational.* In other cases magic and traditional knowledge are victims of war and political unrest.

It is ironic to observe precisely which information appears to be vanishing versus what appears to be preserved for posterity. Once upon a time, very recently, Western magical adepts and elite scholars of magic alike favored the remote "pure" traditions of the Himalayas and Indonesia. Scholars and adepts journeyed with tremendous personal effort to the far corners of the Earth to meet with Ascended Masters while simultaneously scorning magical traditions found closer to the home as superstitious nonsense.

Today it is those previously respected traditions that are rapidly being eroded and are vanishing for a host of religious, political and environmental reasons. Closer to home, Celtic traditions, once reviled as foolishness, have been revived and energized by a massive number of new practitioners. The Romany people, terribly persecuted for centuries, scorned sometimes precisely because of their magical traditions, have recently re-asserted control over those traditions and how they are to be perceived. Hoodoo, once beheld by both academicians and elite occultists with particular scorn, largely for race-based reasons, appears to have its survival assured, thanks to the dedicated efforts of its own scholars, Zora Neale Hurston, Harry Middleton Hyatt, and Catherine Yronwode.

Silver Raven Wolf, modern chronicler of Pow-Wow, once dismissed as ignorant folk-practices that were unworthy of scholarly interest, writes of scouring Pennsylvanian nursing homes, looking for old people with snippets of information that she may then preserve and share. Perhaps others will fulfill this role for other genres of magic in other parts of the world. It takes only one generation for information to be lost forever. How many traditions, how much hard-won human experience and accumulated wisdom from every inhabited continent, have already been lost? This big book that you hold in your hand is but a tiny portion of Earth's magical wisdom.

In keeping with the inquiring, questing spirit of magical practitioners throughout the ages, don't be too respectful with the spells in this book. If you find something that suits you or intrigues you, use it. If something isn't quite right, play with it. Tap into your own magic powers and continue the evolution of our magic repertoire.

PART ONE

Elements of Magic Spells

How do you cast a magic spell? Do you shout *abracadabra*, turn around three times on one foot and shoot sparks from your wand? Or do you stand within a circle of lit candles, magic sword at the ready, attempting to read unknown, unpronounceable words from a dusty grimoire? Will you tuck one single crumb of bread, one single grain of salt, and some burned-out charcoal into a scrap of red fabric, and then make knots in the cloth as if your very life depended upon it? Perhaps you will stand at the crossroads and just … *stand?*

Magic spells come in virtually unlimited form, some dramatic, some shocking, and some perhaps surprisingly mundane. Definitions of exactly what constitutes a magic spell depend a lot upon one's personal history and experience, the stories you were or weren't told as a child, and cultural expectations. What separates a magic spell from just any random series of actions is *you*, your intent, goals and desires.

A magic spell is a conscious formalized attempt to manipulate magic power and energy (heka) in order to achieve your own personal goal.

There are many styles of spells, featuring all sorts of ingredients. If one style of spell doesn't suit you, there are others. Afraid of fire? Cast your spell by creating enchanted baths. Don't have a tub? Brew potions or tie magical knots. If one ingredient is unobtainable, there are substitutes. If you can't afford precious gems and resins, there are plenty of powerful magical materials masquerading as common kitchen ingredients. Magical energy is irrepressible; magic spells are the controlled conduit for directing this magical energy. There is only one component of every magic spell that you cast that cannot be replaced and that is *YOU*. Yours is the unique binding energy that provides the spark of life which transforms actions, words and thoughts into magic spells.

Everyone's secret desire, of course, is to possess enchanted words or objects that achieve our goals for us without even our slightest effort. Just say *"hocus pocus!"* and poof! Your boring date is instantly transformed into Mr. Right. There is a grain of truth in this fantasy: the most magically charged objects will perform a lot of the work for us, although magic spells are *never* completely effortless. Some naturally occurring items inherently possess this type of magic power (iron, menstrual blood, salt, certain botanical plants); in other cases, some extremely intensive spell-casting is required in order to craft a tool of requisite intense magical power (a magic wand, sword, or mirror).

Magic spells take many forms, avail themselves of many powers, and depend upon various elements, tools, and components. Some of these elements, tools and components occur naturally on Earth, whilst others are crafted by people. Sometimes these elements and components can be categorized neatly into categories and sometimes, magic being the unruly, disobedient force that it is, they overlap and merge in a surreal dream-like manner.

Some spells are object-driven; others are dependent upon the power of words. Some require dozens of unusual plants and minerals, while other spells, which rank among the most difficult to cast because you must do all the energy transformation independently, require nothing more than the force of your personal will. Some spells walk a razor's edge between religion and magic on the one hand, and traditional healing and magic on the other. Partly this is because of magic's tendency to appropriate any object, system or method that demonstrates potential for power, and partly this is because, once upon a time, distinctions between various arts and sciences weren't drawn as rigidly as they are today. Awareness of magic power and the desire to use it for one's own benefit is the primordial human art and science. Religion, traditional medicine, astrology, alchemy, aromatherapy, perfumery, music, dance, visual art, and more are all rooted in magic and shamanism.

Before any spell is cast, the initial requirement is that you have a personal goal. What do you want to achieve? What do you wish to prevent? What are your secret desires, your deepest fears? Magic spells are always cast for a purpose, even if it's a generic one like "*personal happiness,*" the proverbial "*peace on Earth,*" or obtaining vague "*good fortune.*" The more specific your desire, the more clearly articulated your vision, the deeper your passion, the more likely it is that your spell will work. There is not one type of spell that is inherently more powerful than another; there are only spells and styles of spell-casting that are more effective for a specific individual. Part of the fun and challenge of spell-casting is finding the spells that best suit you.

In this section we will examine various styles of spell-casting, the various elements of magic, and the tools and ingredients required to cast spells.

✪ Spell-casting

Spell-casting Using the Power of Animals

Spells are cast using the power of animal allies and familiars. Animal allies, familiars and the magic power inherent in specific animal species can help you achieve your spell's goals. (Specific information regarding animal allies and familiars is found within *Animal Spells*, starting on page 105.)

Notice that the above sentence reads "*power of animals*" not "*parts of animals*." If this book included spells utilizing anatomical parts of animals, it could easily have been called *The Element Encyclopedia of 10,000 Spells*. It's not necessary to point any fingers; more cultures than not have engaged in this practice. It's not necessary to discuss whether those spells ever worked or not, either. If they did work, would that make them acceptable today? That discussion veers dangerously close to the opinion frequently expressed about how tragic it is that tigers may soon be extinct in the wild because poachers kill them for medicines and aphrodisiacs that don't work. If the medicines *did* work, would the situation be any less tragic?

Whether those old spells ever worked or not, we now live in an era where the balance of nature is terribly tipped. Those spells are no longer viable. Because spells that rely on any part of an animal, physical or otherwise, are ultimately dependent upon the good-will of its presiding Animal Spirit, those old anatomy-dependant spells will no longer work for us and may even backfire on the spell-caster. Magic is a living, evolutionary art, not a static situation; what worked once must be adapted to present needs.

Whether those old practices (rabbits' feet for money spells, badgers' feet for childbirth spells) were ever as prevalent as some would have us believe is subject to debate. The most sensational, lurid aspects of magic are inevitably emphasized by outsiders and story-tellers. The only thing many know about the vast, sophisticated magical system Hoodoo, for instance, is the infamous black cat bone. Spells using parts of animals are also taken out of context. Once upon a time, people were responsible for killing their own food. Nothing was wasted. What wasn't eaten was utilized for other purposes, including magic. Out of context, a spell can sound terribly cruel. Thus, a

Romany amulet called *"eyes of the crayfish"* implies that only the eyes are used, having been plucked out of the poor creature. In reality, *"eyes of the crayfish"* refers to scrapings from inside the shell, the crayfish itself having been served for dinner.

If you perceive power in this type of spell, however, they can be modernized, adapted, and improved. Candles, charms, and images, for instance, allow us to access the inherent energy of a specific animal species in a manner that retains magic power and is safe for both animal and practitioner. For example, hummingbirds are a frequent component of Central American love spells; a copper or gemstone hummingbird charm allows you to synchronize the inherent animal energy with a compatible material for enhanced spell-casting. For maximum effect, consecrate the charm to the animal spirit, which you would be unable to do if you were using actual body parts obtained through the animal's suffering.

This should not be considered mere New Age fluffy-bunny adaptation. Since ancient days animal image magic has been among the most powerful. What was the Biblical golden calf after all but a magic image? A living calf would have been far less trouble. It was the specific juncture of animal magical symbolism with metal's inherent magical energy, guided by human fear and desire that accurately and potently manipulated and directed magic power.

Animal sacrifice has no place in magic; it is religious ritual entirely and completely, without overlap. All religious traditions at one time or another conducted animal sacrifice, some just further back than others. Some continue these traditions while others do not. What is certain is that *no* religious tradition permits laypeople to conduct these sacrifices. Permission is granted only after strict training and initiation. Where magic approaches the border of religion, symbols are used rather than actual animals. Burn a dove-shaped candle to petition Aphrodite during a love spell or offer her the gift of a figurine, rather than killing her sacred bird. Again, this is not fluffy-bunny magic but ancient tradition. How can you reconcile the idea of a deity who accepts sacrificial offerings of a beloved, sacred creature in one context, but who angrily punishes anyone who harms a hair on the head of that creature in another? Over two thousand years ago, Hecate accepted sacrifices of dogs in her *official* temples, killed only by *official* priestesses in the context of very specific ritual. Even back then, individuals who preferred to make independent, private offerings, or who could not afford to pay the temple the cost of a dog, successfully offered tiny stone dog fetishes to Hecate instead.

There are magic spells contained in this book that require the participation of animals. It's assumed that they'll be treated with the respect one would pay human or spirit partners. It is also assumed that at the conclusion of the spell, the animal will be in as good a condition, if not better, as it was at the spell's beginning.

Several spells require cuts of meat similar to those you might eat for dinner, assuming you are not a vegetarian. Meat for these spells should be purchased in the same manner that you would normally obtain meat for a meal. There are many spells that require eggs, honey, and milk. Vegans may choose not to perform these ones, and there are many more spells in the book that do not use animal products. Magic spells are not divorced from real life. If something offends you in any another context, then it's likely to be inappropriate for you magically as well.

Manipulation of fragrance is an extremely important component of magic spells. As most fragrances derive from botanicals, the topic will be discussed in greater detail in that section. However, certain very famous fragrances have traditionally derived from animal sources, most notably civet, musk, ambergris, and castoreum. Castoreum, derived from beavers, is today only available in synthetic versions. *One* spell featuring *one* drop of civet is included in this book (it is the only ingredient in this sex-magic spell) because, in theory at least, the fragrance may be obtained without unduly harming the animal, and arguments have been made that this may be the only way to guarantee the seriously endangered civet's survival. I can't honestly say that I'm entirely convinced. You, too, may wish to engage in further research.

Frankly, it's unlikely that you'll be able to purchase anything other than synthetic versions of these fragrances, the authentic article being rare and prohibitively expensive. Because they have *always* been rare and prohibitively expensive—and synthetics are a recent invention—historic botanical substitutes have always existed, and those substitutes are used within the spells of this book:

★ For **Musk,** *extracted from the musk deer:* **Ambrette** (Abelmoschus moschatus), *a shrub native to India, also known as musk mallow and treasured for its scented seed*
★ For **Ambergris,** *derived from sperm whales:* **Labdanum,** *a resin excreted from the leaves of the rock-rose* (Cistus creticus, Cistus ladanifer). *Allegedly labdanum from Crete has the closest resemblance to ambergris, although it is also obtained from French, Moroccan, and Spanish sources*

Whether the tendency to utilize animal body parts was ever as prevalent as some believe is debatable. Certainly, grimoires are filled with spells specifically requesting assorted species' feet and hearts and eyes. Many classic grimoires are based largely on various fragments of ancient spell-books that were in circulation throughout Europe, Arabia and North Africa before the development of modern printing. Many of these spells derive from turn-of-the-Common-Era Alexandria. Professional magicians of that time, attempting to keep spells secret yet needing to write them down so that they themselves would remember complex formulas, created an elaborate code, so elaborate that someone had to write it down in order to use it. That list was discovered and translated amid the Magical Papyri (see page 11).

★ *Does a spell call for the* heart of a hawk? *No need to catch that bird, so sacred to indigenous Egyptian religion—what the spell is really asking for is heart of wormwood*
★ *Do you hesitate to cast a spell requiring* lion's tongue? *No need, all that that spell really requires is a "tongue" of turnip*
★ *Wondering how in the world you'll ever extract* Hercules' semen? *Not a problem; just go out to the garden and pick some arugula*

Not every animal reference encoded in the Magical Papyri is a botanical, although (as with magic in general), plants do predominate. The spell that demands a *physician's bone* neither commands you to commit murder or to dig around in the cemetery: a piece of sandstone is what's really being requested.

Many, if not all, of these animal references may originally have referred to botanicals and minerals. Of course, by the time the descendant of a single fragment of papyrus reached Europe, hundreds of years later, copied and re-copied over and over by hand, lacking the accompanying code, and some magician desperate to access the forbidden secret magic of Egypt got his hands on a spell …

The spells recorded in the Magical Papyri are fairly mean-spirited in general, full of commanding and compelling. Were the magicians irresponsible, not caring if others misinterpreted their instructions, or was this just an example of professional secret code, full of in-jokes and personal references, similar to the secret languages (*sim*) still employed by some modern Egyptian entertainers? Across oceans, continents and time, some modern Amazonian shamans also share a secret shamans' language—a professional language only understood by other professionals—in order to protect their information from those who don't know how to use it properly.

Is this what those old Alexandrian magicians intended? We may never know. The moral of the story, however, is never cast spells that aren't comfortable for you. It is not uncommon for botanical and other materials to be named for animals, nor is the practice relegated to ancient history. Many spells in this book, for instance, call for deer's tongue. I assure you, no deer need be harmed. *Deer's tongue* is a type of grass, reputed to provide eloquence: the name is a pun on the plant's appearance and its ability.

Swallow's blood is a red powder that allegedly transmits the magical power of that long-migrating bird; no blood of any kind is required. *Dragon's blood*, an extremely potent magical material, surely ranks among the Top 20 most popular spell-casting ingredients. No need to emulate Saint George, dragon's blood is the resin from *Dracaena draco*, an Indonesian tree. Unlike most resins it's red, hence the name. If you burn it, it does indeed bear a resemblance to blood. (There is also *another* dragon's blood, used in Peruvian magic. This one, too, is a botanical substance, although completely distinct from the Indonesian resin.)

Spell-casting Using the Power of Botanicals

Botanical just means *plant*, however because of the vast variety of forms used (some no longer remotely "*plant-like*") any type of plant-derived power, in its original form or otherwise, is categorized as a botanical. Botanicals, as a category, are probably the most common ingredients in spell-casting. Many people will never cast a candle spell, never work with crystals or wands or magic mirrors, but it's virtually impossible to engage in magic without relying on botanical power to a greater or lesser extent. Plants are ubiquitous in magic. Their power is accessed via many forms, which lend themselves to various styles of spell-casting, so that botanicals are incorporated into virtually every style of spell.

Casting Magic Spells in Partnership with Your Living Plant Allies

Fairy-tale witches reside in huts, cottages or castles surrounded by magically empowered gardens. When Prince Charming seeks Sleeping Beauty in her enchanted castle, the surrounding garden, full of thickets and thorns, actively reaches out to prevent him. Although one must never rely on one's Protection Spell Garden to play the role of armed-response guard, there is a metaphoric truth hidden in this story.

Gardens can be both products of enchantment and independent producers of enchantment; they are a living, on-going magic spell. Gardens may be arranged in any variety of ways—color-coordinated, whatever was on sale at the nursery, even completely haphazardly. If you select, coordinate and arrange plants according to the magic powers they radiate, then planting a garden becomes one style of casting a spell. Thus your desire to draw wealth, protection or fertility to one's home is manifested by carefully arranging the appropriate plants, and vigilantly removing those possessing opposing, contradictory powers.

This obviously is a long-term extended magic spell, rather than the type of quick-fix luck spell you might choose for a spontaneous trip to a casino. How will you benefit from this type of garden spell?

★ *The actual spell-casting, and then time spent among the botanicals and their radiant energy creates the desired adjustment on your own energy*

★ The radiant energy of the coordinated garden draws and/or repels the targeted goal to you and to your home in a more powerful manner than one botanical or amulet could achieve alone

★ This spell is a symbiotic, reciprocal process, which ultimately strengthens all living participants for their mutual benefit. The garden will additionally attract complementary animal and spirit allies who will also contribute to the success of your spell

This type of magic spell is not limited to those with access to personal property or sunny weather. Magic spell gardens may be created indoors in pots. Furthermore, an entire garden need not be created; one or two individual plants may be grown as part of a magic spell or to further other magic spells.

There are several very good reasons to maintain living plants:

★ If you are pursuing a spiritual or magical alliance with a specific plant, this is best accomplished with a living plant, redolent with power and consciousness, rather than processed, dried plants that retain power but lack conscious intelligence

★ You can grow plants necessary for magic spells and/or physical healing. As you nurture the plant, communicate with it: share your fears and desires, let the plant know what you want from it. These plants will potentially provide more power for you than any others. They become your partners in healing and magic. It is a symbiotic relationship: they care for you as you care for them

★ In many cases if you want to work with a plant, you'll have to grow it. That's the only way it is guaranteed to be available. The plant realm is as ecologically devastated, if not more so, than the animal kingdom. Many plants are extinct or seriously endangered. The only way to work with some magical plants (Solomon's Seal or Low John the Conqueror, for instance), the only way to incorporate them into any spell, is to grow and nurture them. It is the only way their power will be available to you

Because there have always been economic, space and climatic reasons why working with living plants is impractical, and because different parts of a plant (roots, leaves, flowers) manifest different magic power and energy and thus are used independently in different spells, various methods of processing plants have evolved over millennia. These include: dried botanicals including incense, flower essence remedies, hydrosols and oils, including fixed, essential, and fragrance oils.

Harvesting Botanicals
In order to maximize botanicals' magic potential, magic rituals and spells are incorporated into their harvesting.

Because plants are alive, removing them from Earth is a risky operation. One has the option of increasing and enhancing their inherent power, or of offending Earth and the presiding Plant Spirits. Once upon a time, all harvesting, for magical or other purposes, was accompanied by spells, rituals and propitiation of various Earthly and Spirit forces. Unless you purchase your botanicals from magically oriented vendors, one can safely assume that modern harvesting is accompanied by no such rituals or spells.

If you practice extensive botanical spell-casting you may wish to incorporate similar gestures in other ways, to enhance your spells and to provide spiritual protection for oneself. If however, one grows and harvests one's own botanicals, ancient spells and rituals may be borrowed or adapted.

Because they're alive, have power and must be treated with respect, it's not appropriate to just go out and grab a handful of plant. Botanical materials are safely harvested through magic ritual. Essentially you cast a spell in order to gain materials to cast more spells. The plant (or its presiding spirit or Earth herself, however you best understand this) must be addressed. The purpose for gathering should be explained. Because of the principle of reciprocity, gifts are exchanged.

WARNING!

Many people exhibit a dangerous tendency to assume that if a plant is used for magical reasons, particularly benevolent ones, it does not also create a physical impact. This is not true, and this assumption can lead to disaster.

Botanicals are an holistic power: they affect us simultaneously on spiritual, emotional, magical *and physical* levels. It is possible to cast word charms, image magic or play with candles and crystals without profound physical effect. This is not so with plants. Plants are the basis of medical knowledge, and even magical plants have a physical effect.

Because something has power, doesn't mean it is always the right power for you. For instance, many magic spell sites on the Internet offer directions for protective spell baths featuring the herb rue with nary a health warning, despite the fact that it has abortifacient properties and the British master herbalist Nicholas Culpeper said that he couldn't recommend that a pregnant woman even walk through a room containing rue, let alone handle or bathe with it.

Be careful. If you have anything that could be perceived as a physical vulnerability, it is your responsibility to verify whether any botanical may aggravate your condition. If you are pregnant, attempting to become pregnant or nursing a child, the potential safety of all botanicals must be determined. This is not obscure information. Many excellent literary sources on herbs and botanicals exist. Knowledgeable, professional herbalists, physicians and medical providers can provide you with information as well. This does not only apply to traditional modes of internal application such as consuming botanicals, but also inhaling fumes or topical application such as bathing, or even perhaps intensive, concentrated handling, depending on the potency of the plant.

Magic is always intended to improve one's life; injuring one's health in the process of casting a spell defeats that purpose. Incorporate your personal needs into choosing the best spells for you.

Libations of water are always appropriate, however different traditions favor different gifts. Native Americans offered pinches of tobacco; Anglo-Saxons once offered oatmeal. The ancient Romans offered bread and wine. Honey, wine, and menstrual blood are popular offerings. Fragrant incense may be burned in the vicinity as a gift.

Magic spells are always as simple or as complex as the practitioner wishes. An involved, formal harvesting spell follows; follow it precisely, if it suits you, or consider how best to adapt for your own personal needs.

Alexandrian Harvest Spell

An elaborate plant-gathering ritual was recorded in Alexandria, Egypt during the first centuries of the Common Era.

1. The harvester first performs personal cleansing spells, while simultaneously *purifying* his or her body, which at that time meant refraining from sexual relations and eating meat, usually for a period of several days.
2. Sprinkle natron (the natural salt used in the mummification process) over the area being harvested. (Baking soda is a close, modern substitute; Dead Sea salt may also be appropriate.)
3. Place pine resin in a censer and use it to fumigate the area around the chosen plant, circling it three times.
4. Burn **kyphi** and pour a libation of milk, while engaged in simultaneous prayer and petition.
5. Finally pull up the plant, simultaneously invoking the name of the deity to whom the herb is dedicated, requesting assistance with the purpose of your spell.
6. The uprooted plant is rolled in a pure white linen cloth.
7. Blend seven wheat seeds and seven barley seeds in some honey. Insert this in the hole left by uprooting the plant and then fill it with dirt.

Sometimes distinct plants demand distinct rituals. Two spells follow, one from Wales, the other from ancient Greece, one for an extremely popular magic plant, the other for a more obscure one. Consider these spells, follow them precisely if you like or consider how best to adapt them for your own harvesting needs.

Virtually any list of Top 10 magical plants will include vervain. Legend says vervain sprang from Isis' tears; the herb is believed to have a special fondness for humans and thus works extra hard to provide happiness and success for us. It is believed to have been one of the crucial ingredients of Cerridwen's Cauldron (see page 6). The Druids insisted that vervain be harvested with an iron knife. An ancient Welsh formula stipulates how vervain must be gathered in order to guarantee its maximum magic power:

Welsh Vervain Harvest Spell

1. The plant must be harvested during the rising of Sirius, the Dog Star, at an hour when both sun and moon are beneath the horizon.
2. Before uprooting the plant, offer a libation of honey.
3. You may only use your left hand during the entire operation, whether you are left or right handed: pull up the plant and wave it aloft.
4. Separate leaves, flowers and roots and dry them separately in the shade. (Each has its own magical uses.)

Ancient Greek Black Hellebore Harvest Spell

Although poisonous, black hellebore, the Christmas rose, is perceived to have magically protective powers.

1. Cast a magic circle around the intended plant, using a magic wand or knife. If you do not work with those ritual tools, consider a respectful way to demarcate the harvest space.
2. Request permission to gather the plant from Apollo and his son Asklepios, the plant's presiding spirits.
3. Burn incense and make offerings to the spirits.
4. Offer a libation to the plant, and then gather it.

Casting Spells Using Dried Botanicals

The most prevalent ingredients of magic spells are processed botanicals, especially dried plants and oils. Drying plants preserves them for extended use, allowing you to work with plants out of season and those that cannot be grown in your personal region. Dried botanicals from all over the world, representing many magical traditions, may be purchased from herbal suppliers.

Dried botanicals are frequently sold already chopped up, cut or powdered. As this frequently needs to be done before spell-casting, purchasing botanicals in this form can be a real time and effort saver—with one caveat. Leaves and blossoms, even chopped, often remain easily distinguishable. Peppermint doesn't smell like vervain or hibiscus, for instance. Roots, on the other hand, often the most magically potent part of a plant, once chopped or powdered, are fairly indistinguishable from each other. It is not uncommon for unethical or ignorant vendors to substitute one root for another. If you are looking for a distinct root, say High John the Conqueror, for whom this is a common problem, buy the whole root and grind and powder it yourself, even though this can be difficult. It is the

only way to guarantee that you are receiving what you want, the only way to maintain control over what may be a pivotal ingredient. Familiarize yourself with botanicals. Know what they *should* look like and what they *should* smell like, and you will be less likely to be fooled.

If you grow plants or have access to fresh plants, it's extremely easy—virtually child's play—to dry them yourself.

Drying Botanicals

Hang botanicals upside down in small bunches, so that they are not too crowded. Professional herb dryers, resembling horizontal ladders, can be used, or attach bunches to a wire hanger. Allow botanicals to hang in a well-ventilated area away from direct sunlight until dry.

Casting Spells by Burning Botanicals

Magic spells are cast by burning botanicals (incense), thus releasing their magic power into the atmosphere (fumigation).

One of the most ancient methods of casting spells is consciously, carefully and deliberately burning botanicals. This method incorporates all four primal elements into one spell. By applying the power of fire, botanical power (which has been nourished by Earth and by water), is transformed into smoke (air) and dispersed into the atmosphere to provide magical solutions and fulfill magical desires. If you burn incense on a metal pan or burner, then you incorporate what many consider to be the fifth element, metal, into your spell as well.

Modern incense frequently takes the form of sticks and cones, which require a little technical know-how. However, incense is an ancient, ancient art. If cave people had the technology to create fine, viable incense, of course you do, too. The original incense was loose dried botanical material, ground and powdered. Most magic spells assume incense will be in this form.

Mortars and pestles are ancient magical, medical and culinary tools. They may be used to break down and blend botanical material. Once upon a time, incense was created by repeated grinding with a mortar and pestle, and then sifting with a sieve (also an ancient magic tool). However, if you desire the fine powder that many spells specify, a coffee or spice grinder, particularly an old-fashioned manual one, can make life easier.

If you prefer stick incense, blanks may be purchased and doctored to your taste.

To Form an Incense Cone

1. Dissolve gum arabica in water, approximately one part powder to two parts water.
2. Allow the material to soak for approximately three hours.
3. In the meantime, pulverize the herbal material to be used until it is finely powdered (using mortar and pestle or other grinding tool).
4. Mix this powder into the liquid until it can be shaped into small cones.
5. Allow to dry completely in a warm area.

Botanical Infusions

An infusion is the process by which one medium (or power) is encouraged to permeate another. The most common are botanicals infused in water or oil. The most famous infusion in the world is a cup of tea. If you make tea with loose leaves rather than a tea bag, you already know a lot about infusions. Infusions allow you to insert specific botanical power into potions, baths, floorwashes, and magical oils, among many other things.

Water-based Infusions

The standard formula for a water infusion is one teaspoon of dried herb, or one-and-a-half teaspoons of fresh herb for every cup of boiling water. Unless otherwise advised, maintain those proportions even when using multiple herbs, adjusting the proportions of the individual ingredients rather than the whole.

1. Place the botanicals into a non-reactive pot or container (glass rather than plastic, for instance).
2. Pour the water over the botanical material.
3. Allow it to brew, usually for between five and fifteen minutes.
4. The plant material may be strained from the liquid or allowed to remain, depending upon the purpose of the spell. For a floorwash, you'd want to remove the botanical; for a particularly potent magical bath, it may be more powerful to retain the botanicals, even though this may leave a mess to clean up.

Sometimes a stronger, more concentrated infusion is desired for a bath or floorwash, but *not* for drinking.

1. Place a more substantial quantity of botanical material into a non-reactive pot or container.
2. Pour only enough boiling water over the botanical material to cover it.
3. Allow it to brew for as long as it takes the water to return to room temperature.
4. Strain the botanicals from the liquid or retain, as desired.

Oil-based Infusions

The process of creating infused oils is slightly more complex, however it is still easily accomplished in the home kitchen. The standard proportion suggested is that for every cup of oil, one ounce of fresh herb or one half-ounce of dried herb is required. Unless otherwise advised, do not exceed these proportions.

1. Place the botanical material in a stainless steel bowl.
2. Cover with the oil.

3. Gently heat over simmering water, either in a true double boiler or in an improvised water bath—a saucepan one-quarter filled with water. The bowl with the herbs must not sit on the bottom of the pan but float in the water. As it is very easy for oil to scorch and burn, this process needs constant supervision for safety. Keep the oil covered.

4. Stir once in a while. Simmer gently for thirty minutes. The oil should not be allowed to get too hot because if it smokes, bubbles or burns, an acrid fragrance will develop, spoiling the infusion.

5. Allow the oil to cool. Then all the botanical material must be strained out through multiple layers of cheesecloth or a fine non-metal strainer. Strain twice, if necessary, or more. If the plant material is not removed, the oil may turn rancid.

6. If an infusion spell includes essential oils or flower remedies for enhancement, add them now, once the oil is strained and cooled.

7. Store the infused oil in an airtight container.

You can substitute a crock-pot for the water bath. Maintain the same proportions. Leave the pot on a low heat for approximately two hours, then strain as above.

Solar-charged Infusions

If you can depend upon consistent warm, sunny weather, extremely powerful infusions may be created via solar power. These infusions contain the power of the sun as well as that of botanicals.

1. Place the botanicals inside a jar with a tight-fitting lid.

2. Pour oil over them (make sure the botanicals are completely covered).

3. Add one tablespoon of apple cider vinegar.

4. Leave the jar to sit exposed to warm sun all day and in a warm cupboard (or exposed to moonbeams, if it's warm) all night, for two weeks. Strain as above.

Flower Oil Infusion

There is also another method of infusing oil that does not require heat. This method is usually used to capture the power-transmitting fragrance of delicate flower petals.

1. Separate the petals.

2. Place substantial quantities of clean, dry petals into an airtight jar and cover with oil. (An oil with minimal fragrance of its own is usually preferred to allow the flower's scent to transmit most powerfully.)

3. Let the petals steep in the oil for three days, shaking the jar occasionally, keeping the jar in the sun in the daytime and in a warm cupboard at night.

4. Strain out and discard the petals, ideally using some cheesecloth or other non-metal sieve, but retain the oil.

5. Fill the jar with a substantial quantity of fresh, clean dry flower petals and cover them with the reserved oil.

6. Again allow the petals to steep, repeating all the previous stages. The oil will retain the fragrance; repeat until the desired intensity of fragrance is achieved (usually three repetitions is needed), then carefully strain out all the solid botanical material and reserve the oil.

If you are creating large quantities of infused oils that will not be used up quickly, it's best and safest to add a natural preservative. One-quarter teaspoon of simple tincture of benzoin, available from many pharmacies, may be added per cup of infused oil. Benzoin is derived from styrax gum, believed to have sacred properties and to create a cleansing, protective action. (Make sure you have simple tincture, not compound tincture, which is also known as Friar's Balsam.)

Vitamin E may also be used as a preservative. However, be aware that much of what is readily available is synthetic. Pierce one Vitamin E capsule and add the contents per every cup of infused oil. Jojoba oil is not a true oil but a plant lipid with antioxidant properties. Blend it with other oils to discourage them from turning rancid. (Maintain the basic proportions of oil to botanicals, however, even when using multiple oils.)

Casting Spells Using Oils

Oils have always been prized components of magic spells. However, not all oils are truly oils, and not all oils are even truly botanical.

Essential Oils

Essential oils are *not* true oils, despite their name. They are volatile liquids extracted by various methods (usually, but not always, by steam distillation) from aromatic botanicals. Modern aromatherapy is the manipulation of these essential oils for therapeutic, cosmetic, magical, and spiritual purposes. The roots of aromatherapy stretch back to ancient China, Egypt, Mesopotamia, and the Middle East. If you would like to access the power of a botanical, essential oils are the most concentrated form and as such have many magical uses. Once upon a time, essential oils were also referred to as *chemical oils*, especially in older grimoires. This relates not to their chemical constituents, which we are only now beginning to understand, but to their previous use in alchemy, the term being a corruption of *al*chemical oils.

Their potential physical impact upon you is as concentrated as their magical power:

★ Never *take essential oils internally without expert supervision*
★ *Even when taken externally, they are used sparingly, drop by drop. Each drop packs a lot of power. More is rarely better*
★ *Because their power is volatile and fleeting, when creating magical baths, potions or oils, essential oils are usually the last ingredients added so as to maximize the intensity of their power and fragrance*
★ *In general, essential oils are not appropriate for use during pregnancy, especially early pregnancy*
★ *Because essential oils are so concentrated (and because some are profound skin irritants) they are usually diluted in true oils (usually referred to as "carrier oils") before using*

Fragrance is an extremely important component of magic, particularly, in romantic spells and, especially, spirit-summoning spells. Each spirit has a characteristic aroma, which calls them and by

WARNING!

Botanical power comes in many forms. These powers are not interchangeable. When a spell requests a dried herb, substituting an essential oil may not be appropriate or even safe.

which they may be identified. In ancient Egypt, this was one way that true spiritual visitation was determined: the deities signaled their presence through the sudden appearance of their characteristic fragrance. Vestiges of this belief survive in folkloric Christianity, where the devil is described as appearing amid the smell of brimstone. (Signature fragrance isn't limited to the spirit realm alone. In the 1944 Ray Milland movie, *The Uninvited*, the ghost signals her presence via the scent of mimosa.) Fragrance, especially as transmitted by true botanicals, is the primary and most effective magical device for communicating between realms.

The human sense of smell remains the most mysterious of our senses. The olfactory system (the part of our brain that processes scent) is near what is known as the *reptilian brain*, the most ancient and least-understood part of the human brain. Scent is our primal sense, the one shared most closely with the animal and spirit realms. Magic is a primordial art; to truly master it, one must access these inherent primordial talents. The sense of smell may be the most concrete, accurate way we have of identifying and accessing *heka*, magic power. Essential oils are frequently the most concentrated, potent and accessible way of accessing an individual plant's *heka*, even though this very power means they must be handled with care.

True Oils

True oils, also known as fixed, carrier or base oils (because they carry essential oils' energies and serve as their base) have always been perceived as precious and sacred. The ancient Egyptians had an astonishing repertoire of true oils, far greater than our own. Although true oils are used as carriers for the magic powers inherent in dried botanicals or essential oils, they also have their own magic power, and spells can be cast using true oils alone. Castor oil has protective, commanding magic

properties, while sweet almond oil is a component of many romantic and erotic spells, for instance. Mineral oil (baby oil) is not a botanical, but a petroleum product: its magical uses are restricted mainly to hexes—malevolent spells.

There are several ways to distinguish essential oils from true oils. Essential oils, also known as *volatile* oils from the Latin *volare*, "to fly away," evaporate completely into air, without leaving a trace. Although they may deteriorate and their power fade, they do not grow rancid. In contrast, true oils will leave a ring or residue and will not evaporate—as anyone who's had to clean out a greasy pan can attest. True oils will also grow rancid over time, although some become rancid more quickly than others.

True oils are, in general, extracted from the seeds or fruits of plants. Cold-pressed oils (which will almost always be labeled as such) are preferable, when possible. (Grapeseed oil, for instance, can only be extracted via the use of solvents.)

Fragrance Oils

Because real essential oils are extracted via expensive, labor-intensive, time-consuming processes, synthetics are often substituted. If an essential oil is too reasonably priced, be cautious. Often we do get what we pay for. Labeling is not always clear and manufacturer's terms may be meant very loosely.

Essential oils cannot be obtained from every botanical. There is no such thing as cherry or cucumber or apple essential oil. Furthermore, essential oils must be derived, by definition, from botanical material. There is no such product as essential oil of rain, although products exist that reproduce the fragrance of a rainy day. Invariably, these products are crafted from synthetic materials, known as fragrance oils, the staples of the perfume industry. Some are real dead ringers for the genuine material and can fool many an expert. However, because no plant material is actually contained, fragrance oils lack true, complete magical power. That said, sometimes, especially for candle magic, fragrance alone may be sufficient to spark *your* magic, to evoke a response from your brain. In general, fragrance oils are fine for dressing candles, but not for the body.

Hydrosols

Hydrosols, also called hydrolats, are the other product of the aromatherapy industry. When essential oils are produced by steam distillation, water is passed through the botanical material and then eventually separated out; that water has also been magically transformed by the distillation process: it is no longer plain water but contains plant molecules. Although other flower waters are sold (usually rose or orange blossom water) these are frequently only flower-scented or flower-infused waters. Hydrosols actually carry the power of their respective botanicals. Hydrosol production is an old alchemical process, although it lay dormant, forgotten and unappreciated for centuries. Now fresh attention is paid to hydrosols; new ones become available every day. They are an increasingly important component of magic spells.

Flower Essence Remedies

Alchemists, witches and herbalists have always painstakingly gathered morning dew from individual plants to access its magic powers. Infused with the specific power of the particular plant, these tiny liquid dew-droplets also contain the perfect balance of the four primal elements: the power of water, the earth radiating through the plant, the surrounding air and fire from the sun.

Once upon a time, if you wanted to access this power, you were limited to the plants growing on your lawn. This is no longer the case. Modern flower essence remedies bring the power of flowers from all over Earth—from the Amazon rainforest to the Australian outback—right to your door.

The pioneer and founding father of modern flower essence remedies was Dr. Edward Bach, a Harley Street physician and homeopath. Dr. Bach eventually came to the realization that true, complete healing was not possible when approached solely from the physical plane. Emotional and spiritual imbalances are the root causes of dysfunction of all kinds. True healing and transformation must be accessed through the soul and emotions. Dr. Bach devoted the rest of his life, at great personal sacrifice, to developing the original Bach flower essence remedies, which provide the vehicle for this healing and transformation. According to Dr. Bach, the flowers communicated to him directly, sharing their secrets and potential for healing with him. Since then, many other flower essence practitioners have followed in Dr. Bach's footsteps to bring us greater access to a wider variety of botanical material than ever before.

It's easy to be confused between flower essence remedies and essential oils: they have extremely similar names and are even packaged in a similar manner (in tiny glass vials). Although they complement each other's powers and work very well together, they are extremely different and *cannot* be substituted for one another.

Essential oils are true plant extracts, with extremely potent and sometimes scientifically documented physical effects. When I taught therapeutic aromatherapy, many of my students were nurses learning to incorporate essential oils into conventional hospital practice. All essential oils are, to a degree, antiseptic; many have potent antibacterial and anti-viral effects in addition to whatever magical power they also hold.

No one completely understands how flower essence remedies work, although they do—profoundly. General consensus is that it is a form of vibrational healing. Flower essences are pure water infused and charged with the plant's energy and vibration. There's no need to kill the plant to access this energy; typically only a few carefully chosen leaves are used. By definition, the remedy won't work if the plant used is not a powerful, healthy specimen. These essences provide a healing bridge between the soul of the botanical and your own. While essential oils may be understood as the lifeblood of a plant, flower essence remedies capture the plant's aura.

Flower essence remedies are the exception to the rule regarding botanicals' impact on the physical plane—there is no direct physical effect. All the effects are felt on the emotional, spiritual and magical planes. They are safe for everyone's use, children, animals, crystals and other plants.

When using flower essence remedies the most common mode of administration is internal. Manufacturers will supply directions, however the standard dose for most is four drops four times a day. Topical administration is also extremely effective: massage the flower essence remedy into the body, particularly into the soles of feet and the thin skin stretched between thumb and forefinger.

Every manufacturer of flower essence remedies has a specific repertoire of botanicals. When flower essence remedies are sited in the text, the name of their manufacturer follows in parenthesis. For example: Mugwort (FES).

Spell-casting Using the Powers of the Elements

In Western magic and philosophy, Earth's power is traditionally broken down into four components, known as the elements: Air, Earth, Fire, and Water. Air and Fire are traditionally considered male or yang energies, while Earth and Water are most typically perceived as female, or yin. Life springs from earth and water but air and fire are necessary to spark the process. Healthy magic power derives from the harmonious balance of these elements.

From a magical standpoint, the power of each element is unique, specific, and alive. Depending upon the purpose of your spell, one element may be invoked or emphasized over the others. Power also derives from the interplay between the elements. Power is enhanced when the elements intermingle and form a threshold. Steam emerges from the marriage of water and fire, for instance, and is a potent force for spiritual cleansing and protection.

Individuals are influenced by these elements, too. One or more elements will predominate in every individual's natal astrological chart and will thus influence not only their character but also the type of magic spell, which usually appeals most to that individual and is most accessible. I have listed the elemental affiliations of the astrological signs below, however an accurate gauge can only be received from a complete birth chart. Someone who is a Taurus, an earth sign, but who has five other planets in a water sign is a very watery person, despite their sun sign.

The elements are easily understood if one considers their qualities.

Air

Air serves as a transmitter and a messenger. Because magic (and some schools of higher physics) asserts that nothing that exists truly disappears, to say that something "vanishes into thin air" is meant very literally when discussing magic spells. Candles that access the power of fire also summon the power of air: what is burned disappears into the air. Air is associated with astral travel; witches fly through the air even if the journey is accomplished with dreams or visions.

Air is considered a masculine, yang energy.

Fragrance is the language of air. Word charms also draw upon Air power.

Air signs: Gemini, Libra, Aquarius.

Earth

Earth is our battery and generator, providing capacity for growth and solidity. Earth is a particularly important element for those journeying into magical realms because earth provides stability, reality, and gravity. Magicians should spend time in the garden, even if not gardening, and barefoot whenever possible. If this isn't appealing, play with real clay (not synthetic), or make mud pies like a child. Go to the spa and take a mud bath.

Earth is considered a feminine, yin power.

Earth's magical power is accessed through the botanicals that are rooted in Earth, figures formed from clay, and dirt itself, as in graveyard dirt or crossroads dirt.

Earth signs: Taurus, Virgo, Capricorn.

Fire

Fire is the most independent of elements, defying all illusions of human control. Fire heals, energizes, cleanses and purifies. Fire is transformative and must always be treated with respect. Although you can get into trouble with any element (think floods, mudslides, tornadoes) fire is commonly the most dangerous. I cannot emphasize enough: *never assume that because you're engaged in magical or spiritual acts that common-sense fire safety does not also apply*. Fire is *never* completely safe. Be vigilant.

Fire is a masculine, yang energy.

Candles are the most popular form of fire magic. Magical bonfires and lamps are also lit. Magic mirrors are sometimes used to access fire's transformative (and potentially destructive) powers.

Fire signs: Aries, Leo, Sagittarius.

Water

Water is the element most affiliated with magic. Water is where life originates, not just as an abstract concept or in Darwinian theory, but literally for each of us as we emerge from our mother's amniotic sacs. Water is the element of psychic power and intuitive knowledge.

Water is a feminine, yin energy.

Water spells are conducted in the bathtub and at the seashore. Water spells include those incorporating lunar charged waters, magically charged waters and captured rainwater.

Water signs: Cancer, Scorpio, Pisces.

Fire and Water, extreme yang and yin, are a matched pair, leaving Earth and Air paired with each other. Like yin/yang forces in general, the elements don't exist in mutual exclusivity. Magic may be performed with only one element (an Air-magic word charm) but is most frequently a combination of two or more forces. For instance, incense combines botanical power (Earth) with Fire, to produce fragrant smoke (Air). A complex spell that involves dressing a candle with botanical oil, and then burning it while you're bathing in a magical infusion combines all four elements simultaneously.

This grouping of the four elements of Air, Earth, Fire, and Water is the traditional Western system and is the one most commonly shared by magical traditions. However, it is not the only system:

★ *Chinese magic traditionally counts five elements. Although metal is important in most other traditions, too, Chinese philosophy emphsizes this importance by counting Metal as one of the elements, alongside and equal to the Western four*

★ *Jewish magic traditionally counts three elements. Air (or ether) is considered so ubiquitous that it doesn't need to be counted as an element. Therefore only Water, Earth and Fire are recognized as elements*

Casting Spells Incorporating the Power of Metal

Although magic in its modern form stems from the discovery of metal and smithcraft, metal today is an under-utilized modern magical material. Perhaps this reflects ancient taboos on the material and the role of the blacksmith.

Each metal, like each stone or botanical, projects a specific magical energy, although as there are fewer metals than the vast quantities of botanicals or crystals, it's easier to sum up these powers.

★ *Brass: protection, love*
★ *Copper: love, healing*
★ *Gold: wealth, vitality*
★ *Lead: domination, binding (the most frequent material for curse tablets)*
★ *Silver: protection, fertility*
★ *Tin: wealth, luck, divination*

The most powerful magical metal, however, and among the most magically charged of all materials on Earth, is iron.

Iron

The metal most associated with magic, worldwide, is iron. Because iron is not found in its pure state except as a meteorite, it was known as the *Metal of Heaven* and perceived as a gift from sacred powers. Meteors were carved into representations of deities: the original cult statue housed inside the Temple of Artemis at Ephesus, one of the ancient world's Seven Wonders, was carved from a meteorite. The most sacred representation of the goddess Kybele was an uncut meteor, believed by many to remain buried under the foundations of Saint Peter's Basilica, which was built over her Roman temple.

Iron provides power and protection. Magically speaking, iron is reputed to restore health, provide vitality, both physical and psychic, and cure impotence. Malevolent spirits are invariably frightened of iron: it repels them and chases them away. Iron boxes protect magical tools the way a lead blanket protects a person during the x-ray process. Because iron is the metal of truth, traditionally in areas of Africa, and perhaps in some areas still, people would swear on iron in the way that others swear on the Bible or Koran. One of the simplest protective spells involves placing an iron knife or tool under one's pillow, not to serve as a ready weapon but to offer spiritual protection while you sleep.

With the exception of menstrual blood, no single item is more associated with magic than iron. In fact the two powers, menstrual blood, and iron, are intrinsically linked. While other metals, like stones, may be perceived as Earth's bones, iron ore is regarded as Earth's menstrual blood.

Despite or because of its great power, iron is a dangerous, volatile element. Iron is used for healing, in magical ritual and also through surgery, dentistry, acupuncture, and any field of medicine that requires metal tools. It is also an instrument of death: knives and guns wound and kill.

Earth's Original Professional Magician: the Smith, Master of Fire

Magic in its modern state arrived with the advent of the Iron Age. The smith's art, the original alchemy, was kept secret for centuries: those who knew it were able to forge weapons that could completely dominate their neighbors. By virtue of their contact with this magic material, and because they alone were privy to its secrets, smiths were more than just artisans: they were the original magicians, the Masters of Fire. Smiths became the first professional magicians (as opposed to shamans), called in to perform spellcasting on behalf of others.

Smiths were simultaneously respected and needed, feared and persecuted:

★ Because the smith is in close contact with the ultimate power substance and, in fact, bends it to his will, he is perceived as possessing more magic power than the average person. He is protected and his personal magical energy continually replenished and reinvigorated by iron

★ However, because iron ore may be perceived as Earth's menstrual blood, a substance typically restricted or taboo, the ironworker who handles it openly and constantly may also be perceived as tainted. On the one hand, the smith is powerful enough to break taboos and thrive, but on the other, this contact makes conservative elements of society uncomfortable. The smith is able to go where others cannot, perform rituals that others cannot: whatever spiritual cleansing or protective rituals the smith requires for his own spiritual survival and protection are unknown to everyone outside the ironworking clan, and thus are suspect

★ Another perception derives from Central Asia's Turkish tribes. They believed that raw metals in general came from Earth's bowels. The raw materials were Earth's waste products, which would ultimately develop into finished metal, by itself, over long periods of time, if they were left undisturbed and buried. The smith's oven is, thus, a substitute for Earth's womb. This artificial womb gives birth to metal. The Master of Fire is thus believed to assert power over Time as he accelerates the process. Because of this he has healing powers and can read the future, but he is also always on the verge of spiritual disaster: digging ore out of the Earth, rooting around in Earth, any kind of digging is akin to rape. Only the ironworker knows if and how he can be purified

The ironworker became a much-needed member of society. Beyond smith craft, he was typically also a healer, herbal practitioner, dentist, surgeon, body artist, and often the sole person permitted to perform circumcision and thus in charge of spiritual initiation. He carves amulets, devises rituals and confers with the Spirits on behalf of others, a combination artisan-shaman. Secrets of metal-working were carefully guarded. Smiths evolved into clans, their techniques into family secrets.

The concept that one can pay someone else to cast a spell for you enters magic as well. A professional class of magical practitioners was born. The smith's wife, the woman who has sex with the Master of Fire, bears his children and may be his professional assistant, becomes transformed into a person of power in her own right, typically performing the role of herbalist, midwife and women's healer, henna artist, (henna being also a substance associated with menstrual blood) and, especially, fortune teller. In some traditional African areas, a wedding may be delayed until the smith's wife can arrive to dress the bride's hair, provide her henna or otherwise bless and attend her.

Societal ambivalence towards the smith cannot be emphasized enough; it will eventually be projected onto magic itself. The history of ironworking to a great extent parallels the history of magic working. Although the smith is required by society, he and his family also remain apart and distinct. People need them, their services are necessary, yet people are afraid to get close to them, or to allow them live as fully integrated members of society. Their very power and skill sets them apart. The Bible associates ironworkers with the Kenites, descendants of Cain, a Jewish tribe that isn't one of the Twelve Tribes of Israel. The most famous Kenite, the otherwise unarmed woman Jael, kills the fleeing enemy general Sisera with a hammer, one of the smith's primary tools.

Ironworkers developed into nomads, traveling from town to town, village to village, staying as long as there was work, and then moving on. This is still true in parts of Africa and Western Asia. There are still Bedouin tribes who await the arrival of the smith to perform circumcisions.

Complicating the picture even further is that the smiths providing services to the majority culture are frequently members of minority groups. It is a complex relationship with tremendous potential for tension: the ironworker performs ritual functions and serves as a repository of spiritual knowledge for traditions that he may or may not share.

In Europe, smithcraft is associated with Tinkers, Travelers and, most especially, the Romany, who traveled with the Tatar and Mongol armies, performing metalwork. Romany culture, as first witnessed by Europeans, is very typical of ironworking clans: the men were metal smiths while the women tell fortunes. In rural Africa and Western Asia, smiths are frequently of Jewish origin, although their personal traditions may have veered far from conventional Judaism. Persecution of the Ethiopian Jewish community, the *Beta Israel*, derives both from their religion *and* from their traditional occupation as ironworkers. The *Ineden*, smiths associated with the at least nominally Muslim Tuareg, are also believed to be of Jewish origin. Distinct clans, they perform the role of general handymen for the majority group: blacksmith, jeweler, armourer, woodworker, healer, herbalist, poet, musician, singer, and general consultant on spiritual and traditional matters. Essential to traditional Tuareg culture, they are simultaneously of low status.

With the coming of Christianity, European ironworkers would be vilified and identified with the devil, who was frequently depicted in the guise of a smith. Some of their traditional spiritual power remained: in the original Gretna Green weddings, the couple was able to cross the border from England and be married by the smith.

Saint Patrick's Breastplate, a famous Irish prayer attributed to the saint, calls on God for protection against *"incantations of false prophets, against the black laws of paganism, against spells of women, smiths and druids, against all knowledge that is forbidden the human soul."*

Because one can safely assume that any modern metal has not been extracted from Earth using respectful, propitiating spells and rituals, any new metal with which you work should be thoroughly cleansed and charged (see pages 74–77). That said, silver and iron are both believed to be incorruptible; although they may be used for ill, malevolent vibrations should not cling to them as they will to other metals or materials.

Metal is incorporated into all manner of spells, from the simple to the complex. Metal steadily, constantly and consistently radiates its power: the spell, thus, keeps going even after initial human participation is ended. Magic rings, for instance, need to be initially crafted, charged and consecrated but once this has been done, they radiate their own power, drawing towards you whatever they have been programmed to pull, even as your attention turns elsewhere.

Basic household and farm tools are often incorporated into magic spells. What we perceive as mundane was once recognized as exceptionally magically charged. The magic remains, it is human perception that changes. Hammers, knives and other metal tools are shared by many occupations. The anvil is reserved for the smith and thus is full of power and sacredness.

An anvil converts to an altar and may be used as such even by someone who is not a smith. That person begins the following spell at Step 3 and assumes the role of the smith in steps 6 and 7.

✳ Anvil Blessing and Magical Activation Spell

1. Before the anvil is made, the smith prays and petitions that it will be reliable, powerful, and will bring luck.
2. When the anvil is complete, it's hidden until its activation ceremony.
3. The owner of the new anvil gives a feast in honor of the anvil.
4. After drinking and dining, the anvil is brought out to receive the crowd's admiration. Placed in the center of the table, it becomes an instant altar.

5. A white candle is placed atop the anvil, with another placed at each side, for a total of three candles.
6. The smith leads prayers that the anvil will bring healing, prosperity and *baraka*.
7. The smith strikes the anvil for the first time, then the crowd showers it with offerings—small metal coins, libations of brandy—so that good fortune will be shared by all.

Spell-casting Using the Power of Minerals

"*Minerals*" includes rocks, crystals and gemstones. Many associate crystals with New Age philosophy, but gemstone therapy and the magic of minerals are about as old age as you can possibly get. Modern magic is profoundly influenced by the power of iron, but prior to the Iron Age there was the Stone Age.

You think you've never accessed gem power? Most of us have, even if unwittingly. The diamond ring placed on the finger of an affianced woman serves to ensure sexual fidelity *and* relieve sexual inhibitions. Jeweled earrings, of all kinds, offer protection to a vulnerable threshold of the body. Many anthropologists assert that all jewelry originally derives from amulets. Alongside shells and seeds, the earliest jewelry was stone. Jewelry may be placed on the body carelessly. However, if it is combined with conscious intent, incantation, petition and/or visualization, something as simple as adorning the body becomes a powerful magic spell. Placing a ring, a bracelet or a locket on someone else's body is potentially a discreet but very powerful method of casting a spell upon them.

Crystals are worn, placed upon altars, added to conjure bags, placed under pillows and used in a wide variety of spells. Beyond specific geologic analysis, distinctions between rocks, crystals and gemstones tend to derive from human perception of value, with the term "*gemstone*" implying greatest value, "*plain rock*" the least. Of course, what's valuable from a financial or aesthetic perspective may not correspond to magical value.

Every specific type of mineral formation, like each specific botanical, has its own hidden powers, attributes and gifts. Like botanicals, from a magical perspective, the mineral kingdom teems with life. The magical quality that characterizes the mineral kingdom (to distinguish it from others) is memory. Stones are believed to retain memories of everything that occurs to them or in their presence. They are Earth's silent witness to history.

Because their nature is so different from our own, even more so than with botanicals, which are clearly born, eat and die, it can be very difficult to perceive minerals as *alive*. Although anyone can access the magic power of crystals superficially just by tucking a crystal into a mojo hand (see pages 86–87), in order to work closely with them, it's necessary to acknowledge that unique memory, that minerals can feel emotions of a kind (the spectrum runs from loyalty and benevolence to resentment of bad treatment) and can communicate their knowledge. Stones have no mouths: they can never learn to speak in the exact manner of a human. However, we can learn to hear and listen to them.

Once upon a time, because of great respect for minerals' magic powers and their formidable powers of memory, as much care, if not more, was taken when gathering (harvesting) stones as it was with botanicals.

Many cultures perceived stones and metals, not as distinct products of Earth for human use, but literally as part of Mother Earth's body. Stones are often perceived as her bones or teeth. From that perspective, great care must be taken when extracting and using them. Only certain people were authorized to gather stones, using very specific propitiatory ritual. Profound cleansing rituals were undertaken before and after their harvest. Stones were removed with care and respect.

Offerings and libations were given to Earth as reciprocal payment and compensation.

Perhaps you have access to a stone that's been treasured for a very long time, a museum piece, as it were. In that case, appropriate rites and care may have been taken. Otherwise, it is fair to assume that the rocks and crystals available today were not removed from Earth with love and care, but yanked out brutally and disrespectfully. As crystals have grown in popularity, the temptation to exploit this popularity for the purpose of some quick cash frequently outweighs any metaphysical concerns.

Assume therefore that crystals may arrive complete with grouchy, resentful attitudes. Furthermore, minerals are the witnesses of human experience too. Minerals are absorbent, absorbing surrounding emotion. Many minerals, particularly the most expensive—diamonds, emeralds, and rubies—are extracted amidst great human suffering. The stones carry these emotions with them as they travel to your hands.

All is not hopeless, however. Stones may be cleansed. Cleansing can remove memory stores, like wiping a computer's memory, allowing for a fresh start. The depth of memory removal depends upon the stone and the cleansing methods used. Cleansing methods are found on page 185.

Stones need to be charged for a purpose or to harmonize with your personal energy, to enhance your partnership.

 ## To Program or Charge a Crystal

1. Cleanse the crystal using the most suitable technique.
2. Hold it in your hands.
3. Clear your mind.
4. When you feel that your energy and that of the crystal are synchronized, state your intention, goal or desire clearly, lucidly and succinctly.
5. Repeat it until it feels right. Speak out loud if possible.
6. When charging feels complete, put the crystal down and consciously detach your attention from it.

Stones are used in their natural state or polished and cut. A specific stone can also be selected and then engraved with a specific design. This creates a talisman, which is then usually worn or carried on the body. There are healing talismans, love-drawing talismans and protective talismans, among many others. This practice brings magic into the realm of professionals. Anyone can find a

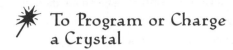

★ Cleanse any new crystals or stones before initial use or immediately upon acquisition

★ It may also be advisable to conduct future cleansings as needed, particularly after intensive spell work or any traumatic, stressful situation

special stone on the beach; not everyone can engrave a gemstone with accuracy and precision.

The following ritual for cleansing and activating gemstones for healing and magic comes from India, birthplace of extremely sophisticated gemstone therapy.

✳ To Cleanse and Activate a Gemstone

1. The night before you intend to wear your stone, immerse it in a cup of fresh milk.
2. Remove it and place the milky stone on an altar, before a sacred image, in the company of quartz crystals and any other objects you hold sacred.
3. Leave it overnight.
4. Arise at dawn and rinse the stone.
5. Raise it towards the rising sun.
6. Pray and petition that the stone fulfills your desires.
7. Wear, carry or use it as needed.

Diamonds, emeralds, sapphires, and rubies have profound magical uses as well as their more conventional role in jewelry. Both magical and conventional uses, however, are limited to those who can afford these expensive gems. Luckily, the absolutely most powerful magic stones are easily affordable and, in some cases, free, if you can only find them. The following are some of the most magically powerful stones.

Quartz Crystals

Quartz looks like beautiful sparkling ice. It is believed tied to that watery trinity of lunar/oceanic/female energy. Clear quartz crystals are used as scrying tools: they are able to enhance the psychic ability and magic power of those who handle them consistently or who are in their presence. Likewise, quartz crystals are used to activate and empower other stones or tools. Quartz crystals may be attached to magic wands. Pack quartz crystals in with tarot cards, runes or any other magical tools to enhance their power. Quartz crystals are used for cleansing purposes. Larger specimens left in a room have a vacuum cleaner effect on negative energy, helping to maintain a fresh atmosphere. (Remember to cleanse the crystal periodically, as if the vacuum bag was full.) It is a protective, empowering stone.

Hag, Witch, Holed or Holey Stones

These names all refer to the same type of stone. Holed stones are exactly as their name describes: small pebbles or stones with naturally occurring perforations, they are gifts from the Earth Mother. They cannot be manufactured. Sometimes you'll just find one: a common pebble with a hole. Pick it up. It is a priceless magical gift. Holed stones provide enhanced magic power, protection against malevolent spirits, humans and the Evil Eye. They are also used to regenerate and protect physical vitality. Wear it around your neck or hang over your bed so that you can absorb its power while you sleep.

Lodestones

Also known as magnetite, lodestones are magnetic iron ore. They are the magical bridge between the realms of stone and iron. They possess transcendentally powerful magic energy. Lodestones attract and draw good fortune: money, success and love. They're also used in healing rituals: lodestones can draw pain from the body in the same manner that they can draw a lover or money towards you.

Lodestones may be used individually or in matched pairs. They are perceived to have gender;

depending on purpose, you may require a male or female lodestone or a pair. It's easier to determine the gender of a lodestone than that of a parakeet. Female lodestones are rounded; phallic-looking lodestones announce their manhood.

Wherever people have been in contact with lodestones, they have used them magically. Alexander the Great distributed lodestones to his troops to protect them from djinn. Chinese magic favors lodestones as wedding rings, to ensure the happy survival of a marriage. In ancient Rome, statues of Venus and Mars were carved from lodestone so as to be magnetically attracted, demonstrating the powerful sexual magnetism between the two forces.

The origins of lodestones are shrouded in mystery. Their use goes back to ancient times. Magnetite, their more scientific name, derives from the ancient city of Magnesia, from whence they were once mined. Lodestones are a positive, benevolent force, always used to draw good fortune. Lodestones, like the root charm High John the Conqueror, are thus not tools for hexing. The worst thing you can do with a lodestone is fail to avail yourself of its power.

Christian legend has it that the stone upon which Christ's body rested for three days following his crucifixion was a lodestone. Its miraculous properties were revealed to Godfrey of Bouillon when he led the first Crusade to Jerusalem. While praying in Christ's Sepulcher a voice whispered to him that his victory was assured if he'd only carry away a bit of the stone. He listened to the voice's advice, which proved true. However, according to this legend, the kings who succeeded him paid no attention to the stone and therefore the Holy Land was lost to them.

In addition to memory, lodestones are acknowledged to possess consciousness, intelligence, even wit, and especially a soul. Although any rock or crystal is alive, lodestones are *really* alive! Because of this perception, lodestones must be replenished consistently by "*feeding*" (though all crystals needs to be recharged periodically). Now you can't just give a lodestone a little bit of your own dinner, the way you'd give a treat to a dog. Lodestones have their own preferred nutritional supplement: fine iron shot, also known as iron filings, iron dust or, in Hoodoo parlance, *magnetic sand*. Magnetic sand is also perceived as possessing a "*drawing*" power all of its own, and is a component of many magic spells, with and without lodestones.

Feeding Lodestones

There are various techniques for feeding lodestones, depending upon different traditions.

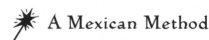

A Mexican Method

Just like people, lodestones have a working week, but then need some time off for rest and relaxation.

1. On Friday evening, place lodestones in a glass of wine, water, or aguardiente (strong liquor), and leave it there overnight.
2. Remove it from the liquid on Saturday and sprinkle it with magnetic sand.
3. Let the lodestone rest until Sunday evening or Monday morning, then send it back to work in a conjure bag, pocket charm or whatever it normally does for you.

Hoodoo Method

1. Dress the lodestone with your choice of condition oils. Coordinate the oil to suit your desired results. Thus if you want the lodestone to draw a new romance to you, choose a love-drawing oil, like **Come to Me, Lover.** Substitute essential oils, true oils or sprinkle the lodestone with a few drops of whiskey or similar beverage.
2. Sprinkle with magnetic sand.

Sometimes, after extensive spellwork or when used to make **Magnet Oil**, a lodestone can become excessively drained.

The following formulas are intended to feed a drastically depleted lodestone:

 ## Overtired Lodestone Spell (1)

1. Anoint the lodestone with olive oil.
2. Place it in a pouch filled with dirt for three days. (Crossroads dirt is best, if possible.)

 ## Overtired Lodestone Spell (2)

1. Place the lodestone in a glass, stone or metal bowl.
2. Cover it with dirt. (Again crossroads dirt, if possible, but any dirt will work.)
3. Keep the bowl inside a closed cabinet for three days.

Gem Elixirs

The power of minerals may also be accessed in liquid form. This ancient method has been revived by manufacturers of flower essence remedies. Modern gemstone elixirs are sold with flower essence remedies and used in the same manner. Commercial preparations are, as of the time of writing, of consistently high quality and provide access to a greater number of gems at accessible prices than most people will ever have access to, in a controlled, safe, easy-to-use manner.

However, this is an ancient technique. Gem elixirs may also be crafted for oneself.

 ## An Ancient Egyptian Method of Creating Gem Elixirs

1. Place crystals on the grass and leave them outside overnight.
2. Collect the dew in the morning.

 ## Modern Methods for Crafting Gem Elixirs

★ *Fill cut-crystal bottles with spring water. Let them charge in the sun and/or moonlight. This water may then be consumed or added to the bath*

★ *Place the crystal in pure spring water in a glass bowl. Energize and activate in the sunlight. The water absorbs the crystal's power and vibrations. Bottle and use as required*

WARNING!

Be very careful regarding internal use of gem elixirs. Some crystals may be toxic: do not use anything internally until you are absolutely sure that it is safe.

Spell-casting Using the Power of People

Yes, yes, of course, this sounds so obvious. Every magic spell is the product of a person. Without the person's intent and direction, magic energy just radiates and isn't channeled into a spell. However, some magic spells draw upon more than the energy, desire and creative properties of one individual.

Not every spell is cast alone. Some spells require partners and participants. In particular, healing and cleansing spells must often be done *for* the person intended to benefit from the spell. Always choose your spell partners wisely. Their individual magical energy radiates through your spell as powerfully as that of any botanical, mineral or element. It's also crucial that those who might undermine the success of your spell, whether willfully or unintentionally, are not chosen as partners. Choose those whose goals are in harmony with your own, those who desire your success as much as you do.

An entire, living, breathing person isn't always required. Various parts of the human anatomy are believed to radiate with magic power, and just as they perform different anatomical functions, so different parts of the body perform different magic spell functions. Typically, the power of the body part is represented symbolically through an image of the particular part: the power of images is an important component of magic spells, and the milagro is a metal charm depicting a specific part of the anatomy. The most commonly depicted parts of the human body include the eyes, genitals, hands, and hearts. These are especially incorporated into healing and protective spells.

Sometimes, however, actual parts are required by spells, although "*part*" may be the wrong word. No pain is inflicted obtaining these parts although they may be obtained for the purpose of inflicting pain. Certain materials generated by the body are perceived as exceptionally magically charged. These materials, which the body sheds, still retain the essence of the body and a connection to the person they come from. By working on these materials, one may profoundly affect that other person. These materials are the *intimate items* deriving from a person's body. Hoodoo refers to them as *personal concerns.*

Because they render the other person vulnerable to magic, in theory, all these intimate items may be used for hexes. However, that is not the only or even their most frequent purpose.

Hair

Most frequently used in love and binding spells, hair is both an object of tremendous power and vulnerability.

Menstrual Blood

Menstrual blood is the ultimate magic power item. If you were forced to reduce magic to its most primal elements, you would be left with menstrual blood and iron (which may be perceived as Earth's menstrual blood).

Menstrual blood is the ultimate controlling mechanism. It provides spiritual protection, allegedly repels demons, and puts out fires. One drop is said to cause others to fall madly in love with you.

Many consider that oppression and discrimination against women stems from perceptions of menstruation as "unclean." An alternative view is that oppression and discrimination stem from the fear of women's power. Menstrual blood is considered the strongest magical substance on Earth. Menstruating women were isolated because of fear of their power. Until recently, for instance, in parts of Thailand, women were discouraged from riding on the top level of double-decker buses because that would place their genitals above men's heads, potentially destroying their power as well as that of their amulets. There are some who feel that all magic stems from menstrual and lunar mysteries. Judy Grahn's book *Blood, Bread and Roses* postulates that all human civilization stems from responses to perceptions of menstruation.

Menstruation may be referred to as a woman's *moon-time*, indicating that menstrual cycles, pregnancy and tides all reflect the phases of the moon. It's also sometimes called *dragon-time*, the dragon being a metaphor for menstruation (which opens up new paths to ponder when considering tales of dragon-slaying heroes, especially those attempting to save virginal princesses).

You don't have any? You used to be able to buy menstrual blood. In ancient Italy, spiritual goods merchants sold used menstrual rags to those who couldn't provide their own.

Nail Clippings

These are used in a similar way to hair, however with slightly less impact. Frequently they are used together, each to reinforce the power of the other.

Saliva

Saliva has profound controlling and protective magical capacities. Like menstrual blood, saliva is believed capable of repelling malevolent spirits and magic spells, hence the custom of spitting in the face of perceived danger. Saliva is also used magically to transmit desire.

Sexual Fluids

Male and female sexual fluids are considered intimate items of extreme power and vulnerability. Although these sexual fluids leave you vulnerable to the most notorious of love spells, they also have other uses. Semen is often invoked in healing spells (topical application allegedly cures headaches), while women's sexual juices provide access to the life-force: it was not an uncommon ingredient in ancient Chinese alchemists' potions. Women's vaginal secretions, both sexual juices and menstrual blood, were frequently the preferred food for vampires seeking increased sexual vitality and/or life-force.

Sweat

Sweat is most frequently used in love and sex spells. It is the closest natural substance men possess that compares to the magical power of menstrual blood.

WARNING!

Spells involving intimate items may rank among the oldest in the worldwide magical repertoire. For this very reason, however, they may reflect a different world with different dangers. Magic is always about improving life and circumstances. Behave responsibly. If you possess any physical condition (HIV, hepatitis, or anything else) that could be passed on by these substances, than these spells are plainly not for you.

Urine

While hair and nail clippings used in spells most frequently derive from another person, urine is almost inevitably your own. Many spells will instruct you to urinate on something. This is not intended as desecration, more in the fashion of a dog marking territory. Urine is believed to create a dominating effect.

There are plenty of spells involving fecal material, too. However, you won't find them in this book. Every author has her limits. The ancient Egyptians cultivated a science that distinguished between the powers inherent in the fecal material of various species—crocodiles, donkeys, humans, cats, all sorts of animals.

Casting Spells Using Names

The magical perspective does not always correspond with the modern scientific view as to what constitutes the human body, or where it begins and ends. Most magical systems acknowledge the existence of a subtle body, the aura, a radiant presence that surrounds the human body, so far undetectable by science. A person's name or names may also be considered magically as part of an individual's intrinsic identity and thus a source of great power and vulnerability.

Knowing someone's true name renders him or her vulnerable to your power. Think about Rumpelstiltskin. Once upon a time (and it still happens in some places), people were given various names, one for public use, one for ritual use, and another to be kept secret. Mothers would whisper names into their babies' ears, never to be repeated, so that one name would *always* be kept secret. In ancient Egypt, to describe someone possessing exceptional magic power it was said that even their mother didn't know their name.

That connection between name and mother is crucial magically. As the ancient world became increasingly male-oriented, patriarchal cultures identified people by their own name and their father's name, so that someone might be called, for instance, Dana, child of Bill. The mother is rarely mentioned. There's one important exception: magic spells and magical documents. There, it's the mother's name that counts. Many consider that this reflects some sardonic humor; for the magical spell to be effective, the name has to be *right*. Because a mother is never suspect but may however harbor unsuspected secrets, the only way to guarantee true identity was to use the mother's name instead of the father's. This tradition is maintained in the directions in this book; follow it if you choose. Unless otherwise advised, the magical formula to write or call someone's name is: "[Name], child of [their mother's name]."

Names of Power

Angels, demons and spirits of all kinds are summoned by calling their true name. Supposedly they can't resist the call. Much summoning magic depends upon this premise.

Of course, there is a caveat; this information was once transmitted orally: to be effective the names are supposed to be pronounced correctly. One has only to observe the conflict between historians, magical practitioners and scholars of all kinds over how the names of relatively famous Greek and Egyptian deities are pronounced to appreciate the inherent problem.

There is a style of spell-casting that incorporates reeling off series of magical names. The Magical Papyri have some of these spells: there's nothing to indicate that the practitioners of their time recognized these names any more than we do. They don't figure in surviving mythology; these names completely lack context.

Call me cautious, but I'm not comfortable summoning someone to enter my home (and life) if I'm not personally familiar with them, or at least have a little background information. Something about not talking to strangers. I wouldn't recommend it to you either. Where the original version of a spell veers off on a tangent of reciting a long list of Names of Power, I've indicated this but omitted the names. My recommendation is to insert your own Names of Power—those Spirits whom you trust, ancestral spirits, even perhaps living people whose assistance would be appreciated and whom you feel you can trust.

Spell-casting Using the Power of Planets

Because they're old systems that pre-date modern astronomy, in magical and astrological parlance, the luminaries, the sun and the moon, are considered planets just like other heavenly bodies, although this does not concur with modern scientific classifications. Modern astrologers *know* that technically the sun and moon are not planets, however both astrology and magic are *geocentric* systems, meaning that everything is perceived as revolving around Earth, even when this is not literally the case.

Some spell-casters rely heavily on astrological wisdom. Every day, every hour, every topic, every category has a planetary correspondence. The same applies to Chinese and Hindu magic, although their respective astrological systems differ from the Western system, which is based on the Babylonian astrology that so influenced Egyptian and Greek versions.

If you would like to synchronize your magic with the planets to this degree, information is easily obtainable from astrological sources and from many traditional grimoires.

Every planet possesses an astrological and magical influence (ancient Greek and Roman curse tablets were under the dominion of Saturn, for instance), however the planets most strongly identified with magic are our own, Earth, and its satellite, the Moon.

Earth

While the moon represents psychic ability, then Earth is our general vitality. Both are required for optimal magic power. According to many worldwide traditions, with little else in common, Earth is the material from which humans are created. Earth is our mother: we are born from her body, and are then returned to her to await rebirth while the corporal body decays and becomes part of Earth once more, in a never-ending cycle. Without actual extended consistent physical contact with Earth our vitality, and hence our magic power, suffers and diminishes.

Earth is also very literally the dirt under our feet. Dirt may be used to empower us and empower our spells. There are various traditions that pursue actual physical healing by packing the patient into heated sand. Moor mud is used to detoxify the body. The dirt at shrines and saints' tombs is perceived as exceptionally charged with power. Bits of dirt are carried as talismans; it may also be sprinkled over items to empower and revitalize them.

Not all dirt is equal. Currently perhaps the most famous dirt in the world comes from the Roman Catholic shrine at Chimayo, New Mexico, although the dirt's miraculous reputation precedes Catholicism in the area. Every year thousands converge on Chimayo for the healing dirt. A testimonial room bears witness to miracles received. This dirt heals more than body and soul. When a good friend's computer crashed, at her wit's end, she placed a canister filled with Chimayo dirt on the computer and it miraculously started working again.

Certain magical traditions rely on the power of dirt more than others. In the twenty-first century, the Afro-Caribbean tradition of Palo Monte probably utilizes more types of dirt than any other. Palo spells may request four handfuls of dirt from a police station, two from a courthouse, three from a hospital, and so on. This magical tradition dates back at least to ancient Mesopotamia.

Although not every tradition pays such detailed attention to Earth, most utilize certain specific types of magical dirt, including:

★ *Crossroads dirt*
★ *Footprint dirt*
★ *Graveyard dirt*

Inherent energy is transmitted through contact with the dirt itself. Each will be discussed in greater detail elsewhere in this book.

The Moon

The moon is considered the ruler of all magical arts, and Magic is timed to the phases of the moon:

★ *Spells intended to increase something (like money), or intended to initiate something new (a fresh romance) are coordinated with the waxing moon. Begin these spells on or just after the New Moon*
★ *Spells intended to decrease something (like debt), or cast for the purpose of banishing (an enemy) are coordinated with the waning moon. Begin these spells on or just after the Full Moon*
★ *The Dark of the Moon, those few days where the moon is not visible, just prior to the rebirth of the New Moon, are controversial. Some traditions will not cast spells during this period. Others, particularly those devoted to Dark Moon spirits like Hecate or Lilith, consider this a period of profound magical power which may be exploited as needed*

In Arabic folk custom, it's recommended that you keep an eye on moon phases. Whatever you find yourself doing at the moment when you first catch a glimpse of the brand new moon is the right thing for you to do.

Although it doesn't eliminate the need to charge items with personal energy, exposing virtually all magical tools, charms and preparations to the beams of the Full Moon provides enhanced magical empowerment.

In general, although not always, magic worked with the moon herself (rather than just by timing via the phases) is women's magic. There is a trinity between the moon, women, the ocean and, by implication, all water. The moon is recognized as having a profound effect upon menstrual cycles and the tides. It is a reciprocal arrangement: since women have a natural affinity for the moon, they may more readily draw on its power.

In many cases lunar deities are female, with Artemis, Diana, Hecate, Selene, Lady Chang'o and Ix Chel only a few of many examples. In other cases, particularly in ancient Egypt, the moon was perceived as male, but this perception was precisely because of the moon's perceived influence on women. The moon was seen as playing a male role. To the Egyptians, the moon was male because it was demonstrated to have profound control over women's fertility. It was believed that pregnancy could occur from exposure to moonbeams, and who else gets a woman pregnant but a man?

Drawing Down the Moon
This term is most familiar today as the title of Margot Adler's influential book, and refers to specific Wiccan spiritual rites by which the Goddess is requested to enter the body of her priestess and speak through her. (Some traditions also possess a parallel *Drawing Down the Sun* ritual, which invokes the male energy of the god.) However, this is a very ancient term that predates modern Wicca and may refer to various other rites or practices,

depending upon magical tradition, and most especially the process of creating moon-infused waters.

Moon-infused Waters

The ancient Greeks called this technique "*drawing down the moon*" or the "*Thessalian Trick.*" The Greeks believed that Thessalian witches held great power and metaphysical knowledge. This was considered one of their most important formulas.

✳ Lunar Slime

1. Fill a jar or dish to the brim with pure spring water.
2. Bring this container outside and position it so that the full moon is reflected within. Maintain this position for as long as possible.
3. This charged water may now be used as an ingredient in potions and spells, substituted wherever a spell demands water, including **Holy Water.** It ranks among the most profound ingredients of the *materia magica,* right alongside menstrual blood and iron.

Despite its power, its name translates to the less-than-romantic *lunar slime.* To fully understand its power, let's jump across the sea to Africa's Mediterranean coast and a more recent Moroccan magic product.

Moon Foam

The stuff of fairy tales, historically prized by Morocco's witches, Moon Foam is a legendary power-substance that captures the essence of the New Moon. It can:

★ *Enforce a husband or lover's fidelity*
★ *Cure or prevent impotence*
★ *Repair male or female fertility*
★ *Instill mad, crazy passion for whoever uses it*

Obtaining Moon Foam entails a complex ritual, a little more difficult than the *Thessalian Trick,* although there are some suggestions that indicate that similar results were expected from the older spell.

1. Approach the cemetery gates at the New Moon and undress completely.
2. Fill a basin or pitcher with pure spring water and place it in the light of the moon.
3. Mount an oleander branch and gallop around the perimeter of the cemetery counter-clockwise seven times, chanting a "special" incantation as you circumambulate. (The incantation, of course, is a well-kept secret. Either find an old wise witch to whom you can apprentice yourself, or improvise.)
4. Ideally by now your actions have succeeded in attracting the attention of the moon's guardian spirits. If all goes as it should, following the seventh circle around the cemetery, a lunar spirit will manifest herself to you and request that you reveal your desire. Tell her that you want Moon Foam. She will not be overly willing to give it to you.
5. You'll have to negotiate. Make various offers; see what works. If the negotiations are successful, the moon will literally drop down into your water.
6. Eventually the water will contain visible silver foam. Strain it off carefully, like oil from water or scum from soup.
7. Take it home and reserve for future use.

This Chinese technique of drawing down the moon is used to create a magic mirror:

✳ Lunar-charged Magic Mirror

A small round mirror is required, ideally one crafted from precious metals such as gold or silver and ornamented with auspicious symbols of protection and good fortune.

1. On the night of the Full Moon, hold the mirror so that it reflects the moon for a minimum of three hours.
2. When you feel that sufficient lunar energy has been absorbed, wrap the mirror in a protective fabric pouch. This mirror is now off limits to everyone but its owner. Although one person may prepare this mirror for another, once given, the mirror belongs to one person exclusively. The remaining steps of this spell must only be performed by the mirror's owner.
3. For the next consecutive fifteen nights, reflect your face in the mirror over substantial blocks of time, so that the absorbed lunar power merges with your own. This is an interactive process, a sharing of essences: gazing into the mirror, you absorb the lunar gifts of radiance, beauty, psychic ability, and fertility, but the mirror simultaneously is imprinted with your personal power and desires.
4. When the fifteen-night period is complete, the mirror is considered charged and in harmony with the individual who owns it. It is now a profound magical tool for obtaining your wishes and desires.

To use the mirror repeat the initial ritual of drawing down the Full Moon, but now use the mirror as a direct communications device, a sort of personal hot line to the moon, to request gifts of love, marriage, psychic power, creative inspiration, personal fertility, or healing.

Spell-casting in Conjunction with the Power and Assistance of the Spirits

This style of spell-casting is unique. In other methods of spell-casting, the practitioner casts the entire spell from beginning to end. Spirit-oriented spells involve inducing, persuading or coercing a powerful Spirit, usually a specialist in a field, to perform the magical action for you, on your behalf. Thus your spell is cast in order to persuade the Spirit to cast the crucial spell or create the needed magical energy transaction.

This area of magic veers dangerously close to religion and sometimes cannot be separated. In some cases, magical practices are what remain of what were once formal and sometimes very important religions. It is worthwhile, when considering the *permanence* of modern religions, to recall that organized worship of Isis, for instance, was not limited to Egypt but eventually expanded further south in Africa, throughout Western Asia and into Europe as far as what is now modern London, and spanned a period of several thousand years.

Spirits worshipped in religion as *"gods"* and *"goddesses"* are incorporated into magic spells. There is a crucial distinction between magic and religion though: religion may involve devotion to and worship of these spiritual entities. Magic invariably requests a reciprocal, cooperative relationship, although it may be a relationship characterized by love, respect and awe. Both spirit and human are perceived as having needs, which, ideally, are mutually fulfilled by a successful magic spell.

Ultimately the most potent, powerful magic derives from spiritual partnership, working with guardian and allied spirits. This is also for many the most challenging, hard to access and *believe* magic, because it doesn't feel *real* to many people.

It may be hard to believe or comprehend that a rock has a memory, but at least you can hold the rock in your hand. When you're working with spirits, are you actually working with *anything* or is this all just the stuff of myth, fairy tale and make-believe?

Discussions about finding the goddess within, although perhaps extremely valuable from a spiritual or therapeutic perspective, present a further magical obstacle. If the goddess (and, by projection, any other magic power) is truly an aspect of oneself, why bother with any of the physical materials at all? Magic spells are, in general, a partnership between inner and outer powers—powers that are part of you, and those that are distinctly independent from you.

Our limited word pool also compounds the problem. Because we approach spirituality *literally*, we also approach religion. Seemingly neutral simple terms like *god* and *goddess* are actually highly charged with personal meaning and resonance. We think that when we use those terms we are all on common ground, but that's not necessarily so. Some use these terms to indicate supreme creators of the world; others use the terms for any type of spiritual entity. So to level the playing field, let's just use the term *spirits* to name those powerful entities that resist human efforts to define them.

Like magic in general, every people, every culture on Earth, has at one time or another practiced some sort of spiritual interaction. Although it might be suggested today that someone claiming to have personal contact with spirits receive psychiatric counseling, at one time this was a common, if never commonplace, human experience.

Spiritual communication of all kinds, but especially the various methods of requesting spiritual participation in magic spells, exists in very consistent ways all around Earth.

If this seems unreal to you or if, based on religious background, you perceive that contact with spirits is potentially evil, there's good news.

Although this is a powerful form of magic, it's easily avoided. Simply skip those spells and find others. Hoodoo, some of the most powerful magic of all, is practical magic devoid of spiritual encounters, as are many other systems. Work with what empowers you and makes you feel comfortable. On the other hand, if you are devoted to a spirit, you may incorporate spiritual petition into virtually every spell.

There is a host of spirits, legions. There are spirits to serve every purpose, and spirits with a vested interest in every topic. In addition to love spirits, protective spirits, healing spirits, etc., there are spirits of the bathroom, beer and perfume. If something can be conceived, then there is at least one spirit attached to it.

Why do they assist us or even pay attention to us? For a variety of reasons, which ultimately may depend upon the nature of the particular spirit in question. Some are benevolent in general, some may have affection for you specifically; however the basic answer is because it is their job to do so. Dentists take care of teeth, doctors treat the ill and spirits have their own department of expertise. It is thus important to petition the correct spirit for a specific purpose, although the spirits who work most consistently and powerfully for you are always your personal guardians and allies as well as your ancestral spirits.

One person's guardian angel can be someone else's demon: I Corinthians 10:20 describes Pagan sacrifices as being made to demons. The Pagans would have disagreed with that assessment. Many of the spirits invoked in magic may seem obscure today, however once upon a time they were huge stars of the spiritual firmament. The emergence of Christianity and Islam demoted many once-renowned spirits to the side-lines. This does not diminish their potential power. If you're willing to believe that a spirit has the power to assist you, then that spirit should be treated with respect and consideration. Never underestimate the power of even the lowest-level spiritual entity. Furthermore, other spirits, depending upon spiritual tradition, are more vital and empowered today than ever before.

At best, this human/spirit alliance creates mutually beneficial relationships of great affection, love and devotion. There is something of a barter relationship involved: we feed the spirits and they care for us, so that we may feed them more and they may care for us more. The key to this relationship, even more than any other kind of magic, is reciprocity. Make an offering when you make a request. Respond with an acknowledgement of thanks when the request is fulfilled, whether by prayer, gesture or through a gift or offering. Spirits, like people, possess preferences. These practices stem back thousands of years; there's a tremendous quantity of accumulated wisdom. It's not necessary to figure everything out for yourself, although intuition may be divinely inspired.

Spirit Categories

Angels

Angel literally translates as *"messenger"* in Greek, a direct translation from the Hebrew. Unlike other categories of spirits, angels do not accept "offerings," or at least not officially. They are customarily called through prayer, petition and fragrance, although High Ritual Magic, based largely on information attributed to King Solomon, compels the presence of angels through sigils and talismans.

Specific angels maintain charge of all matters of life. There is an Angel of Conception, the Angel of Thieves, angels of various specific countries, and individual guardian angels. According to the Talmud, there are eleven thousand guardian angels per person. If you can think of it, it has a custodial agent.

In general, they are dynamic and fierce; creatures of light so blinding you can't help but see them even with your eyes closed. According to Jewish mysticism, angels are beings of light, but when an angel wishes to manifest in physical form, it takes earth, fashions clothing from it and transforms itself.

Angels are discussed before other spiritual entities because they are somewhat different from others, and because (according to Islamic and Jewish traditions), angels are personally responsible for humanity's ability to cast spells. The Creator may have created magic power but angels taught people how to recognize it and what to do with it. They are our magical teachers.

Christian magic, reflecting theology, demands the existence of angels as creatures of pure goodness (with the exception of the fallen angels, who essentially lost their status as angels during the fall), in clear opposition to demons, who are plainly *"bad."* This is not the case in Islamic, Jewish and Pagan perceptions, where angels are just beings of power. There are good angels, "evil angels" and angels who may be persuaded to behave in either direction. Pious descriptions of "good" angels insist that they are asexual and gender-less, although ironically this is in opposition to the Bible, which describes the lust angels feel for human women (Genesis 6:1–4). Because these women conceive children, we can assume those particular angels to have been male with all working parts intact.

Instead of courting these human women with chocolates and roses, the angels bestowed the gift of knowledge—teaching the arts of astrology, magic, witchcraft and cosmetics (not the triviality it may appear today but an ancient magical art). According to the *Book of Enoch* these teaching angels and their subjects included:

★ *Semjaza: enchantments and root cutting*
★ *Armaros: the resolving of enchantment*
★ *Baraquiel: astrology*
★ *Kokabel: constellations*

- ★ *Ezequeel: knowledge of the clouds*
- ★ *Araquiel: earth signs*
- ★ *Shamsiel: sun signs*
- ★ *Sariel: the phases of the moon*

Angels are ranked in various manners: Archangels, Throne Angels, Watchers, Seraphim and Cherubim among others. The archangels command spirit hosts. Various spells request assistance from the archangels, however whether they are personally expected to appear or to delegate another from their host may be subject to interpretation.

There's little agreement among experts or traditions, particularly as regards to the archangels. Are there seven or are there four? And which ones are they?

The standard four archangels are Rafael, Gabriel, Michael and Auriel, also spelled Uriel or Ariel. That much, at least, is agreed upon in Christian, Islamic and Jewish traditions and probably pre-dates all three. But do they serve alone or are there really seven archangels, corresponding to the seven planets visible with the naked eye and to that magic number, seven? If that's the case, who are the other three? Some possibilities include Cassiel/Kafziel, Zadkiel, Samael, Chamuel, Jophiel, Raziel, Metatron, and Iblis. Even Lucifer makes it onto some lists, although obviously he loses his status after his fall. (Most angels, but not all, have names ending with "*-el,*" El being the ancient pan-Semitic name for the Creator, literally "*the Lord.*")

Demons

Demons are most frequently understood to be evil spirits. This is a misnomer, a perhaps deliberate misinterpretation of the Greek "*daemon,*" which merely indicates one's personal guardian spirit, who may be benevolent, malevolent or both, as the case may be. With the emergence of Christianity as a power, any spirit interaction beyond what was

Enochian magic is a system of "angel magic," conveyed to Dr. John Dee, via the medium Edward Kelley. Dr. Dee, that brilliant, prominent astrologer and magician, chose Queen Elizabeth I's coronation date and served as her advisor. He longed to converse with the angels but was unable to achieve personal contact with them, and so was forced to hire Kelley, an alchemist of ill-repute. Unlike Dee, Kelley had excellent shamanic skills and was able to contact the angels via mirrors and crystal balls. Allegedly the angels in contact with Kelley were identical to those who communicated with the biblical Enoch, hence the name. A high degree of familiarity with classical magic is a prerequisite for working with Dr. Dee's angelic system.

authorized by the Church was perceived as evil. Thus the daemon, once a part of one's personality and existence, was transformed into the demonic.

The word demon is frequently understood, within the context of the classical grimoires, to indicate a low-level malevolent spiritual entity and it is used in that context within this book. In general these low-level entities are anonymous, jealous, maliciously mischievous, and stupid.

Orisha and Lwa

These very similar spirit beings emanate from West Africa. The orisha derive from Yoruba-land, part of modern Nigeria. The lwa derive from Fon traditions in Dahomey/Benin. *"Vodou"* means *"spirit"* in the Fon language.

Adored in their homelands for thousands of years, these spirits accompanied their enslaved devotees to the West. Traditional African religions were outlawed under slavery, devotees were persecuted and the spirits were driven underground, but they were not forgotten. Instead they emerged in great prominence in the latter twentieth century as the foundation of increasingly prominent and influential African-derived spiritual traditions.

The orisha are the presiding spirits of the Santeria religion as well as the Afro-Brazilian cults, such as Candomble, Umbanda and Quimbanda. The Portuguese spelling is *orixa*; many of the same spirits are prominent amongst the different cults. Their names may be spelled differently, sometimes the same spirits use different names, their personalities may even manifest slightly differently depending upon location, but underneath the basic nature remains the same. For instance Oya, Spirit of storm winds and the Niger River retains that name in Cuba but is known as Iansa in Brazil. Her mythology and basic personality remain the same.

The lwa are the presiding spirits of Haitian Vodou as well as its descendants, New Orleans Voodoo and Dominican Vodo. *(lwa* is the modern Kreyol spelling; older French texts may use the term *loa*.)* Although there is an entirely different pantheon of spirits, a few are common to both traditions and the behavior and manifestations of orisha and lwa are similar.

The influence of a few spirits was particularly well-distributed in Africa and thus are common to virtually all African Diaspora traditions. This refers particularly to the trickster Master of the Crossroads, Eshu-Elegbara and Ogun, Spirit and Embodiment of Iron. Although their names may vary depending upon location—particularly that of Eshu who, by nature, enjoys tricks, illusion and confusion—their core essence remains consistent.

Conventional wisdom has it that there are thousands of orisha, but only approximately forty have any interest or dealings with people. These forty, however, are passionately interested and involved with humans.

The official, formal African-derived religions, Santeria and Vodou in particular, continue to expand, attracting new devotees. The orisha and lwa, in addition, are gregarious powers. They're eager to work, eager for attention. Because they are constantly fed, they're full of energy. They will also work with independent practitioners and have been assimilated into some Wiccan, Pagan and Goddess traditions. However, ritual possession, the Spirit's use of a person as a medium, common to a vast number of traditions worldwide, only occurs in the formal, official setting, as it should. These are extremely powerful, potentially dangerous practices that should not be attempted by the novice, the unsupervised or the uninitiated. Ritual possession is a shamanic art, not a magic spell.

There is a formal, lucid, structured way of working with the orisha and lwa, which serves as an excellent model for any spiritual interaction. Vodou and Santeria are monotheistic faiths: there is a supreme deity who created all of existence. This creator, however, prefers to be an overseer.

Olodumare, the Yoruba equivalent of God, created the orisha spirits to supervise creation. Each orisha or lwa is responsible for certain departments of life. Conversely every area of life has its own presiding orisha or lwa. Each individual person also has presiding orisha or lwa, typically a male and a female, the *"masters of your head."* They are your patrons, protectors and advocates—providing you don't anger them too much.

Each orisha and lwa has a distinct personality. Each has a color, number, special foods, plants and objects in which they recognize themselves. Attract their attention by manipulating these things: thus spells invoking the power of Oshun, Spirit of Love and Beauty, inevitably draw upon the color yellow, the number five, water, cinnamon and honey, all of which share Oshun's essence. Petitions to Oya draw upon the color purple and the number nine. The spirits will communicate with you with these colors, numbers and items as well. In general, when Spirits perform a service for you, they want the credit. They will attempt to let you know that they have accomplished the miracle or the magic as the case may be. This system may be used to effectively communicate with Spirits of other pantheons as well.

The orisha most involved in human every-day matters are sometimes invoked as a group and known as the Seven African Powers:

1. Elegba
2. Ogun
3. Obatala
4. Oshun
5. Either Oya or Orunmila, depending on individual tradition
6. Chango
7. Yemaya

By petitioning the orisha as a group, you may rest assured that all your bases are covered. The Seven African Powers provide all of Earth's potential blessings and protections. Commercially manufactured Seven African Powers products frequently depict them in their guise as Roman Catholic saints (see Identification/Syncretism, page 63).

The Exus and Exuas (Pomba Giras)
(Singular, *exu* and *exua*, pronounced "Eh-shoo" and "Eh-shoo-ah.")

The West African trickster orisha Eshu-Elegbara is traditionally the first spirit petitioned during a ritual or spell. Because he controls all doors and the access to roads, Eshu determines whether your petition will be blocked or will reach the proper ears. Similar to the Greek god Hermes, devotees contact him first, propitiate him, then request that he invite and escort any other desired Spirits. Although some traditions encourage everyone to simply contact whom they please directly, others consider this initial communication with a gate guardian to be proper Spiritual protocol.

Eshu, more than most, manifests different aspects of himself in different places and to different people. But then, he is a trickster. In his original West African incarnation, he's young and handsome, always ready for sex and romance. In the Western hemisphere, he rarely displays this side of himself, usually appearing as a deceptively frail old man with a cane or as a young, rambunctious, playful child.

In Brazil, Eshu transformed into a completely different type of spirit, into a class all his own, the exus, multiple personalities, distinct from the other orixa (orisha). Powerful, volatile and dangerous, the exus emphasize the extreme trickster aspects of the spirit. Because an exu is closer in nature to humans than the other orixa, he is the spirit most frequently appealed to for mundane matters, like money and love.

By definition, Afro-Brazilian spiritual paths possess this concept of exu.

Each orixa possesses his or her own exu, who serves as the orixa's personal messenger.

Confused? The confusion only increases.

There are a multiplicity of exus, each with a slightly different nature and slightly different role. There are also female exus, the exuas, except that that term is rarely used. The female aspects of exus are instead known as the Pomba Giras, the whirling doves. Despite the fact that these traditions are grounded strongly in West African spirituality, and despite the fact that exus, in particular, clearly derive from Africa, the Pomba Giras are not completely African. Rather they seem to represent a merging of African traditions with those of the Portuguese Romany, deported en masse to the Brazilian colonies, concurrent with the African slave trade. The pre-eminent Pomba Gira, Maria Padilha, is a deified former Queen of Spain, also known in European magic spells. The superficial image of the Pomba Gira, at least, has little to do with the historic Maria de Padilla, wife of Pedro the First of Castile and Leon, but derives from what is at best an outsider's romantic fantasy of Gypsy women and, at worst, an embodiment of every clichéd, negative stereotype: a promiscuous, hard-drinking prostitute/fortune-teller with a razor hidden in her cheek, a rose clenched between her teeth.

In addition to their function as messengers and servants of the orixa, exus and Pomba Giras may also be petitioned independently, specifically for more selfish, malevolent forms of magic in which the orixa may refuse to participate.

Exus and Pomba Giras are frequently perceived as dangerous and volatile, although this is somewhat in the eye of the beholder. Those who approach exus and Pomba Giras from a purely African or Pagan perspective will find them no more or less volatile than many another spirit. Maria Padilha Pomba Gira, in particular, can be a being of great power and generosity. Because many devotees are also either devout or lapsed Roman Catholics, there is often inherent ambivalence towards magic. Yes, it's powerful but is it *good* in the ethical sense? From this perspective, exus are frequently associated with Satan, the Christian conception of the devil. The qualities that most correspond to this concept are emphasized in the Brazilian concept of the exu: lurking at the crossroads, the smell of brimstone, and assistance that brings ultimate doom.

The Pomba Giras in general are perceived as dangerous, disreputable spirits. Their favorite haunt is a T-crossroad. They prefer working with women but will work with men, if requested. Those who fear them suggest that long-term contact will inspire transvestitism in men and prostitution among both men and women.

The traditional offering for exus are plates of yellow manioc flour cooked in oil or drizzled with oil. Pomba Giras prefer flowers to food. Exus drink wine, rum, and cachaca while Pomba Giras prefer anisette or champagne.

Djinn

These Spirits of Arabia and North Africa preceded Judaism, Christianity and Islam, although they have since traveled the world with Islam, and are found wherever Islam has been established. The word may be unfamiliar but it shouldn't be: these are the legendary *genies*. The word *"djinn,"* also spelled *"jinn,"* derives from old Arabic and is thought to mean *"covert"* or *"darkness."*

In one legend, djinn are created before people, to act as intermediaries between angels and people. In another, Adam and Eve actually had thirty children, not just the sons named in the Bible. One day God asked to see all of them. Eve, not trusting God, hedged her bets, by bringing out only fifteen of her children. (In some versions, she hides the fifteen most beautiful children.) Of course God, being God, immediately knows all and announces that the fifteen hidden children must now remain hidden in the shadows forever, while the fifteen brought out for display may live in the light. The visible children become ancestors of human beings; the hidden children become the djinn and other spirits.

Some djinn are benevolent and helpful to people, others are consistently temperamental, treacherous, jealous and malevolent—the proverbial evil spirits. Many djinn may actually be pagan divinities brought down in the world. There is some conjecture that the most famous, the beautiful, seductive yet dangerous Aisha Qandisha may actually be Astarte left without a temple and forced to hang around deserted hot springs.

Although the djinn are little known at present in the West, this was not always the case. In the 1950s, before the occult entered the mainstream, they were discussed in the most important magical texts and spell-books. To some extent their current lack of attention corresponds with the rise in popularity of the orisha. The orisha are not covert Spirits. Even when devotion to them was forbidden, they found ways around prohibitions through the use of identification/syncretization. The orisha and information about them are easily accessible. Many books are available. Practitioners openly proclaim their devotion. Orisha are willing to work with whoever petitions them with respect. There is a harmonious, mutually beneficial relationship between orisha and human devotees.

Unfortunately, this is not so with the djinn, who can be as ambivalent towards people as people frequently are towards them. Unlike the gregarious orisha, djinn tend to be cautious, secretive and ready to fly.

★ *Djinn are most active at night; they maintain nocturnal business hours. In general they avoid appearances during the day, preferring to sleep and, like many other insomniacs, do not appreciate being disturbed*
★ *Djinn hate salt and fear iron and steel, all of which may be used to expel them. They are attracted and pacified by the telling of stories*

★ *Djinn love heat, deserts and hot climates as well as natural springs, ruins and wild places. They despise cold and snow. Some of them like tricks, although others can be very benevolent. Their traditional offering is given by pouring oil over flour*

Djinn are spiritual devotees too. It's believed that there are Islamic, Jewish, Christian and Pagan djinn. Each prefers to assist humans who share their spiritual orientation. The Islamic djinn, in particular, are said to resent and punish petitions from any but the most devout Muslims, who in theory, of course, will not call them. This is the other factor that keeps the djinn from the spiritual spotlight. The orisha survived because human devotees loved them, depended upon them for spiritual sustenance and magical assistance and risked life and limb to maintain their devotion. However, because the djinn are linked to the more disreputable, counter-cultural aspects of Islamic culture especially, a great many might prefer that they disappear. Their human custodians, those most well-versed in djinn lore, in summoning them, appeasing them, sending them packing as necessary and ritually channeling them, in a similar manner to the orisha, are traditionally the Gnawa people of North Africa, themselves descendants of enslaved sub-Saharans. (*Gnawa* or *Gnaua*, as it is sometimes spelled, is believed to derive from *Ghana*.)

Fairies

This is a vast category of Spirits: included are devas and flower fairies (miniature winged plant spirits), as well as human-sized Fairy Folk, some of whom may or may not actually be human. Unlike the terms orisha or djinn, which refer to very specific types of Spirits, Fairy has become a somewhat generic category for a vast variety of Spirits who may or may not be related. Superficially, what appears to connect them is beauty, seductiveness and a temperamental nature, alternating between benevolent and punitive. This category includes *dakini* from Tibet, *apsaras* from India, *peri* from pre-Islamic Iran, Eastern European *vila* and Romany *keshalyi*, *urme*, and *ursitory*. Prettier, sweeter female djinn are sometimes classified as fairies, too.

Like the angels, fairies have recently been sanitized. This has not always been the case. Once upon a time, not too long ago, fairies were perceived as dangerous spirits. Beyond their superficial appearance, what actually connects these diverse spirits are shared associations with wild nature, forests and flowers, love, sex, women's power, and the birth process—all powerful, potentially dangerous magic.

To some extent, this category of Spirits serves as judges of human ritual behavior. They reward those who properly conduct rituals and punish those who do not. Thus the *vila* famously punish cheating, deceitful men, and those who leave women waiting, abandoned at the altar. They also punish interlopers in the forest—presumably those hunters who no longer maintain spiritually correct hunting rituals. In the tale of *Sleeping Beauty*, the disgruntled fairy vents angry judgment because the ritual offering-table was improperly laid: there were an incorrect number of place settings—someone was left out. (See *Fairy Childbirth Spells*, page 852, for further information on this once common European practice.)

This, of course, is the darker side of Spiritual interaction. The Spirits protect us, and take care of us, because they're stronger than us. Once you enter into a mutually acknowledged relationship with them, it's hard to change the rules or terminate the contract. Even the most devoted of Spirit-workers has been known periodically to mutter against this "*mafia*." Because the magic spell is potentially beneficial for the spirit as well as for the spell-caster, once a relationship is established, the spell cast, it may not necessarily be able to be stopped. Payment, tribute, further interaction is expected, on time, with the implicit threat of "*or else …*"

With the rise of European Christianity, of course, these payments and tributes for the most part ceased, leaving some disgruntled, hungry Spirits. In addition, once-powerful Spirits, the proverbial "goddesses," were frequently demoted to Fairy-status, particularly in Ireland. Aine, Spirit of the Sun, a powerful, dynamic, versatile Spirit, for instance, becomes considered one of several Queens of Fairy, as does her compatriot Maeve. These are not Spirits to be trifled with. No wonder the Fairies, for whom Fairy Tales are named, are frequently so grouchy.

In certain parts of Europe, France in particular, witches were accused of consorting with Fairies rather than with the devil. During the French witch craze (basically the period between Joan of Arc and the end of the seventeenth century), a legal conviction for consorting with fairies automatically earned a sentence of hard labor. Attempts were made during her trial for heresy to depict Joan of Arc, herself, as a devotee of the Fairy Folk.

Anthropologists and historians offer yet another possible explanation for Fairies. Based on frequent descriptions of Fairies as nomadic, wandering folk, dwelling in wild forested areas in temporary beehive-like structures, some consider that the Romany were understood to be Fairies by the sedentary people who observed them. Fairies are described as supernatural, dark, small people in an area mostly populated by tall, fair people, brightly dressed in glad-rags during a time of conservative repression. Both Romany and Fairies have associations with magic and divination and suffer accusations of baby snatching and child stealing. Who knows? Perhaps buried within fairy lore are European perceptions of early, fleeting contact with the Romany.

Of course, to complicate matters further, the Romany themselves have a vast, complex, fairy tradition of their own. Their fairies are very clearly spiritual beings. According to Romany fairy tradition, for instance, the history of disease as we know it is largely caused by a series of tragic, sexual assaults inflicted by the King of Demons on the beautiful, fertile Queen of Fairy.

Various other types of spirits are summoned to assist with the casting of magic spells, including elementals (salamanders, undines and similar) and mermaids.

- ★ Offerings depend on the type of fairy invoked. The full-sized ones are said to prefer milk and berries. According to the Elizabethans, fairies revel in thyme. They love the aroma. Thus the best way to see fairies is to surround yourself with the fresh herb: eat it, grow it, and bring it into your home

- ★ Flower fairies, butterfly-sized winged nature spirits, the model for all modern sanitized fairies, are easier to summon and propitiate. They can be petitioned to bestow and enhance botanical powers. All you really need is a garden for an invitation to be extended. (A garden in pots outside may work; flower fairies do not like to venture indoors for extended periods.) Fill the garden with birdbaths, a source of water, charms, statues, witch balls and crystals. Plant the botanicals that they love: berries, chamomile, Corsican mint, forget-me-nots, foxglove, hibiscus, hollyhocks, honeysuckle, lavender, lilac, milkweed, morning glories, pansies, peonies, primroses, vincas and violets. In general, fairies prefer wild flowers to cultivated blooms. Leave the garden a little wild for them. Attract birds and butterflies, the fairies will follow them and help you cast your spells

- ★ A circle of ash saplings is a fairy dance ground. If you don't pull them up, the fairies will remain. Alternately make circles for them from clear quartz crystals

- ★ Romany legend says that stinging nettles guard the doorways to fairyland. Grow some and find out

- ★ Burn Flower Fairy Incense outside to attract them: equal parts dried hollyhock and rosemary

Saints

Whether fairies are spirits or humans may be subject for debate. Many Spirits, from orishas, to those of ancient Greece and ancient Hawaii, may or may not be deified humans. The important orisha Chango, for instance, was once a king in Yorubaland. After death, he was deified and took his place among the orisha. That's one version of his sacred story, anyway. The ancient Greeks demonstrated this process when Heracles and Psyche, both originally mortals, were permitted to shed their human energy and enter the Realm of the Divine.

Saints, however, are resolutely human—or at least they were when they were alive. Because the word *saint* has become so strongly associated with Roman Catholicism, it often comes as a surprise to realize that a concept of sainthood, albeit not an identical concept, exists among many other cultures, including the African Diaspora, Buddhist, Jewish, and Muslim traditions.

Roman Catholic saints are required to fulfill certain expectations before sainthood is officially conferred, and it can be a lengthy, bureaucratic process to prove their miraculous deeds. Other traditions use different criteria: sometimes the magic power (*heka, baraka*) contained by a person is so potent that it defies death, allowing others to continue to access it, for purposes of healing and magic. For many traditions, power of this magnitude is what confers sainthood. It is usually an informal process. There's no official beatification or canonization: word of miracles simply gets around. Shrines spring up and crowds gather.

The behavior of these saints may or may not be exemplary. Many are described as devout, charitable, generous people, although others demonstrate what might be characterized as *profligate tendencies*. Regardless, a saint's great power, *baraka*, is accessible to those in need.

Marie Laveau, the self-proclaimed Pope of Voodoo born in 1792, has ascended to this concept of sainthood. Thousands venture to her grave in New Orleans annually to beseech her for favors. In particular, Laveau has earned an excellent reputation for remedying legal issues, as she did during her life. Attempts to contact her are made by knocking three times on the front of her tomb or by drawing three x's in red brick dust or chalk on the stone. Offerings and payments are left, most customarily salt water or seven dimes.

What is euphemistically called "*folk Catholicism*" has been the bane of the Roman Catholic Church for centuries. The desire to work with a saint, as with a spirit, or perhaps the desire of the saint or spirit to work with the person, is too strong to resist: magical practices creep in. Certain official Vatican-approved saints are also frequent participants in magic spells, particularly Saint Anthony, San Cipriano, Saint Martha the Dominator, Saint George and John the Baptist. A saint's magic powers may have little to do with their official hagiography: Saint Anthony, for instance, is invoked in almost as many love spells as Aphrodite. San Cipriano may or may not have been a reformed wizard in real life, but as far as magic spells are concerned, he's returned to his old profession with gusto. When they are invoked for magic, these saints are treated like any other Spirit: offerings and payment are made for miracles begged and received. Saints, like spirits, have favored numbers, colors, fragrances and gifts.

Unofficial Saints

The impulse to work with saints can be too powerful to wait for permission—or sometimes even to ask for permission. This isn't a problem with traditions with no "*official*" concept of sainthood. In a sense, all Jewish saints, for example, are "*unofficial.*" There's no authority or criteria to make them official, although popularity conveys its own kind of official status. It's between saint and person. What happens, however, within a system where these criteria do exist? What happens when, during what usually starts as a local phenomenon, people begin to recognize a saint's capacity for miracles, without official recognition? Will people be patient and wait for the official verdict or will they create their own rituals? For those who are inclined to magic, the choice is obvious.

So-called *"unofficial saints"* are invariably tied to the Roman Catholic tradition, because it is the only tradition that insists on a lengthy organized bureaucratic procedure of conferring sainthood. There is a vast range of unofficial saints. What they have in common are consistent miracles performed following death. They may be accessed in magic spells in similar fashion to any other Spirit.

Identification / Syncretism

Syncretism is the system by which one spirit is identified or fused to varying degrees with another. Although the process is most commonly and consciously associated with modern African-Diaspora faiths the tradition goes back millennia.

When the ancient Greeks began to travel their world, they encountered other people (Egyptians, Persians) with other pantheons. This frustrated them. Although they didn't insist on one god, they did insist on their own gods. Who were these other spirits? In some cases, spirits from abroad (Dionysus, Hecate) were merged into their own pantheon. In other cases, the Greeks decided, other cultures simply used other names and told other stories about spirits who were the same as the Greek gods. Thus they created a system of identification: Hathor was a beautiful Spirit of love, who liked perfume and music. She must be Aphrodite, also a beautiful Spirit of love, who liked perfume and music. Although sometimes neat, obvious identifications can be made sometimes this leads to confusion. The Persian Spirit, Anahita, was a beautiful deity interested in human romantic and reproductive matters. Obviously she was identified as Aphrodite (identification means

she *was* Aphrodite), but Anahita also had a martial aspect, driving a chariot, leading men to war. Therefore she must be Athena, too.

Identification therefore attempts to identify one spirit within another. Syncretism takes this a step further. One spirit wears the mask of another. When one pantheon is outlawed, the only way to continue devotion to now-banned spirits is to pretend that you're worshipping others. This is precisely what happened to enslaved Africans in the Western hemisphere. Forbidden to practice their own faith, they accommodated it to another. Syncretism permits forbidden spirits to wear acceptable masks. Syncretism also means that acceptable saints are incorporated into magic spells in surprising ways because, in essence, they are fronting for that forbidden someone else. How else can one reconcile the conventional and devout *"official"* Saint Anthony of Padua with the witch-doctor persona he displays so powerfully and benevolently in a multitude of magic spells?

Spirits, like magic in general, are fluid in nature. Shape-shifting isn't hard for them, even without conscious syncretism. Hence India's Durga is an aspect of Parvati. In a moment of terrible stress, Durga unleashed her alter ego, Kali. All three are aspects of one, but all three are distinct beings, too. Confused? Well, you should be, it *is* confusing.

The realm of the spirits is like a journey through a dream landscape. Syncretism only increases the confusion.

Because the syncretism of the African slaves was born of desperation, quick, frequently visual identifications were made. Slaves were forbidden to practice their own religions but were permitted Roman Catholic chromolithographs of saints. They scoured them, looking for coded references to the orisha and lwa. Sometimes these identifications really work: Ogun, Spirit of Iron, was syncretized with the archangel Michael because in his most famous image Michael wields a sword. Yet they genuinely have much in common: both are tireless workers and warriors on behalf of human safety. Michael even has his own associations with iron. Sometimes syncretism is surreal: Chango, that most virile Spirit of Fire and Lightning is syncretized to the virgin martyr Saint Barbara, because her chromolithograph depicts a lightning bolt.

The first generation to engage in syncretization is conscious of what they're doing. After that, though, all bets are off. At what point, if any, do these Spirits genuinely fuse? Perhaps Saint Peter, syncretized to road-opener Elegba because of his keys, really *is* Elegba or vice-versa. And if you're invoking Saint Peter in a magic spell, are you really invoking the saint or Elegba, hiding within, even if, after three generations, the orisha is no longer remembered?

Santeria earned its name, "religion of the saints," because of syncretism. Those who emphasize Roman Catholic ties prefer to emphasize the saints or perhaps a combination. Those who emphasize African roots prefer to emphasize the orisha or perhaps a combination. Others can no longer separate saint from orisha; true fusion has occurred for them. In Brazil, there have been calls to end syncretism as it is no longer necessary.

Were authorities truly unaware of the slaves' subterfuge? It's hard to say. This system of identifying and syncretizing spirits is present whenever one faith demands that another abandon and deny its spirits. Sometimes religious authorities presented syncretism to a population to make the new religion palatable. Hence, Goddess Aine becomes a Fairy Queen. She remains accessible to old devotees in that role, if not in her old one, which was perceived as dangerous to the new religious authority. Celtic Spirit Brigid, the Druid's daughter, becomes identified with Saint Brigid. They merge; where one stops and the other starts becomes very difficult to determine.

Sometimes however this process backfires. In the case of Maximon, also known as Brother Simon, missionaries' attempts to assimilate the Guatemalan spirit Maam with Saint Simon backfired. Maximon, spirit of male primal energy, defied boundaries and took on a life of his own. The Church then attempted to syncretize him with Judas Iscariot or even with the devil. This only enhanced Maximon's outlaw image, making his devotees love him even more. Although intended to merge, to syncretize, with an "*official*" saint, Maximon instead has emerged as a powerful "*unofficial*" saint.

Sometimes syncretism occurred so long ago that the original spirit hiding underneath is completely forgotten. The only way to recognize that syncretism *may* have occurred is the observation that the saint behaves strangely in an *un-saint-like* manner. This applies particularly to the Big Three of Magical Catholic Saints, Saint Anthony, Saint George, and John the Baptist. Although perhaps completely forgotten spirits lurk within, many believe that under their respective masks lie Hermes, Baal, and Adonis.

Spell-casting with Words

Working magical practitioners tend to have a loose definition of what constitutes a magic spell. Once one becomes truly involved with magic and spell-casting, every action of the day can become transformed into a magic spell. Scholars of magic, particularly those who study a topic that fascinates them but in which they don't actually *believe*, may have more rigid definitions. For many, verbal spells are the strictest definition of what constitutes a spell.

Technically, the use of the word "*charm*" to indicate a "*lucky charm*" is a misnomer. Lucky charms are talismans, amulets or magically empowered items. "*Charm*" derives from the same source as "*Carmen*" or "*carol*," as in a Christmas song, and indeed *charm* at its most archaic means a song. To be *en-chanted* literally means to be under the magical influence of a chant. By the strictest, most scholarly definition of a magic spell, every spell should have a verbal component, preferably sung, and perhaps only a verbal component. Certain magical traditions do emphasize this verbal component, particularly traditional Russian magic and modern Pow-Wow. However, this strict definition can only be used in an abstract, theoretical scholarly setting; it doesn't take into account either the realities of magic or the needs of many spell-casters.

Great, renowned systems of magic, such as those belonging to the Finn and Saami traditions, are under-represented in this book. Their magical systems were traditionally based on each individual practitioner's unique repertoire of songs and thus cannot be reproduced in book form. Legendary practitioners were able to sing magic into fruition; any practitioner worth his or her salt, for instance, allegedly possessed a song that could stop a wound from bleeding.

This desire to insist upon a verbal component to every spell is very Eurocentric. This emphasis on the magic power of words doesn't necessarily exist or at least not to the same extent in traditions from Asia and Africa. That said, the power of words in magic spells is profound. Words convey power and intent and can be used to create realities where none existed previously, which is, after all, the goal of many magic spells. Words, sounds and syllables may possess their own inherent power in the same fashion that minerals and botanicals do. Zora Neale Hurston, the author and scholar/practitioner of magic, on considering the origins of magic and magic spells, suggested that God was the original Hoodoo Doctor, having spoken the world into creation with magic words.

Verbal components, like spiritual petition, may be incorporated into any spell. However, words are tricky and subject to individual taste. The classic is *abracadabra*: some perceive it as a word of power, others as an old joke. The verbal component of the spell has to suit the spell-caster's taste, otherwise it can derail the whole spell.

Some tips on spell-casting language:

★ *Repeating the words of a magic spell should never make you feel foolish, stupid, self-conscious or uncomfortable. Change the words to suit your taste and temperament. It will undoubtedly not be the first or last time they are changed*

★ *The majority of the spells in this book are traditional. Not every traditional spell has a verbal component, however where traditional verbal components of spells exist they have been retained. Many spells feature archaic language—language as it's no longer spoken and perhaps never was. An attempt to enhance magical ambience often means resorting to pseudo-archaic language. Some enjoy throwing "thees," "thous," and "forsooths" into spells. This author isn't among them. In general, except where archaic language was somehow intrinsic to the spell or to conveying its specific character, I've used modern language, updating and adjusting where necessary, because magic spells, no matter how ancient their roots, are a modern art, not relegated to the dusty past. However if you like all those "thees" and "thous," if you enjoy archaic language, if it enhances your sense of magical ambience, adjust the spells to suit your taste and put them back*

★ *Many associate the verbal component of spells with rhymes. If you enjoy rhymes, that's fine, however rhymes are not required. The advantage of rhymes is that they're easily remembered, which can be crucial if it's a spell that requires you to exactly repeat incantations at intervals, however what is being said is almost invariably more important than the literary devices used to say it*

★ *It is crucial that the verbal component of a spell express your goals and desires accurately, concisely and without ambiguity, because living magical forces sometimes enjoy playing tricks. Change and adapt as needed. Make up your own words, keeping them simple and to the point or use words composed by others that best express your desires. Psalms are traditionally used in this way; poems or the lyrics of your favorite songs may be able to articulate your desires and goals more accurately than any ancient charm*

USE THE PRESENT TENSE WHEN CASTING A SPELL

Thus a spell for luck proclaims, *"I am lucky,"* not *"I will be lucky."* Keeping it in the present tense serves to create reality, the goal of spell-casting, while the future tense keeps your desires tantalizingly just out of reach. When in doubt, Motown songs are always easily incorporated into spells because the lyrics are direct and almost always expressed in the present tense! (*"Money, that's what I want,"* for instance, or *"He's back in my arms again."*)

Speaking the Spell

Verbal components of spells are usually spoken aloud, however not all spells are spoken the same way. There are different techniques of speaking and enunciating used in spell-casting. Directions are incorporated into the text of the spells but you must understand these directions in order to put them to best effect.

Murmuring and Muttering

In many cases, the verbal component of the spell is not meant to be easily understood by others. This is not necessarily or only because of secrecy. In these spells, you are actually interjecting the power of your words *into* something, even if only the atmosphere, but more frequently into an object. A classic and simple spell is to murmur words over a glass of water, transforming it into a potion. By then giving it to another to drink, you are magically transferring and transmitting your magical message and directions.

Announcing and Chanting

Sometimes, however, words are used to express and announce one's intentions and desires to the universe or towards a specific magic power. In that case, words need to be clearly understood. Articulate distinctly, expressively and at a volume that you deem appropriate.

⬟ Key Concepts for Casting Magic Spells

Although one can just start casting spells, learning by trial and error, understanding certain key concepts boost the chances of a spell-caster's success.

Thresholds

Magic energy radiates from everything and everyone that occurs naturally on Earth to varying degrees, or is derived from naturally occurring parts. Some objects are sources of greater power than others. Frankincense, roses and wild Syrian rue, for instance, permit greater access to magic power than many other botanicals. Certain *areas* are also sources of greater power than others, with "area" meant both in a literal and a metaphoric way.

Thresholds are border areas where one force, power or element encounters another. These meeting areas are potentially the most highly magically charged of all. Thresholds exist everywhere: the seashore, that transitional area where ocean meets land; the foot of mountains, where land begins to rise; and caves, the subterranean thresholds between Earth's outer and inner powers.

There are architectural thresholds: doors and windows. There are thresholds in time: twilight and dawn, where an incoming power approaches before the outgoing power has completely dispersed. Life cycles are thresholds: the birth of a new baby, particularly a first child whose birth transforms someone into a parent. Death is a threshold between one existence and the next. Someone who lingers in a half-life is described as having a foot in both worlds, straddling the threshold. Any transformative ritual is defined as a threshold, by virtue of its very capacity to transform. There are thresholds on the body: the mouth is the threshold between thought and speech.

Thresholds are simultaneously the areas of greatest magical potential and also of extreme vulnerability. A vast percentage of protective amulets, rituals and spells are designed to guard thresholds and the transformative process. In fact, every magic spell can be perceived as a transformative threshold, from a past that has left something to be desired towards the future that the spell hopefully produces.

Most thresholds consist of a simple boundary: with one foot you stand inside the house, with another you stand outside. If your feet are small enough and your balance is good, you can stand poised, neither inside, nor outside.

With one foot you stand in the river or ocean, with the other, you stand on the land. The ancient Egyptians called their country *"the land of the red and the black,"* because there was a distinct division, a visible dividing line between the black fertile land of Nile silt and the stark red land of the desert. You could literally stand with one foot in each color. Each color also typified a different kind of magic and a different spiritual ruler. The black belonged to Osiris, with his arts of orderly civilization; red belonged to his brother Seth, anarchic, chaotic Lord of Magic.

These are simple boundaries: you can hop from one to the other. There are also expanded, exponentially super magically charged thresholds.

The Crossroads

The crossroads are literally where different roads meet and where they separate, where opportunity emerges to change directions. They are unpredictable; you could take any one of a variety of choices. Magically speaking a crossroads is the place where multiple forces converge, where anything can happen, where transformations may occur. Energy is liberated and expanded at the crossroads. Instead of hopping over boundaries, you can stand in the center and be inundated by power, potential and choices.

There are four-way crossroads and three-way crossroads—the proverbial fork in the road. A classic movie scene, albeit one that occurs in real-life if you've ever been lost in the country, shows someone arriving at a fork in the road. With no identifying road-sign in sight, our hero or heroine is forced to choose a road. Choose either one and your destiny may be altered forever. Crossroads offer the opportunity for transformation, for a change of direction, a change in destiny.

Crossroads are ubiquitous in magic. Many spells demand to be cast at the crossroads; others require that the remnants of spells—left-over candle stubs, ashes and the such—be buried at the crossroads, where their energy can safely disperse.

Specific types of spiritual entities, known as *"road-openers"* and inevitably beings of great power, preside over crossroads. These beings can be petitioned for knowledge, information and for a change in destiny. They control thresholds and roads and determine who has free access and who finds roads barred, who will choose the right fork in the road and who will wander hopelessly lost forever.

In ancient Greece, Hermes ruled the four-way crossroads, while Hecate presided over three-way crossroads, her epithet *Hecate Trivia* emphasizing this aspect. *Trivia*, from which the English *trivial* derives, literally means *three roads*.

In West Africa, Eshu-Elegbara rules the crossroads, as does his Western hemisphere incarnations Elegba, Papa Legba and Exu. In Brazil, Exu's female counterpart, Pomba Gira, presides over T-shaped crossroads.

Once upon a time, crossroads were where people met, where nomads rendezvoused, where gallows stood, where the death penalty was enacted and corpses left to hang, where suicides were buried. If magic spells were cast according to direction, then midnight at the crossroads must have frequently been a crowded, busy place, especially on a night like Halloween when the veil that divides the realms of living and dead is at its most permeable, leaving an open road for inter-realm communication.

Christian authorities frequently urged people to avoid the crossroads, particularly at night, as it was the devil's stomping grounds. If you were looking to meet Satan, however, if you had a proposition or a request for him, the crossroads was where you were most likely to find him. When legendary bluesmen Tommy and Robert Johnson journeyed to the crossroads to trade their souls for musical ability, were they looking for this devil or for the sometimes lame, Papa Legba, or could anyone even tell the difference anymore? (See Identification/Syncretism, page 63.)

Unfortunately, the most accessible modern crossroads are traffic intersections. The magic energy remains, however. Think about a busy intersection: on a good day you fly straight through, making a journey faster and easier. A traffic tie-up, however, is an energy build-up with added potential for accidents and road rage.

Faithfully attempting to follow a spell's directions may leave you playing in the middle of traffic. In Rio de Janeiro, Pomba Gira's devotees take this into account: offerings aren't left where you might expect, at the center of the crossroads, but by the side of the road. No matter how powerful your spell, it will have no opportunity to work if you get hit by a car during the casting. Find an appropriate old-fashioned crossroads, a safe area of a modern crossroads, or read between the lines—figure out what the spell *really* requires (*why* you're being sent to the crossroads, for what purpose) and adapt and substitute as needed.

Not all crossroads are literal intersections of roads. Magic spells also emphasize other, very specific crossroads.

The Cemetery

The cemetery is the threshold between the realms of the living and the dead. It too is a place of transformation. Many spells demand that a spell either be cast in the graveyard or that spell remnants be buried there, as if one were conducting a funeral. These include protection, banishing and love spells as well as hexes. Significantly, many necromantic spells, spells for communicating with those who have passed on to the next life, do *not* require a trip to the cemetery.

The cemetery, like the more general crossroads, swirls with energy, albeit of a more specific kind: ghosts, souls of the departed, abstract life and death forces, spiritual entities, protective guardians and those malevolent beings who are attracted to grief or decay all make their home in the cemetery.

Whether the cemetery is a benevolent or a threatening place depends largely on cultural perceptions of what happens to the soul after death. Cultures that depend on protective ancestral spirits rarely fear the cemetery; cultures who believe that human memory and emotion truly dies, leaving nothing but a hungry, destructive ghost will avoid the graveyard except for purposes of malevolent magic.

The Pros and Cons of the Graveyard

The cemetery is the place where dangerous entities lurk, dangerous people, too! Although a Greek word, the term "*necropolis*," city of the dead, stems from ancient Egypt. Once upon a time, the devastatingly poor made their home amongst the graves. This situation still exists in many places, to greater or lesser extent. On the other hand, cemeteries are places of great neutral power (think of all that swirling radiant energy!), which is able to be harnessed for good or evil, as the practitioner intends or desires.

Even in the cemetery, bypassing actual gravesites, certain areas are more packed with power than others. The threshold of the threshold, so to speak, is at the cemetery gates. Older cemeteries traditionally feature iron gates to provide this boundary. Iron, with the exception of menstrual blood, is the single most protective substance on Earth and will repel and contain malevolent spirits and ghosts. Many spells request that items be left at the cemetery gates: this is not because people were afraid to enter the graveyard itself, but because that threshold is so much more powerful.

Many powerful spirits, such as India's Kali and Shiva, Matron and Patron of Tantra, reside in the cemetery, as does ancient Egypt's road-openers, Anubis, the jackal-headed inventor of embalming, and Wepwawet, a wolf deity. (Say the name fast and hear that wolf cry.)

Accessing the power of crossroads and cemeteries is common to most magical traditions, to varying extents. Specific other traditions recognize and incorporate still other crossroads.

The Bathhouse

Prior to the advent of private, indoor plumbing, the public bathhouse was a place of great social importance, a crossroads to which everyone eventually came. Its purpose was not only hygienic and social but spiritual and magical, too.

In the days before privacy, public bathhouses were required for spiritual cleansing rituals as well as physical ones. The bathhouse attendant, now most frequently a lowly janitorial occupation, was once a respected, and perhaps feared, ritual leader who wielded great power. In many cases they might be the only ones privy to occult secrets.

Many traditions still retain the equivalent of a bathhouse: the Jewish mikveh, the Native American sweat lodge, the Aztec temescal. Not all bathhouses feature water, as the sweat lodge demonstrates. Finnish saunas and Turkish steam baths access other methods. In the same way, cleansing spells (see pages 185–223) are as likely to use smoke, sound or other methods as water. The bathhouse, whether wet or dry, was frequently the scene of many threshold experiences:

★ *Babies were born in bathhouses*
★ *Preparation for brides and sometimes grooms occur in the bathhouse*
★ *Cultures that isolate menstruating women frequently have rituals held in the bathhouse to signal her return to society at large*
★ *Bodies are prepared for funeral rites in the bathhouse*

The frequency of these experiences in the bathhouse would exponentially increase the potential power contained within.

The bathhouse is the descendant of ancient springs, each the home of resident magic spirits. Many bathhouses were built on the site of springs, and the spirits took up residence in the new bathhouse. Water spirits, like the nature of their element, are frequently volatile, replete with treasure, but also with dangerous currents. These can be tremendously benevolent spirits (water spirits rank among the most powerful love spirits), but you have to know how to handle them. With the coming of Christianity and Islam, rites of devotion and pacification were forbidden and abandoned. Many spirits packed up and left; those remaining, starved of attention, are frequently grouchy. Thus the bathhouse is both a place of power and danger. Enter alone to access the spirits or avoid entering alone so that the spirits cannot access you!

Russian magic, in particular, manifests this ambivalence and will direct many spells to be performed in the bathhouse, usually at midnight.

Ruins

Ruins of buildings and cities, particularly (but not necessarily) those that met their ruin in violence, are perceived as swirling with power. This is the stuff of fairytale: the European witch convicted purely because she has been gathering herbs amidst the ruins. It's not like there's any other reason to be there, the witch hunters say. Indeed, some of the most powerful magical herbs, mugwort and Syrian rue, thrive best amongst ruins. Many practitioners believe that these botanicals, already more powerful than most, are at the height of their power when picked there, especially at midnight, twilight or just before dawn.

Stone ruins are most powerful because stone, although silent, is in magical terms hardly inanimate.

Stone is believed to retain memories of whatever occurs in its vicinity. Those memories may be accessed by those who know how.

Souls of those who perished in the ruins may linger, as may others drawn to the site. They may be accessed, if you dare. Djinn not found lurking in the desert, behind doorways or at natural springs will be found amidst ruins, the more broken the better. If you want to access them, that's where you'll find them. If you're afraid they'll access you, hurry past without stopping.

Altars

Crossroads and cemeteries are places of power precisely because they allow energy extra space and opportunity to radiate. Sometimes you want the opposite effect, a concentration of energy. The need is to concentrate power and energy in one spot, a focal spot, the very center of the crossroads, if you will. An altar allows you to do this.

Many spells direct that you build an altar.

Although the term is used by many religions to indicate an area dedicated to a deity, this may or may not be the case magically speaking. An altar at its most basic magical definition is a tableau or arrangement of specific articles. Small children are inveterate builders of tableaux, with no conscious conception of religious devotion. They simply pick up power objects and arrange them. For practice, pick any theme, magical or not, and devote a shoe-box diorama or a table top to it.

The simplest ancestral altar consists of a white candle and a glass of water. The most complex Vodoun altar is an entire room, with each object carefully chosen and arranged meticulously. Nothing on an altar, whether simple or lavish, is random or arbitrary. If it's there, it's there for a reason.

Altars are generally erected for one or both of the following reasons:

As a communication device to summon a spirit. By adjusting objects, colors, and fragrances, you send out a specific signal requesting attention. Thus the Yoruba deity or orisha, Oshun, recognizes herself in the spectrum of colors from yellow to orange, in certain types of flowers, in honey and cinnamon. Her objects include peacock feathers and mirrors. Her number is five. The concentration of special themed objects catches her attention and invites her presence. Ideally she'll drop by to see what's going on. Because certain objects may be shared between deities (Aphrodite, Juno, Kybele, and Maria Padilha all love roses, although not necessarily the same color or number, and Maria Padilha prefers hers with long stems but no thorns), the more specific and detailed the tableau, the more likely you are to summon the right spirit.

Altars may be erected in tribute, as an offering of thanks for previous favors or as part of a petition process.

As a means of concentrating energy. An altar can be devoted to a spell, not necessarily to any kind of spiritual entity. Spells that are conducted over an extended period of time, for instance nine-day spells, may benefit from a concentrated area: the spell doesn't blend in to the background but remains distinct, its boundaries and thresholds clear. Thus all objects involved in the spell (and some spells may involve several candles plus assorted dishes and objects) are arranged together in formation.

Altars are most frequently placed atop flat furniture surfaces—dressers, bookshelves and coffee tables. Old-fashioned televisions built into wooden cabinets were once popular altar areas.

There are a wide variety of altars beyond the tabletop tableau. Candle spells require that an altar be kept in plain sight, and many prefer this method because the constant visual presence of the altar empowers many spells. However, it is not necessary. An altar may also be maintained discreetly, within a cabinet or closed box: a shadow box altar. Miniature altars can be created within old-fashioned cigar- and match-boxes.

- ★ One might also consider an altar a method of demarcating sacred space
- ★ A spell may be cast by creating an altar; similar to feng shui, articles and objects are arranged to create a desired energy transformation
- ★ Although some spells specify creating one, even when it isn't suggested, an altar may always be incorporated
- ★ Likewise, if you are seriously challenged for space, remember, magic is always about improving your life. The goal of magic is to eliminate difficulties and stress, not produce new ones. If you have no room for a formal altar, delineate space as possible. Plenty of people burn candles in the bathtub; you won't be the first

Altars may also be created outside. A garden, window box or flowerpot can contain a living altar, an Earth altar. The possibilities are endless.

Altars may be intensely private or public: visualize the roadside shrines frequently erected at the site of fatal accidents. French Caribbean altars are created in sheltered places within tree trunks. If a statue is placed within the tree, passers-by can come with offerings of flowers and candles. Spells of petition dedicated to the Brazilian spirit Maria Padilha invariably begin with directions to lay black and red cloths on the ground: you are demarcating the spell's space, effectively setting up an altar. Spells dedicated to deities of the sea often instruct you to dig a shallow pit in the sand, within which to burn candles. That hole in the sand becomes the altar.

Altars can be created from anything and erected anywhere. Water spirits, for instance, frequently prefer the bathroom to other rooms of the house,

as the most watery place. A shrine (essentially a more lavish altar) dedicated to mermaids belongs in the bathroom rather than in another room that might be considered more "spiritually appropriate." Spirits dedicated to love prefer altars in the bedroom where they can supervise and stimulate activity. Intellectual spirits like Yoruba's Oya or India's Sarasvati prefer their altars to be placed near books. Access the childlike, creative playful part of yourself and it's not difficult to build an altar.

Objects may decorate an altar or serve *as* the altar. Watermelons are sacred to the Yoruba spirit, Yemaya. Place a slice on her altar to call her. Hollow out a watermelon, insert some candles and the watermelon has *become* the altar. Wood may be used as altar decoration but also as the altar. This is particularly true of special sacred woods, such as sandalwood or aloes wood. Sometimes the deity *is* the wood. Hera was represented by the oak in

Greece, while Diana was represented by that wood throughout Europe. A log segment is given center-stage, dressed with oil and adorned with ornaments, small candles or charms.

Unsurprisingly, the bed serves as the altar for many love spells: sheets are sprinkled with powder; power objects are tucked beneath the mattress and the pillows. Botanicals may hang over the bed or candles burn alongside it.

The body serves as an altar in many spells, particularly those for healing, love and protection. Oil and powder may be applied to the body in the same manner as to a candle. Henna and other body decoration transforms the body into a living altar. Next time you get dressed, as you apply cosmetics, jewelry and other ornaments, consider that you are dressing your altar—an altar that serves to communicate with other beings and concentrates your power and energy.

Not every crossroads is a location: a formal magic spell is a crossroads where the inherent magic energies of the spell's components converge. The result of the spell is the symbiotic reaction to that convergence.

Balance

Consider the herbalist's scales: things are carefully weighed out to achieve a desired balance. Magic plays with balance, too. Sometimes the desire is for all forces to be equal and harmonious. At other times goals are accomplished by deliberately, consciously tipping the scales to provide the required effect.

Left and Right

Once upon a time, not too long ago, the concept of Dualism associated the direction *right* with God, high, male, and all those good things. Thus children were forced to use their right hands, *the dexterous hand*, whether that was their naturally dominant hand or not. Children who were naturally left-handed (*the sinister hand*) literally had it beaten out of them until they were dexterous too. Consider various phrases: *in the right, Mr. Right, the left-hand path, a left-handed compliment.*

Connections between genders and these directions, however, predate Dualism *and* Christianity. They exist in completely unrelated cultures, including some that were isolated for a very long time. Hawaiian magic, for instance, associates left with female, right with male as surely as the Chinese and many Asian, African and European traditions. Frequently offerings to female deities are made with the left hand (by both men and women) while offerings to males are made with the right (by both men and women). Feng shui suggests that it's beneficial for women to sleep on the left side of a common bed, while a man should sleep on the right. (Although spells intended to reverse the power dynamic within a relationship may suggest those sides be switched.)

Sometimes spells direct that an action be performed with either your left or right hand. Either one of two things is being requested.

★ *Because left is yin and yang is right, the left side of everyone's body is yin or affiliated with "female forces" while the right side is yang and affiliated with "male forces." Most frequently a spell's success depends upon accessing one force or emphasizing one quality over the other*

★ *Sometimes the spell's success depends upon not using your dominant hand. Because until recently everyone was forced to be right-handed, many older spell books will specify casting a spell with your left hand, because it's assumed that everyone is right-handed. This is, obviously, no longer the case*

Where the importance lies in not using your dominant hand, this is specified in spell-directions.

Left-handed people will be directed to use their right hands. Where no such direction is given, if the only stipulation is to use your left hand, then this applies to everyone across the board.

Materia Magica

Spells utilize various items and materials. Many items occur naturally on Earth (rocks, metals, flowers); others do not, but are creations of people, crafted from one or more of those original materials (magic wands, candles, magic mirrors, etc.).

There is a vast quantity of materials to choose from. It's unlikely that you will need them all. Some will appeal to you, will resonate for you: those are your best tools. If you don't like them, if they fail to hold your interest, it's not likely that they'll work for you, at least not consistently.

Once upon a time, all magic was made by hand from scratch, from soup to nuts. If a spell required paper, you would make that paper, perhaps even gathering the material. You'd make the ink, too. Old-fashioned, you say? Yes, but this soup-to-nuts method has very important benefits, notably, control over your materials and your spell. When you do it yourself, you know that things were done correctly, all powers were properly propitiated, all

ingredients genuine. That said, magic is intended to make your life easier, not more difficult. If you are challenged for time, purchase as much ready-made as possible. The botanicals you grow with love and care will always have more power for you, but if you don't have a garden or green fingers, buy them from someone who does. If you're not "crafty," you can still cast spells. Plenty of other people are and they'll be happy to sell you their wares, oils, candles, wands, and herbs. However, hold these craftspeople to the same high standard that you'd hold anyone else. Don't be afraid to ask questions and specify your needs.

Preparing For Spell-casting

Cleansing

Cleansing is not meant literally but refers to methods of removing spiritual residues. Not everything requires cleansing because not everything retains this residue. Botanicals and candles do not, for instance. Rocks, crystals and magic mirrors may require cleansing, particularly the first time you use them, because they retain memory and impressions. You don't necessarily know everything that's retained within a mirror. (Harry Potter fans:

Remember: Magic spells take many forms, from spoken word to candle burning, to mixing oils to something as simple as posting a specific image on the wall. Your energy, focus and intent are what transform simple actions, words and gestures into magic spells.

remember Tom Riddle's diary. There was a lot hidden within those seemingly blank pages.) Cleansing gives you the opportunity to wipe the slate clean and start afresh.

Most metals fall in a category between rocks and botanicals and so sometimes need cleansing, with the exception of silver and iron, which are impervious to spiritual tarnish. You can still cleanse them, however, if you prefer.

Two areas are typically cleansed prior to initiating any important spell: the ritual space and you—your body. Cleansing will empower you and your spell, removing impediments and obstacles to success.

Further information on cleansing, techniques and spells can be found on pages 185–223.

Charging the Materials

Magic is latent in everything containing life. How is it accessed? How is it directed towards your purpose? By charging the materials.

Charging the materials is magical parlance for imbuing the physical components of your spells, be they stones or plants or fabric or anything else, with your personal energy and the goal of your spell. It is a crucial magical concept, and is akin to charging a battery—a transfusion of energy.

Exactly how necessary it is to charge a substance depends largely upon specific traditions. Some place greater emphasis on charging than others, although no tradition would tell you *not* to charge an item.

Although every spell does not direct you to charge your materials, it is a given that doing so will increase chances of success.

Charging techniques *are* spells; they can be used to imbue any object with your magical energy and power, whether these objects will be used in a formal spell or otherwise.

This is the simplest charging technique of all:

1. Hold the object with two hands, clasped together so that the object or a portion of it is sandwiched between them.
2. Close your eyes and take a few slow, deep breaths.
3. Clear your mind so that there are no conscious thoughts. If thoughts arise spontaneously, consider whether this derives from communication of one sort or another with the object.* Make a note of the thoughts so that you may return to them later, and clear your mind once again.
4. Just hold the object, focusing on energy flowing out of your hands and into the object. (Depending upon the nature of the object, this may be a one-way or two-way energy flow.)
5. When you feel that the object has absorbed sufficient energy or is now in harmony with your personal vibration, place it down and consciously withdraw your attention from it.

If you would like to charge the object with the purpose of a specific spell, follow the instructions up to Step 3. Instead of clearing your mind, visualize the achievement of the spell's desired goal. Hold this steady in your mind. When you feel that the object is sufficiently charged, remove it from your hands and consciously withdraw your attention.

* Sometimes this communication is very desirable, particularly with an object that is intended for divination. Instead of charging the object, follow the thought and see where it leads. If it turns out to be disturbing or undesirable, perform further, stronger cleansing before attempting again to charge the object.

Expanded Ritual Charging

1. Perform appropriate space and personal cleansings, as needed.
2. Prepare an altar dedicated to charging the materials.
3. Hold a white candle between your palms while you concentrate on what you wish from the article you are charging.
4. When you're ready, place the candle on the altar and light it.
5. Hold the article between your palms, charge it with your energy or goals, using the technique explained above.
6. When you're ready, place it down next to the candle.
7. Allow the object to remain there until the candle burns out completely.

Objects can be charged with specific forces, usually sunlight or moonlight, so that they will contain some of this essence. Objects may also be charged with elemental forces.

Blessings of the Elements

Each element can provide ritual blessings for spell tools and materials. Whatever is blessed is empowered and charged with that element's special energy. Choose what is appropriate or desirable, alone or in combination.

★ *Air: Pass the object through or hold within incense smoke. Smudge with a smudge stick*

IMPORTANT CONCEPT: RECIPROCITY

Because magic is an exchange of powers, consistently effective magic isn't all about *me, me, me!* The universe doesn't exist solely to serve you; there is always an exchange of energy, an exchange of gifts. Magic is about *mutually satisfying relationships* between forces and powers, including but not limited to your own. Power and favors must be balanced. You are as much a contributor to the universe as a receiver of its bounties.

When you want something from a power, offer something in return. When you receive a gift or favor, give one in return. This maintains a balance of power in the universe. In some cases, it's necessary. Botanicals work more powerfully for you if you reciprocate, offering libations, when harvesting. Many spirits will not work with you, unless they essentially receive payment of some sort, which may be as simple as devotion or as complex as specific ritual, depending upon the power.

- ★ *Earth: Sprinkle with dirt, particularly specially chosen dirt (crossroads dirt, or dirt gathered from a shrine or holy place)*
- ★ *Fire: Pass through a flame or hold within the flame for a few moments (obviously this is for materials that won't burn or be damaged)*
- ★ *Metal: Allow the object to rest overnight atop the specific metal*
- ★ *Water: Sprinkle with regular water or magically charged formula water (see Formulary, page 1037). Obviously this is for materials that won't be damaged by this technique*

Consecration

Some spells recommend that objects be consecrated. In general, these spells invoke spiritual assistance of one sort or another. Consecrating the object dedicates it to that spirit or deity, enabling it to serve as a conduit to that deity's energy or blessings.

1. Build an altar dedicated to the spirit or deity.
2. Charge the object with your desire.
3. Consciously request that the object receive the needed blessing and energy of the spirit.
4. Allow the object to remain on the altar, in close proximity to the spirit's image if one is used, or else to various power items. Time allotted varies but it is usually at least overnight.

⬠ Ritual Tools and Techniques

Tools, like spells, are creations of people. What may be indispensable to you depends upon your personal traditions and needs. For the practitioner of Wicca, an athame is necessary; in the old Saami tradition it was the drum. If ceremonial "High" magic appeals to you, you may need a lot of "*stuff.*" For others, what's necessary may be as little as what fits into a medicine bag—or even less.

Because so many published works focus on the more ceremonial aspects of magic, there is often an emphasis on tools. These may or may not be necessary to you: poor people's magic, the magic of slaves or nomads who travel light, is no less powerful but may require less *stuff*—or at least different stuff.

There is a tremendous variety of magical tools, demonstrating human ingenuity and creativity at its finest. Some creations serve no other purpose but magic, while others masquerade as common household tools. Get to know your needs, your taste and your own power, and then gravitate towards tools that call to you, that resonate for you.

Amulets and Talismans

"*Amulet*" and "*talisman*" are used somewhat interchangeably, but basically talismans are the archetypal lucky charms, drawing some specific good fortune towards you, while amulets tend to have protective, preventative or curative powers. Confusion derives from the tendency in the English language to skate over these topics very quickly. Other languages have specific names for every specific type of talisman or amulet, all very precise. Our word "amulet" is believed to derive from the Latin *amuletum*, meaning "a method of defense" (reminiscent of ammunition).

There are typically two forms of talismans and amulets:

★ *Those that are written*
★ *Independent objects*

Magic spells are frequently required in order to create talismans and amulets.

Bells

Bells are a multi-purpose magical tool of ancient provenance and international use. They are incorporated into a variety of spells:

★ *Fertility spells (a bell won't* "work" *without the clapper inside it)*
★ *Spirit-summoning spells*
★ *Protective spells*
★ *Space-cleansing spells*
★ *Healing spells*

Church bells derive from magical use, not the other way around.

Bells are crafted from many materials: silver and iron are considered most auspicious, especially for protection, fertility and healing. In addition, bells intended to do double-service as amulets may be crafted for symbolic use: thus bells are found in the shape of pinecones, cats, and frogs.

In some Asian traditions, having been well-used, bells are then melted down and the resulting metal used to create other magic tools, such as ritual cups and plates. The grease from large bells, such as church bells, may also be scraped out and used as a component of banishing and hexing spells. It is a frequent component of **Goofer Dust**.

Books

There was a drastic increase in persecution and prosecutions for witchcraft, sorcery and paganism in late antiquity. Among the charges, besides astrology, divination, the making of love potions and the presentation of petitions at pagan shrines, was possession of magic books.

Books serve many purposes in magic beyond serving as a source for spells. The book may itself be a form of a spell, serving as an amulet. Certain books don't have to be read; their very presence in the home provides protection from a host of ills. Besides the Bible and Koran, other books of this ilk include *The Book of Raziel, Book of Pow-Wows: The Long Lost Friend* and the Russian *Dreams of a Virgin.*

Books serve as magical tools. Specific books are often used as sources of divination. These especially include the Bible, the Koran, Homeric verses and the works of Virgil.

The Book of Psalms possesses an alter ego as a magical book. Psalms are used to cast a host of spells for a variety of reasons. Many assume that this originated with Hoodoo, where recitation of psalms is a common practice, but this is based on the false assumption that the Hoodoo doctors were uneducated and thus must have *"made stuff up."* If fact, it is quite the contrary—incorporation of psalms into magic stems back centuries. The practice was popular enough to stimulate publication of a medieval compilation of the uses to which psalms and their individual verses might be put. *The Magical Use of the Psalms*, a popular work of its time, was frequently reprinted in pocket-sized editions and was translated from Latin into several European languages. It was eventually placed on the *Index Librorum Prohibitorum* of the Roman Catholic Church.

Similarly, spells from the Islamic world may incorporate recitation of appropriate verses from the Koran.

Sacred Texts

The Koran, the Bible and other books are perceived as having inherent magical power because they are sacred texts. Sacred texts are not restricted to monotheistic faiths. The works of Homer and Virgil, the Indian Vedas, and the Chinese I-Ching or Book of Changes are all considered sacred texts. The crucial question, in terms of successful spell-casting, is *"are any of those texts sacred for you?"*

Sacred texts, by definition, are so inherently charged with *baraka* and *heka* that, like a saint from beyond the grave, anyone may access that power. However, magic is both in the transmitter and the receiver; it is a reciprocal process. The most powerful sacred texts for you are those that *you* perceive as sacred. If your sacred texts are Broadway show tunes or doo-wop songs, then incorporate them into your spells in the same manner that you would any other sacred text.

Methods for the magical use of psalms and sacred texts include:

★ *Whispering texts over a cup of water, which is then given to someone to drink (although the spell-caster may also desire to drink it, depending on the purpose of the spell)*
★ *Writing texts down on paper, then dissolved in liquid and drunk (by the spell-caster or the target of the spell: this derives from ancient Egyptian methods)*
★ *Wearing them as amulets, for empowerment and to transmit constant, consistent magic energy*
★ *Tracing them on an apple with a pin; depending on the nature of the spell the apple is then eaten by the spell-caster or fed to the spell's target*

Books of Shadows

Many practitioners like to keep a record of spells cast and created. Blank books are filled with magic spells. Eventually, especially if you incorporate magical inks and designs into your Book of Shadows, the book itself will be highly charged with magic power.

Books themselves sometimes need protection, and mugwort, wormwood and Saint John's Wort are believed to physically preserve books. They provide spiritual protection and keep page-nibbling vermin away.

★ *Place leaves of these protecting botanicals between pages*
★ *Maintain living plants in and around libraries*
★ *Kabikaj is the name of the djinn with dominion over insects. Allegedly writing his name in books and on manuscripts magically prevents their being eaten by worms and other vermin*

Paper

Many spells contain a written component. Something often needs to be written down, if only to be burned. And so, paper is required.

Classical grimoires often suggest that one uses parchment or vellum, especially when creating a talisman. The advantage of these is durability, although they may be difficult to acquire nowadays. Hoodoo often suggests the use of brown paper. Use cut up paper bags or butcher's paper. The advantage of this is the low cost, easy availability and color—brown is the color of justice. This paper thus enhances any spell that demands that justice be done.

It is also very easy to create your own paper with minimal skill and artistic talent. Children's craft kits contain basic paper-making supplies. A spell rarely requires more than a sheet of paper. The advantage of making your own paper is that one can imbue it with desired botanicals and fragrance.

Paper Can Be The Spell

Certain scripts are perceived as inherently powerful, for instance, Arabic, Chinese and Hebrew. If there was a pagan Greek belief that the world was created and activated via the sound of the vowels, in traditional Judaic teaching life is activated through the Hebrew letters. Ancient Egyptians utilized different scripts for different purposes, mystical and mundane. Northern European runes and Celtic Ogham script are specifically for magical and spiritual use. Many contemporary Wiccans and ceremonial magicians use various magical scripts.

Paper can create lasting amulets. The most readily accessible example is the Jewish mezuzah, attached to doorposts. The use of mezuzahs has been adopted by some Hoodoo practitioners. Similar written amulets exist in Chinese, Japanese, Ethiopian, Muslim and Tibetan traditions.

Paper as we know it was invented in China in 105 CE, and China remains the primary home of paper magic. Paper charms are traditionally written in red cinnabar ink on yellow or red paper with a peach wood pen, in special magical script known as *"thunder writing"* or *"celestial calligraphy."* Charms are used in various ways: pasted over the door or on the walls, worn in the hair, or carried in a medicine bag.

Some paper spells are created in ordered to be destroyed, via fire or water. Destroying the paper spell releases its energy into the atmosphere so that the spell can work as intended. Sometimes water and fire are combined: some Chinese charms are burned first, and then the ashes are mixed with tea or water and drunk. Rice paper is particularly effective for this as it dissolves easily in water.

★ *A written spell doesn't necessarily require paper: an ancient custom was to inscribe a clay bowl or plate with spells and incantation. It is then shattered to release the energy into the atmosphere. (If you make your own pottery, the traditions can be combined: insert tiny pieces of paper directly into the pottery, inscribe further, so the magic is contained inside and out, then shatter.)*

★ *Not all paper spells require words. Spells can be cast with images. Chromolithographs incorporate the power and blessing of a Spirit. They may also substitute for a statue. If you can't afford them or locate them, create your own. If you have no artistic ability, a collage of sacred and power images creates an amulet*

★ *A traditional alternative is to write the name of the desired divinity in gold ink on red paper and post it on the wall*

Many spells suggest using "magical ink" formulas. Although this is never required, it can empower a spell. Recipes for creating magic inks can be found within the *Formulary*, page 1037.

Pen and ink are only one form of magic writing. There are many traditions of drawing designs on the ground, particularly to invite, invoke and honor spirits. Materials used include flowers, flour, cornmeal, and special rangoli powder.

★ *Angelic sigils are written on paper or engraved onto metal. Each angel has a specific sigil that can be used to summon them. The vèvè designs of Haitian Vodou have similar purposes. Each lwa or spirit has a vèvè that expresses its essence and is thus worthy of meditation, but the vèvè may also be used to summon and honor the spirit. Vèvès may be drawn on paper but are most frequently drawn on the ground. Candomble and Romany spirits also possess sigils, as do others*

★ *Rangoli, the women's spiritual art of India, utilizes rice flour with brightly colored flowers and spices to create patterns. As Earth's tiny creatures eat the rice flour, they carry imbedded prayers and petitions to the Earth's womb*

★ *In Brazil, pemba, a kind of chalk which may contain pulverized herbs, is used to create invocational markings on Earth. Originally an African practice, the finest pemba is still thought to come from Africa and may be imported and purchased at great cost to a less-than-wealthy practitioner*

Broomsticks

The fantasy image of the witch riding around on her broomstick is actually based on fact. Broomsticks were common ritual instruments in Western

European fertility rites. People rode around fields, women on brooms, men on pitchforks, jumping high in revelry to encourage crops to flourish. The pitchfork, the male tool, would eventually be identified as among the devil's attributes.

Why a broom? It symbolizes the perfect union of male and female energies, with the stick representing the male force plunged into and attached to the female straw. Vestiges of the broom's role in fertility magic survive in the handfasting custom of jumping the broomstick.

In ancient Greece, the broomstick was considered an attribute of Hecate, Matron of Witches and Midwives. It became, for a time, the professional emblem of midwifery, similar to a barbershop pole or pawnbroker's balls.

The use of broomsticks is not restricted to European magic: The symbol arose independently in Mexico as well. The conquistadores, familiar with these images from home, were shocked by images of Tlazolteotl, fierce Aztec spirit of love and witchcraft, riding on a broomstick, naked but for jewelry and a conical bark hat, accompanied by raven and owl familiars.

The broom is used for a variety of purposes:

★ *It has evolved into the emblem of witchcraft as surely as it once represented midwives. They may be displayed as a source of pride and as a device to memorialize the Burning Times*
★ *Brooms serve as an amulet against malefic magic*
★ *Brooms are used in a vast variety of magic spells, especially those for cleansing, banishing and fertility*
★ *The broomstick was the traditional tool used for topical application of witches' flying ointments*

Various types of brooms may be used:

★ *Single use ritual brooms, usually loosely put together from botanical material and taken apart and dispersed immediately following use*
★ *Special ritual magical brooms, only to be used in ritual, as beautifully carved and crafted as any magic wand or sword. These are particularly popular amongst modern pagans and Wiccans*
★ *A plain household broom, the same one used to sweep the floor, the staple of Hoodoo banishing spells. Spiritual and mundane household cleansings may be accomplished simultaneously, through the use of ritual floorwashes*

To Sweep or Not to Sweep?

In some traditions, modern paganism or Wicca for instance, a ritual broom may never touch the floor, let alone dust anything. Brooms, whether single use ones or exquisite hand-crafted tools, are reserved for ritual use. Hoodoo, on the other hand, is practical magic: there's no need for two brooms where one will suffice. A household broom will serve both mundane and magical purposes, often simultaneously, as with the use of ritual floorwashes. Floorwashes accomplish two purposes at the same time: a magic spell is cast *and* the floor is cleaned. Cleaning the floor effectively casts the spell.

This does not really indicate a split between European and African-derived magical systems. Hoodoo's extensive use of the broomstick may in fact derive from its European roots. However, possessing an extensive collection of expensive tools reserved solely for ritual use has certain economic implications. One needs space to keep these items as well as privacy to practice ritual in safety. Instead, mundane activities can camouflage magical ones. Magic spells may be discreetly yet consistently cast, during such everyday activities as sweeping or scrubbing one's front steps.

Whether the fifteenth-century European woman, for instance, who typically resided in a small, crowded house lacking privacy and personal storage space, and who lived in mortal fear of accusations of witchcraft, would have considered it safe and practical to maintain a broomstick reserved for ritual use in addition to a household tool is something we may never know.

★ *The most basic witch's broomstick is constructed from an ash stick, which provides consistent magical protection, bound with birch twigs, meant to entangle low-level malicious spirits*

★ *An alternative choice would be willow twigs, because they are the tree belonging to Hecate, Dark Moon Goddess and supreme teacher of magic (Circe and Medea rank among her finer students)*

★ *Small handcrafted brooms are crafted to be placed and maintained on altars. Embellish the brooms to coincide with their purpose. For instance, decorate a small broom dedicated to sea spirits with sea glass and shells*

Candles

The use of candles as a common ingredient of magic is relatively recent: until recently real candles were very expensive, hence the early popularity of lamp magic. Beeswax was dangerous to obtain; natural plant waxes are very labor intensive. The earliest use of what we would call a candle apparently dates to approximately 3000 BCE.

The first true candles combined a wick with wax, oil or fat that solidified at room temperature, unlike the more ancient and common oil lamps. Beeswax was a luxury item, as rare in its way as sandalwood and frankincense. The most common candle until the development of paraffin was tallow, animal fat, a household item. The downside to tallow is its strong aroma. Still popular in some Latin American magical traditions, you can often find small tallow candles at spiritual supply stores.

Today candle magic has become one of the most popular forms of spell-casting, because of the prevalence of inexpensive candles. Modern candles are most commonly formed from paraffin, a

petroleum wax. There are also beautiful natural waxes: beeswax, bayberry and candelilla. The material is inherently more powerful and benevolent than paraffin, however they are much more expensive. Those who burn candles extensively may find their cost prohibitive. Also those who prefer figure candles may have a very difficult time finding them formed from the finer waxes.

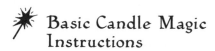 ## Basic Candle Magic Instructions

There are four necessary steps before a candle is burned.

1. *Choose the appropriate candle.* Candles come in a variety of shapes, sizes and colors. Choose what is appropriate for your spell (see Table of Color Associations, page 1063). When in doubt, a white candle will substitute for any other. If a candle must be burned in one sitting, it may be advisable to burn a smaller candle. Likewise, if a candle is to be burned incrementally over seven days, a birthday candle may not be the wisest choice.

2. *Charge the candle.* Follow the basic charging instructions (see page 75). Hold the candle in your hands and focus on the desired goal of the spell.

3. *Carve the candle.* Carving and dressing the candle personalizes it. Using a carving tool, engrave your name, mother's name, birthday, astrological sigil and other information into the wax. That's the typical *identifying information,* however a spell may specify exactly what to carve. Visualize that the candle will ultimately disappear into thin air, carrying your magical message to the Spirit World. Whatever you wish transmitted should be carved into the wax. A carving tool is anything with a sharp point. Because it will likely transmit your most secret fears and desires and may retain this as a kind of "inner memory" it's advisable to keep carving tools reserved for personal magical use. A very traditional carving tool is a rose thorn, which may be disposed of with the spell remnants.

4. *Dress the candle.* No need for little clothes. Dressing the candle indicates that it must be anointed with oil, commonly called a "dressing oil." The spell will specify which type of oil to use. The oiled candle may be dressed more elaborately by rolling it in powdered herbs or color-coordinated glitter.

Common Figure Candles

The following are among the most popular, accessible figure candles and some typical uses for them. These candles are easily purchased in a witch store or spiritual supply store. Candle specialty stores will have a greater variety, although they may not stock candles that are strongly associated with the occult.

Cats
Black: return hexes, negativity and evil intent
Green: good luck, money
Red: sex and romance

Cross or Crucifix
Although they exist in many colors, white is most commonly used
Altar candles
Uncrossing rituals

Devils
Green: fast cash and to have debts repaid
Red: sex spells
Black: domination spells

Human Figure
Use male and female figure candles to represent either yourself or the targets of your spells. They come in a variety of colors that can be coordinated with either the purpose of your spell or the people they are meant to represent.

The typical figure candle is a single naked male or female. There are also special situation figure candles:

★ A Couple Candle *is a single candle depicting a conjoined man and woman, standing side by side, dressed in wedding clothes. Use for marital, binding and other love spells*
★ A Loving Couple Candle i*s a single candle depicting a naked man and woman, entwined in passionate embrace. Use for romantic and binding spells*
★ A Divorce Candle *is a single candle depicting a conjoined male and female, standing back to back. Use for divorce and other separation spells*

Skulls
White: persuasion, communication, uncrossing
Black: domination, hexing, spell-reversals

Witch
For luck, love and reversing spells
To have the witch's blessing on your endeavors

Seven Knob
Black: to prevent and eliminate conflicts of personality, banishing spells
Red: romance, emotional issues
Green: employment, luck, finances

Usually one knob is burned per twenty-four hour period, so that it takes seven days to burn the candle entirely.

Types of Candle

Double Action Candles have two colors, usually red and black or green and black, one column of color atop the other. They are usually burned to increase beneficial forces and dispel harmful influence. *Triple Action Candles* have three layers of color.

Reverse Action Candles are red candles coated with a layer of black wax. Similar to Double Action Candles, although some feel Reverse Actions have a more powerful effect. Use these to reverse negative spells and send them back where they came from.

Seven Day Candles are designed to burn over approximately a seven-day period. They come in many colors and may be used for virtually any purpose. Typically Seven Day Candles are encased in a glass sleeve. Once upon a time, the candles slid out of the sleeves for easy dressing. This is rarely the case any longer.

You can still dress a glass-encased Seven Day Candle: drill holes into the top of the candle to insert your oil. Sprinkle with herbs and glitter dust.

The basic Seven Day Candle is one solid color and comes in a clear glass sleeve. Manufacturers also market Seven Day Candles with special sleeves. These will have special designs on the glass. The design may depict a saint or spirit, such as Saint Anthony, Saint Expedite or the Seven African Powers. The actual candle's color will be chosen to coordinate with the spirit.

The candle may also be intended to coordinate with the goal of a spell: gambling luck candles, for example, will be green and the sleeve may be decorated with images of dice, cards, horseshoes and other lucky charms. Or, the candle may be manufactured to coordinate with a specific formula oil: an Uncrossing Candle to use with **Uncrossing Oil**, for instance, or an Essence of Bend Over candle to be used with that oil.

These decorated sleeve candles essentially become a spell unto themselves. Those dedicated to saints and spirits may have suggested prayers or petitions printed on the back of the sleeve. Use these candles to enhance any spell dedicated to a spirit. Many are available, especially those of the Hindu, Roman Catholic, Santeria, Vodou and Unofficial Saint persuasions. If you can't find one dedicated to the spirit of your choice, or if there is a particular image dear to you, decorate your own sleeve:

1. Obtain a Seven Day Candle in the color of your choice inside a clear sleeve. (Candle supply stores may sell empty sleeves.)
2. Attach your image or a photocopy of the image to the candle. A craft store will sell special glues that adhere to glass.
3. Decorate with glitter glue or with objects appropriate to the purpose of the candle. Attach shiny imitation coins to a candle dedicated to Lakshmi, for instance.

Using this method you can personalize a candle for any purpose: put your ex-lover's image on a Summoning Seven Day Candle to draw him back into your life, for instance.

When a candle has burned down, reserve the glass sleeve. Refill Seven Day Candles are available. Just carve, dress and slip into the sleeve.

Keep an eye on the flames for more than fire safety: they provide an oracular response to your spell. Observe whether the candle burns strong with a bright steady flame or whether it's a moody flame, alternately burning high and low. Sometimes a candle burns very fast while other times it's very slow. If you habitually burn standardized figure candles this becomes very apparent: in theory, candles should burn at a similar rate. If your Seven Day Candle burns out in six, you know you have a speedy candle. Flames may even spontaneously extinguish and then be impossible to relight.

There are many ways to interpret these patterns. However, a bright steady healthy flame is invariably considered auspicious. The way the candle burns may advise regarding likelihood of a spell's success: a candle that burns bright and quick indicates that magic forces are with you. A low, struggling flame doesn't necessarily mean that your spell will fail—it merely indicates that it is working against tremendous opposition.

In most circumstances, unless a spell specifies otherwise, it is considered metaphysical bad manners to blow out ritual candles. Either pinch them out with your fingers, or deprive them of air instead. Beautifully crafted, long-stemmed, mystically themed snuffers exist and may be consecrated to the archangel Michael, the angel in charge of candle magic and fire safety. Alternately, a fire-proof dish may be placed over the flame until it goes out.

The patterns made by melting wax may also be interpreted. Any remains, ashes, or bits of wax, may be significant.

Some common candle wisdom:

★ *If flames shoot high, the spirit you've invoked is now in your presence*
★ *A very low, dim flame, on the other hand, may indicate the presence of ghosts*

Cauldrons

Many older spells assume that you will have ready access to a source of open fire: a hearth, fireplace, wood-stove or even a bonfire, because before the modern stove this was a necessity of life. In the twenty-first century, however, access to open fire may be limited, especially for urban dwellers.

An iron cauldron of appropriate size can often substitute for a hearth or fireplace. A traditional witch's tool, a good cauldron has many uses, from brewing potions, to burning incense, to cooking a meal.

Charm Bags

A magic spell inside a bag. There are a wide variety of names for this most popular spell style, and I've used them somewhat interchangeably in this book. In addition to charm bag, there's conjure bag, medicine bag, medicine hand, mojo bag, mojo hand, just plain old mojo, gris-gris bag, ouanga bag, dilly bag, amulet bag, magic bag, and, for the scholarly, phylacteries. And those are just the English names! These are single-handedly the most popular method of carrying magically charged items around the world.

The charm bag is a bag filled with one or more power items. Some can be seen as a miniature spell or an altar in a bag. Others are work-in-progress: an ever-evolving collection of power objects.

Medicine bags can be extremely simple. A Moroccan spell recommends that an amulet bag be filled with Earth taken from a three-way crossroads and worn around the neck, to ward off the Evil Eye and/or find and maintain true love.

Medicine bags can also be complex. The Brazilian charm bag, the *patua*, is made from leather or cloth might contain a danda root shaped into a figa, the fig hand, and placed between leaves of rue and mucura. Garlic and cloves may be added, then prayers written out, with special ink and sewn into the bag.

Some traditions carry a multitude of items in one bag. In Native North American tradition, a medicine bag is initiated via an activating agent, for instance a pinch of tobacco, pollen, corn kernels, sweetgrass, white sage, or a little bit of Earth, tied into a piece of red flannel. Other traditions insist on one item per bag; magic is forbidden in orthodox Muslim tradition, the exception being the use of Koranic verses as amulets. A separate pouch is needed for each amulet. African nomads may be covered in leather and metal talisman cases.

The variety of this type of magic is endless. The container itself becomes part of the spell. Materials are carefully chosen. Fine Arabic and Tibetan amulet bags are finely crafted from metal and sometimes bejeweled. Other "bags" may be as simple as a knotted handkerchief. The drawstring bag is most familiar. Hoodoo recommends red flannel, while Romany tradition suggests red silk.

Although the words are now used somewhat synonymously, technically a "hand" is a closed bag, rather than an open one. There's a fine line between a sachet and a hand, largely drawn by the fabric it's crafted from (sachets are muslin, hands flannel) and the items they contain (a sachet contains only botanical material, a hand may contain a variety of materials, including botanicals).

Although modern Hoodoo and Conjure magic almost invariably used red flannel drawstring bags, early African-American mojo hands, immediately post-slavery and continuing onwards, were sewn red squares. With the material sewn inside, they resemble an isolated single quilt square. The traditional British mojo hand is very similar: two pieces of red flannel, cut into a heart shape, stuffed, sewn together, and the outside decorated.

Bags possess the advantage of accessibility, however there are other methods of carrying charms. The bag may be sewn into clothes, or individual items sewn into clothing, Romany style, for privacy and for added contact with body. Igor Stravinsky wore his sacred medals pinned to his underwear.

In some traditions the mojo hand is charged before use. The following is a typical ritual, common to Hoodoo and Wicca.

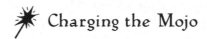 Charging the Mojo

Once the bag is complete:

1. Light a match and plunge it into the bag, extinguishing it. (Do *not* set your bag or its contents on fire. Be very careful if the bag contains dried botanicals or volatile essential oils.)
2. Spit in the bag and pull the string tight.

An alternative version of the mojo bag is the charm vial, popular in Central and South America. Instead of fabric, metal or leather, miniature glass bottles are filled with charms and power objects, essentially a mojo hand-crafted from glass. The items are visible, creating a talismanic, protective effect.

Tiny bottles are recycled for magical use: charms are often made from medical ampoules with yarn or cord attached so that they can be worn or hung. They typically include layers of charms, suspended in oil such as seeds, botanicals, minerals, tiny carvings or votive image cards.

Charm bags are carried in the pocket, worn around the neck or waist. They may also be hung up on the wall like an amulet or kept discreetly inside a drawer or cabinet—a small altar in a bag.

Crystal Balls

Crystal balls are used for divination (scrying), and Spirit summoning.

The art of scrying transcends the stereotype of the fraudulent crystal ball reader. It is an ancient and well-respected technique. In fact, crystal balls are perhaps the most recent evolution in the ancient art of scrying. Scrying is the art of divination through the use of reflective surfaces. It is among the more difficult divination techniques, although perhaps the most ancient. The modern clear round crystal ball is particularly effective because it evokes the image of the moon.

However, the crystal ball is only one of many scrying tools. Presumably the first scryer gazed into a still lake. Roman images of the primal goddess Kybele depict her holding a flat pan of water for divination. A scrying tool may be as simple as that pan of water or as lavish as a star sapphire or star ruby, both famed divination devices. (Should you be privileged enough to have access to either of these precious gems and wish to try your hand at scrying, gaze at their crossed lines and let your mind wander.) Less expensive gemstones are also used: aquamarine and clear quartz stones, as well as polished balls. Smoky quartz is considered particularly beneficial as a device for communicating with spirits or ghosts.

In India, the water in the pan may be replaced by a pool of ink. Egyptian techniques involved gazing into ink held in the left palm. Technically the only tool required is already in your hands: buff your left thumbnail to a high polish and gaze inside.

Unlike pans but like mirrors and gemstones, crystal balls store visions and memories. Cleanse as needed. A new crystal ball must be cleansed and charged prior to its first use.

★ *Charge crystal balls by exposing them periodically to the light of the full moon*

★ *In some traditions, a crystal ball must be fully activated through exposure to the light of thirteen full moons before it's ready to use*
★ *If you use your crystal ball for spiritual communication, you may wish to keep it covered with a dark cloth between uses*

Dolls

These are also known as poppets. "Doll" derives from similar sources as the word "idol" while "poppet" is related to "puppet." The stereotypical witch's doll is made from wax and stuffed with pins to inflict pain and suffering. However, magic spell dolls may be crafted from a variety of materials and serve a variety of spell purposes. Wax dolls have been recovered from ancient Egypt, so they have certainly existed for a long time, but dolls are also formed from fabric, botanicals, wood, clay and bone.

Dolls may be used in positive magic to:

★ *Heal disease*
★ *Induce love*
★ *Unite the estranged*
★ *Promote and enhance fertility*

On the other hand, dolls have also been used to cause injury, impotence, fatalities, pain, insanity, and a wide assortment of other human miseries.

To some extent, modern candle magic, especially the use of figure candles, is an outgrowth of doll magic.

Fabrics

In many cases, spells must be encased in fabric. The fabric itself becomes incorporated into the spell. Many traditions possess "sacred" fabrics. In many cases, the technique needed to create these fabrics derives from magical or spiritual traditions, such as batik or *ikat*. The most common fabrics used in spell-work are red silk and red flannel.

Spells are cast by embellishing fabric: many traditional needle-work arts are intrinsically connected to spiritual traditions. The exquisite traditional embroidery motifs of Baltic, Hungarian, Romany and Slav women confer blessings, power, protection and fertility.

Among the most vital descendants of magic fabrics are flags.

Flags and Banners

Flags are used:

★ *To honor and summon spirits*
★ *As amulets*
★ *As protective devices*

The use of flags and banners in religion and heraldry is rooted in this magical use. The sacred quality attributed to many flags, including those representing nations, derives from this history; the agitation experienced by those who feel that their flag has been "desecrated" also derives from this origin.

Symbols incorporated onto flags are perceived as providing protection—or a threat. Pirate flags weren't limited to the Jolly Roger. The more notorious pirates made sure that a specific flag trumpeted their presence and perhaps provided protection for the pirate himself.

Among the most powerful examples of flags used as a spiritual or magical tool are Haitian sequined flags, so-called Vodoun flags. Sigils, symbols and images of the lwa or their affiliated saints are reproduced onto fabric using sequins.

Magic Belts

This category of magic tool includes anything that circles the waist or hips, and is crafted with magical intent, from the *cingulam* to waist beads. The category could also have been called "girdles," a word that has fallen out of fashion but was once considered seductive and magical: Aphrodite and Ishtar both wear romantic, love-inducing belts or girdles, which they have been known to lend to others in need. The belt is typically a women's magical article, although not always. Even as a woman's article, however, the belt isn't exclusively about love, seduction and babies. Aphrodite and Ishtar both have martial aspects. Belts are also associated with the powerful female warrior orisha, Oya. Belts also indicate that one's loins are girded: they are used in fierce, protective women's power spells.

Magic belts were once far more popular than they are at present. In Cro-Magnon graves, women were buried wearing cowrie shell belts. They lie across the abdominal area, to indicate fertility. Amulets including mojo bags hang from the belts. Ishtar's magic belt finds its descendants among belly dancer's spangled belts. The most powerful belt of all may be shed snakeskins for enhanced fertility and easier childbirth. (Shed is the key word; it's crucial that the skin not be taken by force. Cooperation of the snake powers is needed: fertility as the gift of the snake.)

There is an erotic component to many magic belts. In traditional Africa, waist beads were perceived as very erotic and seductive and thus private. To some extent, beads move to the neck to offset this aspect.

Belts may also serve more public rituals.

The Cingulam

The term "*cingulam*" indicates a cord. The traditional Wiccan belt is a silk cord, nine feet long.

Traditionally used in symbolic binding rituals, it might be a single red braided cord or three cords braided together: red, black and white.

The cord is used to measure the circumference of a coven circle:

1. Hold one end in the center of the circle.
2. Mark the center with a stone or crystal, salt or chalk or other such marker.
3. Rotate the other end around the circle, like a compass.

Magic Boxes

Boxes are used for a variety of purposes.

Cache Boxes

Cache boxes are needed to secure ritual tools and/or small magical items. The size of the box depends upon its purpose: obviously, if you wish to store swords or wands, a full sized chest may be required.

Among the most powerful boxes are the following, in descending order of power:

★ *Iron boxes radiate protective power and serve as a battery, continually re-charging the box's contents*
★ *Spice boxes, crafted from cinnamon and cloves, as originally made in Indonesia*
★ *Wooden or leather boxes embellished with magic designs drawn with alkanet, indigo, woad or henna. (Although a temporary stain on skin and hair, henna is a permanent dye on objects.)*

Spell Boxes

Spells are cast by constructing a spell box, which are enclosed altars or tableaux. In general, a spell box is filled with power items necessary to achieve a goal, although you should follow directions given for specific spells. It may be a cumulative spell done in increments: items are gathered one by one and added to enhance the power of the box. Sometimes a special box lends itself to a magical or spiritual goal. The box itself can become an intrinsic part of the spell:

★ *Attach and incorporate the power items to the box itself, such as charms, shells, beads, and feathers*
★ *Decoupage images on the outside or inside of the box to correspond to the spell's goals*
★ *Embellish with sigils or other fortuitous symbols using magic ink, henna or another natural dye*

Shadow Box Altars

An enclosed altar maintains the advantage of discretion and privacy. Certain spirits, such as dark moon goddesses or some protective spirits may prefer an enclosed altar. Open altars disperse their power through an area; an enclosed altar's power is concentrated within. Each has its advantages; choose which suits you.

What is now called a "shadow box altar" has its roots in medieval Roman Catholic religious cabinets. Shadow boxes range in size from full-size cabinets to miniature altars contained in match-boxes.

Magic Mirrors

Amongst the most popular and beloved of magical tools, the magic mirror is common to many traditions, being especially beloved in ancient Egyptian, Chinese, Western ceremonial, Aztec and Italian folk magic. It is most commonly used for:

★ *Scrying*
★ *Spirit summoning*

★ *Protective magic*
★ *Romantic magic*
★ *Lunar magic (see Drawing Down the Moon, page 50)*

The ancient Egyptian word for *mirror* is a pun for *life*. This is made explicit by the shape of the handle-hand mirror, which echoes the shape of the ankh, the symbol of life held by all the Egyptian deities with the sole exception of Osiris, Lord of the Dead. The visual aspect of the pun remains today, in the *akua'ba*, the fertility producing and thus life-affirming doll from Ghana, whose shape also recalls the ankh.

Although the mirror is a reflective tool, magically it's also believed to possess powers of absorption. Like a crystal, mirrors absorb and store information. Anything once reflected in a mirror, particularly over an extended period of time, is "stored" and may be accessed for future use. Thus the mirror is a primary tool for drawing down lunar and solar energy. It also bears a reputation as a soul catcher. Whether this use is positive or malefic depends upon the intent of the spell-caster.

The earliest mirrors were not made from glass but from natural materials that could be polished until they showed a reflection.

Ancient Egyptian Mirrors

Although mirrors might be created from other precious metals (gold, silver, electrum), the most typical ancient Egyptian mirror was made from polished copper. Copper is under the dominion of Hathor, among the most primordial of the Egyptian deities. Hathor presides over beauty, cosmetics, love, sex, fertility, and magic. She and copper share the same essence—to hold a copper mirror is to hold Hathor in your hands. Depictions of Hathor are typically crafted into the mirror's handle makes this explicit. To gaze into a Hathorian mirror is to absorb her powers of beauty, grace, and love as surely as gazing into a lunar-charged mirror evokes the moon's gifts.

From Egypt, this type of polished hand mirror was exported through the Mediterranean into Europe, where it would meet its finest expression in medieval Italian hand mirrors.

Aztec Mirrors

The most precious Aztec magic mirrors were crafted from obsidian, a rare natural volcanic glass. It was difficult to obtain sufficient quantities of appropriate quality to craft a mirror, and so such mirrors were used for spiritual uses only. More common Aztec mirrors are made from iron pyrite.

The Aztec obsidian mirror is explicitly linked to the deity Tezcatlipoca, the *Smoking Mirror*. Omniscient, all-powerful, all-knowing, a sometimes malevolent figure of temptation (reminiscent of Sauron, the *Lord of the Rings'* ever-present all-seeing Eye), Tezcatlipoca observes *everything* in his obsidian mirror. A preserved idol, recently displayed at the British Museum, depicts a Tezcatlipoca made entirely from polished obsidian, carrying a mirror of polished gold.

Because of the destruction of Aztec culture, we may never entirely know how these mirrors were used. What we do know is that they were used for divination (scrying) and for interactive spiritual communication. This use of magic mirrors is still popular amidst traditional occultists in Mexico and Central America. Following the conquest of Mexico, obsidian mirrors arrived in Europe. The most famous belonged to Dr. John Dee and is now in the British Museum's collection.

Chinese Magic Mirrors

Chinese occult traditions utilize mirrors more consistently and inventively than any other.

Allegedly one man became Emperor of China through the use of a magic mirror. The favored Chinese magic mirror is a small or moderately sized circular mirror attached to a handle, crafted preferably from gold, although other precious metals may be used. Like the Italian mirror, its power is enhanced by decorating the mirror's back with auspicious power symbols.

Mirrors are traditionally used to capture and focus energy. Although the use of mirrors originally derived from lunar magic, the mirror may also be used to channel the power of the sun.

 ## Drawing Down the Sun: Creating a Solar Charged Mirror

This is among the easiest spells in this book. It is also potentially among the most dangerous. If done incorrectly, it can have tragic consequences. It must not be attempted by children. Adults: remember the cautionary tale of Icarus, who underestimated the power of the sun.

1. On a bright, sunny day, hold a small mirror in the palm of your hand, tilted to catch direct sunlight.
2. Maintain this position for no more than a few seconds. Nine seconds is the maximum.
3. That's it: the mirror is charged. The sun is so powerful that nine seconds is all it takes, and half of that is probably more than sufficient.
4. This mirror must be reserved for magical purposes. If it is accidentally used for another purpose, it must be cleansed, reconsecrated and the ritual repeated.

There are many ways to make and use magic mirrors. Any mirror may be converted into a magic mirror; in a sense every mirror *is* a magic mirror.

Reproductions of ancient Egyptian mirrors may be used, as can traditional Italian or Chinese mirrors. It is also not hard to make your own. Consider what you will do with your mirror. The most popular uses are:

★ *Divination*
★ *Spiritual communication*
★ *Spell-work*

IMPORTANT! SAFETY MEASURES WHILE PERFORMING THIS SPELL

★ Do not look into the mirror until the ritual is complete and the mirror is withdrawn from the sun: you must not watch the reflection within the mirror

★ Keep your eyes averted

★ Do not perform this ritual in the vicinity of dried paper, dried leaves or botanicals or anything else that could potentially catch fire

★ Make sure no one is nearby who could be inadvertently blinded or burned

★ *Romantic or protective amulets*
★ *Banishing spells*

If you are using the mirror for casting spells, spiritual communication or as an amulet, you may not wish anyone else to have the opportunity to look into your mirror. Therefore you will need a small, discreet mirror. If used for divination, whether professional or for personal use, a larger mirror may be used and perhaps left out in the open.

Mirrors are sometimes used as negative spiritual entity detectors, something like a metaphysical cross between a smoke detector and a mouse-trap. In theory, any large, powerful mirror is capable of detecting spirits. You may wish to use an antique wall mirror for this purpose, although Chinese tradition recommends that a mirror for such purposes should not be used for any other use, but kept covered when its services are not required.

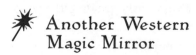

The Basic Western Ceremonial Magic Mirror

This is a good all-purpose magic mirror. It is expected, however, that you will begin the process from scratch. A round, concave piece of glass is required.

1. Coat the back, the convex side, with matte black paint. Apply it thickly but smoothly and evenly.
2. Allow the paint to dry.
3. Mount the mirror on cardboard or similar.
4. Place in a picture frame and embellish as you will.

Another Western Magic Mirror

This mirror is most appropriate for spell-casting. It has the advantage of starting with a commercially manufactured mirror.

1. Purchase a mirror.
2. Inscribe angelic formulas on the back (you may have to carefully pry off the back of the mirror). Formulas may be obtained from many classical grimoires, such as *The Key of Solomon* or *The Black Pullet*. It is recommended that you use your own blood for ink; dragon's blood ink would be a good substitute.
3. Bury the mirror at a crossroads under the full moon, marking the spot so that you can retrieve it later.
4. Dig it up after three days.

Pow-Wow Instructions for Making a Magic Mirror

Pow-Wow magic mirrors are most frequently used for scrying.

1. Obtain clear glass in whatever size suits you.
2. Construct a special three-sided frame, so that the mirror, once inserted, may be easily slid in and out.
3. Cleanse and consecrate the glass.
4. Make a strong infusion by pouring boiling water over chamomile, dragon's blood and eyebright.
5. Let the infusion cool; then use it to "paint" one side of the glass. (Use a paint or pastry brush.) Allow this sufficient time to dry.
6. Paint over the same side, once again, this time with black paint, so that now you have one black side and one unpainted side.
7. When the paint is dry, slide it into the frame with the unpainted side facing up.

If at all possible, when scrying, hold this mirror so that it points towards the physical direction of whomever or whatever you wish to see.

In some traditions no one but you should ever look into your magic mirror. In others, someone else should always have the first peek inside the mirror, preferably your animal familiar.

Consecrating a Mirror

1. Add three spoonfuls of sea salt to a dish of spring water.
2. Stir gently until dissolved.
3. Using a new cloth or a natural sponge, use this solution to cleanse your mirror.
4. Gently wipe it dry with another new cloth.

Milagro

A milagro is a magical object most commonly crafted in the form of an isolated human anatomical part, a heart for instance, or an arm. These objects are today most commonly associated with Latin American magic, however their roots are prehistoric. These objects, known in Latin as ex-votos, have been found in what are today Greece, Italy and Switzerland. The most ancient are believed to derive from Iberia.

Milagros are a very fluid form of magic: most frequently found in miniature form, life-size milagros are sometimes crafted in Brazil. Typically crafted from inexpensive silver colored metals, they may also be carved from precious metals and gemstones, as well as created from wax. Milagros are easily obtainable from spiritual goods stores and from many exporters of Latin American arts and handicrafts. They can also be easily cut from a sheet of tin or copper. Milagros are most frequently used in healing spells, spirit-summoning spells, protective spells and romantic spells.

Mortar and Pestle

At some point it is extremely likely that you will have to grind something or blend some botanicals together. Mortars and pestles are ancient, primal tools. They come in many sizes and materials: glass, brass, marble, volcanic stone. Mortars and pestles are the finest grinding tools for two reasons. First, the tool clearly mimics the sexual act, the act of creation. And what is magic after all but an act of creation, an act of generation? This is made explicit in one of the more obscure Greek myths. Although the more famous story of the discovery of fire involves its theft by Prometheus, in another version, Hermes, the Opener of Ways, first creates fire by vigorously grinding the pestle in the mortar.

Secondly, the very physical act of manual grinding allows you to grind your intentions into the botanicals in a way that pressing the button on a food processor cannot.

If you do not have a mortar and pestle, it is preferable to substitute manual methods rather than a food processor. You can fold a piece of wax paper and place the material that needs to be ground in between the fold. Alternatively, you can smash the material with a hammer, which puts the power of metal in your hand, or roll a rolling pin over it, focusing on your desired results while you work.

The mortar and pestle is also a witch's vehicle: perhaps a hint as to the botanical origins of flying ointments. Baba Yaga, wild Russian forest witch and master herbalist, rides a mortar and pestle through the air, sweeping away her traces with a broom.

Musical Instruments

Did magic adopt the use of specific musical instruments or was the creation of these instruments stimulated by magical need? The earliest magical rituals involved music and dance. Although a spellbook cannot accurately record these rituals, these traditions continue in healing and trance ceremonies throughout the world. Exorcisms and spiritual communication are accomplished through music.

Drums and Other Percussion Instruments

It is probably impossible to separate drums from magic. Drums express the human heartbeat; they are used for a wide variety of magical purposes, including healing, banishing, protective rites and spirit summoning. One type of drum or another is enjoyed by virtually every culture on Earth. The earliest visual depictions of spiritual rituals include drums. The Egyptian protective spirit Bes is almost never seen without his frame drum. Similarly Kybele, perhaps the most ancient deity still familiar to us today, carries a frame drum. The use of percussion instruments are central to both Bes's and Kybele's mythology. Interestingly as opposed to the modern perception of percussion as masculine, drums, particularly frame drums and tambourines

were once identified strongly as women's instruments and were a sacred tool in many women's spiritual traditions.

Drumming remains central to African-derived rituals, as each orisha and lwa possesses their own rhythms and songs, which are used to summon and communicate with the spirits. Drums are also traditional shamanic tools, and tools of divination.

Percussion is easily incorporated into ritual. Many inexpensive instruments are available; they are also easily handcrafted.

Flutes

These are also ancient instruments; flutes appear as a component of many myths and fairy tales. Greek Pan and Athena played different forms of the instrument. Fairy tales abound with stories of magic flutes that may be used to summon spirits, allies, animals or loved ones. The Pied Piper is only the most famous example.

★ *Native American cedar flutes are used for romance and seduction*
★ *Chinese bamboo spirit flutes are used to invoke a specific spirit, whose name may be carved into the bamboo*
★ *European custom suggests that an elder-wood flute played at midnight in a remote, isolated location will summon spirits to you*

Any other instrument may also be incorporated into spell-work. Instruments may be played "live;" recordings may also be incorporated into ritual and spells.

Sieves

This seemingly mundane kitchen tool has a long history of magical use. An old fashioned term for a sieve is a *riddle*, as in riddled with holes.

The term does not refer only to the modern metal strainer, but to any type of sifter, including grain winnows. An example of ancient multitasking—frame drums may have tiny perforations, so that they may be used to finely sift henna and herbs, in addition to their musical uses.

Sieves have fallen out of fashion, exiled to the kitchen cabinets, but they were once considered common magical fare. The sieve is sacred to Isis; she collected Osiris' limbs in a sieve. The sieve is also featured on many Gnostic engraved gems. The Roman Catholic Church would later ascribe the symbol to Satan.

Sieves are used in many spells, especially for fertility, influencing the weather and divination.

Swords

Magic swords have historically played a role in Chinese, Japanese, Jewish and Persian magic, as well as in modern Wicca. Actual functional swords may be used or ceremonial replications. Use of the sword invokes primal metal magic, although just as there are metal wands, there are also wooden swords, particularly in classical East Asian magic.

Once upon a time, each sword was made to order, measured to suit the bearer as surely as a magic wand. Crafting was a secret operation. Master swordsmiths hoarded their formulas: rumors circulated periodically that human blood was needed to forge a magic sword. Vestiges of these legends are still found in Japanese mythology.

A fine sword was considered as much an individual as a person; each had a name, proclivities and was believed to exert a personality. A legendary sword of this type may be observed in the movie, *Crouching Tiger, Hidden Dragon*.

In Chinese tradition, the most valued magic sword would be one inherited from a famous and consistently successful warrior, even if one only intends to use it for magical purposes. The next best bet is either a peach wood or iron blade consecrated in the name of the famed sword it's supposed to represent. Willow and mulberry wood are also favored. Similarly in Western magic, swords of famous warriors held magical associations. Weapons once belonging to the Knights Templar, for instance, that elite knightly order disbanded and doomed because of alleged occult practices, are priceless magical tools.

The sword's power may be enhanced through embellishment. The grimoire, *The Key of Solomon*, recommends engraving Kabalistic inscriptions on hilts and blades. Other powerful embellishments include runes, sacred verses, hieroglyphs and Chinese calligraphy.

Swords are used in various ceremonial rites. They are used for casting circles. They are a protective device and may be used in exorcisms and to repel malevolent spirits. When not in use, swords are kept wrapped in fabric, especially red silk.

Not all magic swords are actual swords. Small Chinese amulet swords are constructed from coins and red silk cord and embellished with a complex series of knots and tassels. Typically inexpensive, they are readily available through Chinatown markets and feng shui sources. These coins swords serve as a protective device as well as talismans to balance and improve finances.

In addition to full-sized swords, knives and daggers also have magical uses.

The most famous ritual knife is the *athame*, the Wiccan ceremonial knife. It is reserved exclusively for ritual use: in particular, it cannot be used to draw blood. In case of accident or emergency, it must be purified and re-consecrated. You may craft one yourself or find an interesting knife or dagger and consecrate it to the purpose. Among its uses are inscribing the circle for magic, mixing potions and charged waters.

Like swords and wands, the power of knives and daggers may be enhanced through embellishment.

Magic Wands

Because magic wands are such an important component in portrayals of fantasy magic, it's crucial to point out that it is not the wand that *works*; it is the practitioner. The wand is merely a tool with which to direct the user's will or intention. Obviously some wands are superior to others; certain wands suit certain purposes, practitioners or traditions better than others.

Historically, magic wands are common to magic traditions all over Earth. Today, they are especially significant in Druid, Wiccan and High Ritual traditions. Wands are used for spiritual and religious ritual purposes as well as a magical tool. Some traditions require use of a wand—it is a mandatory magical tool. Let it be noted, however, that not every practitioner, spell-caster or witch uses a wand. It is not a requirement for magic.

We enter the realm of very personal magic with wands: some practitioners collect wands, preferring different woods for different magical purposes. Others desire only one wand, with which they can forge an intensive relationship, the wand virtually becoming an extension of the body. There are those for whom an exquisitely, meticulously crafted wand is an absolute necessity. Others prefer to work with an unornamented, uncarved branch, a fallen stick or a piece of driftwood.

In some cases, particularly where privacy is an issue, substitutions may be made. A folded-up umbrella serves nicely for discreet, outdoor rituals. In that case, treat the umbrella like the ritual tool that it has become, giving it the same care and consideration as a more traditional magic wand.

Although wands are famously wooden, metal wands can be extremely effective too. Master Magus Aleister Crowley, for instance, typically alternated between two wands: a heavy cast-iron wand and a lighter wooden wand, usually almond wood.

Finding Your Wand

★ *Wands may be inherited from another practitioner, a mentor or coven member*
★ *You may receive a new one as a gift*
★ *You can purchase a pre-crafted one: a skilled artisan can often create an aesthetically more beautiful wand than a layperson, if this is important to you. There are professional wand-crafters who will craft a wand to suit your specific desires and needs*
★ *You can craft your own*

If you inherit or purchase a ready-made wand it is crucial that it be cleansed of previous influences and charged with your own personal energy and vibration. Of course there is always the rare exception: if you have inherited a wand from a particular powerful and revered practitioner—if you've discovered Merlin's very own wand, for instance—you may not wish to erase previous vibrations but to maintain and build upon them.

1. Hold a quartz crystal between your hands and charge it with your energy and power.
2. When the wand is not in use, wrap the crystal around it with a piece of red silk.
3. Roll the wand, with the attached crystal, into black velvet and let them remain together.
4. Periodically, cleanse and re-charge the crystal.

Crafting a Wand

The traditional length of a magic wand is eighteen inches long, or from your elbow to the tip of your forefinger.

To Cut or Not to Cut?

As usual, much depends upon tradition. In the Romany tradition, branches are *not* cut. Instead, one looks for the right branch to appear. Magic wands are gifts of the trees and, in fact, wands are used very specifically in tree magic—magic to call upon the power of the trees and their presiding spirits. If you desire a specific kind of wood or crave a wand from a specific tree, one may request that the tree drop a branch, and return periodically to see if the wish has been granted. If it is, even though no cutting is done, a libation is still offered at the spot where one picks up the branch.

Before you cut a branch, remember to ask permission from the tree. The branch will always contain the essence of the tree and will work more harmoniously and dependably if it is received in a spirit of cooperation.

1. Look for a healthy tree that can afford to give you a branch. Having chosen your tree, should you discover an appropriate branch waiting for you, fallen on the ground, or hanging from the tree, this is an extremely auspicious sign, a true gift of the tree. The wand created from this branch offers you great power.

2. Talk to the tree. Really talk—speak out loud. This enhances the reality of the situation for you. Leave some silence in order to receive answers, as well. Explain why you want a branch and ask permission to take one.

3. Get a response. To receive your answer:
   ★ Use divination: consecrated wooden runes are ideal communication tools, as is the simpler flipping a coin
   ★ Sit quietly by the tree and wait for the answer to become clear to you
   ★ Request a sign: if you see a red bird within the next five minutes, for instance, your request is granted
   ★ Request that the tree or its presiding spirit answer you in your dreams

4. Cut as swiftly and painlessly as possible.
5. Offer a libation: water is a requirement. You may also offer an exchange of gifts: honey, tobacco, wine or spirits, crystals and gemstones are traditional.
6. Take the wood and carve the wand.
7. Embellish, if you like, by carving runes or other magical symbols into the wand. Add a crystal to the tip or enhance with feathers, fabric and stones. Let your personal magical vision guide you.

Choosing Your Wood

Although specific types of wood are favored in various traditions and for various purposes, realistically these may not exist as an option. Most of us have access to only limited types of wood. Neither should we search out endangered or rare specimens.

No wood will work as well for you as the wood from a tree with which you have forged an alliance:

1. Develop a relationship with the tree: visit it, talk to it, bring it gifts, listen to it.
2. When you're ready, either request a branch or wait until one is given to you.
3. Having obtained your wand, if you continue your relationship with the parent tree, you will continue to enhance the power of your tool. Re-energize your wand by resting it against the roots of its mother tree.

Good all-purpose wands include ash, hawthorn,* hazel and rowan. Lightning-struck wood is considered packed with power. Driftwood makes an excellent wand; it does not have to be cut and combines the powers of Earth and sea.

* According to Celtic tradition, hawthorn is one wood that may not be cut without dire consequences. The species belongs to the fairies, who feel very protectively towards it. Unless you are an experienced practitioner of fairy music, find a fallen branch or choose a different wood.

Some woods are favored for specific purposes and thus some practitioners prefer multiple wands for use with different purposes.

★ *Divination: ash, rowan, willow*
★ *Exorcism: date palm, tamarisk*
★ *Healing magic: hazel*
★ *Love magic: apple, ash tree (a.k.a. Venus of the Woods)*
★ *Necromancy: cypress*
★ *Prosperity magic: ash*
★ *Protective wands to ward off malicious spirits and malevolent magic: blackthorn, olive, rowan*
★ *Spirit work: elder*

Favored Woods for Magical Wands According to Tradition

★ *Ainu: bamboo, with leaves remaining. Top carved into spiral designs*
★ *Berber: oleander*
★ *Celtic: hawthorn, hazel*
★ *China: peach, willow*
★ *Druid (British): hawthorn, rowan, yew*
★ *Druid (Gaul): oak*
★ *Romany: Elm*
★ *Russian, Slavic: birch*
★ *Scythian: willow*

Wands are not limited to wood. Metal wands are excellent power conductors. Embellish with crystals, seashells and charms. Copper is a particularly excellent conductor of energy. An iron wand provides power and protection.

Specialized Wands

★ *A wand for love and seduction: copper topped with rose quartz*
★ *Lunar wand: place a moonstone atop a silver wand, for moon, love and fertility magic*

★ *A mermaid's wand: driftwood topped with coral, pearls or shells for lunar, love, fertility and money magic as well as rituals by the sea*
★ *A highly protective ritual wand: wrap copper wire around an iron wand, embellish with hematite and black tourmalines*
★ *A quartz crystal tip empowers any all-purpose wand*
★ *A rose quartz attached to the wand, enhances romantic spells*
★ *Amethysts empower spiritual quests and cleansings*
★ *Black tourmalines, Herkimer diamonds and smoky quartz used to embellish a wand provide added protection during ritual use*

Wrap your wand in leather, red silk or other magical fabric when not in use. Store it in a box for safety, if you like, however wrap it in cloth first.

For optimum power, keep your wand beside you as much as possible to absorb your energy and desires and harmonize your vibrational energies. Many sleep with their wands, either beside them in bed or beneath them.

Staff

The distinction between wands and staffs often has to do with size: a staff is thicker and substitutes as a walking stick. In theory, a staff should be long and solid enough to lean on. Historically associated with ancient Egyptian and Semitic magic, staffs are associated with the Biblical Moses and his Egyptian opponents.

The modern staff is most associated with Obeah, the African-derived traditions native to the British West Indies. The *Obeah Stick*, also called an *Obi Stick*, is a carved wooden staff, usually featuring a serpent motif. The simpler ones are carved so that a snake-like groove encircles the staff. The more elaborate *Staff of Moses* usually features a snake carved from bottom to top. Staffs may be hollowed out and filled with botanicals.

Divining Rods

Hazel twigs and forks cut on Midsummer's Eve are recommended for divining purposes.

Fans

A folding fan, held closed, may substitute for a magic wand. Fans may also substitute for broomsticks. An enchantress in the *Arabian Nights* reveals herself by riding a fan.

Fans are also used in a variety of magical traditions, not as substitutes but in their own right. Chinese magic favors the sandalwood fan, especially for protective purposes. The fan creates a personal psychic and spiritual shield. Sandalwood possesses sacred, benevolent, protective qualities. These may be enhanced through ornamentation: fans are frequently embellished with magical images and/or words. Strengthen and maintain the fan's power by periodically passing it through sandalwood incense smoke.

As with wands or staffs, fans are not tools to be shared. When not in use, the fan should rest discreetly hidden, wrapped in fabric and placed in a magic box.

The powerful Yoruba orisha, Oshun, counts peacocks among her sacred birds. Devotees keep peacock feather fans in her honor. They are used in rituals to honor her and when not they are not in use are kept on her altar. Peacock feather fans are also appropriate for use with other spirits, such as the Hindu Lakshmi and the Roman Juno.

Fans crafted from various types of feather or an intact bird's wing complete with feathers are used in Native American and Native American-influenced traditions as a device for wafting incense, especially for cleansing purposes.

Key Magical Techniques

Bathing

Although this may seem like the magical equivalent of instructions for boiling water, many spells are accomplished through baths. Various magical techniques increase the odds of a spell's success.

★ *In general, it is beneficial to submerge completely in the water at least once, although some spells may specify the number of submersions*

★ *When you want to rid yourself of something—a problem, bad debts, your annoying boyfriend—bathe down and out: start at the top, work your way down your body and out the arms and legs*

★ *When you want to draw something towards you— love, cash, or a job—start at the feet and move in towards your heart. Start at the ends of your hands and move inwards*

★ *Allow yourself to air dry. Drying yourself with a towel wipes much of the residue, the aura of the bath, off your skin. Nothing will happen if you use a towel but you will receive consistently stronger better results if you take the time to air dry*

What may be the most ancient magical techniques of all may be unfamiliar to the modern practitioner—foot track spells and knot magic.

Foot Track Magic

"*Leave nothing behind but your footprints*"—or so go the instructions for today's eco-tourists. Even footprints, however, have their magical uses. Foot track magic, as its modern name goes, is most closely associated today with hoodoo traditions. But it is actually a particularly primal, international magical technique. There are oblique references to it in the Talmud. Instructions attributed to Pythagoras forbade people to pierce footprints with nail or knife, although similar spells are contained in this book.

This ancient practice derives from dry lands, where a footprint lingers. To some extent, men lend themselves more to foot track magic because of their generally heavier, deeper imprints.

There are two varieties of foot track magic: in one, usually used for banishing or hexing, something is done to the actual footprint in the ground. The other method is to scoop up the dirt from the footprint in its entirety. This will usually be later combined with other ingredients for magical purposes, both positive and malevolent.

When gathering up footprints, it is vital to the success of the spell that the entire footprint is gathered. It is also crucial (and not always simple to determine) that one obtains the footprint of the correct person!

Knotting

Knots are so intrinsically and anciently connected with magic that tying knots was once synonymous with magic in general. The art goes back to the Babylonians and who knows how much further back in unrecorded history. The Hebrew word for amulet, *kame'a*, has a root meaning *"to bind."* Knotting is the original binding spell.

Any intension or force can be tied or controlled by the knot. What separates the magical knot from tying a shoelace is the focus and intention of the one making the knot. However, the act of tying a shoelace can be transformed into a magical act: tie a child's sneaker: focus on blessing and protecting as you pull the knot tight.

In a knot charm, it goes without saying that you are focusing and concentrating your energy with every knot. Materials used in knot charms include threads, cord, plant stems, metal wire, animal or human hair.

Knots can be used for positive or malevolent intent. Common uses of knot magic include love, healing, wealth and weather spells (i.e., controlling the wind and rain).

Knots are used to bind intent, and also to remove spells. They are common Celtic, Chinese, Egyptian and Scythian motifs. The concept of the "lover's knot" lies in ancient love knot magic. Some believe that the inspiration for the ring arose from knot magic.

The animal patron of knot magic is the spider.

 ## Basic Knot Spell

1. Focus on your goal and desire, while holding a red cord in your hands.
2. Tie a knot
3. Wrap it in fabric, place it in a magic box and keep it in a safe, secure location.

A Traditional Knot Incantation

This incantation accompanies the tying of nine knots.

By knot of one, the spell's begun!
By knot of two, my spell comes true
By knot of three, so mote it be
By knot of four, power I store
By knot of five, my magic is alive
By knot of six, this spell I fix
By knot of seven, this spell I leaven
By knot of eight, it is fate
By knot of nine, what's wished is mine!

✪ Using this book

Measurements, or the Lack Thereof

Magic is a personal intuitive art. It is crucial that you do not approach it the way you would a chemistry experiment.

What does this mean? It means that a spell cannot be done by rote—not if you expect to see successful results. Magic cannot be reproduced by mechanical means and thus many if not most of the spells do not have precise measurements. Beware of spells that tell you *exactly* how much to add of one ingredient, in proportion to *exactly* how much of another. It is very important that you participate in these decisions, that you determine quantities and proportions. Why? Because this is *your* magical voice speaking, *your* magical participation in the spell. Magic is a sensual, intuitive art. It is vital that fragrances please you, that textures tempt you, that a salt scrub is as wet or dry as you envision.

Don't be afraid to play with your ingredients, to add a little more of one substance or less of another to achieve a result that pleases your senses, not someone else's. (Although if it's a love spell …)

★ *If in doubt, start with equal proportions of all ingredients*
★ *Should specific ingredients dominate the spell, this will be indicated in that spell's instructions*
★ *In the few instances where precise quantities or proportions are suggested, it is because this is a significant factor in that particular spell*
★ *Formulas used for one specific spell are given in the instructions for that spell. Some magical formulas however are extremely popular; many spells depend upon them. Those formulas are included in the* Formulary, *beginning on page 1037. These formulas for magic oils, inks, powders and charged waters are identified in the text by* **bold type**

PART TWO

The Spells

Animal Spells

Is it time to measure the cat for a magic wand? Perhaps the parrot needs to learn some chants? Maybe there is a set of domination spells so that the dog can force you to walk him on the schedule *he* chooses? No, spells regarding animals are still meant for people to perform, although some benefit from some animal assistance. Many of these spells involve protecting animals from physical and spiritual harm. Others benefit humans, through the power and gifts of animals.

Magical Partners

Animals who participate in your spells and rituals, enhancing them with their own powers, tend to fall into one of two categories:

★ *Familiars*
★ *Allies*

The concept of an animal as a *pet* is a modern one. Those who possessed this concept of interspecies friendship ahead of their time often found themselves condemned for witchcraft on grounds of familiarity with demonic creatures like cats, birds, rabbits, black dogs, reptiles, and amphibians. Sounds like what you'd find for sale in any local pet store? Well, familiar animals are exactly that: *familiar*. The classic witch's cat, rabbit or toad, a familiar is an actual, individual animal with whom one can live and share an intense psychic, personal bond. If this characterizes a relationship you have ever had with an animal, then you have had a familiar, regardless of whether you engaged in magical practices together. A dog who won't sleep unless it's under your bed, the cat who follows you from room to room, the bird who spends the day perched on your shoulder: these all qualify as familiars.

A familiar's presence may be sufficient to spark and enhance your magic, whether there is any conscious active involvement or not. For others, the psychic and magical bonds possible between animal and human create profound power and satisfaction.

In general, familiars are creatures who can realistically live with you: cats, dogs, rabbits, birds, toads, and snakes are most typical. Those living and working closely with other species—those species that usually do not live amongst people—may discover psychic and magical bonds, as well. Wild animals that remain wild can also qualify as familiars, though invariably they choose you rather than the other way round. These include those birds or bees that, taking a liking to someone in the family, stop by daily. Scandinavian witches traditionally favored flies as familiars. Wild dolphins occasionally single out an individual human and initiate a relationship. It is not unknown for people living on the edge of woods or in a wilderness place to develop a special relationship with an individual creature.

A familiar is a specific, individual creature with whom you have established a psychic bond. Of course, this limits the creatures with which you can magically interact. What if your magic requires a rhinoceros or crocodile? What if it requires a dragon or unicorn?

A familiar may be considered an animal ally but *animal allies* transcend the boundaries of familiars. Animal allies are a form of spiritual relationship: because the relationship may occur entirely in the realm of spirit, any animal may be approached. The presiding spirit of the animal may also be approached, rather than any individual creature.

A person may have as many familiars and/or allies as needed.

Animal Images

Among the oldest existing human artifacts are the beautifully detailed prehistoric cave paintings, indicating the profound magical link between humans and animals. Small portable images of specific animals, usually crafted from clay or stone, have also been used since ancient times for assorted magical purposes, especially healing, hunting, and protection, and pursuit of enhanced psychic power.

The Zuni, a Native American people from New Mexico, have turned this tradition into an art form. Zuni stone fetishes, miniature carvings of specific animals, were originally created for ceremonial and hunting purposes. Today most are intricately carved, displaying the creator's artistry and skills. Originally, this was not the case: Earth provided the artistry and the magic. Traditional fetish-carvers searched for stones where the shape of the creature was already apparent. At most, minimal shaping was needed to see the animal within. Because the stone charm is discovered, rather than consciously created, the animal spirit is given the opportunity to choose you rather than the reverse.

1. Search for similar stones. You will recognize one when you see it; like holed-stones these are gifts from Earth.
2. Charge and consecrate your stone fetish by placing it in a magic box together with images, food, and magical botanical activators. Traditionally corn pollen was used to feed and activate the fetish; use whatever seems appropriate and sacred to you.
3. When not in use, keep your fetish protected in its box or container. Feed it on schedule to keep it activated and powerful.

 Animal Communication Spell: Eve Oil

Eve Oil may be used to assist and enhance communication with animals.

1. Place apple blossoms, dried pomegranate seeds and snake root in a bottle.
2. Cover with sweet almond and jojoba oil.
3. Dress candles with this oil to accompany visualization as well as actual physical communication.

Familiar Consecration Spell

To cement and/or formalize the psychic bonds between you and your familiar:

1. Cast a circle large enough to hold you, your familiar and any magical tools that you wish simultaneously to consecrate (these may include leashes, collars or similar pet paraphernalia, as well as spell components or ritual tools).
2. Burn frankincense on the periphery of the circle.
3. Sit within the circle, with your familiar, until you feel that it's time to come out.
4. Repeat as needed.

Live dangerously! If your familiar is a cat, cast your circle with dried catnip, and instead of frankincense, burn diviner's sage to enhance your powers of prophesy. Let the cat play, while you allow yourself sudden bursts of inspiration.

Although you can bring any animal into your home, you cannot force it to be your familiar. This profoundly affectionate relationship, built on love, respect and personal chemistry, must develop independently. Likewise, animal alliances cannot be forced.

They may, however, be requested. Many believe that we are each born with the alliances we need, whether animal, botanical or spirit. The key is to discover those alliances and learn how to work with them for maximum power and benefit.

Various methods exist for discovering allies and requesting new relationships. Many card-based divination systems exist. Animal allies also manifest themselves in your dreams. Any animal or species that appears consistently to you, whether in dreams or in waking life, may be an ally, or may potentially become one.

If you desire a specific alliance, request it via a combination of your altar and visualization:

 # Animal Ally Invitation Spell

1. Choose a focal image for your altar, something that represents your ally for you. Use a toy, a photograph or an image. It is more crucial that it resonates strongly for you than that it be a literal depiction.
2. Surround it with objects or images that would normally be used to lure this creature. A dish of honey, for instance, summons a bear. Make the invitation as strong as possible.
3. If you can find candles in the shape of your desired ally or its food, add them to the altar.
4. Grind cinnamon and frankincense together and burn them as a spirit-summoning incense.
5. In addition to Step 2, offer literal food (a dish of milk for a snake, for instance). Alternately, burn images of appropriate food.
6. Relax. Let your eyes go slightly out of focus and await visitations.
7. Try this for up to thirty minutes a day, until you receive results.

Although this spell requests a waking vision, realistically your response may still occur during your dreams: have paper and pen by your bedside to record any significant dreams.

Sometimes familiars and allies are discovered for you.

In traditional Mexico and Central America, many shaman and witches are believed able to transform themselves into animals, known as *nagual*. A coyote observed walking down the road may be a regular coyote or it may be a witch in disguise. In the Mexican state of Oaxaca, however, a different concept exists. The *nahual* (as it is spelled in Oaxaca) is perceived to be a guardian spirit acquired at birth, a sacred gift from parents to their child.

Nahual Baby Ritual

Preparations begin before the birth of the child:

1. The expectant couple obtains some special wood and burns it down to ash. Traditionally, the desired wood leaves white ash, because it will make the rest of the spell easier, however this may be adapted to suit specific desires. Any traditional magic wood, such as birch, ceiba, hazel or rowan would be appropriate, too.
2. These ashes are reserved until the birth.
3. After birth, the placenta is carried to a strategic area, traditionally a mountain crossroads, and placed on the ground.
4. The ashes are sprinkled onto the placenta.
5. The first animal to leave prints either in or with the ash is the child's protector or represents the species.

Of course, this spell obviously derives from a rural area, with little traffic but a lot of wildlife. Adapt to your needs.

The above spell can also be done at any time as a visualization. It may be done for your child but you can also perform it for yourself, to discover your own allies.

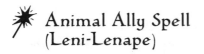

Animal Ally Spell (Leni-Lenape)

Sometimes a more concrete familiar is desired. According to a Leni-Lenape Indian tradition, babies are given a living, tangible animal ally, rather than just an abstract protective spirit. Usually a puppy or kitten is chosen, or some other appropriate companion animal. The animal is treated as a pet and encouraged to be the child's companion. These pets are not shared: every child has his or her own. This is a life partnership.

★ Should the animal die, it is perceived as having been a buffer for the child, essentially having taken the "hit" meant for the child, particularly if the child has been threatened by illness or accident. The animal is buried with ceremonies, releasing the child from the relationship. The child is given another pet immediately
★ Should the child die, funeral rituals release the animal from the bond

Animals may also be dedicated to specific spirits, not just to humans. This creates a profound triangular relationship between human, spirit and animal. In an indigenous Siberian ritual, the animal dedicated to the deity lives a charmed life:

Animal Spirit Dedication Ritual

1. A specific animal is chosen to be dedicated to a specific deity.
2. Purify the animal with juniper incense.
3. Sprinkle it with wine.
4. Decorate the animal with ribbons in colors associated with the specific spirit.
5. The animal is returned home or to its flock. It is now never ridden, worked or eaten, but is instead treated exceptionally well (or at least left alone to enjoy life) as a gesture of sacrificial devotion. This treatment may be extended over the creature's entire natural life or for a specified period of time, although this must be stipulated from the first initiation of the ritual.

Originally a Buriat (indigenous Siberian) custom, traditionally birds, horses or fish were dedicated to the Buriat spirits, the Ongon. The ritual has now been adapted by Mongolian Buddhists, although now, obviously, the animals are dedicated to Buddhist deities. Adapt to your needs. An animal sacred to the specific spirit is most appropriate; hence, a dog would be dedicated to Hecate.

Many spells, especially those that request healing or protection for animals, or those to locate lost animals, suggest consecrating the animal to a spirit. Although there are also many others, the following have earned a reputation as renowned animal-protectors. Incorporate them into your spells as needed.

★ SPIRITS THAT PROTECT CATS: Artemis, Bastet, Freya, Hecate, Lilith

★ SPIRITS THAT PROTECT BIG CATS (TIGERS, LIONS, LEOPARDS, ETC.): Dionysus, Durga, Hathor, Kybele, Sekhmet

★ SPIRITS THAT PROTECT DOGS: Artemis, Hecate, Ogun, Saint Roch

★ SPIRITS THAT PROTECT HORSES: Anat, Demeter, Epona, Poseidon, Rhiannon, Rla-mgrin (Hayagriva)

★ SPIRITS THAT PROTECT TOADS: Agwe, Heket

★ SPIRITS THAT PROTECT SNAKES: Athena, Ezili Freda Dahomey, Lilith, Mami Waters, Simbi, Lady Asherah

★ SPIRITS THAT PROTECT COWS: Brigid, Hathor, Hermes, Isis, Lakshmi, Maeve, Shiva

★ SPIRITS THAT PROTECT FISH: Atargatis, La Baleine, La Sirene, Yemaya

★ SPIRITS THAT PROTECT PIGS: Demeter, Seth

★ SPIRITS THAT PROTECT ANIMALS IN GENERAL: Aphrodite, Artemis, Baba Yaga, Faunus, Hathor, Lilith, Saint Anthony (Saint Anthony is the spiritual detective: request his assistance when anything or anyone is missing)

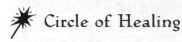

Animal Healing Spells

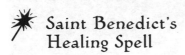

Circle of Healing

Cast a circle with blooming thistles: demarcate the entire circle or place one bloom in each of the four cardinal points. Bring the animal within the circle in order to intensify the effects of any healing or cleansing spells.

Saint Benedict's Healing Spell

In his lifetime, Saint Benedict persecuted pagans and witches. One wonders how he would have reacted had he known that, centuries later, he'd be magically petitioned to assist ailing animals?

Burn a white candle dedicated to Saint Benedict and offer him a glass of brandy or Benedictine. Make your petition of healing; Saint Benedict's animal ally is the crow. Look for the appearance of a crow to indicate a response to your petition.

Masterwort Strength Spell

Masterwort allegedly imparts greater physical strength and has thus been used to assist beasts of burden. Place masterwort in an amulet bag and attach to the animal as desired.

Lost Animal Spells

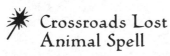

Crossroads Lost Animal Spell

A Russian method for calling lost animals home involves journeying to a crossroads, where, magically speaking at least, roads merge and separate and you never know who or what might turn up from any direction at any time.

1. Go to a crossroads.
2. Face west, the direction of the setting sun.
3. Bow from the waist nine times.
4. Do this three times, for a total of twenty-seven bows, calling the animal as you normally would, and also chant prayers and petitions and recite sacred texts.
5. Don't stop calling and/or petitioning until three series of nine bows each are complete, then take ten steps backward without turning around.
6. Turn around and go home.

When an animal goes missing, one common immediate response is to post signs requesting information and assistance from others. This next Russian spell takes that notion a step further: assistance is requested from Earth's various spirit powers, so that they will locate and send your animal back home. As with standard signs, a reward is posted. Should the spell work, be sure to pay it. (The Forest Tsar is chief of all woodland spirits; the Water Tsar is chief of all water spirits, and so on. Adjust the spell if necessary to suit your circumstances.)

Magical Sign Animal Spell (1)

Write messages on three pieces of birch bark (one for each of the nature tsars) as follows:

I'm writing to the Forest Tsar and the Forest Tsarina and their small children.
I'm writing to the Earth Tsar and the Earth Tsarina and their small children.
I'm writing to the Water Tsar and the Water Tsarina and their small children.
I'm writing to inform you that [INSERT YOUR NAME] HAS LOST A [INSERT COLOR, GENDER, DESCRIPTION] [INSERT TYPE OF ANIMAL INCLUDING AS MUCH DESCRIPTIVE MATERIAL AS YOU FEEL IS NECESSARY TO IDENTIFY AND DISTINGUISH YOUR ANIMAL FROM OTHERS].

If you have him/her please send him/her back without delaying one day, one hour, one minute, one second.

If you don't comply with my wish, I swear to pray and testify against you.

If you comply with my wish, I shall give you [INSERT SPECIFIC PLEDGE].

Fasten one message to a tree in the forest. Bury the second in Earth. Attach a small stone to the third and throw it into some living water.

The animal is expected to find its way home shortly.

 ## Magical Sign Animal Spell (2)

1. Appropriately shaped milagros (images) may be used to locate lost animals. Create one yourself if you can't find an appropriate milagro. Artistic ability is not required: just cut out the basic outline of the body.
2. Hold the milagro in your hands, while concentrating on your desired goal.
3. Give the milagro to the Spirit of your choice as a signal that you need help recovering your familiar.

If you prefer, post the milagro the way you would post a "missing pet" sign. Post it where the animal was last seen or wherever you feel is most appropriate.

Protection Spells for Animals

An animal's collar provides an excellent framework for protection spells; just remember to charge objects before attaching them. You can also incorporate knot magic wherever possible, to make the magic more powerful.

The following may be attached to the collar:

★ *Quartz crystal to enhance the animal's aura and provide protection*
★ *Rose quartz, to bestow the protective properties of your love*
★ *Other crystals, protective amulets, religious medals and similar may be attached to the pet's collar as desired*

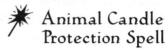 ## Animal Candle Protection Spell

1. Find or create a candle shaped to resemble your companion animal.
2. Carve the animal's identifying information, protective runes or other symbols onto it.
3. Anoint the candle with **Protection Oil** and burn.

If the candle is too cute to burn, get two. Maintain one permanently, while burning the second.

 ## Animal Image Protection Spell

Use an actual photograph of your pet or if unavailable, choose something, another image, statue, or candle bearing a strong resemblance for this spell.

1. Paint protective runes, hieroglyphs or other symbols onto the image.
2. Anoint with **Protection Oil.**
3. Keep the image in a safe, discreet spot, touching up periodically with Protection Oil.

*As an alternative, you could trace invisible runes, sigils or protective hieroglyphs onto the image with **Protection Oil.***

Assorted Spells to Protect Domestic Animals From Malevolent Magic

★ *Build your barn near birch trees*
★ *If the barn is already standing, transplant birch trees nearby*
★ *Adorn the birch trees, or other nearby trees, with red and white ribbons*
★ *Surround the barn with lilies and primroses. (Maintain them, replacing as needed.)*
★ *Bury a hatchet, sharp side up, under the barn's threshold, so that the animals must walk over it as they enter and depart*
★ *Horseshoes protect animals as well as humans. Post them over the barn door. The Hungarian method is to draw a horseshoe over the barn door using black chalk*
★ *Keep a piece of real silver in a dish or bucket of water, out of reach of the animals. This may be a small charm or a real silver coin. Once a week, sprinkle the animals with this water, then replace with fresh water*
★ *Sprinkle the animals with* **Rose of Jericho Water** *once a week*

 ## Animal Conjure Bag Protection Spell

Create this charm for any companion animal that sheds teeth.

1. Collect the animal's baby teeth and place within a conjure bag.
2. Add a coin minted in the animal's birth year if known, otherwise substitute a lucky medal or charm plus a tag with the animal's name or initials scratched into the metal.
3. Keep the bag in a safe place for protection.

This following spell provides a purifying and protective effect, as well as stimulating and activating the pet's role as familiar.

 ## Charcoal Charm Bag

1. Place charcoal in a little pouch.
2. Attach to your pet's collar.

 ## Egg Cleansing Spell

Just like people, animals need periodic ritual protective cleansings. (See Cleansing Spells, page 185.) Fumigations and asperging, the most popular methods for people, are equally effective for animals. However this may be easier said than done: try explaining to horses or cats that wafting smoke over them is really in their best interests. The following may be easier to accomplish:

1. Rub the animal with a whole, raw egg in its shell, working from head to tail and down, rather than up, the legs.
2. Flush the egg down the toilet for a house pet; otherwise, dispose of the egg outside the home or barn.

 ## Forest Tsar Protection Spell

The Forest Tsar cited in the Magical Sign Animal Spell on page 110 is Musail, King of the Forest Spirits. Once among the deities of the Slavic pantheon, post-Christianity he was demoted to an animal guardian spirit, a position he still serves. Request his assistance for any wild animal, as well as any domestic creature that finds itself in the woods.

Musail's sacred tree is the rowan. Hold a piece in your hand and speak to him from your heart. If he provides for you, make an offering on behalf of woodlands or forest animals.

Hair and Wax Protection Spell

1. Collect one hair from the head and one from the tail of every animal you wish protected. (Substitute one feather each from head and tail for each bird.)
2. Melt wax.
3. Add the hairs to the wax.
4. Remove the wax from the heat source and allow it to harden.
5. If possible, now lead all the animals needing protection around the perimeter of their home, in a sunwise direction. A minimum of two people is required for this: the person leading the parade holds the block of wax in one hand and a sacred image in the other. The person bringing up the rear drags an axe on the ground behind.
6. When all animals have safely returned home, bury the wax in a safe, secret place.

Magic Day Protection Spells

Certain days of the year are believed filled with extra magic power. Spells and magic rituals are performed on those days to benefit people, but also to benefit animals. These days traditionally include the following:

Beltane, May Day, Walpurgis (May 1st)

 ## Beltane Bonfire Spell

1. Build a pair of substantial fires.
2. Drive domestic animals between the fires for health, fertility and for maximum production and protection. Although this practice benefits all creatures, it is particularly beneficial for cattle. It's beneficial for people too: make sure you accompany those cows!

 ## May Day Cattle Spell

Place a crystal ball in a tub of water on May Day. Sprinkle the water on your cows to protect them from bewitchment and elf-shot.

Midsummer's Day, Saint John's Day (June 24th)
Although Midsummer's Eve is famous for its aromatic bonfires, water rituals are incorporated as well, especially for animals. (Some substitute the precise date of each year's summer solstice.)

 ## Midsummer's Pig Spell

The circus trick of forcing animals through hoops of fire descends from magic rites. On Midsummer's Day, twist hemp around a wooden wheel and set it on fire, and then lead pigs through the hoop for a year of safety, good health, and fertility.

 ## Midsummer's Protection Spell

1. Light a branch (ideally hazel or rowan wood) in the Midsummer bonfire.
2. Pass it over the backs of horses and cows as well as beneath them.

 ## Midsummer's Salt Water Spell

Take the animals to the ocean and bathe them in the waves. If this is impossible, asperge with salted water or other magical formula water.

Saint George's Day (April 23rd)
In many communities, Saint George's Day was the day animals were lead out into the field, thus protective, blessing rituals abound.

☀ Saint George's Blessing Spell (1)

1. Lead all healthy animals three times around the perimeter of their field, barn or home, always in a sunwise direction.
2. The person leading the parade carries a lit torch, while the person bringing up the rear holds an open padlock in one hand, the key in the other hand.
3. After the third round, the animals are lead back into the barn.
4. Turn the key in the lock.
5. Throw the key in a river or stream, while preserving the now permanently locked padlock.

☀ Saint George's Blessing Spell (2)

1. Preserve a palm blessed on Palm Sunday. (Pagans: substitute a sacred, protective plant, such as wormwood or rosemary.)
2. Place this before a sacred image, together with two whole raw eggs and a pot filled with raw barley.
3. Light candles before the image. (Some versions of this spell specify a church candle.)
4. Use the flame from a candle to light a torch.
5. Group all the animals to be protected in a circle.
6. One person circles around the animals carrying the torch, while a second person sprinkles **Holy Water** or another protective water formula onto the animals, using the palm frond or rosemary or wormwood plant.
7. The animals are then driven to pasture by slapping them with the palm frond or plant.
8. Throw the palm frond or branch into running water.
9. Sow the barley in the ground.
10. Break the eggs on the ground, away from your property.

☀ Magic Incense Protection Spell

Burn elecampane roots, mugwort and Saint John's Wort to calm animals and protect them.

Milagro Animal Spells

Milagros, which translates as "miracles" in Spanish, are votive images, typically cut from metal, although wooden and gemstone milagros do exist. The most famous milagros are formed in the shape of human anatomical parts: eyes, legs, hearts or arms, for instance. They are traditionally donated to a deity or saint in exchange for the healing or protection of whatever is depicted. Milagros are also sometimes formed in the shape of animals, in order to provide protection and healing for the animal depicted.

☀ Milagro Animal Spell (1)

1. Charge a milagro with your desire for protection or healing.
2. Attach it to the animal as appropriate, on the collar or otherwise.

☀ Milagro Animal Spell (2)

1. Charge the milagro with your desire.
2. Carve and dress a candle, charging it with your desires and goals.
3. Stick the milagro onto (or into) the wax candle before burning it.

Milagro Animal Spell (3)

Create a healing (or protection) board:

1. Mount the milagro on the fabric-covered cardboard together with other appropriate images and written affirmations. Incorporate sacred texts as desired.
2. Post this board on the wall or use it as the focal point of a candle-burning altar.

This concept may also be incorporated into a magic spell box. Place the milagro inside the box or use it to decorate the box itself.

Milagros may also be taken to shrines and posted as a request for healing or as thanks for healings already accomplished.

 ## Mistletoe Fertility Spells

Mistletoe allegedly enhances the reproductive capacity of animals. Not only does it promote conception, it's believed to also prevent miscarriage, particularly for sheep and goats. The amuletic part of mistletoe is usually the "wood": be cautious as mistletoe can be toxic, especially the berries.

★ *Hang mistletoe in the barn*
★ *Attach a piece of mistletoe to the animal herself*

 ## Mugwort Protection Spell

Hang bunches of mugwort on gates and field boundaries to protect the animals within from malevolent magic and spiritual danger.

 ## Protection Altar Spell

1. Make an image of your pet the focal item of the altar.
2. If you are requesting assistance from a specific spirit, surround the image with items (candles, images, incense, offerings) that will call that spirit.
3. If you are unsure whom to ask for protection, request it from the animal's guardian spirits: place four white candles in the corners of the altar, with the animal's image in the center. Burn them with frankincense incense.

 ## Purple Loosestrife Spell

The plant purple loosestrife is used to restore peace and maintain harmony amongst animals, as amongst people. (Interestingly, it was also traditionally used to tan leather; perhaps magical, subliminal transmission of the threat of the leather factory is what maintains calm!) Hang it in the barn to maintain harmony and happiness among all inhabitants.

 ## Red Clover Protective Bath Spell

1. Create an infusion by pouring boiling water over red clover.
2. Strain out the solids and used the liquid to bathe animals to keep them protected, healthy and thriving.

Cows

Historically, among the constant and sometimes hysterical accusations against witches was that of bewitching cattle. In general, this means either bewitching the milk away, or obstructing fertility, or somehow mysteriously harming or even killing cows. From a modern perspective, it can be difficult to comprehend this almost obsessive desire to safeguard cattle. However, beyond the economic factor, what one is witnessing, albeit in convoluted fashion, are vestiges of ancient spiritual traditions that once held cattle sacred. These traditions survive in India yet were once common around the world, in ancient Egypt, Greece, Ireland, the Middle East and elsewhere.

Anti-Bewitchment Spell

1. Create an infusion by pouring boiling water over mugwort and allowing it to steep.
2. Detailed instructions for making infusions are found in *Elements of Magic Spells,* pages 31–33. However, be sure to create a sufficient quantity to bathe cows.
3. Strain out the botanical materials and wash the cows with the infusion to break any spells cast upon them.

Should your cows (or goats or sheep) stop giving milk, this Belorussian spell may be worth a shot.

Bewitched Milk Spell (1)

1. Put a sieve over a pot.
2. Fill it with **Holy Water** or pure spring water.
3. Bring it to a boil, stirring constantly with a charged and blessed willow twig.
4. As the water boils, the spell should break.

Bewitched Milk Spell (2)

An alternative British spell to remedy bewitched milk:

1. Place a horseshoe together with some of the animal's hair in a pot.

2. Cover with some of the animal's milk and bring to a boil. (If there's not sufficient milk, mix with milk from other sources.)
3. Allow this to boil, then dispose of it outside of your property.

If the animal has been charmed, this sends the hex back with gusto. Increased milk supply should quickly be witnessed. If the loss of milk is not due to magical causes, this action causes no harm, but will also not improve the milk situation.

Bovine Anti-Bewitchment Spell

If you suspect your cow has been bewitched:

1. Build a fire.
2. Take a little hair from the back of the cow and throw this into the fire.
3. Put a little more of the cow's hair into a pot of the cow's own milk and boil this over the fire.

Cattle Anti-Theft Spell

1. Allow three drops of blood from the smallest finger of the smallest child in the family to drop onto a piece of bread.
2. Crumble this bread and feed it to the cattle. Allegedly this safeguards the cows from being stolen.

Cow Flower Protection Spell

Flowers from Good Friday church services may be used to protect cattle. Good Friday is indicated because of its connection to the resurrection. Because of cattle's intrinsic spiritual connection with human fertility, any sacred day with fertility overtones, such as Beltane or Midsummer's Eve, may be substituted, or a day with personal resonance for you if more appropriate.

1. Collect some of the flowers following the conclusion of the service or ceremony.
2. Burn the flowers, together with seven teaspoons of flour and three teaspoons of salt.
3. Gather up the ashes and sew them into a sachet. Reserve until needed.
4. Should a cow fall ill from natural or suspicious causes, break the sachet open and rub the ashes over the cow's belly three times, always in the same direction.
5. Alternately, place the unbroken sachet on the ground. Lead the cow over it three times, always walking in the same direction.

 ## Heather Torch

Carry a flaming torch of heather around cattle to stimulate their fertility.

 ## Keep the Cows Coming Home Spell

This spell allegedly encourages cows to come home and not wander. Feed the cows out of the pots used to prepare your own dinner. They'll come home.

 ## Milk Production Spells

★ *Hang asafetida in the barn to assure the quality and quantity of milk*
★ *Bathing animals with a watery infusion of mugwort allegedly stimulates them to produce more milk*
★ *Chalcedony and turquoise are used to enhance human mother's milk: use these stones to decorate an animal to see whether it works for it, too*

 ## Mother Sunshine's Anti-Bewitchment Spell

When witches allegedly cursed the cattle of a farmer to whom they owed money in mid-nineteenth-century Devon, the farmer turned to Mother Sunshine, the local "good witch." She recommended taking the heart from one of the four bulls that had died as a result of this curse, sticking it with pins and hanging it in the chimney. History shows this spell to have been a success. Adapt to your needs.

 ## Pow-Wow Cow Botanical Protection Spell

Pow-Wow recommends honeysuckle, rowan and witch hazel as prescriptions for protecting cattle. These botanicals may be used individually or in combination:

★ *Fasten them above the barn doors*
★ *Decorate the barn with them*
★ *Decorate the cows with them*

 ## Rowan Hoop Spell

Rowan is ranked among the most magical of plants. It offers protection from malevolent magic as well as enhancing the user's own psychic, clairvoyant powers.

1. Craft hoops from rowan branches.
2. Drive cattle through them to receive rowan's blessings of protection.

Purple Loosestrife Cattle Spell

Purple loosestrife may also be used to remedy specific personality conflicts: the ancient Greeks hung purple loosestrife around the necks of oxen that were yoked in tandem. Hang it around the necks of any animals that must cooperate with one another, particularly if they're not naturally inclined to do so.

Magic squares are popular devices of enchantment. The famed SATOR square may be the most versatile of the lot. Among its many other uses, it repels malignant spells cast over cows and prevents further bewitchment.

 ## SATOR Spell

1. Write the following on a piece of paper:

S	A	T	O	R
A	R	E	P	O
T	E	N	E	T
O	P	E	R	A
R	O	T	A	S

2. Grind it up and add it to the cattle feed. Have the cows eat the words.

Dogs

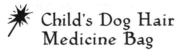 ## Child's Dog Hair Medicine Bag

1. Fill a medicine bag with loose dog hair.
2. Add any other lucky charms, as desired.
3. Give to a child to wear or carry for protection.

 ## Greyhound Spirit Protection

A home where a well cared for, happy greyhound lives will allegedly never be haunted by malicious spirits.

Pacify Threatening Dogs Spell (Christian Pow-Wow)

Pow-Wow strongly incorporates the use of spoken charms. This one is used to soothe a threatening dog and provide protection—excellent for those forced to walk past a snarling, snapping canine.

The charm must be repeated three times before you reach the dog (or the dog reaches you!)

Dog, hold thy nose to the ground!
God has made thee, me and hound.
In the name of the Father, the Son and the Holy Ghost.

Then form the sign of the cross three times.

This spell as recorded in 1820 by John George Hohman in his definitive Book of Pow-Wows: The Long Lost Friend, *omits the last line of the charm, but includes the crosses.*

 ## Pacify Threatening Dogs Spell (Pagan-Friendly Version)

Historically, there have always been two movements within the Pow-Wow community: those who emphasize Christian orientation and those who do not. Rhymes were adapted as needed and continue to evolve. This pagan-friendly version calls upon those Greek divinities that exert great influence over hounds:

Dog, hold your nose to the ground!
Creator made you, me and hound
In the name of the triple goddess, Selene, Artemis and
    Hecate

Repeat three times. The cross, as a pre-Christian symbol of protection, may still be formed. A pentacle, crescent moon, downward facing triangle or other shape may also be substituted, as desired.

 ## Rhodium Oil Spell to Lure Dogs Away

This perfume oil allegedly attracts dogs and was once used by thieves in order to lure dogs away. Play with the proportions until you achieve an effective fragrance.

It may work on other animals, too. Experiment and see. Rhodium Oil consists of:

★ *Essential oil of cedarwood*
★ *Essential oil of rose geranium*
★ *Essential oil of palmarosa*
★ *Essential oil of sandalwood*

Blend with a carrier oil, such as jojoba oil.
Rhodium Oil may be used in various ways:

★ *Wear it as a perfume*
★ *Use the oil to mark a trail*

 ## Stop Dogs Barking Spell

Place leaves of hound's tongue in your shoes, beneath your feet. Alternatively, carry within a charm bag.

Sweet Nature Dog Collar

Sew a piece of flint and a piece of coral inside a dog's collar to protect against illness and ill temper.

Horses

(Charms and spells for horses may also be used for donkeys and mules.)

Evil Eye Spells

From a magical perspective, the horse is the king of beasts. It is universally considered exceptionally powerful magically. Merely being in the presence of a healthy horse regularly enhances your own personal psychic powers, as well as general vitality and libido. Horses, however, perhaps because of their great power, are also considered particularly vulnerable to the Evil Eye as well as attention from malevolent spirits.

Horses provide people with amulets: a horseshoe isn't activated until it's actually been on a horse's foot. However, no animal is considered more in need of its own protective amulet than horses. Decorative horse brasses are now considered objects for collectors; however their original intent is to provide protection for a horse and they may still be used as amulets.

Other amulets for horses include:

★ *Peacock feathers*
★ *Blue eye beads*
★ *Holed stones*
★ *Most protective amulets, even though designed for people, will work for horses in a pinch, particularly the Italian corno and cimaruta*

Remember to magically empower amulets and charms by charging and/or consecrating them before their initial use.

Attach amulets to the horse's mane, tail or where appropriate on the horse's tack, saddle, harness or otherwise.

 Foal's Safety Spell

1. Place a pinch of rue and a pinch of wormwood into a small red charm bag.
2. Attach it to the foal's mane.

Horse Braid Spells

Beyond good grooming, braiding the horse's mane and tail daily serves as a protective, blessing spell. Consider the principles of knot magic and apply. The following suggestions may be combined as desired:

★ *Plait the mane and tail into thirteen braids each, adding straw to the braids*
★ *Entwine red ribbons into the horse's mane and tail*
★ *Braid small bells into the mane or tail*
★ *Attach a piece of rowan wood to the mane or tail*
★ *Place a lump of asafetida into a charm bag and attach to the horse*

Horse Hex

It's crucial that stalls and stable be kept immaculately clean: a traditional method of hexing is to throw coffin nails into the stable as this allegedly causes horses to become lame.

Remove any strange nails or other articles promptly to maintain safety and reverse any malevolent spells that have been cast.

 Horse Love Oracle

For this spell to work, the horses must be in an open barn, not restricted to locked stalls.

1. Stand outside the stable or barn, with your back to the closed door.
2. Kick the door three times with your left foot, while chanting:

If my true love's on the way
Saddle my horse!

If a horse comes running to the door, this is a very good sign. If several horses approach, this is an even more auspicious sign. If the horses ignore you, it's time for stronger love spells.

 Horse Nightmare
Relief Spell

This spell is intended to relieve a horse's nightmares.

1. Pour boiling water over anise seeds, fresh garlic and licorice root (not the candy), making an infusion.
2. Allow this to cool, then strain and feed it to the horse.
3. If the horse won't be induced to drink it, add the infusion to its food or use it to bathe the horse.

Horse Riding Charms

Some talismans serve both horse and rider:

★ *Agate protects the rider from falling and the horse from stumbling.*
★ *Turquoise offers general protection to horse and rider*

Mare Stones

Holed stones are known as *hag stones* or *witch stones*, but also as *mare stones*. Various spirits (including the dreaded *mara*, whose name inspires nightmare) allegedly take pleasure in riding horses at night beyond their capacity. The horse is discovered the following morning, exhausted, glistening with sweat, frothing at the mouth. Holed stones stop these spirits from riding horses.

- ★ *String a holed stone, a mare stone, onto cord and wrap around the horse's neck*
- ★ *Braid holed stones into the horse's mane*
- ★ *Do both; more spiritual protection is always considered preferable to less*

 ## Ride Like the Wind Spell

To protect both horse and rider, carry or wear an amethyst engraved with an image of a winged horse akin to Pegasus.

 ## Smartweed Saddle Spell

For long journeys, place a handful of smartweed under the horse's saddle to enable it to travel extensively without suffering hunger or thirst. This tradition allegedly dates back to the Scythians.

Poultry

 ## Anti-Straying Spell

Feed caraway seeds to your poultry to discourage them from straying.

Hen Laying Spell

The spell allegedly promotes the laying of eggs.

1. Bring hens outside briefly when it's raining and a strong wind is blowing. Remain with them.
2. Hold them up in a tree, if possible.
3. Return them to shelter.

 ## Holed Stone Spell (1)

Hang a holed stone in the center of the chicken pen to protect the hens from spirits and predators.

 ## Holed Stone Spell (2)

To protect poultry from illness and fright, bury a holed stone under their house or coop.

 ## Poultry Protection Spell

To protect chickens from predators, keep a horseshoe (actually a mule shoe is preferable) in the oven. In order to be effective, the shoe must have actually been worn by a horse or mule.

Other variants of this spell suggest hanging the shoe inside the fireplace.

Poultry Protection for People

The benefits of maintaining poultry outweigh just having eggs.

- ★ *Dating back to at least the days of ancient Persia, roosters have been kept to scare away evil spirits. Hopefully your neighbors will appreciate your efforts on their behalf and not object to the rooster's early morning wake-up calls*
- ★ *A more neighbor-friendly approach may be a frizzled, or frizzly, hen. General Hoodoo wisdom states that a frizzled hen scratching in your yard will scratch up any hexes, spells or tricks secretly laid against your household*
- ★ *Should the frizzly hen prove unavailable, the ideal substitute is the black hen, Hecate's holy bird. It too eliminates malicious magic and will keep you supplied with the black hen's eggs so beloved in magic spells*

Fierce Creatures

Not all spells involve domestic creatures. Many spells revolve around protecting humans from fierce, potentially dangerous animals.

In general, carrying or wearing the image of the creature provides a sort of passport of safety. Magically speaking, both fear and affection indicate some sort of alliance. Wear charms or jewelry in the shape of the creature you fear: a snake ring, for instance, or crocodile earrings. Tattoos, temporary and permanent, also provide a measure of protection.

 ### Fierce Creatures Spell

Avens, the blessed herb, is also known as Herb Bennet, a distortion of "benedictus." The presence of avens allegedly protects against all venomous creatures.

★ *Wear fresh avens for safety*
★ *Carry the dried herb in a medicine bag*

 ### Holly Protection Spell

In the Middle Ages, it was believed that if holly wood (the wood, not the leaves) was thrown at wild animals, they would then lie down quietly and passively. Should you find yourself alone with aggravated fierce creatures, this is probably worth a shot.

1. Be prepared: charge the wood with its mission before setting forth into the wild.
2. Carry the wood in your charm bag: in an emergency, toss!

 ### Juniper Protection

Carrying a sprig of juniper allegedly protects against attack by fierce animals.

 ### Mullein Passport

Mullein allegedly transmits the magical message to wild creatures not to molest its bearer while passing through their territory. Carry or wear it for protection.

Protection from Crocodiles and Alligators

 ### Anti-Crocodile Charm (Burma)

Carry iron pyrites as a protective charm against crocodiles.

 ### Anti-Crocodile Charm (Ancient Egyptian)

The Egyptian Book of the Dead *suggests carrying the plant sweet inula to ward off crocodiles, both living ones and those that haunt the spirit realm.*

★ *Wear it in a charm bag to protect against actual visitations*
★ *Sleep with the herb in a dream pillow or beneath your pillow if unfriendly crocodiles are infesting your dreams*

 ### Crocodile Charm Bag

Place a piece of gold pyrite into a drawstring bag together with alligator teeth and/or an image of a crocodile.

Crocodile Teeth

Crocodiles shed their teeth, continually growing new ones. Naturally shed teeth have a prophylactic effect: string them and wear on necklaces and anklets to prevent attack. Alternatively, carry the teeth in a medicine bag.

Papyrus Hieroglyph Spell

Crocodiles, like snakes, are simultaneously fearsome, dangerous creatures and potent symbols of spiritual and psychic protection. Pregnant Isis, after all, hid in the crocodile infested swamps of the Nile Delta. It was the safest spot she knew. In ancient days, the papyrus plant, which once lined the Nile, was a hieroglyphic emblem for Lower Egypt, especially that Nile Delta swampland. It also served as a protective emblem from crocodiles, lending new meaning to Moses' cradle on the Nile, formed from papyrus.

★ *Draw the hieroglyph on parchment and carry it as a talisman*
★ *For intensive protection, draw the hieroglyph onto the body with henna or if danger is constant, consider a tattoo*
★ *Carry a photograph of living papyrus plants as a talisman or post it in a prominent location*
★ *The Beta Israel, the Jews of Ethiopia, are renowned for their beautiful pottery. A traditional motif is a tiny, lidded basket that opens to reveal a happy baby Moses. Carry one as a talisman*

Spirits that protect crocodilians as well as protecting people from them include Isis, Mami Waters and Sobek.

1. Charge a green candle with your fears and desires. Carve and dress it as desired.
2. Place the candle on an altar dedicated to the deity. Images of the deity may be used, however Sobek and Mami Waters may be represented by a crocodile; Isis by a serpent.
3. Articulate whatever it is that you need.

Sharks

Talismans that protect against shark attacks include:

★ *Coral*
★ *Pearls*
★ *Found, naturally shed shark teeth*

Carry or wear as suits you best, however the traditional method is to attach the talisman to a cord and wear around the ankles. Remember to charge magical objects prior to their initial use.

Snakes

Although no animal is more associated with magic than snakes, in general, magic spells for snakes involve methods of repelling them and warding them off.

On the other hand, perhaps you'd like to beckon snakes closer, at least in ritual. Snakes are among people's primary magical teachers and are invoked in spells for childbirth, fertility, healing, protection and financial well-being.

Snake-beckoning Spell

The scent of lavender allegedly invokes the spiritual presence of serpents and the legendary Serpent Spirits.

1. Place an image on an altar, either of a snake or of an affiliated deity—the Minoan Serpent Goddess for instance.
2. Surround this with fresh lavender or warm the essential oil in an aroma burner.
3. Call the spirit. Be prepared to explain why you have issued the invitation.

Do this spell before bedtime, to receive a visitation in your dreams.

 ## Snake Communication Spell

The snake is the totem animal of prophets: it's no accident that the staffs of Asklepios, Hermes, and Moses were embellished with snakes. Over the centuries, magical divining women, from the Minoan snake goddess to Marie Laveau, have danced with serpents. There is even a traditional divination system that interprets the movements of snakes. Because snakes are the repository of Earth's wisdom, there are many reasons why one would wish to communicate with them. That said, it may be easier for most people, for a variety of reasons, to access that knowledge through visions rather than actual contact.

1. Burn yarrow and allow the smoke to permeate the area.
2. Yarrow smoke allegedly stimulates visions of snakes; have your questions or goals ready.

Snake Safety Spells
★ *The aroma of galbanum allegedly repels snakes. Burn it as incense or warm the essential oil in an aroma burner. You may also add it to your perfume*
★ *The aroma of burning juniper wood and leaves also allegedly repels serpents*

★ *Make an infusion of black snake root (black cohosh) and add it to your bathwater, so that your aroma allegedly repels snakes. (Note: Black snake root is not safe for use by pregnant women.)*
★ *Serpentine is named for its affiliation with snakes. Carry it as a charm for safety from them. (This derives from Italian snake-charming traditions. Serpentine may also be used to cement the relationship: it provides safety without repelling.)*
★ *Agates are carried as talismans of safety from both snakes and scorpions. Although plain agate is allegedly effective, the talisman is more potent if engraved with either the image of a snake or of a person, preferably you or at least someone resembling you, riding upon a snake*

 ## Alkanet Spell

Alkanet, also known as bugloss, is most famous as the source for a natural dye. However, among its magic powers, alkanet not only allegedly protects against snakebite but also helps counter and control fears of snakes.

 ## Ashen Boundary Spell

Allegedly snakes will not cross over a boundary formed from mingled ash leaves and twigs. If one lives in snake-infested territory, cast your circle and find out.

Contraveneno Spell

"Contraveneno" is a large black bean, marked on one side with a cross. A staple of Latin American magic, there is apparently no English nickname for Fevellea cordifolia. *The bean is poisonous but is used as a magical weapon to prevent snakebite and attack from other venomous creatures. Carry it in a charm bag around your neck; do not consume it.*

Elder Spell

Elder magically guards against snakes and all manner of fierce creatures, including (allegedly), mosquitoes. Carry elder twigs in your pocket or conjure bag to prevent attack.

 ## Isis Protection Spell

According to legend, the magical botanical vervain sprang from Isis' tears. Because vervain shares in Isis' essence it's believed to protect against the various fierce creatures under her influence.

1. Gently simmer vervain in wine.
2. Strain and let the herb dry out.
3. Carry this dried herb in a charm bag to protect against snakes, scorpions, and crocodiles.

 ## Plantain Snakebite Spell

This spell refers to the common garden herb, not the member of the banana family. Charge plantain with its mission of protection. Carry it in your pocket to guard against snakebite.

 ## Raspberry Leaf Snake Spell

Carry a piece of root from a raspberry vine to magically protect against snakebite.

 ## Shark's Teeth– Snake's Tongues

Fossilized shark's teeth were once believed to be snakes' tongues. They're still believed to have a magical affinity for snakes. Soak a shark's tooth in wine, and then drink the wine to assist in healing snakebite.

Tamarisk Protection Spell

Burning tamarisk branches allegedly wards off snakes.

Wild Dagga Protection Spell

Wild dagga, an African plant, allegedly repels snakes. Maintain living plants in snake-prone areas and burn the dried leaves as needed.

Scorpions

Spirits that protect scorpions and protect against scorpions include Isis and Selket. If you are afraid for the creatures or because of the creatures, set up an offering table. Place an image representing the creature on the table as well as representations of the deity with appropriate offerings. Burn candles and incense as long as you feel is necessary.

Selket (also known as Serket) has particularly strong associations with scorpions. One of the four Egyptian canopic guardian deities, alongside Isis and her sister Nephthys, Selket, a spirit of magic, wears a scorpion crown. She punishes via scorpion stings but she also protects people from her sacred creatures and heals injuries received from them.

1. Create an altar with an image of Selket and/or an image of a scorpion.
2. Burn **kyphi** for Selket and explain what you need.

Tigers

In China, India and elsewhere in Asia, the tiger is profoundly connected with magic power. In many traditional belief systems, the tiger is the creature that embodies the concept of magic power and also possesses the strength and daring necessary to properly implement that power. Tigers provide practitioners with protection and teach magic skills, but obviously this is most often accomplished through magical visualization.

Amber's Chinese name translates as *"tiger soul."* It was believed that when tigers died, their souls became amber. Amber offers the easiest, most accessible method of contacting tiger guardian spirits.

 ## Tiger Guardian Spirit Spell

1. Hold a piece of amber in your left hand, close your eyes and allow your visualization to begin.
2. Do not let go of the amber until the visualization is complete and you have safely returned to your starting point.

Unicorns

Whatever their origins, animals now classified as *"fantasy creatures"* are almost invariably depicted as savage and scary monsters, like the basilisk. The unicorn is the exception. Once understood as fierce, unruly symbols of male primal power, unicorns have been tamed into sedate, docile, often asexual creatures, too pure, gentle, and beautiful to exist. In fact, medieval unicorn legends focus on the capture and murder of unicorns.

Among a unicorn's magical powers is the ability to eliminate and antidote all poisons. Allegedly dipping the unicorn's horn, the alicorn, into any food or liquid automatically removes any trace of poison. That legend has wreaked devastation on narwhals and rhinoceroses over the centuries; at a time when few were aware of fauna outside their immediate area, it was easy to pass off another species' horn as an alicorn. Of course, they didn't work but then, of course, they weren't real unicorn horns. Unicorns allegedly shed their alicorns annually like deer antlers.

 ## Unicorn Spell

1. If the unicorn doesn't actually shed its alicorn directly into your hand, it's a safe bet a horn is not genuine alicorn. If you have reason to be fearful of poisoning, burn a white, black, or red unicorn-shaped candle.
2. Try to transmit your petition of protection to presiding unicorn spirits.
3. Consecrate a unicorn charm by laying it beside the candle while it burns, then wear it afterwards.
4. Should the charm work for you, cleanse, re-consecrate and offer thanks to the unicorn.

Sometimes you need protection *from* fierce creatures, but other times you'd like them to provide you *with* protection.

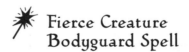 ## Fierce Creature Bodyguard Spell

1. Post the most terrifying images of the most dangerous animals you can envision in areas you perceive as physically or spiritually vulnerable.
2. The goal is not to invoke fear but for the images to serve as symbolic protectors.

 # Banishing Spells

There's often confusion over the difference between banishing spells and binding spells, however it's crucial that you understand this difference.

★ *Binding spells attach something or, more frequently, someone to you with great intensity, often permanently*

★ *Banishing spells remove something or, more frequently, someone from your presence, often permanently*

It's an important distinction. Although magic spells are typically used to manifest something or someone, quite often the reverse is needed. Something or someone needs to be sent packing quickly.

Banishing spells are traditionally timed to coincide with the waning moon, in the hopes that, just as the moon diminishes, so will the unwanted presence.

Also falling under the category of banishing spells are *Avoidance Spells*—those spells required when you wish to avoid contact, for instance with creditors or debt collectors. Banishing spells are used to prevent any unwelcome returns, too. However, you may wish to consider *Protection Spells* to reinforce, or in some circumstances replace, banishing spells.

Banishing People and Other Pests

 ### Ajenjible Banishing Spell

Ajenjible is an herb used in Latin America for culinary and medicinal purposes. Its magical purposes include banishing:

1. Make a strong infusion by pouring boiling water over ajenjible.
2. Strain out the botanical material and use the liquid as the final laundry rinse water when washing your target's clothing. Allegedly this will stimulate the person to move out of your home.

 ### Balloon Banishing

1. Write the target of your spell's name onto a slip of paper.
2. Insert this paper into a balloon, either before or after blowing it up, whichever you find simpler.
3. Take the balloon to an appropriate place and release it.

Banish Evil Spell

Sometimes it's not clear what or who needs to be banished. There's just a prevailing sense of evil that needs to be expelled. This spell is most effective during the Dark Moon. An iron hammer is required, as is a flat rock, and either a coffin nail or an old rusty nail.

1. Hammer the nail against the rock. The goal is not to pierce the rock but merely to score it three times across the face. Visualize what you are dispelling while you hammer.
2. Bury the stone far away.
3. Carry the nail in a red mojo bag, together with some crossroads and/or graveyard dirt.

 Banish Negative Energy

Occasionally what requires banishing is more ambiguous than unwanted guests, mean spirits or vermin: burn chicory to banish negative emotions from the premises as well as negative energy, regardless of the source.

Banishing Powders

The art of the enchanted powder reaches its finest point with banishing spells. Various banishing powders exist, of varying intensity. Some are created from common kitchen ingredients, while others are mixed from more exotic components. Experiment and see which formula works most powerfully for you.

Remember that powders are intended as a subtle form of magic. There's no need to leave a large suspicious pile; a discreet sprinkling is typically sufficient.

Any of the Banishing Powders below may be used to create a Banishing Oil.

 Banishing Oil

1. Grind the ingredients together to create a Banishing Powder (see below).
2. Cover this powder with castor oil, shaking vigorously to distribute.
3. If castor oil is too thick to flow adequately, dilute with jojoba oil.

 Banishing Powder (1) Basic Banishing Powder

Black pepper
Cayenne powder
Cinnamon
Sea salt
Sulfur

Banishing Powder (2) Begone! Banishing Powder

Chopped bay laurel leaves
Black pepper
Cayenne pepper
Powdered hydrangea blossoms
Sea salt

Both formulas above are similar in intensity and may be used in the same manner:

★ *Sprinkle the Banishing Powder on clothes, especially shoes, belonging to anyone you'd like to see gone*
★ *Sprinkle the powder on the ground, so that the target of your spell is forced to step on or over it*
★ *Banishing Powder will enhance the power of any other banishing spell. Sprinkle as an accompaniment, particularly around and over candles*

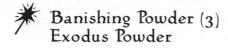

Banishing Powder (3)
Exodus Powder

Asafetida
Cayenne pepper
Sulfur

This is a very concentrated banishing powder, and it's known as Exodus Powder because it allegedly stimulates your spell's target to recreate the exodus—a sudden departure.

Grind all ingredients together to form a powder. Sprinkle this on and around your target's front doorstep to make them move. Actually sprinkling the powder onto your target's shoes should also achieve the same effect.

Banishing Powder (4)
Hot Foot Powder

Black pepper
Cayenne or habanero pepper
Salt
Sulfur

This is the classic Hoodoo version of Banishing Powder. Grind the ingredients together to form a powder.

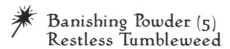

Banishing Powder (5)
Restless Tumbleweed

This is among the meaner banishing powders; your target is not only forced to leave but must wander restlessly like a tumbleweed.

1. If you can catch a tumbleweed, preserve and powder it.
2. Add cayenne or habanero powder and black pepper.

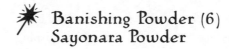

Banishing Powder (6)
Sayonara Powder

Grind and powder black pepper, cubeb peppers, ground dried ginger, and wasabi powder.

The above Banishing Powders are made from what are more or less household ingredients, with maybe a little extra investment. Although not everyone keeps sulfur powder or powdered hydrangea as a kitchen staple, they are both easy, inexpensive items to purchase from an herbalist or spiritual supply store.

The following Banishing Powder has a more complex set of ingredients: obtaining them may take greater effort than the previous formulas. It is, however, considered a stronger, more defiant, and perhaps ultimately a more malevolent banishing agent.

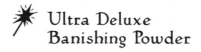

Ultra Deluxe
Banishing Powder

Cayenne pepper
Dragon's blood powder
Filé powder (ground sassafras)
Gunpowder (saltpeter and sulfur may be substituted
   if you cannot get hold of gunpowder)
Habanero powder
Shotgun pellets
A crushed wasp's nest

1. Mash all the ingredients together in a mortar and pestle.
2. Grind in a spice or coffee grinder to reduce to a fine powder.
3. Sprinkle the powder on your target's doorstep.

If you enjoy working with figure candles, black devil candles are considered powerful banishing agents:

Black Devil Banishing Spell

1. Hold a black devil candle in both your hands to charge it with your desire.
2. Dress the candle with Banishing Oil and burn.

Botanical Banishing Spells

The following botanicals possess a banishing effect. Incorporate one or (ideally) a combination of them into banishing spells: angelica, asafetida, basil, bay laurel, citronella, cloves, cumin, devil's bit, dragon's blood, elder, fleabane, fumitory, garlic, heliotrope, horehound, juniper, lovage, mistletoe, mullein, mugwort, oleander, pepper (both black and hot chili/cayenne), yew.

★ *Use in any combination to formulate your own banishing spells*
★ *Living plants grown in quantity around the home discourage uninvited visitors*
★ *Several of the above plants, like oleander and yew, are poisonous. As a general rule of thumb, those plants with toxic properties are used in banishing spells, to varying degrees. However, this may not be appropriate for those with children or animals present*
★ Poison Gardens *are discussed in depth in the* Protection Spells *section; however, if it's safe and appropriate for you, a Poison Garden may provide the privacy-minded with a protective banishing shield*

Change or Else!

This banishing spell targets a trouble-maker. Unlike most banishing spells, which simply encourage the person to depart, this one offers another option. The target of the spell can either reform or else leave peacefully.

1. Add essential oils of patchouli and vetiver to a blend of olive and castor oils.
2. Rub this on the door-knobs of your target's home.

Coffee Grounds Banishing Spell

The most effective way to perform the following spell is via subterfuge. Invite the target of your spell over to your home and serve fresh-brewed coffee. For maximum effectiveness, offer to read their coffee-grounds, turning over their cup. Then when they've left, immediately gather your spell materials.

1. Gather the dirt from your target's foot prints or, alternatively, gather the dirt from under a chair in which they were the last person to sit.
2. Combine this dirt with cayenne pepper, ground sassafras and used coffee grounds. (The most potent coffee grounds are those from the target's own cup.)
3. Sprinkle this on the target's front doorstep.

Cowslip Banishing Spell

Sprinkle cowslip (wild primrose) blossoms over your threshold to turn away unwanted visitors.

A different and very powerful banishing powder is created by invoking Exu's blessing. This Brazilian banishing spell utilizes *pemba*, an ingredient common to both African and Afro-Brazilian magic. Pemba is a type of chalk, traditionally blended with herbs. Each orisha has a specific formula and color of pemba. Once upon a time, pemba was imported to Brazil from Africa. Real pemba is sometimes still available from spiritual supply stores, however common colored chalk is now often substituted instead.

Exu's Banishing Powder

1. Collect seven handfuls of graveyard dirt.
2. Add a package of Pemba de Exu along with the herb corredeira. **Be careful:** corredeira is potentially toxic. Should true pemba be unavailable, red and/or black chalk may be substituted.
3. Grind all the ingredients together until a fine powder is created.
4. Place this powder inside a brown paper bag and take it to a crossroads at midnight.
5. Appeal to Exu. Ask him to bless your enterprise and to bless your Banishing Powder. Tell him whatever you need him to know.
6. Leave him a gift (rum and cigars are traditional) but don't leave the bag of powder. Having been blessed by Exu, you must now maneuver it into the home of your target to effect the banishing.

Foot Track Banishing

Traditional methods of spell disposal are not always possible any longer, for a variety of reasons, ranging from ecological to legal restrictions. In some cases, substitutions are easily made which will not adversely affect the desired outcome, but this is not always the case. The following is a very simple banishing spell, common to various parts of the world such as North Africa, the American South, and Romany-influenced Europe. The disposal of the ingredients effectively *is* the spell: sending your target's footprints downstream causes the banishment. If it's not possible to perform this spell exactly, then try another.

1. Follow the target of your spell discreetly, observing their footprints.
2. When you see a clear, distinct left print, dig it up in its entirety.
3. Take it home in a bag, then transfer the dirt to a glass jar or bottle, being careful not to lose or spill any of it.

4. Seal the bottle very tightly shut, adding a wax seal, if you like.
5. Take this to running water flowing away from you.
6. Turning your back on the water, throw the container over your left shoulder without looking, taking care not to hit anything you shouldn't.
7. Walk away without looking back once.

Four Thieves Banishing Spells

An excellent example of how magic travels and evolves, **Four Thieves Vinegar** arrived in New Orleans, brought by either French or Italians immigrants, who valued it for its illness-banishing properties. In New Orleans, another use was discovered: Four Thieves Vinegar is an excellent banishing agent for unwanted people. From New Orleans Voodoo, this use of Four Thieves entered the modern Wiccan and Pagan magickal community, many of whom are unfamiliar with its original use as a healing agent.

 ## Four Thieves Banishing Spell (1)

To avoid debt collectors or others in hot pursuit of you:

1. Place their business card inside a shot glass.
2. Fill the glass with **Four Thieves Vinegar.**
3. Leave the glass standing in a discreet place as long as necessary.

If a business card does not exist or you cannot obtain one, make one up: write the target's name on a business card-sized piece of paper and place this in the shot glass.

Four Thieves Banishing Spell (2)

Rub front entrance door-knobs with **Four Thieves Vinegar,** *while visualizing your spell target's imminent departure.*

 ## Four Thieves Banishing Spell (3)

The following spell is used to keep someone away from you, as well as to establish healthy boundaries.

1. Write your target's name on a piece of brown paper.
2. Soak this paper in **Four Thieves Vinegar.**
3. Fold the paper and bury in a flowerpot, ideally filled with crossroads dirt.
4. Plant a cactus on top and keep the pot near the front door.

The following banishing spell is traditionally attributed to Marie Laveau. Marie Laveau, born a free woman of color in New Orleans in 1792, may be the individual who has exerted the single most powerful influence over American magic. Until Marie Laveau, Voodoo, African-derived spiritual traditions, and the occult in general, all lingered in the shadows, fearful and disreputable. Laveau took the various strands of magic present in New Orleans and wove them together, creating a coherent, organized metaphysical system, which survived her death as well as subsequent local legal persecution.

Marie Laveau achieved great fame and notoriety in her lifetime. She became a local celebrity, attending church daily, actively performing good deeds and acts of charity while discreetly redeeming slaves and working for abolition. Laveau was the first individual to demand that her metaphysical traditions be openly incorporated into daily life, not hidden behind masks. She demonstrated public pride in her spiritual traditions when it was still dangerous and controversial to do so: Laveau

paved the modern road for anyone who publicly practices magic.

Whether the following spell is actually hers or whether her name was attached to bestow power and glamour, may never be known. It is, however, considered one of the most effective banishing spells.

 ## Four Thieves Banishing Spell (4)

1. Write your target's name nine times on a square of paper.
2. Cover and cross each name with your own, saying
   I cross you, I cover you
   I command you, I compel you to [fill in your desire]
3. Place this paper inside a small glass jar or bottle.
4. Fill the bottle with **Four Thieves Vinegar** and seal it tightly shut.
5. You must now dispose of this bottle. The traditional mode of disposal is to toss the bottle over your left shoulder into running water without looking; however, adapt this to your needs and situation.

 ## Four Thieves Banishing Spell (5)

The following spell may be used as a traditional banishing spell. It allegedly has the added bonus effect of causing the spell's target to cease harassing or bothering you.

1. Sprinkle **Four Thieves Vinegar** over sea salt. (Traditional hoodoo and conjure workers might favor kosher salt instead.)
2. Blend the Four Thieves Vinegar into the salt, then, once the salt has dried, pour it into a conjure bag and carry until your opportunity arises.
3. When the target of your spell next visits you or is otherwise encountered, sprinkle the salt secretly in their wake as they depart from you.

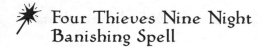 ## Four Thieves Nine Night Banishing Spell

An extra-strength banishing spell:

1. Each night for nine consecutive nights (ideally timed with the waning moon but cast the spell as necessary) write the target of your spell's name on brown paper, together with a brief, explicit message, something like *"Go home!"*
2. Sprinkle one of the banishing powders over the paper.
3. Add one of the target's hairs, a nail clipping or a thread from their clothing.
4. Burn everything; place the ashes in a bottle of **Four Thieves Vinegar.**
5. Following the ninth night, wrap the bottle tightly in black fabric, securing it with cord.
6. Make nine knots in the cord reiterating your desire for banishment with each one.
7. Throw this bottle into running water or a cemetery and return home via a circuitous route.

Four Thieves Quick Banishing Spell

This is a quick-fix version of the Four Thieves Nine Night spell above.

1. Add some banishing powder (any one you like) to a bottle of **Four Thieves Vinegar.**
2. Write the target of your spell's name on brown paper and put it inside the bottle, too.
3. Shake the bottle, then leave it upside down in the corner of your closet or behind your bed overnight.
4. Wrap it in black fabric, securing with cord in which you tie nine knots, reiterating your wish for banishing with each one.
5. Throw the bottle in a garbage can at a distance from your home and return via a circuitous route.

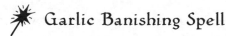 ## Garlic Banishing Spell

Hang a braid of twelve garlic heads over the door to banish jealous people and, by extension, the Evil Eye.

Get Lost and Far Away!

Lost and Away Powder *has various uses, in addition to banishment. It's also used to establish personal and psychic boundaries, as well as to prevent someone else from encroaching on those boundaries.*

1. Write your target's name thirteen times on a square of paper.
2. Sprinkle **Lost and Away Powder** on this paper.
3. Fold the paper up, always folding away from you.
4. Seal it with sealing wax, preferably red.
5. Bury this paper but mark the spot.
6. Leave it buried for thirteen days, watering daily with **War Water.**
7. On the fourteenth day, dig it up and burn it.

Hit the Road and Don't Come Back Spell

1. Fill your pockets with salt in anticipation of the person's departure.
2. Accompany the person as he or she departs, walking just a step behind to the edge of your property, discreetly sprinkling salt in their wake.
3. When the person has gone and can no longer see you, take a broom and sweep the salt away, always sweeping away from your home or the area you wish protected from their presence.
4. Simultaneously murmur your target's name, alternately praying and petitioning that he does not return and commanding and compelling him never to return.

Variations on this spell suggest adding black and/or cayenne pepper to the salt.

Another mode of administering Banishing Powder is via a gift.

 ## I Banish You With A Gift

1. Sprinkle any of the Banishing Powder formulas onto the dirt of a very nice potted plant.
2. Sprinkle some powder under the top layer of the plant's dirt, too, so it isn't so obvious.
3. Give this to your target as a present: the goal is to actually get the powder within the target's home, in order to stimulate them to leave.

 ## A Magical Dis-Invitation

The following spell extends the opposite of an invitation. It's appropriate for getting rid of unwanted potential guests, as well as those who have already outstayed their welcome.

1. Write the name of your target on a small square of paper, one square per unwanted person.
2. Anoint each corner of each square with Banishing Oil.
3. Bury this charm on the path to your entrance door, so that everyone who enters is forced unknowingly to step over it.

 ## Menstrual Blood Banishing

Your own menstrual blood rubbed onto doorknobs allegedly repels anyone who touches the knobs while harboring evil intentions towards you.

 ## Nettle Banishing Spell

Burn nettles while focusing on your desires to accomplish the banishing.

 ## Onion Banishing Spell

The following spell is ideal for unwanted houseguests, or lovers who have overstayed their welcome.

1. Choose an onion whose appearance somehow reminds you of the target of your spell. Traditionally round shapes represented women, while sharp, pointy shapes indicated men but choose whatever resonates for you.
2. Large, fat, tiny, thin, horribly misshapen—whenever you've found your onion, hollow out a hole within it, carefully reserving the piece of onion you've removed.
3. Write your target's name five times on a small slip of paper.
4. Stuff this into the hole in the onion.

Plant lovage in front of and around your home to help ward off all sorts of unwanted intruders, ranging from door-to-door salespeople, to evil spirits, to epidemics, to vermin.

5. Close up the onion by replacing the cut-out piece; this may take a little maneuvering.
6. The next time the target of your spell leaves your home, discreetly roll the onion in their wake, before anyone else has the opportunity to cross the threshold, whether leaving or arriving.
7. Focus your mind exclusively on the person's imminent, permanent departure.
8. Do not bring the onion back into your home but dispose of it outside, preferably as far away as possible.

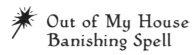

Out of My House Banishing Spell

The following spell is excellent for ridding your home of an unwanted guest, or perhaps even a family member who needs to depart. The spell presumes that you have access to the target's clothing and personal items. Surely you're doing their laundry? The more personal the items are, the more effective the spell.

1. Construct a small doll using personal items belonging to your spell's target.
2. Write the target's name on a small slip of paper. Cross over the name by writing an appropriate message, something like *"Out of my house now!"*
3. Pin this to the doll like a name-tag.
4. Soak the doll's feet in one of the Banishing Oils. (Exodus Oil is particularly appropriate; however, use whichever resonates strongest for you.)
5. Wrap the doll in dark fabric, folding away from you. Keep it in a safe place, anointing the feet daily and secretly telling the doll exactly what you'd like to tell the target of your spell.
6. As soon as the banishment has been effected, destroy or dispose of the doll. Do not keep it in your home.

Poke Root Banishing Spell

1. Carve and dress a banishing candle using any of the banishing oils and/or powders.
2. Wrap some of the melted wax around a poke root and a slip of paper bearing the name of the person to be banished.
3. Shape the wax into a ball and throw it into water flowing away from you.

Pumpkin Magic Lamp Banishing Spell

This time consuming and labor-intensive spell is more suitable for banishing a dangerous, troublesome person from one's vicinity than for banishing houseguests who've outstayed their welcome.

1. Burn **Lost and Away Powder,** creating **lampblack ink** as it burns.
2. Use the ink to write a note detailing who must be banished.
3. Make a magic lamp from a hollowed-out pumpkin.
4. Place the note face up inside the pumpkin.
5. Cover the note with more banishing powder (any one you choose), Grains of Paradise, cayenne pepper, graveyard dust, and soot.
6. Half fill the pumpkin with blended castor and olive oil.
7. Create a wick from cotton and burn this pumpkin outside on seven consecutive Fridays.
8. When the spell is complete, bring the pumpkin to a river or sea and let the water carry it away.

Purple Candle Banishing Spell

Burning a purple candle in the following spell indicates your power over the target of your spell. However, a black devil candle may be substituted if you prefer.

1. Write the name(s) of those whom you wish to banish on a square of brown paper.
2. Cover the name(s) with your own, effectively crossing the first name out.
3. Chant:
   I cover you, I cross you
   I command you, I compel you
   [Name], *child of* [Name] *Get out of my house now!*
4. Dress a purple candle with Banishing Oil.
5. Place the paper on a dish, beneath the purple candle.
6. Burn the candle.

Adapt the chant to your particular situation.

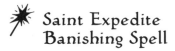 ## Saint Expedite Banishing Spell

1. Write the target of your spell's name and identifying information on a slip of paper.
2. Stick this paper into a balloon, then blow it up and tie it, trapping the name within.
3. Attach this balloon to a statue of Saint Expedite.
4. Offer Saint Expedite a glass of rum and a slice of pound cake and tell him what you need.
5. After you deem sufficient time has elapsed, release the balloon. Allegedly the person will depart in the direction that the balloon travels.

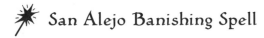 ## San Alejo Banishing Spell

The absolute nicest banishing spell I know invokes Saint Alex or, as he is known in Spanish, San Alejo. *San Alejo is traditionally invoked to keep your enemies at a distance and to protect you from any harm those enemies wish for you.*

This banishing spell is excellent for houseguests who have overextended their welcome or anyone whose presence causes you misery. It doesn't merely send them away; it sends the banished party to a better place, more suitable and happier for them. You're actually doing them a favor!

Incidentally, don't be afraid to plead hard with San Alejo to grant your wish: he's also the patron saint of beggars.

1. Burn a silver candle and chant: *"San Alejo, Alejelo."*
2. Repeat the chant seventeen times, focusing on the target of your spell.

 ## Seven Knob Banishing Spell

Seven-knob candles are used to obtain wishes. Perhaps your wish is to be left alone …

1. Beginning with the bottom knob, carve the name of your spell's target into each knob of a black seven-knob candle.
2. Blend Banishing Oil with Tabasco sauce and ground black pepper. (Tabasco is specifically desirable because it is a simple product with no sugar or other sweeteners, which metaphysically possess a summoning effect, the very opposite of banishing. Check the ingredients on other brands: anything with sugar may neutralize the banishing.)
3. Use this enhanced Banishing Oil to dress the seven-knob candle, being *very* careful not to get any of the oil into your eyes or other sensitive areas. (Wash your hands well immediately after handling the candle.)
4. Beginning at the Full Moon, burn one knob a night. Visualize the person already gone, while chanting something like *"Get Out!"*

 ## Simple Cotton Ball Banishing Spell

Soak a cotton ball in Banishing Oil. Then slip it into your target's pocket.

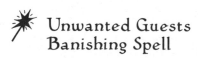 ## Spare Clothing Banishing Spell

1. To encourage someone's imminent departure from your area, obtain an article of clothing belonging to that person. Although any article could be used, an unwashed sock, glove or piece of underwear is best.
2. Cut a strip of fabric from the clothing and stuff it into a glass bottle.
3. Write the person's name, together with the name of an extremely distant, remote location on a piece of paper. Draw a circle around the names.
4. Stick this paper into the bottle, too, along with salt, sulfur and red chili pepper, or any of the Banishing Powder formulas.
5. Seal the bottle tightly shut and allow it to rest in a quiet, dark place for nine days.
6. On the tenth day, take this bottle to a stream or some running water flowing away from you and toss it in. Allegedly you will see results within nine days.

These Feet Were Meant For Moving Banishing Spell

Drizzle Banishing Oil over your target's shoes. Alternately, massaging the oil into their feet, if you can somehow manage this, can also produce desired effects.

Unwanted Guests Banishing Spell

Sprinkle tormentil under the bed to encourage unwanted guests to move on.

Unwanted Guests Banishing Spell Extra Strength

Sprinkling tormentil under the bed is effective but subtle. If you've reached the point of desperation, sprinkle tormentil over unwanted guests' sheets. This is a more powerful, more direct approach but be prepared for questions.

Banishing Bad Habits

Although these spells may be used to target any type of behavior, the term *"bad habits"* is often understood to refer euphemistically to dangerous and/or undesirable addictions. It may be necessary to combine several spells for maximum effect.

Amethyst Anti-Intoxication Spell

Legends surrounding the beautiful purple gemstone, amethyst, suggest that it may be used to prevent intoxication. This is not exactly true: if you're really determined to get drunk, there isn't a crystal in the world that will stop you, nor will drinking from a cup cut from amethyst, the original spell instructions, provide long-term obstruction. What amethysts can do for you are bolster attempts not to drink, whether this means drinking at all or merely to excess. Amethysts reinforce your personal determination and provide a measure of protection.

The amethyst is sacred to Dionysus, Spirit of Ecstasy and Intoxication. It is his power that one witnesses shining through the gemstone. Even gods of intoxication can sometimes be bad drunks, though, as the mythical history of the amethyst points out. Once upon a time, on a morning after, a long, long, time ago, Dionysus, suffering from a hangover and headache, wished to avoid all company. Bothered by every sound, he announced that he would terminate the very next person to cross his path. Who should be passing through the woods at that moment but the lovely young nymph Amethyst, on her way with offerings to present at Artemis' shrine? But before Dionysus could carry out his threat, Artemis stepped in and saved Amethyst by transforming her into a luminous clear crystal. Abashed and ashamed by his bad temper, Dionysus approached with a glass of wine. Pouring it over the now crystallized nymph, Amethyst turned her characteristic purple color. Dionysus swore that whenever he saw this gemstone in the future, he would become an ally in preventing the ill-effects associated with alcohol.

★ *Amethyst's anti-intoxication powers are strongest if one drinks out of an amethyst cup. An amethyst-colored cup may be sufficient*

★ *Wear an amethyst as a ring or over the throat chakra. Remember to charge the gemstone and cleanse it periodically*

★ *Amethysts also have a cleansing effect: metaphysically they will help remove and assimilate toxins, including alcohol*

 Bad Habits Bath

Add the following to a tub filled with warm water:

Essential oil of clary sage
Essential oil of frankincense
Essential oil of lavender
Essential oil of lemongrass or May Chang
Essential oil of rosemary

Enter the bath and inhale the fragrance, and accompany with affirmations and positive visualizations.

 Bury Bad Habits Spell

Among the most famous hexing spells are those involving miniature-sized personalized coffins left on the spell target's doorsteps. This coffin spell is traditionally as much an act of sheer intimidation as it is a magical spell, however it can be put to less malevolent uses. Use the little coffin spell below to lay issues to rest and, in particular, to bury addictions.

1. Create a small coffin. You will need a little box. You can find one or make one, however the imagery should be very clear: there should be no ambiguity regarding the type of box. Inspiration, or a box itself, may be taken from Mexican *Day of the Dead (Dia de los Muertos)* handicrafts.
2. Paint the outside of the box black. Decorate with purple glitter glue if desired.
3. Traditionally the box contains a small doll, which may or may not be personalized so that the identity of the target is clear. Consider how to personify your addiction.
4. Accompany and reinforce this spell with intensive candle burning.
5. The doll may be pierced with pins. Add candle stubs, leftover spell wax, graveyard dirt, asafetida and banishing powder, especially **Lost and Away Powder.**
6. Dress everything with Banishing Oil.

Traditionally the coffin is left on your target's doorstep. Consider appropriate places to leave it, or bury the little coffin within a cemetery.

You may find just making the box therapeutic in itself. In which case, reserve the box for ritual use or destroy it.

Crystal Bad Habit Breaking Spell

Use double-terminated crystals to help break old habits and destructive patterns, and to heal addictions. Other beneficial stones include amethyst and kunzite, which interestingly contains lithium, used medicinally to treat depression and bi-polar syndromes.

★ *Carry the gemstones in a conjure bag*
★ *Lay the stones on or around the body*
★ *Use the stones as a focal point for visualization and meditation spells*

 ## Devil Card Banishing Spell

1. Remove the Devil card from a Rider-Waite tarot deck. (Other decks may work, too. Examine the images closely.)
2. Burn a purple candle. Place the card where you can see it easily.
3. Meditate on the image, observing how loose the depicted chains truly are.
4. Allow spontaneous thoughts and solutions to enter your mind.

Eating Disorder Banishing Spell

For maximum effect, this spell should coincide with a waning moon.

1. Add essential oil of fennel to olive oil or create infused oil of fennel. (See directions in *Elements of Magic Spells*.)
2. Dress a small black candle with this oil.
3. Hold the (unlit) candle in your hands and visualize your pain and bad habits flowing from your body into the candle. Try to purge yourself of all negative urges and emotions, at least momentarily.

4. When you feel this has been accomplished, put the candle down and pick up a moonstone in your left hand, and a clear quartz crystal in your right.
5. Bury the candle, not too close to your home. (If it is buried on your property, make it the furthest point from the house.) Place the crystals in a pretty charm bag and keep them with you constantly, cleansing them frequently, and re-charging as needed.

 ## Eucalyptus Banish Bad Habits Spell

The eucalyptus tree is believed to possess potent banishing properties. If you have a eucalyptus tree, it's simple to make a decoction: place leaves, twigs and loose bark into a pot and cover with water. Bring it to a boil, then lower the heat and simmer gently for an hour or more. Otherwise, you can create an infusion from dried eucalyptus, available from herbal supply stores. Pour boiling water over the botanicals and let them steep until the water cools.

Either way, strain out the botanicals and add the infusion to your bathwater, to destroy evil ties that bind, whether bad addictions, bad habits or bad company.

 ## Everlasting End Banishing Spell

Essential oil of helichrysum, also known as immortelle or everlasting, is believed to magically speed the removal of toxins from the body, thus enhancing any attempt to end a physical addiction.

★ *Inhale everlasting's aroma as needed, either straight from the bottle or added to an aroma burner*
★ *Incorporate full body massage using the essential oil into your recovery program*

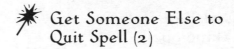

Frankincense Banish Bad Habits Spell

Frankincense is famed for breaking the bonds of addictions and bad habits, as well as those of unhealthy relationships.

1. Explicitly name the tie that needs to be broken.
2. Write this down on parchment, using **Dove's Blood** or myrrh-enhanced ink.
3. Write your full name on the other side of the sheet.
4. Anoint the corners with essential oil of frankincense.
5. Place this in a small saucer, with your name facing upward.
6. Dress a white candle with **Fiery Wall of Protection Oil,** which should contain both frankincense and myrrh.
7. Place it atop the paper on the dish and burn.

Sometimes the condition that requires banishing isn't yours. Perhaps someone else's drinking is causing your life to be miserable. Spells have evolved to *encourage* others to stop drinking.

Get Someone Else to Quit Spell (1)

This Pow-Wow technique is used for curing excessive alcohol intake by another, whether he or she wishes to be cured or not.

1. Scrape the dirt out from under the target's fingernails. (Probably best accomplished while they are in a stupor, unless you are in the general habit of providing a manicure.)
2. Secretly add these scrapings to their favorite alcoholic beverage.
3. When appropriate, serve them some. The person will happily drink this beverage. Allegedly the addition should remove future inclination to imbibe.

Get Someone Else to Quit Spell (2)

1. Bake or roast a black hen's gizzard. Do not boil it, as the correct texture will never be achieved.
2. Let the gizzard dry out, then grind it into a fine powder.
3. Add a pinch of this powder to each of your target's drinks. Allegedly this will cause him or her to lose their taste for alcohol.

There is a price to pay in this Brazilian spell. The person who performs it (i.e., you, not the person being weaned from alcohol) must never eat a black hen again. In effect this means, for most of us who purchase our chickens already killed, plucked, cleaned, and wrapped in plastic, that you must forego chicken altogether, although if the spell works, perhaps this is a small price to pay.

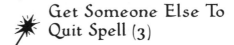

Get Someone Else To Quit Spell (3)

An old English cure for excessive drinking may be the most effective of the lot: keep a live eel in your drink. That would keep most people far from the bottle.

The modern grapefruit is a relatively new species, having apparently evolved in colonial Barbados. Interestingly this fruit which evolved in a place and time plagued by slavery is among the most potent botanicals for breaking personal shackles.

Grapefruit Quit Smoking Spell

A magical plan to stop smoking:

1. Every time you crave a cigarette, have a grapefruit instead.

2. Here's the catch: you must cut and eat the grapefruit completely by hand. You cannot use a knife to cut it or use a spoon to eat it.
3. Peel the grapefruit by hand, and then eat it segment by segment.

 ## Licorice Stick Spell

Who's the boss? You or your habit? Licorice is an herb of domination. Let it help you put that habit in its place. Chew on a licorice stick or twig (not the candy! The real plant is required.) This spell is allegedly extra beneficial for quitting smoking.

 ## Magnolia Bark Spell

Drinking magnolia bark tea supposedly helps one quit smoking.

Maximon (pronounced *Mah-shee-mon*) is an unofficial saint from Guatemala who also answers to the name Brother Simon. His traditional votive image depicts a man with a large moustache sitting at a crossroads, dressed in a black suit. He may hold a bag of money on his lap or display gold coins in his hand.

This unofficial saint is actually the modern manifestation of an ancient Guatemalan spirit, *Maam* or Grandfather. When Roman Catholic missionaries first encountered Maam, they attempted to assimilate him by syncretizing with Saint Simon, often associated with magic in European traditions. They underestimated the power of this spirit. The saintly mask was insufficient for hiding Maximon's true nature—his is the fierce, defiant, wild epitome of male virility and procreative power.

In an attempt to downplay Maximon's influence, further attempts were made to syncretize him with Judas Iscariot, or even Satan. Too late, the damage was done. Attempts to denigrate Maximon and discourage devotion to him only served to enhance his bad-ass reputation as a powerful provider, afraid of nothing. Maximon offers wealth and success to his devotees but he also possesses the power to break even the most powerful addictions.

 ## Maximon's Rehab Spell (1)

1. Build Maximon an altar in order to engage his attention.
2. He accepts offerings of hard liquor, Coca Cola, cigarettes, coins, keys and kumquats.
3. Tell him what you need.

 ## Maximon's Rehab Spell (2)

This and the previous spell may be cast in conjunction or used separately.

1. Carve your name, identifying information and situation into the wax of a white candle.
2. Dress it with **Maximon Oil.**
3. Hold the oily candle in both hands, charging it with your deepest desires.
4. Burn the candle.

 ## Mullein Spell

Burn mullein to help banish any kind of bad habit.

 ## Onion Blossom Spell

Burn onion blossoms while making affirmations to help banish bad habits. This provides a magical cleansing effect too.

Banishing Gossip

 Banish Gossip: Chill-Out Spell

This spell may be used to prevent gossip, slander, and general harassment.

1. Write the target of the spell's name on a slip of brown paper and place within a small glass cup or dish. If one specific person isn't the problem, but rather it's a situation that's gotten out of hand, then explicitly and concisely name the situation instead.
2. Place an ice cube on top of the paper.
3. Break an egg over all and put in freezer to chill out.

 Banish Gossip: Gag Root Spell

Among lobelia's nicknames are "gag root," "puke weed," and "emetic weed," so it's obvious what this plant can do! Carry gag root, don't consume it! It allegedly gags those who talk behind other people's backs and puts a halt to gossip and slander about you.

 Banish Gossip Mojo Hand (1) Put A Lock On It!

Add bay laurel leaves, calendula blossoms, and a small metal padlock to a mojo bag to stop gossip about you.

 Banish Gossip Mojo Hand (2) Sew That Mouth Shut!

1. Place a ginger root and a High John the Conqueror root within a conjure bag.
2. Create a small face from felt and attach it to the bag. Embellish it as you will.
3. Using black thread, sew "x's" across the mouth, sealing it shut. Focus on your desire as you sew.
4. Carry the bag with you.

 Banish Lies

Violets are magically acknowledged as the plant of truth. Ironically, virtually all fragrances purporting to be violet are synthetic reproductions; create your own infused oil from violet leaves. Carve a white figure candle to represent the target of your spell and dress with infused oil of violets. Burn the candle; the truth will allegedly be revealed.

Beef Tongue Banish Gossip Spell

There are many variations of spells utilizing whole uncooked beef tongues. These were once a fairly popular food, but today are somewhat of a specialty item. Although the most notorious versions of these spells derive from New Orleans, these spells, like **Four Thieves Vinegar**, are European importations. This particular genre of spells apparently derives originally from British folk traditions, where pierced organ meats were once not an uncommon magical tool. Most variations of these spells revolve around legal issues. This version aims to stop gossip.

1. Write the name(s) of those whose gossip and slander must cease, as well as any of their allies, onto slips of paper. Each person gets their own slip of paper.
2. Make slits in a whole beef tongue, one slit per slip of paper.
3. Stick the slips of paper into the slits.
4. Close the slits up, using pins and needles.
5. Sprinkle the tongue with cayenne and/or habanero powder plus vinegar, chanting:
   I cross you and I cover you
   I command you to hold your tongue
   Alternate these commands with a straight-forward
   "Shut up!"
6. Wrap up the tongue and place it safely in your freezer for a year or until all danger is gone.

Black Cat Banish Gossip Spell

1. Hold a black cat candle in your hands, charging it with your desires.
2. Burn it, coinciding with the waning moon, to minimize and eliminate gossip.

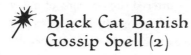

Black Cat Banish Gossip Spell (2)

*Although a black cat candle by itself may be used to end gossip, its power is enhanced by using **Fiery Wall of Protection Oil** with it:*

1. Carve your name and any identifying and pertinent information into a black cat candle.
2. Dress with **Fiery Wall of Protection Oil** and burn.

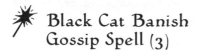

Black Cat Banish Gossip Spell (3)

Alternatively, if you know who is responsible for spreading the gossip:

1. Carve the black cat candle as described above.
2. Dress it with a combination of **Fiery Wall of Protection Oil** and **Command and Compel Oil.**
3. Hold the oily candle in both your hands, charging it with the force of your emotions.
4. Announce, addressing your target by name:
   [Name], *child of* [Name] *I command you, I compel you*
   I command you, I compel you to cease this gossip now.
   [Use your own words to explicitly name your desire.]

The combination of **Fiery Wall of Protection Oil** with the black cat candle is considered most potent for stopping gossip. However, either component of the spell (the oil or the candle) works independently of the other. If that specific type of candle is unavailable, use **Fiery Wall of Protection** to dress any kind of candle.

 ## Clove Banish Gossip Spell

Cloves are used to stifle and end gossip.

1. Grind cloves into powder.
2. Sprinkle the powder onto lit charcoals: fumigate your body, clothing and premises to halt malicious gossip about you.

Fiery Wall of Protection Anti-Gossip Fumigation

*Burn **Fiery Wall of Protection Powder** as incense.*

★ *Fumigate your clothes with the aroma*
★ *Let the scent permeate your skin and hair*
★ *Let the scent permeate your home*

Fiery Wall of Protection Anti-Gossip Powder

*Sprinkle **Fiery Wall of Protection Powder** where the gossip is most active to help stifle it.*

Fiery Wall of Protection End Gossip Bath

*Add **Fiery Wall of Protection Oil** to your bathwater and soak in it.*

Malicious gossip can affect more than an individual: entire families and communities can be harmed. This complex Turkish ritual involves a group intervention to cause gossip to end and restore balance to the community.

Group Gossip Banishing Spell

1. Ritually cleanse the room where the spell will be performed (see page 74).
2. Ritually cleanse the immediate victim(s) of the gossip, too (see pages 207–220).
3. Burn welcoming incense to invite powerful, benevolent, protective spirits to provide assistance.
4. Have the victim(s) sit in chairs in the center of the room, while ritual assistants prepare the spell materials.
5. Gently melt wax in a double boiler or bain-marie.
6. One or more people must hold a white cloth over the head(s) of the victim(s).
7. Someone else must hold a bowl of ice-cold water over this cloth.
8. Pour some hot wax into the water. As it hits the cold water, it will solidify, forming shapes.
9. Remove the shapes, once they've hardened and cooled. (If you remove them too quickly, the wax will still be soft and the initial shape may be altered.)
10. These shapes must be analyzed to shed light on the situation: let the victim(s) of the gossip express their opinions first.

The ritual itself removes effects of the Evil Eye caused by gossip. The shapes displayed by the wax hold the clues to who has started the gossip, who is keeping it going and how best to terminate it. However, wax is a modern substitute: this type of spell originally utilized melted tin, aluminum or lead. Use the original materials if more convenient.

Saint Raymond is invoked to protect against false witness. Outside the courtroom, Saint Raymond may be requested to silence your enemies, ending slander and gossip. The most effective day to petition him is his feast day, August 31st.

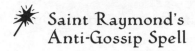 ## Saint Raymond's Anti-Gossip Spell

1. Light a candle in his honor.
2. Offer him a key and padlock and tell him what you need.

Traditional hoodoo condition oils, like **Fiery Wall of Protection**, have entered the lexicons of many other magical traditions, from Wicca to Mexican Santeria, from whence this candle spell derives:

 ## Seven Knob Banish Gossip Spell

1. Carve the gossip's name once on each knob of a white seven-knob candle, beginning with the bottom knob and working upwards.
2. Dress it with **Fiery Wall of Protection Oil.**
3. Roll the candle in a mixture of black pepper, cayenne pepper and chia seeds.
4. Burn one knob every night for seven consecutive nights.

 ## Shut Your Mouth! Anti-Gossip Spell

1. Dress a candle with **Fiery Wall of Protection Oil** and/or a **Commanding and Compelling Oil.**
2. As it burns, create a doll from cloth to represent the person spreading lies about you, ruining your reputation.
3. When the doll is complete, make a slit where the mouth should be. Insert a piece of dumb-cane. (Do *not* touch your own mouth before washing your own hands with soap *very* well. Better yet, wear gloves while handling the dumb-cane—it is potentially very dangerous!)
4. Dribble wax over the doll's mouth to seal it shut.
5. Bury the doll in a secluded, lonely spot where it's unlikely to be unearthed.

Shut Your Mouth Spell: Gris Gris

*Most magical anti-gossip spells take an indirect approach. This doorstep spell brings the point home. Combine stinging nettles and graveyard dust or **Goofer Dust,** depending on how angry and violated you feel. Add a freely shed feather of a noisy bird (a crow or a rooster) and leave it on your target's doorstep.*

Slippery Elm Banish Gossip Spell

Slippery elm, which soothes sore throats, is a common ingredient in cough syrups and cough drops. This spell uses it homeopathically to stop malicious speech.

1. Create a fire in a cauldron or fireplace.
2. Burn slippery elm in the fire.
3. While it's burning, knot a yellow cord, tying your desire and frustration into the knots.
4. Throw the cord into the fire.

Who Cares About Gossip? Spell

*Absolute worst-case scenario? The gossip just can't be stifled? **Crown of Success Oil** prevents gossip from adversely affecting you.*

★ *Add it to your bath*
★ *Massage it into your skin*
★ *Dip a cotton ball into the oil and carry in your pocket or tucked into your bra*

Banishing Harassment

Sometimes it's not the individual who needs banishment; it's their behavior.

Anemone Spell

Carry anemone (windflower) in a conjure bag together with a small silver charm in the shape of a triangle to help stop harassment and bullying.

Black Snake Root Banishing Spell

At least two different roots go by the name of black snake root. Either one may be used in this spell. This spell allegedly causes the person who is harassing you to turn their attention elsewhere and leave you alone.

Obtain intimate items belonging to the guilty party. If these are unavailable, write the person's name on a slip of paper together with his or her mother's name. Place the items in a small iron cauldron with a black snake root and burn them.

Fear of the Devil Anti-Harassment Spell

Oh, they're brave when they're picking on you. Put the fear of the devil into your tormentor. Invoke Satan for protection. In no way does this spell represent Satanism nor does it represent a petition or promise to the devil. What it does is direct a bigger bully's attention towards your personal bully. This spell derives from the American South and rests on the assumption that someone with an easy conscience has nothing to fear from the devil. Satan and his hosts are not depicted as evil but as punishing avengers of evil.

1. Sprinkle asafetida on a lit charcoal.
2. Asafetida is an effective banishing agent precisely because it smells so bad—you will be tempted to leave, too. Instead call your enemy's name aloud. (Call every variation of name that is used by the person. Leave no name for them to hide behind.)
3. *Command* them to leave you alone in the name of the devil and a whole host of powerful, avenging, volatile spirits.

Hand of Power Anti-Harassment Spell

Stop harassment via the use of a powerful amulet. Although various kinds exist, in this instance an open-palmed hand is ideal—something like the Jewish hamsa *or the Muslim* Hand of Fatima. *Strengthen the amulet by anointing it with essential oil of lavender regularly. (If you're serious, invest in superior lavender, grown at higher altitudes. Reputable manufacturers of superior oils will be able to provide this information.) Wear the amulet.*

Holly Spell

Although there is a hex-like quality to this spell, allegedly it will not harm your target. It merely makes them behave well toward you—or to go away!

1. Place a photograph of your target, a paper with his or her name written on it, and/or intimate articles (hair, nail clippings, and so forth) into a jar.
2. Add some holly leaves.
3. Cover everything with very strong, bitter coffee. Murmur your needs and desires over the liquid, then seal the jar shut and hide it in a safe place.

San Cipriano Candle Spell

Among its many versatile uses, **San Cipriano Oil** *is used to stop harassment.*

1. Carve a candle to represent your tormentor. Figure candles in appropriate genders or colors may be used. Brown candles in any shape may be used to represent your plea for justice. Purple candles are used to indicate your power over the situation and the target. White candle may always be used, as blank slates to express your desires.
2. Dress the candle with **San Cipriano Oil** and burn.

Banishing Problems and Situations

Although specific spells exist for many different situations, sometimes a problem doesn't fall neatly into any one category. Perhaps no solution exists: the only possible positive outcome is for the entire situation to be eliminated or banished.

Rotten Apple Banishing Spell (1)

1. Cut an apple in half horizontally, so that the star in the center is exposed.
2. Rub one half of the apple with a mint leaf while visualizing what needs to be banished.
3. Put the two halves of the apple back together again.
4. Stick a skewer through the pieces, so that they will remain joined.
5. Tie the pieces securely together with black silk or satin ribbon.
6. Bury the apple. Your problem should dissipate as the apple rots.

You may also name your problem by writing it on a slip of paper. Dip this paper into essential oil of mint and place between the apple halves, before rejoining them. However, by naming the problem on paper, you take the risk of further manifestation. Cast whichever version of the spell resonates for you.

Rotten Apple Banishing Spell (2)

The following spell may be used to banish either a person or a problem:

1. Using a sharp point (a craft knife or a thorn, for instance) write the name of what or whom should be banished onto a red apple.
2. Place the apple onto an altar and leave it there until it rots.
3. Bury the rotten apple in Earth, far from your home.

Banish Spirits

Sometimes you need to make the spirits leave. Despite the emphasis on *Summoning Spells* placed in the classical medieval grimoires, the bigger problem is often how to force these spirits to leave once you've achieved your own purposes. A good reason for never dabbling in malevolent magic is that it is typically easier to summon than to banish. Exu Marabo, for instance, a powerful yet dangerous spirit, warns that once summoned, he can never be forced to leave.

In many cases, malevolent magic attracts the attention of equally malevolent spirits. Feeling at home, they move right in, regardless of your desires. Once present, bored and restless, they cause destruction and grief.

In general, banishing spirits is work for a shaman. The first choice in all situations would be to hire an effective, knowledgeable professional. That said, hiring a shaman isn't an option for many people in most circumstances. When all action must be taken in your own hands, the following spells are reputed to be extremely potent.

Afrit Banishing Spell

The afrit *or* ifrit *is a species of malevolent spirit, indigenous to Egypt and the Middle East, which rises to the ground wherever the blood of a murder victim is shed.*

The afrit *may be restrained by driving a virgin nail, one that has never before been used, into the ground at the spot where the murder was committed. To release the* afrit, *remove the nail.*

Althaea Banishing Spell

Not only does althaea (mallow) summon benevolent spirits, it also allegedly repels evil destructive ones. Create infused oil of althea. (Follow the instructions in Elements of Magic Spells *to create infused oils.) Anoint your body or add the oil to your bath prior to rituals.*

Asafetida Banishing Spell

When summoning spirits, especially volatile or dangerous ones, keep asafetida at hand, just in case things go wrong. Should you discover you've conjured up more than you can handle, throw the asafetida into an open fire, simultaneously shouting something like "Begone!" or "Go to hell!"

 ## Bamboo Banishing Spell

House spirits are supposed to be helpful; every once in a while a malevolent one turns up. This Korean spell helps banish unwanted house spirits.

Burn bamboo sticks. Allegedly the sound of bamboo's popping knots scares house demons away.

 ## Banishing Incense

The following incense formula allegedly drives away even the most powerful of evil spirits. The ingredients include:

> Asafetida
> Bay laurel leaves
> Galbanum
> Olive leaves
> Rue
> Saint John's Wort
> Salt
> Sulfur

1. Crumble all the ingredients.
2. Blend them together, grind, powder and burn on lit charcoal.

 ## Banishment Bouquet

A bouquet of garlic blossoms and angelica flowers, tied up with red and blue ribbons, repels malicious spirits.

 ## Bean Banishing Spell

Beans are filled with mysterious magical powers: so tiny, yet capable of repelling ghosts and demons. Fill rattles with beans and shake them to repel low-level malevolent entities. (Incorporate into ritual as needed as protection.)

 ## Bell, Book, and Candle

This phrase, the title of a popular play and film as well as the given name of numerous metaphysical stores, evolved from traditional Roman Catholic rites of exorcism and excommunication. This method of banishing malevolent spirits pre-dates Christianity, however and may be used as a framework for exorcists of any spiritual orientation. In order to effectively cast a banishing spell, you must be familiar and comfortable with your tools.

1. The bell is the simplest part of the spell. Bells invoke the combined primal powers of male and female generative energy; the ringing of a metal bell disturbs most malicious spirits. An iron bell will repel most negative entities.
2. The book refers to sacred texts, the introduction of something so sacred that there is no room left for evil to co-exist in the space; hence it's squeezed out. The key is to employ whatever fills you with sacred grace. These might be sacred texts, Gregorian chants, or gospel music, or may even derive from what might be perceived as profane sources: soul music, for instance.
3. Not just any candle will do; the fragrance of beeswax allegedly repels evil. Alternatively rub candles with oils of benzoin and frankincense.

Botanical Spirit Banishing

The following plants allegedly make malevolent spirits feel unwelcome: juniper, maize corn, mugwort, Saint John's Wort, vervain, wormwood, and yarrow. Keep living plants near your home or any area that needs protection, or hang these dried botanicals near doors and windows as amulets.

 ## Dragon's Blood Double Action Spirit Banishing Spell

1. Dress a Double Action candle with **Dragon's Blood Oil.**
2. Burn the candle down completely to keep an area free from malevolent spirits.

Use one candle for every room where you perceive it's needed.

 ## Disperse Evil Incense (1)

Burn benzoin, frankincense, and juniper as a triple threat and triple protection: evil spirits cannot abide any of these fragrances, let alone the combination.

 ## Disperse Evil Incense (2)

Burn benzoin, patchouli, and sandalwood to banish and disperse malicious spirits.

 ## Djinn Banishing Spell (1)

Although there are benevolent, friendly djinn, many djinn have a reputation as troublemakers. Wormwood is the Tuareg recommendation for banishing malicious djinn. Allegedly they will not remain within the presence of its aroma.

★ *Burn dried, powdered wormwood as incense*
★ *Place dried or fresh wormwood in a bowl and cover with boiling water. Use the herbal infused water to asperge an area, repelling resident malignant spirits. Bathe in the infusion for private protection, and add it to laundry rinse water for enhanced protection*

 ## Djinn Banishing Spell (2)

Benzoin is the Moroccan recommendation for repelling djinn: burn it as incense. Benzoin and wormwood combine well together for enhanced protection and banishing power.

 ## Dybbuk Dispelling Spell

"Dybbuk" literally means "attachment." Jewish folklore abounds with tales of these transmigrating souls in trouble who attach themselves to a living body, pushing out the original soul, while asserting their own troubled and often troubling personalities. Shamanic intervention is the required cure, however in case of emergency, fervent repetitions of Psalm 91 allegedly drive out a dybbuk.

 Elegba's Banishing Spell

Hang branches of Abutilon trisulcatum *behind the front door of the home to banish and repel troublesome spirits. This plant, a member of the mallow family and known in Spanish as* escoba cimarrona, *is under the orisha Elegba's dominion. Elegba controls all doors and roads, permitting entry or forbidding it, as the case may be. According to some spiritual traditions, Elegba even determines the capacity and quality of spirit/human interaction. He is, thus, a particularly powerful ally during any kind of banishing spell.*

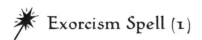 Elf Banishing Spell

Iron or steel tools and implements repel the elven folk.

Exorcism Spells

Sometimes spirits attach themselves to an individual rather than merely haunting an area. The spirit may speak through the individual, refusing to leave. Encouraging or forcing them to leave is a shamanic technique. However, should you find yourself dealing with a case of possession without an exorcist in the neighborhood, the following spells may be attempted. In general, you will still need a ritual assistant to help achieve your magical goals.

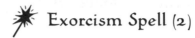 Exorcism Spell (1)

1. Use intensive cleansing methods to purify the area.
2. In addition to whichever methods are employed ring bells, cymbals and sistra loudly.
3. Invoke benevolent protective spirits, like Archangel Michael, Kwan Yin, and/or Isis.
4. Draw up talismans of protection.
5. Summon the demons, demanding that they come forward and depart.

6. Observe for signs of departure. Dramatic spirits will let you know they've gone. Otherwise use divination techniques to determine whether your methods have been effective or, if not, what further action should be taken.
7. If you're sure they've departed, burn the talismans.
8. Mix a teaspoon of the ashes into cooled boiled spring water. Have the person drink it.
9. Close the ceremony.

 Exorcism Spell (2)

1. Fill a new pot with freshly drawn water.
2. Pour some olive oil over the water.
3. Whisper Psalm 10 over this water nine times.
4. Dip a new towel into this liquid to bathe the afflicted person.

 Exorcism Spell (3)

No exorcist available? No friends to help rid you of an unwanted spirit? Do it yourself. Demons reputedly hate the scent of frankincense.

1. Apply essential oil of frankincense to the crown of the head, the forehead, the back of the neck, the throat, chest, palms of hands and soles of feet. Use individual drops of undiluted essential oil for this purpose.
2. Now add some essential oil of frankincense to freshly drawn water.
3. Using a brand new white cloth bathe all of the above body parts, as well as the genital area.
4. Repeat Psalm 145 throughout the entire ritual.

Extreme Yang Spell

In traditional Chinese belief, what we call demons may actually be a manifestation of excessive yin energy. This can be neutralized by applying the opposing force: extremely potent yang energy. The following serve as demon/yin repellants:

★ *Firecrackers*
★ *Mirrors*
★ *The crowing of a rooster*
★ *Swords*

Reading sacred texts and philosophy books is also believed to send malevolent spirits on their merry way because these create order, in which demons (which crave chaos) cannot thrive.

 ## Fenugreek Head Wash

Wash the head with an infusion of fenugreek seeds to protect against demonic possession.

 ## Fire Spirit Banishing Spell

To banish Fire Spirits and prevent their return:

1. Make bundles from any one or a combination of the following botanicals. Be careful, some are poisonous: water lilies, liverwort, spurge, mandrake, leeks, watercress, water mint, plantain, and henbane.
2. Post these bundles as amulets, particularly near doors and windows.

 ## Ginger Banishing Spell

It's traditionally believed that low-level malevolent spirits can enter the body through food. This is the source of many fairy tales where evil is swallowed. Certain foods guard against this as well as expelling any previously swallowed demons, such as ginger. Add it to food to expel and prevent demons.

 ## Goblin Banishing Spell

Goblin *is one of those over-used metaphysical classifications that evoke different images for different people. In the classical sense of the word, however, a goblin is an Earth spirit that may adopt a location or, more frequently, a family and perform services for them, something like a household spirit. Sounds good, doesn't it? Well, it can be, except that goblins have a notoriously stubborn and sometimes malicious streak; what they perceive as performing a "service" may not correspond with the family's perception. As with most guests, spirits or human, it's easier to invite them in than to ask them to leave. However, if an invitation to leave is required, the following spell allegedly works.*

Sprinkle flaxseed on the floor. Goblins have a compulsive streak and will feel obliged to pick every last seed up. It may accomplish this once or twice but will eventually grow bored and frustrated with the task and go elsewhere, hopefully permanently. Repeat as needed.

Incantation Bowl Spell

Incantation bowls were once popular demon-trapping and banishing devices among the Jews, Mandaeans and Pagans of pre-Islamic Mesopotamia.

An incantation bowl is a shallow terracotta dish, typically covered entirely by incantations, written in a spiral design from the outer rim of the dish, toward the center. An image may be drawn at the very center, usually a rough, childlike depiction of an inevitably female demon. The goal is to trap the spirit underneath the dish where the written incantations will disempower it. The dish is then buried under the doorstep of the home.

Incantation bowls are simple to create for oneself. The magic is in the written charm: you may either purchase a shallow terracotta dish or make one. Because it will be buried, advanced pottery-making skills are not required.

With permanent ink, working from the outside edge toward the center, write banishing incantations. The goal is to fill the bowl with words, so there's no need to be very brief.

★ *State in your own words your desire for a demon-free home and existence*

★ *Include phrases like,* "Evil Spirit, Get Out!" *(if you know its name, use it), or* "Get out of the house belonging to [*Name*], child of [*Name*]. Do not disturb her"

★ *Incorporate traditional incantation bowl formulas, for instance the phrase:* "Bound and sealed are all demons and evil spirits"

★ *Sometimes these orders of banishment were written up as traditional divorce decrees, severing the relationship between spirit and human forever and ordering the spirit to depart from the home*

Once complete, the bowl is buried upside down under the doorstep or entry threshold.

 ## Jet Banishing

Powder and burn jet to exorcise malevolent spirits. (Only true jet will burn.)

 ## Low-level Demon Banishing Spell (1)

Low-level demons are easily fooled. A common practice in the Middle East is to paint ceilings sky blue. This completely confuses these low-level, low-intellect entities: they can't tell whether they're inside, outside or where they might be. They have to vacate the premises to think about it.

Low-level Demon Banishing Spell (2)

This general thick-headedness attributed to most demons may be used to your advantage should you wish them to depart. Any inherent contradiction causes the demons to have to think; thinking causes them to stop whatever trouble they've been brewing and depart. Thus a Russian formula for banishing illness spirits doesn't just tell them to go: instead it demands that they come yesterday. Theoretically this confuses the spirit so much it must leave.

Czech and Slovak are unusual languages as it's possible for words to lack vowels. Combined with an aggressive phrase, it's enough to send a demon packing. Lisa Goldstein's novel, The Alchemist's Door, *envisions a collaboration in Prague between the famous magicians Rabbi Judah Loewe, inventor of the golem, and a demon-plagued Dr. John Dee. The stubborn demon is finally exorcised by uttering the Czech phrase,* "Strc prst skrz krk!", *which translates as* "Stick your finger down your throat!"

Low-level Demon Banishing Spell (3)

The key to successful demon banishing and exorcism is creativity and flexibility.

★ *Take advantage of substances that automatically repel them*

★ *Exploit their greediness and lack of intelligence*

For example, author Theda Kenyon recounts the tale of an exorcism aboard a Chinese ship in Singapore, in her 1929 book, Witches Still Live.

It was determined that the underlying cause of the ship's lengthy period of bad luck was an infestation of malicious spirits. A shaman in Singapore proposed the solution: purchase of a deluxe selection of fireworks plus a pair of chickens was recommended. The ship's cook was instructed to prepare the chickens the most delicious, fragrant way possible. The aroma was so tempting that when the chickens were thrown overboard, all the demons followed. Fireworks were then exploded as added inducement for the demons never to return.

 ## Magic Mirror Banishing Spell

Use a magic mirror to capture and banish unwanted spiritual entities. This method is particularly effective for those creatures of the darkness that fear and loathe light.

1. On a bright, sunny day, slowly traverse the infested area, holding the mirror in your hand, tilting it and directing it so that the mirror may capture literally every square inch of the area for at least a few moments each.
2. When you've finished, hold the mirror face down or wrap it in dark fabric.
3. Immediately take the mirror outside and suddenly expose the mirror's face to the sun, for no more than nine seconds. Captured negativity and malevolence are burned out and destroyed. (Capturing the sun's reflection in a mirror is potentially dangerous: refer to page 92 for some crucial safety tips.)
4. Post protective amulets in the now demon-free area.
5. The area, the mirror, and you yourself all now require thorough spiritual cleansing.

This spell derives from Chinese tradition. The Chinese magic mirror needed for this spell is round, golden and embellished with magical charms and images, but you can substitute any of the magic mirrors (see pages 90–94).

It's generally believed that should a malevolent spirit's reflection be caught within a mirror, the spirit's power is immediately curtailed. It is unable to torment whoever possesses the mirror.

Maitre Carrefour's Banishing Spell

The dangerous edge that characterizes most crossroads spirits (Elegba, Hermes, Maria Padilha, Hecate, etc.), that fine line that transforms a trickster into a scary malicious spirit, is especially pronounced with the lwa known as Baron or Maitre Carrefour, the Master of the Crossroads. Maitre Carrefour rules nocturnal crossroads. There is great ambivalence towards this volatile spirit as he can so easily turn dangerous. He isn't summoned without good reason.

Maitre Carrefour permits or obstructs the passage of malevolent spirits as he chooses. If malicious spirits are truly tormenting you, request that Maitre Carrefour deny them access to you. Offer him a very good cigar and fine rum. Speak to him politely and humbly (this isn't the moment to fantasize about commanding and compelling), with no ambiguity as to your request or any payment promised.

 ## Mandrake Banishing

Allegedly no room is big enough for true mandrake root and evil spirits. Bring mandrake in to force malevolent spirits out!

 ## Poltergeist Banishing: Fumitory/Earth Smoke

*Burn **Fumitory** (Earth smoke) to banish poltergeists, demons, and any manner of malicious spirit. (This was the solution allegedly favored in the famed ninth-century geometric gardens of Saint Gall.)*

 ## Poltergeist Banishing: Slamming Doors

Allegedly slamming every door in your residence three times frightens away poltergeists, at least temporarily.

 ## Sage Banishing Spirits Spell

Burn sage—especially white sage—to rid an area of evil spirits and negative entities.

 ## San Cipriano Banishing

During his days as a sorcerer, San Cipriano conjured up spirits at will. According to some legends, he had a host of demons at his personal disposal. Who better to perform an exorcism? Indeed, San Cipriano is the patron saint of magicians and exorcists. Allegedly the condition oil named in his honor possesses a banishing effect.

*Dress brown candles with **San Cipriano Oil**; this should send low-level spirits fleeing. Accompany candle burning with requests for San Cipriano's personal assistance. Allegedly invoking his name scares the mid-level evil entities away.*

 ## San Cipriano Extra Strength Banishing

Faced with full-strength major evil entities, general wisdom suggests that a professional, like San Cipriano in his lifetime, be called in. If this is impossible, invoke the saint's presence.

1. Further empower **San Cipriano Oil** by adding frankincense and benzoin.
2. Dress sufficient brown and white candles with this oil to cast a circle large enough for you to comfortably stand within.
3. Create a circle of alternating brown and white candles.

4. From within the circle, light the candles. Request San Cipriano's presence. Call the spirits' bluff and tell them San Cipriano is on the way. Accompany with the Bell, Book and Candle banishing spell (page 148).
5. When the candles have burned down, continue with extensive *Cleansing Spells.*

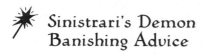 Sinistrari's Demon Banishing Advice

According to Ludovico Sinistrari, a seventeenth-century Franciscan friar, scholar and demonologist, the following are guaranteed to repel and expel demons. Incorporate them into your spells as needed, individually or together.

★ *Castor oil*
★ *Palma Christi, the castor oil plant*
★ *Coral*
★ *Jasper*
★ *Jet*
★ *Menstrual blood*

 Sweet Spirit Oil Spell

This Sweet Spirit Oil is safe for use by most people and smells beautiful. Wearing it endows you with a personal protective aura. Evil spirits will allegedly leave you alone, even if they are lurking nearby.

Blend essential oils of frankincense and vetiver, together with honeysuckle absolute and rose attar into a base of sweet almond oil. Add the oil to bathwater before retiring for the night, or massage it onto the body, to keep malicious spirits far away from you.

Sweet Spirit Powder Spell

To repel evil spirits, while simultaneously beckoning benevolent, kind, protective ones:

1. Grind the following botanicals together to produce a fine powder: frankincense, honeysuckle blossoms, roses, and vetiver roots.
2. Sprinkle the powder onto lit charcoal and burn incessantly, until you're convinced the danger is over.

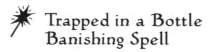 Trapped in a Bottle Banishing Spell

The most famous genie trapped in a bottle may be Jeannie, star of the hit American television show, I Dream of Jeannie. Evil spirits, including but not restricted to djinn, the original "genies," can also be trapped inside a bottle or jar.

1. Drop thirteen rose-thorns into a jar or bottle, one by one.
2. As you drop each thorn, murmur something like *"Evil Presence, I banish you!"*
3. Cover the thorns with the petals from one rose, dropped in one by one as you continue murmuring.
4. Fill the jar two thirds full with salted water, **Holy Water, Rose of Jericho Water** or **Notre Dame Water.**
5. Leave the jar open and unattended overnight.
6. Before sunrise, close the jar tight. Evil should be trapped within.
7. Wrap the jar in dark fabric and bury it far away.

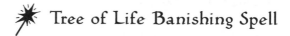 Tree of Life Banishing Spell

Arbor vitae: the name given to this tree means "tree of life." The smoke from its burning leaves allegedly disperses unwanted spirits and sends them packing.

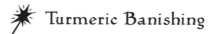 Turmeric Banishing

Sprinkle ground turmeric onto lit charcoals. Malicious spirits allegedly dislike the fragrance enough to leave its presence.

 Witch Balls

Witch balls are globes of iridescent colored glass. Place them around your home and property to disperse malicious spirits.

 Woodlands Banishing Spell

Burn acorns, mistletoe, and oak bark to repel undesirable spirit guests. Murmur your desire for them to leave.

Banishing Stalkers

Sometimes the form of harassment is very specific. You may wish to coordinate the following spells, specifically used to prevent personal stalkers, with reinforcing protection spells.

 Boldo Begone Powder

Boldo is an evergreen native to South America. Its leaves allegedly help repel stalkers. It is combined with traditional components of banishing powder.

1. Grind up boldo leaves and blend them together with asafetida, chili powder and sulfur.
2. Blend this into a base of arrowroot powder.

Sprinkle this powder across the path of the person who must stop pursuing you. Or you can sprinkle the powder across your thresholds as well as any vulnerable areas or points of entry into your home.

 Graveyard Dirt Anti-Stalker Spell (1)

1. Obtain a handful of graveyard dirt, ideally from the grave of someone who loves you and is concerned for your safety.
2. Drizzle **Van Van Oil** over the graveyard dirt.

Use this to paint boundary lines around your home, especially across any thresholds. Women may dip an angelica root into this dirt/oil mixture, wrap it in a white handkerchief and carry it between their breasts.

 Graveyard Dirt Anti-Stalker Spell (2)

1. Grind and powder graveyard dirt extremely finely before adding a combination of **Van Van** and **Fiery Wall of Protection Oils.**
2. Dilute this in spring water or one of the magical water formulas *(see Formulary,* page 1037).
3. Sprinkle this over yourself to set up a protective boundary.

Maneki Neko, the Japanese beckoning cat, is currently perhaps the world's most popular amulet. The charm, available in a vast variety of sizes, from several feet high to no bigger than your smallest fingernail, depicts a cat holding one paw up to its ear, a gesture that in Japan indicates *"come here!"* The images are coded: variations in color and detail create different magical impact.

Initially associated with prosperity spells, Maneki Neko is discussed in greater detail amongst the *Money Spells,* starting on page 804. However, over the years, other uses have evolved: black Maneki Neko cats ward off stalkers.

In magical parlance, *drawing* is the opposite of *banishing*. While a summoning spell draws something or someone specific toward you, drawing spells set up a force of attraction, drawing people or qualities (wealth, fertility, love), in general.

Among the ingredients believed to create a drawing effect are:

★ Sugar
★ Honey
★ Molasses
★ Lodestones

If you are seriously concerned about a stalker, avoid drawing materials, as well as the various Attraction Oils, until the danger has passed.

 ## Maneki Neko's Anti-Stalker Spell

★ *Carry a small one in a charm bag or wear one on a cord around your neck*
★ *Have Maneki Neko stand sentry over your home: place her in a front window, looking outside*

Banishing Vermin

No, not bad boyfriends. Try the regular banishing spells at the beginning of this section for them. Or look through the *Love Spells* for some tips on effectively ending relationships. These vermin are the little creepy crawly kinds that seem to possess magical resistance towards efforts to remove them.

Banishing Powders

*The Hoodoo summoning powder called **Drawing Powder** should contain nothing more than powdered confectioner's sugar. To demonstrate its powers of summoning, sprinkle sugar on the floor and watch ants and other bugs miraculously appear. Yet Drawing Powder is intended to summon people. Try the spell's converse and see if this works on bugs, too. The various Banishing Powders are meant to banish people, just as Drawing Powder summons them: sprinkle Banishing Powder around your home to see if this works as well.*

Banishment By Royal Decree Spell

The single most effective method for banishing assorted vermin is to pay a visit to the Queen of the Species. This powerful spell utilizes no ingredients beyond your powers of visualization. This spell is particularly effective if you would prefer not to utilize conventional extermination methods.

This ritual may be used as a "last resort" before attempting chemical extermination. If you are a tenant rather than the owner of the home, you may have little say in what methods of pest control are used: this ritual gives you the opportunity to sound a warning and perhaps absolve your conscience.

1. Visit the queen of your specific species and issue her an ultimatum.
2. The queen resides in a palace that corresponds to whatever form of home that species naturally uses. Thus the Queen Bee lives in a hive, while the Queen Wasp lives in a wasp's nest, although your visualization may feature luxurious variations.
3. When you enter her palace, you will be met by guards and courtiers. Explain that you have an urgent message for the Queen. Refuse to deliver it to anyone else. Eventually, if you are persistent, you will gain admittance to her presence.
4. Regardless of the size of any other creatures you witness in this visualization, the queen cannot be smaller than you. She must either be comparable in size to you or larger. Because in real life, these creatures tend to be small, you may choose to visualize the Queen as larger than life or, Alice in Wonderland-style, you may temporarily shrink yourself.
5. Approach the Queen. Speak to her as respectfully as if she were the queen of a great nation, yet be firm. Extend a deadline that is reasonable for you: explain that if her creatures have not vacated your premises (you may wish to offer specific boundaries) by the deadline, you are not responsible for the fate that befalls them.

6. If it is not your choice to call for a professional exterminator, you are entitled to request that the queen give you a gift before you leave. Otherwise, be polite, be firm and leave quickly.
7. Depart from the palace via the same route by which you arrived. Wait until the deadline before taking further action.

Eucalyptus Banishing Spell

Botanical methods of banishing may work, too. The scent and presence of eucalyptus allegedly repels cockroaches.

1. Add essential oil of eucalyptus to a bowl of cool water.
2. Soak a cloth in the water.
3. Leave the cloth wherever you'd like to banish the roaches.

If this proves successful, add essential oil of eucalyptus to a spray bottle filled with water and spray wherever needed.

Khonsu's Banishing Spell

The Egyptian lunar divinity Khonsu may be invoked to banish cockroaches.

1. Hold a scarab in your left hand to charge it with your desire.
2. Place it in the light of the Full Moon.
3. Warm essential oil of frankincense in an aroma burner and tell Khonsu what you need.

Ochossi's Banishing Spell

Ochossi, the Yoruba orisha of hunting, never misses his prey. Ochossi is an old-fashioned hunter: he is a master archer, a lover of the forest and has little patience with chemically toxic methods of pest control. Request that he remove your pests. Supplement the spell with traps as needed, so that Ochossi can implement his magic. This spell is meant quite literally: it was given to me by a friend, a resident of New York City, who was plagued by a brave and seemingly unbeatable mouse. Within hours of initiating the spell, that mouse was in the trap.

1. Add cornmeal and honey to a glass of milk and stir it gently to blend. This is your offering to Ochossi: place it on an altar, together with candles and/or other gifts.
2. Leave the offering out for several hours at least.
3. Promise Ochossi more gifts, if the vermin go quickly and stay gone.

 ## Magic Chalk Anti-Ant Circles

Stores in New York's Chinatown sometimes feature Magic Ant Repelling Chalk. The magic may be very effective, but the chalk is just plain chalk. Use white chalk to draw boundary lines and protective circles around your home. Allegedly the ants will not cross these boundary lines.

 ## Valerian Rat Banishing

Allegedly valerian is what the Pied Piper of Hamelin used to lure the rats away from that besieged town. If reports are true, he carried the herb in his pocket. You may, however, wish to try burning it in a portable incense burner or censer. Create a magical path for the rats to follow. Rats, like cats, allegedly enjoy the fragrance and will follow it where it leads them.

 ## Yule Log Banishing

Preserve the charred Yule log and/or its ashes under the bed to keep vermin far away.

Better Business and Professional Success Spells

Although many of these are money spells, they solicit money from a specific source. These aren't spells for conjuring up money from out of the blue; you'd like the opportunity to earn this money. Magic provides financial inspiration, added opportunity and protective buffering from the inherent instability of the marketplace.

Better Business is Hoodoo terminology for more than just increased business, although the desire to stimulate healthy cash flow inspires a large selection of spells. This category also includes anything specifically affecting business, money earned through work or business, employment, and career issues. It is a particularly ancient and universal category: no matter where people come from, they understand the necessity of earning a living, together with its attendant pitfalls, risks, and dangers.

The concept of the "*marketplace*" serves as yet another metaphoric, magical spiritual crossroads, especially if one considers ancient town markets. Roads converged in the marketplace; it was an area of swirling energy and great opportunity for success, loss, transformation, and adventure. More than mere buying and selling of goods went on;

★ Better business spells whose goal is increased profits often rely heavily upon the creation and correct placement of special charms

★ Powders and oils are used to encourage out-going money to return *"home"*

diviners, traditional healers and entertainers including conjurers and professional story-tellers all plied their wares in the marketplace. It was where you went to hear news. Before copyright laws, books were *"published"* by being read aloud in the market square. In many traditional African philosophies the marketplace is a crossroads particularly associated with women's power and opportunity for success.

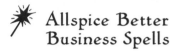

Allspice Better Business Spells

Allspice berries allegedly enhance the fortunes of business ventures. They are also reputed to magically help turn around regrettable investments.

★ *Carry them in a charm bag*
★ *Pierce and string the berries. Wear them as a necklace or more discreet ankle bracelet*
★ *Add allspice berries to a bottle of **Bay Rum**. Massage this enhanced **Bay Rum** into your hands and body*

Almond Tree Better Business Spell

1. Find an almond tree that you can climb.
2. Offer the tree a libation and gift.
3. Murmur your desires to the tree; state your goals and aspirations.
4. Climb the tree.
5. Linger as long or as little as you like; when you come down, offer the tree another libation.
6. Your success will allegedly be achieved; if so, plant another almond tree.
7. Repeat as needed.

Arabka Soudagar Spell

Is business bad? Is a hex or a block manifesting in a financial manner? The Hoodoo formulation Arabka Soudagar *breaks through business blockages to repair and improve finances. Grind bay laurel leaves, cinnamon, frankincense, tonka beans, and vetiver roots together. Burn the resulting powder, allowing the aroma to permeate all areas of the business.*

Basil Better Business Spells

Basil is the botanical most associated with attracting wealth and prosperity. Large, fresh, vivid green basil leaves are believed to resemble cash bills. In addition, basil is strongly identified with various spirits of wealth and good fortune. The presence of the botanical beckons these spirits, together with their blessings of prosperity.

Basil belongs to Maitresse Ezili Freda Dahomey, Vodou spirit of luxury, and features in many of her rituals. Tulsi basil, also known as holy basil, belongs to Lakshmi, the popular Hindu goddess of good fortune.

Basil Spell (1) Lakshmi's Tulsi

In one legend, Lakshmi was transformed into a pot of basil by a rival for her husband's affections. Although she was able to shape-shift back, tulsi still retains her essence.

1. To bring Lakshmi's protection and presence, her essence of luck and wealth, into your home or business, place pots of tulsi basil near the front entrance.
2. Nurturing the basil in turn nurtures your wealth and success.

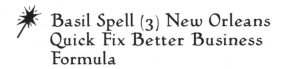

Basil Spell (2) New Orleans Better Business Formula

Maitresse Ezili Freda Dahomey emerged in a region of West Africa known either as Dahomey or Benin. Originally a water snake spirit, she traveled with enslaved devotees to the Western hemisphere, taking root in Haiti, where she has achieved great prominence as the pre-eminent female spirit in the Vodoun pantheon. During the journey, Maitresse Ezili shed her snakeskin to emerge as the breathtakingly beautiful lwa of wealth, luxury, dreams and love. New Orleans Voodoo stands firmly on the shoulders of Haitian Vodou, although the more religious aspects may or may not be emphasized. Basil is a major component of New Orleans-styled better business formulas, although the original connection to Maitresse Ezili may be overlooked.

1. Shred approximately one half cup of fresh basil leaves.
2. Cover the basil with approximately one pint (560 ml) of boiling water. (Play with proportions to achieve the quantity and intensity you desire.)
3. Let the basil steep in this water for three days.
4. On the fourth day, strain out the water, reserving the liquid.

Sprinkle this liquid over the entrances and thresholds of your business, in corners, behind doors and near the cash registers—basically in any spot that might be perceived as vulnerable. It allegedly attracts customers and prevents theft.

Basil Spell (3) New Orleans Quick Fix Better Business Formula

There are two methods of creating this quick-fix version. The most preferred is to add twelve drops of essential oil of basil to one pint (560 ml) of water. This isn't as potent as regular New Orleans Better Business Formula but it's fast. It can be whipped up in seconds. An alternative method is to pour boiling water over one tablespoon of dried basil. Allow it to steep until it cools, then strain and use.

The dried herb lacks the potency of either the fresh herb or the highly concentrated essential oil. However, neither the dried herb nor the essential oil possesses fresh basil's distinctive fragrance. Both Quick Fix solutions lack the visual component of the original spell, too: the soaking basil leaves look a lot like cash. Compensate by adding extra focus and visualization to the spell.

Basil hydrosol may also be substituted. Use it by itself or add it to rinse water. Again, because so little effort is required to use this, compensate by added focus and visualization.

Basil Spell (4) Earth Smoke Enhancement

***Fumitory,** also known as Earth Smoke (because, according to legend, it was believed to have been born from "Earth's vapors"), is a plant with ancient magic uses. Known since Neolithic times, and mentioned by Geoffrey Chaucer in his* Canterbury Tales, *fumitory is used in longevity, cleansing, protection, and prosperity spells.*

1. Pour boiling water over shredded fresh basil leaves.
2. Allow this to cool, then strain out the basil and add the liquid to a bucket of floorwash rinse water.
3. Once the floor has dried, burn Earth Smoke, fumitory incense.

Basil Spell (5)

Fresh basil smells so inviting you may not wish to reserve it for the floor.

1. Chop fresh basil into fine threads.
2. Warm honey gently over the stove. (A double boiler or bain-marie is recommended, as honey scorches easily.)

3. Add the basil to the honey and simmer.
4. Remove the basil-enhanced honey from the source of heat and murmur over it something like this:

   Flies flocks to honey
   Customers flock to me
   Bears flock to honey,
   Business flocks to me
   Ants flock to honey
   Contracts flock to me
   (Adapt to your specific situation.)
5. Run a warm bath for yourself.
6. Rub the honey over your body, and then enter the bath.
7. Soak in the water for a while. When you emerge, before you drain the water, reserve some of the used bathwater.
8. Toss this on the grounds of your business.

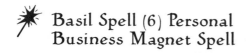

Basil Spell (6) Personal Business Magnet Spell

Sometimes you are your business. Traditionally prostitutes have bathed in infusions of fresh basil to lure customers towards them, a custom believed to originate in Spain, although it has since traveled around the world. Sex workers aren't the only ones whose prosperity is dependent upon selling themselves. This spell is beneficial for anyone whose business depends upon his or her own personal magnetism.

1. Add strong infusions of fresh basil to your bath, together with fresh basil leaves and some basil hydrosol.
2. For extra enhancement, after bathing and air-drying, dust the body lightly with either **Lodestone Body Powder** or Drawing Powder Personal Dusting Powder (see page 166).

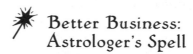

Better Business: Artist's Spell

Artists and steady money: that's frequently a contradiction in terms. Yet even visionaries must eat. This spell assists artists, innovators, and all those ahead of their time to achieve financial stability without sacrificing artistic principles.

Carve and dress one small purple and one small green candle to suit your personal circumstances. Place the candles on either side of a Fool card drawn from the tarot deck of your choice. Burn and trust to inspiration.

Better Business: Astrologer's Spell

Tanit, Queen of the Stars, matron of astrologers, may or may not be Astarte under another name. She is invoked to protect astrologers and increase their business prospects.

1. Dedicate a blue candle to Tanit.
2. Decorate her altar space with Tanit's sacred creatures: dolphins, fish, doves, and snakes plus images of crescent moons and stars.
3. Offer her figs, pomegranates, and stalks of wheat while requesting her blessings.

Better Business: Charm Bag

1. Select one or more of the Money Drawing or Luck oils.
2. Use the oil(s) to anoint five cowrie shells, a High John the Conqueror root and a matched pair of lodestones.
3. Place these into a red flannel draw-string bag. Carry it with you or place it strategically within the business.
4. Anoint with more oil periodically to reinforce the mojo's power.

☀ Better Business: Commanding Spell

*Command and compel business to improve. This spell encourages you to radiate confidence, and others to wish to please you. Rub a drop of **Essence of Bend Over** or another **Commanding Oil** between the palms of your hands just before conferences or when meeting colleagues, bosses, employees, or clients. Shake the target's hand or find an excuse to touch their bare hand.*

☀ Better Business: Drawing Incense

Blend dried basil, benzoin, and ground cinnamon and burn as a business-drawing incense.

Better Business Floorwashes

Floorwashes are a traditional—and discreet—method of casting spells. The botanical infusions are used to radiate magic power, drawing or repelling your desire as the case may be. Floorwashes are used to scrub front steps to provide spiritual protection and attract free-spending customers. Within a building, the term "*floorwash*" is somewhat deceptive; in general, this is more of a "*floor final rinse.*" It is assumed that the floor is clean prior to applying the spell floorwash: the floorwash isn't rinsed off, but should be allowed to dry and radiate its fragrance and power. The physical labor involved in applying the floorwash also enhances the casting of the spell: your effort transmits your intentions and desires.

Applying Better Business Floorwashes
★ *Scrub the walkway and the doorway of your business, beginning at the street and moving toward your front door, just the way customers should*
★ *Scrub the front steps*

★ *Cleanse the interior floors beginning at the front door and corners and working towards the center of each room*

Floorwashes may be created with any of the following or a combination:

★ *Boiled cooled salted water*
★ *Pure spring water (bottled water)*
★ *Strained, collected rainwater*
★ *Plain tap water*

☀ Better Business Floorwash (1)

1. Combine ground cinnamon, brown sugar and red brick dust.
2. Add this to a bucket of water, together with some white vinegar.

☀ Better Business Floorwash (2)

1. Combine **Florida Water, Indigo Water, Van Van Oil,** and ground cinnamon.
2. Add to a bucket filled with salted water, together with white vinegar.

☀ Better Business Floorwash (3)

Add essential oil of citronella to a bucket of water and white vinegar and use as a floorwash. This allegedly drives away negative spiritual entities while drawing in customers to fill the void.

☀ Better Business Floorwash (4)

1. Make a strong infusion by pouring boiling water over a quantity of crushed allspice berries.
2. Strain and add the liquid to a bucket of water, together with white vinegar, and use as a floorwash.

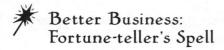 

Better Business: Fortune-teller's Spell

Better Business: Squill Root Spell (1)

Saint Agabus, the patron saint of fortune-tellers, was a compatriot of Saint Paul who correctly predicted Paul's capture and imprisonment as well as his own death. Although this spell may be cast anytime, it is most effective on February 13th, the saint's feast day, the anniversary of his death.

Keep squill root in your cash register to drum up and stabilize business.

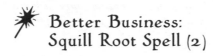

Better Business: Squill Root Spell (2)

Light a purple or white candle. Place something that represents your mode of divination beside it (dice, cards, runes, etc.) and ask for Agabus's blessings on your endeavors and for increased business.

Create an infusion by pouring boiling water over squill root. Add the strained infusion to floorwash and use it to cleanse the floors and walls of your business.

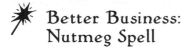 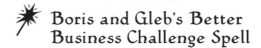

Better Business: Nutmeg Spell

Boris and Gleb's Better Business Challenge Spell

1. Drill a hole through a nutmeg and string it onto green thread.
2. Add one pierced Grain of Paradise, a Jezebel root and a High John the Conqueror. (It may also be necessary to drill the hole through the High John, a particularly hard root.)
3. Tie the thread together and hang over the front entrance to the business.

May 2nd is the feast day belonging to the Russian Orthodox saints Boris and Gleb, who may or may not be those mythological twins Castor and Pollux in disguise. Castor and Pollux are the constellation Gemini's celestial twins; Gemini rules commerce and the marketplace. Coincidentally perhaps Boris and Gleb have some control over the marketplace, too.

Allegedly, if you can manage a successful business transaction on this day, the favorable fortunes of your business are guaranteed for the next twelve months.

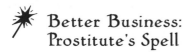

Better Business: Prostitute's Spell

European prostitutes once favored wearing the scent of lavender. Allegedly it attracts men while simultaneously protecting against violence. Add hydrosol and/or essential oil to a tub filled with water and bathe.

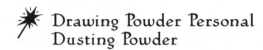

Busy as an Ant Better Business Spell

This is a modern adaptation of a Talmudic-era spell. Jewish spells, like ancient Egyptian spells and modern Chinese magic, often rely heavily on the power of the written word. The original spell might have included sacred words of power, acronyms, notarikon and specially chosen biblical phrases. Incorporate these as you will. There is, however, no substitute for anthill dust.

1. Collect dust from an anthill.
2. On a piece of parchment paper, write your business goals in the present tense. For instance: *"I sell one million units every week."* Use an image or photograph in addition to words, if you wish.
3. Fold up the paper into a very tight little square, always folding toward you.
4. Place the paper, the dust, and a lodestone into a small charm bag.
5. Hang this discreetly in your place of business.

Drawing Powder

Spiritual supply stores sometimes sell really cute little bottles filled with some kind of powdery substance and labeled *Drawing Powder*. It's better business for them if you purchase a few vials, however, it may be better business for you to take a trip to the grocery store instead. Although that name may be used to label a complex, sophisticated Money Drawing Powder full of rare ingredients, technically plain old Drawing Powder is powdered confectioner's sugar. Not sure if it works? Sprinkle some on the floor in a warm climate and watch armies of ants miraculously appear, magically beckoned to draw close to the powder.

To attract customers and financial success:

★ Sprinkle a path of *Drawing Powder* from the street to the front door of your business

★ Sprinkle *Drawing Powder* into your cash register to beckon fresh cash to draw near
★ Sprinkle *Drawing Powder* into and over invitations to your place of business as a magical inducement

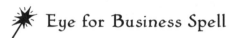

Drawing Powder Personal Dusting Powder

Drawing Powder may be used to draw business toward you yourself, too.

1. Blend powdered confectioner's sugar into cornstarch.
2. Lightly dust this on your body with a powder puff to magically attract personal attention—and open pockets.

For added enhancement, sprinkle the blended powder with essential oil of basil before applying to the body.

Eye for Business Spell

Collect eyes to increase business and provide protection for your enterprise. Assemble four of the following: an Eye of Horus, a blue-eye bead, a silver-colored eye milagro, a black-eyed pea, a cat's eye, or a tiger's eye. Place one in each corner of the room, looking in.

Financial Crisis Better Business Spell

This increased power business bath is considered an emergency spell. It allegedly provides temporary relief in times of crisis. Save it for use during truly hard times and crises. It is most powerful when coordinated with the New Moon. Do not be tempted to perform this spell at every New Moon by rote: it loses its effectiveness when used too frequently.

1. Make a strong infusion from the following materials by pouring boiling spring water over them:
   Dried basil or shredded fresh basil
   Dried parsley or fresh parsley
   Coriander seeds and/or fresh coriander leaves
   Cinnamon
   Brown sugar
   Grated fresh orange zest
   Fresh orange leaves (optional)
2. Allow the liquid to cool.
3. Fill a bathtub half full.
4. Strain out the botanical materials and bring the liquid to the bath.
5. Stand naked in the bathtub and toss the infusion over yourself.
6. Sit or recline in the water, soaking for seven minutes. Pray and petition for help and prosperity for the entire period. Visualize your prayers fulfilled.
7. After seven minutes, drain the water and allow yourself to air-dry.

First Dollar Spells

The first dollar earned by a new business venture is perceived as especially charged with magic power.

 ## First Dollar Ashes Spell

1. Reserve the first dollar earned from a new business.
2. Grind and pulverize it.
3. Blend with frankincense and gold copal.
4. Burn atop a lit charcoal.
5. Reserve the ashes: carry them in a conjure bag.

 ## First Dollar Candle Spell

1. Reserve the first dollar earned in a new business.
2. Sprinkle it with magnetic sand, sugar, and salt.

3. Place a green candle on top of the dollar and burn it.
4. Bury most of the remnants on the property; reserve a few pieces in a conjure bag and hang it near the entrance.

 ## First Dollar Ginseng Spell

1. Reserve the first dollar earned in a new business.
2. Wrap it around a ginseng root with green and red thread.
3. Hold it in your hands and charge it with your hopes and desires.
4. Place it in a conjure bag and keep it in or beneath the cash register to generate further income.

 ## First Dollar San Martin Caballero

San Martin Caballero is invoked in Latin American magic to improve and stabilize business fortunes.

1. Upon initiation of a new business, reserve the first dollar earned and dedicate it to San Martin.
2. Place it beneath a statue of the saint or before his chromolithograph.
3. Sprinkle the dollar with magnetic sand.
4. Burn seven red candles in front of the image.
5. Keep the dollar beneath or affixed to the image (attach it behind the chromolithograph) to encourage increased business and profits.

Garlic Better Business Spell (1)

Garlic provides a combination of increased business with space protection.

1. Make or purchase a wreath formed from heads of garlic.
2. Fill tiny plastic packets or little red flannel pouches with salt. Fill others with yellow mustard seed. (Staple plastic packets shut; sew flannel pouches securely together.)
3. Attach these to the wreath. Decorate with other lucky charms as desired: small horseshoes, crystals, lucky roots or tiny image cards. Should you have a dried snakeskin, it's considered especially fortuitous.
4. Hang over the entrance to your business.

Garlic Better Business Spell (2)

This Italian spell utilizes only one single head of garlic, but the technique involved in forming the amulet maximizes its protective capacities. This charm not only draws business to you but protects your business as well.

1. Stick a brass tack into one side of a head of garlic.
2. Stick an iron or steel nail into the garlic's other side.
3. Stick nine pins into the garlic at various angles and intervals.
4. Attach a corn kernel to the nail with green or red thread.
5. Wind this thread around each and every pin, finally ending by tying and knotting the thread on to the brass tack.
6. Soak this charm into one of the **Money Drawing oils** overnight.
7. Remove from the oil, let it dry out and hang it over the front door.

Anoint with extra oil once a week or after a particularly good day. Should the charm start to rot, dispose of it immediately and replace it.

Has No Hanna Better Business Spell

*Make **Has No Hanna** incense from dried jasmine and gardenia flowers, peppermint leaves and tangerine zest. Burn on lit charcoal and pass business, corporate or legal documents through the smoke for success.*

That "*better business*" is an ancient concern is aptly demonstrated by this Mesopotamian ritual. This spell is thousands of years old; it requests materials (dirt from Ishtar's temple) that may once have been easily attainable but are not necessarily so today. Consider and improvise as needed. The stated goal of this spell, which ultimately evolves into a request for Ishtar's assistance, is increased business. However, Ishtar is a particularly powerful deity, with dominion over love, sex, fertility, justice, and healing as well: the spell format may be adapted to request whatever is needed.

Ishtar's Better Business Spell

1. Obtain a handful of dirt from each of the following places: a bridge, a quay, a ferry, a four-way crossroads, Ishtar's temple, a bordello, the city gates, a gardener's home, a chef's home, and a successful innkeeper's home. Blend and reserve the dirt; there should be ten handfuls in all.
2. Construct a wicker altar for Ishtar.
3. Make or purchase three loaves of bread in the shape of women's breasts. Place these on or beneath the altar.
4. Blend either three or seven distinct sources of spring water together. Place this water in a vessel beside the bread.
5. Fumigate the area with juniper incense.

6. Offer Ishtar some top-quality beer.
7. Consider exactly what sort of assistance you require. Turn your request into an incantation, repeating it *exactly* the same way, seven times.
8. Moisten the reserved dirt with some of the water, blending it with your fingers until you achieve a clay-like texture.
9. Repeat your incantation seven more times.

Use some of the water to wash the front entrance to your home or business. Use the moistened dirt to form the figure of a calf. This is not an art project: do the best you can. Paint the calf gold, if you like. Bury it in Earth on your property, together with Ishtar's beer and loaves of bread.

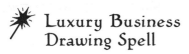

Luxury Business Drawing Spell

This is an extremely deluxe business drawing formula, appropriate for a luxury business. A lavish variety of essences are included, several of which (e.g., neroli, sandalwood) can be quite expensive. It has a sensual, relaxing fragrance, which will encourage customers and business clients to slow down and linger.

1. Blend equal parts pure spring water with **Holy Water, Notre Dame Water,** or **Rose of Jericho Water.**
2. Add essential oils of anise, bergamot, cinnamon bark, lavender, neroli or petitgrain, rose geranium, rosemary, sandalwood, and wintergreen.
3. Warm this formula in an aroma burner. Alternatively, place the formula in a spray bottle and spray throughout the premises, concentrating on threshold areas. Or you can add it to a bucket of water and use it as a final rinse over your floor.

The formula can also be added to your laundry rinse cycle to permeate your clothes with its beautiful aroma and power. (Although in theory you could bathe in the formula, several of the oils can cause severe skin irritation.)

Magic Coin Better Business Spells

An entire school of Chinese magic is devoted to the use of coins. (The use of currency as spell components derives from many traditions, however the Chinese school is most complete and cohesive and also remains extremely vital.) Detailed information may be found among the *Money Spells* (see pages 817–19). In short, coins are used to draw good fortune, protection and increased prosperity toward you or toward an area. Although any metal coin may be used, traditional Chinese coins are best. Beyond the complex metaphysical reasoning, they are simpler to use than most coins: the square hole cut into the center of each coin lends itself to easy stringing, wrapping and hanging. String the coins together yourself for added magical input as this type of spell also relies heavily on knot magic and beautiful, intricate magical knots are incorporated into each spell charm. However, coins may also be purchased already strung and knotted (and if you purchase from a master, blessed) in a variety of numerical combinations from feng shui suppliers and traditional Chinatown vendors.

Magic Coin Better Business Spell (1)

1. String three coins together or purchase them already linked.
2. Place these strung-together coins on top of a yellow or golden cloth.
3. Sprinkle magnetic sand over the coins.
4. Anoint with essential oil of bergamot.
5. Roll and fold the cloth toward you, forming a packet.
6. Tie securely with a red silk ribbon.
7. Place this packet inside or near your cash register for increased business and wealth.

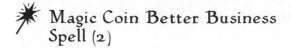 ## Magic Coin Better Business Spell (2)

Two Chinese coins strung together with red thread represents Zhao Gong Ming, Lord of Wealth—someone every establishment would like to welcome as an honored, long-staying guest. Hang this charm above a shop window to attract wealth and good fortune to the business.

Should the actual coins be unavailable, an image depicting this amulet possesses similar powers. Post this instead.

Magic Coin Better Business Spell (3)

Place two coins strung together with red thread underneath the telephone to generate business.

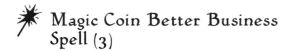 ## Magic Coin Better Business Spell (4)

The concept of "magic money" isn't limited to China. Throughout Africa, cowrie shells were traditionally used as amulets for healing, protection and fertility, as well as a form of currency. Individual cowrie shells may be substituted for virtually any business growth or money drawing charm. Like traditional Chinese coins, cowries may be strung on to cord, incorporating knot magic.

★ Tuck one cowrie shell into your cash register to encourage increased takings
★ String five cowries onto red thread and hang over the front entrance to your business
★ Tie one cowrie on to a silk cord and place within your ledger book

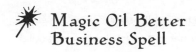 ## Magic Oil Better Business Spell

Anoint invoices, brochures, business cards—basically any stationery with the company-letterhead—with money-drawing oils to generate new and increased business.

Magic Water Spells

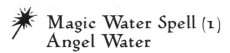 ## Magic Water Spell (1) Angel Water

Sprinkle **Angel Water** (or substitute an infusion of myrtle) around your business premises to encourage cashflow.

Magic Water Spell (2) Glory Water

1. Place frankincense tears (small pieces of frankincense) inside a bottle.
2. Cover them with orange blossom water or hydrosol.
3. Add a few drops of essential oil of bergamot.
4. Asperge **Glory Water** through the premises to increase business, attract blessings and customers, and overcome challenges.

Malachite Merchant Spells

Malachite is the merchant's stone. It's green, like money. It's a stone associated with the astrological sign Libra, the scales. Use malachite to tip the scales in your favor.

★ Place it strategically in your cash register
★ Hang it in the corners of your business
★ Wear it as jewelry while at work
★ Carry it in a charm bag

Malachite gem essence may also be beneficial:

★ *Add it to your bath*
★ *Massage it into the soles of your feet before bedtime*
★ *Add it to floorwash*
★ *Add it to a spray bottle filled with spring water or magical formula water and spray into the corners of your business and over its threshold*

Commercial houses of prostitution descended from and emerged alongside ancient temples dedicated to spirits of love, life, and fertility. With strong ties to spirituality, magic, and financial need, bordellos have traditionally developed their own better business tricks.

 ## Maneki Neko's Magic Spell

Although it's doubtful there will ever be definitive surveys, Maneki Neko, the Japanese beckoning cat, appears currently to be the single most popular amulet on Earth. This distinctive feline image emerged relatively recently in magical history: Maneki Neko was unknown until the end of the nineteenth century. According to one legend, Maneki Neko's career began in the window of its namesake, a struggling cat house. After Maneki Neko arrived, business improved drastically and Maneki Neko's reputation was set. She now appears in the windows of even the most respectable stores and businesses all over the world. A Maneki Neko with an upturned left hand beckons increased business. (The right hand signals the desire for cash.) Although she's very cute and you may wish to look at her face, Maneki Neko works by beckoning others to come to you: place her so that she draws business to you.

★ *Place Maneki Neko in the window, facing outside*
★ *Place Maneki Neko so that she faces the front door*
★ *Although a Maneki Neko in any color will generate income, gold Maneki Neko's allegedly serve most powerfully for this purpose*

Marketplace Spirit Spells

These spirits transcend the mere physical aspects of the marketplace. Although they will help with increased business, they encompass metaphysical aspects as well. The mythical marketplace is a crossroads where women's power, in particular, expands exponentially, given the opportunity. Fittingly, these presiding spirits also manifest as powerful females.

 ## Marketplace Spirit Spell (1) Feronia's Wolf at the Door

Feronia is a mysterious and ancient Italian deity whose rites included fire-walking. Her sacred animal is the wolf, Rome's totem animal. Feronia had various temples including one in the heart of Rome. Slaves who sat on a holy stone within her sanctuary were granted freedom. Among her other roles, Feronia was the spirit of the marketplace and that is the role that remains to her. Post-Christianity, Feronia was transformed from a potent, benevolent spirit of freedom and prosperity into a witch who haunts marketplaces.

Invoke her blessings for a good year. The most effective time coincides with her scheduled festival on November 15th. Set up a brazier and burn basil and rue. Post an image of a wolf at the door.

Marketplace Spirit Spell (2) Oya

Oya is the Yoruba orisha who rules the marketplace. She is most easily contacted on Thursdays.

1. Create an altar for Oya.
2. Offer her red wine and nine purple plums. Request her blessings and advice.
3. If possible, maintain this altar at all times, replacing the plums every Thursday. (The wine may be refilled daily or once a week, as you deem appropriate.) If impossible, keep something purple on the premises as a reminder of her presence.

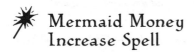

Mermaid Money Increase Spell

The image of the double-tailed mermaid allegedly inspires financial reward. Recently it's been fortunate for Starbuck's coffee houses, however as long ago as medieval times, merchants stamped metal charms with the image and placed these with their wares and cash for protection and prosperity.

1. Draw the image on a square of parchment paper.
2. Place it in your cash box to help the money grow.

Fine iron shot, also known as magnetic sand, is used as a drawing powder, to draw good fortune toward you. Although magnetic sand is naturally dull dark gray, spiritual merchants sell it dyed in various colors for customers with a strong visual sense. If you prefer that visual component, green or gold magnetic sand creates a festive, optimistic-looking powder.

Money Drawing Powder (1)

1. Mix crushed powdered frankincense with dried heliotrope and crushed tonka beans.
2. Add an equal quantity of magnetic sand.

Sprinkle this powder into your cash register over the money, or over your ledger books.

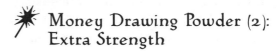

Money Drawing Powder (2): Extra Strength

To draw customers to your door:

1. Blend one tablespoon of Money Drawing Powder with one tablespoon of powdered confectioner's sugar.
2. Sprinkle this across your threshold and front doorstep every Friday.

Alternatively, you can sprinkle the powder to form a path from the street up to your front door.

Money Powder Cross Spell

People's understanding and perception of particular spells may have little to do with the original intent. For instance, the shape of the cross used in the following spell has little to do with Christianity; however, if that added association lends power and comfort for you, incorporate it as you will, as many people have. It is a Conjure spell from the American South and actually relies heavily upon Congolese symbolism. Congolese use of the cross pre-dates exposure to Christianity and describes the successful life cycle, with profound meta-physical implications as well.

Nickels are the traditional coin of choice for this spell, perhaps because five is considered a strong number of protection and generation. However, any coin may be substituted, provided all seven are of equal value.

1. Spread a layer of raw white rice within a baking pan.
2. Cover the rice with a layer of powdered sugar.
3. Sprinkle Money Drawing Powder on top or substitute shredded fresh basil leaves.
4. Lay seven coins on top of the powder in the form of a cross.
5. Dress two red and two green candles with a **Money Drawing oil.**
6. Place one candle at each arm of the cross.
7. Burn the candles completely while visualizing your desired goals.
8. Gather up the nickels, some of the powder, sugar and rice, plus any wax remnants that may have formed vaguely lucky shapes, and place them in a mojo bag, to be worn or kept in your place of business.

 ## Musician's Professional Success Spell

The ancient Egyptian spirit Hathor is the spiritual sponsor of musicians—and dancers, too! Throw a party for Hathor. Play for her (throw a sistrum, her sacred percussion instrument, into the mix to grab her attention), serve wine, beer, and pomegranates and generally have a great time: Hathor is the goddess of joy and pleasure, too. Your happiness honors her. Request her assistance so that happy times may continue indefinitely.

 ## New Orleans Bordello Better Business Spell

While Maneki Neko has shed her risqué reputation, traveled around the world, and has become a great favorite of children, other bordello better business techniques have remained local. The famed houses of the old New Orleans red light district once drummed up business by burning shoes behind their premises. Experiment and see if it works for other businesses, too.

New Orleans Fast Luck Oils

Sometimes you can afford long-term business plans and sometimes you need better business *NOW!* New Orleans-style *"fast luck"* oils provide quick fixes of good fortune. These are short-term solutions; if you discover that these oils work well for you, then reapply consistently and constantly.

 ## Red Fast Luck

Essential oil of cinnamon bark
Essential oil of wintergreen
Vanilla absolute or pure vanilla extract

As its name states, this oil must be red. There are three ways to achieve this:

★ *Blend the ingredients into Turkey red oil*
★ *Blend the ingredients into sunflower and jojoba oils, then use alkanet, a botanical dye to color it. Alkanet bestows its own blessings of good fortune but achieving the correct color is time consuming and labor intensive*
★ *The quick fix method: blend the ingredients into sunflower and jojoba oils, then add red food coloring*

Use Red Fast Luck Oil to anoint anything associated with drawing money into your business: tools, machines, stationery, ledger books, etc. Most especially, anoint all money in your cash drawer, so that it returns to you on the double. If you don't work with cash, then discreetly anoint a corner of all checks paid out.

Red Fast Luck may be used to anoint any other better business charm, to provide enhancement and speed.

Double Fast Luck Oil

Red Fast Luck isn't fast enough? Turn it into Double Fast Luck Oil! Double Fast Luck Oil is used exactly like Red Fast Oil, however it allegedly produces twice the effects at double speed. Double Fast Luck combines the colors green and red. Traditionally red represents luck and life, while green represents growth and prosperity. However, modern associations factor into this oil's power as well. Green and red have evolved into Christmas colors: the goal of this oil is to make every day seem like Christmas. It is an excellent device for shopkeepers and manufacturers who'd like to maintain those Christmas Eve level sales throughout the entire year.

1. Create a green water infusion. This is most powerful if done with cash-drawing botanicals like basil, parsley or mint. However, this will produce a subtle green. If you have visual expectations of bright green, use green food coloring, either alone or as color enhancement.
2. Gently pour this infusion over Red Fast Luck Oil. When at rest, the oil and water should separate, providing two distinct layers of color. Shake it up, dispersing the layers when you wish to use oil.

 ## Personal Salt Mine Better Business Spell

This Japanese Better Business spell takes a less sweet approach than those from New Orleans: place small mounds of salt outside the premises daily to ensure good fortune.

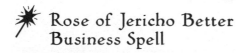 ## Rose of Jericho Better Business Spell

*Among the Rose of Jericho's many blessings are increased business and cashflow. Re-hydrate the rose by placing it in a dish of spring water. Although marketers assure that the rose will bloom overnight or within 24 hours, it is very normal for the process to take several days. Once the rose has bloomed, change its water every Friday (the old water becomes **Rose of Jericho Water** and has many uses), accompanied by the murmuring of psalms or other sacred verses.*

 ## Rose of Jericho Water Better Business Spell

This spell and the spell immediately preceding may be incorporated into one ritual or cast separately, depending upon your circumstances and desires.

*Sprinkle **Rose of Jericho Water** over the premises for increased business; toss it onto your doorstep to provide blessings and protection.*

 ## Rue Better Business Path

Because rue possesses extremely potent protective powers, this spell guards your business's well being too. Grind and powder rue. Sprinkle a path to your business, using this powder to attract customers.

Rue Better Business Protection Smoke

Grind and powder rue; sprinkle the powder on lit charcoals. Pass correspondence having to do with troublesome matters (tax disputes, angry or disappointed clientele) through this smoke for magical protection and happy resolution.

Sex Worker's Better Business Spell

This charm bag, a traditional favorite of those plying the sex trades, allegedly draws free spending, cooperative

people directly to you. It may be adapted by anyone whose business depends upon personal contact.

1. Dress a lodestone with essential oils of basil, bergamot, and lavender. (In theory, the lodestone's gender may be coordinated with the gender of the clientele you wish to draw.)
2. Add **Come To Me, Follow Me Boy** and/or **Attraction Oils.**
3. Sprinkle with magnetic sand and a pinch of ground cinnamon.
4. Carry or wear to charm up added business.

 ## Writer's Better Business Spell

Writers have to eat, too. Wen Ti, Chinese Lord of Literature, is honored by those who earn, would like to earn, or are attempting to earn a living as writers. Wen Ti is usually depicted holding a pen and book displaying four characters that read, "Heaven decides literary success." Perhaps reflecting the instabilities of the career, unlike many spirits who have one annual sacred day,

Wen Ti is honored at various points throughout the year, traditionally during both equinoxes as well as the third and eighth months of the Chinese lunar calendar.

1. Erect an altar honoring Wen Ti.
2. Burn letters of appeal alongside healthy bribes of Spirit Money *(see Money Spells).*

Employment Spells

Many better business spells presume that you own your own business, are an independent contractor or somehow have a share in the business' fortunes. Maybe all you really need is a job.

Employment Spells are less financially oriented than *Better Business Spells*—at least less directly so. Employment Spells encompass enchantments needed to find a job, keep a job, and achieve professional success and happiness. There are also spells for finessing a difficult boss or supervisor and getting along with co-workers—or not, as the case may be.

* Employment-seeking spells are best coordinated with the New Moon
* Coordinate these spells with other more conventional attempts to locate work. No matter how effective the spell, failure to actively seek employment may counteract any chance of success
* Many employment spells, particularly those that assist you in finding work, assume that a certain mobility is required: often some sort of magically empowered object or charm bag must be conjured up that can accompany you to interviews and work

Boss Fix

Is going to work a less than satisfying experience? Perhaps it's not the job that's the problem; maybe you have a supervisor or boss who persecutes you, picks on you, is never satisfied with you and generally makes going to work the equivalent of going to hell? You don't want to leave your job; you'd just like your boss to leave you alone.

The Hoodoo solution is Boss Fix Powder.

According to its most extravagant promises, this spell allegedly causes supervisors to consider you with love and favor. At its more realistic, it offers a boundary line so that at least you'll be left alone to perform your job in peace.

 ## Boss Fix Powder

1. Empty the tobacco from one cigarette. (In order of preference: a cigarette that actually belonged to your boss, his or her favorite brand, any cigarette.)
2. Combine it with some shredded newspaper. (In order of preference: your boss's actual newspaper, a copy of a newspaper he or she favors, any newspaper.)
3. Add some chili powder and grind all the ingredients together into a fine powder.
4. Make sure the powder is fine: this is intended to be a very discreet spell. Your boss already doesn't like you!
5. When the opportunity arises, sprinkle just a tiny bit of powder on or around your boss's chair. If that's too much of a risk, drop a little over the threshold of the office, so that he or she will inevitably step over it.

This is a highly individual spell, tailored toward one target. If more than one person persecutes you, make fresh Boss Fix for each person.

 ## Boss Fix Candle Spell

This spell, cast to receive a raise or promotion, may be a safer, less stressful method of using Boss Fix Powder.

1. Carve and dress a figure candle to represent your boss or supervisor.
2. Place it on a tray covered by aluminum foil and surround the candle with a circle of Boss Fix Powder.
3. Carve and dress another candle to represent you.
4. Dress this candle with a Commanding oil. (Women should also incorporate **Martha the Dominator Oil;** men, use **High John the Conqueror Oil.)**
5. Place this candle on the tray but elevate it so that it is looking down at the first candle.
6. Burn both candles.
7. Sit behind the candle that represents you, facing the other candle. Speak to that candle; tell it what you need.
8. Move the boss candle so that it's resting atop the powder. (Ideally, if possible, dispose of the remnants of this spell in your boss's trashcan.)

Crown of Success Employment Spells

Crown of Success Oil assists you to find a job, land the job and retain the job. It's also used for professional success and advancements, including obtaining promotions and greater financial benefits. **Crown of Success** may be used to enhance any other employment charm or spell: it is an entirely benevolent formula.

 ## Crown of Success Spell (1)

Crown of Success may be applied to the body so that by radiating its magic, you serve as a charm. Add Crown of Success to your bath, or massage it on to your body, especially your hands and feet.

Crown of Success Spell (2)

1. Dress a lodestone with **Crown of Success Oil.**
2. Place it in a red drawstring bag and carry it with you, at work or while searching for employment.

 ## Crown of Success Spell (3)

This spell requires a candle to represent the person seeking employment.

1. Carve the person's name and identifying information into the wax.
2. Dress the candle with **Crown of Success Oil,** holding the candle in both hands to charge it with your desire.
3. Arrange images and items that represent the search for employment around and under the candle.
4. Burn the candle.

 ## Devil's Shoestring Employment Spell

Despite its name, devil's shoestring, there's nothing satanic about this root charm—quite the opposite in fact. Devil's shoestring, the roots of the Viburnum *species, earned its name because it allegedly has the power to trip the devil up, proverbially tying his shoelaces together. Devil's shoestring has an affinity for locating and maintaining employment. Use it to find a job or to improve conditions at the current one.*

★ *Carry it in your pocket*
★ *Pin it within your clothing*
★ *Carry it in a conjure bag*
★ *Attach it to a cord and wear it around your neck*

 ## Don't Sabotage My Success Spell

Are you being set up? Perhaps your boss is unhappy with you or you haven't received your just rewards because you've been maligned and slandered by hostile or jealous co-workers. Although you may wish to supplement with additional Protection, Evil Eye *and* Unblocking Spells, *this particular spell targets co-workers who sabotage your road to career success. Allegedly it will foil any malevolence directed towards you. Prepare a separate mojo for each person who appears to sabotage you.*

1. Write the co-worker's name on a square of brown paper three times.
2. Write your own name over each of the co-worker's names, saying: *"I cross you and I cover you."*
3. Anoint the corners of the paper with essential oils of bergamot, clove bud, and lavender.
4. Fold up the paper, placing it inside a red flannel drawstring bag, together with a devil's shoestring root and some cumin seed.
5. Maintain this discreetly in the workplace, feeding daily with a drop of essential oil of lavender for reinforcement.

 ## Dream Job Spell

1. Write up an advertisement for your dream job.
2. Anoint this "ad" with **Come To Me Oil.**
3. Place it in a conjure bag and carry it with you until your dream is realized (even while employed elsewhere).
4. Anoint with additional oil weekly.

 ## Elfdock Employment Spell

Carry the botanical elfdock at work to receive favors and kindness from others.

Eliminate Jealousy Spell

Wear black gemstones, particularly black tourmaline, to counteract personal and professional jealousy. However, it is crucial that you don't explain why you're wearing them.

 ## Employment Conjure Bag (1)

1. Fill a charm bag with three garlic cloves, nine distinct crumbs of bread, a lodestone and some magnetic sand.
2. Dress with a touch of **Magnet Oil.**
3. Wear or carry to job interviews, adding a new drop of oil prior to each one, if possible.

 ## Employment Conjure Bag (2)

1. Fill a charm bag with the following botanical materials:
   Five finger grass (cinquefoil): to inspire kindness and generosity from others
   Deer's tongue: to provide you with eloquence
   Gravel root: the key ingredient, to provide employment
   Rue: to weed out false opportunities
2. Add a lodestone to draw good fortune towards you.
3. If the bag is to be carried by a man, include a High John the Conqueror root; add an angelica root for a woman.
4. Sprinkle with magnetic sand and **Crown of Success Oil.**

 ## Employment Protection Spell

Tie red ribbons under your desk to provide magical protection at work.

 ## Essence of Bend Over Professional Happiness and Success Spell

Essence of Bend Over, the most concentrated of the Commanding condition oils, takes commanding and compelling into the realm of domination. Indeed, among its other functions, this oil is used in sexual domination spells. However, one of its primary uses is to turn the tables on an employer, particularly for those in menial or service occupations, where continued employment may depend upon the boss's whims and personal satisfaction. Essence of Bend Over enables the employee to discreetly switch the balance of power, so that he or she is able to set professional boundaries and dictate terms of service, although the employer may not realize that this is the case. This is not meant as an evil spell but as a method of preserving a much-needed job and curbing potential abuse and humiliation. And the oil's name? The goal is to have someone else bend over and bow down to you for a change.

Rub the oil onto doorknobs, so that those who open the doors fall under your spell. Or you could rub a drop between your palms and immediately touch the target of your spell.

 ## Find a Job Spell

This is a bit of an arts and crafts spell:

1. Designate a figure candle to represent you.
2. Do basic candle carving (name, identifying information) but then keep going: carve and scratch the wax to represent you in work mode. Create a badge on the candle's chest or scratch the image of a briefcase into the wax.
3. Meanwhile create a model of your ideal workplace from an open-topped box. It can be as specific as you wish or as general. Decorate and embellish as desired. Make sure to create a door large enough for the candle to enter.

4. Have the figure face the workplace.
5. Burn the candle in thirty-minute increments for six consecutive waxing moon days, moving the candle ever closer to the *"job."*
6. On the seventh day, bring the candle within your *"workplace"* and let the candle burn down completely.

Gravel Root Employment Spell

Gravel root has an affinity for those who must earn their living. Carry it within a conjure bag to find and preserve employment.

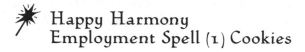

Happy Harmony Employment Spell (1) Cookies

To create a harmonious relationship with bosses and co-workers, rather than to achieve domination, bake cookies for everyone. Murmur your intentions over the batter, focusing on your desires during each step of the baking process.

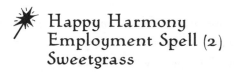

Happy Harmony Employment Spell (2) Sweetgrass

Burn sweetgrass to encourage co-workers to operate harmoniously, without jealousy and backbiting.

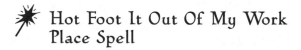

Hot Foot It Out Of My Work Place Spell

If there is still conflict within your office, despite your best efforts to foster harmonious working relationships, encourage unpleasant co-workers to seek other employment, or at least leave you alone, with Hot Foot Powder.

1. Grind equal quantities of black pepper, cayenne pepper, salt, and sulfur together.
2. Sprinkle it on or around the target's chair and desk.

The following spells are used to enhance probabilities of success during employment interviews.

Job Interview Success Spell

1. Charge sea salt with your desire: hold the salt in your hand and murmur your desires into it.
2. Place a little salt in your pocket prior to the interview.
3. If possible, sprinkle a tiny bit of salt on your interviewer's clothes without being observed. (Have a good explanation handy, just in case you are caught!)

If you're unable to sprinkle the person, try and sprinkle a little salt over the threshold to the office or even in the office, preferably near the interviewer's desk or chair.

It is not worth taking undue risks: in theory, merely carrying the salt in your pocket enhances your probability of being hired or promoted, although sprinkling as directed will maximize the effects.

Job Interview Self-Confidence Bath

The following magical bath enhances self-confidence and personal magnetism, and increases chances of success. Take the bath either just prior to the interview or the night before. Remember to allow yourself to air-dry and leave the botanicals in the infusion, for utmost power, if at all possible.

1. Place allspice berries, cinnamon sticks, cloves, whole nutmegs and pieces of sandalwood in a bowl.
2. Cover with boiling water and let the botanicals steep for a while—at least an hour.
3. Meanwhile, draw a bath for yourself.
4. Stand in the tub and toss the now lukewarm infusion over your body.
5. Soak and steep yourself in the bath.

Job's Tears Job Success Spell

Job's tears are the seeds of an Asian grass, much used in spells for improved fortune. They recall the biblical Job who, though sorely tried and afflicted, never lost his faith. Job's tears are almost inevitably used in groups of seven.

1. Place seven Job's tears under your mattress.
2. Place another seven Job's tears within your pillowcase.
3. Replace these every seven days to bring good fortune when searching for employment or when seeking a raise or promotion.

For a really big raise or major promotion, double or even square the quantity of Job's tears you use.

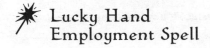 ## Lucky Hand Employment Spell

Lucky Hand root gained its name because it resembles a tiny human hand with too many fingers. Once an extremely popular Hoodoo charm, those extra fingers allegedly enabled you magically to grasp your desires. The more fingers, the more powerful the root is believed to be. As a child, I recall comic books filled with ads for curios like Lucky Hand root, High John and Low John.

The root of a highly endangered orchid species, Lucky Hand root isn't advertised or used frequently anymore. Virtually the only way to have a Lucky Hand root at all today, let alone guarantee that it's been harvested ethically, is to grow one oneself. If you do have a Lucky Hand, it's a treasure. Reputed to help you obtain any desire, it has a powerful reputation as an employment charm, both to find new work and to keep a firm hand on the job you already possess.

Anoint Lucky Hand root with a drop of dressing oil and carry it in a mojo hand.

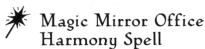 ## Magic Mirror Office Harmony Spell

A magic mirror may be used to counteract jealousy, backstabbing and general negative energy: the proverbial evil vibes. This spell requires a bright, sunny day. Although it is a Chinese-derived spell, it may be understood in the context of the Egyptian spirit Sekhmet, who both heals and destroys with laser beam solar rays.

1. Bring a small round mirror to the scene of the crime or the place of misery. Ideally this is a mirror that can fit into the palm of your hand, for utmost discretion.
2. Slowly, without drawing undue attention to yourself, circulate throughout the room, with the mirror in your hand, reflecting everything in the room for at least several seconds. Include individuals, too, if you feel this is necessary. This spell removes malevolent

energy and intent: it causes no harm. You are essentially vacuuming negative energy out of the room and people.

3. The mirror will store these reflections. When you've completed collecting reflections, face the mirror downwards or wrap it in dark fabric.
4. When the opportunity presents itself, take the mirror outside.
5. Hold the mirror up to the sun for no longer than nine seconds. Negativity is burned away and replaced by positive solar energy.

Note: Before performing any solar mirror spells, read the safety tips on page 72.

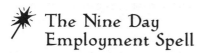

The Nine Day Employment Spell

Allegedly this spell produces results within nine days; however, it must be accompanied by intensive efforts to locate work.

1. Tie a High John the Conqueror root and a cinnamon stick together, with green, red or gold thread, knotting your desire and intention into the charm.
2. Dress the botanicals with **Three Kings Oil** and place inside a red flannel drawstring bag.
3. Each morning, before starting that day's job hunt, anoint the charm with additional **Three Kings Oil.**

Should your situation remain unchanged and unimproved after nine days, this indicates that it's time to reconsider your plans and assess alternatives.

Ochossi's Employment Spell

Ochossi, the divine hunter, may be petitioned for assistance with locating and bagging employment. Traditionally an altar is created for him within a forest. An offering laid before a tree in a park is the best alternative.

If neither is possible, recreate Ochossi's home in your own. Arrange woodland images around an altar. Bring Ochossi offerings:

1. Fill a small terracotta bowl with honey.
2. Place seven silver-colored coins around it (they do not have to be real silver).
3. Ochossi prefers rum or cachaca. Offer him an entire bottle, although it can be a small airline-sized one. Open it for him. (Some take a mouthful of liquor. Without swallowing any, blow it onto the altar.)
4. Add some honey-roasted peanuts.
5. Speak with the orisha; tell him what you need.

Orange Candle Job Spell

1. Write a description of your dream job and/or your employment expectations on the back of a copy of your CV/resumé.
2. Brush the CV with honey and sprinkle it with magnetic sand.
3. Fold the CV nine times.
4. Anoint an orange candle with **Van Van Oil** while you visualize your employment dreams come true.
5. Roll the candle in gold sparkles.
6. Place it atop the folded CV and burn, coinciding with the New Moon.

Pecan Job Retention Spell

You still have your job but you're afraid that there's a genuine possibility that it will be lost?

1. Get a small bag of edible nuts, still in their shells. Pecans are traditional but other nuts may be substituted.
2. Shell the nuts, by hand if possible, and eat them slowly, savoring every bite. If you can eat them in the workplace it's most powerful, however it's crucial that you be able to eat them peacefully, happily and securely. If you must eat them elsewhere in order to accomplish this, then do so.
3. While you're eating maintain a visualization of yourself, secure and happy at work. See yourself holding and cashing your paycheck.
4. When you've finished eating, reserve some of the shells.
5. Hide them at work in a discreet spot where they won't be observed or removed.

 ## Pow-Wow Career Enhancement Spell

Pow-Wow Power Potion *may be used for career enhancement as well as for psychic enhancement. Its vivid golden color and sweet fragrance provide encouragement and self-confidence, as well.*

1. Massage the oil onto your full body or just your hands prior to employment interviews or any stressful meetings.
2. Not only is your personal power boosted but the oil can also sharpen that sixth sense so that you'll know the right thing to say at the right moment.

 ## Saint Anthony's Job Return Spell

You had a job but you've lost it. Saint Anthony the miracle-worker may be petitioned to help get it back. Commercially manufactured seven-day candles dedicated to Saint Anthony are easily available. A plain green candle may also be substituted.

1. On a piece of brown paper, write your name, your workplace (name and address), your position (or former one) and the name of your boss, supervisor or the decision maker who is in the position to re-hire you.
2. Place this under the candle.
3. Petition Saint Anthony for assistance and light the candle.

 ## Saint Joseph's Employment Spell

Saint Joseph is the patron of the unemployed, fathers and step-fathers. He is traditionally appealed to for assistance with finding employment. Should you require work in order to feed a family, he may be helpful and sympathetic.

Although there are various depictions of Saint Joseph, for employment spells he must be shown holding the baby Jesus.

1. Post the appropriate chromolithograph.
2. Keep a vigil candle burning.
3. Request his assistance and search for work.

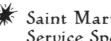 ## Saint Martha's Domestic Service Spell

Saint Martha the Dominator is the matron saint of servants, household staff and domestic workers. In her original Vatican-sanctioned role as Saint Martha of

Bethany, she features in the New Testament as the epitome of the capable housekeeper. According to legend, Martha accompanied Mary Magdalene to southern France, where Martha proceeded to have her own adventures. Most famously she tamed a dragon, leading it on a leash woven from her own hair. She's been taming fierce beasts ever since. Request Martha's assistance in taming your boss, so that you may lead him or her around in the direction that you choose.

Many historians believe that the story of Saint Martha and the dragon conflates Martha of Bethany with another Martha, a Syrian priestess-magician who accompanied the Roman general Marius on his military campaign in Provence. If this is true, it adds credence to Martha's power over bosses. Almost two thousand years later, Saint Martha the Dominator continues to receive countless prayers and petitions daily, but how many recall Marius, her old employer?

1. Dress a green candle with **Saint Martha the Dominator Oil.**
2. Place it alongside an image of Martha, a dragon and/or your employer.
3. Burn the candle as you tell Martha what you need.

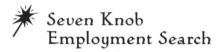

Seven Knob Employment Search

Green seven-knob candles are beneficial for employment magic.

1. Charge the candle with your desire.
2. Scratch a wish or goal on each knob. The name of a prospective employer may also be scratched into the wax.
3. Burn one knob daily for seven days.

Steady Work Spells

Steady Work is a Hoodoo condition formula whose name announces its promise. Steady Work Formula is used to find and maintain steady employment. It consists of:

Benzoin resinoid
Gravel root
Sea salt

Steady Work Spell (1)

1. Grind the ingredients together and burn them.
2. Reserve the ashes, adding them to a mojo hand.

Steady Work Spell (2)

1. Blend the ingredients, but don't burn them.
2. Carry them in a mojo hand while searching for employment.

Steady Work Spell (3)

Sprinkle Steady Work Formula inside your shoes before setting out on a long day's search for work.

Steady Work Spell (4) Steady Work Oil

1. Grind the ingredients used in Steady Work Formula together and place them in a small glass bottle or jar.
2. Cover with sunflower and jojoba oil. *Voila!* Steady Work Oil.

Rub Steady Work Oil on your palms and soles when going to work or looking for employment. Or use it to dress candles and mojo hands dedicated to the job search.

Ten of Diamonds Professional Success and Happiness Spell

Playing and tarot cards may be used to influence your future as well as foretell it. The key, in both cases, is to choose the right cards.

1. Remove the ten of diamonds from a new deck of playing cards and lay it on a dish.
2. Sprinkle it with **Crown of Success Oil** and **Magnet Oil.**
3. Add a handful of coins and/or paper money and/or spirit money.
4. Carve a green candle with your identifying information.
5. Dress the candle with **Crown of Success Oil** and **Magnet Oil.**
6. Place the candle atop the card and burn.
7. Once the candle has completely burned, gather up the ashes, coins, whatever is left of the playing card (it may or may not burn), and any fortuitous-looking wax remnants. Place them in a red mojo hand. Carry with you or keep it in a safe place.

You Need Me Professional Success Spell

Personal success and advancement may be dependent upon the whims of a specific person with power over your career. The following spell encourages that person to think fondly of you. Because the spell is dependent upon your ability to spend at least a little time alone in this person's office, it is an ideal spell for a personal assistant or secretary.

1. Discreetly pick up a much needed object from the person' desk or office.
2. Hold it in your hands and focus your thoughts and desires.
3. Murmur over the object (chant silently, if necessary) something to the effect of: "[Supervisor's name], *you need me like you need this* [name the object]."
4. Replace the object exactly as you found it.
5. Reinforce by repeating as needed.

✪ Cleansing Spells

Isn't the house clean enough? I take a daily shower, isn't that sufficient?

Magical cleansing spells have little to do with actual cleanliness, as defined by the absence of dirt, dust or disorder, although there are spells that accomplish both sorts of cleaning simultaneously. Even the most slovenly, disorganized witch will maintain a regular schedule of psychic cleansing.

At their most basic, cleansing spells remove psychic and spiritual debris. A certain level of this debris accumulates constantly. As you become more psychically aware, you may become more conscious of this and feel a greater need to remove it on a regular basis.

Cleansings remove low-level spiritual entities that are attracted to ritual, if only to feed parasitically off the generated energy. Knowingly or unknowingly, these entities obstruct and weaken your psychic work, lessening your chances of success. In addition, cleansings welcome and make room for more benevolent, helpful spirits.

How do you know when you need to cleanse?

★ *Although it may not be necessary for every quick-fix spell, formal rituals begin with cleansings*

★ *Spells and petitions directed toward spirits are the equivalent of inviting an honored guest to enter your home. Spiritual cleansing beforehand is a measure of respect*

★ *Many magic workers perform cleansings on a regular schedule to suit their specific needs, whether daily, weekly or monthly*

★ *If a room doesn't feel right all of a sudden, if your dog suddenly refuses to enter a room, this may indicate the need for cleansing rites*

★ *Cleanse any areas that feel oppressive, slightly off or creepy. Let your inner voice guide you. Any area that has been the scene of violence or a violent emotional altercation needs cleansing*

★ *Areas that are frequently and/or consistently the scene of violence or altercations need extra-strong cleansing, followed by protective rituals*

★ *Cleansings remove any sense of taint, replacing it with purification and sacredness*

Areas, people, ritual tools or other objects may be cleansed. Various methods and tools of varying intensity exist for cleansing. This is very personal magic: the results are apparent immediately. You must *feel* cleansed. Choose the methods that

If at any level you perceive that magic is inherently evil or bad, yet you continue to cast spells, your need for cleansings is even greater than most. At the simplest level, cleansings remove the proverbial bad vibes. On a more serious note, cleansings provide healing and soothing wherever there has been violence, excessive anger, humiliation and defilement.

resonate most powerfully for you. Your spells will be most effective and potent if accompanied by visualization, affirmation and/or the chanting of sacred texts.

Area or Space Cleansing

Any area may be cleansed, from a tabletop altar area or the inside of a magic circle to an entire home or office building. When cleansing a large area, certain spots are believed to require extra care and attention. Vulnerable areas include doors, windows and other thresholds. Corners, especially dark ones, and the area behind a door, especially one that's consistently propped open, are considered favorite resting spots for malevolent spirits, as are dark closets, bathrooms and any area that feels *creepy*. Do you recall how children often resist sticking fingers and toes out of the covers for fear that something under the bed will nip them? Dark spaces under the bed can accumulate more than dust bunnies. These are all areas requiring extra attention.

Anyone actively involved in the space cleansing process or exposed to the cleansing materials automatically receives personal cleansing as well,

although certain personal cleansing methods cast a more direct and intensive spell.

Animal Allies Cleansing Spells

Scavengers, especially vultures, are the ultimate animal allies of cleansing. Other magical scavengers include crows, jackals and coyotes. Incorporate them into your spells or attempt to establish a magical alliance if spiritual cleansing is a major issue for you.

Spirits affiliated with vultures include Mut and Oshun. Non-scavenger animals affiliated with spiritual cleansing include deer and doves.

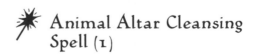

Animal Altar Cleansing Spell (1)

1. Set up an altar space with images of the cleansing animals: rubber toy reproductions are excellent, as are Zuni stone fetishes. Choose one or many, depending upon your taste and cleansing needs.
2. Ring the animals with amethyst, malachite and quartz crystals. This will generate a low-level but constant cleansing action.

3. Whenever you desire a more potent cleansing, hold a white candle in your hands and charge it with your desire. Place it in the center of your altar and light it.
4. Gaze into the flame and envision it as a magnet, sucking all negativity into the fire where it is consumed and purified.

 ## Animal Altar Cleansing Spell (2)

The preceding spell may be adapted so as to maintain a constant, consistent cleansing effect:

1. Place small images of the cleansing animals in all corners of a room.
2. The power may be enhanced by also maintaining one larger image on a central altar.
3. Once a week, "feed" the animals: walking around the room sunwise, greet each one with incense smoke or another offering.

Vulture Spell

Modern vultures possess a bad reputation as filthy scavengers, yet once upon a time, very long ago, they were perceived as holy creatures. Vulture images exist in Paleolithic sacred imagery. Ancient Egyptians considered that vultures, with their wingspan wide enough to embrace an adult, represented the positive ideals of motherhood. Oshun, most beautiful of the orishas, counts the vulture alongside peacocks and parrots as her sacred birds. This profound visualization cleansing spell draws upon this positive imagery. Note: it's not for the faint-hearted.

1. Use either a realistic image of a vulture or an image of the Egyptian vulture deity, Nekhbet. What is crucial is that the image has outstretched wings and a direct gaze.

2. Look the image in the eyes. Request that she come and cleanse you of all spiritual debris.
3. Visualize the vulture enfolding you with her wings.
4. When she releases you and departs, you're cleansed.

Asperging Spells

Asperging means sprinkling with liquid in order to effect spiritual and magical cleansing. These are ancient rites: just like burning loose incense these are techniques known to our earliest ancestors. Asperging spells direct the elemental cleansing power of water and other liquids toward a specific area. Depending upon what is used to direct the water, the elemental cleansing power of Earth may also be incorporated, through the use of botanicals.

★ *Use ritual tools or botanicals to asperge*
★ *Use your fingers to flick the water where it's needed*
★ *Weave an asperging wand of cleansing plants: vervain, lavender, hyssop, and rosemary are favorites. This technique can also incorporate knot magic*

Asperging is the most popular method of liquid-based space cleansing. It is more discreet than smudging or any sort of smoke-based method. Burning botanicals inevitably leaves a lingering fragrance. By definition, it is the aroma of the burning botanicals that provides the cleansing: the inclination of the cleanser is inevitably to strengthen the aroma. This provides the confidence in the effectiveness of the cleansing and its long-term effects. However, aromas tend to evoke highly personal reactions: fragrances favored in cleansings may or may not meet with your neighbors' or housemates' approval.

The issue of fire safety always looms too. Because something is done for positive spiritual purposes does not guarantee that accidents and tragedies will not occur. With water-based cleansings, you are able to maintain tighter control over safety and fragrance. However, different methods resonate for different people: for an intensive cleansing ritual, you may wish to combine several methods.

The most basic cleansing liquid is sea salt dissolved into spring or rainwater. Any of the following formulas also will provide space cleansing. Check the *Formulary* (page 1037) for recipes:

- ★ *Holy Water*
- ★ *Florida Water*
- ★ *Indigo Water*
- ★ *Marie Laveau Water*
- ★ *Notre Dame Water*
- ★ *Pollution Water*
- ★ *Rose of Jericho Water*
- ★ *Tar Water*
- ★ *War Water*

Disperse them through an area. You can intensify the power by combining formulas. **Florida Water**, in particular, empowers any other formula to which it's added. For instance, combine **Florida Water** and **Indigo Water**. Sprinkle through the home or area daily as maintenance cleansing.

 Black Cohosh Cleansing

Make an infusion by pouring boiling water over black snake root/black cohosh; asperge with a rosemary wand to erase evil influences.

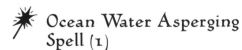 Ocean Water Asperging Spell (1)

Unless you live by the sea, this spell may involve more work and preparation than sprinkling with salted fresh water, however the potential power is also greater.

1. Carry ocean water to the area to be cleansed in a glass or metal flask. (For maximum effect, request permission and offer thanks to the Spirits of the Sea.)
2. Asperge as needed, ideally with a rosemary or sea lavender wand.

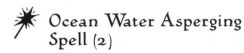 Ocean Water Asperging Spell (2)

*Blend ocean water with **Indigo Water**. Sprinkle as needed using fresh rue as the asperging tool.*

 Peony Root Cleansing

Make a strong infusion by pouring boiling water over peony roots. Asperge as desired.

 Peppermint Asperging Spell

Create an infusion by pouring boiling water over peppermint. Strain and use a peppermint branch to asperge as needed.

 Pine Asperging Spell

Soak pine needles in warm water and asperge as needed.

Ti plant is a sacred and integral component of Hawaiian magical and spiritual traditions. Using a leaf as an asperging tool adds elements of protection to purification rituals. (Ti plant is not the same as either the Australian or New Zealand tea tree but a completely distinct botanical species, despite the similar names.)

Ti Plant Asperging Spell (1)

1. Dissolve powdered turmeric in spring water.
2. Use a ti leaf to disperse the cleansing water as needed. (Turmeric is a potent bright yellow permanent dye; be careful where you sprinkle the water.)

 ## Ti Plant Asperging Spell (2)

Alaea is unprocessed, unrefined sea salt, enriched with small amounts of red Hawaiian clay. It's edible and may be substituted for salt in any formula.

1. Dissolve alaea in water.
2. Asperge with a ti leaf.

 ## Ti Plant Asperging Spell (3)

1. Blend spring water with sandalwood hydrosol.
2. Dissolve both turmeric and alaea in the liquid.
3. Asperge as needed using a ti leaf.

 ## Yarrow Juniper Cleanser

Juniper berry hydrosol
Yarrow hydrosol
Dried juniper berries
Yarrow flower remedy

1. Blend equal parts of the two hydrosols.
2. Add a small handful of slightly bruised juniper berries and a few drops of the flower remedy.

This formula is especially recommended for altar cleansing. However, in addition to space cleansing it may also be used for aura cleansing and to cleanse crystals.

Broom Cleansings

You thought witches' brooms were only for flying? Or perhaps they're for ambience? Think again: a broom is as effective a spiritual cleanser as it is a household cleaning tool. Some maintain special ritual brooms, for magical use only. Some spells call for *really* special ritual brooms, intended to be used only once then destroyed, while other spells utilize any available broom, including the one you use for regular daily sweeping.

 ## Broom Cleansing Spell (1)

1. Use any broom to sweep the dust from the west to the east.
2. Burn this dust and toss the ashes outdoors.
3. Complete the ritual by mopping the floors with a magical floorwash (formulas follow on page 201), followed by a protective incense fumigation.

 ## Broom Cleansing Spell (2)

This spell incorporates a single-use magical purification broom.

1. Use one or any combination of the following botanicals: broom, cedar, fennel, hyssop, rosemary, sage, vervain.
2. Arrange the botanicals and tie them to the bottom of a branch with raffia, visualizing, charging and knotting. (Any branch may be used, however an ash branch is considered particularly powerful.)
3. Sprinkle with salted water or any preferred purification formula.
4. Sweep the area.
5. Disassemble the broom outside, away from the cleansed space.
6. Bury the components in the ground or toss them into living waters, flowing away from you.

Broom Cleansing Spell (3)

Any broom may be used in this spell, homemade or commercial, however it must be discarded at the conclusion of the spell.

1. Add an infusion of lemongrass and some white or rice vinegar to a bucket filled with water. (If you have time to make lemongrass vinegar, this is even more effective than the infusion.)
2. Dip a broom into the bucket of floorwash and sweep the area from the center, working your way outwards. This does not need to be a commercial broom. A branch with attached stiff herbs is fine, however a mop may not be substituted.
3. When complete, dump the wash water outside and discard the broom at a crossroads.

 ## Broom Cleansing Spell (4)

Hyssop and vervain are particularly ancient space cleansers. Hyssop is cited in biblical accounts of Temple cleansings, although there is some doubt as to whether the botanical species now identified as hyssop is actually the same as the one in the Bible. Regardless, what we know today as hyssop has been used as a potent spiritual cleanser for centuries.

Vervain was used to cleanse the temples and altars of ancient Greece and Rome. Effective separately, the two botanicals share an affinity and combine well together.

1. Make a strong infusion from the botanicals.
2. Add this to a bucket of salted floorwash water together with white vinegar.
3. Make a single use broom, particularly from vervain and/or hyssop. Use it to asperge and scrub with the infusion.
4. When you've completed the cleansing spell, dispose of the used water outside your home. Take the broom apart and scatter the parts outside.

 ## Broom Cleansing Spell (5)

When moving into a new home, do not bring your old broom with you. Do not use any brooms the old inhabitants may have left behind. Start with a brand new broom.

1. Obtain a new broom to use exclusively in your new home.
2. The first time it's used, soak it in salted **Florida Water** and sweep away.

Candle Cleansers

Candles deliver the magical space-purifying effects of fire, without the intensity of smoke or the fragrance associated with fumigation cleansings.

 ## Blessing Oil

Create Blessing Oil by adding frankincense and benzoin to a blend of olive and jojoba oils. Use either the ground resin or essential oils. Dress white and blue candles with the oil and burn to purify the atmosphere.

 ## Coconut Candle Cleanser

Coconuts possess an aroma that many find pleasing, sensuous and evocative. Releasing the scent of coconut into the air provides long-term spiritual purification in a relaxed, fragrant manner. Unfortunately what is commercially available is almost invariably synthetic; thus the fragrance may be pleasing but the power is nonexistent. Make your own coconut candles.

The simplest method is to use pour-and-melt wax from the craft store. White or brown are the preferred colors. If you are a skilled candle maker, however, choose any method or wax you prefer.

1. Prepare the candle shell prior to melting the wax. You may use any type of container you choose; however, a hollowed out half of a coconut shell is ideal.
2. Melt the wax until liquid.
3. Stir in pure coconut extract. The quantity depends upon the desired intensity of fragrance.
4. Make sure that the wick is attached securely to the container, either by holding it in place until the wax hardens or by attaching it to a pencil or stick laid across the top of the container.
5. Pour the scented wax into the container.
6. Allow the wax to harden.

Supplement the fragrance with a few drops of ginger, frankincense or lemon essential oils.

Double Reversible Cleansing Candle Spells

1. Burn double reversible candles every week to maintain standard house cleansing.
2. Hold the candle in your hands to charge with your purpose prior to burning.

Cleansing Powders

Powders are sprinkled through an area to radiate a cleansing effect as well as to absorb malignancies in the air. Sprinkle lightly: typically the powders will disperse into the atmosphere quickly. If any powder is still visible after seven days, vacuum it up and replace. If this occurs consistently, you are either applying too much or stronger cleansing methods are needed.

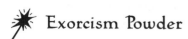

Exorcism Powder

Despite its name, rather than performing actual exorcisms, this powder helps eliminate negative emotions, vibrations and low-level spirit emanations.

1. Blend the following ingredients together and grind into a fine powder:
   Dried basil
   Frankincense
   Rosemary
   Rue
   Yarrow
2. Blend this powder into arrowroot powder.
3. Sprinkle as needed.

Jyoti Powder

*Despite the Hindu name, **Jyoti Powder** is a popular Hoodoo formula, with many uses. Sprinkle as needed: it provides protection in addition to cleansing.*

Cleansing Spirits

Sometimes you need someone else to clean for you. Calling in the spirits to perform a cleansing is like hiring a deluxe cleaning service. They perform a better, more thorough job than the average person could; they are capable of removing spiritual dirt and debris that you weren't aware even existed.

Like a cleaning service, these spirits expect to be paid. Some demand specific gifts or offerings. Others, like the angels, expect a certain atmosphere of respect and reverence: angels feed off the fragrance of precious resins. Fill the room with their aroma—it will enhance the cleansing.

As anyone who's ever hired a cleaning service knows, you must clean prior to the spirits' arrival. Do some basic cleansings first to prepare the area for their presence: smudge sticks or asperging cleansing waters are appropriate.

✴ Four Archangels
Cleansing Service

Summon the archangels; they may arrive alone or leading hosts of lesser angels. The four archangels may be invoked to initiate all rituals and also for the cleansing and protection of ritual space. Angels, most especially the archangels, are not the cute little cherubs one sees depicted on Valentine's Day cards. These are beings of power and majesty. Their presence may remain invisible or they may manifest in various forms, however a typical vision of angels involves a being so bright they remain visible even with your eyes closed. Their presence as cleansing agents burns like purifying fire, yet they leave holiness in their wake, rather than devastation.

1. Cast a circle, with a sword, crystal-tipped wand, flaming torch or other tool.
2. Pause at each cardinal point and invoke the appropriate archangel:
   Raphael to the East
   Michael to the South
   Gabriel to the West
   Uriel to the North

Make the invocation as simple or as elaborate as you choose. Different schools posit which angel has dominion over which direction. If you are familiar with other directions, choose what resonates for you.

Whether the following ritual began in Africa, Haiti, or in New Orleans itself is unknown, however it emerged in New Orleans as an adaptation of Haitian ritual. Extremely popular, it passed into general American magical usage and is now familiar all over Earth. It is difficult to find a botanical, occult or spiritual supply store that will *not* teach you this spell. However, while many are aware of the mechanics of the ritual, few understand the spiritual context of this spell.

The ritual calls upon extremely powerful and prominent lwa to provide cleansing and protection. Although their names are invoked, their identities are forgotten: for many people, this spell is a modern equivalent of the litanies of ancient, forgotten words of power invoked by medieval magicians. However, these are no forgotten spirits: these lwa remain active and vital, invoked daily in Vodoun ritual. If you call them, they may come. If you take the time to understand *who* you're calling, this spell becomes even more powerful.

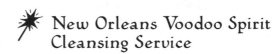

✴ New Orleans Voodoo Spirit
Cleansing Service

This spell may also be used purely as a spirit-banishing spell, however it does a potent job of cleaning up all negative vibrations and debris. It is best performed at midnight during a waxing moon. Be sure proper ventilation is available: the smell of sulfur is pungent and potentially irritating.

1. Place a square of red paper onto a small metal or stone plate. You will need one plate plus its contents for each corner of any room you wish cleansed. Most rooms require four sets.
2. Place a pinch of sulfur on top of each paper.
3. Place each plate in a corner, so that there is one in each.
4. Light the sulfur.
5. Simultaneously, address the four lwa invoked in this ritual, turning to face each new corner as each name is uttered.
   Granbois!
   Baron Carrefour!
   Baron Cimitiere!
   Damballah!
   I invoke you! With the power of your names, I command and compel all evil spirits, spells and vibrations, any negative entities, to leave me and my home and never return!
6. Withdraw from the room, maintaining a vigilant eye on fire safety.

Oya's Cleansing Spell

*Oya, Yoruba orisha of wild storm winds, is the person-
ified tropical hurricane. She has the power to blow away
all impurities, leaving a fresh, cleansed atmosphere in
her wake—ideal for those who wish to begin a situation
completely anew. Oya also is the only orisha who maintains contact and control over the dead; use this ritual
following any sort of unsettling ghost contamination.
This is a complex full night's ritual, with an extensive
list of ingredients. It simultaneously provides space and
personal cleansing.*

The spell requires:

Nine ribbons, each in a different color, long enough
to go around your waist while you're sitting, with
an additional nine inches spare (choose any colors
but be sure to include maroon, purple and
brown)
Nine additional ribbons, each in a different color
Nine small, purple eggplants
One bottle of red wine
A bottle of dark rum
A cigar
Nine coins of any denomination
Wine-colored flowers
White candles
Sea salt

1. Soak the eggplants in the red wine.
2. Divide the nine main ribbons into three groups and
   make a braid from each. You will have three braids.
3. Braid these three together to form one large fat
   braided belt.
4. Tie the additional nine ribbons around the belt so
   that they will fall around your hips when you wear
   the belt. Set the belt aside.
5. Drain and dry the eggplants.
6. Pierce the top of each eggplant.
7. Run one ribbon through each and tie each eggplant
   securely to the braided belt, consciously knotting
   your desires.

8. Take a mouthful of rum and spray it onto the belt.
9. Light the cigar and blow smoke over the belt, all the
   while petitioning Oya to grant your desire.
10. Although this part of the spell is most powerful
    performed in the nude, do whatever is
    comfortable for you: tie the belt around your
    waist. Whirl and twirl through your home,
    visualizing all negativity entering into the
    eggplants.
11. When you feel that the cleansing is complete, take
    off the belt and place it inside a plain brown paper
    bag, together with nine coins.
12. Take this package to Oya's home, the cemetery, and
    leave it at the gates. This is best done at night. If you
    can, without attracting undue attention to yourself,
    rattle and shake the gates. Make your presence
    known. Tell Oya why you've come and what you
    need.
13. Return home via a different route.
14. Light the white candles in the bathroom. Run a tub
    with warm water and add the sea salt to the water.
    Bathe and relax.
15. Put on clean clothes and go to bed in clean, fresh
    sheets.

Cleansing Through Smoke

Burning botanicals releases their powers into the
air, releasing various magical effects. What is actually being released depends upon what is being
burned. This is true in areas outside magic too: up
until World War I, French hospitals burned
juniper and rosemary in order to release the
volatile oils to provide antiseptic, antibacterial
effects.

Smoke cleansings are considered among the
most potent of cleansing spells. Their effect
lingers as long as you can smell any vestiges of the
botanical aroma. Strong, fragrant, visible smoke
that shoots straight up is considered especially
powerful and auspicious.

In order to cleanse an area effectively, the aroma of the burning plant material has to permeate the air. In theory, if the quantities of the botanical cleanser are great enough, there's no need to waft the smoke around. Hence the huge mounds of frankincense and myrrh burned in ancient temples, as well as the traditional Midsummer and Beltane bonfires. If you want to burn such quantities, however, be aware that not only will every corner of your own area be permeated with fragrance, but that aromas spread and are difficult to contain. Your neighbors will be calling to either complain or to thank you, as the case may be.

Few, however, have access to such quantities of botanicals. Therefore, most cleansing smoke needs to be directed towards what needs to be cleansed. Burning releases the magical properties into the atmosphere: actual cleansing comes from direct exposure to the smoke.

✳ Basic Botanic Fumigation Spell

Burning specific botanicals provides magical and spiritual antiseptic effects. These botanicals include: aloes wood, benzoin resin, bloodroot, cajeput, cinnamon, cloves, dragon's blood resin, eucalyptus, frankincense, garlic, harmel (Syrian rue), juniper, mastic, mugwort, myrrh, onions, rosemary, sage (especially white sage), Saint John's Wort, sandalwood, thyme, wormwood, and yarrow. Burn them alone or in any combination.

Many of these plants also radiate a protective aura: maintaining them as a presence, particularly as living plants but also as dried amulets, can only be beneficial. Whatever else these plants do (and many, such as frankincense, dragon's blood and wormwood are extremely versatile magically), they always radiate a cleansing, purifying aura. Although certain methods of use intensify their cleansing effects, those effects are constant: the more these botanicals are used, the more consistent their cleansing power.

The simplest of all smoke-cleansing methods is the **smudge stick**. A smudge stick is a small wand made from dried botanicals. Although today the most famous smudge sticks derive from Native American tradition, this is basically a very simple, universal tool. The old English lavender wand is, in effect, a smudge stick, albeit one that is not frequently burned.

Smudging is the process of using directed smoke to cleanse an area, person or object. Smudge sticks are popular occult tools and easily purchased, but they can be just as easily created:

1. Dry bunches of herbs.
2. When they have completely dried, bind them together with thin cotton thread.
3. When needed, the stick is lit and the smoke directed towards and over whatever needs cleansing.
4. A feather fan is often used to direct the smoke, although you may also use your bare hands.

Be aware of fire safety: smudge sticks tend to smolder long after the flames appear to have died out.

Although a smudge stick may theoretically be created from any dried botanicals, for cleansing purposes, the following are most potent and practical:

★ *White sage or common garden sage*
★ *Juniper*
★ *Desert sage (a different species from the sage above: an* Artemisia, *not a* Salvia)
★ *Rosemary*

The smudge stick has certain advantages: it's neat, compact, easily controlled, discreet and mobile. Loose incense, however, is also extremely effective and offers you the luxury of a wider selection of botanical material.

Many of the most potent cleansing materials are gum resins and wood chips that do not lend themselves to binding into a wand. These are usually burned on charcoal, which is placed on a dish, iron pan or incense censer so that the cleansing smoke may be directed as needed.

Specific cleansing formulas have evolved:

 ## Betony Cleansing Incense

Burning the dried herb betony magically disperses negative energy and lurking entities. This is especially effective if you suspect and fear that the negativity emanates from you.

 ## Birch Cleansing Incense

Burn birch bark and twigs to remove negative energy.

 ## Bloodroot Cleansing Spell

Dragon's blood resin, originally from Indonesia, has fascinated occultists for millennia because of its red color, unusual for a tree resin, and because, when burned, it truly does resemble blood. Bloodroot is, in some ways, the North American equivalent.

Known as bloodroot because of its blood red sap, it is a favored ingredient in North American magic. Used to erect an intensive protective aura, it also has many uses in folk medicine. However, it is potentially very toxic. **Do not take internally without expert professional supervision.**

1. Powder bloodroot with a mortar and pestle.
2. Burn some of the powder for seven consecutive nights at midnight.
3. Conclude the ritual by sprinkling the ashes in an unbroken circle around your home to prevent the approach of evil spirits and malevolent magic.

 ## Cast Out Evil Incense

This powerful formula provides cleansing for areas profaned by evil and/or violence:

1. Blend and grind the following ingredients together into a fine powder:
   Camphor
   Cinnamon
   Frankincense
   Myrrh
   Sandalwood
2. Sprinkle onto a lit charcoal and burn.

 ## Cast Out Evil Extra Strength Spell

For areas that have been truly profaned and need extra-potent cleansing:

1. Do an initial moderate cleansing of the area.
2. Prepare the room by closing all windows and sources of ventilation.
3. Prepare an incense burner with lit charcoals.
4. Place a substantial quantity of Cast Out Evil incense onto the burner.
5. Position the burner in the center of the room.
6. Let it remain there for a minimum of an hour, and overnight at longest. While the incense burns, the room should be closed to all outside ventilation. If it's possible for someone to stay in the room, to attend the incense, they will be rewarded with a powerful personal cleansing. If this is not possible and the incense will be temporarily unsupervised, be extremely vigilant as to fire safety.
7. When sufficient time has passed, open windows, provide ventilation, let the fresh air in.

Cedarwood Cleansing Incense

The cedars of Lebanon were famed in ancient times for their magic powers. Today the cedars of Lebanon are virtually gone. The closest species is the Atlas cedar, native to North Africa. Burn cedarwood chips and needles to purify the atmosphere.

 ## Coconut Cleanser

Coconuts have profound cleansing and absorbing powers. Mainly used in personal cleansings, this variation from the French Antilles is used to fumigate an area.

1. Fill hollowed coconut shells with frankincense, Mecca balsam and chopped vetiver roots.
2. Arrange these strategically around the home: they're typically burned around the outer perimeter but may also be used indoors.
3. Burn the botanicals within the shell.

 ## Coriander Enhanced Cleansing Incense

Blend coriander seeds, frankincense, and gum sandarac. Burn, and waft the smoke as needed.

 ## Desert Sage Spell

Despite its name, desert sage, a Native American botanical, does not belong to the salvia (sage) family but is actually an artemisia, like mugwort or wormwood. Desert sage shares characteristics of both botanical families: true to its artemisia roots, it is a potent psychic enhancer; like the sages, it has profound cleansing powers.

Desert sage lends itself to use as a smudge stick; it was also traditionally tossed into open fire to create cleansing, purifying, protective smoke that allegedly intensifies psychic perception.

 ## Dragon's Blood Cleansing Incense

Dragon's blood is believed to neutralize negative energy. This is a powerful resin, with many magical uses. It is a component of a vast variety of spells for protection, romance, and healing.

Burning dragon's blood alone provides a potent cleansing. However, add dragon's blood to other sacred botanicals for extra enhancement.

Although many enjoy the power of rare, exotic materials, some of the most potent spiritual formulas use common household items, even things that might normally be considered garbage. This cleansing, for instance, utilizes garlic peel.

Although *incensio* technically refers to any *incense*, the word used in many Latin American spiritual traditions to denote special cleansing incense is *sahumerio*. This standard Santeria-derived formula is traditionally performed as regular magical, house maintenance, either weekly or monthly, depending upon how long it takes one to accumulate sufficient garlic peel. Without a sufficient quantity of the peel, only a minimal amount of cleansing smoke will be raised. The goal is to flush out and expel any lingering negative entities.

To prepare for the ritual, whenever garlic is used, whether for cooking or spell casting, don't throw away the peel but retain it until enough has been accumulated.

 ## Garlic Cleansing Spell (1)

1. Place the reserved garlic peel in a mortar and pestle and add brown sugar.
2. Pound and grind them together.
3. Sprinkle the result onto lit charcoal or burn it on a cast iron pan.
4. Waft the fumes over the areas to be cleansed, allowing the aroma to permeate and settle.

Garlic Cleansing Spell (2)

A variation on the theme introduces sulfur, used to add a protective shield in addition to the cleansing:

1. Place the reserved garlic peel in a mortar with brown sugar and sulfur powder.
2. Pound and grind them together.
3. Sprinkle onto lit charcoal and burn.

Garlic Cleansing Spell (3)

This sahumerio *combines the simplicity of reserved garlic peel with rare exotic gum resins.*

1. Place the reserved garlic peel in a mortar together with frankincense, mastic and storax.
2. Pound and grind them together.
3. Sprinkle onto lit charcoal or burn in a cast-iron pan, wafting the smoke as needed.

Garlic Cleansing Spell (4)

This Brazilian variation burns garlic cloves as well as peel. As can be imagined, a much stronger aroma is created:

1. Crush the garlic to release the volatile oils: it may be mashed up with a mortar and pestle, however do not remove the peel.
2. Place it on an incense burner or on a cast-iron pan.
3. Blend brown sugar and good strong ground coffee. Do not use decaf.
4. Sprinkle the blended sugar and coffee over the garlic and set it alight.
5. Carry this, wafting the aromatic smoke where needed.

High Spirit Incense

Very popular among spiritualists, this formula allegedly removes spiritual debris, invites beneficial spirits and offers protection and blessings.

> 3 parts frankincense
> 2 parts benzoin
> 1 part myrrh

Grind the ingredients together with a mortar and pestle and then burn on charcoal.

Juniper-Rosemary Cleansing Spell

A cleansing to precede outdoor rituals relies on the old French hospital stand-by formula. Or does the old hospital formula rely on even older magical traditions?

This must be performed outside: it cleanses ritual space, releases healing energy into the surrounding area, and will provide personal cleansing for anyone exposed to the smoke.

1. Burning juniper branches are the foundation for this formula.
2. Pine branches may also be added as an optional ingredient for additional power.
3. Lay fresh rosemary and lavender stalks on the burning branches.
4. Fragrant resins such as frankincense, myrrh and/or mastic may be added to the resulting bonfire.

Liquidambar Cleansing Incense

Liquidambar (storax), like lavender, has the magical property of enhancing the power of other botanicals when it's combined with them. Blend frankincense, liquidambar, mastic, and sandalwood. Burn and waft the smoke as desired.

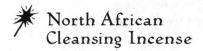 North African
Cleansing Incense

This cleansing formula derives from North Africa. Mastic, a component of ancient Egyptian embalming formulas, is an excellent pre-ritual cleanser especially because it's believed to enhance clairvoyance.

Mastic resin tears or powder
Dried myrtle leaves and berries
Dried rose petals

Mash the ingredients together with a mortar and pestle and burn on charcoal.

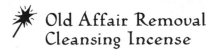 Old Affair Removal
Cleansing Incense

There aren't only spiritual reasons for cleansing spells; sometimes they're necessary to set the stage for new love by removing all vestiges of the past. Burn myrtle and dried rose petals.

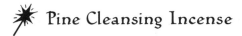 Pine Cleansing Incense

Grind dried pine needles to powder and sprinkle on lit charcoals to cleanse an area of negative energy and entities.

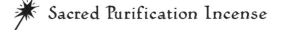 Sacred Purification Incense

This cleansing formula incorporates the botanicals most frequently used in sacred rites. It removes the negative and the tainted, leaving an aura of holiness behind.

Benzoin
Dragon's blood
Frankincense
Myrrh
Sandalwood
Sea salt

1. Blend and grind the ingredients into a fine powder.
2. Sprinkle onto a lit charcoal and burn.

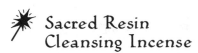 Sacred Resin
Cleansing Incense

Blend dragon's blood powder and frankincense and burn.

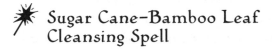 Sugar Cane–Bamboo Leaf
Cleansing Spell

This Brazilian formula utilizes dried pulverized bamboo leaves, which are common in Brazil but may be purchased from herbal supply stores elsewhere.

1. Place the bamboo leaves into a mortar together with some sugar cane and grind them together.
2. Burn the botanicals, wafting the fragrance as needed.

If necessary, substitute granulated brown sugar for the sugar cane, however, it's not exactly the same. You may wish to add a few drops of dark rum in addition, but be aware that rum is extremely flammable and the flames may shoot up higher than is normally the case with incense.

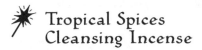 Tropical Spices
Cleansing Incense

Blend cinnamon, cloves, and coriander seeds and burn.

Cleansing Through Sound

Music plays many magical roles. *Charms,* in the most ancient sense of the word, were meant to be sung. Traditional Finnish magicians were famed for their ability to sing things into existence or to heal via songs. Experienced magicians were expected to possess songs that could halt bleeding.

Like botanicals or crystals, perhaps every musical instrument has its magical uses. Violins and flutes are used to cast love spells, while the sounds and reverberations of drums and percussion instruments provide extremely powerful cleansings.

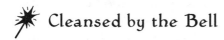 ## Cleansed by the Bell

Among the reasons bells are traditionally incorporated into churches is that bells are powerful space cleansers. Although any bell may be used, the most effective for cleansing purposes include silver bells, iron bells, and brass bells.

Maneki Neko is the amuletic Japanese beckoning cat. Usually a free-standing figurine, Maneki Neko bells cleanse personal and spatial auras, in addition to their traditional function of attracting prosperity and protection.

Ring bells whenever you feel cleansing is required. Hang bells in a breezy spot so that their activity can be consistent.

Bells are interesting cleansers because, unlike other methods, they can operate spontaneously. Should a typically silent bell suddenly ring, especially without obvious cause, pay attention. Further cleansing or protective rituals may be needed.

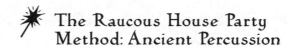 ## The Raucous House Party Method: Ancient Percussion

This method evokes primal spiritual rites. Historically, this method was utilized in ancient Anatolia, Egypt, Nubia, North Africa, the Middle East, and the Mediterranean. This method enhances space cleansing by adding protective, aura boosting and spirit summoning properties.

Preferred instruments include cymbals, sistra, tambourines and/or frame drums. At least some of these instruments are required for effective cleansing, and at least some of the instruments must have metal parts. Supplement with other drums, flutes, rattles and percussion as desired.

Although musical skill and experience certainly never hurts, it's not necessary for cleansing purposes. All that is required is that everyone grabs an instrument and allows the spirits to guide them. Reverberations remove negative debris. In addition, there is an element of banishing: The theory behind the spell is that low-level malevolent entities are frightened by the raucous clatter of percussion and will quickly depart. The sounds also extend a party invitation to sacred revelers like Kybele, Dionysus, the Dactyls, Astarte, Hathor, Isis, Bes and Taweret. Their presence, even if fleeting, provides blessings and protection. The goal, therefore, is to make a joyful noise. Make a lot of noise. This is a party cleansing: it's not solemn and serious. The mood contributes to the ritual. A room that felt uneasy prior to this ritual will feel friendly and inviting once it's over.

This cleansing is an effective ritual itself. It raises a lot of power and energy and is an excellent precursor to spells dealing with love, sexuality, and the more passionate aspects of protection, finances, justice and healing. It may also be a prelude to a great party. It is not the appropriate cleansing to choose, however, if you wish to follow purification rites with serene, controlled, sedate ritual. Try the following method instead.

☀ The Serene Yet Powerful Method: Singing Bowls

The harmonies created by Himalayan singing bowls are used to wash space. Ideally, the goal is to achieve a perfect balance of yin and yang energies. This method is particularly beneficial before ritual. It has a soothing effect on participants as well: beyond cleansing, it is also used to balance and harmonize energies—excellent for the initiation of group ritual.

The singing bowl is a round metal bowl made in varying sizes. It is portable, so that it may be carried directly to any area needing cleansing. Traditionally, the finest singing bowls are crafted in Nepal from seven metals: gold, silver, copper, iron, tin, lead, and zinc. Each metal corresponds to one of the seven visible planets and thus incorporates its energies and blessings.

A small wooden mallet is used to tap the bowl, typically three times for maximum effect. Different sounds are produced depending upon whether the bowl is tapped, rubbed or hit. Try using your fingernail or the tips of your fingers instead of the mallet. Adding varying amounts of water to the bowl also alters the sound. Experiment. Find the sounds that please you, that literally resonate with you. Harmonize the sound of the bowl with your own ears and intuition to achieve the correct sound for your purpose and space.

1. Place a small cushion beneath the bowl as it's carried. A round cushion is traditional. This is not merely a formality: the cushion improves the sound, lengthening the tone.
2. Walk with the bowl, directing the sound as needed.
3. For heavy duty cleansing, place the bowl on its cushion on a table in the center of a room. Strike it, letting its sound reverberate and radiate.

Like any other occult tool, given the opportunity, an individual singing bowl can develop a rapport with an individual person. A fine singing bowl is an exceptionally receptive tool.

It will become attuned to anyone in frequent contact with it. Store the bowl in soft, heavy fabric such as velvet when not in use. Singing bowls improve with age, becoming more powerful with frequent use.

Singing bowls are also used for empowering, energizing and replenishing space following any kind of space cleansing.

☀ Sistrum Cleansing

The sistrum may be used individually as a cleansing agent. A handled instrument, formed from metal, it is shaken so that its small metal discs clatter. An ancient spiritual and magical tool, its ancient Egyptian name "shesheshet" evokes its sound. Sistra are still used in Ethiopian spiritual rites. Simple sistra are available, as are reproductions of ancient Egyptian ones, which typically feature the head of the primal goddess of Earth's delights, Hathor, on its handle.

Among her many functions, Hathor is the Spirit of Music as well as one of the primary guardians of her father, Ra. Ever vigilant, she earned the sobriquet, the Eye of Ra. Hathor is the sistrum. When you wield it, you hold the mighty Eye of Ra in your hands. Shake it in all corners, closets and behind doors to chase away evil and produce a cleansed aura and atmosphere.

Cleansing Vapors

 Blessing Incense

Not all incenses are dry. This is a liquid, steam-based incense formula from Yemen.

1. Gently warm rose water or hydrosol.
2. Add sugar, stirring until the sugar is completely dissolved.
3. Add some or all of the following: aloes wood, rose petals, sandalwood powder, black tea leaves, attars of jasmine, rose, sandalwood, and henna.

4. Simmer, until steam rises.
5. Use the steam to bless and cleanse an area, people and/or objects.

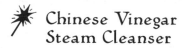

Chinese Vinegar Steam Cleanser

Steam is the result of the merged powers of water and fire; it is an extremely effective spiritual cleanser. This Chinese formula is recommended for a weekly standard cleansing:

1. Boil rice vinegar in a shallow pan until it's steaming (a paella pan or similar is ideal).
2. Very carefully, so as not to burn yourself, carry the steaming pan of vinegar through all the rooms of the home, letting the vapors cleanse corners, closets, all and any areas that don't feel *"right."*

Glittering Coals Vapor Cleanser

There are other ways to merge the powers of water and fire: toss burning coals into a bowl of water. This provides a quick burst of purification for anything (or anyone) in the immediate vicinity. Sizzling, sparking and/or steaming are extra powerful and auspicious signs.

Sacred Resin Liquid Cleanser

Most of the various sacred resins are also available as liquid essential oils, such as frankincense, mastic and sandalwood. Warmed in an aroma burner, they provide space cleansing in this form too, although with not quite as potent an effect as a profound blast of the smoke. It is more discreet, however, and their fragrances are beautiful. Use as general household maintenance.

Follow the directions of your aroma burner. In general, there will be a space to hold water or oil. Fill this partway with the desired liquid and add a few drops of the essential oil. Some method of heating from underneath is required, typically a small candle.

Floorwashes

Floorwashes don't sound as glamorous as incense and asperging, however they are an integral component of the Hoodoo and Conjure magical traditions. They combine actual physical house cleaning with spiritual and magical work, effectively killing two birds with one stone. They are potent yet discreet and perhaps the single most effective use of multi-tasking within magic.

Although the liquid is called *floorwash*, technically it refers to the final rinse used to clean a floor or other interior surfaces. It should not be removed but allowed to air-dry, so that its power radiates into the surrounding atmosphere. In other words, the floor should be clean *before* applying the floorwash. The radiant power of the botanicals is what is crucial: floorwashes are a component of many spells for a variety of purposes, including protection and romance, in addition to their obvious value as a space cleansing device.

There are two standard methods of making a floorwash. Choose which suits you:

★ *Fill a bucket with warm water. Add the magical infusion together with some white vinegar*
★ *Create the infusion and pour it into an empty bucket. Pour enough boiling salted water over it to fill the bucket. Add some white vinegar*

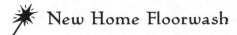 New Home Floorwash

This is recommended for a preliminary cleansing when moving into a new home. This removes old vibrations and emotions lingering from past residents and allows you to begin with a fresh slate.

1. Make a strong infusion from basil, hyssop, and pine needles.
2. Strain and add to a bucket of rinse water, with vinegar.
3. Cleanse floors and surfaces as needed.

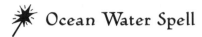 Ocean Water Spell

Fill empty glass bottles with ocean water and bring them home. Use this water to cleanse walls and floors, and whatever requires magical cleansing.

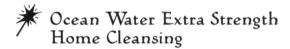 Ocean Water Extra Strength Home Cleansing

Fill empty glass bottles with ocean water. Add **Cascarilla Powder,** agar-agar and powdered kelp. Use this water for magical space cleansing.

Post-cleansing Spell

After other Cleansing Spells are complete, add **Cascarilla Powder** to a bucket of salted water. Wash down floors and walls to seal and enhance your previous efforts.

Full House Cleansings

Special techniques may be needed should you wish to magically cleanse an entire building. Although many cleansing spells assume that a home is being

 Angelica Floorwash

In addition to its cleansing abilities, angelica possesses a strong protective aspect.

1. Make a strong infusion from dried angelica.
2. Strain out the herbs.
3. Add the infusion, together with some white or rice vinegar, to a bucket of wash water to cleanse floors and surfaces.

 Aura Cleansing Floorwash

Agrimony repels and sends back hexes. Peppermint is an aggressive cleanser that beckons the presence of helpful, benevolent spirits. Combined, these botanicals create a particularly potent floorwash.

1. Make a strong infusion from dried agrimony and peppermint.
2. Strain out the herbs and add the infusion liquid to a bucket of water, together with white or rice vinegar.
3. Cleanse floors and surfaces.

Dragon's Tears Floorwash

Make a strong infusion by pouring boiling water over dragon's tears. Add this to a bucket of floorwash rinse water with vinegar and scrub away.

 Four Thieves Floorwash

Add **Four Thieves Vinegar,** black salt, and rosemary to a bucket of floorwash.

ritually cleansed, these spells may also be used for workspaces or any other type of building.

 ## Coconut Cleansing Spell

1. Bring rum, **Cascarilla Powder** and a whole coconut to the corner of your home furthest from the main entrance.
2. Take a mouthful of rum. Don't swallow it; instead spray it over the whole coconut.
3. Next sprinkle Cascarilla Powder on the coconut.
4. Roll the coconut through your home, out the main entrance.
5. Pick it up and bring it to a four-way crossroads at a distance from where you live, a remote crossroads, not one that you pass frequently.
6. Circumambulate the four points of the crossroads, dropping offerings of fruit, coins, and candy as you pass each one.
7. Bring the coconut into the center of the crossroads and throw it to the ground, making sure that it cracks open.
8. Leave it there. Return home via a circuitous route without looking back.

 ## Intensive Space Cleansing

1. Take an entire bunch of peppermint and rub it vigorously against walls, furniture, objects, and whatever else needs to be cleansed.
2. When the cleansing is complete, wrap the peppermint in brown paper and remove it from your home immediately.
3. Dispose of it far from home, returning via a circuitous route.

 ## Jessamine Flowers House Cleansing Spell

Botanicals don't have to be burnt to cleanse: spread day Jessamine petals throughout the house for spiritual cleansing and to remove the residue of any malevolent spells cast against you.

 ## Lodestone Cleansing

1. Hold two matched pairs of lodestones (four lodestones in total) in your hands.
2. Slowly, consciously move through the area in a sunwise direction, encouraging the lodestones to absorb all negativity and spiritual debris.
3. When you have finished, do intensive lodestone cleansing or bury the lodestones in Earth.

 ## Midsummer's Fire Cleansing Spell

Carry burning brands of aromatic herbs from the Midsummer's bonfires through your home to cleanse, purify, and protect.

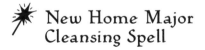

Mother Holle's Cleansing Spell

In fairy tales, Hulde, prominent Teutonic deity of love, sex, birth, and death devolves into Mother Holle, supernal supervisor of women's housework. The spiritual message is subliminal: Mother Holle supervises cleansing rites. Traditionally these twelve herbs were gathered during Midsummer's revels, then preserved, allowed to dry and mature and then used between the winter solstice and January 6th:

> Avens
> Chamomile
> Elder
> Elecampane
> Heartsease
> Mint
> Mugwort
> Mullein
> Slippery elm
> Southernwood
> Vervain
> Yarrow

Grind the botanicals into a powder, and burn, wafting the smoke into all corners and crevices of the home.

New Home Major Cleansing Spell

This cleansing ritual may be used for individual rooms or for an entire house and is an excellent cleansing method prior to moving into a new home.

1. Blend essential oils of frankincense and sandalwood into olive oil.
2. Use this to dress a blue candle.
3. Place this candle onto a disposable saucer or plate.
4. Place this saucer on top of some spread-out sheets of newspaper or a disposal tablecloth.

5. Cast a large circle with sea salt on the paper around the candle and saucer. The circle must be large enough for you to maneuver comfortably within it.
6. Enter the circle; you may either stand or kneel on the paper, and light the candle.
7. Close the doors and let the candle burn out. (Always maintain an eye on fire safety.)
8. When the candle is finished, fold everything up securely inside the newspaper. Do not spill even one grain of salt.
9. Take it to a moving body of water. Slide all biodegradable materials into the water. Throw everything else into a trashcan at a distance from your home. Walk away and don't look back.
10. Repeat in every room that you would like cleansed.

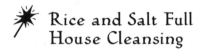

Rice and Salt Full House Cleansing

This Chinese ritual utilizes two potent cleansing agents: salt and rice. This ritual provides a massive cleansing of an entire home or building. Salt ranks among the most reliable magical cleansing agents, while, in addition to absorbing negative energy, rice is also the traditional Chinese offering made to propitiate wandering Earth spirits, in order to promote harmonious coexistence and basically to avoid trouble.

1. Take a cleansing bath before proceeding with the ritual. A salt scrub (see page 218) for personal cleansing is recommended.
2. Blend raw white rice and sea salt in a bowl.
3. First walk around the outer perimeter of the house or property being cleansed, sunwise, tossing small handfuls of the rice/salt mixture on the ground at the base of the house.
4. Repeat this ritual inside each room.
5. The last stop is the front door: toss three handfuls from inside out, then another three handfuls from outside in.

6. Do not clean up for twenty-four hours. Leave everything alone. (If birds eat the rice outside, that's fine, no need to shoo them away.)

The rice/salt outside can remain as a protective circle and as a peace offering to wandering spirits. Vacuum up the rice and salt inside. Do not sweep. Dispose of the vacuum cleaner bag outside the home.

 ## Sain

To sain someone or something is a Scottish method of ritually cleansing and blessing. This spell simultaneously spiritually cleanses and blesses an area and all participants alike:

1. Collect Holy Water, defined in this circumstance as water collected from a local spring or other nearby living source of water, between midnight and dawn, coinciding with a waxing moon.
2. All participants should gather in a circle.
3. Pass the water sunwise for each person to sip and sprinkle over themselves. (It may be more practical for each person to sprinkle their neighbor.)
4. Sprinkle the water in each corner of each room.

Salt Cleansing Spell

1. Make an infusion by pouring boiling water over High John the Conqueror roots.
2. Sprinkle the infusion on salt. (Only moisten the salt; don't melt it.)
3. Allow the salt to dry out.
4. Sprinkle the salt around your home to absorb negativity.
5. Reserve the remaining High John liquid and refrigerate. Repeat the spell as desired, daily or weekly.

Stationary Cleansers

Certain objects are perceived as being similar to magical vacuum cleaners. They absorb malevolence and negativity, removing it from the premises. As a general rule, white foods may be used in this manner.

In general, when the object is full, like a vacuum cleaner bag, it needs to be removed from the premises and discarded. Crystals are the exception: they may be cleansed, effectively emptying them of debris, so that they may be used over and over again. Check page 221 for crystal cleansing methods.

Stationary cleansers are typically left unsupervised in an area; if children and/or pets are present, make sure a safe method is used.

 ## Amethyst Crystal Cleanser

Place large amethysts in room corners to serve as spiritual vacuum cleaners. When they look dull, cleanse and recharge them. Other crystal gemstones recommended for space-cleansing include clear quartz crystal and malachite.

 ## Basic Stationary Cleansing

Sprinkling directs the cleansing, however liquids may also be used as stationary cleansers:

1. Place any of the cleansing formulas recommended in Asperging Spells on page 188 (but especially **Florida Water** and **Notre Dame Water),** in shallow uncovered pans.
2. Situate them strategically through an area, to absorb negative energy and provide a cleansing effect.
3. Replace weekly. If the liquid starts to look odd or smell strange, however, replace it immediately.

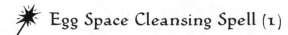# Egg Space Cleansing Spell (1)

Eggs are considered highly absorbent and capable of removing psychic debris. They are also used for personal cleansings and to diagnose and remove the Evil Eye.

1. Place eggs under the bed inside a bowl of spring water. The number of eggs depends upon the number of people sleeping in the bed, one egg per person.
2. Replace all eggs weekly. However should the eggs develop a foul aroma before the week is up, replace them immediately. Essentially, the vacuum bag is full.
3. Do not eat the eggs. Do not break or crack them inside your home. Put them in a brown paper bag and discard them outside your home.

Egg Space Cleansing Spell (2)

Individual eggs may also be placed in the corners of any rooms requiring cleansing. Leave them for seven days or until they begin to smell. This method is recommended for cleansing areas following altercations or minor violence.

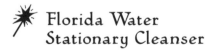# Florida Water Stationary Cleanser

1. Fill a pan with equal parts **Florida Water** and **Marie Laveau** or **Holy Water.**
2. Add one camphor square to the liquid.
3. Keep the pan under the bed or in another strategic location.
4. Change the water once a week or if it should start to smell "off."

Hoodoo Stationary Cleanser

1. Crumble a camphor square into a glass bottle or jar.
2. Cover it with **Florida Water.**
3. Leave the bottle open and strategically placed.
4. When the scent is no longer apparent, dispose of the **Florida Water** and repeat the process.

Onion Space Cleansing Spell

1. Chop one onion into quarters and place one piece in each corner of a room. Don't peel the onion. Don't use a food processor. Chop it by hand.
2. Allow the onion pieces to remain in place overnight.
3. Bury them outside the following day.
4. Repeat the process for a total of five consecutive nights.

Pomander Cleanser

1. Make a pomander from a lime fruit.
2. Pierce it with holes and stick cloves in each hole.
3. Roll the pierced fruit in powdered orrisroot and cinnamon.
4. Tie it with red and black ribbons and hang it strategically to absorb negativity and purify the aura.
5. Replace with a new one when the scent fades.

Rice Cleansing Spell

White foods like eggs and onions frequently possess this absorbent quality. Use white rice for the following spell:

1. Place an uncovered bowl of raw rice out to absorb negative energy and spiritual debris.
2. Replace with fresh rice weekly.
3. Discard the old rice outside the house or feed it to wild birds, whichever is appropriate.

Santeria Stationary Cleanser

Many Santeria space cleansings use water as a defensive mechanism, on the premise that evil and psychic toxins will dissolve in water in the same manner as salt or sugar.

1. Dissolve a square of camphor in a pan of water.
2. Keep it under the bed.
3. Change the water weekly. However, if an unpleasant odor emerges, dispose of the water immediately and replace it.
4. Disposal of the water is part of the spell: ideally it's thrown out the back window. If this isn't possible, flush it down the toilet but smudge the disposal area immediately.
5. Never dispose of the water in the kitchen sink or elsewhere in the house. You want to eliminate any possibility of lingering toxins.

 ## Vinegar Cleanser

Plain vinegar is cheap, easily obtainable and among the strongest cleansing agents of all.

1. Place a cup or bowl of vinegar in every room that needs cleansing.
2. Replace weekly.

*For intensified cleansing, add a square of camphor to the vinegar. To improve the fragrance, add a few drops of essential oils of frankincense, rose or sandalwood or blend with **Florida Water.***

Personal Cleansings

Personal cleansings are done in preparation for rituals and spellwork. They have an empowering effect and will remove accumulated psychic debris that obstructs full expression of personal power. In addition, many who delve into spiritual work perform regularly scheduled cleansings, usually once a week, as general magical maintenance.

Stronger cleansings are needed in special circumstances: they provide psychic healing following violence, violation or humiliation. Personal cleansings can also provide relief after trivial, unpleasant experiences. Should you ever feel somehow *tainted* or *unclean*, to any degree, that's the signal that some sort of personal cleansing ritual is needed. Choose the rituals that resonate most strongly for you.

Personal cleansings have an advantage over many other types of spells: their effects are readily apparent fairly immediately. A successful cleansing spell leaves you feeling refreshed, renewed and *clean.*

Many personal cleansings, particularly the baths, may be performed for oneself. However, some cleansing techniques require that one person performs the cleansing for another. To some extent, that's because many are survivals of shamanic rituals. Shamanic healers provide profound cleansing and soul restoration, beyond the scope of the average layperson. Once upon a time, unlike today, shamanic healing was common and accessible (according to many anthropologists and historians, the true oldest profession is that of the shaman). Perhaps it will be so again: cleansing spells do not replace the need for shamans. However, their methods have been adapted to household use: make sure you choose ritual assistants and cleansing assistants wisely.

 ## Barrida Cleansing

The barrida, *the Latin American ritual sweeping, uses a handmade broom to sweep the body clean, just like a broom sweeps the floor. One person serves as a cleanser for another—you can't really sweep yourself. Make a small broom from branches, ideally flowering branches. Rosemary is the most popular choice, but basil and rue are also effective. These botanicals may also be combined. Tie numerous stalks together. Take apart the barrida (the broom) and dispose of it once the cleansing is over.*

 ## Basil Cleansing Bath

In addition to standard cleansing effects, this bath is excellent for removing negative emotions caused by extended exposure to very controlling people. Basil also enhances luck and the potential for prosperity.

1. Pour approximately one cup of boiling water over one heaped teaspoon of dried basil.
2. Allow this to stand until the water cools, creating a strong infusion.
3. Add this to your bath.

 ## Citrus Bath

1. Obtain as many kinds of citrus fruits as possible: lemons, limes, oranges, tangerines, and so forth.
2. Draw a bath, quarter each fruit, squeeze the juice into the bath and toss the fruit in the water.
3. Add yarrow hydrosol, as much as you like.
4. Get into the bath and rub the fruit over your body.
5. Let yourself air-dry. (You may be sticky but let it remain for as long as possible.)

 ## Cleansing and Energy Balancing Bath

The botanicals frankincense and myrrh are perceived as happily married, perfectly balanced and a matching couple, as are vetiver and patchouli. In addition to aura cleansing, these botanicals also balance yin and yang energies.

1. Add a cup of salt to a dish.
2. Add two drops each of essential oils of frankincense, myrrh, patchouli and vetiver. (You may add more if you wish, but keep proportions equal. Add additional drops in even numbered combinations.)
3. With your fingers, blend this into the salt.
4. Add this to a tub of running water.
5. When the bath has filled and the temperature is correct, adjust the fragrance, if you like, by adding a few more drops of any of the essential oils directly to the water.

 ## Cleansing Oil (1)

Sometimes cleansing means adding something rather than removing it. This Mediterranean formula has a purifying effect. Using either essential oils or fresh herbs add basil, rosemary, and thyme to olive oil and massage this into the body.

 ## Cleansing Oil (2)

1. Create cleansing oil by blending frankincense, benzoin, sandalwood, myrrh, and/or liquidambar into jojoba oil. Use either essential oils or dried botanicals.
2. Anoint at least four white candles with this oil so that you may cast a circle with them wide enough so there's no anxiety about sitting within the circle. (More candles may be used; if only using four, place one in each of the cardinal points.)

3. Light the candles and sit within the circle until you feel cleansed and purified.

 ## Desert Sage Bath

Make an infusion of desert sage. Add it to the bath to cleanse, purify, and alleviate any sense of being psychically or morally "unclean."

 ## Destroy All Evil Bath

1. Add at least one cup of **Florida Water** and at least one cup of sea salt to a tub filled with water.
2. Add a generous splash of **Four Thieves Vinegar.**
3. Just before you enter the water, when the temperature has already been adjusted, add nine drops of essential oil of rosemary.

Reinforce and enhance the bath's potency by keeping a large quartz crystal in the water while you bathe.

 ## Dragon's Blood Bath

Blend dragon's blood powder, crushed frankincense, and sea salt. Add the powder to your bath.

 ## Earth Smoke Bath

*Make a strong infusion by pouring boiling water over Earth Smoke/**Fumitory;** add it to the bath.*

 ## Egg Personal Cleansing Spell (1)

Eggs are believed to be extremely absorbent and are thus able to remove and eliminate all sorts of negative energy and spiritual debris.

1. Pass a whole egg over the body, moving from the top downwards mentally focusing on eliminating any negative psychic debris.
2. When you're finished, take the egg outside, far from your home and smash it on the ground.
3. Leave it there. Return home via a different, circuitous route.

Coconuts are also considered highly absorbent. Some people prefer them and a coconut may be substituted for the egg. However don't overlook the obvious: it's much harder to smash a coconut than an egg.

 ## Egg Personal Cleansing Spell (2)

One person performs this cleansing for another:

1. Pass an egg entirely over the body.
2. Let the person who is being cleansed exhale onto the egg.
3. Break the egg in a dish and examine it. If there is blood or any abnormality present, this indicates that further, stronger action needs to be taken. If the yolk appears normal and is free from blood, the cleansing is considered complete.

In theory, one should use fertilized eggs so that the possibility of blood exists. If blood appears in regular unfertilized supermarket eggs, however, this is an extremely powerful indication that further cleansing is required.

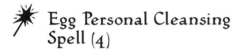

Egg Personal Cleansing Spell (3)

An alternative to the above:

1. Pass an egg slowly and entirely over the person's body.
2. Break the egg into a bowl of water.
3. In addition to observing the condition of the yolk, the patterns made by the egg whites floating in the water are interpreted as a divination technique, to reveal information about the cleansed person's condition and situation.

Egg Personal Cleansing Spell (4)

This cleansing is meant to follow an experience or encounter that leaves you feeling shaken, uneasy or tainted:

1. Strip off all your clothing.
2. Rub an egg over you, working outwards: from the shoulders out the fingers, from the thighs down to your toes.
3. Slap yourself all over with a bunch of parsley.
4. Anoint yourself with rose water. (For an extensive and expensive cleansing, pour a shallow bath of rose water and lie in it, turning over so that both sides of your body are covered with the liquid.)
5. Put on clean clothes. Place the egg and parsley in a brown paper bag and dispose of them far from your home.

Although you can effectively cleanse yourself with this spell, having someone else perform at least the egg-rubbing and parsley-slapping parts is potentially more effective.

Egg Cleansing Spell (5): Invocation to Saint Claire

An extremely popular Cuban Santeria-derived cleansing spell, this is most effective if performed on a Monday.

1. Place a whole raw egg in a glass filled with water, being careful not to break it.
2. Light a seven-day candle dedicated to Saint Claire. (Commercially manufactured candles dedicated to Saint Claire are available. A white seven-day candle may be used or, if these are unavailable, simply burn individual white candles for seven days.)
3. Wait for the candle to completely finish burning, accompanied by prayer, petition and the visualization of one's desired goals. If a significant amount of water evaporates during the seven days, replace it.
4. At the conclusion of seven days, carefully remove the egg. Throw the water out the door onto the street.
5. Carefully carry the egg to a park—never your backyard! Smash it on the ground. As the egg breaks, your troubles disperse.
6. Return home via a circuitous route.

This spell was originally meant to be coordinated with petitions to Saint Claire. A commercially manufactured "Saint Claire candle" will very likely have her prayer written on the back of the glass sleeve. However, this very popular spell has passed into the general magical community; for many the only connection it retains with the saint is its name, although even that may not be recalled. Perform the spell as feels most comfortable for you.

Elder Cleansing Spell

Elder trees possess the magical power to purify and cleanse. Write whatever weighs upon your mind on a

piece of paper—whatever preoccupies you or taints your existence. Bury this paper under an elder tree so that your worries are absorbed and cleansed.

✴ Florida Water Cleansing Spell (1)

Florida Water cleanses the body as well as it does an area. Add at least one cup to bathwater, together with at least a handful of salt.

✴ Florida Water Cleansing Spell (2)

For a fast, spontaneous cleansing, when there is no time to prepare and take a bath:

1. Undress completely.
2. Rub or sprinkle **Florida Water** all over yourself. (Make sure not to neglect the oft-forgotten soles of the feet and top of the head.)
3. Allow yourself to air-dry and get dressed.

*This is particularly effective and refreshing if the **Florida Water** is kept chilled in the refrigerator.*

✴ Flower Remedy Dream Cleansing (1)

Aura cleansing may be accomplished in your sleep using flower essence remedies.

1. Add twenty drops of Antiseptic bush flower essence remedy (Living/Australia) to a bath taken just before you sleep.
2. When you get into bed, rub a few additional drops into the thin skin between your thumb and index finger.

Only repeat the initial large dose in the bath if you haven't performed this spell in months. Otherwise rubbing a few drops into the hand or on the soles of the feet before bed is sufficient.

✴ Flower Remedy Dream Cleansing (2)

Antiseptic bush actually performs the cleansing. However, Wintergreen flower essence remedy (Green Hope) stimulates dreams that will cause cleansing or give clues as to how to seek it. This is particularly beneficial if, despite all attempts at cleansing, you never feel purified.

1. Add twenty drops of the flower remedy to your bath before bedtime. This massive dose will only be done once.
2. Just before bed, rub a few drops of the remedy into the thin skin between thumb and index finger. You may also massage a little into your feet.
3. On subsequent nights start from Step 2.

✴ Garlic Personal Vacuum Service

Sometimes someone else really needs cleansing. If negativity emanates consistently from a single individual, tainting the mood and atmosphere, take matters into your own hands: perform an indirect cleansing. Use a clove of garlic as a personal vacuum cleaner.

1. Peel and crush a single clove of garlic.
2. Place it under the person's bed, chair or under the carpet where they are sure to stand.
3. Remove and burn after twenty-four hours.
4. Replace as needed; an improvement in attitude should be observed shortly.

Herbal Magic Cleansing Bath

Make an infusion by pouring boiling water over fresh lavender, mint, marjoram, oregano, and rosemary. Add the strained liquid to your bath.

 ## Holy Water Bath

*Add as much **Holy Water** to your bathwater as possible. Submerge completely three times.*

 ## Indigo Cleansing Bath

1. Place Turkish blue eye beads into a bottle of **Indigo Water** to provide a power boost.
2. Strain the **Indigo Water** into your bathwater.

Alternatively add large quartz or amethyst crystals to the water.

 ## Kitchen Herb Bath

Magically powerful plants masquerade as common kitchen herbs. Make a strong infusion by pouring boiling water over fennel, dill, and chervil and try adding it to your bathwater.

 ## Lavender Bath

Lavender derives its name from "lavare," meaning "to wash." Laundry comes from the same root source. This bath may be dedicated to Hecate, for whom lavender is a sacred plant. Add essential oil of lavender, lavender hydrosol, or an infusion to the bath for spiritual as well as physical cleansing.

 ## Lodestone Cleansing

Lodestones may be used for personal cleansings. Make sure they themselves are cleansed before beginning. This is an intensive cleansing: someone else must perform it for you. That person should wear iron or silver bangles on both wrists during the cleansing.

With one lodestone in each hand, starting at the head, moving down toward the feet, gently rub the lodestones against skin or aura. Gently shake them periodically. When you have finished, do intensive lodestone cleansing (see Elements of Magic Spells) or bury the lodestones in Earth.

 ## Lovage Bath

This is especially effective for magically cleansing off degrading traces of a failed love affair or an unhappy one-night stand. Grind and powder a dried lovage root. Sprinkle onto your bath water and distribute well.

 ## Mandrake Bath

For emergency, heavy-duty spiritual cleansing, soak a true mandrake root in warm water overnight or for three days. (Don't make an infusion.) Remove the mandrake and preserve it by carefully letting it dry out. Add the liquid to a tub filled with water.

 ## Maté Cleansing Bath

Maté tea, whether as an infusion of the fresh leaves or the dried tea, is considered a strong cleansing agent in Central and South America. Use maté in the bath to remove minor hexes, the lesser Evil Eye and assorted psychic garbage.

1. Create a strong infusion by pouring boiling water over the dried herb.

2. Let the water cool to room temperature and strain, reserving the liquid.
3. Add this strong infusion to the bath or sponge the infusion over oneself following a bath or shower.
4. Allow yourself to air dry.

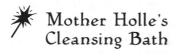

Mexican-style Cleansing Bath

Allow the liquid used to boil stinging nettles to cool and add it to an infusion of rosemary and spearmint. Add the blended liquid to your bath.

Mother Holle's Cleansing Bath

Mother Holle, Germanic Queen of Witches, leads the Wild Hunt. These herbs are traditionally gathered on Midsummer's Eve and used for intensive cleansings between the winter solstice and January 6th.

Blend the following botanicals:

Avens
Chamomile
Elder
Elecampane
Heartsease
Mint
Mugwort
Mullein
Saint John's Wort
Southernwood
Vervain
Yarrow

Make an infusion by pouring boiling water over the botanicals. Let it steep, then strain and add to the bath. For maximum spiritual cleansing and happiness, float heartsease (wild pansy) blossoms in the water.

Nine Flowers Bath

1. Place three white roses, three white carnations, and three white lilies in a dish and pour hot water over them.
2. Strain out the liquid, reserving the flowers, and bring them to the bathtub or shower.
3. Scrub from head to foot with one flower at a time until that flower falls apart.
4. When all nine flowers have been used, get out of the water and air-dry.
5. Dress in clean clothes; don't clean the bathtub immediately. Wait several hours or have someone else do the job.

These next formulas are recommended for spiritual cleansings following abuse, violence, sexual violation or any sort of profound humiliation. They may be performed in combination, for extra enhancement.

Maximum Power Spiritual Cleansing (1)

1. Blend camphor, cinnamon, cloves, frankincense, myrrh, and sandalwood.
2. Burn them in an incense burner, cauldron or cast-iron pan.
3. Fumigate yourself with the cleansing smoke.

Maximum Power Spiritual Cleansing (2)

1. Add copious quantities of sea salt to your bath water.
2. Add essential oils of lavender, rose, rosemary, sandalwood, frankincense, and myrrh, plus some white rose hydrosol.
3. Float rose and calendula blossoms in the water, if possible.

Maximum Power Spiritual Cleansing (3)

This ancient cleansing ritual was originally designed for hunters and soldiers returning to the general community, but may also be used for anyone who has killed someone, particularly inadvertently, to help remove spiritual contamination caused by killing a person. It is a simple but extremely magically powerful spell.

Pour the cooled water from a blacksmith's forge over the person's face three times a day for seven days.

Mucura Cleansing Bath

Petiveria alliacea *is an Amazonian herb popular in South American magic. Known as* mucura *in Peru and* guine *or* tipi *in Brazil, it's believed to possess purifying and protective powers. It protects against malevolent magic as well as attacks from animals and humans. It is a key ingredient in the* limpia *or cleansing bath.*

1. Soak approximately two grams of dried mucura overnight in a liter of water.
2. Add this to your bath to wash off *saladera,* the "salt" that some believe lingers on the subtle body and causes bad luck unless removed.

Mucura earned renown in Brazil as the botanical used by kitchen slaves to slowly but fatally poison oppressive masters. In other words, do not take mucura internally without expert medical supervision, as it is potentially very toxic.

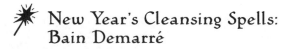

New Year's Cleansing Spells: Bain Demarré

This spell derives from the French Caribbean and is most frequently performed on New Year's Eve. It's intended to cleanse off the previous year's spiritual debris so that one enters the New Year fresh and magically,

spiritually cleansed. Traditionally the bath was taken at the mouth of the river, although now it may be done at home. One may cleanse oneself or, for maximum magical effect, a qualified traditional healer may accomplish the cleansing.

Cleanse the body by rubbing with a cod-fish tail. Follow immediately with a Luck Bath. (See Luck and Success Spells, *page 733.)*

Oak Leaf Bath

1. Crumble five oak leafs.
2. Place in a muslin bag and attach it to the tub's faucet so that the water runs through it.
3. Float five whole oak leaves in the water.
4. Enter the bath and rub your body with the leaves.

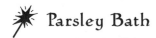

Ocean Cleansing Bath

This bath may be dedicated to Yemaya, Spirit of the Sea.

1. Pour copious quantities of sea salt into a tub filled with water. (Optional: add **Indigo Water.)**
2. Soak in the water, and then allow yourself to air dry.
3. Gently rub your body with long stemmed white roses (remove the thorns!) using an outward, downwards movement.
4. Wrap the roses up in a clean white towel or fresh white tissue paper.
5. Bring them to the beach and throw each rose, one by one, into the sea.

Parsley Bath

This bath is not suitable for use during pregnancy. Make an infusion by pouring boiling water over an entire bunch of parsley and one sliced parsley root. Add the infusion to bathwater.

Peony Root Bath

Create an infusion by pouring boiling water over sliced peony roots. Add the infusion to your bath, together with peony blossoms if possible.

 ## Personal Pine Cleansing

This spell requires a pine branch complete with needles.

1. Have someone gently sweep you with this branch from the top of your head to the soles of your feet.
2. When the cleansing is complete, burn the branch or toss it into running water, flowing away from you.

 ## Pine-Bay Bath

Bruise pine needles; place them in a bowl together with bay laurel leaves. Pour boiling water over them to create an infusion, and add the liquid to your bath.

 ## Rose Herb Bath

Make an infusion of the following: red roses, white roses, yellow roses, pink roses, peppermint, and parsley and add it to your bath.

 ## Verbena Bath

Vervain, sometimes called verbena, and lemon verbena are often and easily confused. The two can complement each other: lemon verbena provides purification while vervain offers magical protection.

Make a strong infusion by pouring boiling water over the combined botanicals. Add the water to your bath, together with a splash of vinegar and slices of lemon.

 ## Yucca Bath

Before the advent of commercially manufactured soap, Native Americans created cleansing suds from yucca plants. Yucca suds have spiritual and magical cleansing effects as well as physical. This cleansing bath is particularly beneficial before and/or after spell casting.

1. Pound dry yucca roots.
2. Whisk them into cold water to create suds.
3. Use to cleanse yourself, especially head and hair.

Personal Fumigation Spells

Personal fumigation means using directed smoke to spiritually cleanse the body and the personal aura. This is also a very ancient method of applying perfume. Perfume literally means *"through smoke."* Although modern perfume is liquid, this is a relatively recent development. For centuries, people stood over burning aromatic materials, wafting it strategically, hoping to permeate skin, hair, crevices and clothing with healing, protective, or seductive fragrances, as the case may be.

Most purifying botanicals also possess a protective aspect. Depending upon which botanicals are used, there may also be a sensual component. For all of their protective and purifying powers, for instance, sandalwood and frankincense are also luxurious, fragrant, even aphrodisiac substances. Cleansings can be sensual rather than medicinal and still be very effective, although this also depends upon personal expectations and preferences.

In ascending order of strength, try these methods:

★ *Have someone else cleanse you with a smudge stick or directed smoke. White sage, desert sage, frankincense and benzoin resin are particularly effective*

★ *Place the incense burner on the ground and straddle it, directing the smoke upwards around the body. Kneel down and direct it over your head. You need greater quantities of botanicals for this to be truly effective*

★ *You can also burn the incense in a small, closed room such as a bathroom. After the room is permeated with the smoke, get undressed and enter the room so that you can bathe in the smoke*

 ## Personal Fumigation Spell (1) High Spirits Fumigation

This removes psychic debris, offers protection and blessings and invites benevolent spirits to pay close attention to you.

> Three parts frankincense
> Two parts benzoin
> One part myrrh

 ## Personal Fumigation Spell (2) Sacred Cleansing Incense

> Benzoin
> Dragon's blood
> Sandalwood

 ## Purification Bath

1. Make a strong infusion by pouring boiling water over nine bay laurel leaves and two tablespoons of anise seeds.
2. Let it reach room temperature.
3. Strain out the botanicals and add the liquid to your tub of water.

 ## Quick Fix Aura Cleanser

*Add one cup of salt and one cup of vinegar to a bath. Lemon vinegar is most potent, however apple cider or rice vinegar is also very effective. Homemade **Four Thieves Vinegar** is also powerful and very effective, however its fragrance is pungent rather than light and relaxing.*

 ## Repentance Powder (1)

This Hoodoo formulation powder does more than cleanse off spiritual debris. It's for use when you feel defiled because of your own actions. For maximum effect, the spell accompanies acts of restitution and good deeds.

1. Write out Psalm 23 and read it aloud.
2. Burn the paper and mix the ashes with hyssop, lavender, and sea salt.
3. Sprinkle the powder on clean white sheets before going to bed.
4. Pay attention to your dreams.

 ## Repentance Powder (2)

1. Create Repentance Powder as above.
2. Sprinkle the mingled ashes, herbs, and salt over burning frankincense.
3. Cleanse yourself with the aromatic smoke.

 ## Rosemary Anisette Cleansing

This personal cleansing invokes the healing powers of massage. Someone else must perform this cleansing on you. The subject of the cleansing focuses on his or her goals or on prayer and petition, while the other person performs the massage.

1. Soak rosemary stalks in anisette.
2. The person to be cleansed lies down comfortably on the floor, bed or on a massage table.
3. The massage is initially performed only with the hands: this is a gentle, easy massage, not a vigorous one. The goal is aura cleansing, not muscle manipulation.
4. With the fingers, repeatedly and rhythmically form the sign of the cross, pentacle and/or other sacred, protective symbols on the body. Start with the palm, and then journey up the arms. Go to the soles of the feet and up the leg.
5. Remove the rosemary wands from the liqueur, shake them out gently and use them to lightly massage the body.
6. Simultaneously request assistance from your favorite spirits. Order any evil entities to leave. Affirm your safety.

Sage Cleansing Spell (1)

Plain garden sage is a profound spiritual cleanser.

1. Dry the sage.
2. Grind it into a fine powder with a mortar and pestle.
3. Sprinkle the powder onto a charcoal and use it to fumigate the body.

Sage Cleansing Spell (2)

California white sage is one of the most powerful magical spiritual cleansers. Unfortunately it is also an endangered species. Luckily it transplants well and grows easily from seed. Grow your own supply, to preserve the plant's existence and to preserve, purify and enhance the power of your aura.

Burn white sage as loose incense or use it to create a smudge stick.

Sage Cleansing Spell (3)

Not only does sage taste delicious, but eating it also provides internal cleansing. There's a reason witches are so frequently depicted stirring cauldrons. Enchanted potions, magical brews and what's cooking for dinner aren't mutually exclusive. Many magic spells, particularly love spells, take the form of meals, as does this cleansing spell, masquerading as poultry stuffing.

1. Make or acquire a cornbread. It must dry out a little before using it in this recipe. Crumble it.
2. Dice one onion, three large stalks of celery and five large, fresh sage leaves.
3. Sauté the onions and celery in butter or oil.
4. Add the crumbled up semi-stale cornbread.
5. Drizzle chicken broth over everything.
6. Add the minced sage leaves.
7. Bake this in a 325°F oven (170°C, Gas mark 3) for twenty minutes, or until done.

Rosemary may be used in similar fashion. Cook with either herb as much as possible to maximize their cleansing potential.

Sage Cleansing Spell (4)

To heal from a friend's betrayal and help remove feelings of violation and humiliation:

1. Soak a photograph in salted water. If the spell is right for you, you will know which photograph to use.
2. Remove the photo from the liquid and let it dry out.
3. Burn the photo on a bed of sage. Smudge yourself with sage, too.

Salt Cleansing Spells

Salt is the single most powerful and consistent aura cleanser. Sea salt, processed as little as possible, is most powerful, although many magical traditions, not necessarily Jewish, prefer kosher salt, as it bears the aura of being blessed. However, *in extremis*, any type of salt is effective.

Salt Cleansing Bath (1)

This is a quick-fix cleansing, perfect for spontaneous needs:

1. Add at least one cup of salt to a bathtub filled with warm water.
2. Soak thoroughly, allowing yourself to air-dry, when the bath is over.

Salt Cleansing Bath (2)

1. Dissolve at least one cup of salt into a tub of warm water.
2. Add at least one cup of vinegar.
3. Slice one lemon and one lime in half. Squeeze the juice into the bathwater. Toss the rinds in also.
4. Rub the squeezed-out fruit halves against your body as you soak in the tub.

Salt Cleansing Spell (3)

There are many ways to benefit from salt's cleansing powers, including bath salts. The basic formula for bath salts consists of two cups of sea salt blended with one-half cup of baking soda. This standard formula, alone, added to the bath provides effective cleansing.

The cleansing may be enhanced and strengthened by adding essential oils. The following increase the potency greatly: frankincense, lavender, manuka, rosemary, thyme *linalool, and sandalwood. Dried powdered ingredients may also be added, especially dragon's blood powder, powdered rosemary, and lavender.*

Salt Scrub

A salt scrub provides a more concentrated cleansing. For maximum effect, add bath salts to the water and then apply the salt scrub directly to the body.

The Standard Salt Scrub formula consists of a blend of approximately one cup of salt and one-half cup of oil. The actual quantity depends, however, upon the desired consistency and the sensitivity of your skin: if you'd like a softer, less abrasive scrub, increase the proportion of oil.

Because salt is purifying and protective, every salt scrub inherently provides aura cleansing. However, the purpose and added effects of a salt scrub may be adjusted through the addition of essential oils. Rosemary, clary sage, frankincense, manuka, benzoin, thyme linalool, and sandalwood all intensify the cleansing effect.

Scythian Cleansing Spell

Once upon a time, the Scythians dominated the European and Central Asian steppes. At the peak of their power, their influence ranged from the borders of China to the borders of Egypt. The Scythians left no written records, only beautiful gold ornaments, much of it in the form of magical animals. What we know of their culture derives from archeological analysis and surviving reports by their literate contemporaries.

According to the Greek observer Herodotus the Scythians didn't bathe with water, instead favoring vapor baths similar to the Russian bathhouse or Native American sweat lodge. Women however also used this cleansing method:

1. Pound cedar, cypress, and frankincense into paste.

2. Apply this to the body and leave on overnight, removing in the morning to impart spiritual cleanliness and beautiful fragrance.

 ## Seven Flowers Miracle Bath

This bath is ideal for when you're very tired, very jaded, very drained or very bitter. Seven different fresh flowers are required for this bath, the magic number associated with hope and miracles. Choose whatever flowers are available or whatever flowers appeal to you. Float the flowers in the bathtub and soak while focusing on regaining innocence and optimism.

 ## Seven Roses Bath

This spell requires:

Seven red roses
A handful of sea salt
A splash of vinegar
A squeeze of lemon juice
A splash of pure spring water or substitute a splash
of either **Marie Laveau** or **Notre Dame Water.**

1. Fill the tub with water.
2. Throw all the ingredients into the tub.
3. Spend seven minutes in the bath, rubbing yourself with the roses, submerging yourself periodically and focusing upon your goals.
4. Dry off with a clean towel, white or unbleached cotton if possible, and put on fresh clothes.
5. Don't clean the tub out right away; let it sit for at least an hour while your aura cleansing stabilizes.

 ## Seven Waves Ocean Cleansing

Immerse yourself in ocean waters to achieve aura cleansing. When seven waves have passed over you, the cleansing is complete.

 ## Spirit of the Sea Magic Spiritual Cleansing (1)

If you suffer from a real sense of defilement, petition the spirits of the sea to provide healing and cleansing. Although there are many such spirits, Aphrodite and Yemaya are particularly powerful and benevolent. Petition either spirit or both. They are compatible with each other.

1. Journey to the beach with a bouquet of roses. (Six yellow roses for Aphrodite and/or seven white roses for Yemaya.)
2. Stand in the shallow water. Dip each rose in sea water and then massage it, gently, one at a time, over your body, stroking downwards: down your legs, down your arms, as if you are removing something. Use a light touch.
3. Toss each rose into the sea after you've used it to cleanse yourself.
4. When all the roses have been given to the ocean, enter deeper water and allow significant waves to pass over you, seven for Yemaya, six for Aphrodite. (If you're afraid of the deep water, sit or recline in the shallows and let the water pass over you.)
5. Ask these beautiful, benevolent spirits to cleanse you and replenish your aura and energy.
6. Turn around and walk out of the water and go home.

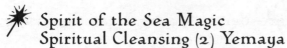

Spirit of the Sea Magic Spiritual Cleansing (2) Yemaya

1. Bring seven empty bottles to the beach.
2. Catch ocean water from a separate wave in each one.
3. Place seven watermelon seeds inside each bottle, together with sprigs of mugwort and mucura and a small clear quartz crystal.
4. Seal the bottles and bring them home. Each bottle will be added to a separate bath to be taken over seven consecutive days. Ideally the bath should be initiated at either 7 a.m. or 7 p.m. and repeated daily at the same time.
5. Add the contents of a bottle to your bath.
6. Accompany by burning a blue or white candle until the final bath, when seven candles are lit.

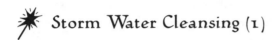

Storm Water Cleansing (1)

Sacred springs, especially steaming hot springs, were the initial primal sources for spiritual cleansing. Unfortunately these are not accessible to all, especially on a regular and consistent basis. The most accessible "wild" water tends to be rainwater.

1. Collect rainwater to provide a similar spiritual effect, especially water from a strong downpour.
2. Pay attention to the after-effects of the storm: if the air feels especially clean, then you know you've collected powerful water.
3. Add this water to your bathwater.
4. Use it to cleanse your hair.

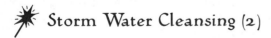

Storm Water Cleansing (2)

1. Collect storm water in an iron cauldron.
2. Heat it up until it simmers and steam is produced.
3. Stand naked beside or over the cauldron, whatever is comfortable and safe, wafting the steam over you, directing it with your hands.

Tlazolteotl's Cleansing Spell

The Spirit of Garbage, Tlazolteotl is the terrible and beautiful Aztec spirit of love and Queen of Witches. A fierce spirit, her domain includes sex, romance, magic and healing. Tlazolteotl cleanses Earth of psychic garbage. She eats it, thus removing it from Earth. Tlazolteotl is capable of absorbing any filth, providing a purified aura instead.

Tlazolteotl invented the temescal bath, the brick Aztec sweat lodge. Outlawed by the conquering Spanish, temescals have recently been revived and are emerging as chic additions to the bed and breakfast inns of Oaxaca and Mexico City, in addition to retaining their traditional healing and spiritual purposes.

Erect an altar dedicated to Tlazolteotl. Decorate it with her attributes: obsidian, smoky quartz, turquoise, spools of cotton thread. Her favorite animals include bats, owls and ravens. Speak to her, describe your experiences in detail and request that she provide cleansing and renewal. This is best done before going to sleep, so that the actual cleansing as well as any messages from the spirit may be received in your dreams. A visit to the temescal may also be in order. If this is not a realistic option, try a steam shower with fragrant herbs, like sage, spearmint, chamomile and rosemary.

Cleansing Objects and Ritual Tools

Any object may be spiritually cleansed using the various cleansing techniques; just make sure that the technique will not harm the object. (Sprinkling **Indigo Water** on a crystal, for instance, is fine. If you soak fabric in **Indigo Water**, on the other hand, it will turn blue.)

- ★ Pass objects through incense smoke
- ★ Fumigate them using a smudge stick
- ★ Asperge with cleansing waters: **Holy Water, Marie Laveau Water** and **Rose of Jericho Water** are particularly effective, however choose what suits your purposes best. Salt water provides a strong cleansing, providing the object will not be damaged by salt
- ★ Singing bowls will cleanse objects as well as areas and individuals

 Balancing Cleansing

Myrrh represents the female principle, frankincense the male. Although most frequently they're blended, this spell suggests alternating between the two.

Burn myrrh and burn frankincense simultaneously but separately. Pass ritual tools through myrrh smoke and then through frankincense, alternating between the two until the spell feels complete, for cleansing, charging, and balancing.

 Desert Sage Cleansing

Pass ritual objects, crystals, and mirrors through desert sage smoke to cleanse and empower them.

Cleansing Crystals

Crystals and gemstones absorb and store energy. Depending upon how they're used, they may need to be cleansed periodically and re-charged.

Various cleansing methods exist:

- ★ Bury the stone in the ground overnight or longer. This is most potent if done outside, but if this is not possible, burying in a flowerpot filled with dirt will work, too. (If you would like to retain the stone, be sure to mark the burial spot.)
- ★ Expose the crystal to sunlight and/or moonlight

- ★ Pass the crystal through incense smoke
- ★ Many clear crystals may be cleansed with salt water: collect ocean water or add sea salt to spring water
- ★ Many of the Charged Waters in the formulary may be used to cleanse crystals, particularly **Florida Water** or **Notre Dame Water**
- ★ Salt may leach color from a vivid crystal or damage a fragile one, like moldavite: bathe crystals in spring water with the addition of a few drops of Dr. Bach's Rescue Remedy or similar emergency flower remedy formula

Cleansing Crystal Balls

It is crucial that crystal balls and scrying glass are kept cleansed, both physically and spiritually. A dusty crystal ball reveals nothing. A crystal ball covered with negative spiritual debris may reveal distortions.

Cleanse with the following:

- ★ A blend of spring water and vinegar
- ★ One of the charged waters: **Holy Water, Marie Laveau Water** and **Notre Dame Water** are particularly recommended
- ★ A water-based herbal infusion made with dried mugwort and/or anise seeds
- ★ Mugwort hydrosol

Add flower essence remedies as desired to any of the above formulas. Mugwort flower essence remedy enhances the crystal ball's powers; Dr. Bach's Rescue Remedy or a similar emergency formula will remove and assimilate disturbing or traumatic visions seen within.

Cleansing a Magic Mirror

Mirrors, like crystals, store information. In theory, anything reflected within a mirror, particularly over an extended period of time, is stored within and may be accessed.

Like cleaning out computer files, cleansing removes the mirror's memory and allows you to start afresh. This is particularly crucial if would like to use an antique mirror of unknown provenance. You have no idea what is in that mirror and what may, thus, emerge.

In addition, if you would like to dedicate a mirror to a new goal or purpose, a thorough cleansing is recommended. These techniques may also be used to consecrate a mirror for any purpose:

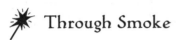 Through Smoke

Pass the mirror through incense smoke, holding it in the smoke for several minutes. Repeat several times. Lillian Too, a world-renowned feng shui authority, recommends no less than a series of three to complete a cleansing or consecration.

Use any of the cleansing incense formulas, or create your own blend from one or more of the following sacred cleansing incenses: dragon's blood, Syrian rue (harmel), frankincense, benzoin, mastic, wormwood, sandalwood.

The Water Method

1. Place the mirror within a basin.
2. Pour bottled spring water or collected rainwater over the mirror.
3. Remove the mirror and dispose of the water. (It may be given to plants but should not be used for bathing or drinking.)
4. Wipe the mirror with a soft, clean cloth.
5. Repeat for a total of three ritual repetitions, gently wiping the mirror in between each.

Living waters are most effective. The ritual may also be performed outside in a stream, waterfall or ocean. However, if necessary, tap water will suffice for the purpose.

Cleansing Magic Ritual Fabrics

If it is safe to cleanse with water, add all or any of the following to the rinse water:

★ *A few drops of Dr. Bach's Rescue Remedy or similar formula*
★ *A few drops of essential oil of cajeput*
★ *A few drops of essential oil of lavender*
★ *A few drops of essential oil of manuka (New Zealand tea tree)*

Fabrics may also be spiritually cleansed, if not actually cleansed, through smoke.

Prepare any of the incense or fumigation formulas in the Cleansing Spells Section. Carefully pass the fabric through the smoke, making sure that it does not burn.

Cleansing a Magic Sword

The following are suggestions for the care, cleansing and consecration of a magic sword based on instructions from the sixteenth century:

1. Build a fire from bay laurel and vervain.
2. Pass the sword through the smoke, actually holding it in the flame if this is safe and appropriate.
3. When it cools, wrap the sword in vervain leaves.
4. Swaddle it in white silk and maintain it this way when not in use.

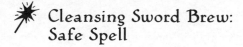 ## Cleansing Sword Brew: Safe Spell

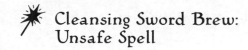 ## Cleansing Sword Brew: Unsafe Spell

This spell is used to cleanse and consecrate metal ritual tools, such as magic swords and daggers. Simmer rue, stinging nettles and vervain in an iron cauldron. When it's steaming, plunge the blades into the water and then remove them.

Dogs, even magical ones, have a tendency to drool. Wolfsbane allegedly grew where Cerberus, the dog of the dead's saliva hit Earth. Also known as aconite, wolfsbane is used to simultaneously cleanse and empower metal ritual tools. This is an old spell and presumably someone has cast it, however incredible caution is advised: even handling wolfsbane can be dangerous. That said, create an infusion of wolfsbane and cleanse metal blades, wands, and other tools in it.

Courtcase Spells: Legal Spells and Spells for Justice

Courtcase Spells

"Courtcase" is Hoodoo terminology for any kind of legal or justice-oriented spell, even if there are no plans to actually venture into the courthouse. Courtcase spells may also be interpreted as an attempt to maintain autonomy (for good *or* bad intent) despite those who would assert unwanted authority over you or interfere with your plans. The courthouse itself may be seen as a metaphoric crossroads: the place where fortunes shift, literally and figuratively. Courtcase spells attempt to seize the spinning wheel of fortune and turn it in the spell-caster's favor.

On the other hand, few things in life are genuinely as stressful as the possibility of landing in jail. As usual, the more dramatic the problem, the greater the number of magic spells. There are spells to get out of jail and to stay out of jail; spells to put someone else in jail; spells to have someone released from prison and spells to keep them locked up. There are spells to invoke the sympathy of judge and jury and spells intended to hinder your opponent's allies. There are spells to enhance testimony and spells to prevent someone from telling everything they know.

You'll find a preponderance of courtcase spells from certain areas of the world and certain magical traditions. This is because only magical practitioners from those cultures where the *possibility* of legal justice exists bother to develop courtcase and legal spells.

Of course, there's one inherent flaw in courtcase magic. Presumably *everyone* in the courtroom has some magic tricks up their sleeve. Does all this spell-casting cancel each other out? Theoretically at least, success goes to the strongest magician or the one with the better spell, the more potent materials, the most powerful spiritual protection. If this doesn't provide enough reassurance, there's also a subcategory of justice spells—spells that petition the universe and various spirit forces to see that justice prevails; if you're completely sure that you're in the right, that isn't a bad place to begin.

There's even magical protection against another party's attempts to magically influence your case: wear a sprig of fresh rue, or a *cimaruta*, the Italian silver charm which mimics rue.

Many spells specifically target judges, attorneys, expert witnesses and members of the jury.

Individuals serving in those roles should perhaps always presume that attempts at magical influence will be made. A sprig of rue automatically worn as part of one's courtroom uniform might be wise.

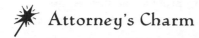

Attorney's Charm

Some babies are born with cauls, *a thin membrane covering the newborn's head, allegedly a sure sign that a child has been blessed (or cursed, depending upon one's orientation) with* second sight, *defined as clairvoyance and extensive psychic power, the sixth sense. Not only does the caul confer power, the caul itself is perceived as being magically charged with power and is traditionally preserved as an amulet. Once upon a time ancient Roman midwives sold cauls as spiritual supplies. Allegedly their best market was the Forum where attorneys paid top dollar.*

Attorneys are advised to wear cauls over their chests during legal proceedings to enhance chances of victory.

Hoodoo-style courtcase spells are fairly simple to improvise. There's a basic repertoire of botanicals, candles and condition oils that magically enhance your chances of legal success and vindication. Each may be used individually or they may be combined—however inspiration strikes.

Basic Courtcase Candle Spells

Brown and/or purple candles are burned for legal success and victories: brown represents justice, while purple represents power.

The most basic courtcase spell is as follows:

1. Obtain an appropriate candle.
2. Hold it in your hands, charging it with your power and desire.
3. Carve and dress the candle as desired, and then burn it.

*To dress the candle use one of the basic courtcase condition oils listed below, a **Commanding Oil** or any combination of these oils.*

Basic Courtcase Condition Oils

The following condition oils are multifaceted and powerful. Among their many uses are legal success, vindication and justice. Formulas are found in the *Formulary* (page 1037). Dress charms, candles and mojo hands with these oils. They may be used to supplement and reinforce other oils as well.

Courtcase Oil
Fiery Wall of Protection
San Cipriano Oil

Basic Courtcase Condition Oil Quick-Fix Spell

1. Dip a cotton ball in any of these condition oils.
2. Carry it in your pocket or tucked into your bra during legal proceedings.

Basic Courtcase Spell Botanicals

Although, as we will see, many other botanicals have beneficial magical courtcase uses, the following are the "*old reliables*" of courtcase magic. Incorporate them into any courtcase spell for extra enhancement. At their most basic, carry one or any combination of these botanicals in a charm bag during legal proceedings.

★ *Black poppy seeds: to sow confusion amongst your enemies and adversaries*
★ *Calendula blossoms: to promote legal victories and to enhance and stimulate self-respect*

★ *Deer's tongue: there's no need to mutilate Bambi; this is a botanical that reputedly provides eloquence to its bearer and the bearer's attorney*

★ *Slippery elm: to protect against false testimony and accusations*

✳ Basic Courtcase Spell Botanical Candle

1. Carve a brown and/or purple candle to suit your situation.
2. Hold it in your hands to charge it with your desired intention.
3. Dress the candle with **Courtcase Oil, Fiery Wall of Protection Oil** and/or **San Cipriano Oil.** If desired, add a **Commanding Oil,** too.
4. Roll the carved, oiled candle into any or all of the dried, powdered basic courtcase spell botanicals.
5. Burn the candle(s).

✳ Basic Courtcase Spell Botanical Mojo Hand

1. Place a pinch of the basic courtcase botanicals into a red or brown conjure bag.
2. Add a pinch of dirt from the grounds of your local courthouse. (If this is not possible, substitute crossroads dirt.)
3. Dress with one drop of one of **Courtcase Oil, Fiery Wall of Protection Oil** or **San Cipriano Oil.**

Beef Tongue Spells

Perhaps the most notorious of all legal success spells, today this genre of spells is strongly associated with the southern United States, however its ancient roots stretch back to Great Britain. Transported to the Western hemisphere, these spells were further developed and refined by the Hoodoo and New Orleans Voodoo traditions.

According to this genre (only possible in cultures where meat is not an unusual part of the diet), specific organ meats are magically dressed and embellished to provide the desired goal. Old spells featured sheep or cow's hearts as frequently as tongues, although only the tongue spells seem to retain their popularity, perhaps for the obvious reason: tongues, unlike hearts, still occasionally remain on the menu.

In no way do these spells require animal sacrifice: they are outcroppings of a meat-based diet. The meat was obtained from professional butchers or from butchering your own livestock: the desired piece of meat could be discreetly purchased or spirited away. Try to purchase a sheep's heart today without drawing undue attention to yourself! Concocting some sort of story about a biology experiment may be required. Raw beef tongue may still be purchased from a butcher, although it's become an expensive luxury item in many areas, rather than a plain kitchen staple.

✳ Beef Tongue Courtcase Spell (1) The Basic Version

This spell is intended to provide legal victory.

1. Write the names of the judge, attorneys, adversaries, anyone who involved in your case who may be perceived as your opponent or an ally of your opponent, on individual slips of paper, about the size of the fortune in a fortune cookie. Each name gets its own piece of paper.
2. Using a sharp knife, cut slits into a beef tongue, one slit per paper.
3. Insert one name paper into each slit.
4. Sprinkle with cayenne pepper and vinegar **(Four Thieves** is recommended, but not necessary).
5. Close the slits with pins and needles.

6. Wrap the tongue up and place it securely in your freezer for at least a year or until you're sure all danger has passed.

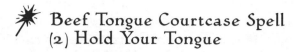

Beef Tongue Courtcase Spell (2) Hold Your Tongue

This spell may be adapted to prevent false testimony, or perhaps to prevent any testimony at all.

1. Write the names of all hostile witnesses, or anyone who needs to either be silenced or encouraged to only speak the truth, on individual pieces of paper.
2. Cross over each name with your own before placing the paper into the tongue.
3. Alternatively, cross over each name with phrases like, *"Keep quiet!"* or *"Shut up!"*
4. Focus on your desire while writing: express it aloud, forcefully telling the individuals in question to shut their mouths.
5. Pin the slits shut. Dress with cayenne and vinegar and either place the tongue in the freezer or follow the next spell's directions.

Beef Tongue Courtcase Spell (3) Cooked Tongue

Should a civil suit be threatened, prepare the beef tongue with name papers and pins and needles as above but instead of putting the tongue on ice, cook and eat it.

1. Write all your opponents' names on individual slips of paper.
2. Make slits in the tongue and insert the name papers.
3. Seal the slits shut with pins and needles.
4. Sprinkle the tongue with cayenne and vinegar, but go easy if necessary because you will have to eat the tongue. It's tempting to smother the tongue in cayenne but don't add so much that it will be impossible for you to eat.

5. Boil the tongue with garlic and salt. Season it as you like it. Some versions suggest adding brown beans, too.
6. Cook everything, including the paper and pins.
7. Eat the papers but carefully remove all pins and needles, placing them in a brown paper bag.
8. Do not reuse the pins and needles or throw them out inside your home. Instead dispose of them away from your home, going and returning via different, circuitous routes.

Beef Tongue Courtcase Spell (4) Hung Jury

The beef tongue spell can be adapted to encourage a hung jury—a split jury unable to achieve a verdict. This version typically requires the assistance of another person as it must be performed while you're present in the courtroom.

1. Write each opponent's name on individual slips of paper.
2. Do not make slits in the beef tongue. Instead cut a hole in the tip of the tongue.
3. Stuff the papers into the hole. They may stay by themselves, however pin the hole loosely shut, if necessary or preferred.
4. Suspend the tongue over a hot fire, with the tip close to but not touching the flames.
5. Maintain this as long as necessary until a verdict is achieved, or not, as the case may be.

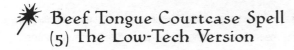

Beef Tongue Courtcase Spell (5) The Low-Tech Version

If the use of beef tongues is as old as it's reputed to be, how was the basic spell accomplished before the advent of refrigeration? Should disaster cause extended power failures, will this genre of spells go the way of the dinosaurs? Luckily an old-fashioned method of preparing this spell exists.

1. Write out all name papers and place them within slits cut into the tongue as in the spells above.
2. Close up the slits with pins and needles.
3. Place the tongue between two large blocks of ice.
4. Wrap up this tongue sandwich in white silk and bury it in Earth.

Once tucked away, whether in Earth or the ice-box, it's not customary to make any further adjustments. However if you feel that it may become necessary for you to go back and play with the ingredients, this version must be done immediately prior to the courtcase because, obviously, without refrigeration, the beef tongue cannot stay secret for long.

Beef Tongue Courtcase Spell (6) The Vegetarian Version

A vegetarian version eliminates the need for refrigeration and *the beef tongue.*

1. Create a name paper for each individual opponent.
2. Cross over the names with your own, if you like, saying something like: *"I cross you and I cover you, I command you and I compel you to tell the truth* [or whatever it is that you wish them to do]."
3. Place these name papers between two red bricks.
4. The spell, up to this point, may be assembled at any time. During the actual trial proceedings, set a metal bucket of ice atop the bricks.

This spell is strengthened by sprinkling the name papers with your menstrual blood or urine prior to placing between the bricks. The bricks may also be ringed by appropriate burning candles.

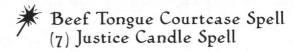

Beef Tongue Courtcase Spell (7) Justice Candle Spell

The beef tongue spells are frequently accompanied and fortified by simultaneously burning brown justice candles, representing a plea for justice. Carve and dress a brown candle so that it complements the theme of your beef tongue spell.

There are as many variations with the candle as there are with the tongue itself.

Namely, when to burn the candle, and where to burn the candle?

★ *Burn the candle while the tongue is cooking on the stove*
★ *Keep dressed brown candles burning from the moment the tongue hits the freezer until the case is resolved*
★ *Burn the candle on the stove near the cooking tongue*
★ *Burn the candle on an altar dedicated to a deity or set up for the specific situation*
★ *Burn the candle atop the toilet tank in the bathroom*

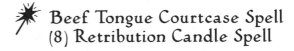

Beef Tongue Courtcase Spell (8) Retribution Candle Spell

Another candle ritual also frequently accompanies beef tongue spells, although this one is an angry plea for protection and vindication.

1. While the beef tongue is cooking or once it's been placed in the freezer, prepare a black pillar candle.
2. Slice off the top of the candle, so that it's flat.
3. Carve the bottom of the candle, so that the wick is exposed and can be lit. You have now reversed the candle.

4. Carve and dress this candle as you find appropriate: **Commanding Oils** should be included.
5. Place powdered sweet flag and licorice root onto a dish.
6. Place the upside-down candle on the dish and burn it atop the toilet tank.

Name papers may be placed under the candle on the dish, so that the wax drips on them. If one person alone is the target of this spell, write that name on a square of brown paper and place under the candle.

*If you are really furious or really terrified and determined to destroy the other party's very capacity to testify, place the candle on a bed of **Goofer Dust,** instead of or in addition to the powdered commanding herbs.*

Although many variations of these spells exist, it is imperative that the candles are burned in the bathroom. They are the descendants of out-house spells: older versions specified that reversed candles, black if at all possible, be left burning all night, stuck into a dish of feces.

 ## Bloodstone Courthouse Charm Spell

The crystal gemstone bloodstone reputedly provides success in legal matters.

1. Soak a bloodstone in rosemary water: either pour one cup of boiling water over one teaspoon of dried rosemary or use rosemary hydrosol.
2. Wrap the bloodstone inside white cloth while the crystal is still a bit damp.
3. Tie the packet together with red thread, knotting your desire into the charm.
4. Carry it in your left pocket while you're in the courtroom.

 ## Cascarilla Keep Away Powder

*This next spell promises to provide safety from law enforcement agencies, bill collectors or any unwanted interference from the authorities. Although authorities may appear and attempt to exert their power, this version of **Cascarilla Powder** allegedly prevents them from succeeding.*

1. Follow the instructions in the *Formulary* for making white **Cascarilla Powder**—dried eggshell powder—with the proviso that the eggs *must* come from a black hen.
2. Place this powder under your front doorstep and/or make an unbroken circle with it around your house or property.

Chestnut Talisman

1. Drill a hole in a chestnut.
2. Fill the hole with sage and tobacco and seal it up with melted black candle wax.
3. Keep it with you while in court; place the chestnut in your left pocket so that you may fondle it constantly but discreetly, internally focused on your desired goal.

Crystal Courtcase Magic Charms

Remember to empower all charms by charging and consecrating them prior to initial use and then cleansing as needed.

★ *Chalcedony, pierced and strung on a donkey hair tail, renders the wearer fortunate in legal matters*
★ *Hematite protects and assists all legal situations. Wear or carry on the body*
★ *A malachite bead necklace protects against litigation, but if that's too late, malachite is still beneficial: it also brings courtroom success*

★ *Too litigious? Wearing moonstones and topaz allegedly relieves one of a fondness for lawsuits. Give one as a gift to relieve someone else of that predilection, too*

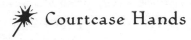

Courtcase Hands

*Rub your hands with **Courtcase Oil** prior to signing important legal documents.*

Courtcase Mirror Box

This spell isolates your adversaries and prevents them from bothering you.

1. Obtain six small square mirrors, placing them together so that they form a box. The reflective side of the mirrors may be inside or outside the box depending upon your desire. If you merely wish to isolate and vanquish your adversaries, keep them in darkness with the mirrors on the outside of the box. If they're a mean bunch and you'd like them to turn on each other, instead of on you, place the mirrored surfaces on the inside of the box.
2. Leave the top open but attach the bottom and sides, using clear tape.
3. Write your adversaries' names and an affirmation of your intentions on a piece of parchment paper.
4. Place it within the box, seal it shut and hide it away.

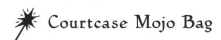

Courtcase Mojo Bag

Carry hickory nuts in a mojo bag to obtain legal success.

Courtcase Root Spells

The botanical most associated with legal victories has earned the sobriquet Courtcase root. This is only one of *Alpinia galangal's* many aliases. Asian cookbooks call it galangal or laos. Keeping company with the botanically distinct High John and Low John, Hoodoo workers also call this root Southern John or Little John to Chew, after its most famous mode of administration. Unlike so many occult roots, this cousin of ginger doesn't have a bitter, unpleasant taste, hence its use in cooking. Its most famous metaphysical use involves chewing, although very definitely not swallowing.

Famous Hoodoo doctors, like Doctor Buzzard, earned reputations by winning courtroom battles for their clients. Once upon a time, not that long ago, Doctor Buzzard was paid a lot of money to sit in the courtroom and chew. At the moment deemed appropriate, the root and/or its juice was spat out in the appropriate direction. Because Doctor Buzzard, in particular, was such a visible, recognizable presence with a powerful magical reputation, an inherent intimidation factor must also be acknowledged.

Courtcase root has earned a wide reputation for providing courtcase success. Try the traditional spell, if you like, although what worked for Doctor Buzzard may get you the wrong kind of attention: public spitting is largely considered déclassé nowadays as well as being illegal in many areas. Luckily there are many other ways to find success with Courtcase root.

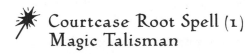

Courtcase Root Spell (1)
Magic Talisman

The simplest method of benefiting from Courtcase root:

1. Hold Courtcase root between your hands, prior to its initial use, charging it with your desires and needs.
2. Carry it as a talisman. Tuck the root into your pocket or carry it in a mojo bag.

Courtcase Root Spell (2)

A reasonably discreet spell, this is among the most basic, traditional methods of Courtcase root magic.

Arrive at court early. Chew Courtcase root while envisioning the desired outcome. Discreetly spit out the root onto the floor before the judge enters. Allegedly proceedings will go in your favor.

 ## Courtcase Root Spell (3) Courtcase Oil

Courtcase root is the primary ingredient in Courtcase Oil.

1. Chop up some Courtcase root.
2. Blend the chopped roots together with black mustard seeds and grind them together.
3. Add any other botanicals associated with legal victories, if you like, such as deer's tongue or slippery elm.
4. Place the ground up botanicals in a bottle and cover with a blend of jojoba and sunflower oils.

 ## Courtcase Root Spell (4) Courtcase Inspiration Incense

Courtcase root may be burned as incense. Burning and inhaling this incense allegedly stimulates legal inspiration and smart thinking.

1. Grind Courtcase root together with High John the Conqueror and cascara sagrada.
2. Sprinkle onto lit charcoal and burn.

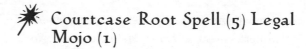 ## Courtcase Root Spell (5) Legal Mojo (1)

1. Place a Courtcase root within a charm bag together with black poppy seeds, calendula blossoms, deer's tongue and slippery elm.
2. Anoint with Courtcase Oil or other dressing oils as desired.
3. Carry with you, especially when in court.

 ## Courtcase Root Spell (6) Legal Mojo (2)

1. Burn Courtcase root for fourteen consecutive nights prior to the court date.
2. Reserve all the ashes, place them in a mojo bag and carry with you to court.

 ## Courtcase Victory Bath

Bathe in an infusion of vervain before appearing in court. Allow yourself to air-dry.

 ## Danda Root Spell

Danda root, popular in Brazilian magical traditions, is also chewed but, unlike Courtcase root, spitting isn't emphasized. It's sufficient to keep a little piece of the root concealed in your cheek. Why would you want to do this? Because allegedly chewing danda root enables you to influence another's words. Concentrate very hard on what should be said, while chewing the root.

El Nino Fidencio is the affectionate nickname given to miracle healer, Jose Fidencio Sintora Constantino (1898–1938). He performed his first miraculous healing when he was a child, on his mother. By his mid-twenties, thousands, including a president of Mexico, were converging on the remote village in Northeastern Mexico, where El Nino performed his cures. He died young, some say poisoned by jealous competing physicians, yet his reputation only continues to grow, fueled by the miracles he continues to produce.

In addition to miracle physical healings, El Nino Fidencio has become a specialist in immigration issues. El Nino speeds the processing and arrival of official papers but may also be petitioned to keep official authorities far away and too busy to pay attention to you.

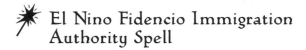

El Nino Fidencio Immigration Authority Spell

El Nino loved flowers, using their powers in many cures.

1. Post his image and offer him a bouquet: he accepts modest offerings made with good intent.
2. Light either a white candle or a commercially manufactured El Nino Fidencio candle.
3. Speak from your heart: tell him what is needed. The customary vow is to offer, that when possible, you too will provide assistance for someone else sharing your circumstances.

If you're asking for a large favor, a vow to make a pilgrimage to El Nino's shrine in Espinazo, Mexico may be in order.

Eloquence Spell (1)

Deer's tongue allegedly provides eloquence. It's nicknamed the lawyer's friend.

Ask your attorney to carry a little, as a special request. If you will be called upon to testify, place deer's tongue in a conjure bag and carry it in your pocket.

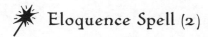

Eloquence Spell (2)

Lapis lazuli performs much of the same function. Should eloquence be required, carry lapis or ideally wear it as a necklace, with the stone lying against the throat chakra.

Fiery Wall of Protection Legal Spells

Fiery Wall of Protection Oil is one of the most powerful and versatile condition oil formulas. Its standard ingredients (including frankincense, myrrh and salt) create a profound protective effect but, in addition, **Fiery Wall** invokes the presence and power of Michael the Archangel, humanity's defender. Like Michael, **Fiery Wall** provides consistent, tireless protection. Although it can be used to dress candles and anoint charms, this formula's name indicates its most powerful use: allow it to create an aura of magical protection.

★ *Add the oil to your bath and bathe in it prior to court dates or other stressful appearances*
★ *Rub the oil onto your body*
★ *Anoint crucial documents with **Fiery Wall***

Follow Me Boy! Legal Spell

*Follow Me Boy! Oil is most frequently a component of erotic spells. However, like most commanding oils, it possesses a protective component. The oil was traditionally favored by New Orleans prostitutes, because of the necessity for both these aspects. Should one already be in hot legal water, put a Courtcase root inside a bottle of **Follow Me Boy! Oil**. Carve candles as suits your situation, then dress with the oil.*

Follow Me Boy! Prevention Spell

Soak cotton balls in **Follow Me Boy! Oil** and slip into your clothing to attract men and avoid trouble with the law.

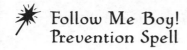 ## Foul-mouthed Powder Spell

Foul-mouthed (Cosearia hirsute) *earned its English nickname from its alleged powers to make the foul mouthed shut up. (Its Spanish nickname is similar,* raspa lengua.) *Those powers make it an integral part of Courtcase magic, although it's usually directed toward attorneys, prosecutors and legal professionals. Foul-mouthed powder doesn't promise victory, per se; it simply weakens your opponents.*

1. Pulverize foul-mouthed.
2. Blend it together with **Cascarilla Powder,** white sugar and cinnamon, creating a fine powder.
3. Sprinkle the powder on or around the chair or bench of the prosecutor or your adversary's attorney. This allegedly makes them quiet and less inclined to speak.

Should the opposing attorney step upon the powder, it allegedly affects his powers of speech: he may lose his voice, or his language may become slurred as if he were drinking. In either case, foul-mouthed encourages the attorney to make verbal mistakes. Foul-mouthed powder also encourages the attorney to become unwilling to represent your adversary.

 ## Gentle Sentence Spell

Carry gravel root and **Cascarilla Powder** *to receive a lenient sentence.*

 ## High John the Conqueror Victory Spell (1)

The root charm High John the Conqueror allegedly promotes victory in any endeavor, while conquering your opposition.

1. Take nine small High John roots or break one large root into nine pieces.
2. Cover it with half of a pint bottle of whisky. Drink the other half or offer it whomever you appeal to for spiritual protection.
3. Zora Neale Hurston's recommendation is to let the roots steep in the liquor for thirty-eight hours although others say overnight is sufficient.
4. Strain the liquid into a bottle.
5. Add approximately an ounce of a lucky cologne. Jockey Club is the traditional choice, however others will work, too, like **Florida Water** or especially **Chypre,** if you're involved in financial proceedings. Wear as needed.

 ## High John the Conqueror Victory Spell (2)

1. Line a small box with bay leaves and stuff it with calendula blossoms.
2. Add one High John the Conqueror root.
3. Remove High John from its magic box and carry with you as a courtcase talisman as needed. When not in use, let it sleep on its calendula bed, absorbing calendula's powers of legal victory.

Legend has it that during the wars between Christians and Moors in Spain, Christians in the town of Atocha were locked in prison and abandoned to their fate. They would have starved but for the daily appearance of a beautiful small boy who brought them food and water to survive. This continued until Christian forces re-took the town, liberating the prisoners. Who was that child? Many thought he was the Christ Child in person. The little boy continues to turn up in Atocha, Spain periodically, performing miracles and emergency rescues. The Holy Child of Atocha has also earned a reputation for responding to magical courtcase appeals.

A votive image has become formalized of a very beautiful, richly dressed child seated on a throne. The popularity of this image spread from Spain to Latin America and then to the various African-derived spiritual traditions that took root in nations that were once Spanish colonies.

This raises a question: when appeals for legal assistance are made to the Holy Child of Atocha, exactly who is being requested to help? Is it the Christ Child himself or is it Elegba, the West African trickster spirit, wearing a mask? This is particularly confusing in Latin American magic, so influenced by both the African Diaspora and Spanish traditions. Arguments can be made on all sides.

However, in either case, the Holy Child accepts appeals for all sorts of legal issues, but his specialty is the prevention and delay of lawsuits.

✳ The Holy Child of Atocha's Legal Appeal Spell

1. Place his image facing your front door, or right behind it, to increase his powers of vigilance.
2. Offer him a golden candle, lots of candy and some rum (just in case he's not a child). The most effective day to request his assistance is Monday.

If syncretism and the associations of African spirits with Roman Catholic saints annoys you, then bypass the masks. Spiritual and magical supply stores sell images of Elegba in the form of a concrete head with cowrie shell eyes and ears. Arrange this head as directed above. Offer him rum but instead of the candy give him a fine cigar.

Invocation of Michael the Archangel

If there's one presence you'd want to have on your side in the courtroom, it's Michael the Archangel. Michael's celestial mission is to be humanity's defender. He epitomizes justice. Request that he come to your assistance.

Post his image, burn fragrant gum resins and use his invocation to call him:

Michael to the right of me,
Michael to the left of me
Michael above me
Michael below me
Michael within me
Michael all around me
Michael with your flaming sword of cobalt blue, protect
*   me today!*

Law Keep Away Spells

In the words of the Bobby Fuller Four, "*I fought the law and the law won.*" Some legal battles are won by not starting the fight at all; maybe your best possible outcome involves keeping the law far away. Law Keep Away spells target legal authorities but also any individuals or organizations that maintain a threat of authority over you: immigration officials, school boards, taxation boards, and the suchlike.

✳ Law Keep Away Oil (1)

1. Place a High John the Conqueror root, a Courtcase root, a tablespoon of dried hydrangea blossoms and a teaspoon of asafetida powder in a jar.
2. Cover the ingredients with a blend of two parts olive oil with one part each castor and jojoba oils.
3. Allow them to soak overnight, preferably exposed to moonbeams, then strain out the solids and bottle the liquid.

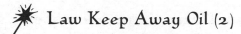 ## Law Keep Away Oil (2)

An alternative method of preparation:

1. Grind the botanicals as given above into a fine powder (this is difficult if working with a whole High John the Conqueror: it's a hard, solid root).
2. Place the powder in a bottle, and cover with olive, castor and jojoba oils in the above proportions.

Use Law Keep Away Oil to dress vigil candles: candles kept burning until all danger has passed. Or rub Law Keep Away Oil on your doorknobs to encourage authority figures who touch them to turn away and leave you alone.

 ## Law Keep Away Powder

1. Grind High John the Conqueror, Courtcase root, hydrangea blossoms, asafetida and black poppy seeds into powder.
2. Sprinkle a boundary line across the path to your home or cast an unbroken circle around your property.

 ## Law Keep Away Spell (1)
Sacred Texts

Recite Psalms 9, 16 and 53, nine times each, daily, to keep the law away from your door.

 ## Law Keep Away Spell (2)
Black Skull Candle Spell

The following spell is considered especially effective for avoiding taxation and immigration authorities:

1. Dress a black skull candle with Law Keep Away Oil.
2. Write your goals and aspirations on a piece of paper.

3. Light the skull candle. Scorch the paper in its flame.
4. Place the paper beneath an upside-down saucer on which you then place the candle, so that it burns over the paper.
5. Burn the candle in consistently timed increments (chosen with regard to your personal situation), pinching it out with your fingers when the time is up.
6. Once the candle has burned fairly low, burn the paper in its flame completely, before allowing the candle to burn out naturally.

 ## Law Keep Away Spell (3)
Conjure Bag Spell

Fennel seeds ward off authority: police and other law enforcement officials, immigration authorities, tax collectors, etc.

1. Place a handful of fennel seeds inside a small bag.
2. Hang it discreetly inside your home, just over the entrance door.

 ## Law Keep Away Spell (4)
Crabgrass

Hang crabgrass in each corner of all rooms to confuse, distract, and disorient the police.

Law Keep Away Spell (5)
Sacred Image Spell

A popular New Orleans-style protection spell involves attaching packets of Grains of Paradise to sacred images. This practice may be adapted into a "law keep-away spell."

1. Place either fennel seeds or a blend of fennel and Grains of Paradise into two small bags. (Use paper bags or cloth pouches: plastic, in theory, is acceptable but has the disadvantage of exposing contents to view.)
2. Attach these packets to the back of an image of Michael the Archangel.
3. Post one image at the front door, the second at the back.

If your fear is very specifically of immigration authorities, an image of El Nino Fidencio may be substituted for the archangel Michael.

Sometimes the problem is not the presence of authority but its absence. Perhaps someone close to you is engaged in activities that are dangerous and should be stopped. Perhaps it would be better for all concerned if someone's activities were brought to the attention of the authorities. Although the obvious response is call the police or inform the appropriate authorities, if only anonymously, magic spells acknowledge the complexities of human situations. Perhaps it's not as simple or safe as just making a phone call. This following spell purports to draw legal attention toward your target without, providing your spell casting isn't witnessed, drawing attention toward you.

Law Please Come Soon Spell

1. A handful of dirt from the actual area that the police need to investigate is required, whether this is the target of your spell's residence or place of business or other.
2. In addition, you'll need a handful of graveyard dirt and a handful of dirt from each of the following places: a crossroads, a prison, a courthouse and four different police stations. If the **Graveyard Dust** does not actually contain dirt, obtain a handful of dirt from a cemetery as well.
3. Blend all the dirt together in a bowl.
4. Use a black seven-day candle or burn each of seven individual black candles daily.
5. Carve and dress the candle with a **Commanding Oil** and **San Cipriano Oil.**
6. Stand the candle within the bowl of dirt and burn it.
7. On the eighth day, when the candle(s) have completely burnt down, sprinkle the remnants of the wax, together with the dirt, onto the targeted individual's property.

 ## Legal Victory Spell (1)

This spell allegedly assures your victory and your opponent's defeat.

1. Blend **Four Thieves Vinegar** with either sea salt or black salt to form a damp paste.
2. Use this to sprinkle a line across your adversary's path.
3. The person must step on or over this line for your goal to be accomplished.

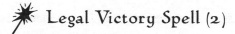

Legal Victory Spell (2)

*In addition to mere success, this spell promises that elusive quality: vindication. Cascara sagrada, the bark of the California buckthorn, translates in English to sacred bark. Once upon a time, it was a frequent component of Native American magic. It's highly endangered today. If you're unable to obtain it or aren't sure whether it's been ethically collected, substitute **Cascarilla Powder.***

1. Pour boiling water over cascara sagrada, making a strong infusion.
2. Sprinkle this infusion on the front steps of the courthouse and/or around the building's perimeter at the midnight prior to your court date.

Allegedly, if anyone witnesses your actions, this spell won't work.

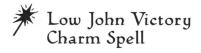

Low John Victory Charm Spell

This charm allegedly guarantees all sorts of victories— romantic and interpersonal as well as legal.

1. Place a Low John root (bethroot) in a shallow dish and cover it with **Notre Dame Water.**
2. Let this sit overnight, ideally charged by moonlight, then carry the root as a charm.

Name Paper Legal Victory Spell (1) Your Enemies

This spell enables you to exert authority over your opponents.

1. Write the names of all adversaries or even potential adversaries on individual slips of paper. Include the judge, attorneys, opponents and their witnesses and so forth.

2. Place these papers on a dish.
3. Cover with honey, strawberry syrup and nine lumps or spoonfuls of white sugar.
4. Carve a candle and dress it with one of the **Commanding Oils,** whichever feels most appropriate to you.
5. Place the candle on the dish and burn it.
6. When the candle has burned completely, bury all spell remnants outside in Earth.

For maximum magical effectiveness, combine this spell with the next one.

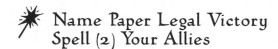

Name Paper Legal Victory Spell (2) Your Allies

1. Several days prior to the scheduled court proceedings, assemble the names of all parties favorable toward you: your allies, attorney, favorable witnesses and so on.
2. Write each name on a slip of paper and place them in a dish.
3. Cover with sweet almond oil, olive oil and/or honey.
4. Burn a white candle beside the dish for one hour daily, then pinch out the flame with your fingers.
5. On the actual day of the trial, don't pinch out the candle but allow it to burn during the proceedings.

Ogun, that prominent and versatile West African spirit, serves as patron of police. Police officers may request his protection. However, depending upon circumstances, Ogun may also be prevailed upon to protect others *from* the police. The iron-handed spirit of justice and righteousness, Ogun is frequently syncretized with archangel Michael. An image of Michael may be used to represent Ogun *providing* Michael is depicted holding his lance or sword. The more traditional method of representing Ogun on an altar is with a piece of iron, such as a horseshoe, knife or tool.

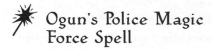 Ogun's Police Magic
Force Spell

1. Place a piece of iron on an altar.
2. Burn a double-action candle and some dragon's blood incense.
3. Offer Papa Ogun over-proof rum and a good cigar and tell him what you need.

 Pomba Gira Cigana Spell (1)

Pomba Gira Cigana specializes in legal matters, including lawsuits, estate distribution, immigration matters, separations, divorces, and custody issues. Cigana is Portuguese for Gypsy, and Pomba Gira Cigana personifies the stereotypical Gypsy fortune-teller. She knows many secrets and divines with a pack of ordinary playing cards. If you can read cards, too, a deck of playing cards serves as an oracle or communication device for Pomba Gira Cigana. To request her assistance:

1. Get a brand new deck of cards. Remove the ace and seven of diamonds and offer them to Pomba Gira Cigana.
2. Make your offering at a T-shaped crossroads: place a red cloth atop a black cloth.
3. Give Pomba Gira Cigana the pair of cards as well as seven red roses, fine cigarettes, a box of matches and a small bottle of anisette.
4. Light a pair of red taper candles.
5. Tell Pomba Gira why you've called her. Tell her explicitly what you need her to do and what you will pay her when the work is accomplished.

 Pomba Gira Cigana Spell (2)

Alternatively, if you have little faith and would like proof of her abilities, merely present Pomba Gira Cigana with the two cards as a down payment.

1. Create a small altar for Pomba Gira Cigana: light two red taper candles and give Pomba Gira a red rose and a glass of either anisette or champagne.
2. Remove the ace and seven of diamonds from a new deck of playing cards.
3. Place the cards on the altar, when the candles have burned down, put the cards safely aside for Pomba Gira. (Do *not* lose them!) Tell her that when she demonstrates her prowess, you will deliver a more extensive, and expensive, offering. Tell her explicitly what and when this will be. She'll know that it's payment for services rendered because the reserved playing cards will be presented as a reminder.

This alternative plan has less chances of success because this small indoor offering may be insufficient to attract Pomba Gira's attention. However, if she's interested in a relationship with you, it may work.

 Red Pepper Name Paper Spell

This spell encourages reconciliation and empathy among parties. Initiate this spell fourteen days before court proceedings begin.

1. Slice a red bell pepper in half and remove the seeds.
2. Write the names of all the parties involved in your legal procedure on slips of paper.
3. Put them inside the pepper and add dillweed and coriander seeds.
4. Fit the halves of the pepper back together, sealing it shut.
5. Place it in the freezer and keep it there until after final legal resolution.

Sometimes you might wish to delay and stall proceedings but sometimes you don't. Delays are not always beneficial. Sometimes expediting matters is in your best interests. If attorneys or others are delaying your case, if you need to cut through bureaucracy and red tape, appeal to the master of speedy deliveries, Saint Expedite.

Saint Expedite Spell (1)

1. Offer Saint Expedite a glass of rum and a slice of pound cake.
2. Inform him that you'll bring him a whole bottle and cake if matters proceed as you've requested.
3. Light a white candle in his honor or a commercially manufactured Saint Expedite candle.

Some like to turn an image of Saint Expedite upside down or even suspend it upside down in the air in the belief that discomfort encourages the saint to work even faster.

Saint Expedite Spell (2)

If a specific opponent is responsible for the delay, bring this to Saint Expedite's attention:

1. Write your opponent's name nine times onto a square of brown paper.
2. Cross over the names eleven time with your own.
3. Place this paper under a candle or offerings made to the saint.

Target Judge Spell (1) Just Judge

At best, this spell allegedly stimulates kindly treatment and verdicts from the presiding judge. At the least, it is a plea for fairness, open mindedness and justice. It is also imperative to remember that this spell appeals simultaneously for two judges to be just: the one presiding over the courtroom but also the ultimate judge on high, whoever you perceive that to be.

1. On a single square of brown paper, write the names of all your adversaries and opponents, plus the names of any decision makers, judge and jury, as the case may be.

2. Drill a hole in a large block of ice.
3. Roll the paper up tightly and insert it into the hole.
4. Fill the hole, covering the paper, with confectioner's sugar. (It may melt quickly; let your intuition tell you when to stop filling the hole.)
5. Arrange nine brown candles around the ice and light them.
6. Rap on the floor with your fist nine times and chant: *"Just Judge, Just Judge, Save me!"*
7. Follow with explicit and precise petitions.

Target Judge Spell (2) Just Judge Charm Bag

1. Anoint a Courtcase root with Just Judge Oil and place it in a charm bag, together with dried carnation, bee balm, rattlesnake root, and yellow dock.
2. Add a coffin nail and wear or carry the bag during courtroom and legal proceedings for victory and mercy.

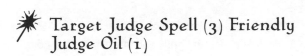 Target Judge Spell (3) Friendly Judge Oil (1)

Two parts dried carnation petals
One part anise seed
One part ground cinnamon

1. Blend the above ingredients together, grinding and powdering.
2. Place the powder inside a bottle.
3. Olive oil beseeches justice, castor oil creates a commanding, protective effect and jojoba oil brings victory as well as serving as a natural preservative. Fill the bottle containing the botanical powder with any one or a combination of these carrier oils.
4. Add a Courtcase root or chip or a hematite or bloodstone to the oil as desired.

Soak a cotton ball in Friendly Judge Oil and then try to maneuver it into the judge's clothing, box or chambers without, of course, getting caught. (It is not necessary for the judge to be physically present for this to be potentially effective.)

Target Judge Spell (4) Friendly Judge Oil (2)

A safer and possibly more effective spell using Friendly Judge Oil may be cast at home.

1. Obtain a brown or purple seven-day candle in a clear glass sleeve.
2. Dress the candle with Friendly Judge Oil.
3. Make a photocopy of an image of your judge or of his/her signature.
4. Attach this image to the seven-day candle.
5. Burn the candle while chanting, visualizing and affirming your desires.

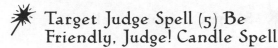 Target Judge Spell (5) Be Friendly, Judge! Candle Spell

1. Obtain a figure candle that best represents your judge. Appropriate male or female figure candles are most typical, especially if this spell is performed merely as a plea for kind consideration. If the judge has a reputation for being difficult, black or red devil candles may be substituted. (If the casting of this spell is stimulated by the judge's prior unmentionably negative attitude toward you, substitute a candle in the shape of a penis, even if the judge is a woman.)
2. Carve the candle with the judge's identifying information, as much as you have. Obviously the judge's birthday and his or her mother's name may not be known to you. Substitute the pertinent information you have: the judge's chamber or courtroom number for instance or a telephone number.
3. Dress the candle with Friendly Judge Oil. Add one of the **Commanding Oils** too, if desired.
4. Begin burning the candle, incrementally, as soon as possible. Continue during the duration of proceedings, starting with a fresh candle if the first burns completely down.

Target Judge Spell (6) Grains of Paradise

Grains of Paradise, with their evocative name, are most associated with love and aphrodisiac spells but are actually quite versatile and are used for legal and protection spells as well. They possess a magical commanding property. A key component of East African magic, they entered Western magical use through African-American traditions.

1. Pray over three Grains of Paradise, murmuring your desires and pleas over them.
2. Discreetly place these three grains on the judge's desk so that he or she will render a favorable verdict.

Target Jury Winning Spell (1)

The following Jury Winning Powder's goals are self-explanatory:

Asafetida
Courtcase root
High John the Conqueror
Dried hydrangea blossoms
Vetiver root

1. Grind all ingredients into a fine powder. This is particularly difficult with High John, which is a harder root than most. Place an entire High John between folded wax paper and smash it into chips with a hammer, before attempting to grind and powder.
2. If you'd like to extend the powder further, blend it into arrowroot powder.

There are two methods of obtaining benefits from Jury Winning Powder: sprinkle it around the jury box so that jurors will have to step on or over it, or cast a ring of powder around brown or purple candles and burn them at home.

Target Jury Winning Spell (2)

Wear celandine to court to inspire sympathy from judge and jury.

Tobacco Courtcase Spell

Use real botanical tobacco leaves for this spell, not the contents of cigarettes and cigars.

Blend tobacco leaves with sea salt. Burn them, accompanied by spiritual petitions and the recitation of psalms or other sacred verses.

Tongue Control Spell (1)

Five-finger grass, alias cinquefoil, is reputed to jog and stimulate memories as well as loosening tongues. This spell encourages a witness to testify, remember and talk.

1. Write the name of the spell's target on a piece of paper.
2. Place the paper on a dish and sprinkle cinquefoil over it.
3. Murmur over the cinquefoil and paper. Describe your needs and desires. Pray and petition as you deem appropriate; reciting psalms at this juncture may be recommended.
4. Carve and dress a white candle with information pertinent to your target and situation.
5. Place the candle over the cinquefoil-covered paper and burn.

Repeat as needed with fresh paper and five-finger grass.

Tongue Control Spell (2)

Sometimes someone's inclination to talk may be an undesirable aggravation, or indeed the very crux of a problem. The following spell offers protection from negative testimony. It also allegedly confuses witnesses scheduled to testify against you.

1. Blend and powder five-finger grass and brown mustard seeds.
2. Mix this powder with **Confusion Oil.**
3. Carve a brown candle to suit the target or situation and dress it with this oil.
4. Write your opponent's name nine times on a square of brown paper. (Each opponent gets his or her own piece of paper.)
5. Cover the names with your own, saying: *"I cross you, I command you, I compel you to* [name your desire].

☀ Tongue Control Spell (3)

The following spell counters gossip, slander and testimony against you. It is most powerful if performed standing at the center of a crossroad, however it may also be accomplished standing at a window. A sudden gust of wind is an extremely auspicious omen.

1. Blend a pinch of white sugar, a pinch of flour and a pinch of fine ground salt.
2. Hold the powder in the palm of your hand while visualizing your desired outcome. Direct your petition to the deity of your choice, if necessary. (If you'd like spiritual assistance but are unsure who to beseech, the archangel Michael and orisha Ogun, warriors who despise lies, are recommended, as is Ma'at, Egyptian dispenser of ultimate justice.)
3. Chant:
   I am innocent of these accusations!
   [Deity's name] *Protect me!*
4. Allow the powders to fly out of your hand.

☀ Trembling Aspen Spell

There are all sorts of legends explaining why the aspen tree trembles, ranging from fear of witchcraft to complicity in the crucifixion. Be that as it may, trembling aspen can be used to strengthen your position during courthouse proceedings.

1. Hold an aspen twig in your hands and charge it with your desire.
2. Murmur over the twig, saying something like: *"As this twig trembles, so trembles my opponent"* (name names if possible).
3. Place the charged twig in a mojo bag, together with other herbs including calendula blossoms, black poppy seeds and slippery elm.

Jesus Christ's twelve apostles are popular figures in Courtcase magic, apparently because of their metaphoric similarity to a twelve-person jury. The list of Apostles' names varies depending upon which Gospel is chosen for information. This list derives from Matthew 10:2–4, however use whichever version suits you best: Simon Peter; Andrew; James, the son of Zebedee; John, his brother; Philip; Bartholomew; Thomas; Matthew; James, the son of Alphaeus; Thaddeus; Simon the Canaanite; and Judas Iscariot.

☀ Twelve Apostles Courtcase Spell (1) Pow-Wow

John George Hohman's Book of Pow-Wows: The Long Lost Friend, *first published in 1820, compiles and chronicles the Pow-Wow canon, a combination of High Ritual Magic, German folk traditions, Romany magic, Kabala, and Native American healing.*

The Book of Pow-Wows' *recommendation for success in a law suit:*

1. Write the names of the Apostles on large sage leaves.
2. Wear these in your shoes, especially when in the courtroom, for legal victory and vindication.

☀ Twelve Apostles Courtcase Spell (2) Hung Jury

The spell suggested in The Book of Pow-Wows *is devout and sincere, suggesting that you bring the Apostles with you to court as allies and support (you literally walk on their strength)—a sort of stronger jury. Other versions of the spell consider the metaphor with historical detachment: if the Apostles are perceived as a jury of twelve, then ultimately a split decision was rendered, with Judas Iscariot insisting upon an independent course of action.*

Use the Twelve Apostles to help produce a divided jury, a jury unable to reach consensus. Perform this spell when called upon to be present in the courtroom.

1. On a small piece of paper, write the names of eleven apostles, omitting Judas Iscariot, in two columns, one of five names and the other of six.
2. Fold this paper up and place it in your right shoe.
3. Write Judas' name on his own piece of paper. Wear this one inside your left shoe.

Twelve Apostles Courtcase Spell (3) Determine the Decision

If you prefer aromatic sage leaves, redolent of justice to using just plain paper, another spell combines sage and the apostles' names to provide justice or a split decision, whichever favors your specific situation:

1. Write the names of eleven apostles, excluding Judas Iscariot, on individual leaves of sage. Place these inside your right shoe.
2. On another sage leaf write the name of the Biblical figure whom most closely relates to your immediate situation: the Biblical character with whom you most identify. For instance, choose Tamar to represent a disenfranchised former spouse or Judith, if you've killed an abusive man. Choose Gideon if you've committed what you perceive as justifiable homicide or Jezebel to represent the slandered and defamed. Venture away from the Bible into other fields of literature if you like (Shakespeare or Homer come to mind), however Biblical figures do lend a consistency to the spell. Certainly the Apostles themselves would be familiar with Biblical names. If your mind remains blank or no one suits your situation, keep the last leaf blank but make sure that it's kept separate from the other eleven.
3. Place this lone sage leaf in your left shoe.

Justice Spells

Perhaps, for one reason or another, it's unrealistic to expect justice to come from conventional sources. Some magical spells bypass official authority for individual pleas, petitions and actions to obtain vindication and justice.

Be careful: justice spells request that justice be done. Some of these spells veer very close to a hex. Make sure that there's no ambiguity about your situation or no other perspective with which to consider the matter, or the spell may just backfire!

Basic All-purpose Justice Spell

This is not a hex, nor a curse, there's no "edge" to this spell at all; it's purely and plainly a magical plea for justice.

Hold a brown candle in your hands, close your eyes and focus on your situation and circumstances: how justice has not been served and why it should. It's not necessary for you to envision the path to proper justice; that's for the powers of the universe to determine. When the candle feels charged and complete, burn it.

Bring a Rapist to Justice Spell (1)

The following spell enables the victim of a rapist to extract justice and perhaps to obtain a measure of closure. It is not necessary to know the identity of the rapist in order to cast the spell. Although it may be perceived as a vengeance spell, this is actually intended more as a prevention spell—to prevent this person from repeating his crimes.

1. Create a penis-shaped candle or purchase one.
2. Carve it as desired (although it must be left intact enough for you to burn it), with as much identifying information as possible.
3. Hold the candle and charge it with your goals and desires prior to dressing, because it may not be safe to hold the candle afterwards. (If you prefer, use plastic gloves.) Visualize the candle, and by extension the organ it represents, shrinking, melting, flopping over and unable to remain erect once the candle is lit.
4. Dress the candle with a combination of **Essence of Bend Over** and Tabasco sauce.
5. Roll the candle in a dish of powdered alum.
6. Burn the candle: in the old days, one would now turn one's back on the candle and depart, however in the interest of fire safety as well as reinforcing the spell with added visualization, remain with the candle and observe the wax melt and shrink.

Be very, very careful not to touch your eyes, mouth or any sensitive areas before washing your hands extremely well.

Traditionally this spell is performed outside and is considered most potent when done in a cemetery. However, it may also be done in your backyard or if, under the circumstances, you are not comfortable traveling alone outside at night, perform it in the bathroom.

 Bring a Rapist to Justice Spell (2)

The spell immediately above may be dedicated to Hecate, Eurasian Mistress of the Crossroads and Queen of Witches. Hecate was the sole spirit to come to Demeter's aid, after the rape and abduction of her daughter, Persephone. When Persephone was finally located in Hades and was forced to stay there part of the year, Hecate decided to remain with her, serving as her handmaiden.

Hecate is believed to witness every crime and may be appealed to for justice. She particularly despises rape and crimes of violence against women and children. Incorporate a petition to her in the spell above or by-pass that spell for a direct approach. She accepts petitions during the Dark of the Moon and on the last day of each month. October 31st is a particularly potent day to call her.

1. Peel three cloves of garlic. Place them on a paper plate or a plate you are willing to lose. Everything offered to Hecate becomes part of the sacrifice; you cannot return for the plate.
2. Cover the garlic with honey and sprinkle with dried lavender.
3. Leave this offering at a three-way crossroads. Tell Hecate what you need.

Should you observe a dog, particularly a solitary or unexpected one, this is a sign that your petition has been accepted.

Justice Spell

This doll-spell represents a plea to the universe for justice and for protection from one's adversaries. Obviously, doll-magic may be taken in many directions: it is the plea for justice that prevents this spell from being considered a hex. If indeed, your plea for justice is undeserved, the spell will benefit the adversary instead. Adjust the spell as needed to suit your situation.

1. On the night prior to the court date, personalize a doll to represent your adversary. (A separate doll is required for each adversary you may have.)
2. Place the doll atop a clean white cloth.
3. Dress the doll with a series of condition oils: **Command and Compel, Courtcase, Fiery Wall of Protection,** and/or **San Cipriano Oils.** Theoretically at least, the more oils, the more powerful the spell.
4. Sprinkle crushed vervain over the doll.
5. Tie a white cotton thread or string around the doll's waist.
6. Burn frankincense and myrrh.
7. Recite Psalm 7 nine times.
8. Wrap the doll up inside the cloth and hide it in the dark in a discreet and private place.

This is a popular spell. Sometimes reciting the psalm is omitted. Other options for disposing of the doll exist, too: for instance, bury the doll in the ground, far from your home, or bury the doll in the cemetery, or burn the doll and scatter the ashes in the wind.

 Soldado Justice Spell

Appeals for justice may be made to Juan Soldado, unofficial saint. According to legend, Juan Soldado's real name was Juan Castillo Morales, a soldier accused of raping and murdering a young girl. A mob turned him over to the authorities and he was executed by firing squad in February 1938. Too late it was revealed that Juan Soldado was innocent: he was framed by his superior, the true perpetrator of the crime. Juan Soldado is buried in Panteon I, in Tijuana, Mexico.

Appeals to Juan Soldado may be made regarding any issue involving justice, not only false murder charges. He is particularly beneficial when others believe the worst untruths about you. Juan Soldado has also evolved into a patron for those who illegally emigrate to foreign lands in search of safety.

Offer him the customary candles, liquor and cigarettes. Vows to visit his tomb should he perform large favors are also appropriate.

Perhaps the issue isn't obtaining justice for yourself. Instead, someone else needs to be brought to justice or justice is required in order to resolve a situation.

The following spell encourages the capture and arrest of a perpetrator of a crime. It is most powerful if performed as a simultaneous group or coven ritual. Somewhere the perpetrator(s) lurks, protected by shadows and anonymity. The goal of the spell is to remove those shadows, exposing the perpetrator so that he or she may be identified.

 Light of Justice Spell

1. Intensely visualize a bright light: appeal to Higher Powers to turn this spotlight on the perpetrator, constantly and consistently, from this moment until justice is served.
2. Do not attempt to visualize the perpetrator. Instead focus on the crime, the location, the victim, and the circumstances. Request that the Higher Powers ensure that all and any perpetrators be exposed, found and brought to justice.

 Ma'at Justice Spell

Ma'at is the ancient Egyptian personification of truth, justice, law and order. Eternal life following death was of the utmost importance to the ancient Egyptians. It was obtained by the successful weighing of one's heart on a scale balanced against the feather of Ma'at. If the heart outweighed the feather, paradise was denied; destruction was assured.

1. Burn a purple candle for Ma'at.
2. Request that you receive justice and vindication.

Murder Victim Justice Spell (1) Actual Murder

Sometimes, in order to see a murderer brought to justice, it's necessary to turn to the victim of the crime.

1. Place an egg in the corpse's hand.
2. Bury him or her like this.

Metaphorically speaking, the victim now holds life in the palm of their hand—very specifically, the murderer's life.

In addition, this practice is believed to keep the murderer tied to the scene of the crime, thus enabling identification, detection and capture. He or she feels compelled to hover or return to the scene of the crime and will somehow draw attention to him or herself.

Perhaps it wasn't literally murder. Maybe no one actually shot a gun, stabbed with a knife or clunked the victim over the head with a large frying pan. Yet survivors may believe that their loved one was magicked, hoodooed or bewitched to death. Because this may never be proved, the best-case scenario is to place methods for justice in the victim's hands. If suspicions are unfounded, nothing will happen. The following methods allow the living to provide the deceased with methods for revenge.

Murder Victim Justice Spell (2) Bewitched to Death Justice Spell (1)

1. Place a cassava stick in one of the victim's hands.
2. Place a knife and fork in the other.
3. Bury the person like this.

Murder Victim Justice Spell (3) Bewitched to Death Justice Spell (2)

1. Slip a razor or small, sharp knife into the deceased's pocket or tuck it within the shroud.
2. Bury the person this way.

Murder Victim Justice Spell (4) Bewitched to Death Justice Spell (3)

1. Wrap broomweed or broom straws in white cloth.
2. Roll the package toward the corpse, saying, *"Go! Sweep it clean!"*
3. Place the package in the coffin.

Murder Victim Justice Spell (5) The Antidote

The antidote spell for the murderer to evade ghostly vengeance? The ghost will have no power over you if you obtain the first handful of dirt turned over by the gravedigger. Of course, your efforts to obtain this dirt may single you out for other attention …

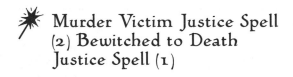

Tarot Justice Spell

1. Remove the Justice card from a deck of tarot cards and place it where it may be clearly viewed.
2. Hold a purple candle in your hands, charging it with your purpose and desires. Carve and dress as appropriate.
3. Place the candle on a dish beside the card.
4. Write your petition for justice on brown paper and tuck it under the candle.
5. Burn the candle, meditate upon the card's image and pay attention to any moments of spontaneous inspiration.

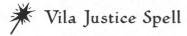 Vila Justice Spell

Not all issues of justice are legal matters. The vila are fierce, beautiful, Eastern European spirits who seek justice for injured, humiliated, and harmed women and animals. They are old, wild forest spirits and may not be verbally articulate.

1. Communicate your pain and passion to the vila by dancing.
2. For utmost power, dance outdoors; however it is your passion and the depths of your psychic wound that calls and activates their power.
3. Request that they provide justice for you; dance until you drop, then leave your burden with the vila.
4. Should pain and feelings of injustice become overwhelming, repeat as needed.

Jail House Spells

It may be a little late for Courtcase Spells. Jail House Spells are designed to prevent or postpone incarceration, win release or at least help you survive the stay.

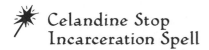 Celandine Stop Incarceration Spell

A spell to prevent imprisonment:

1. Fill a red flannel drawstring bag with celandine.
2. Carry it or wear it so that it is in contact with your skin.
3. Replace the herbs every third day until the matter is completely resolved.

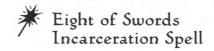 Eight of Swords Incarceration Spell

Because the card in the following spell will be rendered unsuitable for any other use, you may wish to use a color photocopy of it instead. Although the deck designed by that luminary of the Golden Dawn, Arthur Waite, and executed by Pamela Colman-Smith is specified, other tarot decks may be used, if the image on the card is thematically compatible with the spell.

1. Remove the eight of swords card from a Rider-Waite tarot deck.
2. Meditate on the image, observing the blindfolded, bound former prisoner escaping from her confinement.
3. Place a drop of either a **Commanding Oil** or **San Cipriano Oil** on the card.
4. Place it facing up on a dish.
5. Carve and dress either a plain white candle or a white cross candle to express your desires.
6. Place this atop the card.
7. Sprinkle several coins around the candle, as well as dried ground celandine and vervain.
8. Burn the candle.

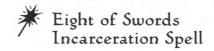 Friendly Judge Stay Out of Jail Spell

Bathe in Friendly Judge Oil (formulas on page 240) for three consecutive nights prior to your court date to stay out of jail.

Get Out of Jail Oil

Magical formula oils, although most associated with Hoodoo and New Orleans Voodoo, are popular in other traditions, too. This formula derives from Santeria and Palo, Latin American spiritual systems deriving from Yoruba and Congo traditions, respectively.

1. Blend dragon's blood powder and fresh ground nutmeg.
2. Place it in a bottle and cover with sweet almond oil and jojoba oil.
3. Add a dash of pure coconut extract.

Carve brown candles and then dress them with Get Out of Jail Oil to win release or prevent incarceration. Alternatively, soak a cotton ball in Get Out of Jail Oil and carry it in your pocket.

Holy Child of Atocha Prison Protection Spell

The Holy Child of Atocha is the patron of prisoners and ensures their well-being. If staying out of jail is no longer an issue, appeal to the Holy Child for protection whilst incarcerated.

1. Post a votive image.
2. If possible, offer him candy and small, inexpensive toys. (Someone else may make offerings on your behalf if you are not in a position to do so.)
3. Tell the Holy Child specifically what you need.

Jail Fix Powder Spell (1) Incense

A variant of Boss Fix (see page 176), designed especially for the House of Correction, this powder allegedly assists one to stay out of prison or to win release.

1. Finely chop one High John the Conqueror root and a Courtcase root.
2. Powder these using a mortar and pestle, then grind them together with dried cloves, rosemary, and sage.
3. Add a pinch of salt and the tobacco from one cigarette. Blend all ingredients together well.

Burn Jail Fix as incense, accompanied by visualization, prayer and petition.

Jail Fix Powder Spell (2) Candle

Jail Fix Oil is the southern American equivalent of the Latin American Get Out of Jail Oil. They may substitute for each other in any spell.

1. Add Jail Fix Powder to a bottle filled with olive, castor, and jojoba oils to make Jail Fix Oil.
2. Carve a brown candle with your name and other identifying information.
3. Dress with Jail Fix Oil. Burn dressed brown candles consistently until the matter is resolved.

Jail Fix Powder Spell (3) Triple Strength

Because sometimes it's best to approach a problem from all angles, this spell utilizes Jail Fix as powder, oil and incense.

1. Start by having a substantial quantity of Jail Fix Powder on hand.
2. Add a pinch of the powder to a bottle filled with oil, while reserving the rest.
3. Carve your name and identifying information into the wax of a brown candle.
4. Reserve some of the powder to be burned as incense.

5. Spread the rest of the Jail Fix Powder onto a sheet of wax paper.
6. Rub Jail Fix Oil over the candle.
7. Roll the oiled candle into Jail Fix Powder.
8. Burn the candle.
9. Simultaneously place the remaining powder on lit charcoals as incense.

Middle Eastern Egg Spell

This Middle Eastern spell is an old one that hearkens back to an era when a prisoner's family was expected to provide his meals—still the case in some places. It also hearkens back to the days before refrigeration, when fresh eggs, hatched that day, were purchased directly from a farmer. Adapt the spell to your circumstances: allegedly it helps win release from prison and alleviates hardships suffered during incarceration.

1. The spell requires three eggs, laid on that very same day.
2. Boil them so that they're very hard and then let them cool.
3. Remove the shells.
4. Write the most potent words of power possible onto the eggs.
5. Eat them.

Ochossi's Jail House Spell (1)

Technically speaking, Ochossi is the orisha of hunting, but like Artemis, his Greek counterpart, his powers encompass so much more than that. In addition to his role as hunter and warrior, Ochossi (Oxossi in Brazil) holds dominion over prisons and prisoners, and all sorts of confinement, especially solitary. As patron of prisons, he may be appealed to for release, improved treatment or just plain staying out of jail.

1. Appeal to Ochossi directly or, if necessary, someone else may make the appeal for you.
2. Ochossi accepts offerings of game, venison or game birds, for instance, but he is also pleased with a dish of honey or honey-roasted peanuts—simple food for a solitary hunter.
3. Offer him an arrow or the image of an arrow. Draw one, if necessary.
4. Tell him explicitly what you need.
5. Should your desires be realized, create a larger, more lavish offering to Ochossi.

Ochossi's Jail House Spell (2) Extra Power Petition

The following ritual actions serve as a petition to prevent incarceration.

Leave a bow and arrow by the prison gates. This could be, in descending order of power, a real bow and arrow, toys, or even an image. You must be bold enough to approach the gate however. For a really supercharged spell, linger long enough to light a white candle dedicated to Ochossi, too. Of course, many spells derive from different eras: make sure that this action doesn't defeat the purpose of the spell by landing you right in jail.

☀ Ochossi Jail House Spell (3) Prison Release Spell

Is it crucial to have someone released from prison? This spell is not cast by the prisoner, but by someone who fervently desires his or her release. Once again, appeal to orisha Ochossi, the Hunter.

1. Obtain a handful of dirt from a forest and also handfuls of dirt from four prisons, keeping each source of dirt distinct.
2. Spread a cloth on an altar.
3. Make a square by placing each handful of prison dirt in a corner of the cloth.
4. Place the forest dirt in the center.
5. Place an image of an arrow or a cross-bow on top of the forest dirt, burn a small white candle or white cross candle beside it, praying and petitioning for your desire. Let it rest overnight.
6. In the morning, blend the dirt together in a bowl, leaving it on the cloth.
7. Place a photo of the target of your spell on top of a white or terracotta plate.
8. Sprinkle it with the blended dirt.
9. Burn either a red seven-day candle on top of the dirt or a single red candle daily for a total of seven days.
10. Sprinkle the candle with a little dirt daily.
11. On the eighth day, or when the candle has burned completely, wrap all remnants, including all the dirt, inside a cloth.
12. Dispose of it as close to the prison where the spell's target is incarcerated as possible.

☀ Prison Guard Protection Spell

Saint Adrian suffered a reversed form of Stockholm syndrome. Allegedly this fourth-century Roman officer became so impressed with the Christian prisoners under his guard that he converted and was jailed with them. Today he serves as the patron of prison guards.

1. Offer him a purple candle on his feast day, September 8th, or as needed.
2. Place a hand-shaped milagro or charm by the candle.
3. Carry the charm with you afterwards.

☀ Sacred Text Prison Release Spell

Recite Psalm 91 seventy-two times each day to win release from prison.

Jail House Spells aren't reserved for prisoners, nor for those who wish to win their release. Sometimes, whether in the name of justice or safety, it's important that someone remain in jail. This spell helps keep that person locked up.

☀ Stay Locked Up Spell

1. Write the targeted person's name on brown paper.
2. Place it inside a clear bowl, glass or Pyrex™ for instance, so that when looking from the outside the bowl's contents are visible.
3. Cover the paper with a layer of black pepper.
4. Cover this layer with another layer of cayenne pepper or similar ground up hot chili pepper; habanero powder is even hotter and thus more desirable.
5. Add a nail, preferably a rusty one, or a coffin nail, if it's important that the person fulfill a life sentence.
6. Cover everything with ammonia.
7. Place a key in the bowl, standing upright, leaning against the side of the bowl. It will fall down; you must be vigilant and keep it standing.
8. Every day at noon turn the key a quarter-turn to keep the person locked up.

Death Spells: Death, Ghosts, Necromancy, and Vampires

Death spells are not hexes nor are they meant to cause death. There are no *"killing curses"* here. Instead, *"death spells"* as a category revolves around the topic of death, death's aftermath and death's magical effect on both the departed and the living left behind. Although magical practitioners may be buried with their ritual tools, for a variety of reasons, most typically death spells are spells for the living. Ghosts, vampires and other denizens of the next-world will have to discover their own new repertoire of enchantment in the Summerlands.

This was not always the case: ancient traditions from Egypt and Tibet for instance required that spells and rituals be learned in life so that they could be performed after death. The books, known in English as *The Tibetan Book of the Dead (The Book of the Great Liberation)* and the *Egyptian Book of the Dead: The Book of Going Forth by Day*, record these traditions. Spiritual adepts trained for years, so that they would be prepared and show no fear when they finally faced their after-life examinations, sort of like the application process to a university with extremely tough admissions standards. (Although eventually in Egypt this practice degenerated into merely being able to present the appropriate spell or sacred text. Thus the wealthy were buried with *Books of the Dead* as amulets—or glorified hall passes!)

This is another of those spell categories that fall along the razor's edge between religion, spirituality and magic. Cast these spells (or adapt them) as they correspond to your personal spiritual realities.

Death spells tend to fall into a few categories:

★ *Spells to prepare and propitiate the dead so that they will not bother the living. Ritually correct* respectful funeral rites are crucial so that the dead will pass on peacefully to their next existence. Incorrect or absent rites may produce ghosts, demons, vampires or just general trouble*
★ *Spells to protect the living from the dead*
★ *Spells that permit the living to avail themselves of the dead's special powers, with or without the dead person's co-operation, including necromancy*

---

* Where there is ambiguity as to what is *"ritually correct,"* the expectations of the dead person set the standard.

Many of these spells are extremely ancient, so many presume that preparations for the dead person will be conducted at home, typically by someone who is either familiar with the deceased or familiar with correct magical procedure. However, for modern people in industrialized nations, death is primarily a topic to be avoided at all costs. Death has become a mystery, tended to by professionals. People no longer die at home: they die in hospitals or hospices. Families and loved ones no longer prepare the body: professionals whisk away the corpse and perform all functions discreetly away from the eyes of loved ones left behind. It is perhaps the area where magical cultures diverge most strongly from surrounding conventional ones. Magical cultures are concerned deeply with preparation of the body and the funeral rites. This is an extremely important threshold; if errors are made, there are potentially disastrous consequences for both living and dead:

★ *Incorrect or absent funeral ritual leaves the soul of the deceased vulnerable to capture by a sorcerer who may use the soul as a tool for nefarious ends or as a work-slave. This belief dates back at least to ancient Babylon and survives in the duppies of the West Indies*

★ *The spirit of the deceased who cannot transition properly to the next realm has nothing better to do than hang around this realm and, depending upon their frustration level, make life miserable for the living. This applies particularly to unidentified homicide victims*

★ *In many cultures, the "next life" means becoming an ancestor and serving and protecting descendants. If proper burial rites as well as later propitiatory offerings aren't available, neither is the potential power of an ancestor, leaving the dead angry and frustrated and the living vulnerable and unprotected*

Death Spells also incorporate spells involving those who may be dead: ghosts or vampires. There's overlap between spell categories; it can be difficult to distinguish between a "ghost spell" and a "death spell."

Death Spells

Death Spirits or *Spirits of Death* sound so threatening compared to a *Healing Spirit* or a *Spirit of Love*. This isn't mere modern squeamishness but an attitude shared with the ancients. Death Spirits,

NOTE

For purposes of organization, spells to *prevent* formation of ghosts and vampires, particularly those involving funerary rites and immediate post-death rituals, are grouped with Death Spells. Spells involving already formed "*mature*" ghosts and vampires are classed under their own headings.

although they play a necessary function, made our ancestors nervous, too.

Death Spirits tend to fall into one of two categories:

★ *Spirits who are involved in the dying process or who serve to ease the transition to the next life*
★ *Spirits who are guardians of the dead, who preside over the realms of the dead, or who rule cemeteries and cremation grounds*

Many Spirit Guardians of Death's Doors remain unnamed. As with Disease Spirits, there's some reluctance to name many of them, just in case they actually come when called, thus epithets and euphemisms are frequently substituted. Often, a Death Spirit's true name remains secret. Hades literally means *"the unseen one."* Should that name become too familiar, other euphemisms may be substituted: Polydegmon means *"the hospitable one"* because, after all, *everyone* is welcome in his realm. Pluton means *"wealth,"* because ultimately he owns everyone and everything.

Despite the fear they instill, these Spirits can be very needed, helpful and welcome—at the right moment, of course. Their assistance is incorporated into many spells for a variety of reasons and purposes.

Guardians of the next world and of the cemetery gates include:

★ *Baron Samedi, leader of the Vodoun Ghede spirits, and his consort, La Grande Brigitte*
★ *Dongyue Dadi, Lord of Tai Shan (China)*
★ *Erishkigal/Lamashtu (Mesopotamia)*
★ *Hades, Persephone (Greece)*
★ *Hella (Norse)*
★ *Kali, Shiva, Yama (Hindu)*
★ *Mictlantecutli and Mictecacuiuatl (Aztec Lord and Lady of the Dead)*
★ *Oya (Yoruba)*
★ *Osiris (Egypt)*
★ *Yambe Akka (Saami)*

Appeal to these guardian spirits to protect the souls of the dead, and also to maintain control over the souls of the dead, keeping them in line, so to speak. Petition them also for access to the spirits of the dead, should this be desired.

Psychopomps

Psychopomp means *"conductor of souls"* in Greek. The term refers to a specific type of spirit, entrusted with a specific type of function. These are the spirit guides who lead the soul between the lands of the living and the dead. (In addition, they sponsor, protect and guide shamans who journey back and forth between the realms.) You will recognize them in your dreams or waking visions by the attributes they carry; traditional emblems for this class of spirits include a key, a cutting instrument and/or a torch. Culso, an Etruscan psychopomp, for instance, awaits the arrival of all souls. He carries scissors in one hand to sever ties with the realm of the living and a bright flaming torch to light the way toward new adventures.

Psychopomps include:

★ *Angels: Gabriel, Azrael and the unnamed "Angel of Death" (Jewish)*
★ *Anubis, Hathor, Wepwawet (Egypt)*
★ *Baron Samedi, Baron La Croix and Baron Cimitiere (Vodoun)*
★ *Culso (Etruscan)*
★ *The Valkyries and Freya (Norse)*
★ *Giltine (Lithuania)*
★ *Hecate, Hermes (Greece)*
★ *Jizo (Japan)*
★ *Mother Holle (German)*

Animals serve as psychopomps, too. The most famous are dogs, jackals and other canines. Many spirit psychopomps manifest in these forms. These include Anubis and Kali (jackals), Hecate (dog) and

Wepwawet (wolf). Other animal psychopomps include butterflies, snakes, and birds, especially ravens, crows, hornbills, and frigates. It is considered extremely auspicious if any of these creatures make a spontaneous appearance at a funeral or similar post-death rites. This indicates that the escort service for the soul has arrived and is intended to comfort and reassure the living.

Psychopomps may be petitioned to ease the travails of the dying, by the dying person or their loved ones alike.

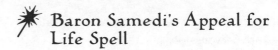

Angel of Death Intervention Spell

Foil the angel of death by changing a person's name! Death angels in Jewish tradition, similar to Chinese death spirits, possess a bureaucratic nature. Instructions must be followed to a "t," thus they come prepared with a magical warrant naming the specific person whose soul is scheduled for harvest. (It's believed dangerous to have too many people—like more than one—bearing the same name in one family. The Angel of Death might get confused and take the youthful one instead of the aged.)

1. In case of life-threatening illness, should a visit from the Angel of Death genuinely be feared, change the afflicted person's name. Traditional choices are Raphael for a boy, interpreted to mean *"The Creator heals"* or Eve for a girl, which literally means *"life."* Other options are names of animals, especially *"Bear," "Lion"* or *"Wolf"* because these creatures are perceived as holding onto life particularly fiercely and tenaciously.
2. Should the illness and threat of death abate, it's considered wise to maintain the new names, even changing names legally, on the off chance that the Angel is still searching.

Baron Samedi's Appeal for Life Spell

There are many magic spells for healing illness. From a certain perspective these may be understood as spells that indirectly seek to prevent or forestall death. There are very few spells, however, that openly and directly target prevention of death, perhaps because most magical philosophies understand death as part of the process of life.

In an emergency, however, a rare exception is an appeal to Baron Samedi. The Ghede are the Vodoun spirits of death and the guardians of the cemetery. They control the crossroads between life and death. Baron Samedi is their leader, owner of the metaphoric and literal cemetery; ultimately no one can die if Baron Samedi refuses to "dig the grave." You'll have to have a very good explanation of why a life must be spared, however Baron Samedi has been known to be sympathetic to appeals made on behalf of dying children.

1. Offer Baron Samedi a piece of dry toast, a cup of black coffee and some dry roasted peanuts. He drinks rum in which 21 very hot peppers have been steeped. Cigarettes and cigars are appreciated as well.
2. Give the Baron a pair of black sunglasses, with one lens popped out, demonstrating that he can see in two worlds, the realms of the dead and the living. (Once you've given the gift, they're his; don't put them on afterwards.)
3. Set up an altar, make your offering and start talking, explicitly, respectfully and frankly about what you need and what will be offered in exchange for a miracle.

Brigitte's Appeal for Life Spell

If you perceive that a woman may be more sympathetic, appeals may also be made to La Grande Brigitte, Maman Brigitte, Baron Samedi's Scottish-born wife. She co-owns the cemetery with the Baron.

1. Offer La Grande Brigitte nine purple eggplants together with a glass of red wine.
2. If possible, set up her offering by the central cross in a cemetery or under a willow or elm tree. Given the choice, the most auspicious day to petition her is on a Wednesday.
3. Light a white or purple candle for Maman Brigitte, make your appeal and explain why it should be considered.

 Burial Protection Spell

Drive or carry the deceased around the cemetery sunwise (either one or three times is recommended) before burial, for protection and luck during the next journey.

 Epidemic Lock and Key Spell

There's only so much one family should have to bear; however, epidemics are greedy and know no boundaries. This spell can only be performed after at least one member of a family has succumbed to an epidemic. It must be cast during that person's burial in an attempt to protect other members of the immediate family. Someone in the family casts the spell.

1. Lock a padlock while focusing on your desired goal.
2. Throw the closed padlock into the grave so that no further members of the family will follow the deceased into the grave.
3. Bury the padlock under Earth together with the coffin. It must not be removed under any circumstances, nor ever opened.
4. If there is a key, put it in a small bag filled with stones and drop it into a river, arriving and leaving via a circuitous route, without looking back.

 Escort Service to the Beyond Spell (1) Tarot Card

To request this sort of escort service, either for yourself during the dying process or for a loved one immediately following death, remove the Moon card from a Rider-Waite tarot deck or a thematically similar deck.

1. Place it where you can meditate on the image. The two canines are the awaiting psychopomps; the crab or lobster is the soul beginning its next, long journey.
2. Try to go into the card, jump inside and see what happens. Practice jumping in and out of the card; it's important to the success of the ritual that you're confident that you can emerge safely. The subject of death is a mystery and so to some extent is this spell.
3. Enter the card and see what assistance you can bring back with you.

 Escort Service to the Beyond Spell (2) Spirit Intervention

If, for any reason, the soul of the deceased seems to be lingering or doesn't seem to be in a hurry to make the next journey, appeal to one of the psychopomps to provide an immediate pick-up service. Any of the spirits may be petitioned, although one dear to the deceased would be the kindest choice.

If you're unsure what to do, burn white candles and provide one of the fragrances that call in spirits best: benzoin, cinnamon, frankincense or sandalwood. Call the spirit by name and request that it comes to collect the recalcitrant soul quickly.

Escort Service to the Beyond Spell (3) Psychopomp Spell

Knowledge that a psychopomp awaits, that the journey won't be made alone, can be very comforting. Some like to be surprised but others prefer to choose their own tour-guides. This spell allows you to magically place your order.

1. Gather images to represent assorted psychopomps: assorted deities may be represented as well as canines (dogs, jackals, wolves), snakes (especially aspects of the Vodou lwa Simbi), and birds (corvids, hornbills, seagulls). Flames may be used to represent angels.
2. Place them on an altar or cast a circle with the images. Accompany by burning candles and incense, especially benzoin.
3. If you find one particular image calls to you, intrigues or comforts you, keep it by your bedside or sleep with it under your pillow.

Escort Service to the Beyond Spell (4) Hecate

*Toss wolfsbane/aconite into a simmering cauldron to invoke Hecate's escort service to the beyond. (**Beware:** wolfsbane is very toxic!)*

Escort Service to the Beyond Spell (5) Canine Intervention

Many spiritual traditions believe that a dog psychopomp awaits the newly dead, waiting to lead the way to the next existence. Without the dog, it was believed, the dead soul was doomed to wander and never find the right path. Trusting souls know that their loyal spirit dog awaits them, however, not everyone has faith. Perhaps out of anxiety, different traditions tried to compensate: sometimes a familiar pet was

killed following a person's death so that they could be buried together, with this pet dog assuming the role of psychopomp. The ancient people of what is now Mexico came up with a happier magical solution:

1. Create or obtain a clay image of a dog; it can look like a specific breed or individual dog or just be a generic canine.
2. Incorporate this figure into funeral rites, either burying together with the person or cremating them together.

 ## Fiery Ring of Protection

1. Until funeral rites occur, maintain lit candles around the body to create a fiery wall of protection.
2. Irish tradition designates a dozen candles steadily burning; other traditions suggest two (one each at head and foot), four (marking the body's cardinal points) or as many as can be squeezed around.
3. Light a new candle, every time one burns out.

Guardian of the Dead Spell: Osiris

Osiris, Lord of the Dead, presides over the Western Lands, the ancient Egyptian after-life. He may be petitioned to guard the soul of a loved one. Burn frankincense and gum arabica in Osiris's honor; light black and green candles. Osiris accepts offerings of spring water, flowers, and grain.

 ## Iris Spell

Popular Greek mythology indicates that Iris was a messenger for the Olympian spirits until she was supplanted by Hermes. Iris had other roles, too: she served as psychopomp for women's shades. Plant purple irises on women's graves to ensure Iris's help and blessing.

Funeral Cleansing Spells

Once upon a time, the first magic spell one encountered, immediately after birth, was an enchanted cleansing bath. One's final Earthly magical activity (at least in this body) was similarly a magical bath. Just as childbirth rituals frequently incorporate cleansing spells (specifically, cleansing baths), so last rites usually incorporated a magical/spiritual cleansing bath. The body is bathed, typically with spiritually cleansing, protective materials. Incense may also be burnt to cleanse and comfort.

 ### Chervil Incense

Chervil, also known as Sweet Cicely or British myrrh, was among the ancient Egyptian funerary herbs. Remains of the herb were found within Tutankhamun's tomb. Burn the dried herb as incense to comfort the bereaved and also to enable them to contact the deceased if desired.

 ### Copal Incense

Copal is traditionally burned during Mexican Day of the Dead rituals but it may be used anytime. Its fragrance allegedly pleases, pacifies, and honors those who have passed on, while protecting and cleansing the living at the same time.

 ### Funeral Cleansing Spell (1)

Different traditions emphasize different cleansers. Select one or any combination of the following:

★ *Juniper*
★ *Lavender*
★ *Lime (fresh slices, rather than the essence)*
★ *Mugwort*
★ *Nutmeg*
★ *Rose*
★ *Sandalwood*

 ### Funeral Cleansing Spell (2)

According to Seneca tradition, the oils of two evergreen trees, Canadian hemlock and balsam fir are used to wash and prepare the body. Bodies are then laid out for funerary ceremonies on boughs of the trees.

 ### Funeral Garland (1)

This garland offers immediate comfort and spiritual cleansing. Each tear is charged with blessings and may be burned at a later stage for protection or in attempts to contact the deceased. Pierce tears of frankincense and myrrh and string onto thread. Give the garlands to funeral attendees to take home as a talisman to burn as needed.

 ### Funeral Garland (2)

Pierce cloves and string them onto a necklace. Wear or hang to comfort the bereaved.

 ### Hyacinth Spell

Fill the home with fresh hyacinths to comfort the bereaved and assuage their grief.

 ### Jasmine Incense

Burn jasmine incense to protect and purify, comfort the bereaved, and honor the deceased.

☀ Ocean Cleansing Spell

Life emerges from salt water, both metaphorically speaking and literally. Each person begins their Earthly incarnation swimming in their mother's salty amniotic fluid. Ocean water is also used to signal rebirth in the next realm.

Gather ocean water; add essential oil of lavender and bathe the deceased's body with this liquid. If real ocean water is impossible for you to get, place as much salt in spring water as possible, preferably Dead Sea salt, and use this instead.

☀ Sandbox Cleansing Spell

No, not that *kind* of sandbox; sandbox tree is the popular name given to euphorbia, a member of the spurge botanical family. Make an infusion of its leaves with which to intensively spiritually cleanse a house from which a corpse has been removed.

☀ White Sage

Burn white sage to comfort the bereaved and to provide simultaneous spiritual cleansing.

☀ Funerary Preparation Spell (1)

Create an infusion by pouring boiling water over myrtle, mugwort, and rue. Use this liquid to bathe the body.

☀ Funerary Preparation Spell (2)

Place a fresh sprig of basil over the deceased's chest to provide safe passage to the next realm.

☀ Funerary Preparation Spell (3)

Place fresh rosemary in the deceased's hands, for protection against any coming dangers.

☀ Funeral Protective Spell (1)

Amulets and travel-charms may be sent along for the journey, for luck and protection, as exemplified by the ancient Egyptians who filled the tombs of the wealthy with every object needed to maintain the lifestyle to which the dead person was accustomed, including magical models of people to serve them and do their bidding in the next life. Even the poorest person, however, was buried with basic protective amulets and an eye-makeup palette, necessary for magic as well as maintaining appearances.

The Egyptians cultivated a magical science of amulets and talismans for a variety of purposes. There were over thirty styles of funerary amulet alone. These included:

★ Eyes of Horus
★ Scarabs
★ Tet amulets (Buckle of Isis)
★ Djed amulet (Pillar of Osiris)
★ Vulture shaped amulets

☀ Funeral Protective Spell (2)

The body may be decorated after death. In particular, henna is used to provide good fortune and protection in the next realm. Different traditions use different designs; choose what resonates for you. Drawing the image of an amulet, if accompanied by the chanting of sacred texts and charging through magical focus, was believed to equal the actual amulet in ancient Egypt.

Using henna, decorate the deceased's hands and feet, incorporating Egyptian funerary amulet designs.

Funeral Protective Spell (3)

Place sulfur in the coffin to protect against evil and danger.

 ## Funeral Protective Spell (4)
Dog Amulet

Craft a dog from paper and place it within the coffin for protection and guidance.

 ## Ghost Prevention Spell (1)

1. Immediately following a death, brew substantial quantities of bayberry *(Myrica cerifera)* tea, in order to follow a Seminole recommendation to prevent ghosts.
2. Family and friends of the deceased should drink this tea, as well as bathing their heads and arms with it for three days following the death.

 ## Ghost Prevention Spell (2)

Bury the body in the same spot where the deceased's placenta and/or umbilical cord were buried: allegedly this prevents the soul from returning as a ghost.

 ## Hair Girdle Spell

It is customary in many traditions to remove a lock of the deceased's hair as a keepsake or memento. An Australian aboriginal custom suggests the metaphysical origins of this tradition. Think of "girdle" in terms of a magic belt or "girding your loins," rather than as a figure-shaping undergarment.

1. When a man dies, his hair is cut off by a male relative.

2. It's woven into a belt and presented to the deceased's eldest son. Wearing this magic belt transmits all the positive masculine qualities of the deceased and enhances the wearer's psychic skills.

 ## Madame Death Spell

Central Europe's Madame Death is a unique spirit. When she arrives, she actually teaches you how to die, demonstrating how to do it, and then serves as escort during the transition. If it's time to contact her, look for Madame Death sitting at the crossroads or in apple and pear trees. It's unnecessary to bring her gifts or offerings, and you can't see her until she's ready to see you.

 ## Passport to Death

In many disparate magic and spiritual traditions, a tattoo serves as the passport to the next world. The tattoo serves as an identifying mark for the psychopomp and gains one admittance to the afterlife, in the sort of way some clubs and museums stamp one's hand when allowed entrance. It's believed that this reason was among the initial stimuli for the concept of permanently tattooing the body.

This tattoo is applied when one is still living, typically on the hand or inner wrist. Geometric patterns are typical; however, consider what your passport should look like. If you're not sure but would like one, turn to the Divination Spells to help you determine what sign is needed.

Mysteries of Death Contemplation Spell (1) Baba Yaga

Baba Yaga is the Russian spirit who rules the conjunction of magic and harsh reality, of limits and possibilities. This Death Spirit provides fertility when she chooses, but she also consumes those who disappoint her. Baba Yaga, iron-toothed and boney-legged, wears a necklace of human skulls; her home is surrounded by a fence crafted from human bones. She offers comprehension, not comfort.

Like her compatriot spirits, Kali and La Santisima Muerte, Baba Yaga encompasses all the mysteries of life and death; contemplate her in order to begin to comprehend these mysteries. This spell doesn't suggest contacting her (the Baba has little patience; don't waste her time without good reason), but this kind of magical contemplation instead.

1. Build an altar featuring birch wood and leaves, animal imagery, a mortar, pestle and broom, and, *especially,* food and drink. Baba Yaga is always voraciously hungry. Offer her real food or cut out photo images for the altar: she's especially fond of Russian extravagances like coulibiac. Offer her a samovar with blocks of fine Russian caravan tea and perhaps a water pipe.
2. Sit with the altar, gaze at it from different angles, play with the objects and see what comes to mind.

Mysteries of Death Contemplation Spell (2) Sheela na Gig

The sheela na gig *is the crossroads where fertility and sterility, birth and death meet. The* sheela na gig *is a genre of ancient Celtic images depicting a naked wizened crone holding her legs open as if she were giving birth, although she is clearly too old to do so. The* sheela na gig *stretches her parturient vagina open with her hands as if it were a gate, while looking the viewer in the eye: many traditional belief systems perceive the Earth Mother as the ultimate source of life and death. One returns to her after death only to emerge again. The* sheela na gig *invites you to contemplate these mysteries.*

1. Create an altar of contemplation with a *sheela na gig* as the focal point.
2. Combine images of fertility and death: include pomegranates, bones, seashells and feathers.
3. If one is brave or curious enough, visualize stepping through the gate the *sheela na gig* holds open.

Discussions of death inevitably leads one to consider one's own mortality and the mysteries of what happens after death. Many traditions believe in reincarnation. Rituals are performed to discover previous identities.

Past-life Spells: Crystalline Memory Bank

Stones and crystals contain the memories of the world. Certain crystals allegedly evoke long-buried memories in others, especially past-life memories. Brown crystals, in general, are believed beneficial to this purpose. Among those considered especially effective are: cuprite; garnet; jasper, especially brown jasper; serpentine; and variscite.

Crystal Past Life Spell: the Passive Method

Simply wear, carry or sleep with the crystals and allow memories to arise of their own volition.

Crystal Past Life Spell: the Active Method

Place one crystal onto the Third Eye area, above the point where one's brows meet, and consciously try to remember. Be aware, however, that these memories cannot be forced or commanded.

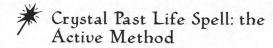 ## Past Life Spells: Magic Mirror

Do not expect immediate success with this spell. It takes practice; an extended period of time may be required before results are achieved. It is more difficult than it seems; do not perform the ritual for more than fifteen minutes at a time, until a successful momentum is achieved. You will need a chair and a table, with a white candle and either a fixed or hand-held mirror.

1. Take all spiritual precautions. Cast a circle around the table and chair.
2. Burn mugwort and sandalwood within the circle.
3. Light the candle and place it between yourself and the mirror.
4. Keep your mind clear and calm.
5. Gaze at your face in the mirror neutrally—this is not the moment to count pimples, wrinkles or despair at your nose.
6. Call your own name clearly and distinctly three times.
7. Eventually you may be tempted to call another name or another name will simply fall from your lips. Try it: ask the mirror to show you who you were.

Petrified Wood Past Life Spells

Pieces of petrified wood are typically sold alongside crystal gemstones. Like crystal gemstones, they're believed to retain memory and are used to help access those buried within you.

 ## Petrified Wood Past Life Spell (1)

Hold a piece of petrified wood in your hand during conscious attempts at past-life regression.

 ## Petrified Wood Past Life Spell (2)

Place a piece of petrified wood in a charm bag. Wear it around your neck while sleeping for information to appear in your dreams.

 ## Sandalwood

Burn sandalwood to stimulate past-life recall.

 ## Wisteria Past Life Spell

Hang wisteria over your bed to access past-life memories while you sleep.

Following removal of the body, it's recommended that any rooms where it was kept be swept out completely. (See also *Cleansing Spells*, page 185–223.)

 ## Post-Death Cleansing Spell

1. Sweep the house thoroughly using a single use ritual broom or any other broom that you're not sorry to lose.
2. Dispose of any dust and debris outside the house, ideally by burning.
3. Dispose of the broom immediately, outside the home, preferably at a crossroads unless, of course, you'd like return visits; then keep the broom as a summoning device.

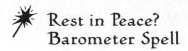 ## Rest in Peace? Barometer Spell

Do the dead rest easy? Flowers and flowering shrubs may be planted on the grave to serve as barometers. Allegedly if the flowers thrive and bloom, there's no need to worry about whoever's in the grave. Of course, some plants are considered better barometers than others. Marjoram is believed to provide a good guarantee: if it thrives on a grave, the person within is certain to be content.

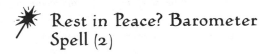 ## Rest in Peace? Barometer Spell (2)

A Jewish variant of the above suggests planting a cutting of elder on the grave. If it flourishes, this is a sign that the soul of the deceased is peaceful and happy. (It's not necessary to be a passive spell participant in this or the spell above; do whatever is necessary to keep the plants alive and thriving.)

Rest in Peace Aloe Vera Spell

Plant aloe vera on the gravesite in order to soothe the deceased, ease any sense of loneliness or abandonment, and prevent their longing for the living.

Rest in Peace Chamomile Spell

A carpet of chamomile planted over a grave encourages the dead to sleep and also eases their passage to the next realm.

Rest in Peace Floral Spell

Cover graves with a carpet of daisies and bluebells to bring peace to the deceased and joy to the bereaved, and to invite the presence of benevolent guardian spirits.

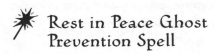 ## Rest in Peace Juniper Spell

Burn juniper berries at the gravesite during the funeral to ward off any malicious or mischievous spirits.

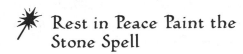 ## Rest in Peace Ghost Prevention Spell

Drive iron arrowheads into the ground at the foot and head of the deceased's body to prevent the formation and return of a ghost.

Rest in Peace Paint the Stone Spell

Alternatively, keep the deceased content by dressing their tombstone:

1. Powder dried henna blossoms, roses and pinks together and grind them into a fine powder.
2. Add water to make a paste and paint the headstone with this mixture.
3. Repeat as needed.

Rest in Peace Rowan Spell

Plant rowan trees in the cemetery, especially overlooking graves, to watch over the spirits of the dead.

 ## Rest in Peace Sleep Well Spell

To encourage the dead to sleep peacefully and deeply, strew wild poppy seeds throughout the cemetery.

Rest in Peace Willow Spell

1. Place willow branches on the side of a grave to drive away mean spirits and meddling, troublesome ghosts. These willow branches will also prevent the deceased's ghost from rising, protect living visitors from *"ghost sickness,"* and attract benevolent, protective spirits of the dead.
2. Replace the branches as needed.

 ## Rest in Peace Just try to Get Out Spell

Planting thorn bushes on graves allegedly prevents either vampires or ghosts from rising.

 ## Rest in Peace Final Amends Spell

Ideally one has the opportunity to say a final farewell to the deceased and depart on good terms. This is not, unfortunately, always the case. This can stimulate great pain and regret for the one left behind. According to a Romany tradition, however, it's never too late to make amends. This spell should relieve your heart and also forestall any possible difficulties with a testy, still-resentful ghost.

1. Go to the grave.
2. Offer a libation of spring water or whatever would be the beverage of choice. A small gift of some kind might not be a bad idea either.
3. Talk to the person. Be frank and familiar. The standard speech goes something like this:
   I forgive you. Don't harm me, don't haunt me.
   I behaved badly towards you [or specify the situation]
   Please forgive me. I forgive you.

Ideally a response is received shortly, in dreams if not in waking life.

 ## Rest in Peace Food of the Dead Spell

Although it's customary in many traditions to spend time at the gravesite, cleaning, caring and sometimes bringing offerings of food and drink, a more direct method was used in ancient Greece.

Create a blend of olive oil, honey and spring water. This may be poured directly onto the grave, or poured through a tube into the grave. Meanwhile, the living should picnic nearby.

 ## Rest in Peace Menu of the Dead Spell

Asphodel is allegedly among the favored foods of the dead. Asphodel is sometimes planted on graves, however the legend is also taken literally. Prepare asphodel—it's typically roasted—and leave it atop a grave to comfort and satisfy the deceased within.

 ## Rest in Peace Tansy Eternal Life Spell

Tansy is described as an herb of life everlasting. It allegedly comforts the bereaved while assuring the dead that they will not be forgotten. Sprinkle ocean water or **Holy Water** *over the deceased's body using a tansy branch as an asperging tool.*

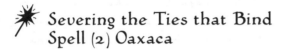

Severing the Ties that Bind Spell (1) French Caribbean

When two people were very much in love and one dies, especially suddenly, both parties may continue to cling to each other intensely. This creates a type of paralysis for both: the living person isn't really living, while the deceased can't completely depart. A spell from the French Antilles attempts to sever these unhealthy ties between living and dead.

1. Cut acacia branches into either three or nine wands.
2. The living person must go to the grave and whip the ground repeatedly with these wands until they feel a release.

Severing the Ties that Bind Spell (2) Oaxaca

A ritual from Oaxaca helps create healthy boundaries between a living woman and her deceased husband:

1. Immediately following death, the widow sits alone at home, grieving for nine days. She neither communicates with nor looks at anyone. Food is brought to her but she's left alone.
2. On the ninth day, she's brought fresh, clean clothes.
3. Carrying the clothes, she hurries immediately to a river or ritual bath, stopping only three times to draw breath. She must not talk on the way.
4. A complete bath is taken, submerging entirely three times.
5. When she puts on her fresh clothes, her mourning is complete and she is free from the influence of the dead.

The most complex, organized system of modern after-life offerings may derive from Taoist traditions. The Chinese after-life is organized like a bureaucracy. Huang Feihu, a warrior prince who was deified after death, eventually transformed into Dongyue Dadi, Supreme Ruler of the Underworld. He is responsible for maintaining the registry that contains every individual's expiration date, the day of their death. When the due date arrives, underlings are dispatched to collect the soul.

Souls ideally are transformed into loving, guiding ancestors. A system of reciprocity exists: ancestors protect the living, the living feed and care for the deceased, keeping them strong and well provided for so that the deceased can continue to care for them in turn. The dead live in a parallel universe and they, too, have needs that descendants must provide. Although edible offerings may be included, many Chinese spirit offerings take the form of burned paper.

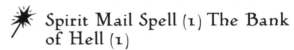

Spirit Mail Spell (1) The Bank of Hell (1)

Once upon a time perhaps real cash money was burned, as it was elsewhere in the world. Obvious flaws may be observed with this system. If the ancestors really care about you, do they want you to go broke?

Special spirit money was designed instead, specific currency to be used by ancestors in the next realm: it is delivered to them, through the air, by burning. This spirit cash, typically drawn on the Bank of Hell, is easily and inexpensively obtained from feng shui suppliers and Chinatown vendors.

Because even the afterlife modernizes, and no doubt the cost of living increases in the other realm just as it does here, Bank of Hell checkbooks are now available, as are credit cards so that the ancestors may shop for themselves. The reference to Hell doesn't insult ancestors, by the way, implying that their behavior on Earth was less than exemplary or requiring of punishment: there's no connection with the Christian concept of Hell. It's merely a somewhat sardonic reference to everyone's fate in the afterlife.

Burn spirit money as you will. If you need your ancestors to work harder for you or perhaps you'd like to do something for them, set up an ancestor altar.

1. Arrange photographs, if you have them, or place objects on a tablet that remind you of your ancestors or would remind them of their connection with you.
2. Place a white candle on the altar, together with a glass of pure spring water or **Spirit Water.** Make any other offerings you deem fit.
3. Light the white candle and burn generous quantities of Bank of Hell notes.

 Spirit Mail Spell (2) The Bank of Hell (2)

The immediate presence of death sometimes opens portals between this realm and the spirit realm, causing a sudden awareness of hovering spirits and hungry ghosts. Toss or burn Spirit Money at crossroads to assuage and please lurking ghosts and spirits. This is especially beneficial during funeral processions.

Spirit Mail Spell (3) Next Realm Post Office

The ancient Egyptians had a sort of spirit mail, too, also delivered through smoke, although theirs took the form of an actual letter to the deceased. Their tradition is very easily adapted.

1. Write a letter to the person you'd like to contact. Write down exactly what you need to say.
2. Place this letter inside an offering bowl or on an altar.
3. Cover the letter with food offerings. The Egyptians would have used bread, but use whatever is appropriate for your precise situation.
4. Embellish the altar as needed: offer candles, food and libations.

5. Eventually burn the letter: it will be received via smoke and air.

Death is one of life's major thresholds: there are spells for the periods immediately preceding and immediately following death.

Scarab Spell

The scarab, the most popular amulet of ancient Egypt, still retains its popularity. The amulet depicts a scarab beetle and is usually crafted from faience or gemstones. The scarab represents the Egyptian deity Khephra (an aspect of Ra) "He Who Turns," representing the eternal return of the sun. The scarab, a lucky health-bestowing amulet, was used to replace the heart during mummification and is a meditative symbol of everlasting life.

The scarab serves as an instrument of the divine: to heal and promote longevity or to promote peaceful, graceful transitions to the next realm. Whisper words, blessings, sacred verses, names of power, or wishes into the scarab. Give it as a gift to someone who stands near the threshold of life and death.

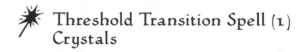 Threshold Transition Spell (1) Crystals

Crystals can help ease the tradition: place aquamarines strategically on the body.

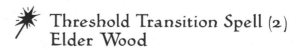 Threshold Transition Spell (2) Elder Wood

Elder wood eases the transition to the beyond and may be used to unlock various paths, speeding the journey. Either place a branch of elder wood within the coffin, or cremate elder wood with the body.

Threshold Transition Spell (3)
Flower Essence Remedies

Among flower essence remedies' finest expression is their ability to ease the transition from life to death. Flower essence remedies are either given internally or gently massaged into the dying person's feet. The following are especially recommended:

★ *Angels' trumpet (FES), to ease the process and promote spiritual surrender*

★ *Angelica (FES, Pegasus), to connect with the angels and psychopomps and to beseech their protection and benevolence*

★ *Blackberry (FES), which eases depression and fear*

★ *Chrysanthemum (FES), which stimulates the courage to contemplate the journey ahead*

★ *Grape (Master's Flower Essence), which eases the sense of abandonment during the dying process and following death*

★ *Purple Monkeyflower (FES), which eases and resolves the terror of dying*

★ *Scarlet Monkeyflower (FES), to help resolve rage and anger about death and dying*

★ *Sweet Chestnut (Bach), to relieve the bitter isolation of the soul*

★ *Tobacco (Pegasus), which promotes spiritual surrender*

Threshold Transition Spell (4)
Midsummer's Ashes

Midsummer's ashes bring fertility but also assist the dying to cross the threshold into the next realm.

1. Place ashes from the Midsummer's bonfires in a charm bag.
2. Give it to a dying person (have them wear it or place under the pillow) to ease the transition to the next realm.

Threshold Transition Spell (5)
Pennyroyal Spell (1)

Pennyroyal, a member of the mint family, serves as a botanical magical bridge between life and death. (As befitting its magical usage, pennyroyal is unsafe for pregnant women to handle.) Pennyroyal aids in the transition from one realm to the next.

Pour boiling water over pennyroyal to create an infusion. Strain and use the liquid to bathe the deceased.

Threshold Transition Spell (6)
Pennyroyal Spell (2)

Sprinkle dried, powdered pennyroyal on and within the coffin.

Threshold Transition Spell (7)
Protect the Living

The period immediately following death, from a magical standpoint, is perceived as being as vulnerable for the living as for the deceased. One way of looking at it is to recognize Death as one of the pre-eminent thresholds, with as much attendant vulnerability as the Birth process. Everyone immediately present at that threshold, whether they are the dying individual or not, is exposed to some metaphysical danger.

Another way of looking at it is that when death occurs one of the psychopomps is present and may still be lingering. Is anyone else scheduled for the pick-up service or could mistakes be made? Various customs have evolved to ensure the safety of living and recently deceased alike.

★ *Immediately turn mirrors to face the wall or cover them entirely. It is considered harmful to capture the reflection of any angels of death. In addition, it's believed dangerously shocking should the soul of the deceased view their post-death reflection, or lack thereof*

★ Traditionally, the deceased is never left unattended. Someone must stay with them, from the moment of burial until funeral rites are complete. In places where malevolent sorcery attempts to exploit the dead, a vigil may also be kept following burial in the cemetery for specified periods of time, allowing the soul to depart and decomposition of the body to begin

★ Burn candles near the deceased. Some traditions ring the body with candles; others place one candle at the foot, another at the head while other traditions keep the candles burning beneath the deceased's bed

1. Offer whatever was the person's favorite drink as a libation. Share a glass, too.
2. Burn sandalwood, frankincense and/or benzoin.
3. Think of the departed and light white and/or silver candles.
4. Say, clearly and aloud if possible:
   I light this candle for [name].
   I remember [name] *and will always remember* [name] *even though* [name] *has departed.*
   I wish [name] *peace and love and safety.*
   May [name] *rest in peace.*
   Our love journeys with you forever.

 ## Threshold Transition Spell (8) Iron Safety Spell

Should death occur at home, iron is used to secure and ground the living. Death is believed to infect water and food.

1. Thrust a piece of iron, like a nail or a knife, into every item of food (meat, cheese, canisters of flour and sugar, for instance) to prevent and combat this contagion.
2. Standing water should be thrown out of the house.
3. The iron may be thrust into open bottles; securely sealed bottles, like beer and wine bottles, are generally considered safe from contamination.

 ## Threshold Transition Spell (10) Walking Papers Spell

The ritual above may be performed after funeral rites. A similar Tibetan-derived spell must be done before the body is removed from the home.

1. Serve a meal to the deceased, before the body's removal from the home.
2. An elder or other authoritative member of the family then speaks firmly to the deceased, in clear, calm, no-nonsense language, saying something like:
   [Name!] *Listen! You're dead. Don't have any doubts about this.*
   There's nothing for you here anymore.
   Enjoy this meal. It's the last one.
   Eat a lot. You have a long journey ahead of you.
   Good luck. We love you.
   Fortify yourself and don't come back.

 ## Threshold Transition Spell (9) Travel Assistance

In order for their journey to be successful, the dead soul may require some ritual assistance from the living. A lingering soul may need reassurances as well as explicit instructions to leave. It's important to be very clear in this ritual, repeating the deceased's name, calmly but frequently, so that there's no confusion about who is being discussed.

Threshold Transition Spell (11) Threshold of Time

Sometimes the home must be brought back to order following the inherent trauma caused by a death in the family. An Obeah ritual creates a healing threshold period for the living as well as for a lingering soul.

1. Maintain a dish of plain spring water and burning candles in the room where the death occurred and/or the body was prepared for burial for nine days.
2. Change *nothing* in that room during those nine days except for replacing candles as needed and substituting fresh water daily.
3. When the nine days are complete, dispose of the water, the pan and the candles outside the home.
4. Redecorate the room: rearrange the furniture, change pictures and ornaments, even purchase new furniture.

Threshold Transition Spell (12) These Shoes were Meant for Leaving

According to some traditions, the shoes belonging to a dead person must be removed immediately. It's not auspicious for a living person to step into these shoes, nor should they be left to tempt the deceased to return.

1. Gather up all shoes belonging to the deceased.
2. Take them to the woods.
3. Throw shoes in every direction and leave them there.

Threshold Transition Spell (13) Willow Spell

Willow trees are among those sacred to Hecate. Among their other magical uses, they ease passage to the next realm. Plant a willow tree to assure easy passage after death; although this may be done any time, for the spell to be effective, the willow must be alive when you die. For added enhancement, have leaves or small branches of this tree placed within the coffin.

Transition Incense

This incense blend has healing, strengthening, and empowering properties but also opens the road to the next realm, if this is inevitable. Burn cypress, angelica, and juniper. (Use the dried powdered botanical, whole botanicals, or essential oils as desired.)

Transition Incense Myrrh

Burn myrrh to ease and illuminate a person's transition between life and death.

Death's Gifts: Magical Ingredients

Death offers magical gifts to the living. Certain magical ingredients, incorporated into countless spells all over the world, are the products of death.

Coffin Nails

Technically, *"coffin nail"* is a straightforward description: a coffin nail should be pulled from a casket, ideally a used one. Any iron nail demonstrates the magical power of iron; coffin nails are basically extra-strength regular nails, their inherent power enhanced by their encounter with the threshold of death. Although to modern ears this sounds like a malevolent ingredient, coffin nails are used in benevolent spells as frequently as they are in hexes, particularly protective spells.

Real coffin nails are no longer easy to obtain, if they ever were. Trying to get an authentic one will probably land you in a lot of trouble. You may be able to explain away a handful of graveyard dirt but tampering with coffins constitutes illegal vandalism in most places. A nail picked up from a casket manufacturer or a funeral parlor may suffice even if it's never actually been in a used coffin. The associations with death may be powerful enough.

✷ Coffin Nail Transformation Spell

Regular nails may be transformed into coffin nails through the process of magic.

1. Hold the nails in your hand and charge them with your desire and intent.
2. Place them in a bag or box filled with graveyard dirt for seven days or during the Dark Moon phase, periodically murmuring your desires and sacred texts over them.
3. For maximum intensification, bury the bag or box in Earth during this period, marking the spot with a "headstone."

✷ Quick Fix Coffin Nail Transformation Spell

Sometimes you need ingredients right away. If a spell requiring coffin nails needs casting immediately:

1. Place some graveyard dirt on a plate or in a box.
2. Hold the nails in your hand, charging them with your desires and intent.
3. Roll the nails in the graveyard dirt prior to use.

Corpse Water

Modern people have concerns about hygiene and contamination that would probably preclude using a product like corpse water. Corpse water is the reserved liquid that has been used to bathe the deceased, usually in preparation for funeral rites. Contact with the dead body transforms water into corpse water. Like coffin nails and graveyard dust, corpse water is an ingredient shared by magical traditions all around the world.

Unlike coffin nails, there is no way to transform regular water into corpse water.

Since bodies are now only rarely privately prepared for burial at home, this is now an ingredient that's virtually extinct. However, the water used to bathe a corpse may be reserved for various magical uses:

★ *Mixed into his food or drink, it prevents another man from having sex with your wife*

★ *An abusive man who can be induced to wash his hands with this water, is deprived of strength and vigor, making him unable to beat his wife, or at least as badly as usual*

★ *Used as an anti-love potion, it can destroy someone's feelings of love*

★ *Fed to a woman, it can induce her to stop weeping over a deceased friend*

Corpse water is also used both to provide and prevent personal fertility. In parts of the Middle East, this water is believed to retain some of the life essence, the last sparks of life as it were, of the deceased. In that case, drinking it may repair fertility. This is particularly true if this life-potion is drunk immediately following the bathing of a corpse who died suddenly in the vigorous, vital prime of life. Those protesting, disbelieving sparks of life are looking for someplace to go to be *alive*.

In North Africa, however, surreptitiously feeding corpse water to a rival is believed to cause her to become infertile, especially where the corpse was old, feeble and took a long time to die, so that no life essence remains. (This hex should be understood in terms of a polygamous society, where one woman's status and quality of life may depend on the outcome of rivalry with others.)

Because so many uses of corpse water are malign and controlling, great care is taken to be sure that it remains distinct from other, innocuous water. Prescribed methods of disposal exist, too. (Because these are old-fashioned spells, they presume that the body is attended to by loved ones at home. Adapt to your own needs.)

In many traditions, the water used to bathe the body is kept under the bed as long as the body remains present or at least kept in the same room. Because the water is believed to contain some of the dead person's essence, it is traditionally removed either with or after the body, not before. Suggestions for safe, proper disposal include:

★ *Throw the water into or onto the person's grave*
★ *Toss the water out on the ground, outside the home property, behind the coffin or body, as it departs from the home*
★ *Toss the water on the ground where the deceased's placenta and/or umbilical cord was buried*

Graveyard Dirt/Graveyard Dust

Wherever there are burials, there are cemeteries. Wherever there are cemeteries, graveyard dirt is used in magic spells. (Ashes and dirt from cremation grounds are used too.) Graveyard dirt is among the most crucial, important magical ingredients and a prime component of many, many spells.

The use of dirt dug from cemeteries or graves is fairly standard universal magical practice; where traditions differ is whether this practice is considered entirely malevolent or not. Graveyard dirt, by the very nature of where it comes from, will be used as a tool of cursing and hexing spells, however, is the material inherently malicious and toxic? In general, the answer to that question depends upon what role, if any, the dead play toward the living. Cultures who perceive ancestral spirits as being positive and helpful, such as many deriving from Africa and Asia, cultures who aren't fearful of the dead, in general (as opposed to an individual threatening ghost), often use graveyard dirt for benevolent purposes.

On the other hand, those who perceive the dead as malevolent and threatening will simultaneously perceive the cemetery as a place of toxic, perilous power. For instance, among certain Native American cosmologies, the soul is entirely transformed by the dying process. What remains accessible on Earth has no benevolent purpose and retains no specific memory of past relations with the living. In that case, any contact with a dead body or with cemeteries is potentially contaminating, both spiritually and physically. The power may be harnessed but only for evil: the sorcerer who delves into graves is contaminated and potentially contaminating as well.

What actually is graveyard dust? At its most basic, it's dirt from a cemetery or from a specific grave. However, graveyard dirt or dust is also a nickname for various botanicals, with no actual relationship to death. Valerian, for instance, a strong insomnia aid with a foul smell, is called graveyard dust because it promises that you'll sleep like the dead. Patchouli is often called graveyard dirt, because of its unique wet earth aroma.

★ *Some practitioners pick up a handful of surface dirt from the cemetery*
★ *Some practitioners obtain dirt by digging within a grave. An entire science exists of precisely whose grave suits which magic spells, ranging from that of your mother's grave to that of a murderer to that of a young child*

★ *Some practitioners wouldn't be caught dead with actual dirt: they use either one or a blend of several botanicals: powdered mullein, powdered patchouli, or powdered valerian.*

These aren't arbitrary choices. In addition to the reasons given above for patchouli and valerian, mullein is under the dominion of both Hecate and Oya, two powerful spirits with strong associations with death and cemeteries

★ *Some practitioners like to combine botanicals with dirt. Sometimes real cemetery dirt is used, while other practitioners feel that the addition of graveyard dirt botanicals transforms any dirt into graveyard dirt*

Graveyard dirt must be seen within the context of all kinds of dirt being used as amulets and spell ingredients. Dirt from shrines and sacred areas was painstakingly preserved and carried. People carried bits of dirt from graves of saints, holy people and loved ones, perhaps purely as souvenirs and talismans, perhaps for other reasons. For millennia, Jews carried pouches of dirt from Jerusalem, laying it in the grave after death. Romany collected dirt from the legendary seven lucky mountains. Dirt from North African shrines is brought home and sprinkled over hand-made fabrics and carpets to imbue them with the power and protection of the saint. Perhaps the most famous modern example is the Shrine of Chimayo in New Mexico, where thousands of pilgrims converge each year to receive a bit of miraculous healing dirt.

Looked at from that perspective, the use of botanicals instead of real Earth seems euphemistic. On the other hand, perhaps *dirt* itself is a euphemism. What exactly is being collected in the cemetery under the guise of graveyard dirt? If one digs deeply for dirt within an old grave, particularly one conforming to spiritual traditions that bury the body in nothing more than a shroud or a wooden coffin that disintegrate quickly, there is an inherent implication that one is really looking for some part of the body that has returned to Earth. People used to be far less squeamish than they are today nor were they necessarily as concerned about sanitary hygiene. Relics, purportedly pieces of a saint's actual anatomy, were prized, collected and sold. It wasn't even necessary to dig in graves for relics. Public executions created a whole other venue: following the execution of Jacques de Molay, last Grand Master of the Knights Templar, spectators gathered up his ashes, as was done with Joan of Arc and countless others. What exactly was done with those ashes?

Methods of graveyard dirt collection vary. Some believe there's no need to dig; dirt from Earth's surface, provided that it's contained within the cemetery walls, is sufficient to constitute graveyard dirt. Some like the dust clinging to a tombstone. That's not sufficient for everyone. Some commercial purveyors of graveyard dirt advertise different levels of dirt, taken from varying depths, depending upon the purpose of your spell. According to British magical traditions, graveyard dirt is ideally taken from the top of the coffin, just above where the heart of the deceased would be. According to Hoodoo traditions, three scoops of graveyard dirt should be taken, one from over the head, one from over the heart and one from below the feet of the deceased.

There are discreet methods of collecting graveyard dirt in broad daylight:

★ *If you only require a handful, gather it and carry it home in your pocket or in a talisman bag*
★ *If you need more substantial quantities, rather than cut flowers, bring potted plants to transplant onto the grave. Dig a hole for each new plant, reserving the dirt. Carry the graveyard dirt home in the plant's emptied container, creating a dirt transfer if you will*

In some traditions, gifts of coins or libations are made to appease the spirit of the dead whom you may have disturbed, particularly if one is doing some serious digging. Remember to drop the gift into the hole.

Graveyard dirt is used for both benevolent and malevolent purposes. Some examples are offered here in order to give a sense of the nature, power and scope of the material, however graveyard dirt spells will be found amongst every possible magical category.

Benevolent Uses of Graveyard Dirt

☀ Protection From a Loved One Beyond the Grave Spell

Gathered from materials from a loved one's funeral, this creates a memento mori *as well as a protective charm.*

1. Fill a red flannel bag with a pinch of dirt taken from the gravesite, one flower from the funeral and a pebble picked up at the cemetery.
2. Anoint with a drop of the deceased's favorite perfume or signature scent.

☀ Protection From a Stranger Beyond the Grave Spell

Romany spiritual traditions combine a dislike of disturbing the dead with a desire for the protective capacities cemetery dirt offers. Although one might not want to disturb one's own ancestors or someone one knows, there's no actual fear of the cemetery, thus an anonymous, unknown grave is chosen. This spell harnesses abstract, protective qualities inherent in graveyard dirt to protect a child embarking on a long journey.

1. The parent takes a little dirt from any grave, balancing it on the back of the left hand.
2. When the departing child isn't looking, this dirt is tossed over his or her head to provide protection.

Malevolent Uses of Graveyard Dust

Many malevolent uses of graveyard dirt may be observed among this book's Hexing Spells. Perhaps the simplest hex involves throwing a handful of graveyard dirt at someone's back as they walk away from you. How does this differ from the benevolent Romany spell where dirt is tossed over your beloved child? Your intent. Your desire, energy and personal power are the unnamed component of every spell you cast. Your personal energy transforms a loving spell into a spell of hatred. Merely tossing the dirt isn't enough to hex anyone: what turns the trick is the suppressed rage and anger that precipitates the action.

In Java, graveyard dirt is used in spells to induce deep sleep, whether for the purposes of robbery or for a romantic rendezvous—where it's used to prevent parents or spouses from awakening.

Frequently graveyard dirt is transformed into a destructive force by the addition of other ingredients, as in **Goofer Dust**.

☀ Waste Away Hex

A popularly recorded spell, although not necessarily popularly performed (if only because of the time and expense demanded), the following was no doubt invented by the owner of a spiritual supply store wishing to drum up business quickly. Deriving from New Orleans, this spell has now passed into the general Western magical lexicon.

1. Graveyard dirt is combined with a host of standard formulas: Asafetida powder, Babel Powder, Black Cat Oil, Damnation Water, Four Thieves Vinegar, Goofer Dust, Jezebel Root Powder, Lost and Away Powder, Mummy Oil.
2. This blend is mixed with some item belonging to the spell's target, as intimate as possible.

3. Placed in a small bag, it's buried or hidden near the target's home. The goal of this hex is to cause the victim to gradually waste away, becoming listless, passive and losing vitality and life force.

✸ Eternal Life Spell

In modern Western magical traditions, only Palo Mayombe acknowledges the use of human bones. This was once not unusual however. Despite all the Halloween skeletal imagery, few today have actually seen exposed, bare human bones. Once upon a time this was not so unusual (and the practice still survives amongst some isolated traditions). Bodies were disinterred for various reasons having nothing to do with vandalism.

★ *Certain traditions disinter ancestors periodically to invite them to rituals and celebrations, returning them to the grave at the conclusion*
★ *Other traditions retain ancestral bones to honor and communicate with them*
★ *Particularly in areas where land is scarce, bodies may only remain underground as long as flesh remains. Bones are permanently moved to catacombs or ossuaries*

Bones are also disinterred so that magical rituals can take place to preserve the deceased's soul for eternity or to activate the reincarnation process.

Paint human bones red to magically provide the deceased with eternal life, of one sort or another. Menstrual blood was the most ancient activation material; however red ochre has also been used since prehistoric times.

✸ Eternal Life Spell (2)

You'd really like Great Grandpa Phil to have eternal life but you're not ready to paint his bones, menstrual blood, watercolour or otherwise? Never fear, other magical solutions exist.

Determine a proper waiting period; this spell is not cast immediately after death. A year and a day is appropriate, as may be anything with significance to you or the deceased. Paint the grave marker, headstone or monument red. Cover it in its entirety or decorate with magic symbols, especially diamonds, downward-facing triangles, hexagrams and eyes.

Ghosts

The understanding of what constitutes a ghost depends largely on what one believes happens to the soul after death or, in fact, on how one views the soul during life.

To discuss the human soul as singular contradicts many metaphysical beliefs. Many believe that each person has multiple souls, each with a special function. Thus the dream soul travels and wanders, when released by sleep. Perhaps one of these souls or facets of the soul lingers on Earth after death.

Perceptions of souls and what happens to them following death vary according to spiritual tradition and individual belief. As one example, in traditional Hmong belief, the soul exists as a kind of trinity: one part stands guard at the grave, another journeys to the realm of the dead while a third part is subject to reincarnation.

In traditions that revere and communicate with ancestors, death forms a different kind of crossroads: will the soul take a positive turn and accept the responsibilities of an ancestral spirit or will it transform into a ghost? If it does transform into a ghost, will this be a helpful, benevolent or at least unobtrusive, quiet ghost content to linger near the living, or will it transform into a malevolent, spiteful, resentful, mischievous, trouble-making ghost?

The road taken at that crossroads may depend on the actions of the living: were proper funeral rites given? Was the body treated with respect and care? Were any needed spiritual precautions offered?

Among many traditional philosophies, those who die violently far from home or whose funerals and/or graves are neglected have the capacity to evolve into wandering semi-malevolent ghosts or worse. (See Vampires, page 291.)

It is never too late to lay a ghost, however, and many rituals exist worldwide for propitiating those who were laid to rest without proper rites. For example, the Festival of Hungry Ghosts: during the seventh month of the Chinese lunar candle, paper offerings are burned for one's own personal ancestors. However, extra offerings may be given to placate any hungry, wandering ghosts. In Mexico, November 2nd, the Day of the Dead is a national holiday. Families congregate in cemeteries, visiting loved ones, repairing and caring for graves. In addition to offerings made for ancestors and relatives, many add candles for forgotten souls, those who have no one to welcome and care for them. These candles, with additional offerings, may be placed on the family altar or as independent offerings by the roadside, for passing ghosts.

If a ghost isn't causing trouble, how do you know it's there?

★ Candles that burn dim, low or blue may indicate the presence of a ghost
★ An unexpected chill in the air may indicate a ghost: A frequent observation is that the presence of ghosts is indicated by a significant decrease in temperature—a cold spot
★ Ghosts may signal their presence through specific fragrance, a sort of aromatic calling card

Peaceful, mutually beneficial coexistence may not require any spells. Many homes feature the presence of a ghost who wants nothing more than to linger in the presence of loved ones. If the ghost isn't bothering you, there is generally no need to exorcise it; actions to do so may in fact antagonize the ghost and cause trouble.

There are basically two types of ghost spells:

★ Spells to provide protection from troublesome ghosts and keep them far away
★ Spells to obtain access to ghosts and their powers

Spells where you wish a ghost to do something for you are included in this section. Spells where you wish a ghost to provide you with information are included in the Necromancy section (see page 284).

 ## Samhain Hungry Ghost Spell

Samhain, the Celtic roots of Halloween, marks the beginning of the dark, incubatory half of the year. It's also the moment when the veils between realms of living and dead are sheerest. Thus it's the time around the world to contact one's ancestors, pay tribute and honor to them, and engage in necromantic practices of various kinds. Hungry ghosts are also believed to abound—those without family or friends to feed and remember them.

Place offerings of milk and barley outside under the stars to ease the ghosts' hunger, prevent their mischief, and to accrue their blessings.

 ## Boneset Ghost Spell

Boneset guides ghosts elsewhere, attracting protective, benevolent spirits instead. Boneset may also be used to protect people and animals from "ghost sickness," the illness that some believe may emerge after extended contact with the dead. The most potent boneset is found growing on or near graves. Supplement it with white pine for added enhancement.

Hang fresh boneset branches over doorways, or burn young boneset branches and twigs within a cauldron to drive away existing ghosts.

Duppie Repelling Charm

In Jamaican folklore, duppies are harmful, mean-spirited ghosts. Allegedly they'll stay away from someone wearing the following conjure bag:

1. Place asafetida, camphor and garlic inside a black cloth.
2. Tie it up with a black silk ribbon.
3. Wear this around your neck or waist using another black silk ribbon.

 ## Fragrance Communication Spell

Because a ghost may be identified by a specific fragrance, this can be used as a communications device. The ghost may be identified by that specific fragrance. If you are on compatible terms, ask the ghost to use that fragrance as a communications device and identifying factor.

1. Choose a specific aroma to identify your desire to communicate with the ghost.
2. The next time you apprehend the ghost's fragrance, communicate aloud with the ghost.
3. Explain that you'd like to set up a formal system of communications, where you are an equal partner, rather than a passive partner, subject to the whims of the ghost popping in and out.
4. Demonstrate your chosen fragrance to the ghost and explain that when you wish to initiate communication, that fragrance will be wafted into the atmosphere. It will not be used at other times.
5. Ask the ghost for a sign that he or she is in accordance with this plan.

 ## Get Away Ghost Spell Backwards Candles

1. Light a white candle after dark.
2. Carry it in your right hand while holding a handful of salt in your left.
3. Walk backwards through every room of the haunted house from bottom to top, sprinkling salt through your fingers. (Keep additional salt in your pockets for refills if your house is large: do not backtrack.) Simultaneously tell the ghosts to get lost, aloud or silently as you deem appropriate.
4. At the topmost, furthest point of the home, extinguish the candle.

 ## Get Away Ghost Bean Spell

Scatter beans around your property to deny entry to ghosts for a year. (If plants result, this banishing effect may last even longer!)

 ## Get Away Ghost More Beans Spell

This spell has its roots in ancient Greece, and involves spitting or throwing beans at ghosts to make them go away.

 ## Get Away Ghost Yet More Beans Spell

To prevent hauntings, surround your home with living bean plants. Not only do beans repel ghosts but allegedly, the plants sing to wandering ghosts, guiding them to the next realm. If you'd like to hear these songs, a shamanic art, sit under the vines while they're in bloom. Meditate or allow yourself to fall asleep.

Get Away Ghost Spell Bistort

Burn dried powdered bistort to banish ghosts, wafting the fragrance as needed.

 ## Get Away Ghost Bistort Extra Strength

Hit the ghost with a double-whammy by burning and asperging with bistort.

1. Burn bistort, waft the fragrance through the home and reserve the ashes.
2. In the meantime, create a strong infusion by pouring boiling water over the powdered herb.
3. Sprinkle the bistort infusion throughout the home.
4. Sprinkle the ashes over thresholds.
5. Repeat regularly—at least once weekly—to send stubborn, persistent ghosts packing.

 ## Get Away Ghost Coffee Spell

Tell those ghosts to wake up, smell the coffee and leave! Burning ground coffee (rather than brewing it, although you can try that, too, having a cup in the process) allegedly repels ghosts as well as malevolent spiritual entities. It's important to use real ground coffee, the stronger the better, and especially not decaffeinated.

 ## Get Away Ghost Fennel Door-blocker

This spell may be used to ghost-proof individual rooms or an entire building. It only works on some ghosts but may be worth trying. Stuff keyholes full of fennel to prevent ghosts from entering the room (or leaving, too. If the ghost is already in the room, it may be trapped.)

 ## Get Away Ghost Juno's Brew

Despite its Roman name, Juno's Brew is reputedly a Greek formula. Juno is the firm mistress of her home. She determines who has permission to stay and who must leave immediately. This formula allegedly banishes all ghosts from your premises:

1. Cover half a cup of vervain leaves with boiling water.
2. Let it steep for ten minutes, then strain it.
3. Add the liquid to a bucket of wash water together with some white vinegar.
4. Wash your floors and thresholds; wipe up the walls and window areas. Concentrate on sending strong mental messages: this is your home; you choose who stays within its walls.
5. When cleansing is complete, leave doors and windows open for thirty minutes.

 ## Get Away Ghost Genitalia Spell

Botanicals are by no means the only way to banish ghosts, nor are they even necessarily the strongest. These methods also have the disadvantage of requiring preparation. What if you are suddenly surprised by a threatening ghost? The ultimate weapon may be used spontaneously, requires no preparation and costs nothing (beyond a jail sentence, if performed at the wrong time and place).

The human genitalia are perceived as the ultimate sign of life and thus the ultimate ghost-repellant. Sudden visitations may be removed merely by quickly and aggressively flashing your private parts at the ghost. It is effective for women to do this at any time. Men: if it's not erect, don't bother; that's the only way to impress a ghost.

Because there are many good reasons, apart from threat of legal action, against exposing your genitals, a host of amulets deriving from human genital imagery has evolved. Be prepared; wear as needed:

- ★ Downward facing triangles
- ★ Cowrie shells
- ★ Penis beads, cornos and other phallic amulets
- ★ A red, firm chili pepper worn on a cord around the neck
- ★ The fica, or fig hand amulet

Get Away Ghost The Fig Hand

Merely making the gesture of a fig hand in the direction of the ghost should be sufficient to send it packing. Tuck the thumb between the first two fingers and thrust it aggressively in the appropriate direction.

Get Away Ghost Pine Trees

According to Hildegard of Bingen, ghosts hate pine trees and avoid places where they grow. If it's not possible to surround your home with living pines, bring small living trees within it and situate them strategically. Decorate with images that resonate strongly of life: ankhs, hexagrams, and imagery (abstract or otherwise) depicting human genitalia. (In case you weren't sure what to do with that Thai penis amulet, this is the perfect opportunity.) This allegedly drives away the ghost, or at least makes it feel extremely unwelcome.

Get Away Ghost Tiger Lilies

Tiger lilies planted near doors and windows allegedly prevent the entry of ghosts.

Get Out Ghost!

If the ghost has taken up residence in your home or within another building, hanging alyssum up in every corner of a house will allegedly exorcise it.

Ghost Co-existence Spell (1) Lilies

Do you have ghosts? Can't get rid of them, no matter what you do? Keep lilies in your home and garden. They won't repel ghosts or banish them but they will keep the ghosts well behaved, preventing them from causing harm or mischief.

Ghost Co-existence Spell (2) Incense

Keep ghosts happy and good-natured by maintaining the fragrance of benzoin and sandalwood in the home.

Ghost Good Behavior Spell: Hecate's Supper

The Eurasian spirit Hecate guards the frontier between the realms of the living and the dead, negotiating the sometimes divergent needs of both parties. Although she may not banish ghosts entirely (you can ask, though!), she can enforce their good behavior. Hecate is traditionally depicted having one body but three faces, sometimes that of women but most typical that of a dog, a horse and a lion.

1. Each month, at the full moon, bring a three-headed image of Hecate to a three-way crossroads.
2. Place the image so that each face points toward a road (or as close as possible).
3. Place food on the ground including fish, honey and a round cake with candles.
4. Make an invocation to Hecate requesting that she make the ghosts behave.
5. Leave the meal at the crossroads for whoever takes it.

✷ Ghost Keep Away Spell (1) Don't Cross that Line, Ghost!

Create a boundary line over which ghosts allegedly will not cross.

1. Place three peeled cloves of garlic in a bowl, together with one handful of sea salt and one handful of fresh rosemary leaves.
2. Grind and mash the ingredients together.
3. Sprinkle them to create a boundary, as needed.

✷ Ghost Keep Away Spell (2) The Wreath of Life Spell

A wreath of fresh bay laurel leaves posted on your entrance doors signals "No Trespassing" *to ghosts.*

✷ Ghost Keep Away Spell (3) Caribbean Fumigation

The following herbs are burned in some Caribbean traditions to ward off malevolent ghosts and other troublesome spirits:

★ *Epazote*
★ *Grannybush* (Croton linearis; *known locally as rosemary, this is botanically distinct from the rosemary native to the Eastern hemisphere,* Rosmarinus officinalis)
★ *Guinea weed*
★ *Spiritweed*
★ *Water marigold or waterweed*

Burn one or a combination of these herbs in a pan, wafting the smoke as needed.

✷ Ghost Keep Away! (4) Roman Talisman Ring

An iron ring, containing a splinter of wood from a gallows, forms a magical talisman to frighten away ghosts. The ancient Roman formula suggested that the ring be formed from a bent nail, used in a crucifixion. (Not the crucifixion! It was a popular ancient practice; the Romans had plenty of nails to choose from.)

✷ Ghost and Poltergeist Protection Spell

To provide relief from destructive and mischievous ghosts and poltergeists:

1. Maintain fresh bay laurel branches and/or leaves within the home.
2. Replace them as their green color fades.

✷ Ghost Safety Spell: Knife and Fork

That ghost may clank its chains as much as it wants but at least this spell will guarantee you a safe night's sleep.

1. Get into bed.
2. Open the Bible or whatever sacred text gives you comfort or the ghost pause.
3. Begin to read backwards from wherever the book was opened.
4. When the page is concluded, fold that page over.
5. Insert a knife and fork as a page marker then place the book with its "bookmarks" under the pillow.

✷ Ghost Sickness Spell (1)

In many metaphysical beliefs, particularly Native American ones, the problem isn't that ghosts clank their

chains at night or pop out at inconvenient moments to say "boo!" Rather, ghosts need to be avoided or banished because it's believed that contact with ghosts causes illness in the living, something specifically known as "ghost sickness." If you fear this type of unhealthy contact, burn desert sage and white sage to repel and remove these influences as well as strengthening the defenses of the living.

 ## Ghost Sickness Spell (2)

Ghosts of those who died by violence are believed able to roam and cause aggressive forms of "ghost sickness." As diagnosed in traditional Mexican magical belief, ghost sickness is characterized by chills and excessive nervousness. The patient jumps at the slightest provocation. Ghost sickness may also be characterized by coma or the loss of the ability to speak.

The patient may be cured by rubbing the body with a live black hen. (The intent of the cure is not to kill the hen; if anything efforts are made to preserve the hen from harm, however many curers believe that exposure to ghost sickness may be too much for the hen and result in death or injury.) Patient and chicken should then undergo ritual fumigation using smoke derived by burning a combination of bay laurel leaves, frankincense, copal, and crossroads dirt. (Curers with Roman Catholic orientations would also include palm leaves blessed on Palm Sunday in this blend.)

 ## Ghost Vision

Are those ghosts really there? Carrying a lavender wand allegedly allows you to see ghosts for yourself.

 ## Haunted House Prevention Spell (1) Anti-Ghost Garden

Ghosts may be prevented from haunting houses by surrounding the home with specific botanicals. Create an anti-ghost garden by maintaining a substantial quantity of bay laurel trees, rowan (mountain ash) trees and lilies.

 ## Haunted House Prevention Spell (2) Fumigation

Fumigating an area with camphor and mint is used to send unwanted ghosts in search of new housing. One application may not be sufficient, however. Use repetitions of mystical numbers for reinforcement. Repeat for three, seven, nine, eighteen, twenty-one, or twenty-seven days as needed.

 ## Haunted House Prevention Spell (3) Bayberry

Sprinkle a strong infusion of bayberry inside and around the perimeter of a house to exorcise existing ghosts and repel new ones. For added power, asperge with a bay laurel branch.

 ## Haunted House Prevention Spell (4) Raspberry

Hang raspberry vines over the entrances to the deceased's former home to prevent the ghost from re-entering.

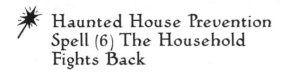

Haunted House Prevention Spell (5) Angelica

1. Make a decoction of angelica roots or pour boiling water over the dried, powdered root to make an infusion.
2. Sprinkling this within and around the home is an Iroquois recommendation for exorcising and preventing ghosts.

Haunted House Prevention Spell (6) The Household Fights Back

A Russian method of repelling ghosts from a home involves a coordinated household attack. At midnight, kosher or other blessed salt must be aggressively thrown from all windows and doors.

Apparently the presence of unwanted ghosts was a matter of some concern for the ancient Mesopotamians; ghost prevention, expelling and appeasing spells abound. As elsewhere, ghosts most likely to cause trouble were those with irregular funeral rites or those who no longer received post-funerary offerings, perhaps because no family members survived to perform this function.

Other potentially difficult ghosts included those who died violently, in sudden accidents, criminals sentenced to death—particularly unrepentant ones—and those who were not buried at all. Although this is specifically the ancient Mesopotamian perception, it's one shared with more magical traditions than not.

The Mesopotamians possessed an elaborate, sophisticated science of either repelling or appeasing ghosts, depending upon circumstances and the individual ghost. Spells may be complex or simple, aggressive or propitiatory. Adapt these to your own needs.

Mesopotamian Ghost Spell (1)

An ancient Mesopotamian formula to drive away ghosts allegedly works against either actual physical manifestations or disturbing, consistent dream visitations:

1. Blend vinegar, rainwater, well water, ditch water and river water.
2. Asperge the ghost-infested area with this liquid.
3. Ring a bell vigorously.
4. Hold a lit torch in the left hand and a cattle horn in the right. (If you're out of cattle horns, substitute a *shofar,* the Jewish ritual horn, available from Judaic religious supply stores.)
5. Announce in a firm, clear, steady voice:
   My goddess, * look upon me!*
   My god, * watch over me!*
   Let angry hearts be calm
   Satiate and appease anger
   Establish protective boundaries for me
   Establish well being for me.

Mesopotamian Ghost Spell (2)

Another Mesopotamian formula to drive away ghosts bypasses the realm of spirits to take banishing into one's own hands. This method is suggested if a ghost sighting has you spooked.

The original spell might insist that one spin one's own woolen threads. If you can spin, the spell will be strengthened by incorporating that process.

1. Braid a strand of unbleached wool and a strand of red wool together, so that the colors stand out from one another, remaining distinct. Use red wool that will not bleed into the other strand. The finished braid must be long enough to tie around your forehead.

* Substitute names as desired.

2. Make seven knots in the braid, while focusing upon your desires.
3. Bind the braid around your forehead, while chanting an incantation, something like this:
   Until red turns white and white turns red,
   That ghost that appeared to me can't come back again.
4. Sleep in the braid overnight (and whenever deemed necessary in the future).
5. Afterwards, carry it as a talisman, in a charm bag.

 ## Mesopotamian Ghost Spell (3)

Burn an image of the ghost, however you understand this. Whether or not this is sufficient to expel the ghost, it is a threatening gesture indicating that stronger action will be taken.

 ## Mesopotamian Ghost Spell (4)

Sometimes attempts to expel the ghost or take aggressive action aren't necessary or wise. Peaceful coexistence may be the best possible goal.

Keep the ghost happy by pouring out regularly scheduled offerings of flour and water. (Traditionally the water was poured from an ox horn or hoof: horn shaped beakers may be appropriate as well.)

 ## Mesopotamian Ghost Spell (5)

Laying the ghost can be a cooperative process. Why should you have to presume the needs, intentions or desires of the ghost? Negotiate with the ghost: find out why the ghost is present. What are the ghost's personal cultural post-death expectations? What can you do to transform a troublesome ghost into a protective ally? If direct negotiation is difficult, check the Necromancy Spells below for some tips on communicating across the realms.

 ## Pacify Ghost Halloween Spell

At midnight on Halloween bury apples at crossroads to feed hungry ghosts.

 ## Rest in Peace Spell (1) The Unknown Ghost

An ancient Greek method to lay a ghost to rest is especially beneficial if not only the identity but also the gender of the ghost is unknown.

1. Make distinctly male and female dolls from wood or true earthen clay (not synthetic substitutions as typically found among art supplies). It's crucial to the success of this spell that the dolls be formed from biodegradable materials, so that they can decompose entirely without leaving traces.
2. Give the dolls a feast, a party in their honor. Have real food and drink, real fun.
3. When the party's over, explain that their wanderings are over, too. Bury them in uncultivated land, where they are unlikely to be disturbed for a long time.

 ## Rest in Peace Spell (2) The Proper Send Off

Restless ghosts may be laid to rest by giving them the proper funeral they may never have had.

1. Place a small doll in a tiny coffin.
2. Have a great send-off.
3. Bury the coffin in a remote area or even in a cemetery itself.

Summoning Ghosts and Extracting Cooperation from Them

Not all ghostly visitations are unwelcome. For all the emphasis placed on exorcism and separation, sometimes the proper boundaries between living and dead can be maintained, for mutual benefit, while still permitting visits or even co-existence.

For every malevolent ghost, there's another who visits out of care and concern and whose help may be very useful. Before automatically repelling ghosts, especially if they haven't already proved hostile, it may be wise to determine who they are and why they've appeared before you bar opportunity and protection from your door. Further information on communicating with the dead may be found under Necromancy (page 284).

Sometimes the desire for contact doesn't emanate from the ghost. The dead may be summoned for protection or to perform various functions perhaps impossible for the living to accomplish. Spells for summoning the dead for purposes of divination or obtaining information are included under Necromancy.

Calling Up The Dead Incense

> Dried amaranth flowers
> Dittany of Crete
> Wormwood

An incense made from the above botanicals is traditionally burned in the cemetery, to simultaneously invite the dead to arise while offering protection to the living.

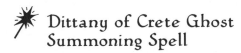

Dittany of Crete Ghost Summoning Spell

Just as certain botanicals summon spirits, others may be used to beckon ghosts. Dittany of Crete, named for a Greek divinity, perhaps an aspect of Artemis, is used to communicate with those who have passed on to other realms. Traditionally it's burned in the cemetery, although it may be used to call the dead to come to you. Legend has it that the image of the deceased will appear in the smoke just above the flame.

Sprinkle dried, powdered Dittany of Crete onto lit charcoals. If you are outdoors, burn substantial quantities of dried Dittany of Crete within a cauldron.

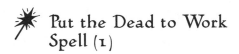

Put the Dead to Work Spell (1)

An extremely ancient metaphysical practice that still survives involves setting the dead onto somebody. Recorded practice goes back to ancient Egypt. Technically, one is merely requesting assistance from the deceased, over a specific situation, problem or person. However, there is an inherent intimidation factor involved with receiving a visitation from beyond the grave: frequently there's an element of something akin to calling in thugs to work over your enemy.

A trip to the cemetery is not required. If you know whose assistance you need, an altar may be erected at home, so that you may discreetly request personal aid.

1. The minimum offering is a white candle plus either a glass of spring water or **Spirit Water.**
2. The altar may also be personalized so as to strongly attract the person whose assistance you seek: offer a favorite libation or meal. Set out photographs or objects that will beckon attention.
3. Write a brief, clear, concise statement of your desire on a piece of brown paper.
4. Place this within a conjure bag, together with graveyard dirt and seven coffin nails.
5. Carry this with you, retain it in a safe place in your home or bury it in Earth immediately.
6. If and when your petition is granted, bury the bag in Earth.

⁕ Put the Dead to Work Spell (2)

In a traditional Chinese belief, the dead may be empowered to rise for brief periods and perform evil deeds, as desired by another, if a dog is beneath the bed containing the corpse while a cat is simultaneously on the roof of the building within which the corpse lies. (In other words, for everyone's protection, keep cats and dogs away from the corpse, enclosed and supervised, until the body is gone.)

⁕ Put the Dead to Work Spell (3)

A spell derived from ancient Alexandria suggests having a ghost deliver your unrequited lover. Whether that person will be pleased to be "delivered" in this fashion is subject to debate. More romantic love and seduction spells may be found elsewhere in this book.

1. Make a wax figure to represent the object of your desire.
2. Pierce the image with thirteen needles. No sharp pains or other harm is intended to befall your target. Instead the spell's goal is to make him or her burn with desire for you.
3. Put one needle each through the brain, the eyes, the ears, mouth, hands, feet, anus, genitals and abdomen. (These are the traditional spots; however if others are more fitting for your situation, use those instead.)
4. As you pierce the brain, murmur: *"You can't stop thinking about me,"* or *"You think about me all the time."* As you pierce each eye, murmur something like: *"You only have eyes for me."* Continue with each stop along the anatomy, personalizing your chant as much as possible. No need to be shy, the ancients were quite explicit. You can be, too.
5. At sunset, place the fully pierced doll on (or within) the grave of someone who either died young or violently or preferably both. The spirit emerging from this type of death is allegedly restless and filled with resentment and thus willing to accept a commission from a stranger.
6. Call on the corpse in the name of those spirits with authority over the dead, those who supervise their comings and going, and those whose legends somehow involve the realm of the dead. The original spell suggests Adonis, Anubis, Erishkigal, Hecate, Hermes and Persephone; however, use whichever spirits you think will be most effective under the present circumstances. There's little real spiritual invocation here: instead it's a pyramid of intimidation. The dead soul is called upon to intimidate the object of your affections, while the spirits are called upon to intimidate the dead.
7. Announce:
   By the spirits of the afterworld,
   By the spirits of those snatched from life too soon,
   I command you, Spirit of the Dead, arise!
   Go to [give the address] *and bring me* [Name], *child of* [Name] *to be my lover!*
8. Go home and await results.

Put the Dead to Work Spell (4)

The spell above attempts to exploit the inherent restless energy stimulated by a certain type of death. An Obeah ritual requests more personal assistance. Aid is sought from someone who loves you and is loyal to you from beyond the grave.

1. At night, visit the grave of someone with great love and loyalty toward you: your mother is considered the ideal but another family member or good friend also works.
2. Bring raw eggs, cooked rice and a libation. (Rum is the traditional Obeah libation as it is in many other traditions, not only because it's what's available but because rum derives directly from sugar, which has profound summoning properties. Whiskey, aqua vitae, is also popular; however choose what's most suitable for your circumstances.)
3. Pour the libation onto the ground.
4. Break the egg onto the dish of rice and mix them.
5. Leave the offering at the grave.
6. Move away for a few minutes, then approach and explain why you've come and what you need.

Spiritweed Spell

Spiritweed is an herb, originally native to the Amazon. Often called false coriander *because of its resemblance to that herb, it has culinary and magical uses. As its name indicates, spiritweed is used to maintain control over the dead, whether for exorcising or summoning. Different motivating factors are used to persuade a ghost to accept a mission from the living: intimidation, love, sometimes bribery.*

1. Bring two bottles of rum and some spiritweed to the cemetery.
2. Attach the spiritweed to a stick and be prepared to initiate the spell at midnight.

3. Take off your clothes.
4. Place one bottle of rum at the head of the grave.
5. Strike the tombstone three times with the spiritweed stick and call the deceased:
   "[Name], *child of* [name]. *Come out! I have work for you!*"
6. Leave the second bottle at the foot of the grave. Strike the ground beside it three times with the stick and repeat your call.
7. In clear, concise language—no murmuring and muttering now—explain precisely and exactly what you need.
8. Open the bottles but leave them at the grave. Don't turn around until you get home. At some point that you deem appropriate, with your back to the grave, you may put your clothes on.
9. Don't speak with anyone until daylight.

Stinging Nettles Ghost Safety Spell

Wear gloves for this spell! Hold stinging nettles in your hands to ward off ghosts.

Necromancy

Technically necromancy is a divination system that exploits the special powers of the dead. It has come to encompass contacting the dead by various means to extract information, about the future or otherwise. Necromancy is a word frequently misused and misunderstood: it's been used as a catch-all label for any sort of cemetery desecration. Although desecration may occur in the name of communication (and one person's ritual is another person's desecration), vandalism and desecration for its own sake or for destructive purposes is not necromancy under any definition, and there are many methods of contacting and speaking with dead souls that do not involve a trip to the graveyard, nor require any contact with a corpse at all.

Necromancy exists because the end of life does-n't necessarily end the need for one person to talk to another. Necromancy also exists because some metaphysical systems believe that dead souls are the only ones both privy to certain information and able to share that information in a lucid man-ner with the living.

Because it's believed that the dead are no longer bound by the limitations of the mortal physical realm, they are able to foresee events, understand the past and be either persuaded or compelled to reveal these details. Necromancy may be used to reveal the future or to gain understanding of a past or current situation.

Two kinds of souls may be summoned:

★ *Those with ties of love and loyalty to you, who are probably inclined to be helpful*
★ *Those who must be compelled to appear and provide assistance*

Different methods of summoning exist for differ-ent souls. Whether there must be contact with the corpse depends upon the method chosen.

The ancient Greeks believed that the recently deceased were more coherent than those who had been dead for a while. In essence, the long-deceased are out of practice. The longer one has been dead, the further away from the land of the living one has drifted. It becomes harder for the living to under-stand the dead and likewise for the dead to compre-hend the living person's needs, desires and even language. Hence the Greeks' inclination to use fresh corpses in necromantic ritual.

Of course, all of this depends upon whether you believe that love, loyalty and consciousness tran-scend death. For some cultures, all semblance of human feelings and memory immediately ceases at death, therefore there can be nothing benevolent about contacting the dead. Any contact with the dead is thus, by definition, malevolent sorcery.

The most famous modern necromantic device is the ouija board, available at toy stores amongst the board games, and its relative, the planchette. This begs another point of consideration. Some philosophies consider that wisdom and foresight are acquired during the death process. Others believe that nature and intelligence after death remains what it was during life. In other words, if Aunt Sophie never gave you good advice while she was alive, what makes you think that she'll do any better now that she's dead?

Be cautious whose advice is relied upon, whether it derives from living sources or those beyond the grave. The ouija board is considered something of a portal to the next realm: an open telephone line, as it were. Consider who speaks with you before continuing and maintaining any conversations.

These are all remnants of shamanic rites, out of context. When shamans are banished, people attempt to do needed jobs themselves, as best as they are able, whether or not they have been extensively trained.

Necromancy should be preceded by intensive cleansing and protective spells. Fasting probably wouldn't hurt and may make the process more suc-cessful to boot. Wear or carry protective amulets and charms.

 ## Bugleweed Spell

Old-school séances often featured bugles, reminiscent of Gabriel's horn. Bugleweed encourages contact between realms more quietly: burn it as incense during the séance.

 ## Cemetery Stroll

Circle around the cemetery three times, staying calm but focused on your desire. The dead should become visible to you and you will be able to communicate.

Dreams of the Dead Incense

This incense blend allegedly allows you to contact those who have gone on ahead in your dreams.

Burn dried powdered acacia, althea, and star anise before bedtime. Permeate the room with the aroma. As you go to sleep, visualize the dream that you need. Try to "begin" the dream before you fall asleep and see what happens.

 ## Dream Summons to the Beyond

1. Create an infusion by pouring boiling water over *yerba santa, "holy herb."*
2. Bring the strained liquid to the cemetery and sprinkle it over the grave belonging to the person whom you wish to see and perhaps communicate with.
3. Allegedly the person will appear in your dreams that very night, although the extent to which one can communicate may be dependent on your dream skills.

Dumb Supper Spells

Do you wish to dine with Dr. Dee, Madame Blavatsky and Mamzelle Marie Laveau? Invite them! Perhaps you'd rather share a meal with your late great-grandmother. Invite her, too! Dumb Suppers are ritual meals enacted between living and the dead. *"Dumb"* indicates not lack of intelligence but that these meals (and any communication) are conducted in silence. While the dead are formally invited to attend, all cooking and serving is done by the living. Although a dumb supper may be served at any time, traditionally they are scheduled to coincide with Halloween, the time of year when the veil between realms is thinnest. Extend specific invitations, or allow yourself to be surprised by who shows up.

 ## Dumb Supper for One

1. Set the table for two (or more, depending upon the number of guests anticipated or invited).
2. Serve yourself and the other party.
3. Don't utter a sound until the meal is over.

 ## Dumb Supper for Two

1. Set the table for three (or more).
2. Serve both living people and also the departed. (Make sure there are enough chairs so that the departed may sit.)
3. After the meal is over and cleared away and you have left the table, both people may discuss their experiences and perceptions.

 ## Dumb Supper Extravaganza

1. Set a table for a banquet.
2. Invite a number of people, both living and otherwise.
3. Dress for dinner. Set the table beautifully. Make sure there are sufficient chairs and place settings for the unseen guests.
4. Do not speak at all. Do not serve yourself. Everyone must serve others, living or otherwise. Allow yourself to become sensitive to the desires of others. (You may also designate specific people to serve as waiters.)
5. When the meal is over, dishes cleared away and everyone has left the table (and the dead have presumably departed), discuss experiences, perceptions, and insights.

 ## Dumb Supper Baltic Version

This Dumb Supper is celebrated on the third, ninth, and fortieth days following a funeral.

1. The souls of the deceased are publicly invited to share a meal with the living.
2. This meal is eaten in silence. The table is set without knives.
3. Any food that falls should not be picked up but remain for hungry ghosts to enjoy.
4. Presumably once upon a time, libations and offerings were made; incorporate as desired.

Golden Bough Spell

Mistletoe allegedly works as a key to unlock the doors between the realms of the living and the dead. Hold a branch of mistletoe, "the golden bough," in your hand during necromancy for inspiration, protection and success.

Greek Necromantic Spell (1)

For the ancient Greeks, a fire made from privet opened the gates to the afterlife. To summon and speak with ghosts, burn wormwood on a bed of privet fire.

Greek Necromantic Spell (2)

Shamanic methods are retained by this Greek necromantic spell, with its echoes of Odysseus' journey to Hades. The ritual should be accomplished at the Full Moon, the Dark Moon or the days in between.

1. Dig a ditch deep enough to stand within.
2. Surround it with incense. (Dittany of Crete, mugwort and/or wormwood are recommended.)
3. Cast a protective circle around it to keep everyone away except the one(s) you summon.
4. Pour a libation of equal quantities of honey, milk and wine into the ditch.
5. Make a figure of the person you wish to communicate with from bread dough.

6. Ornament it with bay laurel leaves and fennel. Throw it into the ditch.
7. Nick your little finger and sprinkle a few drops of blood into the ditch. (This is sufficient: do not injure yourself or cut yourself severely.)
8. Drum, dance, work yourself into an ecstatic state and speak.

Interview With a Corpse Spell

An old Greco-Egyptian spell for questioning corpses is reminiscent of the spell used to create the legendary golem of the Prague Ghetto.

1. Create ink from red ochre, burnt myrrh, fresh wormwood juice and either powdered evergreen leaves or the essential oil of an evergreen species.
2. Write the following on a flax leaf: *"AZEL BALEMACHO."* (This is the English transliteration. Ideally the formula is written using the Greek alphabet, so that it will have twelve letters.)
3. Place this leaf in the mouth of the corpse.
4. Ask your question. Listen patiently. Modern literal minds may expect the corpse to start speaking. Although nothing is impossible, this isn't necessarily the way answers are received. Allow yourself to receive spontaneous mental revelations. In addition, the response may come from another person, who may or may not realize that they are serving as an oracle.

Interview With a Loved One Spell

Eliphas Levi was the magical name adopted by the French master magus Alphonse Louis Constant (1810–1875). This complex, lengthy necromantic spell is based on his instructions. This spell allegedly enables contact with someone with whom the spell-caster shared a close, loving relationship. It extends over fourteen consecutive days although the actual conversation doesn't occur until the final day.

1. Choose a significant date for communications to occur, whether a birthday, anniversary or some other date of significance for both you and the deceased.
2. Intensive preparation for necromancy must begin fourteen days prior to the chosen date and continue for the duration. Undergo extensive cleansing spells daily for the fourteen days: refrain from sex, alcohol and eating meat. Only simple, minimal food should be consumed during this period.
3. The spell must occur in a room belonging to the deceased. If this is not possible, reproduce another room so that it resembles the actual room as closely as possible. A *museum-quality* reproduction must be realized and must be ready fourteen days prior to the chosen date.
4. Place a portrait of the deceased in a prominent position. Veil it in white fabric.
5. Arrange flowers around the portrait. Choose the individual's favorite flowers or those that hold significance towards the personal relationship shared together. Change the flowers for fresh ones daily.
6. Every night during the fourteen-day period, go to the room alone, maintaining total silence. Ideally enter the room at the same time each evening, as if keeping an appointment. For a minimum of an hour, contemplate the portrait. The only light permitted is one candle or magic lamp placed behind the spell-caster.
7. Fumigate the room before leaving. Choose a fragrance beloved by the deceased or one that holds personal significance for your relationship. If the choice puzzles you, choose benzoin or mimosa, to invite benevolence and ward off mean spirits.
8. Leave the room by walking out backwards, never turning your back on the portrait.
9. On the actual day designated for communication, dress up in a celebratory manner. Do not see or communicate with anyone else but the deceased on this day.
10. Earlier in the day, before the time scheduled for the regular "appointment," set a table for two in the room. Eat a meal of bread, fruit and wine while facing the portrait. Place half the food and a glass of wine before the portrait but do not unveil it. Eat your own food and then leave.
11. Come back at the appointed time in total silence.
12. Build a fire of cypress wood, and cast frankincense upon the fire seven times.
13. Call the person's name.
14. Extinguish the candle or magic lamp. Allow the cypress fire to burn out.
15. When the fire is reduced to mere embers, add more frankincense.
16. Call upon the Creator of the Universe in a manner pertaining to the spiritual beliefs of the departed. Speak from the perspective of the deceased.
17. Be silent for fifteen minutes, then talk as if the person is present. Pray aloud for them to arrive, then silently cover your face.
18. Call the person's name three times from a kneeling position, in a strong voice with your eyes closed. Call again very gently.
19. Open your eyes: the spirit should materialize or their presence should at least manifest to you.

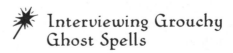

Interviewing Grouchy Ghost Spells

Burn three parts wormwood to one part vervain when summoning ghosts who were suffering from a state of depression when they died. This formula may also be

used when communicating with ghosts who haven't realized that they're dead, especially if you're planning to break the news. Alternatively, to raise grumpy and/or unwilling ghosts, you can burn three parts wormwood to one part Solomon's Seal.

If you anticipate that the ghosts may not be so delighted to see you, and that they may have preferred undisturbed eternal rest, offer honey immediately as a peace offering, to sweeten the experience for all concerned.

Jewish Necromantic Spell

1. Spend the night at the grave, clothed in *distinctive garments.*
2. Burn spices and incense.
3. Concentrate on your question, whether one asks it aloud or silently.
4. Wave a myrtle wand, until one *hears* the answer to your query. The myrtle wand must be held continuously while conversing with the deceased at the gravesite.

Iron Necromancy Spell (1)

If iron protects against ghosts, it also enables communication between the realms of the living and the dead.

1. Bring an iron wand to the cemetery.
2. Point it in the direction of a grave.
3. Speak and listen.

Iron Necromancy Spell (2)

If a trip to the cemetery is impossible, the spell may still be accomplished. Face a portrait of the deceased or conjure up a vivid mental image. Hold the wand; speak and listen. When you wish to terminate the session, lay down the wand.

Mugwort Ghost Spell

Desires may be complex. Although you may wish to consult with a ghost, you don't necessarily want that desire to be misinterpreted as an invitation to follow you home. Mugwort both facilitates communication with the dead and protects you from them.

1. Burn an offering of mugwort: this enhances your psychic senses, enhancing your powers of reception with other realms.
2. Keep the mugwort burning following the ghost's apparent departure.
3. When you depart, step over the burning mugwort; this allegedly stops a ghost from following you.

Necromancy Ritual Trident

The magic fork or trident sometimes used in medieval high ritual necromancy must be fashioned from almond or hazel wood. Traditionally the wood is severed from the tree with one blow from a virgin knife—a knife that has never before been used. To guarantee that this is so, the old magicians observed the manufacture of the knife, purchasing it directly from the smith, or they crafted the knife themselves. The knife can only be used to craft the wand. The trident's three prongs will be crafted from its blade.

Osiris Incense

Osiris is the Egyptian Ruler of the Dead. Blend acacia and frankincense together, and burn this incense to reach someone in his realm.

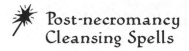

Post-necromancy Cleansing Spells

After communicating with ghosts, strong cleansing is recommended.

★ *Get into the tub and scrub vigorously with salt*
★ *Make a paste using salt, **Holy Water** or one of the other formula waters and cleanse the body*
★ *Form a paste with olive oil and salt and scrub the body*
★ *Create a paste with salt, olive oil and fresh rosemary leaves. Scrub the body*

Scottish Necromantic Spell

In order to perform this Scottish necromantic spell, one must arrange to have a room with total, complete privacy.

1. Meticulously spiritually cleanse the room and oneself prior to beginning the spell at nightfall.
2. Using a compass, cast a circle in the middle of the room, large enough for you, a table and chair.
3. Place objections of protection on the table. The traditional spell calls for a Bible and/or a crucifix. Substitute as needed. If the Bible doesn't work for you, substitute another lengthy spiritual work, both for protection and to occupy you until the ghost shows up.
4. Light a white candle: this is your only source of light.
5. Sit down and concentrate on your desires. Call the specific ghost you need. Read the book. Wait for the ghost to show up, perhaps in person. Should you fall asleep, be prepared to speak with the ghost in your dreams and remember and record the conversation.

Séance Incense

Grind frankincense resin and sandalwood powder together and burn. The fragrance lets ghosts know they're welcome, while simultaneously beckoning angelic and other protective powers.

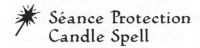

Séance Protection Candle Spell

This candle provides protection during séance proceedings.

1. Slice the top off a small white votive candle.
2. Carve the bottom of the candle so that the wick is exposed and may be lit.
3. Fill a glass half-full of spring water.
4. Place a saucer on top and quickly flip it over so that the glass rests on the saucer but no water is spilled. (This becomes easier with practice.)
5. Place this on the floor, behind the door.
6. Place the reversed candle on top of the glass and light it.

Tree Necromancy Spell

Trees are traditionally planted atop graves, in the same manner that they're planted over a newborn's buried placenta or umbilical cord. This serves multiple purposes: in essence, the tree roots the deceased in the grave, but it also serves as a communications device between the dead and those left behind. This is commemorated in fairy tales like The Juniper Tree *and various versions of* Cinderella *where the dead mother magically communicates with her children through a tree planted on her grave. Trees most commonly and effectively used include cypress, juniper, and pine.*

1. To communicate, bring a libation and/or other gift for the tree, which serves as the portal.
2. Bring something for yourself, too. If you'd like to bring a gift to the deceased, do so as well. Sit down, eat, drink, and talk to the tree.
3. The response may come in dreams or unexpectedly.

Tormentil Safety Spell

Tormentil tea allegedly offers protection while journeying to the realms of the dead. It ensures that you'll return—and return alone! Drink a cup of tormentil tea before embarking on your journey or any other necromantic methods.

Wisteria Dream Spell

Wisteria may be used to communicate with those who have passed on. Consider whom you wish to speak with:

1. Place a photograph of the person you want to contact under your pillow. If a photograph isn't available, write their name on a piece of paper as a substitute or, better yet, use their signature written in their own handwriting.
2. Hang wisteria over the bed or keep it beneath the pillow; whichever is more convenient and comfortable.
3. Concentrate on what you wish to discuss and go to sleep.

Wormwood Spell

Allegedly if wormwood is burned in the cemetery, the souls of the dead will rise and speak.

Vampires

No after-death spirit retains as much fascination for the living as does the vampire. Popularly known as the *un-dead*, many understand vampires to exist on a plane somewhere between the realms of the living and the dead. Are vampires tortured souls of the dead, compelled to feed upon the living? Or are they souls rewarded with eternal life, able to achieve the alchemist's ultimate fantasy without spending endless hours shut up in a laboratory?

Who or what exactly are vampires? Interpretations differ; *"vampire"* is a catch-all word that encompasses many concepts. However, one quality is held in common by all vampires: they suck vitality from others. The most notorious literary and cinematic vampires, like Bram Stoker's *Dracula*, Sheridan Le Fanu's *Carmilla*, or the inhabitants of Anne Rice's novels, are blood-suckers. Some vampires kill their victims by draining them of all their blood immediately. More sensuous vampires prolong the process: it isn't the loss of blood that ultimately kills the victim. The blood is merely the means for the vampire to drain the victim's life force away.

How does one become this type of vampire? Different traditions cite different causes, some much crueler than others if one considers the implications.

★ *Inadequate, improper funeral rites potentially create vampires*

★ *There is a contagious quality to being a vampire. One vampire infects, initiates and creates another. Having been attacked by a blood-sucking vampire, according to this school of thought, one either becomes a vampire oneself or dies*

★ *Bram Stoker conflated his Dracula legend with tales of Vlad the Impaler, Ruler of Transylvania. In actual Transylvanian folklore, illegitimate sons, born outside Church-sanctioned marriages, are doomed to become vampires*

★ *Ukrainian folklore perceives vampires as the inevitable result of sexual relations between witches and werewolves*

★ *According to other legends, those born on Christmas Day are potentially future vampires*

★ *Some spirits are believed to be innately vampiric, transcending rhyme or reason*

Traditional antidotes to vampires include bells, bright light or sunlight, garlic, onions, and silver bullets or bullets created from melted down bell metal. Whether crosses and Church-blessed Holy Water also repels vampires or whether this is merely Christian propaganda is subject to debate. Devotees of Japanese anime will recall that these methods have no effect on *Vampire Princess Miyu*.

More specialized, occult charms to repel vampires exist.

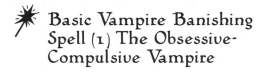

Basic Vampire Banishing Spell (1) The Obsessive-Compulsive Vampire

1. Place fishing nets over entrance doors and windows of the place you'd like to protect.
2. Allegedly the vampire must compulsively count all knots before entering. He or she will either be caught in the sunlight or simply give up and find another home.

Fishing nets may be replaced or supplemented with sieves: the vampire will be forced to count the holes instead.

Basic Vampire Banishing Spell (2) Magic Ring

A recommendation from the Gypsies of India:

1. Wear an iron ring set with pearls.
2. Remember to charge and consecrate the ring prior to its initial use.
3. Cleanse the ring in incense smoke following any encounters or close calls.

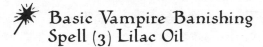

Basic Vampire Banishing Spell (3) Lilac Oil

Lilac oil reputedly repels vampires and is certainly more fragrant than garlic. It's very difficult to find real lilac oil, most of what is commercially available is synthetic; presumably vampires can tell the difference. Make your own, the lingering aroma should keep the vampire out of the house, too.

1. Infuse olive oil with lilac blossoms. (Check *Elements of Magic Spells,* page 31, for reminders on making infusions.)
2. Rub the oil on the body as needed.

Vampires similar to those in literature and movies, who spend their nights on the prowl but their days in the grave, may also be destroyed. However, it's necessary to identify the gravesite.

Destroy Vampires Spell (1)

Pour boiling water over any cracks or holes visible on the gravesite.

Destroy Vampires Spell (2)

Walk a horse back and forth over the grave repeatedly.

Get Away Vampire!

Perhaps it's sufficient to banish a vampire, albeit from a greater territory than just your private home and presence. Simple enough—provided you have his sock.

1. The vampire's left sock is specifically needed, although perhaps this vampire interchanges socks like many people do.

2. Stuff it with graveyard dirt, preferably from his or her own grave, blended with rocks from the cemetery.
3. Toss this outside the limits of the area you wish to protect into running water, flowing away from the area.

Peppermint Vampire Banishing Spells

Peppermint allegedly repels vampires as effectively as garlic, and can be easier to administer.

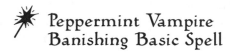

Peppermint Vampire Banishing Basic Spell

Hang fresh peppermint leaves around one's neck at bedtime. (This is also reputed to have an aphrodisiac effect, so maybe you'll be too busy to worry about the vampires.)

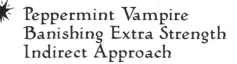

Peppermint Vampire Banishing Extra Strength

Grind dried peppermint leaves and garlic cloves together, forming a powder. Place some of this powder in a bag and wear around your neck. (This is no longer an aphrodisiac.)

Peppermint Vampire Banishing Extra Strength Indirect Approach

Make a powder by grinding dried peppermint and garlic together. Cast a circle with this powder around your bed just before bedtime; allegedly infernal beings will not enter this circle.

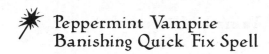

Peppermint Vampire Banishing Quick Fix Spell

Traditional vampires always seem to go for the neck.

1. Add essential oil of peppermint to a vial of grapeseed oil.
2. Keep the bottle beside your bed. Anoint your neck with the oil before retiring for the night or as needed.
3. If you like the fragrance (and this one *can* work as an aphrodisiac!) anoint your pillow too.

Trap-A-Vampire Spell

Vampires, like genies, may be trapped in bottles. Choose a glass or metal bottle; presumably the vampire can bite through a plastic one. This spell works on the same principle as a fly-trap.

1. Place some kind of food the vampire likes inside the bottle, but not blood. This spell works on a vampire who is understood to have once been a regular person with predilections for human food. Find something particularly tempting and put it in the bottle.
2. You will know when the vampire is in the bottle when you observe a bit of straw or fluff within. Seal the bottle up securely.
3. The bottle and the vampire may be destroyed by throwing the sealed bottle into a fire.

Vampire Diagnostic Spell

This spell to determine whether a cemetery is infested with vampires derives from Transylvania, the cinematic, if not necessarily the actual, heart of vampire country.

1. Place a young virgin boy onto a young virgin black stallion.
2. The boy must ride this horse around the cemetery.
3. Should the horse halt at any spot and refuse to go further, suspicions are confirmed.

Wherever the horse stops is a clue to the vampire's abode and identity, not necessarily the actual home of the vampire. Clues may need to be analyzed for a complete revelation and understanding.

Vampire Pacification Spell

In Macedonian tradition, vampires can be prevented from causing harm by scattering millet seed throughout the cemetery. Any passing vampires are compelled to obsessively pick up every tiny seed, leaving them vulnerable to the banishing rays of the sun.

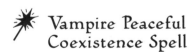 ## Vampire Peaceful Coexistence Spell

If you are unable to beat, destroy or banish a vampire, what other option is there? No, you don't have to join them. Sometimes peaceful co-existence can be arranged. A practical Romany method involves creating a regularly scheduled offering table for the vampire and providing food. In exchange, the vampire promises not to bother an agreed-upon list of people. In addition to blood, Romany vampire lore says that the creatures of the night crave milk. Offer dairy milk, coconut milk and rice balls boiled in milk. Those vampires with a sweet tooth accept offerings of halvah.

 ## Vampire Prevention Spell (1)

Scatter iron over the suspected grave.

 ## Vampire Prevention Spell (2)

Scatter garlic cloves over the grave.

 ## Vampire Prevention Spell (3)

Spindles are an ancient symbol of life and death. The Fates traditionally wield a spindle with which they spin the thread of life—and a pair of shears to cut that thread. Three days after a burial, stab nine spindles into the grave to prevent a vampire from rising.

 ## Vampire Prevention Spell (4)

Hammer iron nails into Earth over the grave—as many as possible, and at least a hundred.

 ## Vampire Prevention Spell (5)

Grow briar roses over the grave to prevent a vampire from rising.

 ## Vampire Protection Spell (1)

Blackthorn sticks may not repel a vampire but they protect against harm from them. If involved with magical activities that may accidentally or deliberately summon vampires, use a magic wand crafted from blackthorn.

Vampire Protection Spell (2)

Some vampires allegedly prefer infants and children. To protect them, place the following in a small bag: a safety pin, mustard seeds, rosemary, and an image of San Cipriano. Tie this around the child's waist.

Vampire Repellant Powder

Grind and powder dried hawthorn and rowan leaves. Blend this powdered mix with either fresh or powdered garlic. Carry the powder within a charm bag for protection, and sprinkle it to create boundaries as needed.

Special Vampires: Incubi and Succubi

Vampirism can be understood metaphorically as well as literally: that may not be just any old blood the vampire is draining. Menstrual blood may be perceived as symbolizing women's mysteries and magic powers. (Traditional magical wisdom considers this to be more than just metaphor and symbol.) The male vampire depicted preying upon a young woman may be perceived as either attempting to appropriate or annihilate her special power. (And when you consider those vampires who also crave milk …)

Literary and cinematic vampires typically possess a sexual element. To some extent that type of vampire combines the blood-sucker with the more ancient incubus (male) and succubus (female). Incubi and succubi are spirits, vampiric creatures who suck and drain sexual vitality, often through sexual intercourse, whether actual physical intercourse or through dream hauntings. Although the visitations may occur in dreams, the severe devitalization is apparent upon awakening.

These may be the original vampires, once more famous and prevalent than the notorious blood-suckers of today. These legends converge in the Semitic spirit Lilith, often diabolized as both a blood-sucking vampire and as a seductive but dangerous succubus. Other famous succubi include Lilith's daughters, Herodias and her daughters, La Diablesse of the French Caribbean and the djinn, Aisha Qandisha and the Karina. Incubi apparently prefer anonymity, perhaps because so many more spells are devoted to banishing them.

 Avoid Succubi

The standard magical recommendation for men who wish to avoid succubi:

★ *Never sleep alone and never sleep in an empty house*
★ *Don't respond to sexual advances from solitary, beautiful, mysterious women who linger alone amidst ruins or near deserted fresh water springs*

Banish Incubus Spell (1)

Ludovico Maria Sinistrari (1622–1701), a Franciscan friar, is widely acknowledged as the last of the "gentleman demonologists." The incense formula he recommends to ward off an incubus largely consists of a combination of aphrodisiac and commanding ingredients. Perhaps the goal is to attract other company to keep busy with at night, so that the incubus is denied his opportunity?

1. Place the following ingredients in a cauldron: sweet flag (calamus), cubeb seeds, roots from two different aristolochia species, cardamom, ginger, long pepper, pink cloves, cinnamon, cloves, mace, nutmeg, frankincense (Sinistrari's formula calls for only resin; I've interpreted this to refer to frankincense, however interpret as you will), benzoin, aloeswood together with its root, and sandalwood.
2. Brew all ingredients in three and a half quarts (approximately four and a half liters) of brandy and water.
3. The steam from the simmering brew repels the incubus.

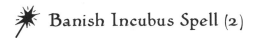 Banish Incubus Spell (2)

This spell repels an incubus and prevents his return.

1. Wrap three thorn apple seeds in a white handkerchief.
2. Use a safety pin to fasten this handkerchief to the underside of your pillow.
3. Leave this attached for seven nights then either throw the seeds out the back door or bury them in the ground at a distance from your home.
4. As soon as the seeds have been disposed, immediately wash the handkerchief. Use **Indigo Water,** if appropriate and essential oils of lavender and cajeput in the final rinse water.

Banish Incubus Spell (3)

An Anglo-Saxon defense against an incubus may represent a Christian overlay over an older spell.

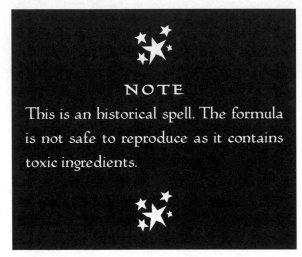

NOTE
This is an historical spell. The formula is not safe to reproduce as it contains toxic ingredients.

1. Collect hops, wormwood, lupine, bishopwort, henbane, harewort, garlic, fennel, heathberry plants, ashthroat, viper's bugloss and githrife.
2. Place the botanicals in a jar and place beneath an altar.
3. Sing nine masses over them.
4. Boil them in butter and mutton fat.
5. Add salt.
6. Strain the mixture through cloth.
7. Take the strained herbs and dispel of in running water.
8. Anoint yourself with the salve as needed.

Incubus Protection

1. Weave fresh dill, Saint John's Wort and vervain into a garland and wear it for protection while you sleep.
2. Should dried herbs only be available, place a pinch of each in a medicine bag and wear it around your neck.

Incubus Repellants

The following worn around your neck repel and protect against incubi: coral, flint, or a necklace woven from peony roots. For maximum effectiveness, all ingredients may be combined. Charge and consecrate all items prior to initial use. Remember to knot your goal into the necklace.

While there seem to be fewer generic succubi spells, individual succubi have earned great renown, unlike incubi. (Who remembers the name of Merlin's father, allegedly an incubus?) One succubus, Meridiana, allegedly advised Pope Sylvester; it was her influence that supposedly allowed him to attain the pontificate. In exchange he remained faithful to her throughout his life. (Whether sleeping with a succubus breaks vows of celibacy is an interesting theological dilemma.) Other succubi, however, are more malevolent.

 ## La Diablesse

La Diablesse, a Caribbean vampire, resembles Lilith and Aisha Qandisha, as well as some other vampiric, alluring djinn. La Diablesse usually appears as an exceedingly beautiful, charming woman; she may appear in traditional Creole costume but betrays herself with her one cloven goat's foot. Her anger is towards men: she seduces them then kills them.

1. To save yourself, should you have a close encounter with La Diablesse, take off all your clothes.
2. Turn them inside out, then put them back on again.
3. Walk home backwards, never once during this entire process taking your eyes from La Diablesse.

East Asian Fox Spirits are a special sub-genre of incubi/succubi. Shape-shifters, they appear to the victim in the form of extremely handsome or beautiful men and women, although when traveling incognito they tend to use the form of a fox. They are seductive, charming and frequently the most exciting lover the victim has ever had, therefore blinding the victim to potential danger. Some fox spirits are in fact benevolent, however most are vampiric creatures that suck the life-essence from those they seduce sexually. The victim wastes away, traditionally becoming tubercular.

Fox Spirit Exposure Spell

In general, fox spirits can only retain their power over an individual as long as their victim refuses to recognize the potential danger. Once exposed, the malicious spirit generally flees in search of another victim.

1. Fox spirits love wine and crave intoxication. Given the opportunity, they tend to over-indulge but just like any other drunk, this causes them to be sloppy and careless.
2. When drunk the fox spirit will reveal their true identity, breaking their spell.

The Sukuyan

In Trinidad and elsewhere in the Caribbean special vampiric spirits are known as sukuyan. *During the day, the sukuyan appears as an innocuous, frequently charming or even beautiful person; at night however she is transformed into a dangerous, bloodthirsty spirit. To determine her true identity, empty 100 pounds (45 kg) of rice at a crossroads. The sukuyan, an obsessive-compulsive like so many low-level spirits, will feel compelled to pick it up grain by grain, leaving herself vulnerable to identification.*

She (and the sukuyan seems inevitably to be a "she") gains admittance to a home by coming to the door and requesting the loan of matches or salt. If you give them to her, you are at her mercy. To escape the sukuyan's clutches:

1. Murmur *"Thursday, Friday, Saturday, Sunday"* three times.
2. Mark a cross over every door or window in your home.
3. Hang a mirror on the outside of entrance doors.
4. Leave it there until all danger has passed.

Special Vampires: Psychic Vampires

There is also another type of vampire, perhaps the most common of all. This one neither craves your blood, nor haunts your dreams. This vampire enhances its own personal power by absorbing that of another. This may be deliberate or completely inadvertent. This vampire is a living person and typically means no harm. You will know these vampires by their effect upon you: no matter how much you like the person, no matter how much you enjoy their company and conversation, you are always exhausted and drained after spending time in their presence. Perhaps every individual has moments of unconscious psychic vampirism, in times of stress and need. However, if this is a consistent reaction to someone's presence, protection must be taken. One doesn't necessarily have to avoid the other person; instead one needs to learn how to shield and protect one's own energy.

It is crucial not to leak psychic energy, which subliminally attracts these vampires like a bleeding wound summons sharks, or those other kinds of vampires. A weak or damaged aura signals your psychic vulnerability. If you are in contact with a psychic vampire, check the *Protection* and *Psychic Power Spells* and immediately begin to fortify your defenses.

 ## Psychic Vampire Defense Spell (1)

Rosemary provides emergency relief. Drink rosemary tea. Or create strong infusions by pouring boiling water over fresh or dried rosemary, and add substantial quantities to your bath for aura repair and to relieve psychic exhaustion.

 ## Psychic Vampire Protective Shield

Black tourmalines and labradorite crystal gemstones provide a shield of protection against psychic vampires. Wear them or carry them in a pocket so that they are close at hand, rather than tucked into a mojo bag.

Psychic Vampire Repair

Flower essence remedies may be used to repair the damage done. They will also assist you to manifest new behavior so that you are no longer as vulnerable. Recommendations include:

- ★ *Apple(FES), for depletion of sexual creative forces and energy (also excellent for incubi/succubi repair)*
- ★ *Fringed Violet (Australian Bush), to repair damage to the aura caused by other individuals*
- ★ *Garlic (FES), repels parasitic entities of all kinds and repairs any damage done*
- ★ *Rue (FES), heals and empowers those whose energy and life-force is easily depleted or is overly absorbent of negative forces*

Special Vampires: Accessing Healing Energy

There is one other kind of unintentional vampirism: the victim doesn't necessarily "leak" energy nor does the stimulus to drain vitality originate in the vampire. Psychic energy and vitality are offered. This type of vampirism possesses no inherent malevolence, selfishness or diabolism; instead it may be necessary for Earth's proper functioning and one way magic power, *heka*, is transmitted. That said, this type of vampirism is not without dangers.

Those with plentiful magic power and a strong life-force feed others with their own energy and essence, although they may be unaware that they do so. These include healers and counselors of all varieties, psychic practitioners, soul singers and assorted individual caregivers. These individuals may forget or not realize how crucial it is to replenish their energies.

The flower essence remedies recommended above may be used, as well as Leafless orchid (Living/Australia), suggested for those in service to others who suffer feelings of depletion. Others should not be encouraged to feed at will but as invited and permitted.

If you suffer from this type of vampirism, create boundaries essentially determining when the pump is open and when it's closed.

- ★ *Wear black tourmaline*
- ★ *Wear dark sunglasses and headphones as needed to demarcate private space*

Special Vampires: Sorcerers

There is yet another kind of vampire, also resolutely human. However, unlike the psychic vampire, this type of vampirism is not inadvertent but construes a category of sorcerer.

Although the phenomenon occurs elsewhere, the fullest analysis of this type of vampire comes from Chinese magical and alchemical traditions. Vampires figure prominently in Chinese magic, although they rarely have anything to do with blood. These practitioners of malevolent magic are known as soul stealers. The goal of the vampire-sorcerer is to extend personal power, health and longevity by tapping into another's life force. Someone whose *chi* or soul force was stolen would waste away, eventually falling ill and dying prematurely, their life literally stolen to enhance that of the vampire.

There are various methods of soul stealing, some explicitly sexual, although the most common technique involves absconding with some of the victim's hair. This, combined with proper technique and incantation, makes soul extraction possible. In this circumstance, the victim may be saved by getting the hair back, combined with shamanic intervention.

Another method targets a child, and also demonstrates why there is such a profusion of children's protective spells.

✳ The Operation for Drawing Out Life

1. Collect peach wood and "prime" it by concealing it in or near the home of a pregnant woman. It must remain until the baby is born and, for reasons that will become obvious, the mother cannot know of the wood's existence.

2. When the baby is born, the wood is removed and the practitioner uses it to create a doll made to resemble this new baby as closely as possible. All the while, incantations are chanted, beseeching a spirit to come and enter the doll.

3. When complete, the doll is placed discreetly behind or underneath an altar. The practitioner will continue to invite a spirit to reside within the doll.

The baby's spirit may thus be lured into the doll. Unfortunately, as it gradually enters the doll, it is gradually leaving the baby, leaving a weakened, listless child who fails to thrive. Should the baby die, the spirit will come entirely under the practitioner's power.

The sorcerer desires such a doll because it can be used to serve him or her. It can especially be called upon as an agent of divination.

✪ Divination Spells

Before you can choose a spell, sometimes you need to choose a course of action. In order to do that, sometimes you need more information than you already have—or than seems humanly available. That's where divination comes in. Divination is the magical art of receiving information about future events right now in the present. (It is also used to achieve greater understanding of past and present happenings.) *Diviners*, also known as *readers*, use tools, rituals, spells, and systems to reveal hidden information. Diviners thus practice prophetic arts, the *mantic* arts, after the Greek word *"mantikos,"* meaning "prophet." Words concluding with the suffix *-mancy* indicate some form of divination.

Once upon a time, as with shamans, every town had a respected professional diviner or two providing these prophetic services. Persecuted, driven underground, forced to practice secretly in back rooms or not at all, the loss of professional readers didn't stop people from requiring their services. People learned to provide those services for themselves, sometimes as highly structured ritual, sometimes in the guise of party games.

The divinatory methods included here descend from those homemade arts. They do not require special texts, years of study or, in theory at least, a professional reader: in other words, complex systems like tarot, playing cards, runes, the I-Ching, and similar are not included. Some systems are obviously more suitable for some households and individuals than others, but theoretically all can be reproduced by the magical layperson.

Methods included offer the opportunity to access other realms, other beings, and other people in order to receive needed information. Some offer a source of divine inspiration; others encourage you to discover your own hidden fonts of psychic or subconscious knowledge.

Systems of divination and fortune-telling operate according to the principle of synchronicity, as do magic spells in general. Synchronicity rejects the concept of coincidence. Events occurring at exactly the same moment share something in common and may be used to reveal something about each other. The trick is learning how to recognize and understand these revelations.

As its name indicates, divination puts you in direct contact with the divine. There is a sacred, magical aspect to even the most raucous party method. Divination should be treated with the respect shown to other spells. Appropriate cleansing and protective rituals should be considered. Divination tools, even the simplest pebbles, shells or dice, *are* ritual tools and should be treated with similar care and respect.

How do you choose the right system for you? In some cases, the choice is obvious: certain spells were designed for specific situations. The very question needing answers, the very information required, determines the method. In some cases, your own abilities set directions: it takes a different kind of personality to scry patiently in a pan of black ink than it does to pierce a Bible passage with a needle. In other cases, let the choice choose you: the desire the spell awakens within you is its invitation to perform.

It goes without saying that every method and every incident of divination begins with a question. The most difficult part of divination may come in formulating that question. Don't leave it vague: oracles delight in tricks, especially puns and word games. Take the time to formulate exactly what it is you wish revealed in clear, lucid, *precise* language. Write down the question, so that you can later compare it to the response, better interpret its nuances and implications and also eliminate arguments if performing group divination!

Alphabet Divination Spells

Books are formed from words; words are formed from letters. One school of Kabbalah suggests that the Creator formed the entire world from Hebrew letters. Individual letters, of any alphabet, may be used to provide an oracle.

Alphabet Divination (1)
Basic Method

This particular method is popular in both Asia and Italy.

1. Write the letters of the alphabet, several times each, on individual squares of paper. Playing pieces, like Scrabble™ blocks may also be used.
2. Place all pieces inside a jar, ideally one with a tightly fitting cover.
3. Shake them up and spill the letters on the floor or table.
4. Look for words to provide the answer to your query.

Alphabet Divination (2)
Alectromancy

Alectromancy *lets a rooster choose your words for you.*

1. Make a circle using the letters of the alphabet: use chalk to mark them on the ground or cut out letters and lay them in a circle.
2. Place an equal quantity of grain on top of each letter.
3. Put a rooster in the center of your alphabet circle and turn him loose.
4. Observe the order in which the rooster picks up the grains. Words may be formed or suggested, providing the oracle.

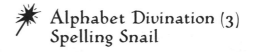

Alphabet Divination (3)
Spelling Snail

Snails can spell as well as roosters can. This divination method traditionally uses fireplace ashes. A more potent version might involve writing your queries on paper, burning them and using those ashes instead. For a quick-fix method, use flour.

1. Make a smooth, even bed of ashes or flour.
2. Gently place a snail in the center of this bed.
3. Allow the snail to wander as it will and leave the circle when it chooses.
4. The shape of its trail will indicate initials, letters or images to provide your oracle.

Arrow Divination

Known as *belomancy*, this is an ancient method of divination mentioned in the Bible and especially popular among Babylonians, Scythians, Slavs, and Germans. Various methods are used.

Arrow Divination (1)

Attach inscriptions to an arrow and shoot it. Distance or other predetermined signal determines which inscription forms the oracle.

Arrow Divination (2)

In this version three arrows may be used; one designates an affirmative answer, the second, a negative answer and the third is left blank, because not all fates can be revealed. Separate messages can be attached to each arrow or the arrows may be distinguished in other ways.

Augury

The ancient system of *augury* is the ancestor of modern bird watching. Augurs foretell the future by observing birds and their flight. Although ancient Roman augurs had a codified, rigid system, it is easily adapted into a spontaneous system, especially if you feed birds regularly.

Formulate your question, and then scatter birdseed or crumbs on the ground. Step back and watch the birds partake and depart.

★ *If the birds fly off toward the right, your answer is affirmative*
★ *If the birds fly off toward your left, the response is negative*

★ *If they scatter and fly all over the place, you lack the information needed to make a decision. The situation is more complex than it may appear*

If the birds reject the food, it doesn't mean that the oracle didn't work. This is also a response: your question holds more significance and greater implication than you realize. Reconsider the question as well as all possible consequences, actions, and solutions.

Axe Head Divination

Divination via axe head is an ancient Middle Eastern system.

1. Heat the axe head until it's red hot.
2. Make the axe stand so that the edge is perpendicular.
3. Place an agate on the edge.

If the agate stays on the axe head, this constitutes a negative response. If it rolls away, leaping off, as it were, this is a positive confirmation of your query.

Repeat up to three times for confirmation.

Bibliomancy

Although the Bible is a frequent medium for this method, *bibliomancy* merely means divination via the use of a book. Traditional sources for *bibliomancy* include the Bible, the Koran, the Vedas and Homer and Virgil's respective Trojan War sagas. Any large book may be used; many prefer sacred texts filled with spiritual depth and vision, although dictionaries and encyclopedias, even really large catalogs, also provide great oracles.

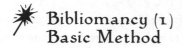

Bibliomancy (1)
Basic Method

1. Formulate the question.
2. Close your eyes.
3. Flip open the chosen book.
4. Stick your finger on a word or passage.
5. Read and interpret the oracle.

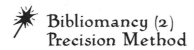

Bibliomancy (2)
Precision Method

Pinpointing a verse with your naked finger can be clumsy and ambiguous. Did your finger actually point to those biblical lines about punishment of sins or did it just accidentally slide off those verses about reaping justly earned rewards? The following method may be more accurate.

1. Formulate the question while holding a needle in your hand.
2. With your eyes closed, randomly flip open the book.
3. Keeping your eyes closed pierce the page with the needle.
4. The needle marks the spot where your oracle begins.

Bibliomancy (3)
Lord Thoth's Trio

Thoth, Egyptian lunar god, is given credit for inventing books, magic, and dice. All are combined in the following method.

1. Formulate your question, while holding dice.
2. Close your eyes and flip open the book.
3. Gently, with eyes remaining closed, toss the dice onto the open book.

Read the passage indicated by the location of the fallen dice. An alternative is to read the passage indicated by the numbers shown on the dice—thus you might begin at the sixth line, third word or similar. If using numerical coordination, it's not necessary for the dice to actually land on the page, although both methods can be integrated.

Bibliomancy (4)
The Control Method

Ancient books frequently took the form of loosely bound pages or scrolls. This type of book may lend itself to bibliomancy with greater ease than the tightly bound shape of modern books. Even post-Gutenberg and standardized printed and bound books magicians still copied Homeric verses onto vellum or papyrus scrolls specifically for purposes of divination. This method also allows you to eliminate any fortunes you really don't want to receive.

1. Select a sufficient quantity of text to fulfill the purpose of your divination.
2. Copy it onto a parchment scroll or, if for one-time use, onto a large square of paper.
3. Verses are selected by throwing dice or pricking pages with a needle.

Botanical Divination

Take nine thorn apple seeds. (Be careful; thorn apple, although a frequent magical component, is poisonous.) Pass them through wormwood smoke and then toss them out on a tray and interpret the patterns made.

Calendar Oracles

Some oracles are only delivered during specific days or, more typically, nights of the year.

✳ Calendar Oracle (1)
Candlemas

The Candlemas Bull flies through the air on February 2nd. The bull appears in the sky in the form of a cloud early in the morning on Candlemas. If you can find it, it will give you information regarding the year to come.

If the bull faces east, a bountiful year is anticipated. However, if the bull faces south, expect grain shortages. And if the bull faces west, tighten your belt. The entire year will be needy.

✳ Calendar Oracle (2) Christmas Eve Mirror Divination

If the following Russian Christmas divination is done correctly, allegedly your future will be shown to you in a mirror.

1. On Christmas Eve, sit in a darkened room containing two mirrors and lit by only two candles.
2. Arrange the mirrors so that one reflects the candlelight into the other.
3. If you can determine the seventh reflection, visions of your future should follow.

✳ Calendar Oracle (3) Christmas Eve Onion Oracle

The onions used in this German oracle must be gathered on Christmas Eve. An onion is required for every possible solution or alternative to your dilemma. An extra one may be added to represent an unknown solution, one that awaits discovery.

1. Consecrate the onions to your purpose and place them on an altar.
2. Write your various alternatives and options on small pieces of paper.
3. Place each paper under a different onion.

4. Let this rest overnight, then the next day, plant each onion with its paper inside its own flowerpot. Mark the pots so that you know which suggested plan is contained within.
5. The first onion to sprout indicates your significant response.

✳ Calendar Oracle (4) Halloween/Samhain

Allegedly any question asked during this ritual will be answered, while any wish made will be granted.

Simmer basil, rosemary, Saint John's Wort and wolfsbane in a cauldron (wolfsbane is highly toxic; it may be wiser to delete it from the formula). Interpret the patterns made by the steam; scry by gazing into the gently bubbling liquid.

☀ Calendar Oracle (5) New Year's Eve

This Russian New Year's Eve women's divination ritual foretells the fortunes awaiting in the New Year. In the days before private bathrooms and indoor plumbing, the bathhouse was a place of social as well as hygienic significance. It is also often a place of great magical and spiritual significance. What is now only a "bathhouse" was once the home for spiritual, shamanic, and magic rites. Babies were born in the bathhouse, healings performed, men and women readied for marriage. Post-Christianity, the bathhouse retained its power but also developed an aura of the forbidden.

In Russia, the bathhouse maintains a magical aura akin to a crossroads. The bathhouse is also the home of powerful spirits, ancient pagan deities now demoted to bathhouse guardians. Forgotten spirits tend to be grouchy spirits, although not always. This ritual takes place at night, ideally at midnight, the threshold of the New Year.

Taking turns, women remove their underwear and approach the bathhouse backwards, skirts lifted over their heads. The bathhouse door is left partially open: each woman sticks her naked bottom through the door and waits.

If the resident spirit slaps or scratches her, this is not a good sign for the coming year. If, on the other hand, she receives a gentle and pleasurable caress, with hands rather than claws, her future shines bright, while a kiss is auspicious enough to go buy some lottery tickets.

☀ Calendar Oracle (6) New Year

Another divination method is based upon Russian New Year's fortune-telling games. One person is needed to supervise this group ritual.

1. Each individual invited to this divination party brings some sort of spring or magical formula water plus a ring or small metal charm. These trinkets should not be identical but distinctive and readily identifiable.

2. Each person places their charm or ring into a cauldron.

3. Traditionally a crucifix is also placed in the cauldron, although a pentacle, horseshoe or other sacred metal object could be substituted.

4. Each person pours their water into the cauldron, simultaneously making a secret wish.

5. When all the water has been blended together, it's sprinkled with mugwort and oats.

6. Toss in one lit charcoal per participating person.

7. The supervisor stirs the cauldron with her or his left little finger.

8. The cauldron is covered.

9. One by one each person chants a rhyme, alluding to his or her secret wish.

10. Following each rhyme, the supervisor reaches into the covered cauldron and fishes out a charm. The charm provides clues as to the success of each person's desire.

When the ritual is complete, charms and rings may be exchanged or returned to the original owner as desired, however the water cannot *remain in the house. It must be immediately emptied out at a crossroads.*

Ceromancy—Divination by Melted Wax

☀ Basic Ceromancy

1. Carefully melt wax: it may be necessary to use a double boiler or bain-marie.

2. When the wax has liquefied, pour it gently into a dish of ice-cold water. The wax will harden upon impact with the water, typically forming shapes.

3. Allow time for the wax to solidify before removing it from the water, as it's initially very pliable and the original shapes may be changed or destroyed by handling too quickly.

4. Remove the wax and interpret the shapes.

The number of shapes formed may also bear significance. Particularly auspicious-looking shapes may be transformed into amulets, preserved or carried as needed.

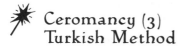

Ceromancy (2)
An Italian Method

1. Place three rose hips, three nettle leaves, some cumin seeds, and a few sprigs of rue in a bowl or pan of icy water.
2. Bind two candles with scarlet ribbons. (The original formula specifies tallow candles, but this may be because that's what was available.)
3. Place these candles within the pan of water.
4. Light the candles and observe the wax dripping into the water.

Lucky shapes should be carried within a red mojo bag.

Ceromancy (3)
Turkish Method

A Turkish method involves group participation.

1. The person(s) posing the query sits in a chair, while wax is carefully melted.
2. One or two people hold a white cloth over the querent's head.
3. Someone else holds a dish of ice water over this cloth.
4. The melted wax is carefully poured into the dish of cold water.
5. Once the wax hardens, shapes are analyzed, with the querent offering the first interpretations.

Lucky shapes are given to the querent as a lucky charm. Inauspicious, negative forms are disposed of in running water.

Children as Oracles and Mediums for Divination

Perhaps because of their innocence, perhaps because they haven't forgotten how to access their magic powers, perhaps because of greater psychic power, children have always been favored oracles.

The earliest testimonials come from ancient mythology. Isis, searching desperately for Osiris' body, has no success until children tell her their observations. This story epitomizes the strength and use of children in divination: the children do not understand what they have seen, they merely describe their observations. It is Isis, an adult and an experienced magician, who is able to interpret that information.

Children, in general, do not make good fortune-tellers. They lack the life experience to understand the client's problems or to deliver needed information in a constructive, graceful manner. Their strength instead comes from purity of heart and vision. Like the child who reveals the truth in the tale of *The Emperor's New Clothes*, children are often able to see clearly and name what they see, without self-delusion, fear or subterfuge.

That said these are historic methods of divination and perhaps should not be used, or only under very special circumstances. The potential for abuse and exploitation is great when a child serves as an oracle. If done at all, it should be approached as a game, with no pressure placed on the child. This is both for the sake of the child *and* for the success of the divination. An unwilling, oppressed medium *cannot* deliver a true and accurate message.

Even the most experienced, accomplished diviner sometimes finds psychic vision blocked. Sometimes an oracle refuses to appear. Some futures just cannot be revealed. If a child says that they see nothing, then that is what they see. That is the sole answer of the oracle and the child must not be pressured to try to see harder or provide additional information.

✳ Child Oracle (1) Basic Method

The simplest method of obtaining an oracle dates back to ancient Egypt and Greece. Because the child is completely unaware that he or she is an oracle, it may be the purest, most powerful method: the child is not swayed by desires to please or displease the querent. It is also the safest system, with the least potential for abuse.

Formulate your question in your mind but do not articulate it aloud. The first spontaneous words heard from a child's voice form your response.

✳ Child Oracle (2) Invocation of Anubis

This spell, based on practices from Alexandria in Egypt, requires a bronze bowl engraved with an image of the jackal-headed inventor of mummification, road-opener Anubis. The original spell might have expected you to actually create the engraving as part of the ritual.

1. Fill the bowl with water.
2. Float a film of oil on top.
3. Have the child sit on top of four bricks beside the bowl.
4. Place a sheer veil over the child's head, through which he or she can see, until the divination is ready to begin.
5. Consecrate a magic lamp to the divination.
6. Place the lamp on one side of the child, incense on the other.
7. The querent should chant an invocation to Anubis, requesting a vision and a response to the questions. It is not necessary to state the question aloud, in the child's hearing.
8. When the invocation is complete, have the child gaze into the water until he or she sees something, then have them describe it.
9. If this is insufficient, gently and with soft voice, request further description from the child.
10. The oracle ends when the child says it is over.

✳ Child Oracle (3) Cagliostro's Method

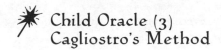

One can observe the evolution of magical methods by contrasting the above method, dating from the early centuries of the Common Era to the following, suggested by Alessandro, Count di Cagliostro (1743–1795), a renowned and notorious alchemist, charlatan, magician, and perfumer. Although the bottom-line method is virtually identical, the specially engraved bowl is no longer part of the spell, and neither are the four bricks, reminiscent of Egyptian childbirth practices. The magic lamp has been replaced by candles, a luxury accessible to Cagliostro because of his wealthy patrons, including a king of France. Details come from his trial documents.

1. Arrange the ritual room.
2. Although the child should observe preparations, the querent should perform all needed cleansings, protection spells and other ritual.
3. Prepare a low table with a pan of water and a number of white candles. (Keep the atmosphere neutral so as not to influence the child diviner: you neither want to scare or intimidate the medium nor do you wish to encourage "fluffy-bunny" magic.)
4. Have the child sit on the floor and look into the pan of water.
5. Place your hand gently on the child's head. If you haven't already, explain what you wish done.
6. Step back but keep a vigilant eye on fire safety at all times. (The adult is responsible for all safety issues during ritual.) Bid the child look into the water again and just describe what he or she sees. There is no need for trance or possession. Don't lead or influence the child's vision, simply copy down whatever he or she says, for later analysis.

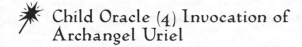

✳ Child Oracle (4) Invocation of Archangel Uriel

Technically this oracle will not be provided by any human means but by angelic revelation. The oracle is directed towards the archangel Uriel, Master of Information, who may or may not ultimately appear in person to deliver the oracle. The ritual should be preceded by cleansing, summoning the angel, and burning fragrant incense.

1. Mix walnut oil with liquid tallow and/or lampblack.
2. Place this within your right palm or onto your right thumbnail.
3. The direction faced depends upon the question posed. If inquiring about money or missing treasure, face east; if robbery, face west; for murder or any other crime, as well as love and romance, face south.
4. Whoever holds the liquid must repeat the first seventy-two psalms in order. Allegedly wonders will then occur.

Coin Divination

Oracles tend to deliver complex responses, requiring consideration and analysis. Most methods are thus more suited to equally complex issues. Maybe you only have a simple dilemma. You really need a *yes-or-no* answer; choose A or choose B without discussion or ambiguity. If you need to choose between two distinct alternatives, but are unable to ascertain which choice is wiser or advisable, why don't you just flip a coin? Determine which alternative is represented by the coin's head and which by the tail. Flip and see which choice is yours.

This is not a flippant suggestion. Coins are closely identified with principles of metal magic and have been used for divination since time immemorial.

★ *Although you can fish any coin out of your pocket, many readers retain one special coin for purposes of divination, treating it with the care shown to prized tarot cards or runes. I-Ching coins are recommended, as are antique coins*

★ *Metal religious medals may substitute for a coin, as can some gambling chips or any round, small disc, providing the sides are distinct*

★ *For added enhancement, request blessings and assistance from spirits devoted to metal: Brigid, the Dactyls, Hephaestus, Ogun or Scatach, for instance*

Coin divination isn't limited to simple *yes-or-no* questions. More complex decisions may be rendered using multiple coins, usually a set of three, sometimes thrown multiple times. Answers are determined by analyzing the number of coins that fall face up or down. Determine the question and the method of analysis before tossing the coins.

Copal Divination

Copal is a tree resin indigenous to Mexico, Guatemala and elsewhere in Central America. Used in sacred rites by the Aztec and Maya, it retains popularity for magic, healing, and spiritual use. Inhaling its aroma allegedly enhances powers of clairvoyance, however copal is also used to provide systematic oracles.

✳ Divination by Copal (1) Guatemalan Method

1. Burn copal incense.
2. Pass fourteen kernels of corn through the smoke.
3. Toss the corn on the ground, then read and analyze the patterns made.

Divination by Copal (2) Mexican Method

Although it is frequently purchased ground up and ready to burn as incense, copal is also available in the form of small balls.

1. Burn copal incense.
2. Formulate your question
3. Toss small balls of copal into a pot of water.

If they float, the answer is affirmative. If the balls sink, the response is negative. The likelihood of success is ascertained depending upon whether more balls or less float.

Divination by Copal (3) Fire

With your left hand toss corn kernels into a fire, and with your right hand toss copal into the fire. Observe the resulting smoke and flames.

Cowrie Shell Divination

Cowrie shells are the medium for sacred divination systems throughout Africa. They serve as the oracular voice of the orisha. However, cowrie shells may also be used in simple household divination. Cowries, once used as currency in Asia (including in China) and Africa, are frequent substitutes for coins. Substitute cowries for any coin divination spell, particularly if you'd prefer to invoke the elemental power of water instead of metal.

1. Slice the rounded, closed side of the cowrie off, so that the shell lands flat when tossed. (Cowries for divination may also be purchased pre-sliced.)
2. Determine your question and also which side of the cowrie is heads, which tails.

Crossroads Divination

Crossroads divination is based on an old Persian tradition.

1. Go to a crossroads on a Wednesday and just loiter.
2. Hang around discreetly, listening to the words of passers-by, little one-liners or snippets of conversation.
3. Try to apply them to your situation, considering whether the words are auspicious or not.

Dactylomancy

Dactylomancy involves divination via a suspended ring. Traditionally a wedding ring is used, although any magic ring would be equally suitable. Otherwise any metal ring may be used—gold, silver, copper, iron, or lead.

 Dactylomancy (1) Basic Method

1. Pluck a few strands of hair and suspend the ring from those hairs. The ring will answer questions from the person whose hair it is suspended from or from anyone that person suggests.
2. Put a glass on the table so that the ring is suspended above it. The ring may fall within or outside the glass, whichever you prefer and is most comfortable. The ring may assert its own preference.
3. Gently begin to swing the ring. This divination method is something of a cross between a pendulum and table-rapping. Pay attention to the sounds the ring makes as it brushes the glass. Establish a code so that it will answer your questions.

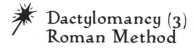

Dactylomancy (2)
Identifying the Hex

Dactylomancy may also be used to help determine who has bewitched someone, especially to the point of illness.

Suspend a snake ring from strands of the victim's hair. (It is not necessary for the victim to be present, although it helps. The hair however is critical.) Use this ring as a pendulum to determine from which direction the bewitchment was initiated. A code may also be established, as in the preceding spell, to determine the existence of the bewitching party.

Dactylomancy (3)
Roman Method

In 371 CE, the Roman historian Ammianus Marcellinus described this method of divination, a sort-of ancient cross between a ouija board and a pendulum.

1. Create a disc with letters of the alphabet encircling the rim.
2. The disc is placed on a small table or tripod. (The tripod, a three-legged table, evokes the Oracle of Delphi's pythoness who sat upon a tripod while delivering her prophesies.)
3. Suspend a ring on a light thread.
4. Pray, petition and allow the ring to form a pendulum, spelling out answers to questions.

Daphnomancy

Those prophesying pythonesses of Delphi were reputedly stimulated to deliver their predictions by inhaling fumes emanating from a geological fissure beneath the shrine. These fumes remain a mystery: archeologists and geologists have been unable to identify traces of natural emanations. Some believe that special vision-inducing botanicals were burned, although if so, that formula remains mysterious, too. General consensus is that whatever else was in the formula, it also contained bay laurel leaves.

Daphnomancy refers to divination using bay leaves. Bay leaves have profound associations with divination. According to legend, the Delphic pythonesses delivered their oracles with bay leaves clenched between their teeth. According to another very famous legend, Daphne, Delphic pythoness, was transformed into the very first bay laurel tree when she tried to escape Apollo's attempt to rape her.

Adding complexity to the sexual dimensions of the Daphne-Apollo myth, another famous oracular shrine was named after and presided over by Daphne herself. The oracle at Daphne, near Tarsus, was obtained by dipping bay leaves or branches into a sacred spring. The shrine at Daphne, maintained within lush, beautiful groves, was renowned or notorious, depending upon one's perspective, for its carnal pleasures and *"licentious"* sexual rites. The shrine, together with its surrounding groves, was an early casualty of Christianity's rise to power. Bay leaves, however, remain an ingredient of many magic spells and a tool for divination.

Concentrate on your question while holding bay leaves in your hand. Then either place a single bay leaf onto a lit charcoal or toss a few leaves into an open fire.

★ *If the leaves crackle loudly and burn brightly, the prognosis is positive*

★ *If leaves sputter, refuse to burn or, worse, all flames die out, consider postponing or adjusting your plans*

★ *If flames shoot straight from the bay leaves, the signs are auspicious: all powers and blessings are with you*

Divine Oracles

Oracles were once associated with shrines to deities. One of the functions of ancient shrines or spiritual centers was specifically to provide a source of divination, presumably under the auspices of the presiding spirit. Delphi, the most famous oracle of the ancient world, was originally dedicated to Gaia, Mother Earth and served by snake priestesses, who actually delivered the prophecies. Amidst great violence, Apollo, an arrival from the North, forcibly took over the shrine. The pythonesses, the snake priestesses, were retained, although their prophesies were now filtered through male priests. Delphi was not Apollo's only oracle. Although he is most famous as the solar-affiliated lord of medicine, music and prophesy, in the guise of his familiar, a mouse, Apollo also guards grain. He provides another oracle through this venue. Once upon a time, this system of divination, known as "*aleuromancy*," was available if one made a donation at Apollo's shrine. The ancestor of the fortune cookie, it is easily reproduced at home.

Whether this oracle tastes good or is even completely baked depends entirely on whether you plan to eat the oracle once its answer is received.

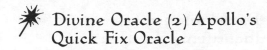

Divine Oracle (1) Apollo's Grain Oracle

1. Make very simple bread dough, from approximately one cup of flour, one egg and one quarter cup of water.
2. Write your choices or alternatives on slips of paper.
3. Place each within a ball of dough. Each ball must appear reasonably identical.
4. Bake these balls so that they're sufficiently hard.
5. When they cool off, select a ball and an oracle.

Request Apollo's blessings before initiating the oracle, if desired.

Divine Oracle (2) Apollo's Quick Fix Oracle

A quick-fix version bypasses the connection with grain:

1. Write your choices onto slips of paper.
2. Slip these papers into identical balls rolled from kitchen foil.
3. Place the balls in a bowl and shake them around.
4. Choose your fortune.

Divine Oracle (3) Hermes

Apollo was not the only divinity with an oracular shrine. They were common to many spiritual entities. Zeus gave answers through the whispering oaks of Dodona. Ammon held forth in the Libyan dessert. The simplest oracle of all, and extremely easily reproducible, comes from that trickster master of the crossroads, Hermes.

1. The original oracle involved making a donation to Hermes and then postulating a question within his shrine. Incorporate Hermes as you will or merely formulate your question in a still, quiet location.
2. Stop up your ears and go outside.
3. When you are ready or at some predetermined signal (after sixty seconds, after observing the color red—you choose the signal), open your ears.
4. The first words heard provide your oracle. Words spoken by children hold added impact.

If venturing outdoors is impossible or inadvisable, wait for the predetermined signal and then turn on the radio. Lyrics of a song are as powerful as spoken words, if not more so.

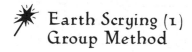

Divine Oracle (4) Conduit to the Spirit Realm

Smoke, wax or flames from altar candles dedicated to a deity may be interpreted to provide an oracle from the actual spirit. A candle flame shooting high and bright indicates that the spirit you've invoked has arrived.

Drum Divination

Drums are used for summoning spirits, psychic enhancement and shamanic journeys, but also may be used for straight-forward divination. The most famous divining drums in the world once belonged to Saami shaman. Beautifully decorated, ritually enhanced and consecrated, they were standard equipment, as necessary as another tradition's wand, broomstick or athame. During forced conversions to Christianity, the drums were outlawed and destroyed. A few original drums were preserved and remain on view in Swedish museums.

Although drums are musical instruments, the visual component is as important as the aural one when used in this method of divination. Magical designs were painted on stretched skin drumheads. Each shaman's drum was unique, painted according to personal vision and spiritual direction in addition to common traditional motifs. Small objects were then place on the drum. As it was beaten, to the accompaniment of divining songs, the objects jumped and danced and revealed the future.

Hungarians and Saami share Finno-Ugric ancestry. Until recently a similar drum was used for divination by Hungarian country people as well as resident Romany women, although typically without the complex shamanic ritual. Improvise the basic system until it works for you.

1. Paint three black and three white circles onto a frame drum.

2. Chant and beat the drum.
3. In the process toss shelled cranberry beans onto the drum.

The future or the response to the oracle is determined from the patterns made by the dancing beans and painted circles.

Earth Scrying

Although it lacks the hypnotic luminosity of water, moon, glass and some gemstones, Earth provides a surface on which to scry, too.

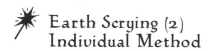

Earth Scrying (1) Group Method

This Native American system is deceptively simple.

1. Clear a patch of ground so that you have smooth dirt: no grass, weeds or garbage.
2. Four people sit, one at each cardinal point.
3. The person seated in the west casts a circle with a stick, cane, wand, or knife.
4. Then the four individuals study and analyze the surface within the circle in order to make predictions. Observe any life-forms, insects or other, that make an appearance. Take your time; this is a leisurely system.

Earth Scrying (2) Individual Method

This Russian Earth oracle may be performed solo:

1. Cast a circle on the ground.
2. Chant:
   Circle, circle, tell me true
   Show my fate for me to view
3. Look down and see what is revealed.

Egg Divination

1. Paint an egg with symbolic imagery: it should be as beautiful as possible, however the design is meant to stimulate the oracular process. The eggshell will not be preserved.
2. Boil it.
3. Unpeel the egg and cut it open. Predictions are made according to the shape and hue of egg and yolk.

 ## Fig Divination (1)

Figs were considered by many to be the tree of life. This ancient method of reading fig leaves to determine the future of your life is known as sycomancy.

Write your question, scheme or proposal on a fresh fig leaf. Retain the leaf and observe it. A leaf that shrivels up quickly provides a negative response, while a leaf that dries slowly, retaining a fresh, green appearance provides encouragement.

Fig Divination (2)

Sycomancy may be used to compare options and explore choices.

1. Write a distinct scheme, plan or proposal on a fig leaf, one leaf per option or choice.
2. Retain the leaves so that they are together under exactly the same conditions but not touching.
3. The leaf that remains fresh, green and youthful looking the longest represents the oracle's choice.

If all leaves age at exactly *the same pace, the indication is that there is yet another, more appropriate choice that has been overlooked. Consider your options further before making a choice.*

 ## Fire Reading (1)

Flames may be interpreted without candles or containers, although even greater fire safety vigilance must be maintained: a Slavic method creates and then burns a paper fan.

1. Fold paper into an accordion-style fan.
2. Stand it up in a vertical direction.
3. Set it on fire.
4. The oracle is received by interpreting the flames as well as shadows cast.

 ## Fire Reading (2)

A slightly different version observes which part of the fan burns versus which part doesn't.

1. Fold paper into an accordion-style fan.
2. Write desires or choices on each fold of the fan.
3. Place the paper in a fireproof receptacle and set it alight.
4. Only light the paper once: should the flame go out without burning the paper in its entirety, analyze remaining words versus destroyed words to receive your oracle.

Should the entire fan go up in smoke, this is an extremely auspicious sign, a blessing on your future plans.

 ## Fire Reading (3) Capnomancy

Large ritual fires and bonfires also supply divinatory information. Capnomancy *divines using images appearing in the smoke of ritual fires. Enhance the divinatory power by burning herbs associated with psychic vision: mugwort, wormwood, Syrian rue (harmel), diviner's sage.*

Fire Reading (4) Tephramancy

Tephramancy *divines from what's left in the fire's aftermath. Ashes, cinders, and soot are examined for clues to the future. The more sacred the fire, the more seriously the information should be taken.*

Sometimes the ashes reveal words and clues to your future without any added assistance. When either hearth fires or ritual bonfires go out, examine cooled ashes to see whether letters, words or shapes may be observed. This is a powerful oracle; it's not necessary to formulate a question but merely to receive information.

 # Hibiscus Divination

Designate cut blossoms as a person or situation, particularly when choices must be made. Float the flowers on a bowl of water and observe.

 # I Spy Oracle

This Scottish spell, believed to derive from Norse sources, is used to gain information regarding the well-being of another person far away. This game of "I spy with my little eye" can only be performed on the first Monday of the month, before sunrise, on an empty stomach and with bare feet.

1. Walk sunwise around your home with your eyes closed until you arrive full circle at the entrance once again.
2. Without opening your eyes, make a circle with your finger and thumb.
3. Put it up to your eye, open your eye and look through the circle.
4. The omen is the first object or sight that meets your eye. A sacred symbol is especially auspicious.

Lampadomancy

Lampadomancy is the ancient art of divining via a lamp. Magic lamps may be crafted from brass or stone, however the most common traditional lamp is formed from earth, terracotta. The oracle is determined by the appearance and duration of the flame. Lampadomancy was once a very common form of divination, dating back to the days of ancient Egypt and Mesopotamia. Because candles were once rare and expensive, magic lamps were more commonly used.

Magic lamps haven't changed much, basically consisting of a terracotta dish filled with oil, the sides proportionately high so that oil and flames are contained. A coiled linen strip resting in the oil and hanging over the edge creates a wick. Similar lamps, reproductions as well as ancient artifacts, are available through antiquarians, but this is a very simple, even child-like design, easily crafted or improvised. The outside of the lamp can be painted or otherwise embellished if desired.

The type of oil used in the lamp varies. Although olive oil evokes associations with *The Arabian Nights*, Aladdin, genies in bottles and magic lamps, actually in ancient days olive was among the more expensive oils in Arabia, Mesopotamia, and Egypt. The Egyptians, who even by modern standards possessed an extensive repertoire of oils for perfumery, cooking, sacred healing and magical purposes, apparently favored palm oil for lamps: an oil still popular in many African and African-derived spiritual traditions.

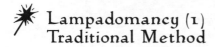

Lampadomancy (1) Traditional Method

1. Charge and consecrate a magic lamp.
2. Formulate your question.
3. Light the wick and read the response.
4. Gaze at the lamp, focusing on the flames, as well as any shadows cast behind the lamp.
5. Watch the flames: analyze the number of points of flame. Observe in what direction the flame leans, whether it's high, low, dim, bright, noisy and sputtery or silent. This is a patient art. Does the flame burn clean or is it smoky? If the flame goes out abruptly, this is not a positive sign.

Lampadomancy (2) The Louisiana Magic Lamp

Although lampadomancy retained its popularity in India and Arabia, it fell out of favor in the West. With the arrival of kerosene lamps in America in approximately 1869, lamp magic was revitalized. The revival was strongest in Louisiana, where it still retains some popularity. The Louisiana Magic Lamp is typically a hurricane or kerosene lamp, fueled by some blend of castor oil, olive oil and kerosene—usually two parts kerosene to one part oil. It is read in similar manner to the ancient oil lamp.

Lotus Root Divination

Lotuses, beautiful, pristine blossoms emerging from mud, invoke images of purity and fairness so this method has more nuances than a mere tossing of the coin.

1. Write or inscribe the letter *"N"* (for *"no"*) on one side of the root.
2. Write or inscribe the letter *"Y"* on the other side to represent the affirmative response. (Adapt this spell to suit your specific query, if needed.)

3. Toss the root up in the air; the side that lands on top delivers the response.

Love Oracles

"He loves me, he loves me not!" All you have to do is count the petals before beginning that rhyme to receive the desired oracle. Other oracles are not as easily controlled. Romance is so vital a topic special divination systems have evolved solely to chart its progress.

Love Oracle (1) Acorns

Will a couple remain together?

1. Gather well water and place it in a crystal bowl. (Substitute spring water if you have to.)
2. Take two acorns; name one for each member of the party. Charge them with your query.
3. Drop the acorns into the bowl of water.
4. If they remain together, so will the couple.

Love Oracle (2) Apples of Love

Should you be lucky enough to have a choice of wonderful lovers, this spell helps you choose wisely between them.

1. One red apple is required to represent each potential love.
2. Carve a person's name into each apple using a rose thorn.
3. Place the apples in a dark secret place where no one else will disturb them. They must not touch each other.
4. Check the apples daily: the apple that resists rotting, that stays freshest longest is your true lover.

Once the decomposition process starts you may wish to maintain a more frequent eye, to prevent confusion and mistakes.

Apples are sacred to Aphrodite, Genius of Love. Invoke her assistance and blessing on this oracle if you wish.

✳ Love Oracle (3) Apple Alphabet

Peel an apple while simultaneously reciting the alphabet. When the peel breaks, the letter reached is your true love's initial. (Keep reciting the alphabet until the peel either breaks or is removed completely.)

✳ Love Oracle (4) Apple Peel

1. Peel an apple in its entirety: the peel can't break, the entire peel must be removed in one long slice. If the peel does break, begin again with a fresh apple.
2. While peeling, concentrate on your query: who is your true love? Who will you marry? And so forth.
3. When the apple has been completely peeled, throw the peel over your left shoulder without looking.
4. Once it's landed on the floor, turn around and consider the shape: the apple peel should land in the shape of an initial or some other oracular response to your query.

✳ Love Oracle (5) Barking Dog

This oracle depends upon a barking dog. Ideally this will be a strange dog, either within a building or behind a gate. It cannot however be a dog that barks without provocation.

1. Provoke the dog to bark: knock at the door or the gate with a silver or stainless steel spoon, while saying, *"Bark, dog bark! Fetch me my true love!"*

2. Pay attention: the direction of the very first bark indicates where your true love may be located. The nature of the bark also indicates something of the nature of your love: a big, strong, healthy bark is an auspicious sign.

✳ Love Oracle (6) Boneset

Two boneset roots are required in this Cayuga spell to determine whether love will flourish.

Designate each to represent one person. Hold the roots together to see if they will intertwine. If they will, the signs are auspicious for relationship and romance. If they do not, reconsider this romance (or keep looking for better bonesets).

✳ Love Oracle (7) Boneset Love Amulet

Intertwining boneset roots may be transformed into an amulet to draw and preserve the love indicated by the previous spell:

1. Wrap them toward you in a piece of red cloth.
2. Tie securely with red thread or ribbon.
3. Wear as a charm or hide in safe place.

✳ Love Oracle (8) Christmas

After dinner on Christmas Eve, take your tablecloth to a crossroads and shake it out. A man will pass by and say something to you as he passes; it might be something as innocuous as "Good evening" or even "Merry Christmas." No, this isn't your true love, at least not necessarily, however something about this man—his build, height, general nature—should reveal something about the soul mate for whom you search.

Love Oracle (9) Daphnomancy

Bay leaves provide a barometer to assess a relationship's future prognosis. Place two bay leaves side by side on burning charcoal.

★ *If they're reduced quickly to ashes, your relationship is harmonious and your future looks bright*

★ *If the leaves crackle while they burn, this will be a tempestuous, volatile love affair*

★ *Bay leaves that crackle fiercely and jump apart, warn that another partner should be found, or perhaps one should consider the advantages of solitude*

 ## Love Oracle (10) Dark Moon Spell

1. Go to a deserted hut, ruined building, or bathhouse during a Dark Moon night.
2. Bring a mirror and a torch with you; the torch will serve as your sole source of illumination.
3. Place the mirror opposite the open door and gaze into it.
4. At midnight, the image of your true love should appear in the mirror.

 ## Love Oracle (11) Mystery Dinner Date

Choose the place and time for this enchanted dinner date carefully. This is a Russian spell and that magical tradition suggests casting the spell in the bathhouse; consider what serves as a magically charged threshold for you. Choose an auspicious date too: May Eve, Midsummer's Eve, Halloween, or maybe a date with special significance for you.

1. Set a romantic table for two.
2. Place a mirror and a candle on the table. (This should be your only source of light.)

3. Seat yourself at the table; gaze into the mirror and the flame.
4. At midnight, your true love should appear, whether in person or in a vision.

 ## Love Oracle (12) Irish Halloween Cabbage Patch Game

This oracle benefits those wishing to have the identity of future husband or lover revealed, as well as providing a good party game. This ritual must be accomplished on Samhain/Halloween.

Participants are blindfolded and set loose in a cabbage patch. Everyone is allowed to pull up one—and only one—cabbage. The size and shape of the cabbage head and stem reveals details concerning your future lover's body. The quantity of Earth clinging to roots foretells his financial status: a rich lover's root is packed with dirt, and the taste of the cabbage heart reveals his temperament.

After eating it, if this cabbage satisfies and pleases you, put the stem over your front door to guide your lover toward you.

 ## Love Oracle (13) Halloween Daphnomancy

A more private Halloween love oracle/ritual:

1. Sit before a low but steady fire in the fireplace. Gaze into the flame.
2. Focus on your beloved or on your desires. Formulate your question.
3. Have a small supply of bay leaves at hand. Without taking your eyes off the fire and your mind from your desire, toss a small handful of bay leaves into the fire.
4. Chant:
   Laurel leaves that burn in the fire.
   Draw to me my heart's desire.

5. Once the flames die down, repeat again for a total of three repetitions.

If flames shoot up, or leaves crackle and pop, you've received very auspicious signs: your wishes will be fulfilled. However, quiet leaves and dim flames counsel patience or perhaps a change of plans.

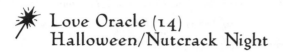

Love Oracle (14) Halloween/Nutcrack Night

Halloween was once nicknamed "Nutcrack Night" in Great Britain; this spell echoes that old name.

1. Find a matched pair of chestnuts; designate one for yourself, the other for the other party.
2. Place them side-by-side in the burning fireplace.
3. Keep an eye on your beloved: if it burns bright, so does his or her love. If the nut cracks and jumps, it signals infidelity, inconstancy, nervous, unsure or untrue intentions. If the nut doesn't burn, his or her heart is cold towards you. However, if both nuts burn together at a harmonious, steady pace, this relationship could be a keeper.

Love Oracle (15) Knot Spell

Is Love True? A simple spell helps you find out.

1. Make seven knots in a thread.
2. Set it on fire.
3. If the flame passes several knots, your love is true and strong, the more knots passed, the stronger.

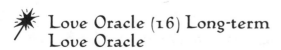

Love Oracle (16) Long-term Love Oracle

Allegedly a very accurate spell for those possessing the patience to await its results:

1. Plant a bed of pansies in the shape of a heart.
2. If they thrive and flourish, your love will too.
3. If not …

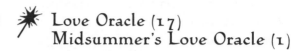

Love Oracle (17) Midsummer's Love Oracle (1)

1. On Midsummer's Eve place a piece of wax in an unwashed sock.
2. Sleep with it under your pillow.
3. In the morning, remove and melt the wax.
4. Pour it into a dish of cold water.
5. The shape the wax assumes as it hardens will reveal something of your future love life.

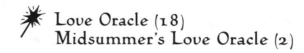

Love Oracle (18) Midsummer's Love Oracle (2)

"Midsummer men" refers to the plant, orpine, so called because these plants are symbolic of people in this Midsummer's divination spell. (Yes, those people may be women, however that doesn't seem to have been taken into account.)

1. On Midsummer's Eve, plant two cuttings of orpine side by side, designating one to represent you, the other to represent your lover.
2. Keep an eye on them: if the plants flourish and especially if they grow towards each other, your love is strong and future happiness and stability is predicted.
3. If one or both plants does not flourish, this is not an auspicious romantic sign. Clues may be interpreted by the orpine's behavior.

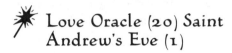

Love Oracle (19)
Midsummer's Love Oracle (3)

1. Journey to a crossroads on Midsummer's Eve.
2. Sprinkle hempseeds while repeating nine times:

   Hempseed, hempseed
   Hempseed I sow
   Hempseed, hempseed
   True love, come help me mow!

3. Allegedly one of two things should now happen: either your true love will genuinely pass by, or a vision of your true love carrying a scythe will appear.

Love Oracle (20) Saint Andrew's Eve (1)

Sit alone in your bedroom on Saint Andrew's Eve, November 30th. At precisely midnight fling the door open to catch a vision of your true love.

Love Oracle (21) Saint Andrew's Eve (2)

1. Sit in a dark room across from two mirrors, with a candle placed in between.
2. Stare into the candle flame maintaining complete silence.
3. As you focus on the candle, choose a number and begin to count backwards.
4. As you finish, turn to the nearest dark corner and study the shadows. The shape or form of your true love should be apparent.

Love Oracle (22) Seven Bean Spell

This spell simultaneously sets a snare to capture your heart's desire but also serves as an oracle to advise whether your target will ever love you. Does romance stand a chance?

1. Arrange seven beans in a circle on a path where your target is certain to walk. (Tonka beans are most effective but you may use any other beans at hand.) Conceal them under leaves and dirt, or, if the path is inside, under newspapers or socks on the floor.
2. You can watch as long as you're hidden from view.

If he steps on the beans, brushes up against them or in any way comes in contact with them, the romance will be a success. If he steps over the beans, this is especially auspicious; if he misses the circle completely, starts on the path but then deviates from it, the charm is ineffective. He is not the lover for you. Reconsider your desires and actions.

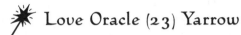

Love Oracle (23) Yarrow

Although the oracular system the I-Ching now uses coins, the original system used stalks of yarrow to reveal one's destiny. In this spell, yarrow reveals whether love is reciprocated.

1. Walk barefoot at midnight in a patch of yarrow under a Full Moon.
2. With your eyes closed, pick a bunch of flowers. Offer a libation or small exchange at the spot where the flowers were picked.
3. Take them home and place them under your bed, your pillow or in a bedside drawer.
4. At dawn, or when you awake, check your flowers. If the flowers remain fresh, this is a positive sign: your love is reciprocated. If even the dew remains, this is *extremely* auspicious. If the flowers have dried, withered or faded, try again at the next Full Moon, or consider another lover!

Lunar Divination

A particularly bright full moon, shining low on a cloudless night provides an extremely powerful scrying surface. When the moon presents this face, venture out so that you are exposed to the moonbeams. Although the divination may be performed indoors or in the shadows, your own psychic reception is enhanced by exposure to moon light.

 ## Lunar Divination (1)

1. Gaze up at the moon.
2. Pose your question in your mind.
3. Keep gazing and let answers and inspiration come to you.

 ## Lunar Divination (2)

Lunar scrying may be enhanced:

1. Reflect a pan of water, magic mirror or crystal ball in the moonlight.
2. Gaze within the medium, rather than or in addition to the moon, for the desired information.

 ## Lunar Divination (3)

1. Place a dish, bucket or pail of water so that it captures the light of the full moon.
2. Surround the water with four lit torches, creating a circle or magical area.
3. Gaze into the water but also pay attention to the interplay of the candle flames, to reveal the information required.

Lunar divination enhanced by water simultaneously draws down the moon, producing lunar-charged water (see page 51). Reserve the water for future spell-casting.

Lychnomancy—Divination by Candle

Candles not only accompany or constitute magic spells. Any candle, lit for any purpose, can simultaneously serve as an instrument of divination. Candles can also be used purely as instruments of divination.

Candle flames, wax, shadows, smoke, and ashes provide running commentary on a spell's likelihood of success. Although *lychnomancy* involves divination by flame, it is also always worthwhile to observe patterns made by melting candle wax as well. In addition to flame and wax, candles provide another oracle: patterns made by smoke. Experienced diviners can coordinate oracles received from all three sources. Beginners may wish to choose one venue of divination to start with.

 ## Lychnomancy (1) The Simplest Method

1. Light a white candle.
2. Gaze into the flame.
3. Allow visions, words, and inspiration to enter your mind.

This simple method may be enhanced:

★ *Place the candle between you and a mirror*
★ *For purposes of direct communication, place the candle between you and an image. This may be a sacred image, a votive statue for instance, or the image of an actual person or animal, who may or may not be currently alive. Gaze at the image through or over the flame*

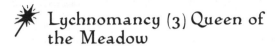 Lychnomancy (2) Ivy

This method is traditionally used to discover who is working malicious magic against you.

1. Charge a yellow candle with your query and desires.
2. Wrap ivy around the candle.
3. Burn the candle: the person should become known to you, although this may occur in dreams.

 Lychnomancy (3) Queen of the Meadow

Botanicals can enhance this method:

1. Place a Queen of the Meadow root inside a glass of water.
2. Place this glass beside a burning white candle.
3. Gaze into the flame, to obtain visions of the future.

✹ Lychnomancy (4) Multiple Candles

Multiple candles may also be used. Divination in this case is achieved by analyzing the appearance and behavior of the flames and the relationships between them.

Arrange three candles, so that they form a tight triangle or pyramid.

★ *Should one flame burn particularly high, vivid and bright, this is extremely auspicious, a sign of good fortune*
★ *Should one candle abruptly go out before the others, the situation may be detrimental for the person involved*
★ *Rising and falling flames indicate a cautionary warning*
★ *Back and forth movement generally indicates evolving circumstances, perhaps the inherent changeability of the situation*

★ *Flames twisting in spirals indicate a warning to beware of hidden plots and false friends*

Mirrors

The most ancient mirrors were not crafted from glass but from smooth metal surfaces, typically copper, polished so that reflections appeared. Reproductions of ancient Egyptian mirrors are available and lend themselves very well for divination. A metal mirror must be polished sufficiently to display a reflection when one looks within. This may require some maintenance.

Modern glass mirrors are more readily available and also more obviously mimic the reflective power of water. Traditional Italian magic mirrors possess a glass face but a highly ornamented metal backing, enhanced by depictions of spirits and other sacred images. These may be used to communicate with the specific deity or deities depicted. Because many display Turanna, the Etruscan Venus, they are also excellent for receiving information and spiritual advice regarding romance.

Mirrors in general have potent associations with spirits of love like Hathor and Aphrodite, as well as mermaid spirits. They are wonderful love and romance oracles. Images of Hathor form the handle of most ancient Egyptian mirrors: these may also be used as a device to communicate with this most primal, powerful spirit.

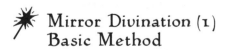 Mirror Divination (1) Basic Method

Gaze within the mirror and allow your mind to wander.

✴ Mirror Divination (2)

A Chinese mirror divination combines scrying with aural oracles. The first part of the spell must be conducted in private, while the second half requires the unknowing participation of another.

1. Place a sieve upon a cold, unlit stove.
2. Place a basin of water and/or a mirror within the sieve.
3. Focus on your query.
4. When you have achieved the correct frame of mind, go outside.
5. The first words that you hear, whether positive or negative, provide your response. Analyze as needed.

If it is impossible to go outside into the presence of others, turn on a radio instead.

✴ Mirror Divination (3)

Catoptromancy, *a specific type of mirror divination, is used to answer medical queries. Enhance clairvoyance with burning incense.*

1. Hang a mirror by a thread over a fountain or pool of water.
2. Slowly lower the mirror until its base barely touches the surface of the water.
3. Gaze within the mirror to receive information regarding a patient's recovery or to receive recommendations for treatment.

This method is based on rituals practiced at a Greek shrine to Demeter. It was originally accompanied by prayers and petitions directed towards her. Incorporate these as you will.

✴ Mirror Divination (4)

Determine what it is you wish to see before initiating this spell. Although it is most frequently cast as a love oracle, any request may be made.

1. Place two mirrors opposite each other on a table.
2. Place two candles on either side of each mirror.
3. Sit between the mirrors with their candles.
4. Gaze into the mirrors until the desired image appears.

For romantic divination, to view a love oracle, get undressed prior to sitting between the mirrors, either completely or just down to sexy lingerie. Loosen your hair, have a glass of wine, if desired: the goal is to seduce the image into appearing for you.

Molybdomancy

Ceromancy, the oracle of melting wax, actually derives from an older form of divination, *molybdomancy*. Molybdomancy uses identical methods, however the medium used is metal, typically lead or tin. Once upon a time, wax was a far more precious, expensive commodity than scrap metal, particularly in ancient Rome, where metaphysical texts recommended that practitioners steal lead from sewer pipes. Wax is much easier to work with, however metal has its own advantages. Metal has specific magical and astrological associations. Tin is under the dominion of Jupiter, traditionally the planet of expansion and good fortune. Lead carries the attributes of Saturn, a planet with a somewhat dour, stern, even malefic reputation.

Substitute either metal for wax in any ceromancy spells.

Ophiomancy

In addition to their role as teachers, guardians and inspirers of magic, snakes are also tools of divination. *Ophiomancy* refers to divination by snake: theoretically it requires more than one snake to accomplish. Those with access to a snake pit, filled with writhing snakes will find this a profound method.

Formulate your question. The response comes from observations of the snakes' movements and especially from the display of their skin's color and geometric patterns. Use the same methods as if you were scrying from water, oil, or ink (see below).

 ## Oracle Sage

Oracle Sage's Latin name, Salvia divinorum, *"diviner's sage," indicates its use as an oracle. It's believed to be the legendary oracular substance of the Aztecs.*

This is not a divination system; instead oracle sage allegedly opens the gates of psychic ability, similar in effect to whatever Delphic pythonesses were inhaling. Burn, breathe and see what you discover.

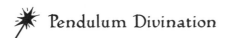 ## Pendulum Divination

Certain botanicals allegedly create excellent pendulums. Try it: attach an orrisroot or angelica root to a cord and use as a pendulum.

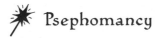 ## Psephomancy

Psephomancy is the art of divining with pebbles. Mark beans or pebbles with signs or colors to indicate your different choices, place them in a drawstring bag and shake them up. Either toss them all out and interpret the manner in which they fall or randomly draw them out, as a response to your query.

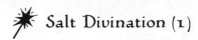 ## Salt Divination (1)

Toss the salt or let it dribble through your fingers. Interpret the patterns it makes in the air as it falls.

 ## Salt Divination (2)

Pour salt through a sieve, shaking and moving the sieve while the salt is poured. Afterwards, observe and interpret the patterns created.

 ## Salt Divination (3)

Throw salt into fire. Interpret the resulting flames, their color, height, patterns, and so forth.

Scrying

At its absolute most basic, scrying means divination via a smooth surface. Perhaps scrying was invented when someone, gazing into a lake's smooth surface, fell into a trance and received visions and psychic messages. Lakes aren't always tranquil nor are they accessible to all. Other more consistently available techniques were developed.

Ancient images of Kybele, the Magna Mater, perhaps the most primal deity of all, show her holding and gazing into a pan of water. This method remains as effective as ever. Its major requirement is patience and the ability to still one's mind: this isn't a quick-fix method. The mind needs time and freedom to float and explore. These methods are particularly suited for those born under the astrological water signs (Cancer, Scorpio, and Pisces) as well the watery air sign, Aquarius.

Scrying (1) The Original Method

If one has access to a particularly tranquil lake, this method remains extremely effective. Sit beside the water and gaze into the glass-like depths. Let your mind be still and see what happens.

Scrying (2) Kybele's Method

1. Fill a shallow pan with water.
2. Allow it time to achieve stillness and tranquility.
3. Gaze within the water or gaze at the surface, whichever suits you.

Scrying (3) Oil

Some prefer other materials for scrying:

1. Fill a shallow pan with oil.
2. Gaze at the surface or into the oil and allow inspiration to approach.

Scrying (4) Ink

An alternative is ink: some find black ink's stillness and depth soothing. Fill a small shallow dish with black ink. Gaze into the ink to receive an oracle.

Scrying (5) Oil and Water

Oil and water don't mix. This detail creates patterns that enhance divination:

1. Fill a shallow pan with water.
2. Once it is still, add several drops of oil.
3. Observe the behavior of the oil: does it form a shimmery surface or create a rainbow? Patterns formed by the oil may also be interpreted. This method is particularly beneficial for queries regarding the Evil Eye.

Scrying (6) Egyptian Method

An ancient Egyptian variation instructs specifically how and what to observe. Although it may be performed for oneself, the Egyptians, at least during the early years of the Common Era, preferred using a child, ideally a pre-pubescent boy, as a medium. Contact with spirits may be established as well as revelations of future events.

1. Fill a flat dish with water.
2. Spread a thin film of oil over the water.
3. As the film thins out, the colors will disappear. Follow them.

Scrying (7) The Vessel

Although the oracle is obtained from whatever is poured into the dish, the vessel itself is not inconsequential. A special vessel, charged and consecrated, or perhaps embellished with sigils, texts and images, may produce a clearer, more potent oracle. In addition, any vessel that the diviner likes or finds attractive may simply be more effective for that person. On the other hand, the simplest vessel, the one at the end of your arm can be extremely effective:

1. Cup the palm of your left hand.
2. Pour some black ink into the palm of your hand.
3. Gaze into the ink to receive an oracle.

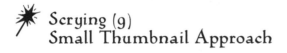

✴ Scrying (8) Thumbnail Approach

Many methods of divination demand peace, privacy and (sometimes) expensive materials. Oil was once a luxury item: to fill a pan or dish with it, perhaps solely for the purposes of divination, was for many an extravagant gesture. A very ancient divinatory system minimizes expenses and can be performed fairly spontaneously:

1. Place one small drop of oil on your thumbnail. (Traditionally the left thumbnail is used.)
2. Shine it so that it is smooth.
3. Gaze within to see the future or receive information.

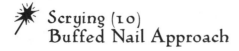

✴ Scrying (9) Small Thumbnail Approach

Children are favored oracles for thumbnail divination. The child may accomplish the first two steps independently.

1. Place a bit of oil on a child's thumb.
2. Polish it until it's shiny and smooth.
3. Have the child gaze at the nail.
4. Pose your question directly to the child or simply allow the child to describe what he or she sees. It is not necessary for the child to know or understand the question.

✴ Scrying (10) Buffed Nail Approach

To really cut down on expenses or to maximize the potential for spontaneity, buff your thumbnail to a high polish. No oil is now required. Gaze at the nail, turning it a bit, if necessary, so as to catch the light. Allow inspiration to reach you.

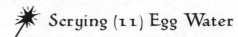

✴ Scrying (11) Egg Water

Because of the symbolism of the egg, this divination system is particularly beneficial for questions having to do with fertility, pregnancy, and children.

1. Fill a jar or glass three-quarters full with cold water.
2. Using a pin, make a small hole in the top and bottom of a raw egg.
3. Let a few drops of egg white fall into the water.
4. Watch and wait. During the next several hours, the egg white will spread through the water, forming images that can be interpreted.

To enhance this method, place the glass before a lit white candle.

✴ Scrying (12) Pegomancy

Scrying may be accomplished by observing movements of water. This method, known as pegomancy, *requires beginning with a reasonably smooth surface, although it's not necessary for it to be as mirror-like as needed for regular scrying.*

Drop or toss stones into still, living water, such as a lake or spring. Interpret the resulting ripples, rings and movement. Appearances of living creatures stimulated by your actions should also be noted and interpreted. In other words, a sea monster or even a turtle or fish, appearing in response to your toss of a pebble should be considered significant.

✴ Scrying (13) Crystal Vision

Scrying is also accomplished by gazing into mirrors, crystal balls, and polished and uncut gemstones: the use of polished round crystal balls was, according to legend, popularized by Romany diviners. Clear quartz, smoky quartz, and aquamarines may be read in similar manner. Among the more difficult skills to be achieved with

scrying is getting the gaze right: look intently, but also leisurely, with eyes just slightly out of focus. Try using peripheral vision instead of a direct gaze as a starting point.

1. Gaze within the crystal.
2. When shadows or shapes appear, follow them.

 ## Scrying (14) Gemstone Vision

The most luxurious tools of divination may be star sapphires and star rubies. If you have access to one, allow it to reveal secrets to you.

1. Gaze at the center of the gemstone's cross, with eyes slightly out of focus.
2. Allow your mind to wander.

This method may also be attempted with staurolite, alias cross-stone or fairy-stone. These crystals possess profound magic power yet lack the luminosity of star sapphires and rubies, making scrying more difficult.

 ## Scrying (15) Scrying with Cups

Once upon a time, diviners used cups in the manner of crystal balls.

1. Fill a large wine glass with spring water or **Holy Water. (Marie Laveau Water** may be used as well providing it's made with lavender water not lavender essential oil.)
2. Add a few drops of liquefied palm oil.
3. Place a white candle behind the glass.
4. Calmly gaze into the glass until visions appear.

This next method of divination requires a matched pair of stones, pebbles, crystals or sea-shells. They must be of roughly the same size and texture but of distinct colors or patterns, thus easily distin-

guishable by sight, not touch. This method is easily spontaneously performed in the woods or at the beach, wherever natural materials are readily available. Should you find a successful, matched pair, keep them in a mojo bag, preferably together with powdered mugwort for psychic enhancement.

1. Determine which of the pair represents an affirmative response, which the negative.
2. Close your eyes and don't peek.
3. Let your fingers play with the stones, rearranging them, as you formulate and focus on your query. Move them around, don't try to keep track of which one is where; just focus on the question, with your eyes closed.
4. When you're ready, pick one up, then open your eyes and see your answer.

Sideromancy

Sideromancy involves divination by heated iron. Traditionally iron was heated in the fire until red-hot; the method was once reserved exclusively for iron-workers, proficient in magic but also able to safely heat and handle iron. This has evolved into a household divination, although great care must be taken.

Cast iron pans are heated over a fire or placed in the fire of a hearth.

1. Heat the iron to whatever temperature is safe and realistic for you.
2. Remove the iron from the fire.
3. Drop an odd number of straws onto the pan. Broom straws are traditional, although dried yarrow stalks make a powerful substitute, because of their connection with the I-Ching.
4. Interpret the resulting movement and shapes as well as the nature of the smoke and flames.

Sieve Divination

Although now typically considered nothing more than common kitchen tools, once upon a time, sieves held powerful associations with magic and were identified with magic as frequently as broomsticks or cauldrons. (Although witches may have flown through the air on broomsticks; they set out to sea in sieves.) Divination by sieve is particularly ancient.

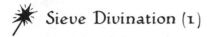

Sieve Divination (1)

Coscinomancy *refers to a specific form of divination via sieve. Ancient Athenians called it "the trick of sieve and scissors." It is most often used to help identify a thief.*

1. The sieve must be suspended in air. This may be accomplished by several methods: attach string or threads to the sieve, use a pair of shears to hold the sieve up, or hold the sieve aloft by balancing on two fingers or two fingers belonging to two different people.
2. Pray for sacred guidance.
3. While holding the sieve aloft, begin chanting the names of those held in suspicion. Allegedly the sieve, shears or both will swirl at a significant person's name.

Sieve Divination (2)

Trick of sieve and scissors, indeed! At least as far as this experienced diviner is concerned, coscinomancy may be the single most convoluted, unwieldy system of divination of all. I can barely visualize it, let alone describe it. Another ancient method, still in use throughout the Middle East, puts a sieve to better use.

Pour sand through the sieve. If reading for another person, the reader pours the sand, while the querent holds and shakes the sieve or vice versa. The result will be hills and valleys of sand. If reading for oneself, interpret the way the sand lies. If reading for another, have them draw a line through the sand with a finger. Observe how the sand shifts, watch the patterns and read.

Sieve Divination (3)

This method works best with a flat bottom sieve, a grain winnow or finely perforated frame drum. This method is excellent when one needs to analyze or choose between two different options or actions.

1. Cover half of the inside of the sieve with white flour.
2. Cover the other half with charcoal powder.
3. Use an existing pendulum or create one with a stick and some string. (A mugwort or wormwood twig is ideal.)
4. Let the pendulum swing within the sieve and watch lines and patterns appear.

Smoke Divination

1. Toss a handful of poppy seeds into a fire.
2. Observe the smoke.

If the smoke ascends, straight and light, this is an auspicious, positive response. However, if the smoke hangs low, heavy and dark, this is an ominous, negative response.

Steam Oracle

1. Focus upon your question while boiling thistles in water.
2. Lower the heat, but allow it to simmer.
3. Keep your ear near the steam and listen carefully for sounds and answers to emerge.

Alternatively remove the pot from the heat source. Place it on a flat surface where you can sit or lie beside it as the steam rises. However, this way, you must be quick: the steam won't last long.

Tongue Stones

"Thunderstones" and "lightning stones" are names used to refer to small meteorites, actual lightning-struck stones, various odd rocks or unearthed ancient artifacts. Amongst Bulgarian and Serbian Romany, these are known as "tongue stones," because they can speak with you.

Tongue stones are sacred, charged with tremendous power and are reserved for use during an emergency. This is not an everyday method of divination for trivial decisions but only for a genuine crisis. When the path is crucial but unclear, a tongue stone provides council.

1. At night, the stone is smeared with animal fat, such as lard or other cooking fat.
2. Bury the stone deeply under earth and grass, forming a mound.
3. Urinate on the little hill and let it sleep overnight.
4. Next day, dig up the tongue stone.

If the stone still feels greasy, your undertaking should meet with success. If it feels rough, all the grease has gone, your plan won't work. Find another. Should the stone display reddish marks, this warns of a dangerous undertaking. And if plenty of earth and grass cling to the stone, your plan will bring good luck and fortune, although it may not work out exactly as you've anticipated.

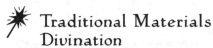

Traditional Materials Divination

Let Earth bestow the gift of divination upon you: in North Africa, the media used in this system of divination are described as "traditional materials" to distinguish them from tarot, playing cards, dominoes or other commercially manufactured methods. Materials are collected over time, as they turn up: small stones found on the ground or washed from the sea, abandoned snail and crab shells, sea shells, roots, clavicle or other sheep bones, the upper and lower jaws of animal carcasses taken from food sources or from road kill, etc., etc.

Collect materials as they appear, cleansing and preparing as needed, and keep them in a basket, covered by a silk scarf. When you wish to read the oracle, gently shake the basket or mix it by hand, but do not allow anyone to see the materials within the basket. Should anyone uncover the basket or observe how the items are falling before they have been tossed to the ground, the process must be halted.

Eventually throw the traditional materials onto the ground. Using your finger, a knife or stick, draw a cross through the materials and interpret the patterns in quadrants.

This method combines excellently with an Earth Oracle.

⬟ Spells of Domination, Persuasion, and Influence

These are among the spells that give magic a bad name: spells that convince others to do your bidding, spells that allow one to exert one's will despite opposition, spells that enhance one's influence beyond natural limits, spells that persuade others to bend over and ask what they can do for you.

Domination spells are *not* hexes: no harm is intended towards your target. Ideally everyone lives happily ever after, just according to *your* rules. Obedience, cooperation and compliance, perhaps a little flexibility, is the desired goal. In today's magical climate, these are not politically correct spells. Modern Wicca and Wicca-influenced magic frowns upon the entire topic of domination magic because the goal of these spells is to deprive another of free will. Practitioners of other magical traditions might say that that's the whole point of spell-casting, so this has evolved into a major philosophical issue within the occult community. Many desist from casting any spell on another in the belief that it is morally wrong to prevent another person from exercising free will. In other words, it's fine to cast a spell requesting that love come to you but wrong to cast a spell on

John Doe because you're sure he's the man for you, although he doesn't know it yet. Understandably then, from this perspective, spells that explicitly set out to dominate are abhorrent.

On the one hand, this is extremely commendable: an example of the genuine goodness and moral high standards to which people aspire. The dawning of the Aquarian Age has sparked discussion of the ethics of magic perhaps never before considered, at least as far as surviving documents demonstrate. Read magical texts from 500 years ago or 1500 years ago or even further back and you will quickly discover that considerations of *fairness* were not major topics of concern. But, on the other hand, total disdain and contempt for domination spells also demonstrates a misunderstanding of the subject. It's true: these are not *nice* spells. However, it's not always a *nice* world. The suggestion that spells of domination should *never* be performed suggests at best naively idealistic, at worst ignorant, protected, Ivory Tower sensibilities. Images of powerful wizards in castles to the contrary, magic spells have always served as weapons of the disempowered.

Societies where every individual is free, has enough to eat, isn't dependent on others and is able to retain control over one's own body, sexuality, family, and personal destiny, do not develop domination spells. They don't need them. Although any spell may be abused, domination spells, as a rule, did not spring from evil, selfish intent. Instead these are protection spells of a very specific kind.

Domination spells were created by women whose quality of life, sometimes whose *very* life, was dependent upon the whims of husbands, fathers, brothers, or sons, whose life might end, literally or figuratively, if unable to produce a child on schedule, who might lose her home if her husband became sexually infatuated with another. Other domination spells were created by slaves whose very lives belonged to others, whose bodies were subject to the desires of others, whose families remained intact only by the grace of another. Under circumstances like these, influencing another becomes a crucial art indeed.

Dominant people don't need domination spells. Those with money and power have faster, more efficient methods at their disposal. Why play around with sweet flag, the primary ingredient of domination spells, when you have enough money to buy whatever or whomever you want? Magical domination spells, in general, are the attempts of the dispossessed and disempowered to turn the tables and, as much as possible, level the playing field. For the truly disempowered, magic may be the only recourse. Wherever slavery exists, wherever power imbalances or severe oppression exists, you will find spells to provide safety, protection, and balance.

Socio-political history is revealed in magic spells. There is a good reason why many involve women's attempts to dominate the men in their lives, but not the reverse—and it's not because, as the witch hunters suggested, women are evil. Men haven't needed magic to enforce economic dominance or generally submissive behavior: historically, other methods have proved very effective.

Before resorting to these spells, as perhaps with any, personal motivation must be examined. If

DOMINATION SPELL-CASTING TIPS

★ Domination spells are in general fueled by the inherent dominating properties of specific botanicals, most notably sweet flag/calamus, licorice root, bergamot, High John the Conqueror, and vetiver

★ The other crucial component of domination spells is the intensity of the spell-caster's desire and desperation

★ Purple is the color of power and dominance. Incorporate that color into candle spells or wherever appropriate

your goal is to assert control for selfish reasons, than these spells truly should not be cast, both for ethical considerations and because malevolent magic invariably attracts the same back to its sender, with potentially dire results for everyone around you.

These old spells—and their roots are ancient—should not be forgotten, however. Should you ever find yourself in *real* trouble, in desperate straits, power reduced, your options for self-preservation and protection severely limited, perhaps your very life and future dependent upon the goodwill of others, then these spells are for you.

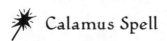

Agrimony Sleep Spell

Allegedly the herb agrimony, placed within a dream pillow, induces incredibly deep sleep and so is used magically by those wishing to slip from the house unnoticed.

Stuff a dream pillow or sachet with agrimony, charging it with your desire. According to European folk-magic, one waits until the target of the spell, usually a spouse or a parent, is already asleep and then the agrimony pillow is tucked beneath their head. If all goes according to legend, they will be unable to awaken until you return and remove the pillow.

Calamus Spell

Vetiver is sometimes confused with sweet flag. Both may be called calamus. Sweet flag is usually partnered with licorice; vetiver's customary "spouse" is patchouli. Once in a while, let them swap. Both calamus herbs are believed to possess profound commanding powers and both are sometimes aphrodisiac. Take this spell bath when you wish to radiate personal power.

Make an infusion by pouring boiling water over sweet flag and vetiver. Add this infusion to your bath together with your favorite perfume. Allow yourself to air dry.

Commanding and Compelling Spells

Modern commanding spells most frequently make use of standardized-formula condition oils. Hoodoo and New Orleans Voodoo evolved a complex repertoire of what are called *Commanding Oils*. These are marketed under various names: *Commanding Oil, Compelling Oil, Commanding and Compelling Oil, All High Powerful Conquering Oil*, and many others. All are reputed to enable you to exert your will over others.

Despite its massive influence, for a variety of mainly racial but also class-based and gender issues, Hoodoo, Voodoo, and their sub-genres receive little respect from the public, from the media, and even from other metaphysicians. Masters like Marie Laveau, Dr. John Montanet, and Henri Gamache have been denied credit, while the average Hoodoo doctor has been painted as an ignorant, superstitious charlatan with little knowledge of true occult science. This is untrue: many of the founding mothers and fathers of Hoodoo were extremely well-versed in a wide variety of metaphysical schools. Their standardized commanding oils prove their knowledge. Despite all the variations in name, these oils rest securely on foundation materials whose use can be traced back at least as far as ancient Egypt.

The most famous and powerful commanding materials are not a heavy club, a sharp sword, or a magic staff with a hidden blade. Instead all that force is contained within two rather innocuous botanicals: sweet flag (also commonly called calamus) and licorice root. (Licorice is a botanical, not the candy named in its honor. The candy cannot substitute for the root.) Each may be used for commanding purposes independently. Married together their powers are believed to increase ten-fold. These two botanicals are the foundation stone of all the standardized commanding oils; their age-old partnership may also be witnessed among the *Magical Papyri* found at Alexandria, used for identical goals.

Commanding oils are very easily purchased. Every metaphysical supplier, every occult or spiritual goods vendor, every botanica sells some version. However, because what is marketed rarely contains true herbs, it's crucial to purchase from reputable manufacturers or to blend your own oils. Formulas are found in the *Formulary*.

★ *In general, condition oils named with variations of the words **Command** and/or **Compel** are of similar strength and potency*

★ *All **High Conquering Oil** or any variant using the term "conquering" suggests the addition of High John the Conqueror, although this may be nothing more than a suggestion*

★ *Essence of **Bend Over**, also marketed as Bend Over Oil, is the most concentrated and potent of the commanding oils. Its inherent promise is to strongly encourage another to bend over and do your bidding*

In addition to their ability to influence others, commanding oils also contain an inherent protective quality: they protect against hexes, other people's bad intentions, and attempts to dominate you.

Commanding Candle Spell (1) Basic Spell

This spell enhances your charismatic powers and makes you a generally more forceful, commanding presence. It does not target any specific person to be submissive toward you. This is perhaps the most politically correct of all domination spells, unlike the next one.

*Carve a candle to represent you. Dress it with **Command and Compel Oil** and burn it.*

Commanding Candle Spell (2) Do My Bidding!

This spell requires two candles, one to represent you, the other to represent the target of your spell. Figure candles in the appropriate genders are most appropriate, though any candle may be used. A white candle is used to represent your target. Use a purple candle to display your power. If purple is unavailable, substitute either red or black. Do not use two white candles.

1. Carve your target's name and identifying information into the white candle.
2. Carve the second candle to represent you. Dress this candle with a **Commanding Oil** and then decorate it with red, purple, and gold glitter.
3. The white candle is not dressed with oil. Instead, take nine pieces of black thread and knot them around the white candle, about one inch apart.
4. Concentrate on a vision of the other person's pliability and cooperative attitude toward you.
5. Elevate the purple candle. Position the white candle so that it looks up toward the other candle.
6. Light the candles. As the white candle burns and the strings break, the person's will submits to your own.

Clues as to whether the spell will work will be given by the candle flames. Observe and analyze.

✴ Commanding Candle Spell (3) Tell the Truth!

Use a commanding oil to compel a liar to confess:

1. Dress a purple candle with **Command and Compel Oil.**
2. Write your target's name on brown paper, nine times.
3. Cross over these names nine times with your own name.
4. Place this paper under the candle and burn it incrementally for seven days, coordinated with a waxing moon.
5. Each time you light the candle, call the person's name aloud, demanding
   I command you, I compel you
   I command you, I compel you
   Tell me the truth!
6. When the candle burns all the way down, wrap any leftover wax in brown paper and dispose of it at a crossroads.

✴ Compelling Bracelet

Before you can get your way, you may have to encourage someone to come closer. This charm both beckons and produces cooperation. There is a sexual aspect to this spell, which is not contained, despite their name, in all domination spells. It may also be adjusted for use as a binding spell.

1. Obtain a little hair from your target.
2. Soak the strands in **Command and Compel Oil.** (You could also make an infusion by pouring boiling water over sweet flag and licorice and soak the hair in this instead.)
3. Add one drop of essential oil of bergamot and one drop of essential oil of vetiver.
4. Let the hair dry out.
5. Braid it together with a strand of your own hair.

6. Knot them together, ideally creating nine knots. (If this isn't possible, the hair isn't long enough, wrap red or black thread around the braid and tie nine knots in this instead.) Murmur your desires into the hair while knotting.
7. Make this charm into a bracelet, supplementing with red and/or black thread for additional length, if necessary. Wear this bracelet on your right wrist, if you're right handed, your left one, if that's the dominant hand. Constantly, consciously will the spell's target to come to you and fulfill your desires.

✴ Commanding Oil Spell

*Anoint a piece of ginger root with a drop of **Commanding Oil.** Carry it in a conjure bag to maintain a dominant presence.*

Commanding Oil: Do As I Say Oil Spells

Sweet flag (calamus) is prized for its aphrodisiac properties as well as its powers of command. Both influences are at play in Do As I Say Oil, also known as As You Please or As I Please Oil. Although it may also be used in business relationships, many spells using Do As I Say Oil possess an erotic component, as it combines the effects of a Commanding Oil with that of a seduction oil. Do As I Say Oil is one of the milder commanding condition oils; its intent is to make others wish to please you.

✴ Do As I Say Oil

1. Grind sweet flag (calamus), myrrh, cedar chips, and peppermint.
2. Place them in a bottle and cover with safflower, jojoba, and apricot kernel oil.
3. Add a few drops of essential oil of bergamot.

Do As I Say Oil Spell

This spell is particularly effective when the candle is burned in the presence of the target. (No need to explain why the candle is being burned; just have it blazing.)

1. Should someone resist your advances, write their name on a piece of brown paper.
2. Anoint it with a drop of Do As I Say Oil.
3. Carve a purple candle or a figure candle that represents the target of the spell, and then dress it with Do As I Say Oil.
4. Place the candle atop the paper and burn.

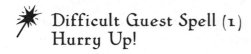 ## Difficult Guest Spell (1)
Hurry Up!

To encourage a late guest to finally show up, stick a needle into the top of a broomstick. Allegedly the missing guest will feel this like a sharp pain in the backside and feel compelled to arrive quickly.

Difficult Guest Spell (2)
Behave Yourself!

Perhaps you have a guest you wish had stayed home. There are some guests whose arrival you dread. Not all guests are welcome, not all behavior is exemplary. You'd prefer to maintain some control over this guest's behavior while in your home. Keep a vigilant eye as the person makes his or her initial appearance:

1. Watch where their right foot first touches your threshold or the inside of your home.
2. Immediately, as soon as the opportunity arises, before anyone else can step on this same spot, drive an iron nail into the exact place.

 ## Dish of Persuasion Spell

This spell intends to charm and enchant someone, in all senses of the words, so that they desire to please you. A romantic component to this spell potentially exists; make it more or less romantic, as desired, by manipulation of botanical material. (In other words, if you'd like this spell to cast a romantic influence, incorporate basic botanicals of love, as found in Love Spells.*)*

1. Place a photograph of your target face-up in a casserole or similar dish. (If you don't have a photograph, write the target's name and identifying information on a piece of paper.)
2. Add a matched pair of lodestones, magnetic sand, honey, sugar syrup, ground licorice root, and carnation petals.
3. Cover everything with olive oil until the dish is approximately three-quarters filled.
4. Create a simple cotton wick, insert it in the oil, and burn.
5. Stir this *"magic brew"* up at least once daily.

Doll Domination Spell

1. Gather your target's complete footprint.
2. Moisten the dirt with **War Water** and your own urine but don't allow it to get too wet.
3. Create a figure from the footprint. Add intimate items from your target (nail clippings, strands of hair) if possible or add a slip of paper with the person's name written on it.
4. Wrap a red thread or ribbon around the figure and pierce it with a nail. The person it represents will allegedly do as you command.

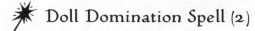 Doll Domination Spell (2)

1. Hold a small candle in your hands while you concentrate on what you wish the target of your spell to do.
2. Dress the candle as appropriate and burn.
3. While the candle burns, make a clay or wax image of your target.
4. Hollow out a hole in the doll in the abdominal region.
5. When the candle burns out, stick the candle stub into the hole.
6. Dress with **Commanding Oil** if you like or roll the doll in powdered herbs.
7. Bury it near your target's home.

 Domination Candle Spell

Burn white candles alongside the image of the Strength card drawn from the tarot deck of your choice. (Different decks feature different interpretations of the image; choose one that resonates for you.) Contemplate the image while the candle burns, then place the card under your pillow where it should remain until the spell is no longer needed.

 Domination Powder

Grind and powder the following:

Cayenne or habanero pepper powder
Dragon's blood
Licorice root
Stinging nettles
Sweet flag/calamus root

Sprinkle the resulting powder in your target's path or on his or her shoes.

 Elder Domination Spell

Elder is an extremely powerful, magical tree. Ask permission of the tree before removing any bark and remember to bring gifts and libations.

1. Write the name of the person whom you wish to dominate on brown paper, ideally with **Dragon's Blood Ink.**
2. Burn the paper; mix the ashes with an equal quantity of elder bark.
3. Mix this magical blend into seven little fabric bundles.
4. For the next seven consecutive nights, bury one packet on the path between you and your target.
5. By the last night, your target will allegedly be under your spell.

 Essence of Bend Over Spell (1) Traditional Use

*Rub **Essence of Bend Over** on your doorknobs so that all who enter will be submissive to you.*

 Essence of Bend Over Spell (2) That Kind of Domination

Use a commanding oil to achieve sexual dominance:

1. Carve a red devil candle with information pertinent to the target of your spell.
2. Dress the candle with **Essence of Bend Over** and burn the candle.

If you'd prefer that your target show some enthusiasm for this domination, you may wish to add erotic oils as well (see page 714).

Expose the Truth Spell

The aroma of copal allegedly forces liars to expose themselves.

1. Burn enough copal to permeate a room's aura.
2. Allegedly anyone attempting to lie will give themselves away, either verbally or through some action that permits others to recognize the lie.

 ## High John Domination Spell

1. Soak a High John the Conqueror root in **High John Oil** and then let it dry.
2. Write the name of the person as well as their mother's name on a strip of paper.
3. Cross over it with your own name twice saying, *"I cross you, I cover you, I command you to _____."*
4. If desired, add a drop of **Commanding Oil.**
5. Wrap the paper around the root and tie with purple thread.
6. Wrap it in a piece of purple cloth and hide this charm in a safe place.

 ## Hollyhock Domination

Hollyhocks are frequently the tallest, most dominating flowers in the garden. Allegedly they help you achieve that dominance, too. Dry and powder hollyhocks, especially black blossoms. Carry the powder in a conjure bag.

 ## Hollyhock Extra Strength Domination Spell

Blend powdered hollyhock, sweet flag, and licorice root. Anoint with a drop of essential oil of bergamot and carry in a conjure bag.

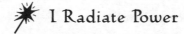 ## I Radiate Power

This spell allegedly enhances your powers of persuasion.

1. Place coriander, licorice, and sweet flag (calamus) in laundry bluing* at the New Moon.
2. Let it remain in the bottle for seven days, then strain out the botanicals.
3. Use the bluing in your laundry with appropriate clothing; the goal is not to decimate your wardrobe. Wear these clothes in the presence of others when making a request.

 ## In My Hands!

*Rub your hands with one of the **Commanding Oils**. Immediately touch the person you wish to control.*

* This spell can theoretically be done—and will be stronger—with true indigo also, but be aware that indigo is a profound and permanent dye. Make sure you are familiar with its effects before applying to clothing.

Kick a Stone Spell

1. Find a small stone. Designate it as the person you need to dominate. If you can find something reminiscent about the person in the stone, whether color or shape, this makes it even more effective. Location also produces an excellent link: locate the stone near the other person's favorite haunts or, if you're daring, pick it up in the other person's presence.
2. Bring the little rock home. As soon as you enter your home, throw the rock on the floor.
3. Kick it, reasonably gently (your goal is submission, not injury), through your home until it rolls under your bed.
4. As you kick the stone, visualize the rock as your spell's target; actually see the person as if they were the size of the rock, running before you.
5. Address the rock by the person's name. Tell it what you need. Visualize the person doing your bidding, extending cooperation, fulfilling whatever is your key need and desire.
6. Leave the rock under your bed.
7. Should you ever need to reinforce this spell, bring the rock outside, urinate on it, and start the kicking process all over again.

 Lodestone Needle Spell

1. Dress a lodestone with **Command and Compel Oil** and then place needles upon it.
2. Alternately, dip the needles in **Command and Compel,** before placing them on the lodestone.
3. Whenever some cooperation is required, remove one needle and discreetly attach it to your target's clothing. Hems, cuffs, and creases in the backs of clothing are traditional target spots.

 Love Domination Spell

*Soak long peppers in safflower oil. (Blend safflower oil with a **Commanding Oil** for added effect.) Rub the oil on your hands and then touch your lover to put him or her under your command.*

 Mandrake Domination

Legendary mandrake root is associated with such powerful female characters as the biblical Rachel, Circe, Medea, and, not least, Isis.

1. Obtain or create an image of open-legged Isis riding upon a sow.
2. Write the name of the person you wish to dominate on paper.
3. Cover it with your own name, twice.
4. Place this paper beneath the image.
5. Charge the mandrake root with your desire; wrap it in dark cloth and place it near or beneath the image, too.

Menstrual Domination Spells

In these Chinese spells, a woman's menstrual power is turned against her.

 Menstrual Domination Spell (1)

Bury a woman's menstrual rag under her threshold to ensure that she will never run away.

Menstrual Domination Spell (2)

Burn a woman's menstrual rag on the seventh day of the seventh month of the Chinese lunar calendar. Sprinkle the ashes over the threshold to keep her tied to the home.

Mummy Candle Spell

The use of mummy figure candles derives more from movie imagery than from any basis in true Egyptian magic, whether ancient or modern. The mummy in this spell is more akin to a Hollywood zombie than to Tutankhamun; an example of the mindless, walking dead so easily dominated by a sorcerer.

Carve a red mummy candle to represent the target of your spell. (Each mummy candle may only be used to dominate one person; if you have the need to command a host, you'll have to carve a candle for each individual.) Dress it with your choice of **Commanding Oils** and burn.

My Will Be Done

Rub your entire body with one of the **Commanding Oils,** so that you radiate influence and power. Allegedly, reading appropriate psalms, for instance Psalms 12, 14, and 32, enhances this method.

Open Hands Spell

A Mesopotamian charm necklace serves to pry open clenched hands. Wear it when you need someone to be generous toward you, or when you want something from another that they may not be inclined to give.

Place head and hand shaped beads on a blue cord, knotting your intentions within. Wear this necklace in the presence of the one from whom you need something.

Persuasion Spell

This is a reasonably gentle spell, falling closer to persuasion than domination on the influence spectrum. It requires a personal touch.

1. Blend red brick dust with powdered deer's tongue.

2. Place this in a jar and cover it with olive oil.
3. Add a lodestone. (You may also add essential oil of patchouli, which will enhance this spell's power, providing that the spell's target doesn't hate its very characteristic aroma.)
4. Close the jar, shake it up, and let it sit overnight.
5. Rub a bit on your palms and touch the hand of the one you wish to influence.

For a more intensive spell, cut the euphemisms and substitute a sprinkling of menstrual blood for the red brick dust.

Putty in My Hands Spell

No need for obscure materials deriving from ancient civilizations. Modern materials possess magic too:

1. Write your target's name, identifying information, and your desires on Silly Putty or Plasticine.
2. Play with it: roll it into a ball, stretch it, bounce it. When the spell feels complete, toss the ball into a body of water.
3. The target should become putty in your hands.

Sealed Up in a Jar

This spell targets a specific person whom you wish to influence:

1. Write the name of the person whose cooperation is required nine times on a piece of paper.
2. Cover each name with your own name.
3. Wrap the paper around twigs of licorice, sweet flag, and vitex agnus-castus, with the written side on the inside.
4. Dress this with a drop of **Command and Compel.**
5. Tie it with a devil's shoestring root and place it within a jar. (If devil's shoestring isn't available, substitute red thread.)
6. Add a camphor square or a drop of essential oil of white camphor.
7. Roll a High John the Conqueror root in over-proof rum, bourbon, or other whiskey and then add the root to the jar.
8. Cover all the contents with honey.
9. Seal the jar and keep it in a discreet place.

Slippery Elm Persuasion Spell

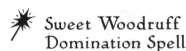

Powder slippery elm bark. Place it in a bag around a child's neck to encourage development of a persuasive tongue.

Sweet Woodruff Domination Spell

*Sweet woodruff is most famous in European folk tradition as the key ingredient in **May Wine**, the May Day potion. Its use as an herb of domination emerges in its nickname "waldmeister" or "Master of the Woods." Sprinkle the powdered root over a path where someone is sure to walk over it in order to dominate that person.*

Thoth's Tool of Command

Master Scribe, Lord Thoth, ancient Egyptian inventor of writing and magic spells, reputedly writes with a calamus reed pen, the better to enforce his spells. Take a tip from Thoth: use a similar pen for spellwork and important messages. To enhance the commanding power even further, add a drop of essential oil of bergamot to ritual ink.

 Underfoot Spell (1) Ancient Method

Some spells require hands, while others require feet. While many domination spells are of necessity secret and discreet, the ancient Egyptians possessed a very defiant, very public one. Your enemy's image or name was painted on the soles of your shoes, so that you could scrunch him or her into the dirt with every single step, keeping the person underfoot, under control, and under your power.

Underfoot Spell (2) Modern Method

A modern update may not be as evocative or soul-satisfying, but it is far more discreet: place your enemy's photograph within your shoe.

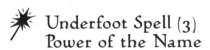 Underfoot Spell (3) Power of the Name

If you lack a photograph and don't trust your artistic skill to be effective:

1. Write the target's name together with his or her mother's name on a piece of brown paper.

2. Ideally **Bat's Blood Ink** or **Raven's Feather Ink** is used; however, plain red ink can be doctored with a drop of essential oil of bergamot, or a commanding oil.
3. Place this within your shoe, underfoot.

Women's Domination Spells

Because women's lives were once so dependent upon men's cooperation, and still are in some places, a sub-genre of Domination Spells evolved to serve these needs. The traditional target of these spells was a man, usually a husband as the person who exerted most control over a woman's life. However the bottom-line goal of these spells is to improve the woman's life.

There is a metaphysical belief that certain botanicals, like hormones, affect men and women differently. Angelica and rosemary, two primary components of women's domination spells, may be used for healing and protection by both men and women. They provide personal power, however, only to women. (Comparable plants for men include High John the Conqueror, Master root and Sampson snake root.)

Spells designed for men to dominate women almost invariably target sexuality: the desire to bend a woman toward one's desires, to make her more sexually agreeable in general, or to persuade her to engage in specific acts. Because their motivation is sexuality not survival, these spells will be found amongst the Love, Sex, and Seduction Spells (pages 628–732).

 Angelica Spell

*Dip an angelica root in **Command and Control Oil**. Carry it in a charm bag, reinforcing with further oil as needed.*

 Corpse Cooperation Spell

The desperation required to perform this spell would alone charge it full of magic power. Has anyone actually cast this spell? Requirements include nerves of steel and access to a fresh corpse.

The corpse must be the same gender as the person you wish to dominate. Obviously the freshest possible corpse, with minimal rigor mortis, is desired.

1. Raise the upper half of the corpse so that it is kind of sitting.
2. Get behind the corpse so that it now leans and reclines upon your lap. (This is an ancient Egyptian/Middle-Eastern birthing position.)
3. Because this is a North African spell, it's suggested that a bowl of couscous now be placed on the corpse's knees but any similar mild-flavored, absorbent food will do: orzo, a nice risotto …
4. Place a wooden spoon in the corpse's hand. Take its hand in your own and together stir the food.
5. Lay the corpse back down. Its job is over.
6. Bring the food home, providing you are not already there, and allow it to dry out.
7. Periodically add small portions to your mate's food. After he eats it, he should become as docile as a corpse.

Corpse Vision Spell

Once upon a time, for millennia, it was customary to bury people with coins over their eyes to pay the passage to the next realm. This Balkan magic formula to blind a lover (husband) to your infidelities or perhaps provide the spell-caster with a measure of freedom depends upon that old tradition. Those coins must be stolen in order to cast this spell or at least borrowed for a little while.

1. Steep copper coins from a dead man's eyes (if the spell is to be cast on a man; the gender of the corpse must match the gender of the spell's target) in wine or water.
2. Give the liquid to your partner to drink so that he'll be just as blind and compliant as the corpse.

 ## Dust Under My Feet Spell

1. With a broom, sweep dust from the street, through your main entrance door and toward your bed.
2. When it reaches the bed, stamp on the little pile of dust.
3. Call out your lover's name and announce, *"Come to me as humbly and pliant as what's beneath my feet."*

According to legend, Martha, the meek, mild housewife from Bethany, traveled to France by boat with Mary Magdalene during the chaos of the Roman conquest of Judea.

In Provence she evolved into Martha the Dominator, tamer of dragons. During the centuries, she has also evolved into one of the most petitioned miracle-working saints, her specialty being, as her title advertises, domination. She is particularly beloved by domestic workers attempting to hold their own with employers, and by wives, suffering under the yoke of authoritative, or worse, husbands.

A cautionary tale regarding domination hides within Martha's most famous legend. When Martha tamed the dragon, she thought everyone, including the dragon, would live happily ever after. Instead as soon as townspeople realized it was no longer a threat, they killed the pacified dragon, over Martha's protests and tears. She could command the dragon but not a lynch mob. Successful pacification had rendered the previously fierce dragon unable to protect itself—or willing to die; a spell's consequences can be unpredictable.

 ## Martha the Dominator Spell (1) Basic Spell

*Maintain a shrine to Martha with an image of the saint, a dragon or both. Dress green candles with **Martha the Dominator Oil** and burn as needed.*

Martha the Dominator Spell (2) Extra Strength

A stronger appeal to Martha the Dominator utilizes intimate items.

1. Obtain hair and/or nail clippings from the target of your spell.
2. Place them on a small green cloth.
3. Pull a few strands of hair from your head and soak them in **Martha the Dominator Oil.**
4. When the hair dries, braid it.
5. Use this braid to tie up the cloth.
6. Hide the packet in a secret place, dressing with oil as needed.

Although some of these spells may seem anachronistic, relics of a past age, many women still find themselves the submissive partner in a marriage or relationship, perhaps because of age, ethnic or cultural background, or simple good nature. What may not start out as a problem can evolve into one.

What happens when one's dearly beloved develops Alzheimer's—but refuses to hand over the checkbook because he remembers just enough to know that he's *always* paid the bills before? What happens when the guy who looked like Mr. Right before you pooled your assets turns out to need a sponsor in Gamblers' Anonymous? It might be easier if you wanted or were able to leave him. Perhaps all you wish to do is adjust the balance of power.

The promise inherent in the women's formula below is that it will transform the woman into the ruling mistress of her domain. This oil also possesses a moderate aphrodisiac effect (more than moderate for those strongly affected by orrisroot) so, theoretically at least, imposition of will may be welcomed as a pleasant surprise.

 ## Mistress of the House

Powdered sweet flag
Powdered rosemary
Powdered orrisroot
Devil's shoestring root
Jojoba oil
Sweet almond oil

1. Add the powdered botanicals to a glass bottle or jar.
2. Add the devil's shoestring root.

3. Blend two parts sweet almond oil with one part jojoba oil and fill the bottle with this blend.
4. Let the oil steep for several days to achieve full strength. Empower by exposing to full moonlight if possible.
5. Administer by various methods: massage Mistress of the House Oil into your loved one's feet, sprinkle it within his shoes, or sprinkle it on him, while he's sleeping.

 ## Rosemary's Empowerment Spell

Allegedly women's power thrives in the presence of living rosemary. Grow abundant quantities in your garden or in pots in your home.

 ## Scarlet Ribbon Spell

This Mexican spell allegedly pacifies abusive men.

1. Measure the entire length of his body with one single length of red ribbon.
2. Slice the top off a candle and carve the bottom so that the wick is exposed.
3. Dress, carve, and charge this candle.
4. Tie the ribbon around the center of the candle and burn it upside down.

Dream Spells: Dreams, Insomnia, Nightmares, Astral Projection, and Witches' Flying Potions

It's only a dream, some say, implying that something is ephemeral, unreal, unworthy of attention. Those subscribing to that notion are not occultists. For the spell-caster, nothing holds more significance than a dream. Dreams are your passport to magical realms and the ticket to your own power. Because dreams come naturally doesn't mean that dreaming isn't also a skill that can be learned and enhanced. From a magical perspective, dreaming isn't a passive state. Dreaming is a primary activity of the soul. Dreams aren't something that happens *to* us; dreaming is something we *do*. Magic spells encourage you to consciously guide and control the dream process.

Dreams are how we most frequently receive communiqués from other realms. Spiritual entities communicate in dreams, as do guardian angels, animal allies, ancestral protectors, and those who have departed. Dreams are where we receive responses to petitions; where we receive the answers to oracles. Spells are cast in dreams, healing occurs, spontaneous past-life regressions and visions of the future are achieved. Dreams replenish our psychic ability and strengthen our personal power.

During the dream state, divisions between psychic knowledge and conventional wisdom grow thin or even disappear. Psychic receptivity increases. Without dreams psychic power is minimized or even curtailed, physical health suffers; we are cut off from needed spiritual advice and intervention.

Everyone dreams. Like a running cinematic program, the average person with sufficient sleep has approximately five dreams every night. The last dream, the one that occurs just at the threshold of awakening is usually the most spiritually and magically significant.

You object: you're sure *you* don't have any dreams at all, let alone a series of five.

Most likely you're wrong. Few of us truly don't dream, although it's very common not to remember dreams. Some people, unfortunately, only remember unpleasant dreams, leading to negative associations and fear of sleep. This fear, as well as trauma and stress, sometimes result in dream suppression.

True failure to dream frequently derives from chronic lack of sleep, or sometimes from medication, especially, ironically, medication taken to enhance sleep. That irony is furthered when one considers the possibility that the whole function of sleep may exist so that dreaming occurs. In other words, it's not *sleep deprivation* that's potentially a problem; it's *dream deprivation.*

Because dreams are so crucial to the magic process, an occult science has evolved to control, nurture, and enhance dreaming. If you think you don't have dreams, there are botanicals that will coax them out of the shadows. You can produce the dreams you need and desire, teach yourself to recall your dreams, and receive visitations from desired persons and spirits alike. You can control and understand nightmares so that they no longer plague you.

What actually happens during dreams?

Although there are various scientific explanations, according to many spiritual/magical traditions, each person has not one but multiple souls, including a distinct dream soul that can journey during dreams and have true experiences before returning to the body when it awakens. The dream soul then sleeps when the body is awake. This dream soul can pursue information, journey to other realms, rendezvous with other dream souls and have magical adventures impossible when awake. What happens in dreams, thus, really occurs, at least in that special realm, Dreamland.

Dreams serve as the bridge between daytime reality and Dreamland, offering information to assist us during waking hours, to improve life and provide protection.

Dreams cannot always be taken literally: they are fluid, hallucinatory, full of secret codes, private languages, and inner jokes. Dreams can be overwhelmingly joyous and ecstatic. There are those whose most transcendent sexual, spiritual, creative, and magical experiences occur in dreams. I play the piano beautifully in dreams—an ability I cannot reproduce in waking life.

Dreams can also be a source of terror: horrible things happen in dreams, worst nightmares and deepest fears are realized. Suppressed memories emerge or are they *just dreams?* Loved ones turn into enemies in dreams; we engage in behavior we would never countenance while awake.

The Talmud states that, *"An uninterpreted dream is like an unread letter."* According to general worldwide metaphysical wisdom, dreams may be harbingers or omens; however, they rarely, if ever, cast a sentence of inevitable doom. Instead dreams carry warnings, messages of protection from watchful ancestors and guardian spirits that must be interpreted correctly in order to avert danger and disaster. Looked at from this perspective, even a bad dream may be welcomed; clues in dreams often indicate your best attempt to fix or preempt an unhappy situation. Nightmares signal some sort of imbalance or else a potentially dangerous situation, of varying degrees: usually imbedded in the nightmare are clues for preventing or remedying disaster, as opposed to submission to the inevitable.

Dream Spells

According to the Talmud, three kinds of dreams come true:

★ *The dream in the morning*
★ *The dream that someone else has about you*
★ *The dream that is interpreted by another dream*

Spell-casters' Dream Tools: Mugwort

If an alarm clock is a dream's worst enemy, then mugwort is a dream's best friend. Mugwort is a member of the *Artemisia* family, botanicals named in honor of the Greek lunar deity Artemis. Artemis protects women, wild nature of all kinds, fertility and creativity, witchcraft, magic, and psychic ability. No other plant has more powerful associations with magic in general and dreams in particular.

Mugwort doesn't give you psychic ability; instead it unearths what's hidden within you and drags it, kicking and screaming if necessary, to the surface. Mugwort is not a gentle plant. It is not for everyone, for a variety of reasons. ***Mugwort should not be used by pregnant women or those actively attempting to become pregnant.*** A traditional medicinal herb for stimulating menstruation, mugwort may cause violent uterine contractions. Nor is it for children's use. Children typically produce vivid-enough dreams, without further stimulation.

Mugwort doesn't produce dreams for you; instead it flings open the gates to Dreamland. Even if you swear you *never* dream, mugwort will very likely stimulate the process. Most commercial herbal dream teas, baths, and products contain mostly mugwort. Other ingredients are required, not to enhance mugwort's magic powers, but to make it palatable. Like its close cousin, wormwood, mugwort is among the original bitter herbs.

Mugwort stimulates the production of dreams. It also enhances clarity, vividness, and your ability to remember dreams. In addition, dreams allegedly linger longer: you may receive a little extra time to hold onto the dream and record it. Because mugwort simultaneously enhances and stimulates psychic power, your ability to understand dreams may also be enhanced. Mugwort also provides spiritual protection during dreams, encouraging acts of bravery and daring you might not otherwise attempt.

Despite these benefits, not everyone likes mugwort. Some find dreams produced under its influence too vivid, too intense, or too frequent. Some complain that all that dreaming prevents a good night's sleep! Experiment and test your personal reactions. Mugwort may be most valuable for jump-starting the dream process: a psychic enhancement to be used only as needed.

Mugwort, as is true for many plants, is available in a variety of forms. Even more than for most other plants, these forms are not interchangeable. In other words, the flower remedy, dried herb, and essential oil all produce different effects.

★ *Essential oil of mugwort, also marketed under its French name, "Armoise," is not safe for use by anyone. Mugwort's chemical constituents are more highly concentrated in the essential oil than in any other form: it is potentially neurotoxic*

★ *The dried botanical herb is safe in moderation for most people, other than pregnant and nursing women, women actively attempting to conceive, and children. A general rule of thumb for mugwort, long considered to be a women's herb, is that if you're not old enough to menstruate, you are not old enough for mugwort. The dried herb is used in teas, baths, herbal pillows, and various spells. An infused oil may be made from its blossoms*

★ *Living mugwort plants are a powerful dream and magic ally. Mugwort, which grows rampant on wasteland, is not necessarily an easy plant to cultivate, just like its namesake goddess. If it grows for you, this indicates the plants willingness to work magic with you and to encourage your psychic powers. Mugwort may be grown from seed; however, it is best propagated by taking cuttings or by root division in the fall. Surround your house with it; grow mugwort in pots indoors. A witch's garden isn't complete without this witch's herb*

★ *Mugwort flower essence remedy is the safest, most accessible method of use. However, be cautious: a bottle of mugwort essential oil is easily mistaken for the flower remedy. Be sure you have the right product, especially if you plan to take the flower remedy internally. Follow the manufacturer's directions for internal dosage or add to baths and massage oils*

Dream Stimulation Flower Essence Remedies

Flower essence remedies are strongly beneficial for the dream process because they work upon soul and emotions most easily expressed through dreams. The effects of any flower essence remedy may be perceived through dreams, but the following specifically stimulate and facilitate dreaming.

★ *Apple (FES)*
★ *Chokecherry (Pegasus)*
★ *Gum plant (FES)*
★ *Jimson weed (Pegasus)*
★ *Mugwort (FES, Pegasus)*

Take in combinations of up to six remedies at a time, as per manufacturer's directions. Place a few drops in a glass of spring water and drink before going to sleep, or rub flower remedies into the thin skin between your thumb and forefinger.

Dream Stimulation: Holed Stone

Humble holed stones facilitate dreams as much, if not more, than precious gemstones. Should you find a naturally perforated pebble or small rock, treasure it: it's a priceless gift from Earth. These stones provide protection, and clairvoyance, and enhance all facets of the dream process.

To access a holed stone's dream power:

★ *Wear it around your neck*
★ *Attach it to the headboard or bed post*
★ *Post it on the wall above the bed*
★ *Tuck it under the pillow*

Dream Baths

These baths are intended to be relaxing, sensuous, and soothing. Don't toss botanicals over your head; just relax in the tub. Warm water is generally more conducive to sleep and dreams than either hot or cold. Simultaneously burning candles and dream incense in the bathroom may facilitate the process, too.

Take these baths just prior to going to sleep. Add essential oils to a bath after the water has been drawn and the temperature has been adjusted. Unless advised otherwise, adjust quantities to suit your nose, but remember: when using essential oils, *less is always more*.

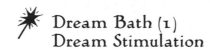

Dream Bath (1)
Dream Stimulation

This dream-stimulation bath doesn't work on a regular basis. It's for use as a single-use jump-start only. This bath is most beneficial for the following purposes:

★ *To initiate your first forays into the dream-world*
★ *To stimulate a specific, new course of dreaming*
★ *To initiate a new dreaming process, after an extended period of not having or recalling dreams*
★ *To kick off any dream healing, dream oracle, or intensive dream spell*

Add twenty to thirty drops of mugwort flower essence remedy (never, never, never the essential oil!) to a bath before bedtime. Follow the manufacturer's recommendations for internal use also, if so desired. This dosage is for single-use only. If you'd like to continue using the flower remedy in the bath, reduce the dosage to no more than five drops after the initial foray.

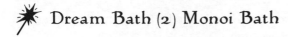

✴ Dream Bath (2) Monoi Bath

Monoi is gardenia-infused coconut oil from Tahiti and one of the few commercial sources of genuine gardenia fragrance.

1. Draw a warm bath.
2. Generously massage monoi into your body.
3. Add a few drops of essential oil of lavender to the bath.
4. Get into the bath; let the water disperse the monoi.
5. Relax, air dry if possible, but if not pat yourself dry, rather than vigorously toweling.
6. Go to bed and dream.

✴ Dream Bath (3) Mugwort Bath

Bathing in mugwort tea may be more pleasant than drinking it and equally effective.

Pour boiling water over one teaspoon of dried mugwort. Allow the infusion to cool to room temperature, then strain and add to the bath. Enhance by adding a few drops of mugwort flower remedy to the water, too.

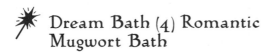

✴ Dream Bath (4) Romantic Mugwort Bath

A plain mugwort bath is potent but medicinal. This bath packs an equivalent punch but is sensual and romantic, too, not to mention excellent for enhancing love-dream oracles and erotic dreams. Take:

One handful of dried hibiscus flowers
One tablespoon of orange blossoms
One tablespoon of red rose petals
One teaspoon of dried mugwort
Three dried bay leaves

1. Place the botanicals in a bowl and cover with boiling water.

2. Allow this infusion to cool.
3. Strain the botanicals, if desired, and add the liquid to the bath.

Dream Incense

Dream incense is *not* burned while you sleep and dream; the burning process should be complete just prior to actually going to bed.

1. Close doors and windows prior to burning the incense, to intensify its effects and fragrance.
2. Place the incense burner on a nightstand or on a safe area near the bed.
3. Burn the incense.
4. When the incense has completely burned, provide ventilation by opening doors and/or windows as appropriate and then go to sleep. Don't wait too long or the fragrance may dissipate.

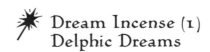

✴ Dream Incense (1) Delphic Dreams

Powdered bay laurel leaves
Cedarwood chips or shavings
Storax gum resin

This incense is a traditional formula, with all ingredients having associations with the Oracle at Delphi. The botanicals included cover all bases in order to provide you with an enhanced dream experience:

★ *Bay laurel leaves assist dream recall and enhance prophetic ability*
★ *Cedarwood clarifies dreams and sharpens awareness of detail*
★ *Storax promotes peaceful sleep and soothes insomnia*

Grind the ingredients together. Sprinkle on lit charcoal and burn.

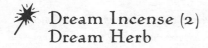

Dream Incense (2) Dream Herb

Mugwort derives from the Eastern hemisphere. Other plants served similar purposes in the Western hemisphere, including one that earned the nom de plume, *"Dream Herb."* Calea zacatechichi *is a native of the Mexican rainforest. Burning dream herb as incense extracts its power.*

1. Burn it in the bedroom before going to sleep, allowing enough time for the incense to burn completely.
2. Do not go to sleep until the incense has completely burned, inhaling the aroma instead and concentrating upon the dream adventures one wishes to experience.
3. Keep doors and windows closed while the incense burns, but then immediately provide ventilation before going to sleep.

Dream Incense (3) Mugwort Incense

Sprinkle ground mugwort on a lit charcoal and burn right before bedtime. Go to bed and dream.

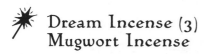

Dream Incense (4) Next Realm

Burn the following incense in your bedroom before going to sleep in order to contact someone who has passed over into the next realm or just to see them in your dreams.

Acacia leaves
Myrrh
Star anise

Mash the botanicals up in a mortar and pestle and burn before going to sleep.

Dream Incense (5) Psychic

Blend copal, mugwort, and mastic and burn for psychic, visionary dreams.

Dream Incense (6) Rainforest Blend

Sometimes having vivid dreams isn't enough. Other abilities must be enhanced in order to take advantage of dreams received. Copal enhances clairvoyance and reception, while providing spiritual protection as well. Combine it with dream herb (zacatechichi) *and burn in the bedroom before going to sleep for maximum benefits.*

Dream Incense (7) Shadows of the Past

Sometimes the dream you need to incubate doesn't pertain to the future; the information you require is buried in your past. These botanicals are specifically used to facilitate past-life recall and also to access this lifetime's hidden memories:

Chopped bay leaves
Honeysuckle blossoms
Lilac blossoms
Juniper

Burn the powdered ingredients on lit charcoal before bedtime.

☀ Dream Incense (8) Triple Strength Dream Incense

Mugwort's closest botanical friends are wormwood, also under Artemis' dominion, and Saint John's Wort, associated with Artemis' brother, Apollo. Both enhance mugwort's power as well as providing additional spiritual protection. All three plants are considered most powerful if picked on Midsummer's Day.

1. Grind mugwort, wormwood, and Saint John's Wort together, blending into a fine powder.
2. Sprinkle on lit charcoals and burn.

Dream Incubation Spells

Dreaming can be an adventure; one never knows what will happen, who we'll meet, what adventures we'll have. Although that can be very exciting, sometimes we need more from our dreams. We need dreams to be a source for specific information that we're unable to access in any other fashion.

A dream incubation spell requests a specific dream. The technique of dream incubation becomes easier with practice; initially it may be challenging. Do not give up if the dream doesn't occur on first attempt; persist, repeating as needed. Different dream incubation spells work for different people. Play about and experiment until you find those that work for you.

Dream incubation is an ancient technique, pioneered in early temples of healing, Earth's first hospitals. Following spells, rituals, counseling, and healing, one went to sleep within the shrine with expectations of receiving a healing dream: either an actual healing within the dream, a visitation from the resident spirit, often in the form of a snake, individual diagnoses or treatment recommendations. Dreams may be incubated for any purpose, however.

Two types of spells for requesting dreams exist:

★ Spells cast to receive a specific dream. The dreamer knows exactly what dream or what type of dream is needed: Dream Incubation Spells
★ Spells and procedures to increase clairvoyance and psychic ability. Dreams are prophetic; however, the dreamer is content to receive dreams as they appear, not specify the exact one. These spells are classed among Prophetic Dreams (see page 366)

☀ Dream Incubation (1) Archangel Michael Dream Oracle

Michael the Archangel's flaming sword illuminates dreams and provides safety as you linger in Dreamland. This dream oracle affirms whether a spiritual petition or request is appropriate or not. This spell is based on surviving remnants of Alexandria's Magical Papyri. The request for the dream is made using a magic lamp.

1. Cleanse and purify yourself thoroughly, using whatever methods you prefer.
2. This spell doesn't assume that you have a special ritual lamp. Oil lamps were once common household articles, like a table lamp is today: it wasn't a big deal back then for a spell to suggest using one, any more than a modern spell's request for a spoonful of salt is an inconvenience. An *"everyday"* magic lamp may be used, or create one following the instructions in Ritual Tools (see pages 83–6).
3. Light the lamp.
4. Speak to the lamplight, observing it, reacting to it, until it burns out.
5. Repeat the following incantation periodically throughout the vigil, and it must be recited at the very conclusion:
   Lamp, light the way to Archangel Michael,
   If my petition is appropriate, show me water and a grave
   If not, show me water and a stone.
6. Be silent, go to sleep, and dream.

The symbols of water and grave and water and stone were used at the dawning of the Common Era. Use them if you like or select others that suit you better; just announce explicitly the identities of the symbols.

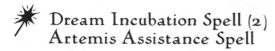

Dream Incubation Spell (2)
Artemis Assistance Spell

Divine assistance may be requested to receive the dreams you need.

1. Build an altar for Artemis.
2. Decorate it with images of the moon and the animals she loves, especially dogs, wolves, and deer.
3. Light silver and/or white candles.
4. Sprinkle dried mugwort onto lit charcoals and burn as incense.
5. Describe the type of dream you need to Artemis.
6. Go to sleep.

Should you receive your dreams, Artemis accepts gifts of toy animals, your old childhood toys, living Artemisia plants, and moon-shaped cakes lit with candles.

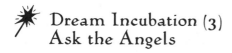

Dream Incubation (3)
Ask the Angels

Russian magic favors beautifully poetic incantations. These incantations follow specific formulas, usually placing the spell-caster in the heart of a mythological dreamscape (an island in the sea, the hills of Zion) before incorporating information pertaining to the specific spell. Although this formula may be used to incubate any dream, it's believed particularly beneficial for diagnosing and identifying mysterious health ailments.

1. Place an object under your pillow that pertains to the question you need answered in the dream.

2. Chant aloud:
   I lie on the hills of Zion
   Three angels surround my bed
   One hears all
   One sees all
   One tells me what I need to know.
3. Conclude the chant by incorporating your question, as succinctly and specifically as possible.
4. Go to sleep.

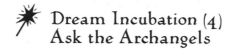

Dream Incubation (4)
Ask the Archangels

Sometimes you need dreams to get in touch with the spirits. Sometimes you need spirits to help you receive the right dream. This dream divination is based upon traditions from Alexandria, the great Egyptian city of Alexander the Great, and dates from the first centuries of the Common Era. It invokes assistance from angels and clairvoyance from bay laurel.

1. Write the following incantation on bay laurel leaves:
   I call upon you Uriel, Michael, Raphael, and Gabriel
   Don't pass me by
   Don't disregard me
   As you bring your nightly visions, please enter and reveal to me what I wish to know.
2. State your wish clearly, concisely and explicitly.
3. Place the leaves beside your head and go to sleep.

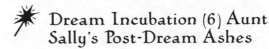

Dream Incubation (5) Aunt Sally's Dream Powder

A famous Hoodoo formula, designed to induce all kinds of dreams, Aunt Sally's was believed especially effective for dreaming up lottery numbers. It was produced and marketed to work in conjunction with Aunt Sally's Policy Player's Dream Book and Wheel of Fortune, *a dream book first published in the 1890s and still in print.*

Dream books have circulated for centuries, the theory being that everything you dream is not only symbolic but also corresponds to a number. Thus according to Aunt Sally's Policy Player's Dream Book, *to dream you are playing a violin indicates that you will soon receive good news. It also indicates the numbers 8, 12, and 28. Using a dream book, you could pick up apart your dreams, analyzing them for meanings, but also hopefully come up with some winning combinations of numbers for the lottery.*

Assorted dream books and systems have been around for centuries. Aunt Sally's, which seems to be an amalgamation of various older books, remains the most popular.

Aunt Sally's Dream Powder consists of the following:

Cardamom
Cinnamon
Coriander
Licorice

1. Grind all ingredients into a fine powder.
2. Sprinkle on charcoal and burn before bedtime.
3. Record your dreams, when you awake. Pay attention to any numbers in your dreams (count things, if necessary) or make correspondences using a dream book.

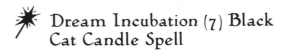

Dream Incubation (6) Aunt Sally's Post-Dream Ashes

If there aren't any numbers in your dreams, don't despair. There's another way to access numbers from dream incense.

1. In the morning, when you awake, using either your bare fingers or a sieve, sift the ashes of Aunt Sally's or other dream incense.
2. Interpret the results to receive your message.

Dream Incubation (7) Black Cat Candle Spell

Sometimes you know exactly what kind of a dream you need. This spell is used to incubate a specific dream:

1. Prepare your bedroom. Do everything necessary so that once the candle is pinched out, you can go straight to sleep.
2. Hold a black cat candle in your hand while you consider explicitly what dream you need.
3. Write this down succinctly and clearly on a small slip of paper.
4. Slip the paper into the cat's mouth. (Use a knife to cut a slit into the wax if necessary, or attach it with oil and bit of acacia gum.)
5. Charge the cat with its mission and light the candle.
6. While the candle burns, have a relaxing bath with dream-inducing oils. Drink a dream-stimulating tea.
7. Keep an eye on the candle; once the paper has been reduced to ash, pinch the flame out and go to bed.
8. If you need to revisit this specific dream or dream-issue, because the dream wasn't received, you weren't able to recall details or the whole dream, or you require further information from the same dream, use the same candle. If the surface of the candle has flattened, you may rest the paper atop. If not, attach it with gum resin or make a slit into the wax and insert it.

For a totally new dream, a totally new situation, start with a new cat.

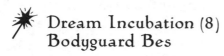 **Dream Incubation (8) Bodyguard Bes**

Often described as a cross between a lion and a dwarf, although Bes doesn't figure into the grand cosmologies favored by mythology books, to the average Egyptian person he may have been the most popular spirit of all. Bes's image was everywhere in ancient Egypt: decorating walls, spoons, cosmetic jars, tattooed onto dancers' bodies, carved onto beds to serve as a night watchman. Typically the only male member of the spiritual entourage surrounding Isis, fierce little dancing Bes serves as a spiritual guard-dog. This ritual requests more than nocturnal protection from Bes:

1. Begin by preparing the ink and consecrating a black strip of cloth or a scarf to Isis.
2. Doctor up **Dove's Blood** ink with an extra drop of myrrh and a little raspberry or pomegranate juice or grenadine syrup.
3. Draw an image of the protective spirit Bes on a piece of papyrus with your left hand, if you're right-handed; the reverse, if not.
4. Write out the question requiring a dream answer, while reciting a *Names of Power* incantation. The ancients favored repetitions of long strands of magical names that they may or may not have understood. Create your own Names of Power invocation. Invoke those whom you believe will protect you and who will help send you the needed dream. Begin the incantation with: *"Send the truthful seer out of the holy shrine."*
5. Chant your Names of Power and conclude with the words: *"Come this very night!"*
6. Take the black strip of cloth, wrap one end around your left hand and the other around your neck. Go to sleep. Bes may appear in person with your answer or you may just receive the answer.

 Dream Incubation (9) Magic Lamp Spell

A magic lamp is used to stimulate this dream revelation, based on traditions from Alexandria. The original spell demanded several days of purification, at least three, in order to obtain optimal results. This means no alcohol, no meat, and no sex. Although an everyday lamp may be used for this spell, it should be ritually consecrated before use, charging it with intent and fumigating with incense.

1. Set up a magic oil lamp. If it's terracotta, you may wish to decorate the body of the lamp with appropriate symbols or sigils.
2. Consider explicitly what you require from the dream.
3. Work out an incantation, which addresses your needs and requests assistance from the deity of your choice.
4. Place a mat on the ground to sleep on; the original spell called for a rush mat, modern versions are sometimes sold as beach blankets although perhaps any mat or blanket of natural material will suffice.
5. Using ink that has been scented with myrrh, write down whatever it is you need to conjure, your dream requirements, onto a strip of white linen.
6. Wrap this strip around an olive branch, with the words facing in.
7. Place it on the mat, so that when you are ready to sleep it will be by the left side of your head.
8. Fumigate the room and yourself with **kyphi** or frankincense and myrrh.
9. Kneel on the floor beside the lamp and repeat your incantation seven times, gazing into the flame.
10. Go to sleep and dream.

✴ Dream Incubation (10) Mystery Tour

Who's sending those anonymous letters? How to discover where your mysterious lover really lives? This Russian oracle allegedly provides identifying dream visions of specific doorways or displays directions to the location of your choice. Of course, first you have to get to sleep. Why is it that dream-oracle food always tastes so bad and dream-oracle animals are inevitably those that leave us sleepless? This spell would be so much easier if you could just borrow a little kitty-cat instead.

1. Take a cockroach from your neighbor's house. (Because, of course, the dreamer's house doesn't have any, or because it must be a traveling cockroach?)
2. Put it under your pillow before bedtime and say, *"Cockroach! Lead me to the door of _____* [Name your desire]."
3. Go to sleep. You should see the door in your dreams. You may be able to follow the cockroach's route. If so, consciously try to pay attention to directions in your dreams so that they may be analyzed or reproduced.

Really squeamish about having that cockroach crawling around under your pillow? Other versions of this spell suggest keeping the cockroach in a locket around your neck. Much more reassuring, isn't it?

✴ Dream Message Spell

Send a message via dreams. The goal of this German spell is to magically induce someone else to have a specific dream.

1. Determine the exact dream that needs to be transmitted in as much detail as possible.
2. At the New Moon, place a clear quartz crystal within a glass of spring or **Holy Water** and create lunar-infused water by leaving it exposed to moonlight overnight.

3. During the waxing moon, dress your bed with clean white sheets and sprinkle the lunar water over them.
4. Place yarrow, wormwood, and thyme inside a muslin bag or tie up within a handkerchief.
5. Hold the herb packet in your hand; concentrate on the person for whom this dream is intended.
6. Place the packet within your pillowcase; as you go to sleep visualize the dream you'd like to send as if you were watching a movie.

Dream Oil

Dream Oil (1) Gardenia

The fragrance of gardenias inspires abundant, prophetic dreams, beckons benevolent spirits and enhances psychic ability. That's the good news. The bad news is that the scent of genuine gardenia is rare. Commercially available products are almost invariably synthetic; what's in the bottle smells like gardenia but doesn't actually possess the botanical's magic powers. If at all possible, if you possess fresh gardenia petals, create your own gardenia infused oil to spark intensely powerful dreams. (The alternative is the Tahitian gardenia-infused coconut oil known as monoi.)

1. Infuse gardenia petals in coconut oil (see Infusion Instructions in *Elements of Magic Spells,* page 31). (It may require as many as six weeks to achieve the desired intensity of fragrance.)
2. Strain the infused oil and discard the flowers.
3. Reserve the oil. Add approximately one tablespoon to a bath before bedtime to stimulate prophetic dreams.

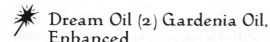

Dream Oil (2) Gardenia Oil, Enhanced

1. Create gardenia-infused oil as directed above.
2. Take a finger-full of this infused oil and add a few drops of mugwort flower essence remedy (FES).
3. Rub onto the soles of your feet before bedtime to kick-start dreaming.

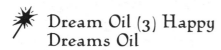

Dream Oil (3) Happy Dreams Oil

Add essential oils of frankincense, myrrh, and petit-grain to a bottle of blended sweet almond and jojoba oil. Massage this into the body before bedtime.

Dream Oil (4) Hidden Access

This oil is infused from honeysuckle blossoms and lilac blossoms. The fragrance of lilac unlocks the door where hidden memories, from this lifetime and those long past, are stored. Unfortunately there is virtually no version of commercially available lilac fragrance that is not synthetic. If you'd like to access lilac's power, you'll have to infuse your own oil.

1. Follow the instructions in *Elements of Magic Spells* for making flower petal-infused oil.
2. When the oil is finally complete and all botanical material has been strained out, for added enhancement add a few drops of mugwort flower essence remedy (FES).
3. Massage onto the body before bed or add to the bath to unlock buried memories from this lifetime or others.

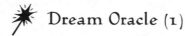

Dream Oracle (1)

1. Write your query lucidly and concisely on a slip of paper.
2. Slice a slit into a poppy seed head and place the paper within it.
3. Sleep with this beneath your pillow to receive a response in your dreams.

Dream Oracle (2) Doll Divination

This method, which resembles something from a fairy tale, traditionally uses a mandrake root, though ginseng or any human shaped root may be substituted.

1. Embellish and dress the root so it looks like a person. (German folk tradition suggests using millet for eyes.)
2. Wrap the root doll in silk when not in use and keep in a safe place.
3. Unwrap the doll and talk to it before bedtime. Tell it your concerns and questions.
4. Perch it on your pillow or tuck it beneath while you go to sleep and dream.

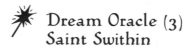

Dream Oracle (3) Saint Swithin

1. On Saint Swithin's Eve, July 14th, cut the corners off a square of fine paper and burn them.
2. Using a new pen with red ink, write down the three things you most wish to know on the corner-less paper.
3. Fold the paper up; wrap three hairs from your head around it. Make a knot with each, reiterating one query with each.
4. Place this paper under your pillow for three nights and allegedly all will be revealed to you.

Dream Pillows

Dream pillows are an excellent venue for botanicals to stimulate and enhance dreaming. Botanicals are placed within a bag, which is then either laid under the cheek or placed beside you on the pillow. The bag should be smooth and comfortable. Botanicals are ground to a fine powder so that nothing protrudes and irritates. A dream pillow that prevents you from sleeping defeats its purpose.

Dream pillows serve all sorts of uses:

★ *Basic dream stimulation*
★ *Incubation of specific types of dreams: erotic dreams or financial dreams, for instance*
★ *Sleep enhancement*
★ *Nightmare prevention*
★ *Spiritual protection while you sleep*

Specify your goal by adjusting the botanicals stuffed within the pillow. Every botanical has its own power: select those that correspond to your desire. Crafting the dream pillow is a spell: remember to charge and consecrate materials as desired. Focus on your desire and intent while you're crafting. Every knot tied is an opportunity for an individual knot spell.

The typical dream pillow is made from muslin or some other soft material. Natural fabrics breathe better, allowing better access to the pillow's fragrance. The pillow's power is delivered to you via its aroma. The standardized dream pillow is 12 inches by 8 inches (30 cm x 20 cm) and requires approximately 8 to 10 ounces (around 300 g) of dried herbs. However, craft whatever pillow suits you best. A small sachet made from highly absorbent material works beautifully. Resist the temptation to stuff the pillow with herbs in the mistaken belief that increased quantity always means increased power: a flat, loosely filled pillow is more comfortable, more conducive to sleep, and thus most likely to be more effective.

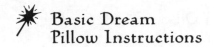

Basic Dream Pillow Instructions

For the pillow, cut two matching pieces of fabric and sew them up together on three sides.

Fill the bag from the open end, and then sew this last side up, too.

1. Botanicals must be completely, thoroughly dry before sewing into the pillow or sachet because otherwise they may rot, producing an acrid fragrance liable to stimulate nightmares, rather than the desired dreams.
2. Unless they are very soft, grind ingredients to a fine powder. Comfort is the key element: rose petals are preferable to buds, which are pointy and must be finely ground. Bay leaves are superb dream enhancers but must be at least crushed. Otherwise they will protrude from the pillow and are liable to poke you in the eye.
3. If adding essential or fragrance oils, blend them into the dried material well, using a twig or wooden chopstick. Allow the material time to dry *completely* before sewing into the pillow.
4. If adding charms or harder roots, place them carefully in the center of the pillow and surround with softer material.
5. Ideally, if only for maximum effectiveness, the pillow's fragrance should be pleasing to you. Dislike of any botanical's aroma may signal that this plant is not beneficial for you. Irritation is liable to keep you awake, defeating the purpose. At the very least, make sure you find the fragrance neutral. Adjust the fragrance to suit your taste, keeping in mind that when you're lying in the dark, deprived of other stimulation, especially if unable to sleep, the fragrance may be more intense than initially realized.

Crystal Dream Pillows

Many crystals enhance dreaming, but because they must be cleansed periodically (for maximum potency but also in the aftermath of disturbing visions and nightmares), don't sew them up inside a pillow or sachet.

1. Place a crystal on a clean white handkerchief together with some dream herbs.
2. Tie it together with a blue silk ribbon.
3. Sleep with this under your pillow or cheek.
4. Take it apart and cleanse as needed.

 ## Doctoring a Dream Pillow

Although beautiful commercial dream pillows are available, the herbal stuffing is rarely as potent as the one that you can create at home, nor as specific to your needs. Have the best of both worlds. When someone falls in love with a commercially manufactured dream pillow, usually it's the fabric that truly attracts. If a dream pillow is too pretty, evocative or cute to leave behind, buy it, bring it home, and enhance its power.

1. Carefully, open the seams and remove the herbs.
2. Dress the original herbs with dream-enhancing oil and allow them to dry before replacing, or substitute fresh herbs of your choice.
3. Sew the bag back up and enjoy it.

 ## Quick-fix Dream Pillow

Sometimes you have the herbs but lack the time or patience to sew. Maybe you just really hate sewing. In that case place dream botanicals in a white handkerchief and tie them up in a bundle with a red, blue or silver ribbon. This is not as comfortable to sleep with as a smooth, flat pillow, and the herbs do have a tendency to spill out. However, purely from a spell-caster's perspective, this is equally as effective as a full-blown dream pillow.

Alternatively, fill a drawstring bag with dream herbs and use it as a dream pillow. Muslin is preferable to flannel, as the fragrance is released with greater intensity.

 ## Dream Pillow (1) A Basic Dream Pillow

The simplest dream pillows contain one ingredient only: mugwort. Fill a pillow with dried mugwort to stimulate your dreams.

 ## Dream Pillow (2) Artemis' Dream Herbs

Fill your dream pillow with a divinity's special botanicals to request their protection as well as their presence in your dreams. Artemis is an obvious choice because she rules the night as well as the herbs so intrinsically connected with dreaming.

Dried Dittany of Crete
Dried mugwort
Dried southernwood
Dried tarragon
Dried wormwood

1. Fill a white bag with a combination of the above herbs.
2. Add a tiny smooth silver charm to the center of the bag.
3. For maximum strength, create and inaugurate the pillow on a Full Moon.

 Dream Pillow (3) Baby

A dream pillow to encourage a baby to sleep:

1. Construct a sleep pillow by placing dried dill weed and seeds inside a flannel bag.
2. Use a few layers of flannel, so that the pillow will be extra soft.
3. Keep the pillow near the crib rather than inside it, to make sure the baby doesn't choke on any materials.

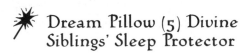 Dream Pillow (4) Children

Fill a very soft flannel dream pillow with one or a combination of the following: chamomile flowers, hops, lavender blossoms, and linden flowers. (Avoid chamomile where there's a possibility of ragweed allergy.)

Dream Pillow (5) Divine Siblings' Sleep Protector

Those who sleep, unpredictably, at all hours of the day or night, need 24-hour vigilant protection. Mugwort represents Artemis, Spirit of the Night, while Saint John's Wort belongs to her twin Apollo, who radiates the power of the sun. Master archers both, have them train their vigilant eyes over you while you sleep.

1. Use equal parts of dried mugwort and dried Saint John's Wort to fill a dream pillow, to obtain their unwavering protection both day and night.
2. For added enhancement, add small, smooth silver charms in the shape of dolphins or moons.

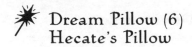 Dream Pillow (6) Hecate's Pillow

Hecate provides protection at night as well as psychic enhancement, so that you can journey safely during dreams. Appeal to Hecate to block nightmares too.

Dried lavender
Dried mullein
Essential oil of lavender
Optional: tuberose absolute

1. Blend two parts lavender to one part mullein.
2. Sprinkle a few drops of the essential oils over the dried botanicals.
3. Allow this to dry thoroughly and use it to fill a black pillow.

For optimum results, create and inaugurate the pillow during the Dark Moon or on Halloween/Samhain.

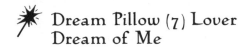 Dream Pillow (7) Lover Dream of Me

Sometimes it's not your own dreams that are so crucial. Give this dream pillow as a gift to someone whose dreams you'd like to enter.

1. Grind allspice berries and orrisroot to a fine powder.
2. Place them in a bowl together with dried honeysuckle blossoms, red rose petals, and hibiscus flowers.
3. Add a lock of your hair.
4. Dress with one drop of essential oil of pine and one drop of essential oil of sandalwood.
5. If you'd like, add one drop of menstrual blood.
6. Stir gently to blend thoroughly.
7. Allow the mixture to dry completely.
8. Use this blend to fill a small dream pillow and present it to the one you love.

Pillows covered in red silk or satin are most powerful.

Dream Pillow (8) Morpheus

Who can forget the sleep-inducing field of poppies in The Wizard of Oz? Poppies, the source of some of the earliest anesthesia, represent the healing, renewing power of sleep. Sacred to many deities from Demeter to Hathor, poppies are the special emblem of Morpheus, Greek spirit of dreams, hence the name morphine, *derived from the opium poppy. Stuff a red dream pillow with poppy seeds, dried poppy flowers, and mugwort for sound sleep as well as prophetic, visionary dreams.*

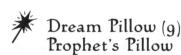 ## Dream Pillow (9) Prophet's Pillow

Stuff a dream pillow with heather for prophetic and financially insightful dreams.

Dream Pillow (10) Restless Spirit

Fill a dream pillow with two parts lavender blossom to one part each of agrimony and mugwort to ease restless spirits and still fitful dreams, and to encouraging clairvoyant ones instead. (If you are a very sensitive sleeper, a mere pinch of mugwort may be sufficient.)

Dream Pillow (11) Romantic Dreams

Fill a small pillow with peppermint leaves, rose petals, and ground cloves for restful sleep and happy, romantic dreams.

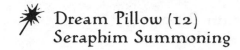 ## Dream Pillow (12) Seraphim Summoning

Dried henna powder calls in the seraphim, the fire angels. If you'd like to experience or communicate with them, fill a muslin drawstring bag or a dream pillow with the powder and place it under your cheek while sleeping.

Dream Potions

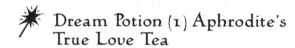

Don't confuse magical dream potions with medicinal sleep aids. Most of these potions are ancient recipes; whether or not they've since been discovered to have sedative properties is incidental. Their goal is to promote dreaming, not to forcefully sedate you into sleep. In general, drink these potions just before bedtime.

Dream Potion (1) Aphrodite's True Love Tea

Aphrodite's sacred tree is the apple and thus its fruit is the fruit of love.

Make apple blossom tea. Sweeten it with honey and bring it to bed. Before drinking make an invocation to Aphrodite, requesting that true love dreams be sent to you.

Dream Potion (2) Basic Mugwort Tea

Plain mugwort tea is very potent. A cup before bedtime should stimulate dreams. Unfortunately it tastes so unpleasant few will drink it. Adding honey may be sufficient to sweeten the taste for some.

Place one teaspoon of dried mugwort in a cup and cover with boiling water. Allow this to steep for ten minutes, then strain and drink.

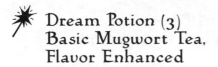

Dream Potion (3) Basic Mugwort Tea, Flavor Enhanced

A more palatable blend:

> One tablespoon dried mugwort
> One teaspoon dried lemon balm (melissa)
> One teaspoon dried hibiscus

1. Place the ingredients in a tea pot. (This is more herb than necessary for a single cup of tea. Adjust quantities to suit your needs.)
2. Pour boiling water over the herbs and let them infuse for ten minutes.
3. Strain and drink.

Sweeten with honey if desired.

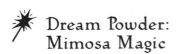

Dream Potion (4) Mugwort Power Potion

If you're able to drink plain mugwort tea, you may be able to stomach this even more bitter brew. One single cup, no more than once a week, should be sufficient to stimulate powerful dreams.

Place one teaspoon of dried mugwort and half a teaspoon of dried wormwood in a cup. Fill the cup with boiling water. Allow the tea to steep for ten minutes, strain and drink.

Dream Powder: Mimosa Magic

Mimosa Magic Powder serves three purposes:

★ *To banish bad dreams*
★ *To stimulate good dreams.*
★ *To encourage good dreams to come true*

1. Grind up rose petals, lilac petals, and acacia gum in a mortar and pestle.
2. Blend this with cornstarch.
3. Add a few drops of essential oils of mimosa and bay laurel. (If you like a sweeter, more floral aroma, also add one or two drops of rose attar.)

Sprinkle Mimosa Magic between the sheets, or around the bed. As an alternative, powder the body with it following a bath.

Dream Protection

While some perceive the dream-state's hallucinatory fluidness as an opportunity for spiritual growth, excitement, and adventure, others fear sleep and dreams. Surrender of consciousness leads to feelings of extreme vulnerability. That *anything* can happen in a dream may be an invitation for some, a nightmare for others. That sense of exposure and vulnerability is no illusion: all sorts of defenses are surrendered together with consciousness when you lie down to sleep. Standard physical precautions are taken: doors are locked, windows bolted, the stove turned off, and burning candles extinguished to avoid danger and risk. Special magical security measures may also be taken to provide spiritual safety whilst you sleep—a wise plan for nervous and intrepid dreamers alike.

These spells are specifically designed to ward off spiritual night dangers rather than scary dreams or nightmares. (For protection against these, see the section on *Nightmares*, page 380.) You may wish to supplement with general *Protection Spells* too.

Dream Protection (1) Artemis

Use Artemis' herbs to invoke her nocturnal protection.

1. Set up a shrine to Artemis within sight of your bed.
2. Use a statue of the goddess as the shrine's focal point or designate a white candle or a lunar image to represent her.
3. Place a dog beside her: either a rubber toy model or a photograph works well.
4. Place wormwood and mugwort at her feet. Supplement with other herbs she favors: Sweet Annie, southernwood, Dittany of Crete.
5. Add pieces of silver, smooth white stones and/or empty wooden thread spools.
6. Tell Artemis what you need: before you retire at night, light a white or silver birthday candle to remind her of your need.

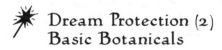 Dream Protection (2) Basic Botanicals

The following botanicals enhance sleep, or at least won't disturb it, whilst simultaneously creating a spiritual shield to protect you while you sleep:

Angelica
Anise
Black mustard seeds
Cloves
Henna
Mugwort
Purslane
Rosemary
Rue
Saint John's Wort
Southernwood
Sweet Annie
Sweet flag (calamus)
Vervain
Wormwood
Yarrow

Use one or any combination of the above to fill a dream pillow.

 Dream Protection (3) Basic Botanical Potpourri

Place any combination of dried dream protection botanicals (see list above) inside a closed magic box. Keep the box closed except when you're sleeping; then open it so that the fragrance radiates a protective shield around you.

 Dream Protection (4) Basic Botanical Protective Circle

If you're really fearful, cast a circle with any one or combination of the above dream protection botanicals around the bed where you sleep.

 Dream Protection (5) Dream Pillow

Fill a small dream pillow with coriander seeds and dillweed to enhance sleep and dreams, and to provide spiritual protection at the same time.

 Dream Protection (6) Five Finger Grass

Wrap cinquefoil (five-finger grass) in red cloth. Tie with a silver or red ribbon, knotting in your desired goal, and place this under your pillow to ward off malevolent nocturnal spirits, or hang it over the bed.

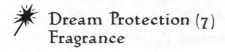 Dream Protection (7)
Fragrance

Not all protective fragrances come in the form of dried herbs. Fragrances that confer protection include coconut, frankincense, gardenia, hyacinth, mimosa, and myrrh.

Position one or more of these fragrances so that it wafts over your bed. Either place the botanical beside your bed (potted plant, bouquet or cut fruit), or warm the fragrance within an aroma burner. If you do this, make sure you have the real item, not a synthetic reproduction. Synthetics may be dead ringers for the superficial aspects of fragrance but they lack the botanical's spiritual and magic protective powers.

 Dream Protection (8) Iron

Nothing protects against the terrors of the night better than iron.

Place a knife, dagger or horseshoe under your pillow while you sleep, or keep a magic sword under the bed.

 Dream Protection (9)
Iron Enhanced

Wrap mugwort and/or wormwood around an iron implement. Place this under your pillow for maximum spiritual protection while dreaming.

 Dream Protection (10)
Mugwort and Wormwood

Those botanical siblings, mugwort and wormwood, have each earned strong individual reputations as guardian amulets. Operating together, however, they're able to provide massive-strength spiritual protection, especially while you're sleeping.

Sleep with them under your pillow, tucked into your nightclothes or hanging from the bedpost.

 Dream Protection (11)
Mugwort and
Wormwood Shield

Place twigs and roots of mugwort and/or wormwood across your chest while you sleep for intensified protection. Another method is to cast a circle of mugwort and/or wormwood roots around your bed.

 Dream Protection (12)
Sea Spirit

Sea Spirit, also known as Ceylon Moss, is a type of seaweed. When it's dehydrated and powdered, it's called agar-agar, and is used as a food thickener in many Asian cuisines.

1. Stir a pinch of agar-agar into a glass of whiskey or rum.
2. Place it on a nightstand beside your bed to ward off (or sedate) any visiting dangerous spirits of the night.

 Dream Protection (13) Sea
Spirit/Florida Water

Add a pinch of agar-agar to a bottle of **Florida Water**. Keep the open bottle near your bed while you sleep.

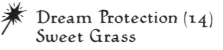 Dream Protection (14)
Sweet Grass

A Cheyenne method used for children and adults alike is to tie a piece of sweet grass root onto a necklace, blanket, clothing or cradleboard to ward off malevolent night spirits and to sweeten dreams.

Dream Rendezvous

This spell assists dream assignations. This spell may be easier to accomplish if the people wishing to meet in Dreamland work out the dream details in advance. (In other words, make plans where to meet.)

Grind and powder linden flowers and blend with rice flour. Both parties must dust their bodies from head to toe with this powder before going to sleep.

Erotic Dreams

Aphrodisiacs create erotic enhancement while you're awake; certain botanicals stimulate sensual dreams and pleasures while you sleep.

The following botanicals provide that special effect:

Aloes wood
Anise
Cardamom
Catnip
Cloves
Coriander seed
Damiana
Gardenia
Henna
Hibiscus
Jasmine
Myrrh
Orchids
Rose
Tagetes-marigold*

* Tagetes is the botanical classification for what are popularly called French marigolds, Aztec marigolds or African marigolds, basically anything other than calendula, the common pot marigold, which is the only completely safe marigold. Tagetes are potentially toxic: do not ingest or apply to the body. Inhaling the spicy, sexy flowers is sufficient. An essential oil is available but fresh flowers are safer.

Tuberose
Vanilla
Vervain

★ *Fill a dream pillow with any one or combination of the above herbs*
★ *Instead of filling a pillow with the herbs, place them loose in a covered box kept by your bedside. Inhale this potpourri before bedtime*
★ *Make an infusion from any combination of these botanicals, except tagetes, and add to your bath*
★ *Dried plants aren't necessarily more effective. Place a bouquet of cut flowers on the nightstand or keep living plants close enough to waft their aroma over you while you sleep*

Erotic Dreams (1) Angel's Water Bath

*Add substantial quantities of **Angel's Water** to your bath for aphrodisiac effect and to provoke erotic dreams.*

Erotic Dreams (2) Aphrodite's Dream Bath

If a real lover isn't in your bed, summon a dream lover instead. Aphrodite's favorite botanicals incite dream-time revels. Allow yourself to air-dry; the botanicals will linger on your skin and attract real-life lovers, too.

Use six drops of essential oil of myrtle and six drops of rose attar in your bath.

Erotic Dreams (3) Cat's Tail

Place a cat's-tail plant in a glass of water on a nightstand by your bed. This not only inspires erotic dreams but allegedly helps transform those dreams into reality. In the morning, toss the water out in your front yard.

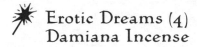 **Erotic Dreams (4)
Damiana Incense**

Sprinkle powdered damiana and powdered sandal-wood on lit charcoals and burn.

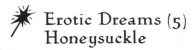 **Erotic Dreams (5)
Honeysuckle**

Some erotic-dream inducing botanicals are particularly powerful. Honeysuckle, in particular, is strong enough to create the desired reactions independently.

★ *Add honeysuckle flower essence remedy (Bach flower) to the bath before bedtime*
★ *If you're fortunate enough to possess real honeysuckle, place some on your pillow or by the bed so that its aroma wafts over you*

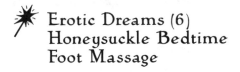 **Erotic Dreams (6)
Honeysuckle Bedtime
Foot Massage**

1. Gently warm a little hazelnut oil.
2. Remove the oil from the source of heat and add one or two drops of jasmine absolute and a few drops of honeysuckle flower remedy (Bach flower).
3. Massage this into your feet and ankles when you get into bed.

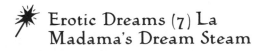 **Erotic Dreams (7) La
Madama's Dream Steam**

Aunt Sally's Dream Powder is also used to stimulate erotic dreams. Considering her powder possesses such power, it seems so disrespectful to refer to this mistress of dreams as "Aunt Sally." The image on her book resembles the Espiritismo spirit La Madama, unofficial matron saint of fortune-tellers, and offers a title of respect.

Cardamom
Cinnamon
Coriander
Licorice

1. Mash up the ingredients in a mortar and pestle.
2. Add them to a pot of water, wine or apple cider.
3. Gently warm until the fragrant steam permeates the area.
4. If the aroma doesn't reach the bedroom, carefully place the steaming liquid into a pan and waft the fragrance around the bed with a feather fan.
5. If desired, pour yourself a glass of this erotic-dreams elixir to drink before going to bed.

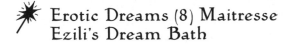 **Erotic Dreams (8) Maitresse
Ezili's Dream Bath**

Maitresse Ezili Freda Dahomey is the beautiful lwa of luxury, dreams, and love. This bath blends all three of her domains.

1. Fill a tub with warm water.
2. Add three drops of rose attar, three drops of neroli, and three drops of jasmine absolute.
3. Add fresh white roses, basil leaves and gardenia blossoms to the bath.
4. Pour yourself a glass of champagne, if desired; relax and luxuriate in the tub.

 **Erotic Dreams (9) Myrrh
Alone Incense**

Burn myrrh as incense in the bedroom to stimulate erotic dreams, if you're sleeping solo.

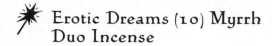 **Erotic Dreams (10) Myrrh Duo Incense**

Burn myrrh together with frankincense, if you're not alone.

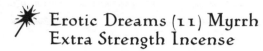 **Erotic Dreams (11) Myrrh Extra Strength Incense**

Burn myrrh together with storax and labdanum (rock rose), for erotic inducement and sound sleep.

 Erotic Dreams (12) Rose Bath

One cup of rose hydrosol
Five drops of rose attar
Five drops of neroli or essential oil of petitgrain
Five drops of honeysuckle flower essence remedy
   (Bach flower)

Add all the above "ingredients" to a tub filled with water and luxuriate before bedtime.

For maximum effect, float fresh rose petals and/or orange blossoms in the bath, too.

Financial Dreams

There are all kinds of *prophetic dreams*. That term is sometimes used euphemistically to refer to dreams of financial inspiration. Sometimes this means a dream advising the most profitable future investment, real insider's information. Sometimes it refers to the desperate need to dream up a financial plan to rescue you from dire straits. Other times you just need to conjure some lucky numbers.

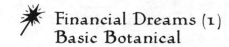 **Financial Dreams (1) Basic Botanical**

Herbs to facilitate financially providential dreams include basil, chamomile blossoms, cinnamon, coriander, High John the Conqueror, parsley, and vervain.

★ *Place any one or combination into a dream pillow*
★ *Place herbs in a charm bag and hang it around your neck while you sleep*
★ *Place loose herbs in a covered magic box. Uncover this potpourri just before bedtime so the fragrance is released while you sleep*

 Financial Dreams (2) Financial Solutions

Answers and solutions to your financial dilemmas are just out of reach. Perhaps they reside within you, if only they would rise to the surface. This ritual attempts to draw them out during dreams.

1. Sprinkle either infused basil oil or essential oil of basil onto a lodestone, just before going to sleep.
2. Get into bed, turn out the lights and gently rub the scented lodestone in a sunwise direction on your forehead. (When you awake, your forehead will probably be dirty. Don't panic; lodestone dust is lucky.)
3. Keep the lodestone near the bed, so that you can inhale the basil fragrance.

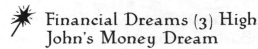# Financial Dreams (3) High John's Money Dream

1. Just before going to sleep, break up a High John the Conqueror root into chips and shards. (A hammer may be required.)
2. Place the chips into a dish.
3. Grind nutmeg and dried basil over these chips.
4. If the aroma is strong, just place the dish by your bedside.
5. If not, grind the blended materials into a finer powder. Sprinkle on lit charcoals and burn before going to sleep.

Lucid Dreaming Spell

Lucid dreaming is the technique of staying conscious while dreaming, thus being able to actively navigate through Dreamland rather than being the passive recipient of dreams. Various methods teach mastery of this shamanic art; however, many people have spontaneous, if brief, lucid dream moments.

Jasmine's fragrance encourages this spontaneous lucid dreaming. For maximum effectiveness, maintain living jasmine plants in the bedroom. If this is not possible, incorporate jasmine attar into a pre-bedtime massage, or sprinkle the sheets with jasmine water.

Marriage Dream

This is more than a soul mate or true love dream. Bridewort has an affinity for marriage; allegedly this spell produces dream visions of the one you'll marry.

Create infused oil from the blossoms of the Druid's sacred plant Queen of the Meadow, also known as bridewort. (Instructions are to be found in Elements of Magic Spells.) *Rub it on your body before bedtime to dream of the one you'll marry.*

Prophetic Dreams

The floodgates of psychic ability are completely open while we sleep. Stimulate prophetic dreams, enhance and encourage clairvoyance with various spells. Experiment to discover which ones best enhance your own innate power. Many of these techniques also encourage dreams to linger, be more vivid, and more easily recalled.

Prophetic Dreams (1) Bay Laurel Quick Fix

Bay leaves stimulate clairvoyance while awake or asleep. They are also a common, inexpensive kitchen ingredient. As a quick fix, when you desperately need a prophetic dream but don't have time or materials for other methods, tuck some bay leaves under your pillow.

Bay leaves can be sharp: if they prick you or scatter during the night, safety pin one to each corner of your pillow.

Prophetic Dreams (2) Basic Psychic Enhancement

Certain botanicals stimulate clairvoyance, psychic perceptions, and prophesy:

Angelica
Anise
Basil
Bay laurel
Copal
Dittany of Crete
Dream herb (zacatechichi)
Gardenia
Mimosa
Mugwort
Peppermint
Roses

Sandalwood
Syrian rue (harmel)
Wisteria
Wormwood

Use any one or combination of these herbs to stuff dream pillows. Or place any combination of them in a conjure bag, to be worn around the neck at night.

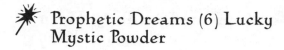

Prophetic Dreams (3) Botanical Blast

1. Choose any combination of the prophetic-dream botanicals listed above.
2. Place the loose botanicals inside a covered box, kept beside your bed.
3. Uncover or inhale this potpourri before sleeping, to receive a blast of its power.

Prophetic Dreams (4) Gardenia

Gardenia's fragrance potently invokes clairvoyant dreams, as well as inviting benevolent spirits to visit. Place fresh gardenias by your bedside so that you may inhale the fragrance while you sleep.

Prophetic Dreams (5) Gardenia Crown

An intensified version of the method above, this dream incubation spell draws its inspiration from Hawaii.

1. Weave fresh gardenias into a lei or crown, focusing on the desired dream and knotting your goals and intentions into the garland.
2. Wear it while you sleep or place it beside you on the pillow.

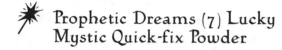

Prophetic Dreams (6) Lucky Mystic Powder

A Hoodoo formulation said to induce psychic dreams:

1. Grind dried basil and vetiver root together, creating a fine powder.
2. Blend this powder with silver magnetic sand, until you achieve a fragrance and appearance that pleases you.
3. Sprinkle this powder around your bed before bedtime.

Prophetic Dreams (7) Lucky Mystic Quick-fix Powder

Sprinkle essential oils of basil and vetiver on silver magnetic sand. Let it dry out and then cast a circle around your bed with the powder.

For a really quick-fix, place magnetic sand in a dish by your bedside and add the essential oils just before you go to sleep. Don't bother casting a circle; just turn off the lights and inhale the fragrance.

Prophetic Dreams (8) Mary Magdalene Rosemary Wand

This British dream oracle is simple to accomplish but reserved for one night only: the Eve of Mary Magdalene's feast day, the night of July 21st.

1. Blend wine, vinegar, and water in a bowl beside your bed.
2. Soak a rosemary wand in the bowl; then gently shake off the excess liquid.
3. Place this wand between your breasts and go to bed without saying another word, to produce prophetic dreams.

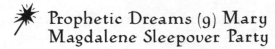

Prophetic Dreams (9) Mary Magdalene Sleepover Party

Mary Magdalene's Eve is considered especially fortuitous for prophetic dreams. Even without deliberate request or ritual, pay attention to any spontaneous dreams received. The following British dream spell is, traditionally, performed by three women, preferably sisters, on Mary Magdalene's Eve. This ritual was also once a sleepover party game, perhaps instigated by parents desiring peace and quiet, since the participants can't talk!

1. Blend wine, rum, gin, vinegar, and water.
2. Use a rosemary wand to asperge this liquid around the room(s) where you'll sleep.
3. Sprinkle in all the corners, on the bed and, finally, on yourselves.
4. Go to bed without speaking another word until after any dreams are recorded.

Prophetic Dreams (10) Mugwort

Burn mugwort and vervain before bedtime for prophetic, truthful dreams and the ability to recall and comprehend them.

Prophetic Dreams (11) Pigpen Incubation

An ancient Italian method of incubating prophetic dreams involved sleeping in the pigpen together with the pigs. The sole requirement was that the pen contained a nursing sow with her piglets. This is obviously no longer an accessible method for most people, but if you raise pigs or know someone who does, try it and see what kind of dream this produces. If living pigs are an impossibility, or you doubt you'll be able to sleep soundly enough to dream in their midst:

1. Collect pig figurines. The nursing sow with piglets is a popular image; make sure you have at least one.
2. Arrange them around you on the bed and tell them what type of dream you need or the information required.

This spell was traditionally combined with a petition to Saint Anthony to help you receive and remember your dream.

Prophetic Dreams (12) Rose Tea

Roses are often heavily sprayed with pesticides making them unsafe to drink. Make sure your roses are organic, and drink a cup of tea brewed from them before bedtime to stimulate clairvoyant dreams.

Prophetic Dreams (13) Saint Anthony

Saint Anthony accepts petitions for prophetic dreams on his own, without the pigs.

1. Place Saint Anthony's image on your nightstand or close to the bed.
2. Place at least one fresh cut lily in a vase beside it.
3. Tell Saint Anthony what you need.
4. Turn off the lights; inhale the fragrance of the lily and dream.

Prophetic Dreams (14) Sweet Flag

Burn sweet flag and liquidambar (storax) beside the bedside when prophetic dreams are required. Before going to sleep, describe the dream you will have.

Remembering Dreams

The dream was desperately needed. Perhaps you needed to see your true love's face before you accepted what might be the wrong marriage proposal. Maybe you needed a dream consultation with your grandmother regarding some vital family secrets. You ground the dream incense by hand, forced yourself to drink that bitter, bitter mugwort tea, and surrounded yourself with dream charms and pillows. You tried and practiced for weeks and finally you had the *exact* dream you needed! You were so excited you promptly woke up—and forgot the dream.

It's happened to all of us. A dream is so vivid, so vital, so important we swear we can never forget it even if we try. We're so sure of this that we see no reason to record the dream and within hours precious details are gone forever.

Dreams are by nature elusive: if you move abruptly when you awake, you will lose all or part of your dreams. Nothing prevents dreams from being recalled more than a loud, sudden alarm clock. Dreams are always retained and recalled better if one wakes naturally, whenever one is ready. If you must wake up *on time*, gently transitioning awake, perhaps to soft music, rather than being abruptly jolted awake, increases the likelihood of retaining your dreams.

Keep pen and paper by your bedside. Some prefer a special dream journal. As you become an experienced dreamer, you may awaken briefly following every dream, in order to record it, before returning to sleep. This shouldn't disturb your rest: "*awaken*" may be the wrong word. A sort of half-sleep state is achieved, just awake enough to fuzzily perform the function of writing. This semi-comatose state is the best state in which to recall and record dreams. Some learn to write in the dark, some learn to write with their eyes closed. Dream pens are sold containing tiny lights, so as to provide just enough to write by. As long as you

can understand your own writing later, it's not important to write neatly now. Transcribe dreams into a proper journal later.

Record dreams immediately: even minutes later, details disappear forever from memory. Don't believe me? Experiment: when you awake, write down your dream immediately, then go back to sleep or about your business. Several hours later, without reading what you've written, recall your dream or write it down again. Go back to your first record: most will discover that the initial description included details, some crucial, no longer remembered.

Other methods assist dream recall too.

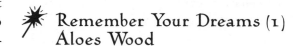

Remember Your Dreams (1) Aloes Wood

Aloes wood (not aloe vera, a different plant) is believed to deepen sleep and to create access to other realms while dreaming. It is also supposed to enable you to better remember your dreams. Aloes wood is rare: burn splinters of it at a time, while wishing for profound, magical dreams.

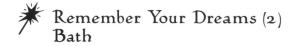

Remember Your Dreams (2) Bath

This fragrant bath encourages dreams to linger longer so that you can remember them better.

Four drops essential oil of juniper
Four drops essential oil of lavender
Four drops essential oil of mimosa

Add the essential oils to a full tub of water.

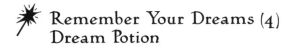 ## Remember Your Dreams (3) Deluxe Bath

Rare, luxurious oils create an air of sensuous pleasure. This is a fairy-tale bath, suitable for Circe or Morgan le Fay. Lush and fragrant, the botanicals also stimulate vivid dreams. Keep costs down by substituting petitgrain, extracted from an orange tree's unripe fruit and twigs, for its sister scent, neroli, extracted from orange blossoms. The fragrances are similar and petitgrain may even have greater sedative effects.

Three drops of honeysuckle absolute
Four drops of jasmine attar
Four drops of essential oil of lavender
Three drops of neroli
One drop of tuberose absolute

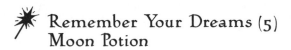 ## Remember Your Dreams (4) Dream Potion

This deceptively simple technique is highly effective, although it may take a little time to get the hang of it. Practice and persistence will be rewarded. Mugwort tea or any of the Dream Potions are deemed most effective; however, any beverage may be used.

1. Bring a cup of tea or glass of water to your bedside before going to sleep.
2. Have a sip and tell yourself, *"When I awake, I will have another sip and remember my dreams."*
3. When you wake up, do so.

Remember Your Dreams (5) Moon Potion

This enhanced method not only helps you recall dreams but also promotes understanding and clarification.

1. Charge a bottle of spring water in full moonlight. Refrigerate the water.
2. Before going to sleep, pour a small glass of water.
3. Take a few sips; leave the rest beside the bed to sip as needed.
4. Reserve a little bit to drink just before recording any received dreams.

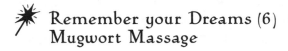 ## Remember your Dreams (6) Mugwort Massage

A sensuous method, which not only assists dream recall, but also helps clarify dreams so that you are better able to understand them.

1. Gently and carefully warm a tablespoon of walnut or hazelnut oil.
2. Bring it to your bedside.
3. Add two or three drops of mugwort flower remedy (FES) and/or morning glory flower remedy (FES) and massage into the soles of your feet.

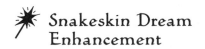 ## Snakeskin Dream Enhancement

Hang a freely shed snakeskin over the bed to ensure prophetic dreams and banish nightmares.

Spirit-summoning Dream Spells

Dreams are the simplest, most convenient venue to converse with Spirits of all kinds. Responses to petitions of all kinds most frequently occur in dreams. The spirits may not wait for you to make the first move; often their initial approach to you comes in dreams. Maybe they've been approaching you for years but you've been unable to pick up the messages. Allies and familiars of all kinds reveal themselves to you in your dreams: another good reason to maintain that dream journal.

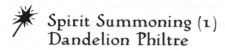

Spirit Summoning (1) Dandelion Philtre

Although rare, exotic botanicals earn seductive magical reputations, one of the most potent spirit-summoners is as common as a weed:

1. Place a cup of steaming, hot dandelion tea beside your bed, just before you go to sleep.
2. Watch the steam waft up and call in the desired spirits.
3. Have a sip, when it cools, turn off the lights and go to sleep.
4. A sip of cold tea when you awake may stimulate enhanced dream recall.

Spirit Summoning (2) Divine Conversation

Now that you've summoned spirits, you'd like to talk. The following botanicals encourage and facilitate communication between people and spirits: anise, bay leaves, gardenia, mimosa, mugwort, roses, Saint John's Wort, and wormwood. Fill a dream pillow with any combination of these.

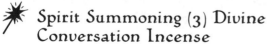

Spirit Summoning (3) Divine Conversation Incense

Grind and powder any one or combination of the botanicals listed above. Sprinkle the powder on lit charcoal and burn as incense before bedtime.

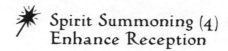

Spirit Summoning (4) Enhance Reception

Angelica flower essence remedy (FES) encourages receptivity to spiritual guidance within dreams. Forget-me-not flower essence remedy (FES, Alaskan) also encourages and enhances communication with spirits in dreams. Administer both internally as per the manufacturer's directions, or use in baths or massage oil.

Spirit Summoning (5) Potted Plants

Potted gardenia and heliotrope plants, placed close enough to the bed that their fragrance wafts over you, summon friendly, protective spirits while simultaneously enhancing your powers of reception.

Spirit Summoning (6) Spirit Water

*A glass of **Spirit Water** placed beside the bed calls in ancestors and spirits alike.*

1. **Spirit Water**'s power may be enhanced by drinking a small glass of anisette or sambuca before going to sleep.
2. Leave another glass as an offering for a spirit or an invitation for an ancestor.
3. Finish your own glass but toss the contents of the other glass away when you awake.

Stop Dreaming

Because sometimes you've had enough: hang a sprig of lemon verbena around your neck to halt the dream process, should you need to take a break.

Sunflower Truth Spell

If you suspect lies have been told, have the truth revealed in your dreams.

1. Before taking the next step, talk to the sunflower plant and explain what is about to occur and why.
2. Pull up an entire sunflower and gently shake it free of dirt. Otherwise leave the plant whole.
3. Place an offering (coins, honey, tobacco) in the hole left by the plant.
4. Place the sunflower beneath your bed. The truth should be revealed within your dreams.

True Love Dream Spells

Fairy tales are filled with princesses determined to wed none but their one true love, their soul mate. They've never actually met the guy, but he visits frequently in dreams. Perhaps the princesses tried one of the following spells:

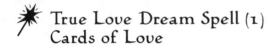 ## True Love Dream Spell (1) Cards of Love

1. Remove all four playing cards corresponding to the gender of the person you desire from a deck of playing cards: kings for men, queens for women.
2. Place the four cards under your pillow to dream of your true love.

If for any reason, one card, not necessarily a court card, holds special romantic significance for you, substitute that card instead.

 ## True Love Dream Spell (2) Cinquefoil

Burn powdered cinquefoil (five-finger grass) in the bedroom before bedtime to dream of your true love.

 ## True Love Dream Spell (3) Daisies

After you've established whether or not he loves you by pulling the petals off daisies, place daisy roots beneath your pillow to dream of your true love.

 ## True Love Dream Spell (4) Dinner for Two

After everyone has eaten dinner and left the table, discreetly pick up a knife and some salt and bread that have been left behind. Place these under your pillow to dream of your beloved.

 ## True Love Dream Spell (5) Dumb Cakes

Cast this dream spell on a solitary evening. However, it's a lot more fun to cast it the traditional way: during a sleepover party with sisters or good friends.

1. Combine one cup of flour, one cup of salt, and a sprinkle of fireplace ashes. (Scrape any ashes from out of the fireplace, but leftover ashes from some love incense or from a fireplace romance divination are most powerful.)
2. Add enough water to form a *"batter."*
3. Ladle the batter onto a heated, greased griddle, so that there is one dumb cake per participant. Pretend you're making pancakes. Flip them with a spatula.
4. Before each dumb cake is completely done, scratch a name or initials or some identifying mark onto the

cake, so that everyone knows to whom each cake belongs.

5. Each time you flip a cake, add an additional sprinkle of salt. (If there's a party, make sure everyone gets the chance to flip a dumb cake.)

6. What's the next step? Eat them? Oh no, that would be too cruel! Instead, each person must place her dumb cake under her pillow to dream of her very own true love.

Why are these called dumb cakes? *Not because these pancakes taste so bad you'd have to be severely intellectually challenged to eat them, but because the ritual demands total silence (not a peep!) from anyone involved, from start until the conclusion the next morning after all dreams have been recorded!*

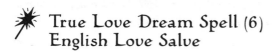

True Love Dream Spell (6)
English Love Salve

Blend calendula, thyme, marjoram, mugwort, honey, and white vinegar to form a salve. Anoint your breasts, hips, and belly with it just before going to bed, to dream of your true love.

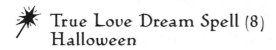

True Love Dream Spell (7)
Garter Belt

Place a garter belt under your pillow on Midsummer's Eve to dream of your true love.

True Love Dream Spell (8)
Halloween

As the fire is burning down on All Hallows Eve, drop hair and nail clippings into the burning embers. Do not speak once you begin this process until after any dreams have been recorded in the morning. After the fire burns out, go to bed and dream of your true love.

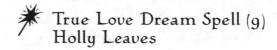

True Love Dream Spell (9)
Holly Leaves

Pick nine holly leaves at midnight on a Friday. Wrap them in a white handkerchief and place this under your pillow.

    Total silence must be maintained from the time you venture out for the holly until awakening in daylight, or the spell won't work.

True Love Dream Spell (10)
Honey Paste

1. Grind dried marjoram, thyme, and wormwood into fine powder.
2. Gently warm some honey in a bain-marie.
3. Add a dash of vinegar and the powder, creating a paste.
4. Bring this paste to the bedside.
5. Before going to sleep, anoint your Third Eye area with the paste while requesting a dream to reveal your true love's identity.

True Love Dream Spell (11)
Love Dream Pills

These "pills" reputedly enable you to dream of your true lover or your future spouse, whichever the case may be ...

1. Grind one hazelnut, one nutmeg, and one walnut and blend them together.
2. Cream butter and sugar together and add the ground powder.
3. Form nine *"pills."*
4. Take one every night for nine consecutive nights. Keep your dream journal handy. He or she should appear.

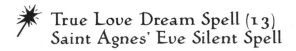
True Love Dream Spell (12)
Saint Agnes' Eve Shoe Spell

In Great Britain, Saint Agnes' Eve, the night preceding her feast day on January 21st, is traditionally a time for young women's romantic divination spells. Rituals exist to receive visions of one's true love or one's future husband—hopefully, but not always, one and the same.

1. Before retiring for the night, place a sprig of thyme in one shoe and a sprig of rosemary in the other.
2. Place one shoe on either side of your bed.
3. Just before going to bed, chant:
   Sweet Saint Agnes, to lovers so kind,
   Please come and ease my worried mind
   Show me the one with whom my heart will bind
4. Remain silent until morning. Your destiny should be revealed within your dreams.

True Love Dream Spell (13)
Saint Agnes' Eve Silent Spell

Another ritual for Saint Agnes' Eve allegedly reveals your soul mate:

1. Fast all day and concentrate on your desire.
2. Before you begin the next part of the ritual, get ready for bed: put on your nightclothes, fix your bed.
3. The following part of the spell demands total silence. You may not utter a word or a sound until it's time to chant the incantation.
4. Hard boil an egg. Cut it in half and remove the yolk. Fill the cavity with salt. Now eat the entire egg with salt, including, traditionally, the eggshell.
5. Walk backwards to bed uttering this invocation aloud:
   Sweet Saint Agnes, work your fast
   In my dreams, let this spell be cast
   If ever I am to marry a man, or a man to marry me
   I hope tonight him to see!
6. Maintain silence until morning: the oracle is revealed in your dreams.

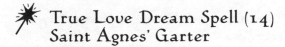
True Love Dream Spell (14)
Saint Agnes' Garter

1. Get into bed.
2. Twist your left garter around your right stocking making a knot.
3. As you knot, petition Saint Agnes, murmuring:
   This knot I knot
   Helps me see
   The face of who my true love will be.
4. Place it under your pillow and go to sleep.

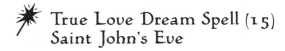
True Love Dream Spell (15)
Saint John's Eve

Hang Saint John's Wort over your bed, or place it beneath your pillow, on Saint John's Eve to dream of your soul-mate.

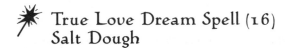
True Love Dream Spell (16)
Salt Dough

This Jewish ritual requires a little finagling in order to obtain dreams of your true love. The end result probably tastes as bad as the Saint Agnes' Eve egg. Why is that aphrodisiacs designed to be served to a lover inevitably taste seductively delicious, while magical concoctions used to reveal that lover's identity force the spell-caster to suffer?

1. Obtain salt from one house, some flour from a second, and an egg from a third.
2. Bring them to your home and knead them together secretly.
3. Eat the mixture before going to bed to dream of your love.

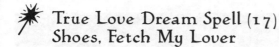

True Love Dream Spell (17)
Shoes, Fetch My Lover

1. Sprinkle a pair of your beloved's shoes with spring water or **Angel's Water.**
2. Place a sprig of thyme in one shoe, rosemary in the other.
3. Place a shoe on either side of your bed.
4. Crawl in and dream.

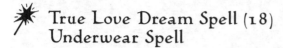

True Love Dream Spell (18)
Underwear Spell

This spell, at least from Step 2 onwards, is cast under a Full Moon.

1. Obtain an undergarment appropriate for the gender of the one of whom you wish to dream.
2. Perform appropriate personal cleansing spells.
3. Take a bucket of pure spring water or **Angel's Water** and go outside at midnight under the Full Moon. (The traditional recommendation is that you should be naked, however adapt to your needs and circumstances.)
4. Gaze at the moon: make a petition for true love and a request to see your lover in your dreams. Show the moon the underwear.
5. Toss the bucket of water over your left shoulder.
6. Go to bed without looking back.
7. Place the underwear under your pillow and say aloud: *"Lover, come get your underwear!"*
8. Go to sleep.

Reserve the underwear afterwards. The spell may be repeated, as needed. Should your dream lover arrive, fumigate with Dreams of Delight or other erotic incense and have him or her wear the item for you.

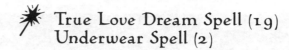

True Love Dream Spell (19)
Underwear Spell (2)

A Russian version of the underwear dream spell simplifies the actions but insists that the spell can only be cast on the Eve of Saint Andrew, November 30th.

Obtain an undergarment suitable for the person of whom you wish to dream, and put it under your pillow on Saint Andrew's Eve to dream of your true love.

True Love Dream Spell (20)
Wild Roses

Drink a cup of tea made with wild rose petals before bedtime to conjure a vision of your true love.

True Love Dream Spell (21)
Winter Solstice

On the eve of the winter solstice peel an onion. Wrap it in a handkerchief and sleep with it beneath your pillow. The face of your true love should be revealed to you.

Insomnia

If you can't sleep, you can't dream, it's that simple. Of course, chronic insomnia causes other troubles too: you're grouchy, irritable, and inefficient at work. Unable to sleep when you want, you may find yourself unable to stay awake at inconvenient moments. Your immune system may suffer. Because so much growth and healing occurs during sleep (or is it during dreams?) you may find yourself feeling stagnant and blocked. Many turn to sleeping pills, which can force sedation but tend to suppress dreams. Is this a problem? Consider whether you wake up feeling refreshed and ready to go and you'll have your answer.

These are traditional magical remedies; they may or may not also have sedative or other sleep-enhancing properties. However just because remedies are magical doesn't mean that they don't also have profound physical impact, particularly botanical-based spells. Insomnia can be an adjunct of various physical ailments: discuss your remedy plans with your professional health-care provider before initiating any course of action.

There are sleep scientists and dream researchers who consider that the whole reason for sleep is to provide an opportunity for dreaming. It's the dreaming part that's really the necessity. Without ample rest and sleep, one's psychic and magic powers suffer and weaken. Because sleep and dreams are so crucial to magic, a host of magical remedies exist to ease your way into Dreamland.

 Insomnia Bath

This bath provides the soothing equivalent of milk and cookies before bedtime. Its power is proportionate to the quantity of milk used.

1. Gently warm goats' or, ideally, sheep's milk (as in counting sheep).
2. Blend true almond extract and several drops of essential oil of lavender into the warm milk so that the fragrance pleases you.
3. Add to a tub filled with warm water before bedtime.

 Insomnia Incense (1)

Blend pine, juniper, and ledum and burn as incense. This soothes an insomniac to sleep while stimulating prophetic dreams at the same time.

 Insomnia Incense (2)

Blend frankincense, myrrh, and sandalwood for sound peaceful sleep accompanied by clairvoyant dreams.

 Insomnia Spell (1) Ancient Formula Sound Sleep Incense

Blend frankincense resin, storax resin, and rose petals together. Then burn the blend over lit charcoal near the bed before going to sleep.

Insomnia Spell (2) Basic Botanicals for Sweet Sleep

The following herbs allegedly promote sound, deep sleep:

Bee balm *(Monarda didyma)*, also sometimes called bergamot or bergamot mint. It is not a true mint nor should it be confused with essential oil of bergamot, which is extracted from a type of Italian bitter orange.

Calendula blossoms

Catnip

Chamomile blossoms

Henna

Hops

Linden blossoms

Marjoram

Mullein

Patchouli

Poppies and poppy seeds

Tuberose

Valerian

Vervain

Vetiver

Place any one or combination of these herbs in a dream pillow.

Too sleep-deprived to sew? Try one of the quick-fix dream pillows instead (page 356).

Insomnia Spell (3) Basic Botanical Magic Box of Sleep

1. Place any combination of loose herbs in a closed magic box and keep it by your bedside.
2. When you can't sleep, open the box and inhale deeply several times.

Insomnia Spell (4) Burton's Sound Sleep Pillow

Sir Richard Burton, translator of the Arabian Nights *and the* Kama Sutra, *recommended a pillow stuffed with dried wormwood to combat insomnia.*

Insomnia Spell (5) Crystals to Enhance Sleep

Crystal gemstones can stimulate sleep as well as dreams. Blue crystals in general are particularly beneficial. Other stones believed to encourage sleep and dreams include amber, amethyst, emerald, jet, and smoky quartz.

Charge the crystal with your desired goal prior to its initial use. Crystals' magic power may be accessed any of the following ways:

★ *Place one or more crystals under your pillow*
★ *Wear as jewelry against your skin while attempting sleep*
★ *Create sleep charms: hang them from your bedposts or keep a larger stone on the nightstand*

Insomnia Spell (6) Datura-leaf Shoe Spell

This is an old spell, but be cautious: not only is datura poisonous, it's also a skin irritant. Place datura leaves in your shoes, then place these shoes under the bed facing the wall to encourage sleep.

Insomnia Spell (7) Freya's Sleep Potion

Beautiful Freya rules love, sex, and magic. Queen of Witches, original sponsor of Scandinavian shamans, Freya journeys through the sky in her falcon-feather cloak. Simple cowslip, a wild primrose, ranks among her sacred plants. It allegedly permits dream visitations from the land of the fairies, too.

Steep cowslips in wine or milk, and drink this before bedtime. Back in the good old days, wine was actually made from cowslip, ostensibly to prevent and heal insomnia. If you have some, try it!

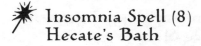 Insomnia Spell (8)
Hecate's Bath

Once upon a time, according to legend, Hecate had a temple in the ancient city of Colchis, surrounded by vast botanical gardens. Her priestesses, including her most famous devotee Medea, were famed for their botanical knowledge. No doubt they could concoct a sleeping potion or two. This simple bath uses two of Hecate's sacred materials—honey and lavender—to soothe the way to sleep and encourage healing dreams.

1. Gently warm some milk. The quantity is up to you: the more milk, the more luxurious and soothing the bath.
2. When the milk is warm, carefully add honey, stirring so that it blends. (Otherwise the honey will just settle at the bottom.)
3. Remove from the heat; add several drops of essential oil of lavender.
4. Add to a tub filled with warm water.

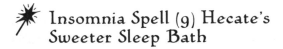 Insomnia Spell (9) Hecate's
Sweeter Sleep Bath

This bath has a sweeter fragrance: see which suits you better.

> One cup of milk
> One quarter cup of honey
> One teaspoon pure vanilla extract
> Four drops essential oil of lavender
> Four drops essential oil of chamomile

1. Warm the milk gently over a low heat and stir in the honey.
2. When they are blended, remove from the heat and add the vanilla extract and essential oils.
3. Disperse the mixture in warm running bath water.

You can increase the quantities if desired, but maintain the proportions.

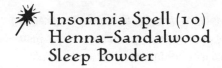 Insomnia Spell (10)
Henna-Sandalwood
Sleep Powder

Sift henna powder and sandalwood powder together until the mix is fine and smooth. Sprinkle onto lit charcoals and fumigate the bedroom before sleep.

If the powder is very fine, try sprinkling onto your sheets instead of or in addition to burning.

 Insomnia Spell (11) Henna
Sound Sleep Pillow

Henna is most frequently associated with body art and temporary tattoos. However, it has a long medicinal and magical history as well. It's used in love spells, to reduce fevers, and, especially, to provide deep, restful, restorative sleep. Fill a dream pillow with powdered henna to promote a sound night's sleep.

 Insomnia Spell (12) Hops
Sound Sleep Pillow

A tenth-century Saxon prescription suggests filling a pillow with hops for sound, restful sleep.

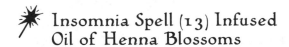 Insomnia Spell (13) Infused
Oil of Henna Blossoms

1. Follow the instructions in *Elements of Magic Spells* for making infused oils. Remember that it may take weeks to achieve the desired intensity of fragrance.
2. If possible, use ben oil for the infusion. Also known as moringa oil, this was the ancient Egyptian's favorite for perfumery and is now, after centuries, being marketed in India. If ben oil is unavailable, try safflower or sweet almond oil, instead.

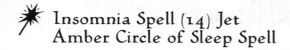 ## Insomnia Spell (14) Jet Amber Circle of Sleep Spell

Jet and amber, crystallized botanical material rather than true minerals, work well in partnership. Beware of plastic replications with both.

Cast a circle around your bed with alternating pieces of jet and amber.

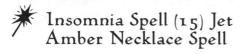 ## Insomnia Spell (15) Jet Amber Necklace Spell

A necklace is just a circle cast around one's self.

1. Create a necklace from alternating amber and jet beads, focusing on your desires.
2. Create as many knots as possible, tying your intentions into each knot.
3. Wear your necklace to sleep.

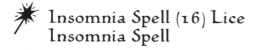 ## Insomnia Spell (16) Lice Insomnia Spell

Many dream and sleep spells are romantic, but not all: a medieval spell that allegedly encourages sleep relies upon an infestation of lice, which might perhaps explain the insomnia in the first place …

1. Obtain a louse from the insomniac's head.
2. Induce it to crawl into a bone with a hole.
3. Plug up the hole.
4. Hang the imprisoned bug around the patient's neck.

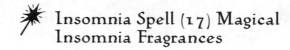 ## Insomnia Spell (17) Magical Insomnia Fragrances

Sometimes fragrance alone is sufficient to soothe you and send you to sleep. Try the following essential oils:

Bergamot
Chamomile
Frankincense
Lavender
Manuka (New Zealand tea tree)
Myrrh
Neroli
Petitgrain
Pine
Rosalina
Sandalwood
Tuberose
Vetiver

This is very individual magic. Play with the fragrances until you find one that you enjoy and that works for you. (Write down formulas and proportions as you're working so that should you discover a winner, you'll be able to reproduce it.) There are different ways to experiment:

★ *Blend a few drops into a tablespoon of carrier oil, such as jojoba or sweet almond. Massage into temples, soles of feet or any other areas of the body*
★ *Add several drops to a warm bath before bedtime*
★ *Place several drops in an aroma burner or essential oil diffuser and inhale the fragrance*
★ *Use any of these oils to dress a dream pillow or dream potpourri*

Insomnia Spell (18) Sleep like You're Dead Pillow

So tired and sleep-deprived, you're starting to look at the cemetery with envy? The following botanicals have earned the nickname graveyard dust *because they allegedly encourage you to sleep as soundly and peacefully as the dead: patchouli, mullein, and valerian.*

1. Grind the botanicals together to create a fine powder.
2. For extra enhancement, add another botanical strongly associated with sleep—poppy seeds—the first anesthesia.
3. Fill a dream pillow with the botanicals and sleep.

For enhanced dreaming, add chopped-up bay leaves too.

 Insomnia Spell (19) Spikenard

Warm essential oil of spikenard in an aroma burner; its scent allegedly eases fears, soothes sleep, banishes malicious spirits, and provides happy, peaceful dreams.

 Insomnia Spell (20) Violet Wreath

Make a wreath from violet leaves and/or flowers; wear it for a sound night's sleep.

Nightmares

The problem isn't that you *can't* sleep; you're just too scared to close your eyes.

Going to sleep, a welcome relief for some, a palace of delight for others, is the living equivalent of going to hell for those afflicted with chronic nightmare. Because sleep is a place of persecution and misery, those afflicted with nightmares often avoid it at all costs, driving themselves to stay awake as long as possible. Temperament suffers, work suffers, health suffers, and magic power also suffers as a result.

Everyone has a bad dream once in a while. The occasional disturbing dream may be a warning signal of some sort, worthy of attention and careful interpretation. For those afflicted with chronic nightmare, every dream is a horror, the only good night a dreamless one. What should be a source of pleasure and power feels like being cursed and haunted instead.

There are various magical interpretations for nightmares. In some cases, it is perceived as a haunting or curse. The actual word *"nightmare"* derives from the German *"mara,"* a type of evil spirit, which squats on a sleeper's chest, causing frightening dreams and the sensation of suffocation. Spirits haunt Dreamland, sometimes from good intent but sometimes not. Ghostly visitations may be desirable after that necromantic ritual you performed because you need to ask Great Aunt Maud that important question which only she can answer,

Spells to banish dream visitations from incubi and succubi are found amongst the Vampire Spells; see pages 291–300.

but nightmarish when the ghost makes the first move. Then there are assorted vampires, incubi, succubi, etc.—creatures of the night that revel in creating nocturnal disturbance. Sometimes spiritual portals are accidentally opened, allowing us to witness things we should not. Sometimes, as we will see, an act of malice allows one person to send another a frightening dream.

Typically chronic nightmares indicate some sort of spiritual and emotional imbalance (magic, a holistic system, cannot separate the two) or even some kind of extended, unpleasant spiritual test. Avoidance of sleep and suppression of dreams isn't the solution. Dreams must be analyzed (by professional dream diviners, if necessary), untangled, and faced, so that they will disperse and make room for sweeter, more desirable dreams.

Dreams deliver messages to us, from Earth, from Spirits, from ancestors, allies, other dreamers, and our own subconscious. What happens if someone tries to call you on the phone and can't get through? Sometimes the caller gives up, but if it's important and the caller is responsible and persistent, they'll keep trying. If you fail to pick up or properly understand a dream message, that dream or recognizable variations will repeat itself until you do.

Next time, someone chases you in a dream, whether loathsome ex or fearsome creature, turn around and confront it. Calmly, firmly, ask it what it wants. Odds are those animal dreams involve an animal ally trying to get in touch with you. Animal allies come in all forms, not just cuddly bunnies. Deep fear is as much an indication of an alliance as deep love and attraction. The ally may misunderstand your reactions in the same way that you misunderstand theirs. Anxious to reach you, the more you run, the faster they chase and the more eagerly they await your return to Dreamland. The creatures don't necessarily mean to scare you; they may even mean to assist you.

Yes, this sounds easier said than done, but it can be accomplished, although taking control of your

dreams may take time. As usual, there are magical tools to assist, to provide protection, and to place bad dreams in perspective and abeyance.

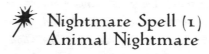

Nightmare Spell (1)
Animal Nightmare

According to Roman Catholic legend, Saint Margaret faced Satan who appeared in the form of a very scary, giant serpent. Was this in real life, during a waking vision or in a dream? Did Margaret run? No, she did exactly what every dream therapist tells a nightmare victim to do: she confronted that serpent and called his bluff. The snake promptly fulfilled the worst fears of every nightmare victim: mouth open wide, it swallowed Margaret in her entirety. But the story isn't over: Margaret's goodness and purity of heart was so powerful and distasteful to the snake that she was immediately spat out, whole, well, redeemed, and on her way to sainthood.

There's another way of looking at that story. Saint Margaret is matron saint of childbirth and pregnancy. Snakes are the creatures most associated with that topic as well as with female reproductive health in general. Snakes are women's spiritual and magical teachers. Perhaps Margaret wasn't disgorged because she was just too good to die; maybe she emerged because she passed her test. Only by facing and surviving this spiritual trial by serpent was Margaret able to acquire the needed wisdom and secrets to perform her new role.

If you suffer from lurking or chasing animal dreams, keep Saint Margaret in mind.

1. To receive her support and assistance during your own dream trials, build her a small shrine by your bedside.
2. Display Saint Margaret's image, together with that of the serpent who is now her familiar companion.
3. Not everyone is a saint. It can take many attempts before one is able to face one's worst nightmare with grace and courage. Should you awaken, shaken by failed attempts, look at Saint Margaret for reassurance and then go back to sleep.

Nightmare Spell (2) Anti-Nightmare Garden

Why start a nightmare protection plan in the bedroom? Target the whole house. There's a reason everyone in Sleeping Beauty *slept so soundly. That wild overgrowth of surrounding botanicals banished bad dreams. This isn't a suggestion to banish the gardener, too. The plants can still be manicured if you wish; however, certain botanicals provide nightmare blocking. Cast a living circle around your house.*

The primary botanical nightmare-repellant is rosemary. Given the opportunity it flourishes and grows wildly. Other suggestions include:

Mimosa
Mint
Mugwort
Poppies
Roses
Rowan
Saint John's Wort
Snake plant
Wormwood

 ## Nightmare Spell (3) Anti-Nightmare Bedroom Garden

If a full garden is unrealistic for you, there's nothing wrong with keeping nightmare maintenance in the bedroom.

Place potted rosemary plants in the bedroom near the bed to create a magical anti-nightmare shield. Add any of the other plants listed above, too.

Nightmare Spell (4) Banishing

This spell is most beneficial immediately after a nightmare although it can be used to disperse lingering effects long after the dream is over, too. If possible, keep a

window open for the duration of the spell, to encourage dream visitations to fly away.

1. Write the nightmare down in detail on a piece of fresh paper.
2. Light a white, silver, black or red candle.
3. Hold the paper in the flame until it catches fire.
4. Let the paper burn down in a saucer or cauldron.
5. Cover it if necessary with a second upside-down plate so that the ashes don't escape into the house. This is tricky because you can put the fire out. If so, just light it again. It's vital that the entire dream is burned to ashes and removed from your home.
6. If possible, dispose of the ashes immediately through an open door or window. If not, place the ashes inside a brown paper bag and dispose of it outside the house as soon as possible.

 ## Nightmare Spell (5) Banish Nightmares Oil

Create infused oil of hyacinth and lavender blossoms. Rub onto the body before bedtime to ward off nightmares.

 ## Nightmare Spell (6) Betony

Gather betony in August without the use of iron. Dry the plants and then grind the leaves and roots. Cast a circle around your bed with this powder to protect against nightmares.

 ## Nightmare Spell (7) Candle

1. Charge a yellow or golden candle with your desire for sound, peaceful, untroubled sleep. Place a glass of spring water beside it while it burns.
2. When you're ready to sleep, place this glass of water beside your bed to absorb any bad dreams. (There's no need to keep the candle burning.)

3. In the morning, flush the water down the toilet, whether you recall bad dreams or not. Repeat as needed.

 ## Nightmare Spell (8) Coffee Banishing

The aroma of coffee brewing, as well as fumigation by burning coffee beans, allegedly banishes nightmares. (It also allegedly banishes sleep for many people, but that's another story.)

A bedside coffee-maker, ready to go as soon as you push the button, may be all that's required to banish fear-filled nights. Otherwise, sprinkle good full-strength (not decaf) ground coffee onto lit charcoals and fumigate the bedroom area before you sleep.

 ## Nightmare Spell (9) Crystals

Certain crystal gemstones repel and relieve nightmares:

★ *Blue crystals in general, especially angelite, lapis lazuli, and turquoise*
★ *Black crystals, with the possible exception of onyx*
★ *Chrysolite*
★ *Citrine*
★ *Topaz*

How to access the crystal's nightmare-repelling powers:

★ *Wear while sleeping so that they are in contact with your skin*
★ *Place one or more on or beneath your pillow*
★ *Put one or more in a small flannel drawstring bag; wear it like a shield across your chest or place it beneath your cheek for comfort*
★ *Cast a circle around your bed or on your bed around you with crystal gemstones*

Onyx is a stone that evokes unpredictable personal reactions. Although it is used to halt nightmares, it occasionally causes them. If you habitually wear onyx and also habitually have bad dreams, remove the stone(s) and observe any reactions.

Many magical approaches to nightmares consider the long-term results: spells for banishing them, preventing them, understanding them, and minimizing them. What action can you take when you've just awakened from a nightmare? Nightmare dispersal spells are intended to disperse and nullify a specific nightmare's effects immediately upon waking.

 ## Nightmare Spell (10) Nine of Swords Dream Dispersal

The nine of swords card in the Rider-Waite tarot deck depicts the end of the nightmare, that breakthrough moment of understanding that forever banishes a specific nightmare.

Contemplate the image to help resolve and dismiss your own horrible dream. Post it by your bedside for encouragement.

Nightmare Spell (11) Silver Bell Dispersal

Keep a bell made from real silver on the nightstand, and ring as needed to dispel a nightmare and cleanse the atmosphere.

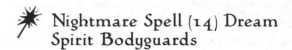

Nightmare Spell (12) Dream Animal Bodyguards

Post protective guards in your bedroom to watch over you while you sleep. Images of your own personal animal allies and guardian angels and spirits are best; however, if you're unsure where to turn, the following creatures may be invoked:

★ *Snakes*
★ *Dragons*
★ *Crocodiles*
★ *Bears*
★ *Dogs, wolves or other canines*

Yes, they're fierce: that's the point. Do you want a protector with less courage and ability?

If anyone of them strikes a particular note of fear in your heart, explore the reasons why carefully and consider—it may be the most powerful ally for you.

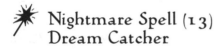

Nightmare Spell (13) Dream Catcher

Spiders weave dreams as well as spinning webs. In the indigenous traditions of the Native American Plains, circular webs resembling a spider's web, known as "dream catchers," are hung over the bed to facilitate the arrival of desired dreams while preventing disturbing dreams from reaching the dreamer. Not only are nightmares prevented, but the dreams received are happier, more vivid and exciting.

Charge the dream catcher with your desires and needs before hanging over the bed. If disturbing dreams suddenly start arriving, it may be time to cleanse the dream catcher (emptying out the vacuum bag, so to speak) by passing it through cleansing incense smoke.

Nightmare Spell (14) Dream Spirit Bodyguards

Post images of the following protective guardian spirits to watch over you while you sleep. Although the image is sufficient, the magic is stronger if you talk with them and tell them your fears and what you need.

Archangel Michael
Archangel Gabriel
Bes
The gorgon Medusa
Morpheus
Taweret
Thoth
The various spirits of iron: Brigid, Dactyls, Hephaestus, Ogun, Scatach, and Wayland the Smith

If you feel nightmares are stimulated by spiritual attack, coordinate anti-nightmare spells with general magical protective measures. (See Protection Spells, page 876.)

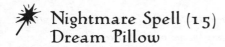 Nightmare Spell (15)
Dream Pillow

This pillow soothes the effects of nightmares, minimizes their frequency, and hopefully banishes them. Blend anise, black mustard seeds and mullein. Fill the pillow and sleep in peace.

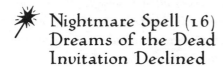 Nightmare Spell (16)
Dreams of the Dead
Invitation Declined

One particularly distressing nightmare involves a visitation from someone who is no longer alive, who invites you in the dream to come live with them. Sometimes the invitation is less explicit but no less pointed: the deceased requests that the living person hold their hand. It is an inappropriate request and makes for a very disturbing dream, especially if you knew the person well. It's never polite to ignore an invitation. To put an end to persistent visits, you must RSVP promptly. Although the invitation comes during dreams, the response must be delivered fully awake.

1. Go visit your would-be host's grave.
2. Take off your shoes, lie down beside the grave and cry aloud something similar to this response three times:

   By God's will and by my own will,
   I'm not going with you or with any other dead person.
   Don't come after me!
   Leave me alone!
   Don't come after anyone I love either—you, your friends, allies or messengers
   I live in this world and not in any other.
3. Put your shoes back on, get up and go home, without looking back.

If journeying to the actual grave is impossible, reproduce the spell in visualization.

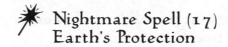 Nightmare Spell (17)
Earth's Protection

Metaphysically speaking flint is perceived as Earth's bones, coral is perceived as the ocean's menstrual blood, and turquoise as a piece of the sky. Gathered together they provide you with unfailing, perpetually vigilant magical protection from every corner of the universe. Together they also create a potent anti-nightmare amulet.

1. Collect at least one small piece each of coral, flint, and turquoise.
2. Charge each one individually by holding in your hands and focusing on your desires.
3. Attach them to a cord or place them within a medicine bag.
4. Hang over your bed or around your neck.

Nightmare Spell (18) Flower Essence Relief

Because flower essence remedies heal on the level of soul and emotion, they are particularly beneficial for healing and relieving nightmares. They will not banish them but will help you understand, assimilate and cope with them. Once a nightmare is truly understood, it loses its power over you and is usually dispersed. However, be aware that flower remedies typically work by bringing hidden secrets to the surface: there may be an intensive healing crisis. In other words, the darkest hour comes before the light. In the process of healing, flower remedies may force you to face issues long avoided and suppressed. Make sure you choose a safe time and place to initiate the process.

The following flower essence remedies relieve nightmares:

Amaranthus (Pegasus) calms and soothes disruptions caused by disturbing dreams

Grey Spider Flower (Australian Bush) relieves terror and panic and helps to assimilate mysterious nightmares

Saint John's Wort (FES, Green Hope) relieves fear of dreams, darkness and/or sleep, and offers spiritual protection

These flower essence remedies help you understand your nightmares:

Black-eyed Susan (FES, Green Hope, Australian Bush)

Scarlet Pimpernel (FES)

Snap pea (Green Hope, Perelandra)

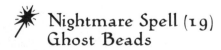 Nightmare Spell (19) Ghost Beads

Ghost beads are the name of a traditional Apache and Navajo charm for warding off children's disturbing dreams. String juniper berries on yucca thread to make bracelets for the child to wear. Originally desert juniper was used, but any species of juniper could work.

 Nightmare Spell (20) Hex

A true nightmare, this is not recommended for reproduction, but to consider the causes of nightmares. It's one of the cruelest hexes of all. The sorcerer strikes at his victim through dreams. The following instructions are merely the mechanics; great magical skill is required to target the specific victim with the specific dream.

To send someone a nightmare, write a charm on red paper using a few drops of blood drawn from a perfectly black male goat as ink. The charm is then passed through the smoke of coriander seeds and storax.

 Nightmare Spell (21) Iron Clad Protection

Iron, and to a lesser degree silver repels evil spirits, malevolent magic and low-level spiritual entities. Iron never rests. It works when you're awake and it continues to do so when you sleep.

★ *Place an iron, steel or silver knife under your pillow. Either a real knife or an amulet may used*

★ *A small amulet knife may also be worn around the neck on a chain, as can tiny scissor charms or any representation of a sharp stabbing metal device*

★ *Arrange scissors so that they're open and place them under your pillow*

★ *An iron horseshoe placed under the pillow wards off nightmares. If you're really scared, place it across your chest*

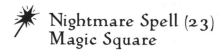 **Nightmare Spell (22) Iron Fortification**

Long-term bad dreams create a detrimental effect on the dreamer. Both physically exhausted and spiritually drained, the nightmare produces a wasting effect, similar to that imposed by the Evil Eye. This spell doesn't necessarily repel the nightmare; it strengthens, empowers, and heals the afflicted dreamer instead. Perform the spell in conjunction with other steps to understand, unravel or banish bad dreams.

1. To heal those afflicted by nocturnal hauntings, take an iron nail from a coffin or sepulcher.
2. Drive it into the lintel of a door, ideally that of the afflicted person's bedroom. The lintel of the main entrance is the second best choice.

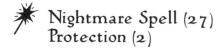 **Nightmare Spell (23) Magic Square**

Do you sleep in a four-poster bed? Create a magical protective square. Hang a different amulet from each corner. Hang another from your neck as the final touch; otherwise place a piece of wormwood under the mattress or a piece of metal, like a magic sword, under the bed.

Nightmare Spell (24) Peony Roots

Twist peony roots together, forming a chain long enough to wear as a necklace, and tie your goals and desires into any knots. Allegedly this prevents nightmares or minimizes their impact.

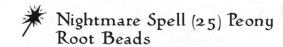 **Nightmare Spell (25) Peony Root Beads**

Beads formed from peony roots also repel nightmares.

1. Slice dried peony roots; as you cut each slice, visualize the abrupt, final termination of the nightmare, never to return.
2. Pierce each slice with a needle, forming rough bead and string these onto red cord.
3. Incorporate visualization and knot magic as appropriate to your situation.
4. Wear this necklace as a protective shield and nightmare repellant.

Peony roots are frequently sold pre-sliced. If this is the case, incorporate Step 1's visualization into Step 2.

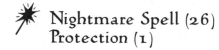 **Nightmare Spell (26) Protection (1)**

Grind and powder dried agrimony. Cast a circle with the powder around your bed to prevent bad dreams and provide protection in case any slip through the circle.

Nightmare Spell (27) Protection (2)

Betony protects against fearful visions whether sleeping or awake. Place a handful of the dried herb within a conjure bag, which may be placed in a pocket, under a pillow, or hung around one's neck.

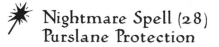 **Nightmare Spell (28) Purslane Protection**

Grind and powder purslane, which is also known as portulaca. Sprinkle this powder around your bed to prevent nightmares.

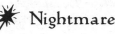

⁕ Nightmare Spell (29) Sleepwalker's Talisman

Sometimes it's not your dreams but one's compulsive behavior during sleep that really comprises the nightmare. Allegedly a topaz worn on a chain around the neck serves as a charm against sleepwalking.

⁕ Nightmare Spell (30) Turpentine Protection

Turpentine has fallen out of favor, even among many artists. Make sure there's proper ventilation if casting this spell as reports suggest that inhaling turpentine fumes may not be beneficial for one's health. Turpentine is certainly not safe for consumption so this spell must be cast cautiously, if at all, in the presence of children, animals, and those adults who'll gulp anything in a shot glass. (Ironically, this spell was once a common magical remedy for children afflicted with nightmares.) Turpentine also allegedly benefits anyone whose dreams are filled with torturous demonic visions.

1. One shot glass is required for each corner of the bedroom.
2. Fill each glass with old-fashioned turpentine and place each one in a corner overnight.
3. Empty it in the morning, disposing of the turpentine carefully and responsibly.
4. Replace as needed.

⁕ Nightmare Spell (31) Vervain

Suspend vervain over the bed to prevent nightmares.

⁕ Nightmare Spell (32) Water Absorption

1. Leave a glass of water by your bedside.

2. For extra strength, add camphor, but be sure not to drink the water!
3. In the morning, flush the water down the toilet.
4. Reserve the glass for this use only and repeat as needed.

⁕ Nightmare Safety Spell

Fleeing from nightmares doesn't make them go away. This conjure bag helps you face and explore your nightmares through enhanced dream skills and the confidence that comes from magical protection.

Fill a red charm bag with agrimony, mugwort, and peppermint. Add a round iron or silver bead and wear around your neck while sleeping.

Astral Projection

The dream soul is liberated to journey during dreams. Astral projection attempts to reap the benefits of the dream-state yet also retain memory of the experience, together with conscious control of all situations. For some it is the ultimate form of travel.

According to some occult theories, the journeying soul and body remain connected by a thin silvery cord, sort of a permanent *"astral umbilical cord."* Thus the soul can confidently wander with full assurance that that cord will lead back to the body, as surely as Ariadne's thread lead Theseus safely from the labyrinth. Easier said than done; the dream soul often resists travel as long as waking consciousness remains. Sleep is what unlocks the gate for the soul. Because of this astral travel during sleep, *if* you can learn to stimulate and control the process, this provides the best of both sleeping and waking realms.

Astral travel can occur while awake or during sleep. Practice during waking hours, together with the study of lucid dreaming techniques, enhances

Astral projection should not be attempted under influence of intoxicants of any kind, or any pharmaceuticals. The extremely aged, frail or ill, and also those who've suffered sexual abuse or post-traumatic stress, are extremely vulnerable to soul loss. Astral projection can potentially be harmful in any of the above situations. If you generally possess a sense of being out of focus or of being estranged from your body, do not attempt astral projection, at least not without experienced, reliable, expert shamanic supervision. (Get references for a shaman the same way you would for a doctor, plumber or other professional.)

the chances for successful dream astral travel. Some find it an extremely challenging process, while others take to it naturally. The soul consciously journeys, flies to a chosen destination, while the body rests passively below. Descended from shamanic rites, there are various methods to accomplish astral projection and various tools to encourage success. Even when traveling while awake, astral projection mimics the dream-state. Take whatever protective precautions you would use in dreams.

The end of the journey, the return to the body, is typically effortless. As soon as you awake, body and soul are automatically re-joined, although ideally this is a natural, gradual process. If you waken naturally, there are usually no re-connection difficulties.

If abruptly awakened, some actually feel a jolt. Others experience a brief moment of shock, panic, or disorientation, which may **lead to soul loss** (see page 562 for more on this).

Beginning Astral Travel Techniques

Basic Astral Projection

A practice method, to be performed initially while you're awake. Repeat as needed. Some show quick aptitude for astral projection but it's not unusual to require years of practice. Sometimes initial success is followed by a long period of challenge.

1. Lie down; relax; shut your eyes.
2. Visualize yourself standing at the foot of your bed, exactly as it is, looking at yourself.

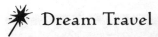 ## Dream Travel

Astral travel in your dreams:

1. Before sleep, fix in your mind where you want to go, whom you want to visit. Fix the image of it and the image of yourself—what do you look like? What are you wearing?
2. Pay attention to details. Charge yourself with a mission.
3. Practice!
4. Keep a diary of your journeys.

 ## Waking Dreams

1. Envision a dream before going to sleep.
2. Decide where you will go, and what will happen in the dream.
3. Then just as you feel yourself falling asleep, *walk into the dream.*

Practice by stepping into images: tarot cards, paintings, whatever—just pick safe appealing ones, rather than scary nightmare images. Practice emerging and returning from the images too.

There are various magical methods of enhancing and stimulating astral travel:

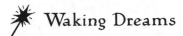 ## Astral Projection Spell

Surround the bed with fresh (potted) mugwort plants to help achieve lift-off.

 ## Astral Travel Powder

Cinnamon
Mugwort
Sandalwood

1. Grind the botanicals to a fine powder.
2. Blend with arrowroot powder.
3. Sprinkle on your sheets before setting out on your journey.

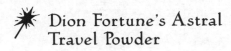 ## Dion Fortune's Astral Travel Powder

Dion Fortune, renowned author and occultist, suggested the following formula for astral traveling:

Benzoin
Dittany of Crete
Sandalwood
Vanilla bean

1. Grind all the dried ingredients into a fine powder.
2. Burn it on lit charcoal to accompany your travels.

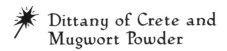 ## Dittany of Crete and Mugwort Powder

Dittany of Crete and mugwort, two herbs closely associated with Artemis, offer assistance with accomplishing astral projection, and protection during the journey.

★ *Burn the herbs as incense to accompany your journey*
★ *Fill a dream pillow with the combined herbs*
★ *Simultaneously appeal to Artemis for assistance with your goal*

 ## Jasper Astral Projection

Jasper crystal gemstone has strong associations with astral travel.

Lay the crystals on your chakra points, or cast a circle of jasper around you while you journey.

Moldavite Astral Travel Enhancement

When a meteorite struck rock in the Moldau Valley, rock and meteorite both melted and merged, producing the delicate green gemstone moldavite—or so goes the theory of its origin. Because moldavite combines terrestrial and extraterrestrial energies, it provides grounding while simultaneously assisting astral travel. Place a moldavite over your Third Eye (brow) chakra when attempting astral travel.

ROLOR Square

*This magic square allegedly enables you to fly like a crow. Write the following onto parchment, preferably using **Raven's Feather Ink**:*

```
R   O   L   O   R
O   B   U   F   O
L   U   A   U   L
O   F   U   B   O
R   O   L   O   R
```

Pin this paper to your chest. Close your eyes, relax, and see whether you fly.

Yellow Gemstone Astral Projection

Astral projection is allegedly assisted by yellow crystal gemstones. Hold them in your hand while practicing, and place a crystal on your Third Eye chakra.

Witches' Flying Ointments

Modern astral travel is basically a mental and magical exercise; botanicals and crystals are used to enhance the process, but they do not produce the experience. Botanicals may also be used to produce similar, although not identical, experiences. Keeping control over the experience is among the key goals of unassisted astral travel; however, once botanical substances become the source of the journey, that control is, to varying extents, ceded.

Botanically assisted soul journeys, just like astral projection, are surviving vestiges of shamanism. Ointments to produce visions—including group visions—exist in many traditions. Many are accompanied by the sensation of flying. These ointments are the medium of shamanic journeys. The most famous may be medieval witches' flying ointments.

What were witches' flying ointments? Did they fly?

Allegedly, special ointments and salves, when applied to the body, allowed one to mount a broomstick and fly to witches' sabbats.

Two theories exist, not mutually exclusive. One is that the witches, if some were really witches, were on shamanic journeys. The other theory is that the ointments provided erotic adventures instead, with the broomstick serving for those lacking more conventional dildos, not a standard household item in medieval Europe. Ointments were applied where the skin is thin and permeable: the wrists or vagina.

Flying ointment formulas revealed under torture have since been tested, and the results from scientific testing indicate that many formulas, when applied topically, will produce the sensation of flight.

Medieval witches' flying ointments have three types of ingredients not always mutually exclusive:

★ *Those with actual vision-producing propensity*
★ *Those that are poisonous*
★ *Those that are disgusting*

Many botanical components of these salves were highly toxic: a very precise, trained hand was needed to determine exactly how much would provide a shamanic experience, as opposed to how much would kill you. In other words, either those formulas were a lie, or whoever successfully used them was a person of skill and knowledge.

Dangerous items (and they *are* dangerous; do not consider reproducing these formulas) used safely could indicate shamanic skill and botanical knowledge, if one is inclined to think that way and if one is inclined to respect that skill and knowledge. However, looked at from another perspective, their use could also point to a person's *"supernatural"* ability to withstand poison or, perhaps, if one is inclined yet another way, to indicate the devil's protection.

Disgusting ingredients are almost inevitably dead babies, typically unbaptized. Information was extracted under torture. It's very hard to judge how much was genuine information from witnesses and how much was derived from the torturer? Under the circumstances, if the torturer asked whether you used baby fat, would you disagree?

Technically speaking, baby fat was only needed for a base. (The constant suggestion that it was used also points to early abortion wars and the identification of midwives with witches.) Every ointment or salve needs some base for other materials. Fat is merely a carrier for the potent ingredients. Any animal or vegetable fat will serve.

Despite all the pictures of witches literally flying around on broomsticks, a report from 1435 indicates that there was appreciation that the journey was shamanic, not actual: "A woman allegedly rubbed herself with ointment while seated in a large kneading trough. She immediately went to sleep and dreamed of flight. However she shook so vigorously that she fell out and injured her head."

Basic Witches' Flying Ointments

Among the ingredients cited in witches' flying ointments are:

Aconite (wolfsbane)
Baby fat
Belladonna (deadly nightshade)
Betel
Cantharides (Spanish Fly)
Cinquefoil (five-finger grass)
Foxglove
Hashish
Hellebore root
Hemlock
Hemp
Mandrake
Opium
Parsley
Poplar
Poppies
Soot
Thorn apple (datura)
Tobacco
Water parsnip juice

Water parsnip is believed to refer to water hemlock, which is extremely poisonous, as are most of the other ingredients.

Russian Witches' Flying Ointment

1. Rub autumn gentian into the armpits and backs of knees to be enabled to fly.
2. The most potent autumn gentian is allegedly picked on Saint John's Eve at Bald Mountain.

Don't run out and get autumn gentian. That may not be the exact plant used. Russian magic placed greater

emphasis on the process of gathering botanicals ("during the seventh minute of the fourteenth hour, under a dark moon, in the thirteenth field, wearing a red dress, pick the twelfth flower on the right") than on precise identification of the botanical itself. This isn't meant to be completely sarcastic. Different traditions place emphasis on different aspects of magic. Ritual, as remains true in Amazonian ayahuasca preparations, is of no less importance than ingredients.

 ## Witches' Flying Potion

This potion is far more innocuous than the average witch's flying ointments. Basil tea or juice was once considered sufficient to enable a witch's flight. (This is not a spell for pregnant women or those actively attempting to conceive, although neither are the rest of the witch's ointments …)

 ## Witches' Flying Potion: Through the Clouds

Basque witches also allegedly created flying ointments although, perhaps because Mari, Basque Queen of Witches, flies on a fire bolt, the associations of flying on broomsticks are lacking. Instead of brooms, incantations are needed: rub the ointment on the body while repeatedly chanting something like: "Above all the thorns, through all the clouds …"

 ## Safe Modern Flying Potions

Modern flying potions, far less toxic, may be able to reproduce the sensation of witches' flight. Possible herbs include cinquefoil, Dittany of Crete, and mugwort. Experiment; add other herbs as you will.

1. Chop up fresh leaves. In order to get fresh herbs, you'll likely have to grow them. Attempts may be made with dried herbs. But *do not* work with essential oils: mugwort essential oil, for instance, is extremely toxic.
2. Melt cocoa butter, shea butter or similar in a double boiler or bain-marie.
3. Add fresh leaves, as many as you can, mashing them down and adding more. The goal is to permeate the base fat.
4. Simmer, then remove from the heat.
5. Add approximately two teaspoons of lanolin.
6. Strain into a jar. The traditional tool was a sieve, however they didn't have cheesecloth back then. Use what works best.
7. If the ointment is too hard, add more lanolin. Reserve and use as desired.

 ## Stop a Flying Sorcerer

Allegedly maintaining air potatoes (Dioscorea bulbifera) on your property prevents any journeying souls, whether astrally or botanically projected, from landing without invitation.

The Evil Eye

Oh, that Evil Eye! Is there really such a thing? Is it a constant dire threat, a secret universal force or nothing but cliché, the worst use of magic and superstition as a repressive force? And is there really an eye involved?

The answer is a qualified yes to all of the above.

Although it may be delivered by people, the Evil Eye is not the same thing as a malevolent spell. A malevolent spell is targeted deliberately and intentionally: the spell must actually be *cast*.

The Evil Eye is not a spell at all, although there are many spells to oppose it. Instead the Evil Eye is an ill-defined, somewhat nebulous, but entirely malefic force naturally present in the universe—a different kind of magic power. Although there is general agreement on what constitutes the Evil Eye, who is vulnerable and the nature of its destructive effects, exactly *where* the Eye emanates from is subject to heated metaphysical debate.

Some perceive the Evil Eye as an abstract destructive force, like an infectious cloud that one must attempt to avoid, ward off, repel, minimize, or remove. Many other traditions, however, believe that *people* deliver the Evil Eye, sometimes knowingly, sometimes completely innocently and unintentionally. Sometimes they just can't help it.

From that perspective, the Evil Eye is a destructive force that emanates from certain or potentially all people. Every one of us, according to some theories, is able to cast the Eye. It is the human ability to scorch with a glance. The Evil Eye is the force of envy, jealousy, and resentment that shoots out of the human soul like a heat-seeking missile.

The Eye reference may be understood in two ways, which are not mutually exclusive:

1. The Evil Eye as omnipresent destructive abstract force, somewhat similar to *The Lord of the Rings'* all-seeing Eye. Try as you may to hide happiness and good fortune, the Evil Eye is attracted, sees all and spoils it.
2. The Evil Eye is cast with the human eye, either intentionally by those who are jealous, destructive, and malicious by nature, or involuntarily in other circumstances.

There are also two methods of avoiding the Evil Eye:

1. Don't boast, brag or call undue attention to your good fortune.
2. Protection via the use of magically empowered amulets and spells.

Because the secrets of other hearts are unknown, believers council discretion regarding personal matters. What you might never construe as bragging may still invoke the Eye from another. The bereft, lonely, heartbroken woman, overhearing another complain that there are just *too many* men in her life, may involuntarily shoot her with the Evil Eye. The person unable to conceive or whose children have died, overhearing someone complaining about how hard life is because her babies won't sleep at night, may be unable to resist casting that Evil Eye. It just shoots out.

Then there is the southern Italian *jettatura*. This person knows he or she is casting the Eye because they do it all the time. They can't help it; they don't mean to do it. It is just a force that emanates from them: everything they look at turns to disaster. Glance at a building, within 24 hours it burns down. Glance at a champion cow, by nightfall it's sick and dying. Glance at a pregnant woman …

They're not necessarily bad people, these *jettatura*. They may even be very good people. Even a pope was once branded a *jettatura*; people ran from him, hoping to avoid that fatal glance, no matter how benevolently it was intended. (If you fear you

are or know a *jettatura*, don't worry. There is a magical solution. Keep reading.)

Although anyone may be struck by the Evil Eye, not everyone is equally vulnerable. Some are more at risk than others: Brides, babies, pregnant women, children, and horses are all exceptionally vulnerable. Men are not inherently vulnerable to the Evil Eye, but their sperm, genitals, and capacity for fertility are.

The connection with eyes is not limited to the English language. In Italian, this force is called "*mal d'occhio.*" In Hebrew, it's "*ayin hara,*" literally "*evil eye.*" In Arabic it's just "*ayin*" or "*the eye.*" Anti-Evil Eye amulets invariably take the form of eyes, usually, in Mediterranean lands, blue eyes.

These blue eyes indicate something else about the Evil Eye. People's abstract conception of the Evil Eye, the concept of its existence rather than the Evil Eye itself, has historically been used to target minorities and individuals who are different from what is perceived as mass culture, although one could say that the persecutors are manifesting the destructive force of the Eye even as they accuse others. Thus in the Mediterranean, blue eyes are suspect. In Northern Europe, dark skin is suspect. Redheads, frequently a minority, are often targeted as possessing the Evil Eye.

Exploiting the Evil Eye as a tool of discrimination by a dominant culture indicates little true magical knowledge, little understanding of the

There is some belief that the Tenth Commandment that forbids *coveting* actually refers to deliberate casting of the Evil Eye.

Eye as a phenomenon, or else the complete degeneration of a magical system. The Evil Eye either emanates from the universe and not from any individual, or else every individual potentially casts the Eye. *Real* magic makes discrimination and persecution unnecessary. It's a waste of time, only increasing tension and resentment within a society. Real magic has much more powerful means to avoid and remove the Evil Eye.

Traditional signs of attack by the Evil Eye include:

★ *Sudden disaster. Everything was going really well and then, all of a sudden … a major problem or series of problems hits like a bolt of lightning. A perfectly normal pregnancy suddenly isn't normal any longer. A perfectly healthy child suddenly has a health crisis*

★ *Not all manifestations are so sudden: the Evil Eye also manifests as malaise, characterized by consistent lack of energy and lack of interest, and by wasting illnesses that resist conventional diagnosis and/or treatment*

★ *Stubborn, persistent head or body lice*

★ *Sudden, excessive biting of the lips, especially while sleeping*

★ *The Evil Eye can also block fertility, although it is but one of many other potential metaphysical reasons given for the inability to conceive or deliver a healthy, living child*

There are several issues involved when dealing with the Evil Eye: *prevention*, so that the Eye cannot be cast; *repelling*, so that even if cast it bounces off the target without causing harm; and the *removal* of the Eye and its effects. There are many methods employed to prevent being a victim of the Evil Eye, probably the most common being the carrying of charms and amulets.

★ *Many Evil Eye amulets also ward off other dangers: malevolent magic, spiritual attack, etc. Each type of disaster leaves you vulnerable to others. There is an entire category of general* Protection Spells *(see*

pages 876–938); however, these may not ward off the Evil Eye and they will not remove it

★ *Because the Evil Eye is typically inflicted during personal contact, most frequently outside the home, many Evil Eye repelling charms and spells are mobile, like amulets and conjure bags*

★ *Because one can never be sure when the Eye will be cast and from what direction, many magical anti-Evil Eye spells take the form of amulets that, once charged, will repel the Eye independently without further action from the spell-caster*

★ *Anyone (babies, brides) or anything (new cars, new houses) perceived as exceptionally vulnerable to the Evil Eye may be protected* before *the Eye falls upon them*

★ *Like healing and cleansing spells, Evil Eye removal spells frequently require the participation of another to perform the spell on behalf of the afflicted. Always select ritual assistants carefully. The "target" of the spell is generally the person who is afflicted with the Eye*

☀ Antler Charm

1. Attach a piece of antler to a cord made from hair drawn from a black mare's tail.
2. Enhance the power of this amulet by adding a silver tip to the antler. (This balances male and female forces: the male antler, the female silver.)

If the antler breaks or snaps, this indicates that it has intercepted a powerful Eye. Bury it respectfully and replace.

Body Defiance Spells

Just as certain people and objects are inherently vulnerable to the Eye, certain images, objects, and botanicals are perceived as the Evil Eye's natural enemies, repelling, removing, defying, and destroying the Eye by power of their very nature, none more so than images depicting parts of the human anatomy.

It takes an eye to defeat an eye.

Eye shaped amulets match the Evil Eye's glance, distract it, and overpower it.

Natural stones or crystals that vaguely or literally resemble eyes are valued but rare, a problem when the Evil Eye is so omnipresent, therefore people developed more accessible talismans. Glass beads that look like tiny, perpetually open eyes are favored worldwide, especially blue eye beads. Although this association has caused trouble for the blue-eyed in certain parts of the world, the original intention was not to point fingers at certain people or ethnic groups. Instead blue is an important color indicating spiritual protection. Doors, ceilings, and amulets are customarily painted blue for the same reason. That blue eye beads protect from the Evil Eye does not indicate that blue-eyed people are any more likely to cast it.

The most famous and accessible blue eye bead is the Turkish *"nazar boncuk."* These round blue beads may be used independently one at a time, or they may be strung together to form shapes, especially horseshoes.

 Blue Eye Bead Spells

Blue eye beads' power will be enhanced if you cleanse, charge, and consecrate them before use and whenever you perceive that they've "worked" for you.

★ *Wear a single bead around your neck*
★ *Pin individual beads all over using safety pins*
★ *Sew them onto clothing or anything else that needs protection*
★ *Hang them from the rear-view mirror of an automobile*

If a bead cracks, it's understood to have worked. Its demise is considered death on the field of combat, a

direct hit from the Evil Eye. Bury it with honor and replace it.

 Deer's Eye Charm

Deer's eye, like deer's tongue, is obtained without cruelty to animals. "Ojo de venado," the deer's eye, is a bean that closely resembles an eye. It's used in Latin American magic to protect against the Evil Eye. Although it will innately oppose the Evil Eye, if you're genuinely afraid and would like to depend on enhanced power, charge and consecrate beans before their initial use.

An ojo de venado *is often the centerpiece of special hanging charms.*

1. String an *ojo de venado* onto red wool, together with amber, coral, and jet beads, glass blue eye beads, religious medals, and other lucky, protective symbols.
2. Finish off the charm with a big red pom-pom on the bottom and hang it.

The power of the ojo de venado *is sometimes enhanced by gluing spiritual images, such as tiny votive cards, onto the bean.*

Other methods of accessing the power of deer's eye include adding the beans to protective charm bags, or gluing one to wall amulets or wrapped horseshoe charms.

Because the Evil Eye can be understood as the anti-life force, as a withering force of sterility and destruction, powerful, assertive, potent signs of life repel and prevent it. What more powerful signs of life are there than those parts of the anatomy that initiate the life process in the first place?

The defiantly life-affirming energy implicit in the human genitals is among the most important elements in Evil Eye amulets. Does this mean you should unzip your jeans and flash someone you suspect has hit you with the Evil Eye? Even in ancient days, this was recognized as *not* a viable solution.

Amulets in the form of genitals are among the most ancient and prevalent of all charms. They are not meant to be prurient but to affirm life, energy, vitality; the very antithesis of the Evil Eye. Sometimes they are very literal, easily recognized images: penis beads or breast beads, plus an entire genre of international phallic amulets, ranging from life-sized, realistic depictions to tiny, pocket sized, heavily embellished versions.

In order to be effective, most Evil Eye amulets must be visible. If hidden away, its capacity to do its job (search out and deflect that Eye) is limited. As it's not always appropriate to walk around with a silver penis hanging from your neck, more subtle versions abound.

★ *Downward-facing triangles represent the vulva, upward-facing ones the penis. The downward-facing triangle is considered among the most potent anti-Evil Eye amulets of all. It is ubiquitous in beads, in tribal tattoos and in tribal ornamentation. (Take another look at that priceless Oriental carpet.)*
★ *Diamond and lozenge shapes can also stand in for the vagina. (They sometimes represent eyes, too.)*
★ *Seashells are metaphors for the vulva*
★ *The horseshoe may be the most subtle rendering of the female genitalia*
★ *A pair of horns is used to represent women's internal reproductive organs. A single horn, or even anything vaguely similar, is used to represent a penis*

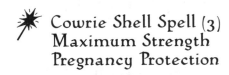

Chili Pepper Spell

This is among the simplest but most potent anti-Evil charms, recommended especially for guarding sperm count, virility, and male reproductive capacity.

1. Pierce a fresh, firm red chili pepper; ideally it should appear as phallic or horn-like as possible.

2. String it from a cord and wear it around your neck.
3. Its effectiveness lasts as long as it remains firm and hard. A temporal amulet, replace as needed with a fresh one.

Cowrie Shell Spell (1) General Protection

1. String cowrie shells onto red cord, charging each shell as you pick it up and tying your desire into every knot.
2. Wear around your neck to repel the Evil Eye.

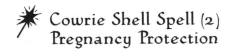

Cowrie Shell Spell (2) Pregnancy Protection

1. String cowrie shells onto red cord, long enough to wear around a pregnant belly.
2. Wear this belt outside your clothes to repel any envious, malevolent eyes.

Cowrie Shell Spell (3) Maximum Strength Pregnancy Protection

1. Sew cowries and blue eye beads onto a freely shed snakeskin.
2. Wear it as a belt. (The protective capacity is so powerful that this could be worn secretly under clothes.)

Mutiny Against the Eye

Winged phalluses, the symbol of the Roman spirit Mutinus and found in the ruins of Pompeii, serve as a prophylactic against the Evil Eye. Wear or hang as needed.

The shape of the human hand is a ubiquitous, international magical protective charm. The hand depicted may be realistic or extremely stylized; sometimes only the five fingers are implied using five dots, or a pentagon. Five fingers poke out the Eye. These hands are shared with general protective magic, however other hand images specifically target the Evil Eye.

★ The "fica" or fig hand, an ancient Italian amulet, repels the Evil Eye. This amulet depicts a hand, with the thumb poking between the first two fingers. This is intended to duplicate the reproductive act. To make matters more explicit, the word fig is ancient slang for vulva. The hand, thus, re-creates the power of the genitals

★ The "mano cornuto" or horned hand, another old Italian Evil Eye charm, displays a hand making the sign of the horns, first and last fingers thrust out from the otherwise clenched hand

Should you find yourself threatened without recourse to an amulet, take your hands off your belt: it's not necessary to resort to the genuine article. Magical gestures made with the hands ward off the Eye. In general, this is not a confrontational act: the gesture is made behind the suspect's back as they depart from you or under cover, out of sight. The goal is to stop the Eye, not start a fight.

These spells will repel the Evil Eye if you catch it as its being sent or immediately after; they will not remove its effects, however. Stronger spells are needed.

 ## Fig Hand Spell

Make the fig hand. Stick your thumb through the first two fingers and thrust in the direction of the Eye.

 ## Horned hand Spell

Make the sign of the horns, the mano cornuto, *by holding down the two middle fingers with your thumb and thrusting out the little finger and forefinger in the direction from which you perceive the Eye, straight ahead if in doubt.*

General Evil Eye Protection Spells

 ## Bean Spells

Grow jack beans or sword beans as a border surrounding your home and property to repel the Eye.

 ## Camelweed Spell

The plant Alhagi camelorum *is indigenous to the Mediterranean region. Naturalized in the United States, it's considered a pest, and called "camelweed," the bane of bicycle riders. In Azerbaijan, on the other hand, it's known as the "camel's needle," because it can be used to pierce the Evil Eye.*

Hang the needles above the front door. Or hang the needles from a car's rear-view mirror, depending on where you want protection.

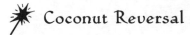 Coconut Reversal

1. Carry a coconut to your front door.
2. Hold it in your hands and visualize the forces of evil plaguing you passing from your body out of your hands and into the coconut.
3. Visualize the coconut's eyes as the Evil Eye and the coconut head grinning at you.
4. When you're ready, open the door, drop kick or place the coconut on the floor and kick it out on the street, yelling aggressively, *"Get the hell out!"* or something stronger.
5. Go inside and immediately perform cleansing and protective rituals for yourself.

This may also be used to reverse any kind of malevolent spell.

Conjure Bags

These bags, in general, provide protection from the Eye, a measure of security. They will not necessarily remove the Eye that's already been cast.

 Anti-Evil Eye Conjure Bag (1)

Anti-Evil Eye recommendations from India suggest filling a red bag with some or all of the following:

★ *Crocodile teeth*
★ *Pottery shards or bits of terracotta pottery found in a cemetery*
★ *Protective verses and sacred texts*
★ *Chili peppers, lemons or limes, to be replaced with fresh ones weekly or as needed*

Wear or carry the bag with you.

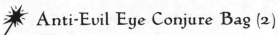 Anti-Evil Eye Conjure Bag (2)

Place at least one pinch of each of the following in a red conjure bag:

★ *Henna powder*
★ *Red dirt, iron oxide powder or ochre*
★ *Tar*

Add one or five blue eye beads and carry it with you.

 Anti-Evil Eye Conjure Bag (3)

Even when not decorating your eye, traditional kohl powder has amuletic power against the Eye. Carry the powder in a red mojo bag.

 Anti-Evil Eye Conjure Bag (4)

Combine at least a pinch of any one or combination of the following: antimony powder, henna powder, ground malachite powder, or iron oxide powder. Add one cowrie shell and carry in a charm bag.

 Anti-Evil Eye Conjure Bag (5)

1. Gather dirt from a three-way crossroads.
2. Place it in a blue, red or mirrored conjure bag.
3. Wear it around your neck to avoid and repel the Eye.

 Crescent Moon Charm

Underscoring the similarity between horns and crescent moons, according to ancient Hebrew practice, wearing the crescent moon shape repels the Evil Eye.

Daghdaghan Spell

Various parts of the daghdaghan *tree repel the Eye. Small twigs and branches may be hung on cords and worn. The tiny fruits can be dried, pierced, and treated like beads; sew them onto clothing, fabrics, and amulets.*

Dill Evil-Eye Repellant

Hang dill over all entrances and windows to ward off the Evil Eye.

 ## Disarm Yourself! (1) Evil Eye

Are you afraid that you're *sending the Evil Eye? To disarm:*

1. Unroll one cigarette.
2. Sprinkle the tobacco onto freshly lit charcoal.
3. Stand over this incense or waft it toward you with your hands or a fan, so that the smoke creates a fumigation for you.
4. Repeat as needed.

 ## Disarm Yourself! (2) Jettatura

The jettatura *is the unwilling but constant sender of Evil Eye rays. If you're afraid that you're one, allegedly focusing your vision onto your left nostril incapacitates the Eye. You may look odd but no one gets hurt.*

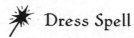 ## Dress Spell

The clothing worn when the Eye is encountered can help you remove and repel its effects. This Northern European technique of averting and removing the Evil Eye should be attempted as soon as possible following contact with the Eye. The dress in the spell is understood to be the one you were wearing when you met the Eye.

1. Pull your dress over your head as if you were removing it, but instead, with it held over your head, twirl three times sunwise.
2. Remove the garment.
3. Holding it open and, leaving it inside-out if this is how it has come off, drop a burning coal through it three times.
4. Put the dress back on.

✹ Evil Eye Diagnosis (1) Cloves

Illness caused by the Evil Eye manifests as genuine physical illness. The complicating factor is that a cure cannot be obtained without both conventional healing methods and removal of the Evil Eye. Thus sometimes the Evil Eye must be diagnosed in order to plan and complete the proper course of treatment.

1. The curer takes nine cloves in the right hand and passes them over and around the target of the Eye's head.
2. Light a candle. (This is a traditional Italian spell and the recommendation is for a church candle, but adapt this to your needs.)
3. Insert a needle through the head of one clove and then insert it into the candle flame to ignite it.
4. Use the burning clove to make the sign of the cross over the afflicted person.
5. Chant:
   Three saw you. Three bewitched you
   From your mother you were born
   In the name of the Father, the Son and the Holy
      Spirit
   All evil away!
   (Pagans may easily substitute the triple goddess for the Christian trinity. Alternately, Selene, Artemis, and Hecate, or the Irish warriors, the Morrigan are very suitable.)
5. Drop the burned-out clove in a glass of cold water.
6. Repeat with another clove. If a clove bursts, this is an indication that the person has been hit by the Evil Eye. If the person flinches from the snapping sound, then the spell has been broken. (It's the departing evil that caused the involuntary motion.) If no cloves snap, then there is no Evil Eye influence; any ailments stem from other causes. The entire ritual may end now.
7. If the clove that snaps is the ninth and last one, three more cloves must be burned. If the third or last clove snaps, repeat with another series of three cloves. Repeat until the last clove does not snap.

8. The victim now takes three sips from the glass of water containing the burned out cloves, drinking each sip from a different spot on the glass's rim.
9. Facing the victim, the curer dips his or her fingers into the glass and shakes the water in all directions. This must be repeated twice more, for a total series of three.
10. The curer dips his or her fingers into the water again and now forms three crosses on the victim's forehead and three more on the back of the neck.

✹ Evil Eye Diagnosis (2) Olive Oil

This basic method may be used to diagnosis the Evil Eye and determine whether it still lingers. It may also be used to determine whether an illness is rooted in the Evil Eye.

1. Drip three drops of olive oil into a dish of water.
2. Examine what happens.
3. Oil and water don't mix. If the drops remain distinct, everything is fine. There is no Eye.
4. If, however, they disperse, the Evil Eye is present.

Perform anti-Evil Eye spells. After each spell, repeat this ritual to verify whether the Evil Eye has been lifted. When the oil behaves as it should, the Eye has been removed.

✹ Evil Eye House Protection Spell

Protect your new home from the Evil Eye and other envious glances, particularly while it's under construction.

1. Create a doll to divert the eye. In India, from whence this ritual derives, the doll is usually made from fabric and stuffed with straw; however, what the

doll is made from isn't as important as what the doll looks like. The crucial point is that it must be eye-catching. Usually the dolls are vivid in color, funny or sexually suggestive: long protruding red penises are customary, although this may not play well in the suburbs.

2. Charge the doll with its mission, then set it on scaffolding or hang it above the front door. When observers glance at your house, their eye is irresistibly drawn to the doll; they never see your house.

3. Remove the doll, if you like, following protective rituals for the home.

Evil Eye Oil

Although the concept of the Evil Eye and many anti-Evil Eye spells are ancient, modern versions exist, too. This Hoodoo spell draws upon a blend of Egyptian and British magical traditions.

1. Draw a blue eye onto a white plate using indigo or blue food coloring.
2. Fill a dish with **Van Van Oil.**
3. Using water, rinse the blue eye off the plate into the **Van Van.**
4. Rub the resulting concoction onto your hands and the soles of your feet daily for seven consecutive days.

For best results, accompany with recitation of Psalms and/or other sacred texts.

Evil Eye Removal Spells

A typical Evil Eye removal spell involves one person holding something in their hand which is then passed around the victim's head three times. The substance held in the hand must be magnetic and absorbent.

★ *The substance serves as an Evil Eye magnet: it pulls the Evil Eye off the victim*
★ *Because it is absorbent, the Evil Eye goes into the substance*
★ *The substance is then usually immediately thrown into a fire, destroying the Evil Eye and its capacity to harm*

This ritual can be in response to an attack of the Evil Eye, suspicion of attack or even just as a nightly precautionary method. The person doing the removal (versus the target of the spell, the victim of the Eye) magically concentrates and focuses on removing the Eye and blessing and protecting the victim. The spell may be accompanied by murmuring blessings, sacred texts and/or defiant comments towards the Eye. Although the spell may work even if done mechanically, it lacks the potency and blessing-quality of a consciously empowered spell.

Evil Eye Removal (1) Alum

1. Pass alum over the person who is afflicted.
2. Throw the alum into fire to dispel and destroy the spell.
3. Should the pieces come together in the fire in some semblance of a male or female shape, this is a clue as to the gender of the spell-caster.

Evil Eye Removal (2) Black Cumin

1. Wrap an odd number of black cumin seeds in paper or place them inside a small paper bag.
2. Pass this packet around the victim of the Eye three times.
3. Burn it in fire.
4. When you hear the seeds snap, crackle, and pop, you'll know the Evil Eye has cracked too. If no sounds are heard, consider whether further action is needed.

Evil Eye Removal (3)
Date Leaves

1. Collect 21 date palm leaves.
2. Knot them together, envisioning your goals and desires as you form each knot.
3. Wave this garland around the afflicted person.
4. Place it in a covered terracotta pot in the corner of the afflicted person's room overnight.
5. Put an old shoe, a broom or a piece of iron on top of the pot.
6. In the morning dispose of the pot's contents at a crossroads or burn the garland outside the home.
7. Spiritually cleanse the pot before further use.

 ## Evil Eye Removal (4) Dragon

1. To remove particularly persistent Evil Eye infestation, erect a dragon altar using an image of a fierce dragon with wide-open staring eyes.
2. Create a lair to invite the dragon's presence. Offer treasure to guard: crystals, replica coins and gold ingots, gemstone beads.
3. When the dragon is happy and comfortable, explain your dilemma and that he is the only one strong enough to destroy and consume the Eye. Visualizations before you go to sleep are especially effective.

 ## Evil Eye Removal (5) Egg

1. Pass one egg around the afflicted person three times, muttering blessings, sacred texts, and defiance towards the Eye.
2. Take the egg outside, ideally off your property and smash it on the ground.
3. Check for signs of blood; if any appear, continued magical action is required.

 ## Evil Eye Removal (6)
Egg and Oil

1. Fill a dish with olive oil and reserve.
2. Rub the body from head to toe, using a downward, outward motion, with five whole raw eggs.
3. Use one egg at a time; after each turn, place the used egg in the oil.
4. When all eggs are in the bowl, sprinkle them with cayenne pepper and ground cinnamon.
5. Insert cotton wicks into the oil and burn the oil.

 ## Evil Eye Removal (7)
Egg and Thorn

1. Gently rub an egg over the afflicted person, especially over their eyes.
2. Break the egg into a bowl.
3. Pierce the yolk with seven sharp thorns.

Evil Eye Removal (8) Iron

1. Heat a bar of iron until it is red-hot.
2. Holding it with tongs, pass the iron bar around the afflicted person three times.
3. Drop the bar into a dish of turmeric water.
4. Leave it there until the water cools, then dispose of the water outside the house.

Evil Eye Removal (9) Is It
Gone Yet?

To determine whether the Eye has been removed, follow spells to remove the Eye by dropping three fresh drops of oil into a pan of fresh water. When the drops remain round and distinct, the Eye is gone.

Evil Eye Removal (10) Novena

The concept of the "Novena," a nine-day candle spell, pre-dates Roman Catholicism. Burn a new candle for nine consecutive evenings, murmuring over it, reciting sacred verses, and charging the candle with your desires. Each morning throw the wax remnants as far from your home as possible.

Evil Eye Removal (11) Salt

1. Prepare a fire.
2. Pass a handful of salt around the afflicted person's head three times.
3. Toss the salt into the fire.

Evil Eye Removal (12) Sizzling Water

1. You need to create a hot surface: either place hot coals onto a plate or heat up a metal plate.
2. Place an overturned jar on top of the plate.
3. Fill a bowl with water. Pass it over the afflicted person. Empty the water over the jar so that it spills onto the plate. (If the water hisses or sizzles or somehow makes noise, it's attempting to communicate with you regarding the spell and the success of the removal. Try to interpret.)
4. Place a metal implement across the now-empty bowl until you can properly cleanse it.

Evil Eye Removal (13) Three Hot Peppers

1. Pass three red chili peppers around the affected person's head three times.
2. Each time you make a rotation, chant: *"I pull off the Eye, be it man, woman or spirit!"*

3. Throw the chilies into an open fire and burn them.

Evil Eye Removal (14) Uzarlik

1. Prepare a fire.
2. Take a handful of uzarlik (Syrian rue, harmel) and sea salt.
3. Pass it around the target's head in a circle, making three complete rotations while chanting:
   Uzarlik, uzarlik
   You are air
   You are against every grief
   Pluck out the Evil Eye and place it in my hand.
4. Throw the handful of herbs and salt into the fire. Popping and spluttering is a very good sign.

Evil Eye Remove and Repel

This Palestinian spell may be used to remove or repel the Evil Eye or any other malevolent spell:

1. Place a piece of tamarisk wood and either a pinch of salt or a pinch of alum in a pan over the fire.
2. The patient must walk around it seven times.
3. As soon as a crackling sound is heard, the spell is broken.

Evil Eye Waters

The following formula waters repel the Eye:

Holy Water
Indigo Water
Marie Laveau Water
Notre Dame Water

Formulas may be found in the *Formulary* (page 1037).

Add substantial quantities of one or a combination of these waters to your bath. Alternately, asperge an area using a rue wand to cleanse the place of the Evil Eye's influence.

 ## Eyebright Evil Eye Repellant

The dark spot in the center of the eyebright flower is often interpreted as an eye. Grow the flower around your home to repel the Eye.

 ## Five Eye Spell

Five pairs of glass beads, each pair in a different distinct color, are required for this amulet. Dizzying colors dazzle the Evil Eye.

1. String the beads in a double row.
2. Arrange them in a circle.
3. Post or wear.

 ## Five in Your Eye!

Sometimes dazzling the Eye isn't sufficient. Just as people attempt to protect themselves from the Eye, so the Eye is believed to possess instincts of self-preservation and will recoil from potential harm. How many times have you heard adults admonish children, "Don't play with sticks! You'll poke someone's eye out!" or "Don't point your finger! You're liable to poke out an eye!" Sharp, pointy objects and plain human fingers serve as potent Evil Eye amulets.

Many Evil Eye spells feign aggressive action and mimic destruction of the Eye. Don't touch or get near anyone's actual eyes! It's that big abstract malevolent invisible force that must be stopped, not anyone's actual glance or their ability to glance.

1. When the threat of the Eye is perceived aggressively mutter or shout, as appropriate, the Moroccan saying *"Five in your eye!"*
2. Add a thrusting motion of the hand with splayed fingers in the direction that the Eye is believed to come from, or straight ahead of you if unknown.

 ## Four Corners Dirt Spell

This quick-fix pan-Semitic spell is extremely effective for removing all traces of the Evil Eye.

1. Take dirt from the four corners of your home.
2. Mix it together and throw it on a fire within the house shouting fiercely *"Get the hell out, Evil Eye!"*

Henna

Amulets are left at home, lost, forgotten, or given to others as emergency protection. Permanent amulets that can't be lost create another option: one of the primary primal reasons for tattooing is the creation of such a permanent amulet.

Once upon a time, and sometimes still, throughout Africa and Asia, women's faces were tattooed with small blue downward facing triangles and/or a series of five dots, representing the protective energy of the human anatomy.

North African tattoo designs were particularly intricate, each detail filled with symbolic value. After the Islamic conquest, Berber women were forbidden their traditional tattoos. So that the shapes would not be forgotten, the women turned to henna.

Henna, in itself, is an extremely potent enemy of the Evil Eye. Even carrying the powder in an amulet bag repels the Eye; however its power is magnified when combined with anti-Evil Eye imagery.

Most other botanicals demonstrate their power ephemerally or through aroma. Henna does both and adds visual impact too. Henna creates a temporary dye on the skin. The color ranges from orange to brick red to deep brown, all metaphysically powerful colors, particularly in regards to spiritual protection. Magical, amuletic, and talismanic designs are displayed on the skin. Henna's primary associations with weddings and fertility may derive from its reputation as a potent anti-Evil Eye weapon.

Use the powder to create henna paste in order to decorate hand and body. (Check the *Formulary* for further instruction.) The most efficacious anti-Evil Eye designs to be incorporated into henna decoration include:

★ *Downward facing triangles*
★ *Dots grouped together in series of five*
★ *Pentagons*
★ *Eyes, especially an eye inside a triangle*

These designs may also be incorporated into tattoos and other body art.

 ## Home Protection Spell

Envious neighbors? Too many passers-by gazing at your house? This spell is particularly effective when undergoing construction work on a home.

1. Attach a red ribbon to a hand of bananas and some rue. Add Evil Eye beads or a *cimaruta,* the Italian Evil Eye amulet, for maximum effect. (The *cimaruta* is usually crafted from silver or a silver-colored metal, and has evolved into a complex, fabulous amulet.)
2. Hang outside the house until the bananas are completely rotten.
3. Burn or bury everything; do not bring within the home.
4. Repeat as needed.

 ## Horn Charm Spell

Fill a small horn or cornucopia with sage leaves to protect against the Eye. Wear it or situate it strategically.

 ## Iron Anti-Evil Eye Spell

Found nails protect against the Evil Eye. If you find one, pick it up and carry it in a red conjure bag.

 ## Make-up Spell

Among the arts the angels taught those early Daughters of Men were the use of cosmetics. Although there may have always been an erotic component intrinsic to make-up, its initial use was magically protective: to shield against the Evil Eye.

Heavily ornamented eyes distract the Eye from the vulnerable iris. Power is enhanced by using kohl (kajal) powder, which, like henna, is believed to possess inherent anti-Evil Eye properties. One can carry the powder discreetly in a bag to receive its benefits, however its power is magnified when used to decorate your eye.

Outline the shape of your eyes in black: genuine kohl is most powerful, however more conventional black eyeliner or modern "kohl pencils" also work.

Bold red lipstick diverts the Eye from vulnerable eyes toward the more aggressive (the teeth!) mouth.

Maximon Anti-Evil Eye Spell

Maximon (pronounced "mah-she-mon") is the primal Guatemalan spirit of the crossroads and male phallic energy. A modern unofficial saint who emerged from the juxtaposition of an ancient Mayan grandfather spirit with Saint Simon, fearless Maximon offers his devotees many gifts, not least protection from the Evil Eye. Sprinkle a circle of tobacco around a black candle and burn it in front of Maximon's image to repel and remove the Evil Eye.

 ## Mirror Charm

Supplying your own eye may not be necessary. Mirrors reflect the Evil Eye straight back where it came from and, as with the fabled basilisk, can prove fatal.

Mirrors are incorporated into other amulets. Or they can be strategically arranged so best to repel the Evil Eye; sew small mirrors and reflecting surfaces onto your clothing.

 ## Moroccan Anti-Evil Eye Incense (1) Basic Version

Benzoin incense, called "jawi" in Morocco, destroys the effects of the Evil Eye.

1. Mash up benzoin resin or use benzoin powder.
2. Sprinkle onto lit charcoals and fumigate an area or a person.

Benzoin comes in different colors; for maximum power, blend darker and lighter pieces.

 ## Moroccan Anti-Evil Eye Incense (2) Extra Strength Version

Benzoin is also a component of complex protective incense formulas.

1. Gather the following ingredients:
   Alum
   Benzoin
   Coriander seeds
   Garlic
   Gum ammoniac
   Harmel (Syrian rue, uzarlik)
   Juniper
   Sulfur
2. Blend the ingredients together, mashing with mortar and pestle.
3. Grind them to a fine powder and burn.

 ## Nine Nail Lemon Charm

1. Pierce a lemon with nine nails.
2. Wind red thread around these nails.
3. Knot the end of the thread around one of the nails.
4. Place this charm above the door to repel the Evil Eye.

 ## Pomander Anti-Evil Eye Spell

Pomanders are presently most associated with old-fashioned Christmas crafts, though their roots lie in magical and herbal healing. There is an implicit aspect of Evil Eye removal involved in crafting a pomander.

1. Choose an eye-shaped fruit if possible: a lemon, lime, or citron may be more effective than an orange.
2. Completely pierce it with holes. Visualize piercing the Evil Eye simultaneously. (It's not necessary to imagine literally piercing an eye; visualize piercing the damage done, like removing the air from a balloon.)

3. Fill each hole, each vacuum, with a clove. Cloves are magical *"nails,"* the traditional botanical Evil Eye repellant.
4. Bind the pomander with blue or red ribbons and hang it as a warning symbol of what will happen to the Eye should it return.

Quick-fix Evil Eye Spells

Although many anti-Evil Eye spells and rituals are lengthy and complex, in a pinch, quick-fix anti-Evil Eye spells can be very effective, especially when you need to remove the Eye from oneself without assistance.

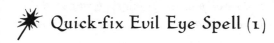

Quick-fix Evil Eye Spell (1)

Drip olive oil into water, especially boiling water. Let the water cool, and then bathe yourself with it, focusing on the face, back of the neck, and the soles of your feet.

Quick-fix Evil Eye Spell (2)

Drop glowing coals or lit matches into water. Watch them hit the water. Expose yourself to any steam. Visualize the Eye extinguished.

Quick-fix Evil Eye Spell (3)

Pierce a lemon with iron nails. Visualize yourself simultaneously piercing the Evil Eye.

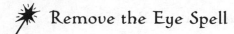

Remove the Eye Spell

This Italian spell removes the Evil Eye.

1. Add spring or **Holy Water** to a saucer.
2. Add three drops of olive oil to the water plus seven small leaves from an olive branch that has been blessed on Palm Sunday.
3. Dip your finger into the dish, swirl it in the ingredients, then use your finger to make a cross on the victim's forehead, saying:
   Jesus, Joseph and Mary
   Evil Eye Away!
4. Repeat two more times for a total of three crosses and three chants.
5. Repeat on three consecutive mornings. Here's the catch: oil and water don't mix; if they do, something is wrong. The drops of oil need to remain visibly distinct within the water. Should they at any point disperse completely into the water, dispose of the ingredients. Wait 24 hours and repeat the entire ritual.

An alternative rhyme is sometimes used:

Two eyes have overlooked you
Two saints have enjoyed you
By the Father, Son, and the Holy Ghost
Evil Eye Away!

Rue, the herb of grace, is one of the most powerful weapons in the arsenal used against the Evil Eye

Rue Spell (1) Basic

Pin a single fresh sprig of rue to your clothing or hair to repel the Eye. Remember to replace it with a fresh one daily.

Rue Spell (2) Bath

1. Mash up some fresh rue.
2. Cover this with boiling water.
3. Let the infusion cool and use it to bathe the afflicted person.

Bathing in an infusion of rue is a common recommendation for removing the Eye and for cleansing spells in general, however rue is an extremely potent and potentially dangerous botanical. ***It is not safe for pregnant women or those actively attempting to conceive to use rue.***

 ## Rue Spell (3) Charm

A safer method to benefit from rue's power is available: the cimaruta. *The amulet derives its shape from the rue plant ("ruta" in Italian). Different amuletic shapes are hung from the ends of the stylized sprig of rue.*

1. Charge and consecrate a *cimaruta* before wearing.
2. For maximum effectiveness, cleanse and empower the amulet by passing through rue smoke. (Someone else can cleanse the charm for its wearer, if exposure to rue is problematic.)

 ## Rue Spell (4) Culinary

It's no accident that witches are so frequently depicted stirring a cauldron. Cauldrons double as magic ritual and culinary tools. Once upon a time, spells were frequently administered through meals. Emulate the old Romans and add rue to the diet to protect against the Evil Eye. (But remember, rue is unsafe for pregnant women.)

 ## Rue Spell (4) Discreet Version

Hide sprigs of rue in your clothing or carry it in a charm bag to foil the Eye.

 ## Rue Spell (5) Incense

Grind and powder dried rue. Sprinkle onto powdered charcoal and burn as incense to cleanse an area of the Eye's influence.

 ## Saint John's Wort Infused Oil

An infusion of Saint John's Wort blossoms and/or leaves in olive oil protects against the Evil Eye. Rub on the body, concentrating on the soles of the feet and the back of the neck.

 ## Secret Red Ribbon

Tie a red ribbon to your underwear. (Just wearing red underwear may be effective, too.) For maximum effectiveness, magically charge all items prior to use.

 ## Send it Back! (1)

This ritual either neutralizes the Eye or sends it back from whence it came.

1. If you know or suspect who cast the Eye, secretly cut a small bit of the suspect's clothing.
2. Burn it together with frankincense resin.
3. Brandish either the burning incense or the dish with the cold leftover ashes in front of the suspect with an aggressive gesture.

There's no need to explicitly inform the other person of the intent of the ritual: the effect is subliminal.

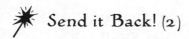

Send it Back! (2)

Caught them at it? Sometimes you can feel the Evil Eye right away. It can be neutralized immediately, too, with a simple ritual from modern Egypt: toss a handful of Earth in the suspect's wake as they walk away from you.

 ## Shark's Tooth Spell

Wear a fossilized shark's tooth to repel the Evil Eye. Cleanse periodically by passing through protective incense smoke.

 ## Three-fork Stick Spell

This Romany spell requires a three-forked stick. Finding one quickly when you need it is very auspicious. If you can't find one, you may carve one. The ritual is ultimately dedicated to a protective deity. Choose one who gives you confidence. If in doubt, Michael the Archangel is divinely charged with the role of humanity's protector and may always be petitioned in time of need.

1. Fill a pot or cauldron with water from a stream. The water must be taken with the current, not against it.
2. Add the following items to the pot: seven glowing coals, seven handfuls of cornmeal, seven cloves of garlic.
3. Place the pot over a fire to boil.
4. When the water begins to boil, stir it with a three-forked stick, chanting:
   Hey! Evil eyes look here!
   Your power is gone
   Seven ravens come.
   Seven ravens pierce all evil eyes, every one.
   Evil eyes look here!
   Your power is now gone!!
   Dust in your eyes!
   Five fingers stab your eyes!
   You are blind!

Hey! Evil eyes look here
You are extinguished now
Burn, burn, burn in the fire of [Deity's name]

A Tuscan anti-Evil Eye remedy benefits from the synergistic magic power of specific plants: mugwort, rue, vervain, and wormwood.

 ## Tuscan Formula (1) Bath

Create an infusion by pouring boiling water over the combined herbs. Add this infusion to the bath.

This spell is absolutely not for pregnant women or those actively trying to conceive.

 ## Tuscan Formula (2) Emergency Spray

1. Create an infusion by pouring boiling water over the combined herbs.
2. Once it cools, strain out the botanical material and add the liquid to a spray bottle; apply as needed.

 ## Tuscan Formula (3) Incense

Grind and powder the dried botanicals. Sprinkle onto lit charcoals and burn.

 ## Tuscan Formula (4) House Charm

1. Tie a bunch of the fresh herbs together with scarlet ribbons.
2. Enhance by adding anti-Evil Eye charms, like blue eye beads, fig hands, *cornutos* or the *cimaruta*.
3. Hang over the door or any spot perceived as vulnerable.

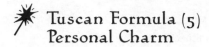

Tuscan Formula (5) Personal Charm

1. Tie a few sprigs of the fresh herbs (at least one of each) with red ribbon.
2. Add anti-Evil Eye charms (blue eye beads, *cimaruta*, etc.) as desired.
3. Wear in your hair.

Uzarlik Spells

Peganum harmala is known in English as Syrian rue. While there is no botanical relationship to true rue, what the two plants share in common is their aura of sacredness and their traditional use as an extra-potent weapon against the Evil Eye. Known as *"harmel"* in Arabic, Syrian rue is one of the most frequently used North African and Middle Eastern magical and shamanic herbs. In Azerbaijani, it's called *"uzarlik."*

Not only will the ambient smoke and aroma of burning uzarlik remove the Evil Eye, it also prevents those in its vicinity from casting it. Where uzarlik is present, the Evil Eye is immobilized. As you can imagine, amuletic use of uzarlik is ubiquitous. Uzarlik provides protection wherever and whenever vulnerability is perceived, at weddings and births, for instance, or in the presence of a new car or home.

Uzarlik Evil Eye Spell

Throw handfuls of uzarlik into an open flame or sprinkle the herb onto lit charcoals. The goal is to produce smoke. Sufficient quantities will permeate an area; otherwise direct the smoke in the direction of whatever needs to be protected.

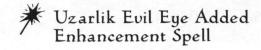

Uzarlik Evil Eye Added Enhancement Spell

Burn uzarlik and benzoin together as above.

Uzarlik Evil Eye Protection Spell

Uzarlik doesn't stop being effective after it's been burned but may also be used as an amulet to protect against the Evil Eye.

1. Once uzarlik has burned, allow the ashes to cool and then collect them.
2. To protect a specific person, spread the ashes on the forehead and the back of the neck.
3. Chant:
   Uzarlik, uzarlik
   You are air
   You are against every grief
   Keep me young and powerful
4. Ashes may also be preserved as a permanent amulet in a charm bag. Include the chant anyway.

Although some traditions believe that the Evil Eye is cast unwittingly and uncontrollably, others disagree. Some perceive that the Eye is cast deliberately, making it similar to casting a malevolent spell. Various methods exist to determine the identity of the spell-caster. This Hungarian sieve divination spell below is used to identify who cast the Eye or any other malevolent spell.

Who Cast the Eye? (1)

1. Place nine different power objects of your choice inside a sieve.
2. Rest a dish with ice-cold water on top.
3. Pour liquid molten tin or wax into the water.

4. As the wax or tin solidifies, it forms shapes identifying who or what has caused the bewitchment, and why.

 ## Who Cast the Eye? (2)

A Turkish spell seeks to identify the exact perpetrator.

1. Light a candle.
2. Stick a needle through a clove and pass it into or just over a fire.
3. As the clove roasts, recite the names of individuals suspected of casting the Eye.
4. If the clove should explode as a name is said, this indicates that the culprit has been identified.

 ## Who Cast the Eye? (3)

This Greek spell uses cloves to perform a diagnosis as well as to receive information regarding treatment:

1. Light a candle.
2. Stick a needle through a clove and pass it into or just over a fire.
3. Ask questions regarding the affliction, the cure and/or the possible Eye-caster. For instance, questions could include: *"Is it a man?" "Is this his occupation?" "Should we call this curer?" "Should we cast this spell?"*
4. Should a clove pop immediately following or during a question, this is an affirmative reply.

 ## Witch Balls

Witch balls *are more than an evocative name. Hang these iridescent glass balls in the window to ward off the Evil Eye.*

Children's Evil Eye Cures

Infants and children are considered especially vulnerable to the Evil Eye. Precautions for babies are somewhat simpler, if only because they're smaller, less mobile, and thus less easily targeted. Infants in societies that fear the Evil Eye are kept sequestered at home as much as possible. They are swaddled when outside. Baby, crib, or carrier is guarded with powerful amulets. Children, on the other hand, are out and about in the world. Who knows what they'll come home with? Spells to protect children from all sorts of dangers, especially the Evil Eye, are legion. Some are for prevention, others for diagnosis and removal of the Eye.

Because of their inherent vulnerability children cannot remove the Eye for themselves. An adult must perform the spell on their behalf.

 ## Child's Diagnosis Spell

This spell performs a diagnosis but does not remove the Eye.

1. To determine whether a child is under malign influence, fill a washbasin with water.
2. *Gently* place three glowing embers of wood and two broom straws on the surface of the water.
3. If at least one straw sinks to the bottom, malign influence is indicated. Take appropriate further action.

Magic spell baths remove and repel the Evil Eye:

Evil Eye Bath (1) Glowing Coals

1. Fill a tub with spring water. (A metal washtub is suggested, rather than a conventional bathtub, although that can be used, too.)
2. *Don't* put the child in the water but let him or her watch.
3. Toss glowing charcoals into the tub.
4. Dip a fresh, clean white cloth into the water and bathe the child with it.
5. Dump the water out in an isolated place where no one is likely to step over it.

Evil Eye Bath (2) Silver

1. Borrow silver from a neighbor. Because the Evil Eye lurks everywhere and probably for a variety of other reasons, it's considered wiser *not* to explain exactly why you need the loan. (Traditionally a coin was borrowed, which was very discreet. However modern coins are invariably silver-colored metal, not true silver. Borrow an antique coin, a piece of jewelry, or a piece of silverware: it will be returned.)
2. Place the silver inside a tub filled with pure spring water.
3. Intensify the action by adding some quartz crystals.
4. Bathe the child in the tub. Return the silver, with a small gift.

Evil Eye Bath (3) What's Cooking in the Kitchen?

Removing the Evil Eye can be fun. This Hungarian spell, effectively a game of charades played to foil the Eye, demands participation from at least two people besides the afflicted child. Time the spell so that it's in full swing at midnight.

1. Bring a big tub into the kitchen as if you were preparing an old-fashioned bath.

2. Put wood under the tub. Pretend it's the olden days when you actually had to heat the water. (But don't light it; it's never actually lit. Go through the motions as if you were. It's a game.)
3. Make the child sit in the tub. There's no water in the tub, but you can go through the motions of washing, stirring, and basting. (*Basting?* Think of fairy tales where the witch tricks the child into a big pot in the guise of bathing, when she's really about to be cooked.)
4. Someone else must then enter the room and ask, *"What are you cooking?"*
5. You reply something like, *"Mmm, mmm … delicious meat on the bone!"*
6. Repeat parts 1 through 5 for a total of twelve times.
7. Then the person doing the *"cooking,"* the cleanser, so to speak, runs around the entire house or the area twelve times sweeping with a broom. Make aggressive gestures with it, thrusting it away from the house.

Complete the ritual by placing an amulet on the child. Eat something and go to sleep.

Evil Eye Cure Spell

This spell originates from Denmark.

1. At midnight, gather up three scoops of Earth from a crossroads.
2. Wrap the dirt up in red fabric.
3. Wrap this around the child's neck.

Evil Eye Illness Spell

The Evil Eye is blamed for children's mysterious, lingering, wasting illnesses—those illnesses that defy medical diagnosis and medical treatment. This is particularly true for those patients whom logic and convention say

should be improving but for some unknown reason they are not. This spell draws the illness out of the child and lets wild creatures destroy it.

1. Place seven flat breads underneath the child's pillow.
2. Leave them there under the sleeping child overnight, or an equivalent amount of time.
3. When the child awakens, remove the bread from your house; leave it for birds or stray animals.

Evil Eye Potion

A modern Syrian custom suggests that an Evil Eye-afflicted ailing child drink water blended from seven distinct wells or cisterns. It can be difficult to locate one well or cistern. As if you didn't have enough trouble, now you have to locate seven? Update the spell, itself an adaptation. There is a very ancient pan-Semitic belief in the magical healing power of water blended from seven springs. When the springs became unavailable, cisterns were substituted.

1. Blend seven different bottled spring waters, each from a distinct source.
2. Give the child a glass to drink and apply a compress soaked in the blended water, too.

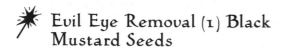

Evil Eye Removal (1) Black Mustard Seeds

This spell from India removes all traces of the Evil Eye. It can be used as a precautionary method, just in case the Eye has been cast, by incorporating it into a child's bedtime routine, like brushing teeth and telling a story.

1. Before children go to sleep at night, heat a cast-iron pan so that it is extremely hot.
2. Hold a handful of black mustard seeds over the child, while making a blessing or wish.

3. Then toss the seed into the pan and pop them over high heat.
4. Throw them away or burn the remnants.

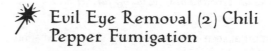

Evil Eye Removal (2) Chili Pepper Fumigation

This smoke can be profoundly irritating, although I suspect that the tears induced were once considered part of the cure. If attempting, be sure to provide proper ventilation.

1. Gather dust from a crossroads.
2. Sprinkle this on lit charcoals.
3. Burn a chili pepper on top of the crossroads dirt.
4. Let the smoke pervade the room so as to envelope the afflicted child and the area.

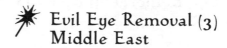

Evil Eye Removal (3) Middle East

There are slight variations in this Middle Eastern spell depending upon the religion of the caster. Muslim tradition suggests adding a piece of tamarisk to the pan, while Christian tradition recommends palm blessed on Palm Sunday.

1. Place chunks of alum, salt, frankincense, and the wood into a hot pan on the fire
2. Lead the child around the pan seven times.
3. As soon as anything pops or cracks in the pan, the spell has been broken.

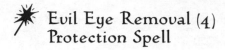

Evil Eye Removal (4) Protection Spell

If you feel the Evil Eye has been cast on a child, this spell removes the Eye and also wards off further attack.

1. Cut off a piece of the clothing the child was wearing at the time of attack. (If you're not sure what he or she was wearing, cut a small piece of cloth from an undergarment.)
2. Burn this together with salt. (Optional ingredients that will intensify the spell are alum, coriander seeds or any botanical used to repel the Eye, such as rue or henna. However, only salt is necessary in order to be effective.)
3. Fumigate the child with the resulting smoke and/or sprinkle the child with the cooled ashes.

Evil Eye Removal (5) Red and Black Rice

Dye white rice red and black in order to cast this spell.

1. Pluck three straws out of a new, unused broom.
2. Light them.
3. Pass the smoking broom-straws around the child's head; then let the straws burn out.
4. Rub your fingers in the broom straw ashes and use them to mark the child's forehead.
5. Mix the dyed rice with some white camphor, salt, and chili peppers. Add some of the victim's hair and nail parings. (If you know for sure who inflicted the Eye, you may add their intimate articles, too.) Lastly

add some Earth, either taken from beneath or near the front door or graveyard dirt from the grave of an advocate for the child.

6. Pass all the items around the child, and then throw them into a fire. The resulting aroma should be thick, pungent, and irritating. If it behaves as expected, this means the cure has been affected. If, however, there is no aroma or if it's weak, you're facing a tough case. Further action must be taken.

Evil Eye Removal (6) Salt

1. Take a handful of salt.
2. Pass it around the child's head and body.
3. Throw a bit into each corner of the home and the rest over the threshold and out the door.

Evil Eye Removal (7) Seven Pebbles

1. Take seven pebbles from a three-way crossroads.
2. Heat them in a fire.
3. Have the ailing child sit before this fire.
4. Place a brass dish containing turmeric water between the child and the fire.
5. With tongs, remove each pebble from the fire and pass it around the child. Then place the pebble into the dish. When the water becomes red, the spell has been broken.

If the water doesn't become red, further action is needed.

Fertility: Spells for Conception and Contraception

Magic spells are cast to obtain many benefits: wealth, luck, true love or a passionate lover, renewed health, enhanced psychic power. However, the subject it is most primordially and intrinsically involved with is human fertility.

Although it's often suggested that religion and mysticism emerged in response to the mysteries of death, the very opposite may be the case. The earliest religions, characterized by veneration of images of the human genitals, were fascinated by the mysteries of birth and life and generative power. Clues are imbedded in our language: the word "venerate" stems from the same roots as Venus, venerable, and venereal.

This fascination with generation remains crucially integral to magic. After all, what does a magic spell usually attempt to do but create something new, something that previously didn't exist? The Spirits most involved with magic (Hecate, Artemis, Yemaya, Baba Yaga, Freya, Oshun, Aine, and so many others) invariably are involved with human reproductive capacities as well.

Themes of sexual reproduction echo throughout magic. Magical instruments most frequently double as fertility motifs as well: mortars and pestles, sieves, cauldrons, broomsticks, not to mention phallic wands ands staffs, derive their power from associations with human generative power. Humans can generate babies and humans can generate magic.

To some extent, even the term *sex magic* is redundant: ultimately the sexual act *is* a magical act, although like everything else, it can be performed badly, degraded, abused, and unappreciated. Violence and coercion destroy all trace of the sacred.

This isn't to suggest that magic is all about being fruitful and multiplying. The emphasis is on control over reproductive cycles so that the individual retains health and happiness. Magic provides a vast repertoire of spells for fertility. The earliest magical systems are also intrinsically connected to the earliest medical systems: holistic systems don't rigidly distinguish between the two. Great emphasis was also placed on botanicals to prevent and sometimes end pregnancy when it wasn't desired. Many of the most famous and ancient witch-spirits like Hecate, Kybele, Artemis, and Baba Yaga are also master herbalists. Perhaps fertility spells are best understood as reproductive

Despite all this talk of sex and procreation, fertility spells aren't limited to people wishing to have children. They may be used to enhance and stimulate artistic creativity as well as actual conception and birth. Adapt these spells to suit your needs.

control spells; spells designed to permit conception when and if one desired.

Fertility is a capacity that exists so that it may be drawn upon as desired and when desired. In a sense that capacity for fertility is synonymous with one's capacity for magic. You may not wish to cast magic spells every day but you want the power to do so when you choose. Likewise you may not wish to become pregnant this year or ever, but if you change your mind, you want the capacity to fulfill your desires.

Despite tales of legendary fish with such intense fertility power that even virgins and men who consume them conceive, there is not one spell here for a virgin birth. Fertility magic requires sex: it is a given that any spells are accompanied by the actual act of procreation. No matter how powerful your magic, no matter how splendid and rare your materials, if you're not accompanying fertility spells with well-timed sex, they can't work.

Spells for Conception

The boundaries between magic and traditional botanical medicine are often fluid; nowhere is this more true or crucial than in fertility magic. Please consult the section in the *Elements of Magic Spells* regarding botanical safety. Botanicals, unlike

visualizations for instance, always have an actual physical effect on the body. Many botanicals used to promote fertility in the seriously infertile are unsafe during pregnancy, especially early pregnancy. Be very careful and choose your spells wisely. Topical application of an herb, for instance in baths or massage oils, may have effects as strong as or even stronger than internal application. *As a general rule, essential oils are not safe during pregnancy, especially early pregnancy.*

Animals of Fertility

Animal of Fertility Spell: Fly

I know an old woman who swallowed a fly,
I don't know why she swallowed a fly …

Well, yes, we do know why. It was once believed that women could conceive by swallowing flies. Fairy-tale heroes are often conceived in this manner.

Flies were understood as souls of the dead looking for a new incarnation. Souls were once believed able to travel between lives in insect form. The original Baal-Zebub, Philistine spirit and psychopomp, later demonized as Beelzebub, was not only Lord of the Flies but also Shepherd of Souls, leading them to new incarnations.

1. Incorporate this imagery into spell visualization, to help manifest your desires in reality. No, don't swallow real flies: find more appetizing ones.
2. Mold marzipan or chocolate into the shape of flies.
3. Swallow one per visualization and see yourself filled with the soul of the child you desire.

 ## Animal of Fertility Spell: Frog

A more active fertility spell incorporates the use of Zuni carved fetishes. A frog fetish is required; one carved from shell is especially potent for this purpose.

1. Bring the frog to bed with you; otherwise keep it in a jar or bag.
2. Feed it at regularly scheduled intervals to activate and maintain its power. Traditionally corn pollen was offered but bits of food may also be used, or whatever inspiration suggests.
3. Speak to the frog; tell it your heart's desires.

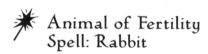 ## Animal of Fertility Spell: Rabbit

Modern Halloween cards invariably depict the witch accompanied by a black cat, but once upon a time witches' familiars were a varied lot. The most popular familiar during the Burning Times was believed to be a rabbit. This association derives from the rabbit's perceived affinity with the moon (many cultures see a rabbit in the moon) and as the totem animal belonging to many spirits of women's primal power. And we all know the habits of the rabbits …

This is an easy, discreet spell: begin to collect rabbit images. Surround yourself with them. Keep silent about your intent, why *you're collecting them. Discussing it weakens the spell. Others collect images of bears, pigs, dwarfs or fairies, so why not rabbits? The rabbits will eventually begin to come to you, multiplying as rabbits are wont to do. During the Full Moon, take your rabbits*

outside, *cast a circle of them, sit inside, exposed to the moonbeams, and see yourself multiplying, too.*

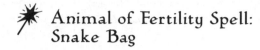 ## Animal of Fertility Spell: Snake Bag

In the tale of Adam and Eve in the Garden of Eden, the snake isn't necessarily the third party. Once upon a time, some say, snakes were believed, metaphorically and magically at least, to possess the power to impregnate women and activate conception. Whether that's true or not, snakes remain profoundly affiliated with women's fertility and general reproductive health. A woman's snake power is her fertility power. This amulet bag attempts magical activation.

Very many botanicals are named in honor of serpents, so many they lead to confusion. Many are used therapeutically to remedy various aspects of women's reproductive health; however, this is a magic spell. Merely carry the botanicals, do not consume. Many of these botanicals are unsafe if consumed by pregnant women and no medicine should be used without expert supervision.

Gather as many as you can and carry in an iridescent beaded bag. Botanicals include the two black snake roots—black cohosh and Serpentaria—rattlesnake root, rattlesnake master, adders tongue, snake weed (bistort), snake head, and many others. If you find an unnamed root or twig that resembles a serpent, add that too. Snake charms and carved stone fetishes may also be incorporated. A piece of freely shed snakeskin may be added as well. Carry the bag to enhance and boost fertility and psychic power. Sleep with it beneath your pillow.

✳ Animal of Fertility Spell: Snake Bag Extra Strength

Carrying the bag described above is allegedly sufficient. However, a more active spell may also be cast.

1. Carry the bag during the day and sleep with it at night, as described above.
2. Once a week, however, preferably on a Friday, take the items out of your bag and play with them. Examine them, handle them, murmur over them, make wishes with them.
3. Dress with one drop of milk or red wine and then put the objects back for the week.

✳ Animal of Fertility Spell: Snake Bag Spirit Spell

Creation of the bag and handling it may both be extremely effective; however, you can up the ante by incorporating spiritual petition.

1. As you create your bag, simultaneously create a snake altar.
2. Use serpentine images as a focal point, whether of the Minoan snake goddess, Mami Waters, a naga, Maitresse Ezili in her water snake form, another of the serpentine lwas or any other image that resonates with you. A photograph, candle, or statue of an actual snake may also be used.
3. Burn coiled snake candles on the altar. Offer the snakes dishes of milk and treasure.
4. Put doll babies on the altar to help manifest your desire. Activate your charms and conjure bag by leaving them on the altar overnight.
5. If the snakes inspire you to dance, do so.

Astarte Oil

The name "*Astarte*" is believed to mean "*the filled womb.*" The name may refer to an independent deity or it may be another name for the Semitic deity, Anat. Either way, the authors of the Bible viewed her with reprobation; she held a notorious reputation for encouraging erotic rites and independent women. The oil named in her honor is believed to promote personal fertility.

> Essential oil of coriander
> Essential oil of jasmine
> Essential oil of myrrh
> Essential oil of petitgrain or neroli
> Rose attar

Blend all the ingredients above into a bottle filled with sweet almond and jojoba oils. If desired, add cowries or henna twigs and blossoms to the oil.

Because many essential oils are not safe during pregnancy, especially in the first months, reserve this oil for magical uses such as dressing candles and charms.

✳ Astarte Oil Spell (1) Candle Dressing

1. Obtain a human figure candle that represents you.
2. Carve it with your name, birthday, identifying information, affirmations, and desires.
3. Dress the candle with Astarte Oil, particularly the abdominal and genital areas.
4. An optional step is to roll the candle in henna powder.
5. Burn the candle.

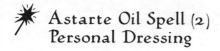 ## Astarte Oil Spell (2) Personal Dressing

Many botanicals that influence fertility appear to create a balance: they encourage fertility if you're not pregnant but can have the opposite effect if you are. If you're sure you're not pregnant, rub the oil on your thighs prior to sex to magically enhance possibility of conception.

All Astarte Oil spells may be accompanied by spiritual petition directed towards Astarte.

Basil Spells

Basil is considered a fertility promoter both physically and symbolically. A tea made from its leaves relieves suppressed menstruation. It is also a traditional component of infertility repair magic spells.

 ## Basil Spell (1) Living Plants

Basil's very presence is believed to enhance fertility. Plant basil around the home or maintain abundant potted plants. Place basil plants in window boxes or beside the door to signal your wish for fertility to Earth's spirit forces.

 ## Basil Spell (2) Basil Boughs

Hang fragrant boughs of basil over the bed to enhance successful conception. Keep the basil fresh, green, and aromatic: replace with fresh boughs as needed.

 ## Basil Spell (3) Fertility Diet

Add basil to your diet—a perfect excuse for pesto. Dine on basil and make love by the light of red candles.

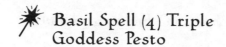 ## Basil Spell (4) Triple Goddess Pesto

An even more potent fertility pesto is concocted from three types of fertility-associated herbs. Each of the herbs is associated with at least one powerful fertility goddess.

Basil (Ezili Freda Dahomey, Lakshmi)
Lemon Balm (Aphrodite)
Parsley (Persephone)
Pine nuts or walnuts
Garlic
Olive oil
Optional: Parmesan cheese

1. From the perspective of a traditional spell-caster, to maximize the symbolic value of the spell, the herbs should be ground the old-fashioned way, using a mortar and pestle, whose parts and process mimic the procreative act. However, if you lack the patience, blend and chop the herbs using a food processor.
2. Add the nuts and as much garlic as you like.
3. When these dried ingredients have been processed, add olive oil a little bit at a time, mixing and blending until the desired consistency has been achieved. Some prefer a paste-like pesto while others prefer it more liquid and oily.
4. Traditionally served over pasta, pesto may also be used to dress fish and meat. Cover with plastic and store in the refrigerator until you're ready to use it. Mix Parmesan cheese into the blended sauce, if desired, just prior to serving.

Bed Spells

The bed is the altar on which magical rites occur. Treat it the way you would any sacred altar: spiritually cleansing, ornamenting, and empowering it, demarcating it as enchanted space. Spells incorporate the conjugal bed as a way of promoting fertility.

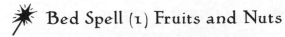 Bed Spell (1) Fruits and Nuts

A recommendation from the time of the Chinese Han dynasty (206 BCE–220 CE) is to scatter dates and chestnuts on the bed to stimulate conception. The presence of the dates and chestnuts on the bed stimulates the aura of fertility; however, making love on the bed before removing them or changing the sheets can be incorporated into the spell.

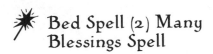 Bed Spell (2) Many Blessings Spell

Another legendary tradition is attributed to one of the emperors of the Tang Dynasty: gold and silver coins were thrown onto the marriage bed of his favorite daughter to stimulate fertility, magnetically attract wealth, and provide protection.

Bed Spell (3) Talisman

Making love amidst nuts and coins may not be that comfortable. Incorporate coin cures in a more convenient way.

Tie strings of Chinese replica coins (I-Ching coins) to the bedposts or hang them on the wall beside the bed. Coins are easily purchased already strung together, however the spell will be more potent if you attach the coins to red silk thread, tying your desire and affirmation into each knot. Either way, hold the coins in your hand and focus to charge them.

Bed Spell (4) Cowries

Cowrie shells were once used as currency in Asia and Africa. They were also used as coins in China before metal coins. Substitute cowries for metal coins, and string them onto red silk cord, tying desires into every knot. Hang the string of shells from bedposts or over the bed.

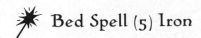 Bed Spell (5) Iron

The bed itself can impact fertility. An iron bed offers spiritual protection against all dangers of the night while generating and radiating fertility energy while you sleep.

For maximum effectiveness fumigate the bed with cleansing incense, hang charms and talismans from the bed, and spend a lot of time lying in it.

Berber Herbal Spell

In traditional Berber herbalism, Spanish lavender and/or germander gathered in the morning prior to sunrise, especially on New Year's Day, provides many health benefits.

They may also be used to concoct a women's fertility remedy.

1. Dry the herbs in the sun, pound them, and mix them with honey.
2. Eat them in the morning on an empty stomach.

Bloodstone Spells

Bloodstone, despite its name, is neither bright red nor the faded brown of dried blood. It's a green stone, flecked with red, and earned its name because it was believed beneficial to various blood disorders as well as to halt bleeding. The stone is the talisman of Isis and is among the crystal gemstones most associated with fertility. It is especially potent as a magical fertility charm when carved into a Tet amulet (the Buckle of Isis); however, even uncut bloodstone emits radiant fertility power.

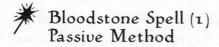 Bloodstone Spell (1)
Passive Method

Keep bloodstone close to the body to absorb its fertility energy.

★ Wear bloodstone jewelry
★ Carry it in your pocket
★ Carry it in a charm bag

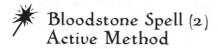 Bloodstone Spell (2)
Active Method

1. Lay pieces of bloodstone directly over the womb and ovaries to heal and stimulate fertility.
2. Lie quietly and leave the bloodstone in place for at least 30 minutes.
3. This is most potent if timed to coincide with the exact phases of the moon—New Moon, Full Moon, and quarters.

Botanicals of Fertility

Plants containing extra magical fertility-boosting power often reveal themselves by their resemblance to human genitalia, affiliation with the moon, or by the extravagant quantity of their seeds. These plants include: assorted snake roots, black-eyed peas, corn, figs, jasmine, lilies, lotuses, melons, moonflowers, mugwort, assorted nuts, olives, pomegranates, poppies, pumpkins, roses, and wheat.

 Botanical Fertility
Bistort Spell

Bistort is also known as dragonwort or snakeweed. Carry the dried root to promote conception.

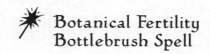 Botanical Fertility
Bottlebrush Spell

Place bottlebrush blossoms in the bedroom to promote fertility.

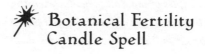 Botanical Fertility
Candle Spell

Hollow out the inside of a vulva-shaped candle. Stuff it full of a selection of basic botanicals of fertility. (Fruits and vegetables are highly represented among these; use leaves, flowers, and dried seeds rather than the fruit or vegetable itself.) Then burn the candle.

Candle Spells

Candle magic may be used to stimulate fertility and pregnancy. Red candles are typically chosen for fertility spells. Any candle may be used, but figure candles may be particularly appropriate: either an individual human figure, to represent the spellcaster, or a joint male-and-female figure candle. Other powerful candle choices include red cats and red witches as well as snake candles and candles in the shape of hearts or genitalia.

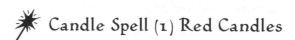 Candle Spell (1) Red Candles

British folk healers recommend burning red candles before, during and after sex to enhance chances of conception. (If you're really serious about getting pregnant, just keep those red candles burning whenever it's safe and appropriate.) Although you can if you like, it's not even necessary to carve and dress the candles; just keep them burning brightly.

Although this spell stands alone, it can also be incorporated into any other fertility spell as extra enhancement.

Candle Spell (2) Red Witch

The traditional image of the Halloween witch still proudly displays the emblems of women's reproductive magic: womb-like iron cauldron and triangular peaked hat. When witches weren't riding on broomsticks, whose form unites the principles of male and female generative energy, they rode through the sky in mortars and pestles like Baba Yaga, or set sail at sea in sieves, oyster shells and egg-shells, all images of women's reproductive power, and all components of fertility spells.

Candles in the shape of red witches may represent a literal woman or witch, but they are also used to represent women's primal magical powers, the metaphysical traditions deriving from the mysteries of birth and menstruation. The red witch possesses long forgotten and suppressed magical secrets that might perhaps assist you in your quest, whatever it is. Burn red witch candles to tap into that power and discover the magical secrets and power hidden within you.

1. Write your deep needs or desires on a piece of paper.
2. Carve and dress a red witch candle, using Astarte Oil or another oil of your choice.
3. Place the paper under the witch and burn the candle.
4. When the candle has burned down completely, bury all spell remnants in Earth or carry them in a mojo bag tied around your waist.

Cowrie Shell Spells

Because seashells come from the sea, and because the sea is perceived as a font of fertility power, any seashell radiates and transmits that power. However, some shells are more powerful than others, especially those bearing the closest resemblance to the vulva.

No shell has more associations with fertility than the cowrie. Cowrie shell belts worn over the reproductive area are among the most ancient human artifacts. Because they've been unearthed still adorning the remains of prehistoric bodies in Northern Europe, as well as in Asia and Africa, we know how they were used, as well as that they were valued objects of trade.

Cowrie Spell (1)

String cowrie shells into a belt long enough to wear over your hips. (They should fall over the ovaries and inner reproductive organs.) Tie your intentions into each knot. Wear the belt whenever and however you like, but for maximum effectiveness wear your belt under the Full Moon.

Cowrie Spell (2)

Stitch cowrie shells onto a strip of scarlet silk long enough to wear across your reproductive region.

Cucumber Spell

There's a whole genre of jokes regarding why cucumbers are better than men. In this case, however, the cucumber can only enhance fertility, not substitute for a male partner.

1. Keep a cucumber in the bedroom.
2. Replace with a fresh cucumber every week or whenever the cucumber stops looking or smelling fresh and healthy.

This spell only works if the cucumber is kept whole.

Date Spells

This is a two-part spell for a couple that wishes to conceive. Either part of the spell may be cast independently, but they work best in conjunction.

 Date Spell (1)

This allegedly boosts a woman's reproductive capacity: a man feeds dates by hand to the woman he hopes will be the mother of his children. Reserve and cleanse the date pits to be used in Date Spell 2.

 Date Spell (2)

The man should now carry the cleansed date pits in a red conjure bag for enhanced fertility and sexual power. (Although a similar spell exists for enhanced virility alone, his fertility is allegedly unaffected unless he has actually put the dates into the woman's mouth.)

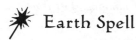 Earth Spell

Once upon a time, women engaged in magic ritual to enhance the fertility of the Earth. If you're in need, Earth can repay the favor. However, not all dirt is believed to possess equal fertility-activating magic power.

1. Gather a handful of dirt from near the doorway of a bordello.
2. Gather a handful of dirt that's been dislodged (dug up) by a bull's horns.
3. Gather a handful of dirt that's been dislodged by a boar's tusks.
4. Place them in a red conjure bag and carry with you.

 Earth Spell Enhanced

This spell derives from traditional offerings to the Hindu deity, Durga. Durga, warrior spirit of protection, rides upon a tiger, doing battle with demons.

Create the bag as above, but as part of a petition of fertility directed toward Durga. Bring it to one of her shrines or dedicate it to her upon a personal altar.

Egg Spells

Eggs, for obvious reasons, rank among the most ancient and powerful of fertility symbols, and are incorporated into many spells.

 Egg Spell (1) Candle

Create your own strong, powerful egg.

1. First make the candle mold: gently punch a small hole in the large end of a raw egg.
2. Use a cuticle scissor to cut a small circle of eggshell. (Buy a dozen eggs; you may have to practice a bit.)
3. Empty the egg into a bowl: use as desired.
4. Gently wash the inside of the shell with water. The membrane and all contents must be thoroughly removed. Allow it to dry completely.
5. Prepare the wax. (You may also add tiny fertility charms or herbs.)
6. Use the egg carton as a holder. Place the eggshell, hole-end up, in the carton.
7. Pour in liquid wax, reserving a little. (When it's half full, you may add tiny seed beads, charms or herbs if you choose, although the candle is effective without them.) Let the wax harden overnight.
8. Next day: gently heat the reserved wax until liquid.
9. Gently chip away the shell, exposing your candle.
10. Heat an ice pick or similar sharp thin tool: put it through the center of the candle and quickly thread with a wick.
11. Fill the hole with the hot wax.
12. Decorate. Keep as an amulet or to burn in a spell.

Egg Spell (2)

1. With a pin, carefully pierce each end of a raw egg. (In some variants of this spell, the male partner must pierce the holes.)
2. The man and woman kiss.
3. Place the egg between you, holding the egg gently in both mouths, each taking an end. (No hands!)
4. The man blows egg out of the shell into the woman's mouth. (How easy or difficult this is, depends upon egg and people.)
5. She swallows the egg.
6. Carefully set the shell aside. (Don't break it.)
7. Have sex.
8. Whenever you're ready—there's no rush—take the empty eggshell outdoors together and bury it in Earth, at least seven inches deep. (If not possible, bury it in its own flower-pot and enhance with fertility plants.)

 ## Egg Spell (3)

1. Place a pair of eggs in a bowl and cover them with spring water.
2. Place these eggs under your bed.
3. Replace weekly or as soon as they smell bad.

For extra enhancement, add two porcelain frogs to the bowl of water. Keep the water level high enough to keep the frogs immersed.

Egg Spell (4)

Eating an egg with a double yolk, if you can find one, allegedly produces fertility. Likewise, finding a fish within another fish bestows tremendous fertility power. (And if there's a magic ring inside that fish, you're the star of your very own fairy tale and should expect miracles to occur!)

 ## Egg Spell (5)

The creation of an Egg Tree allegedly brings children to the childless. Birch and cherry trees are the traditional choices; however, work with what you have.

1. Decorate eggs and hang them from the tree.
2. For maximum effect, decorate the eggs with images of fertility symbols like triangles, snakes, fruits, and nuts, or dye the eggs red, using conventional paint or food coloring, henna paste or menstrual blood.

 ## Egg Spell (6)

A Greek variant of the Egg Tree makes the goal of the spell very explicit. Instead of hanging eggs from the tree, hang dolls.

1. Collect small baby dolls or handcraft dolls that express your desires.
2. Hang them from the tree and leave them there. They're a gift to the tree, don't take them back; hopefully the tree will use its power to give you a similar gift.

 ## Egg Spell (7)

1. Whisper your secret needs and desires into a raw egg.
2. Talk to the egg or talk into the egg like a tape recorder, however best suits you.
3. Bury the egg in Earth to transmit your desires to the magical powers that be.

*If you prefer, write your wishes onto the eggshell, using either invisible ink or **Dove's Blood ink.***

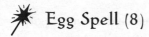 Egg Spell (8)

Write incantations, affirmations, and verses from sacred texts onto hard-boiled eggs before eating them.

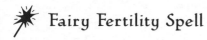 Fairy Fertility Spell

Hawthorn trees are sacred to fairies. Do not remove leaves or wood from the living tree.

1. Gather fallen hawthorn leaves.
2. Make an invocation to the fairies: name your desire. Promise that if this spell works, you'll set up an offering table for them in the birthing room (See *Pregnancy and Childbirth Spells*.)
3. Bring the leaves home and place them beneath your mattress.

 Fertility Crystal Bath

Fill a bath with as much rainwater as possible. Place moonstones and quartz crystals in the tub (make sure the crystals are large enough so there's no danger of falling down the drain!) and bathe, ideally in the moonlight.

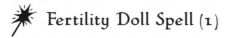 Fertility Doll Spell (1)

The use of dolls to magically enhance fertility and activate conception was once common around the world, from native North America to China, Italy to India. Vestiges of these traditions survive, not least in the dolls that traditionally ornament the wedding cake. Fertility doll magic remains most vital, however, in traditional Africa. Although the style of doll varies, the spell is virtually identical wherever fertility doll magic is practiced.

Create or obtain a doll baby. The doll does not have to be life-like unless it's important to you. Dolls are crafted from wood, clay, nuts, bones, corn cobs, fabric, metal: any conceivable material. If working with a mass-produced doll, embellish it with seashells, beads, seeds, and fertility charms to enhance its power.

This doll is your baby. In Africa, dolls accompany their "mothers" everywhere, sometimes discreetly, sometimes not. The doll is fed, bathed, and cared for every day, never left unattended, as if it were a flesh and blood child. This may be understood in various ways:

★ *The doll is the seed from which the actual child grows*
★ *The spell magically stimulates conception*
★ *Your actions indicate your desire to the spirit powers and also demonstrate what a good mother you'll be, given the opportunity*

Like a real baby, the doll is not abandoned, whether pregnancy occurs or not. The doll may be treated as the resulting child's sibling, or given to the child as a toy or amulet. A successful doll may be passed on to another infertile woman to work its magic, while a doll that is not successful may be buried with its "mother" when she dies.

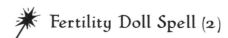 Fertility Doll Spell (2)

This doll may be treated like the doll in the spell above or one may consider it to be a doll-shaped conjure bag.

1. Create a doll from red fabric.
2. Stuff the doll with basic fertility botanicals.
3. Sew the doll up; embellish the outside of the doll with beads, seashells, little mirrors and charms. These may also be buried within the doll.

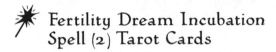

✵ Fertility Dream Incubation Spell (1) Four Jacks

Sometimes the conventional information available regarding your situation isn't sufficient. You need a dream to divine exactly what's going on or to plan your solutions. To incubate a fertility dream remove the four jacks from a brand new deck of playing cards. Place them under your pillow and wish for a dream before going to sleep.

Repeat, using the same cards (you don't need new decks), until you've received the dream required, or until the issue is resolved.

✵ Fertility Dream Incubation Spell (2) Tarot Cards

If you prefer the power and symbolism of the tarot deck, place the following cards under your pillow and follow the directions above:

> The Empress
> The Sun
> The ace of cups

✵ Fertility Incense

1. Gather a pinch of dirt from a fertility shrine or use graveyard dirt from your ancestor's grave.
2. Mix with dried crumbled red rose petals and hibiscus flowers.
3. Sprinkle on lit charcoal and burn.

✵ Fertility Mojos

Conjure bags designed to enhance and empower fertility are treated slightly differently to the standard bag. The standard mojo hand is a red flannel drawstring bag; however, for fertility enhancing purposes, red silk or beaded bags are most potent. You should wear the bag hanging between your breasts or over the abdominal area, rather than carrying in your pocket, and sleep with the bag beneath your pillow or hang it over the bed in which you make love.

✵ Fertility Mojo (1) Shrine Dirt

Create a fertility mojo hand from items radiant with fertility power.

1. Collect pinches of dirt from shrines associated with fertility. These may be shrines dedicated to Spirits of Fertility or areas that naturally radiate fertility power (the menhirs, standing stones, Hawaiian phallic rocks).
2. Place these in a red flannel or silk bag, together with silver charms, seashells, and bits of coral.

For maximum effect, wear this bag around your waist or hips.

✵ Fertility Mojo (2) Dirt Bag

1. Fill a red silk or flannel bag with dirt: pinches taken from a crossroads, graveyard dust from sympathetic ancestors' graves, and also from sites associated with babies: birthing centers, a house with a lot of happy, healthy children, or a successful midwife's home for example.
2. This is a work in progress; begin to carry your bag as soon as you've collected the first pinch of dirt.
3. Supplement with other fertility charms if you like— bits of coral, shell, or silver charms.

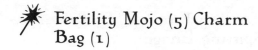 Fertility Mojo (3) Root of
Balance Bag

*Certain botanicals radiate female generative power
while others transmit male power. Sometimes you might
want one or the other, but for purposes of fertility, perfect balance is desired. Charge roots with your magical
intentions and place them in a conjure bag together and
see what transpires.*

1. Add female fertility botanicals to a red silk or flannel
   bag: angelica root or Queen's Delight.
2. Add the male botanicals next: ginseng root or High
   John the Conqueror.
3. Add a plain gold ring to symbolize the union of
   roots. (Use a real wedding band or a dime-store ring:
   the key is that it is gold colored and not
   ornamented.)
4. Carry the bag with you or keep it under your
   mattress.

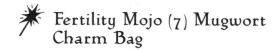 Fertility Mojo (4) M is
for Mother

*Their first initial isn't what really links these particular
botanicals; rather it's their association with fertility and
the moon.*

1. Add the following to a conjure bag:
   Mandrake
   Mistletoe
   Motherwort
   Mugwort
2. Wear or carry as desired.

*Be cautious with mandrake and mistletoe, both are
potentially very toxic.*

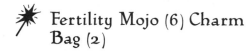 Fertility Mojo (5) Charm
Bag (1)

1. Fill a mojo bag with fertility charms: acorns,
   mistletoe twigs, cowrie shells or pearls, or silver
   charms in the shape of rabbits or moons.
2. This is a spell-in-progress. Add charms as they
   appear.
3. Dress with Astarte Oil for fertility and **Van Van** to
   make your dreams come true.

Fertility Mojo (6) Charm
Bag (2)

*Fill a conjure bag with black-eyed peas, silver fish charms,
iron beads, a Low John root, and jasmine flowers.*

Fertility Mojo (7) Mugwort
Charm Bag

*In Uganda, women carry mugwort in a red silk bag for
enhanced fertility.*

Fertility Potion (1) Couple

*A Romany fertility potion is designed to be shared by
prospective parents together. Time this spell to coincide
with either the New or Full Moon, whichever suits your
reproductive cycles best.*

1. Make an infusion with spring water and comfrey.
2. Combine with equal parts brandy.
3. Pour into a single glass, which the man and woman
   drink together.
4. Drink it in bed; make love immediately afterwards.
5. Repeat three nights in a row.

*If it doesn't work, wait until next month's correspond-
ing moon phase before attempting this method again.*

Fertility Potion (2) Dad's
Spitting Image

A prospective father may choose one of two ways to pre-pare this fertility potion for the prospective mother of his child:

1. Either drop burning hot coals into spring water or spit into it (think of *"spitting image of his father"*).
2. While the woman drinks the water, the man chants:
   I am the flame, you are the coals!
   I am rain, you are the water!

 Fertility Potion (3) Gourd

Sometimes it's not merely the ingredients but the means of preparing the potion that generates magic fertility power:

1. Make a hole in a gourd.
2. Fill it with milk.
3. Bring the milk to a boil. (A double boiler may be required to avoid scorching the milk.)
4. When it cools, drink it or use it to bathe the body, abdomen or vulva.

 Fertility Potion (4) India Moss

The woman who drinks this water as a fertility potion will allegedly never be sterile.

1. Place an India moss crystal gemstone in a glass of water.
2. Leave it overnight.
3. In the morning, remove the crystal and drink the water.

 Fertility Potion (5) Men

A Moroccan potion to increase male fertility and sexual vigor invokes the fertility-inducing prowess of the egg.

1. Break a raw egg every morning and swallow it before breakfast for 40 consecutive days.
2. Immediately after consuming the egg, fill the shell with olive oil and drink.

Results should be apparent at the conclusion of the 40 days.

If the possibility of salmonella gives cause for pause, a different Moroccan recommendation is for men to drink just olive oil alone to enhance the procreative powers.

 Fertility Potion (6)
Rose Hydrosol

True rose hydrosol is used as a woman's fertility potion. You can either drink small portions by itself, or blend rose hydrosol with spring water or champagne and drink.

 Fertility Potion (7) Ruby

1. Place a ruby in a glass and cover it with spring water on the night of the Full Moon.
2. Leave it overnight, exposed to the moonbeams.
3. In the morning, drink the water.

 Fertility Potion (8) New
Well Water

The first water of a new well is charged with extra power and baraka. Therefore the first drink is custom-arily offered to a childless woman as a fertility potion.

Fertility Spell (1) Coconut

Place a coconut on an altar or situated in a focal position in the bedroom to enhance female fertility.

 ## Fertility Spell (2) Fruits

Placed dried longans and lichee fruit under your bed.

 ## Fertility Spell (3) Jack-in-the-Pulpit

Carry the dried root of a Jack-in-the-Pulpit plant as a fertility charm.

 ## Fertility Spell (4) Poppies

Today, poppies are most associated with opium and illicit drugs, however in ancient days poppies' associations with fertility were equally strong. Poppies demonstrate their affinity for human reproduction via their bulging seedpods.

Dry the seedpods. Pierce and string them onto red cord and wear or hang over the bed as a fertility enhancer.

Fertility power, like magical energy is contagious and may be obtained via enchanted methods of transference.

 ## Fertility Transference (1) Birth Process

If you are childless but would prefer not to be, be present in the delivery room during a birth. Allegedly your presence in the room stimulates your own personal fertility. (Conversely, pregnant women should keep away from delivery rooms as their own birth process may be stimulated too soon.)

 ## Fertility Transference (2) Clothes

If you are childless but would prefer not to be, borrow and wear clothing from fruitful women—those with happy, healthy children.

 ## Fertility Transference (3) Death Soap/Corpse Water

Other transference methods have nothing to do with pregnancy and birth; quite the contrary, in fact.

Bathe with the soap and/or water used to cleanse a corpse. Allegedly this transfers some of the recently departed but still lingering life to you. It's crucial for the success of this spell that the deceased was youthful, vital, and clung to life, or that death occurred as a shocking, surprising, traumatic incident.

 ## Fertility Transference (4) Dead Men's Ghosts

Associations between conception and recent death are based on ancient Middle Eastern magical practices. Once upon a time, women wishing to conceive but having trouble doing so would step over freshly executed men, especially hanged men, or walk between rows of murdered men. It's crucial that the corpse cannot have died a peaceful, natural death. The interrupted lifeforce allegedly swirls around looking for a place to re-enter and re-emerge. The woman desiring to conceive provides safe haven.

Similar rites existed in Anglo-Saxon Britain, although, as far as we know, without the stipulation that the death could not be natural.

Fertility Transference (5) Grass Spell

A Hungarian Romany spell for women desiring children but unable to conceive combines a host of fertility powers.

Eat the grass growing on a grave where another woman, who bore children, is buried. Ideally the woman should have died in childbirth. (The child is alive, only the mother is dead.) Grass transmits the integration of lunar and earthly generative power—the moon shines on grass all night; the grass derives earthly power from the dirt.

Even though the woman is dead, her death from childbirth underscores the fact that she could get pregnant, which is the goal of the spell-caster. (Of course, you'll be obliged to perform massive protection spells before delivery, but you'll cross that bridge when you come to it.)

Fertility Transference (6) Bed

According to Ozark Mountain belief, laying babies on a bed is a sure harbinger of new babies to come. If you want a baby, invite family and friends to lay theirs on your bed.

Conversely, if a baby is the last thing you want, do not ever allow anyone to use your bed as a changing table, or permit babies to nap upon it.

Fertility Tree Spells

Trees are particularly associated with fertility. Any tree may have fertility power because of its phallic appearance rising from Earth (or entering her); however, some trees are more associated with generative power than others.

★ *Trees most associated with fertility bear fruit or nuts. The most potent, such as the orange tree, flower and*
fruit simultaneously. Trees bearing fruits and nuts resembling genitalia or somehow suggesting the sexual act are the most potent of all: figs, peaches, pomegranates, and walnuts for instance. Trees with milky sap also radiate fertility power

★ *Willows have particularly strong fertility associations because of their affinity for water, the element most associated with fertility, and also because they are under the dominion of Hecate, Spirit of magic, fertility, and healing*

★ *Certain trees are redolent of fertility because of their associations with specific Spirits of Fertility; the tree is a conduit to the Spirit's power and blessings. Examples include apple trees (Aphrodite) and pines (Dionysus)*

 ## Fertility Tree Spell (1) Basic

To avail yourself of the tree's fertility power, make love under it by the light of the Full Moon. The ritual may be that simple, or you may embellish as you please.

 ## Fertility Tree Spell (2) Personal Relationship

Enhance and intensify any spell by developing a relationship with a specific tree.

1. Choose an existing tree or transplant a grown specimen.
2. Nurture the tree. Develop a relationship with the tree, or with the resident tree spirit or presiding spirit, however you best understand it.
3. Embellish and decorate this tree.
4. Charge fertility amulets, charms, and spell ingredients by hanging them on the tree or placing them at its base overnight, especially in the light of the Full Moon.
5. Offer libations to the tree.
6. Sleep under the tree.
7. If possible, make love under the tree.

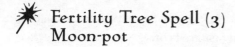
Fertility Tree Spell (3)
Moon-pot

To inaugurate the partnership between yourself and a tree, bury a terracotta pot filled with menstrual blood at the foot of the tree.

Fertility Tree Spell (4)
Transference

This method may also be used to transfer a tree's fertility to you.

1. Bury a terracotta pot filled with menstrual blood at the foot of a particularly fertile tree.
2. Respectfully explain to the tree, in your own words, what you want in return and why you admire this particular tree.

Fertility Tree Spell (5)
Lunar Water

Should a pot filled with menstrual blood be unrealistic for you for any reason, a potent alternative exists.

1. Follow the instructions in the *Elements of Magic Spells* for creating lunar-charged water.
2. Bury a terracotta pot filled with this water at the foot of the tree instead.

A lunar-charged magic mirror into which you've expressed your deepest desires may also be buried at the foot of the tree, although this should be accompanied by some sort of libation as well.

Fertility Tree Spell (6) Apples

Apple trees are sacred to Aphrodite and figure prominently in all spells that fall under her dominion, especially those for love and fertility. Mix water with apple tree sap and wash your face and hands with it.

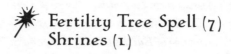
Fertility Tree Spell (7)
Shrines (1)

Miracles may be accomplished at a fertility shrine by speaking with the presiding Spirit and receiving blessings and favors. Sometimes, however, fertility is promoted merely by being in the shrine and Spirit's presence. The goal is to absorb the radiant fertility power present at the shrine into one's own body. Merely being on site may be sufficient; however, other magical means to encourage the transmission and absorption of this power exist.

1. Make a "cradle" from a towel.
2. Place a stone within this cradle, to represent the child of your dreams.
3. Hang the cradle with child on a tree at the shrine, making a personal vow to the saint to be fulfilled if and when your desire is fulfilled.

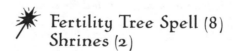
Fertility Tree Spell (8)
Shrines (2)

The Berber spell above makes one's desires very clear and explicit. Conservative Christianity and Islam might frown on such explicit methods: a similar tradition, popular all over Asia and Europe, may derive from older rituals.

1. When you journey to a shrine, bring a rag from home.
2. Carry it in a charm bag around your waist or tucked into your bosom.
3. Keep it with you while you pray, petition or perform spells and rituals.
4. Before you leave, tie it to a tree at the shrine.

Fertility Tree Spell (9) May Pole

The May Pole derives from ancient fertility rites. Create your own rituals with living trees. This spell is extra potent if cast during one of Earth's fertility power days: May Day, Midsummer's Day or Valentine's Day.

1. Wrap scarlet ribbons around a tree, visualizing your desire all the while.
2. Enhance the spell by ornamenting the tree with fertility-inspired charms, small dolls or decorated eggshells.
3. For maximum effect, make love under the tree.

 ## Fertility Tree Spell (10) Rowan

Making love under a rowan tree is allegedly a cure for infertility.

Fertility Tree Spell (11) Willow

Place a willow branch beneath your bed for enhanced chances of conception.

Fig Hand

The fig, an ancient and powerful symbol of fertility, also lends its name to a gesture and amulet: the *"fica"* or fig hand. The fig hand is made by closing the fist and inserting the thumb between the first two fingers. This is both a representation of sex and simulates a pregnant woman. The gesture protects against spiritual dangers, and can be used as a protective device against any danger.

Depictions of the fig hand are also a popular amulet. The material it's carved from determines the purpose of the charm. To serve as a men's amulet for protection of genitals, sperm, virility, and general procreative capacity, wear a small fig hand carved from red coral.

 ## The Real Fig-hand Spell

This spell is allegedly beneficial for either female or male infertility. However, the carving should be done by a woman. Carve a phallus from fig wood and carry it with you.

Gender Spells

Sometimes conception isn't enough. For one reason or another, a child of a specific gender is desired. Various magic spells attempt to fulfill your desires:

★ *To conceive a boy, place a dagger in your headboard*
★ *To conceive a girl, put a dagger in the headboard with a bay laurel wreath around it*
★ *To conceive a boy, place arrows under the bed*
★ *To conceive a boy, charge a small gold knife charm with other yang materials. Wear it as a charm around your neck*
★ *To conceive a girl, place a spindle under the bed or mattress*

 ## Grow-a-Seed Spell

The most basic fertility spell of all may not seem particularly magical to our jaded eyes: grow plants from seed. What has evolved into a child's kindergarten project was once perceived as an act fraught with mystery and magic. Do not transfer mature plants or cuttings: it is crucial that you sprout the seeds and nurture the plants. This may be done directly on Earth or in pots within your home.

The choice of plants is entirely up to you; however, plants that are metaphysically associated with fertility

will increase the power of the spell. Furthermore, time spent in the presence of plants radiant with fertility power can only be beneficial.

Grow plants that can assist you in the quest for conception or plants that will serve as herbal remedies. By doing this, you set up a symbiotic relationship, a true alliance; each of you depends upon the other. Talk to the plant; tell it what you need it to perform for you. Herbal remedies grown in this manner will be more potent than anything you can purchase. Faithfully keep a gardening diary. Eventually within its pages you may discover parallels and clues to your own condition.

Holed Stone Spells

The precious gem most associated with fertility is the ruby. However, precious gems are not the only potent magical fertility tools. The humble holed stone is a powerful fertility booster. Holed stones, also called holey stones or hag stones, are pebbles or small stones containing natural perforations. Only Mother Nature can create them. If you have a holed stone, for fertility purposes:

★ *Wear it around your neck on a red or silver cord*
★ *Hang it from your bed on a red or silver cord*
★ *Carry it in a medicine bag*

✷ Holed Stone Spell (1) Extra Enhancement

1. Sprinkle rosemary on a holed stone, especially in the hole.
2. Carry it in a medicine bag or wear it around your neck.
3. Repeat the ritual to coincide with the New Moon.

✷ Holed Stone Spell (2)

Not all holed stones are small enough to wear around your neck. Europe and the British Isles are dotted with huge standing stone formations, some erected, some natural, some with holes. These holes have traditionally been used for all manner of healing but particularly for providing and enhancing personal fertility. Getting to one of these fertility power spots may be difficult; the ritual is simple.

1. Journey to a holed standing stone.
2. Make your wish, prayer and/or petition.
3. Climb through the hole.

Khonsu's Spells

In myths, the moon is usually perceived as female and represented by female spirits. The ancient Egyptians saw things differently. To them, the moon was male. Many lunar aligned deities were male, too—for example, Thoth and, especially, Khonsu. This doesn't mean that the Egyptians didn't recognize the lunar influence on women's reproductive cycles and pregnancy. Quite the contrary, the moon's powerful effects are precisely *why* they perceived it as male. Who else gets a woman pregnant but a man?

Sleeping exposed to Khonsu's moonbeams was believed to provide the activation necessary for successful pregnancy. That doesn't mean you don't need ordinary sex, too. The moonbeams are the bonus touch that makes pregnancy most likely to occur and be successful. (In medieval Europe, unmarried girls were cautioned against sleeping in moonlight. Now you know why.)

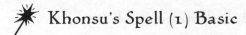 ## Khonsu's Spell (1) Basic

Sleep naked exposed to moonlight, as frequently as possible. Having sex in the moonlight won't hurt either.

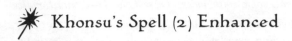 ## Khonsu's Spell (2) Enhanced

The fertilizing influence of moonlight is enhanced by direct petition to Khonsu, Egyptian Lord of the Moon:

1. Build an altar for Khonsu, ideally situated so that it's exposed to moonlight.
2. Offer him lunar-charged waters, dice and images of the moon, baboons, crocodiles, and falcons.

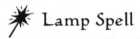 ## Lamp Spell

Lamps are a traditional Chinese symbol of fertility. It's traditional to place a lamp under the nuptial bed to enhance the possibility of conception.

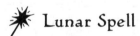 ## Lunar Spell

This spell must be accomplished at the first sighting of the New Moon.

1. Look up at the moon and talk to her.
2. Explain that although she's but a tiny sliver now, you know that she will quickly fill out and grow, charged with power.
3. Tell her that you would like to emulate her and become large and filled with life. (Be explicit: tell her you want to be pregnant and bear a healthy child. The moon also rules water and bloating diseases: if you don't explain precisely how you wish to enlarge, you could be unpleasantly surprised.)
4. Go home and make love.

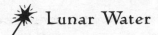 ## Lunar Water

The powers of moon and water are combined and brought into the bedroom.

1. Coinciding with the New Moon, fill a bowl half-full of water. Natural living water is best: sea, river or rain. Use bottled spring water if these are unavailable.
2. Take it outside to absorb moonbeams.
3. Leave it outside for three hours.
4. Bring the bowl inside and place it under the bed, approximately under where the woman lies.
5. Make love over this lunar-charged water.
6. Repeat until the Full Moon.
7. Begin again with fresh water at the New Moon.

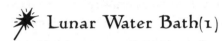 ## Lunar Water Bath(1)

Charge spring water in full moonlight. Toss it into your bathwater or use the direct method: place it in a basin and bathe the vulva.

Lunar Water Bath (2)

1. Bring a tub or pool large enough in which to bathe outside underneath the full moonlight.
2. Fill it with spring water. (If this is unaffordable, at least add substantial quantities of pure spring water to regular tap water.)
3. Get undressed, get into the pool and bathe in the moonlight.

In an ideal world, you'd have a silver basin, with a large seashell for a ladle.

Magic Cake Spell

In Jewish magical traditions, magical cakes are prepared for brides or other women to ensure fertility.

Decorate a round cake or a triangular slice with the woman's name, magic spells, names of power, and sacred texts. The woman should then eat the cake all up.

A favored sacred text to counteract sterility is **Deuteronomy 7:12,** *chosen perhaps for its name* Akriel, *which evokes (or defies?) the Angel of Barrenness. Also the word* berit, *occurring in this verse, is often understood to refer to genitals.*

 Magic Circle Spell

Magic circles provide protection as well as enhanced fertility and romance.

1. Make a circle sunwise around the bed with brandy.
2. Make another circle with coal dust.
3. Make a circle with powdered chalk (or white clay or white flour).
4. Get in the bed and make passionate love.
5. Repeat for three nights consecutively.

 Magic Diagnosis Spell

Testing to determine causes and sources of infertility are far more refined today than ever before; however, a high percentage of infertility is classified as idiopathic, *meaning no known reason can be determined. If that's your situation, magical diagnostic tests may put you on the path toward discovering personal solutions. This magic fertility test derives from North Africa and is reminiscent of fertility tests from ancient Egypt. It attempts to determine which partner is the source of the obstacle.*

1. Make two small piles of sawdust.
2. Each partner urinates on only one pile. Remember which is which.

3. Wait seven days then examine the piles.

If a pile exhibits any signs of life—worms, insects or such—don't be disgusted. This is a positive response, indicating excellent potential for fertility. In contrast, a barren, lifeless pile indicates the need for work to remove and heal obstructions. If both piles are barren, this indicates that both systems need some serious warming up.

Mandrake

Mandrake root has extremely ancient associations with fertility, with its use recorded in ancient Egypt and the Bible. It is under the dominion of powerful spirits: Aphrodite, Hathor, and Hecate. Mandrake also has aphrodisiac properties. However, in all cases it is used as a charm. Mandrake is potentially very toxic: do not take it internally or apply it to the body.

True mandrake is extremely rare: other plants, most typically May Apple, are sold under the name *mandrake* and substituted for the authentic article. The real root bears a strong resemblance to the human anatomy. There are male and female mandrakes: which one you possess should be immediately, visibly identifiable.

 Mandrake Spells (Basic)

★ *Carry mandrake root as a charm*
★ *Place a mandrake under the bed, mattress or pillow for enhanced sex and fertility*

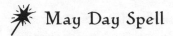 Mandrake Spell Enhanced

An ancient image of Hathor, spirit of magic, pleasure, fertility, and women's power, depicts her wearing an enchanted necklace formed from mandrake and poppies (which is also a fertility plant, because of its abundant seeds; both plants also have narcotic properties, in addition to other similarities, although they are botanically distinct).

Reproduce and wear Hathor's magic fertility power necklace, either with real plants (incorporating knot magic into the necklace's creation), with a henna design, or you could create a beaded or bejeweled version. For maximum effectiveness, wear the necklace while making love.

May Eve/Beltane/Walpurgis Spells

Earth's sexual forces are at their peak on May 1st, May Day, and the preceding Eve, also known as Walpurgis Night. Both night and day are associated with witchcraft, spells, and the successful accomplishment of fertility rites. Celts celebrated this day as Beltane, the festival that honors the fertility power inherent in all life. It is an excellent time to attempt conception. Even without immediate success, you are harmonizing your own fertility energy with all Earth's natural powers.

 Beltane Bonfire Spell

Beltane rituals are still held. Traditionally bonfires are lit. To heal infertility, people creep through bonfires, jump over them, and run between them. Once upon a time, they also made love amongst the bonfires, although to avail yourself of this power you may have to build private, personal fires.

May Day Spell

May Day is the holy day belonging to the Roman spirit of flowers and happy sex, Flora. She may also be petitioned for fertility, especially if infertility treatment and sex on demand has dampened the joys of the sexual experience.

1. Request healing, happiness, and access to life's pleasures.
2. Flora is beckoned with fresh flowers: she especially favors lupines. Her sacrament, the gift that you can give her, is blissful sex. (All rites for Flora are traditionally performed nude.)

Melon Spell

A Chinese fertility spell requires the assistance of sympathetic friends. Friends of an infertile couple steal a melon (and apparently it must be a theft), dress it in baby clothes, and give it to the couple. This must be secret, not prearranged, although in exchange the couple is supposed to provide a reasonably lavish dinner for the helpful thieves.

This is most powerful if performed on the fifteenth day of the eighth month of the Chinese lunar calendar, the birthday of Lady Chang'o, the resident woman on the moon.

Midsummer's Spells

Midsummer's Eve coincides with the Eve of the feast day of Saint John the Baptist. The date also coincides with the Summer Solstice, the height of the sun's powers, and the ancient Roman festival of Ceres, spirit of Earth's generosity. The date has powerful associations with fertility rites, as exemplified by the bonfires traditionally lit on Midsummer's Eve or Saint John's Day.

These bonfires and accompanying fertility rites were once common throughout Europe.

Midsummer's Eve is also sacred to the Irish solar deity, Aine, a spirit of love and fertility, and the day has strong Celtic associations. The fertility aspect of the holiday, especially the bonfires, was very popular throughout the Mediterranean, especially in Greece, Italy, and Spain but also across the water in Algeria, Morocco, and Tunisia, although there associations are made with Fatima rather than Saint John.

Among the reasons given for the bonfires during the Middle Ages was that they prevented dragons of the air from their annual revelry, which inevitably concluded in wanton copulation in the skies and the subsequent pollution of springs and wells from drops of dragon ejaculate.

Another theory is that the John the Baptist celebrated amidst fertility rites is not the ascetic John the Baptist who wandered the Judean wilderness wearing his mugwort belt, living on locusts and wild honey, and performing baptisms in the Jordan River. Instead the ancient Semitic fertility spirit Adonis may be lurking underneath, wearing the syncretized mask of the respectable saint.

Although the date itself is propitious for any fertility magic, it's the bonfires, the revelry among them and the attendant herbs that hold particular value.

✳ Midsummer's Spells (1) Basic

Making love among the bonfires is believed extremely auspicious for fertility. However, as public sex hasn't been condoned in centuries, build your own private bonfire to celebrate the day and conduct private revels.

✳ Midsummer's Spells (2)

Customarily at least one pair of large bonfires is built. These bonfires are also beneficial for other forms of healing, but their associations with fertility are strong.

Couples or individuals desiring fertility run between the fires.

Jump over the bonfires; childless couples should jump over bonfires together, holding hands, to repair, rejuvenate, and revitalize fertility.

✳ Midsummer's Spells (3)

Not just any random plants are arbitrarily chosen for the bonfire. Traditionally specific, strongly aromatic plants are used: chamomile, chervil, pennyroyal, rue, Saint John's Wort, thyme, geranium (the fragrant herb, not the bright red flower), and mugwort. When burned, their smoke radiates fertility power.

1. Expose yourself to the smoke of the bonfires.
2. If this isn't possible, choose a selection of Midsummer's herbs, grind and powder them and burn them as Midsummer's Eve incense.

Warning: Make sure that you are not pregnant; several of the herbs may positively influence obstructed fertility but are not safe for use or exposure during pregnancy itself.

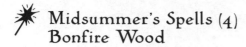 ## Midsummer's Spells (4)
Bonfire Wood

Although bonfires are built from herbs in the Mediterranean region, Celtic regions of Europe may build bonfires of carefully chosen wood. This version, for example, suggests nine sacred Druid woods.

Build the fires using the following woods:

> Apple
> Ash
> Birch
> Elm
> Hawthorne
> Hazel
> Oak
> Rowan
> Thorn

Collect the ashes once the fires have burned out.

 ## Midsummer's Spells (5)

Midsummer's bonfire ashes retain magic power. Fill charm bags with the ashes and carry them for good fortune, healing, and renewed fertility.

 ## Midsummer's Spell (6)

Midsummer's ashes can also be incorporated into more active magic spells. Gather some up and bring them home. Sprinkle them on the sheets and make love. Or use the ashes to cast a circle around the bed and make love.

 ## Midsummer's Spells (7)

If bonfires are not realistic for you, fertility power is also traditionally gained by walking around naked in your vegetable or flower garden on Saint John's Eve.

 ## Midsummer's Spells (8)

Balkan Gypsies suggest that if you gather flowers on Midsummer's Eve and burn them that night, their ashes will substitute for Midsummer's bonfires.

 ## Midsummer's Spells (9)

Many plants are believed at the height of their powers on Midsummer's Day. Gather them on that day for future use.

1. Gather mugwort on Midsummer's Eve.
2. Wind it into a girdle or crown and wear it during revelries.
3. At some point, when you're ready, make a wish and throw the mugwort garland into the bonfires.

Menhirs

Many believe that erected standing stones were placed (obviously with tremendous effort) over specific spots to mark the special powers emanating from that point on Earth. This is also believed true for that other stone formation, the *menhirs* of France. Rather than passing through stones, however, power is accessed by sitting on the menhirs.

 ## Menhir Spell (1)

Once upon a time, the recommendation was to sit on menhirs while naked, but once upon a time, there was more privacy and fewer legal restrictions. Sitting on the stones in a loose skirt without wearing underwear may provide the best of both worlds.

✳ Menhir Spell (2)

Midsummer's Eve revels were once held among the menhirs and sometimes still are. Making love amidst the stones on that night is said to bring tremendous fertility power and Earth's blessings on your union.

Milagros

"*Milagros*" means "*miracles*" in Spanish. It's the term now most popularly used to refer to the ancient custom of *ex-votos*. The magical concept of reciprocity figures extremely prominently in the Spiritual petition process:

★ One requests a favor or blessing, sometimes offering a gift to mark the request but always specifying what will be paid for receipt of the requested "miracle"
★ Having received the favor or blessing, one then renders payment

It is wisest to maintain control over two areas of this process: inform the Spirit precisely what blessing or favor is desired. Inform them specifically and explicitly in what form payment will be made and precisely when.

Milagros are used for both purposes. Milagros are tiny depictions, usually but not always formed from metal, of the part of the anatomy that needs repair or healing. These are traditionally brought to the shrine at the same time as a petition is made. The concept of the milagro or ex-voto is ancient. They have been found in Greek, Celtic, and Iberian healing shrines. Prehistoric objects that are dead ringers for ex-votos have also been discovered, although without context or explanation it's impossible to prove what they are. The custom remains most vigorous in Latin America. Shrines typically have an area reserved for you to pin your own ex-voto, either a velvet-covered board or sometimes on the votive image itself, particularly if the image is associated with miracle cures.

Milagros are also offered to offer testimonial of miracles received. This often evolves into payment for the desired miracle. A cheap metal or wax charm is initially offered, with the promise that if the miracle is received, a golden charm, miniature or life-sized, will be then presented.

Specific milagros represent specific ailments. A pair of metal eyes is donated for eye trouble. A leg or an arm is offered in exchange for healing the appropriate appendage.

Shapes representing fertility and the quest for a child are both literal and metaphoric:

★ *Uterus*
★ *Ovaries*
★ *Heart (not an anatomically correct heart but the Valentine's Day shape), because it can be synonymous with vulva and because it represents the love you'd offer a child*
★ *A baby*
★ *A hedgehog (because of the old European belief that the womb resembles a hedgehog)*

If you have no access or belief in shrines, tie rags or milagros to your own tree or well.

Charge the charms with your desire by any or all of the following methods:

1. Holding them in your hands and concentrating hard on your desire.
2. Sleeping with them under your pillow.
3. Weeping onto them until they're wet from your tears.
4. Carrying in a mojo bag for seven days and nights, until charged with your personal energy.

Mistletoe Charms

According to Pliny, a piece of mistletoe carried as amulet helps woman conceive. This corresponds with other traditional beliefs regarding this botanical parasite. Mistletoe was perceived as being in a category all its own. Although it lives on trees, it's not a tree. Although it's like a plant, it doesn't grow in either Earth or water. It is potentially very poisonous and should not be taken internally, but it has myriad uses as a fertility charm. Mistletoe berries resemble tiny golden moons enhancing the lunar and fertility symbolism.

★ *Carve fertility charms from mistletoe wood; carry them or attach a pin and wear as a brooch*
★ *The most powerful mistletoe jewelry is embellished with pearls*

⁕ Mistletoe Spell

Mistletoe hung over doorways at Yule is for kissing. Mistletoe hung over the bed anytime is for pregnancy. Be careful: mistletoe's berries and leaves can be poisonous. This is not an appropriate spell for households with children and pets.

⁕ Moon Blood Fertility Spell

Women who hope not to be pregnant feel relief when their monthly period arrives. For women who had hoped to finally be pregnant the first stirrings of menstruation lead only to grief and depression. Modern Western culture perceives menstruation as the antithesis of pregnancy, its opposite. Once upon a time, however, menstrual blood was understood as the force that activated conception. Menstruation was the flower, the necessary precursor to the fruit of the womb.

1. Create a doll baby from real, not synthetic, clay. If you can dig it out of the Earth yourself, so much the better.
2. Dab it with your own menstrual blood to magically activate the doll.

3. Allow the doll to dry. The doll may be carried as a fertility charm; it may also be incorporated into doll magic spells.

Moon Magic Fertility Spell

The ancient's noticed that not every sexual act resulted in conception. The moon was considered the magical third party in the conception equation; pregnancy was believed to occur as a result of the moon's powers of fertility activation. Thirteen is the number of months in one lunar year and is a number sacred to many spirits of primal female power.

Once upon a time priestesses danced widdershins (anticlockwise) around the New and Full Moon, often in groups of thirteen. Dance among friends or dance by yourself to draw down the moon's fertility power.

Mugwort Spell

1. Pick mugwort from nine fields.
2. Bind the plants together and post as an amulet and/or carry in a charm bag.

Mugwort is most powerful picked under a Full Moon or during the Summer Solstice/Midsummer's Eve festivities.

Nut and Seed Spells

Nuts and seeds represent the property of germination. Eat them if this is healthy and appropriate for you. Carry them in charm bags. Place bowls of nuts in plain sight to radiate fertility power.

Any nuts or seeds may be used in fertility magic, though as usual some are more potent than others:

★ *Oak galls, known as* serpent eggs, *are transformed into magical charms and amulets*

★ *Acorns gathered at night hold the strongest fertility power. The Full Moon enhances the power; look for an oak with particularly abundant acorns*

★ *Chinese magic exploits puns and other word games, for instance the derivation of Chinese word for peanut: hua sheng. Hua alludes to "great variety," sheng to "give birth." Bowls of peanuts are thus frequently displayed at weddings or in the home to radiate fertility power*

1. Make a necklace from acorns, sunflower, pumpkin and melon seeds, and dried corn kernels in a variety of colors: red, yellow, blue, and black.
2. Soak the material in warm water until softened. (At least an hour.)
3. Using a sharp needle, string them on strong thread, ideally red, black, or green (It may be necessary to drill holes in the acorns.)
4. Pass the charms through the smoke of frankincense and myrrh to further empower, if you wish, although this isn't necessary.
5. Wear your charms.

 ## Nut Spell (1) Jupiter's Nuts

The Latin designation for walnuts, "juglans," refers to Jupiter's testicles. Walnuts and chestnuts are particularly beneficial for men's fertility magic.

1. Place bowls of nuts in plain sight, to radiate and transfer their energy.
2. Eat them as appropriate.
3. Replenish with fresh nuts as needed.

 ## Ocean Immersion Full Moon Spell

The Full Moon shining over the ocean encompasses the most potent fertility forces here on Earth. Be a mermaid: enter the ocean, naked if possible, under the light of the Full Moon. Completely immerse yourself at least once.

 ## Nut Spell (2) Bath

The transfer of fertility energy is also attempted via a bath, for the purpose of boosting either male or female fertility.

1. Steep five chestnuts in a pot of water for five hours.
2. Strain, burying the nuts outside, but reserving the liquid.
3. Add this to your bathwater.

 ## Nut and Seed Charms

Seeds and nuts may also be used for adornment. These simple charms make powerful amulets: the process of making them is as magically charged as wearing them.

 ## Ocean Waves Spell

Infertility derives from many causes. Where physical causes are elusive, spiritual causes may be seen. While some spirits heal infertility, others cause it, sometimes one and the same spirit. Ocean water, as well as that from healing springs, is believed to cure infertility inflicted by djinn and other spirits.

Go to the sea. Let seven waves pass over your body to remove evil influences and obstacles. (The number of waves depends upon which side of the Mediterranean you're on. Moroccan magic favors seven. Identical spells exist in Spain but nine waves are required to accomplish the same purpose.)

Ocean Waves Spell (2)

This Moroccan spell benefits either male or female fertility.

1. Go to the sea.
2. Let seven waves pass over your body. Take a sip from each wave. Gather water from each wave in a bottle.
3. Take this water home; drink it and add it to your bath for the next seven days, accompanied by affirmation, visualization, and spiritual petition.

Ocean Waves Spell: Wash the Slate Clean

Moving into a new home can be an opportunity for a fresh start. This Moroccan spell takes advantage of the occasion to wipe the slate clean and remove obstructions to fertility.

1. Forty days after moving into a new home, journey to the ocean, arriving before sunrise. The journey and arrival at the shore must not be witnessed by anyone or the spell won't work. (My interpretation of this traditional spell is that it's important that no one recognizes or notices you. Don't call attention to yourself. A quick, anonymous passer-by should not nullify the effects of the spell.)
2. Upon reaching the ocean, throw a loaf of bread into the sea.
3. Allow seven waves to pass over the body.
4. Address the presiding spirits of the sea. The traditional incantation goes like this:
   Oh my uncle, the sea. I'm troubled with spirits.*
   Give me children and health.

* This is an ambiguous but potentially significant line. Does "troubled with spirits" indicate that you suffer emotionally or that literal Spirits are troubling and obstructing your goals and desires? Consider how this applies to you.

5. When you're ready, turn around and return home, without looking back.

This spell appeals to the legendary King of the Sea, but other marine spirits may be petitioned—whoever is most real and most meaningful to you.

Pinecone Spells

Pinecones look phallic; they're also associated with Dionysus and Kybele, both powerful providers of fertility. Dionysus' magic wand, the thyrsus, is topped by a pinecone. Pinecones are beneficial for both male and female fertility. Because pine trees are also magically identified with happy marriages, pinecones are especially beneficial for those relationships strained by the stress and anguish of infertility.

Collect baskets of fallen pinecones; look for strong healthy ones filled with seeds. Place them in bowls and baskets in plain sight, to radiate their power and transfer it to you.

Pinecone Spell (1)

1. Make a wish on a pinecone. Hold it in your hands and charge it with your desires.
2. When you're ready, toss it into a fire to transmit your appeal to the Spiritual powers that be.

This method may also be used to make a petition to either Kybele or Dionysus or both.

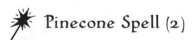

Pinecone Spell (2)

1. Collect pinecones.
2. Decorate them by dipping them into wax and glitter.
3. String them onto red cord to make necklaces.

✴ Rainwater Sieve Spell

Although terrestrial water, oceans, springs, lakes, and rivers are perceived as female powers, rain is metaphysically likened to semen. It's difficult to understand at first why masculine "thunder gods" (Zeus, Baal, Thor, Chango) are associated with fertility. It's not the thunder and the lightning; it's the accompanying showers that fertilize the Earth. Thunder gods are invariably promiscuous: strong rain fertilizes a lot of land at the same time.

Spells that emphasize immersion in the ocean seek to draw on female fertility power. Spells involving rainwater draw on the masculine powers, although both types of spells benefit women in particular. Many spells combine yin and yang, charging rainwater in moonlight, for instance.

Sieves have traditional associations with fertility. They are used similarly in personal fertility spells as well as weather spells to end drought.

1. Collect rainwater.
2. Keep the container tightly sealed in the refrigerator until you have a bright moonlit night.
3. Place the water outside, exposed to the moonbeams.
4. Pour this water through a sieve onto a woman who wishes to conceive. (If she is naked, this is even more potent.)
5. Water may be poured over the head, over the genitals or directed over the breasts, accompanied by petitions to have a healthy child to nurse.

✴ Saint George Fertility Spell (1)

Saint George's Eve is an extremely potent night for fertility rites. Crusaders encountered Saint George in Semitic West Asia and brought him home to Europe, where he is most famous for killing the dragon. Or did he? And why is he so helpful to women who wish to conceive? Some believe Saint George to be Baal in disguise. Baal, Semitic weather deity and bane of the biblical prophets, exemplifies male thunder gods who rain down fertility on a parched region. The image of the dragon or great snake is often used to represent menstruation, the monthly heartache of women wishing but failing to conceive.

Women once flocked to a Syrian shrine devoted to Saint George. Its attendant priests developed such a reputation for working miracles of conception that suspicious husbands soon forbade their wives to go, preferring no children at all to these "miracle" children.

There's no need to discover the ruins of this shrine: Saint George can assist your quest in the privacy of your own home.

1. Hang a new white nightgown from a fruitful tree on Saint George's Eve.
2. Leave it overnight.
3. Inspect the garment in the morning. If any living creature is found within it, the woman can expect to conceive before next Saint George's Day.

To activate the spell put the nightgown on immediately. Having sex while wearing it wouldn't hurt either.

✴ Saint George Fertility Spell (2)

The most common form of life discovered in the chemise is a bug or worm. Should you discover a snake wrapped up in your clothing, this is a powerful blessing and promise. A variation of the spell from Kurdistan actively seeks the snake's blessings.

1. Lay your nightgown at the foot of a tree or in its branches in an area known to be infested with snakes, the more venomous the better.
2. Leave it overnight.
3. Return to get the clothing the following day. If a snake is sitting on, or is in any way touching your nightgown, you should be pregnant within the year.
4. Take the clothing (not the snake!) home, put it on and make love without laundering it first.

Secondary Infertility Spells

When one is unable to have more children, having already successfully borne at least one child, this is known as *"secondary infertility."* Because the theoretical ability to have children has been proven, different magical methods are used to heal this condition.

Magically speaking, who heals infertility? The list includes angels, orishas, and other fertility spirits, midwives, witches, shaman, traditional herbalists, santeros, marabouts, and miracle rabbis.

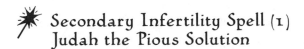

Secondary Infertility Spell (1) Judah the Pious Solution

Among the most famous miracle-working rabbis was Judah the Pious (1150–1217), author of the influential Book of Angels. *Although many other rabbis are credited with miracle cures, usually their methods aren't revealed—just vague tales of prayer and ritual. A legend, however, explicitly explains how Judah the Pious effected a cure and why it worked. Adapt to your own situation.*

In the story, a woman who had previously borne children, now older (old enough to perform the ritual for their mother), wished to have another child but found herself unable to do so. She petitioned Judah the Pious for help.

His prescription? He had her children dig a grave for her and place her within it and pretend to mourn for her. Unknown to the woman, children, and other participants in the ritual, Judah had hired armed men to make a sudden show of attack. The children were so terrified that, forgetting their mother and the ritual, they immediately scattered and ran off, at least temporarily.

For that moment it was as if the woman didn't exist, which caused the spirits, blocking her fertility, to mimic the children and scatter also, searching for other hosts.

The woman arose from her grave, fresh and reborn, and according to the legend, very quickly conceived.

Secondary Infertility Spell (2) Romany Home Bread Crumb Spell

A Romany ritual doesn't wait for secondary infertility to assert itself. It is performed as soon as a new baby enters its home for the first time.

1. The mother, carrying the baby, lays it on the threshold.
2. She picks it up, then carries it to the hearth where she lays it down again. (If there's no hearth, place by or on the stove or the home's chief source of heat.)
3. Lay the baby down in every corner of every room in the house.
4. Each time the baby is placed down, beginning at the threshold, the father sprinkles breadcrumbs around it in a circle.
5. During the ritual both parents focus on a vision of a house full of love and happy children.

Do not sweep up the crumbs or vacuum for 24 hours or overnight.

Secondary Infertility Spell (3) Romany Home Thorn Apple Spell

An alternative version of this spell requires a little bit more pre-ritual preparation.

1. Before the baby is brought home, thorn-apple seeds are scattered in all the spots where the baby will be laid.
2. First the baby is placed on the thresholds and in the four corners of each room.
3. The baby is then placed on the hearth, which has been smeared with goose fat.
4. Then the baby is placed on the table where the family customarily eats.

5. A circle is made around the baby with breadcrumbs and drops of brandy and the ritual is complete.

Beware: *thorn apple is toxic; make sure that Baby doesn't put the seeds into his or her mouth!*

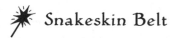 Snakeskin Belt

The most famous fertility creature is the snake, whose shape alludes to both male and female genitals. (The male resemblance is obvious; the female reference derives from the snake's unhinged jaws. It's able to expand its jaws to swallow prey logic insists is too large for it, just as the vagina expands to disgorge a baby's head.)

Shed snakeskins are potent fertility charms. Because you are beseeching assistance from the snake, the skin can't be taken by force. The snake's blessing is paramount to activating the magic. People who keep snakes will have a ready supply, although a found snakeskin is believed to be extra magical, as it is a direct gift and blessing from the snake spirits.

Wear a shed snakeskin as a belt or girdle. The most powerful skins come from venomous snakes, although shed snakeskins discovered on Saint George's Eve are exceptionally blessed and potent too.

Spider Web Spell

A Hungarian Romany fertility cure is puzzling unless one understands the spiritual reasons underlying it: a barren woman gathers spider webs and eats them, together with her male partner. Spider webs are more poetically known as gossamer thread and gossamer is reputed to be spun by the fairies.

Spirits of Fertility

Sometimes you need personal assistance. There is a tremendous variety of Spiritual sponsors, healers, and nurturers of fertility. Themes of infertility are central to many of their myths and holy stories.

Spirit Petition (1) Aphrodite

In addition to her more famous role as Spirit of Carnal Delight, Aphrodite also provides fertility and heals both men's and women's reproductive woes, although this bath is more beneficial for women, and its flowery aroma is probably more to their taste. On the other hand, benefits may be shared. Aphrodite has many departments of expertise: this bath is also an aphrodisiac.

> Lemon balm
> Myrtle
> Rose geranium
> Roses

Use either hydrosols, dried botanicals or essential oils or a combination. (Lemon balm essential oil may be prohibitively expensive and is marketed under the plant's other name, melissa. Unlike other forms of the botanical, it's also a profound skin irritant.) Add the botanicals to a tub filled with warm water. Float rose petals on top for added enhancement.

Spirit Petition (2) Armisael

Armisael is the Angel of the Womb. Request that he heal or fill yours. Call him with frankincense and myrrh.

✴ Spirit Petition (3) Bastet

Ancient Egyptian couples commissioned special statues of the cat deity Bastet to fulfill their wishes for children. A specific number of kittens, designed to correspond to the number of children desired, were incorporated into amulets and images of Bastet.

The most powerful image of Bastet for use in this spell depicts her as a cat-headed woman wearing a dress and carrying a basket and sistrum. Place kittens in the basket or by her feet.

✴ Spirit Petition (4) Bossu

The lwa Bossu is depicted as a three-horned bull. A sacred bull, he represents primal male vigor, similar to the biblical Baal. Like Baal he can be a wild, dangerous, volatile spirit: imagine the effects of way too much testosterone. Be that as it may, he responds to women's pleas for fertility. Create an altar for him; a horn may be used to substitute for his standard image. His colors are red and black.

What Bossu eats, what he'd like as an offering, is subject to debate. Some, especially those who'd like to keep the wild bull gentle, suggest grain offerings including beer. Others recommend spicy foods and rare beef.

✴ Spirit Petition (5) Demeter

Demeter presided over the Eleusinian mysteries, once the most prominent religious rituals in Greece. Demeter's mythology is fraught with tales of fertility versus barrenness, sacred sexuality, and the loss of women's personal and political power.

1. Build an altar to Demeter. Decorate with poppies and pomegranates and images of snakes and horses.
2. Dedicate a small gold or silver pig to her as a votive offering.

3. Wear it for fertility and luck. If and when you bear a healthy child, place a larger, more valuable one permanently on the altar.

✴ Spirit Petition (6) Freya

Friday the 13th has come to be considered an evil, unlucky, dangerous day because it combines the day most associated with deities of primal female power with their number, the number of months in the lunar year. It is a powerful day to request spiritual assistance for healing and enhancing reproductive power. Friday is sacred to many potent female spirits, from Aphrodite to Oshun, but the day's English name especially summons Freya.

Freya, a powerful, multifaceted spirit, serves as psychopomp in her capacity as leader of the Valkyries. But she also offers magical blessings of reproductive fertility, which is among her many dominions. Carve, dress and burn cat candles for Freya on Friday the 13th and request her assistance.

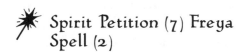

✴ Spirit Petition (7) Freya Spell (2)

Freya, "She Who Shines Over the Sea," has associations with cats as powerful as Bastet.

No forgotten goddess, Freya particularly irritated Christian authorities. More details survive regarding Freya than any other Northern European female deity, specifically because the Church focused so much negative attention on her. She became their model for the seductive version of the stereotypical witch. (Hecate was used to represent the crone.) Freya had periodic revivals of popular devotion, including one in fifteenth-century Germany. In an Edict of 1484, Pope Innocent VIII declared all female worshippers of Freya be burned at the stake, together with their cats.

Build Freya a beautiful altar featuring amber, feathers, gold and silver charms, and images of the moon. Light white candles for her on the ninth and

thirteenth day of each month and request assistance with fertility.

 Spirit Petition (8) Freya Cat Spell

The old Norse tradition of paying tribute to Freya involved feeding milk to cats.

1. Put out milk for stray cats. If you don't live in an area with stray cats, bring contributions to a shelter or adopt a gray stray cat.
2. Feeding isn't done by rote but as a conscious offering; speak with Freya simultaneously, explain your needs, desires, and broken heart, and request assistance.
3. Pay attention; the response may come through the cats.

 Spirit Petition (9) Frigg

Mistletoe has strong associations with Norse mythology. It's dedicated to Frigg, Lady of Fertility. At Yule, a boar was sacrificed to Frigg, and it's head decorated with bay leaves, mistletoe, and rosemary.

Frigg may be petitioned for personal fertility. Her sacred bird and messenger is the stork, subject of many jokes regarding where babies really come from. Her old Yule offering may also be replicated. Create a clay boar's head and embellish it or, if you eat whole roasted pig, offer her the genuine article.

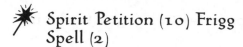 Spirit Petition (10) Frigg Spell (2)

An Anglo-Saxon fertility charm may be used independently; however, it originally represented an offering to the divine mother and provider of fertility, Frigg.

1. Use a sheaf of corn or a corn dolly to represent Frigg.
2. To invoke her power, mark a piece of birch wood with Frigg's rune, *ger,* which bears the meaning *"fruitful year."*
3. Hang it over your bed for nine nights. This rune represents love and fertility. The doll is an offering to Frigg. When nine days are over, place it on an altar or wrap it in cloth and bury in Earth.

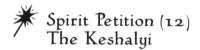 Spirit Petition (11) Gabriel the Archangel

Gabriel, the Archangel of the Moon, performs miracles of conception. Call him with myrrh and lilies.

Spirit Petition (12) The Keshalyi

Call on the Keshalyi, Romany fairies traditionally invoked to prevent and heal infertility. This phrase calls them: "Keshalyi lisperesn," which literally means "Fairies spin."

1. Write the words with glue on cardboard.
2. Sprinkle powder or glitter over it so that the phrase is visible.
3. Let it dry and post it where it's visible.
4. Make an offering of milk, fruit brandy, and/or cakes.
5. Then begin to chant the words aloud, until you have a sense of the Keshalyi's presence.
6. Speak with them, bargain for their services.

Spirit Petition (13) Kwan Yin

Kwan Yin, the Buddhist Heart of Mercy and Queen of Compassion, is no forgotten deity but among the most popular on Earth today. Kwan Yin achieved nirvana but refused to leave Earth as long any person still suffers. Kwan Yin vows that if you call her name in times of anguish, she will come and assist you. Her assistance is not limited to fertility; however, themes of infertility resonate through her myth. Kwan Yin and her two sisters were, in fact, born after her parents suffered an extended period of infertility, only relieved by petition to the Taoist deity, the Lord of T'ai Shan. Petition Kwan Yin to relieve your drought.

1. Erect an altar for Kwan Yin. Although she has many votive images, the most powerful in this instance depicts her holding a baby.
2. Offer her incense and baby shoe charms.
3. Tell her what you need.

It's customary to make a vow in exchange for Spiritual gifts given. Kwan Yin is protector of women, children, and sailors, and also animals. Offerings on their behalf would conceivably be appreciated.

 Spirit Petition (14) Kwan Yin Spell (2)

Although there are some advantages to a personal shrine, it doesn't replace a trip to an official shrine. Kwan Yin has thousands, great and small alike. Those desiring fertility traditionally bring Kwan Yin a gift of baby shoes as part of the petition.

1. Bring a new pair of baby shoes to the shrine.
2. Remove a pair already present and take it home as an amulet.

Should you conceive and bear a healthy child, it's traditional to donate yet another pair of shoes (or bring the

borrowed pair back) to the shrine, although this time there's no need to take another pair home.

 Spirit Petition (15) Lailah

Lailah is the Angel of Night and Conception. He blesses and activates nocturnal lovemaking. Call him with night-blooming jasmine.

Spirit Petition (16) Lord and Lady of the Bed

Lord Ch'uang-kung and Lady Ch'uang-mu are the Lord and Lady of the Bed—Chinese presiding spirits. They have power over what occurs in bed and what does not. As may be imagined, they are frequently petitioned for fertility.

Hang prints of the Lord and Lady on the wall over the bed, to receive their blessings and good fortune. Such image-posting spells must, of course, be accompanied by charging the images, consecrating them, and consciously affirming your desires.

Spirit Petition (17) Lord and Lady of the Bed Offering Ritual

For maximum magic power present offerings on the final day of year and/or on the day following the full moon in the first month of the Chinese lunar calendar, the Lantern Feast. Women wishing for enhanced fertility attempt to procure one of the ends of the candles used to light up the dragons carried through the streets. This is the most potent, auspicious candle for this spell; however, if unavailable, light candles as you normally would.

1. Place offerings directly on the bed, on a tray placed on the bed, or on a table brought beside the bed.

2. Use the candle stub or other method to light another candle on the edge of the bed.
3. Ceremoniously present the offerings. Typically, couples make offerings together. Personal offerings include cakes and fruits, with a cup of fine tea for the Lady and a glass of wine for the Lord. Offerings of fertility fruits and eggs dyed red are placed on a table beside the bed.
4. Petition the Lord and Lady for what you desire, explain it to them explicitly.

Spirit Petition (18) Oshun

Oshun is the youngest, sweetest, and most beautiful of the orisha. She ranks among the most powerful spirits of love, right beside Aphrodite and Inanna-Ishtar, and like them is affiliated with the planet Venus.

For all her youth and sweetness, Oshun is also a spirit of major power and maximum generosity. As spirit of love, romance, and sex, fertility naturally falls under her domain. In addition she rules the abdomen and female reproductive organs, so reproductive disorders are also under her power. She may be petitioned for physical healing, too.

*Oshun is the spirit of sweet waters: rivers, streams, and waterfalls. Her number is five. Her colors are the spectrum including yellow, gold, and orange. She may manifest as a mermaid or as a glowingly beautiful woman. Her sacred birds are peacocks and vultures. Although Oshun is the spirit of precious fresh water, she is also the embodiment of honey. Call Oshun with her two emblems: a glass of spring water and a dish of honey. This is her traditional offering. However, it is crucial always, every time, to taste the honey. Once upon a time, someone tried to kill her with a dish of poisoned honey and ever since then she looks upon untasted offerings **with suspicion.***

Oshun performs many spells using one of her favorite plants, the pumpkin. The seeds are her children. Those who petition her for fertility traditionally refrain from eating pumpkin or any type of yellow squash in any form.

1. Hollow out a small pumpkin.
2. Write your name and any message to Oshun on a piece of paper.
3. Smear it with honey (taste it!) and place it flat inside the pumpkin.
4. Hold a yellow votive candle between your hands and charge it with your desire.
5. Place the candle inside the pumpkin, on top of the paper, and light it.

This is most effective if repeated for five consecutive days with fresh materials.

Spirit Petition (19) Oshun Spell (2)

1. Obtain a cantaloupe or honeydew melon specifically for this spell.
2. Place it on an altar to Oshun, petitioning her for a child.
3. Write your request onto a slip of brown paper.
4. With a knife, make a slit in the melon and insert the paper.
5. Wrap the fruit up in yellow fabric.
6. For five days leave the melon on the altar surrounded by constantly burning gold, yellow, orange or white candles and accompanied by prayer and petition.
7. When the five days are over, dispose of the melon in a river.

Spirit Petition (20) Thor

Thor, Lord of Thunder, also has some involvement in the issue, as storm gods are wont to do. His sacred tree is the birch; he avows that those who hang it outside their home are protected from infertility.

If you have done this and still are not conceiving, petition him and hold him to his promise. Do it on a Thursday.

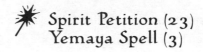 Spirit Petition (21) Yemaya

Yemaya, orisha of the Sea, represents the epitome of motherhood, and manifests all aspects of maternity to the finest and fullest degree. She is associated with the ocean and salt water. Yemaya resides in the sea, she is the spirit of the sea and she is the sea, especially its upper, most accessible surfaces. Yemaya's association with the ocean also reminds us that all humans have their origins in the sea—not in an abstract sense, but swimming in their mother's salty amniotic fluids.

Yemaya rules all issues pertaining to women and may be petitioned for fertility and to heal specific physical reproductive disorders. She is most powerfully petitioned at the beach. If this is impossible, call her with a goblet filled with salted water and enhanced with seashells and sea glass. Decorate her shrine with ocean motifs: ships, anchors, fish, shells, and nets. Many spells beseech her assistance with reproductive fertility:

1. Burn a blue seven-day candle dedicated to Yemaya once a month, coinciding with the start of your period.
2. Should you become pregnant, maintain a shrine for her during the pregnancy. She may also be petitioned for good health during pregnancy and an easy delivery, too.

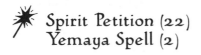 Spirit Petition (22)
Yemaya Spell (2)

1. Take a watermelon to the beach as a gift for Yemaya.
2. Make your petition.
3. Send the watermelon out to sea.

 Spirit Petition (23)
Yemaya Spell (3)

1. Take a watermelon to the sea.
2. Cut a well into it large enough to fit a candle. (Make sure it's a biodegradable candle or something environmentally safe. Sending garbage out to sea won't gain you points with Yemaya.)
3. Make your petition and light your candle.
4. Send the watermelon out to sea.

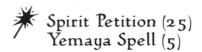 Spirit Petition (24)
Yemaya Spell (4)

1. Fill a dish with water tinted blue. Use **Indigo Water** in any of its forms, true indigo or blue food coloring.
2. Hold a floating candle in your hand and charge it with your desires.
3. Place it on the blue surface of the water and light it.
4. For maximum effectiveness, repeat for seven days with a total of seven candles.

★ Spirit Petition (25)
Yemaya Spell (5)

1. Cut a pomegranate in half.
2. Spread honey over both halves.
3. Write the name of the person wishing to conceive on a piece of paper together with any messages to Yemaya.
4. Place the paper between the pomegranate halves and stick them back together.
5. This message is traditionally delivered to Yemaya at her home the ocean. Her daughter (or sister, depending on legend) Oshun, Spirit of Sweet Water will also pass on messages for Yemaya at rivers, streams or waterfalls. (Yemaya is the elder; she does not return the favor.) If this is the venue of delivery, it's also customary to bring Oshun a gift.

It's not necessary to invoke a specific spirit. Fertility spirits in general share specific attributes: roses, lilies, and pomegranates. In essence the following are *generic* fertility spirit spells; however, the botanicals alone are charged with magic power (that's *why* they're attributes) and if you're personally unfamiliar with the spirits, generic spells may be more comfortable than calling on a spirit you don't know. Use pomegranate leaves and blossoms for these spells rather than the fruit.

 Spirit of Fertility Generic Spell: Indirect Approach

Surround yourself with fresh bouquets.

 Spirit of Fertility Generic Spell: Direct Approach

Add the blossoms and leaves to your bath. (Make sure you're not *pregnant.)*

 Well Spell

Wells, especially in areas where drinking water is scarce, evoke radiant fertility power. This is particularly true of open wells, fed by rain and constantly charged by moonlight.

Charge a rag with your desire for fertility and attach it to the well.

 Yarrow Spell

Basil boughs over the bed are a Middle Eastern recommendation to promote fertility. European magical tradition suggests hanging boughs of fresh yarrow over the bed for enhanced romance, sex, and conception.

Hedge your bets by weaving garlands of both yarrow and basil, and hanging them over the bed. A really supercharged version adds mistletoe and mugwort, too.

 Yule Log Spell

The Yule log has associations with fertility, apart from connections with Frigg. These may stem from worship of Diana and Hera in the shape of a log or merely from the fertility power implicit in trees. In France and Switzerland, the burning of the Yule log is accompanied by fervent petitioning for children, should they be desired.

Contraception Spells

The repertoire of contraceptive spells is far smaller than that devoted to successful conception. Until recently, the emphasis was on being fruitful and multiplying as much as possible, rather than the opposite.

Traditional cultures, the source of so much fertility magic, have also had access to herbal methods of birth control, making magic spells unnecessary. Magic is a mysterious process: you ask for one thing, sometimes you get it and sometimes you get something else. Conventional methods of contraception are usually more reliable and definitely more predictable than magical means.

Magical contraception is intended to supplement and enhance more conventional methods of birth control, not replace them. Perhaps they should be considered historic spells or what the old Hoodoo drugstores called *"curios."* Those unable to use other forms of contraception for one reason or another may find these methods useful, although they should still be accompanied by close monitoring of reproductive cycles, if you genuinely care about not getting pregnant.

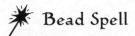 ## Bead Spell

1. Mix menstrual blood into clay and form a bead, piercing it with a needle.
2. When the bead is ready, hold it in your hand, and focus upon remaining childless.
3. Keep this bead in a safe place. Don't lose it.
4. Whenever you're ready to conceive, toss the bead into a river or spring and let the water dissolve the bead.

For absolute utmost power, use a girl's first menstrual blood.

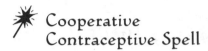 ## Cooperative Contraceptive Spell

A Moroccan contraceptive spell's success depends upon cooperation between a man and a woman. A few drops of menstrual blood plus either one dried fig or one bead is required.

1. Cut the dried fig lengthwise.
2. Sprinkle the blood into the slit or place inside the bead's hole.
3. The man then hides the fig in a place unknown to the woman. Ostensibly a period of sterility will remain for as long as the fig is hidden.

To break the spell, the man removes the fig from its hiding place and with a flourish, displays it to the woman.

 ## Death Spell

To avert pregnancy, linger at a burial site after others have left a funeral. Step three times over the grave, always in the same direction, not back and forth. Focus on your intention—similar spells are used to repair and reinvigorate fertility.

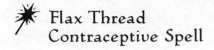 ## Flax Thread Contraceptive Spell

The original spell would have required the woman to spin the thread, in the manner that fates, fairies, and goddesses spin, wield and sever the thread of life. Flax is sacred to such spirits of fertility as Frigg, Hulda, and the Russian spirit who sometimes masquerades as Saint Paraskeva.

1. Soak flax thread in menstrual blood.
2. Tie ten knots in the thread.
3. Wear it non-stop for nine days and nine nights, sleeping with it at night.
4. When the nine days and nights are complete, bury the thread in a corner saying, *"I bury you for* [insert the time desired to stay pregnancy-free].*"*

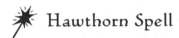 ## Hawthorn Spell

Tuck hawthorn leaves under the mattress to magically enhance contraception.

 ## Knot Spell

1. Make knots in a cord for contraception, knotting in your desires, goals, and intentions.
2. Reserve the cord in a safe and private place.
3. Place the cord in a glass of water.
4. Let it soak overnight, then drink the water.
5. When you're ready to conceive, untie the knots.

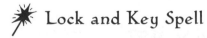 ## Lock and Key Spell

1. Place a lock and key on the floor.
2. Walk in the space between them. Turn around. While turning state: *"When I open this lock again, I will successfully conceive."*
3. Turn the key and lock the lock.

4. Keep the lock and key in a safe place. Prior to attempts at conception, you must ritually open the lock.

 ## Mill Contraceptive Spell

Slip out of the house at midnight and go to a grain mill. Turn the wheel of the mill four times backwards as a contraceptive charm.

 ## Placenta Pregnancy Delay Spell (1) Hills and Valleys

Many contraceptive spells are cooperative ones between a man and a woman, with much of the action traditionally performed by the father, as with this Cherokee ritual. If the father is unavailable or unable to do this, someone else may be delegated by the mother to perform the spell. This spell is intended to prevent pregnancy following too quickly upon the heels of a birth. The spell must be cast immediately following that first birth.

1. Carry the placenta, with respect and reverence, far from home.
2. Ideally several hills are crossed, with each hill representing another year before a new baby is born. (If there are no hills, designate and articulate other landmarks as substitutes.) Consider how many hills to cross.
3. When the proper destination has been found, the placenta is buried in Earth.

 ## Placenta Pregnancy Delay Spell (2) Porcupine

Another spell to prevent another pregnancy occurring too quickly after a birth involves the placenta, and again must be performed immediately following birth.

Take the placenta and fill it with porcupine quills (available from traditional henna supply stores; the quills are a traditional applicator tool). Bury it in Earth.

 ## Roasted Nut Pregnancy Delay Spell

This spell is traditionally cast during a wedding. The bride must consider how many years she'd like to remain child-free.

1. Obtain one roasted walnut to represent each desired child-free year.
2. Tuck all the roasted walnuts into the bodice of the wedding dress.

Too late? The wedding's long over? Never say it's too late. Renew your vows, this time with walnuts.

 ## Umbilical Cord Pregnancy Delay Spell

This spell must be accomplished immediately upon delivery. Traditionally the woman makes prior arrangements with the midwife, who is the one who actually performs the spell: tell her or whoever will cast the spell what you need before the birth.

1. Make as many knots into the umbilical cord, still attached to placenta, as the number of years you'd like to remain without another pregnancy.
2. Bury the knotted cord and placenta in Earth.

Witch Bottle
Contraceptive Spell

This spell assumes the guise of a witch bottle to enhance contraception.

1. Wash clothing stained with menstrual blood.
2. Fill a bottle with the bloody rinse water.
3. Seal the bottle with red wax.
4. Bury the bottle in a safe place where it will not be disturbed.

Hexes: Spells to Render Someone Infertile

Because women's status and well-being was historically so dependent upon their capacity to give birth, some of the meanest hexes target that ability. These spells are not intended for use but for historical knowledge alone, or perhaps information given so as to protect yourself. Whether they may also be used as contraception is anyone's guess; however, these tend not to be spells one would voluntarily cast on one's own behalf.

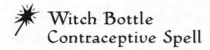 ## Hex (1) Dead Bee Bread

This hex takes a spell ingredient normally associated with healthy fertility (bees) and twists it so as to provide the opposite.

Make bread with a piece of honeycomb containing dead bees and secretly feed it to a woman to allegedly harm her fertility.

 ## Hex (2) Dressed Egg

Like the hex above, this spell perverts an ingredient normally used to provide enhanced, healthy fertility.

*Roll a guinea hen egg in cayenne pepper and **Goofer Dust**. Place it in a pot filled with rainwater and boil it for a long time.*

 ## Hex (3) Mule

Mules are the animals most associated with sterility, for obvious reasons. Their influence is believed to exert a contraceptive force, in the same way that consistent exposure to fertility animals like bees and rabbits enhances a woman's capacity to conceive.

Make bread with flour blended with the charred hoof parings of a mule. Feed it to a woman so that she will become barren as the mule.

 ## Hex (4) Mule Spell (2)

Mix charred mule hoof parings into honey and feed it to a woman. She will become barren as the mule, allegedly.

⊕ Fire Safety Spells

Watch that candle! Keep an eye on that incense! There's too much smoke coming from that cauldron! Magic spells are fraught with opportunities for fire disaster. Those who favor candle magic must always bear in mind that even rituals performed for the most spiritual reasons remain subject to all physical laws of Nature.

On the other hand, magic powers are also invoked to provide fire safety, usually, but not always as a method of prevention. Magical fire safety measures include invocations to saints and angels, magic books and squares, and the miracle-working protective capacities of great sex and menstrual blood.

Fire safety spells do not replace the urgent need for water or the fire department. Consider these spells as methods of enhancing other, more conventional, fire prevention measures, or perhaps keep them reserved for that absolute worst-case scenario when there is no help or water available but you're not ready to give up hope.

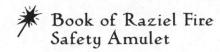

Archangel Michael's Department of Mystic Fire Safety

According to Jewish magic, the entire department of candle and other fire magic falls under the rule of Michael, Archangel of the Flaming Sword. Good thing, because he's also the angel in charge of fire safety. If you work extensively with candles or if fire causes you particular concern, encourage Michael to lend his ever-vigilant eye.

1. If you like, place an image (statue or chromolithograph) of Michael near the main candle-burning area or the area you perceive as most vulnerable.
2. Call him with the aroma of frankincense and through his invocation:
   Michael to the right of me,
   Michael to the left of me
   Michael above me
   Michael below me
   Michael within me
   Michael all around me
   Michael with your flaming sword of cobalt blue,
       protect me today!
   [Add personal requests at the end]

Balm of Gilead Fire Prevention Incense

Balm soothes scorched skin; this incense allegedly prevents fire.

1. Steep balm of Gilead buds in red wine.
2. Let them dry out and burn them as incense.
3. Coat your finger or, if you have enough, your hands with the sticky residue. According to legend, this residue creates an aura of fire protection and fireproofing.
4. Rub it on your body or hair. If there is an object or area that you're particularly concerned about, rub your hands over it.

Book of Raziel Fire Safety Amulet

According to legend, Michael was the adamant angel with the revolving fiery sword posted at the front gates of Eden to keep Adam and Eve out and prevent anyone else's entry. Another angel proved more sympathetic. As Adam passed through the gates, the angel Raziel gave him the first book ever, a book of magic.

That first Book of Raziel was engraved on sapphire and allegedly now rests on the ocean floor. Luckily copies were made, although for centuries no two versions of the Book of Raziel were necessarily identical. The edition circulating today was first published in Amsterdam in 1701. It is a difficult, dense, dry work, hardly light reading, filled with astrology, amulets, and arcana. It may be the only book ever published with the expectation that buyers wouldn't and couldn't read it.

Far beyond the ken of even many scholarly readers, the Book of Raziel was sold as an amulet. The amulets depicted within may be removed and posted. However, the presence of the book in its entirety was believed to bring special benefit to the home, especially regarding fire safety: allegedly fire will not damage or harm a home containing the Book of Raziel.

1. For safety's sake, keep the *Book of Raziel* out in the open, not tucked behind other books, to make sure the Fire Angels are well aware of its presence.
2. Although the book is believed powerful enough to provide protection without added input, if you are particularly concerned with fire safety, holding the book in your hands and charging it with your desire can only enhance its magic.

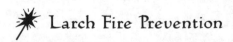

Larch Fire Prevention

Pieces of larch wood kept in the house allegedly prevent fires.

Menstrual Blood Stop the Fire Spell

Most fire safety spells target prevention but this one aims to stop the fire itself. Throw a menstrual-blood soaked rag onto the fire. If you keep pads soaking in a moon-pot, just toss the entire contents onto the flames.

 ## Midsummer's Ashes Fire Protection

Sprinkle ashes from the Midsummer's bonfires on your roof and around your property to protect against fire.

 ## Midsummer's Fire Safety Spell

The following seven botanicals are known as "the herbs of Saint John": hawkweed, mistletoe, mullein, orpine, vervain, wormwood, and, of course, Saint John's Wort. Gather them either at midnight on Saint John's Eve (Midsummer's Eve) or at noon on Saint John's Day. Dry them and hang them within your home to magically protect against fire.

 ## Perfect Balance Fire Safety Spell

According to general occult theory, specific Chinese yin-yang theory, as well as mathematics, providing something's perfect balance, its perfect inverse, neutralizes it, canceling its effects. Water puts out fire. Fire is about as yang as you get, while water is maximum yin. Makes sense? Let's take it a step further.

Fire is a destructive, consuming force leaving waste and void in its wake. What could possibly neutralize acts of destruction better than acts of creation?

Perhaps because the goal is constant vigilance, or maybe because the ancients realized that under the circumstances, with your house in flames, you might lack the immediate ability to perform this spell yourself, image magic is used.

Your first task is to obtain illustrations of men and women extremely happily engaged in sexual intercourse. These may be photographs or drawings. Now hang them on the wall. Traditionally, this is done in the kitchen but may be done wherever there is legitimate fear of fire.

Your own sexual preferences are irrelevant: this isn't about what you like to look at or what you'd like to do. The image(s) must be of men and women and they must both appear equally happy. Any hint of bondage, domination, or sadomasochism will negate the spell. The goal is to display the perfect balance of yin and yang. With these elements so perfectly balanced, it's believed impossible for fire, a yang power, to dominate.

Your grandmother refuses to believe that's why you have that picture hanging in the kitchen? Trade a little bit of power for discretion. Post symbolic depictions of this balance: the yin-yang symbol, perhaps, or the six-pointed Star of David, or an entire collection of mortars and pestles.

Rainwater Mistletoe Spell

Wouldn't it be convenient if torrential downpours could be magically harnessed to miraculously appear on cue whenever a fire needed extinguishing? This spell attempts to achieve that miracle.

1. Collect rainwater and let it chill in the refrigerator.
2. Place mistletoe in a white or blue bag.
3. Soak this bag in the rainwater.
4. Squeeze out excess moisture and hang the bag up in your home to dry. It will now serve as a protective amulet against fires.

Other amulets that allegedly prevent house fires include:

★ *A resident happy, content tri-colored cat*
★ *An image or statue of Maneki Neko, the Beckoning Cat*
★ *Dried shed snakeskin hanging from the roof*

 ## Rooster Fire Protection

A picture of a little red rooster allegedly provides a home with magical protection against fire. Post the image in the kitchen or near the hearth.

 ## Saint John's Wort Fireproof Spell

Burn Saint John's Wort in an iron cauldron. Carry it through the home so that the smoke permeates all corners, to serve as magical fireproofing.

 ## Saint John's Wort Fire Safety Spell

Gather Saint John's Wort on Midsummer's Eve and dry the plant. Place within a glass jar or bottle kept near a window to protect against fire.

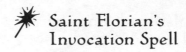 ## Saint Florian's Invocation Spell

Saint Florian is the patron of firefighters. It's his job to guard them, protect them, and bring them home safely. If you're a firefighter, request his assistance.

Saint Florian is a spiritual firefighter himself. His invocation spell signals your request that he protect your home or property from fire. His annual feast is on May 4th, an excellent opportunity for petition. However, his ritual may be initiated, repeated, and reinforced at any time during the year. Given the choice, the best day to petition Saint Florian is a Sunday.

1. Find an image of a burning house or building.
2. Burn a red candle in front of it and speak to Saint Florian.

Saint Florian may also be invoked during any crisis for emergency aid.

The SATOR square is the most ubiquitous of magic squares, and is a tool used in a variety of magic spells for all kinds of purposes, from physical healing of humans to removing hexes from cows, although fire safety is its most famous use.

SATOR has been found wherever the Roman legions traveled; it apparently traveled with them. No one knows exactly what it means. There is conjecture that it refers to the Mithraic rites so popular with Roman soldiers, although another school of thought considers it to be a Christian charm, the words being an anagram of *Pater Noster.* Either way, it is as follows:

S	A	T	O	R
A	R	E	P	O
T	E	N	E	T
O	P	E	R	A
R	O	T	A	S

For fire protection:

1. Write the magic square carefully on parchment, making sure that the letters line up neatly but that no letters touch.
2. Place it at the highest point within the home.

To put out a fire when there is no water:

1. Etch the magic square onto a wooden plate.
2. Throw it onto the fire.

Don't laugh. In 1742, not *that* long ago, the state of Saxony ordered that plates bearing this formula be kept handy for firefighting. (There are also versions suggesting that the square be engraved on silver tablets for the same purpose, which, to the modern mind, may be less troubling than the thought of throwing wood onto a blazing fire one wants to put out.)

 ## Stinging Nettle Fire Safety Spell

This spell doesn't promise to extinguish a fire but, according to legend, it will minimize or prevent damage being done. Throw stinging nettles on the fire.

 ## Yule Log Fire Prevention

1. Keep the remains of your Yule log in the home all year long to prevent fires.
2. Light the new log with the remains of the old one.
3. Once the new one exists, grind up the old ashes and sprinkle them around the perimeter of your home for extra protection.

 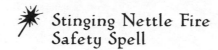

Gamblers' Spells and Charms

Thoth, that over-achieving Egyptian, not only invented magic and writing, he invented dice and wagering, too. Baccarat allegedly derives from Etruscan spiritual rites; nine priests, or so the rumor goes, convened to observe a young, virginal blonde roll numbers in what might be called Etruscan roulette. High numbers earned her the prestigious position of priestess; the wrong numbers forced her to take a one-way stroll into the sea. The magical roots of gambling run deep.

Next time you shake up dice and call on Lady Luck, do so with reverence. You're actually invoking the once very prominent Roman goddess, Fortuna, the original Lady Luck. The Wheel of Fortune, also the name of a tarot card, is among Fortuna's sacred emblems. Dice, cards, roulette wheels, all these gambling devices also double as tools of divination. Every hand, whether loser's or winner's, may be simultaneously read as a message about the future.

Divination serves as a conduit to the divine and, as some see it, gambling does too. After all, isn't every card, number, winning horse or roll of the die ultimately determined by the Hand of Fate? Like that fated Etruscan blonde, gambling offers the gods an opportunity to reward you—or not.

According to theories of divination and synchronicity, it's impossible to choose the wrong card, pick the wrong straw or roll the wrong number. Whatever hand Fate deals is the one you're meant to play. Gamblers, a notoriously superstitious bunch, invoke divine favor with ritual, spell, and charms. Gamblers' Spells are a sub-genre of Luck Spells, developed and refined to fulfill a special need.

 Angelica Charm

Carry an angelica root in your pocket as a gambler's talisman. This is especially beneficial for women.

Chypre Magic Gamblers' Cologne

Many types of cologne, like liqueurs, have their origins in magic potions and formulas. **Angel's Water**, for instance, began its incarnation as an aphrodisiac while **Hungary Water** earned its initial fame as a youth potion. These magical formula waters and colognes are in a sense the old-world version of magical formula dressing oils.

Perhaps because for so long gambling was considered an exclusively male pursuit, many fragrances targeted at men derive their roots from gambling luck formulas. Jockey Club and **Bay Rum** for instance, provide luck and financial good fortune. **Chypre**, however, is the gambler's favorite. Named after Aphrodite's island of Cyprus, this formula allegedly also brings luck in business, the stock market, and anything having to do with money and finance. Legend has it that the scent was brought to England by returning twelfth-century Crusaders in powder form. It could be used like that or added to oil as needed.

Although the word "*chypre*" is now used to designate a class of perfume, those fragrances may lack any connection with the magical formula beyond the name. To be true magical **Chypre**, this earthy fragrance should contain rock rose (labdanum), strongly associated with Cyprus. Oakmoss is also a frequent component because of the belief that it draws cash to its wearer. (See page 1040 for the formula.)

 ## Chypre Spell (1) Modern Use

Wear the cologne to attract wealth and general good fortune anytime but especially when gambling. Close your eyes while applying it and make a quick wish or invocation.

Pay attention to the fragrance while playing; normally you don't smell fragrance worn on your own body. If the fragrance suddenly, unexpectedly intensifies, pay even closer attention: it just may be giving you a few players' tips.

 ## Chypre Spell (2) Traditional Use

For traditional use, carry the dry perfume in a conjure bag, and rub it on your hands just before playing.

 ## Chypre Oil

*Add **Chypre** powder to jojoba oil. Rub a drop of this oil between your palms especially before playing games where you actually handle the materials (cards, dice, etc.)*

Devil's Shoestrings Spells

Among its many other uses, the root devil's shoestring is used to magically enhance gambler's luck.

 ## Shoestring Bag

1. Put a whole devil's shoestring inside a red bag together with patchouli and vetiver.
2. With your desire firmly in your mind, spit in the bag.
3. Tie it together with a real shoestring.

 ## Shoestring Paper Spell

Rub devil's shoestring onto lottery tickets, racing forms, and other gambling cards and papers.

Shoestring Powder

Grind devil's shoestrings, patchouli, and vetiver and blend with cornstarch. Sprinkle within your shoes when on your way to a game of cards.

Sometimes the way the chips fall depends upon in whose good graces *you* fall. Oh, knowing a pit boss or a croupier may get you some free drinks, but the type of help many prefer to rely upon comes from the spirit realm. Request divine intervention, winning numbers, or at least some advice as to whether it's wise to play.

Ironically, although gambling's symbols belong to her and even though she is probably invoked more during one day in Las Vegas than all year anywhere else, Lady Luck herself, Fortuna, is not associated with gambling as much as she is with plain, everyday good fortune. One of her most significant roles in old Rome was helping married women maintain their husband's sexual interests.

You've been invoking the wrong goddess? Don't despair. Plenty of other spirits patronize gamblers, providing them with lucky numbers and good fortune.

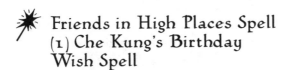

Friends in High Places Spell (1) Che Kung's Birthday Wish Spell

The earliest documentation of gambling comes from China. Che Kung, Patron of Gamblers, is a deified general dating from the Sung dynasty, with a temple maintained near the Hong Kong racetrack. Demonstrating the oft-blurred line between gambling and divination, Che Kung's temple is popular for its resident fortune-tellers.

Che Kung's blessings manifest as gamblers' luck. His festival celebrates his birthday: the second day of the first month of the Chinese year. Wish Che Kung a happy birthday to receive good fortune and especially gamblers' luck in the New Year.

If you're in Hong Kong on Che Kung's birthday, get in line to spin the sails of the copper windmill within his temple. Allegedly three spins earns the spinner Che Kung's blessings in the year to come.

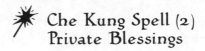

Che Kung Spell (2) Private Blessings

A trip to Hong Kong isn't realistic? Honor the general at home:

1. Offer Che Kung incense.
2. Burn paper spirit money in his honor. Be as generous to him as you'd like him to be toward you.

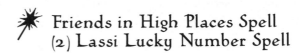

Friends in High Places Spell (2) Lassi Lucky Number Spell

The Lassi are Italian protective spirits and household retainers. Survivors of Roman paganism, they languish ready to serve. One pair of Lassi traditionally serves each household, the successful performance of their career contingent upon the success of their respective households. Wake them up and put them to work. Request their assistance with the lottery or with gambling in general.

1. Dedicate three candles to the Lassi.
2. Burn the candles at midnight.
3. While the candles burn, call the Lassi, request their presence; chant something similar to this aloud:
   Lassi! Come here now!
   I'm calling you. I need you!
   Do me this special favor!
4. While calling, hold up three playing cards in your hand: the ace of spades, the ace of clubs, and the ace of diamonds.
5. When you feel the Lassi's presence, close your eyes and toss the cards up into the air.
6. Open your eyes: observe and analyze the way the cards land, which ones turn face up or which appears most prominent. The ace of diamonds is an extremely favorable response, while the ace of spades is not. The ace of clubs offers moderate, qualified encouragement.

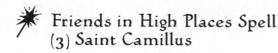

Friends in High Places Spell (3) Saint Camillus

Sometimes you need a different type of help with gambling. Petition Saint Camillus to help you stop gambling. Saint Camillus (1550–1614) was a Neapolitan solder; a nobleman's son, whose addiction to gambling was so severe that he literally lost his shirt and ended up begging in the street. Camillus took a job doing construction work for the Capuchins, the only ones who would hire him. This attempt to rebuild his life resulted in spiritual epiphany and ultimately his sainthood.

Petition Camillus when you need him; light a white candle in his honor. Offer him a little cash and a sample of your poison: playing cards, dice, racing forms, or whatever represents gambling to you. His feast day is July 14th.

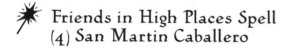

Friends in High Places Spell (4) San Martin Caballero

San Martin Caballero is Saint Martin of Tours in his guise as Saint Martin the Horseman. A spirit of exceptional generosity, he rewards devotees with luck and money. Burn white or red candles for Saint Martin. Place a horseshoe charm beside the candles; wear it to carry his blessings and power with you.

Friends in High Places Spell (5) Saint Simon's Lucky Number Spell

Saint Simon, the hero of Tuscan magic, may be an apostle. He may also be that Simon (or Simeon) who performed Christ's circumcision, tying him to the magical traditions of smithcraft—ironsmiths even today serving as wandering circumcisers in traditional areas of Asia and Africa. He may also be that bane of the early Christian Church, the competing magician Simon Magus, hiding under the ultimate disguise.

Whoever he is, Saint Simon has earned a reputation for providing all sorts of needed information, especially winning lottery numbers. You just have to ask for them the right way.

1. For three consecutive nights, just prior to going to sleep, repeat Simon's novena three times in a row at midnight.
2. After the third night, Saint Simon will allegedly manifest himself to you. This may be while you are awake but he usually appears in dreams. His appearance varies: he has been known to appear as a Roman Catholic priest, or as a friar, or in the guise of an ancient Egyptian. He might surprise you. His demeanor, however, is consistent: sullen, grouchy, and bad-tempered.
3. He will demand to know what you want and why you've called him. If you respond truthfully and without fear, he usually grants your wish. If, however, you're not quick and fearless, he's been known to slap petitioners and immediately vanish.

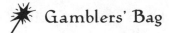

Friends in High Places Spell (6) The Venus Throw Spell

"Lucky at love, unlucky at cards," or how does that old saying go? With assistance from Turanna, the Italian Venus, perhaps you can have both. This beautiful sponsor of lovers also favors gamblers and fortune-tellers. Her number is six and that's why throwing sixes with dice is called "the Venus throw."

Turanna deals out cards and the hands of fate. She may be appealed to for assistance with any matter in addition to her traditional domains. As an act of hopeful devotion and as a communications device, build an altar in Turanna's honor.

1. Instead of a statue, remove the queen of hearts from a new deck of playing cards and use it to represent Turanna.
2. Place three dice, all displaying the number six before the card.
3. Offer Turanna the gifts she likes: sweet liqueurs, perfume, and/or flowers.
4. Request her aid.
5. If and when she comes through for you, give her more presents.

Galangal Root Spell

Galangal root, also known as Courtcase root, also known as Little John to Chew, also known as Southern John, is most closely associated with legal victories. It's also helpful for gamblers.

1. Chew a piece of the root when you need to place a bet, make a selection or a decision.
2. Pay attention to inspiration and intuition.

Gamblers' Bag

Chop an onion into pieces, concentrating on your desire. Put them into a red charm bag together with alder bark and six juniper berries.

Gamblers' Candle Spell

The popular perception of magic spells worked with figure candles is similar to that of spells using dolls; people often presume that these spells are malevolent hexes worked on someone else. However, figure candles can also be used to draw good fortune toward you.

1. Obtain a human figure candle that represents you.
2. Carve the candle with your name, identifying information, and any potential lucky numbers.
3. Dress the candle with **Magnet Oil** and **Black Cat Oil.**
4. Put extra **Magnet Oil** on the candle's hands or wherever else you think is appropriate.
5. Burn.

Gamblers' Doll Spell

Dolls, like candles, are as easily used to draw good fortune as bad.

1. Pin together two pieces of red fabric.
2. Draw a human figure meant to represent you onto the top piece of cloth and then cut it using scissors or fabric shears.
3. Embellish the outside of the doll as much as you please, adding lucky symbols and numbers, as desired.
4. Sew three sides together, leaving a hole to stuff the doll.
5. Fill the doll with dried parsley and basil, adding tiny charms as desired: miniature dice, cards, horseshoes, wishbones, and four-leaf clovers, for instance.

6. Completely sew up the doll and finish decorating the surface as you please. Personalize as much as possible. Draw or place a lot of money in your hands.
7. Anoint the doll with **Magnet Oil** and any other Gamblers' Dressing Oils (see below) you choose.
8. Place the doll atop a square of gold-colored fabric together with lots of play money—Chinese spirit money or Monopoly money or similar.
9. Wrap everything up, rolling towards you. Safety pin the packet together and keep in a discreet, secure place.
10. Whenever you've won or whenever your luck needs reinforcing, anoint with more **Magnet Oil.**

Gamblers' Dressing Oils

Gamblers' Dressing Oils are magic formula oils created to enhance a gambler's luck. Many of the most potent condition formula oils are extremely versatile and used for a variety of purposes, for instance, **Black Cat Oil**, **Magnet Oil**, and **High John the Conqueror Oil** have many uses, gambling and otherwise. Find instructions in the *Formulary* (page 1037). Other oils are used somewhat exclusively for gambling. This is a popular magical category: choose whichever dressing oil best resonates for you. Select one or several: they combine well together.

Use the dressing oils to:

★ *Anoint mojo hands and lucky charms*
★ *Anoint cards, dice, chips, and other paraphernalia, if possible*
★ *Anoint corners of lottery tickets, race cards, and similar*
★ *Rub a drop between your palms before playing*
★ *Anoint candles during spells to increase and enhance good fortune*

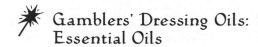

Gamblers' Dressing Oils: Essential Oils

Essential oils are used to blend magic formula oils but can also be extremely potent independently, if you've got the right oil. Essential oils of basil and bergamot are most strongly associated with financial luck.

Rub one single drop of either or both oils between your palms before playing, or use them to anoint candles, charms, and lottery tickets in the same way that condition dressing oils would be used.

Gamblers' Dressing Oils: Fast Luck Oils

Fast Luck Oils bring money and love fast, as promised, but be aware that this is "quick-fix magic." Don't count on it to last. Fast Luck Oils are designed for those living in the moment or desperate for a quick hit of good fortune. They are believed to be particularly beneficial for those playing slot machines or any sort of fast-paced game involving dumb luck, versus more complex games of chance. Place a drop of Fast Luck Oil onto the slot machine or anoint your hands just before playing.

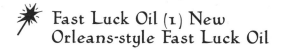

Fast Luck Oil (1) New Orleans-style Fast Luck Oil

Cinnamon
Vanilla
Wintergreen

1. Use essential oils or grind up a cinnamon stick and a vanilla bean and then anoint the resulting blend with essential oil of wintergreen (rarely available in other forms).
2. Add them to jojoba oil.

✺ Fast Luck Oil (2) Fast Luck Bingo

Add agar-agar (Sea Spirit) to New Orleans-style Fast Luck Oil; rub it between your palms before playing, or anoint the card.

✺ Fast Luck Oil (3) Red Fast Luck Oil

This is basically the same formula as regular New Orleans-style Fast Luck Oil except that this dressing oil is red, to intensify the luck. Traditionally the red color was obtained with alkanet root, an ancient natural dye. Alkanet bestows its own gifts: it protects money and draws luck towards you. Unfortunately, like other those other natural dyes, woad, madder, and indigo, it's not easy to use. Add it carefully and slowly. Red food coloring lacks the power of alkanet but, like the promise of the oil, it is fast, and easy.

✺ Gamblers' Dressing Oils: Gamblers' Oil

Essential oil of bergamot
Essential oil of basil
Essential oil of sandalwood

1. Add the essential oils to a bottle filled with jojoba oil.
2. Add allspice berries and powdered nutmeg.

✺ Gamblers' Dressing Oils: Has No Hanna

*Zora Neale-Hurston described this as "jasmine lotion," and an adequate **Has No Hanna Oil** may be made by adding jasmine essence to unscented hand lotion. However, this limits its applications to rubbing on the hands and body. If you'd like to dress candles, charms, and conjure bags, use essential oils or botanical material instead, blended into carrier oil. Some versions of **Has No Hanna** also contain essences of tangerine and gardenia. This rendition adds some dried lucky herbs, too:*

Essential oil of jasmine
Essential oil of tangerine (mandarin orange)
Dried powdered oakmoss or the essential oil
Dried powdered vervain
Optional ingredients: fresh jasmine blossoms; dried tangerine zest.

1. For maximum power, add the above ingredients to Tahitian monoi or infused gardenia oil. Monoi is coconut oil infused with Tahitian gardenia, and is one of the only methods of purchasing genuine gardenia fragrance. Monoi solidifies in cooler temperature. Place the bottle inside a pot of warm water to liquefy the oil. (If true gardenia-scented oil is impossible, use jojoba oil as a carrier base.)
2. Roll the bottle gently to distribute the essential oils.
3. Place an open safety pin in the bottle.

✺ Gamblers' Dressing Oils: Lucky Dog Oil

Dried carnation petals
Dried oakmoss
Dried powdered vervain
Dried five-finger grass (cinquefoil)

1. Grind and powder the dried ingredients.
2. Place them in a bottle and cover with jojoba oil.
3. Add allspice berries, a nutmeg and/or a Low John root.

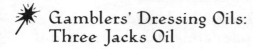

Gamblers' Dressing Oils: Three Jacks Oil

As its name implies, this dressing oil is most beneficial for card players.

Dried patchouli
Dried vetiver
Galangal root
Optional ingredients: cardamom; cinnamon; cloves

1. Grind and powder all ingredients.
2. Add to jojoba oil.
3. If you can find itty-bitty playing cards, stick a jack, preferably one-eyed, into the bottle. Otherwise or in addition, add whole cardamom pods and cloves.

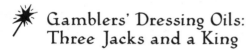

Gamblers' Dressing Oils: Three Jacks and a King

Dried patchouli
Dried vetiver
Galangal root
High John the Conqueror

This is basically a more potent version of Three Jacks Oil. However, whichever resonates strongest for you will provide the best luck.

1. Powder the ingredients and add them to jojoba oil.
2. Add cardamom, cinnamon or cloves as desired.
3. Use similarly to Three Jacks Oil. If you want to add a tiny playing card, choose the king of diamonds.

Gamblers' Hand Spells

What's in a gambler's hand anyway? Loaded dice? A palmed card? "*Hand*" is another term for a mojo, medicine, charm or conjure bag. Sometimes a hand is a work in progress, a collection of lucky charms accumulated along the way. Some spells, however, specify exactly what goes into a hand.

Traditionally items are charged and consecrated prior to being placed in the bag. Reinforce the spell by anointing with one of the Gamblers' Dressing Oils. When you need the hand to work at full strength for you, re-charge the items and anoint with more oil.

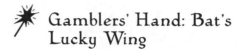

Gamblers' Hand: Bat's Lucky Wing

1. Place a holly leaf, five red holly berries, and a cat's-eye gemstone in a drawstring bag.
2. Add dried, powdered ginger.
3. Spit in the bag gently.
4. Close the bag and tie it shut with nine knots, visualizing luck and success with each knot.

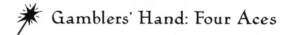

Gamblers' Hand: Four Aces

*Place four aces, one representing each suit, in a mojo bag together with a High John the Conqueror root and a matched pair of lodestones. Anoint with **All High Conquering Oil** as needed.*

Gamblers' Hand: High John's Snake Charm

Wrap a rattlesnake root and a High John the Conqueror root up in a piece of freely shed snakeskin. Place this within a conjure bag, adding seven tonka beans for good fortune.

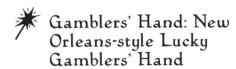 ## Gamblers' Hand: Lucky Spirit Guardian

Place a galangal root, a matched pair of lodestones, a four-leaf clover (either real or a replica charm), and seven tonka beans in a conjure bag, together with a medal of Saint Anthony and/or a charm depicting a fork-tailed mermaid.

Gamblers' Hand: New Orleans-style Lucky Gamblers' Hand

1. Add the following to a red flannel drawstring bag:
   One Lucky Hand root
   One High John the Conqueror root
   A pinch of cinquefoil (five-finger grass)
   Miniature dice (a pair), horseshoe and/or playing cards
2. Use essential oil of basil, **Magnet oil** or any other gambling or money-drawing oil to dress the bag
3. Pull the red flannel bag closed. Place this bag inside a leather pouch or drawstring bag and carry it with you when needed.

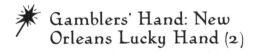 ## Gamblers' Hand: New Orleans Lucky Hand (2)

1. Dress a lodestone and a High John the Conqueror root with **Black Cat Oil** and Lucky Dog Oil.
2. Sprinkle them with magnetic sand. (Some prefer magnetic sand dyed green or gold but regular is fine, too.)
3. Place inside a red flannel drawstring bag together with a pair of miniature dice.
4. Place this bag inside a second leather pouch or drawstring bag.
5. Anoint the lodestone and High John with dressing oils weekly or as needed.

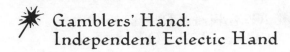 ## Gamblers' Hand: Independent Eclectic Hand

Let inspiration and the Hand of Fate help you create your own hand, by collecting gamblers' charms as you find them, charging them with your intention, anointing them with dressing oils and placing them within a bag.

Look out for the following Gamblers' Lucky Charms:

★ *Amazonite*
★ *Cat's eye crystal gemstone*
★ *High John the Conqueror root*
★ *Lodestone*
★ *Lucky Hand root*
★ *Magnets, especially magnetic horseshoes or other charms*

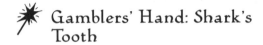 ## Gamblers' Hand: Shark's Tooth

Sometimes very specific goals must be achieved.

1. Add pinesap to **Bat's Blood Ink.**
2. Write the amount you need to win or the goal needed to be achieved on a piece of parchment.
3. Place this talisman inside a piece of red fabric with a shark's tooth.
4. Sew it up with cat hair. (Anyone who lives with a cat has hair a-plenty on sweaters, sofas and coats and will be delighted to share it with you. There's no need to bother the cat nor will doing so bring you good luck. Quite the opposite, in fact.)
5. Carry this charm in a left pocket over your heart or wear it within your left shoe.
6. Once the charm has worked, take it apart and burn the parchment. Reserve the shark's tooth for future use.

Gamblers' Handwash

The term *"handwash"* is deceptive: it makes you think of soap and water. These are actually liquid hand *rubs*, a sort of lingering final rinse, perhaps. They are intended to remain on the hands, radiating luck and power, while the gambler plays.

★ *Apply handwash just before playing so that it retains its strength*

★ *Carry it into a casino, bingo parlor or other venue in a flask or bottle (although, as we will see, other traditional methods of application also exist)*

★ *Do not wash the handwash off until it's no longer needed. If you must wash your hands, reapply as needed*

 ### Gamblers' Handwash (1) Galangal

1. Boil galangal roots in rainwater and then let this cool.
2. Strain the roots and reserve the liquid.
3. Place the liquid in a flask: use it to wash your hands before gambling.
4. Let them air dry or shake them dry.

 ### Gamblers' Handwash (2) Girlfriend Handwash

According to one old New Orleans formula, the best gamblers' luck doesn't come from celestial goddesses of good fortune but from the mortal woman who really wants you to win. The most powerful mode of application is believed to be direct application:

1. The gambler's female companion urinates either directly onto his hands or onto his mojo bag to provide him with luck. (Urine is considered a profound controlling mechanism.)

2. Again air or shake dry.

If preferred, urine may be kept in a bottle or flask and applied as needed.

 ### Gamblers' Handwash (3) Girlfriend Double Dose Handwash

1. Blend the gambler's female companion's urine and **Chypre** in a flask, for a double-dose of power.
2. Use this to dress the gambler's hands just before playing.

 ### Gamblers' Handwash (4) Girlfriend-Won't-Do-It Handwash

Because you could really use the luck but one or both of you was appalled by and absolutely rejected the previous suggestions, a substitute has evolved:

1. Make a strong infusion by pouring boiling water over dried chamomile blossoms.
2. When it cools off, have your girlfriend stir it with her little finger.
3. Strain the liquid, carry it in a flask, and use it as a handwash just before playing.

 ### Gamblers' Handwash (5) High John Handwash

1. Place seven large High John roots in a gallon (4.5 liters) of rainwater.
2. Bring this to a boil, and then simmer it for twenty-one minutes.
3. Let it cool.
4. Place the liquid in a flask or bottle.
5. Use as a handwash prior to gambling.

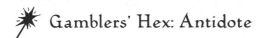

Gamblers' Handwash (6)
Gambler's Lucky 7 Handwash

Make an infusion by pouring boiling water over alfalfa, allspice, calendula, chamomile, cinnamon, clover, and Irish moss. Allow the infusion to cool, then strain out the botanical material and use as needed.

Gamblers' Handwash (7)
Hawthorn Handwash

Hawthorn allegedly draws good fortune. Create an infusion by pouring boiling water over hawthorn leaves and berries. Strain out the botanicals and bottle the liquid. Rub it on your hands and allow them to air-dry as needed.

Inevitably, if someone wins, someone else loses. The temptation to hex a competitor can be very strong:

Gamblers' Hex: To Keep a Horse from Winning a Race

1. Collect dirt from the horse's hoof.
2. Wrap it in cloth together with asafetida.
3. Tie the package up with a twisty vine.
4. Place it under a heavy stone or something of comparable weight.

Gamblers' Hex: Antidote

The antidote to the above spell? Keep your horse's hooves immaculately clean, and be aware of who has access to your horse.

Gamblers' Incense

The advantage of incense is that the power inherent in the botanicals can permeate an entire area. For maximum effect, use the incense to fumigate clothing, tools, and anything else that could use some magical assistance.

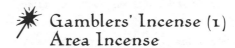

Gamblers' Incense (1)
Area Incense

This classic formula is just known as Gamblers' Incense:

Dragon's blood
Frankincense
Mastic pearls

Grind all materials to a powder. Sprinkle it on lit charcoals and burn weekly for luck and inspiration.

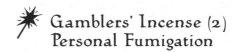

Gamblers' Incense (2)
Personal Fumigation

Gamblers' Incense may also be used as a personal fumigant.

1. Create Gamblers' Incense as above.
2. Launder the clothes you intend to wear while gambling.
3. Hang them from the bathroom shower curtain rod to dry, while burning the incense in the bathroom, so that they are permeated with fragrance.

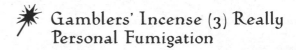

Gamblers' Incense (3) Really Personal Fumigation

Fumigate yourself instead of or in addition to your clothing.

1. Create Gamblers' Incense as above.
2. Burn it on lit charcoals in a brazier or burner placed on the floor.
3. Permeate hair and skin with the fragrance by standing over the incense.

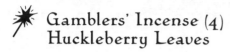

Gamblers' Incense (4) Huckleberry Leaves

Grind and powder dried huckleberry leaves, and then burn them before bedtime for dreams filled with lucky numbers.

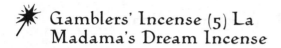

Gamblers' Incense (5) La Madama's Dream Incense

Allegedly inhaling the aroma of this incense stimulates dreams of winning lottery numbers. (This Dream Powder may also fulfill other dreams; it is reputed to be an aphrodisiac.)

> Cardamom
> Cinnamon
> Coriander seeds
> Licorice root

Grind the ingredients into a fine powder. Add a pinch to a lit charcoal on an incense burner placed beside your bed right before going to sleep.

Gambling Horses

Horses are Poseidon's sacred creatures. The King of the Sea allegedly created horses from rolling, breaking waves. Horse races were given in Poseidon's honor in the same manner that the Olympic games were held to honor Zeus. Request Poseidon's aid for gambling luck with the ponies.

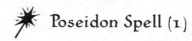

Poseidon Spell (1)

Aquamarine and beryl are Poseidon's sacred stones. Carry these gem talismans with you to the race track.

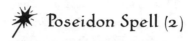

Poseidon Spell (2)

Carry ocean water in a flask and wash your hands prior to placing bets.

Gambling Powders

The difference between powders and incense is largely in their mode of use: typically incense is burned while powders are sprinkled, used as dry perfumes or stuffing for mojo hands. Arrowroot powder is traditionally an extremely auspicious base for gambling powders, though rice powder or cornstarch are also suitable. Do not substitute talcum powder.

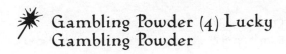

Gambling Powder (1) Algiers Powder

A traditional gamblers' formula, Algiers Powder evokes whispers of Hedy Lamarr, Pépé le Moko, and the labyrinthine Casbah. Those whispers would be wrong. Algiers Powder isn't named after the capital of Algeria but instead for a town in the southern United States. During a nineteenth-century period of intense legal harassment and persecution, New Orleans voodooists fled en masse *across the Mississippi River to Algiers, which eventually developed a magical reputation equal to its sister city.*

    Cinnamon sticks
    Dried patchouli leaves
    Vanilla beans

Grind all the ingredients together with a mortar and pestle. Carry the powder in a conjure bag and sprinkle and rub as needed.

In addition to providing gambling success, Algiers Powder promises increased money, in general, and luck in love.

Gambling Powder (2) Algiers Spell

1. Write the amount of money needed on a piece of brown paper.
2. Sprinkle Algiers Powder over the paper.
3. Fold it up and burn it.
4. Sprinkle the ashes on your shoes before going out to play.

Gambling Powder (3) Lottery Luck Powder

Grind black pepper and cinnamon together and sprinkle them in the corners of your home, around your bed, and in your wallet for good luck with the lottery.

Gambling Powder (4) Lucky Gambling Powder

    Sandalwood powder
    Dried powdered carnation petals
    Ground cinnamon
    Frankincense
    Myrrh

1. Grind and blend into a fine powder.
2. Leave the powder as is or blend it into cornstarch or rice powder for a smoother consistency.
3. Sprinkle and rub as needed.

Ginger-root Charm

Anoint pieces of ginger root with Lucky Dog Oil and carry them in a mojo bag.

High John's All Conquering Lucky Spells

High John the Conqueror, the root of a morning glory, indigenous to Mexico, draws luck and good fortune.

High John (1) Basic

1. Dress a High John root with essential oil of bergamot once a week for gamblers' luck or whenever you have a large win.
2. Carry it in your pocket or in a gamblers' hand.

High John (2) Incense

1. Grind and powder High John the Conqueror.
2. Burn it as incense once a week and especially before gambling.

High John Spell (3) Candle Spell

1. Once a week, carve a green candle with your name, identifying information and lucky numbers.
2. Dress the candle with **Magnet Oil** or other gambling oil of your preference.
3. Sprinkle powdered High John the Conqueror over and around the candle.
4. Burn it for blessings of luck, good fortune, and winning numbers.

Lottery Numbers Spell

1. Obtain one small (birthday candle-size will do) green or gold candle for every number needed. In other words, if your game has six numbers, six candles are required.
2. Charge each candle with its mission of discovering winning numbers.
3. Dress the candles with Fast Luck, Lucky Dog or **Black Cat Oil.**
4. Burn one candle at a time. Gaze at the flame and let the number pop into your head. Fill in the lottery ticket as you cast your spell.
5. Repeat until all the candles are lit.
6. Sprinkle the ticket with Money Drawing Powder or magnetic sand.
7. Place a dry lodestone on top of the ticket. (You don't want your ticket to be stained with oil.)
8. Pinch out the candles, if they haven't burned out already.
9. Let the ticket sit with the lodestone overnight, then play.

After you've burned a candle, what do you do with the leftover wax? Although many spells specify that you dispose of it, the temptation to hold on to it can be powerful, particularly when the spell was potent or when, as in days gone by, wax and oils were precious and expensive. These wax balls may also be understood as conjure bags carried in wax rather than cloth. In Hoodoo, they're categorized as "*jack balls.*" Well known in European occult traditions, they were particularly popular in Spain, where they are referred to as *luck balls, love balls, money balls* or whatever the specific purpose of the spell may be.

 ## Luck Ball

1. Burn gambling luck candles: plain purple or green candles, or perhaps one of the cat candles. More than one candle may be used. (Carve the candle, if you wish, but don't dress it heavily with oil, as this may affect the eventual texture and consistency of the wax.)
2. If you have a specific monetary (or other) goal, write it on a piece of paper and slip it under the only or most prominent candle. Burn it.
3. Gather up a small handful of warm soft wax.
4. Roll it into a ball. (The size depends upon what's comfortable for you and what you wish to insert inside it.)
5. Push lucky charms into the wax: little dice, little magnetic horseshoes, four-leaf clover charms, etc.
6. Roll the wax in powdered herbs such as basil, vervain or parsley, or in one of the gambling powders.
7. Carry this as a mojo hand or in a mojo hand Anoint with dressing oils as needed.

As gambling occurs outside the casino, too, this is also good for general good fortune, for playing life's Wheel of Fortune.

Lucky Cat Spells

Lucky dogs to the contrary, cats are the animal allies of gamblers and games of chance.

Lucky Cat Spell (1) Big Cat!

If you want lots of luck, you may require a larger cat. In traditional Chinese magic, the tiger is the animal ally of gamblers. This fierce animal drives away bad luck.

1. Post the image of a rampant tiger clutching cash to provide enhanced gambling success.
2. Contemplate the image before playing.
3. Burn incense or spirit money before the image for extra success or to give thanks as needed.

 ## Lucky Cat Spell (2) Big Cat (2)

There are also more active methods of accessing tiger-power, albeit without injuring the tiger.

1. Charge tiger's eye crystal gemstone with your desires.
2. Pass it through gamblers' incense and carry within a conjure bag.

 ## Lucky Cat Spell (3) Cat's Eye

Small cats are powerful, too. In addition to general gambling luck, cat's eye gemstones are believed especially fortuitous for lottery players and speculators in the stock market. Carry them in your pocket or charm bag. Keep one on your desk or by your telephone, computer or most frequent method of transaction.

 ## Lucky Cat Spells (4) Candle

Candles in the shape of cats are the figure candles most associated with gambling magic. Red, black or green candles may all be used. Let your intuition guide you.

1. Inscribe the candle with your name, identifying information, and any lucky numbers.

2. Dress it with **Black Cat Oil** or another gamblers' luck oil.
3. Burn the candle.

 ## Lucky Hand Oil

Grind and powder the following ingredients: cinnamon, cloves, five-finger grass (cinquefoil), and peony roots. Add them to sunflower and jojoba oils and rub the oil on your hands as needed, or use it to anoint cash or chips.

 ## Make a Wish Easter Sunday Spell

Although many spells demand discretion, if that's a concern for you, you'll never be able to cast this Russian gambler's spell. It can only be accomplished at church on Easter Sunday.

1. Be alert and pay attention.
2. When the priest announces, *"Christ is risen,"* immediately shout out loud something like, *"I've got an ace!"* or *"I have a full house,"* or whatever it is that you need. Allegedly whatever you call out will be yours for the year.

Spit Spell

Saliva, like urine, is believed able to transmit your will.

Spit forcefully (with intent!) *but lightly (you need to be able to turn them in) on lottery tickets, race cards or similar. Spitting on your palms before applying handwash or dressing oils, or spitting into your mojo hand, may also be effective.*

Thoth's Roll of the Dice Spell

Invoke Thoth for success with games of dice. After all, he invented them and won the very first game. Place a pair of dice atop the Magician card pulled from a tarot deck and light a candle beside it.

 ## Toad Spell

The name of the game "craps" allegedly derives from the French word crapaud, *meaning "toads." Frogs and toads have symbolized the concept of increase and generation since at least the days of ancient Egypt.*

Just before rolling the dice, discreetly touch them to the genitals to endow them with generative power.

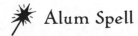 Happy Home Spells

Home sweet home. Sounds nostalgic, but nowhere as exciting as gambling, wild sex, fame and fortune—the usual goals of magic spells. That may be true but when all isn't peaceful on the home front it can be hard to concentrate on anything else. Sometimes what you need more than anything is a peaceful home and a family that doesn't argue. Magic offers advice for pouring oil on troubled waters.

Some Happy Home Spells concern themselves with who's in the home; they allegedly provide peace in the family and create an aura of tranquility. Other spells are concerned with the home—the residence or dwelling—itself. In many cases, in accordance with the belief that it's easier to prevent trouble than fix it, Happy Home Spells are meant to be performed as soon as or before one moves into a new home.

☀ Alum Spell

Alum magically "eats" negativity. That said, let alum do all the eating. Do not consume it yourself, and make sure it's kept away from children and animals.

1. Place alum in dishes.
2. Discreetly arrange to eliminate negative feelings and behavior.
3. Replace at least once a week.

☀ Alum Extra Strength

*Blend alum and **Florida Water** and arrange strategically around the room. Replace weekly.*

Anger Powder

If **Peace Water** encourages peace and **War Water** is a tool of psychic warfare, what does Anger Powder do? Wrong! Anger Powder is used as a banishing agent to dispel angry emotions. Asafetida and sulfur are both components of various exorcism formulas, so one could say that Anger Powder exorcises anger. Of course, another reason it may work is because Anger Powder smells so foul everyone will desert the area, leaving no one left to be angry.

Asafetida
Black pepper
Chili powder
Sulfur powder

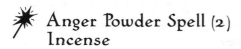

Anger Powder Spell (1) Sprinkle

Sprinkle the powder as needed, in areas where tension and anger occurs or where you anticipate it strongly. To make the powder more "powdery" blend it with rice powder or cornstarch.

Anger Powder Spell (2) Incense

Sprinkle Anger Powder onto lit charcoals and burn as incense. Be sure to provide proper ventilation, as it isn't advisable to inhale sulfur fumes.

Ashes Spell

For this Russian spell to protect and maintain the stability of the home, gather ashes from seven wood stoves and sprinkle them on to your stove, hearth, or cauldron.

Basil Happiness Spells

Surround your dwelling with fresh basil so as to draw and increase joy within the home, and to stimulate tranquility, harmony, cooperation, and peace.

★ *Grow basil in your garden and around the house*
★ *Place pots of fresh basil by your front entrance and around the perimeter of your home*
★ *If it's not possible to grow basil, then place fresh basil in a vase in a prominent spot in your kitchen, replacing it weekly or as soon as it starts to spoil*

★ *Cook with it as much as possible, or incorporate it into spellwork. (Since basil also draws love and money towards you, this isn't a painful, difficult recommendation!)*

Blessed Water Spells

Certain magically charged formula waters simultaneously provide house blessings with space cleansing spells.

Blessed Water Spell (1) Notre Dame Water

Notre Dame Water promotes peace, calm, and serenity; summons benevolent spirits to your home and disperses any malevolent ones lingering about.

Place a few spoonfuls into open dishes and distribute through the house. Add more as it evaporates.

Blessed Water Spell (2) Notre Dame Maximum Strength

1. Sprinkle **Notre Dame Water** through the home using a white rose as an asperging tool.
2. Concentrate on corners, closets, thresholds, and any areas that are frequent sites of tension and dissension.

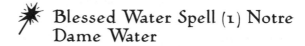

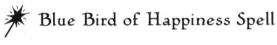

Blessed Water Spell (3) Rose of Jericho Water

Rose of Jericho Water has many uses including healing, cleansing, and protection. Its presence also encourages serenity and tranquility.

1. Rehydrate a Rose of Jericho flower, by placing it into a dish and covering it with water.
2. After the rose blossoms, retain the flower but change the water weekly.
3. Don't throw out the old water—it's packed with magic power. Use it to attract blessings of peace, protection, and prosperity to your home.
4. Pour the old water out onto your front doorstep, in an auspicious shape. Choose a pentacle, hexagram, crescent moon, cross or other. Sprinkle the shape of a sigil or rune, if you prefer.

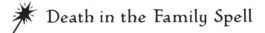

Blue Bird of Happiness Spell

Rare blue flowers confer peace and protection on a home. Grow cornflowers, delphinium, bluebells, and hydrangeas. Reserve the blossoms; dry, grind, and powder them, and then sprinkle the powder discreetly through the home.

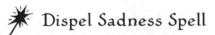

Death in the Family Spell

In the event of the death of the "head of the family," the main protector or income provider, preserve a lock of her or his hair. Nail it beside the lintel of the main entrance with an iron nail to maintain the household's prosperity and protection.

Dispel Sadness Spell

When a home is filled with oppressive, contagious sadness, this spell can be very effective.

1. Hold a white candle in both hands while you think of all your sorrows and the causes for them.
2. Write these sorrows onto a piece of white paper. Ideally **Dove's Blood Ink** or myrrh-scented red ink should be used, but don't give yourself further cause for stress and grief. Just use red ink if that's easiest or whatever you have.
3. Anoint the page with honey.
4. Fold it up.
5. Light the candle. Use the candle flame to burn the note, while chanting something along the lines of:
   I give my sadness to the flames
   The Spirit of Fire eats my grief and pain
   (Substitute goddess, god, lady or lord of fire— whatever corresponds to your beliefs. You may also substitute the name of a fire spirit, if you choose.)

Djinn Happy Home Spells

Although some djinn have a reputation for taking over homes, creating a haunted house effect, others help maintain home peace, tranquility, good fortune, and home security. The first spell is beneficial for new homes or those that have recently undergone major construction; follow it with spell two—considered beneficial for every home.

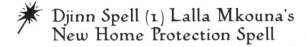

Djinn Spell (1) Lalla Mkouna's New Home Protection Spell

Because nature abhors a vacuum, a vacant home, especially one just fixed up and improved, is very inviting to spiritual visitation. In much the same way that nosy neighbors can't wait to get inside and look around, so low-level spirits hover, eager to see what's new and perhaps make themselves at home. Lalla Mkouna bent Mkoun, daughter of the Sultan of Demons, is an extremely powerful but unusually benevolent djinn. As befitting the daughter of royalty, she serves in a

spiritually supervisory capacity: She keeps an eye on other rowdier spirits. Invite her to supervise spiritual proceedings in your new home and keep the riff-raff out.

1. Invoke Lalla Mkouna with offerings of fragrant incense to serve as the guardian of a new home before the family moves in, to ensure that no malevolent djinn or other spirit moves in with you.
2. After you've called her with incense, appeal to her verbally and tell her what you need.

 ## Djinn Spell (2) The Three Stones of the House

Lalla Mkouna and her two retainers are called the "three stones of the house" because they provide a foundation of stability and tranquility. Invite these three benevolent female djinn to linger in your home, providing blessings of peace and prosperity. "Lalla" literally means "lady" and is the title of respect used to address virtually all female djinn—at least the nicer ones.

1. Use actual stones to represent them in their rightful places at the hearth.
2. Regularly scheduled, consistent offerings keep them working on your behalf; offer them a little extra when they've performed substantial work or favors. The traditional offering is oil drizzled over a plate of flour.
3. Place the plates in the djinn's respective spots in the fireplace: Lalla Haniya brings peace. She sits at the right side of the hearth. Lalla Guiya brings wealth. She sits to the left of the hearth. Lalla Mkouna holds the center; she assists with everyday maintenance and well being of the home.

Dragon's Blood Spells

Dragon's blood is a resin derived from the fruit of an Indonesian palm tree. Among its myriad other magical uses, dragon's blood is believed to neutralize negative energy and provide spiritual protection.

 ## Dragon's Blood (1) Basic Happier Home Incense

1. Blend dragon's blood and frankincense together in a mortar and pestle.
2. Burn it over lit charcoals, wafting it in specific areas as needed.

 ## Dragon's Blood (2) Discreet Peace Protection

1. Pulverize dragon's blood resin.
2. Blend the resulting powder together with salt and sugar.
3. Put this powder inside a matchbox.
4. Place the matchbox in a white envelope and seal it.
5. You may wish to decorate the envelope with magical seals, sigils and/or runes, if only to help you distinguish this envelope from others.
6. Hide the envelope so that you alone know where it is. You should be able to maintain control and peace in the home.

 ## Dragon's Blood (3) Public Peace Protection

1. Mix sugar, salt, and dragon's blood powder.
2. Place it in a small bottle.
3. Seal the bottle with red wax and keep it in the kitchen to maintain peace in the home and between family members.

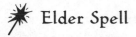 ## Elder Spell

Here's a cheerful spell: keeping elder (meaning elder twigs, leaves or berries, rather than elderly people) in the home allegedly ensures a happy, peaceful death for all the inhabitants.

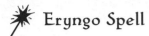 ## Eryngo Spell

Eryngo (sea holly) allegedly stops couples from quarreling. Keep eryngo in rooms where peace is needed.

Fairy Blessing Spell

Leave a bouquet of primroses on your doorstep or threshold overnight to invite the fairies to bless your home with happiness, luck, and prosperity.

Family Unity Spells

The nature of a magic spell, whether positive or malevolent, is determined by intent rather than mechanics. Although many associate hair and nail clippings with malevolent manifestations of magic, vindictive figure spells, for instance, they also have benevolent applications. Although these spells ask for major blessings, they generally use only modest ingredients—typically intimate items, usually collected under a mother's direction, to provide safety, peace and harmony amongst family members.

Family Unity Spell (1)
Hair Clippings

1. Take a small hair clipping from every member of the family.
2. Roll it up in a leaf, rolling toward you.

3. Fasten it with the strand of the mother's hair (or the father, or whoever is the unifying focal point of the family).
4. Bury it under a tree.

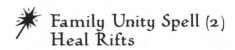 ## Family Unity Spell (2)
Heal Rifts

To heal rifts and maintain the unity of the family, you will need one hair from the head of each person in the family or each person involved in the rift, whatever you deem appropriate.

1. Braid them and tie together with red silk thread
2. Wrap the braid in more red silk thread, winding it and making seven knots in it.
3. Wrap this in a small square of white silk.
4. Bury this packet at a crossroads.

Family Unity Spell (3)
Paper Doll Spell

Make paper dolls, one to represent each member of the family. Tie them together and place them in a basket to signify the unity of the family. Keep them safely as charms or use them in the following ritual, as needed:

One person, usually but not always the mother, is designated leader of this ritual. She takes out the little puppets, one by one, from the basket and begs each to take on any bad luck coming to the individual it represents. When the ritual is complete, in the presence of everyone, the dolls are burned and pass into the spirit realm.

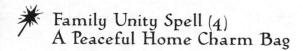 ## Family Unity Spell (4)
A Peaceful Home Charm Bag

The ingredients for this spell are:

A single strand of hair from each member of the
family (add animal hairs from pets if you like, too)
Blue thread
A piece of angelica root
Essential oil of German chamomile
Balm of Gilead buds
Flax seeds
Lavender blossoms
Pink and white rose buds

1. Make a braid with the hair and thread.
2. Use the braid to tie a bow around the angelica root.
3. Anoint the root with one drop of chamomile oil for
   every member of the family.
4. Place the root together with the other ingredients
   into a sachet or conjure bag.

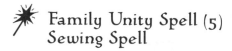 ## Family Unity Spell (5)
Sewing Spell

*Magic can be created from the humblest articles: this
spell derives from a time when sewing, mending, and
needlework were constant, everyday practices.*

1. Keep a little jar beside you as you sew.
2. Every time you finish a thread, toss the bit into the
   jar, saying something to the effect of *"Bless this
   house. Protect all within from harm and hardship."*
3. When the jar is full, seal the blessings within by
   laying one protective leaf or root on top.
   (Suggestions are bay laurel leaf, angelica root,
   bethroot or wormwood.)
4. Close the jar tightly and store it near the top of the
   house, in the attic, or hang it from the rafters.

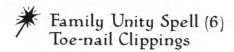 ## Family Unity Spell (6)
Toe-nail Clippings

1. Gather toe-nail clippings from each member of the
   family.
2. Wrap them in cloth and bury at the foot of a tree.

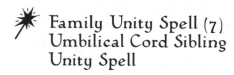 ## Family Unity Spell (7)
Umbilical Cord Sibling
Unity Spell

1. Dry and reserve your children's umbilical cords.
2. Save them in an amulet bag.
3. As each new child is born, tie the umbilical cord to
   that of its siblings to keep the children close, united
   and harmonious.

 ## Flax Seed Spell

*Sprinkle flax seed over the threshold to end dissent and
preserve harmony.*

 ## Gardenia-Mimosa Spell

1. Make an infused oil of gardenia and mimosa.
2. Rub it on woodwork as appropriate.
3. Soak cotton balls and place strategically in rooms, to
   promote serenity and family harmony.

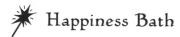 ## Happiness Bath

This one is not for pregnant women!

1. Make an infusion by pouring boiling water over a
   bunch of parsley.
2. Strain out the parsley while the liquid remains hot
   and stir in cinnamon honey.
3. Add to your bath.

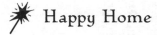 Happy Home

1. Place dried motherwort in a jar.
2. Surround it with family picures.

 Happy Home Charm Bag

1. You'll need one bay laurel leaf and one garlic clove for each member of the family. (Four people means four cloves and four leaves, for instance.)
2. Place these in a charm bag and add a pinch of salt, a pinch of five-finger grass, and an iron nail.
3. Dress with **Van Van, Protection** and/or **Saint Martha the Dominator Oil.**
4. Hang in a discreet place within the home; anoint with fresh oil once a week.

 Happy Home Floorwash

Holy Water or **Marie Laveau Water**
Florida Water
White vinegar
Crushed sweet basil leaves
Crushed lavender blossoms
Cascarilla Powder

1. Pour boiling salted water over the lavender and sweet basil.
2. Let the botanicals steep for an hour, then strain out the solids.
3. Add the liquid, together with all other ingredients to a bucket filled with floorwash rinse water.
4. Use this water to cleanse all entrance areas as well as floors and windowsills.

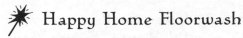 Happy Home Floorwash

Create an infusion of lavender and passionflower. Blend **Cascarilla Powder** *into the strained liquid and add to a bucket of salted floorwash to eliminate disagreements and tension.*

Happy Home Fragrance Blends

Commercially prepared room fresheners are typically crafted from synthetic materials. Who knows what type of powers they possess, if any? Happy Home Spells include what might be considered magical room fresheners; their fragrances range from pleasant to beautiful, though their true goal is the encouragement of happiness, harmony, and cooperation.

 Happy Home Fragrance: Lunar Power Blend

Add essential oils of aloes wood, white camphor, and myrrh to an aroma burner and diffuse through the home to encourage a tranquil, happy atmosphere.

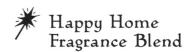 Happy Home Fragrance Blend

Add essential oils of coriander, Roman chamomile, and spearmint to an aroma burner and diffuse the fragrance through the home.

 Happy Home Herb Blend

Blend yerba santa, spearmint, and cascara sagrada in an open dish to encourage happiness and cooperative behavior.

Happy Home Kitchen Blend

Fill the home with the aroma of cinnamon and cloves. Brew the dried spices in water or cider to bring an aura of happiness and tranquility to the home.

Happy Home Incense

Blend frankincense, myrrh, and liquidambar (storax) resins. Burn them to clear away negative energy and to encourage happy spirits, in all senses of that word.

Happy Home Oil

Add gardenia petals, myrrh, and a pinch of five-finger grass to blended jojoba and coconut oil, together with a pinch of salt.

Hazel Twig Spell

Gather fallen hazel twigs on May Day. (Even though they've fallen, thank the tree; libations are not a bad idea.) Collect a strand of hair from every resident of the home (even pets) and tie the hazel twigs up with them for a year of harmony.

Hearth Spell

That happy feeling of security and contentment so frequently derived from simply sitting beside a burning hearth or roaring fireplace indicates that magically more is going on than just burning some wood. The subliminal conjunction of male and female primal energy is extremely potent, protective, and full of blessings. Examples include nailed horseshoes, hexagrams, mortars and pestles, locks and keys. However, a subtler example was once ever-present: the blazing hearth. The hearth itself, or the fireplace, or its modern replacement the cauldron, represents the female principle; fire represents the male. A roaring hearth fire is thus a magical cauldron of transformation, full of power and blessings. Hence the desperate fear of ever letting the fire go out.

At one time, the hearth was the heart of the home. Various benevolent spiritual household guardians made their homes in or under the hearth. Unfortunately today an ever-present, ever-burning hearth fire is rare.

Light the fire, either in the hearth if you have one, or in a cauldron, and magically evoke feelings of happiness and security. Intensify the blessings by tossing magical botanicals into the fire; include any or all of the following: angelica, anise, pine, rosemary, and wisteria.

Home Construction

Although China's *feng shui* is internationally the most famous school of metaphysical home arrangement, it isn't the only one. India's *Vastu shastra* is a similarly complex, cohesive system. Its name translates as *"the science of the environment"* or *"the science of structure."* Other traditions may place less emphasis on structural organization; however, most offer at least a few isolated tips and suggestions for maintaining your happy home. According to Jewish metaphysical wisdom, if you're rebuilding your home or involved in some major construction, if at all possible don't alter the position of doors and windows. Doing so aggravates angels, demons, and other spirits, making them grouchy and spiteful rather than helpful and benevolent.

Home Protection Oil

Home Protection Oil provides spiritual protection and encourages a serene peaceful atmosphere to prevail in your home.

Home Protection Oil Spell (1)

1. Anoint areas of the home, especially areas perceived as vulnerable or areas that have suffered tension and arguments.
2. Reapply the oil once a week or as needed.

 ## Home Protection Oil Spell(2)

1. Use the oil to dress candles, burning them to preserve peace, tranquility, happiness, and security at home.
2. Keep these candles burning as needed, whether once weekly or constantly.

Home Protection Spell

1. Collect rocks and pebbles from your travels, especially places where you felt safe and happy.
2. Charge them in your hands.
3. Keep them in open terracotta pot.
4. Use to cast circles, for ritual or protection, as needed.

House Blessing Incense

The advantage of incense is that its fragrance permeates an area, leaving a lasting, lingering fragrant aura. Burn sufficient quantities to achieve that effect. Concentrate on troublesome areas first or fumigate the whole home. Benzoin is a resin deriving from Sumatra and Thailand. The ancient Egyptians imported it, favoring it for incense blends they considered *"joyful."* Benzoin encourages a relaxed, tension-free atmosphere and is frequently the primary component of what are called *"house blessing incenses."*

 ## House Blessing Incense (1) Basic Benzoin

Burn benzoin incense to create peace, while simultaneously cleansing the atmosphere and providing protection. Benzoin is also reputed to drive off harmful, malicious spirits.

 ## House Blessing Incense (2) Extra Strength Formula

This formula combines benzoin and dragon's blood to ward off malicious spirits, invite benevolent ones, clean out old lingering psychic debris, and encourage a happy, tranquil atmosphere.

Blend benzoin, dragon's blood resin, and dried lavender blossoms together. Sprinkle the powder on lit charcoal and burn.

 ## House Blessing Incense (3) Lighten up the Home Front

Which came first, the chicken or the egg? Depression and low energy are contagious. Sometimes people's energy suffers because the energy in the house is listless. Sometimes, however, the general energy of the home may be dolorous because it has absorbed and retained elements of depression suffered by one or more of the residents. This fumigation simultaneously lightens up the home atmosphere while helping to relieve an individual's feelings of depression.

1. Combine and blend equal parts benzoin, brown sugar, and dried powdered garlic.
2. Burn it in a cast iron pan.

House Blessing Incense (4)
Slavery Era Incense

Although fragrant gum resins were available for burning in the pre-Civil War South, they weren't available to slaves. Among the enslaved Africans brought to the Western hemisphere were magical practitioners, very familiar with those precious resins. Denied access to these materials, they adapted new formulas to fit their needs. This formula, attributed to African-American slaves, is said to sweeten the atmosphere in the home and draw good fortune toward it.

1. Blend several drops of honey with approximately one-quarter pound (100 grams) of brown sugar.
2. Place some of the paste onto lit charcoal or burn it on a cast iron pan and let the fumes circulate through the home.

 ## Joy and Laughter Oil Spell (1)

Add essential oils of sweet orange, lime, and pink grapefruit to a base of jojoba oil. Dress candles with this oil and burn throughout the home to instill joy and laughter.

 ## Joy and Laughter Oil Spell (2)

Spread the joy! Make someone else's home happy, too. Soak cotton balls in Joy and Laughter Oil and carry them in your pockets, so that joy travels with you.

 ## Joy of the Mountain Happy Home Spell

The Origanum *family of botanicals may derive its name from the Greek words* oros, *"mountain," and* ganymai, *"I am joyful." Blend, grind, and powder oregano, marjoram, and Dittany of Crete; sprinkle on* lit charcoal and waft the fragrance through the home to stimulate joy.

 ## Lima Bean Serenity Spell

This spell is called for following or in the midst of domestic arguments: pierce three lima beans and string them onto red silk thread. Carry them for three days, then burn the beans and thread for renewed peace and harmony and to resolve conflicts.

 ## Low John Spell

Low John the Conqueror, also known as bethroot, is an indigenous American plant, now extremely endangered. Traditionally used as an ingredient of love spells in Native American magic, it entered African-American materia magica *as a happy home charm, encouraging peace, tranquility, and the well-being of the family.*

1. Dress Low John with Home Protection Oil or **Van Van Oil.**
2. Place the root within a bag and hang discreetly in the home.

This can be combined with an angelica root for enhanced blessings.

 ## Low John Happy Home Spell

Low John the Conqueror allegedly stimulates family peace, happiness, and harmony. Hang it within the home to radiate its influence.

Middle Eastern House Blessing Incense

Blend myrrh and galbanum resins. Burn, wafting the fragrance throughout the home.

 ## Motherwort Charm Bag

Place motherwort in a charm bag. Hang over entry doors to guard those in the family.

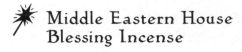 ## Negativity Begone!

Cast this spell on a happy day, whose ambience you'd like to preserve forever. Blend cumin with sea salt and scatter a circle sunwise around the perimeter of your property to banish negativity and dissension.

 ## New Home Oracle

Use this Russian oracle to determine whether your new home will be fortunate:

1. Take a handful of dirt from your new home.
2. Wrap it in cloth.
3. Place it under your pillow to dream how happy (or not) life will be in the new home.

 ## New Home Spell

Lu Pan is the Chinese divine patron of carpenters, builders, and inventors. In real life he was a contemporary of Confucius. Following his death and deification, Lu Pan provides peace in the family and builds protection right into a new home. It is particularly auspicious to invoke him after building a new home or if you are the first resident in a new building.

1. When construction is complete or when you are ready to move in, have a party in Lu Pan's honor.
2. Burn Spirit Money and incense in his honor.
3. Set off fire-crackers to get rid of any malevolent spiritual party-crashers, who might wish to linger in your home. (Loud, percussive music works, too. It's hard to say which will annoy the neighbors more.)

Peace is notoriously difficult to maintain, while an aura of arguing, divisiveness and general unpleasantness spreads all too easily. The Bible suggests pouring oil on troubled waters. Although the recommendation is usually interpreted as metaphoric, some occultists have traditionally taken the suggestion literally.

 ## Oil on Troubled Water Spell (1) Literal Spell

1. Pour olive oil on the exact spot where an argument, unhappy confrontation or scene of humiliation occurred.
2. Let it stay for a little, to absorb the tension and negative energy, before cleaning it up.

 ## Oil on Troubled Water Spell (2) Peace Water

*This New Orleans Voodoo formula oil derives its inspiration from that same biblical reference to pouring oil over water. However, unlike the previous spell, **Peace Water** will not increase chances of a broken neck, nor is someone ultimately forced to clean oil off the floor, perhaps leading to yet another argument as to who is responsible for cleaning up. **Peace Water** has another advantage. Purchasing most condition oils from commercial vendors leaves you wondering what's in the bottle, whether there are any real botanicals in there or whether you've been had. **Peace Water** is a visually distinct oil: one look and you'll know whether it's real.*

Peace Water exists under the premise that oil and water won't mix. It should have three (sometimes two) distinct layers of oil and blue liquid. True **Peace Water** is visually beautiful; when looked upon, it should evoke a sense of serenity and pleasure.

To provide and maintain peace within in the home, keep a bottle of **Peace Water** prominently displayed in each room of the house, to encourage peaceful, happy coexistence. In the event of tension, violence or altercation shake the bottle of **Peace Water,** dispersing the layers. Sprinkle as needed, wherever needed.

 Peaceful Home Oil Spell (1)

This condition oil allegedly ends familial quarrels and encourages reconciliation. An excellent spell to coincide with a family reunion!

1. Create Peaceful Home Oil by grinding brown sugar, bee pollen, orrisroot, and peppermint leaves together.
2. Place this in a bottle together with pink rose petals.
3. Cover with sweet almond and jojoba oils.
4. Soak cotton balls in the oil and tuck them strategically through the room.

 Peaceful Home Oil Spell (2)

1. Carve blue candles to suit your personal situation.
2. Dress with Peaceful Home Oil and burn after arguments and before attempted reconciliations, to encourage happy resolutions.
3. Use the oil to dress candles, too.

 Onion Vacuum

1. On a Friday night when everyone else in the house is asleep, cut an onion in half.
2. Hold it up, visualize it as a psychic vacuum cleaner. Let it suck up all negativity.

3. Let it rest on table.
4. Hold up one peeled crushed garlic clove.
5. Leave out for little while.
6. Put it in a paper bag and dispose of it outside the home.

 Pennyroyal Happy Home Spell

Because pennyroyal has for centuries been used as a dangerous abortifacient it's difficult not to observe sardonic humor hidden within this spell. Place pennyroyal in a bowl to maintain serenity in the home.

 Relocation Spell: Comfrey Root

Tuck bits of comfrey root into possessions and furniture before loading them onto the moving van, to ensure their safe arrival at their destination.

 Relocation Spell: Horseshoe Easy Relocation Spell

This popular Latin American spell is used for financial stability (see Money Spells) *but also to magically ease relocation and bring good fortune to a new home.*

1. Wrap a horseshoe in red thread so that only the tips are left exposed.
2. Attach the horseshoe, with tips facing downward, to a square of cardboard.
3. Decorate with sequins, glitter glue, lucky seeds and beans, and votive images of San Martin Caballero (Saint Martin of Tours).
4. When the physical aspect of the spell is complete, activate its blessings of good fortune by repeating the words *"Citron nueve" ("nine fruits")* twenty-one times.

Sometimes tension in the home isn't caused by people or relationships; the root of the problem may be the home or residence itself. Fear of being forced to leave one's home as well as the fear of being unable to leave one's home when desired can be incredibly stressful. Magic spells attempt to solve these dilemmas.

☀ Residential Stress Spell (1) Home Oracle

Perhaps stress derives from not knowing whether one will change residences or not.

This winter solstice ritual strives to forecast whether you'll still be in the same house come same time next year.

1. On the eve of the winter solstice, stand inside your home with your back to the front door.
2. Throw one shoe backwards over your shoulder.
3. Leave it where it falls without looking at it. Ensure that no one disturbs it.
4. The next morning, check your shoe. If the shoe is facing away from the door, you'll move during the next calendar year. However, if the shoe lands with the toe pointing inside, no change of residence is indicated.

☀ Residential Spell (2) Landlord Cooperation

It's easier to cooperate than fight. This spell invokes a landlord's cooperation, kindness, patience, and good nature.

1. Write your landlord's name nine times on a square of brown paper.
2. Tuck this paper into an empty bottle together with one shot each of gin, rye, rum, brandy, vodka, and whiskey. (Feel free to add anything else you have at home; it won't hurt.)

3. Add two tablespoons of sugar.
4. The original spell now requests one tablespoon each of river water, well water, and cistern water. If you can replicate this, do so. My suggestion is to substitute spring water for the well water and rainwater or water from a storm drain for the cistern water. If you can obtain the third tablespoon from a source of living water, such as a river, stream or lake, in that order of preference, do so, or substitute spring water from a different source than the other tablespoon.
5. Cap the bottle tightly. Keep it turned upside down in a dark, peaceful corner behind your bed or deep within a closet.
6. Reinforce the spell by shaking the bottle at least once a day, at noon or midnight, or both.

If this spell seems to work for you, reinforce it further by giving your landlord a gift of a bottle of one of the included liquors, once a year, as appropriate, but usually in the winter holidays.

☀ Residential Spell (3) Landlord's Retaliation

The rent is never on time; the carpet is ruined; they've trashed the place; the police keep visiting; and all the neighbors are complaining—but the lease is air-tight. What to do? This landlord's spell allegedly stimulates troublesome tenants to move.

1. Offer to clean the bathtub drain. No doubt you will find at least a few hairs. Reserve them.
2. Twist or tie the hairs to a black cohosh root (black snake root) and burn everything.
3. Gather up the ashes and place them inside a jar that can be closed tightly.
4. Sprinkle the ashes with a few drops of **Four Thieves Vinegar.**
5. After dark, preferably at midnight, bury the jar at a crossroads.

Residential Spell (4) Root Yourself Within Your Home

Perhaps the problem is that you really don't wish to move from your home. This spell is beneficial for anyone concerned about forced eviction. It serves to ground you firmly in your home. In my experience, it is a very reliable spell, but be forewarned: if you only wish to stay long enough to find another dwelling, this spell may ground you so securely that you'll be unable to discover alternatives. Only cast this spell if you are truly determined to stay.

You will need a rock from the property (if you can dig it out from underground, this is especially potent) plus benzoin (either powdered or what is sold as essential oil) and charcoal.

1. Grate a little bit of rock and charcoal into a mortar. (An ordinary metal grater works on most rocks.)
2. Add the benzoin and mash everything together. The consistency depends upon what form of benzoin you use.
3. Scatter this mixture across all thresholds to the outside: all venues of entry, doors, gates, windows—anything large enough to permit someone to enter.
4. Reserve the materials and repeat whenever threat appears, using the same rock. Other materials may be replaced but once the rock is gone, you must consider leaving or other alternatives. (Choose your rock wisely: if you fear it will be a long haul, choose a large one.)

Residential Spell (5) Sell a Home

Has stress within the home developed from the need to sell that home? Saint Joseph has earned a potent reputation in folk Catholicism for helping to unload property quickly.

You must signal your need correctly, however.

1. To sell your home, bury a small statue of Saint Joseph somewhere on your property, upside down and facing away from the home.
2. Don't dig him up, even after the sale, but leave him there.

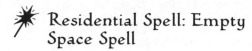

Residential Spell: Empty Space Spell

*To successfully rent out a home or apartment, rub **Attraction Oil** onto the woodwork, always rubbing into the house, from the entrance into the house rather than in the opposite direction.*

Saint Martha's Trouble-free Home Spells

Saint Martha epitomizes the strong, serene matron of the house. Martha feeds messiahs and walks killer dragons on a leash. Invoke her to keep your home serene and peaceful and trouble free. Her annual feast day is July 29th. Her day is Tuesday.

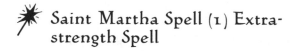

Saint Martha Spell (1) Extra-strength Spell

1. Blend **Martha the Dominator Oil** and **House Blessing Oil.**
2. Place an angelica root into the bottle and allow it to rest overnight in front of an image of Saint Martha.
3. Obtain a strand of hair from each member of the family or from anyone on whom you wish Martha to maintain a vigilant eye and firm hand.
4. Braid or twist the hairs together.
5. Soak them in the blended oil and place the braid under a statue's feet or beneath a chromolithograph's supervising eye.

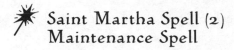 ## Saint Martha Spell (2) Maintenance Spell

To truly bring Saint Martha's peaceful organizing presence into your home, create an altar for her.

1. Place images of Martha and her dragon on the altar.
2. Burn green candles for her every Tuesday to maintain her good influence.

 ## Saint Martha Spell (3) Special Assistance

1. Carve a green candle with your name, address, and identifying information.
2. Dress the candle with **Martha the Dominator Oil.**
3. If you need special assistance from Martha, write your request on a square of brown paper and place it under the candle.
4. Burn the candle.

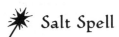 ## Salt Spell

Toss a handful of salt into your cooking fire (stove, grill or similar) every Monday morning to keep your family happy and good-natured.

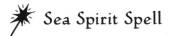 ## Sea Spirit Spell

Place the botanical Sea Spirit (agar-agar) in a jar. Cover it with whiskey, sea salt, and water. Keep the jar in the kitchen to attract blessings to all members of the family.

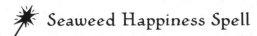 ## Seaweed Happiness Spell

Sprinkle powdered dulse around the home to sweeten the atmosphere.

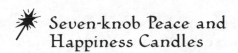 ## Seven-knob Peace and Happiness Candles

Seven-knob candles draw happiness to you while deleting hardship from your life. Inscribe blessings on each knob of a white seven-knob candle and burn one knob daily.

Sweet Dove Powder

Dove's blood, dove's eyes: magic spells are filled with references to doves. Doves are among the creatures most beloved by spirits of primal female powder, from Aphrodite and Asherah to Maria Padilha's black doves. Grind and powder bay laurel leaves, carnations, cardamom, cloves, marjoram, myrrh, and rose petals. Sprinkle the powder throughout the home to help create joy.

Sweet Dove Powder Intensified Version

Create Sweet Dove Powder as above. Sprinkle on lit charcoals and burn, wafting its fragrance throughout the home, particularly in areas that were previously the site of disputes.

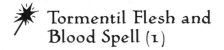 ## Tormentil Flesh and Blood Spell (1)

Tormentil, also known as "flesh and blood" promotes family happiness and harmony. Hang it over entrance doors as well as over bedroom thresholds.

Tormentil Flesh and Blood Spell (2)

Introduce tormentil to its own flesh-and-blood, its kissing-cousin, five-finger grass (cinquefoil). Place tormentil and five-finger grass in a conjure bag, together with an angelica root, for extra protection and happiness.

 ## Tranquil Times Oil

Add crumbled white rose petals, cumin, and caraway seed to jojoba oil. Dress blue and white candles with this oil and burn daily or as needed.

 ## Triple Happiness Luck Charm

1. Place three garlic cloves, three yellow rose buds, and three golden coins in a white bag. (The coins must be gold *colored;* anything ranging from real gold to chocolate coins in gold foil works.)
2. Tie the bag up with gold ribbon.
3. Holding the bag, dance around the perimeter of your home three times sunwise.
4. Dance around the perimeter three times counter-clockwise (moon-wise).
5. While dancing envision sealing in love and happiness.
6. Hang the bag over the front entrance using an iron nail.

Vanilla Spell

1. Stick a vanilla bean into a tightly sealed canister of sugar.
2. The aroma will infuse the sugar: use it in your cooking and feed it to your family, to instill feelings of peace, contentment, and happiness.

 ## Vervain Happy Home Spell

Vervain is considered the friendliest botanical. Unlike other botanicals, which display ambivalence towards people, vervain is believed to love us, crave our presence, and delight in bestowing its blessings and gifts. Surround the home with it; vervain's magical protection is desirable plus you'll always have a fresh supply. Create an infusion by pouring boiling water over vervain. Sprinkle this liquid throughout the home to enhance and maintain happiness and good cheer.

 ## Vervain Happy Person Spell

Add infusions of vervain to your bath as well as those of other family members so that you'll all radiate happiness within the home and outside it.

 ## Vetiver Mattress Spell

Vetiver, also called khus khus, is one of the more powerful commanding botanicals. Surprisingly perhaps it's also known in India as the "plant of tranquility." It has a deep, earthy scent with mild sedative effects for many. Command some serenity, peace and tranquility! Traditionally used as roofing material in India, when it rains the scent is released and intensified. A more accessible method for most comes from the French Antilles:

1. Place vetiver roots together with citronella leaves under your mattress. Heat and movement will encourage release and intensification of the fragrance. (These ingredients are also primary components of **Van Van,** which leaves so many blessings in its wake.)
2. Should the fragrance lose its intensity, it's time to replace the old botanicals with fresh ones.
3. Burn or bury the aged leaves and roots.

Wisteria Spell

Place a piece of wisteria root in a bottle of **Florida Water** or your favorite fragrance. Anoint yourself daily for joy, happiness, and a peaceful heart.

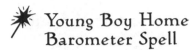 ## Yarrow Happy Home Spell

Decorate the home with boughs of fresh yarrow to banish sadness and negativity.

Young Boy Home Barometer Spell

There is a Taoist belief that boys under the age of seven embody so much pure yang energy that simply bringing one into the home and observing his behavior and reactions serves as an atmospheric barometer.

Invite a small boy to visit your home to provide you with a home-happiness diagnosis. Obviously you must choose your boy wisely; however, the following are the indicators to watch out for:

★ A smiling, happy, playful, energetic, vigorous (but not destructive or overly hyperactive) child indicates positive energy. Things are fine

★ A child who falls asleep or is sluggish indicates that the energy in the home needs revitalizing

★ A tantrum, crankiness, major hissy fit, destructive impulses or general bad behavior indicate that something is amiss. Instead of, or in addition to, rejuvenating the energy, some good cleansing spells may be in order

How do you revitalize that energy?

★ Yang energy may be boosted by at least once a day opening blinds and shutters and allowing sunlight to stream in

★ Temporarily and simultaneously opening all outside doors and windows encourages circulation of air and magical energy

★ Consider using the raucous Sound House Cleansing spell on page 199 to liven up the atmosphere

✪ Healing Spells

Even those who swear that they don't believe in magic, don't approve of magic, and would *never* participate in magic will make an exception for a healing spell. It's amazing what illness or affliction, especially those that defy diagnosis or conventional treatment, will stimulate us to do.

Healing spells are not intended to be used *instead* of conventional, traditional, or other methods of healing. Instead they work best in conjunction with them, reinforcing other systems, enhancing their power and the likelihood of recovery. Many spells are intended to be cast after one has already exhausted other more conventional resources.

Magical healing spells may be particularly beneficial for those ailments that resist conventional identification because magic possesses a broader definition of the origins of illness:

★ *Illness or disability may derive from purely neutral physical causes*
★ *Illness or disability may derive from spiritual and/or magical causes*
★ *Illness or disability may derive from a combination of physical/spiritual and/or magical causes*

Straightforward physical illnesses are no more than what they appear: you got stuck in the rain; you caught a cold. You ate too much sugar and didn't brush your teeth; now you have cavities. You smoked four packs a day; now you have emphysema. Although the cause of illness is physical, magic may still be used to enhance recovery. In general, however, cure matches source. Straightforward ailments demand straightforward treatment.

Spiritual and magical ailments are more complex. In order to determine the correct course of treatment, it must be determined whether an ailment's ultimate source is human or spirit-derived.

★ *Magical ailments of human derivation may be the result of a malevolent spell or the Evil Eye*
★ *Spirit-sent ailments are more complex: was illness caused intentionally? Illness may have been sent as punishment, as an attempt at communication, or simply inadvertently*

There's also another magical way to consider illness: health, the state of harmonious balance, is the natural state. Thus illness, by definition, indicates magical workings or spiritual imbalance, the intensity of the illness defining the intensity of the magical or spiritual situation. Sudden surprising severe illness (particularly when fatal) tends to be interpreted as either deriving from human sources (a hex) or from minor low-level spirits. Major diseases, especially smallpox, may be identified with specific well-known spirits. Ailments that are curious, hard to pin down, resist diagnosis, and are incurable (the person never gets better or worse but lingers in a malaise) are also often attributed to major spirits. In this situation, the reason behind the illness may be to stimulate the afflicted person to contact the spirit, not to kill that person. Once spiritual interaction occurs, the illness passes or is controlled.

Healer's Spells

Although concern is focused on the patient, the healer is considered vulnerable during treatment, too.

 ## Archangel Raphael Spell for Protection

The archangel Raphael sponsors and protects nurses, physicians, pharmacists, and healers of all kind. Request his assistance to accomplish your healing and also to protect you before, during, and after.

TIPS FOR MAGICAL HEALING SPELLS

★ Where illness derives from bewitchment, particularly where a hex was cast using some sort of tool like a wax figure, it may be necessary to find and remove the trick for healing to be accomplished. There are also usually specific magical antidotes and jinx-reversing spells. (These issues are dealt with amongst Hexes and their Antidotes, page 568.)

★ In general, one must cast one's own spell. However, healing spells are unusual in that it's very likely that someone else must cast the spell on behalf of the ailing person. The person who needs or desires the spell may be in no condition to perform the spell. Most, although not all, healing spells demand the presence and sometimes the participation of the patient, however

★ Given the opportunity to choose, many traditions assert that the full moon is the best time to initiate healing spells because as the moon diminishes, so should pain and illness

1. Dedicate a white candle to Raphael.
2. Hold the candle in your hands to charge it with your desire.
3. Place a small silver or iron fish charm near the candle.
4. When the candle has burned completely, carry or wear the fish charm. Reserve any auspicious looking remnants of wax in a mojo bag or magic box.

Distance Healing Spells

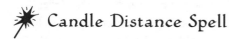 ### Candle Distance Spell

This candle spell, although intended to assist in another's healing, may also be cast for oneself.

1. Carve a white candle (plain, human figure, cross or "praying hands" shape) to reflect the person for whom the healing spell is intended. (In other words, carve the other person's name, identifying information, and so on.)
2. Soak hyssop in olive oil and then use the oil to dress the candle.
3. Burn the candle; this is traditionally accompanied by the recitation of psalms or other sacred verses.

 ### Doll Distance Healing Spell

Because once upon a time Chinese women wouldn't undress before a doctor (even today a visit to a traditional Chinese physician rarely involves undressing), beautiful, anatomically correct naked dolls were carved from ivory. These dolls served as a communications device between doctor and patient; pain, illness, affliction, and methods of healing could be demonstrated on the doll with minimum embarrassment. These dolls are still sometimes found in antique shops; reproductions are also available. Use this type of doll or craft or use a less realistic one to perform magical distance healing.

1. Hold the doll in your hands to charge it with your intentions and healing energy.
2. Murmur healing incantations and blessings over the doll.
3. Massage the doll with blended castor and olive oils, scented with essential oil of lavender.
4. Place the doll within a ring of burning healing candles.
5. Repeat as needed until the healing is complete.

 ### Job's Tears Distance Healing Spell

Bless and charge seven Job's tears individually, one at a time. Place them in a white charm bag containing powdered everlasting and ivy. This bag is taken to the patient and placed under their pillow or mattress.

Peppermint Distance Healing Spell

1. Place peppermint leaves on top of a photograph of the patient.
2. Charge a blue candle with your desire.
3. Carve and dress the candle as desired.
4. Burn it beside the photograph.
5. When the candle has burned down, dispose of the peppermint leaves.
6. Repeat as needed, with fresh leaves each time.

Psalm Distance Healing Spell

1. Write out a petition of healing and/or blessings of improved health on a piece of parchment.
2. Place this in a dish containing **Holy Water** or **Marie Laveau Water.**
3. Murmur psalms over this dish.
4. When the spell feels complete, remove the parchment, and allow it to dry. It may be preserved, buried or given to the spell's target as a protective talisman.

 ## Talisman Distance Healing Spell

To promote distance healing, charge stones with healing energy, then give them to the spell's target as a talisman. Choose any crystal that feels best to you; however, traditionally alexandrite, Herkimer diamonds, lodestones, moonstones, pearls, and quartz crystals are considered most effective.

 ## Dr. Jose Gregorio Healing Spell

Born in 1864, the Venezuelan physician Dr. Jose Gregorio Hernandez was renowned in his lifetime for his generosity to the poor, often waiving his fees for treatment. He was struck by a car in 1919 and killed while bringing medicine to a patient. After death, his miracle healings began.

Jose Gregorio is perhaps the most prominent of the unofficial saints (and also perhaps the one most likely to become official, following in the footsteps of Padre Pio).

He is an unofficial saint everyone can agree on, and there is a strong movement to have Dr. Jose Gregorio declared an "official" saint; as of this writing, he is apparently well on his way to canonization. Many devotees assume that he has already been canonized. Numerous Venezuelan orphanages, clinics, and hospitals are named in his honor. Spiritual supply stores around the world sell his votive cards, images, and candles.

Dr. Jose Gregorio may be petitioned directly by those ailing. He also sponsors, protects, and inspires healers. Officially, Dr. Jose Gregorio is not petitioned directly. Instead, God is requested to send the good doctor to the petitioner's aid. The following is the typical format for a request; adapt the words to fit your personal situation:

Dear God,
I am grateful for your healing blessings transmitted through your servant, Jose Gregorio, to whom you gave the power to heal the sick people of this world. Lord, by your Grace, please grant Jose Gregorio divine power to help me heal, body and soul, mind and spirit. Lord I pray that I may follow the example of Jose Gregorio in my life and be a channel for humility, healing charity, and loving kindness.

However, it must also be said, that, despite protestations, direct offerings to Dr. Jose Gregorio have been witnessed.

1. Burn a white candle near Dr. Jose Gregorio's image, or burn a commercially manufactured Jose Gregorio Hernandez seven-day candle.
2. Place offerings in front of his votive image. Cigarettes are perhaps an inappropriate offering for a medical doctor; however, the standard offering of a glass of water or rum would probably not be refused.

 ## Gemstone Shield Spells

Certain crystal gemstones create a protective shield so that the healer may accomplish his or her mission without fear.

1. Carry or wear bloodstone, clear quartz, and/or black tourmaline during healing spells and rituals.

2. Anoint with **Protection Oil** if desired.
3. Cleanse after each magical session.

This is particularly effective for spells or other attempts to heal using body-working therapies, such as massage.

Healer's Spell Crystal Protection

Crystal gemstones can be extremely beneficial in healing; however they are also very appealing to fairies. Do your valued crystals keep disappearing? To prevent the fairies from filching precious crystals:

1. When not in use, keep the crystals safe in an iron box.
2. Fairies can be beneficial in healing too: to remain in their good graces, offer them a gift of glass marbles instead.

Rosemary Infusion of Power

Washing your hands with an infusion of rosemary magically empowers and enhances all healing.

Create an infusion by pouring boiling water over rosemary. Allow it to cool, then strain. This may be done immediately prior to healing or the liquid may be bottled and refrigerated for later use.

Rosemary Infusion of Power: Quick Fix

Add several drops of rosemary essential oil to water and cleanse your hands with it.

Diagnostic Spells

As we have seen, according to general metaphysical wisdom there are three sources of illness:

★ *Those attributed to neutral, i.e., completely physical causes*
★ *Those caused by some sort of spiritual and/or magical force*
★ *A combination of the two*

Sometimes in order to determine the correct approach to an illness, especially when other conventional methods have failed, a magical diagnosis may be in order.

Bear Diagnosis Spells

Bears are closely identified with herbal medical systems. A popular magical theory regarding how people acquired herbal knowledge is that bears taught it to us.

Appeal to Bear Spirits to help establish a diagnosis or determine treatment.

1. You will need a full-frontal image of a bear's head, a sort of portrait, although a photograph of a real bear is more powerful than a drawing. Whether the rest of the bear is in the photo is irrelevant. The crucial element is that you can look directly into the bear's eyes.
2. Just before turning out the lights to go to sleep, gaze into the image bear's eyes. Take your time. Treat this as a meditation. In your mind, elucidate what information you require, while continuing to gaze into the bear's eyes.
3. When you feel ready, place the image under your pillow; turn out the light and go to sleep.
4. Insights and inspiration sent by the bears, although you may not necessarily see the bears, should emerge in your dreams. Repeat as needed.

Action on behalf of bears' welfare and habitat may enhance chances of success or serve as a reciprocal gesture.

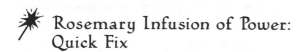

Perhaps you'd like a more direct approach. Well, it's not advisable to directly approach bears. Contact with humans typically ends in tragedy for person and bear alike. However, dreams permit access not possible in waking life.

 Bear Dream Journey Spell

A traditional European fairy-tale image depicts a person, usually but not always a woman, riding on a bear's back. Let a dream bear take you on a healing journey. This visualization is excellent when you know what ails you but don't know how to treat it. Bears are repositories of traditional medical wisdom.

1. Take the image of a bear to bed with you. Three dimensional images are best, something like a Zuni stone fetish or even a toy bear, providing that it's *"bear-like"* rather than too cute. The advantage of the 3-D bear is that you can hold it in your hands while you journey (or if it's a big enough stuffed animal, even ride it) but if all you have is a photo image or similar, use what you have.
2. Prepare yourself for sleep. Turn out the light but begin your dream while you're awake.
3. Visualize your bear—the dream bear doesn't have to look like the image.
4. Visualize the scenario where you meet the bear, mount the bear and tell the bear what you need to find (a remedy). Then let the bear take over.
5. At some point you will probably fall asleep, although some people achieve waking visualizations. The journey should continue in your dreams. Repeat as needed until the information you require is received.

Make sure that at the end of the visualization the bear returns you to where you began. If this doesn't happen in your dream, work with it while awake.

 Egg Diagnostic Spell (1) Mexican

This diagnostic spell offers possibilities of divination, also.

1. Gently rub a whole, raw egg (the original spell suggests a freshly laid egg) all over the ailing person's naked body.
2. Break the egg in a dish.
3. Whatever forms are assumed by the egg or the broken shell will reveal causes of illness, diagnosis, and/or advice on how to get rid of it or cure it.

 Egg Diagnostic Spell (2) Pow-Wow

A Pow-Wow diagnosis is intended to determine whether an illness is caused or aggravated by malevolent influences. Pass a whole raw egg over the individual's body.

Break it into a bowl: if there are traces of blood, this is evidence of psychic malfeasance.

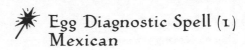 Healing Party Spell

As long as you're holding a vigil for someone who's ailing, you may as well do something constructive. This ritual is intended to shed light on mysterious, serious illness so that a cure may be determined. Do not be fooled by the description of the offerings as "humble," this is modesty in the face of the Spirits. In reality, each element is derived from the sacred.

This ritual is performed by seven people—no more, no less—on behalf of another who is ailing. (The person who is ailing does not count as one of the seven and is not expected to be present.) One person is designated the leader of the ritual, the official "curer," the stand-in for what was once a shaman's job. This person serves the others and addresses the Spirits.

1. Prepare a large dish of spicy tamale.
2. Burn copal to cleanse the space.
3. Illuminate the room with candles.
4. Each of the seven participants is given a glass of brandy, a cigarette, and a slice of tamale. Each places a little of what he or she has received in a clay pot, placed near an item of clothing belonging to the sick person.
5. The leader speaks, addressing the Spirits:
    You, Masters of the Seven Airs* and the Earth, heal and help this child of God,
    [Name] *child of* [Name].
    Make him/her well. Remove illness from him/her.
    In exchange, I bring this humble offering of brandy, tobacco, candles, copal, and tamale.
    I bring you the fire so that you can bring illumination and show the exact spot where [he/she] *met this illness.*

This ritual blends pre-Columbian tradition with Roman Catholicism, and so is accompanied by fervent prayers and petitions to God and the saints, especially Mary Magdalene. Repetition of psalms would not be inappropriate. (Incorporate your own spiritual belief and petition.)

 ## Hot Pepper Diagnostic Spell

If the Evil Eye has been cast, this diagnostic method from India detects and removes it.

1. Prepare a fire.
2. Pass a whole chili pepper over the ailing person, as if it were a smudge stick.
3. Throw the pepper into the fire.

*Among many indigenous people of Mexico, the Aires are extremely powerful wind spirits. They can cause illness and damage, although they are usually not thought of as being deliberately malicious. They are simply so powerful that contact with them can be overpowering and profoundly debilitating to people.

4. If the resulting smoke smells of the chili, the illness is definitely not attributable to the Evil Eye. Continue to search for a diagnosis and remedy.
5. If the chili burns without creating a distinct aroma, the person *was* afflicted but the influence has now been broken.

 ## Hot Stone Diagnostic Spell

A Scottish diagnostic method attempts to determine from which part of the body an illness derives.

1. Designate individual stones to represent parts of the body. Traditionally three are used, one for the head, one for the heart, and one for the body but you can designate any number or system that suits your situation, providing the stones are distinctive and identifiable.
2. Place them overnight to rest in the hot ashes of the hearth. (No hearth? Burn incense in cauldron and use that instead.)
3. In the morning, drop the stones one at a time into a basin of cold water.

The one making the loudest sound on contact with the water provides the diagnosis.

Popping Clove Diagnostic Spell

A Greek ritual determines whether an illness derives from magical or conventional sources. Before you begin, select a set number of cloves: twelve is customary, but choose what is most significant. Otherwise, this spell may be performed endlessly.

1. Insert a needle or pin through a dried clove.
2. Hold it over a candle flame.
3. Murmur psalms. If you fear the illness is caused by malevolent magic or the Evil Eye, verbally send it back and reverse the hex.
4. Once that first clove has burned down, repeat with another. Keep burning cloves one at a time, while petitioning and chanting until finally one clove snaps and makes noise. If the sound makes the petitioner jump, flinch, or start, the spell is considered broken. If no cloves snap, the illness is deemed organic. There is no magical influence. Other causes and treatments must be sought.

 ## Snake Dream Diagnosis

It's no accident that the caduceus, the staff entwined with double serpents, is the modern symbol of the medical profession. Snakes are the primary animals of healing and have been so since ancient days. Once maintained in the temples of healing that were the first hospitals, their venom both heals and harms. Their old skin fades and grows dull, only to be shed painlessly as the snake emerges vivid and youthful once again, revived and refreshed. Because they lack limbs, snakes are always in contact with Earth. They burrow in Earth's crevices, live in the sea and in trees: they are privy to all Earth's secrets. Snakes are the guardians and sometimes sharers of Earth's wisdom, the guardians of her treasures, including secrets of healing.

This magical diagnostic technique is especially suited for conditions that defy conventional identification or treatment. An image of a snake is required. It may be a photograph, a stone fetish, or other artistic rendering; however, it must fit comfortably under your pillow and not disturb your sleep.

1. Bring the image to bed with you before going to sleep.
2. Gaze into the snake's eyes and charge it with its mission: to reveal the mysteries of your ailment and its required treatment.
3. Place the image under your pillow, then go to sleep. The goal is to incubate the required dream.
4. Repeat this ritual until the dream has been received, clarified, and understood and no further dreams are required.

Warning Alarm Spells

Certain vigilant magic materials provide diagnoses and health warnings, so that action may be taken immediately, before a health problem becomes obvious.

 ## Crystal Gemstone Warning Spells

Crystals and gemstones offer warning service in addition to their other gifts. However, in order to provide this information, they must actually be in contact with your skin. Check that the backs of jewelry allow for this.

★ *Rubies allegedly fade or grow dull in the presence of anemia or blood-related disorders*
★ *Turquoise fades and/or cracks in the presence of ill-health*
★ *Coral grows paler and less vivid in the presence of illness*

✳ Unicorn Warning Spell

Allegedly the alicorn, the unicorn's horn, has the magic power to cure any illness. If only one could buy genuine powdered alicorn at any pharmacist. Unicorn-shaped talismans, however, bestow other magic powers: they help detect poisons.

Wear or carry a unicorn charm. Should the charm suddenly call attention to itself, it is sounding a warning. Pay attention and take action as needed.

Spirit Healers and Disease Spirits

Although spirits may be approached to prevent or heal disease, they are not all the same type of spirit. There are extremely powerful, generally benevolent (everyone has a testy moment once in a while) spirits who may be appealed to for virtually anything. Isis is the classic example. Appeal to her in your hour of need, whether it's illness, financial, or otherwise. Disease Spirits and demons of diseases are specifically affiliated with illness, although the most powerful disease spirits can transcend this role to become someone's primary spiritual patron.

An important distinction between Spirit Healers and Disease Spirits is that Spirit Healers only cure diseases; they do not, as a rule, inflict them. Disease Spirits, on the other hand, go both ways. Transcending the concept of inflicting the illness, Disease Spirits *are* the illness. A visit from one of the Smallpox Spirits means being in the presence of the actual illness. However, whether one is actually infected and the magnitude of the infection depends upon the Disease Spirit. Because they are Geniuses of their particular disease, the Disease Spirit is also able to prevent and heal their illness. Disease Spirits, especially those of the more virulent diseases, are among the most feared and

respected of all. A few are actually beloved by their human devotees, most especially Babalu-Ayé.

Low-level disease demons tend to remain anonymous and are similar in nature to mosquitoes: since they exist, they must serve some higher purpose but it's difficult to determine what that might be. Disease Spirits, however, are stars. Each has an identity, a personality, specific physical manifestations, personal tastes, and predilections, just like any other spirit. Although they are addressed by specific names, these may not in fact be their real names. Similar to the distaste for calling the devil because he might answer, a Disease Spirit's true names are rarely used, on the off chance that it will provoke an unwanted response. Euphemisms, typically loving and respectful, are substituted instead.

A crucial point: those spirits who cause disease know *everything* about that ailment. Frequently they *are* the disease; therefore no one is more qualified than they are to heal this particular disease. Although it is dangerous to approach them because contact with them is contact with the illness itself, in a metaphysical sense if not a literal one, in times of crisis, an appeal to the Disease Spirit may be perceived as necessary in order to *prevent* illness. To actually have the disease is akin to a kind of spirit possession. Eliminating the disease can be understood as an exorcism.

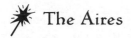 The Aires

In Mexican and Central American magic, the aires are literally the winds, but they're more than just a weather phenomenon. The aires aren't just any light breeze. Some winds contain spirits that others don't. How will you know you've met such a wind spirit? Typically, you'll get sick.

Although the aires are specific to Latin American magic, dangerous wind spirits exist worldwide. Even the wind spirit Oya, counted among the protective Seven African Powers, is noted as the orisha who controls the cemetery gates. Dating back at least to ancient Mesopotamia, wind spirits have spread disease, sometimes deliberately and maliciously, sometimes not. The aires—who are sometimes perceived as an abstract force, at other times personified, usually as dwarves—can't help themselves. They are typically amoral and neutral in intent; however, their natural force is so strong it may be too much for people. Contact with them, as with radiation, may lead to disease. Although the disease manifests physically, because its root cause is metaphysical, it typically won't dissipate without magical curing methods.

1. To heal illnesses caused by the aires, clay figures, usually black, are created. The healer determines what shapes are required; however, animal figures are typical, as are images of holy beings such as archangels. Abstract *"towers"* representing wind and water are also used. A group of figures may be needed for one healing. Creation of the figures is accompanied by the murmuring of incantations, chanting of sacred verses, prayer, appeal, and spiritual negotiation.
2. Take these figures, together with a food offering, to the area where the ailing person is believed to have contacted the aire.
3. Cleansing rituals, such as barrida sweeping (see page 208), are conducted there.
4. Food and figures are buried on the spot or hidden in the area, then patient and healer return home, by a circuitous route, if possible, without looking back.

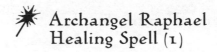 Archangel Raphael
Healing Spell (1)

The archangel Raphael is the angel in charge of healing. He is the special patron of physicians, nurses, pharmacists, the ailing, and the blind. He watches over travelers and supervises the guardian angels. Raphael is believed present, at least fleetingly, at every birth.

Raphael, whose name is given to mean "Healer of the Lord," "the Lord's remedy," "the Lord heals," or "the Lord has healed," is the hero of the apocryphal Book of Tobit, accompanying travelers to safety, healing the blind and vanquishing demons. Visual images of Raphael tend to draw on elements from the Book of Tobit. Raphael's emblem is the fish. He wears a flask of medicine tied around his waist. Allegedly he manifests on Earth disguised as a handsome, bright young man, in both senses of the word "bright," offering healing advice and instructions.

Call Raphael for assistance with his invocation:

Archangel Raphael filled with mercy
Please hear my call
Vanquisher of demons
Protector of travelers
Endowed with healer's grace
Help all who implore your assistance
Please help me with [fill in the blank].

 Archangel Raphael
Healing Spell (2)

Many visual depictions of Raphael exist, from votive imagery to masterpieces of art. Choose an image that resonates for you, and meditate upon this image or use it as a medium of communication with the archangel. For added enhancement, burn frankincense and red candles near the image.

Blame the Ancestors Spell

Yet another possible source of illness exists. According to traditional Chinese philosophy, some illnesses or other misfortunes (particularly those of a chronic nature) may be caused by Ancestral Spirits. Ancestors may be aggrieved because a grave is neglected, or perhaps illness and disaster result from a lack of sufficient sacrificial offerings to sustain beneficial energy. These ancestors aren't necessarily malevolent; they just lack enough energy and power to keep harm from your door. What can be done?

★ *First of all, feed them. And feed them well*
★ *Verify whether a grave needs tending. Make improvements if you can. If this is impossible, if a grave is situated in a location beyond reach, in parts unknown or does not, in fact, exist, then explain this to the Ancestors in detail, including what your plans are for compensation. Divination may be in order to receive their opinions on the matter, too*
★ *Build an ancestral altar or enhance one that already exists*
★ *Burn paper offerings. The traditional offering is Bank of Hell cash, but Bank of Hell checkbooks and credit cards are now available, too. (See Death Spells, page 264, for more information.)*

It may be beneficial to obtain a shamanic diagnosis, particularly in the case of an illness that resists conventional diagnosis and/or does not respond to treatment.

 ## Candle Spell

Offer any spirit, deity, or saint a candle as tall as the person for whom the healing is requested. This European custom of the Middle Ages remains viable and is still practiced. It is particularly effective when petitioning fiery spirits, like Brigid or Diana.

 ## Disease Demon Banishing Spell (1)

According to Ainu and Japanese magical tradition, disease demons despise mugwort. Therefore hang bunches of mugwort throughout the home, concentrating on vulnerable areas, to disperse and repel these malevolent spirits.

 ## Disease Demon Banishing Spell (2)

This method will also repel the Evil Eye.

1. Take seven glowing coals from the hearth.
2. Circle each one around the head of the afflicted person seven times. (There will thus be 49 circles.)
3. Toss each coal into a bowl of water following use.
4. Either a post-menopausal woman or a pre-menstrual girl must take the bowl to a crossroads and dump out the contents.
5. Don't look at the water or return home by the same route.

 ## Disease Demon Banishing: Bunch of Chives Spell

Hang bunches of chives around the home to repel disease demons—or any other kind for that matter.

 ## Disease Demon Dispelling Incense

Burn Dittany of Crete to drive away illness-provoking spirits.

Djinn Healing Spells

In traditional North African magic, when an illness is mysterious and if it fails to respond to conventional treatment, focus turns on the djinn, for two reasons. First, because illness, whether physical, emotional, and/or spiritual may indicate foul play on the part of the djinn, stimulated perhaps by genuine anger or just by the impulse to do mischief. Illness may also be a manifestation of spiritual possession. If this is the case, ultimately healing must come through elimination (exorcism) or propitiation of the djinn.

The second reason is that although the djinn are implicated in causing many illnesses (and worse), they are also master healers. Djinn can heal illnesses other djinn have caused as well as diseases of all other derivation, including purely physical ones.

Basically when all else fails, it never hurts to approach the djinn for healing, although perhaps one might not wish to wait that long. Many spells and rituals exist, some to be performed by the afflicted person; others reserved for their caregivers.

Djinn Healing Spell (1)

Faced with a stubborn illness that won't improve? Make an offering to the djinn.

1. Buy your own oil but borrow a cup of flour, without explaining why you need it, from a married woman who has only been married once and who has never been widowed or divorced.
2. Mix the oil and the flour together.
3. After dark, leave small portions of this mixture in various places—basically all the djinn's favorite haunts: bathrooms, doorways, crossroads, ruined buildings, near springs.
4. Accompany offerings with an invocation to Simday, Sultan of the Djinn, requesting his assistance. He has

control of a host of spirits. Surely one of them is causing the illness or has information.
5. Go home, but don't discuss your mission. Go to sleep and prepare to receive answers in your dreams.

Djinn Healing Spell (2)

On the other hand, if you like, instead of going to find the djinn, you can lure them to you.

1. Spread sweet butter on sweet bread. (There can't be *any* salt in either the bread or the butter; the djinn will refuse the offering.)
2. Talk to the bread, murmur over it, tell it all your troubles and physical concerns.
3. Place the bread on the roof of the house, announcing aloud: *"God! I complain of my illness to this bread!"*
4. Leave it exposed overnight so that the spirits can partake of its essence.
5. In the morning dispose of it by either holding a funeral for the bread; bury it in Earth, complete with funeral rites. Alternatively, give it to a dog to eat.

Djinn Healing Spell (3)

This method of requesting healing and protection was developed in North Africa specifically for the djinn, but the format could be used for any spirit.

1. Pass handfuls of cumin and coriander seeds around the patient's head.
2. Holding the seeds in your hands, talk to the Spirits. (Although this may be accomplished for oneself, it is a descendant of shamanic rites and traditionally one person performs the ritual on another's behalf. Also, it is understood that the person requiring this cure may be in really bad shape and in absolutely no condition to cast the spell.) Say something like:

"I place myself under your protection, under the protection of all the great ones and the small ones among you.

I place myself under the protection of [Begin invoking names–whose protection, patronage, and healing skills do you seek?]

If [name] child of [name] has wronged you, if she has offended you, if she has angered you, if she behaved badly, if she was angry, resentful, selfish, rude [keep going], please seek out the one who has done harm to her. Implore him to release her." [You can also ask the Spirit to intercede with God.]

3. Try to get the patient to chew the seeds now. If she is unable or unwilling, you chew them and spit them out. Lick the patient's hands immediately.

 ## Djinn Healing Spell (4)

A variation of the above spell may be cast without the patient's presence.

1. Chew coriander and cumin seeds while composing a letter to the Spirits. Use the same format in as the spoken chant above. Don't stop chewing yet or if they're all chewed out, keep the seeds in your mouth.
2. Place the letter in an envelope. Spit the seeds out and lick the envelope to seal it.
3. Burn the letter together with fresh coriander and cumin seeds.

 ## Djinn Healing Spell (5)

This spell attempts to bribe or pay off an invading, disease-causing spirit.

1. Soak a coin of reasonably large denomination in spring water, **Holy Water, Angel Water, Carmelite Water** or similar.
2. Burn black and white colored benzoin.
3. Pass the coin through the incense smoke and place it under the patient's pillow.
4. Should the patient begin to recovery, ask a spirit worker to divine who (which spirit), caused the illness. Donate the coin to a cause dear to that spirit's heart. Feel free to supplement with additional cash.

In Morocco, where this spell originates, the coin would be given directly to the Gnawa shamans who traditionally would have officiated at a formal ceremony.

✳ Djinn Healing Spell (6)

This incredibly complex, elaborate Moroccan spell is designed to remedy spirit caused illnesses. Symptoms might include any or all of the following: fever, hallucinations, lethargy, malaise, pains in the head, and/or knees. The patient may talk to him or herself, or to others invisible to everyone else.

The spell demands the participation of four women besides the person performing the ritual on behalf of the patient. (Unless specified otherwise, all steps of the spell are performed by this person acting on behalf of the patient.) One woman, who plays an extensive role, must be post-menopausal; the other three must be married women, who have each only been married once and who have never been widowed or divorced. If they have living, healthy children (and have never lost a child), this is even better.

1. Each of the married women must donate two handfuls of flour.
2. Blend all the flour together and place it in a white cotton handkerchief.
3. Fumigate this medicine bundle by burning white-colored benzoin.
4. Place it under the patient's head (or pillow) overnight.
5. In the morning, the post-menopausal woman/crone opens this handkerchief, removes three handfuls of flour and makes a small loaf of bread with it, using no salt.
6. Use the other half of the flour to make a loaf with salt but no yeast. Put seven grains of barley on the loaf with no salt, and bake both.
7. Purchase five varieties of fish. The spell requires five pieces plus enough for the household to eat. (If using individual large fish, then use the fish entrails for the ritual and offering to the djinn. Eat the rest.)
8. Cook the five varieties of fish (one of each, for a total of five pieces of fish) in a brand new baking dish with butter, onions, and black peppercorns, but no salt.
9. Give a little piece of each fish and some of the resulting sauce or cooking liquid to the patient to eat. Rub a little sauce on the patient's wrists, elbows, knees, and ankles. Put a little under the bed and in each corner of the patient's room. (If you have a lot, you can do each corner of all rooms, but the patient's room is most crucial.)
10. The crone now puts the salt-free loaf in a basket, plus a container with the remainder of the fish and sauce.
11. Decorate the container with four small flags: one black, one white, one red, and one yellow. (You can use cocktail flags, children's toy flags, or make some up out of fabric or paper.)
12. Add three small dolls, representing a man, a woman, and their daughter. (The dynamics of your own family are irrelevant.)
13. Put a small silver coin into the container and say aloud: *"Forgive us if we have forgotten anything you like. Here's some money to buy whatever you want."*
14. The crone then places another silver coin into her mouth (she must keep it in her mouth until her return in Step 16), and takes the basket to an isolated place—the seashore is preferred, but any remote place, any place with the reputation of being "haunted" or where djinn might linger, is appropriate.
15. On the trip there and back, she must not speak to anyone or ever look behind her. Everything inside the basket should be left at the haunted place but the basket may be taken home if desired. Should dogs or other animals be attracted to the offering, don't give it to them, but don't stop them from eating either. This is actually an auspicious sign.
16. On her way back, the crone picks up seven stones from the road. She throws them down, one at a time, on the doorstep of the sick person's house so that the people within (who have been holding a vigil) will let her in. She can't talk yet nor can she knock at the door. She must keep the silver coin in her mouth until she has entered the house, then she must keep it, not give it away.

17. In the meantime, the remaining fish should have been prepared. Prepare them anyway you like but make sure you add salt. This fish and the loaf of bread with salt are now eaten by the household. If the patient is a child, then no one but immediate family members and other children may eat. However, if the patient is an adult, anyone may participate in the meal. If someone else isn't feeling well, eating the salted meal should have a beneficial effect.

Elf Shot

Elves, like fairies, have been sanitized over the centuries. Once upon a time, great ambivalence existed toward them. The original elves were not miniature artisans laboring in Santa's toy factories. Instead, true elves are beautiful woods dwellers, skilled at archery, well versed in forest-lore, and equally ambivalent toward people. Unlike Santa's elves, they are not petite, but human-sized or even taller. They have a cool nature, with a dangerous edge. The elven-folk of J.R.R. Tolkien's *The Lord of the Rings* are an excellent depiction of these true elves.

Like fairies, once upon a time, relations between people and elves may once have been more harmonious. However by the time Christianity was established in Anglo-Saxon England, elves were perceived as a root cause of illness. Elves shot victims with magical arrows or spears, inflicting wounds or disease with no other apparent cause; hence to be so afflicted was to be *"elf-shot."*

Should you perceive yourself as being elf-shot, never fear, remedies exist.

✳ Elf-Shot Basic Remedy

1. Gather betony, garlic shoots, fennel, rue, and wormwood.

2. Bind them together while murmuring sacred verses.
3. Wrap the herbs in white cloth and bind to the wound or site of affliction.

✳ Elf-Shot Intensive Magic Remedy

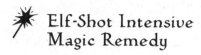

Nine is the sacred number of Anglo-Saxon magic and spirituality. Should these specific herbs not be available, substitute others as required in order to maintain that magic number. Although the basic spell might be accomplished for oneself, this intensive spell requires another to perform the healing ritual.

1. Gather the following nine herbs:
   Betony
   Chervil
   Dill
   Fennel
   Garlic shoots
   Mugwort
   Plantain
   Rue
   Wormwood
2. Bind them together while murmuring sacred verses.
3. Bless the herbs and the patient nine times.
4. Wave the herb bundle over the patient's body or gently rub it on the body.
5. Burn the bundle, wafting the smoke over the patient as a fumigation.
6. Dispose of the ashes in living water, flowing away from you.

✹ Exu Marabo Spell

Many consider calling on Exu Marabo to be like calling on Satan for help. Petition this dangerous, volatile (perhaps malevolent) spirit for miracle healings as a last resort, when all else has failed. There is no illness he cannot cure, although he has been known to kill as well. For what it's worth the exus tend to deliver whatever expectation devotees have of them. The more fearful and ambivalent you are, the worse they tend to behave.

Exu Marabo has a tendency to make spontaneous appearances; he signals his presence through the scent of sulfur. He cures with wormwood. Here's the catch: once invited, you cannot ask him to leave, whether he provides your miracle or not. When Exu Marabo arrives, he moves in permanently. You will feed him forever; your only option to keep him happy and pacified is with gifts and prayers.

1. Crush and grind wormwood twigs, leaves, and/or roots.
2. Sprinkle this wormwood on lit charcoal.
3. Carve Exu Marabo's sigil into red and white candles before burning them. (Red devil candles may be used, if preferred.)
4. Have some *really* good cigars and fine rum waiting in case Exu Marabo accepts your invitation. You will know that he is present by the scent of sulfur (brimstone). Tell him what you need.

✹ Hecate's Living Altar Spell

Hecate is most famous today as a Dark Moon Spirit and Queen of Witches. Those are but two aspects of this multifaceted deity. Hecate was once the chief deity of the Carian nation, now in Western Turkey. She is matron of the city of Istanbul. She has dominion over life and death and who makes the journey in between, indicating her power as a healing deity. Hecate is matron of midwives and herbalists.

Her priestesses (the most famous was Medea) were trained herbalists. Those in need of healing or solace journeyed to the gardens attached to Hecate's shrine in Colchis on the Black Sea, home of the Golden Fleece pilfered by the Argonauts.

Hecate's assistance may be accessed by building a living altar in her honor:

1. Plant a garden outdoors or create a living altar inside with potted plants.
2. Add some or all of the following: dog roses, garlic, lavender, mandrake, Queen of the Night, roses, thorn apple, and tuberoses. Hecate's trees include: black poplar, date palm, pomegranate, willow, and yew.
3. Place votive images of Hecate, together with her favorite creatures—dogs, dragons, and snakes—in the garden.
4. To petition Hecate directly or to receive spontaneous magical inspiration regarding your healing needs, sit in or beside your living altar in the dark.

✹ Obatala Healing Spell

Obatala is Yoruba's gentle healer. Obatala's powers of healing are so miraculous he isn't syncretized to any ordinary saint but to another miracle healer, Jesus Christ. Obatala's color is white. He owns everything of that color (including bones) and heals through that color, hence the eggs and camphor in this spell.

Although Obatala may be invoked for any sort of healing, his specialty is cooling, in all senses of that word. Invoke Obatala to remedy any over-heated situation or condition, whether physical, emotional, or spiritual. Known as Oxala in Brazil, Obatala's days are Sundays or Thursdays, depending on tradition. He is traditionally offered white things: milk, coconut, rice, **Cascarilla Powder,** *white shea and cocoa butter, and white candles.*

Every person involved with this spell is assigned an egg, whether that person is ill or is serving in the capacity of healer. Maintain this spell as a vigil until healing

occurs. When and if the eggs start to smell, dispose of them outside the home and replace.

1. Write the appropriate name on each egg, so that they may be distinguished from one another.
2. Fill a clear, sparkling clean, crystal bowl with spring water.
3. Dissolve a square of white camphor in the water.
4. Place the eggs within the bowl.
5. Change the water morning and evening, adding additional camphor.
6. Burn two white cross candles or plain white candles on either side of the egg-filled bowl. Enhance with dressing oils as you deem appropriate.
7. Accompany the spell with prayers and petitions as desired.

 ## Obatala Two-In-One Healing/Cleansing Spell

This ritual petitions Obatala for healing. It simultaneously performs a spiritual cleansing.

*Place **Cascarilla Powder,** a few pieces of coconut and a few chunks of cocoa butter into a white drawstring bag. Pass this bag over the body of the person in need of healing. This ritual is beneficial for enhancing mental stability and serenity as well as physical healing.*

 ## Spirits of Healing: Fairies

Fairies are botanical masters with detailed knowledge of magical herbs. They may be petitioned for miracle cures and to prevent illness.

1. Accompany your petition with small gifts of milk, berries, crystals, and similar.
2. The fairies express their power through their favorite botanicals. Gather seven different species at noontime, during a summer full moon. Fairy herbs include althea, eyebright, foxglove, ragweed, Saint John's Wort, self-heal, speedwell, thyme, toadflax, and yarrow. Choose what suits you; obviously if you have allergies, ragweed isn't for you.
3. This spell intends magical use of the herbs, not medicinal: arrange them in bunches and hang throughout the home to protect against illness and speed healing.

General Healing Spells

The following are spells to maintain good health, enhance immunity, provide general healing, and practice preventive magic.

 ## Acorn Good Health Spell

Acorns are sacred signs of life. Carry an odd-numbered quantity of acorns in a green or red charm bag to maintain good health.

 ## Agrimony Bath

This cleansing provides psychic and magical healing.

1. Make a strong infusion by pouring boiling water over agrimony.
2. Let it cool, then strain out the botanical material.
3. Dip a white cloth into the infusion and gently bathe the patient.

 ## Amber Beads Disease Prevention

Amber beads are perceived as bolstering health; however, not just any amber beads will do. Amber beads carved into the shapes of genitals, whether very literally or just vaguely reminiscent, allegedly provide protection, especially regarding health. Wear or carry as needed.

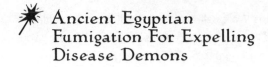

Ancient Egyptian Fumigation For Expelling Disease Demons

Calamus/Sweet Flag
Coriander
Juniper
Myrrh

Blend all the ingredients and burn them together. Grind and powder the botanicals, if you are using small quantities in small space. However, during a mass emergency, burn large quantities. In such cases it's not necessary to grind ingredients. (Juniper would be burned in French hospitals many, many centuries later as a disinfectant.)

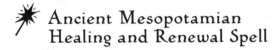

Ancient Mesopotamian Healing and Renewal Spell

This Mesopotamian method provides spiritual cleansing and purification for a person suffering from illness. It may also be used as a preventive measure, performed on a regular schedule (once a week, once a month or as needed) to avoid and repel disease demons. There is a remarkable similarity to modern healing rituals associated with Afro-Caribbean healer and Disease Spirit, Babalu-Ayé.

Rub the body with oil, and then rub the body with bread or dough.

Anemone Healing Spell

According to legend, anemones (wind flowers) sprang from Aphrodite's tears as she wept over the wounded Adonis. According to other legends, anemones spring from those wounds. The very first anemone of the year allegedly has amazing magical healing properties. Keep an eye out for it. Should you find this flower—and the first one of the season you see may be it—wrap it up in

red cloth. Bind this cloth around an ailing person's arm with prayers, blessings, and affirmations. An accompanying petition to Aphrodite may be beneficial as well.

Astrological Healing Waters

Each part of the body is under the dominion of an astrological signs, from the head (Aries) to the feet (Pisces). The sign influences that part of that anatomy. In days long gone by, medical physicians were expected to have strong working knowledge of astrology.

Create twelve bottles of lunar-charged healing water, corresponding to the astrological signs:

1. Each month, on the night of the Full Moon, expose a glass bottle filled with pure spring water to the moonbeams.
2. In the morning, label the bottle with the appropriate astrological sign (or place in smaller bottles, then label).
3. Apply these waters to the parts of the body ruled by that astrological sign for healing purposes. (See the Tables of Correspondences on page 1064.)

Banish Affliction Spell

Touch the relevant part of the body, wherever healing or relief is needed, with three fingers: the thumb, middle, and ring fingers. Stretch the other two out straight and chant:

Go away!
It doesn't matter whether you originated today or
  earlier or anytime
This illness, this pain, this swelling, this tumor, this rash
  [fill in as appropriate]
I call it out, I lead it out, I speak it out,
I call it gone, I lead it gone, I speak it gone,
I call it vanished, I lead it vanished, I speak it vanished
Through this spell, from my limbs and bones, my flesh
  and blood
Vanish pain, vanish illness, vanish suffering!

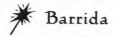

Barrida

The barrida *is a method of spiritual, magical cleansing, indigenous to Mexico, that may be used to heal and "sweep away" illnesses caused by enchantment.*

1. Construct a small broom from branches. The exact botanical is chosen based upon availability and the nature of the healing; however, for illness caused by bewitchment rosemary is most common. Small pepper tree branches and red geraniums may be tied up together with the rosemary to form a broom.
2. Someone must cleanse (sweep) the patient; once upon a time (and still, in some places) this was a shamanic rite. The cleansing is accompanied by prayer, petition, incantation, and spiritual negotiation.
3. When the sweeping is complete, the broom must be taken apart and destroyed.

Bear Fetishes

Bears are acknowledged as the totemic animals of shamanic healers. When ill or when engaged in healing work, pay particular attention to dreams featuring bears. Bear figurines, particularly Zuni stone fetishes, may be used to stimulate magical healing.

Pick a fetish that "calls to you," the one that stimulates a craving for possession. The fetish that chooses you will always work most powerfully for you, but white bears and bears carved from turquoise are considered especially powerful. In fairy tales, real bears become actual around-the-clock companions. Treat the fetish like that fairy-tale bear. Keep it with you all day, tucked into your pocket or carried safely in a charm bag. Sleep with it under your pillow or by your bedside. Feed it on schedule: although actual substances are offered, the bear eats the essence. A traditional Native American offering would be corn pollen but don't do this by rote: think about what your bear needs to eat.

Most importantly, talk and listen to the bear: once activated, it will eventually offer healing advice and recommendations for maintaining health.

Bezoar Stones

Bezoar derives from the Persian "pad-zahr," "poison expelling." Bezoar stones are concretions found in the stomachs of animals, usually goats, credited with antidoting poison and removing illness. The typical method of use is to bind the bezoar to the afflicted area.

Bloody Stick Transference Spell

According to magical theory, illness may be removed via methods of transference. The following ritual must be accomplished in complete and total silence.

1. Position yourself by a stream so that the water runs away from you.
2. Take a hazel or elder stick.
3. Carve your name into it.
4. Make three small slices into the stick.
5. Fill these slices with your blood, either menstrual blood or a few drops obtained by pricking your finger.
6. Throw the stick over your left shoulder or between your legs into water that must be flowing away from you, ideally rapidly.
7. Walk away without looking back.

✴ Clothing Spell

Among various Dravidian traditions of India, the concept of the contagious aspect of illness extends to the magical. Thus the sick person's clothes and bed linens become impregnated by the disease and are thus dangerous. This is a magical impregnation, beyond what laundering with antibacterial soap can cure.

To counteract, bring fabrics to a place with extreme baraka *or benevolent sacred magic power, to regenerate, revitalize, and make them safe. Hang the clothes or linen on a sacred tree, in holy place, or in shrine. (This is also beneficial for new linens or ritual clothing. Beyond safety precautions and preventive measures, this creates highly charged talismanic fabrics.)*

Once a year, during the month of May, masses of Romany people converge on the French town of Les Saintes-Maries-de-la-Mer, at the shrine of their matron saint, Sarah Kali. Sarah Kali's identity is subject to interpretation. She may be the Egyptian servant who accompanied Mary Magdalene, Mary and Martha of Bethany and Mary Salome to France; she may be a Romany priestess of Ishtar who greeted them upon arrival in Provence; she may be the daughter of Mary Magdalene and Jesus Christ; or she may be the Hindu deity Kali in disguise, having accompanied the Romany from India.

A beautiful statue of Sarah Kali is enshrined within an ancient grotto, believed to have once been a venue for celebrating the mysteries of Mithras. During her festival, the statue is carried in procession to the sea where it is immersed and bathed. Brought back to her shrine, she is then dressed in finery.

It is traditional to bring offerings to the statue in conjunction with petitions asked and received. However Sarah Kali also accepts offerings of clothing from those suffering from illness or in need of healing. The clothing is placed on her body and creates the connection between the deity and the petitioner. As the clothing absorbs the deity's power, the healing is transmitted to the petitioner, who may have attended the festival or may be far away. This principle may also be applied to a personal shrine and a votive image close to your heart.

Color Therapy

Every color has the capacity to heal. Each color has specific magic powers best suited for certain ailments or physical conditions. Expose yourself to concentrated doses of the appropriate color(s) to avail yourself of their healing energy. Surround yourself with the needed color; wear it, gaze, and meditate upon it.

Access the healing magic of color through:

★ *Crystals. Although each crystal gemstone possesses its own specific healing powers, generalities may be drawn based on color. Select crystals in the color range most beneficial for you: use them in massage, meditation, and other healing rituals*

★ *Color baths. Tint the water so that it coordinates with your healing needs. There are commercially available "color baths." In addition, the nineteenth-century Bavarian cleric and healer, Father Sebastian Kneipp, pioneered a system of hydrotherapy. Although there seems to be no evidence connecting Father Kneipp's theories to color healing, his baths, now commercially available,* are *vividly colored and may be the most accessible color bath, although this may not have been their original intent. However, you can also tint the water yourself with food coloring and various natural plant dyes. Just make sure whatever you use is safe and non-toxic*

★ *Candle magic. Coordinate candle colors with your particular ailment*

★ BLACK: physical and mental exhaustion
★ BLUE: emotional imbalance, post-traumatic stress, throat disorders, speech disorders, headaches, toothaches, insomnia, susto
★ BROWN: vertigo, disorientation, psychic torpor
★ GREEN: physical healing, cancer, ulcers, high blood pressure, heart trouble
★ ORANGE: bowel and digestive disorders, arthritis, asthma, fevers, bronchitis and related bronchial ailments
★ RED: physical disabilities, blood disorders, HIV and AIDS, anemia, vitamin deficiency, impotence, infertility
★ YELLOW: stomach problems, skin disorders, depression due to heartache

 ## Colored Water Spells

1. Fill clear glass or cut crystal bottles with spring water.
2. Tint the water the desired shade.
3. Place the bottle(s) in a sunny window.
4. Sit, relax and gaze at the color(s).

 ## Color Spell: Maximum Intensity

Different methods of accessing the magic healing power of colors aren't mutually exclusive but may be used in conjunction. The following combination of colors, candles, crystals, and chants allegedly helps prevent illness as well as overcome it.

1. Choose the appropriate color.
2. Burn candles in the corresponding color.
3. Surround them with color-coordinated crystal gemstones and color-water bottles.

4. This spell may be further empowered by chanting sacred verses, especially Habakkuk 3:3–5.

 ## Color Spell Romany

Wear red clothing when ill because red is the color of life, health, and vitality. A vigorous, defiant color, it does fervent battle against illness on your behalf.

Convalescence Spells

Maintain the magic during convalescence to speed healing and protect a vulnerable aura.

Convalescence Spell: Coffee

Coffee allegedly invigorates and empowers magically. Brew good fresh strong coffee. Add an odd number of cups to the bath and bathe.

 ## Convalescence Spell: Rue

Wear a sprig of fresh rue pinned to your clothing during convalescence for protection and to magically speed healing.

 ## Coriander Spell

Coriander allegedly decreases the power and lessens the effects of disease demons.

Burn the seeds and waft the fragrant smoke over the ailing person.

 ## Crossroads Healing Spell

One never knows exactly whom one will meet at the crossroads. Crossroads are perceived as a magic junction full of swirling energies, powers, and spirits. This spell presumes that at least some of those forces will be sympathetic to your plea.

1. Bring bread and a libation to a crossroads.
2. Pour out the libation and place the bread on the ground.
3. Turn in all applicable directions, each time making a request for healing and improved health.
4. Return home without looking back.

 ## Doll Spell (1) Healing Doll Spell

Illness may be transferred by using dolls and figurines. This ancient Assyrian formula, intended to restore good health to someone who is ailing, requires the creation of a clay or wax figurine. It should look anonymous and not resemble either the person suffering from the ailment or anyone else.

1. Someone other than the ailing person is appointed to communicate with the Disease Spirit. The goal is to entice the illness to leave the human and enter the doll instead. Consider how this is to be accomplished before beginning the spell. Remember, low-level spirit entities, which include many of the lesser disease spirits, are not overly blessed with intelligence.
2. As soon as it's apparent that the disease demon has taken the bait and entered the doll, immediately remove the doll from the premises and dispose of it far from home.
3. Return via a circuitous route.
4. Both the target of the spell (the patient) and the person who communicated with the Disease Spirit should undergo extensive cleansing and protective rituals.

 ## Doll Spell (2) Demon Doll Spell

An alternative doll magic technique is to have the doll actually represent the illness itself in an abstract sense, or a specific disease demon, however you best understand the situation.

1. Make a figure from clay, dough, wax, or pitch. Any other material that seems appropriate may be used with the proviso that whatever is used can be completely and entirely destroyed. This is not the moment to pull out fancy arts and crafts materials that boast the ability to last forever.
2. Personalize the doll as needed.
3. When you're ready, destroy it by either tossing it onto a fire or tossing it into running water, flowing away from you. The illness is expected to depart also. The demon feels uncomfortable and unwelcome and so goes elsewhere.

Doll Spell (3) Dream Doll

Stuff dolls with dried eucalyptus leaves to serve as healing dream pillows.

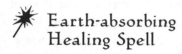 ## Earth-absorbing Healing Spell

In theory, this spell is dedicated to a deity, the "you" referred to in the chant. Leave it ambiguous or substitute the name of your choice. The spell may also be dedicated to the powers of Earth. The end result is that the illness or affliction magically departs from your body and is absorbed by Earth.

Chant the following nine times:

I think of you.
Heal my___ [fill in the blank].
Let Earth retain the illness.
Let health remain with me.

Put your hands flat on Earth and spit.

 ## Emergency Spell

This emergency healing spell works exclusively on the magical plane.

1. If you fear you've been exposed to illness, take whatever medical actions and precautions are needed. In addition, peel and bruise one clove of garlic.
2. Rub it on your naked body from head to foot. One clove should be sufficient but use more if necessary.
3. Throw the used garlic into living waters flowing away from your home.

 ## Evil Eye Healing Spell

*A method of healing illness caused by the Evil Eye: remove the influence by massaging the body with a whole raw egg, and then bathe the person with **Holy Water**.*

 ## Filipino Life Binding Spell

Encircle the wrists and ankles of a dangerously ill person with brass wire, to bind their soul to Earth.

 ## Five Poisons Image

Imagine being stung by the five most venomous creatures on Earth. Now imagine that this venom didn't kill or incapacitate you but inoculated you from danger instead. This is the magical theory underlying the image of the Chinese Five Poisonous Creatures.

Create or obtain an image of the Five Poisonous Creatures: centipede, lizard, scorpion, snake, and toad. Post it to provide magical protection against disease and the effects of poisoning.

Four-leaf Clover Healing Spell

Four-leaf clovers allegedly possess magical healing powers. If you can't find one, create one. This spell is especially beneficial if one person does it for another.

Cut a four-leaf clover shape from paper or a sheet of copper or tin. Empower it with blessings of healing than hang it near the patient or within their line of sight to magically ease pain, bring joy, stimulate healing, and speed recovery.

Forest Blackmail Spell

This mean-spirited Russian spell is not dissimilar in tone and method to many from early Common Era Alexandria.

1. Write a letter on parchment paper to Musail, the Forest Tsar, Guardian of Nature, demanding to know why [*Name*], child of [*Name*], servant of the Lord, has become ill.
3. Attach this note to a rowan tree.
4. Announce your unhappiness.
5. Threaten the tree with dire action: you'll cut down the tree if healing doesn't occur quickly.

Fumigation Against Illness and Infection Spell

Grind small amounts of dried juniper and dried rosemary together. Sprinkle the resulting powder on lit charcoal.
For greater intensity, an outdoor ritual may be effected, to transmit the healing fumes into the greater atmosphere. Build a small fire with juniper wood, and feed it with rosemary branches.

Good Health Maintenance Spell

To maintain and preserve good health, place a crumb of bread and a grain of salt on top of a burned out piece of charcoal. Wrap everything up in a square of red fabric, tying knots to close it, focusing upon your wishes and desires.

Good Health Mojo Hand

Place an angelica root, an ankh charm, a piece of jade, and the botanicals betony and everlasting in red bag. Murmur sacred verses, incantations, and blessings over it.

Hathor's Myrrh Healing Spells

Among the primeval spirit Hathor's epithets is Lady of Myrrh. Hathor's sacred essence is expressed through fragrant myrrh. Once upon a time Hathor's temples also served as centers of healing, similar to those of Asklepios. Less information survives regarding Hathor's holy hospitals; apparently some form of hydrotherapy was performed. The following magical therapeutic spells are enhanced by petitioning Hathor directly for healing. The two spells complement each other.

Hathor Myrrh Bath

Add essential oil of myrrh to the bath to invoke Hathor's healing presence.

Hathor Myrrh Fumigation

Burn myrrh tears. Waft the resulting smoke over the person and/or the room.

Healing Candle

Arrange a circle of silver-dollar eucalyptus around an appropriately carved and dressed red candle. Burn the candle to speed healing.

Healing Herb Candle

This spell involves crafting your own candle.

1. Gather the herbs traditionally used to heal or treat your condition (whether you are going undergoing herbal therapy or not). Incorporate them into a candle.

2. Grind and powder the herbs.
3. Melt the wax and blend in the herbs.
4. Your relative skill and enthusiasm for candle making determines the type of candle crafted. Feel free to make it as elaborate as possible, incorporating shapes associated with healing or with your personal situation. (Don't become attached to the candle however; it is *crucial* that is burned, not retained.) Otherwise, follow standard candle-making directions.
5. Burn the candle; visualize your ailment dissipating and disappearing along with the melting wax.

 ## Healing Garden Spell

Because different botanicals radiate different magic powers, they may be arranged to provide a needed effect. The following botanicals are believed to create a protective aura that shields against disease spirits and illness in general. Spending time within their presence is also believed to transmit healing energy and vigor to the human body. The effect of these botanicals is magical; they may or may not have corresponding physical healing effects. This spell is particularly beneficial for convalescence or for chronic ailments.

1. Fill a garden with all or any of the following: anemone, angelica, balm of Gilead, basil, chamomile, coriander, fennel, garlic, heliotrope, henna, lavender, melissa (lemon balm), mint, mugwort, onion, peony, poppy, rose, rosemary, rue, Saint John's Wort, thyme, tobacco, and wormwood.
2. Trees that radiate magic healing power include apple, bay laurel, birch, cedar, olive, and willow. Ideally trees should form a circle so that you may sit within their midst.
3. Sit and relax within your garden to access its healing power: it's as simple as that. Sit on Earth if it's comfortable or place a bench in a strategic spot. Arrange crystals, glass witch balls, and inspirational, uplifting images as desired.

4. Enhance the magical healing energy with crystals, witch balls, and votive imagery.

 ## Horehound Spell

The botanical horehound derives its name from Horus, Isis' son. Place it beside the patient's bed to assist healing.

 ## Illness Absorption Spell

This spell allegedly helps cleanse and remove the aura of illness.

1. Blend equal parts of **Florida Water** and **Marie Laveau Water.**
2. Add a pinch of sea salt.
3. Place under the bed to absorb the emanation of illness.
4. Replace once weekly, or in intense situations replace daily.

 ## Iron Healing Spell (Forge Water)

Iron is believed to magically energize and empower everything with which it has contact, thus the water used for cooling either an anvil or iron is filled with magical potency and can be used for treating illness. Collect the water and allow it to cool to a safe temperature. Bathe the patient with this water.

 ## Iron Healing Spell (Forge Coal)

Coal used for heating iron is also considered filled with healing energy. Let the coal cool to a comfortable warmth. Wrap the coals in red flannel, and tuck them in next to the patient.

Knot Healing Spells

Many healing spells utilize the principles of knot magic. Remember to focus your intent and desire as you pull the knot.

 ## Knot Healing Spell (1)

This spell comes from Central Asia.

1. Spin or obtain a three-colored cord: blue, green, and red.
2. Tie one knot in the cord for seven consecutive days.
3. After the seventh day and the seventh knot, bury the cord in an inaccessible spot. The disease should disappear as the cord rots.

 ## Knot Healing Spell (2)

Sometimes you have to tie, but sometimes you have to untie. Visualize the illness and suffering as you tie the initial knots. You're not wishing the illness—quite the opposite. You're essentially transferring the illness into the knot. Then visualize relief as the knots are untied; the illness's terrible energy dispersing into the atmosphere.

1. Tie seven knots in a string.
2. Make it into a bracelet for the patient.
3. Untie one knot each day.
4. On the last day, unravel the thread and throw everything into running living water, flowing away from the patient's location.

Originally this spell began with the spinning of the thread, accompanied by sincere prayer and the repetition of sacred texts.

 ## Knot Spell: Heliotrope

Although today "heliotrope" indicates a specific flower indigenous to Peru, the ancient Greeks and Romans used the name to indicate any plant that followed the sun. Either may be used in this formula attributed to Pliny. Tie knots in a heliotrope stem, murmuring a prayer over each one. Petition that the patient will recover to untie the knots.

 ## Knot Spell: Peony Roots

Peony, the healing plant of the ancient Greeks, is allegedly a plant of divine origin formed from moonbeams. It's associated with the divine healer, Asklepios. According to legend, Asklepios was the child of Apollo and his priestess, a princess. While pregnant she fell in love with a mortal man and attempted to marry him. Apollo, jealous and infuriated, killed her but saved baby Asklepios from her funeral pyre. Or so goes the story. Bad things seem to happen to women who catch Apollo's romantic interest, if we recall some other priestesses, such as Daphne and Cassandra.

In any case, Apollo nurtured his son and taught him secrets of healing. Asklepios became such a good doctor that he revived the dead. This upset the balance of nature and upset the gods; Hades in particular was livid, so Asklepios was immediately killed and deified.

Fashion a necklace from peony roots and have the patient wear it around his or her neck. This allegedly wards off illness and evil and is also beneficial for soothing, preventing, or minimizing seizure disorders.

 ## Kyoto Powder Spell

*The Hoodoo formulation, **Kyoto Powder**, is used to provide healing. Although, unlike so many other magical healing spells, this is accomplished through topical application, still all healing is done on the magical plane, not physical. Sprinkle **Kyoto Powder** on the*

patient, or on the sheets, or in a circle around the patient's bed.

 ## Magic Circle Spells

Allegedly, casting circles around afflicted areas magically contains an ailment. Circles may be visible or invisible as safe, appropriate or desired. Use magic wands, fans or knives to cast invisible circles, and cast visible circles with charcoal, magic chalk or henna paste.

 ## Magic Circle using Magnetic Sand

Circle afflicted areas with olive oil or shea butter, and sprinkle with magnetic sand.

 ## Magic Iron Circle Spell

Allegedly creating or placing iron rings around all manner of ulcers, sores, and skin disorders will magically prevent them from spreading. If this will cause no harm, this old magical remedy may be worth a shot. Charge the iron with your desire before initiating the spell.

 ## Magic Wood Healing Spell

Although any wood, like any herb, contains some sort of power, certain woods are perceived as more magically charged than others, for instance oak, thorn or rowan.

1. Create a fire with magically powerful wood.
2. Concentrate on your desired goals while gazing into the fire.
3. When the fire has almost died out and the wood has been reduced to charred fragments, pick one piece up using metal tongs.

4. Drop the wood into an awaiting pot of cold water; simultaneously envision the illness breaking up, dispersing, and disappearing.
5. Repeat for seven consecutive nights.

 ## Magic Wood: Oak Healing Spell

Oak is traditionally amongst the most powerfully magical of trees. Build a fire from oak wood on the hearth or within fireplace or cauldron. Toss rowan and/or stinging nettles into the fire to heal and eliminate illness within the home.

 ## Magical Healing Aromas

Add essential oils of frankincense, lavender, and mastic to an aroma burner and disperse the fragrance through the area, to magically strengthen the body as well as inner resolve, while at the same time summoning benevolent spirits and putting others to flight.

 ## Magical Immunity Enhancing Incense

This simple fumigation formula allegedly boosts immunity to illness. Grind chopped bay laurel leaves and frankincense resin together. Sprinkle on lit charcoals and direct the smoke as desired.

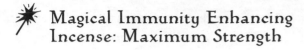 Magical Immunity Enhancing Incense: Maximum Strength

Chopped bay laurel leaves
Benzoin
Frankincense
Juniper berries and/or wood
Thyme

Grind these ingredients together into a powder. Sprinkle on lit charcoals and direct the smoke as needed.

Milagros

The milagro (Spanish for *"miracle"*) is a magical tool that may be used as a charm, amulet, votive offering, or spiritual communications device. Although milagros may be used in other types of spells, they are most frequently dedicated to healing.

They may also be formed from any material, from precious gems to wax, but most milagros are cut from inexpensive silver-colored metal. The shape of the milagro is chosen to correspond with an ailment or affliction. Milagros take the form of isolated body parts, the most common being hands, heads, feet, legs, arms, eyes, male and female genitals, breasts, eyes, ears, noses, and hearts. Uteruses are traditionally represented by images of toads or hedgehogs, reflecting medieval conceptions of the female reproductive system.

The purpose of the milagro is to either strengthen or heal the corresponding part of the body, to prevent, or to heal a disorder. Milagros may be used in ritual to help extract ills afflicting the corresponding part, but they are most commonly used as a spiritual communication device.

Milagro Spiritual Petition Spell

1. Determine to whom your petition is to be directed and thus to whom the milagro will be presented. Milagros may be presented at a shrine (many Latin American cathedrals have special areas reserved for such petitions) or upon a home altar. Determine what you will give in exchange, should the healing be effected.
2. Light candles and do whatever is necessary to draw attention toward your petition.
3. Hold the milagro in your hands to charge it with your desired goal.
4. Make your request and your vow.

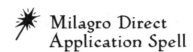 Milagro Direct Application Spell

Representations of anatomical parts are believed to strengthen the corresponding part of the wearer's body. Hold the milagro in your hands and charge it with your desired goal and pin it to your clothing, close to the applicable body part. Spiritually cleanse the milagro periodically, re-charging and re-consecrating it as needed.

 Milagro Good Health Maintenance Spell

Because milagros strengthen corresponding parts, they may also be used to maintain a state of good health. Collect assorted milagros, corresponding to parts for which you may have concern. Pin them to a fabric-covered board. Maintain quartz crystals nearby to further empower the milagros, just in case the Direct Application Spell above should ever become necessary.

Mistletoe Ring

Carve a ring from mistletoe (and wear it!) to ward off illness.

 Notre Dame Water

*Asperge the patient, bed, and room with **Notre Dame Water**.*

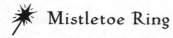 Pentacle Spell

The five-pointed star or pentacle may be understood to represent a human shape: feet apart, arms extended, and the head represented by the star's point. This spell is cast by one person on behalf of another.

1. Visualize the pentacle's shape while measuring a person using a single red thread.
2. First measure from each foot to the opposite hand, then from each foot to the head and finally across the arms to reproduce a pentacle.
3. Analyze the measurements: allegedly they contain clues as to treatment and final outcome.
4. Finally burn the thread, encouraging the patient to breathe the fumes.
5. Add the ashes to water (this may be the perfect moment for **Seven Sisters Water**) and give it to the patient to drink.

 Pearls of Health

An expensive prescription for maintaining good health suggests you keep a bowl filled with real pearls in easy reach. Periodically run your fingers through them. This allegedly enhances the immune system, stimulates health, and encourages longevity.

 Pliny the Roman's Iron Knife Spell

In addition to its use as surgical tools, iron also bestows a sort of magical immune system enhancement, considered particularly beneficial for young children and the elderly. This formula comes from Pliny. It's also used as ritual protection against poison.

1. Take a knife or dagger, the crucial point being that it is crafted from iron or steel.
2. Cast an imaginary circle three times around body of patient with the point always facing toward them.

 Pomanders

Pomanders have devolved into an old-fashioned, somewhat archaic craft, typically reserved for Christmas decorations; however, their roots lie in magical healing. Clove-studded citrus fruits (the cloves and orrisroot used to craft the pomander preserve the fruit indefinitely) were used as amulets against illness and were especially popular during infectious epidemic.

1. Choose a beautiful, healthy orange or grapefruit.
2. Carefully pierce it with holes: ideally only the rind is pierced, not the underlying fruit.
3. Stick a clove into each hole.
4. The above are the mechanics: to actuate a spell, focus on your desired goals while piercing and adding the cloves. Murmur sacred verses, affirmations, and blessings.
5. Roll the pomander in orrisroot and ground cinnamon.
6. Tie it up with red ribbons and hang it to repel and remove illness.

Potato Health Preservation Spell

Potatoes possess an absorbing quality, similar to eggs or coconuts. Use this spell to maintain good health or to magically absorb and eliminate lingering minor ailments.

1. Carry a small potato, such as a fingerling, in your pocket or medicine bag, to ward off disease and other evils.
2. Carry the potato until it begins to smell, rot or somehow become distasteful. (If you don't want to touch it, then it's time to stop carrying it.) Essentially, it's full like a vacuum bag.
3. Discard and replace.

 ## Preventive Magic Spell: Pine

Arrange boughs of fresh pine over the bed to dispel illness and enhance healing.

Preventive Magic Spell: Violet

Pick violets in the springtime; dry and preserve them. Place them in a charm bag together with marjoram in the winter to guard against illness.

 ## Radiant Health Oil

1. Grind and powder angelica root, calendula, eucalyptus, lavender, juniper, and rosemary.
2. Cover with two parts jojoba oil to one part castor oil.
3. Carve candles to suit your situation and dress with Radiant Health Oil to achieve and maintain a healthy condition.

 ## Rose of Jericho Water Spell

The Rose of Jericho is also known as the "Resurrection Plant" because of its powers of revival. Let those powers be transferred to you. **Rose of Jericho Water** *provides general vitality and allegedly prevents illness. Experiment and see what it can do.*

1. Once the rose has blossomed, play with it and the water. Touch the rose very gently, let your fingers play in the water, in the meantime praying, petitioning, and visualizing good fortune and radiant health.
2. Add **Rose of Jericho Water** to your bath or use it in compresses to bathe the brow.

 ## Russian Witches' Midsummer's Eve Harvest Spell (1)

The healing property of herbs is believed greatly empowered if they are gathered on Saint John's Eve/Midsummer's Eve or on the following morning. The belief that harvesting botanicals on Midsummer's Eve increases their magical properties is common to many traditions. The sun is at the height of its power, near the summer solstice, and the plants radiate this increased potency.

Russian witchcraft suggests that following these directions will further empower herbs harvested on Saint John's Eve. As you venture out to harvest, stop at the threshold of your front door and bow six times toward the sun. Bow an additional six times toward the sun when you've reached the plants, just before you gather them.

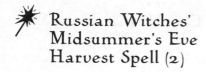

Russian Witches' Midsummer's Eve Harvest Spell (2)

According to Russian folklore, although any herbs are more powerful when picked on Midsummer's Eve, the most powerful herbs are those gathered on Bald Mountain near Kiev during the witches' annual revels celebrated there. Venture out to gather herbs, alone, naked, and without fear of any Spirits you may encounter. Ask Earth for her blessings before harvesting herbs.

Saint John's Eve Healing Spell

Among mugwort's many nicknames is Saint John's girdle, causing frequent confusion with Saint John's Wort. Allegedly John the Baptist wore a girdle (belt) woven from mugwort while in the wilderness. A similar magic belt allegedly provides you with good health.

In time for Saint John's Eve, weave a magic belt from mugwort, knotting your hopes and intentions into the girdle. Wear it while dancing around the bonfire; at some point before the night ends and the bonfire burns out, toss the belt into the flames to receive a year of good health.

Send the Disease Out to Sea Spell

Every magical tradition on Earth has its personal quirks and predilections that distinguish it from others. Russian magic is characterized by incredibly poetic, evocative word-charm formulas. They are formulaic because the beginning of the chant is standardized, something like the "Once upon a time" or "Once there was and once there wasn't" traditional beginnings for fairy tales. When you hear those openings, you know you've entered the realm of fairy tales. Similarly, these standardized word charms signal that you've entered the realm of enchantment. Inevitably the formula allows you an opening at the end to personalize the spell. Chant aloud:

> On Earth there is an ocean
> In the ocean there is a sea
> In the sea there is water
> In the water there is an island
> On the island is land
> On the land is a forest
> In the forest there are woods
> In the woods there are trees
> In the trees there is one tree
> On that tree is a bough
> On that bough is a branch
> On that branch is a creature
> That creature is a [name it]
> Illness! Go into that _____ [name the creature].

(If you want to diminish it even further, give the creature a parasite.)

Snake Bag

This is a magic evocation of the old-fashioned doctor's black bag. Wrap the following up in a freely shed snakeskin: adders tongue (not the real thing, the herb), a piece of rattlesnake root, and a snake stone fetish or an image of Medusa's head. Hang or carry to speed recovery and to maintain good health.

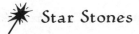 Star Stones

Quartz pebbles are known as "star stones" in ancient British folk tradition.

1. Search a running stream to find star stones.
2. Collect nine as well as some water from where they were found.
3. Boil the stones in the water.
4. Let the water cool and give some to the patient to drink for nine consecutive mornings.
5. When the patient recovers, return the star stones to the stream where you found them.

 Stinging Nettles Spell

Keep fresh stinging nettles under the patient's bed. Replace them daily, burning the old nettles.

 Sweet Grass Health Protection Spell

Wear sweet grass roots as necklaces or sew them onto blankets and clothing. This Cheyenne charm also allegedly works as a disease preventative.

 Three Angels' Health Spell

Chant:

Three angels stand on the far side of Jordan
One binds, one resolves,
One cries out, Kadosh, Kadosh, Kadosh!

Continue with further chants and recitations of sacred texts. Tell the three angels what you need.

 White Cow Healing Bath Spell

While they remain so in modern India, once upon a time, cows were sacred all around the world. The bull and the cow respectively represented the ideal state of male and female health and vitality. The cow's healing power was transmitted through her milk. This healing bath is based on the ancient magic traditions of Celtic Ireland and Scotland.

1. Gently warm milk, ideally from a white cow or a white-faced one.
2. Pour this into a bowl over dried healing herbs and let them steep together.
3. Strain out the solids and add the milk to your bath.

Any herbs suitable for your health may be used. For general vitality, try a combination of chamomile, lavender, and rosemary.

 White Sage Healing Spell

White sage, indigenous to North America, is considered one of the most potent cleansing and protective botanicals. Once common, it is now endangered; for maximum benefit and to preserve this botanical wonder, grow and use your own. Burn quantities of white sage to magically drive away illness.

 Widdershins

"Widdershins" is the ancient word indicating a counter-clockwise motion, the opposite of deasil. When you circle deasil, whatever you are circling remains on your right side; when circling widdershins, what you are circling remains on the left, traditionally the female side. Deasil reflects the circling of the sun; widdershins was associated with the lunar path.

In militantly Christian Europe, widdershins, the left-hand path, became known as the "witch's way."

Witches were believed to dance widdershins at their nightly revels; spells for contacting fairies involve circling widdershins. To be observed circling a building widdershins was sufficient evidence for charges of witchcraft. In light of the cruelty and terror of the witch craze, circling widdershins may be perceived as an act of defiance against the witch-hunters and an affirmation of the old ways.

Fascinatingly, although other such evidence of witchcraft (brooms, cauldrons, familiars, etc.) has since been embraced, modern Wicca has largely absorbed this Christian prejudice against the left-hand (sinister) motion, associating it with "black magic." Many covens advise against ever circling widdershins; others recommend it only for banishing spells. In fact, the widdershins motion has traditionally been used to successfully banish and disperse illness.

Walk widdershins around the ailing person or the perceived perimeter of the illness with a torch or asperging material thirteen times.

 ## Witch's Food Remedy Spell

If you fear your illness is caused by a malevolent, deliberate spell, instead of reversing it and sending it back, in a kind of magical volleyball, use the power of the original spell-caster to remove this hex. (This is particularly effective when one suffers from a malaise or wasting illness that doesn't respond to conventional cures.)

The magical remedy is to eat and drink some of the witch's food in his or her own house. Now, this is not about breaking and entering and stealing food from the kitchen. Voluntary participation by both parties is crucial to effect the cure. Request that the person you suspect of casting the spell serve you a meal in their home. There's no need to explain why, but you can always make up a surreptitious reason. Once upon a time, of course, the implications would have been understood. Traditionally the suspected spell-caster served a simple meal: bread, salt, and cheese. If the person's health fails to improve, this indicates that the suspect is not the culprit.

 ## Wonder of the World Root

All kinds of magical claims are made for ginseng root, so many that in Hoodoo parlance, it's known as Wonder of the World root. Consuming this tonic herb reputedly enhances longevity, libido, and performance. Used as an amulet, it allegedly stimulates miracle cures. Wrap it in cloth and place it beneath a patient's mattress to magically effect recovery.

 ## Woodbine Spell

Create a garland of twining woodbine. Pass the patient through the garland nine times.

Yerba Santa Spells

Erictyon californicum, a California native, is most popularly known as *yerba santa*, literally "*sacred herb.*" Another name for this botanical is "*bear weed,*" indicating its use as a miracle healer.

 ## Yerba Santa Prevention Spell

Wear the herb around your neck to prevent illness and injury.

 ## Yerba Santa Healing Spell

Burn yerba santa in the sick room to disperse disease demons and to psychically empower the ailing person.

Specific Ailments

Asthma

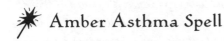 Amber Asthma Spell

Wear amber around your throat to heal asthma and prevent attacks.

 Asthma Cherry Spell

Place a lock of your hair within a cherry tree to cure and relieve.

Autism

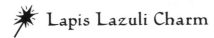 Lapis Lazuli Charm

Lack of speech or speech disorders may be improved by placing or wearing lapis lazuli over the throat chakra.

Sugilite Charm

The crystal gemstone sugilite allegedly benefits those suffering from autism. Wear or carry as appropriate. If this is unrealistic, place sugilite near the person while he or she sleeps.

Back Problems

 Feng Shui Spell

Place a bamboo flute lengthwise, underneath the body, between the box spring and the mattress.

Blood Disorders

This category includes any affliction association with blood including anemia, AIDS, hemophilia, high and low blood pressure, and leukemia.

Bloodstone Healing Spell

Bloodstone is not red but a green stone flecked with red. It gained its name because of its believed affinity for blood. The stone is sacred to Isis and draws its essence from her. It has been used to remedy blood disorders since the time of the ancient Egyptians.

Bloodstone allegedly benefits all disorders of the blood, including halting or minimizing bleeding, both external and internal. Wear or carry it, cleansing and empowering the stone frequently.

Buckle of Isis Spell

Although bloodstone is beneficial in any form, it is most powerful when carved into a Tet amulet, the so-called Buckle of Isis. The amulet represents the healing power of Isis's sacred blood and may have magical benefits for blood even when not formed from bloodstone. For example, carve a tet amulet onto a red candle. Hold the candle in your hands and charge with your desire, then burn.

Iron Blood Invigoration Spell

Place a horseshoe or other piece of iron under your pillow while you sleep.

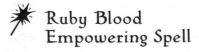 Ruby Blood Empowering Spell

Wear rubies to magically strengthen and empower the body's blood system. Allegedly rubies fade and grow dull

when blood is not at optimal health. Wear rubies against your skin to maintain a visual commentary on the state of your blood. (The gemstone itself must be in contact with your flesh; make sure that jewelry setting allow for this.)

Bronchial Complaints

Shave the patient's hair. Hang this hair on trees and bushes so that the birds will carry it away and put it to good use feathering their nests. Allegedly the illness is transferred with the hair to the birds, which know how to process it in a positive manner.

This is a European spell. There is a school of African-derived magic that specifically warns against birds getting hold of your hair and using it for nests, because it will either give you headaches or make you crazy. Choose which system resonates for you.

Spells for Healing Burns

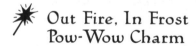

Out Fire, In Frost Pow-Wow Charm

Murmur the following charm over the burn:

You look east
You look west
You look south
You look north
Three angels appear
One brings fire, one brings frost
Blow out fire!
Blow in frost!

Christian Pow-Wows would conclude this charm with "In the name of the Father, Son and Holy Ghost."

Out Fire, In Frost British Charm

Although the imagery is slightly different and a botanical component is retained, this British spell is recognizably the same as the preceding Pow-Wow charm.

1. Gather nine bramble leaves.
2. Place them in spring water.
3. Murmur over each leaf:
   Three ladies came from the east.
   One with fire, two with frost
   Get out with you fire!
   Come in with you frost!
4. Pass the leaves over the afflicted area. (It's not necessary for actual physical contact. Passing over the aura is sufficient.)

Topaz Healing Spell

Gently place topaz over the burned or bandaged area. Let your open palmed hand (palm facing the injured area) rest several inches above the topaz and the burn, transmitting healing energy. This allegedly speeds healing.

Bubonic Plague Spells

See also Epidemic/Plague

Opal Safety

Wearing opals allegedly prevents one from succumbing to bubonic plague.

These spells specifically target bubonic plague, not any other kind of infectious disease. A genre of anti-bubonic plague spells, mainly from Eastern Europe and the Balkans, is dependent upon ritually ploughing furrows around the area requiring protection.

Twin Anti-Plague Spell

Identical twin brothers must carve the wooden parts of a plough from the wood of twin trees, preferably ash. These brothers must then plough around the perimeter of the area to be protected, driving identical twin black oxen.

 ## Virginal Ploughing Spell

One dozen naked virgins of each sex must plough the perimeter of the area. Seven circumambulations must be made; no one may glance at anyone of the opposite sex for the duration of the spell or it won't work.

Children's Healing Spells

Although any safe, applicable spell may also be used to benefit children, because children are perceived as particularly vulnerable to all sorts of danger, including completely physically-derived illnesses as well as the Evil Eye, certain rituals have evolved specifically for their benefit.

(Spells for the general protection of infants are found in *Pregnancy and Childbirth Spells,* page 869.)

 ## Bait and Switch

Children's diseases that resist diagnosis and treatment are sometimes understood as having an underlying spiritual cause: malicious spirits seem unable to leave children alone. This African method of playing bait-and-switch *with the spirits is meant to provide a cure.*

1. Make an offering of fragrant food to the spirits. Serve whatever is perceived as appropriate: the key is it must *smell* tantalizing and alluring. Communication with the disease demons is conducted via aroma.

2. Quickly, while the spirits are feasting, preoccupied with the food, attach iron ankle bracelets and necklaces with bells to the child. (The feet and the back of the neck are the magical jugular spots.) This prevents re-entry of the spirits. (Any other persons in the home, adults included, should also take precautions so that the now homeless demons have no other venue to go to.)

 ## Blacksmith's Water Healing Spell

A remedy to cure an ill or debilitated child regardless of the derivation of the illness.

Fill a small vessel with pure water and bring it to a blacksmith, who dips a piece of red-hot iron into it. Give this water to the child to drink.

 ## Briar Rose Healing Spell

According to British folk magic, a very specific type of plant has the power to heal and revitalize a child. The plant must be searched out by the child's mother, and the child's mother alone. The spell is only valid if she finds the plant (motherless children are out of luck with this one) and she must look for it and initially locate it completely on her own.

The goal is to find wild roses, briar roses that have bent to ground and become rooted, forming an arch. Once found, the child is then taken to the plant on nine consecutive mornings and passed through the arch each time, for a total of nine distinct passes.

Jade Health Protection Spell

Jade protects against childhood diseases. Place a jade charm on a red cord and have the child wear it around the neck. (If the jade's cut into auspicious shapes, it's even more powerful.)

 ## The Licking Cure

Do you suspect that a child's illness is really a manifestation of bewitchment? The following spell attempts to break the spell with the magical vitality transmitted through saliva.

Lick the child's forehead upward, then across, then up again. Spit behind the child's back. If you taste the distinct flavor of salt, this indicates that the diagnosis of enchantment is correct, however, further, stronger action may then be beneficial.

 ## Magic Pin and Chicken Soup

Chicken soup is often teasingly referred to as "mother's magic." This Italian spell, however, creates a soup that serves as a spell remedy for a bewitched child, whose enchantment is characterized by a lingering illness that will not depart.

1. Reserve the liver but make soup from the rest of a chicken.
2. Stick the liver full of pins and put it in a casserole dish together with the sick child's shirt, preferably an undershirt.
3. Simmer them in the chicken broth until you hear the ringing of steel, the chiming of bells or singing. If you hear any one of those sounds, the spell has been broken. Your ritual is complete.

If after three days none of these sounds has been heard, a spell was indeed set, but very professionally: it's beyond home repair. Call in a professional.

 ## Padlock Spell

An ailing or particularly vulnerable child may be held to Earth with an iron padlock charm worn on a red cord around the neck. Of course, every parent perceives their child as being particularly vulnerable, so what was once an emergency measure became stylish. Ornate tiny padlock charms, formed from gold or other precious metals, will perform a similar function; however, for utmost magic power the padlock should be formed from either iron or peach-wood.

 ## Poisonous Five Healing Spell

A Chinese ritual specifically protects female children from illness.

Decorate red paper flowers with images of the Poisonous Five: snake, scorpion, lizard, toad, and centipede. (In addition to being venomous creatures, these animals are fertility emblems as well; creatures that can survive, thrive, and multiply under the worst circumstances.) Attach these to the child's hair.

Soul Calling (1) Coma and Convulsions

This Chinese-derived ritual, now spread throughout Eastern Asia, is used for a child in a coma or child suffering convulsions. This is really a shamanic method and, in theory, those who could afford them would hire a professional soul-caller. However, this has also (if only out of necessity) been accomplished by families for themselves for centuries. The method is dependent upon the belief that the affliction ultimately derives from soul loss—loss of a piece of the soul, usually in response to sudden severe shock or fright—and thus cannot be really cured until that piece of soul is retrieved.

1. Call the child's name. Then something to the effect of "wherever you're having fun, come home now!" Or "wherever you're scared and hiding, it's safe to come out, come back now!"
2. Assure the child that they will not be in trouble, bribe them, whatever would be most effective for your child. This may be done at home but traditionally, especially for a child in a coma, soul-calling was performed by walking streets calling for the child.
3. If you're walking the streets calling the child, a second person follows announcing that he or she has returned. (Whether there has been improvement or not: this can be understood as positive visualization and affirmation.) Some suggest bringing the child with them and/or the child's favorite clothes: the clothes call the child.

Soul Calling (2) Failure to Thrive

In contemporary Taiwan, soul-loss is blamed for a child's listlessness, fretfulness, or sickliness. The proverbial "failure to thrive" may actually be a sign of soul-loss. This is confirmed if you can identify a moment of intense fright that precipitated the decline.

If you suspect that the soul was driven out by fright:

1. Return the child to the scene of the initial fright.
2. Perform soul-calling rituals.
3. Bring favorite toys or clothes to lure the soul back.

Cholera Spells

The Romany Disease Spirit Bibi may also bring or heal tuberculosis and typhoid fever but cholera is her primary manifestation. Her euphemistic name literally means "Aunt." In addition to her manifestation as the disease, Bibi also appear as a tall, thin woman dressed in red with long black hair and bare feet, sometimes accompanied by two small girls, her daughters, and two white lambs. Bibi may also manifest as a hen: each of her accompanying chicks represents a different disease.

Those who actively honor and venerate her believe themselves able to either avoid her diseases or to receive a cure, if afflicted. This active veneration is not only insurance against illness; Bibi allegedly draws prosperity to her devotees too.

The key towards propitiating Bibi comes from her notorious love of immaculately clean houses. There are two ways to approach this:

★ *Keep your house really spotless so that she will be pleased and not harm you*
★ *Keep your house incredibly messy. Bibi will be so appalled she'll move on and have nothing to do with you, sparing you the disease*

Bibi Healing Spell

To exorcise Bibi (in other words, heal and eliminate the disease):

1. Take dirt from a stranger's grave, an insect found within the crevice of a tombstone and a heap of small grains (wheat, millet, barley, or similar).

2. Mix these with water taken from three different wells at the midnight hour.
3. At sunrise, bathe the sick person with this mixture, reserving the water.
4. Blend this water with fresh clean water taken from a running stream, placing the blended waters in a bottle, jar, or other container.
5. Whoever is responsible for administering the cure takes this container outside, travels a distance from the patient via a circuitous route, then faces east, still holding the liquid, and utters an incantation giving Bibi back the disease she owns and has caused.
6. Throw the liquid on the ground.
7. Do not return via the same route.

 ## Bibi's Prevention Spell

1. Set a table with a white cloth.
2. Serve white cake.
3. Each participant is given a slice of cake in exchange for an offering to Bibi.
4. Don't eat the cake but preserve it for an emergency as it has magical healing powers, especially beneficial for children, for whom cholera is an extremely dangerous disease.
5. Light candles and incense.
6. Place all Bibi's offerings on an altar or underneath it.
7. Have a party in Bibi's honor: eat, drink, toast her, and request her blessings.

 ## Slavic Cholera Spell

This Slavic ritual is intended to stop an outbreak of cholera; however, it may also be effective against other plagues. This ritual is for women only. Although men will ultimately benefit from the ritual's success, they are not allowed to participate or even witness the ritual, on pain of death.

1. At midnight, nine virgins and three widowed crones, who are at least temporarily celibate, go to the outskirts of town. (Other women are welcome and encouraged to join them.)
2. There the core group undresses down to their shifts, slips, and undergarments. The widows cover their hair with white shawls or turbans while the virgins wear their hair loose.
3. A plough is hitched to one crone and driven by another.
4. The nine virgins carry scythes.
5. The remaining crone carries animal bones and skulls.
6. The procession circumambulates the perimeter of town, ploughing a furrow to permit the Earth spirits to emerge and fight off disease. A noisy, raucous atmosphere is encouraged; the women should chant and sing and howl.

Common Cold

 ## Amber Temperature Control Spell

Minimize and ward off chills by wearing tightly beaded amber necklaces. Amber is believed to absorb body heat and retain it, thus magically creating a balancing effect.

Ruby Water Spell

Astrologically aligned with the sun, rubies are believed to radiate hot red cosmic rays that cure illnesses caused and aggravated by cold. Steep a ruby in a clean vessel filled with pure, spring water. Remove the ruby and drink the water.

Ruby crystal gemstone elixir (Alaska Flower Remedies) may be substituted, although do not exceed the manufacturer's recommended dosage. Wearing a ruby is also supposed to help.

Ruby Water is also recommended for anemia and other ailments associated with blood, including circulatory deficiencies, low (but not high, which it will aggravate) blood pressure, infertility, and (my favorite) stupidity.

Digestive Disorders

Gimme a Pig-foot Spell

1. Go to a butcher and buy a pig-foot. Take it home.
2. Boil the pig-foot until the meat is so tender, it falls from the bone.
3. Do with the meat whatever you will: eat it, give it to the cat, throw it away but strip it clean to the bone because *that's* what you really want.
4. Wash the bone well, dry it, and then rub your abdomen with it in a clockwise motion.

Repeat as needed.

Moonwater Healing Potion

1. Place sacred objects in an iron cauldron or glass bowl.
2. Cover them with pure spring water.
3. Expose this water to moonlight overnight.
4. In the morning drink the water or use it to bathe with.

Although this spell is specifically recommended for digestive disorders, it may be beneficial for other health ailments as well.

Epidemics/Plagues

This category covers the entire gamut of infectious disease. These spells target any infectious disease capable of instilling fear in the collective heart of a population.

A large percentage of epidemic-oriented spells involve fumigation and the magical plant angelica. Fumigation (burning botanicals as incense on a grand scale) is one of the primary tools against epidemic. Its basic use is similar to private fumigations performed as personal cleansing ritual spells, but on a much grander scale. When plague and epidemic threatened a city, fumigations were frequently government-sponsored. Metaphysical wisdom suggests that an invisible aura of illness surrounds and emanates from the ailing person, like a malevolent, infectious force-field. To prevent infection and the spread of epidemic, this aura must be contained and eliminated. Fumigations, magic via the element of air, pervade the atmosphere and help contain this destructive aura.

During London's Great Plague, massive fumigations were undertaken using sulfur and saltpeter, with ambergris added to improve what must have been an unbearable scent. (If you feel the need to reproduce this formula, substitute labdanum resin for ambergris; however, be aware it's not advisable to inhale sulfur fumes. Consider Dr. Atkinson's Formula first; see page 536.)

Many, if not most, anti-epidemic spells feature angelica, the botanical named in honor of the angel who first demonstrated its magical anti-epidemic properties.

Be warned—do not use wildcraft angelica. It resembles a species of hemlock and mistakes have been made. Harvest only from a home garden where its identity is secure, or purchase it from reputable vendors.

Angelica Spells

According to legend, in the midst of a terrible, lingering plague, an angel appeared to a monk in a dream and showed him a botanical remedy guaranteed to rout the plague and heal the ill. It worked and the root was named angelica or archangel root in the angel's honor. General consensus says Michael, humanity's defender, was responsible for this angelic intervention, although a few dissenting voices insist that it was Raphael, God's healer.

Angelica is a frequent component of magical healing spells. Add angelica root to **Four Thieves Vinegar**, in addition to the four ingredients reserved for each thief, especially in times of genuine epidemic. Angelica root may also be carried as an amulet, to promote healing and preserve health.

Angelica was considered a primary weapon against periodic epidemics of infectious disease or plague, as this formula from Great Britain demonstrates:

Angelica Potion (1) The King's Majesty's Excellent Recipe for Plague

Angelica water
Treacle
Nutmeg

Simmer over heat and serve to plague victims twice daily. Modern experimenters may wish to substitute angelica hydrosol for angelica water, for increased potency.

☀ Angelica Potion (2)

Many modern liqueurs and cordials originated as healing potions, many formulated by monks. Angelica is a frequent ingredient. It was a primary component of the banned liqueur absinthe, the inspiration for Baudelaire, Toulouse-Lautrec, and so many French painters and poets. (Angelica wasn't the controversial component, which was wormwood, a herb with narcotic properties.) Angelica is also a flavoring agent in Benedictine, Chartreuse, and vermouth. A simple angelica liqueur, for healing purposes of course, is easily concocted, providing you have a little patience.

The ingredients are as follows:

Three green cardamoms
Five anise or fennel seeds
One teaspoon dried marjoram
One-sixteenth teaspoon dried allspice
One-sixteenth teaspoon ground cinnamon
One-sixteenth teaspoon ground coriander
One-sixteenth teaspoon ground star anise
An angelica root or dried ground angelica
A shot of vodka plus one cup of vodka
One half cup of sugar syrup
Optional: Green food coloring

1. Grind the cardamoms and anise or fennel seeds with a mortar and pestle.
2. Add the dried herbs and grind them all together. It's not necessary for the powder to be overly fine.
3. Place the powder in a glass jar or bottle with tight fitting lid.
4. Add the shot of vodka, seal the bottle and let it sit in a dark, cool, quiet place for one week.
5. After a week, strain through cheesecloth and discard the solids.
6. Blend the reserved liquid with one cup of vodka and one-half cup of sugar syrup, stirring to dissolve the syrup.
7. Place this in a bottle or jar with a tight-fitting lid and let it rest undisturbed in a cool, quiet, dark place for two weeks.

8. Strain the liquid through cheesecloth once more.
9. Begin to add bits of angelica until the desired flavor is achieved.
10. Put this in a bottle or jar with a tight fitting lid and let it sit undisturbed in a cool, quiet, dark place for two months.
11. Taste it. Add more vodka, sugar syrup or extract of angelica if desired.
12. Tint with food coloring if desired.

Adjust the proportions of spices to suit personal taste.

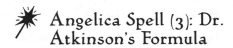

☀ Angelica Spell (3): Dr. Atkinson's Formula

Dr. Atkinson's Formula, a remedy used during the Great Plague of London, combines the principle of fumigation with angelica's magic power.

1. Powder dried angelica roots. (You can purchase them already powdered, which will save time and effort; however, the advantage of powdering your own roots is the sure knowledge that you have the correct botanical and the ability to grind intent into spell.)
2. Steep the powdered angelica in white vinegar for three or four days.
3. Pour the liquid into a pan and heat gently.

Use it as an inhalation, and to fumigate auras, clothing, people, and rooms.

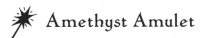

☀ Amethyst Amulet

Wearing amethysts allegedly offers magical protection against plague. Spiritually cleanse the amethysts frequently.

☀ Beeswax Epidemic Prevention Spell

Prevention is always the best medicine. The metaphysical wisdom of the Andaman Islanders suggests that the scent of beeswax offends those demons responsible for epidemics.

★ Burn beeswax candles
★ Maintain blocks of beeswax or beeswax candles in the home. The aroma is strong (and pleasing to most) even without burning
★ The Andaman prescription is to dip stakes into melted beeswax. Stick them into the ground around the home to serve as guards and sentries

Cornelius Agrippa's Magical Recommendations
Master magician Cornelius Agrippa, although not formally trained as a physician, served much of his life in that capacity. Agrippa won renown for remaining to treat patients during epidemics while other doctor's fled. Luckily for his patients, Agrippa didn't follow his own number one tip for staying healthy during an epidemic: if at all possible, get out of town until all danger has passed. For those, like him, who must stay in town, Agrippa had other magical recommendations.

☀ Agrippa's Bath Spell

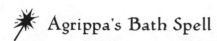

If it is not possible to leave town until the epidemic has abated, bathe with combined vinegar and rosewater.

☀ Agrippa's Vapor Spell

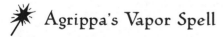

Simmer rue in vinegar. Allow the vapors to permeate home and clothing.

☀ Epidemic Hex

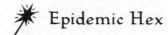

Wind spirits have been associated with danger from various sources, including disease, since at least the Mesopotamians, indicating at least some consciousness of conventional theories of contagion. This spell takes advantage of an infectious situation to send a hex.

Wait until the wind is blowing in the right direction, i.e., toward the one the curse is intended for. Pick up a handful of dust, dirt or snow and blow it into the wind, chanting:

"Wind! Wind! Blind [Name] child of [Name]." Describe explicitly what you want done. Typically someone is targeted with the effects of a current airborne epidemic.

☀ Four Thieves Magic Bath

Add **Four Thieves Vinegar** to the tub in quantities proportionate to how threatened you feel by the epidemic. Repeat daily until the threat has passed.

☀ Four Thieves Quick-Fix Bath

Soak a handkerchief in **Four Thieves Vinegar** and cleanse the body with it, with motions moving up and in (bringing the protection into the body) rather than down and out.

☀ Gentian Epidemic Spell

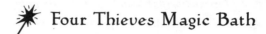

Legend has it that a king of Hungary used belomancy (divination by arrows) to end a rampaging plague. He shot an arrow into the air with a prayer that it would lead him to a cure. The arrow was found in a gentian bush and indeed, the legend says, gentian cured the plague. Gentian is traditionally crafted into liqueurs, some of which may still bear a medicinal reputation, however easier magical methods exist. Dry gentian and hang it in the home to preserve against illness.

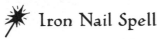

Hyssop Spell

Hyssop, sacred herb of the ancient Greeks and Hebrews, was used for ritual cleansings but also to forestall epidemics. It was once used as a strewing herb for this purpose; however, the practice of covering one's floors with botanical material is a fashion not likely to be revived. Instead, keep hyssop above your head: place bunches of hyssop over doors, windows, and room thresholds to prevent entry of infectious disease. Carry small hyssop bouquets if you must venture out.

Iron Nail Spell

The Romans believed themselves to be descendants of a priestess of Mars and perhaps children of that divinity, too. Certainly they were under his protection. Thus in times of trouble, they turned to iron, the metal ruled by Mars, to prevent plagues and illness. Of course with so many vulnerable to disease, there wasn't enough forge water to go round. The Romans discovered a protective measure, viable for all: at the first sign of illness, or whenever fear strikes, drive an iron nail into the wall.

This practice bears similarity to the Hoodoo technique of nailing Indian Head pennies to a wall to serve as "watchers." Indian Head pennies serve as symbolic "Indian scouts," alert for danger. However, it's possible that the iron nails used to fix them may be what activates and empowers the coins.

Magical Anti-plague "Perfume"

This sixteenth-century European formula is built on a foundation of that luck-bringing fragrance **Chypre***. Remember that until recently, fragrances were frequently sold in the form of powders, rather than alcohol-based liquids. The word perfume itself literally means "through fire." What the folks then understood as perfume would today be described as fragrant incense.*

1. Begin with powdered **Chypre** and then add the following ingredients: aloes wood, ambrette seed, cloves, elder, frankincense, juniper, mace, mastic pearls, myrrh, nutmeg, rue, and wormwood.
2. Blend all ingredients well, using a mortar and pestle. The ingredients are a combination of dried botanicals and gum resins. Once blended, a sort of paste should form. Adjust proportions until the material holds together; if it's too dry, add more of the resins.
3. Form the blend into little cakes.
4. Burn it to perfume, fumigate, and magically cleanse a room and its inhabitants.

Mugwort Anti-infection Spell

Hang mugwort over entry doors to ward off infectious disease and epidemics.

Papua New Guinea Semen/Coconut Remedy Spell

Grate some coconut into a dish. Mix it with a little semen and feed it to those wishing to receive magical safety from the epidemic. (Presumably whose semen is served affects the likelihood of the spell's success.)

Scarlet Pimpernel

Scarlet pimpernel's other name is "Cure All." Make a chain of scarlet pimpernel and hang it to ward off epidemics and pestilential disease.

Thyme Anti-infection Spell

Thyme's name derives from the Greek thumos, "to smoke" or "fumigate." Burn thyme so that its aroma permeates an area to ward off infectious disease.

 ## VSR Spell

Allegedly born in 1293, Saint Roche spent much of his lifetime nursing plague victims. After death, this saint developed a magical reputation for warding off epidemics and performing miracle cures. Place the letters "VSR," for "Vive Saint Roche," above doorways to guard against infectious disease in general, and cholera in particular.

Eye Disorders

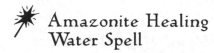 ## Amazonite Healing Water Spell

Place an amazonite crystal gemstone in pure spring water overnight. Use the water to bathe sore, weak eyes.

Emerald Green Stone Spell

Green stones are allegedly beneficial for weakness of the eyes. Ancient craftsmen, the engravers whose work was so demanding on the eyes, kept green stones (preferably an emerald) on their workbenches so that they could periodically rest their eyes to refresh and protect them. This may be beneficial for those who labor long hours in front of a computer screen or in any other profession that threatens to render you blind.

Emerald-green Eyes

Steep an emerald in spring water overnight, exposed to moonlight ideally. Use the water as an eye-wash to heal and strengthen eyes.

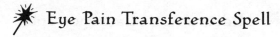 ## Eye Pain Transference Spell

This Hungarian healing charm must be chanted while standing barefoot on bare Earth. It was originally intended to diminish eye pain and discomfort; however, the chant may be amended for any other part afflicted with pain. Adjust as necessary.

I have two eyes.
I have two feet.
Pain from my eyes, go into my feet!
Go from my feet,
Go into Earth!
Go from the Earth,
Go into death!

Iron Flower Water Spell

For weary eyes and to relieve eye strain:

1. Fill a cast iron pot with spring water and set it to boil.
2. Add nine grains of barley, nine elderflowers, and nine sprigs of rue.
3. Let these botanicals simmer for fifteen minutes, then allow the water to cool.
4. Dip a white cloth in the cooled liquid and make a compress to place over the eyes.
5. Then place the barley, elder, and rue on top of the compress and relax.

Midsummer's Eve Eye Potion

Midsummer's Eve dew allegedly possesses special powers and is believed especially beneficial for afflicted eyes. Collect dew from plants gathered on Midsummer's Eve.

Use this dew as safe and appropriate for healing and soothing afflictions of the eyes.

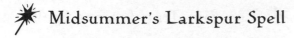 ## Midsummer's Larkspur Spell

Look at Midsummer's bonfires through larkspur flowers to strengthen eyesight.

 ## Saint Lucy Eye Spell

Saint Lucy may be a Christian martyr. She may also be Juno Lucina hiding behind a respectable mask. She may be both. According to legend, Saint Lucy, determined to remain chaste and never to wed, tore out her eyes to discourage a suitor. Her plan worked: the horrified suitor high-tailed it out of there, she maintained her virginity, and God was so impressed at her determination that he not only restored her vision but also gave her the power to cure eye diseases, including those caused by the Evil Eye. Petition her for any assistance needed.

1. Dedicate white candles to Saint Lucy: one for an affliction in one eye, two for both eyes, and five candles arranged in the shape of a cross for the Evil Eye.
2. Hold something that represents eyes in your hands and charge it with your purpose. Use eye beads, glass marbles, an eye milagro, or an Eye of Horus charm. A photograph or a homemade drawing of an eye works, too.
3. Place this "eye" beside the candles.
4. Once the candles burn down, post or carry the eye as a healing, empowering charm.

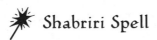 ## Shabriri Spell

This Jewish formula can either be posted as an amulet, or recited. It benefits vision (and water-borne illnesses, among others), and in this instance it must be recited rather than written. A person in danger of losing vision says:

My mother told me to beware of

```
S  H  A  B  R  I  R  I
A  B  R  I  R  I
R  I  R  I
R  I
I
```

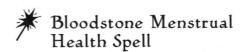 ## Willow Spell

Charge a sprig of willow and wear it in your hair to help stave off blindness.

"Female Problems" Magical Remedies

A historic euphemism for what could be called reproductive disorders except that this assumes desire to reproduce. Spells specifically targeting reproduction (pregnancy, enhanced fertility, healing infertility, and miscarriage) may be located in the sections on *Fertility Spells* and *Pregnancy Spells*. The following spells target health disorders in the reproductive region regardless of any desire for fertility or the lack thereof.

Bloodstone Menstrual Health Spell

Bloodstone, the gemstone identified with Isis, is recommended for menstrual problems by many healers including Hildegard of Bingen. Wear around the neck or, most powerfully, suspended around the hips.

Other red stones can also be very beneficial: string red stones or beads on red cord or a silver chain long enough to wear as belt. Cornelian, red coral, rubies, and garnets are all suitable. Just look for the color red.

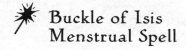

Buckle of Isis Menstrual Spell

The Egyptian tet amulet is especially helpful when carved from bloodstone, a crystal under the dominion of Isis. Euphemistically known as the buckle of Isis, the tet represents the goddess's menstrual pad, soaked with her talismanic blood. Wear one or carry it in a red bag.

The shape of the tet amulet holds its own magic powers, even without bloodstone.

Using henna paste, draw a tet amulet over the abdominal region or on the thighs.

Drowned Doll Spell

This Hungarian spell is intended for women's reproductive area disorders, though it could be adjusted toward any other condition, if desired. The spell presupposes that you can name your ailment. If unable to do so, you can still do the spell; just adjust the incantation.

1. Take nine pieces of white cloth. Manipulate each by folding, knotting or tearing into a small doll, so that at the end you have nine small dolls.
2. Go to a river carrying the dolls under your skirt or tucked into your underwear near your groin
3. Slip each doll into the water, one by one, while chanting:
   Dolls, swim away!
   [Malady: identify it with a name] *swim away!*
   [Malady] *Don't come back until I fish these dolls from the water.*

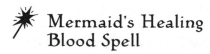

Mermaid's Healing Blood Spell

Coral is sometimes understood metaphysically as the ocean's menstrual blood—or the collective menstrual blood of mermaids—with great potential for healing and protection.

Wear smooth coral beads or charms, ideally red, near the groin area to stabilize and regulate menstrual flow and ease discomfort or pain.

Mugwort Moon Spell

Mugwort flower essence remedy (FES) may be used to coordinate one's own menstrual cycle with the moon. Follow the manufacturer's directions for internal administration or add to massage oils and baths.

Nopales Ovarian Health Spell

Nopales are cactus paddles. Produce markets often sell them, with prickles removed to be pickled or added to salad. Use them to assist healing ovarian difficulties. Soak nopales in gently warmed olive oil and place these over the ovaries as compresses.

Oshun's Women's Healing Spell

Depending upon the legend, Oshun is either Yemaya's daughter or sister. She specifically has dominion over the abdominal area, including all female reproductive organs. Petition her for healing. Offer Oshun a glass of pure spring water and a dish of honey, tasting the honey before giving to her. Light five golden candles and request her assistance.

Ovarian Shield Spells

According to metaphysical wisdom ovarian disorders are linked to intense criticism, whether from others or self-criticism. Every sharp criticism is an arrow aimed straight at the ovaries. Erect a psychic shield.

★ Dilute one drop of rose attar into sweet almond oil and massage it over the ovarian region, for protection and to promote self-love and acceptance
★ Make a magic girdle: string charms, amulets, and cowrie shells on red cord
★ Place red or quartz crystals over the area. Visualize a shield that lingers after the crystals are removed

Red Roses Menstrual Spell

This spell, intended to bring on a period or to stabilize the menstrual cycle, must be performed when roses are in bloom. Wash all over with rose water, then toss your used bathwater over a blooming rose bush. (Obviously, red roses are ideal.)

 ## Serpentine Magic Belt

Snakes are the animals that represent healing in general, but they are specifically affiliated with women's reproductive health.

1. Obtain a freely shed snakeskin. Because this spell essentially requests blessings from the Serpent Realm, it's vital that the skin not be gained by force. People with pet snakes have ready access to the skin; animal shelters and zoos may provide them, too.
2. Wear this skin as a belt against naked skin, draped around the afflicted area, for healing and regeneration.

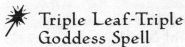 ## Triple Leaf-Triple Goddess Spell

A three-leaf clover represents the three stages of a woman's life: maiden, mother, and crone. Carry a real one or a replica charm as a talisman for optimum health at all stages.

 ## Uterine Creativity Unblocking Spell (1) Athena's Healing Spell

Metaphysically, uterine problems are thought linked to suppressed or repressed creativity—creativity with no outlet for expression. In conjunction with whatever treatment is taken, consider what avenue of creativity may be blocked. Start a project. If you draw a blank and are sure you don't have frustrated desires or don't know how to begin, build an altar to Athena, Deity of Crafts and Creativity.

1. Decorate an altar with images of snakes, gorgon's heads, spiders, looms, and olive leaves.
2. Offer Athena a glass of retsina and a dish of olive oil.
3. Burn white candles and make your appeal.

 ## Uterine Creativity Unblocking Spell (2) Brigid's Healing Spell

The prominent Celtic divinity Brigid is affiliated with water, fire, fertility, smithcraft, and human creativity. She is a sponsor of writing and poetry. Request that she unblock your creativity and simultaneously heal your health disorder.

1. Request her assistance for stalled projects or build her an altar to request inspiration.
2. Decorate her altar with burning candles and dishes of magically charged waters.
3. Display images of cows, pigs, bees, and bee-hives.
4. Offer Brigid a bowl of milk and blackberries.

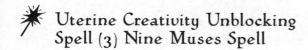 Uterine Creativity Unblocking Spell (3) Nine Muses Spell

For further magical assistance with uterine disorders:

1. Build a shrine to the muses. Let this be a work in progress.
2. Each muse represents a different human art: give each one something applicable to her area of concern or, better yet, create it for her, mining and discovering your own talents.
3. Burn a candle for each muse and petition for your healing.

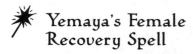 Yemaya's Female Recovery Spell

The orisha Yemaya has dominion over all women's issues, therefore she may be petitioned for renewed and rejuvenated health. Offer her a glass of water with sea salt and a slice of pound cake covered with dark molasses. Dedicate a blue seven-day candle to Yemaya and tell her what you need.

Fever

Today, the term *"fever"* very specifically refers to elevated body temperature. Once upon a time, medical terminology wasn't necessarily as specific as it is today. Spells for fever target a whole host of ailments united only by a shared tendency towards elevated temperature. These spells are indicated for any ailment that even loosely falls under that category, including outbreaks of flu.

 ABRACADABRA!

Perhaps the most famous spell in the world still retains its mysteries. What does the word mean? Various theories regarding its derivation are offered and hotly debated. Is it related to the Gnostic Spirit, Abraxas, recalled fondly by fans of Hermann Hesse's novel, Steppenwolf? *Is it from the Chaldean* abbada ke dabra, *"perish like the word?" Is it derived from Hebrew* Abreq ad Habra, *"hurl your thunderbolt even unto death," or is it a corruption of the Hebrew words* bracha *("blessing")* and dabar *("action, word")? Maybe it's none of the above but the name of a now-forgotten spirit.*

Despite its modern usage as a joke magical word charm, something like hocus pocus *or* bippety-boppety-boo, Abracadabra *is, in fact, a written charm intended to provide physical healing. It is the most famous of a series of diminishing word charms, most common to Semitic magic. Presumably, as the word diminishes, so does the fever, pain, or illness.*

Instructions appear in the first written reference to the spell in the second century CE, *from* Quintus Serenus Sammonicus, *the personal physician to the Roman Emperor Septimius Severus. For relief from fever:*

1. Inscribe the word "abracadabra" on parchment or metal lamella.
2. Attach this word charm to a piece of flax long enough to be worn around the patient's neck.
3. The charm must be worn around the neck for nine days then thrown away over the left shoulder into water flowing east.

Tips for writing "abracadabra:"

★ *Write neatly and carefully, focusing on intention as you write. Don't let your mind wander*
★ *The letters are not supposed to touch each other*
★ Abracadabra *is believed most effective when written with Hebrew letters because the word in Hebrew contains nine letters, nine being the supreme number of power*

There are various methods of using the charm. The inverted triangle is recommended for fever:

```
A  B  R  A  C  A  D  A  B  R  A
B  R  A  C  A  D  A  D  A  B  R  A
R  A  C  A  D  A  B  R  A
A  C  A  D  A  B  R  A
C  A  D  A  B  R  A
A  D  A  B  R  A
D  A  B  R  A
A  B  R  A
B  R  A
R  A
A
```

An upward facing triangle is used to heal and relieve asthma:

```
A
A  B
A  B  R
A  B  R  A
A  B  R  A  C
A  B  R  A  C  A
A  B  R  A  C  A  D
A  B  R  A  C  A  D  A
A  B  R  A  C  A  D  A  B
A  B  R  A  C  A  D  A  B  R
A  B  R  A  C  A  D  A  B  R  A
```

Abracadabra may also be written as a parallelogram, consisting of two triangles, for enhanced healing and empowerment:

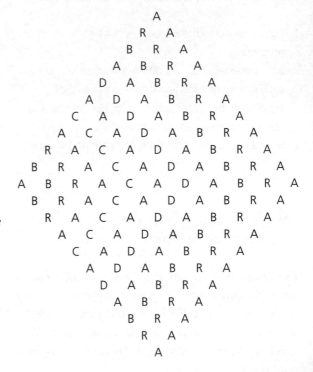

```
            A
          R  A
        B  R  A
      A  B  R  A
    D  A  B  R  A
  A  D  A  B  R  A
C  A  D  A  B  R  A
A  C  A  D  A  B  R  A
R  A  C  A  D  A  B  R  A
B  R  A  C  A  D  A  B  R  A
A  B  R  A  C  A  D  A  B  R  A
B  R  A  C  A  D  A  B  R  A
R  A  C  A  D  A  B  R  A
A  C  A  D  A  B  R  A
C  A  D  A  B  R  A
A  D  A  B  R  A
D  A  B  R  A
A  B  R  A
B  R  A
R  A
A
```

Abrakala Spell

This is another word fever charm. This one is written and worn around the sufferer's neck like an amulet. The concept is to build heat to the breaking point and then gradually diminish it in a controlled, safe manner.

Ab Abr Abra Abrak Abraka
Abrakal Abrakala Abrakal
Abraka Abra Abra Ab Ab
And the people called unto Moses
And Moses prayed to God and the fire abated
May healing come from heaven for all kinds of fever
*   and consumption, heat and pain*
To [name] child of [name]
Amen Amen Amen
Selah Selah Selah

Berber Healing Spell

1. Blend and grind bay laurel leaves, pennyroyal, rosemary, and thyme.
2. Sprinkle on lit charcoals or burn on a brazier.
3. Fumigate the patient and his or her immediate environment. This allegedly breaks the fever and promotes healing.

*(Note: this spell is **NOT** safe for pregnant women.)*

 ## Chelidonious Spell

Wrap a chelidonius gemstone in yellow linen. Wear it around the neck to soothe and heal fevers.

 ## Chili Pepper Fever Spell

1. Break two chili peppers each in half.
2. Place them on an old cloth.
3. Sprinkle them with black mustard seeds and tamarind.
4. Wrap up the packet, knotting it shut.
5. Pass this over the afflicted person three times.
6. Have him or her spit on the bundle three times.
7. Throw the packet into a fire.

 ## Coconut Cooling Spell

Coconut juice (not the milk squeezed from the flesh, but the actual coconut liquid) is believed to have cooling properties. These properties may be enhanced by chanting sacred verses.

1. Cut a small hole in a coconut.
2. This spell derives from Malaysia so Koranic verses are traditionally recited, especially Surah XXXVI. The crucial point is to imbue the liquid with blessings and protection. Choose verses or texts that best suit your purposes and philosophy. Murmur it over the liquid.

3. The patient then drinks the liquid, straight from the coconut if possible.

 ## Cross of Caravaca Fever Relief

Allegedly, replicas of the miracle Cross of Caravaca will break a fever. Accompany with prayer, petition, and recitation of psalms. Have the afflicted party hold the cross in his right hand; if this is not possible, lay it on his chest.

 ## Egg Fever Spell

Gently rub the feverish person's entire naked body with a whole raw egg. When the massage is complete, bury the egg within cool living water (a stream or lake) or place it in the icebox, to cool off the body.

 ## Fever Drainage Spell

Place a piece of amber in the patient's hand. Amber allegedly drains a fever, breaking it.

Henna Fever Removal Spell

Henna is believed to crave heat. Traditionally, while the person whose hands have been decorated waits for the henna paste to dry, she will place her hands near a source of heat (a candle, a brazier filled with coals, a cup of tea) so that the henna can draw in the heat and become empowered. Because henna loves heat, it absorbs it and so serves the function of a cooling plant. This can be meant very literally. Henna is considered an excellent fever remedy because it will allegedly suck out the heat.

★ *Mix it with water to create a paste and apply this to the forehead of the feverish person. (Any resulting reddish color is considered very auspicious and protective.)*

★ *Roll henna paste into a small ball, so that the feverish person, especially a child, may hold it in the hand for relief*

Herod's Daughter's Fever Spells

In Russian magic, fever demons are personified as the daughters (sometimes the sisters) of Herod. The numbers vary: there may be forty sisters, seven sisters or seventy-seven daughters, although a dozen daughters is the most popular version. These magical sisters or daughters bear no relation to historical facts about King Herod's family. For what it's worth, they do, however, resemble the legendary demonic daughters of Lilith, who is sometimes identified with Herod's wife, Herodias. (In other legends Lilith is unable to bear children at all.)

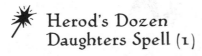 ## Herod's Dozen Daughters Spell (1)

Each one of Herod's twelve daughters manifests disease in a slightly different fashion. Once upon a time, spirit workers examined the patient, plying them with questions, in order to determine which daughter was responsible so that they could prescribe a cure. Allegedly the daughters as a group will cause no harm where they see their names posted, similar to a famous legend regarding Lilith. (See Childbirth Spells, page 854.)

To dispel and ward off fevers, find or create an image of a gorgon's head with twelve snake tresses. Write the names of Herod's daughters on or beside this image and post it prominently on the wall. The daughters are:

Neveia (identified with Salome)
Gladeia
Glukheia
Gneteia
Grynusha
Korkusha
Ledeia
Lomeia
Ogneia
Pukhneia
Triaseia
Zhelteia

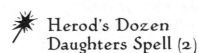 ## Herod's Dozen Daughters Spell (2)

Another method of appeasing Herod's dozen daughters is to pay them off.

1. Bake twelve pies (you determine the size).
2. Wrap each pie individually in fabric.
3. Leave them at a crossroads saying, *"Here you go, twelve daughters! This is for you. Now leave me alone."*
4. Depart without attracting the attention of anyone.

Repeat as the situation demands.

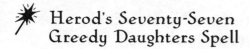

Herod's Seventy-Seven Greedy Daughters Spell

This spell subscribes to the notion that there are seventy-seven daughters. Steps 1–4 must be accomplished before sunset. Unlike many illness spells, it's assumed that the afflicted party will perform this spell for him or herself.

1. To heal a fever, collect and blend water from three distinct sources.
2. Place the water in an iron pot and hard boil an egg in it.
3. Cut this egg into seventy-seven pieces.
4. Tie these pieces up into a cloth.
5. At sunset, take the packet to a river or stream.
6. Throw it over your left shoulder, without looking, into the water flowing away from you.
7. Mutter how you wish the fever would leave you.
8. Go home without looking back, because if you catch the sisters in action not only will the spell not work, there could be further danger. Allegedly as soon as the packet hits the water, the sisters will each fight for their individual share of the egg. In the feeding frenzy, the victim is forgotten and the fever can disperse.

Isis Healing Spell

Isis, the Egyptian Mistress of Magic, is so all-powerful and all-knowing that she may be appealed to for any cause. Her myth contains specific references to healing. On two occasions, one to heal her own son Horus, Isis saves children from deadly scorpion stings. This healing invocation makes reference to that myth. It's intended to minimize or eliminate fever.

Oh Isis, Great of Magic,
Free me, liberate me.
Release me from all evil red things, from the fever of the god and the fever of the goddess,

From death and death from pain and the pain that comes over me
As you freed, as you released your son Horus
Free me, liberate me
As I enter into the fire and go forth from the water.

Ochnotinos Spell

Another fever-diminishing word charm, like "abracadabra." This one allegedly refers to a fever demon, with the theory being that one diminishes a fever by diminishing a fever demon's name. However, unlike abracadabra, *this spell is not a written charm but is said aloud, with the final sibilant hissed like a fierce, healing, protective snake:*

O	c	h	n	o	t	i	n	o	s
C	h	n	o	t	i	n	o	s	
H	n	o	t	i	n	o	s		
N	o	t	i	n	o	s			
O	t	i	n	o	s				
T	i	n	o	s					
I	n	o	s						
N	o	s							
O	s								
S									

Ochnotinus Candle Spell

The "ochnotinus" diminishing fever charm has been adapted to a candle spell.

Starting near the top, inscribe a red candle with the OCHNOTINUS *fever charm.*

Burn the candle. When it has burnt down past the final "s," quench the candle with ice water for magic fever relief.

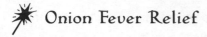 ## Onion Fever Relief

Place a cut onion beneath the bed to relieve fevers. Replace it daily until all threat has passed.

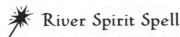 ## River Spirit Spell

This spell pays off the river spirits so that they'll remove a fever. It may easily be combined with a doll spell, similar to that on page 516. Before sunrise, place a coin on the stream bank (or toss it in) with the water going away from you (or the ill person). Let the water carry away the disease.

Although this spell was originally intended to remove a fever, it may also be used to remove other illnesses, too.

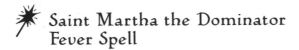 ## Saint Martha the Dominator Fever Spell

Saint Martha the Dominator may be appealed to for assistance and protection from fevers.

1. Carve a green candle with your name, birthday, identifying information, and your desire.
2. Dress it with **Martha the Dominator Oil.**
3. Place a small dragon charm near the candle as it burns. (If you craft your own candles, metal dragon charms may also be hidden inside the candle.)
4. Burn the candle. Once it burns down, carry the dragon as a protective amulet.

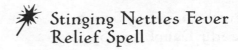 ## Stinging Nettles Fever Relief Spell

This spell is traditionally cast by one person on another's behalf:

1. Dispel fever by pulling up a stinging nettle by its roots using your hand rather than a gardening tool.
2. While holding the plant, chant or sing aloud the name of the feverish party, his or her parents and any other ancestors whose name you know. (Patient and parents are required; the others are extra enhancement.) Allegedly the fever should break.

Headache/Migraine

 ## Amethyst Headache Remedy

Because of amethyst's associations with Dionysus and alcohol (see Banishing Spells, *page 127*), presumably this magical cure is especially beneficial for those morning-after headaches.

1. Immerse an amethyst in moderately hot water for seven minutes.
2. Gently pat it dry.
3. Carefully rub the amethyst over affected areas plus the back of the neck.

Because rubies are believed to have a warming effect on the body, it's recommended that ruby jewelry be removed from those suffering fever.

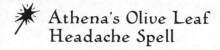 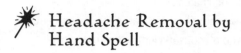

Athena's Olive Leaf Headache Spell

Athena was born not from a woman, but from her father Zeus's head. His labor pains took the form of a pounding explosive headache. Summoned to perform a healing, Hephaistos, the divine smith, took his axe and split Zeus' head open. Out popped Athena, fully grown and fully armed for battle.

An ancient Greek headache remedy is to scratch Athena's name on an olive leaf. Attach the leaf to a ribbon or scarf and tie it onto your head, with the leaf placed over the throbbing spot to ease the headache.

Headache Removal by Hand Spell

Potatoes, coconuts, and eggs are all considered "absorbent" powers used to remove illness and spiritual debris. The human hand has similar properties. Test your powers of healing. See if you can magically remove someone else's headache. Eggs, coconuts, and potatoes are thrown out following use; however, in this case, so as to avoid you being saddled with the headache, other methods of transference and disposal are used.

1. Lay your hand on the brow of the person suffering from headache.
2. Try to draw the headache into your palm but don't allow it to travel past your palm, not up your arm or any farther. You don't want to inherit the headache.
3. As soon as you feel it or the other person expresses relief, immediately drive a nail into the wall.

It's not safe to use this technique for anything other than a minor ailment, without extensive magical preparation. If you fear inheriting the headache, use a lodestone as a tool instead of your palm. Alternately, use a flat hand charm, such as a hand of Fatima or a hamsa, ideally crafted from silver.

Hematite Magic Charm

Place a hematite crystal gemstone over the spot where your head throbs. Amazonite and jet may be used in a similar fashion.

Henna Heat Headache Spells

Henna's magical affinity for heat may help soothe headaches specifically caused by a reaction to intense heat. Try one of these options:

★ *Cover fresh henna blossoms with boiling water. Let the infusion cool, strain it and make a compress*
★ *Crush fresh blossoms and add them to white vinegar. Use this as a compress*
★ *Fresh blossoms are most effective, but if they are unavailable a drop of hina attar in water may substitute*

Horseshoe Headache Spell

Horseshoes transmit the magic power of iron, the vigor of horses, and the protection of ancestral female spirits. To relieve headaches, hold a horseshoe against the painful area.

Visualize the pounding of your headache leaving you and being drawn into the horseshoe, just like nails.

If it's too much for you, don't strain yourself visualizing. Just place the horseshoe on the spot and let it do its stuff. A horseshoe is the best tool; however, any piece of iron or steel, such as a knife, will transmit iron's healing powers.

 ## Magic Grass Spell

1. Pluck a few blades of grass.
2. Chant the following charm while making the sign of the horns behind you:
   It isn't this grass I take,
   But its magic power
   Go away, headache! Begone!
3. Wrap the grass against your brow with a white cloth.

Marcellus' Knot Spell

This recommendation comes from Marcellus of Rome who suggested, in 380 CE, that to relieve migraine or "pain in the eye," tie as many knots as you have letters in your name into a piece of flax at the first sign of pain, pronouncing each letter as you make the knot. Tie the flax around your neck.

Mugwort Midsummer's Eve Headache Spell

Weave a garland of mugwort on the day of Midsummer's Eve (Saint John's Eve). Wear it the next day and throughout the holiday as a crown around your brow, or view the Midsummer's bonfires through it, to prevent, heal, and minimize headaches and migraines until the following Midsummer's Eve.

Oya's Headache Remedy Spell

The orisha Oya cures headache. This spell is particularly beneficial for chronic migraine.

1. Oya wears a crown with nine charms. Collect them for her as a petition for ending your headaches: hoe, pick, gourd, lightning bolt, scythe, shovel, rake, axe, and mattock.
2. Burn a small purple candle each time you collect a charm.
3. When you have all Oya's charms, burn a purple seven-day candle in her honor. Offer her a glass of red wine and the charms, and make your request.

 ## Romany Headache Cure Spell

A Romany recommendation for healing chronic debilitating headache:

1. Obtain water from nine distinct sources and mix them together.
2. Add glowing charcoals.
3. If you have enough water, bathe the target's entire body. If there's not sufficient water, bathe the person's head, neck, and feet.
4. Repeat daily for up to nine days.

To cement the cure, embroider symbolic designs on the patient's clothing and bed linens. Traditional Romany designs would include roosters, roses, suns, cakes, knives, snakes, and acorns but choose whatever symbolizes health and vitality to you. You must embroider these motifs by hand, not purchase them ready-made. Like knotting, you are inserting intent and blessings into the design. If needlework is not your forte, hand painting the images would be the second-best choice.

 ## Rose of Jericho Headache Relief Spell

*Soak a white cloth in **Rose of Jericho Water** to create a compress. Place it onto your forehead or the back of the neck to provide relief.*

Skull Necklace Headache Relief Spell

Certain fierce female spirits demonstrate their wild power by wearing necklaces of skulls around their neck, such as Anat, Baba Yaga, and Kali. These goddesses' skull necklaces do more than just strike horror into the hearts of those that view them; they also have profound magical healing properties, especially for headache relief. Take that pain out of your head and get it under control! No need to collect real skulls. Skull beads will provide you with the same gift.

1. Collect skull-shaped beads and charms.
2. String them together onto red cord, knotting your desire after every bead.
3. When you feel headache approaching, wear your necklace as a prophylactic charm. Place the skulls against your brow for extra power.
4. When not in use, store your skull necklace in a magic box, ideally with a small crystal skull for empowerment and revitalization.

 ## Stony Head Headache Spell

Pick herbs that are growing on the head of a stone statue. Tie them up with a red thread and place them on the spot where your head hurts. This allegedly removes the pain. Mugwort and/or peppermint are considered the most efficacious of the herbs.

If you suffer from frequent headaches, you may want to train your herbs to grow this way, even if you have to knock the statue's head onto the ground. Both the preferred plants are hardy growers who like stony soil.

 ## Walnut Leaf Magic Cure

Stick walnut leaves in your hat to prevent headaches.

 ## Watery Crossroads Spell

For chronic headache take water from the spot where two streams or rivers merge, essentially the water's crossroads. Sprinkle this water on the patient.

Heart Condition Healing Spell

 ## Heart of Steel Spell

1. Go to a smith and get a piece of steel directly from the smith's hands.
2. Take yarn and saffron and place them, together with the steel, in a pint (half a liter) of stale ale.
3. After they've soaked for a while, remove the yarn and wrap it around your wrist.
4. Drink the ale. (If there's any possibility of choking, remove the steel first.)
5. Keep the yarn around your wrist. If, after three days, it's lengthened this is an auspicious sign. You should recover.

 ## Rose Quartz Heart Spell

Sew a rose quartz within a thin muslin sachet. Add healing herbs as desired. Wear this sachet next to your heart for healing and vitality.

Kidney Function

 ## Jade Spell

Attach a piece of jade to a red silk cord. A kidney-shaped piece or one carved into an auspicious shape is most powerful. Wear this slung around your hips, under your clothes.

Spells to Relieve Mental Health

 Crossroads Possibilities Spell

To relieve feelings of depression, helplessness, and hopelessness, journey to a crossroads and absorb the power. The crossroads is the juncture of powerful energies, where all possibilities meet. Don't go to a traffic intersection—the most common modern crossroads. Excessive yang energy will only worsen the situation. What you need is a traditional witch's crossroads, ideally the intersection of remote streets but at least roads with minimal traffic. You don't have to do anything: just linger, keep your mind open and absorb the converging energies. (Make sure you don't get in trouble for loitering!)

Depression

 Eyebright Anti-depression Spell

Does everything appear dismal, dark, and hopeless? The botanical eyebright is used therapeutically for various eye ailments but also to help one see the sunny side of things, especially when it is extremely difficult to find. Create an infusion by pouring boiling water over eyebright. When it cools use the liquid as an eye wash.

 Has No Hanna Spell

*Allegedly bathing in **Has No Hanna Oil** or using it in full-body massage alleviates depression.*

 Has No Hanna Candle Spell

*Designate a figure candle to represent you. Place the candle on a bed of crushed bay leaves and poppy seeds. Anoint it with **Has No Hanna Oil** and burn.*

 Has No Hanna Candle Spell Extra Strength

1. Carve a seven-day candle to represent you and your situation.
2. Dress it with **Has No Hanna** and **Wall of Protection Oil.**
3. Roll the candle in powdered bay leaves and poppy seeds.
4. Burn the candle in its entirety.

 High John's Spell

*Add a pinch of powdered vervain to **Van Van Oil** and use this to dress a High John the Conqueror root. Carry this High John root to alleviate depression, confusion, and melancholy.*

 Stinging Nettles Spell

Allegedly stinging nettles disperse darkness. Consume them in order to be able to perceive light. This spell operates on a magical level. Stinging nettles may be cooked or brewed into tea. (Once cooked, they no longer sting; however, handle with gloves during preparation.)

 Thyme Pillow

Stuff dream pillows with thyme to ward off melancholia.

 Dr. John Montanet's Spell for Jangled Nerves

Whether known as Bayou John or Dr. John, John Montanet's life was an adventure. Born a prince in what is now Senegal, he was captured and enslaved as a boy. Transported to Cuba, he labored as a slave until he eventually earned his freedom. Signing on for a nautical

life, he sailed around the world, until he finally settled in New Orleans where he became an extremely prominent Voodooist, a contemporary and compatriot of Marie Laveau. Dr. John was a pivotal, influential figure in the history of magic, uniting direct experience of West African magic, with early Santeria and New Orleans Voodoo. The following magic remedy for soothing frazzled, jangled nerves is attributed to him.

1. Add a teaspoon of ground cumin to **Peace Water.**
2. Shake it up so that the layers disperse.
3. Let it sit quietly for three days in a dark, cool, serene place, then strain the liquid.

Use the water as a cool compress on the forehead, or sprinkle it throughout the room, especially in corners and areas of tension and darkness.

 ## Hypochondria Potion

This magic potion allegedly relieves the stress and anxieties of hypochondria. Steep lemon balm (melissa) in wine for several hours. One glass allegedly helps stabilize the condition.

 ## Moonlight Water Spell

Collect rainwater during the full moon and use this water to bathe your head and wash your hair, to magically relieve stress and depression.

 ## Peony Lunacy Spell

Peonies, classified as lunar flowers, are used to magically soothe mental agitation or "lunacy." Gently cover the person with peony blossoms. Allegedly this creates a miraculous soothing effect. Peony flower essence remedy may have similar powers and will definitely be easier to administer.

 ## Saint Dymphna's Mental Relief Spell

Have you read too many of these cures? Are you obsessing about the Evil Eye or developing an unhealthy interest in Disease Demons? Maybe you work with the terminally ill and now you see illness everywhere, even where it doesn't exist?

Petition Saint Dymphna, Matron Saint of Mental Disturbances for relief Saint Dymphna, believed to have been a seventh-century Celtic princess from either Britain (or Brittany), or Ireland, had tremendous personal familiarity with mental disturbance. Her father was obsessed with her, sexually molested her, and then pursued her tirelessly when she escaped from him, eventually locating her in Belgium, where she died, either directly at his hands or because he turned her into authorities to be killed as a Christian martyr.

Petition Saint Dymphna to heal debilitating obsessions. Her magic emblem is a downward-pointed sword. Carve this image into the wax of a blue candle, along with your name, birthday, and any other identifying information you perceive necessary. Hold the candle in your hands to charge it with your desires and light it. The best day to petition her is Monday.

Similar magic rituals and spiritual appeals may be made to Saint Dymphna on behalf of incest survivors or anyone suffering from a mental health crisis or their families.

 ## Wodaabe Mental Health Spell

A Wodaabe recommendation to drive away evil spirits that induce madness in a person is to burn cassava seeds on a charcoal brazier. The patient inhales the smoke and the body is fumigated with it.

Pain Relief Spells

 ## Chestnut Pain Relief Spell (1)

Horse chestnuts are reputed to absorb physical pain, and are especially effective for joint pain:

1. Place a bowl of horse chestnuts in the afflicted person's room.
2. Wash the nuts daily in cool spring water to enhance their capacity to absorb pain, and then dry them well.
3. Should a nut crack, decay or appear damaged, discard it immediately and replace.

Enhance the power of the chestnuts by ringing the bowl with clear quartz crystal.

 ## Chestnut Pain Relief Spell (2)

Carry a buckeye or horse chestnut in your pocket, or in a conjure bag around your waist, to soothe and protect against arthritis.

 ## Copper Garter Spell

Copper's affinity for healing the aches and pains of arthritis go beyond the popular bracelet. For maximum effectiveness, attach copper charms to a red garter and wear it.

 ## Lodestone Pain Withdrawal Spell

Lodestones, magnetic iron ore, are most frequently used to draw good fortune toward you; however, their magnetic properties may also be used to draw illness and physical pain out of the body. This is particularly beneficial for pain or illness that manifests in a specific spot on the body, rather than a general aura of illness.

1. Charge the lodestone with your purpose prior to beginning the healing session.
2. Visualize the illness or pain drawn out of your body and into the lodestone.
3. Two techniques may be used. Use either or both in conjunction as appropriate for you. Either place the lodestone on the area of illness or pain and leave it there for a while, or gently massage it over the afflicted area.
4. Shake the lodestone out periodically. It's vital to cleanse and feed the lodestone after each extensive session. Repeat as needed.

 ## Murder Weapon Pain Removal Spell

This is a simple spell provided you have easy access to a murder weapon. To heal someone afflicted with sharp pains or stitches that come on suddenly, particularly in the side or breast, lightly prick the person with the point of a dagger, sword, knife or similar tool, which was once used to kill someone.

 ## Potato Spell

Place a potato in your pocket to draw out the pain and stiffness of rheumatism.

 ## Raw Beef Anti-pain Spell

This magical transference method allegedly helps remove pain or illness concentrated in one isolated area. Place raw fresh beef on the afflicted part until the body starts to sweat. The sweat must be in contact with the meat; this is how the pain and illness is transmitted. Give this meat to a cat or dog to eat.

Stone Pain Removal Spell

1. Hold a rock in your hand and visualize it absorbing your pain.
2. Wrap barley straw around the stone, while maintaining this visualization.
3. Throw the stone into living water flowing away from you.

Scars

Intensive scarring is believed to have a detrimental, damaging effect on one's aura, the invisible shield of protection surrounding one's body. Various psychic repair spells may also be in order. (See *Psychic Power Spells*, page 939.)

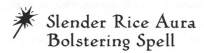 ## Slender Rice Aura Bolstering Spell

Slender rice flower remedy (Australian Bush) specifically targets damage caused to the aura by scarring. This repairs and defends the invisible aura; it has no impact on the visible appearance of scars.

1. For initial use, add twenty drops of slender rice flower remedy to a bath before bedtime. This intensive dose will only be used this one time. Pay attention to your dreams afterwards.
2. Apply a few drops twice daily to the skin between thumb and forefinger or rubbed into the feet. In addition, follow the manufacturer's recommendations for internal administration if desired.

Seizure Disorders

From a metaphysical standpoint, there's a tremendous historical ambivalence toward those afflicted with seizure disorders. On the one hand, the experience is perceived as being similar to involuntary ritual possession. Thus in some cultures, those possessing these disorders carry an aura of sanctity: predictions, visions, even isolated words uttered during a seizure are highly prized. On the other hand, not every culture thinks ritual possession is desirable, particularly those who assume that the only kind of possession that exists is possession by demons. In those situations, to possess a seizure disorder is to suffer on two counts: from the ailment and from discrimination and persecution.

 ## Amber Seizure Charm

A medieval European recommendation was to wear amber over one's heart to prevent and relieve epilepsy and other seizure disorders.

 ## Anti-seizure Conjure Bag

1. Place a piece of coral, a jasper gemstone, and a nux vomica root onto a square of linen.
2. Wrap into a bundle, knotting your intentions into the packet.
3. Carry in your pocket or in a larger leather bag, magically cleansing the jasper periodically.

Note: Nux Vomica, the rat poison plant, is the source of strychnine, the deadly poison. Use only with extreme caution if one must use it at all.

 ## Aries-Vervain Bag Spell

A medicine bag created especially to provide relief for seizure disorders: gather vervain when the sun and/or moon are in Aries. Carry the botanical in a bag with a kernel of corn or a piece of grain, plus a one-year-old penny or another coin of trivial value.

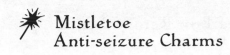

The Bachelors' Anti-seizure Spell

This very old, once very popular English spell, intended to avert and avoid seizures, remains mysterious. What is the significance of the bachelors? Is it vestigial memories of an all-male healing cult? Or is it that because bachelors aren't married, they're understood to have little sexual contact with women? Or perhaps as bachelors, playing the field, they're assumed to have more? Maybe "bachelor" is a euphemism for a man with no sexual interest in women, or for those young virginal boys so valued in divination?

1. Create a ring from five silver sixpences (or substitute five other real silver coins) collected from five bachelors, one coin each.
2. Have another bachelor, a sixth one, collect the coins and convey them to a smith to make the ring, who must also be a bachelor. None of the five persons from whom the coins are initially obtained can know purpose behind their collection.
3. The sixth bachelor will then convey the ring to the afflicted party, who should wear it.

Elderwood Spell

Break an elder twig into nine pieces. Thread them together and wear them to minimize and prevent seizures.

Golden Rooster Spell

Bury a golden rooster charm beneath the bed to relieve, minimize, and prevent seizures.

Mistletoe Anti-seizure Charms

Mistletoe is believed to possess a magical affinity for seizure disorders.

★ *Carry a piece of mistletoe in your pocket or within a conjure bag*
★ *Jewelry and charms are carved from mistletoe wood: wear or carry*
★ *The most potent mistletoe seizure charm is a magic knife with an iron blade but a handle carved from mistletoe wood*

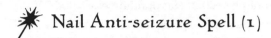
Nail Anti-seizure Spell (1)

Obtain three coffin nails or three screws from a coffin dug up from the cemetery (they need to be used nails, in other words, not just extras picked up at the undertakers). Craft them into a ring to form a charm against convulsions and seizures.

Nail Anti-seizure Spell (2)

If the thought of digging around cemeteries is enough to induce a seizure, another type of nail is also believed to be beneficial towards seizure disorders.

Obtain a nail recovered from a shipwrecked vessel. (It is not necessary for the person with the ailment to perform the recovery personally.) Craft into a ring or carry in a charm bag worn around the neck.

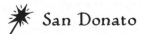
San Donato

San Donato, an Italian saint particularly popular in Naples, is described as the Patron Saint of Epilepsy; however, his behavior may, in some instances, perhaps be likened to that of a Disease Spirit. To be afflicted with a seizure disorder may indicate San Donato's

wish for personal communication. Relief or at least a spiritual understanding of one's situation will allegedly arrive following devotions to the saint.

San Donato also has many devotees who do not suffer from these ailments, just as most of Babalu-Ayé's devotees have never had smallpox.

1. Dedicate an altar to San Donato.
2. Traditional offerings include candles, small containers filled with grain, and an iron key.
3. San Donato's traditional image depicts him standing on a crescent moon. Decorate the altar space with images of moons and frogs. Although any of these may be empowered and charged as a healing charm, the key is most frequently used as such.
4. Appeal to San Donato as desired.

 ## Shattered Plate Seizure Spell

A spell from the Jews of Galicia, intended to drive the Demon of Convulsions far from a child, is simple to perform. Suddenly, without warning, break a clay pot or dish in front of the child.

 ## Thyme Pillow

Dream pillows stuffed with powdered thyme allegedly relieve and prevent seizure disorders.

Skin Disorders and Afflictions

 ## Babalu Bread Spell (1)

Babalu-Ayé, Father of Smallpox, will heal any skin disorder.

1. Place a glass of dry white wine on a raffia cloth, together with a bowl of milk in which you've soaked two slices of bread.

2. Place an additional piece of white bread on this altar.
3. Light a white candle and petition Babalu-Ayé to remove your affliction.
4. Leave everything overnight. The next morning, dispose of everything but that additional slice of bread.
5. Soak that bread in palm oil and use it to cleanse the afflicted skin, then dispose of the bread outside the home.

 ## Babalu Bread Spell (2)

A simpler version of the above:

1. Dedicate a slice of bread to Babalu-Ayé. (Leave it on his altar for a minimum of seventeen minutes.)
2. Put palm or olive oil onto the soft bread.
3. Use this as a sponge to gently cleanse the affected area.

 ## Oshun's Healing Skin Spell

Although Babalu-Ayé is the orisha most associated with skin disorders, Oshun may also be petitioned for assistance, particularly for wet sores or any sort of "weepy" skin ailment. Oshun has beautiful skin; allow her to heal yours.

1. Make an offering to Oshun of a glass of spring water, yellow flowers, and a dish of honey, remembering to taste the honey before giving it to her.
2. Light a yellow candle and tell Oshun what you need.
3. Consecrate a plain brass bangle to her, leave it beside the candle until it burns out, and then wear it as an amulet.

Pebble Magic Bath Spell

1. Heat pebbles, especially auspiciously shaped ones, until they're red hot.
2. Throw them into a basin of water.
3. This water, when cool, is considered magically charged to enhance healing of skin disorders or bruises.

 ## Saint John's Eve Meadow Dew Skin Spells

Water was believed charged with extra healing power on Saint John's/Midsummer's Eve. Choose either or both of the following to prevent ailments of the skin. (Even if you don't have problem skin, allegedly these spells enhance youthful appearance and beauty for all.)

★ *Roll naked in meadow dew on Saint John's Eve*
★ *Bathe in the sea, dressed or otherwise, on Saint John's Eve*

These are old, old customs. St. Augustine himself denounced this pagan practice of his youth.

 ## Saint John's Eve Siberian Skin Enhancement Spell

The power generated on Saint John's Eve is accessed by this Siberian spell. Unlike the preceding spells, which derive from the warm Mediterranean, no nakedness is required or even suggested.

Lay a white cloth on the grass during Saint John's Eve or day. When it's wet, place it on the face or other afflicted areas to heal skin disorders.

 ## Sapphire Skin Charm

Allegedly, sapphires serve as a preventive/curative amulet for skin disorders.

Although a sapphire may be carried as a charm, for maximum magical effectiveness periodically lay the gem on the area that requires healing.

*Place the sapphire in a glass of pure spring or **Angel's Water** and expose to the light of the Full Moon. Remove the sapphire in the morning. Place on the afflicted area. Use the lunar/sapphire-charged water to bathe the area as well, if this is appropriate.*

Smallpox

No other disease has such powerful associations with Disease Spirits. Smallpox Spirits roam Earth delivering the disease but also preventing and healing it.

Babalu-Ayé Spells

Few spirits are as beloved and simultaneously as feared as West Africa's Obaluaiye or Babalu-Ayé, as he is popularly known. Babalu is a humble, simple, modest, unpretentious spirit. He has been ill himself, he understands suffering, and can be tremendously compassionate. On the other hand, when he is angered his methods of punishment are terrible. Babalu-Ayé has dominion over pestiltial illness, most especially smallpox, although any epidemic falls under his domain. He has dominion over AIDS.

Call upon Babalu-Ayé for healing and prevention. He has modest tastes. Overly lavish offerings may offend him; keep it simple. Babalu-Ayé accepts offerings of dry white wine (never water, which irritates his sores), popcorn (because the individual popped kernels are perceived as resembling smallpox pustules), and/or a bowl of milk with bread soaking in it to feed his loyal companions, the dogs who lick his sores.

Babalu-Ayé Spell (1)

1. Create a simple shrine by laying down raffia cloth.
2. Make an offering to Babalu-Ayé.
3. Pour palm oil over a bowl of popcorn.
4. Place this on the cloth and allow it to stand for seventeen days. (The offering however may be removed as you deem appropriate. It's usually not considered wise to maintain altars to Babalu-Ayé for longer than necessary. Although you want him to like you, you don't necessarily want him to become so enamored that he moves in, if you get the drift.)
5. Use the shrine as the focal point for prayer and petition.
6. After seventeen days, take the popcorn outside, to a park, perhaps, and feed it to the birds. (If the popcorn disappears quickly, this is a very favorable sign.)

 ## Babalu-Ayé Spell (2)
Saint Lazarus

Babalu-Ayé has been syncretized to Saint Lazarus, although not to the Lazarus you might expect—the Lazarus, brother of Martha and Mary of Bethany, the man resurrected by Jesus Christ. Although connections regarding illness could be drawn, the reason for this particular syncretism is based on a visual image. There is another Saint Lazarus, based on a parable, formalized in chromolithographs as a poor man who walks with crutches, accompanied by dogs. It is the dogs that provide the link between Lazarus and Babalu-Ayé. Dogs are the creatures that, in various worldwide spiritual traditions, most frequently guide souls to the Realm of the Dead. This identification of Saint Lazarus and Babalu is extremely powerful in Cuban traditions.

1. Purchase a special charm, usually small gold-plated crutches or something similar.
2. Light a white seven-day candle placed on raffia cloth together with a glass of good dry white wine.

3. Tell Saint Lazarus that the candle is payment for your good health. If your health remains strong, next year at this time, you will get him a solid gold charm instead. (Make sure that you do, if it does and you promise.)
4. When the candle is gone, lose the charm near a hospital.

Many present the solid gold charm at Saint Lazarus's shrine in Cuba, although a private shrine may also be maintained.

The various Afro-Brazilian traditions refer to the Smallpox Spirit as Omolu, Babalu-Ayé's Brazilian incarnation. Omolu accepts petitions and requests via special ritual popcorn, doboru. Not only don't people like to utter the spirit's name, many don't even like to call his popcorn by name, preferring to refer to it as *"the flowers of Omolu."* Omolu's other flowers are, of course, the red smallpox blisters that decorate the body.

 ## Omolu's Disease Repelling Charm

Omolu's Umbanda ritual greeting serves as a verbal magic charm to repel illness. Repeat as needed: "Atoto."

Doboru: Omolu's Flowers

Different traditions use different formulas for preparing Omolu's doboru: either white or red popcorn may be used. Some sprinkle with garlic salt, others say no salt should be used—it irritates Omolu's sores. Some dress the popcorn with dende (palm oil).

One formula is as follows:

1. Cover the bottom of an iron pot with beach sand.
2. Heat it over an open fire.
3. Add the corn and pop.

This spell is used as a petition for healing or prevention; however, it may also be used as a general cleansing spell.

 ## Flowers of Omolu Spell (1)

1. Sit naked on new white cloth.
2. Let others cover you with popcorn.
3. Pray and petition Omolu.
4. When you feel ready, rise from the popcorn and dress in white.
5. Wrap the popcorn up in a cloth. Disperse it onto Earth for the birds to eat.

Either dispose of the cloth or reserve it for similar or sacred use.

 ## Flowers of Omolu Spell (2)
Popcorn Space Cleansing Spell

Prevention or healing is directed towards an entire area, including all those who approach and all those already within.

The cleansing ritual is technically simple: pop vast quantities of doboru. Cover whatever needs to be cleansed with Omolu's flowers: fill a room, let it rest overnight, then dispose of the doboru on naked Earth.

For an entire building, cover the roof with doboru and let birds and Mother Nature take care of disposal.

 ## Hungary Powder

Snake Oil or Hungary Powder? This very expensive magic powder allegedly relieves smallpox and measles. It was once prescribed by physicians, although only to the wealthy, no doubt.

Hungary Powder is composed from emeralds, rubies, sapphires, jacinth, pearls, red and white coral, Armenian bole, terra Lemnia, hartshorn, raspings of ivory, cinnamon, cloves, saffron, sorrel seeds, sandalwood, red sandalwood, lemon zest, and gold leaf. Powder all the ingredients and blend together. Once upon a time, the standard dosage was between twenty and thirty grains.

 ## Mango Leaf
Anti-welcome Spell

Allegedly fresh mango leaves will repel and relieve smallpox. Hang fresh mango leaves over and around the doorway and gates of the home. When the leaves begin to wither or droop, replace immediately with fresh ones.

 ## Mariyamman Basic
Smallpox Spell

India possesses two important smallpox spirits, albeit with very different natures. According to various legends, Mariyamman, like Babalu-Ayé, was once a victim of smallpox herself. Mariyamman literally battles smallpox; an epidemic indicates that Mariyamman herself is under siege, having been attacked by smallpox demons. The epidemic will not lift until and unless she is victorious. Offerings to Mariyamman thus simultaneously empower her and beseech her for mercy.

Hang neem leaves over entrance doors and windows to repel smallpox.

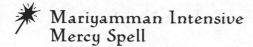

Mariyamman Intensive Mercy Spell

1. Place a brass pot filled with water and ornamented with neem leaves on an altar.
2. Burn yellow candles around it.
3. Offer Mariyamman pumpkins and request her protection and mercy.

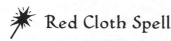

Red Cloth Spell

Lay the person suffering from smallpox in red bed clothes (pajamas, linens and sheets).

Alternately, wrap the person up in red fabric to magically enhance healing.

Sunflower Smallpox Spell

Weave and knot dried sunflowers into necklaces and wear them to magically repel smallpox.

Sitala

Sitala, Northern India's Mother of Smallpox, has a sardonic nickname: *"The Cool One."* Sitala and her sisters preside over pustular diseases. Sitala's specialty is smallpox: she both causes and prevents the disease. According to legend, she is the youngest of the sisters, born considerably later than her siblings. Human beings paid little attention to her. In order to force humans to create rituals in her honor, Sitala invented smallpox. The tactic worked. Her most famous manifestation is as smallpox. However, smallpox is only a manifestation of Sitala, as with Babalu-Ayé, not the sole, defining characteristic. Sitala also appears in female form, typically dressed in red. She roams the countryside, riding a donkey, searching out victims, but she also responds to pleas for prevention and healing of smallpox. If one has survived smallpox, then one may consider oneself under

Sitala's matronage and may request other favors and general protection from her.

Sitala Spell (1)

1. Create an offering table for Sitala.
2. Offer her flowers and cooling foods such as cold rice, coconuts, cucumbers, plantains, and yogurt.
3. Do not burn candles; instead maintain a "cool" aura in Sitala's presence. In addition, during rituals for Sitala, *"heating"* foods are avoided—foods that possess a heating effect upon the body and also food that has been literally warmed up. Rice is eaten cold, for instance.
4. Make your petition, and maintain offerings, replenishing as needed, as long as the perceived threat remains.

Sitala Spell (2)

Attach a cowry shell, a small gold charm, a piece of turmeric root, and a lock of the patient's hair to a cord. (They may be wrapped up in white fabric.) Tie this cord to the right wrist of the patient, blessing as knots are formed.

Sitala Spell (3)

Use pure cool spring water to bathe an image of Sitala. Give this water to the patient to drink.

Thousand Flower Anti-smallpox Charm Bag

Charge a lump of asafetida with your desires. Carry it within a red charm bag together with an iron nail.

T'ou Chen Niang Niang

T'ou Chen Niang Niang, Chinese Lady of Smallpox, is known as the "Lady of the Thousand Flowers." She travels accompanied by two servants. Unlike Sitala and Babalu-Ayé, she is almost exclusively identified with smallpox and so is traditionally beseeched to travel else- where and stay far away. Should she arrive, however, magical steps are taken.

Burn incense, offer her cooling foods, and burn huge quantities of Spirit Money in T'ou Chen Niang Niang's honor. Petition her very politely (she's touchy and gets offended easily), to oversee the patient's recovery.

Should the patient recover:

1. Place the Lady of the Thousand Flower's image on a paper boat or chair.
2. Place these upon a paper phoenix.
3. Burn all on a pile of straw to give the Lady a polite goodbye and hopefully send her on her way.

Should the patient die, however, dispose of all offerings as you deem appropriate. T'ou Chen Niang Niang is traditionally cursed off the premises in these circum- stances.

Successful Surgery Spells

 ## Babalu-Ayé's Milagro Spell

This spell combines petition to Babalu-Ayé with what is essentially a milagro.

Request that Babalu-Ayé watch over you before, dur- ing and after surgery so as to guarantee its outcome. It's customary that should everything turn out fine an offer- ing will be made to him of a solid gold replica of the piece of anatomy involved in the surgery: heart, lung, brain, whatever. The charm may be miniature if this is all you can afford, however wealthy people will offer a life-sized replica.

Ogun's Iron Nail Spell

Ogun, the spirit of metal, is by extension patron of metal workers, including surgeons, and patients anticipating surgery. Make offerings before surgery with a promise of additional tribute should things proceed as desired. Ogun's day is usually given as Wednesday, his numbers are three and seven, and his colors are red and black. He accepts the perhaps un-medicinal gifts of fine cigars and over-proof rum.

Soak seven iron nails in a dish filled with salt water. Burn a red and black double action candle next to the dish. Following surgery, bury the nails in Earth and spill the water on the ground.

Susto: Remedial Spells for Soul Loss

"Susto" is the name for what is perceived in Latin America as a specific ailment with a very specific cause: a moment or brief period of intense fright that leads to the loss of a piece of one's soul. Some- times the condition rights itself but typically the piece of soul must be retrieved as long-term soul loss can lead to dire circumstances. Young girls are perceived as being particularly prone to this condi- tion. Anxiety, sleeplessness, and a continued state of fright or agitation following the initial shock are all indications of susto. Prolonged absence of the piece of the soul may produce disease, trance states, mental disturbance, eating disorders, and/or death. Serious cases need shamanic intervention, however there is a remedy that may be attempted at home.

 ## Soul Loss Spell (1)

1. Pass an egg over the patient's body, concentrating on drawing malignancies into the egg.
2. Break the egg into a bowl.
3. If blood is observed, this confirms a serious situation. Take stronger action.

4. If there's nothing but a plain old egg, prepare a strong infusion of spearmint and chamomile.
5. Give the patient some of the infusion to sip.
6. Dip a clean cloth into the infusion, squeeze out any excess liquid and use it as a compress on the patient's head.

 ## Soul Loss Spell (2)

In Peru, an infusion of ajos sacha *leaves is added to a child's bath to relieve susto, or the extreme fright that may lead to susto. (The kids may not like this bath; it has a strong garlicky odor.)*

 ## Soul Loss Prevention Spell

Adults can suffer from sudden, overwhelming fear too. This spell must be done at the moment of fear or immediately afterwards in order for it to be effective. Name the Dactyls: Celmus, Damnameneus, and Acmon to regain courage and calm and to preserve vitality. For extra magical empowerment, clang cymbals.

Toothache/Dental Health

 ## Abracadabra/Sator Full Strength Combination Dental Health Spell

To remedy toothache, chant the Abracadabra spell (instead of writing it) three times, followed by three repetitions of the SATOR square (see page 118).

 ## Alligator Healthy Teeth Spell

No one has healthier teeth than an alligator: they naturally shed old teeth to grow new ones. (Thus the alligator does not need to be killed or harmed to obtain teeth.)

Carry some in a mojo hand or string a necklace of alligator teeth. Many teeth have a natural hole near the top from which they may be hung, otherwise pierce gently.

 ## Carnelian Dental Health Spell (1)

Arabic recommendation suggests that one wear or carry carnelian to prevent or improve loose teeth. That's the basic spell. The following spell includes some unusual embellishments.

 ## Carnelian Dental Health Spell (2)

1. Cut a tiny bit of bark off a young oak.
2. Cut a tiny bit of the sufferer's hair.
3. Spin or braid these together with a hair from a dog and a hair from a lion. (No need to injure either; the spell requires no more than a single hair from each.)
4. Thread three carnelians onto this braid.
5. Wear it around the wrist for relief of tooth pain.

 ## Coffin Nail Tooth Spell

Coffin nails allegedly ease toothache. Carry one in a conjure bag.

 ## Double Hazelnut Tooth Relief

Find a double hazelnut and carry it within a red drawstring bag to relieve dental pain.

Iron Dental Health Spell

The following is a German recommendation to soothe a toothache. Heat a horseshoe or other piece of iron until extremely hot. Pour oil onto the heated iron. The rising fumes will allegedly ease the pain. If it is safe to do so (there's no need to exchange toothache for a painful scald), bend over the fumes, exposing the tender spot.

 Shark Healthy Teeth Spell

Shed shark teeth are often found amongst seashells. Tie onto red cord and wear around the neck or ankles.

Tumor Relief Spell

 Crossroads Cake Spell

Ancient diagnoses weren't as accurate as they are today. This spell is meant for any sort of "wasting" illness, by which many cancers may be understood but interpret as seems appropriate:

1. Borrow flour from nine houses.
2. Bring it home and blend it.
3. Bake a cake with this flour.
4. Bring the cake to a crossroads, say a prayer or petition and leave the cake there.

 Obatala's Tumor Relief Spell

To assist dissolving tumors:

1. Melt tallow gently over the stove.
2. Crush cotton seeds and add them to the tallow, mixing gently so that they are well distributed.
3. Apply this salve to the afflicted area.

This derives from a Santeria petition to Obatala. For maximum effect this should be combined with a petition to that orisha.

Water-derived Illness

 Shabriri Spell

The safety of drinking water may be suspect, whether because of parasites or, as the ancients feared, because of water demons. When you really have doubts about the safety of water but have little alternative but to drink it, this incantation allegedly provides safety and wards off illness-causing water demons. This is excellent for travelers: campers fearing lurking parasites, as well as more serious water-born illness like cholera.

This Jewish formula is traditionally murmured over the water in question. Amulets depicting the protective triangular form may also be worn or posted.

My mother told me,
Beware of

```
S  h  a  b  r  i  r  i
B  r  i  r  i
R  i  r  i
I  r  i
R  i
I
```

I am thirsty for water in a white glass.

 Tibetan Serpent Spell

Lu and Luma, male and female serpents respectively, are vigilant guardians of ecological balance, specifically that of Earth and water. Water pollution offends them incredibly. Even digging holes in Earth or moving rocks around displeases them, let alone any unethical harvesting of Earth's precious gems and metals. Are they in a good mood lately? What do you think?

When certain other large snake-like creatures get

angry, they allegedly thrash around causing earth-quakes or breathe fire. Not Lu and Luma. When they get mad, they emerge as disease. Their broad spectrum of illness includes tuberculosis, leprosy, skin disorders including ulcers, itches, and acne. However, their illnesses are most frequently characterized by water imbalances, like swelling, bloating, edemas, or dehydration. A complete cure cannot be achieved until they are appeased. Traditionally shamanic healing is required; however, if this isn't possible, steps may still be taken.

1. If you suspect you've offended them or they are the root cause of an illness, designate an altar area with which to communicate with these spirits.
2. Burn herbal incense and offer dishes of milk.
3. Burn white and/or gold snake-shaped candles; request inspiration so that you will know best how to compensate for past actions.

Gestures to repair ecological imbalance, in Tibet, the Himalayas, or elsewhere, may gain favor.

Whooping Cough Spells

 ## Whooping Cough Dog Spell

This whooping cough remedy from Devon, England, perceives the disease as the result of a spell that needs breaking. Butter two slices of bread. Place one of the patient's hairs between the slices as if in a sandwich and feed it to a dog. If the dog coughs, the spell is broken and the child will recover.

 ## Whooping Cough Ferret Spell

This spell requires assistance from a cooperative ferret. Pour a bowl of milk and let the ferret lap up a little bit. Remove the ferret from the milk (without allowing it to scratch you), and give the remainder of the milk to the patient to drink.

Wound and Fracture Healing Spells

 ## Adder's Tongue Spell

This spell, for wounds and bruises that refuse to heal, attempts to transfer pain and injury into Earth, where it will dissipate.

1. Soak the botanical adder's tongue in warm water.
2. Place it on bruised skin.
3. Cover it with a clean white handkerchief.
4. When the herb grows warm, remove it and bury the herbs and handkerchief in mud or a swamp. The wound or bruise will allegedly now heal.

 ## Binding Spell (1) Odin's Knot Binding Spell

An extremely ancient Scandinavian incantation refers to a long lost legend of Odin, the All Father, and his son, Baldur the Beautiful. It has several variations.

It's particularly beneficial for injured fingers, limbs, and also for bone-deep wounds, where one fears infection. However, it may be used for any type of fracture and even minor cuts.

1. Apply healing salve or medication, as needed.
2. Then make seven knots in a black thread, while murmuring one or more of the following incantations. (Traditionally, these chants are meant to be mumbled and barely intelligible.)
3. Tie the thread around the fracture while chanting:
   Baldur rade.
   The foal slade [i.e. slipped].
   He lighted and he righted.
   Set joint to joint, bone to bone, sinew to sinew.
   Heal in Odin's name.

The above version survived in the Orkney Islands. However, the spell and its incantation traveled, evolved, and survived, as the next spell shows.

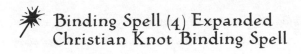

Binding Spell (2) Woden's Knot Binding Spell

A tenth-century English alternative: Woden is Odin's Anglo-Saxon alter-ego. Baldur has vanished from this version, perhaps because the specific legend had already disappeared, or perhaps Baldur's remaining associations with death did not appeal. Maybe what caused the spell to survive is Woden's reputation as a Master Healer and Magician.

Believed most effective if done on Wednesday, Woden's Day, although, obviously, this is a ritual performed as need arises. Make seven knots in a black thread. Wrap it around the injury or close to it, muttering:

Then charmed Woden
As well he knew how
For bone sprain
For blood sprain
Bone to bone
Blood to blood
Limb to limb
As though they were glued

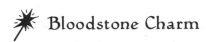

Binding Spell (3) Christian Knot Binding Spell

This incantation survived further adaptation to Christianity, where it now allegedly refers to an incident during Jesus' triumphal ride into Jerusalem when his donkey slipped. Although the incantation varies, knotting the thread, which may be pulled right out of one's clothing in an emergency, and wrapping it around the injury survives.

In later Christian versions sometimes only a single knot is used, rather than the magic seven.

The Lord rade.
The foal slade.
Set joint to joint, bone to bone, sinew to sinew
Heal in the Holy Ghost's name

Binding Spell (4) Expanded Christian Knot Binding Spell

Our Lord rade
His foal's foot slade
Down he lighted, his foal's foot righted.
Bone to bone, sinew to sinew,
Blood to blood, flesh to flesh
Heal!
In the name of the Father, the Son, and the Holy Ghost.

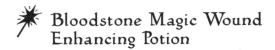

Bloodstone Charm

Bloodstone is reputed to encourage wound healing, and also to prevent wounds.

★ *Wear a bloodstone for prevention*
★ *Apply to the wound as appropriate (gently bind to bandages?)*
★ *Carry a bloodstone within a red charm bag*

Bloodstone Magic Wound Enhancing Potion

Place a bloodstone in a glass of pure spring water overnight, exposed to the light of the Full Moon. Use this water to bathe wounds, as appropriate, for magically enhanced healing.

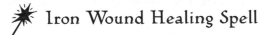

Iron Wound Healing Spell

Allegedly the magic power of iron encourages and enhances healing. If appropriate, periodically ring open wounds with iron to avail yourself of this power.

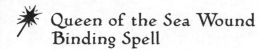
Queen of the Sea Wound Binding Spell

Russian magic is filled with beautiful, powerful word charms. The one below may be dedicated to the deity of you choice. This version cites the Queen of the Sea; devout Christians would dedicate the same charm to the Virgin Mary.

Chant:

On a rock, on an island, in the sea, in the ocean, the
    Queen of the Sea sits on her golden throne.
With her silver needle she threads scarlet silk thread,
She binds the bloody wound.
Wound, you do not hurt!
Blood, you do not flow!
Blood, you are staunched!
Wound, you heal clean!

Melissa Wound Healing Spell

If melissa (lemon balm) was bound to a sword and if that sword was touched to a wound caused by that very same sword, allegedly bleeding would be quickly staunched and healing would be miraculously enhanced.

Vervain Spell

Vervain allegedly enhances the healing of wounds. Wrap it in white cloth and place over the injury if possible.

Yarrow Spell

Carry yarrow stalks in a medicine bag for magical wound prevention.

Yaws

Mama Jo's name is an English corruption of the French Maman de'leau, "Mother of the Water." This beautiful mermaid spirit of the West Indies cures diseases, especially yaws, once a much-feared illness. Mama Jo travels. Her spell need not be cast in the Caribbean; it will require a trip to a beach, however. It may be cast by one person on behalf of another.

1. Dig out a flat altar space within the sand.
2. Place silver candles in the sand, one for every year of the ailing person's age. (Silver birthday candles may be used.) Light the candles.
3. Place a small image of a black goat or black chicken near the shore, such as a child's farm toy or similar. (Create your own from wax, wood or wool if desired.)
4. Step into the water, so that at least your feet are wet, and call Mama Jo. Tell her what you've brought and what you need. Leave whenever you're ready. Whatever happens to the image is up to Mama Jo, whether waves pull it into the water or another person picks it up.

⬟ Hexes and their Antidotes

Admit it: this is the first page to which you turned. With the exception of love and money spells, nothing fascinates like a mean, wicked spell. Magic power used so benevolently to draw health, wealth, stability, love, and fertility can also be used as aggressive, punishing conduits of frustration, anger, and resentment toward others, hence the hex. These spells define why some fear magic.

These are not socially respectable spells, to say the least. Lest you take them to represent the state of modern magic, let me emphatically add that in the current cultural climate of twenty-first-century witchcraft, hexes, curses, and other malevolent spells are incredibly depasse. Modern Wicca passionately emphasizes the three-fold law: as you reap, so you shall sow. Whatever magical intention and energy you put forth will come back to you at least three times over, if not seven, nine or twenty-one times. Many modern Wiccans hesitate before casting a reasonably innocuous love or employment spell on the off-chance that the other party's free will might be compromised. In that context spells that deliberately attempt to cause someone strife, misery, and unhappiness are perceived as abhorrent indeed.

These are the spells that have earned magic its evil reputation—or are they?

In fact ethical considerations of what constitutes *"wicked magic"* date back to that proverbial time immemorial. According to the purest magic theory, power is neutral. Malevolence or benevolence depends entirely upon what is done with this power. Any power can be used for good or ill. This theoretical concept hasn't always satisfied people. Since the very earliest times, there's been debate about *"good magic"* versus *"bad magic."*

According to conventional, traditional European Christian traditions, *all* sorcery and magic is evil, regardless of intent. Therefore even those who try to fight sorcery with sorcery should be punished because all sorcery, no matter how benevolent its purpose, harms the soul, which is worse than harming the body.

The Saxon Law Code of 1572 prescribed the death penalty for both harmful and harmless witchcraft. The victimless crime remains a crime. These laws decreed that even *"good"* witches were to be burned. Even if no one was harmed, even if some were helped, witches were a potential danger to be rooted out.

The view taken by the Vatican since the early Middle Ages is that magic is inherently evil regardless of the worker's motivation: all rites are evil in themselves, except natural magic. *Natural* magic is theoretically acceptable because it isn't really *"magic,"* it's merely the result of having secret knowledge of herbs, gems, and other substances. You're not a witch or a worker; you just know more than other people. So you could, theoretically anyway, wear a gemstone talisman for good fortune but you couldn't consecrate that talisman to even the most benevolent angel or fairy, because by definition any spirit that will bother to deal with you is at best a demon in disguise.

That's one point of view. Medieval rabbis took the opposite approach. Natural magic was *not* permitted. The only officially approved magic involved working with spiritual forces—angels or other spirits—because technically people aren't doing the magic: you're just summoning the angels or demons who will actually do it for you, although you may request, direct, and benefit. This philosophy would eventually have a tremendous impact on what is now called High Ritual Magic and explains the emphasis on summoning and commanding (or attempting to command) spirits.

There's a pattern here: the only acceptable magic is magic that's not really magic.

For Islam, all magic is forbidden. Summoning and attempting to command djinn, the goal of many sorcerers, was officially discouraged. What outsiders to that culture might consider magic, because in *their* own cultures it *is* magic—the use of sacred verses as amulets—was historically not considered *"magic"* by devout Muslims but religious devotion.

These debates aren't limited to the Big Three of Monotheism. Plato acknowledged the existence of natural magic, asserting that it was of neutral morality. Aristotle, on the other hand, denied that natural magic exists. Hence any magic must stem from either a divine or demonic source. In ancient Mesopotamia, magic itself was acceptable as a source of comfort and healing, *if* it was performed from positive intentions. Magic for the purpose of deliberately causing harm was perceived as evil. Roman law distinguished between divination and magical healing, which were not defined as crimes and thus not punished, and malevolent magic, which was subject to legal prosecution.

In contemporary Africa, roots of malevolent magic are perceived as stemming from unresolved anger as well as the usual jealousy and envy. Positive magic derives from love while negative magic derives from anger, the desire to ruin, to spoil, and to inflict damage. Thus the difference between an aggressive spell deriving from the desire for protection and an aggressive spell meant to harm may be nothing more than the practitioner's intent.

Debates about the appropriate use of magic power have existed as long as there has been awareness of this power, and show no sign of abatement. Some fear magic in its entirety, some fear aspects of magic, while others recognize its inherent sacred quality. According to medieval master magician, Cornelius Agrippa, a theologian whose time coincided with European witch hunts, the practice of magic was one of the lawful ways to attain knowledge of God and nature.

At some point, in the Common Era, *"good"* and *"bad"* magic transformed into *"white"* and *"black"* magic, terms that still retain popularity. Those terms are not used in this book. The straightforward terms *"malevolent"* or *"benevolent"* are used instead. At best, it's disingenuous to use those terms (white and black magic) today, pretending that they don't have racial and ethnic connotations. People protest that they don't mean the phrase *that way* but it's difficult to understand how else to interpret it in the context of a world where, historically, darker-skinned minority groups have been discriminated against or persecuted for magical practice and witchcraft by the lighter-skinned majority, whether in Europe (Jews, Romany, Saami), North Africa (Gnawa) North America (Native Americans, those of African descent) or South America (indigenous Americans, those of African descent).

Why would anyone send a hex or a curse anyway?

The first reason is the obvious: bad people do bad things. The destructive impulse can be extremely potent.

Other answers are more complex and ambiguous. In some cases, there may be an extremely fine line between a hex and a justice spell. We're very quick to jump to conclusions these days and automatically brand every hex-caster as evil; however, this perception may derive from the luxurious vantage of comfortable times. People don't create or cast courtcase spells unless there's at least a remote possibility of legal justice. What if you exist in a time or place where you or your loved ones are at the mercy of others more powerful than you and there is no recourse, none, not at all, to justice? What do you do then? Hexes are not an uncommon response. Hexes may be cast as a desperate attempt to end persecution and abuse.

In the same manner that Witch Wars escalate, with witches lobbing spells at each other until it's impossible to determine who cast the first spell, one shouldn't always assume that the hex is the initiating action. It may be cast in response to a terrible violation, crime or injustice.

Many of the most powerful hexes ultimately call on sacred—or infernal—powers to deliver the punishment. It isn't the mechanical action of the spell that makes the successful accomplishment of a hex possible. It's the passionate anger, hatred, and rage that fuel it. Yet for all that hatred and rage, the spell-caster is plotting a hex, not committing murder. The average hex-caster, or at least those who initially derived these spells, was either not in a position to act on these impulses or was leaving it in the hands of divine justice. Those

extreme situations (and there are fine lines; the Justice spell against a rapist on page 244 could conceivably be interpreted as a hex, as could the Green Devil Spell to regain a cash debt owed) are perhaps the only situations that could justify some of these spells.

Hexes also sometimes serve a function that transcends magic: enforcement of social order. Many of the most malevolent hexes are secret: black candles burned in private or funeral services chanted over your enemy. Other hexes, however, are extremely public: the spell is activated by "dusting" the target's doorstep. Something is left on the target's front doorstep for them to find when they open the door. It's quite likely that by the time the target discovers the hex, all the neighbors and passers-by have already witnessed it. Although these spells are nominally anonymous (the identity of the spell-caster is reputedly unknown), realistically many in the community will know exactly who cast the hex. If someone is behaving in a manner that is perceived as dangerous or undesirable, dusting their doorstep is traditionally a way of informing them that others are unhappy, giving them an opportunity to change their ways or leave. In these cases, hexes may be understood in terms of intimidation rather than magic. And some of them are threatening indeed.

There are essentially two types of hexes:

★ *those created from materials that are inherently malevolent; the fact that the material is even used indicates a hex.* **Goofer Dust** *spells fall in this category*

★ *those created from neutral materials or even from material that is inherently sacred, benevolent, and beneficial. The spell-caster's intent is what transforms it into a hex. Thus a handful of graveyard dust may be tossed in someone's wake to provide a blessing or a curse*

IMPORTANT:
A WARNING SPELL BEFORE BEGINNING

Should one for any reason (and, of course, yours is a good one) attempt to cast a malicious spell using oils or powders, and should some of that hexing material somehow get onto you, forget about the original spell and focus immediately on cleansing yourself instead.

★ Cleanse thoroughly using rosemary hydrosol or appropriate quantities of the essential oil. (Remember less is always more with essential oils. Don't be tempted to use excessive amounts because you've scared yourself.)

★ Wait at least 24 hours before considering whether to return to the original spell

This cleansing may also be used if you are the target of a malevolent spell.

 Anthill Hex

This spell allegedly causes financial discord: gather dust from an anthill and sprinkle it on your target's doorstep.

 Betel Nut Hex

Betel nuts are the stimulant of choice in many parts of Earth. They're also used magically.

To cast a hex with betel nuts, wrap your enemy's photograph, a piece of paper with your enemy's name on it, and/or intimate articles belonging to your target in a black cloth. Add betel nuts and cubebs. Wrap everything up and bury it, ideally where your target is sure to pass.

Black Arts Oil

A traditional condition oil used to cast hexes:

1. Grind up black mustard seeds, black pepper, mullein, stinging nettles, and valerian.
2. Put it in a bottle and cover with mineral (baby) oil.
3. Float whole peppercorns in the oil and if you have a black dog, add one single hair. (Pick it off the sofa or your clothing. Don't bother the dog; annoying the dog will cause the spell to backfire on you immediately even before the Rule of Three kicks in.)

So now that you've concocted this mean-spirited oil, what do you do with it?

☀ Black Arts Oil Spell (1)
Candle Spell

Carve a black or purple candle to suit your situation. Dress with Black Arts Oil and burn.

☀ Black Arts Oil Spell (2)
Direct Approach

This is potentially a stronger spell than the one above. Soak a cotton ball in Black Arts Oil and drop it into your target's pocket.

☀ Bladderwrack Hex

Bladderwrack is normally carried as a protective botanical but it can be used to provide a particularly nasty hex, too. If hidden in a bathroom that your enemy uses, it allegedly causes uterine tract infections.

☀ Blueberry Hex

Even something as innocuous as blueberries has been used to cast malicious spells. Create an infusion of blueberry leaves and sprinkle over your target's doorstep.

☀ Bottle Hex

1. Place your target's photograph inside a bottle.
2. Write the target's name on a piece of paper and put this inside the bottle, too.
3. Stuff holly and ivy into the bottle.
4. Add some black ink and **War Water.**
5. Seal the bottle shut and bury it upside down.

☀ Candle Hex (1) Black Cat
Crossed Your Path

*The condition oil **Black Cat Oil** is most frequently used for benevolent purposes, to draw protection, good fortune, and attention from the opposite sex. However, it may also be used to turn a trick. The combination of wax and pins requires no doll.*

1. Hold a black candle in your hands and charge it with your intention.
2. Carve it with your enemy's name and any identifying information pertaining to that person.
3. Dress the candle with **Black Cat Oil.**
4. Pierce the candle with five pins placed vertically, approximately one inch apart.
5. Light your candle and let it burn until the first pin drops out.
6. Pinch out the candle and reserve it.
7. The following night, light the candle again and let it burn until the next pin drops out.
8. Burn in nightly increments until the final pin drops out.
9. Pinch the candle out yet again but this time take what remains of the candle and throw it against your enemy's front door.
10. Walk away without looking back, returning home via a circuitous route.

☀ Candle Hex (2)
Black Powder

1. Grate charcoal until you have coal dust. (True coal may be used too.)
2. Blend the coal dust with **Black Salt** and **Goofer Dust.**
3. Carve a purple candle as desired, then slice the top off and expose the wick on the bottom of the candle so that it may be burned upside down.
4. Roll the candle in the powder, set it on a plate, and light the candle.

5. Get completely undressed, remove all jewelry, and loosen your hair.
6. Get in touch with all your rage and anger.
7. Stick one hundred pins into the burning candle. Scream, shout, and curse as you deem appropriate.
8. Leave all spell remnants, including the plate, on your enemy's doorstep.

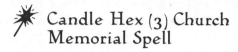

Candle Hex (3) Church Memorial Spell

The memorial prayers in this hex may be considered metaphorically as if one is burying success, happiness, vitality, or whatever has been targeted. For this hex to be effective, the religious ritual and candle used must possess significance for the spell-caster.

1. Obtain a church candle.
2. Slice the top off the candle, flattening it.
3. Carve the bottom of the candle, so that the wick is exposed, effectively reversing the candle.
4. Carve and dress as you deem appropriate.
5. Burn while reciting memorial prayers dedicated to your adversary.

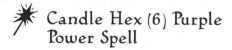

Candle Hex (4) Devil's Bit

1. Blend asafetida, cayenne pepper, ground devil's bit, and sulfur.
2. Carve a black candle as desired with a rusty nail or a coffin nail. (For maximum strength, use a rusty coffin nail.)
3. Dress the candle with baby (mineral) oil.
4. Roll the candle in the botanical powder and burn.

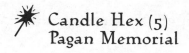

Candle Hex (5) Pagan Memorial

An alternative version of Candle Hex (3) for those with different spiritual orientations:

1. Carve and dress a black candle rather than a church candle.
2. Chant what you envision happening to your target rather than reciting memorial prayers.

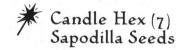

Candle Hex (6) Purple Power Spell

1. Carve a purple candle with your enemy's name and identifying information.
2. Dress the candle with a combination of **Commanding Oil** and your urine.
3. Burn.

Candle Hex (7) Sapodilla Seeds

Sapodilla is a tropical fruit with many magical uses.

1. Grind and powder Grains of Paradise and sapodilla seeds.
2. Place them in a bottle and cover with olive oil.
3. Use this oil to dress a carved black candle.

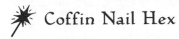 Candle Spell (8) Skull Candle

Although modern metaphysical people, including this one, bend over backwards explaining that candles in the shape of skulls can be used for benevolent purposes, they can also be used to cast a hex.

1. Carve a skull candle with your target's name and identifying information. Dress it as desired.
2. Write the same information on a piece of brown paper, together with any other information you feel needs to be expressed to the universe.
3. Place the paper underneath the candle and burn it.
4. Stay with the candle while it burns; look into the skull's "eyes" and focus on your desire.
5. Dispose of the spell remnants outside your home.

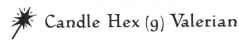 Candle Hex (9) Valerian

Blend asafetida, cayenne pepper, and valerian and sprinkle over your enemy's photograph. (If you lack a photo, write the enemy's full name, variations on his or her name, and his or her mother's name on a piece of paper.) Place a black candle atop the photograph or name-paper and burn.

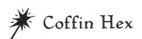 Coffin Hex

This Russian coffin spell is superficially similar to the New Orleans-based one discussed later under Public Hexes (see page 584), but is actually very different. The goal is not intimidation but genuine, unadulterated malevolence. The coffin, and hence the hex, is not made public but kept hidden; the hex is more insidious and harder to lift.

1. Work a strand of the target's hair into wax or some clay. (If the clay can be crafted from their gathered footprint, this hex is believed to be even more effective.)

2. Mold the wax or clay into something resembling your target.
3. Place this image inside a little coffin.
4. Bury the coffin and cover it with a rock.

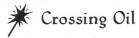 Coffin Nail Hex

Pound a coffin nail through a piece of fabric soaked with your target's sweat. Simultaneously, articulate a curse.

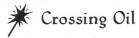 Crossing Oil

*Of course, if **Uncrossing Oil** exists, there must be Crossing Oil, too. Use this formula to cast a hex:*

1. Grind cayenne pepper, Grains of Paradise, and wormwood.
2. Place it in a bottle together with a pebble from the cemetery.
3. Cover with mineral (baby) oil.

Curse Tablets

The most common hex of the ancient world appears to have been Curse Tablets. At least they're the most common artifacts found. Created from metal, curse tablets survive, as no doubt intended, for millennia, unlike more ephemeral wax, paper, and fabric methods. Curse tablets are small sheets of metal, inscribed with specific curses naming the target and what destiny is wished for him or her. Having been inscribed, the tablets were traditionally tossed into wells or springs, and are frequently dedicated to the Spirit of the spring as if expecting the Spirit to actually carry out the curse. There were professional curse tablet makers; we know this because blanks have been found, standard formulas with spaces left to incorporate a name. However, because soft metal is used and little skill is required, this was always also easy do-it-yourself hexing.

The most favored metal is lead, for two reasons. First, lead is under the leadership of Saturn, a planet with a dour, unforgiving reputation. Saturn, once known by astrologers as the Greater Malefic, is where one discovers life's harsh limits, which is what the target of the spell is expected to discover. Second, and on a more prosaic note, lead is heavy. It sinks and doesn't rise. As the best way to undo a curse tablet is to discover and destroy the tablet, using lead virtually ensures the success of the spell.

In ancient Rome the most powerful curse tablets were believed created on lead stolen from sewer pipes. If you wanted to play around with the form, and a blessing tablet could just as easily be created, curse tablets are even more easily created from tin or wax.

1. Determine the desired effects you wish the tablet to deliver.
2. Cut out a sheet of metal or wax.
3. Inscribe it with your desire, naming your target and his or her identifying information as explicitly as possibly.
4. Traditionally tablets are dropped into springs or wells or attached to sewer walls. A blessing tablet might be affixed to a shrine or altar.

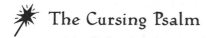 The Cursing Psalm

The power to heal can be the power to harm. Even something as intrinsically good and sacred as a psalm may be used malevolently. Psalm 109 has been called "the cursing psalm." It may be chanted to harm an enemy.

The psalm itself is inherently benevolent. It's your emotion and intention that transforms it. Therefore the first step is to be in the right mood. Then start chanting and visualizing.

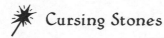 Cursing Stones

Charging a stone with malevolence is an ancient Celtic method of delivering a curse. Charge the stone by holding it in your hands while allowing yourself to be engulfed by feelings of rage, jealousy, anger, or hatred. The stone will store this emotion. When charging is complete, terminate the process by setting the stone down and consciously changing your train of thought. Reserve the stone for future use.

Should one wish to curse someone or something, hold the stone within your hands, stroking it, while turning it counter-clockwise and murmuring curses.

 Damnation Powder

Consider whether casting this spell is worth it. Although it's believed to be a potent hex, the hex-caster allegedly is left with hell to pay.

Refer to the Formulary and create the powder base for **Damnation Water.** *Drop nine pinches of* **Damnation Powder,** *one at a time, into a flaming cauldron, intoning the target's name as each pinch falls.*

Damnation Water Hexes

These are revenge spells, spells cast from anger. Because **Damnation Water**, like **War Water**, can either confer a hex or break one, the emotional intent of the spell-caster determines the outcome.

 Damnation Water: Basic Hex

Sprinkle **Damnation Water** *on the path where your enemy is sure to walk.*

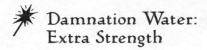

Damnation Water: Extra Strength

1. Soak parchment in blended **Damnation Water** and **Four Thieves Vinegar**.
2. When the paper dries, write every variation of your target's name on it. (For maximum strength, use **Bat's Blood Ink**.)
3. Carve and dress a black candle against your enemy.
4. Burn the paper in the flame of the candle.
5. Reserve the ashes of the parchment to sprinkle on your enemy's property.

Dead Man's Rope Curse

The Renaissance magician, Cornelius Agrippa, discussed this hexing tool. Use a rope to obtain nine measurements from a dead man's corpse. Measure each of the following three times each:

★ *from the elbow to the longest finger*
★ *from the shoulder to the tip of the longest finger*
★ *from the head to the toe*

Keep the rope. Anyone subsequently measured with it will suffer misery, misfortune, or worse.

Dissension Spell

Blend cayenne or habanero pepper powder with powdered wild ginger (not ginger root; this plant is also known as asarum or Canada snakeroot). Sprinkle this mixture on your target's doorstep or on the path where he or she will walk, to create dissension and discord.

Dog Hex

This spell allegedly destroys your target's peace and harmony, sowing enmity and discord instead.

1. Hang out in a dog park. Eventually, inevitably, some dogs will have a fight. This is what you're waiting for: look for a mass free-for-all, complete with gnashing teeth and wild barking.
2. Don't get between the dogs when they're fighting, but when the battle ends gather up a handful of dirt from where the dogs were fighting.
3. Pick some cat hairs off a cat-lover's sofa or clothing.
4. Grind the dirt and hair together with salt, black pepper, and cayenne or habanero pepper so that a fine powder is created.
5. Sprinkle this powder wherever you wish to sow enmity.

Doll Hex (1) Basic Pins and Needles Doll

The term "voodoo doll" has entered the English language but maligns the Vodou religion. The magical tradition of pierced wax dolls, for both positive and negative purposes, is ancient and international, dating back at least to the days of the Egyptians and appearing virtually around the world. Here is a Hungarian Romany version:

1. Create a figure to represent your target from melted candle wax.
2. Add bits of the target's clothing and any intimate items that you may possess—hair, nail clippings, and so forth.
3. When the doll is finished, allow the doll to harden.
4. Prick it with a needle as the spirit moves you but always in a series of three or nine.

Doll Hex (2) Cactus Needles

Create a wax or clay image of your enemy. Instead of pins and needles, stab it with cactus thorns, while murmuring curses.

Doll Hex (3) Foot Track Spell

This Malay spell combines wax doll and foot track magic to craft a potent hex.

Measure your enemy's footprint. Make a wax effigy of your target corresponding exactly in length with the footprint. Personalize and pierce as desired.

 ## Doll Hex (4) Lost and Away

This is technically a banishing spell, but one delivered with malice. **Lost and Away Powder** *is made from crossroads dirt and various agents commonly used in exorcisms.*

1. Personalize a rag doll. Label it with your enemy's name; add intimate items if possible.
2. Put the doll inside a paper bag or a shoebox.
3. Sprinkle it with **Lost and Away Powder.**
4. Melt black wax gently in a double boiler or bain-marie on the stove.
5. Pour the wax over the doll and sprinkle it with more **Lost and Away Powder** before the wax hardens.
6. Bury the doll in the ground away from your home.
7. Visit the doll's grave once a week and sprinkle the spot with **Lost and Away Powder.**

Your enemy should be too preoccupied with his or her own troubles to bother you.

 ## Doll Hex (5) Malay

Who needs wax? A Malay spell suggests making a paper doll to represent your husband's girlfriend or another romantic rival. A drawing or photograph may work too. Stick a needle in the heart or head, with wishes for misfortune to distract her from your man.

 ## Dragon's Blood Hex

Many botanicals such as dragon's blood are usually relied upon for their protective properties, but they can be twisted toward malevolent purposes too.

In the Solomon Islands, the dragon's blood tree, Dracaena, is believed to have sprung from the grave of a sea spirit. A powerful plant, whose resin is most frequently used in protection rituals, this hex utilizes the tree's leaves.

1. Wrap a lime and a piece of ginger root in a dracaena leaf.
2. Lay it in the path of your target.
3. Should he or she step on or over it, his or her life will be filled with great distress.

Enmity Spells

Sometimes hexes are vague: the spell-caster simply wants the target to suffer. General misery, in any form the universe wishes to dole out, is acceptable. Sometimes, however, a hex is very specific; a specific end result is desired. Frequently the desire is to transform love into its opposite.

 ## Enmity Spell (1) Break Up Spell

This spell is intended to cause enmity between two who currently love each other or are closely attached. There may be desire to break up a marriage, a romantic attachment, a business partnership, or a friendship.

Boil a black hen's egg in your own urine. Feed half the egg to a dog, the other to a cat, saying: "As these two hate one another, so may hatred fall between [Name] and [Name]."

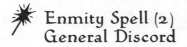

Enmity Spell (2)
General Discord

To sow general discord within a home, bury a found crow's feather in the target's house. (It must be a found feather; take it by force and watch the spell backfire on you.) This spell, from India, derives from a region with thatched roofs and so was easily accomplished. You never actually had to get inside the home. However, any other discreet place in the residence will do. Under the front step, where the target is bound to step over it, should be equally effective.

Enmity Spell (3)
Separation Powder

Black pepper
Cayenne or habanero powder
Cinnamon
Galangal
Vetiver
Metallic sand

Separation powder allegedly does what its name promises: separates formerly devoted lovers or partners. Sprinkle it where the targeted couple will be together.

Enmity Spell (4) Seven
Ant Hills

To specifically cause enmity between a married or romantic couple, collect dirt from seven ant hills and slip the dust between their bed sheets.

Empty Wallet Hex

Some hexes are subtle, such as this Romany spell intended to create a negative financial impact.

Give a new wallet as a gift, straight from the store, in a nice box, with nothing in it. Doesn't sound like a hex, does it? The target of the spell will probably be happy to receive it, unless they're sophisticated enough to realize they've just accepted a wish for a perpetually empty purse.

The moral of the story? Always stick at least a penny into a wallet before giving it as a gift—and be wary of gifts received.

Flying Devil Oil Hex

Carve your enemy's name into a black or white candle, ideally using a rusty coffin nail. Dress the candle with **Flying Devil Oil**. Roll it in powdered patchouli and valerian and then burn the candle.

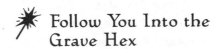

Follow You Into the
Grave Hex

Keep tormenting your enemy even after death. The original stimulus for the system of feng shui comes from the necessity of arranging funeral sites. A Chinese hex plays havoc with feng shui's best intentions: insert slivers of ailanthus and peach wood into a grave to destroy the positive feng shui.

Foot Track Hexes

Although foot track magic can be used for positive means as easily as negative, it has something of a bad reputation, one it has retained for millennia: Pythagoras warned against its misuses.

Foot Track Spell (1)
Australian Aboriginal

Place a sharp stone or piece of broken glass into the footprint.

Foot Track Spell (2) Curse of the Running Feet

Cheating men who've abandoned their sweethearts at the altar should be wary of the vila. If these Eastern European Fairies catch them, they'll dance these men to death as a form of justice. (This is the mythological basis for the ballet, Giselle.) Hoodoo, on the other hand, has the curse of running feet.

Mix the dirt from your target's footprint with cayenne pepper, and throw it into running, living waters. This allegedly causes your target to run from place to place, unceasingly, without rest, ultimately with disastrous results.

Foot Track Spell (3) Estonian

No need to dig up the footprint or even to do anything visible to it. Instead, measure the footprint with a stick. Slice off that measure of the stick and bury it, preferably in the cemetery.

Foot Track Spell (4) Hobble their Steps

A German foot track spell is intended to render someone lame, although whether literally or figuratively is subject to debate.

1. Gather Earth from the footprint.
2. Place it in a pot together with a nail, a needle, and some shards of broken glass.
3. Heat the pot until it cracks.

Foot Track Spell (5) Nail Them Down

Hold metal or coffin nails in your hand and focus on your desired end result. Hammer the nails crosswise above or over the footprint of the one whom you wish tormented.

This is the spell Pythagoras didn't like!

Foot Track Spell (6) Russian

Measure the footprint with thread, and then burn the thread.

Foot Track Spell (7) Walk into Danger

Burn someone's footprint to cause illness or worse. This spell derives from Russia, where for maximum power it would be burned in the bathhouse at midnight, the point being that it was burned in a sacred yet dangerous place.

Foot Track (8) Wind

1. Dig up your enemy's footprint.
2. Carry it with you until a windy moment presents itself.
3. Let the wind carry the foot print dirt away.

To Prevent Someone from Casting a Foot Track Spell on You

These spells are to protect against danger from either foot track spells or any malicious magic absorbed through the feet—powders or secret tricks one walks over, for instance. Their goal is to prevent rather than break an already-cast spell: hex-breakers or spell reversals are required in that unfortunate circumstance.

✳ Prevent a Foot Track Hex (1) Devil's Shoestrings

Devil's shoestrings are roots derived from the Viburnum botanical family. Their name confuses people who think that the roots must be used for evil purposes. Quite the contrary: devil's shoestrings allegedly tie the devil's shoes together to prevent him, or evil in general, from successful pursuit. Worn as an ankle bracelet, devil's shoestrings repel foot track curses. This spell requires nine devil's shoestring roots of equal length. They cannot be cut to size but must be chosen carefully.

1. Knot, braid or weave the roots together to form an ankle bracelet.
2. Attach a tiny piece of real silver, whether a coin, bead or lucky charm and wear it for protection.

✳ Prevent a Foot Track Hex (2) Henna

Henna creates a protective shield when applied to the soles of the feet. Although beautiful patterns are always a pleasure and decorating with auspicious, protective symbols will no doubt enhance the potency, they're not necessary for the purpose. If you're pressed for time, dip your sole into henna paste for a solid coat of henna.

✳ Prevent a Foot Track Hex (3) Pepper

Sprinkle black pepper and cayenne pepper in your shoes. You may also rub it directly into the soles of your feet.

Goofer Dust Spells

Goofer Dust is the malevolent derivation of graveyard dust. (See the *Formulary*, page 1037, for more details.)

✳ Goofer Dust Spell (1) Basic Direct

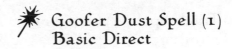

*Toss a handful of **Goofer Dust** behind someone's back as he or she walks away from you.*

✳ Goofer Dust Spell (2) Basic Indirect

*Sprinkle **Goofer Dust** over your target's front steps or across their path, where they are guaranteed to walk over it.*

✳ Goofer Dust Spell (3) Candle

1. Slice the top off a black pillar candle so that it is flat and will stand.
2. Carve the bottom of the candle so that the wick is exposed and may be lit, effectively reversing the candle.
3. Carve and dress the candle as you wish.
4. Place the candle on a plate covered with **Goofer Dust** and burn it, concentrating on your desires.

✳ Goofer Dust Spell (4) Jack Ball

Jack balls are usually made to draw love, luck, and prosperity. This one is designed to deliver a hex.

1. First carve and dress a black candle to suit your purpose.
2. Take some of the melted wax and roll it in the palms of your hand.
3. Add identifying items to the little ball: your target's fingernail clippings, hair, bits of their clothing, etc.
4. Add a couple drops of your own urine, as a controlling mechanism.
5. Add some **Goofer Dust.**

6. Roll everything into a smooth ball.
7. Unlike other jack balls, don't carry this one around with you. Instead, bury it on the other person's property.

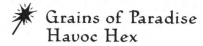 Grains of Paradise Havoc Hex

Although Grains of Paradise are most frequently used in romantic spells, they also possess powerful commanding properties, which may be turned toward malevolent uses.

To create havoc in someone's life, and not *the fun romantic kind either:*

1. Grind up Grains of Paradise.
2. Sprinkle the powder over your target's threshold so that he or she will walk over it.

 Hand Hex

1. Collect dirt from the victim's footprint, nail clippings and/or strands of hair.
2. Place these within a red flannel drawstring bag.
3. Add graveyard dirt or **Goofer Dust,** red pepper, needles, and pins.
4. Bury the bag on the person's property or at a crossroads, ruin or cemetery.

 Heart Hex

Who needs wax for pins and needles to be effective? This British spell derives from a time before people bought their meat in supermarkets. This type of spell is the ancestor of New Orleans-style courtcase beef-tongue spells (see page 226). Those spells use the cow's tongue to either quicken or quiet a human tongue. This hex allegedly causes "heart trouble," although whether this is meant metaphorically or literally is open to debate.

1. Obtain a cow or sheep heart from a butcher.
2. Make nine slits in it.
3. Write the target's name on nine slips of brown paper.
4. Place one in each slit.
5. Close each slit with a pair of crossed pins or needles. (You will need a total of 18.)
6. Wrap the heart up with baker's string or cord.
7. Blend equal parts pure grain alcohol with your target's favorite beverage. (If unsure, use whiskey or absinthe.)
8. Place the heart in a jar and cover it with the alcohol.
9. Burn one black candle in its entirety on top of the jar every night for nine nights, for a total of nine candles.
10. When the spell is complete, dispose of all spell articles and remnants far from your home and return via a circuitous route.

 Hemlock Hex

Hemlock is another very poisonous plant; handle with care, if you must handle it at all.

Write your target's name on a piece of paper; this is most powerful if using hand-crafted magical ink or drops of blood from your smallest finger. Tie the paper around a piece of hemlock and bury.

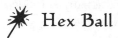 Hex Ball

1. Burn a candle against your enemy, carving and dressing as desired.
2. Reserve some melted wax.
3. Add algae or any kind of mold to the wax. Scrape mildew off the shower curtain and add that too.
4. Roll the doctored wax into a ball.
5. Add black pepper and valerian.
6. Toss the ball onto your enemy's property.

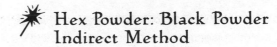

Hex Conjure Bag

1. Rip up a photograph of the target of your spell and place the pieces inside a charm bag.
2. Add sharp things like tacks, pins, needles, and shards of broken mirror.
3. Sprinkle graveyard dust or **Goofer Dust** inside the bag.
4. If you've burned candles against your target, add any wax remnants to the bag.
5. Spit in the bag and close it up.
6. Bury it at the crossroads, in the cemetery, or on your target's property.

Hex Packet

1. Write your enemy's name in black ink on red paper.
2. Sprinkle asafetida, **Black Salt,** camphor, and **Goofer Dust** onto the paper.
3. Fold the paper away from you, knot it shut with red thread, and wrap it in black fabric.
4. Pierce this packet with nine pins.
5. Bury this packet where your enemy will walk over it or on their property.

Hex Powders

Hexing powders are most traditionally sprinkled where the target will walk over them. They are also used in candle spells and conjure bags.

Hex Powder: Black Powder Direct Method

*Blend **Black Salt,** black pepper, and black mustard seeds. As you talk with your target, sprinkle this powder on them or directly in their path.*

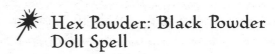

Hex Powder: Black Powder Indirect Method

If you don't have access to your target, or would prefer a less direct method of application, create a candle to represent them. Sprinkle the powder over the candle and burn it.

Hex Powder: Black Powder Doll Spell

1. Create a doll to represent the target of your spell.
2. Sprinkle Black Powder over it.
3. Wrap the doll in fabric or place it within a box (coffin).
4. Bury the doll or leave it on your target's doorstep.

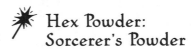

Hex Powder: Crossing Powder

1. Obtain ashes from the target's cigarettes or cigars. (*Another* reason why smoking can be dangerous to your health!)
2. Grind the ashes up finely, then spit on them.
3. Add **Goofer Dust** and use as desired.

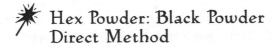

Hex Powder: Sorcerer's Powder

Grind and powder the following:

Asafetida
Black pepper
Patchouli
Peppermint
Valerian
Vetiver

Blend all the botanicals together and add graveyard dirt. Sprinkle as desired.

Hex Your Enemy Spell

Because illnesses are so dreaded, hexes attempted to specifically inflict them, like this one: brew nine types of grain, then pour it out at a crossroads or outside the home of the one you wish to bewitch.

If the target of your spell steps over the potion, he or she will fall ill, typically with an irritating skin disorder. If you feel you're the one who's been bewitched, this may also be used as an antidote.

 ## Jezebel Root Anger Spell

Jezebel root is considered an excellent conduit for focusing anger at someone. It may be used against an enemy, whether as a malicious hex or to prevail in an emotional or legal conflict. The following spell is extremely popular but frequently misunderstood. Even those who are unfamiliar with the Bible associate Jezebel with the proverbial wicked queen. Thus this spell, using the root named in her honor, is often perceived as inherently evil. That's not the point. The point is that Jezebel imposes her will in difficult situations. Her desires are accomplished, after the nice, ethical methods have failed. This spell is about prevailing at all costs:

1. Hold the root in your left hand. Close your eyes. Concentrate on your target, on your situation, on your desire. Hold the root for as long as necessary; don't rush.
2. The traditional recommendation is to now place the root in a jar filled with water. Because of the connection with the biblical Jezebel, I'd recommend filling the jar with red wine.
3. Seal the jar tight. Keep it in a secret, dark place for three days.
4. Remove the root, throwing it away far from your home.
5. Empty the liquid from the jar out on the ground and dispose of the jar, too.

 ## Jinx Powder

Allegedly this powder creates havoc and turmoil in your target's life. Blend magnetic sand (fine iron shot) and dried, ground stinging nettles carefully together. (Add to talcum powder if you'd like a more "powdery" texture.) Sprinkle over your target's threshold or where he or she is guaranteed to step over it.

 ## Knot Hex

Take three threads, each one of a different color. Tie them together, making three knots, cursing as you form each one.

Name Paper Spells

Who needs intimate items when you have a name? Once upon a time (and sometimes still today), it was believed that if you possessed someone's true name you also possessed control over that person.

 ## Name Paper Hex (1) Active Spell

1. Write the name of your target clearly on a piece of paper as well as any other identifying information.
2. Dress it with a drop of **Commanding Oil.**
3. Hold it in your hand, close your eyes and focus your desire.
4. Now do something to the paper to demonstrate injury to the target. For instance, placing the name paper under drums while they're played allegedly causes the victim to suffer headaches. Can you imagine what taping it inside a pair of cymbals might do?

Name Paper Hex (2) Oak Gall

1. Write your adversary's name, including their mother's name as well as any identifying information on a strip of brown paper using **Raven's Feather** or **Bat's Blood Ink.**
2. Wrap the paper around an oak gall, with the name on the inside.
3. Bury this in a very remote spot.

 ## Name Paper Hex (3) Lemon

A simple piece of fruit may be as effective as a wax image: write the full name of the victim on a slip of paper. Stick pins through the paper into a lemon, to cause bitterness and a sour existence.

 ## Name Paper Shoe Hex

This hex derives from Central American magical traditions.

1. Capture one of your target's shoes.
2. Write the target's name, mother's name, and any identifying information on a slip of paper.
3. Place this paper within the shoe—lift up the sole so it doesn't fall out, if necessary.
4. Do to the shoe whatever you visualize happening to your target.

Peppermint Candle Spell

Peppermint oil, usually a benevolent component of romantic and healing spells, is also used as a hexing agent in candle spells to bring harm and unhappiness to one's enemy.

1. Write your enemy's name and your desires for him or her on a piece of brown paper.

2. Carve a black candle as you deem appropriate.
3. Add some peppermint essential oil to mineral (baby) oil and use this to dress the candle.
4. Hold the candle in your hands, charging it with your intentions.
5. Place the paper beneath the candle and burn the candle.

Public Hexes

Most hexes, like magic spells in general, are cast privately and discreetly. In many cases this discretion is considered vital to the potential success of the spell. A few hexes, however, are extremely public, which begs the question—is the purpose of these hexes genuinely magical or rather attempts at intimidation and crowd control?

 ## Public Hex (1) Coffin Hex

This is the spell that scares everyone—the dreaded little coffin. It's difficult to determine whether this spell's potential success derives from magic or from its intimidation factor. Although in theory this is an elaboration of a wax doll spell, many are titillated by the coffin imagery and so the entire spell frequently consists of nothing more than dumping a tiny coffin in front of the target's front door, without candles or powders or anything that might remotely require magical skill. The sheer nastiness and threat implicit in the spell may be enough to achieve its purpose.

Like other doorstep-dusting spells, this is also very public magic. Although the person who sent the spell may or may not be known, with the coffin conspicuously laid before someone's door, it's very possible that all the neighbors and passers-by will see the hex before it's discovered by those for whom it's intended.

This, of course, is the crux of the spell: if someone really intended serious spiritual harm to another, a personalized coffin might be created but it wouldn't be

necessary to leave it on the doorstep. There are a lot of other potentially more effective methods of disposal. The coffin must be publicly deposited because the goal of the spell is really to let the target know how angry and hateful someone is toward them, whether justifiably so or not. It is, in essence, a public declaration of war or a warning of murderous intent.

1. Traditionally this hex is delivered by crafting a small (only two or three inches long) black coffin. The coffin may be made of wood, metal, wax, or papier-mâché and then painted black, if necessary.
2. Inserted inside is usually a doll pierced with needles and pins plus a burnt black candle stub, apparently the remnants of a spell worked on the target.

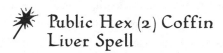 Public Hex (2) Coffin Liver Spell

This is a very "traditional" public hex:

1. Craft a miniature coffin.
2. Instead of inserting a doll, however, place a raw chicken liver within the casket.
3. Sprinkle asafetida powder and cayenne pepper over the liver. Add candle stubs if you want.
4. Leave the casket on your target's doorstep.

Public Hex (3) Egg Hex

Write your target's name on a whole, raw egg, using your menstrual blood as ink or, if unavailable, obtain a few drops of blood by pricking your smallest left finger. Toss the egg on their doorstep.

Public Hex (4) Slavic Hex

This Slavic hex is one of the most public. Imagine how full of resentment and hate you must be to cast this spell.

1. Prepare a candle and journey to your target's home.
2. Undress down to your underwear.
3. Circle the target's property with a burning candle muttering hexes and curses.
4. Then break the candle in half and bury it upside down.

Rue Curse

Rue, the herb of grace, supreme protector against the Evil Eye, may also be used to deliver a hex. Throw rue at your target while uttering the curse.

Rune Curse/Rune Blessing

Although there are some substances that are perceived as totally benevolent magically and a few other substances believed to possess the opposite effect, in general anything used to bless may also be used to curse and vice versa. The intent and actions of the practitioner determine the effect of the spell. Runes, for instance, can be used to deliver a blessing or a curse.

Runes are symbols ascribed with various magical, mystical, and divinatory properties. Magical alphabets, runes are most associated today with Northern Europe. Early rune symbols have been dated as far back as c. 8000 BCE. Individual runes literally represent something; however they also radiate mana, *magic power.*

1. Choose the rune that best represents—and transmits—your desire.
2. Write that rune onto a slip of paper.
3. Maneuver it so that the target of your spell thinks that he or she dropped this paper, or else place it within other papers that the target then picks up. The target has to accept the rune willingly, if unknowingly.
4. When the target takes the rune-paper, especially if it's then placed in his or her pocket, he or she is effectively accepting the rune—curse or blessing, as the case may be.

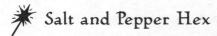 Salt and Pepper Hex

Low-level hexes cause low-level misery. Sprinkle salt and pepper on your target's clothes, while thinking or chanting:

I put salt and pepper on you,
From now on you'll be sorry, miserable and itchy too!

 The Smith's Curse

The flip-side of the power to heal is the power to curse. It was once a traditional belief in Western Ireland that should a smith become angered, by turning his anvil upside down and speaking malicious, harmful words he could deliver a potent curse.

Spoiling

The Russian magical concept of *"spoiling"* lies somewhere between the Evil Eye and a hex. Like the Evil Eye, the root cause is envy, jealousy, and malice. Also like the caster of the Evil Eye, the spoiler may not be able to help him or herself, thus necessitating constant protective magic from others. Various methods of spoiling exist, including this one:

1. Place the following into a packet: a bone dug up from the cemetery, some of the target's hair rolled up into a ball, three wooden splinters burned at both ends and several herb Paris berries.
2. Sew this packet into your victim's pillow.

Herb Paris berries are *extremely* poisonous. Do not handle or use without great caution.

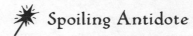 Spoiling Antidote

The antidote to this spell necessitates discovering the packet. Remove it from the pillow, handling it as little as possible. Scorch the packet in fire then toss it in a river flowing away from you.

 A Teeny-Weeny Little Hex

You only want to hex someone a little bit? Sprinkle dried safflower on your target's doorstep to cast a mild hex.

Tseuheur

Following her illness and death, there's been debate and conjecture regarding whether the American author, Jane Bowles, a long-time resident of Morocco, was literally cursed via traditional North African magic. Many apparently believed she was. Allegedly a poisonous packet was found in one of her houseplants, placed there by a close companion. The type of packet in question, a *tseuheur*, is filled with power items, coordinated to create a magical effect. Instead of a mojo bag intended to create one's own good fortune, this is a secret conjure bag intended to cause another person harm.

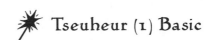 Tseuheur (1) Basic

The standard malevolent tseuheur includes antimony (kohl powder), menstrual blood, and pubic hairs. Fold the items up into a cloth and somehow hide it among your target's belongings or in the target's home.

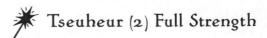 Tseuheur (2) Full Strength

A sample tseuheur intended to bewitch those who live in a house.

1. Fill a packet with seven pebbles, seven sharp shards from a broken mirror, seven large seed pods, antimony powder, and the hex-caster's pubic hairs, together with menstrual blood clots. (Of course with those ingredients, there is the risk that if the packet is found, the spell-caster is *extremely* vulnerable to a spell-reversal.)
2. Find a way to secrete it in your target's home. (A houseplant is an extremely popular way to administer a wide variety of spells, not just hexes.)

War Water Spells

War Water, also known as Water of Mars, is a classic formula that harnesses the power of iron to send a hex, repel a hex, or protect against all sorts of malevolent energy. Different recipes may be used to create benevolent or malevolent **War Water**; check the *Formulary* for details (page 1037).

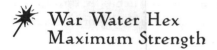 ### War Water Hex
Maximum Strength

Gather Spanish moss. Add it to the aggressive form of ***War Water*** *and use as desired.*

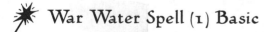 ### War Water Spell (1) Basic

The most common mode of administering ***War Water*** *is to splash your target's doorstep with it. However, as this is the most common method of casting any* ***War Water*** *spell targeted at another for whatever purpose, it's crucial that while splashing, all of your attention is intently focused on the desired outcome of your spell.*

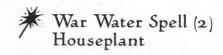 ### War Water Spell (2)
Houseplant

A Hoodoo houseplant jinx suggests that the hex-caster sprinkle ***War Water*** *on the leaves and roots of a really nice plant and give it to the target as a gift.*

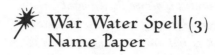 ### War Water Spell (3)
Name Paper

1. Write your adversary's name and identifying information on a strip of brown paper.
2. Place it in a jar and cover it with **War Water.**
3. Seal it tight and hide it in a dark, secret place.
4. Shake the jar periodically.

✳ Warning Hex

Fine lines sometimes exist between a hexing spell and a protection spell. Rather than examples of spontaneous malice, hexes may sometimes be understood as warnings to malefactors, a message to back-off. The hex may be a response to violence and evil, especially where more direct action or protest is denied the wronged party.

A classic example comes from the American South, where slave masters and overseers who mistreated slaves might discover gris-gris on their doorstep, within their home or even in their clothing. Although it might be impossible to identify for sure who was specifically responsible for the hex, the warning was clear. The hex thus serves two purposes.

The hex may indeed work as desired and may be the only way to disable or remove the target of the spell. However, secret, hidden hexes are equally effective and safer for the spell-caster. Gris-gris that the target is guaranteed to discover thus serves an additional purpose. This hex subliminally indicates that a boundary of intolerable behavior has been crossed; continuation of this intolerable behavior may stimulate further desperate action. The awareness that a spell has been cast, that the victims are not entirely helpless or passive, may persuade the target of the hex, the true wrong-doer, to amend his or her evil behavior.

The traditional Southern American slave's hex-bag contained salt, pepper, gunpowder, and dried, pulverized manure.

✳ Weeping Willow Hex

This spell allegedly makes your enemy cry, weep, and moan.

1. Obtain a weeping willow branch.
2. Water it for nine days, retaining any water that doesn't evaporate. (Just keep adding more water.) This gives you nine days to consider and reconsider your plan of action.

3. Pour the water on the front doorstep of your target to stimulate tears in that home.

Wind Curses

Powerful winds have been traditionally greeted with ambivalence. Some revel in them, perceiving them as powerful spiritually cleansing forces; others, particularly in agricultural communities fear their volatile, uncontrollable nature, some even perceiving winds as a source of evil. This ambivalence dates back at least to ancient Mesopotamia. Volatile *"wind spirits"* like Lilith or Pazuzu could bless or harm as they chose. In modern Central America, the *Aires* are a potent natural, metaphysical force so powerful that, like radioactive material, merely being in their presence may cause illness. Russian magic, however, takes advantage of the inherent power of the winds to craft a magical tool.

Russian sorcerers and witches fly through the air, not only on broomsticks or in mortars and pestles like Baba Yaga, but also transformed as whirlwinds. They can be stopped by stabbing a knife into the winds.

✳ Wind Curse Spell

This type of magic is heavily dependent upon personal perception. If you revel in strong winds, if they hold no inherent malevolence for you, you'll be unable to cast a hex with them. If, however, powerful constant winds fill you with irritation and loathing, whatever malevolent potential exists is at your fingertips.

1. Stab a knife into the wind.
2. Do not clean or wipe the knife but carefully wrap it in fabric and reserve for future use.
3. The knife may be used to cast wax image or foot track hexes by stabbing the material.

4. One malicious stab is contained in the knife before it must be replenished.

Witch Bottle Hexes

Witch bottles became popular protective spells based on the fear that witches cast malevolent curses with bottles themselves. Hexing and reversing witch bottles became a form of *"witch warfare."*

 ## Witch Bottle Hex (1)

1. Fill the bottle with intimate items belonging to the victim (hair, nail clippings, and so forth).
2. Cut red felt into a heart shape and stab it with pins, focused intently on the curse.
3. Stuff the heart inside the jug and seal it tightly.
4. Bury it or throw it into a river.

 ## Witch Bottle Hex (2)

Technically a "vengeance spell," witch curse bottles were allegedly created when justice wasn't served in any other fashion.

1. Fill a bottle with shards of broken mirror, pins, needles, coffin nails, and your own urine.
2. Using **Bat's Blood Ink,** write the target's name on a slip of brown paper and put it in the bottle.
3. Seal the bottle with wax from a purple or black candle.
4. Bury it as close to your target's front door as you dare.

 ## The Witch's Ladder (1)

The most potent hex needs no more than hatred and a piece of string. Knot hatred into a cord: make nine knots focusing all your rage and anger.

 ## The Witch's Ladder (2) Enhanced Version

Create the witch's ladder as above. This time, however, embellish it by tying one black hen feather into each of the knots.

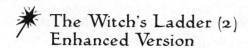 ## Wormwood Hex

Wormwood, used in so many protective and hex-breaking spells, can also be used to cast a hex. Wormwood is incredibly bitter; this spell literally brings bitterness to someone's door. Grind wormwood leaves and roots into powder. Sprinkle them over your target's threshold or in their path.

Reversing Spells

Originally I didn't intend to include hexes amongst the five thousand spells in this book because it's really not necessary: if you are angry, frustrated, bitter or resentful enough, virtually any spell you cast can be converted to a hex. However, for every formal hex or malevolent spell that exists, there are at least two to repel or remove the spell. It is impossible to understand Reversing, Protection or Uncrossing Spells without considering the malevolence of hexes.

Antidote spells or spells to break a hex take various forms, although there can be considerable overlap between them.

★ Hex-breakers *generally focus on breaking the malevolent spell only*
★ Uncrossing spells *generally focus on removing the effects of what might be a hex. The effects are real but the cause may be only suspected. If misfortune is indeed caused by a hex, some uncrossing spells will reverse it back to its sender, although if this not the case, no harm will be done*

★ Antidotes *are exactly what they promise to be: they counteract the effects of a specific type of spell*

★ Reversing spells *break the hex and return it to its sender*

Some of these return-to-sender spells are dependent on your knowing the identity of the spell-caster, while others will automatically return-to-sender without that knowledge. You can rest assured that the spell has been returned; however, you may never know the identity of your oppressor—not for sure, anyway.

There is also a spell to transform negative energy sent your way into the positive energy that you truly desire instead.

Beyond the three-fold law and beyond basic ethics, there is another excellent reason for not engaging in hexes. Should your hex be effective, eventually the target of your spell will suspect that they have been victimized. Although people will swear that they will only resort to hex-breakers and uncrossing spells, if someone gets sufficiently angry and afraid, the standard response tends to be a reversing spell and often the most malevolent kind. What's the difference between many reversing spells and hexes? Well, the reversing spell-caster wasn't the one who initiated the situation and frequently that's about it. After a while, frankly, it can be very hard to remember who actually started the whole malevolent affair. Initiating a hex is rarely a quick-fix, effortless method of removing an enemy. What initiating a hex usually does instead is to initiate psychic warfare—a witch war—with detrimental, damaging effects to all involved as well as their loved ones and many innocent bystanders.

Antidotes

According to sociologists and non-magic practicing scholars, the reason hexes are frequently so effective (particularly intimidating public doorstep

ones like coffin spells) is that the target believes him or herself to be doomed and thus wastes away. There may be a grain of truth to this: why is it that so many have a hard time taking love and good fortune spells seriously yet at the same time live in mortal fear of hexes? A hex doesn't necessarily spell doom; it just sets a process in motion. Don't be passive. Just as every poison has its antidote, so does every spell.

These antidotes specifically target a genre of spell; if you're unsure how the spell was cast or if there isn't an antidote to suit your situation, choose hex-breaking, uncrossing or reversing spells instead.

 ## Antidote: Bewitched Food

To remove and repel a spell cast when you accepted a gift of bewitched food:

1. Throw any remaining food into fire.
2. Slap the fireplace chimney with a broom.
3. Slap all windows with a broom.
4. Slap all entrance doors with a broom.
5. The removal is complete. Follow up with strong house and personal cleansings.

 ## Antidote: Bewitched Food or Drink

Create an infusion by pouring boiling water over tormentil. Strain out the botanical and drink the tormentil tea to repel and remove a hex that was administered in food or drink, the proverbial evil potion.

 ## Antidote: Curse Tablets

This amulet, from Asia Minor, what is today modern Turkey, is essentially an anti-curse tablet. In use

around the dawning of the Common Era, the amulet's form, engraved writing on a small metal plate is known as a "lamella." It's not hard to cut out tin and scratch an incantation into its surface. The original was addressed to a deity or protective spirit. Adapt as inspired.

The ancient text reads something like:

Drive away the curse from [Name] *child of* [Name].
If anyone harms me in the future, if they attempt to
    harm me in the future,
Throw that curse back where it comes from!

An alternative version: "Free [Name] child of [Name] from all hexcraft and all suffering and all magical influence by night and by day."

Keep the lamella in a safe, secret place or throw it down a deep well.

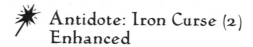 Antidote: Foot Track Magic

Obtain your own footprint. Carry it until a windy moment presents itself then toss the footprint down the wind.

Antidote: Iron Curse (1) Basic

*This German spell antidotes curses cast with iron, including **War Water** spells. How do you know whether you're a victim of such a spell? Signs that such a spell has been cast are when a person suddenly and consistently begins to have accidents with small metal implements, such as knives or scissors, which become progressively more serious, graduating to car accidents or industrial accidents.*

This is the bare-bones spell and the version most popularly circulated. The antidote is easy to accomplish any time. The rings may be re-used and many perform this spell as a regularly scheduled preventive measure.

1. Place three small iron rings in spring water overnight or for 24 hours in a serious case. (By rings, jewelry isn't necessarily meant, although this could be used, but rather any circle formed from iron: hardware stores often sell small metal rings for various purposes.)
2. After the time has elapsed, remove the rings and drink the water.

Antidote: Iron Curse (2) Enhanced

If you find yourself really scared, the basic antidote's power may be enhanced:

1. Cover the glass containing the rings with a white cotton, linen or lace handkerchief.
2. Leave it exposed to the full moonlight.
3. The next day, immediately, on an empty stomach, drink the water.

Antidote: Knot Magic

The very simplest antidote to knot magic is to find the string and untie the knots. Should you be unable to locate the string, reciting the Koran's Surah CXIII allegedly undoes any evil worked via knot magic.

Sometimes you can't miss a trick. Has your doorstep been *"dusted?"* Did you open the front door to discover evidence of a spell laid against you? Tricks may be laid via various powders, **Goofer Dust**, **War Water**, nasty little coffins, chicken parts, black candle stubs, rotten eggs or worse. Don't despair; you're not doomed. There are several remedies, which may also be combined for maximum coverage if desired.

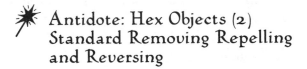 Antidote: Hex Objects (1) Standard Removal and Repelling

This Hoodoo spell can be used as an antidote to any type of object-driven hex, whether the items were left on your doorstep, buried in your garden, or secreted within your home.

The first step is removal: find all the pieces and gather them up, wrapping them in a fabric packet and folding away from you. Then take the packet to a crossroads at midnight, and burn everything.

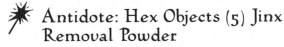 Antidote: Hex Objects (2) Standard Removing Repelling and Reversing

Chinese magic tradition recommends that should you find hex objects don't touch them with your hands.

1. Heat up an iron pan filled with hot oil.
2. Pick any hex objects up with metal tongs.
3. First toss them into hot oil, "frying" them a little.
4. Then throw them into a fire to be destroyed.

This negates the effect upon you and automatically reverses the hex to whoever was the sender. It's not necessary to know the identity of the hexer for this to be accomplished.

Antidote: Hex Objects (3)

1. Urinate on a trick immediately or have a child do it, to neutralize it.
2. Using metal tongs, discard any pieces: do not bring them into the house.
3. Scrub the doorstep with a floorwash that includes red brick dust immediately.

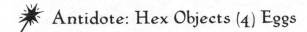 Antidote: Hex Objects (4) Eggs

If eggs have been broken on your doorstep or property, do not *touch them with your hands.*

1. Craft a ritual broom (see *Elements of Magic Spells*) to remove the egg.
2. Sweep away eggshell with the broom, moving it as necessary with metal tongs.
3. Cleanse the wet part of the egg using protective floorwash.
4. Do not bring the broom or any of the egg inside.
5. Ideally burn everything outdoors.

Antidote: Hex Objects (5) Jinx Removal Powder

1. Place arrowroot powder in a bowl.
2. Sprinkle the powder lightly with essential oils of chamomile, peppermint, and wintergreen. (Don't let the powder get too wet.)
3. Stir the powder to blend the essential oils.
4. When the powder dries, sprinkle it as needed.

Antidote: Hex Objects (6) Wash it Off

This method may be used to counteract object-driven hexes as well as those that are harder to clean up: powders, waters, and **Goofer Dust.**

1. Make a strong infusion of dill, Saint John's Wort, trefoil, and vervain.
2. Do not strain it.
3. Rub or sprinkle on anything suspicious or threatening to neutralize their effect.

Of course not everything can be picked up and removed. Although object-driven hexes are among the most emotionally upsetting spells (and frequently the most grotesque) they are actually relatively easy to clean up and repel compared to other methods. Object-driven hexes are also an open threat rather than an insidious hex. However, **War Water** for instance is quickly absorbed. Within minutes, especially in warm climates, you may never know it was there. **Goofer Dust** or other curse powders may be indistinguishable from any other dust (although the tell-tale scent of sulfur tends to reveal magical workings!). Don't despair: powders, dust, and waters must simply be thoroughly washed off rather than picked off.

 ## Antidote: Red Brick Dust (1)

Red brick dust is a powerful magical remedy. It's a modern update for henna powder, ground hematite, and red ochre, themselves modern updates for the protective power of menstrual blood. Use any of these instead if they are easier or resonate more deeply for you. Red iron oxide powder should work, too. However, red brick dust is cheap, potent and accessible.

Smash an old red brick with a hammer to obtain the dust. Add it to a bucket of water and cleanse wherever you know or suspect a trick was laid.

 ## Antidote: Red Brick Dust (2) All Around

If you suspect that more than the doorstep was targeted:

1. Spread red brick dust around the perimeter of your home (or inside, if you feel it's necessary).
2. Sweep it out with a ritual broom.
3. Dispose of the broom after sweeping or reserve it for similar use.

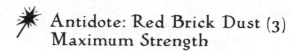 ## Antidote: Red Brick Dust (3) Maximum Strength

1. Dissolve red brick dust and lye in a bucket of water.
2. Add your own urine, focusing your intent: remember urine is a powerful commanding agent.
3. Use this water to cleanse the area where you found the spell or any area that you suspect has been targeted.

Perhaps you suspect someone has hexed you via a wax image spell, whether a candle or a needle-pierced doll:

 ## Antidote: Wax Image Spell (1) Seven Limes

This antidote requires seven limes. Although it may be performed for oneself, it is most effective if you have an assistant doing the squeezing and bathing.

1. The target of the hex must stand within a large metal washtub.
2. Cut the limes in half and squeeze the juice into the tub.
3. Dump the squeezed-out fruits, the lime peel, into the tub as well.
4. Wash your body with lime juice.
5. When the bath is complete, step out of the tub, let yourself air-dry and put on fresh, clean clothes.
6. Leave the lime peel in the washbasin until evening when it is deposited, preferably in the sea, but at least far from home. There should be no further bathing for 24 hours.

✳ Antidote: Wax Image Spell (2) Twenty-one Limes

An ancient Semitic formula to antidote a curse cast with wax.

1. Twenty-one limes are required. Pray over them, charge them with their purpose.
2. Fumigate them with benzoin and frankincense.
3. Ideally the victim should stand on large leaves. If this is not possible, stand on brown paper.
4. Squeeze the fruits into a bowl.
5. Bathe the person with the fruits and juice.
6. Drop the squeezed out limes onto the brown paper.
7. When the ritual bathing is complete, have the person hop off.
8. Wrap up the limes in the paper.
9. The limes and leaves may be deposited in the sea. Alternatively, sprinkle them with salt and deposit far away from home via a circuitous route.

Another version of this spell suggests using three limes each of seven different species or variants. In theory, this is possible. In reality, what is available to most of us is severely limited. Try varying the spell by using seven different citrus fruits, with an emphasis on sour, bitter or acidic ones rather than sweet ones.

Hex-breaking

✳ Angelica Hex-breaker

Make an infusion of angelica root. Add this infusion to your bath to remove curses, hexes, and bad spells. Essential oil of angelica may be used instead of an infusion; however, be aware that it has phototoxic properties. Avoid exposure to the sun following use.

✳ Anti-Sorcery Headwash (1)

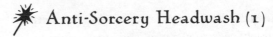

This is not a preventive measure but is effective if you've already been hit by a malevolent spell. In the traditional Chinese formula, the head is entirely shorn before the head wash. If this is not desirable, make sure the scalp is cleansed as well as the hair.

Wash the scalp and hair with an infusion made from mugwort, garlic, honeysuckle, and broomstraws.

✳ Anti-Sorcery Headwash (2)

1. Moisten your head with warm water but do not shampoo.
2. Blend salt and your regular hair conditioner to form a paste; it should be on the dryer side of moist.
3. Add essential oils of rosemary and ylang ylang.
4. Use this paste to scrub your scalp.
5. Visualize your troubles falling away. Leave it on for as long as is comfortable but try for at least seven minutes.
6. Rinse.

✳ Ash Hex-breaker

Gather fallen ash leaves. Murmur your concerns and fears over them and then take them to the crossroads and disperse them in all directions.

✳ Bamboo Hex-breaker

Inscribe your goal, wish, or prayer onto bamboo wood. Grind it into powder, then burn it to break a hex.

✳ Bastard Cedar Hex-breaker

The bastard cedar tree, also known as West Indian Elm, can allegedly break any spell that any human can create.

Make an infusion by pouring boiling water over seeds and leaves and add it to your bath.

 Cayenne Hex-breaker

Sprinkle cayenne pepper throughout the home to break any malevolent spells.

 Chamomile Hex-breaker

Sprinkle chamomile around the perimeter of your home and property to break spells against you.

Compelling Curse Breaker Spells

Command that hex to bow down and crawl away! Powerful botanicals, like spirits and people, tend to be multifaceted. Strong **Commanding** formulas, most frequently used for *Domination Spells* may also be used for hex-breaking, as they also possess a protective aspect. **Essence of Bend Over** is particularly strong but use whichever formula appeals to you most.

 Compelling Curse Breaker Bath

Massage **Essence of Bend Over Oil** *into your skin and then enter a bath containing salted water.*

 Compelling Curse Breaker Extra Strength

Burn the powder formulation of **Essence of Bend Over** *as incense: allow its aroma to permeate the area and your clothing. Stand over the incense naked and allow the smoke to permeate you as well. Remember to lift up your feet and expose your soles to the smoke.*

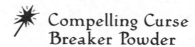 Compelling Curse Breaker Powder

Use this powder to supplement any other hex-breaker spell as an extra magical enhancement. Grind and powder sweet flag/calamus, licorice root, peppermint, and vetiver. Blend with arrowroot powder and dust your body.

 Curse Removal

Legends tell of individuals innocently obtaining objects, typically ancient idols, jewels or magical weapons, marked with a curse. Ever worsening misfortune accompanies possession of the object. Sometimes malevolent individuals give gifts like this on purpose. If you are merely the innocent recipient of this curse (in other words, you're not the one who broke into the tomb, stole the object, and activated the curse), this technique may lift it, enabling you to be safe and perhaps even retain the object, if you still want it.

Pass a handful of salt around the object three times. Then throw the salt into an open fire, without looking into the fire.

 Curse Removal Powder

1. Grind and powder sandalwood, red sandalwood, frankincense, myrrh, and pine needles.
2. Burn the resulting powder on lit charcoal, wafting the smoke as needed.
3. Go to a crossroads and scatter the ashes to the winds in all directions, praying and affirming that the curse is lifted.

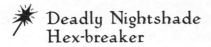 ## Deadly Nightshade Hex-breaker

Allegedly wearing a crown crafted from deadly nightshade leaves breaks a hex. Be careful: deadly nightshade is indeed deadly. Make sure the cure doesn't add to the curse.

 ## Doboru All-Night Vigil

Doboru is the special ritual popcorn dedicated to the Brazilian orixa, Omolu. (See page 559 for more information.)

1. Pop the doboru on a Sunday night so that you are able to begin the ritual very early on Monday, after midnight.
2. Pour the doboru over your naked body.
3. Petition compassionate Omolu to remove and repel all evil worked against you.
4. When you feel the popcorn bath is complete, pick *all* the doboru up and spread it on the ground at a crossroads or cemetery before daybreak

 ## Doll Hex Removal

Just as generally benevolent magical materials (dragon's blood, peppermint, psalms, etc.) can be used to lay a curse, so the items most frequently associated with hexes can also be used to remove and reverse them.

Construct a doll to remove a persistent, stubborn hex:

1. Make a doll to represent you. A doll constructed from rags is fine or whatever you prefer.
2. Pin a name tag on the front and the back of the doll.
3. Blend equal parts **Four Thieves Vinegar** and either spring or some sort of magically charged water.
4. Put the doll in a dish and cover it with this solution. Let it soak overnight. (If it can be exposed to full moonlight, this is extremely beneficial.)

5. In the morning, dispose of the liquid and let the doll dry out in the sun.
6. When the doll is dry, place it on a white cloth.
7. Pour **Uncrossing Oil** or similar over the doll.
8. Wrap it up in the cloth, folding away from you.
9. Bury the doll in the ground, chanting throughout the burial: *"Here I lie! The curse on me dies!"*
10. The spell should leave you and settle into the ground with the doll.
11. Go home. Take purification and protection measures.
12. Keep an eye on that grave. Don't dig it up. You might want to plant protective plants over it, like nettles or a cactus. Feed weekly with *Uncrossing Oil, Black Cat Oil,* menstrual blood, and/or urine.

 ## Doll: Hex-breaker Spell

This doll not only removes a hex—it returns it where it came from. To make a return-to-sender doll, you will need:

> Two pieces of red flannel
> Stinging nettles (for stuffing)
> White paper
> Gloves
> Pen, needle, thread, pins and scissors

1. Pin one piece of cloth atop the other.
2. Draw a simple outline of a human body on the top piece to serve as a pattern.
3. Cut out two figures.
4. Sew the two pieces of flannel together, leaving a small opening at the head. Do not add features or identifying information. This is not an attempt at a hex; it's merely an anonymous return-to-sender, whoever the sender may be.
5. Stuff with stinging nettles. (Wear gardening gloves; stinging nettles have earned their name for a reason.)
6. Sew up the hole.
7. Write *"Return to Sender"* on a tiny piece of paper and pin it to the poppet.

8. Talk to the doll; charge it with its mission.

9. To conclude the spell, either take it to a trash can a distance from your home via a circuitous route and throw it away, or leave it in the center of a four-way crossroads, not too close to your home. Whichever method you use, return via a circuitous route.

Dragon's Blood Bath

There is no essential oil of dragon's blood; create dragon's blood oil by blending dragon's blood powder into jojoba oil. Add this oil to your bath, together with a handful of salt, every day for fifteen days to be rid of a clinging curse.

Dragon's Blood Hex-breaker

Burn dragon's blood resin or powder near an open window for seven consecutive nights at midnight to remove a hex.

Dragons' Tears Bath

Dragons' tears are the name given to annatto seeds. They are a potent dye; the red color will wash off your skin but not towels or other fabrics. Make an infusion by pouring boiling water over dragons' tears. Add it to a tub filled with water and bathe.

Draw Back Evil!

To rid yourself of evil magic:

1. Bring an offering to the Full Moon. This is based on old Mesopotamian rituals: their offerings might include beer, wine, incense, or perfume. Offer what you feel is appropriate.

2. Tell the moon the deep secrets and fears of your heart.

3. Chant:
   Evil Magic, draw back!
   Evil Magic can't come near!

Family Full of Trouble

Sometimes a whole family seems to be under a dark cloud of misfortune. This Romany ritual from Hungary aims to lift that cloud. Central and Eastern European Romany have a concept of "lucky mountains." Specific mountains are believed to be sacred, powerful places. Consider what would be the comparable place for you: a place where Earth's spiritual and magic powers are magnified and accessible.

One person needs to be the ritual leader; the identity of this person may be obvious. If not, one person must be delegated although the other family members must accompany and participate.

1. Approach the power spot.

2. The leader offers a libation of donkey's and sow's milk.

3. One piece of meat is buried for each member of the family (four people, four pieces of meat, for instance).

4. Pray, petition, and visualize the desired outcome.

5. Kindle a small fire.

6. Each person expected to benefit from this blessing/uncrossing spits three times into the fire.

7. Let the fire die out.

8. Collect the ashes, and distribute them in small bags to each member of the family as protective amulets.

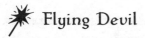 Flying Devil

Considered dependable and fast-acting, this traditional hoodoo formulation is used for uncrossing and to return a hex to its sender.

> Black pepper
> Cinnamon
> Dragon's blood
> Patchouli
> Vetiver

1. Grind and powder all ingredients.
2. Burn them on lit charcoals.
3. Repeat daily for seven consecutive days, for safety's sake.

 Flying Devil Candle Spell

Flying Devil Powder may also be used to dress a candle. Add the blended powder to a mixture of olive and castor oil and rub this mixture onto a candle. Any type of candle may be used although it is believed to be extra effective if it is a black devil figure candle.

 Ginseng Hex Removal

Burn ginseng to break a hex.

 Hermes Hex Removal

The identity of "moly," the plant that preserved Odysseus from Circe's spell, remains hotly debated. Was it garlic? Mullein? Something else? What is certain is that this magical remedy and advice came from the Greek crossroads spirit, Hermes. If you fear that you're under a spell or are in danger of falling under one, petition him for assistance.

1. Explicitly, lucidly, and distinctly, write your question or need on a piece of paper. Leave Hermes as little room for tricks as possible.
2. Erect a cairn of pebbles over the paper.
3. Light a white candle and place it on or beside this cairn.
4. Wait for inspiration—Hermes' voice—to strike.

Hex-breaking Baths

Sometimes it's most crucial to wash a hex off of oneself. Hex-breaking baths may be combined with any other measures or they may be used independently. Follow the magical bathing instructions below to maximize the potential of these baths:

★ *If at all possible, do not strain botanicals from their infused liquids but add everything to the tub*
★ *Submerge entirely at least once, if possible*
★ *Allow yourself to air-dry followed by no further bathing for 24 hours*

 Hex-breaker Bath (1) Agrimony Reversing Spells

The herb, agrimony, is prized in magic circles for its ability to repel and return a hex.

Make an infusion by pouring boiling water over angelica, agrimony, chamomile blossoms, hydrangea flowers, lovage, and either tormentil or five-finger grass. When it cools add everything to your bath.

 Hex-breaker Bath (2) Gentian

Bathe in gentian to break a hex or curse. Use this bath against spells cast by angry ex-lovers.

Hex-Breaker Bath (3) Lemons and Limes

1. Draw a full tub of bath water.
2. Squeeze as many lemons and limes into the water as possible, dropping in the squeezed-out rinds too.
3. Throw in nine bay leaves.
4. Get into the water and bathe, rubbing your body with the fruit.

If you need some inspiration, whether about your situation or who caused it, chew on a bay leaf (but don't actually eat it).

 ## Hex-breaker Bath (4) Lime Bath

A Malay recommendation to wash off an evil spell is to bathe with limes, and to sip the water that slides off your hair.

 ## Hex-breaker Bath (5) Marie Laveau Bath

This spell is attributed to Marie Laveau.

1. Draw a bath of warm water.
2. Make an infusion by pouring boiling water over a dish containing one head of garlic (broken into cloves, but not peeled), one bunch of basil, one bunch of parsley, and one bunch of sage.
3. Let the infusion stand. Do not strain.
4. Add eight fluid ounces (about 250 ml) of geranium hydrosol.
5. Stir in one teaspoon of saltpeter.
6. The bathroom should be cleansed and fumigated.
7. When you're ready, get into the tub: either pour the entire dish of cleaning materials over you or ladle it gradually. Then soak in the tub.

8. Let the water out. Air-dry, let the water dry on you. Don't worry about cleaning up the tub for at least an hour, and preferably wait until the next day.
9. Rub your body with **Bay Rum.**

 ## Hex-breaker Bath (6) Mimosa Magic

A simpler hex-breaking bath involves adding essential oil of mimosa to the tub. Soak in the water and then air-dry.

 ## Hex-breaker Bath (7) Notre Dame

*Add substantial quantities of **Notre Dame Water** to your bath to provide a hex uncrossing. Immerse yourself completely seven times.*

 ## Hex-breaker Bath (8) Seven Waves

Discreetly travel to the sea at sunrise or before, and let seven waves pass over your body.

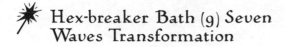

Hex-breaker Bath (9) Seven Waves Transformation

If the ocean is inaccessible or you are unable to go, transform your bathroom into a magical substitute:

1. Pour quantities of sea salt into the bathtub.
2. Add blue and/or green food coloring, if you like.
3. Add quartz crystals to the water.
4. Submerge yourself seven times if possible.

This spell may be enhanced by its dedication to the orisha Yemaya. Build her an altar in the bathroom.

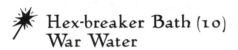

Hex-breaker Bath (10) War Water

War Water *causes hexes but it also repels and removes them. Add* ***War Water*** *to your bathwater. Soak and focus upon your desires.*

Hex-breaker Candle (1)

1. Write out a magical declaration:
   The hex is broken
   The curse is lifted
   I am lucky, happy, fortunate and healthy
   I am free from all evil
2. Carve a red candle as appropriate and dress it with
   Uncrossing Oil.
3. Sprinkle it with powdered agrimony and hydrangea blossoms.
4. Place the candle on top of the paper and burn it.

Hex-breaker Candle (2)

Black candles may also be used to remove curses. This is an entirely benevolent spell; it removes the hex but doesn't reverse it.

Carve a black candle as appropriate to your situation. Dress it with **Uncrossing** *and* **Black Cat** *oils. Roll the candle in powdered hydrangea and burn it.*

Hex-breaker Conjure Bag

Place a piece of broken chain, a piece of jet (a bead or fig-hand), some rue, agrimony, and five-finger grass (or its botanical cousin tormentil) inside a conjure bag. Murmur your desires over it and wear it to break a hex and repel new ones sent your way.

Hex-breaker Incense

Blend bay leaves and sandalwood and burn them together. Waft the fragrance to remove malevolent spells, hexes, or curses.

Hex-breaker Spell (1) Angelica Leaves

Most spells utilizing angelica demand the root; this spell uses angelica's leaves. Place seven angelica leaves in a square of white silk. Fold it or sew it into a packet and wear it over your heart.

Hex-breaker Spell (2) Babylon

Based on an ancient Babylonian spell, this spell is for someone who perceives him or herself as under psychic attack or siege—but doesn't understand why and doesn't know what he or she did (or didn't do) to warrant this punishment. The Babylonians had a tremendous awareness of what we would call "sin," although that doesn't describe it accurately. Spiritual transgression might be a more accurate term: You could "sin" absolutely unconsciously and yet be punished for it. This spell removes that punishment.

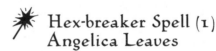

1. Consecrate a fire.
2. The subject of the spell peels an onion and tosses the peel into the fire. (Crying in this spell is good.)
3. Chant incantations in which the undoing of one's "sins" are compared to this activity.
4. Finally the fire is extinguished, as are the person's sins.

✳ Hex-breaker Spell (3) Cast Off Evil

1. Take four candles to a deserted crossroads.
2. Dress three candles with **Protection Oil** and line them up in a triangle shape with the point farthest away from you.
3. Light the candles; petition and pray.
4. Dress the fourth candle with **Uncrossing Oil.**
5. Break it. (You want to snap it with your hands so that it's still held together by the wick, not cut it with a knife so that the pieces are completely severed.)
6. Set the broken candle in the midst of the others and light it.
7. Chant:

   May the evil worked against me be broken and vanish.
   Just as I have broken this candle and it's smoke is vanishing,
   So the evil worked against me disappears in defeat!

✳ Hex-breaker Spell (4) Chili

1. Crush one dried hot red chili pepper using a mortar and pestle.
2. As you grind the pepper, envision the spell breaking, its effects dispersing far from you.
3. Once the pepper has been ground to powder, use it to cast a protective circle around yourself, your bed or your home.
4. Repeat as needed.

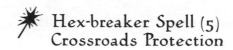

✳ Hex-breaker Spell (5) Crossroads Protection

This spell removes evil caused by malevolent magic or the Evil Eye; it also provides a shield of protection.

1. Take seven small stones from a crossroads.
2. Place them on a censer, in a cauldron or cast-iron pan.
3. Cover the stones with salt, crushed garlic cloves plus garlic peel, onion peel and leaves or shoots, chili peppers and black mustard seeds.
4. Set the botanicals alight.
5. Waft the resulting smoke over the afflicted person.
6. When the material cools off, return the stones and ashes to the crossroads and leave them there. Return home without looking back.

✳ Hex-breaker Spell (6) Pow-Wow Style

This is particularly effective for spells that prevent economic growth and/or stability.

1. Fill a small white cup half full of dirt.
2. Place it in the corner of your bedroom.
3. Pray that Earth absorbs any spells sent against you.
4. Leave the dirt in a corner for a week. Then toss the dirt out of your house, through a back door or window.
5. Wait 24 hours before washing the cup with cold water.
6. Reserve the cup for similar purposes; don't use for regular drinking any longer.

Hex-breaker Spell (7) Salt Bar

Transform a bar of salt into an oil lamp to break the effects of a spell cast against you.

Although you can use any kind of bar soap in a pinch, the spell can be further empowered by carefully considering what kind of soap to use. An olive oil soap, a salt bar, or pure Castile soap may be used, or perhaps an herbal soap containing sage. Soap-makers may be able to craft soap with the **Uncrossing** *or* **Protection Oil** *formulas or with one of the charged waters.*

1. Lay the soap down flat.
2. Drill three holes into it, not going all the way through the soap.
3. Pour oil into each hole. Add a cotton wick.
4. Sprinkle fine salt over the soap.
5. Focus on your desires. Light each wick. Speak your desire out loud.
6. Let the wicks burn out.

You can dispose of the leftover soap or you may wrap it up and save it as a protective amulet, but don't use it for washing.

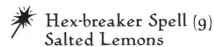 Hex-breaker Spell (8) Salt and Dill

Blend salt and powdered dill. Scatter it around your home, office, property or other vulnerable areas, to counteract any magic worked against you.

 Hex-breaker Spell (9) Salted Lemons

1. You will need a lemon, a dish of salt, **Holy Water** or other charged water.
2. Light one black, one white, and one red candle.
3. Light uncrossing incense.

4. Chant your request for a spell to be broken or for your path to be unblocked.
5. Pass a knife through the incense smoke, hold the blade in each of the candle flames, and then pass it through the water.
6. Slice the lemon into three sections.
7. Dip each into the water, then into the dish of salt.
8. Leave the slices out. When they are completely dried out, you may dispose of them.

If any of the lemon sections start to rot, repeat the spell from the beginning.

Holy Water *will only break the spell; if you're angry and feel it's appropriate to return the hex, substitute* ***War Water.***

 Hex Reversing Psalms

Repeat Psalms 10, 13, 15, and/or 91 to bring about reversal of a hex, focusing upon your desired goals.

 Hydrangea Hex-breaker

This spell focuses on removing the hex only; if you wish to return it, a more complex hydrangea powder may be used. See Reversing Spells, *page 607.*

Grind and powder hydrangea blossoms. Sprinkle around the perimeter of your home, in your clothing, on candles, and on you.

 Jinx Removing Powder

This formula specifically antidotes Jinx Powder, but it is also used to remove any malevolent spells, hexes, or crossed conditions:

Dried ground hydrangea blossoms
Dried agrimony
Dried wisteria

Grind and powder all the ingredients together. Blend with rice powder if a more "powdery" texture is desired. Sprinkle throughout your home, over your thresholds, and wherever you sense vulnerability.

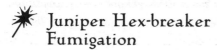

Juniper Hex-breaker Fumigation

Burn juniper berries, fumigating with the smoke, to break a hex.

Kupala's Hex-breaker

Kupala is the Slavic spirit of water, magic, and fertility. The summer solstice is her sacred day. If you can wait that long, Kupala rewards those who honor her by breaking spells cast over them.

1. On the eve of the summer solstice, light a candle in honor of Kupala.
2. Add fresh flowers and a bottle of spring water to a tub filled with water and bathe. (If you have access to spring or lake, this part of the spell may be cast outdoors.)
3. When you emerge from the bath, jump over the candlestick.
4. Allow yourself to air-dry and put on fresh, clean clothes.
5. First thing in the morning roll around in the morning dew so that your clothes and body are suffused with moisture. Visualize all curses and negative enchantment clinging to you being washed away.

Lucky Spirits Oil

Let the spirits break the curse! This oil allegedly sends out an SOS to benevolent spirits. Combine this spell with intensive spiritual petition.

Add essential oils of bergamot, citronella, frankincense, and sandalwood to sweet almond oil. Use this oil to dress candles.

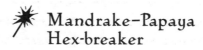

Mandrake–Papaya Hex-breaker

1. Create an infusion by pouring boiling water over papaya leaves and seeds.
2. Add a true mandrake or white bryony root to the water.
3. When it cools, strain out the botanicals. Discard the botanical material, if you choose, however since real mandrake is so rare and expensive, one might prefer to let it dry out for further use.
4. Add the infused liquid to your bath to break a curse.

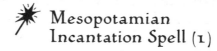

Mesopotamian Incantation Spell (1)

Every power has its place in the cosmos, including yours. This chant from ancient Mesopotamia affirms the value of the individual to the Universe, thus calling on powerful protection and repelling bewitchment.

I am pleasing, I am pleasing
Heaven takes pleasure in me
Earth takes pleasure in me
The ocean takes pleasure in me
The sky takes pleasure in me
[Deity's name] takes pleasure in me
The sun takes pleasure in me
The moon takes pleasure in me
My mother takes pleasure in me
[Ad infinitum …]

Create your own spontaneous chant but conclude with:

May any evil magic on me be dispelled
May any evil magic on me be removed!

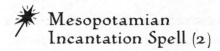 ## Mesopotamian Incantation Spell (2)

Another Mesopotamian anti-malevolent magic formula is as follows:

Evil man
Evil Eye
Evil mouth
Evil tongue
Evil spell
Witchcraft, spit, saliva, evil deeds, evil thoughts
Get out of the house now!

If you suspect the hex was cast by a woman rather than a man, amend first line.

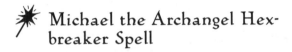 ## Michael the Archangel Hex-breaker Spell

Archangel Michael vanquishes hexes, demons, and curses with his flaming sword. Have you heard the legend that a spell can't be removed if the one who cast it has since died? Or that a hex can't be removed unless you find the object used to cast it? Michael can remove them.

1. Grind frankincense, dragon's blood, and salt and add them to a base of sweet almond oil.
2. Dress red candles with this oil and burn them in petition to archangel Michael.
3. Add some more of the oil to a bath and soak in it, visualizing yourself surrounded by the cobalt light reflected from Michael's sword.

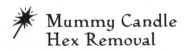 ## Mummy Candle Hex Removal

Inscribe a black mummy candle with your name and identifying information and burn it to break a hex.

 ## Nine Twigs Hex-breaker Spell

Time this spell to coincide with the waning moon. Gather nine twigs, ideally rowan or some other magically protective wood. Whisper your fears over them as well as explicit descriptions of your crossed condition. Burn one twig daily; once the twigs are all gone, the hex should be gone, too.

 ## Poke Root Hex-breaker

The real reason Poke Salad Annie was gathering those greens? Maybe she was really digging up poke roots to break a hex. (Poke root is highly toxic; definitely not for consumption.) This is a strong hex-breaker; use only as needed.

Make a strong infusion by pouring boiling water over poke roots at the New Moon. Wash your home with this infusion to break free from hexes, jinxes, and curses.

 ## Ragweed Spell Repellent

Few modern plants have as bad a reputation as ragweed. Once upon a time, its power to stimulate what is now understood as allergies was considered a testament of its magical powers. Fairies were believed to ride upon ragweed, earning its nickname "fairy's horses." Witches allegedly rode upon it as well, just like a broomstick. Ragweed will not work with everyone; if its presence makes you ill, the plant is telling you something. Choose another spell. However, if you can, carry ragweed to break hexes and repel them.

 ## Rue Hex-breaker Bath

This bath is not safe for pregnant women or those actively attempting to conceive.

1. Create infused oil of rue.

2. During the waning moon, add nine drops of this oil plus a handful of salt to a bath.
3. Repeat for eight more nights consecutively, for a total of nine baths.

Rue Hex-breaker Conjure Bag

*Place a sprig of fresh rue together with a nail or other piece of iron in a red bag. Anoint with **Uncrossing** and **Protection Oil** and carry.*

Rue Hex-breaker Extra Intensive Spell

Vigorously rub a bunch of fresh rue against walls, floors, doors, thresholds, objects, and people as needed to break a malign spell. Simultaneously, command the spell to go away in a firm, angry voice. Shout if necessary. Accompany with prayers, petitions and the recitation of psalms or other sacred verses.

Sloe Hex Fizzle

Sloe berries, the fruit of the blackthorn tree, are used to concoct mixed drinks and break curses. This is a seven-day uncrossing spell.

*Add fourteen sloe berries to a bottle of **Uncrossing Oil**. Burn one berry at noon and another at midnight for seven consecutive days.*

Squill Root Hex-breaker

Hold squill root in your hands and charge it with your desire. Allegedly, if you then carry it with you constantly, all hexes and curses will be broken.

Stinging Nettle Hex-breaker Spell (1)

The princess in the Grimm fairy tale The Twelve Swans *is almost burned as a witch while crafting nettle shirts to break a curse laid on her brothers. It's largely the nettles that condemn her; in Christian Europe, stinging nettles developed powerful associations with witchcraft. Despite the obvious care needed to gather them (wear gloves!), nettles are very beneficial: they are extremely nutritious and can also be used to create a sort of fabric, as in the story.*

If you're willing and able to spin and weave nettles, an effective quick-fix hex-breaker spell exists.

1. Carve a figure candle to represent the afflicted party, whether yourself or another.
2. Spin and weave a nettle shirt large enough for the candle.
3. Literally dress the candle with the shirt and burn *everything* under the light of the Full Moon.

Stinging Nettle Hex-breaker Spell (2)

An easier way to use the hex-breaking power of nettles: grind and powder them (carefully). Blend the resulting powder with graveyard dirt and burn some of this blend, wafting the smoke where desired; carry the rest in a conjure bag.

✷ Stinging Nettle Hex-breaker Spell (3)

This spell removes a hex but also returns it. It's not necessary to know who, if anyone, cast a spell against you: if someone has, the spell will find him or her.

1. Stuff a red cloth doll with stinging nettles. (Wear gardening gloves.)
2. Write *"Return to Sender"* on a slip of brown paper.
3. Pin it to the doll.
4. Dispose of the doll outside your home, returning via a circuitous route.
5. Immediately take cleansing, protective actions.

✷ Sweep Away that Hex!

Based on shamanic ritual, someone else must perform this spell on the afflicted person. Use a pine branch complete with needles to sweep the body from head to toe while murmuring affirmations, prayers, and sacred verses.

✷ Thistle Hex-breaker

1. Spin and weave thistles into *"fabric."*
2. Create a garment from it—any kind—to break a hex. Shirts are traditional, but any garment will do.
3. The entire creation process from start to finish constitutes the spell. The garment is created with *intent*. Once the garment is placed on the body the spell is complete and the hex is broken.

✷ Ti Plant Protection

Ti plant is the sacred plant of Hawaii, not to be confused with either Australian tea tree or New Zealand tea tree (manuka). Ti plant flower essence remedy (FES) helps repel and remove malevolent magic directed to you.

1. Initiate the spell with an intensive bath: add 20–30 drops of the flower remedy to a tub full of water just before bedtime. Pay attention to your dreams. Any subsequent baths should use no more than half-a-dozen drops of the remedy.
2. Follow manufacturer's instructions for internal administration or apply topically until you feel that your curse has been lifted, your spell broken.

Van Van Spell Removal Spells

Van Van Oil is associated with the acquisition of good luck; it can also be used to break a spell of malevolently inspired bad luck.

 Van Van House Hex-breaker

*Add a strong concentration of **Van Van Oil** to floorwash rinse water. Scrub the house with it to remove a strong curse.*

✷ Van Van Personal Hex-breaker

*Van Van can also be used on the individual indirectly by using it to launder clothing. Do not use the oil however. Take the botanicals crafted to create **Van Van Oil** and make an infusion of it instead. (See the* Formulary.*) If using essential oils, these may be applied directly to rinse water. Strain out the botanical material and add the liquid to laundry rinse water.*

 Van Van Uncrossing Oil

*Uncrossing Oil and **Van Van** are combined to break hexes while simultaneously bestowing good fortune.*

1. Grind and powder hyssop, rue, sweet flag (calamus), and peppermint.

2. Add them to a bottle of **Van Van Oil,** together with a bit of broken chain.
3. Bathe in this oil (if you're not pregnant) or use it to dress candles.

 ## Wisteria Hex-breaker

Hold a dried wisteria seedpod in your hands and concentrate on your situation and the desired results. Burn the seedpod to break the hex.

 ## Witchgrass Spell Removal

Pour boiling water over witchgrass to create an infusion. Add the liquid to your bath to break malign enchantment.

Spell Reversals

Spell reversals do more than just break a hex and remove its effects; these spells create a boomerang effect, returning the spell wherever it came from.

 ## Absinthe Oil

This is not essential oil of wormwood! Essential oil of wormwood is among the most dangerous essential oils and should only be used under the most expert supervision (and most experts avoid it!).

Soak wormwood roots, leaves and stems in castor oil. (If you really despise your target, use mineral oil as a base instead.) Castor oil does not flow easily; dilute with jojoba or olive oil as needed. This is an oil of revenge, an oil of justice: it sends harm back to an evil-doer. Secretly apply it to the body of your enemy so that the harm they have caused will revert back to them.

 ## Black Cross Reversing Spell

*Dress a black cross (altar) candle with **Uncrossing Oil** and **Flying Devil Oil.** Visualize the hex leaving you and flying toward its original sender.*

 ## Black Skull Candle

Use a Black Skull Candle to reverse a spell.

1. Carve the candle as desired.
2. Dress with **Flying Devil Oil.**
3. Focus on your hopes and desires as the candle burns.
4. Dispose of the candle remnants outside of your home, returning via a circuitous route.

 ## Black Snake Reversing Spell

Burn black snake candles to reverse a hex. Accompany with prayer, petition, and the recitation of sacred texts. If you feel inspired to hiss, do so.

 ## Blackthorn Reversing Spell

1. Collect five thorns from a blackthorn tree.
2. Create a wax image; it can be a generic image. It doesn't have to represent any specific person. It's not necessary for you to know who wished you harm; if someone did, this spell will find them.
3. Stick one thorn through each hand saying, *"The evil that you have crafted returns to you."*
4. Stick one thorn through each foot saying, *"The evil that you visit upon me returns back to you."*
5. Stick the last thorn into the image's head saying, *"The evil that you think and conceive returns to you."*
6. Burn or bury the image.

 ## Coffin Spell

That little coffin is also used to reverse a spell. Send it back.

1. Create a petite coffin, no more than a few inches long: it may be made from any material but it should be painted black.
2. Focus on the coffin containing the hex that has been placed upon you, rather than the person who sent it to you. Allegedly this spell will reverse the hex without any further action from you.
3. Surround the coffin with small black candles and burn them.
4. Visualize your hex, misfortune, and sorrow burning away, too.
5. When all the candles have burned out, wrap up the coffin together with any wax remnants in a red or black cloth, folding it away from you.
6. Bury or dispose of the spell remnants at a crossroads or a cemetery. Or cremate the coffin, if you prefer.

If you are very sure who cast the spell, the temptation, of course, is to send the coffin back; however, this will inevitably lead to the escalation of psychic warfare. Trust the spell to do whatever is best without further input or destructive behavior.

Draw Back Powder

Combine dragon's blood powder, dried, powdered rue, and dried, ground nettles. Sprinkle this powder around your home to prevent and send back a hex. (At a pinch, sprinkling plain dragon's blood should also be effective.)

Elm Reversing Spell

Elm is a magical tree, associated with both elves and fairies and considered under the dominion of Mother Holle. It may be used to remove and reverse a hex.

Grind and powder elm twigs and leaves. Add it to your bath water to break a hex and return it.

Eyebright Reversing Spell

This spell requires that you know the identity of your hexer although, in theory at least, if you're mistaken, no harm will be done. Blend eyebright with graveyard dirt. Sprinkle on the hex-caster's property to send that spell right back.

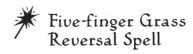 ## Five-finger Grass Reversal Spell

Five-finger grass, also known as cinquefoil, allegedly removes any damage five fingers can create. Burn five-finger grass and allow the smoke to waft over you and around the area to remove a malicious spell.

Foot Track Reversal Spells

If you know or suspect the identity of the person who crossed you, gather all the dirt from their footprint carefully in a bag. Sprinkle it on whatever has been hexed. This is especially effective when there are actual physical manifestations of the hex—actual objects to sprinkle it on.

If you're wrong in your identification of the perpetrator and that person has not hexed you, no harm will be done.

Galangal Root Reversing Spell

Chew galangal root (Chewing John) while intently focused on your crossed condition. (As if you could think of anything else!) When you feel ready, spit the root out hard in the direction the hex came from. If you're unsure who hexed you, spit to the west.

Spell Reversal: Gullah-style

Deliberately, consciously, chew the root Little John to Chew (also known as Southern John, Laos root, or Galangal root). Concentrate on the hex laid upon you, its detrimental effects upon you, and your troubles. Once the root has been reduced to pulp, spit it out vigorously. If you know for certain who laid the trick on you and have an image of that person, you may spit the root toward or onto it.

Reinforce the reversal by carrying a piece of (unchewed) root in a red flannel bag for seven days. Then throw that root on the ground and stamp on it.

 ## Haitian Spell Breaker

This popular spell-reversing formulation is known as Haitian Spell Breaker. It's not completely clear what it has to do with Haiti, other than vetiver is a component and Haiti is the source for some extremely fragrant, beautiful vetiver. Perhaps the formula came from Haiti to become part of the New Orleans voodoo repertoire, which then became part of the general American magic spell repertoire? Perhaps manufacturers of condition oils found the name evocative?

Regardless of its origin, you may use powdered herbs or essential oils.

For a powder-based oil, add sea salt to the following dried and powdered herbs: lavender, lemon zest, peppermint, patchouli, vetiver, and vervain. Mix the powder with almond, palm or jojoba oil.

For an essential oil-based formula add essential oils of lavender, lemongrass, patchouli, peppermint, and vetiver to the oil. Add some salt. Use either dried powdered vervain or the flower essence remedy. (There is no essential oil of vervain.)

Rub the final product onto your body while standing outside under a Full Moon.

 ## Horseradish Hex Reversal

Grate or grind dried horseradish root. Sprinkle it over your thresholds, corners, windows, and any areas perceived as vulnerable, to reverse any malevolent magic cast against a building's inhabitants.

 ## Hydrangea Hex Reversal

Burn dried hydrangea to reverse spells and remove hexes. Blend the ashes with more dried, ground hydrangea and scatter around the home.

 ## Identity Well Known Hex Reversal

To send a hex back to someone you know is hexing you, you will need something that belongs to the person— ideally hair or fingernails, but any object will do.

1. Lay down a black cloth.
2. Put a small mirror onto it.
3. Put the jinxer's personal item atop the mirror.
4. Write their name on a slip of paper.
5. Write your own name over that name, while chanting:
   I cover you, I cross you,
   I cover you, I cross you,
   You put a spell on me,
   Now it returns to you
6. Cover the mirror and paper completely with sea salt.
7. Wrap it up in the black cloth, folding away from you.
8. Bury it at a crossroads, ideally at sunrise, and ideally under the Full Moon.

Kapo's Reversal Service

The Hawaiian spirit Kapo, older sister of famed volcano spirit Pele, is an expert on all sorts of magic, especially malevolent. She's been known to teach hexing skills; she's also an expert on antidotes and removals, too. Matron of powerful Hawaiian sorcerers, she may be petitioned to reverse any spells cast against you.

Kapo is a tempestuous spirit—contact her out of doors, ideally in stormy, windy weather. Tell her what you need and what price you will pay. (Some recommendations if she lifts your spell: learn her sacred rite, the hula, or make generous offerings to preserve Hawaii's wild nature, especially on Kapo's home turf, Molokai.)

Mummy Reversing Spell

Black mummy candles are burned to break a hex, but they may also be burned to reverse one, providing you know who cast it.

Inscribe the candle with the hex-caster's name and identifying information. Burn the candle; while it's burning, tell the mummy what to do. Use simple, commanding language ("Send it back!"); anything too complex will stymie the mummy and neutralize the spell.

Pine Bark Reversal

Reverse malevolent spells by burning pine bark and wafting the fragrance as needed, being sure to permeate yourself with the fragrance. For maximum strength, crumble pine bark into **Uncrossing Incense** or combine with benzoin.

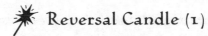 Reversal Candle (1)

A Reversal Candle to reverse a spell cast against you:

1. Get a new seven-day candle.
2. Turn it upside down. Carve the bottom of the candle so that the wick is now exposed and may be lit.
3. Slice the top off the candle so that it can stand.
4. Dress the candle. If you know the name of your jinxer, carve it into the wax.
5. Light the wick and chant: *"Candle, let the evil done against me reverse itself as I have reversed you."*

Reversal Candle (2)

This more complex reversed candle spell derives from Brazil.

1. Fill a cup with dirt.
2. Place a small candle in this dirt and light it. Let it burn for a little while.
3. Abruptly, grab the candle, lifting it from the cup, turn it upside down, and extinguish the lit end in the dirt.
4. Bite the burned end off and spit it out away from you.
5. Light it again and chant:
   As this candle is reversed, so is all evil targeted towards me,
   The flame is dead in the dirt.
   Attempts to oppress me are extinguished!
6. Now let the candle burn all the way down. Place the dirt, the candle stub, and any remnants of wax in a brown paper bag and dispose of them far from your home.
7. Return home via a circuitous route. Complete the ritual with a cleansing bath.

Reserve the cup but use it only for similar purposes. (In Brazil, some recommend that this spell be repeated monthly as a preventive measure.)

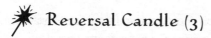 Reversal Candle (3)

This is a reasonably mild reversal; if you were mistaken and there's been no hex, this candle will do no harm.

Carve the top off a white candle, flattening it, and then trim the bottom of the candle so that the wick is exposed and may be lit. Dress this candle with essential oils of patchouli and vetiver to send a hex back where it came from.

Revocation Spell of Elegba

"Revocations" recall, revoke or annul something. In this case, you'd like a curse revoked. Elegba owns the roads, permitting or forbidding passage as he sees fit. So, technically speaking, the hex that reached you did so with his permission. Of course, perhaps that one slipped right by him without catching his attention. Draw his eye toward the hex; explain the injustice and request that he send the curse back to its sender, simultaneously erecting a shield of protection around you.

1. Fill a cup two-thirds full with **Indigo Water.**
2. Top it off with **Florida Water, Flying Devil Oil, Protection Oil, Uncrossing Oil,** and turpentine.
3. As this is being done, petition Elegba, owner of all roads, to send the evil that is afflicting you on its way quickly.
4. Take a small mouthful of rum: hold it in your mouth, then blow it into the cup.
5. Blow cigar smoke into the cup. (If you don't smoke, just waft the cigar smoke over the cup.)
6. Add three nails.
7. Add a camphor square to the cup.
8. Write the name of your enemy, if you know who it is, on a piece of brown paper.
9. Put the paper over the cup with the name facing in.
10. Place a plate on top of it.
11. Quickly reverse the cup so that it is now upside down on the plate.
12. Place this near a door.

13. Knock three times on the floor, calling *"Open the door Papa Legba!"*
14. Place a white candle on top of the cup and burn it. Explain your predicament to Elegba.

Revocation of Archangel Michael

The Revocation of Archangel Michael provides protection and returns a hex.

1. Write your enemy's name on a small piece of paper.
2. Place it inside a glass.
3. Cover the paper with sea salt.
4. Fill the glass with spring water, **Carmelite water,** angelica hydrosol or any combination of these.
5. Cover the glass with a saucer.
6. Turn it over quickly so that it rests atop the saucer, making sure no water spills or leaks out. (If it does, start completely from scratch.)
7. Slice a white candle into nine pieces, pulling out the wicks, so that each becomes a distinct little candle. Every night for nine consecutive nights, place one candle slice on top of the reversed glass and burn it.
8. Petition Michael for assistance while it burns.

Rompe Zaraguey Reversal Spell

Rompe zaraguey is the Spanish name for the herb eupatorium, a close relative of agrimony. Rompe zaraguey cleansing baths are a popular product in spiritual supply stores catering to a Latin American clientele, as it's believed to remove hexes, jinxes, and curses as well as any lingering traces of evil. It will reverse a hex without your knowledge of the sender.

Make an infusion by pouring boiling water over eupatorium. Add to the bath.

Be careful: eupatorium is potentially toxic.

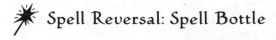 Spell Reversal: Spell Bottle

To send a hex back when you know exactly where it came from.

1. Obtain personal items from your persecutor: hair, nails, what have you.
2. Put them inside a jar or a bottle with a cork.
3. Cut a piece of red flannel into a heart shape.
4. Stick pins into it: visualize all the negative energy and enmity leaving you, like arrows, going back where they came from.
5. Stuff it into the bottle.
6. Add nails, pins, or needles.
7. Throw it in running water, flowing away from you.

 War Water Reversal Spell

*Boil pins or nails in **War Water**. Allow it to cool, strain out the solid material and throw the liquid in your target's home to return a bad spell.*

 Other Direction Reversal Spell

1. To reverse a reverse, put your clothing on backwards.
2. Walk backwards while concentrating on sending the curse back.

Transformation

Living well is the best revenge against a hexer. There are spells to neutralize malevolent magic. There are spells to reverse and send back malevolent magic. However, this spell takes the malevolent energy someone has deliberately aimed toward you and changes it into your chosen good fortune.

1. Hold a small black candle in your hand and envision all the negative effects of the curse that has been laid upon you.
2. When you're finished—and you should really think deeply, even if it isn't pleasant—place the candle on a tray covered with brown paper.
3. Wash your hands by rubbing them with either a salt scrub or dry salt, then rinsing.
4. Hold a white candle in your hands and concentrate on a vision of your life as you would like it to be. See yourself happy, stable, and secure, with all that negative energy transformed into positive.
5. Place this candle on the tray too.
6. Consider what you need to make that happy vision a reality. Write down your requirements or a plan of action on a piece of brown paper.
7. Place a small flat sheet of copper between the two candles, so that one is at each end. (Copper sheets are available through hardware and art supply stores.)
8. Place the paper on top of the copper sheet.
9. Light the black candle and say aloud, something like: *"Negative energy transform into good. Transform into [name your desire]."*
10. Light the white candle and say aloud, something like: *"My dreams and desires are accomplished. Nothing and no one obstructs me."*

Remember, copper is an excellent conductor of heat and energy!

Uncrossing Spells: Removing a Crossed Condition

New Orleans Voodoo and Hoodoo have incorporated Christian iconography in unorthodox manners. Any visit to a spiritual supply store will turn up white candles shaped like crosses or crucifixes. Magic is in the eye of the beholder. These candles may be used in any way that makes sense to the candle burner and so these candles are frequently used as altar candles; however, they're really intended for uncrossing rituals. The terminology derives from that old metaphor about one's cross being too heavy to bear. In hoodoo terminology—and hoodoo is a genre that loves to play with words—this is known as a *"Crossed Condition."* Uncrossing candles, oils, and rituals aim to remove that cross *and* uncross that crossed condition.

A crossed condition may derive from any number of sources, although a malevolent hex is most common. The Evil Eye may also cause it. Uncrossing spells are less concerned with where misfortune came from and where it should be redirected then simply making sure it leaves you for good, although some will reverse a spell. All uncrossing spells are most effective when accompanied by hex-breaking baths, prayer, petition, and/or fervent repetition of psalms.

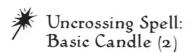

Uncrossing Spell: Basic Candle (1)

How do you get rid of a cross? You burn it. Dress a white cross candle with **Uncrossing Oil,** *light it and burn.*

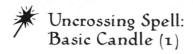

Uncrossing Spell: Basic Candle (2)

Some manufacturers sell special "Uncrossing" seven-day candles.

1. Dress with **Uncrossing Oil** (drill holes in the top of the candle if it won't slide from the sleeve and drip the oil into the holes).
2. Burn the candle.

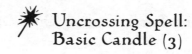

Uncrossing Spell: Basic Candle (3)

Combine a purple candle, indicating personal power, with a white cross candle. Dress both with **Uncrossing Oil,** *burn and pray.*

Uncrossing Spell: Black Cat Candle

1. Dress a black cat or witch candle with **Uncrossing Oil.**
2. When the candle has burned out completely, wrap up and bury any wax remnants, ideally in a cemetery or a very remote location.
3. Mark the spot by sprinkling with asafetida powder.

Uncrossing Oil may be used on any kind of candle for similar results.

Uncrossing Spell: Black Cat

Let a black cat uncross your path. **Black Cat Oil** *is used to attract the opposite sex, garner luck, and break hexes too! Sprinkle it at all entrances to your home to reverse, repel, and remove malign influences.*

Uncrossing Spell: Ending Oil

Almost identical to Evil Eye Oil, this version repels spells set deliberately and ends a crossed condition.

1. Draw three blue crosses onto a white china plate with indigo, food coloring or blue water-soluble ink.
2. Rinse it off completely with water into a container filled with **Van Van Oil.** The crosses must dissolve completely if you anticipate success.
3. Funnel the solution into a bottle and use Ending Oil to massage your body, especially the soles of your feet. You may use it in the bath or on uncrossing candles.

Uncrossing Spell: Gamache-style Candle Spell

Henri Gamache, author and prominent master of magic, may be the pre-eminent influence on modern candle magic; his classic work The Master Book of Candle Burning or How to Burn Candles for Every Purpose *remains an all-pervasive influence, although his name is little known. Gamache's spells are complex enough to require diagrams, simultaneously using various candles and dressing oils. This spell approximates his style although it is not as complex or as detailed as his actual spells. Gamache recommended a combination of the elements water and fire in a seven-day ritual to unblock a crossed situation. This spell for instance uses eight candles and a minimum of three dressing oils, and gives a flavor of his candle magic.*

1. Place four candles on an altar, three white and one black. Light the black candle last.
2. Two cross candles dressed with a **Blessing Oil** are placed on the back corners.
3. Dress a black seven-day candle with **Confusion Oil** and a white seven-day candle with a **Commanding Oil.**
4. While the candles burn, take a hex-breaking bath.

Gamache suggests that the additional candles (not the seven-day ones, which may burn around the clock, should you choose) burn only when the person is bathing, then be extinguished, although this potentially lengthens the duration of the spell. My recommendation is to use a different uncrossing oil or ingredient in the bath daily, including **Black Cat Oil, Four Thieves Vinegar** *and* **Uncrossing Oil.** *Read verses from the Book of Job daily and the crossed condition should be removed by the end of the seven days.*

Uncrossing Spell: Rosemary

This spell breaks a curse and will also lift the Evil Eye.

1. Put nine drops of essential oil of rosemary in a glass of rainwater.
2. Add nine drops of **Uncrossing Oil.**
3. Stir it up and place it in the window. Leave it there for three days.
4. On the fourth day, sprinkle this water throughout the house, concentrating on corners, dark spots, and any areas that feel "creepy."
5. At the same time, add rosemary essential oil and **Uncrossing Oil t**o your bathwater.

Uncrossing Mojo

Add the following to a red flannel drawstring bag: a scoop of crossroads dirt, a rusty iron nail, a small magnetic horseshoe, and a real silver bead or charm. Dress the bag with **Uncrossing Oil** *and carry with you.*

You can incorporate other charms or religious medals as desired.

The plant, wahoo, also known as "bleeding heart" and "burning bush," is indigenous to North America. Once a not-uncommon medicinal herb, European-Americans learned its therapeutic use from Native Americans. Does this famous uncrossing spell also derive from Native American tradition or, replete with Christian symbolism, does the *"wahoo"* verbal component represent an attempt to incorporate the Tetragrammaton?

 ## Wahoo Uncrossing Spell (1)

Wahoo bark may be used to uncross (remove a curse) from oneself.

1. Create an infusion by pouring boiling water over wahoo bark.
2. Bathe your head with the infusion seven times, calling out *"wahoo!"* each time.
3. Reserve the used infusion and dispose of it at a crossroads.

 ## Wahoo Uncrossing Spell (2)

A stronger uncrossing is accomplished if one person performs the uncrossing for the other. Once upon a time every locale possessed a magical professional capable of removing (and perhaps casting) a hex. Choose your person wisely.

1. Create a strong infusion by pouring boiling water over wahoo bark.
2. The crossed person's head is bathed with this infused liquid seven times.
3. Each of the seven times is marked by the healer passing their hands over the crossed person's head (similar to Evil Eye removal) and calling out *"wahoo!"*
4. While this is done, the crossed person stands very still with their arms crossed over their chest.
5. Following the final *"wahoo!"* the healer abruptly pulls the previously afflicted person's arms straight, effectively uncrossing them.
6. The wahoo infusion should be dumped on the ground at a crossroads.

7. Healer and the now uncrossed person should take further cleansing and protective steps to complete the spell.

Witch Bottles

Spells can be cast within fabric pouches, cigar boxes, and furniture cabinets. Once upon a time, spells cast in sealed glass bottles were very popular. Witch bottles, as these spells are known, derive their name from two sources.

The most obvious is that witches were assumed to cast spells using glass bottles. In addition, witch bottles were a popular method of breaking hexes allegedly cast by witches. Whether witch bottles were ever as popular as some claim is worth pondering. They've largely fallen out of favor because, in general, witch bottles favor extremely dangerous methods. Frankly, you're far more likely to be seriously injured from one of these bottles than from a curse. These traditional witch bottles spells are reproduced for historical value only. ***I strongly recommend against casting any of them.*** Safer, modern adaptations are presented following the old ones.

Witch bottles basically exist for one of two purposes:

★ *To provide spiritual protection*
★ *To reverse a malicious spell*

Protection Bottles

 Protection Bottle (1)

To protect against malevolent magic:

1. Place a single castor bean in a small glass bottle.
2. Seal it tightly. Keep one bottle and bean in each room of the house.
3. Replace the beans at every new moon.

Warning! Castor beans are poisonous. Do not leave the bottle where a child or animal (or an unknowing adult) has access to it.

 Protection Bottle (2)

1. Fill a tiny vial with mercury.
2. Seal it tightly shut.
3. Place this bottle inside a second larger bottle or jar.
4. Fill this second container with water and seal tightly shut.
5. Place this second bottle into an even larger jar or bottle.
6. Fill this with sea sand, seashells, and pebbles from the beach.
7. Seal tightly shut and bury it. Traditionally this is buried in the hearth or by the home's front entrance.

Warning! Mercury is an extremely toxic substance.

Spell Reversing Bottles

These are the most famous—or notorious—witch bottle spells. It's hard to imagine that anyone actually cast them, as the potential for harm to those within the spell-caster's house is so strong.

 Spell Reversing Bottle (1)

1. Place nine pins, nine needles, and nine nails in a small glass bottle. Fill the bottle with water and seal it tightly shut.
2. At midnight, place the bottle over the fire.
3. Accompany by burning frankincense. *Don't let anyone stay anywhere near the bottle.*
4. If you know for sure who placed the curse on you, call the name out loud three times and demand that the curse be returned. If you're not sure of the identity, just focus on the spell-reversal.
5. When the bottle explodes, the spell is returned.

WARNING!

The Spell Reversing Bottle spells are dangerous, and involve exploding glass and flying sharp implements. They are included here for historic value only. Please do not attempt to reproduce them.

Spell Reversing Bottle (2)

This version was allegedly used for reversing spells cast through water as well as for reversing unwanted love spells.

1. Place at least a dozen needles or straight pins in a small glass bottle or jar.
2. Fill it with water. (An even more potent version suggests filling the bottle with your urine.)
3. Seal it tightly shut and place it in a pot on the stove or in a fireplace.
4. Heat the bottle until it explodes. The needles and pins will go all over the room. Stay out of the way.
5. Pick up every one of them plus every bit of broken glass, and dispose of them away from the home immediately.
6. Return home via a circuitous route; take a cleansing or protective bath and put on fresh clothing.

If you like the concept of the witch bottle, frankly these modern safer variations are the only ones that could possibly be recommended.

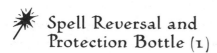 ## Spell Reversal and Protection Bottle (1)

1. Fill a bottle or jar with sharp items: nails, needles, pins, broken glass, etc.
2. Cover it with your urine. You may also add menstrual blood.
3. Seal it shut tightly. (You may want to create a red wax seal as well.)
4. Bury it deep and leave it undisturbed.

 ## Spell Reversal and Protection Bottle (2)

1. Go through your home or any area that you feel has been hexed.
2. Pick up any sharp, stray items you find, such as pins and bits of broken glass, and use these and only these to fill the bottle.
3. Cover with urine and/or menstrual blood, seal the bottle tightly shut and bury deeply.

 ## Hoodoo Jinx Removal

Hoodoo is sensible, practical magic: there are no flying shards of glass, although this method of jinx removal is based on the same theory as witch bottles.

1. Place equal parts, approximately one ounce each, of cornmeal, salt, and your own urine into a can.
2. Put the can on the stove at midnight.
3. Cook it until it's scorched and burned and starts to smell very foul.
4. Dispose of the can and its contents outside your home.

Invisibility and Transformation Spells

Oh, to have an invisibility cloak!

Invisibility spells are the stuff of magic dreams. Who wouldn't want an invisibility cloak or a special potion to render you impervious to sight, for as long as one wanted? Are there such spells? Well, yes and no.

Here's the deal: there are reputedly some excellent, very effective magical invisibility spells; *however*, in general they will not render you literally invisible. What these spells accomplish is a kind of selective invisibility. These spells obscure the vision of those in your midst. You're there; technically you're visible; but somehow people don't notice you, provided of course that you don't draw attention to yourself. If you can be still, these spells permit you to be the proverbial *"fly on the wall"* or to lie extremely low, if that's what's needed. If, on the other hand, you talk, fidget, or generally make a noise, these spells won't work. Stillness, silence, and calm are as intrinsic to these spells as any other ingredient.

 ## Amaranth Invisibility Spell

Weave a wreath of amaranth flowers and wear it to create an aura of invisibility.

 ## Bay Leaf Opal Spell

Albertus Magnus, the thirteenth-century alchemist and magus, recommended wrapping an opal in bay leaves for invisibility. Hold it in your hands for the period you wish to escape detection. Although you will not become invisible, if all goes correctly, on-lookers should be blinded.

 ## Black Box Invisibility Spell

Allegedly this spell enables you to maintain a low profile, especially when there is threat of danger from another.

1. Make a figure representation of yourself (or the person desiring invisibility) from black clay (available from an art supply store).

2. Blend intimate items (hair, fingernail clippings, and similar) into the clay for maximum power.
3. Adorn the figure with black stones—anything other than black tourmaline. Obsidian is an excellent choice.
4. Cover with black feathers or wrap it in black velvet.
5. Place the figure within a small black box or a box made from mirrors or lined with mirrors. (If the box is large, place the figure in the center and surround it with black velvet.)
6. Place the box in a dark, quiet place.

 ## Cat's Eye Invisibility

Charge a cat's eye gemstone with your intent and desire, and then carry it inside a mojo hand to promote invisibility.

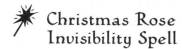 ## Christmas Rose Invisibility Spell

Be careful! Christmas rose, which is really hellebore and not a true rose, is poisonous. Dry the flowers and leaves, and crumble them before you to promote invisibility.

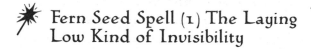 ## Fern Seed Spell (1) The Laying Low Kind of Invisibility

What are known as "fern seeds" are actually spores on the leaves of the common fern. They are easily visible, and to gather them you just scrape them from the leaves. Carry fern seeds in a mojo hand to promote invisibility.

Fern Seed Spell (2) The Real Deal Invisibility Spell

The Fern Seed Spell above has entered the general magical lexicon but actually derives from a more complex magical tradition. The original spell demanded fern seed gathered on Saint John's Eve, and not just any fern seed either. John the Baptist is unusual, as a saint with two feast days—not only the usual anniversary of his death but also his birthday. Allegedly John was born at midnight at the Summer Solstice. According to legend, on the eve of his birth, at the very moment of his birth, ferns bloom and seed. If you can obtain that seed, this will work as a charm to render you truly invisible.

1. On the night of Saint John's Eve, search out growing ferns.
2. Watch them closely.
3. At midnight, if seeds appear, gather them and carry as needed.

Russian magic suggests that the most powerful fern seed, for purposes of invisibility or otherwise, is picked on Bald Mountain on Saint John's Eve. The Synod of Ferrara in 1612 forbade the gathering of fern seeds on Saint John's Eve.

 ## Fern Seed Spell (3) Witch's Privacy Spell

Making less dramatic claims but easier to obtain, the fiddlehead fern also offers a kind of invisibility. Most magical practitioners require secrecy and privacy. Fiddlehead fern (bracken) seed spores allegedly prevent others from observing your personal business.

Gather fiddlehead ferns on Saint John's Eve. Gently, carefully scrape the spores into a thin cotton sachet, and wear this upon your body as needed.

Fumitory-Earth Smoke Spell

Why are there so many "invisibility spells" that aren't true "invisibility" spells? In essence, these are privacy spells and sometimes their effectiveness can mean life or death.

Huge numbers were killed during the Burning Times, the European witch craze. Estimates range from the hundreds of thousands up to millions (lack of consistently accurate records lends itself to debate). At least one town in Germany reportedly had only one woman left in it. Thus the women (and men, too—however victims were disproportionately female) captured, tortured, and killed during the Burning Times reflected a wide variety of backgrounds and experiences, many of course with absolutely no connection with witchcraft.

However, what of those genuinely involved in the broad range of practices that fell under the category of witchcraft? The very actions one believes can save you, perhaps the only actions in one's arsenal, are the very same actions that, if observed, will condemn you to the stake. To be caught walking widdershins around the churchyard, to be seen gathering nettles and mugwort among the ruins where they grow, immediately brands one a witch. Herein lies the paradox of witches' invisibility spells: the great danger of being observed yet the real need for magic in a time of great danger.

Allegedly witches could become "invisible" with **Fumitory** *smoke. Throw* **Fumitory** *in the fire. Let the smoke envelope you, and then quietly and discreetly go about your business.*

 ## Golden Knife Invisibility Spell

Once upon a time the magically correct harvesting of plants meant carefully choosing the right tools. The Druids gathered mistletoe with a golden sickle, vervain with an iron one. Sampson snake root allegedly despises metal; it must be gathered by hand alone or with only the most primitive wood or stone tools. The following specifically directs when and how to gather the needed botanical.

Using a golden knife, gather chicory at either midnight on Midsummer's Eve or noon on Midsummer's day. Dry and preserve it; allegedly carrying chicory promotes invisibility.

 ## Hand of Glory

Although the Hand of Glory is most famous for its sleep-inducing powers, some believe that when carried it also promotes invisibility. A detailed description of the Hand of Glory is contained in Spells for Thieves, *page 1002.*

Heliotrope, as we know it today, is a specific plant indigenous to South America. What the ancient Greeks and Romans knew as heliotrope was any flower that revolved around the sun. Allegedly heliotrope blossoms carry the power of the sun and are thus able to dazzle the eyes of beholders, lending its carrier a certain anonymity.

 ## Heliotrope Spell (1) Bloodstone

Wrap a bloodstone in fresh heliotrope blossoms, and carry it to promote invisibility.

 ## Heliotrope Spell (2) Crystal

To confuse matters further, heliotrope also refers to a type of crystal gemstone, also known as hyacinth, which is of course the name of yet another flower. Heliotrope the gemstone bestows the same powers as heliotrope the flower. So again, carry a heliotrope gemstone to enhance powers of invisibility.

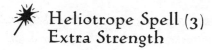 Heliotrope Spell (3)
Extra Strength

For double the power, wrap a heliotrope gemstone in a fresh heliotrope leaf and carry it to enhance your powers of invisibility.

 Heliotrope Spell (4)
Heliotrope Oil

You'll notice that heliotrope spells for invisibility require access to a living plant. This may be equally true for the next spell. There is no commercial source for heliotrope oil. No essential oil is produced; what is commercially available is almost certainly synthetic.

1. Create infused oil of heliotrope blossoms following the instructions on page 31. (Remember it may take as long as six weeks to complete the process. Once completed, however, the oil will grant longer access to heliotrope's magic powers than when you are dependent on fresh blooms.)
2. Anoint a bloodstone or heliotrope crystal gemstone with heliotrope oil and carry it with you.

 Magic Mirror Invisibility Spell

1. Holding a small magic mirror, cast a circle around you. The circumference of the circle may define your area of invisibility so don't make the circle too small.
2. Holding the mirror so that it faces away from you, revolve counter-clockwise.
3. Visualize that those who look in your direction see only the mirror and hence themselves, not you.
4. Step out of the circle: go about your business quietly with calm, smooth, minimal movement. Speaking or abrupt movements break the spell.

 Mistletoe Invisibility Spell

Wear mistletoe around your neck to promote invisibility.

Poppy Seed Invisibility Spell

Soak poppy seeds in red wine for fifteen days. Strain and then drink the wine over a period of five consecutive days. Allegedly once this is accomplished you will be able to make yourself invisible.

Raven Feather Spell

You must be still, quiet and discreet for this method to work. The first step is to practice stillness: try to increase the intervals of time that you can sit completely motionless and silent.

1. Find a raven feather. In order for this spell to work, it must be a freely given raven feather. In other words, you can spontaneously find it but you can't trap the raven or otherwise take it by force. The spell is essentially a blessing from the ravens.
2. Charge the feather with your desire.
3. When you wish to be rendered virtually invisible (unnoticeable) hold the feather in your hand. This doesn't actually make you invisible but promotes the inability of others to see you. This is an extremely effective technique but practice is required.

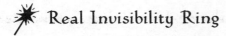 Real Invisibility Ring

Abbot Trithemius of Spandau (1462–1516) claimed to have manufactured a ring that gave the wearer the power of becoming invisible—really invisible. Reproduce if you can and verify whether his claims were true.

1. This ring must be crafted from amber-colored electrum, a natural alloy of silver and gold, favored by the ancient Egyptians. To possess the requisite power certain requirements have to be met:
   - ★ The ring must be cast at the precise time the person wishing to wear it was born
   - ★ It must be inscribed with the Hebrew letters of the Tetragrammaton, the four letters of the Ineffable Name
2. Wear the ring on the left thumb to provide invisibility.
3. Don't hide this ring away when you don't wish to be invisible. Worn on any other finger, it allegedly antidotes poisons. It also changes color in the presence of the wearer's enemies.

 Sea Spirit Spell

No, this isn't a petition to Aphrodite, Yemaya, Thetis, or any of the vast host of sea spirits. Sea spirit is a botanical, a type of seaweed, better known as agar agar, which is the name used to designate the dried product popular in Asian cuisine. In its form as a whole plant, the name Sea Spirit is used instead. Very similar to the raven feather spell, the same ability to maintain silence and stillness is required.

Practice maintaining utter stillness. When you wish to remain unnoticed, hold a bit of sea spirit in your hands and be still.

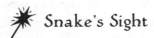 Snake's Sight

Perhaps it's not that you wish to be invisible. Visibility is fine; instead you'd like to be able to see invisible realms.

Allegedly, if you eat the remains of a snake's meal, without bothering the snake, you'll have that power or at least be able to catch a glimpse of the invisible world.

Wolfsbane Invisibility Spell

The poisonous plant wolfsbane, allegedly a frequent component of witches' flying ointments, has powerful associations with invisibility and transformation spells. It's a problematic botanical; although referred to in many grimoires and folk spells, wolfsbane is potentially so toxic that not only must it not be consumed, but even inhaling its fumes or just handling the plant can be extremely dangerous. The safest wolfsbane spell may be this one for invisibility.

Carry wolfsbane seeds in a conjure bag to achieve invisibility, or at least escape other's notice. No need to handle the plant or obtain the seeds for oneself; wolfsbane seeds are available for sale, especially from magical or Gothic-oriented seed catalogs. There's no need to even open the seed packet: place the whole thing within a black conjure bag and wear.

Transformation Spells

The animals that sponsor invisibility magic are cats, ravens, foxes, wolves, and mice. Even though they are present, they can be virtually invisible when desired. Promote your powers of virtual invisibility by emulating theirs.

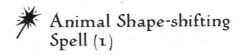 Animal Shape-shifting Spell (1)

The desire to shape-shift, to transform into animal shape, is a relic of shamanism—or stimulus for the art. Most famously incorporated into sorcery and hunting rituals, transforming into a specific animal-shape allows one access to secrets of Earth normally denied to

human beings. Choose your animal based on your desired goals:

★ *Abundance, creativity, and fertility: fish, frogs, cats, pigs, rabbits*
★ *After-life mysteries: bears, dogs, jackals, ravens, seagulls, swans, vultures, wolves*
★ *Occult secrets: snakes, crocodiles (crocodilians pre-date dinosaurs and have survived them. They know everything.)*
★ *Secrets of Earth: badgers, bears, snakes*
★ *Spiritual pursuits: birds, lizards*

The most important thing is to practice! Access the childlike aspects of yourself and play. When you have some privacy, pretend to be the creature you choose. Do this regularly and see what happens.

1. Learn to shape-shift and prevent detection by imitating the creature.
2. Practice "becoming" one or several and see what transpires.
3. For added enhancement, build an animal ally altar dedicated to the creature you choose and request personal assistance and tutoring in your quest.

Don't be surprised if another creature shows up; be prepared for the unexpected. Given the opportunity (and this exercise essentially offers this opportunity) animal allies may reveal themselves in the same manner that orishas, lwas and other spirits take ritual possession of a person.

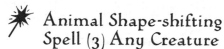

Animal Shape-shifting Spell (2) Russian Wolf

Spontaneous, intuitive practice can teach you to shape shift; however more formal magical techniques also exist. Russian magic has some tips, although gymnastic talent seems to be as much of a requirement as magical. These spells are specifically intended to transform some-

one into a wolf (whether this means a real wolf or a werewolf is open to interpretation).

1. Go into the woods and locate a smooth tree stump. Pay attention to which direction you have used to approach it.
2. Stick a copper knife into the stump.
3. Somersault over the knife.

To transform yourself back to your original form, approach the tree stump from the opposite direction. Somersault backwards. If the knife has been removed, you're out of luck.

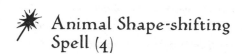

Animal Shape-shifting Spell (3) Any Creature

Another Russian spell apparently allows you to choose what form you will take.

1. Stick twelve knives in the ground at intervals.
2. Somersault over each one.

Again, to transform back to your own form, approach from the opposite direction and somersault backwards.

Animal Shape-shifting Spell (4)

Twist yucca fibers into a hoop. Jump through it to shape-shift into animal form. Jump through it backward to transform back into yourself.

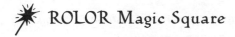

ROLOR Magic Square

Allegedly this magic square enables one to fly like a crow. Will it also transform one into a crow? Experiment and find out.

```
R   O   L   O   R
O   B   U   F   O
L   U   A   U   L
O   F   U   B   O
R   O   L   O   R
```

For maximum effect, concentrate on your desire and hold onto a freely shed crow feather.

Samovila, Matron of Transformation

Samovila, Eastern European deity, leader of the vilas and protector of animals, is a famed shape-shifter. She can transform into whatever she wants; however her most famous forms include a swan, snake, horse, and a whirlwind, the shape in which Russian sorceresses still hide themselves. Samovila, who also serves as a psychopomp, has been known to teach her skills to humans, at least those whom she likes. However, if you've ever harmed animals, if you've hunted without proper magical and spiritual ritual, and especially if you've hunted deer, stay away from her for your own safety.

1. Enter the forest during the Full Moon.
2. Find a natural clearing of trees.
3. Approach Samovila just before dawn, as the moon is departing. Bring her gifts, speak from the heart and request what you need.

Self-transformation Spells

Sometimes the desire for transformation is more subtle than shape-shifting into animal form.

Sometimes one's desire is to completely transform one's basic reality, to *truly* become the person one secretly desires to be.

Self-transformation Spell: Apple Spell

Apples are the fruit of self-transformation and this spell may be used for any kind of transformation.

1. Hold an apple in your hand.
2. Consider who you want to be—or who you truly are.
3. Take as long as you need but don't put down that apple.
4. When you're ready, line up a mirror, a yellow candle and that apple.
5. Gaze into the mirror while the candle burns.
6. After the candle has burned out, consider whether you still desire this transformation.
7. If so, eat the apple.

Medusa's Transformation Spell

Medusa's name derives from a root word meaning "wisdom." Originally a Libyan snake spirit, she is the magical matron of transformation, positive or negative. Medusa enables you to determine who you wish to be and then helps you attain your vision of yourself. This spell is a long-term spell; do it for fifteen minutes at a time. The effect will linger longer. It's most powerful if performed before going to sleep and if you possess a mirror with an image of Medusa on the back.

1. Greek mythology warned that gazing into Gorgon Medusa's face was liable to turn one to stone. Take the chance. Gaze closely at one or more images of Medusa.
2. Now gaze into a mirror.

3. Make faces at yourself, emulate Medusa, but don't look away. Gaze into your eyes and see who looks back. Consider whether that person pleases you or whether you'd prefer to see someone else. Switch back and forth between the image of Medusa and your own until you're sure who you want to be.

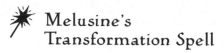

Melusine's Transformation Spell

A not uncommon folk-tale motif describes powerful, magical women who must secretly retreat once a week to spend the day bathing in private. When their privacy is inevitably breached, as it is in these stories, it is revealed that she is really a mermaid in disguise; during the six other days of the week she represses her fish or water-snake tail. In order to survive as a woman or to successfully cohabit with other people, that tail requires a regularly scheduled 24-hour period to emerge. The most famous of these mermaid-women is Melusine.

Once a week, lock the door and forbid anyone from disturbing you. This is your day to be whoever you wish to be, to shed the masks you must sometimes wear, even if these are masks you've chosen and enjoy. Run a fragrant, magical bath for yourself. Spend all day in it, like Melusine, if you like; however "immersing oneself in water" can also be understood metaphorically to mean immersing oneself in magic, spirituality, or women's primal power.

 ## Phoenix Transformation Spell

According to legend, each phoenix eventually explodes in flames, only to be reborn from its own ashes. Sometimes change doesn't come easily. Frankincense is the botanical most associated with the phoenix; according to another legend, perhaps initiated by protective incense merchants, frankincense was a magical substance, a gift from the phoenix, which carried it to people in its talons.

Surround yourself with the aroma of frankincense (resin or essential oil) to assist and ease inner and outer transformation.

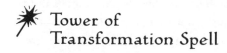

Tower of Transformation Spell

The Tower tarot card indicates unpredictable events that shake one's reality and self-identity. Rebirth, as the phoenix surely knows, may be periodically necessary and ultimately beneficial, but it rarely comes without pain.

Contemplate the Tower tarot card (some older decks name this card The House of God) while burning cinnamon and frankincense. Sleep with the card under your pillow.

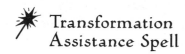

Transformation Assistance Spell

Not all transformations are easy, physical, self-initiated or voluntary. Life has a way of forcing us to grow and transform whether we choose to or not. Helichrysum, also known as everlasting, assists the process of emotional transformation as well as providing the illumination that enables the metaphoric caterpillar to transform into a butterfly. Add essential oil of helichrysum to an aroma burner and inhale its fragrance as needed. For more direct application, add a few drops of the essential oil to your bath or to massage oil.

Werewolf Spells

Fear of werewolves once ran rampant throughout Europe, causing panic and persecution. Between 1520 and 1630, there were thousands of werewolf trials in France alone. If those burned as witches were disproportionately female, those condemned to die as werewolves were disproportionately male.

The tendency when considering trials for witchcraft, consorting with fairies and werewolves is to mock and denigrate the intelligence of the hunters and inquisitors. What idiots could believe in werewolves and witches? If our ancestors had the intelligence, education, and *rationality* of modern people, or so the thinking goes, these tragedies would never have occurred. The issues are more complex; it's not a coincidence that the werewolf-craze was concurrent with the witch-hunts.

What are werewolves anyway? Werewolves in stories and movies are inevitably tortured souls, unable to control their actions at the Full Moon. Why ever would anyone wish to be one? However, werewolves can be understood, not in terms of Lon Chaney and Hollywood movie werewolves, but as relics of shamanism, as worshippers of shape-shifting lunar deities, especially Diana whose worship was once prevalent throughout a great swathe of Europe. The shamanic werewolf is not out of control but in perfect harmony with the moon, planet of magic.

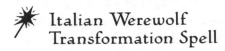

Basic Werewolf Transformation Spell

This spell will only work if you love *the moon and wolves.*

Stand outside so that you're bathed in the light of the Full Moon. Some might suggest you undress completely, although depending where you live, this may be unrealistic. Carefully choosing your adornment—a crescent pendant, or a wolf T-shirt for example—may assist the transformation. Gaze at the moon and howl.

Diana Altar

1. Create an altar to Diana: decorate it with images of the moon, the forest and her favorite animals: hounds, wolves, and deer.

2. Place a dish of water or a mirror onto the altar to represent Diana's sacred spring: if you can, position it so that it reflects moonlight.

3. Gaze at the altar and howl.

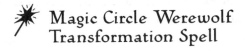

Italian Werewolf Transformation Spell

The wolf, now virtually extinct in Italy, was once the totem animal of Rome, sacred to many Italian deities including Diana, Faunus, Feronia, and Mars. This spell is reminiscent of shamanic initiation rituals; although not specified, presumably one should fast or otherwise purify oneself in the days leading up to the spell.

Sleep outside during a Full Moon Friday. You will either transform into a werewolf or be attacked by one.

Magic Circle Werewolf Transformation Spell

This method underscores the reality that historically those condemned as werewolves were virtually always men.

1. Get undressed under the Full Moon.

2. Concentrate on your goal. With this fixed in your mind, urinate while revolving in a circle. This allegedly activates the transformation.

3. Leave your clothes in the circle. When you wish to transform back, return to your clothing, urinate while revolving in the opposite direction, get dressed and go home.

Werewolf's Full Moon Ointment

Movie werewolves transform involuntarily at the Full Moon, inevitably during a first date or while baby-sit-

ting or some other embarrassing, inconvenient moment. Wouldn't you think they'd invest in a decent Almanac listing accurate moon phases? Real life werewolves allegedly sometimes created ointments, similar to witches' flying ointments, to aid in transformation. Also like witches' flying ointments, many of these formulas were highly *toxic* and skin irritants to boot. Stick to howling at the moon; do not attempt to reproduce this spell.

1. Go to the woods during the Full Moon with your cauldron and supplies.
2. Cast a circle around the cauldron.
3. Typical werewolf-transformation ingredients included belladonna, hemlock, henbane, opium, wolfsbane, and the surprisingly innocuous parsley.
4. Smear the body with the resulting salve and wait.
5. Either transformation should occur or a spirit will arrive to provide guidance.

Werewolf Safety Spells

You're not buying that line about werewolves not being out-of-control? Perhaps you're right. Perhaps werewolves, like Dionysus' maenads, are so completely transformed that they're incapable of controlling themselves during ritual possession. Silver bullets hurt people. Luckily, other spells to keep one safe from a werewolf exist too.

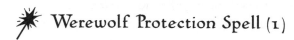

Werewolf Protection Spell (1)

Should you encounter a werewolf, calling out his or her real name provides you with safety.

Werewolf Protection Spell (2)

This spell protects you so that you can sleep while the werewolves are out on the prowl. Keep a mirror by your bedside alongside sharp iron or steel implements like a knife or scissors (keeping doors and windows locked might not be a bad idea, either). Should a werewolf show up the sight of these objects (or presumably his own image in the mirror) is either enough to transform him back into a person, or at the very least make him leave and find another victim.

Werewolf Protection Spell (3)

Safety-pin fresh rue to your clothing to protect yourself against rampaging werewolves.

Wolfsbane

Wolfsbane is among Hecate's sacred plants, however it earned its name because it was used to poison Europe's once plentiful wolves, now virtually eradicated. Werewolves allegedly avoid it, and so grow wolfsbane in the garden to prevent werewolves from visiting. Wolfsbane can be beautiful and is a component of the traditional poison garden. However, it is poisonous and although werewolves know to avoid it, children may not.

✪ Love Magic: Spells for Romance, True Love, Seduction, and Sex

The universal stimulus for magic, there are more love spells, more different types of love spells than any other kind of magic. There are spells to find love, lose love, repair love, and to discourage one love but encourage another. Basic Love Spells are grouped together, followed by more specialized concerns:

★ *Binding Spells*
★ *Break-Up Spells*
★ *Fidelity Spells*
★ *Love Potions*
★ *Notorious Potions*
★ *Heartbreak and Disappointment Spells*
★ *Sex and Seduction Spells*
★ *Male Virility Spells*
★ *Summoning Spells*

Some of these spells are a lot of trouble to cast. Some may be perceived as "*disgusting*" or demand that the spell-caster do humiliating or unpleasant things. Although theoretically most spells are cast in secret, in many cases, it's almost impossible for the target of some genres of love spells not to know a spell has been cast or at the very least to think that you're doing something crazy. (Consider the spell that demands that you bathe the spell target's private parts with a potion while they sleep: how can the other party not wake up mid-spell?)

There are two things to remember: first, it can be very flattering to have someone go through so much trouble out of love and desire for you. This may even account for a portion of the effectiveness. And second, spells that are a lot of trouble, particularly those that are a lot of trouble over an extended period of time, invite you to examine the crucial question, is he or she worth it? Particularly with binding spells where you are, in effect, binding yourselves together for eternity, if it's too much trouble, maybe you shouldn't be performing a binding spell.

Basic Love Spells

These are spells to find new love as well as preserve and protect existing romance.

TIPS FOR SUCCESSFUL ROMANTIC MAGIC

★ TIMING: In general, all things being equal, a Friday coinciding with a New Moon is considered the most auspicious time to perform love spells. Fridays in general are the best days for love spells. The day is named in honor of Freya, Northern Lady of Love. It is also the day associated with other powerful spirits of love, Aphrodite and Oshun

★ COLORS FOR LOVE MAGIC: Yellow, orange, pink, and red

★ NUMBERS:

    Two: the standard number, for the obvious reason

    Five: if you'd like to invoke the power of Oshun, Orisha of Love

    Six: if you'd like to invoke the power of Aphrodite, Lady of Love

    Eight: if you'd like to invoke the power of Inanna-Ishtar, Queen of Heaven. Eight is also the number of infinity and eternity

★ Bathe your hands with rose water prior to mixing up any love potions or powders to intensify their effects

★ If you find that your love spells are consistently not working, place a strand of your target's hair under a continuously dripping faucet to magically wear away resistance

Adam and Eve Root Spells

Adam and Eve is the name given to the roots of the family of orchids that grow from a pair of conjoined roots. The root has two forms, male and female (hence Adam and Eve), believed to resemble the respective genitalia. Once upon a time they were extremely popular, advertised in the backs of comic books and commonly sold as curios in spiritual supply stores. Today, the plants are endangered and the roots are thus very scarce. They are considered very powerful and are featured in many love spells.

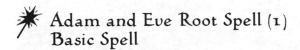

Adam and Eve Root Spell (1) Basic Spell

Carry the roots in a mojo hand. Take them out periodically, hold them in your hand and charge them with your desire.

Adam and Eve roots like their private time together; they don't play well with other botanicals. Don't add other roots or plants to an Adam and Eve conjure bag.

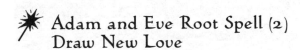

Adam and Eve Root Spell (2) Draw New Love

Begin this spell at the new moon to draw new love into your life.

1. Choose Adam and Eve roots to represent the appropriate gender and dress them with love-drawing oil, something like **Come to Me Lover.**
2. Place the roots facing each other on opposite ends of a mirror.
3. Each night, dress the roots with an additional drop of oil and move them a little closer to each other. They should be touching when the full moon arrives.

If you are unable to find Adam and Eve roots, substitute lodestones or figure candles.

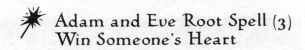

Adam and Eve Root Spell (3) Win Someone's Heart

This is not a spell for casual relationships; it's essentially a commitment charm.

1. Give the appropriate root to one you desire: an Eve root to a woman, an Adam to a man.
2. You keep the other.

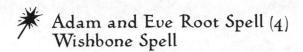

Adam and Eve Root Spell (4) Wishbone Spell

Instead of breaking a wishbone, preserve it in a conjure bag to help make your wish for true love a reality.

1. Clean and dry a wishbone.
2. Decorate it with red or gold glitter glue. (Or dip it into glue and then into powdered glitter.)
3. Make a braid from a few strands of your hair and tie it to the wishbone.
4. Place these in a red charm bag together with an Adam and Eve root.
5. Sprinkle everything with a love drawing powder.

Amber Spells

Virtually every mythological explanation for amber's origins involves a love story.

Beautiful Freya is the Norse spirit of love. Like many another Genius of Love, Freya knows all about the topic because she hasn't been so lucky. One day, her beloved husband just left. The tears Freya weeps turn to amber. According to Lithuanian legend, Juraste, a mermaid princess betrothed to the King of the Sea fell in love with a mortal fisherman and brought him to live in her underwater palace made of amber. When her father the thunder god found out, he blasted her palace to bits and chained her to the ruins. Amber washing to the shore commemorates her forbidden love. Another Lithuanian legend is happier: a mermaid prince fell in love with a mortal woman, Amberella, bringing her to spend happy eternity in their immortal life beneath the sea. Although she found true love, occasionally Amberella has regrets: when this occurs she sends gifts of the precious resin to the people she left behind.

Amber is potentially a powerful love charm, although you may have to activate that potential. Romany magical traditions particularly value amber as a love-drawing charm.

✸ Amber Charm (1) Romany Dreams of Desire

1. On a Thursday night, make a list of the qualities you desire in a romantic partner or visualize and name a specific person. Before you go to sleep that night, leave a piece of amber by your bed or under your pillow.
2. On Friday morning, first thing upon awakening, clutch the amber in your left hand, holding it close to your heart.
3. Close your eyes. Visualize your desire: make it as real and tangible as possible. Take as much time as you need.
4. Kiss the amber and wrap it up in a small piece of silk, wrapping or rolling toward you.
5. Keep this with you for seven days, carrying it by day, sleeping with it at night, beside your heart, between your breasts, wherever.
6. Repeat the process every morning. At the conclusion, you will have a highly charged love-drawing amulet.

✸ Amber Charm (2) Romany Magic Mirror

This spell creates a small, unbreakable variation of a magic mirror.

1. Look at the full moon through a piece of amber, holding it in your left hand and focusing on all your heart's desires.
2. Place this under your pillow before you go to sleep.
3. When you awake, you will have a potent love charm. Use it to draw those desires to you. Replenish its power by repeating the ritual at subsequent full moons.

✸ Aphrodite Oil

Add essential oils of myrtle and rose to a base of sweet almond oil. Add to a bath, or use as a massage oil or on candles honoring and petitioning Aphrodite.

The arrows of love go straight to the heart, and arrows are frequent components of love spells.

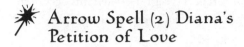

Arrow Spell (1) Arrow of Love

A spell intended to arouse passionate love from a woman is adapted from the great scholar of magic and spirituality, Idries Shah, who in his turn adapted it from the ancient Sanskrit magical text, the Atharva Veda. *Kama, Hindu Lord of Love, wields a bow and arrows, just like his European counterparts Eros, Amor, and Cupid. The spirits referred to in the incantation, Mitra and Varuna, are legendary soul mates, each the other's perfect complement.*

1. Craft a ritual arrow, accompanied by the following incantation. The incantation, reminiscent of Aretha Franklin's song, "Dr. Feelgood," is chanted repeatedly while the arrow is made.
2. Insert the target of the spell's name into the chant; personalize it as you desire.
   With this all-powerful Arrow of Love, I pierce your heart
   Love, love that causes unease, love overcomes you
   Love for me!
   This arrow, flying straight and true
   Strikes you with burning desire for me and me alone
   My love is its point
   My determination to possess you is its shaft
   Your heart is pierced!
   The arrow has struck home
   This arrow overcomes your reluctance
   You love me now!
   Come to me lover!
   Submissive, without pride as I have no pride
   But only longing for you
   Your mother can't stop you from coming to me
   Your father can't stop you from coming to me
   Your sister can't stop you from coming to me
   Your brother can't to stop you from coming to me
   Your friends can't stop you from coming to me
   You are completely in my power!
   Oh Mitra, Oh Varuna!
   Strip [Name], *daughter of* [Name] *of resistance*
   Only I have power over the heart, soul and mind of
       [Name], *daughter of* [Name] *my beloved.*

3. Once the arrow has been crafted, the maker holds it and gestures with it, setting up the magical vibrations, all the while continuing the chant.
4. Repeat from step 3 as needed.

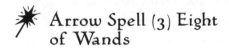

Arrow Spell (2) Diana's Petition of Love

Diana, the Roman lunar goddess and mistress of magic, to whom this spell is dedicated, has excellent archery skills. Don't try this spell unless your skills are worthy of the goddess. The spell requires that you shoot a flaming arrow. This is potentially a dangerous spell for more than one reason. Diana will not look favorably upon your petition if you burn down her forest.

1. Write out your petition of love.
2. Affix it to an arrow.
3. Set the arrow aflame.
4. Quickly shoot it towards the moon.

Arrow Spell (3) Eight of Wands

One of the traditional meanings of the eight of wands tarot card is love at first sight. The eight wands represent the arrows of love.

1. Carve and dress a red candle as desired, using love-drawing oils.
2. Burn the candle.
3. Place an eight of wands Card upright near the candle so that it is easily visible.
4. Place a rose quartz beside the card and candle.
5. Once the candle burns down, place the card underneath your pillow so that it can provide romantic insight and inspiration while you sleep.
6. During the day wear the rose quartz in a charm bag, pocket or tucked into your bra to attract and maintain the love you desire.

Basic Botanicals of Love

Although there are many plants associated with love and romance, the following have all earned a powerful reputation as love-drawing botanicals. In combination they're even more potent. Incorporate them into your spells as inspired: basil, carrots, catnip, chamomile, cardamom, coriander, cubeb, gardenia, grains of paradise, hibiscus, hyacinth, iris, jasmine, lady's mantle, lavender, lovage, mint, onion, orchid, poppy, rose, rosemary, Saint John's Wort, southernwood, strawberries, thyme, tormentil, vervain.

Surround your home with one or more of these living plants as an open invitation to true love.

Basic Botanicals of Love Candle Spell

1. Select basic botanicals of love that please you.
2. Choose a pink, red, yellow, or orange candle.
3. Hollow out the base and pack it full of botanicals.
4. Burn the candle.

Bethroot Love Spell

Rub a bethroot (Low John the Conqueror) over one's naked body to attract romance.

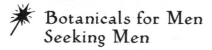

Botanicals for Men Seeking Men

The botanicals hyacinth, deer's tongue, and Sampson snake root are believed to hold special affinity for gay men. Place the three botanicals within a charm bag and carry to attract love. The bag is most traditionally worn against skin, within underwear.

Birch Spells

Birch is the tree of new beginnings and is used to magically draw and initiate new relationships.

Birch Love Candles Spell

Dress candles meant to draw love with oil of birch.

Birch Message of Love

Birch bark was traditionally used to craft "paper" in North America and Russia. Find a shed piece of bark or request one from the tree. (Give the tree a chance to say no.) Offer a libation. At the New Moon, write a message in red on white birch bark. Prick your little finger for a few drops of blood or use one of the magic inks in the Formulary. Write your hearts desire, "Bring my true love to me," or whatever you like. Then burn the message.

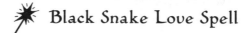

Black Snake Love Spell

Carry a black snake root (Senicula) within a red bag to attract a lover.

Bouquet Spells

Presenting someone with a bouquet of flowers was once a method of delivering a spell right into your target's hands. The "Language of Flowers," whereby each type of flower represents a specific message, originated in the harems of the Middle East, where secrecy regarding romantic intrigues was crucial. That floral code would ultimately be formalized in Victorian England. Some floral bouquet spells, however, transcend any code.

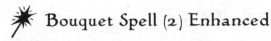 Bouquet Spell (1) Basic

The simplest, yet extremely effective, love spell is the gift of roses, either one single bloom or a bouquet of a dozen.

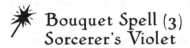 Bouquet Spell (2) Enhanced

Combine roses with myrtle for an especially powerful bouquet. Both plants are sacred to Aphrodite, and together they transmit her power and beseech her blessing. For extra enhancement, combine with conscious petition to Aphrodite.

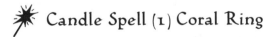 Bouquet Spell (3) Sorcerer's Violet

The addition of vincas, also known as the sorcerer's violet, transforms any bouquet into an instrument of seduction.

1. Sprinkle a bouquet of romantic flowers with dried powdered vinca flowers, the sorcerer's violet.
2. Give them to the woman you want.

Candle Spells

Candle Spell (1) Coral Ring

1. Ring a gold candle, a red witch candle or a candle in the shape of a heart with pieces of coral.
2. Surround this ring with another circle of small red or pink candles.
3. Visualize the fulfillment of your desire.
4. Light the central candle first, then light the rest.

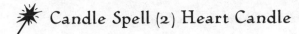 Candle Spell (2) Heart Candle

1. Scratch your lover's initials into a heart-shaped candle.
2. Dress it with love drawing oil and sprinkle with a love drawing powder.
3. As it burns, chant:
   As this candle burns, so your heart burns with love for me
   As this wax melts, so your heart melts with love for me
   When this spell is complete, your heart belongs to me!

Candle Spell (3) New Moon

This spell is most effective if using handcrafted candles, because you can actually embed the magical material into the wax. However, a store-bought candle may be doctored as well.

1. Prepare the candles so that this spell is ready to begin in conjunction with the New Moon.
2. Make two wax figures or purchase figure candles to represent you and your beloved.
3. Place a few strands of his or her hair in the candle representing the other party. (Pubic hair is most powerful, with underarm hair a close second. However if all you have are a few strands picked off a jacket, this will do.)
4. Place a few of your own hairs in your candle.
5. Begin burning the candles at the New Moon. Face the candles across from each other. Burn them in timed increments, a little bit every night, gradually bringing them increasingly closer and closer to each other.
6. When the candles are finally touching, let them burn all the way down, so that the waxes intermingle.
7. Any remaining wax can be saved as a love talisman, especially if it's melted into an auspicious shape.

Win Your Heart Candle Spell

This spell allegedly enables you to win the heart of the one you desire.

1. Carve your name and that of the desired party nine times each on one pink seven-day candle.
2. Gently warm honey in a bain-marie and then blend in rosewater and powdered orrisroot.
3. Roll the candle in this mixture and then burn it.

 ## Chamomile Wash Spell

Wash your face and hair with chamomile hydrosol or infused water to attract true love.

Copal Spells

Copal is resin deriving from trees held sacred in the Aztec, Mayan, and Incan traditions. Most frequently used for spiritual, cleansing, and oracular purposes, copal, like those other sacred resins frankincense and myrrh may also be used to draw romantic attention from the opposite sex.

 ## Copal Spell (1) Basic

1. Obtain a solid lump of copal, rather than copal that's been already ground into powder for incense.
2. Carry the lump in your pocket or in a charm bag, especially when the opportunity to meet someone arises.

 ## Copal Spell (2) Locket

1. Grind a lump of copal into powder using a mortar and pestle, visualizing your desires coming true while you're grinding.

2. Carry a sprinkling of powder inside a locket around your neck.

 ## Dandelion Love Letter

Blow on a dried dandelion's head and scatter the seeds to the winds? Most people do it for fun, however the dandelion will also provide magical messenger services. Allegedly the seeds will carry loving messages and wishes to the one you love. Focus hard on your desire and blow!

Doll Spells

The description *"doll spell"* tends to invoke images of stereotypical *"voodoo dolls."* However the use of dolls in magical spells is incredibly ancient and fairly universal. Dolls are used for hexing but they're also used for healing, protection, fertility, and romantic spells. The piercing of wax figures with pins goes back at least as far as ancient Egypt, however those pins weren't meant to cause bodily injury. Instead they were intended to stimulate pangs of love and desire from whatever part of the body was pierced. Methods of piercing are frequently more inventive than just sticking needles into the doll.

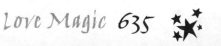

 ## Doll Spell (1) Binding Spell Soft Dolls

The advantage of these doll spells over some other binding spells is that these spells aren't permanent. Should you change your mind about this romance, just separate the dolls to terminate the binding effect.

1. Create a pair of dolls from fabric, one to represent each partner.
2. Stuff them with dried love-herbs (see page 633 for some recommendations).
3. Rub them with aromatic romantic oils.
4. Dress and ornament them. Add beads if possible, forming a knot with every bead.
5. Tie the dolls together, face to face, to protect and preserve romance.
6. Wrap them in fabric and keep them in a safe place, for as long as you wish this romance to last.

Doll Spell (2) Binding Spell Hard Dolls

1. Create two small dolls from a hard material: roots, wood, or bone.
2. Embellish the dolls: decorate with beads and fabric.
3. Anoint with love oils and with any available sexual fluids.
4. Bind them together with red cord, creating knots.
5. Hide them safely, for as long as you wish the romance to last.

Doll Spell (3) Go Fetch!

Who says figures have to be human? In this spell a paper dog is charged with fulfilling your romantic desires. Japan possesses its own genre of paper magic. Instead of imbuing the paper with sacred images or with words to be preserved, posted or destroyed, the paper itself becomes the medium for magic. Beautiful, handcrafted

paper is carefully manipulated into different shapes, including figures just as powerful as those made from wax or clay.

1. Articulate the purpose of the spell. What exactly do you want the little dog to bring home to you?
2. Roll and twist two small pieces of paper into a ribbon, then manipulate it into a dog shape (or the best that you can do).
3. Stick a needle into its upper left leg, where the thigh should be.
4. Talk to the dog, explain that the needle will not be removed until your desire is fulfilled. However if it is fulfilled you will feed the image food and saké or whatever you think this little dog likes.
5. Place the image on a shelf or in a cabinet and remember to deliver its offerings if your desire comes true.

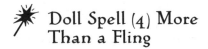 ## Doll Spell (4) More Than a Fling

To turn a sexual relationship into something more:

1. Cut out dolls to represent each party from an unlaundered bedsheet, stained with sexual fluids.
2. Personalize as much as possible. Embroider or draw names onto the dolls if secrecy isn't an issue.
3. Fill each poppet with love-herbs: roses, rosemary, orrisroot, heartsease, and vervain.
4. Bind the dolls together, face to face, belly to belly with scarlet ribbons.
5. Wrap the dolls in red or black velvet.
6. Slip this packet under the mattress on the side the other party usually sleeps on.

 ## Doll Spell (5) Pierced Doll

Perhaps for secrecy's sake, the original version of this fifteenth-century spell to evoke a woman's love was written backwards in a blend of Hebrew and Yiddish.

1. Craft a female figure from virgin wax. Emphasize the female parts of the anatomy; try to make it resemble the object of your intentions. Carve her name over the doll's breast and onto her back, between the shoulders.

2. Chant:

   May it be your will, Oh God
   that [Name] daughter of [Name]
   burns with passion for me and for me alone!

3. Bury this figure in Earth for 24 hours, being careful not to damage it.

4. Dig it up and hide it under the eaves of a house, covered with a stone for 24 hours.

5. Disinter her yet again.

6. Dip her in spring water three times, ritually invoking a different archangel each time: Michael, Gabriel, and Raphael.

7. Finally, dip the doll into your urine.

8. Dry her gently. The doll is complete.

9. When you wish the woman she represents to feel the pangs of passion for you, pierce appropriately.

 ## Doll Spell (6) Pinned through the Heart

1. Make a doll from malleable materials, such as wax, clay, dough, or similar.

2. Personalize it: if you possess any intimate items, incorporate them into the doll. Otherwise, decorate as you please.

3. Scratch a name onto the doll or pin a name-tag on it.

4. Push a brass pin or an ornamented hat-pin (especially one with a romantic motif) through the heart. This pin is thought to open the heart and induce love for the maker of the doll.

 ## Doll Spell (7) River Spell

In ancient Egypt, the figure in this spell would have been created from Nile clay, which was perceived to have magical connections with various spirits of love, especially Isis and Sobek. Enhance the power of your spell, by invoking Isis or any another riverine love spirit: Aphrodite, Maitresse Ezili, Oba or Oshun. Mermaids, whether specific ones like La Sirene or just as a generic power, may also be invoked.

1. Create a figure from clay, making it resemble the object of your desire as much as possible. If you possess any intimate items, such as hairs or nail clippings, these may be incorporated into the doll.

2. When you are ready, stick needles in all the areas where you wish him or her to desire you.

3. As you pierce, announce aloud: *"Your heart feels pangs of love"* or *"Your ears burn for the sound of my voice"* or similar. Be creative; express your desires explicitly.

4. Massage the doll with a soothing but erotic oil, but do not remove the needles.

5. Write love spells or your wishes and desires on fine paper.

6. Attach this note to the doll with the protruding needles.

7. Wrap everything in a cloth and bury in Earth, ideally by a riverbank.

Fairy Knot Spells

There's a Romany belief that fairies sometimes tie knots in the boughs of willow trees. These knots are a powerful source for love magic. Should you find such a knot, preserve it.

 ## Fairy Knot Spell (1) New Love

If you desire someone, sleep with the knot under your pillow.

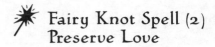 ## Fairy Knot Spell (2) Preserve Love

Use your knot to preserve an already existing love:

1. Dress the knot with love oils.
2. Make a braid from a few strands of your hair and that of your lover.
3. Tie it to the knot with red thread, place it inside a red silk conjure bag and keep it safe.

Should you ever change your mind about this romance, untie the willow knot.

 ## Friendship into Love Spell

Turn friendship into something more:

1. Obtain a Lover's Candle, a usually red candle depicting an entwined naked couple or, if you're a candle-crafter, create one of your own.
2. Carve the woman's name on the man's body and the man's name on the woman's.
3. Anoint with the love oil you like best **(Amor, Jezebel, Come to Me Lover!** for instance) and burn the candle.

 ## Forget-Me-Not Spell

Slip a forget-me-not into someone's pockets so that you will remain on their mind.

 ## Freya's Love Spell

Cowslips, the wild primroses also known as fairy cup, are Freya's sacred flowers.

1. Collect cowslips in the morning, still wet with dew.
2. Put them in a pot of clean rainwater.

3. Murmur your desires and intentions over them.
4. Leave the pot exposed to sunlight.
5. Sprinkle some of the water over your beloved's pillow at night for hours of passion.

 ## Garnet Soul Mate Magnet

Wear garnets to attract the love of your life.

 ## Goddess of Love Spell

Grind up pink rose buds, peppermint leaves, and ambrette seeds. Blend this powder into rice powder and dust onto your body; rub some between your palms and touch the one you want.

Grow a Lover Spells

Having trouble finding a lover? Grow one. Oh, if it was only that simple! However, these basic spells allegedly stimulate the arrival of love.

 ## Grow a Lover Spell (1) Avocado

Grow an avocado from a pit to draw love to you.

 ## Grow a Lover Spell (2) Basil

Grow basil in pots at home to draw love and also to counter lack of erotic interest.

 ## Grow a Lover Spell (3) Bleeding Heart

Grow the flower Bleeding Heart in a flowerpot. Stick a coin in the pot to activate the spell and draw love to you.

Grow a Lover Spell (4)
Female Lover

Plant a tulip bulb in a flowerpot to draw a female lover. Allegedly watering the plant with your tears enhances your chances of success.

 ## Grow a Lover Spell (5) India

Etch the name of your lover or the one you desire on a seed and then plant and nurture it.

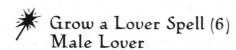 ## Grow a Lover Spell (6)
Male Lover

To draw a male lover near, place an onion in a flower-pot. Again, watering it with your tears allegedly enhances the chances of success.

 ## Grow a Lover Spell (7) Slavic

1. Dig up your beloved's footprint, ideally from your own property, if possible.
2. Put it in a flowerpot, together with other dirt if necessary.
3. Grow marigolds in the pot.

 ## Halloween Spell

1. Write your romantic affirmations and aspirations on a piece of paper.
2. Fold it up over either a lump of dragon's blood resin or some dragon's blood powder.
3. Toss it into the fire on Halloween night.

 ## Heart Charm

Corazon de buey ("Heart of the ox") is a large heart-shaped seed used in Latin American magic to attract love. Charge a seed with your desire. Carry it in a locket or conjure bag to draw love toward you.

 ## Hibiscus Love Spell

Find one perfect hibiscus flower. Wear it for a little while if possible and then offer it to the one you desire. If the person accepts it and holds onto it, he or she will be yours.

 ## Hidden Charms Spell

Pin hummingbird, mermaid, and/or broomstick charms to your underwear to draw a lover.

Holly and Ivy Spells

Holly and ivy, like frankincense and myrrh, are a natural couple. Holly represents Dionysus while Ivy symbolizes his true love, Ariadne.

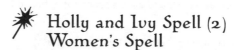 ## Holly and Ivy Spell (1)
Men's Spell

Men seeking to attract women should carry a conjure bag filled with holly leaves and berries.

Holly and Ivy Spell (2)
Women's Spell

Women seeking to attract men should carry a conjure bag filled with ivy.

☀ Holly and Ivy Spell (3) True Love Spell

Should you discover your true love, mingle holly and ivy together. Place half of the blended botanicals in one red conjure bag, the other half in a second bag, one to be carried by each member of the relationship to keep love strong and true.

☀ Horseshoe Spell

In Latin American magic, horseshoes are wrapped in colored thread and ornamented with power objects to create a magical talisman. In order for it to be effective, the entire process must be perceived as a spell: focus on your desires, goals, and intentions during every step of creation.

1. Wrap a horseshoe with red thread so that it is completely covered.
2. While you wrap, visualize your desires, knotting them in.
3. Once the horseshoe is all wrapped up, mount it onto cardboard and start decorating.
4. Ornament the horseshoe directly or attach charms to the backing cardboard.
5. Place grains of paradise in tiny bags and attach them. Add beads, charms, amulets, and sacred texts and images as desired. Consider what you wish the horseshoe to draw toward you:
   ★ Attach dried rose buds for new love
   ★ Attach tiny bags of cumin and caraway seed for fidelity
   ★ Add phallic beads, cubebs, cardamom, grains of paradise and pieces of vanilla beans for enhanced sex
6. When it's complete, hang this talisman so that it reminds you of its purpose.

Hummingbird Spells

Hummingbirds are prized ingredients in Mexican love magic. Dried hummingbirds are often found amongst the oils and botanicals of the famed witch markets. A modern method of accessing this love magic is through the use of metal and gemstone hummingbirds.

☀ Hummingbird Spell (1) Altar of Love

1. Post an image of a hummingbird as the focal point of a love altar.
2. Burn copal in front of the image and visualize your desires.
3. If you wish, for maximum intensity, coordinate this altar with a petition to Xochiquetzal, beautiful Aztec spirit of love. Offer her vivid flowers and spring water and request her assistance.

☀ Hummingbird Spell (2) Charm

1. Attach a hummingbird charm to a red silk cord.
2. Surround it with other lucky love charms as well as turquoise and silver beads.
3. Knot your intentions into the cord as you string the beads.
4. When complete, dip the hummingbird charm into **Come to Me Lover!** or other love drawing oil.
5. Wear it to attract and maintain love. Reinforce by periodically anointing the charm.

Hummingbird Spell (3) Found Feather

A found hummingbird feather is a potent promise of future love.

1. Save it as a love drawing and preserving charm.
2. Place it within a red silk charm bag and wear it hanging between your breasts.

Hungarian Crossroads Love Spell

1. Obtain some hairs from the one you desire.
2. Bury them at a crossroads, while concentrating on your wish.
3. He or she should return your affections.

Jezebel Root Spell

Place a Jezebel root in a red conjure bag. Add one Grain of Paradise every Friday until you have the love you desire.

Juniper Spells

Juniper is most commonly associated with protection spells. However, juniper berries possess tremendous love drawing and sexuality enhancing powers.

Warning: Juniper spells are not safe for use during pregnancy.

Juniper Spell (1) Hot Mama Douche

Soul mate? Perhaps all you desire is to find a fun, vigorous, exciting lover. This hoodoo formulation takes a little while to prepare but promises quick, exciting solutions.

1. Make juniper vinegar: warm apple cider or wine vinegar on the stove. Add a handful of bruised juniper berries. Let it simmer for a little while, then bottle in an air-tight container. Allow this to sit for at least two weeks, and then strain out the berries.
2. When you're ready to use it, dilute with warm water or a hydrosol.
3. Used as a douche, this is said to draw men like the proverbial flies.

Juniper Spell (2) Woman Seeking New Love

A quicker spell to prepare, ironically it solicits long-term love, romance, and commitment.

1. Soak juniper berries in vinegar for several hours.
2. Strain out the berries, reserving some, and add a generous quantity of the infusion to your bath water.
3. Enjoy your bath. Vividly visualize the end results of a very successful spell.
4. Emerge from the bath but don't drain the water yet.
5. Toss some used bathwater plus the reserved berries outside onto the Earth near your home to signal your desire for love and your available status.

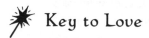 Easy Juniper Spell

Pierce, string, and wear juniper berries to attract lovers.

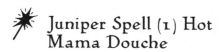 Key to Love

1. Find a key; pick it up.
2. As you pick it up, call out the name of the one you desire.
3. The person will be yours.

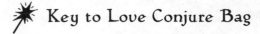

Key to Love Conjure Bag

Place an arrowhead, a key, and six coral beads inside a red silk bag together with Grains of Paradise and orrisroot.

Lodestone Love Spells

Lodestone's magnetic properties inspire their use in love spells. Lodestones are used to draw love toward you and then keep that love close at hand. According to traditional Chinese mysticism, the luckiest wedding bands are crafted from matched lodestones.

Lodestone Love Spell (1) Attraction

Lodestones are believed to have genders, just like other living creatures. Their gender is determined by appearance: the rounder-looking ones are female, while the males bear a phallic resemblance. Choose lodestones to match your desires. Use one to represent yourself and another to represent the person you would like to draw into a romance.

1. Choose a lodestone to represent you and soak it in **Come To Me Lover Oil!**
2. Sprinkle it with magnetic sand and place it on the edge of a mirror.
3. Choose a lodestone to represent the person you wish to draw into romance. It is not necessary for the lodestones to be of opposite sex; males may draw males, and females may draw females.
4. Soak this one in **Amor Oil.**
5. Sprinkle with magnetic sand and place it on the mirror, on the opposite edge from the first lodestone.
6. Carve a candle dedicated to romance and dress it with **Lucky Lodestone Oil.**

7. Light it, focus on your wish for romance and move the two lodestones slightly closer to each other.
8. Pinch out the candle.
9. Repeat this daily until the lodestones meet in the middle, then allow the candle to burn all the way down.

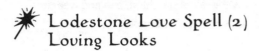

Lodestone Love Spell (2) Loving Looks

Gently rub your eyelids with lodestones to attract loving looks.

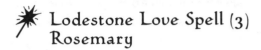

Lodestone Love Spell (3) Rosemary

1. Sprinkle dried ground rosemary onto a lodestone.
2. Carry it in a charm bag to draw love and attract favorable attention.

Lovage Spells

The herb lovage lives up to its name: it allegedly inspires love and amorous attention.

Lovage Spell (1) Bath

1. Draw a tub of warm water.
2. Sprinkle fresh or dried lovage into your bath to attract romantic attention.
3. Let yourself air-dry.

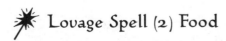

Lovage Spell (2) Food

Sprinkle lovage on food—fish or chicken is recommended—ten minutes before serving the meal to your beloved.

Love Attraction Bath Spell (1)

Create an infusion by pouring boiling water over fresh basil and dill. Strain out the botanicals and, while the liquid is still hot, stir in cinnamon honey. Add this to your bath.

 ## Love Attraction Bath Spell (2)

Make an infusion by pouring boiling water over gentian and lavender. Add the strained liquid to your bath. Allow yourself to air-dry before venturing out in search of love.

 ## Love Attraction Spell (2)

1. Write your target's name on a small piece of paper.
2. Sprinkle it with the most fragrant fresh flower petals available.
3. Fold the paper toward you.
4. Hide it within your underwear drawer to magically lure the person closer to you.

 ## Love Attraction Spell Extra Strength

1. Select, carve, and dress a candle to represent the object of your desire.
2. While the candle burns, write your own name on a piece of paper. (If you're shy, use invisible ink.)
3. Sprinkle the most fragrant flower petals available over the paper and fold it toward the candle.
4. Hide this billet-doux in your target's underwear drawer.

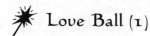 ## Love Ball (1)

1. Soften beeswax.
2. Add powdered dragon's blood, frankincense, rosemary, chopped straw, and a little hair of the one you desire. Roll this into a ball between your palms and carry it with you.

 ## Love Ball (2)

Some plants are considered perfectly matched romantic couples: frankincense and myrrh, vetiver and patchouli, for example.

Add them to softened beeswax, together with a few drops of your sweat, urine and/or menstrual blood, plus some hair taken from the one you desire. Carry the charm over your heart or in your pocket.

 ## Love Candle Spell

This spell requires two candles, one to represent you and one to represent the object of your desire.

1. Carve the candles as desired.
2. Dress the candle that represents you with **Magnet Oil** and **Come to Me Lover!**
3. Light that candle; it will remain in one place.
4. Dress the other candle with plain olive oil and sprinkle magnetic sand over it.
5. Burn it in increments, drawing it ever closer to your candle and sprinkling with magnetic sand.

Love Conjure Bags

Create your own bag using romantic charms, botanicals, and symbols, or follow one of these formulas.

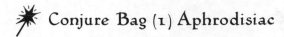 ## Conjure Bag (1) Aphrodisiac

This bag promotes faithfulness as well as romance.

1. Take a whole spikenard root or a piece of one, together with a little bit of hair taken from the tail of a goat.
2. Wrap it in fabric or carry it in a bag.
3. Reinforce periodically by dressing with essential oil of spikenard or a drop of oil infused from the root.

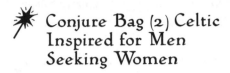 ## Conjure Bag (2) Celtic Inspired for Men Seeking Women

Fill a bag with holly leaves and holly berries.

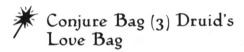 ## Conjure Bag (3) Druid's Love Bag

Fill a bag with elecampane, mistletoe, and vervain.

Conjure Bag (4) English

1. Cut out two matching red velvet or flannel hearts.
2. Sew them together, forming a sachet, leaving a hole so that it may be stuffed.
3. Fill the heart with love herbs and a lock of your hair. Add either a bead, a piece of coral or a pearl dipped into sweat or menstrual blood. Don't stuff it too much; you want this charm to stay reasonably flat so that the outside is easily embellished.
4. Complete sewing the bag.
5. Decorate the outside with more beads and/or sequins. Sew on your initials, the initials of the one you desire, your wishes, the words *"I love you."*
6. Give this as a gift to the one you love.

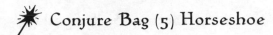 ## Conjure Bag (5) Horseshoe

1. Place at least one small magnetic horseshoe into a bag.
2. Combine with lodestones and magnetic sand.
3. Dress with love drawing oils.

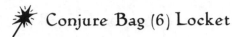 ## Conjure Bag (6) Locket

A locket worn around the neck serves as an elegant charm bag. The chain also gives it the air of a binding spell.

Place a photo of your beloved inside a locket together with a strand of hair and a tiny piece of moonwort (Botrychium lunaria).

 ## Conjure Bag (7) Love in my Pocket

In Romany, a conjure bag is known as a "putzi," literally a "pocket."

Fill a red silk bag with all or some of the following ingredients to draw and maintain love and romance: amber, cinnamon, cloves, acorns, rose buds or petals, orrisroot, a magic ring and an old coin, re-engraved with new sigils.

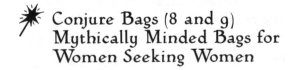 ## Conjure Bags (8 and 9) Mythically Minded Bags for Women Seeking Women

Don't combine the materials into one bag; the divinities they're consecrated to are both very independent, autonomous ladies who don't necessarily play well with others. Two distinct bags may be created, however, for maximum intensity, each carried on a different area of the body.

Artemis' Charm Bag

Fill the bag with a silver charm in the shape of the moon, plus wormwood, mugwort, and southernwood.

Athena's Charm Bag

Fill the bag with olive twigs and leaves, a snake charm and a charm version of the gorgon's head. Anoint with a drop of menstrual blood or vaginal juice.

Love Drawing Bag

1. Sew up three sides of a red silk sachet.
2. Fill it with henna powder, a heart charm, and a rose quartz crystal.
3. Sew up the remaining side and carry the sachet near your heart to attract love.

Love Drawing Sachet (1)

Fill a sachet with catnip leaves and rose petals and wear it near your heart.

Love Drawing Sachet (2)

Fill a sachet with vervain, rosemary, lavender, and rose petals. Wear it within your clothing to draw romantic attention.

Love Incense

Love Incense (1) Aloes wood

Burn aloes wood on the Full Moon for a new lover by the New Moon. Repeat as needed.

Love Incense (2) Deluxe Love Drawing Powder

To find a new love, grind the following ingredients into a fine powder and blend them together. Allow your nose to determine the proportions that are correct for you.

- Aloes wood
- Camphor
- Frankincense
- Mastic pearls
- Myrrh
- Orrisroot
- Patchouli
- Red sandalwood
- Saltpeter
- Sandalwood
- Vetiver

1. Place this powder in a red flannel bag.
2. Carry it between your breasts for seven days; sleep with it beneath your pillow for seven nights. This may be enough to attract new love.
3. If there are no results or promising leads after seven days, burn a pinch of the powder every morning for seven days.

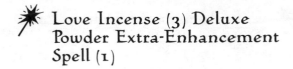 Love Incense (3) Deluxe Powder Extra-Enhancement Spell (1)

Just because you've found love, don't abandon the deluxe drawing powder above. It may also be used to enhance sexual relations with a lover you already have. Burn the powder as incense while preparing the boudoir for romantic assignations.

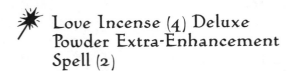 Love Incense (4) Deluxe Powder Extra-Enhancement Spell (2)

The difference between powder and incense is frequently only its mode of use:

1. Blend the above deluxe powder with rice or arrowroot powder.
2. Dust it between the sheets or onto yourself.

✳ Love Incense (5) La Madama's Dream Powder

Aunt Sally's Dream Incense calls in more than lucky numbers. It also allegedly draws your one, true love.

1. Grind cardamom, cinnamon, coriander seeds, and licorice root into a fine powder.
2. Place it on charcoal and burn before bedtime.

✳ Love Incense (6) Vanilla Bean

How vanilla has earned a reputation for blandness is a mystery. Indigenous to Mexico, vanilla orchids were cultivated by the Totonacs as sacred plants, gifts of the spirits, as well as aphrodisiacs. When the Aztecs conquered the Totonacs, they acquired vanilla's sacred gifts. When in turn the Spanish conquistadors conquered the

Aztecs, they brought vanilla back to Europe, nicknaming it the "little sheath," a euphemism for vagina.

1. Pierce a whole vanilla bean with a pin.
2. Burn one every Friday to attract, hold, and enhance love.

Magically enhance the power of your love letters. For maximum effectiveness cast these three spells in conjunction with each other.

✳ Love Letter Spell (1) Bay Leaf

Write an invisible wish on a bay leaf and enclose it in the envelope.

✳ Love Letter Spell (2) Bay Oil

Dab a tiny bit of essential oil of bay laurel onto the corners of the letter's pages.

✳ Love Letter Spell (3) Perfumed Bay Leaf

Place a drop of jasmine attar or your favorite perfume on a bay leaf before placing it in the envelope.

✳ Love Oil: Spellbound Oil

This allegedly holds those who behold you spellbound. Add the following essential oils to a blend of apricot kernel and jojoba oils:

Bergamot
Frankincense
Jasmine
Myrrh
Petitgrain

Place a piece of wisteria in the bottle and wear as perfume, or soak a cotton ball in the oil and carry it in your clothing.

Love Powders

Once upon a time most perfumes were dry. They were easier to transport, both in terms of trade and in terms of personal use: a conjure bag could easily be filled with perfumed powder and carried with you to use as needed.

Powders are versatile and can be used in various ways:

★ *Dust powders on the body*
★ *Sprinkle them around the bed*
★ *Sprinkle them around a lover*
★ *Cast a circle for a love spell*

Sprinkled on the sheets, any vigorous activity that heats up the bed will simultaneously cause the erotic fragrances to intensify. Sweat encourages the powder to adhere to the skin.

The advantages of edible powder cannot be overemphasized: avoid talc and replace with food quality powder.

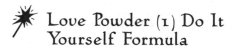 Love Powder (1) Do It Yourself Formula

Customize your own love powder.

1. Choose one or any combination of the following:
   Cinnamon
   Cloves
   Chocolate powder
   Cubeb
   Dried ginger
   Essential oil of cypress
   Grains of Paradise
   Orrisroot
   Peppermint
   Rose petals
   Vanilla sugar
2. Grind the ingredients into a fine powder.
3. Blend them with rice powder, cornstarch, potato starch or arrowroot powder, distributing the botanical material evenly.
4. Use a sifter to help you achieve a smooth, even consistency.
5. Test it on your skin to make sure that you have a comfortable dilution: some of the powder ingredients (cinnamon, cloves) can irritate sensitive skin.
6. Place in a covered container and use.

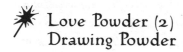 Love Powder (2) Drawing Powder

1. Grind the following botanicals to a fine powder:
   Basil
   Lavender
   Rose petals
   Yarrow
   Optional: ginger blossoms
2. Blend with rice powder.
3. Sprinkle around your home, your bedroom, on your sheets and on you.

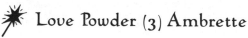 Love Powder (3) Ambrette

Grind and powder ambrette seeds and then blend with rice powder. Sprinkle a path to your door to attract a lover.

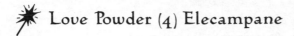

Love Powder (4) Elecampane

A Russian spell utilizes elecampane for love, however this can't be just any elecampane. For best results, hand-pick the botanical on Midsummer's Eve.

1. Dry the botanical.
2. Grind and powder it and then pound it with rosin.
3. Place this powder within a small sachet.
4. Wear this next to your body for nine days and nights.
5. Secretly sew it into the clothing of the one you love.

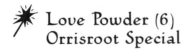

Love Powder (5) Orrisroot Unknown Lover

Orrisroot derives from the roots of certain species of iris. It's extremely fragrant, serves as a botanical preservative and is a famous aphrodisiac. To draw an unknown lover toward you:

1. Blend approximately one tablespoon of ground, powdered orrisroot into approximately one cup of powder (e.g., rice powder).
2. Dust yourself with it.

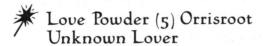

Love Powder (6) Orrisroot Special

When you know whom it is that you want, dust powdered orrisroot on his or her clothes or body to arouse interest and ability.

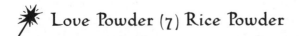

Love Powder (7) Rice Powder

Plain old rice powder allegedly enhances sexual attractiveness in women and virility in men. It also allegedly heightens passions for both: use by itself as dusting powder or as the preferred basis for other love powders. Sprinkle it between your sheets.

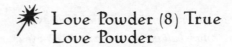

Love Powder (8) True Love Powder

This is a very ancient formula. Some recommend mixing it in food or water, as a love philter. Mistletoe has toxic properties—perhaps this is taking too much of a chance with romance. However, grind dried elecampane, mistletoe and vervain into a fine powder.

★ *Sprinkle the powder around the bed*
★ *Use it as drawing powder*
★ *Decorate an altar*
★ *Dress a candle*
★ *Carry it in a charm bag*

If your heart is set on that love potion, a safer and perhaps even more powerful method of drawing on the powder of the botanical blend is to substitute the flower essence remedies made from each plant. Add a few drops of each to champagne or sparkling water.

Love Safety Spell (1)

According to Arabic magical traditions, eating pistachio nuts breaks the effect of love spells and prevents others from casting them upon you.

Love Safety Spell (2)

Do you suspect attempts to enchant you? Carrying a water lily allegedly renders a woman immune to the effects of undesired love potions and spells.

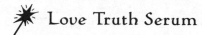

Love Truth Serum

1. Gently, place an agate on the left breast of a sleeping woman.
2. Quietly, so as not to waken her, ask what you wish to know.
3. Allegedly she will speak the truth while sleeping.

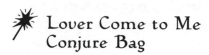

Lover Come to Me Conjure Bag

*Anoint cubebs, patchouli, and vetiver with **Come To Me Lover Oil!** Place the botanicals in a red silk bag and carry to attract and keep love.*

Lunar Love Spells

Around the world, the moon is the planetary body most invoked in love spells.

Lunar Love Spell (1) Full Moon Circle

A Full Moon spell to draw new love:

1. Dress aloes wood with **Come to Me Lover Oil!**
2. Place some on each of four charcoals.
3. Place each charcoal on an incense burner or plate and take them outside with you.
4. Arrange them in a circle, with each charcoal at one of the cardinal points. Stand inside the circle.
5. Light the incense, stand in the center, dance for the moon and request a lover to dance with you by the time the next full moon arrives.

This spell is considered most effective if performed naked, while exposed to strong moonbeams.

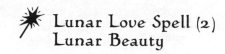

Lunar Love Spell (2) Lunar Beauty

1. Go out underneath a beautiful shining Full Moon.
2. Bathe yourself in the moonbeams.
3. Chant:
   Moon, beautiful Moon
   You look so beautiful to me, shiny and bright
   Let [Name], child of [Name] see me as I see you
   Let me look as beautiful to [Name], child of [Name]
   as you look beautiful to me.

Lunar Love Spell (3) New Moon Spin

At the first sight of the New Moon, spin sunwise on one foot, murmuring, "Moon! Twist a man [or give a name if you have one] around me just like I'm twisting around you!"

Magic Lamp of Love Spell

Create a magic lamp to turn on the love-light of the one you desire.

1. Rub a photograph of the person you desire all over your naked body. (If you don't have a photo, substitute a piece of paper with the person's signature on it or else write your target's name, birthday, and other identifying information on paper and use that.)
2. Place the photograph face-up in a casserole or similar dish.
3. Sprinkle ground peppermint, cinnamon, basil, Grains of Paradise, cubebs, cloves, cardamom, and damiana over it.
4. Add a real iron horseshoe and Jezebel root.
5. Blend honey into red wine and cover the ingredients of the dish with it.
6. Add vegetable oil until the dish is approximately three-quarters full. (Don't fill it to the top; it's not safe.)
7. Create a cotton wick, place it in the oil and light it.
8. Traditionally this love lamp is kept burning until your desires are fulfilled, with the ingredients being stirred daily.

 ## Magic Mirror of Love

This Jewish love spell invokes the Pagan deity Mother Holle, a powerful, wild Northern European forest spirit, Queen of Witches and Provider of Love. Mother Holle is Holland's namesake and the star of the Grimm's fairy tale that bears her name. As the days of rural markets are mostly long over, you may have to invoke the assistance of a friend to symbolically "buy" a three-day-old dirty egg from you.

1. You'll need an egg laid on a Thursday by a jet-black hen, which has never before laid an egg. This is the easy part of the spell.

2. Bury it that same day after sunset at a crossroads. Mark the spot because you'll be back for it.
3. Let the egg remain buried in Earth for three days then dig it up after sunset.
4. Sell it. Use the proceeds toward the purchase of a small mirror, which must be buried that same night at the exact same spot where you buried the egg.
5. Invoke Mother Holle, tell her your desire.
6. Sleep over that spot for three nights. Remove the mirror. Whoever looks into it will love you.

Magic Ring Spells

Fairy-tale heroes and heroines possessed magic love drawing rings. Merely placing it on your finger or twisting it three times once it was on was usually enough to draw one's true love. Try these rings and see if they work.

 ## Magic Ring (1) Helen of Troy

Legend has it that Helen of Troy owned a powerful magic ring that responded to the wearer's desires. It forced anyone who piqued the wearer's romantic interest to immediately fall in love with her. Helen's ring reportedly was a signet engraved with the image of Pan. Reproduce this if you wish.

 ## Magic Ring (2) Love Drawing

1. Collect your materials so that you are ready to begin this spell at the New Moon.
2. Purchase a simple gold wedding band, possessing no markings, engravings or decoration. Do not haggle over the price.
3. Drop the ring into a large glass filled with champagne or rose water.
4. Add one oak leaf, one willow leaf, two bay leaves, and two bamboo knots.

5. Write the name of your intended on a piece of silver paper.
6. The ring needs to be magically activated by moonlight: place the glass on top of the paper, by a window so that it's bathed in moonbeams from the New Moon until the Full Moon.
7. By the light of the Full Moon, remove the ring. Hold it near your heart and speak your desires aloud.
8. Wear the ring on a red silk cord around your neck. Enhance with copper or rose quartz beads or other love charms.

For optimum power, do not reveal the purpose of your spell to anyone.

 ## Magic Ring (3) Venus

This magic love ring derives from The Lapidario, *an astrological treatise on stones written for Alfonso X, the Wise, King of Castile (1221–1284), ostensibly a translation of a Chaldean manuscript. The Chaldeans were devotees of Ishtar, Spirit of Love who is identified with the planet Venus. Her sacred gem is lapis lazuli. Lapis summons Ishtar's blessings of love. If worn in a ring, it allegedly attracts the opposite sex. (Supposedly it draws women with blue/gray eyes to men who wear this ring. What it draws to a woman is left a mystery.)*

1. Charge the ring with your desires before wearing.
2. For maximum effect consecrate the ring to Ishtar.
3. This love charm is even more potent when crafted under harmonious aspects from the planet Venus.

 ## Magic Three Times Seven Love Bath

This bath is recommended before going someplace where you hope to meet someone new.

1. Blend seven pink or red rosebuds with seven lovage leaves and seven Grains of Paradise.
2. Pour boiling water over the botanicals and allow them to steep.
3. Do not strain out the botanical material but add everything to your bath.
4. Let yourself air-dry afterwards to radiate your desire for a new love.

Magical Matchmakers

Once upon a time, in fairy tales anyway, fairy godmothers ensured that true love would find a way, the slipper would find the right foot, and each true heart would meet its match. Fairy godmothers and fairy queens were often storytellers' devices to describe now-forbidden spirits.

Sometimes we still need a little assistance—to find love, to keep love, to navigate love's treacherous waters. The following spirits, many among the most powerful of all, are the geniuses of love. Choose your ally.

✴ Anima Sola Spell

Anima Sola *translates as the "Lone Soul" or "Lonely Spirit" and refers to a very specific votive image. Based on Roman Catholic votive statues (but now a standardized chromolithograph), this image is particularly popular in Latin American magical traditions. It depicts a woman standing amidst flames, eternally burning yet never consumed. She gazes upwards, holding her chained hands towards heaven. Is her soul burning in the fire of Hell or does her heart burn with the fire of love?*

Allegedly unrequited love is what drew this poor soul into her predicament: the Anima Sola traded eternal salvation for the joys of temporal love. She is invoked in only the most desperate love spells.

1. When you want someone's love so bitterly that nothing else matters, gaze at the image.
2. Make a vow that, in exchange for this person's love during this lifetime, following death you will assume the place of that poor burning soul.

Aphrodite Spells

The most celebrated love spirit of all, aphrodisiacs are named in her honor. The finest are believed to share in her essence.

Aphrodite most commonly manifests as either a mermaid or as an impossibly beautiful woman. She shines so brightly that she dazzles the eyes. She is the Queen of Wild Beasts and the Lady of Flowers, and she accepts devotion from both men and women. A friendly, sociable although temperamental spirit, she is usually accompanied by a host of lesser spirits as well as her companion animals. She likes a party. Love is her sacrament. To say that you're too busy for love or uninterested in romance is to offer her grave insult. To acknowledge the need and desire for sex and romance is to honor her and acknowledge her authority: request her assistance so that you, too, may worship at her altar.

Aphrodite is at the height of her power during the Summer Solstice. Her planets are the sun and Venus. Her day is Friday. Call her with myrtle, myrrh, and roses. Ancient worshippers offered her triangle-shaped honey cakes. Aphrodite is a versatile spirit and her altars take many forms. The bottom line is that they, like the spirit that they honor, must be beautiful. Decorate with seashells and other motifs from the sea.

✴ Aphrodite Spell (1) Apples of Love

Aphrodite is a bountiful spirit; she has not one but many sacred creatures and a multitude of sacred botanicals. Apple trees are among her favorites, however, and apples figure prominently in Aphrodite's magic spells.

1. Place three yellow apples on Aphrodite's altar and request that Aphrodite bless them.
2. Ask her to charm the fruit so that whoever eats these apples will fall madly in love with you.
3. Give an apple to the one you choose.

This may be considered the most "ethical" love spell of all, as the other person retains the choice to eat the apple or not.

✴ Aphrodite Spell (2) Bower of Love

Aphrodite revels in wild nature, human and earthly. Draw her presence and assistance with an outdoor living altar, a bower of love.

1. Decorate an area with statues of Aphrodite, her mermaid friends and her favorite animals.
2. Plant apple, myrtle, and pomegranate trees. Add scented geraniums, marjoram, poppies, roses, roses, and more roses.

3. A bench or a hot tub strategically placed so that you can best enjoy the atmosphere, preferably with someone you love, is the finishing touch.

4. If this other party hasn't yet manifested in your life, request that Aphrodite send him or her along quickly so that her bower of love will be complete.

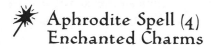

Aphrodite Spell (3) Dream Lover Bath

Make an infusion by pouring boiling water over rose petals, marjoram, and myrtle; add the liquid to your bath. While bathing, conjure up a vision of your dream lover. Repeat for six consecutive days; allegedly he or she should appear to you.

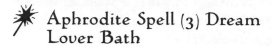

Aphrodite Spell (4) Enchanted Charms

Have Aphrodite empower your love charms so that they will become romantic talismans to draw, maintain, and protect love.

1. Create an altar for Aphrodite.
2. Consecrate it with offerings to her such as flowers, fruit, perfume, or jewelry.
3. In addition, place upon the altar something that you'd like her to empower for you as a love charm. A belt or waist beads are traditional but any small charm or piece of jewelry is effective.
4. Be very clear and explicit as to what belongs to Aphrodite and will remain hers forever versus what she's empowering for you as a charm.
5. Let the charm rest on the altar overnight. Give it to your beloved as a gift or use it to draw new love.

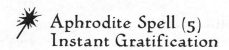

Aphrodite Spell (5) Instant Gratification

Who has time to build an altar? You've been hit by love at first sight and opportunities are fleeting. Use Aphrodite's apples of love for a spontaneous spell.

1. Make a quick silent invocation to Aphrodite while holding an apple.
2. Take a bite.
3. Pass it to the person you desire.
4. If he or she bites into it, your wishes will be fulfilled.

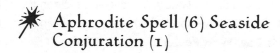

Aphrodite Spell (6) Seaside Conjuration (1)

Conjure Aphrodite by the sea.

1. Dress aquatic colored candles, blue or green, with the fragrance of myrrh and roses.
2. Create an altar in the sand.
3. Offer Aphrodite myrtle and roses (toss them into the sea) and light your candles as you petition for love.

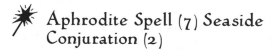

Aphrodite Spell (7) Seaside Conjuration (2)

If you're unable to travel to her home, invite Aphrodite to yours.

1. Cast a circle with sea salt.
2. Use shells to demarcate the four directions.
3. Light candles within the circle, sit inside and talk to the Genius of Love.

Apollo Spell

Apollo is a spirit of omnivorous sexuality. His romantic desires for men and women are equally strong; what seems to be the bottom line of attraction for him is beauty, intelligence, and talent, rather than gender. His is a complex myth. Classical Greek mythology paints him as the handsomest, most talented, most clever spirit of all, yet the women he pursues inevitably run from his embrace. Apollo had better luck with male lovers, with whom he had happy, successful relationships. Request his assistance, especially with someone who's hard to get.

1. Carve and dress a large yellow or gold candle and dedicate it to Apollo. Use any of the love drawing oils. **Pow-Wow Power Oil,** although it wasn't intended for this purpose, may attract Apollo's attention because it's so *sunny.*
2. Roll the candle in powdered Saint John's Wort.
3. Burn it and make your appeal.

Apollo's sacred creatures include crows and mice. Significant or surprising appearances may signal your response.

Artemis Spell

Women seeking other women may request assistance from Artemis and Athena.

Artemis's happiest times are spent in the company of other women. She has deep-seated doubts about men, although she's partial to the very few special ones who come along. If you've discovered one of those unique men, Artemis may also be petitioned for assistance.

1. Petition Artemis at night.
2. Offer her cool spring water and white or silver candles. Small images of the wild animals that she loves are appropriate offerings.
3. Tell her that if she will grant your wish you will make a contribution toward the preservation of wild life.

Athena Spell

Athena is a complex spirit, torn between her roots in the ancient Libyan religion of the Great Mother and her later fervent embrace of conservative patriarchy. Appeal to her earlier instincts:

1. Call Athena with a dish of olive oil dressed with olive flower essence remedy and a glass of wine.
2. Decorate her altar with images of snakes and gorgons.
3. Speak to her lucidly and articulately and tell her what you need.

Bastet is the ancient Egyptian spirit of love, joy, magic, sex, fertility, perfume, and the pleasures of life. Once an extremely popular divinity, she may manifest as a cat or as a human woman with a cat's head. Invoke her powers to find and keep true love.

Bastet Spell (1) Love Incense

1. Gather the following ingredients: catnip, myrrh, rose petals, and Grains of Paradise.
2. Grind all the ingredients into a fine powder and burn on lit charcoal.

Bastet Spell (2) Seduction Candle

1. Carve your desires into a green cat candle.
2. Dress it with **Come to Me Lover!, Cleopatra** and/or **Queen of Sheba Oils.**
3. Sprinkle with a little catnip and damiana and burn.

Maitresse Ezili Spells

Maitresse Ezili Freda Dahomey, Haitian lwa of love, derives from Dahomey where she began her incarnation as a water snake spirit, the embodiment of the Azili River. She accompanied her enslaved devotees to Haiti, where she evolved into a powerful spirit of love, beauty, and dreams, the most prominent of the female lwa.

Maitresse Ezili epitomizes the capacity to dream, to imagine and to desire beyond what is reality, beyond what is merely adequate. Maitresse Ezili prefers to live in an idealized dream world, where everyone is beautiful, benevolent and well-mannered, a world full of love, laughter, and luxury and devoid of poverty, meanness, ugliness, and unpleasantness. Inevitably reality intrudes on her and she cries a river of tears. Maitresse Ezili's symbol is the heart and inevitably it is a heart pierced with disappointment.

She sleeps with whomever she chooses and she chooses a lot, yet she is chaste rather than promiscuous. Instead she is so full of love and desire, that she transcends any concept of fidelity or promiscuity. She wears three wedding rings: one life, one reality, one husband isn't enough.

Maitresse Ezili isn't particularly impressed with simple gifts: she is a queen and expects lavish offerings. She loves champagne and French pastries. She rewards devotees by assisting with matters of health, love, and finances. Her sacred plant is basil. Maitresse Ezili sends healing and messages through erotic dreams.

 ## Maitresse Ezili Love Oil

For women looking for romance:

1. Create an infused oil of fresh basil leaves using sweet almond oil.
2. Use this oil to dress candles dedicated to Ezili to accompany petitions for love.

 ## Maitresse Ezili Perfume Oil

1. Create an infused oil of fresh basil leaves using sweet almond oil as above.
2. Add red hibiscus flower essence to the oil once the infusion process is complete.
3. Use this oil in the bath or as massage oil to radiate an invitation for love.

 ## Maitresse Ezili Pierced Heart Spell

Because magic appropriates anything possessing power for individual use, sacred images are frequently taken out of context. Images of the Mater Dolorosa, the Mother of Sorrows, depict a beautiful woman's heart pierced with a sword. The image may be understood as Maitresse Ezili.

Traditionally an altar of love, using this image as a focal point, is created to petition for the return of a lover at any cost. Commercially manufactured seven-day candles also bear this image. Gaze at the woman, experience your own pierced heart and consider whether the spell's success is worth it.

 ## Maitresse Ezili Potion

This allegedly serves as an aphrodisiac as well as a request for Maitresse Ezili's blessings.

Steep fresh basil leaves in wine. Strain and drink the potion.

✴ Maitresse Ezili Talisman

This written talisman emphasizes the fluidity of the world of spirits. La Baleine is a whale spirit who may be the mother or the sister of the beautiful mermaid, La Sirene. Or perhaps they are merely distinct aspects of one being. To make matters more complex, perhaps they are really only facets of Maitresse Ezili. By linking these three spirits together, this talisman captures the various facets of love, romance, desire, and sexuality. Its possession allegedly helps you win the love of the one you desire and retain the attention of someone you already have.

*Use **Dove's Blood Ink** to write the following on a piece of parchment or fine ivory stationary:*

```
L A B A L E I N E
A
S
I
R
E
N
E Z I L I - F R E D A - D A H O M E Y
```

Carry it with you or post it over a bedroom altar.

✴ Mary Magdalene's True Love Spell

The beloved disciple is invoked to find one's true love. Her feast day, the most advantageous day for petitions, is July 22nd.

1. Create an altar with an image of Mary Magdalene as the focal point.
2. Offer her flowers, perfume or perfumed oils and salves. Spikenard, which is also believed to ensure fidelity, is especially associated with her.
3. Request your desire.

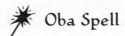 Oba Spell

Oba, another beautiful Yoruba river orisha, is often overlooked and under-appreciated. It's the story of her life. Her efforts to overcome this and claim her glory culminates in her chief claim to mythological fame as the butt of a rival's joke.

Chango is the Yoruba orisha who epitomizes dynamic male beauty and virility. Oba was his first and thus presumably official and chief wife. However, with Chango one woman is never enough. As long as her position as his acknowledged partner remained unchallenged, Oba could deal with simple infidelity. But when Chango began passionate romances with the dynamic orishas Oshun and Oya, Oba was devastated.

To regain Chango's undying love and attention, one of Oba's rivals suggested using a spell that involved garnishing his favorite dish with her ear, which would grow back. After all, pointed out the rival Orisha, this worked for her: she possessed Chango's adoration as well as both her ears.

Oba took the advice. When her turn to host Chango finally arrived, she offered this grisly dish. Appalled and disgusted, Chango ran from Oba, never to return. The moral of the story is that if a spell makes you uneasy for any reason, don't cast it.

In Africa, Oba has emerged as a protector of prostitutes; however in Brazil she is venerated as a goddess of love. Oba understands what it means to be willing to risk all for love. She is generous, knows all about heartbreak and appreciates attention. Do not invoke her simultaneously with Oya or Oshun. She is particularly beneficial should you require information and direction regarding an already existing relationship.

1. To resolve queries regarding love, bring candles and flowers to a lake, together with food for Oba. She's partial to beans with onions and shrimp.
2. Light the candles, toss the flowers into the water and pose your questions.
3. Leave all offerings behind at the lake for Oba.

Oshun Love Spells

The spirit of sweet waters, Oshun, is the very embodiment of love and romance. She has tremendous magical knowledge and power. Among the most versatile, powerful, and prominent spirits, she also assists in financial matters as well as with physical healing. She is a miracle worker; there's little she can't do.

Oshun is the spirit of Nigeria's Oshun River. She traveled to the Western hemisphere with enslaved Yorubans, emerging as a beloved force in Santeria, Candomble, and other African Diaspora traditions.

Oshun may manifest in the form of her sacred birds: vultures and peacocks. She may appear as a mermaid. Her most common manifestation is as a breathtakingly beautiful woman, usually dressed in yellow or gold. She wears five brass bracelets and a mirror at her belt, the better to stop and admire herself whenever she wishes. Oshun bears a pot of river water, her gift of healing magic and love.

Her sacred areas are the bedroom and near fresh flowing waters, such as rivers, streams, and waterfalls. A talented chef, she also likes the kitchen. She likes the bathroom, if you transform it into a luxurious healing spa. Spells, offerings, and supplications are most effective if performed in these places. For maximum effect, perform rituals for Oshun beside a river by the light of a full moon.

The standard offering to Oshun is a glass of pure spring water and a dish of honey.

A crucial point: *taste the honey. Everytime* it's offered. Once upon a time, someone tried to poison Oshun with honey. She's been suspicious of offerings ever since. Untasted honey evokes her hostility, not generosity.

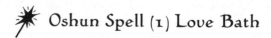 Oshun Spell (1) Love Bath

1. Draw a bath filled with warm water.

2. Add the petals from five yellow roses plus a handful of Grains of Paradise, some cinnamon sticks and cloves and some warmed honey.
3. Offer Oshun a glass of spring water and some honey, remembering to taste it.
4. Enter the bath and tell her what you need.

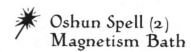 Oshun Spell (2) Magnetism Bath

Oshun is completely irresistible when she chooses to be. This bath attempts to share in a little of that magnetic essence.

1. Offer Oshun her spring water and honey, remembering to taste it.
2. Fill a bath with warm water.
3. Standing on a towel, completely paint yourself with warmed honey.
4. Enter the bath and soak.
5. When you emerge from the bath, dust yourself with cinnamon powder blended into cornstarch.

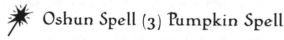 Oshun Spell (3) Pumpkin Spell

Pumpkins are a major component of Oshun's magic spells. If she helps you, it's customary to refrain from eating pumpkin and all yellow or orange squash out of respect for her sacred food.

1. Hollow out a small orange pumpkin as if you were making a jack o'lantern.
2. Carve the name of your beloved on the underside of the pumpkin. (If you can carve out a jack o'lantern that resembles your beloved, do so.)
3. Rub the inside of the pumpkin with love drawing oil.
4. Hold a candle in your hands to charge it with its purpose.
5. Place it inside the pumpkin and burn it.

✳ Oshun Spell (4) Water Shrine Love Spell

Most people will find this ritual easiest to accomplish in the bathroom, however you may also take the materials to a river or stream. It needs to be performed on five consecutive days beginning on a Friday.

1. Build a shrine to Oshun in the bathroom. Suggestions for decorations include candles, shells, mermaids, hand mirrors, and coconuts.
2. Offer Oshun spring water and honey. Light white and/or orange candles.
3. In the meantime run a bath.
4. Place five cinnamon sticks, five different types of perfume or perfume oils, some love drawing powder, and yellow and orange flowers in a bucket, and cover them with warm spring water.
5. You need a photograph of your beloved, the target of this spell. Write his or her name and birthday as well as his or her mother's name on the back of the photo. Place the photograph on the altar or where you can see it from the bath.
6. Coat your body with honey.
7. Stand in the tub. Pour the ingredients in the bucket over you.
8. Recline, relax and concentrate on your desires.

The photograph and the altar remains standing in the bathroom for the duration of the ritual. Feel free to maintain lit candles for the duration, if it's safe and appropriate.

✳ Pan Spell

Children's mythology books typically depict the half human male-/half goat-shaped spirit Pan in hot pursuit of women. This may be true. However, he may have varied tastes; since ancient days Pan has been the traditional patron of men who desire other men.

1. Request his assistance directly. His altars are most effective if built outside.
2. Call him with music from the pan pipes. Offer him wine and grapes.
3. Burn a purple candle in his honor.
4. Tell him what you need.

Pomba Gira Spells

The most famous, prominent Pomba Gira is Maria Padilha. That Maria Padilha is evoked in many love spells is not surprising. She knows a lot about the complexities of love. She began her incarnation on Earth as a living woman, Maria de Padilla, the wife of Pedro the Cruel, fourteenth-century king of Castile and Leon. Although she was her husband's unquestioned soul mate, the love and passion of his life, he simultaneously entered into other, more politically advantageous marriages.

Maria de Padilla refuses to die. Invoked in Romany spells for centuries, serving as the inspiration for a nineteenth-century French novel and a Donizetti opera, Maria's most surprising incarnation is as Queen of the Pompa Gira in Afro-Brazilian spiritual and magical traditions, where her name is spelled Portuguese style, Maria Padilha.

✳ Maria de Padilla's Lodestone Spell

This Spanish spell evokes Maria Padilla together with Asmodeus, King of Demons. A dangerous malevolent spirit, he is an angel of malice and destruction. This is a real crossroads spell; one can identify Romany, Jewish and Christian influences within it. Asmodeus is also sometimes identified with the Christian concept of Satan, so perhaps this spell invokes the devil to bring you your love, albeit in exchange for cheese rather than souls.

1. Powder a tiny bit of lodestone or obtain a little lodestone dust.

2. Add the powder to some aguardiente and drink it before going to sleep.
3. Chant the following:
   To the Mount of Olives one day I did ride
   Three little black goats before me I spied
   Those three little goats on three carts I laid
   Three black cheeses from their milk I made
   One I bestow on the Lodestone of Power
   So that it will save me from all ills this very hour
   The second to Maria Padilla I give
   And to all of her ladies about her who live
   The third I fetch for Asmodeus lame
   That he fetch for me whomever I name!
4. Name your lover out loud.

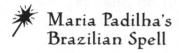

Maria Padilha's Brazilian Spell

A Brazilian ritual invokes Maria Padilha in order to attract a lover.

1. Go to a crossroads at midnight. (Most likely this is a traffic intersection. The modern Maria Padilha is an urban spirit, no remote country roads are necessary. Like Hecate, Maria Padilha prefers a three-way crossroads, the T-shaped ones are her favorites. Make your offering safely on the side, not in the center of the crossroads, in the midst of traffic.)
2. Make an altar on the ground with a red scarf.
3. Offer Maria Padilha seven long-stemmed roses, from which you have removed the thorns by hand and a small bottle of anisette.
4. Open a fresh box of matches. Arrange seven matches so that they are sticking out and place them near a pack of expensive cigarettes.
5. Light red candles and tell Maria Padilha what you need.
6. You should see results after seven, fourteen, or twenty-one days. If so, Maria Padilha will expect a second, more elaborate offering as payment due.

Maria Padilha Pomba Gira Oil

1. Grind and powder red rose petals, red carnation petals, dragon's blood, and three or seven saffron threads.
2. Blend this powder into jojoba oil.
3. Use this oil on candles, in the bath and on yourself to attract love and desire, and to talk with Maria Padilha.

Pomba Gira Seven Crossroads' Spell

Maria Padilha is the most famous of a host of Pomba Giras. There are others, who may or may not be aspects of Maria Padilha. **Pomba Gira Seven Crossroads** *is a powerful road opener and a magician of love. Petition her for the recovery of a lost love or to discover new love.*

1. Obtain seven beautiful, bright red roses. If they have thorns, remove them by hand.
2. After dark, visit seven crossroads.
3. At each one, repeat your petition to Pomba Gira Seven Crossroads. Leave a single rose by the side of each crossroad.
4. If she comes through for you, give her a more substantial offering including anisette, champagne, roses, and deluxe cigarettes.

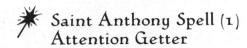

River Spirit Spell

Traditionally, river spirits rule affairs of the heart. Perhaps one lives near you:

1. Stand on a riverbank holding a leaf.
2. Prick your smallest finger and smear one side of the leaf with it while repeating your own name, all possible variations of it, over and over and over.
3. Repeat on the other side of the leaf but chant your beloved's name instead.
4. Toss the leaf into the river.

This offering is a petition to the presiding spirit of the river. Feel free to combine with other offerings, as enhanced bribery.

Saint Anthony Love Spells

A much beloved *official* son of the Roman Catholic Church, Anthony of Padua is amongst the most popular saints. Born in Lisbon in 1195, he became a Franciscan, traveled to Morocco, and eventually resided in Italy where he died at age thirty-six.

Saint Anthony is renowned in folk Catholicism as the supreme finder of missing things. What is ever more challenging to locate than real love?

Saint Anthony is a tireless provider of miracles. He specializes in resolution of particularly difficult situations. In Brazil, Saint Anthony is called *the marrying saint* because of his skill with matchmaking.

Saint Anthony's emblems are fish and lilies, suspiciously reminiscent of pagan fertility imagery. His number is thirteen, the number of months in the lunar year. Indeed, he is traditionally depicted holding an infant. He is the patron saint of the spice trade, sponsor of the European importers of rare Asian and African gums, resins and spices, so integral to the magical arts. African-derived traditions syncretize Saint Anthony to a variety of powerful spirits: Elegba, Exu, and Ogun. He shares Exu's feast day, June 13th. Tuesday evening is traditionally the most effective time to contact him. He responds to petitions made on behalf of yourself or another.

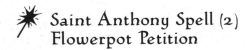

Saint Anthony Spell (1)
Attention Getter

1. Create an altar dedicated to Saint Anthony decorated with his image and favorite attributes.
2. When you wish to attract the saint's attention, blend rice and rose petals and toss this onto his statue.
3. When you feel his presence, tell him your desires.

Saint Anthony Spell (2)
Flowerpot Petition

1. You'll need two flowerpots containing basil and a third containing rue.
2. Wrap each flowerpot with a crimson silk ribbon made with three knots and pierced with pins.
3. Petition and pray to Saint Anthony as you work the spell.
4. At midnight, place the pots on an open windowsill with the rue in the middle.
5. Listen for the first words or sounds you hear: this is the response to your petition.

Traditionally, favorable signs include:

★ *Knocking at the door*
★ *Barking dogs*
★ *People whistling, laughing or singing*

Unfavorable signs include a hearse or a dark horse. This indicates that the saint will not work this petition. The appearance of a white horse is favorable, but indicates that a considerable amount of time and effort are needed. Pre-arrange other signals with Saint Anthony.

Saint Anthony Spell (3)
Ritual Substitution

In order to work the following spell you must be familiar with Roman Catholic ritual.

1. Take a rosary and wherever an *"Our Father"* would normally be said, instead say: *"Saint Anthony asked, Saint Anthony prayed, Saint Anthony delivered."*
2. At each bead where a *"Hail Mary"* would normally be recited, instead say: *"I ask, I pray, I receive."*
3. When you've finished, tell Saint Anthony precisely what—or whom—you desire.

Saint Dwyn's Love Spell

Saint Dwyn was a fifth-century Welsh girl, madly in love. After a serious argument with her beloved, to the point of break-up, Dwyn cried a river of tears and engaged in prayer desperate enough that an angel responded, offering Dwyn a potion to ease her heartache. Dwyn drank it but the results weren't exactly what she desired: her beloved was instantly transformed into stone. The angel offered Dwyn three wishes as consolation.

Her first wish was that her lover be returned to living flesh-and-blood. Her second wish was that she herself be spared the pangs of love (and indeed Dwyn became a nun and abbess of the convent at present-day Llanddwyn), and finally Dwyn wished that all true lovers who invoke her name will either receive their heart's desire or get over it quickly! Allegedly calling out Dwyn's name is sufficient, however as she is also the matron of ailing animals a vow to contribute to that cause may be appropriate if she helps you.

Santa Elena Spells

In Latin American magic, the saint most invoked for assistance in romantic matters is Saint Helena or, in Spanish, Santa Elena. At first this is puzzling: why is Santa Elena considered a genius of love? After all, the historical Santa Elena is most renowned as the mother of Constantine, the Roman Emperor who converted to Christianity and made it Rome's official faith.

No one knows more about love than someone who hasn't had a lot of luck with it. Santa Elena knows a lot about love. A former bar girl and courtesan (other professions have also been suggested), she captivated Constantine's father who, having fathered her son, repudiated her and sent her into exile when a more politically advantageous marriage became possible for him. Santa Elena is renowned for piety. Her most famous act was discovering the True Cross while on a pilgrimage to Jerusalem at age seventy. The part usually left out of the story is where she found it—in a crypt beneath the recently destroyed Shrine of Aphrodite.

 ## Santa Elena Binding Spell (1)

Santa Elena is much petitioned in matters of the heart. The following Cuban spell, a binding spell, requests her assistance.

1. Build an altar or a shrine of love.
2. Fill a small bowl halfway with spring water.
3. Add a splash of **Florida Water,** a tablespoon of honey, sugar, five cloves, five sticks of cinnamon, and five sprigs of mint.
4. Dress a white candle.
5. Tie a white ribbon around this candle and stand it in the center of the bowl. Request that just as the ribbon is tied around the candle, so two people will be tied together; that you be given the opportunity to wrap your arms around your lover like the ribbon wraps around the candle. Finally, ask for the opportunity to burn with passionate happiness.
6. Burn the candle.
7. When it's burned down, add the liquid and contents of the bowl to a bath.
8. Repeat in its entirety for seven consecutive nights, by which time you should see results.

Santa Elena Binding Spell (2)

According to legend, when Santa Elena found the True Cross, she also discovered three nails used for the Crucifixion. Two were used reasonably conventionally (one was preserved as a relic, the second was thrown into the sea for the salvation of drowned sailors), but Santa Elena dedicated the third nail to the lovers of the world so that they would be preserved from heartache. This legend forms the basis for various love spells dedicated to Santa Elena. This one derives from the sixteenth-century grimorio, The Book of San Cipriano and Santa Justina:

1. Place a medal or other votive image of Santa Elena atop a piece of green silk.
2. Hammer three golden nails into the silk.
3. Pray, petition, and burn candles to Santa Elena. Tell her what you need; remind her that one nail is meant for lovers.
4. Remove one nail from the silk and place it into an object, portrait, or figure (wax) dedicated to the person who is to be bound to you.

Santa Elena Candle Spell

Burn a large white candle to honor Santa Elena. While the candle is burning, carve and dress a figure candle to represent the one you love. Put a nail through the candle's heart and burn.

Santa Elena Invocation of Love

This traditional invocation may be used alone or in conjunction with any other spell dedicated to Santa Elena.

    Say aloud:

Most loving mother of the Roman Emperor Constantine,
To the Mount of Olives you did go,
The three nails of Our Lord Jesus Christ:
One you threw into the sea for the salvation of sailors,
Another you nailed into a dedicated object
The third I drive into [Name, child of Name's] heart
So that he [or she] may be unable to eat, sleep, or rest
Be unable to converse with women or men
Nor have a moment of rest
Until he [or she] surrenders at my feet
Please Santa Elena, if this desire is received
I will be your most sincere, loving devotee.

Santa Elena's Love Spell (1)

This spell is traditionally cast using a milagro or charm depicting a heart pierced by a knife. A nail or other metal heart charm may also be used.

1. Dedicate a red candle to Santa Elena.
2. Pierce it with the charm or nail.
3. While the candle burns, petition that the target of your spell be unable to rest, eat, sleep, or have any peace until they surrender to your desires.
4. When the candle has burned down, wear or carry the charm.

Santa Elena's Love Spell (2)

1. Dedicate a red candle to Santa Elena.
2. Place a photograph of the one you love before the candle.
3. Place a nail on top of the photograph.
4. Express your desires to Santa Elena explicitly and lucidly.
5. When the candle has burned down, wrap up any wax remnants together with the photograph and nail and hide them in a safe place, like under your mattress.

Saint Martha the Dominator Spell

In the New Testament, Saint Martha exemplifies the busy, happy housewife, who maintains steady control of her home. Saint Martha accompanied Mary Magdalene to France, where a different aspect emerged. According to legend, Martha was able to pacify a local dragon, the tarasque. Although countless knights had already perished in attempts to slay this creature, Martha, small, alone and unarmed, was able to tame the dragon through the power of love. The dragon peacefully emerged and allowed Martha to lead it on a leash, thus earning her the title Saint Martha the Dominator.

Among her many other magical roles, she may be invoked in matters of love. She is especially sympathetic to those involved with difficult people or difficult situations.

1. Burn a green candle in Saint Martha's honor for nine days. (Special Martha the Dominator candles are also sold.) Use **Martha the Dominator Oil** and/or love drawing oils to dress the candle.
2. Each day request that the target of your spell be so enchanted with love that they are unable to eat, sleep or rest until they have approached you.

In recent years, Martha the Dominator has become identified with the most famous image of the African Spirit Mami Waters, which depicts a beautiful snake charmer with her snakes. Incorporate this image if it resonates for you.

 ## Santisima Muerte

Perhaps the most unusual of the unofficial saints, La Santisima Muerte, Holy Death, is the spiritual matron of Mexican witches. La Santisima Muerte is essentially Death herself, the Grim Reaper dressed up in robes and carrying a scythe. Why is she here amidst the Love Spells? Because La Santisima Muerte is traditionally

petitioned to magically return errant lovers and husbands back to the women who await them.

Statues of La Santisima Muerte robed in red are traditionally used when invoking her for love. Build an altar in her honor and burn red candles dedicated to her. Because she is a dangerous spirit—you are, after all, essentially conjuring up death—invocations to La Santisima Muerte are traditionally accompanied by simultaneous petitions to protective saints, those who've demonstrated that they can handle and pacify her, especially Michael the Archangel, San Cipriano, and Santa Elena. Incorporate other saints into the altar as appropriate.

Spells to Make Her or Him Love You

In the same manner that certain medicines or hormone treatments affect men and women differently, so some botanicals have different impacts upon the different genders. With the following spell categories (*Make Her Love You* and *Make Him Love You*) in general the gender of the target of the spell is what is significant. Thus these are spells to attract a man or a woman. The gender of the spellcaster may or may not be significant so unless told otherwise, assume that these spells are equal opportunity spells.

Make Her Love You Spells

 ## Aroma of Love Spell

Fumigate your clothing with the scent of aloes wood, cinnamon, and myrrh to attract women's romantic attention.

Basil True Love Spell

Hand a woman a sprig of basil. Allegedly if she accepts it, she'll fall in love with you and remain faithful forever.

Devil's Bit Spell

Carry the botanical devil's bit to attract women.

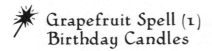 ## Grains of Paradise Bath

This spell benefits men searching for a new woman.

1. Pour boiling water over seven Grains of Paradise.
2. Let them steep.
3. When it cools, add the infusion with the Grains to your bath water.

Grapefruit Spell (1) Birthday Candles

1. Cut a pink or red grapefruit in half horizontally.
2. Place half on a dish.
3. Sprinkle cayenne pepper, Grains of Paradise, sugar, and sea salt over the top of the grapefruit.
4. Write the woman's name on a slip of paper and push it into the center of the grapefruit.
5. Top it with a cherry or strawberry.
6. Stick nine pink, yellow, gold, and/or white birthday candles into the grapefruit as if it were a birthday cake.
7. Light the candles.

Repeat this ritual for six nights.

 ## Grapefruit Spell (2) High John

Because of the use of High John the Conqueror root, this spell can only be performed by men. A woman wishing to seduce another woman should substitute an angelica root.

1. Cut a grapefruit in half, horizontally.
2. Place one half in a pan.

3. Sprinkle it with salt, sugar, pepper, and Epsom salts.
4. Write your beloved's name on a strip of brown paper.
5. Roll up the paper and tie it with red thread.
6. Insert it into the center of the grapefruit.
7. Arrange nine candles (red, pink, yellow, and/or gold) around the grapefruit half.
8. Light them.
9. While the candles burn, circumambulate around them sunwise while rolling a High John root in your hand, praying and petitioning.
10. Pinch each candle out.
11. Repeat for a total of nine nights (nine minutes a night for the first eight nights should be sufficient). Then on the last night, let the candles burn out.

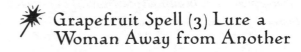 ## Grapefruit Spell (3) Lure a Woman Away from Another

1. Cut a grapefruit in half
2. Write the woman's name and her present lover's name on a piece of brown paper.
3. Write your own name over the lover's name, so that the original lover's name is now illegible.
4. Stick this paper into the center of the grapefruit.
5. Put it inside disposable pan or baking dish or line a permanent pan with foil.
6. Sprinkle the grapefruit with salt, pepper, and brown sugar.
7. Arrange five golden candles around the grapefruit in the dish and light them.

It's no accident that High John the Conqueror root is called by a man's name. It has powerful associations with men's magic. Many women find success with it as a charm for luck, money, and general good fortune. When it comes to love and sex, however, this charm works best for men.

High John, like lodestones, is divided by gender: there are male and female High John's. Shape determines gender: the round ones are female; the phallic-looking ones are male. For love, sex, and romantic domination spells, obviously the more phallic the High John the better.

High John has heterosexual proclivities: it draws women to men. Men seeking other men traditionally substitute Sampson snake root.

 ## Basic High John Spell

1. Hold a High John root in your hands and charge it with your desire.
2. Anoint it with a love drawing oil and carry it in your pocket or within a mojo bag.

 ## High John Attraction Spell

To attract a specific woman:

1. Steep High John in a jar of olive oil for seven days.
2. Remove the root and bury it under the steps of your target's home.

Reserve the oil for use as dressing oil.

 ## High John Bend Over Spell

*Allegedly **Essence of Bend Over** encourages enthusiasm towards anal sex. Soak a High John the Conqueror root in the condition oil; carry it with you and see what happens.*

 ## High John Cooperation Spell (1)

*Soak a High John the Conqueror root in **Command and Compel Oil**. Carry it to encourage women to cooperate with your desires.*

 ## High John Cooperation Spell (2)

Soak High John the Conqueror in a solution of sugar water, to attract women who'd really like to make you happy.

 ## High John Conjure Bag

1. Obtain matched male and female High John the Conqueror roots.
2. Steep dried damiana and catnip in sweet almond oil overnight, then strain out the botanicals.
3. Dress the female root with this infused sweet almond oil.
4. Dress the male root with **Magnet Oil** and **High John the Conqueror Oil**.
5. Place them both inside a red flannel drawstring bag.
6. Sprinkle with a love drawing powder until your desire is fulfilled.

Lodestones may be substituted for High John the Conqueror. Sprinkle with magnetic sand instead.

 ## High John Domination Spell (1)

Because it works to fulfill desires, High John is also used in romantic domination spells, although since High John is so intrinsically benevolent, the effect ideally is to persuade the other person to share your desires, whatever they may be.

Blend powdered High John the Conqueror with sugar and cayenne pepper and use it to fill a charm bag. Hide it under your woman's bed. This allegedly causes her to become more sexually cooperative and good-natured.

High John Domination Spell (2)

Blend sugar and cayenne pepper on a plate. Drizzle **High John Oil** *over it and hide it under the woman's bed to encourage sexual cooperation and generosity.*

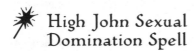 ## High John Love Drawing Spell

1. Obtain a few strands of hair from the head of the one you desire.
2. Wrap it around a High John the Conqueror root, making knots.
3. Anoint with a love drawing oil and place it inside a red drawstring bag.
4. Sleep with this under your pillow, and carry it with you during waking hours.
5. Anoint with one drop of the love drawing oil daily.

High John Sexual Domination Spell

In addition to stimulating sexual generosity, this spell also allegedly produces a compliant nature

1. Add a few drops of tuberose absolute to a bottle of **Command and Compel Oil.**
2. Use this oil to dress a High John the Conqueror root.
3. Place the dressed root into a red charm bag and sprinkle it with powdered confectioner's sugar and cayenne pepper.
4. Keep this bag under the mattress on the side where the woman usually sleeps.
5. Dress the root once a week with the oil to ensure cooperation. (And also to ensure that she hasn't yet discovered and removed the bag!)

 ## High John Sugar Spell

1. Soak a High John root in sugar water for 24 hours.
2. Remove the root and carry it in a red flannel bag to make yourself attractive to women in general.
3. Add the remaining sugar water to your bath.

 ## Isis Invocation: To Lure a Woman From Another Man

This spell requests assistance from Isis. It invokes famous lovers in the hopes that you too will achieve their ecstasy.

1. At midnight on Saint John's Eve, pick a handful of vervain leaves, the plant that allegedly sprang from Isis's tears, when she lost her true love.
2. As you pick them, call on her:
   Isis, Great of Magic!
   Make [Name] daughter of [Name] love me like I love her.
   Make her love me like you love Osiris!
   Make her love me like Penelope loves Odysseus!
   Make her love me like Ariadne loves Dionysus!
   Make her love me like Aphrodite loves Adonis!
   Make her love me like Juliet loves Romeo!
3. From the moment you grasp the leaves, until your arrival home, keep up your chant and petition. Improvise, speak from your heart, invoke other lovers, but don't stop.
4. Carry the leaves home inside your shirt against your skin.
5. Place the leaves in new green silk.
6. Leave this packet in a dry, well-ventilated place for 21 days.
7. Then grind the leaves into a powder. Keep them in a mojo bag. When the opportunity presents itself, dust your hands with the powder. Touch the woman's hands and ideally her face.

Lodestone Sweat Spell

1. Soak a lodestone in your sweat, then dress it with one drop each of essential oils of cardamom, frankincense, and sandalwood.
2. Wrap this charm up in red fabric, rolling it toward you.
3. Carry this in your pocket, within easy reach, until your next encounter.
4. When you see her, rub your hand on the lodestone packet: touch her with that hand immediately.

 ## Lovage Bath

Lovage is used in general romantic magic spells throughout Europe, however in Poland this herb is considered especially beneficial for men seeking to attract women to them.

Make a strong infusion from lovage. Men should add this to their bath to attract women. Remember to air-dry so that the botanicals linger on your skin.

 ## Male Sexual Domination Spell

Waldmeister, Master of the Woods, magically encourages a man to be a master, *whatever that may mean. For many men, it means mastery over the women in their lives and, indeed, Master of the Woods is used for this purpose. Carry Master of the Woods (woodruff) in a conjure bag at all times.*

 ## Myrtle Oil Spell

When Aphrodite first emerged naked from the sea, she was clothed in myrtle leaves. Ever since then it's been one of her sacred plants and a potent tool in romantic spells.

Crush myrtle leaves and use them to create an infused oil, following the directions on page 31, Elements of

Magic Spells. *Rub this oil on your body to attract the woman of your dreams.*

 ## New Needle Spell

1. Murmur your desires while threading a brand new needle, which has *never* been used, with unbleached thread.
2. This must be passed through the clothing of the woman you love near the heart three times. (She does not have to be in the clothing at the time, although no doubt if she is that will enhance the strength of the spell!)

 ## Nutmeg Spell

1. Carry a whole nutmeg in your armpit for 48 hours.
2. Grind it up, add it to a bottle of red wine and serve to your heart's desire.

Alternatively, prepare a romantic Italian meal and sprinkle it over the food.

 ## Rue Shoe Spell

1. Obtain a shoe that belongs to the woman you desire—the older and more used the better.
2. Stuff it with rue.
3. Hang it over your bed to draw her to it.

 ## Sandalwood Seduction

Men are advised to wear sandalwood to elicit a positive sexual response from women.

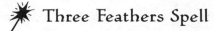 **Three Feathers Spell**

You will need three feathers from a rooster's tail, given freely. (This can't be a food rooster, a fighting cock or a sacrificial rooster. He must be a proud, living, successful, barnyard rooster with a harem of hens or the spell won't work. The feathers lend you his essence, so if you humiliate the rooster by taking the feathers by force, the spell will backfire on you.)

1. Charge these feathers with your desires.
2. Hold them in the smoke of love drawing incense, if desired.
3. When you have the opportunity, press them into a woman's hand to gain her love.

 Three Hairs Spell

1. Steal three hairs from the woman, one at a time, on three separate occasions, while the woman is sleeping. For maximum effect, the hair should be taken from near the nape of the neck.
2. Braid the hairs.
3. Hold onto this braid for a little while, don't rush this spell.
4. Keep it in a charm bag worn or carried on the body, to absorb your power and desire.
5. When you're ready, push it into a crack of a tree so that it may grow with the tree from then on. (A romantic tree is ideal, such as an apple, other flowering or fruit tree, hazel, ash, hawthorn, or elder.)

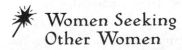 **Women Seeking Other Women**

A gift of whole orrisroot allegedly serves as the key to love. Anoint with myrrh, menstrual blood, and/or vaginal juices and wrap it in a beautiful charm bag.

Make Him Love You Spells

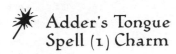 **Adder's Tongue Spell (1) Charm**

No need to worry about the safest mode of collecting an adder's tongue. Adder's Tongue (Ophioglossum vulgatum) is a fern used in Polish magic by women to attract male romantic attention. Carry it within a red silk charm bag to attract, maintain, and protect romantic love.

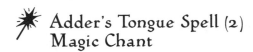 **Adder's Tongue Spell (2) Magic Chant**

Adder's Tongue is magically empowered if, while gathering, the following spoken charm is incorporated into the harvest ritual. Adder's Tongue gathered in this manner may be used in any spell.

1. As you reach for the plant, chant aloud:
   Adder's Tongue I pluck you with my hand
   Five fingers reach, my palm the sixth
   Let the men I desire pursue me
   Let the men I desire, desire me.
2. Gather as you've described with a full hand, rather than by pinching with fingers.

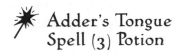 **Adder's Tongue Spell (3) Potion**

This spell isn't necessarily for drawing one specific lover; instead it's intended to draw men toward you en masse so that you can best make your selection.

Make an infusion by pouring boiling water over the herb. When it cools, strain the botanicals out and drink the potion, to bring success with men.

Baked Goods Spell

1. Bake bread, a cake, or cookies for the one you love.
2. As you knead the dough, press it against your private parts or squeeze it beneath your underarm.
3. If you are baking multiple items simultaneously, mark whatever is intended for your beloved, to avoid confusion and trouble.
4. Feed it to him.

Follow Me Boy!

Follow Me Boy! is the name given to a traditional condition formula. It is considered one of the Commanding formulas but is virtually always used in romantic or erotic situations. Sweet flag creates the commanding effect, which is reinforced further if you add licorice, however damiana is a potent aphrodisiac. He may be forced to follow you but he'll be happy to do it!

The basic formula consists of:

Dried sweet flag (calamus)
Dried catnip
Dried damiana
Optional: add licorice if you like the fragrance. For a more potent seductive oil, also add essential oils of bergamot, sweet orange, and tuberose, plus essences of any red flowers.

1. Powder the dried ingredients together.
2. Add them to sweet almond oil, shaking to blend.
3. Finally add any essential oils.

To use, dip a cotton ball in the oil and tuck it into a bra or pocket.

Follow Me Boy! Fumigation

1. Wash clothing and hang it in the bathroom to dry.
2. Grind and powder the basic botanical formula: sweet flag, catnip, and damiana.
3. Sprinkle on lit charcoals.
4. Place the incense so that your clothing is permeated with the fragrance.
5. Wear these clothes to draw men to you.

Follow Me Boy! Perfume

Wear the oil as perfume: it is reputed that this will draw men to you like flies so be selective. (This formula was once allegedly a staple business necessity for New Orleans male and female prostitutes looking for male clientele.)

☀ Follow Me Boy! Spell

Follow Me Boy! is also used in a more elaborate New Orleans ritual to draw a specific individual toward you. This spell utilizes a water-based infusion rather than oil.

1. Begin by making a strong infusion from the main ingredients: pour boiling water over dried, ground sweet flag, catnip, and damiana. Allow it to cool.
2. Light red candles in the bathroom. You may also light incense, if you feel it empowers you. (Follow Me Boy! powder may be burned as incense.)
3. Add red flower petals to the bath. Red carnations, roses, and hibiscus are popular but any bright red flower will do. (You may also add the essential oils suggested for the condition oil formula directly to the bath.)
4. Strain the infusion, reserving the liquid.
5. Carry it over to the bathtub. Enter the tub and toss the infusion over your head.
6. Soak. Focus on your desire.
7. Get out of the tub but don't drain the water yet.
8. Toss a bowlful of the used bathwater out the back door or window.
9. Bottle up some of the rest, together with the flower petals.
10. Carry them to your target's home and splash it on his doorstep. Announce out loud: *"Follow Me Boy!"* and then return home by a straightforward, simple route without looking back.

☀ Follow Me Romany Spell

This European spell does not use the classic condition formula, preferring more intimate items instead. It targets a specific individual rather than attempting to draw a crowd, however the magic ritual's stated goal is identical to the New Orleans spells.

1. Make a paste from your beloved's intimate articles: hair, saliva, nails, blood, semen, whatever you've got—the more the merrier.
2. Mold a little figure from the paste.
3. Bury it at a crossroads under the first quarter moon.
4. Urinate over the spot, while chanting:
   [Name], *son of* [Name] *I love you!*
   As this image becomes one with Earth,
   You follow me like a dog follows a bitch in heat and are one with me!

☀ Mermaid's Conjure Bag (1)

Few can resist the legendary seductive power of a mermaid. Place a mermaid charm in a conjure bag, together with seven water-lily seeds. Carry the bag to attract your soul mate.

☀ Mermaid's Conjure Bag (2)

1. Place a mermaid charm in a red conjure bag. (It may also be pinned to the bag.)
2. Add seashells, some rosemary, and a pinch of agar-agar.
3. Carry to draw a man towards you.

☀ Shoe Spell

To turn a sexual relationship with a man into something more:

1. Pick up his shoes as soon as he takes them off.
2. Place your own shoes inside his, your left inside his left, your right inside his right.
3. Buckle or tie them together as securely as possible.
4. Leave them like this until morning.

Sugar Spell (1) Candle

Hydrosols or flower waters may be used in this spell.

1. Blend honey, jasmine flower water, orange flower water, and rose water in a saucer.
2. Place a pink votive candle in the center of the saucer.
3. With a pin or a rose thorn, scratch your initials and that of your beloved, encircled together within a heart on each of five sugar-cubes.
4. Arrange these sugar cubes around the candle in the saucer. They will immediately start to merge with the flower waters, which is fine.
5. Visualize your goal. Light your candle.

For maximum effectiveness, repeat with fresh materials for five consecutive nights.

 ## Sugar Spell (2) Clothing

1. Secretly, or at least very discreetly, obtain an unwashed glove or sock from the one you desire.
2. Fill it with sugar and magnetic sand.
3. Tie it shut with a knot.
4. Sleep with it under your mattress.

 ## Vetiver Attraction

The fragrance of vetiver allegedly attracts men, whether worn by women or other men.

    Wear it on the body or soak a cotton ball in the essential oil and tuck it into a pocket or bra.

 ## Women's Conjure Bag

Place mermaid, hummingbird, and broomstick charms in a red silk bag. Add geometrically shaped charms, like diamonds and triangles, as well as angelica and orris-root and cubeb peppers and carry to attract the love you want.

 ## Wrap a Ring Around You Spell

1. Create a wreath or hoop from vines or love drawing plants, knotting your intentions and desires into the hoop.
2. Burn it.
3. Gather the ashes and sprinkle them around your heart's desire in a ring.

 ## New Love Initiation Spell

Magically signal your readiness for love to the universe. This spell allegedly beckons true love near.

1. Pulverize splinters of acacia and aloes wood together with three hairs from your head.
2. Take the resulting blend to a crossroads on a breezy day.
3. Let the powder slip from between your fingers as you revolve in a circle, murmuring an invocation of love.

 ## New Lover Magnet Bath

Add cubebs and hibiscus blossoms to your bath. Reserve some of the used bathwater and sprinkle it around your home to signal your magical invitation to a new lover.

 ## Old Love Spell

A proverb suggests that love is wasted on the young. Orrisroot preserves the pleasures and passions of romance throughout one's life. Create this powder by grinding orrisroot and blending with rice powder. Dust on your body and the bed sheets as desired.

Oils of Love

Other oils will be found in *Formulary*, including **Black Cat**, **Cleopatra**, **Come to Me Lover!**, and **Queen of Sheba**.

 Amor Oil

1. Place a balm of Gilead bud and a piece of coral inside a bottle.
2. Cover these with sweet almond and jojoba oils.
3. Add a few drops of either neroli or petitgrain essential oil plus a drop of tangerine essential oil.
4. Add a bit of ground cinnamon or *one* drop of essential oil of cinnamon leaf.

 New Orleans-style Fast Luck Oil

As far as love goes, Fast Luck Oil is a pick-up oil. Expect to draw a surprise one-night stand or even a great weekend, but not true long-lasting lingering love. The ingredients are cinnamon, vanilla, and Wintergreen, with a jojoba oil base.

 Orrisroot Spell (1)

Place a pinch of ground orrisroot in each corner of every room of your home to attract new love.

Orrisroot Spell (2)

Carry whole, unadorned orrisroot for success with the opposite sex.

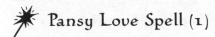 Pansy Love Spell (1)

Look for pansies with little faces that please you. Weave them into chains and hang them in the bedroom to capture the love you desire.

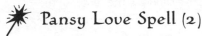 Pansy Love Spell (2)

This spell evokes shades of A Midsummer's Night's Dream.

1. If the one you desire is sleeping, place or pass pansies over their eyes, then linger near.
2. Allegedly he or she will fall in love with the first person seen upon awakening.

 Q Perfume Oil

What does "Q" stand for? No one remembers anymore. However, this famous hoodoo formulation allegedly causes you to be romantically irresistible.

1. Use carnation absolute, the hydrosol or powder fresh carnation blossoms.
2. Blend with myrrh and peppermint and then add to sweet almond oil.

 Red Witch Candle Spell

Candles in the shape of red witches are particularly beneficial for love magic.

The imagery is always positive: the red witch may represent the power of the witch as an ally or she can transcend the entire concept of human witches, to represent primordial female power. The red witch is symbolic for the menstrual blood that figures in so many love spells.

Red Witch candles are used to draw love:

1. Anoint her with love drawing oils.
2. Chant your invocation:
   Red witch, red witch
   Bring me my lover
3. Light the candle for a set period of time nightly. Choose a number that has significance for you—six minutes, nine, an hour. What is crucial is that this increment of time be maintained faithfully.
4. Burn nightly until consumed.

This spell may be used for an unknown lover or for someone whom you already desire. If you know the person's identity, insert their name into the chant.

 ## Red Witch Love Spell (1)

1. Place a beautiful red apple beside a red witch candle.
2. Burn the candle while murmuring incantations of love.
3. Feed the apple to your heart's desire.

 ## Red Witch Love Spell (2)

1. Scratch your beloved's name beneath the witch's feet (the base of the candle).
2. Dress the candle with the fragrance of roses.
3. Burn the candle while chanting: *"Red witch, red witch, bring my love to me!"* or whatever best expresses your own situation.

 ## Red Witch: Wisteria Spell

1. Charge a red witch candle with your desires.
2. Place a wisteria root beside her while she burns.
3. When the candle has burned down, tie a red thread around the root and carry it in a red charm bag to attract happy love towards you.

 ## Re-ignite Love Spell

"Nothing's cold as ashes after the fire is gone …"

Allegedly vervain can re-ignite spent passions and past love. Create an infusion by pouring boiling water over vervain leaves. Add the infusion to your bath and allow yourself to air-dry when meeting your old love— although presumably for maximum effectiveness one bathes together.

 ## Right Person Love Spell

*You don't want just any love; you need the right one. This spell is beneficial for a long-term love search. Add **Attraction Oil** to your bath every Friday until you've found the love you want.*

Romantic Maintenance Spells

 ## Romantic Maintenance (1) Angel Powder

Grind and powder pink rosebuds, red carnations, vervain, and spearmint. Sprinkle this powder on your sheets to keep your lover interested and true.

 ## Romantic Maintenance (2) Bath

This romantic love bath for seduction and sharing is based on the herbal traditions and lush flora of the French Antilles. Make a strong infusion of hibiscus, mignonette (reseda), and orange blossoms and then add it to your bath, together with some pure vanilla extract.

✴ Romantic Maintenance (3)
Beryl

Beryl gemstones are used to cement and solidify romance. They are also used to renew and rescue fading love. They are most effective when worn as a ring or a necklace.

Wear beryl to attempt control over the situation. Alternately, give as a gift to your partner to provide some romantic insurance.

✴ Romantic Maintenance (4)
Candle

1. Melt some candle wax.
2. Remove from the heat and stir in honey, sugar, romantic flower petals, and your favorite perfume.
3. Pour this enhanced wax into a hollow half of a coconut shell, complete with a candle-wick.
4. Burn the candle to entice your lover and maintain his interest as well as to provide a sweet, protected atmosphere.

✴ Romantic Maintenance (5)
Cinnamon

Grind pieces of cinnamon or cassia bark together with hair from your head and that of your partner's. Burn and place the ashes in a glass vial. Keep the vial in a safe place for as long as you wish love to last.

✴ Romantic Maintenance (6)
Conjure Bag

1. Fill a medicine bag with small magnetic horseshoes, a lodestone (or a matched pair), and some love drawing powder or herbs.
2. In addition, a photograph of your lover is needed: either solo or ideally a photograph of the two of you together, looking happy. A photo of you kissing is even better.
3. On the back of the photo, draw a heart and write your names inside five times, something like *"Jon and Jennifer Together Forever."* Anoint with **Come To Me Oil!** or similar.
4. Keep the bag safe under your mattress.

✴ Romantic Maintenance (7)
Elder Spell

Place a branch of elder wood beneath the bed to preserve love, stimulate passion, and encourage fidelity.

✴ Romantic Maintenance (8)
Love Protection Spell

Blend lavender blossoms with violet leaves and flowers. Carry in a charm bag to protect your love from challenges and danger.

✴ Romantic Maintenance (9)
Mistletoe Kiss Spell

Why do people kiss under the mistletoe? Because it's fun? Well, yes but also because doing so allegedly magically preserves love and ensures that the relationship lasts (providing there is a relationship to begin with). Don't take the mistletoe down once the Yule season is over; hang it throughout the home and repeat the spell as needed!

✴ Romantic Maintenance (10)
Pansy Bag

Carry pansies in a charm bag to ensure that your lover remains enamored of you.

Romantic Maintenance (11)
Perfume

1. Entwine a strand of your own hair with that of your beloved.
2. Place this braid into a bottle filled with your favorite perfume.
3. Add an Adam and Eve root.
4. Wear this perfume daily.

 ## Romantic Maintenance (12)
Plum

Share one single plum to keep love fresh and lively.

 ## Romantic Maintenance (13)
Protection

Sprinkle an infusion of hawthorn berries together with whole berries around the perimeter of your home to foil those who would lure your partner away.

 ## Romantic Maintenance (14)
Spikenard

Make an infusion of spikenard or add a few drops of the essential oil to some warm water.

Carefully sprinkle this on a photograph of your lover, or on his shoes, or even on him (although this can be hard to explain). This allegedly keeps love constant and true.

 ## Romantic Maintenance (15)
Sugar

To inspire a romantic, loving ambience—because the only good part of an argument is making up:

1. Fill an air-tight canister with fine granulated sugar, either white or brown is fine.
2. Imbed a vanilla bean, a cinnamon stick, cardamom pods, some dried hibiscus blossoms, and some orange blossoms in it.
3. Visualize love flowing out of the canister and spreading through the room. Seal the canister. Use it as a powder sprinkle or feed it to your lover and yourself in times of tension.

 ## Romantic Maintenance (16)
Tormentil

Tormentil's nickname is "flesh and blood." Hang it within your home and bedroom to keep you and your partner's flesh and blood together.

 ## Romantic Maintenance (17)
Yarrow Heads

1. Bind nine dried yarrow flower heads still on the stalks together with green silk ribbon.
2. Hang this over the bed to ensure pleasure and happiness.

This charm is most powerful when created on a waxing moon Friday.

Roses Spells

Roses are a metaphor for the human heart. No flower represents love more vividly. Perhaps nothing does. Roses are sacred to the most powerful spirits of love: Aphrodite, Juno, Isis, Kybele, Maitresse Ezili, and Maria Padilha. Oshun loves yellow roses.

Cleopatra, the living embodiment of Aphrodite and Isis, seduced Marc Antony in a scented bedroom, packed knee-deep with rose petals.

Red Rose Powder

Red Rose Powder is used to heal lover's quarrels.

1. Grind red rose petals and peppermint leaves into a fine powder.
2. Sprinkle Red Rose Powder on your partner, on a gift of a bouquet of flowers, or on the sheets.

Better yet, add Red Rose Powder to rice powder to create a body dusting powder. Apply it to your own body with a powder puff so that no one can stay mad at you.

 ## Rose Love Beads

The original love beads are crafted from rose petals.

1. Process rose petals in a food processor or grind them with a mortar and pestle until they form a paste.
2. Roll small amounts into tiny beads with your fingers. Concentrate on your desire as you roll, utter a petition of love as you form each bead.
3. Let the beads dry, ideally on a screen that allows air to circulate.
4. While they are still slightly damp, before the bead has completely dried, pierce each bead with a large needle, so that it may be strung on a cord. Visualize your heart pierced with love as you wield the needle.
5. String the beads on a red silk cord and wear it or hang it over your bed.

Red Rose Spell

1. Place a long stemmed red rose between two red taper candles dressed with a love oil.
2. Burn the candles.
3. When the candles have burned down, give the rose to the one you want.

Spells to initiate love emerge from different needs. Perhaps you await your soul mate, whose identity remains unknown, or perhaps soul mates and true love aren't an issue: you'd just like a companion, a new lover or relationship. Or maybe you have your heart set on someone special, whose identity is known to you. Now if only this person shared your desires …

 ## Seeking New Love Spell

A spell to find new love, particularly following a long period of solitude, loneliness and bad luck:

1. Add a few strands of hair from your head plus some thumb nail clippings to dried rose petals, Grains of Paradise, and vervain.
2. Burn them over lit charcoal like incense.
3. Stand over the rising smoke wearing outer garments but no underpants. Inhale the smoke's fragrance as it wafts up toward you.
4. Still wearing no underpants, travel to a cemetery.
5. Walk through the cemetery in two directions, forming the shape of a cross, to destroy evil from all directions.
6. Go home via a different route than the one by which you arrived.

 ## Seeking New Love: Catnip

1. Soak catnip in good whiskey overnight, ideally in the light of the Full Moon.
2. Strain it out and sprinkle the liquid on your doorstep for 21 days in the shape of a new crescent moon.

Seeking New Love: Grains of Paradise

Grains of Paradise allegedly incite passion, erotic thoughts, and actions. They also possess a commanding element. Originally a popular East African magical ingredient, they are now renowned worldwide.

Use them to draw new love into your life: add an infusion of Grains of Paradise to your bath water; sprinkle the used bath water together with some extra powder around your home to signal your availability.

 ## Seeking New Love Shoe Spell (1) Gullah

Burn your former lover's shoes and you'll have more new loves than you'll know what to do with. (Conversely, folk wisdom states you should never give a lover a gift of shoes: he or she will only use them to walk out on you.)

 ## Seeking New Love Shoe Spell (2) Violet Leaf

Violet leaves resemble hearts. Place some in your shoe to attract new love and to guide you towards the right lover.

 ## Snake's Friend Love Spell

The flower Indian Paint Brush is also known as Snake's Friend. Place the blossoms in a sachet to draw love near.

Seeking Someone Special Spells

Spells for when you know who you want.

 ## Someone Special: Altar of Love Spell

This is a spell to persuade someone to return your affections. Three candles are required: one to represent you, the second, the object of your affections and the last candle, the potential state of romance. Use figure candles to represent the people plus a large pillar or heart-shaped candle.

1. Arrange the two figure candles six inches apart.
2. Place the third at the apex of the triangle.
3. Dress the candles, petition, and light.

 ## Someone Special: Clothing Spell

1. You'll need a piece of your lover's clothing, ideally intimate apparel but anything, a glove or a scarf, will do.
2. Gather seven acorns and wrap them in the clothing.
3. Knot the packet shut with red thread.
4. Sleep with it under your pillow for seven nights.
5. On the eighth day, take the packet into the woods (or the closest semblance you have). Find a natural cleft, a cleft in a tree, a hole in the ground. Look for an appropriate place and slip the packet inside.
6. Walk around the spot three times sunwise, calling your beloved's name each time you do a rotation. Walk away and don't look back.

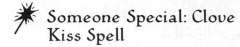

Someone Special: Clove Kiss Spell

1. Arrange for the person you desire to visit you at your home.
2. Stir a spoonful of brown sugar into a glass of rainwater. Have it waiting by the back door or a back window while you wait for your potential lover to arrive.
3. When the person arrives, before you answer the door, pop a clove into your mouth and suck on it.
4. Toss the rainwater out the back and spit the clove out after it.
5. Pop another clove in your mouth and answer the door.
6. Kiss your intended, with the clove still tucked into your mouth, touching his or her tongue with your own.

Someone Special: Conjure Bag

1. Write both your names together (*"Morgan and Merlin Together 4-Ever"*) seven times on a heart-shaped piece of paper.
2. Place this paper in a red silk bag together with a lock of the other person's hair or some threads from their clothing.
3. Add a lodestone, love-drawing powder, a rose quartz, and seven rose buds.
4. Carry this bag to draw the love you want.

Someone Special: Dream Ashes Spell

For this spell, you will need an object that fulfills two criteria: first it must carry the vibration of the person the spell targets. Thus it must belong to him or preferably have been in extended contact with him. And second, it must be possible to burn it.

1. At night place this object between your legs and dream of happiness together with your lover.
2. Do this for nine consecutive nights.
3. Then burn the entire object or part of it, reserving the rest for later use, on a Friday morning, as the sun rises.
4. Reserve the ashes. Whenever possible, sprinkle these on the man, his shoes, or his underwear.

Someone Special: Footprint Spell (1) Buried

1. Dig up the entire footprint of the one you love.
2. Whisper over the dirt, telling the feet exactly where you'd like them to come.
3. Bury the footprint dirt under your front doorstep.

Someone Special: Footprint Spell (2) Hung Up

1. Gather up the entire footprint of the one you desire.
2. Tie it up in a cloth and hang it over your door to draw the person to you.

This spell will be enhanced if you dress the dirt with an appropriate oil, such as **Come to Me Lover!** *or* **Follow Me Boy!**

Someone Special: Foot Track Love Spell

Dig up the footprint of the person you desire. Place it within a bag and carry it with you. The other person should feel obliged to follow you.

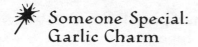 Someone Special: Garlic Charm

To inflame a heart with passion (and dominate them too!):

1. Puncture two garlic cloves, one on top of the other, with a steel nail, so that they are held together. (You may also wrap a red thread around them for reinforcement.) The clove on top represents the person making the charm. Make sure that one stays on top.
2. Hide this charm in a dark, private place at least until the other person begins to demonstrate signs of affection (or you no longer want them).

Should the bottom garlic sprout, this is a very auspicious sign.

 Someone Special: Hair Spell

Procure a lock (or even a strand) of hair from the one you desire. Wear it in your hat to turn their heart toward you.

 Someone Special: Heart Spell

1. Write the name of the person you desire on parchment paper seven times.
2. Draw a heart around these names by writing your own name in script, without picking up the pen or pencil. Lengthen each letter or write your name repeatedly, the key is not to pick up the pen until the seven names are completely enclosed by your own.
3. Chant something like: *"You are in my heart"* or *" My heart encompasses you."*
4. Preserve this talisman of love in a safe place. (Should you change your mind, rip up the paper, breaking the heart, and destroy it.)

 Someone Special: Magic Ring Spell

1. On a New Moon Friday evening, fill a wine glass with either red wine or spring water.
2. Suspend a ring from a red ribbon that is long enough so that the ring may be comfortably suspended like a pendulum within the mouth of the glass. Traditionally, this sort of spell uses your mother's wedding ring or similar sentimental ring but any ring may be transformed into a magic ring.
3. Initially keep the pendulum as still as possible. First say your own name, then call out the name of your desired one. Repeat this three times.
4. Focus your mind on your beloved. Let the pendulum begin to sway until it clinks against the glass one time for every letter of his or her name.
5. Tie the ribbon around your neck, letting the ring fall over your heart or between your breasts.
6. Repeat the spell for the next two consecutive Fridays for a total of three Fridays, wearing the ring continually in between. You should see results by the conclusion.

 Someone Special: Name Paper Ashes

1. Write the desired one's name on a strip of paper or parchment.
2. Write your desired goal upon another one.
3. Cover the other person's name with your own.
4. Place both in a cauldron, fireproof bowl or pan, together with orange blossoms and/or orange leaves and/or orange zest.
5. Burn everything.
6. Gather up the ashes. Slip them into a small box or perfume vial. If it's a bottle, seal shut with wax. If a box, use knot magic (silk threads) to close.

If you find that someday you no longer desire this relationship, break the seal and scatter the contents to the winds.

 **Someone Special: Name Paper Candle Spell**

Although this spell did not originate as a petition to Oshun, it does use her materials and is very easy to dedicate to her. If so desired, use a yellow candle instead of red and burn it for five days.

1. Cut two slips of paper, approximately the size of a fortune in a fortune cookie.
2. Write your name on one and the name of your beloved on the other.
3. Pin them together in the form of a cross, with your name on top.
4. Put them in a glass containing water, orange flower water, and sugar.
5. Burn a dressed red candle before the glass for nine days.

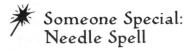 **Someone Special: Needle Spell**

1. Take two needles.
2. Charge, empower, and consecrate them.
3. Name one for yourself and one for your beloved.
4. Traditionally the point of the male needle is inserted into the eye of the female needle, however this may be adjusted to suit your circumstances.
5. Preserve in a safe place as a love charm.

 Someone Special: Picture of Love

Cover a small photo of the one you love by wrapping it in strands of your hair. Wrap this up in red thread. Wrap this up in red velvet and bury the whole packet in Earth.

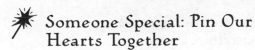 **Someone Special: Pin Our Hearts Together**

1. Cut two hearts from red wax.
2. Scratch your name on one, your beloved's on the other.
3. Pin them together with three pins and carry near your heart.

 Someone Special: Pin Our Hearts Together Deluxe Version

To create an intensified version of the above spell, scent the wax with jasmine. Sandwich a little powdered orrisroot and/or rose petals between the two hearts before pinning with the three pins.

 Someone Special: Pin Our Hearts Together Love Charm

1. Cut two hearts from red wax.
2. Designate each heart to represent a person.
3. Using needles attach the hearts together and wear them next to your heart.

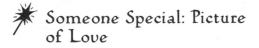 **Someone Special: Rattlesnake Master**

*Rattlesnake master root allegedly enables you to capture the love you desire. Anoint the root daily with a drop of love-drawing oil, such as **Come to Me Lover!** until your goal is achieved.*

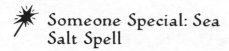

Someone Special: Sea Salt Spell

To win the love of the one you desire, walking naked make a circuit around a field or your home in the light of the Full Moon. With each step, toss a handful of sea salt behind you.

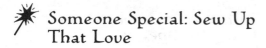

Someone Special: Sew Up That Love

To have and keep the object of your desire:

1. Obtain some stray hairs belonging to your heart's desire: extract them from a comb or brush, or pull some out of the bathtub drain.
2. Sew them into your mattress or into a dream pillow stuffed with love-herbs.

Someone Special: Shoe Spell

1. Obtain a lock of hair from the one you desire.
2. Wrap it in a small square of silk, folding the cloth toward you.
3. Wear it in your shoe.
4. The object of your desire should soon approach and give you the opportunity to make a favorable impression.

Someone Special: Snail Shell Spell

To win love, abandoned snail shells are converted to love charms. Gently carry a snail shell on your body. Give it to the one you love and get him or her to carry it.

Snail shells are fragile. If it's crushed too quickly, consider whether this is a sign.

Self-Love Spells

Before you can receive love from another, you must love yourself. Roses, hibiscus, and calendula stimulate and teach self-love, self-forgiveness, and self-acceptance.

★ *Add fresh blossoms to your bath*
★ *Make infusions from dried flowers and add to your bath*
★ *Surround yourself with bouquets and living plants*

Talismans of Love

Fairy tales are full of magic power objects that draw love and good fortune toward their bearers. What the stories sometimes neglect to mention is that you can craft your own.

Talisman of Love: Chinese Coins

Traditional Chinese coins have square holes in the center. They are customarily strung together with red thread for good luck and protection. Hair should be substituted for love spells.

1. Obtain several hairs from the head of your beloved.
2. Braid them together.
3. String two coins together with this hair. (If the hair is long enough, wrap the coins in the hair, too.)
4. Wrap this charm in red silk or sew it onto the red silk.

Talisman of Love: Coral Earrings

In ancient Rome, coral earrings were believed to beckon men and draw love. Wear a pair at strategic opportunities.

Talisman of Love: Needle and Shroud

1. You'll need a needle that has been stuck into a dead human body.
2. Place the needle onto a small piece of cloth cut from a shroud or winding sheet.
3. Cover the needle with dirt in which a corpse has been laid. (This does not have to be the same corpse as Step 1.)
4. Wrap the needle and dirt up in the cloth and preserve it. You now possess what is allegedly a very powerful love charm. Pierce someone's clothes with the needle to make them fall in love with you.

 ## Talisman of Love: Peyote

Peyote may be used to create amulets for love and romantic happiness. Peyote, like lodestone, is distinguished as being male or female: they're visibly distinctive. Women need a male peyote while men need a female one.

1. The peyote must be kept whole.
2. Bathe the peyote in ritual corn beer.
3. Sing to the peyote. Dance for it. Tell it your desire.
4. Wrap it in a small piece of red silk and carry it near the heart or wrapped around the right knee.

 ## Talisman of Love: Red Ribbon Spell

To discover a bit of red ribbon, string, wool, or piece of fabric indicates luck in love and a change in romantic fortunes. Pick it up and make a wish. (If you can't think of one, requesting luck and happiness in love is more than appropriate.) Carry the ribbon as an amulet.

 ## Talisman of Love: Rose Quartz

Rose quartz allegedly draws lovers towards you. Wear it as jewelry or carry it with you.

Should it draw too many, too fast in an overwhelming manner, add an amethyst for a stabilizing effect.

 ## Talisman of Love: Sweet Lotus Petal Spell

Carry lotus petals and flowers (real or replica) in a charm bag together with sugar cubes and a scarab charm to attract love towards you.

Vervain Spells

 ## Vervain Spell (1) Bath

1. Make an infusion of vervain by pouring boiling water over the botanical.
2. When it cools off, add the entire infusion (liquid and plant material) to your bath, ladling it over your body.
3. Rub the vervain over your body and soak in the bath for luck in love.

 ## Vervain Spell (2) Oil

Vervain is another of those plants where no essential oil is produced. What is commercially available tends to be lemon verbena, a South American native that bears a confusingly similar name but is botanically distinct. Create your own infused oil of vervain to obtain its profound magical benefits.

Create an oil-based infusion of vervain leaves following the directions in Elements of Magic Spells, *page 31. When the oil is complete, massage it onto your body or add it to your bath.*

Vervain Spell (3) Sweet Touch

Crush some fresh vervain leaves in your hands. Rub the juice over your hands; don't wash it off before touching the one you love. The results are reputedly very sweet.

 ## Window box Spell

Plant a love window box with love-attracting flowers and herbs: pansies, poppies, marjoram, rosemary, lovage, thyme, and miniature roses. This magically signals your availability and your desire for love.

 ## Wishbone Love Spell

Paint a wishbone gold. Carry it in a red charm bag together with six Grains of Paradise and some red rose petals.

 ## Witchgrass Spells

Witchgrass, also known as couch grass, may be used to draw love toward you. Carry it in a charm bag to attract new love. Or grind the dried botanical into powder and sprinkle it under your bed to stimulate fun, romance, and commitment.

 ## Yarrow Love Bath

Add yarrow hydrosol to your bath to locate a new lover.

Binding Spells

It's crucial to distinguish between banishing and binding spells, a not uncommon source of confusion.

★ *Banishing spells repel something or someone, removing it from your presence, perhaps permanently*
★ *Binding spells bind another person to you through eternity and perhaps beyond*

Occasionally the term "*binding*" is meant to indicate that someone has been incapacitated ("*bound*") and is no longer able to harm you. However it is *not* used in that context in this book. Think "*ties that bind*" rather than "*bound and gagged.*"

There are two types of love binding spells:

★ *Mutual binding spells that couples cast together to preserve, enhance, and protect love. In a sense these are magical soul weddings, affirmations of true love. These bindings are entered into consciously and with free will and desire*
★ *Binding spells that one party casts on the other, frequently without their knowledge. These bindings are often desperate attempts to salvage a relationship or prevent another from leaving. In a sense, these spells assert romantic ownership over another party. As such, they can be malevolent spells, which rarely work out happily for either party*

How do you know if a binding spell has been cast over you? If every effort to leave a relationship fails, there's reason at least for suspicion. Never fear; as with hexes, antidotes exist.

There is a key difference between menstrual blood potions and classical binding spells: a successful menstrual potion causes the other person to love you forever. You, however, remain a free agent. Binding spells bind you as surely as they bind the other party. Use them judiciously.

Wait! Before the binding spells begin below, how do you know you have the right person? Are you binding yourself to true love or to living disaster? These two spells will help you determine the answer.

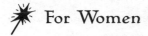 For Women

*Rue attracts love but also eliminates women's romantic illusions. **It is not safe for use by pregnant women or those actively attempting to become pregnant.** (In which case, other issues and factors may be at hand.)*

Simultaneously burn rue, inhaling the fragrance, while drinking rue tea. Bathing in an infusion of rue, at the same time, will maximize the potential of this spell.

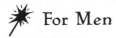 For Men

An amethyst carried as a talisman attracts women. It specifically draws honorable women.

Mutual Binding Spells: True Love Spells

These binding spells are entered into freely and with mutual intent. They produce a magical wedding of souls and affirm commitment to one another. At their best, these are the most romantic spells of all.

Ancient Irish Hair Binding

In ancient Ireland, it was customary for a man to braid a bracelet from his hair and give it to the woman he loved, a gift of trust in the context of what we've seen can be done magically with hair. The binding is not activated unless she accepts the gift, thus accepting him and agreeing to the spell. This is not a binding that can be imposed on another.

Conjure Bag Binding (1) Amazon

1. Create two ritual pouches: bead and decorate them with love.

2. Fill with combined Amazonian herbs, *mucura* and *ajos sacha*.
3. Exchange and carry to protect your love.

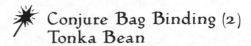 Conjure Bag Binding (2) Tonka Bean

1. On a New Moon Friday, dress a pair of tonka beans with a love drawing oil.
2. Place them in a conjure bag to be kept in a safe, secure place.
3. Re-anoint every Friday, ideally together. Nothing should break you apart.

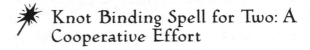 Knot Binding Spell for Two: A Cooperative Effort

This binding spell ensures that a couple remains together. It will also counter efforts to sunder your love, thus serving as a simultaneous protection spell.

1. One partner takes a handkerchief or square of cloth and ties two knots in it.
2. The other partner ties two more knots.
3. Both parties together now take these four knots and tie them together to make one big, tight knot: both parties pulling so that the knot is as tight as possible.
4. Keep the charm in a safe place. Dress it with a love oil periodically.
5. If at some point you do wish to separate, untie or break the knot.

 Lodestone Binding

The most successful binding spells stem from mutual desire and intent.

1. **Lodestone Oil** is required as well as some privacy.
2. Create Magnetic Sand Dusting Powder: combine

rice powder with magnetic sand. You'll need a powder puff or a feather for application. (A shaker bottle will work but doesn't quite have the same effect.)

3. Massage the **Lodestone Oil** onto one partner's body.
4. The other partner should apply the Magnetic Sand Body Powder.
5. Make love.
6. The binding spell is complete; repeat as desired.

 ## Magic Mirror Binding

A binding charm from Hungary: these magic mirrors were once sold in the marketplace and just needed to be cleansed and charged to put into practice. You, however, may have to make your own.

1. You'll need gingerbread dough, whether from scratch or a mix, is irrelevant. The cookie will not be eaten but preserved as a charm: gingerbread lasts virtually forever.
2. With a cookie-cutter, cut the dough into a heart shape.
3. Push a small mirror into the center of the cookie.
4. Bake in a low, slow oven.
5. When it has cooled, decorate with red beads and other charms. Make your charm as elaborate or simple as you like. (Truly elaborate ones place small shutters over the mirror.)
6. When you're ready, you and your beloved should gaze into the mirror together and swear your devotion to each other.
7. Wrap it in red silk cloth and keep in a safe place, perhaps bringing it out whenever your vows need reaffirming.

An almost identical charm is found in Croatia where it's used as a Mother's Day gift. The goal remains the same, however: unswerving devotion.

 ## Pomegranate Binding

"How do I love thee?" Let me count the seeds …
  To effect a binding:

1. Break open pomegranates; two should be sufficient:
2. One partner eats 220 seeds, the other eats 284.
3. Count them and eat them together.

 ## Thumbelina's Love Spell

Thumbelina was famously put to bed in a walnut shell, however the connection between beds and walnuts transcends Thumbelina. Walnuts are used to affect sexual and romantic attraction, either strengthening or breaking those ties that bind. This spell allegedly binds sexual magnetism and fidelity into a relationship.

1. Anoint Adam and Eve Root with a drop of **Come to Me Lover!** or **Amor Oil.**
2. Place within a hollowed-out walnut shell.
3. Lay some spider web over it as a gossamer blanket.
4. Place the other half of the walnut shell on top and seal together with red candle wax.
5. Secrete this charm into your lover's clothing inside a closet or drawer. (Allegedly this charm shouldn't be discovered so don't slip it into a pocket of clothing in active use.)
6. Alternatively, borrow a used sock and place the walnut within that.
7. Make a knot, sealing in your intentions and place the sock under your mattress.

If an Adam and Eve Root is unavailable, miniature figures may be crafted from wax.

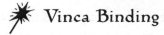
Vinca Binding

According to master herbalist Nicholas Culpeper, if men and women eat the leaves of vinca, the sorcerer's violet, together, this will bind them together forever.

Other Bindings

Any of the following binding spells may be converted into Mutual Binding Spells, although historically one person frequently casts the binding so as to control another. Many of these spells have a malevolent, threatening air rather than a romantic one.

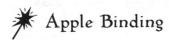
Apple Binding

1. Cut an apple in half horizontally to reveal the star hidden in the center.
2. Spread each half with honey.
3. Take a lock from each person's head, braid them together and place on top of one half of the apple.
4. Bring the two halves together, sandwiching in the honey and hair. Bind them together securely with a red silk ribbon, making several strong knots.
5. Bury this apple in Earth, preferably in a romantic spot.

This may be accompanied by an invocation to Aphrodite, although be warned: if casting the spell against another's will, know that Aphrodite is a rule-breaker with more sympathy for true love, sexual freedom, and attraction than mere ties that bind.

Conjure Bag Binding

A conjure bag to bind a lover:

1. Draw or cut out a paper heart.
2. Write both your names inside it.

3. Anoint the paper with **Come to Me Lover!**, **Cleopatra Oil** and **Command and Compel Oil.**
4. Place it inside a red conjure bag.
5. Add a photograph of your love or one of the two of you together and happy. Also add a lodestone and a small magnetic horseshoe.
6. Add two roots: use angelica to represent women, High John the Conqueror to represent men. Tie them together with red thread, knotting securely.
7. Keep this bag securely beneath your mattress, anointing with more oils, as needed.

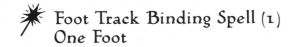
Foot Track Binding Spell (1) One Foot

Obtain a needle which has been used to sew a shroud. Thrust it into your lover's footprint found on your property (the closer to your front door, the more powerful the binding).

This is done with the intent of forcing the lover to stay with you, regardless of his or her desires. This is a mean-spirited binding: according to Ozark legend, if the lover resists the spell, he will gradually fall ill and will only recover in your presence. If he stays away, ultimately he will die.

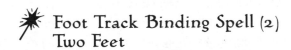
Foot Track Binding Spell (2) Two Feet

1. Find a good footprint left by your partner.
2. Place your foot beside it and make a matching footprint. If it's his left foot, you use your right and vice-versa.
3. Carefully dig both up in their entirety and place in a bag.
4. Add it to a flowerpot with additional Earth if necessary. Mix up all the dirt so it can't be separated.
5. Plant marigolds in the pot.

Graveyard Dirt Binding

1. Take some graveyard dirt with the back of your right hand.
2. Slide it into a charm bag.
3. Place it under the intended one's bed: *"till death do us part …"*

 ## Lamella Binding

A combined binding/enforced fidelity spell. The goal is not only to bind your target to yourself but also to prevent him or her from successfully maintaining a relationship with another. Lamella is the technical name given to small, engraved sheets of metal. The most famous lamellae are ancient curse tablets and this allegedly romantic spell essentially follows the curse tablet format.

1. Inscribe your desires on a tablet of wax or a sheet of copper or tin: You can make this about yourself or you can focus on the threat of a third party. For example: *"May [Name] child of [Name] have no desire for anyone but me, [Name] child of [Name]. Let him only have sex with me. Let us grow old together in happiness and health."* Or: *"Keep [Name] child of [Name] away from [Name] child of [Name]. There is no desire between them. There is no pleasure between them. There is no sex between them. There is no affection between them. There is nothing between them."*
2. Roll it up tightly and pierce it with a nail.
3. Place this in an underground place: a well, a grave, a cave, or a sewer, where it will not be disturbed for eternity.

 ## Magic Mirror Binding (1) Broken

This binding spell also allegedly ensures fidelity. It keeps him planted safely at home.

You will need a small hand mirror in which your lover is the last person to look. Important: *do not look inside the mirror!*

1. Smash the mirror into tiny pieces.
2. Bury these in your yard if you have one; if not, bury it in within a flowerpot filled with dirt and keep it inside. Plant a love drawing flower to mark the spot.
3. On Fridays, anoint the ground above the shards with oil of spikenard (the essential oil, or you can make an infusion from the root) or shave a piece of root onto the spot while repeating an invocation including your lover's name.

 ## Magic Mirror Binding (2) Preserved

1. Place a photo of yourself, face up, beneath a small mirror.
2. Take a photo of your heart's desire and place it face down in front of the mirror, so that the faces in the photographs are looking at each other with the mirror in between.
3. Wrap the three objects together with red cord or thread, focusing on each knot.
4. Wrap the bound mirror in red silk cloth.
5. Now wrap this package in thread once again, so it's very tight and secure.
6. You must now hide this packet: the traditional Romany spell recommends burying it somewhere in the target's home. If you'd like to do this, bury it inside a plant and give it as a gift (and hope that the gift isn't passed on). But this may not be possible or even desirable; what if they find it and unwrap it? What if you change your mind and can't get it back?
7. Consider burying in Earth, ideally besides apple trees, roses, or other plants of love, or even in a flowerpot filled with Earth and plants, kept under your control in your home.

 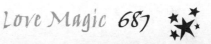

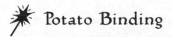 ## Potato Binding

1. Take two potatoes of similar shape and size.
2. Slice each in half vertically.
3. Retain one half of each potato. (Cook the other halves as you will. Garnish with basil and parsley and eat them together with your lover.)
4. Designate one half potato as you, the other as your partner. Carve the appropriate names, initials, birthdays, and identifying information into the cut sides of the potatoes.
5. Spread honey over the cut sides.
6. Place the two halves together so that they appear to be one potato. Stick either a new nail or a coffin nail horizontally through the potatoes, connecting them together. Drive it through the potato representing your partner first, so that the head of the nail is on his side and the point is coming through you.
7. Bind the potatoes together further with red silk cord.
8. In the moonlight, bury this tied-together potato. If you have no access to land, bury it in a flowerpot and grow either love herbs or a cactus.

 ## Secret Sortilege of the Seven Knots of Love

Once upon a time, this Secret Sortilege Spell was extremely popular: religious goods supply stores sold kits containing the complete ingredients. Someplace, stacked in a warehouse, those kits must still exist.

This elaborate spell, combines knot magic, medieval high magic, as well as appeals to the saints. It's an interesting spell, combining the simplicity of knot magic with all the "stuff" and precision of high ceremonial magic. There are also extremely detailed lengthy incantations. I've adapted the language so that it's reasonably simple while maintaining the poetry. More arcane versions also exist if you prefer, or just re-phrase to your own satisfaction. The spell reflects a jumble of traditions: the original makes reference to "Cabalistic circles" although there's little here to do with Kaballah.

Saint Anthony is invoked for miracles and love magic, Saint Martha for her commanding powers.

1. You will need a red silk ribbon approximately 12 inches long. Seven knots will be made in this ribbon, each knot approximately an inch apart.
2. The initial knot is made in the center of the ribbon. While knotting say: *"With this first knot, I tie you up [Name], child of [Name] in a magic circle, enclosed by the force of my love and will."*
3. Make the second knot about an inch to the right of the first knot and say: *"This second knot binds your will [Name], child of [Name] with mine with the force of steel. You will not say or do anything that does not correspond with my desire."*
4. Make the third knot about an inch to the left of the initial center knot and say: *"With this third knot I tie up your love and hold it firmly to mine. You will not be able to break this love, regardless of your intention. You will not break it. You will not loosen it. You will not shake it. I do not wish your energy to be weakened."*
5. The fourth knot is tied to the right of the initial knot, an inch past the second knot and you should say: *"Your thoughts are completely bound to my own. You will never be able to remove from your mind the image of me that follows you lovingly wherever you go and wherever you are. My love and my just desires are executed as I desire now. I demand this by the force and power of the Secret Sortilege. I demand this by the ardent petition of love that I dedicate to Saint Martha the Dominator and to Saint Anthony, so that they are my proponents in what I wish with all sincerity, with justice and without bad intentions."*
6. The fifth knot is tied to the left of the center, one inch past the third knot. Say: *"With this fifth knot, I imprison your heart. You will be unable to fall in love with any other person. You will not desire to fall in love with any other person. You will not attempt to fall in love with any other person. Your heart is entirely dedicated to my love and happiness."*

7. The sixth knot is tied to the right, an inch past the fourth. Say: *"From this day forth, your words, your thoughts, your desires, your actions are on me because of this well-placed Secret Sortilege and the knot-work that I do."*

8. The final knot is tied to the left, past the fifth. Say: *"Your love is entirely and completely mine. With this knot I close the circle. I enclose you in my magic circle, formed from this Magic Ribbon. With this circle, I surround your heart, I enclose your heart. With this circle I love you. With this circle you and I are bonded as one through these Seven Knots of Love. We are as one from this day forward. We will stand together for each other. Nothing will be able to break, interrupt, or destroy our happiness and unity."*

9. Tie the two ends of the ribbon together to form a circle. Snip off the left-over ribbon. Use this ribbon to tie two silver charms to the circle. A male or female silver head, representing the target of your desire, is tied to the seventh knot; the one representing yourself is tied to the center.

10. Build an altar featuring Martha and Anthony.

11. Every other night, for a total of seven times (so over 14 nights) place the circle around your left arm, above the elbow before you go to sleep. (This instruction presupposes the size of one's arm: if necessary put it on the left wherever you can.)

12. When you awake hide the charm behind or beneath your altar.

13. Once the 14 days are over, the charm remains there. This presupposes that you will maintain this altar. From then on, carry a special charm: a silver heart pierced by a sword with three crosses, engraved with the word *"Blessed."*

The Spell of Nine

1. Carve your name and that of your beloved on a candle. Add any identifying information or anything else you deem necessary.

2. Blend honey, rosewater or rose hydrosol, and rose petals. (You want this to be on the dryer, sticky side; don't add too much floral water.) Optional ingredients: menstrual blood, henna powder, or ground cinnamon.

3. Roll the candle in this mixture.

4. Light the candle at exactly 9 p.m. for exactly nine minutes for nine consecutive nights. (The more you can incorporate the number nine the better; initiate the spell on the ninth day of the ninth month, if you can.)

5. On the ninth night, take whatever is left of the candle and wrap it up in fabric.

6. Tie it with a red ribbon.

7. Bury this package at a crossroads, in a cemetery, at a crossroads within the cemetery or, prosaically but equally effectively, under your front doorstep.

Allegedly no one can witness any part of this spell or it won't work.

Wax Image Binding

You will need a wax image representing the couple you intend to bind together. You may use commercially prepared candles because they are the easiest to obtain, however this image will ultimately be buried not burned. Because one doesn't need to worry about a functional wick, it's easy to sculpt a wax figure.

Using one single wax figure to represent the couple intensifies the binding, however individual figures may also be used.

1. Make a garland by knotting flowers together.

2. Wrap this around the wax figurine, especially around the target of the spell.

3. Carve your desires and intentions into the figure with a rose thorn.

4. Write your desire on a piece of parchment or carve it into a wax tablet.

5. Tie it to the wax figure with 365 knots, knotting your intentions into every single knot.

6. Bury the statue at a crossroads or in a cemetery.

To Break a Binding Spell

You've discovered that someone has bound you without your knowledge or permission and against your desires. All is not lost. Binding chains can be broken.

 ## Antidote Spell

1. Powdered sassafras bark is required. Take a bit from your own tree and grind with a mortar and pestle or purchase from an herbal supplier. Ground sassafras is also a staple of Cajun cuisine, sold under the name filé powder—think filé gumbo. It may be purchased under that name from spice companies.
2. Add the ground powder to a blend of castor and jojoba oils. (Do *not* use essential oil of sassafras; it is highly toxic.)
3. On seven squares of paper, write the following using **Dragon's Blood Ink:**

   I break your power; I destroy your force [Name], *child of* [Name]
   You have no control over me [Name], *child of* [Name]
   You have no power over me [Name], *child of* [Name]
   I am free from your binding spell.
4. Every morning for seven consecutive mornings, soak one paper in the oil.
5. Tear it into either three or five pieces. Add the pieces to frankincense and myrrh resin and burn them.
6. Every day, as you complete this spell, the power of the other person over you diminishes. It should be completely broken by the spell's conclusion.

Break Up and Romantic Discouragement Spells

Sometimes the romantic issue at hand isn't attracting or maintaining love, rather it's terminating a relationship. *Break-Up Spells* include:

★ Spells to terminate an established, existing relationship
★ Spells to discourage unwanted attention from strangers and also from those who imagine a relationship exists where it does not. If that attention is extremely persistent and aggressive, check out Banishing Spells *(page 127)* for those that discourage stalkers

 ## Anti-Love Potion

Turnips are allegedly the anti-love food. Set a dish of turnips before an unwanted suitor to send him on his way.

 ## Black Snake Root Spell (1) Bath

This magical bath is recommended when you wish that someone would reconsider their present romantic interest in you, and especially to help terminate an abusive relationship or to discourage someone whom you perceive possesses the potential for abuse. **Black snake root is not safe for pregnant women.**

1. Make an infusion by pouring boiling water over chopped black snake root, also known as black cohosh.
2. Fill the bath with water.
3. When the infusion cools, do not strain it but bring it to the bathtub.
4. Enter the bath and ladle the infusion over your body before soaking in the water.

Black Snake Root Spell (2) Protection

Black snake root protects against repeat involvement in abusive relationships. Carry it with you or bathe in the infusion to protect yourself.

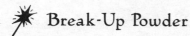 Break-Up Powder

Sometimes a significant relationship may have ended for you. Now you're waiting for the other person to come to the same understanding.

1. Grind and powder the following dried botanicals: lemongrass, mullein, patchouli, valerian, and vetiver.
2. Sprinkle the powder in the pockets and shoes of the one whom you'd like to send packing.

Warning: this is not a secret spell. The ingredients are derived from **Van Van** *and (botanical)* **Graveyard Dust***. The powder will have a strong aroma. Questions will be asked.*

 Camphor Spell

Unfortunately, sometimes attention drawn is the wrong kind. Magic spells help you discourage unwanted attention: during the days of the polio epidemic, mothers hung camphor balls around children's necks to ward away illness. This spell works under the same premises, except that what you're warding off is the metaphysical virus of an unwanted romantic attention.

Choose one of these options:

★ *Reproduce the old childhood remedy*
★ *Dip a cotton ball in essential oil of white camphor* and keep it in your pocket or tucked into a bra*

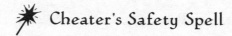 Cheater's Safety Spell

This spell allegedly protects a cheater from detection. It allows you to go from one lover's arms straight into those of another without having those cheating vibes subliminally betray you.

Rub your cleansed genitals with an egg. Flush the egg down the toilet.

 Post Break-up Cleansing

According to general metaphysical wisdom, any sexual relationship creates vestigial ties that bind, the more intense, passionate, and lengthy the relationship, the more intense, passionate, and lingering the bonds. This cleansing spell is beneficial whenever you wish to sever and erase those bonds, whether from a long-term relationship or a one-night stand.

Gently rub a whole raw egg against your naked body, from head to toe and outwards from shoulders to fingers, with extra emphasis placed on the genitals. When complete, break the raw egg into the toilet and flush it away.

* Be sure not to use any other variety of camphor. Only essential oil of white camphor is safe for use.

✳ Quitting Powder

This Hoodoo formula could be called "Love Fix Powder." It allegedly forces someone to quit bothering you and leave you alone, halting unwanted romantic and sexual advances. As a bonus, it may also be used to stop any attempts at placing a hex on you.

1. Blend and powder the following ingredients: ground cinnamon, ground nutmeg, powdered newsprint (preferably from the spell's target's favorite publication or even a newspaper that has been in their possession), plus the tobacco taken from one cigarette (ideally obtained from that person, but their favorite brand would be a close second-choice). Some formulas recommend that tobacco be left whole; others that the cigarette be smoked (or just burned, if you don't smoke) and only the ashes used.
2. Use the resulting powder in any of the following ways:
   ★ Sprinkle it where your target is sure to sit on it or step over it
   ★ Sprinkle it to create a boundary of safety for yourself
   ★ Carry it in a mojo bag as a protective talisman

✳ Relationship End Powder

This powder is more subtle than Break-Up Powder.
  Grind the following botanicals into fine powder: camphor, pennyroyal, and slippery elm. Sprinkle into the shoes and pockets of the one who should depart.
  Warning: Pregnant women or those actively attempting to become pregnant should not handle pennyroyal.

✳ Walnut Bath

Metaphysically speaking at least, all sexual relationships are significant because they cause subliminal bonds between people. Having had sex with someone, especially on a consistent, frequent basis, you carry part of their essence with you and vice-versa. This can make ending relationships difficult. This bath helps remove all ties that bind and may also be used to break a binding spell.

1. Simmer one dozen walnuts, still within their shells, in an iron pot filled with spring water.
2. Simmer for three hours. (Add more water if necessary.)
3. After three hours, turn off the heat and let the water cool to room temperature.
4. Remove the walnuts and add the infusion to your bath. (Do *not* eat the walnuts; bury them in Earth instead or burn them within a cauldron, then scatter the ashes at a crossroads.)
5. Visualize your goals, resolutions, and desires while soaking in the bath.

Do not perform this ritual unless you are sure that the relationship is over. Following this bath, it's believed that you should never have sex with the other person again.

Heartbreak and Disappointment Spells: Pre-Break Up

Do you sense love slipping away? These spells attempt to restore and revive lost or fading love. The relationship isn't completely over; your partner hasn't left … yet. (Under those circumstances, consider *Summoning Spells* to help bring the other party back.)

 ## Baby Please Don't Go Spell

There's no need for a Summoning Spell. He or she hasn't left yet. You, however, foresee with fear and dismay that the date of departure seems imminent. This variation of a floorwash attempts to forestall that departure, revive love and happiness, and make that Summoning Spell you've already picked out completely unnecessary. This is a version of a classic condition formula known as Stay With Me.

1. Pour boiling water over the following ingredients to create a strong infusion:
   Bloodroot
   Cardamom
   Coriander
   Cumin
   Forget-me-not
   Rosemary
2. Strain out the botanical material, and add the liquid to a bucket of water together with some vinegar.
3. Use it to cleanse your home, concentrating on thresholds to the outside and the bedroom.
4. For maximum power, cast the spell in conjunction with many repetitions of the sacred sounds of Lorraine Ellison's recording, "Stay With Me Baby." Sing along or just listen as inspired.

 ## Has No Hanna Staying Power Spell

*Wearing **Has No Hanna Oil** as perfume allegedly prevents loved ones from leaving you. Make sure they inhale its fragrance on you.*

 ## Love Me Again Spell

It matters little that your partner hasn't left; love seems to be gone.

Burn dragon's blood while chanting petitions for love to be restored and resurrected. Keep chanting continuously for as long as the dragon's blood burns.

Magic Moon Spell

This spell is intended to recover and revive lost love. The spell was originally aimed at regaining a husband's love, the loss inspired by the woman's failure to bear a child. The situation implicit in this spell is that the man hasn't physically left, he's still sleeping in the marital bed, still taking at least the occasional meal at home but he's withdrawn his affection, love, and interest. (He may also have a new woman or be looking for one, creating a dimension of "time running out" for the spell-caster.)

All the details, however, are ultimately extraneous: the key is that the spell-caster wants her partner's full love and attention and the security of knowing that the relationship will endure.

It's from Morocco, where houses traditionally have an inner courtyard, creating the privacy required for this spell. Adapt it to your own needs and circumstances.

You will need a cloth steeped in the man's seminal fluids, although as this is a different kind of spell, there isn't that emphasis on making sure none of your own sexual juices are intermingled. Cut a strip from an unlaundered bedsheet if an item of clothing doesn't exist.

1. On a moonlit night, do whatever you would do to prepare for an evening of seduction: remove or shape body hair. Apply oils, make-up, clean your teeth, freshen your breath. Get ready for a hot date.
2. Go to the courtyard, bringing a pot filled with spring water and the cloth. Remove your clothes and dishevel your hair so that it looks like you've been lying in bed.
3. Place your clothes near a pot of water. Sit beside them and talk to the moon.
   Oh, Moon, if you're in the mood for love and if I
      look good,
   Come on down,
   Come to me!
   The intent is to induce the Moon to enter the water and impart its magic power.

4. Sprinkle some of the lunar-charged water onto a cloth soaked with the man's sexual fluids.
5. Place seven pieces of harmel (Syrian rue), seven myrtle twigs, four lumps of alum, one piece of rock salt and one piece of sulfur onto this cloth.
6. Wrap them up and hide this packet under the man's pillow for three nights.
7. After three nights grind up its contents.
8. Make a homemade loaf of bread, adding these ground packet contents.
9. Break this loaf in half. Slip one piece under where his head lies in the bed, the other under his feet and leave it there for three nights.
10. Finally grind this bread into a powder. Use it to make a porridge-type cereal and feed it to the man, by hand if you possibly can.

 ## Reconciliation Sachet

Blend eucalyptus leaves with rose petals inside a small sachet to encourage reconciliations. Carry it or give it to the one you love.

 ## San Cipriano Spell

San Cipriano allegedly made the transition from master sorcerer to devout Christian when the love spell he was conjuring on behalf of a client was foiled by its target's purity of faith. The condition oil named in his honor is reputed to reconcile lovers.

*Carve a conjoined couple candle to represent you and your beloved. Dress it with **San Cipriano Oil** and burn, accompanied by prayers, petitions, and affirmations.*

 ## Stick With Me Spell

"Pega-pega" is the Spanish name for the botanical Desmodium obtusum. Pega-pega literally means "stick-stick" or "attach-attach."

★ Add pega-pega to conjure bags to mend damaged relationships and stay together

★ Sew it into the other person's clothing

Heartbreak And Disappointment Spells: Post-Break Up

Sometimes it's not about the other person; it's about repairing and soothing your own broken heart.

 ## Apple Romantic Cleansing Spell

A cleansing spell for when a bad love affair has left you feeling tainted, humiliated, or defiled.

1. Dice an apple and douse the pieces with honey and cayenne pepper.
2. Let it sit until it rots.
3. Flush the pieces down the toilet.
4. Affirm that you will learn to love again but more wisely this time.

 ## Ariadne Bath

Ariadne thought her life was over when she was cruelly abandoned by Theseus but her love-life was really only beginning. If she hadn't been abandoned on that island, perhaps she would never have met her soul mate, Dionysus.

Add essential oils of labdanum, mastic, myrrh, and rose to a bath. Enter the bath, inhale the fragrances, and concentrate on believing that the best may yet to be.

 ## Broken Heart Bath

1. Add white rose petals, honeysuckle blossoms, and rose attar to a bath filled with water. Substitute hydrosols for the fresh flowers if necessary.
2. Place a rose quartz large enough not to go down the drain in the bath too.
3. Soak in the scented bath.
4. Following the bath, carry the rose quartz with you. Sleep with it under your pillow until you don't need it anymore.

Broken Heart Bath: Broken Blossoms

1. Blend calendula, hibiscus, and jasmine flowers.
2. Make an infusion by pouring boiling water over two-thirds of the flowers.
3. Add this infusion to your bath; float the remainder of the blossoms in the water.

Broken Heart Bath: Water of Mercy

*Add copious quantities of **Notre Dame Water** to your bath and float white rose petals on the water.*

Broken Heart Healing Sachet

1. Cut out two matching squares of red silk or white muslin.
2. Place one atop the other and sew three sides together with pink thread, leaving one side of the square open.
3. Fill the sachet with balm of Gilead buds, honeysuckle blossoms, tonka beans, and rose quartz.
4. Carry it with you during the day; sleep with it under your pillow at night.

 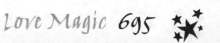

Broken Heart Potion

1. Steep balm of Gilead buds in red wine overnight. Leave a rose quartz in the wine, too.
2. Strain; drink and toast future possibilities.
3. Enhance the power of the potion by adding honeysuckle (Bach, Healing Herbs) or boronia (Australian Bush) flower remedies.

Heartsease Spell

Heartsease are wild pansies. Their name reveals their secret power to soothe heartache. Float fresh blossoms in your bath or add the flower essence remedy.

Honeysuckle discourages unhealthy nostalgia and attachment to the past, enabling you to move forward in a whole, healthy manner. These spells require traditional fragrant honeysuckle rather than Cape Honeysuckle, which is beautiful but lacks scent.

Honeysuckle Spell (1) Flower Essence

Honeysuckle flower essence remedy (Bach Flower, Healing Herbs) heals a broken heart and encourages you to look forward to a happier future, rather than being preoccupied with what is past and gone.

1. Initiate this spell when you feel frustrated, lonely, and miserable: add 20–30 drops of the flower essence remedy to a bath filled with warm water. This bath will be taken only once; any further baths require at most half-dozen drops of the flower essence.
2. Dry yourself with a fresh, clean white towel.
3. Drink a healing heart potion: a glass of spring water, fruit juice, champagne, or wine to which two drops of honeysuckle flower essence and two drops of red hibiscus flower essence have been added.

4. Drink this potion daily until you don't need it anymore.

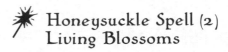

Honeysuckle Spell (2) Living Blossoms

Fresh, fragrant honeysuckle blossoms, preferably with at least a little bit of stem still attached, are required. This spell is most effective if cast just before retiring for the night.

1. Gather the blossoms and bring them to your bed.
2. Twist and knot the blossoms together, creating a garland. Focus on your desire for healing and happiness as you knot.
3. Wear this garland around your head or neck, inhaling the fragrance. Sleep with it if possible. You should feel better when you awake. Repeat until your heart no longer needs solace.

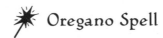

Oregano Spell

The scent of oregano allegedly helps you forget old lovers. Ordering a pizza may be of some use once in a while, however burning the dried herb as incense or heating a few drops of the essential oil in an aroma burner are much more effective.

Yarrow Heartsease Bath

Among yarrow's meanings in the Language of Flowers *is "cure for heartache."* Add yarrow hydrosol to your bath water.

Love Potions

At its most basic, the exact nature of the simple love potion beverage is less crucial than your magic power with which you've charged it.

1. Pour out the potion.
2. Whisper and murmur your desires and intentions over the liquid in the glass.
3. Serve it to your lover.

Black Snake Root Potion (1)

Allegedly, this is an aphrodisiac. I say allegedly because a traditional method of getting rid of unwanted romantic attention (or snakes) is to bathe in lots of black snake root (Cimicifuga serpentaria). Perhaps it's homeopathic: a tiny bit stirs the fires, while a lot puts it out? Either way, black snake root, more popularly known as black cohosh, is not safe for use by pregnant women.

1. Make black snake root tea.
2. Add some rum or whiskey.
3. Serve this to the one you love.

Black Snake Root Potion (2)

The botanical nickname, black snake root, also refers to Senicula marilandica. *Is this the plant of love? Create an infusion and find out.* Like black cohosh root, this black snake root is also used to remedy "female troubles" and is not safe for pregnant women.

Create an infusion by pouring boiling water over black snake root. The strained liquid may be added to the bath or served as tea.

Caraway Potion

Not the alcoholic beverage or herbal tea type? Not to worry. Bake caraway seeds into cakes, breads, and cookies and serve to the one you desire to stimulate mutual emotions.

Chestnut Love Fix

Allegedly hand-feeding someone chestnuts stimulates them to love you.

Chicory Potion

Grind and powder chicory seeds and leaves. Sprinkle over someone's food or drink to inspire feelings of love.

Chocolate Potion

Following the conquest of Mexico, chocolate was exported to Europe. In Aztec Mexico, chocolate was served as a ritual drink, with chili peppers rather than sugar. In Europe, chocolate's aphrodisiac properties were exploited instead. The Inquisition was not pleased: some Spanish women got into trouble for allegedly using hot chocolate to cast love spells. Interestingly, chocolate is now known to contain phenylethylamine, a stimulant similar to those released during sex. For what it's worth, Casanova's recommended pre-sex menu was a cup of chocolate and a plate of oysters.

Serve hot chocolate to the one you love and see if it works. For extra enhancement, top with powdered aphrodisiac spices, like powdered cinnamon or cardamom.

Dreams of Delight Love Potions

The basic formula includes cardamom, cinnamon, coriander seeds, and licorice root. Two different techniques provide different effects.

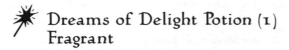

✷ Dreams of Delight Potion (1) Fragrant

The aroma of simmering Dreams of Delight may be so inviting that drinking may not be necessary. Merely inhaling the fragrance with its subliminal message of love and seduction may be sufficient for the purpose.

1. Fill a pot with wine.
2. Add the dried botanicals and warm to a simmer.
3. Strain the solids out and serve the warm potion to the one you love.

✷ Dreams of Delight Potion (2) Mobile

Of course, simmering the formula over the stove implies that you wish to cast a love spell at home. Perhaps you were planning a picnic or a road-trip. This version of Dreams of Delight offers possibilities of mobility and spontaneity.

1. Bruise the botanicals in a mortar and pestle. (Don't grind them finely as this causes difficulty in straining the mixture.)
2. Add these botanicals to a bottle of wine.
3. Let it steep for several hours or overnight, then when you're ready strain and share.

✷ Elderberry Potion

Fairy tales tell of fairies so infatuated with mortal lovers that they seduce them and carry them away to Fairyland, where no doubt this potion is served. Gather elderberries on Midsummer's Eve, whispering your desires over them. Make them into elderberry wine, or just steep the berries in wine and serve.

✷ Elecampane Love Sachet

1. Gather elecampane on Midsummer's Day.
2. Dry and powder it.
3. Place it within a cotton or linen sachet.
4. Wear this between your breasts for nine consecutive days.
5. Open the sachet and sprinkle the powder into the food or drink of the one you love.

✷ Flowers of Love Potion

Add a few drops of hibiscus flower essence remedy to jasmine tea and serve to the one you love.

✷ Honeyed Words Potion

1. Dip your finger into honey and use it to write your desires inside a cup.
2. Fill it with red wine, so that the honey clinging to the sides isn't too obvious, and serve to the object of your affections.

✷ Hydromels

Beverages made from fermented honey may be the most ancient intoxicating drink of all. As a category, they're known as hydromels. Ancient formulas survive: one can still find mead, various French offerings as well as tej, the Ethiopian honey wine allegedly shared by the legendary lovers Solomon and Sheba.

Hydromels are prized ingredients in spells for seduction. The magic power is inherent in the drink, however

this ancient Roman recommendation serves to enhance even further:

1. Pick three leaves of arugula with your left hand.
2. Pound them in a mortar and pestle.
3. Add them to hydromel, serve and drink.

 ## Hydrosol

Hydrosols may be blended to create quick, simple elixirs d'amour:

1. Blend cardamom and cinnamon leaf hydrosols.
2. Serve to the one you love.

 ## Job's Tears Potion

Job's tears are tear-shaped pearly seeds of an Asian grass. Powder some of these seeds and slip them into your lover's drink to retain their affections.

 ## Lady's Mantle Love Potion

Alchemilla vulgaris, *the Latin designation for Lady's mantle, underscores that plant's deep connection to alchemy and magic. Collect morning dew from the leaves and pollen from the flower and add to any other love potion for extra enhancement. Lady's mantle dew and/or pollen will also transform any food or beverage into a love potion. (Avoid during pregnancy.)*

 ## Lady's Tresses Potion

Lady's tresses are orchids of the Spiranthes *family. Approximately 300 types exist worldwide, many extremely endangered. They have traditionally been used as aphrodisiacs and as love potions.*

1. Steep lady's tresses in water.
2. Give the water to your beloved to drink.

 ## Lavender Potion

Lavender is one of those interesting substances that may serve as an aphrodisiac—or create the opposite effect. The only way to find out how someone will react is to serve it.

Add fresh lavender to a bottle of white wine. Allow it to steep several hours or overnight, then strain and serve.

 ## Licorice Potion

Licorice refers to the botanical root rather than the candy named after it. **Licorice is not recommended for those with blood pressure problems.**

1. Blend one teaspoon of powdered licorice into a glass of sparkling water.
2. Murmur your desires over it and serve to the one you love.

 ## Liverwort Potion

Although its name doesn't sound very romantic, allegedly the drinker will have thoughts only of the one who prepared the potion. The name makes more sense when one recalls that in ancient days the heart wasn't the anatomical organ associated with love and romance; instead it was the liver.

1. Make an infusion from liverwort (Marchantia polymorphia).
2. Serve it to the target of your spell, or blend with more conventional black tea or herbal tisane.

 ## Love Potion #2

A potion for two intended to enhance, stimulate, and preserve true love.

1. Pour a bottle of red wine into a pot or cauldron.
2. Add the following botanicals (adjust quantities to suit your taste or that of your intended): cardamom pods, cinnamon sticks, and clove buds.
3. Allow to simmer gently for an hour, then strain.
4. Pour the wine into glasses and add one drop of red hibiscus flower essence per glass.

 ## Love Potion #9

Today any spiritual supplier worth its salt sells some sort of love-drawing oil called Love Potion #9 but, as anyone who's ever actually listened to the song knows, the original was a drink. The earliest Love Potions # 9 seem to have been infusions of herbs, i.e., herbal teas or tisanes, relying on aphrodisiacs rather than alcohol to deliver the passion.

1. Choose nine love herbs. Consider these:
   Damiana
   Ginger
   Grains of Paradise
   Hibiscus
   Lovage
   Melissa (lemon balm)
   Peppermint
   Red clover
   Rose petals
   (Other options might include adder's tongue, cardamom pods, catnip, cubeb, lavender, red raspberry leaves or rose hips.)
2. Make a strong infusion of all the herbs, strain, and serve.

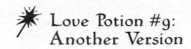 ## Love Potion #9: Another Version

Lovage, a plant whose associations with romance are indicated by its name, is also known as "nine-stem." Some consider that lovage tea is the true Love Potion # 9. Experiment and see which is most effective.

1. Blend all parts of the plant: flowers, stem, leaves, and roots.
2. Grind them into powder (don't make it too fine as it becomes difficult to strain the botanical out of the liquid).
3. Pour boiling water over the ground lovage.
4. Strain and serve.

Technically a potion need not be a drink but any magical edible substance. (Philters on the other hand *must* be beverages.) These three spells feature powders to be added to one's lover's food.

 ## Potion Powder (1) Chicken Heart Spell

1. Cook a chicken heart. Do not boil or cook in soup as this will produce a rubbery texture; bake, roast or broil.
2. After it's cooked, let it dry out and then grind it into a fine powder.
3. Add some powdered coriander seeds. Add little bits of this to your beloved's food: it inspires passion but also instills docility.

 ## Potion Powder (2) Coriander Seed

Powder coriander seeds in a mortar and pestle while chanting:

Warm seed, warm heart
Never let us be apart

Reserve this powder and sprinkle a little bit into food or drink periodically to keep love true and passions high.

 ## Potion Powder (3) Slice of Pie Spell (2)

Sprinkle ground cardamom onto apple, peach, or cherry pie to inspire erotic longing.

 ## Papaya Potion

Share a papaya. This not only induces erotic feelings but allegedly stimulates true love.

 ## Sugar Cube Potion

1. Place a sugar cube in your armpit. (Women may choose to insert it into the vagina, instead.)
2. Wear it as frequently as possible for a period of nine consecutive days.
3. Add what's left of it to any love philter and serve it to the one you love.

 ## Sweat Drop Potion

Some potions were never meant to be consumed:

1. Explicitly engrave your desires onto a small copper sheet. The spell should silently transmit this message of love to the target of your spell.
2. Fill a shot glass with your sweat and perhaps a drop of menstrual blood.
3. Hide this in a place where the target of your spell is sure to pass, placing the glass atop the copper sheet.
4. Once he or she has passed, the spell has been initiated and the materials may be removed.

 ## Tea for Two

Brew loose-leaf black tea. Add cloves, cinnamon, and cardamom and serve.

 ## Tea of Love

Simple ordinary black tea allegedly induces lust and erotic inclinations. After all, tea does derive from the beautiful camellia family. Drink it by itself or use it as a base for more complex potions.

Brew black tea from leaves, incorporating fresh mint, rose petals, and/or jasmine blossoms for added enhancement. Add one drop of essential oil of bergamot before serving and murmur your desires into the steaming liquid.

 ## Truth Serum Potion

This romantic truth serum helps you discover whether your lover is telling the truth.

Cumin and caraway encourage fidelity while caraway also allegedly forces any falsehoods to be revealed.

1. Steep caraway and cumin seeds in wine.
2. Feed him or her the potion and wait for revelations.

The simplest potion of all is wine. It invokes the blessing of Dionysus, Patron of Intoxication and the only Olympian spirit happily wed to his soul mate. Wine also invokes the precision required by magic: just the right quantity kindles passion and ability. Too much and erotic power is removed, replaced by sleep, obnoxiousness, erectile dysfunction, and general unpleasantness.

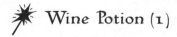 Wine Potion (1)

Choose a wine that suits you and the object of your affections. Pour out a glass, murmur your desires over it and serve.

 Wine Potion (2) Amber and Essence

1. Steep amber in red wine.
2. Remove the amber before serving.
3. Add wild rose (Bach Flower) and hibiscus flower essence remedies (FES, Pegasus, South African Flower) just before serving.

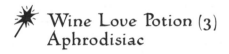 Wine Love Potion (3) Aphrodisiac

1. Steep the following ingredients in wine:
   Cinnamon
   Cloves
   Coriander seeds
   Grated lemon zest
2. Add hibiscus flower remedy (FES, Pegasus, South African Flower) at the last moment, two drops per glass.

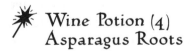 Wine Potion (4) Asparagus Roots

To arouse lust and vigor, boil asparagus roots in wine. Strain and drink for seven consecutive mornings on an empty stomach.

 Wine Potion (5) Dill

Steep dill seeds in wine. Strain and serve.

 Wine Potion (6) Melissa

Soak fresh melissa (lemon balm) and coriander in wine. Strain and serve.

 Wine Potion (7) Spiced

1. Pour red wine into a pot or cauldron and add anise, cloves, rosemary, ground cumin, honey, and orange zest.
2. Add two candied rose geranium leaves. (Substitute candied violets, angelica, or ginger if the geranium isn't available.)
3. Stir the pot, let the wine come to a boil, then reduce the heat and simmer gently while you focus upon your desire.
4. When it starts steaming, turn off the heat and let the potion cool off.
5. Strain the solids out using a fine sieve.
6. Warm up the wine once more. When the aroma is arousing, pour it into glasses and serve it to the one you love.

 Wine Potion (8) Vanilla

1. Start with a base of good red wine placed into a pot or cauldron.
2. Scrape a vanilla bean with a pin and add it to the wine.
3. Add ginseng root, a piece of rhubarb, cinnamon sticks, cloves, and a sliced orange.
4. Let the potion steep, then strain through a fine sieve.
5. Serve as is or place the strained wine back in the pot and heat to simmer.

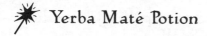 Yerba Maté Potion

Maté tea, the national beverage of Argentina, a powerfully caffeinated beverage akin to coffee or tea, has strong romantic associations. Allegedly the couple who drinks maté together out of one cup will stay together, weathering all challenges that come their way.

The Notorious Potion: Intimate Spells for Eternal Love

We'll never know if these are the most ancient spells of all but they're undoubtedly the most widespread. They exist wherever there are women. The basic premise: if someone consumes even as little as a drop of a woman's menstrual blood, that person will love her passionately forever. It is the ultimate binding spell, the most powerful love charm of all.

These spells can be spontaneous, although traditionally a few drops might be stored in a small perfume bottle or a *"poison ring,"* thus allowing the elixir to be secretly administered anytime. (Secrecy may be required for the spell to be administered; it is not required for it to work. If someone *wants* to love you forever, you may not need to go through all the machinations of these spells.) If menstrual blood was reserved, then the ability to administer this spell could survive even menopause.

Menstrual blood is the single most potent magic spell ingredient. In addition to love spells, it's used in healing, protection, and banishing. A rag soaked with menstrual blood repels the fiercest demons. (The ancient Roman equivalent of today's spiritual supply stores sold used rags, for those without personal access.) Menstrual blood is not the only love-binding substance, however, nor is this type of spell reserved solely for women to

cast. Sexual secretions, as well as sweat, hair, and/or nail clippings administered orally should have a similar, if not quite as powerful, effect.

Notorious potions have two things in common: the spell's power is generated by the magical workings of the human body, and it is administered orally.

Menstrual Potions

 Basic Spell

The classic potion consists of that single drop of menstrual blood. However, the mode of administration is also important. Allegedly, a cup of good strong coffee is the vehicle of choice. The best alternative is a glass of red wine. Tomato-based sauces are also used, if only because this is an easy camouflage.

 Brazilian Variation

1. Blend sugar with some menstrual blood clots.
2. Brew it with coffee and serve.

Hungarian Variation

You'll need one Orchis maculata *root. In English this plant is known as* "gander-goose" *or* "spotted orchis." *In Romany, its name is the more evocative* "devil's hand." *This spell is considered most potent if the root is gathered on Saint George's Eve or Midsummer's Eve.*

1. Dry the root, then pound and powder it using a mortar and pestle.
2. Add a little menstrual blood.
3. Camouflage it in your beloved's favorite food and serve.

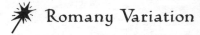 ## Romany Variation

This spell is believed most effective if cast on New Year's Eve.

1. Burn apple seeds.
2. Mix the ashes with menstrual blood and add this concoction to food.
3. Serve to a man to inspire undying passion.

 ## Snail Water Version

1. Mix menstrual blood with the water with which you have boiled snails. (Escargots are perceived as a potent aphrodisiac; presumably you're serving them as well.)
2. Serve to your beloved as a true love potion.

Underwear Spells

Underwear notorious potions serve as the bridge between menstrual spells and other bodily variations. Although some underwear spells specify that the underwear be stained with menstrual blood, others leave the subject ambiguous. It is crucial, however that the underwear be used and unwashed.

 ## Underwear Spell (1) Boiled Water

1. Boil your unwashed underwear, stained with menstrual blood if possible, in a pot or cauldron filled with water.
2. After removing the underwear, reserve the boiled water to make tea or coffee to serve to your lover.

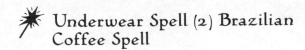 ## Underwear Spell (2) Brazilian Coffee Spell

1. Sleep in a panty or tight pajama bottom for two nights. Don't wash it.
2. Strain coffee through the crotch.
3. Serve a man one cup at breakfast, another at dinner. Reinforce as needed.

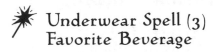 ## Underwear Spell (3) Favorite Beverage

Strain a glass of whiskey, rum, champagne or whatever his favorite beverage might be through your unwashed underwear. Serve it to your lover with a smile.

Other Notorious Potions

Menstrual blood isn't the only bodily product to magically provoke true love and/or passion.

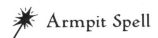 ## Armpit Spell

This spell dates back to Shakespeare's time.

1. Carry a peeled apple slice in the armpit for a little while. (The more you perspire, the less time is required.)
2. Feed it to your beloved.

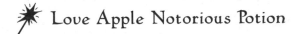 ## Love Apple Notorious Potion

1. Prick a red apple full of holes with a needle, invoking the name and image of your beloved as you pierce.
2. Sleep with this apple between your legs, as high as you like.
3. The next day, dress the apple with honey and sprinkle it with cinnamon.

4. Place it on an altar dedicated to Aphrodite and/or surround the apple with burning red candles.
5. When the candles have burned down, incorporate this apple into pie, cake, or pastry and serve to the one you love.

The following spells are for the fastidious among us. It isn't only modern sensibilities that can be sensitive; these botanical substitution spells are centuries old. Certain botanicals allegedly provide similar effects as the more noxious options: if prepared and fed to the one you love, he or she will love you forever.

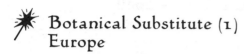

Botanical Substitute (1) Europe

The European plant of choice is tormentil, which allegedly inspires permanent torments of love. Brew an infusion or grind the dried herb. Add it to your lover's food or drink to instill undying love as well as fidelity.

☀ Botanical Substitute (2) North America

The most famous botanical substitute is bethroot, also called Low John the Conqueror. Be careful: Native American legends contain many descriptions of what can happen when the wrong person accidentally gets the potion.

1. Simmer the root in water.
2. Mingle tiny portions of the root and the cooking water into the target of your spell's food and drink, so that it is consumed.
3. Only do this once a day, but repeat daily for several days if desired.

Plants are not the only substitute substances— fish are too. How do these constitute notorious potions? Just wait.

☀ Fish Spell (1) Medieval

This medieval love spell allegedly produces one of the most potent aphrodisiacs. This spell lingered throughout Europe for centuries. Its practice was condemned by a Latin penitential dated from the tenth or eleventh century. If you are in the habit of purchasing live fish to personally kill prior to cooking, then perhaps this spell is for you.

1. Insert the live fish into your vagina.
2. Keep it within until you are absolutely sure it's dead.
3. Cook the fish as you will. Presumably using other aphrodisiac ingredients, such as saffron, champagne or cardamom, can only enhance the power of this spell.
4. Serve it to your beloved. Beyond stimulating great passion and sex, it is also supposed to keep him faithful.

☀ Fish Spell (2) Pagan Russian Bride's Spell

A variation on this spell was part of ancient pagan Russian marriage customs.

1. The bride was given a ritual bath before her marriage in that place of power, the bathhouse.
2. Her sweat was wiped from her body using a raw fish, which would then be cooked and fed to the groom.

Fish Spell (3) Medieval Man's Love-Binding Spell

The fun isn't reserved for the ladies, although preparation is less dramatic. A medieval fish spell for men serves to bind a woman, keeping her entranced by the relationship.

1. Do you fear your lover will leave you? Cook a whole fish in donkey's milk.
2. Strain, reserving the liquid, because that's what you need for the spell. What you do with the cooked fish is irrelevant.
3. Let the liquid cool.
4. While the woman is sleeping, gently bathe her vaginal area with some of the cooking liquid.

 ## Hair Spell (1)

This spell, cast to win a love, combines notorious potions with foot-track magic.

1. Gather up your target's footprints.
2. Take a few strands of your own hair and mix it with the collected dirt.
3. Burn everything to a powder.
4. Camouflage this in food: secretly induce your intended to eat it.

 ## Hair Spell (2)

1. Snip off a tiny bit of pubic hair from the right side.
2. Snip off a little hair from under your left arm.
3. Grind these with fresh coffee beans and brew.
4. Serve to the one you love. (This is most effective if you also add chocolate to the cup. Add lots of sugar, cream, and aphrodisiac liqueurs.)

 ## Hair and Nail Clippings Spell

1. Trim your pubic hair, your finger, and toenails.
2. Burn them to a powder.
3. Add this to spring water.
4. Let it stand for nine days, strain and serve as a love potion.

Although this is the original medieval Jewish spell in its entirety, realistically you must combine this water with some sort of delicious love potion. No one will possibly drink it otherwise.

 ## Nail Parings Spell

1. Soak nail parings in red wine.
2. Strain them out.
3. Serve the wine to the one you love for extra affection.

 ## Sugar Spell

1. Prepare to take a romantic bath to put yourself in the mood for love.
2. Walking backwards, from the kitchen to the bathroom, pour sugar on the floor.
3. Bathe, then allow yourself to air dry, letting yourself remain slightly damp.
4. Walk barefoot on this sugar path back to the kitchen.
5. Take a bowl and scrape the sugar off your feet into it.
6. Use this to bake something sweet for your beloved.
7. Unless you have other ideas, vacuum up the remaining sugar.

Sweat spells recall that once upon a time the bath-house (which frequently meant a sweat-bathhouse) was a magically charged arena for planning and initiating spells.

Sweat Spell (1) Basic

In order to accomplish this spell to ensure love and devotion, you must sweat. It is thus easiest to accomplish if your home has a sauna, steam bath, or steam shower although, in theory, any bathroom can be converted into a steam shower by running the hot water long enough. (This is not recommended as it may also remove the plaster from the ceiling.)

1. Keep a bag or canister of flour near at hand.
2. When your body is completely covered with sweat, powder yourself all over with this flour.
3. Scrape the flour off your body and into a mixing bowl. Supplement with additional plain flour if needed.
4. Incorporate this flour into a cake recipe and serve it to your beloved.

 ## Sweat Spell (2) Enhanced Power

This spell incorporates sweat, hair, and nails and no doubt anything else you can think of.

1. Take a hot, aromatic steam bath. The goal is to sweat a *lot*.
2. Dust your body with cake flour.
3. Wipe the sweat off with clean white linen and squeeze this into a dish.
4. Mix in an egg.
5. Trim your finger and toenails. Snip hair from all over your body, a little from any distinct part that has any. Blend hair and nails together and then burn them down to a powder.
6. Add this powder to the sweat-flour and egg. Add whatever else you need to bake it into an appetizing cake and serve it to your beloved.

 ## Sweat Spell (3) Romany

Who needs the trouble of the steam bath and scraping off all that flour? This simple spell bypasses those steps:

1. Do not launder a dress or garment that has been soaked with sweat or perspiration. (The underarm is typically best.) Instead, let the sweat dry into the fabric.
2. Burn the sweat-soaked piece to ashes. Should one of your hairs somehow end up in the fire, all the better.
3. Add these ashes to any love potion or to the food and drink you serve your beloved.

Men's Notorious True Love Spells

Women aren't alone. Men have spells to make women love them forever, too, although the mode of administration tends to differ.

 ## Men's True Love Spell (1) Acacia Honey

No other kind of honey may be substituted. Acacia gum is perceived as being the tree's menstrual blood complete with similar romantic powers, therefore lending men a magical power that biology deprives them. Acacia honey is produced in France.

1. Anoint the penis with acacia honey.
2. Make love.

This action not only ensures that she will love only you but allegedly guarantees fidelity as well.

Men's True Love Spell (2) Civet

Place one drop of civet on the tip of the penis just prior to sex. Allegedly this causes a woman to desire you continually and exclusively forever.

Men's True Love Spell (3) Oral Administration

Of course, the above two spells presume that you have reached a certain stage in a relationship. If this is not yet the case and you have the ability to be discreet, the following spell may be administered orally.

1. Dip something sweet, such as a sugar cube, a date, raisin or fig into your semen.
2. Dip into sugar or chocolate or something similar if camouflage is needed.
3. Feed it to the woman you love to invoke passion and desire.

Sex, Seduction, and Aphrodisiacs

These are very specific spells: a romantic or true love component may also exist but that's not the main focus of the spell. Just like regular love spells, this category is vast, with spells to suit every taste and desire. If *Notorious Potions* and *Fidelity Spells* are associated with women's magic, a high percentage of *Sex and Seduction Spells*, especially the more ancient ones, are designed to enable men to magically seduce women. This may be because for millennia women's spells went unrecorded or it may reflect historical social sexual dynamics.

During the European witch-craze, the fear of witch-caused impotence reached states of hysteria. In other cultures, other concerns were more prominent. The fear-inducing magical figure of *The Arabian Nights* or Jewish fairytales isn't that notorious female witch, it's the evil male sorcerer intent on seducing young virgins and devout, faithful wives alike with irresistible mystical charms, amulets, and spells.

For happiest results, cast these spells cooperatively.

Angel's Water Spells

Angels make their earliest appearances on the Biblical stage not as androgynous, sex-less, genderless beings but as passionate seducers of mortal women. Perhaps those angels inspired this magically charged aphrodisiac water.

Angel's Water Spell (1) Bath

*Add large quantities of **Angel's Water** to a bath to maintain romance and excitement, whether bathing solo or together.*

Angel's Water Spell (2) Laundry

1. Add substantial quantities of **Angel's Water** to the final rinse when washing sheets or pillow cases.
2. Reserve these scented linens for special occasions.

Basic Aphrodisiac Ingredients

Aphrodisiacs tend to be foods or fragrances. Because they evoke very personal, unique responses, experimentation is required to discover which aphrodisiacs work for you or your lover. Incorporate any one or combination of the following into your very personal spells:

Caviar

Champagne

Chocolate

Coriander

Fruits: apricots, peaches, cherries, grapes, figs,
pomegranates

Garlic

Hibiscus tea

Honey

Hot peppers

Mint

Onions

Radishes

Saffron

Shellfish especially, but all fish in general

Spices: cardamom, cinnamon, cloves

Sushi

Vanilla

 ## Copal Path of Seduction

*Make a path by sprinkling copal powder to create an
aura of romance.*

 ## Cyclamen Spell

*In the Language of Flowers, cyclamen represents
voluptuousness.*

*Soak the root in sweet almond oil for three days.
Strain and reserve the oil to serve as a dressing oil for
charms and candles. Cyclamen flower remedy (Pegasus)
may have aphrodisiac properties too. Experiment.*

 ## Diamond Spells

*Diamond refers to both a gemstone and a shape. In the
metaphysical language of geometry, the diamond shape
may stand in for the human eye or for the vagina. Is this
why Western marriages are typically initiated with*

*diamond rings? Emeralds are the gemstones that attract
and stabilize love and fidelity. So why are diamonds
such popular engagement rings?*

*Diamonds, whether carried or worn, promote self-
confidence in sexual matters. They relieve root causes of
sexual dysfunction. They are a cleansing, releasing,
purifying stone in matters of sexuality. These are spells
that will, no doubt, please the target:*

★ *To stimulate someone to be more sexually receptive
toward you, bestow the gift of a diamond, magically
charged with your own desires*

★ *To heal your own sexual inhibitions and dysfunction,
don't wait for someone else to bestow the gift. Provide
your own diamond: charge it with your desires, bathe
it in spring water enhanced with hibiscus flower
essence remedy (FES) and wear it*

 ## Dress for Seduction Spell

*What does the goddess of love wear to cast a seduction
spell? A magic cloak with nothing underneath? Once
upon a time, like Aphrodite or Ishtar, she wore a magic
girdle but that magical garment seems to have lost some
power over the ages. Another item of clothing however,
once associated with witchcraft, retains its magic powers of seduction.*

*Wear a crimson garter belt to enhance your powers of
seduction, create an aura of irresistibility (it works
without anyone seeing it, unless you want them to), and
to discover wells of primal female power.*

 ## Erotic Incense

*Grind and powder ginger lilies, jasmine, myrrh, and
tuberose. (Essential oils may also be warmed in an
aroma burner.) Waft the fragrance where desired.*

Flowers of Desire Oil

Blend essential oils of jasmine, tuberose, lavender, and ylang ylang to render yourself irresistible and to inspire passionate feelings.

 ## Fruits of Love Spell

Eve seduced Adam with an apple. Or did she? As apples aren't native to that part of Earth, there's been much debate as to the actual identity of the forbidden fruit. Other possibilities include apricots, pomegranates, quince, and figs (hence the fig leaf). A simple display of fruits allegedly magically tempts even someone determined not to be seduced.

1. Find the most beautiful examples of the above fruits you can and place them in an equally attractive bowl.
2. Offer them to the target of your spell. If he or she eats the fruit, they will be yours.
3. If they decline, merely leave the bowl close at hand and see what happens.

 ## Grinding Spell

It's your choice! Choose whether this spell serves as an aphrodisiac—or the opposite!

1. Put a sheet flat on the floor and cover it with wheat.
2. Undress completely and coat yourself with honey.
3. Lie down on the sheet and roll around in the wheat.
4. Now stand up and scrape off the wheat, catching it in a bowl.
5. Grind the wheat in a hand-mill. Ultimately, you will bake it into bread or cake and feed it to the target of the spell.

The crucial moment comes when you grind the wheat:

★ *If you turn the handle in a counter-clockwise motion, your advances will be received with vigor and passion. To intensify this reaction, knead the dough between your thighs, as high as possible*

★ *If you grind the wheat clockwise, however, your man will lack sexual desire and be unable to perform, even if he tries*

Horseshoe Spells

Horseshoes are most commonly associated with luck, prosperity, and protection but they're also extremely powerful components of love spells. There's often conjecture about which way a horseshoe should be hung to keep the luck from running out. This sidesteps the issue of why the horseshoe is so potent. It is partly about the horses, but not entirely.

The horseshoe incorporates several elements that reinforce each other, all bearing sexual overtones:

★ *The power of iron, associated with male sexual vitality*

★ *The shape is reminiscent of a crescent moon, which is associated with love as well as primal menstrual power*

★ *The shape of the horseshoe evokes the shape of female genitalia*

★ *Hammering an iron nail through a horse shoe completes the picture*

★ *When it comes to sex magic, horses also add an additional component. Stallions are perceived as exceptionally virile animals: the horseshoe is expected to transmit that power*

Use horseshoes to enhance your sex life:

1. String blue and gold beads on red silk thread, knotting in your intentions, desires, and lascivious thoughts.
2. Hold a horseshoe in both hands, charging it with your desires.
3. Wrap the beaded chain around the horseshoe. Enhance with other love charms if you want.

4. Anoint the horseshoe with the scent of tuberose and gardenias.
5. Hammer the horseshoe above your bedroom door, while envisioning your desires.

Lavender Spells

Lavender is an unusual plant; some find it to have aphrodisiac properties while others find it to be the opposite. Test its effects on lovers.

 ## Aphrodisiac Lavender Honey

1. Warm one cup of honey in a bain-marie.
2. Add approximately one-quarter cup of fresh or dried lavender blossoms.
3. When the honey begins to bubble, remove it from the heat. (Don't let it scorch!)
4. Let it sit for thirty minutes, then strain out the lavender.
5. Use the honey while warm.

 ## Aphrodisiac Lavender Sugar

1. Add at least half a cup of fresh or dried lavender blossoms to one pound of granulated sugar.
2. Blend the sugar and the lavender and keep in an airtight container for at least one month.
3. Strain out the lavender, reserving the scented sugar.
4. Sprinkle bits of it on your lover's food.

 ## Lavender Irresistibility Spell

Pin fresh lavender to your underwear; allegedly this renders you sexually irresistible. Alternatively, add essential oil of lavender to final rinse water when washing your underwear; this may be as effective and will certainly be more comfortable.

 ## Love Drawing Sachet

1. Make a small sachet or charm bag from linen or muslin.
2. Fill it with dried rosemary leaves and/or flowers.
3. Wear it over your genitals to attract lovers.

 ## Love Lettuce

Certain botanicals lend themselves to controversy; consider the humble lettuce. Is it an aphrodisiac or the opposite? In ancient Egypt, a particularly phallic-looking lettuce was sacred to Min, primordial deity of male primal power.

1. Create a salad for seduction: include endive, uncut carrots, cucumbers, and asparagus.
2. Sprinkle powdered basil over the top.
3. Whisper your desires and intentions over the salad; serve and see what happens.

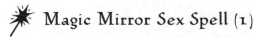 ## Magic Mirror Sex Spell (1)

1. Purchase a small hand mirror. Many modern mirrors are double-sided; this is an old spell. A mirror with some sort of a back to it is required.
2. Pay whatever is the asking price; don't haggle.
3. Remove at least some of the back of the mirror and write your beloved's name three times in that space. That's the easy part.
4. Now you need to find a pair of copulating dogs. Don't disturb them; just hold the mirror so that their image is reflected within it. Don't look inside it yourself or allow anyone but the object of your desire to gaze within.
5. Somehow you must induce him or her to look into the mirror.
6. Having accomplished this, hide the mirror for nine days in a spot where your beloved is guaranteed to pass by frequently.
7. When the nine days are over, carry the mirror on your person.
8. Allegedly this will now cause the object of your desire to become sexually aroused whenever she or he is in your presence.

Magic Mirror Sex Spell (2)

These two magic mirror spells are almost identical, however there are slight differences. This second spell is easier because your beloved is not required to look within the mirror, however other aspects of the spell may be more challenging. The first spell only requires that the mirror be hidden where your heart's desire is sure to pass; this spell insists that it be secreted within his or her home and preferably the bedroom!

1. Obtain a new small mirror.
2. Carefully remove the mirror from the frame.
3. Etch or write the name of your target on the back of the mirror.
4. Carefully replace it in the frame.

5. Use the mirror to reflect dogs or horses having sex. Do not look in the mirror.
6. Wrap it in velvet cloth and conceal it for nine days in a room belonging to, or at least much frequented by the object of your desire. (Ideally you want the room he or she sleeps in.)
7. You must now manage to remove the mirror and carry it on your body as a charm until the desired results are obtained.

Magic Seduction Tips

These tips set the stage for magical seduction spells. Very effective independently, you may also incorporate these suggestions into any other spell.

1. To increase the odds of seduction scatter carnelians and garnets around the bedroom.
2. Light red candles and sprinkle a love drawing powder on the sheets.

Myrrh is considered among the most erotic of resins. It was used in ancient Mediterranean seduction spells to make a woman burn with passion.

Mandrake Spell

Place a mandrake root under the bed for purposes of seduction and better sex.

Myrrh Spell (1) Book of Proverbs

The Book of Proverbs warns men to beware of women who perfume their beds with myrrh, aloes wood, and cinnamon. Wonder why? There's one way to find out.

Myrrh Spell (2) Isis Ointment

Myrrh shares so much of Isis's power and essence that effectively myrrh is Isis.

1. Blend essential oil of myrrh into shea butter to make an ointment.
2. Anoint yourself, while visualizing and chanting:
   You are the myrrh that Isis anointed herself with when she joined with Osiris, her true love.
   Myrrh, make [Name], child of [Name] love me like Osiris loves Isis,
   Make him desire me like Osiris desires Isis
   Make him long for me like Osiris longs for Isis [and so on and so forth …]

Myrrh Spell (3) Sizzling

1. Place a piece of myrrh on a hot surface (preferably iron) so that it sizzles and melts.
2. Chant to it, something like this:
   Myrrh as you burn, so [Name], daughter of [Name] burns for me
   As you melt, so her heart melts for me.
3. Improvise. Ancient spells were quite explicit. Take this wherever you want it to go.

Myrrh Spell (4) Shoe Spell

The women of ancient Israel placed myrrh and what is now known as Mecca balsam inside their shoes. This accomplishes more than providing fragrant feet.

1. To accomplish a seduction: when you spot the one you want, quickly slip off your shoe and kick up your feet towards your target.
2. Ideally, he'll think it's his idea.

Name Paper Spell

*Allegedly burning a person's name causes them to burn with passion for the one wielding the flame. This can only be more effective if the paper is burned in the flame of a candle carved to express your own desires and dressed with passion-inducing oils. (**Come To Me Lover!**, **Black Cat**, **Cleopatra**, or **Amor**, for instance.)*

New Orleans Parfum d'Amour

1. Blend and gently warm the following ingredients:
   Florida Water
   Rose water or hydrosol
   Cinnamon hydrosol
2. Dissolve honey in the liquid, stirring to distribute.
3. Allow it to cool.
4. Place in a bottle and wear the fragrance.

Peppermint Spells

Persephone wasn't Hades' only love. His true love apparently was the nymph Mentha. This relationship pre-dated his abduction of Persephone and continued after their marriage. When Demeter discovered that not only had Hades kidnapped and raped her daughter, he was also cheating on her, she was outraged and in a classic example of blaming it on the woman, transformed Mentha into the lowly peppermint plant. Mentha had the last laugh: Hades was rendered unable to perform sexually without mint. (Of course, the fact that peppermint was once used as a contraceptive might also have influenced the Lord of the Dead.) To this day mint is considered among the most potent aphrodisiacs.

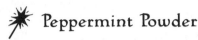 Peppermint Romantic
Floorwash

Pour boiling water over a bunch of peppermint to make a strong infusion, strain and add the liquid to floorwash rinse water. Use it to cleanse any room intended for romance or seduction, so that the room encourages romance from the ground up …

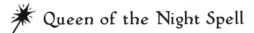 Peppermint Powder

Grind dried peppermint leaves and lavender blossoms into fine powder. Blend with rice powder and sprinkle between the sheets.

Queen of the Night Spell

Night blooming jasmine's nicknames "Queen of the Night" and "Moonlight of the Grove" indicate its power. Wear fresh blossoms after dark to attract a new lover, romantically hypnotize one you already have, and to transform yourself into a nocturnal queen.

Road of Love

Blend hibiscus and rose petals. (Grind, powder, or leave whole as you choose.) Use these flowers to sprinkle a path to the bedroom or wherever you choose. You may create a lavish carpet or be extremely discreet, as long as the path is unbroken.

Seduction Incense

Grind and powder aloes wood, clover, dried ginger, and sandalwood. Waft the fragrance as desired.

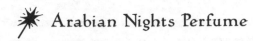 *Seduction Oils*

Arabian Nights Perfume

The compilation of stories known as The Thousand and One Nights *or* The Arabian Nights *is filled with details of magic spells and formulas for seduction. Because stories that fall under the broad category of fairy tales are now relegated to children, the erotic material contained in* The Arabian Nights *is typically excised. Add essential oils of aloes, ambrette, jasmine, liquidambar, myrrh, and rose to your bath in preparation for nights of love.*

Cleopatra Oil Spell

*Place five drops of **Cleopatra Oil** in each corner of the bed and another five in the very center for enhanced erotic enjoyment and powers of seduction.*

Jezebel Oil, like the queen in whose honor it's named, is a complex, multifaceted oil. Mainly used in money, love, and seduction spells (and especially those spells that bridge all three concerns), the key to **Jezebel Oil** is that it is used for getting what you want, in the face of all odds. Jezebel root, a cousin of orrisroot, possesses both seductive and commanding properties.

Jezebel Seduction Spell (1)

*The spell may be used to initiate a relationship or to hold an already existing lover spellbound. Intensify standard **Jezebel Oil** by adding cinnamon, damiana, jasmine, and/or rose petals. Dress purple taper candles with this oil and burn it in your intended's presence.*

Jezebel Seduction Oil Spell (2)

*Perhaps the relationship hasn't progressed far enough for the other person to be present. In that case, use standard **Jezebel Oil** or doctor it up as suggested above. Carve your target's name and identifying information into a purple seven-day candle, dress it with the oil and burn.*

 ## Laka's Love Oil

Laka is the beautiful Hawaiian spirit of dance and love.

1. Blend and grind pikake, frangipani, gardenia, and hibiscus flowers.
2. Add them to a blend of jojoba and liquefied coconut oil.
3. Add to the bath or massage onto the body to transform into a magnet for love and desire.

 ## Oil Spell (1) Erotic Oil

Make a flower infusion with the following botanicals using sweet almond oil: frangipani, gardenia, and honeysuckle. When the oil is complete, gently warm as much as is needed and massage freely to incite passion and desire.

 ## Oil Spell (2) Isis and Osiris Eternal Love Oil

1. Gently warm one-quarter cup of grapeseed oil.
2. Remove from the source of heat and add six drops each of essential oils of myrrh and frankincense.
3. Massage as desired or add to a bath.

 ## Oil Spell (3) Jasmine

Allegedly this oil arouses desire and ability and reduces resistance.

1. Blend a few drops of jasmine attar into sweet almond oil.
2. Use it to massage the one you love.

 ## Oil Spell (4) Seduction Oil

1. Powder sandalwood and aloes wood, or use their essential oils.
2. Blend these into sweet almond and sesame oils.
3. Massage as desired or add to the bath.

 ## Oil Spell (5) Night of Love Oil

Blend cubebs, damiana, Grains of Paradise, red rose petals, and sweet flag (calamus). Add the blend to apricot kernel and jojoba oils. Anoint yourself with the oil or give your intended a massage with it.

 ## Oil Spell (6) Queen of Sheba Oil

***Queen of Sheba Oil** is used when you wish to seduce or be seduced:*

★ *Dress romantic taper candles with this oil*
★ *Anoint yourself with **Queen of Sheba Oil***
★ *Put a drop of **Queen of Sheba Oil** on a lightbulb and let it heat up*

 ## Powder Spell (1) Better Sex

Grind cubeb peppers into powder and sprinkle it around the bed to magically inspire better sex.

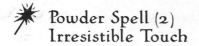 Powder Spell (2)
Irresistible Touch

Powder orrisroot and mix with cinnamon powder. Rub just a little bit between your hands and touch the person you desire.

 Powder Spell (3) Spicy
Love Powder

Grind and powder the following:

  Cayenne pepper
  Cubeb peppers
  Dried ginger root
  Cinnamon
  Grains of Paradise

Sprinkle the resulting powder around the bed, candles, or within billets-doux. Keep it out of the sheets, off your skin, and definitely out of your eyes or other sensitive areas because this powder may burn as hot as the love it's intended to inspire.

 Powder Spell (4) Triple X
Powder

Grind Grains of Paradise, damiana, and cubeb peppers together. Sprinkle this powder around your bed to enhance all activities within it.

Powder Spell (5) Triple X
Powder Candle Spell

1. Grind Grains of Paradise and cubeb peppers together.
2. Charge a red candle with your hopes and desires. (Any shape candle may be used, however Entwined Lovers or those candles formed to resemble genitals are believed to be extra-effective.)

3. Sprinkle the powder over the burning candle to initiate a spell of romance.

 Saffron Seduction Spell

Saffron, Earth's most expensive spice, is also one of the famed Tantric perfumes. Allegedly if someone was fed a diet featuring saffron for an entire week, he or she will be unable to resist erotic advances from the person administering the sex potions. For maximum benefit, add to love potions and shellfish dishes.

Only little bits of this expensive flower are needed to flavor a dish; this is a case where less is definitely more. Significant amounts of saffron are not safe during pregnancy.

 Seduction Bath

For maximum power, use lunar-charged water to create this infusion.

1. Pour boiling water over cinnamon, cloves, coriander seeds, and cardamom.
2. Strain and let it cool.
3. Dip a white cloth into the pot of water and bathe the body, concentrating on the neck and thighs.
4. Let yourself air-dry so that you radiate the botanical powers. This allegedly enables the bather to seduce whomever is desired.

 Sewing Needle Spell

To draw someone into a sexual relationship:

1. Lay two sewing needles together, with the eye of one beside the point of the other.
2. Wrap them in a mint or basil leaf, wrapping it toward you.
3. Secure with a red thread, knotting in your desire.

4. Wrap this in a piece of red silk or satin, again rolling or folding toward you.
5. Place this in a red flannel bag and wear it around your neck or waist.

To end the spell: remove the charm, take it apart and break both needles.

To reinforce the charm: feed it with three drops of dark rum added to the open bag.

 ## Sex Conjure Bag

Make someone desire you.

1. Obtain hair from your target, preferably pubic hairs.
2. Place them in a small red charm bag together with bethroot (Low John the Conqueror) and seven cloves.
3. Hide the bag under your mattress, anointing it weekly with a love drawing oil.

 ## Sex Sheet Spell

1. Toss a sheet over copulating dogs and then get it back. Don't wash that sheet!
2. Find an excuse to wrap the sheet around to the one you desire. This will allegedly arouse amorous feelings.

 ## Shoe Spell

Obtain his or her shoes and hide them under your bed. Allegedly this stimulates him or her to walk straight toward that bed.

 ## Southernwood Spell

Southernwood's nickname is "lad's love," perhaps reflecting its reputation as a tool for magical seduction. Place it under the mattress to arouse passion and performance.

 ## Sweat Spell

What's the difference between this Sweat Spell and Sweaty Notorious Potions? Easy. There's no need to convince your spell's target to eat anything!

1. Work up a sweat.
2. Wipe the sweat with a cloth.
3. Reserve the cloth; don't wash it.
4. Use this sweat-soaked cloth to rub the person you'd like to seduce, while thinking something like:
   My sweat on your skin
   Your sweat on mine
   My love is yours
   Your love is mine

 ## Sweet-talking Seduction Spell

For sweet, persuasive speech, chew a bit of cinnamon just before speaking.

Peppermint (real peppermint leaves, not breath mints) may work, too.

 ## Switch Lovers Spell

Use a red and black double-action candle to get rid of one lover, while simultaneously drawing another.

1. Carve the name of the lover you'd like to see vanish onto the black wax.
2. Carve the name of the lover you'd now like to have onto the red wax.
3. If necessary, carve the bottom of the candle, exposing the wick, so that both ends may be burnt at the same time.
4. Stick the candle horizontally onto a spiked candlestick, or pierce the border between red and black with a long pin, something like an old-fashioned hat pin, then balance the candle over a bottle and burn both ends simultaneously.

Thyme for Irresistibility

According to legend, thyme derives from Helen of Troy's tears, and thus shares her essence. Bathe in an infusion of fresh herbs to radiate the power of a love magnet. Use carefully: remember Helen was kidnapped twice!

 ## Torment Them With Love Spell

Tormentil, a very close botanical relative of five-finger grass, earned its name because allegedly it stimulates the torments of love. Carry it to make someone burn for you.

 ## Tuberose Seduction Spell

Once upon a time women were warned not to inhale the seductive, languorous fragrance of tuberose, also known as Mistress of the Night, *because it might put them in a dangerously romantic mood. Tuberose's fragrance intensifies after dark. Set the magical scene for seduction by artfully arranging fresh tuberoses.*

 ## Vanilla Seduction Spell

Cast this spell to attract or seduce a lover. Add genuine vanilla extract to your bath. Allow yourself to air-dry, then dust with rice powder blended with a little ground cinnamon.

 ## Wild Thyme Spell

Wild thyme for wild times: thyme is associated with Aphrodite, Helen of Troy, and reveling fairies. Carry thyme in a conjure bag together with staurolite crystal gemstones to attract passion and pleasure.

 ## Women's Inhibition Free Erotic Bath

Make an infusion of hibiscus flowers and Grains of Paradise and add it to the bath. Allegedly this unleashes a woman's erotic thoughts and abilities, while removing inhibitions.

It's all getting too much? Need to cool down?

 ## Camphor Cool-Off Spell

Camphor is a substance frequently taken for granted. It's used in many lotions and cosmetics because of the cooling sensation it provides. Camphor, botanically related to cinnamon, is considered a sacred lunar plant; in Marco Polo's time it was bartered for with gold.

   Camphor allegedly reduces sexual desire. Burn camphor or add one or two drops of essential oil of white camphor (other forms are toxic) to your bath when you need to cool off.

 ## Chill-Out Spell

Add a few drops of essential oil of hops to a bath to cool off desires.

 ## Passionate Balance Spell

A fourteenth-century talisman is recommended to balance overwhelming passions and emotions. Astrological symbols of the sun and the moon are engraved onto white zircon, and the talisman is worn as needed.

Virility: Enhancing, Maintaining, Reviving, and Repairing

In addition to general aphrodisiacs, there is a special category of spells designed to enhance, strengthen, and remedy male sexual performance. Male sexual performance spells fall into two categories:

★ Spells to magically counteract and remedy impotence
★ Spells to enhance sexual performance, so as to transform a regular guy into a magically empowered lover

Spells to Heal and Remedy Impotence

 ### Impotence Diagnosis: The Hand of Ishtar

According to ancient Mesopotamian belief, all-seeing, all-knowing spirits punish a host of infractions, some of which you may not even have realized you had committed until you received the punishment. Mesopotamian deities typically communicate their displeasure by inflicting disease. Each possesses its own specific illness. Thus you will know by the disease, whose displeasure you have evoked. Ishtar, Divine Spirit of Love, Life, and Sexual Delights, punishes via sexual dysfunction. If impotence is a result of her anger, then the only way it can be resolved is through rituals to evoke her forgiveness.

However, a problem of ambiguity exists: impotence may also be the result of malevolent bewitchment cast by another person, or of a mangled Fidelity Spell cast by your wife to stop you playing around on the side. (The notion of a purely physical cause may or may not have existed.)

The root cause of impotence affects the nature of its cure. This diagnostic spell seeks to determine whether lack of sexual ability stems from human hands or from the Hand of Ishtar. As with many healing rituals, someone else performs the spell for the patient.

1. Form dough from emmer wheat and potter's clay.
2. Use it to create male and female figures.
3. Place one on top of the other, however you're inspired.
4. Place them near the afflicted man's head.
5. Recite an incantation seven times, blessing Ishtar and requesting that the needed information be clearly revealed.
6. Remove these figures and place them in the vicinity of a pig. If the pig approaches the figures, this confirms that Ishtar is responsible for the ailment. A cure may be made through offerings and rituals of appeasement. If however the pig does not approach the figures, if they do not attract its attention, the man has been bewitched by a person. In order to undo the spell, he must find the charm and undo it or take other magical measures.

I've left the ancient spell's original instructions as per materials, on the off chance that emmer has some magical qualities distinct from other wheat and that this ingredient may be possible for some to find. However, feel free to substitute a more convenient wheat if needs be.

 ### Impotence Remedy (1) Dandelion

Early American colonists recommend dandelions to counteract impotence based on magical and folk-healing traditions. Interestingly dandelion leaves have since been discovered to contain extremely high quantities of Vitamin A, essential for production of male and female sex hormones.

A glass of dandelion wine serves as a restorative potion. Alternatively add dandelion leaves to salad. Before consuming, murmur your desires over the food and visualize successful accomplishment of the spell.

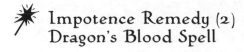 Impotence Remedy (2)
Dragon's Blood Spell

Place a chunk of dragon's blood in a red bag and keep it under the mattress, to reinvigorate male sexual prowess.

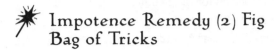 Impotence Remedy (2) Fig
Bag of Tricks

Carve a phallus from fig wood. Carry it in a mojo bag together with any of the various snake roots.

 Impotence Remedy (3) India

Onions, a botanical associated with male vigor, are incorporated into an Indian potion to remedy erectile dysfunction.

1. Blend white onion juice and freshly grated ginger into honey.
2. Take a tablespoon daily for three weeks. Results should be apparent within that time.

Iron represents primal male power. It is invoked in spells to remedy erectile dysfunction because of this inherent magic power, but also in hopes that its enduringly hard, stiff nature will be transmitted through enchantment.

 Iron Spell (1) Iron Bath

Water used for cooling off iron or an anvil is an impotence cure. Allow the water to cool to a safe, comfortable temperature and then bathe the afflicted parts. Better yet, have someone else bathe them.

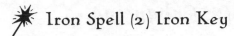 Iron Spell (2) Iron Key

1. Obtain seven keys, each from a different house, each from a different town.
2. Heat them until red-hot on an anvil. (A cast-iron pan will substitute.)
3. Blend water from seven different sources: the original Moroccan formula requests water from seven different wells, in itself an adaptation of the ancient pan-Semitic miraculous water from seven springs. If either option is a possibility, follow the original directions. Otherwise, seven types of bottled spring water, each deriving from a different source is a realistic modern update.
4. Pour this blended water over the red-hot keys. The patient is then exposed to the steam. (Be careful not to scald yourself; the goal is to improve the situation, not worsen it.)
5. Catch the water as it comes off the anvil or pan.
6. When it cools off, use it to bathe the afflicted parts.

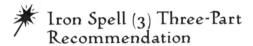 Iron Spell (3) Three-Part
Recommendation

There are three components of this Moroccan magical impotence remedy, any of which may be used independently. However for best chances of success, allegedly the three parts should be performed in conjunction.

1. Drink a potion concocted from rosewater, sugar, and pounded almonds.
2. Observe the copulation of horses. (Keep your eyes on that stallion!)
3. Take ritual baths, as prescribed by a herbalist.

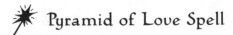 Pyramid of Love Spell

Keep the key, candles, oil, and dragon's blood powder used in this spell handy; this, the candle-worker's version of Viagra is intended to be cast as needed.

1. Carve three red candles as desired.
2. Dress them with **All Night Long** and/or **High John the Conqueror Oils.**
3. Roll the candles in powdered dragon's blood.
4. Arrange them on a tray in triangle formation with the point at the top.
5. Charge one large antique key with your desires and place it in front of this pyramid of candles.
6. Sprinkle some powdered dragon's blood over the key.
7. Light the candles; extinguish all other illumination and see what happens.

 ## Strong as an Oak Spell

Oaks are traditionally associated with primal male power. This spell may be used to remedy impotence or just enhance sexual capacity.

1. Look for an older, strong, powerful-looking oak.
2. Talk to the tree: whisper your situation to it, describing your needs and desires. Request assistance.
3. Look down: if the tree is sympathetic, you'll find twigs or acorns on the ground.
4. Actually seeing the twig or acorn fall—or even being hit on the head by one—is a profound assurance of assistance.
5. Leave a gift and libation for the tree; gather up your acorn or twig and carry it with you.

Super Sexual Ability Spells

As the Marvellettes sang, *"My baby must be a magician because he's sure got the magic touch!"* These spells may benefit someone suffering from erectile dysfunction, it doesn't hurt to try; however their real goal is to transform regular sex into nights (and days!) of unflagging ecstasy.

Male Super Sexual Ability Spells tend to take the form of potions or virility charms. In many cases the magic symbolism inherent in these spells evokes female sexual symbolism in order to enhance male sexual ability (almonds, honey, clams, and more.)

 ## All Night Long Oil

Add essential oil of jasmine, ideally jasmine sambac, to sweet almond oil. Use this oil to dress candles or the body, to magically fulfill the promise inherent in its name.

 ## Date Super Sex Spell

Make a date with some dates: carry cleansed, dried date pits in a conjure bag, for enhanced sexual ability.

 ## High John the Conqueror Virility Spell

Create an infusion by pouring boiling water over High John the Conqueror roots. Use this liquid as the final rinse water when laundering your underwear.

 ## Johnny-Jump-Up Sex Power Spell

Carry dried Johnny-Jump-Up blossoms in a conjure bag to enhance male sexual potency.

Juniper is invoked in various sexually oriented love spells for both women and men.

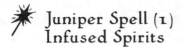 ## Juniper Spell (1)
Infused Spirits

This formula combines two spells in one: the potion produced allegedly enhances sexual pleasure, vigor, and ability, while the juniper berries used to create it can magically impact your love life.

1. Steep a handful of juniper berries in rum or whiskey for at least one month.
2. Strain out the berries and reserve them. You can either toss the used berries in your front yard to attract a new lover, or toss them into your backyard to keep the woman you already have extra satisfied and happy.
3. Drink one tablespoon of the infused spirits every day for enhanced virility.

 ## Juniper Spell (2) Wine Potion

A simpler variation on the above, this spell can be cast virtually immediately, without waiting the month. Steep juniper berries in red wine, and drink a shot glass daily for increased virility.

 ## Lion's Ear Spell

Lion's ear, an East African botanical also known as lion's tail and wild dagga, reputedly endows men with the positive qualities of a lion, including their legendary sexual prowess. Eat it and see.

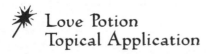 ## Love Potion
Topical Application

1. Grind and powder aloes wood, dried basil, and thyme.
2. Add the resulting powder to **Bay Rum.**
3. Massage into the body for added vigor and vitality.

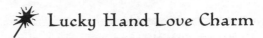 ## Lucky Hand Love Charm

Different botanicals sometimes share nicknames. The Hoodoo root charm Lucky Hand derives from an orchid and is prized by gamblers. The European root charm Lucky Hand derives from male fern and is prized by lovers. "Male" fern is so designated because of its erect, robust appearance, versus the droopier female fern, and also perhaps because historically male fern has been a component of herbal contraceptives. Male fern's root—known as Lucky Hand or Hand of God—is used to bolster and enhance virility.

Male fern root is believed most powerful if gathered on Midsummer's Eve. Dry and carry it in a mojo hand for virility and sexual charisma. (Lucky Hand also conveys magical protection in case all that machismo lands you in trouble.)

The viagra of ancient Rome, satyrion root, is named in honor of the satyrs. Legend had it that satyrion root was a mainstay of the satyr's diet and was responsible for their incredible powers of prowess. Satyrion remains available in herbal supply stores as well as those specializing in spiritual goods. The only problem is that the exact identity of the root beloved by the ancients hasn't been determined; no one is entirely sure exactly which plant it was. Satyrion was some sort of orchid but exactly which member of that large family is no longer known. As best as we can tell, satyrion was a double-rooted plant with smooth leaves. It may have been modern salep root, which is what is frequently marketed as satyrion today. It may not be. For what it's worth, satyrion root remains a mainstay of magical virility spells and retains its magical sexual stimulating reputation.

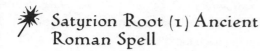 Satyrion Root (1) Ancient Roman Spell

Steep the root in goat's milk. Drinking this potion allegedly provides the goods for 70 consecutive acts of copulation.

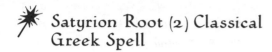 Satyrion Root (2) Classical Greek Spell

Pound satyrion root. Eat it together with arugula and eggs to provide enhanced, prolonged erections.

 Satyrion Root (3) Oil

Soak satyrion root in warm olive oil. Strain, and use the oil to anoint the penis.

Satyrion Root (4) Potion

1. Pulverize satyrion root.
2. Add it to wine and allow it to steep overnight or for the equivalent number of hours.
3. Strain and drink.

Sexual Prowess Potion (1) Arabic

Drinking camel's milk blended with honey daily for a week allegedly stimulates male potency dramatically.

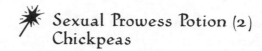 Sexual Prowess Potion (2) Chickpeas

To enhance male sexual prowess:

1. Soak chickpeas (garbanzo beans) in water. They will swell.
2. When they are completely soft and swollen, strain out the chickpeas and drink the water. This allegedly makes a man so virile he can deflower 72 virgin cows in one night.

Sexual Prowess Potion (3) Fenugreek

Fenugreek earned its magical reputation as the herb of increase. It's used in money spells, fertility spells and even spells to enhance a woman's bust line. This potion increases male sexual ability and vigor and may magically remedy impotence as well.

1. Place two teaspoons of dried fenugreek in a cup and cover with boiling spring water.
2. Steep for five minutes, then strain.
3. Add lemon and honey to taste.
4. If the flavor remains too medicinal, try combining with peppermint, also a strong aphrodisiac.

 Sexual Prowess Potion (4) French

Add one egg yolk to a glass of fine cognac, and drink daily for potency and prowess.

Sexual Prowess Potion (5) India

Blend coconut milk and honey together and drink. This may be taken as frequently as desired.

Sexual Prowess Powder (1)
Arabic

Grind and blend cardamom pods, cinnamon, and dried ginger. Sprinkle this powder over boiled onions and eat for added passion and virility.

 ## Sexual Prowess Powder (2)
Breakfast of Champions

Before breakfast on three consecutive mornings, eat shelled almonds pounded with cinnamon and then mixed into honey. Three mornings is allegedly enough to provide a long-lasting effect.

 ## Sexual Prowess Powder (3)
Grains of Paradise

Grind Grains of Paradise into a fine powder and add it to honey. Take some right off the spoon or add it to a drink to create a passion-arousing potion

 ## Sexual Prowess Spell

Keep male fern and High John the Conqueror roots stored amongst your clothing. When you wear the clothing, you will allegedly radiate sexual magnetism.

Sexual Restorative Spell

A Japanese formula to restore sexual vigor following extensive, exhaustive sexual activity:

1. Bake a dozen clams in the oven at low heat for approximately two hours. Take them out of the shell, if you like; it's the meat that counts here.
2. Remove the clams from the oven and let them cool.

3. If you haven't already, remove the clams from their shells and discard the shells.
4. Pulverize the dried clams with a mortar and pestle, visualizing your desired goals.
5. Dissolve one-half teaspoon of this powder in water and drink nightly for seven consecutive nights.

 ## Virility Charm (1) Horns

Double horns evoke primal female power, reflecting the appearance of women's internal sexual organs; a single horn manifests male primal power and sexual vigor for obvious reasons. Although men aren't inherently vulnerable to the Evil Eye, their sexual power and reproductive capacity are among the Evil Eye's primary targets. Charms representing horns, traditionally worn around the neck, potently protect male genitalia and virility.

 ## Virility Charm (2) Coral

Magically speaking, coral is perceived as the sea's menstrual blood, offering powerful sexual, reproductive, and romantic protection.

1. Wear a single jagged piece of red branch coral around the neck to protect sexual functioning and sperm count from the Evil Eye.
2. This allegedly enhances performance too.

 ## Virility Charm (3)
Italian Amulet

1. The Italian *corno* amulet may be used, too. Its shape echoes peppers and animal horns.
2. Traditionally carved from red stone, plastic versions are most common now.
3. Hang an extra one from the bedpost for added magical enhancement.

Virility Charm (4) Sampson Snake Root

Sampson snake root allegedly restores virility.

1. The herb has an antipathy to iron: do not cut it with a knife. Doing so will render the charm ineffective.
2. To separate the root or a portion of the root from the plant, you may twist, bite or rip, but do not use any metal tools. A crystal or stone knife may be used.
3. Carry it in a mojo bag.

 ## Virility Charm (5) Sea Horse

1. Charge a metal sea horse charm, ideally crafted from steel or iron, with your desire.
2. It is activated as a virility charm if carried in the pocket or worn in the vicinity of the genitals.

 ## Virility Charm (6) Thistle Arts of Love Spell

Carry thistles in a conjure bag; allegedly the botanical bestows not only increased sexual vigor but also enhanced skill and sensitivity with the arts of love.

 ## Ya Ya Powder

Grind, powder, and blend the following: cinnamon, peppermint, red sandalwood, and vetiver. Dust the sheets or dust yourself to inspire your partner.

Summoning Spells

Summoning spells are exactly what they promise: magic spells to bring someone to you. Most often used for lovers, a summoning charm may be effective for anyone with whom there is a strong soul connection or emotional bond.

In some cases summoning spells beckon a new lover or someone who is a friend, acquaintance or who has perhaps expressed casual romantic interest but the spell-caster wants more. Usually these spells target someone whose identity is known as opposed to the abstract new love drawing spells found amongst *Basic Love Spells*.

Many of these spells, however, are specifically cast to summon a spouse, partner, or ex-partner who has abandoned the spell-caster or with whom there has been a substantial disagreement. Their whereabouts may or may not be known. Many older spells specifically target a husband; women may have been less likely or able to leave or perhaps there were more direct means of bringing them back.

 ## Acorn Cup and Ashen Key

1. Find an empty acorn cup still attached to an oak leaf or twig.
2. Gather ash seeds (the *"keys"*).
3. Murmur over them *"Acorn cup and ashen key bring my true love back to me."*
4. Place them under your pillow on three consecutive Friday nights, repeating the incantation each time.
5. If your beloved has not returned by then, it's time to consider the possibility that this is not your true love.

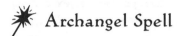 Amethyst Bedroom Spell

Encourage a spouse or lover who has abandoned a relationship to return.

1. Charge a substantial amethyst crystal with your desires.
2. Attach this activated amethyst to the right side of the bedpost or headboard.
3. Seduce him into sleeping with you in that bed; ultimately he should fall asleep on the left side of the bed.
4. Encourage him to stay. Repeat from Step 3 as needed.

Archangel Spell

1. Simmer cardamom, cinnamon and cloves in rosewater within an iron cauldron, until the potion steams and the aroma is potent. Traditionally, this is accompanied by reading sacred texts and reciting sacred verses.
2. Remove the cauldron from the fire.
3. Write your beloved's name in the center of a piece of parchment.
4. Write the names of the four archangels in each corner of the parchment: *Michael, Raphael, Gabriel, Uriel* and add the parchment to the steaming cauldron.
5. Throw in a piece of the beloved's clothing, a shirt or an undergarment, or something similar.
6. Allow everything to steep for at least an hour.
7. Return the cauldron complete with contents to the fire.
8. As the mixture boils, your lover's affections should return to you.

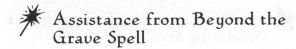 Assistance from Beyond the Grave Spell

1. Take an article of his clothing to the cemetery, specifically to the grave of someone who is sympathetic towards you and potentially has power over your beloved. (His mother, if you think she likes you, is ideal.)
2. Bury the clothing within or in the immediate vicinity of the grave. Talk with the spirit in the grave: communicate, express your desires, explain why they should help you.
3. Leave it there for three days. On the third day, resurrect the clothing. Do not shake off the dirt; in fact, take a little extra. Leave a small gift for the spirit (water, honey, cigarettes, candy, alcohol, whatever you think they'd like).
4. Add some sea salt to the clothing and graveyard dirt and place it in a bag or packet.
5. Place this near or above a door where your beloved is sure to pass.
6. Allegedly you should see results in nine days.

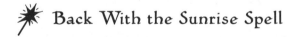 Back With the Sunrise Spell

For the return of an absent lover:

1. Buy peppercorns and coriander seeds from a store that faces west.
2. Burn them at sunset.
3. Turn to the east and let a towel with which you have cleansed yourself after sex flutter in the wind.
4. Pray and petition that when the sun returns, your beloved will return also. If necessary, repeat at sunrise.

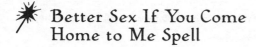

Better Sex If You Come Home to Me Spell

This spell was inspired by men who took younger second wives. This is the old wives' retaliation. It may also be used to lure a man back from another lover.

1. Sleep with one date inside your vagina for seven nights. Use the same date; you may remove it during the day, reinserting at night.
2. After this point, the target of your spell is invited for a meal.
3. Chop up the date very finely and feed it to him in his food. If the spell goes as planned, it will not be a brief, businesslike meal.

The spell has two effects: first, to induce him to return to you, and second, to make sex unsatisfactory with anyone but you in the meantime. The second aspect allegedly kicks into action as soon as the date is inserted.

 ## Cleopatra Oil Summoning

*Bring an errant lover back with **Cleopatra Oil.** The oil may be worn as perfume; otherwise saturate a cotton ball with it to wear or carry when you anticipate running into your ex.*

 ## Come Back Powder Spell

1. Put salt in a dish.
2. Drizzle it with **Come to Me Lover!** or similar.
3. Sprinkle it with powdered sugar and blend everything together.
4. Take a pinch in your hand and turn to each direction, north, east, south, and west. Utter an invocation, requesting, or commanding, as the case may be, that your lover return to you.
5. Blow the powder in each direction. He or she should

be drawn back to the place where the spell is performed, so choose your place wisely.

6. Repeat daily until your lover returns.

 ## Commanding Doll Spell

1. Make a rag doll to represent the target of this spell or use another kind of doll.
2. Write your beloved's name on a piece of paper.
3. Attach it like a name-tag to a doll.
4. Anoint the doll with **Command and Compel Oil.** Lay it on a piece of red silk or satin. Sprinkle it with **Come to Me Powder.**
5. Chant:
   I command you, I compel you,
   I command you, I compel you.
   I've covered you with powder
   I command you, I compel you,
   I command you, I compel you
   Hear my voice!
   I command you, I compel you:
   Return to me now!
   This very instant, this very minute, this very hour!
6. Repeat for three consecutive nights.
7. Following the third repetition of the entire ritual, wrap the doll in silk, and hide it in a dark closet or secret space.

Damiana Potion Spell

1. Soak damiana in your lover's favorite wine or other beverage for seven hours.
2. Sprinkle this outside your doorstep and petition for his or her return.
3. Repeat for 21 days. If there are no signs of return by the conclusion of this period, the spell's message is that you should consider other romantic choices.

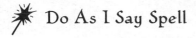

Do As I Say Spell

This summoning spell demands personal contact with the target.

Create Do As I Say Powder by grinding and powdering cedar chips, myrrh, sweet flag/calamus, and peppermint leaves. Sprinkle the powder on the ground in your target's path; allegedly this will magically induce your ex- to return to you.

Drawing Powder

Spiritual supply stores often sell a product called **Drawing Powder,** *intended to draw someone or something into your life. If the bottle is really cute and clever, it may be worth purchasing. If not, you may be better off looking for* **Drawing Powder** *in the supermarket. You'll have to look under a different product name, however.*

Although occult manufacturers may place anything in the bottle, talcum powder most frequently, **Drawing Powder** *should be powdered confectioner's sugar. Disappointed? Were you hoping for something more mystical, elusive, or rare? Don't be. Sugar is among the strongest beckoning, summoning, drawing forces on Earth. If you've ever spilled sugar on the floor and wondered how on earth the ants streaming in to the kitchen could discover it so quickly, this is why. It's not the salt and butter in pastry that draws customers to the bakery: it's the sugar.*

Sprinkle a fine path to your door to summon the one you love or, better yet, sprinkle a little **Drawing Powder** *into a letter to attract only your spell's target and not the ants!*

Fireplace Spell

This spell possesses a diagnostic aspect that will allow you to determine your odds of success.

1. Make a fire in the fireplace with ash, cedar, pine, and oak.
2. Soak juniper berries in **Come To Me Oil** or similar (you may also substitute dark rum) and throw them into the fire.
3. Petition, request, pray, affirm, focus: stay with the fire while it burns.
4. When the fire is low but before it completely burns out, toss some bay leaves in to see whether the beloved is likely to return. If the flames shoot up out of the bay leaves, if there's loud crackling—this is a positive sign. Leaves that barely burn or else burn very quietly do not indicate success.

Foot Track Summoning Spell

1. Obtain your lover's footprint, ideally from your property.
2. Place it in one of his socks, unwashed is best, if possible.
3. Add a devil's shoestring root.
4. Knot the sock. Keep it in a safe, secret place, for instance, under your mattress. He should be back soon.

Love Written in Blood Spell

1. With a needle, draw a drop of blood from the wedding-ring finger. Use the needle as a pen, the blood as your ink.
2. Write your initials and those of the other party in your blood on a chip of wood. (In the Ozark Mountains of the United States where this spell originates, ironwood is the wood of choice.)
3. Draw three concentric circles around the initials.
4. Bury the chip within Earth.
5. He should be back within three days.

Lover Come Back Incense!

Grind cardamom and dragon's blood into a fine powder. Sprinkle on lit charcoal and burn.

Lover Come Back Spell

This spell allegedly returns a departed lover within twenty-one days. It possesses a protective aspect as well as a summoning one. If the spell doesn't work and he's not back in the prescribed time, this may mean you're better off without him. Start making new plans.

1. Create an infusion by pouring boiling water over damiana and red rose petals.
2. Bathe in it. When you're done, reserve some used bathwater in a bottle.
3. Add a little of your own urine and sprinkle some of this liquid in front and back of your home for twenty-one days.

Magnet Oil Spell

*Anoint the corners of a photograph of someone whom you wish to draw into your life with **Magnet Oil**.*

Magnetic Summoning Spell

Sprinkle magnetic sand onto a magnetic horseshoe to encourage the return of a lost love.

Mallow Summoning Spell

This is a gentle summoning spell.

1. Gather mallow (which is also known as althaea) while focusing on your heart's desires. Silently call your lover's name.

2. Place this mallow bouquet in a glass or vase and leave it on your doorstep overnight. (Alternatively, place it in an open window.)
3. This should call your beloved back.

The Moorish Charm

This spell is from Spain. "Charm" is meant in its classical sense as a magical incantation, chant, or song rather than the popular usage indicating a magically empowered object.

1. Gather your materials:
   Caraway seeds
   Coriander seeds
   Cumin seeds
   Mastic resin
   White lime (not the fruit, but burned limestone preparation once very easily obtainable through any pharmacy; substitute oyster shell calcium tablets if easier)
   Verdigris (the green coating which forms on brass or copper; it can be created or secured from art supply store or pharmacist)
   Myrrh resin
   Dragon's blood
   Broom straw
2. Take your materials to a crossroads or cemetery.
3. Make a fire.
4. Toss in the ingredients, one by one, chanting over each something to the effect:
   Oh magic caraway: bring him to me!
   Oh magic coriander: blind him with love for me!

The order of the first eight ingredients doesn't much matter but leave broom straw for last, chanting: "Oh magic broom, fly him to me!"

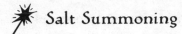 Pierced Heart Spell

This is a particularly old charm, well-distributed amongst Earth's magic traditions. This version with a pierced candle is British. Once upon a time, instead of candles, a sheep or cow's heart was used, and still could be if you normally cook organ meats.

Stick two new pins through a lit candle in such a way that they pierce the wick and form a cross. Then chant:

It's not this candle alone I stick
But [Name]'s heart I prick
Whether he be asleep or awake
I'll have him come to me and of love make!

Other versions of this spell pierce the wick before lighting the candle.

Other possible materials and their origins include:

Onion (England)
Nut (India)
Lemon (Sicily)
Plantain sucker (Fiji)

If not using a candle, then amend the first lines of the rhyme to: "It's not this [whatever] that I wish to stick but [Name]'s heart I mean to prick."

Rosemary Summoning Spell

1. Gather rosemary stalks before daybreak on Midsummer's Day.
2. Light a fire. Add three rosemary stalks.
3. Chant three times:
   I burn rosemary.
   But I'm not burning rosemary.
   What do I burn?
   Your heart—the heart belonging to [Name], *child of* [Name] *that's what I burn*
   That he may neither be able to stop or stay away
   Until he comes to be with me and stay

Salt Summoning

1. Throw salt on an open fire on three consecutive Friday nights.
2. Each time chant:
   It isn't this salt I wish to burn
   But [Name], *child of* [Name]'s *heart I need to turn*
   Let him not rest nor happy be
   Until he comes back to stay with me
3. If he is not back by the Friday following the third Friday, or if there has not been any positive response by then, it may be time to look for another.

Salt on the Fires of Love Spell

Toss salt on the fire for seven consecutive mornings to summon your absent lover home.

San Cipriano Spell

San Cipriano Oil *is used to locate lost articles and also to summon lost lovers.*

Carve and dress a candle to represent your beloved. Dress it with ***San Cipriano Oil*** *and burn to help persuade them to return to you.*

Sugar Summoning Spell

Sugar has profound summoning powers; allegedly this spell will draw someone quickly. Chew fresh sugar cane while keeping your mind's eye fixed on your beloved.

Summoning Powder (1)

1. Grind bay leaves, cinnamon, lavender, and star anise together.
2. Blend with an equal amount of sugar.
3. If personal belongings have been left behind,

especially underwear and socks, sprinkle them with powder. If there are no belongings, try to meet him, and sprinkle him surreptitiously with a little powder. As a last option, write him or her a letter, adding some powder to the envelope.

 ## Summoning Powder (2)

Blend dragon's blood powder, saltpeter and sulfur. Throw the mix on the fire (it will blaze!) while chanting a wish for the return of your beloved.

 ## Twenty-seven Day Spell

This spell comes with a time limit; if success isn't shown by the end of 27 days, it's time to consider a new romantic start.

1. Cut out a paper heart.
2. Write your lover's name on this paper nine times.
3. Cross over each name with your own.
4. Place the paper in a saucer or small dish and cover it with sugar.
5. Stick a white birthday candle in the center of the sugar. Burn it. (Make a wish if you want but don't blow out the candle.) Keep the dish with the sugar, paper and any wax drippings.
6. Add a fresh birthday candle the next day. Repeat for a total of nine times, nine candles altogether.
7. If he's not back by the end of the ninth try, burn the sugar and the paper.
8. Start again the next day, repeating with all new materials. If after nine days and candles, he or she is not back, burn the materials again.
9. If you like, try it one more time, for another nine days.

Three times is the charm: if he's not back after this, he won't be.

 ## Wax Doll Summoning Spell

1. Make a wax image of your beloved, if possible adding personalizing items: sweat, saliva, semen, blood, what have you.
2. Prick your wedding-ring finger with a needle. Using this bloody needle as a pen write the person's name on the forehead of the doll and your name over the heart.
3. With four new needles, ideally silver, pierce the figure in the back, head, heart, and through the groin. Visualize all these manifesting as pangs of love and desire for you.
4. Sprinkle the figure with powdered rosemary.
5. Kindle a fire with a piece of paper bearing the target's handwriting.
6. Burn the image in the fire.
7. When the fire is out, with your fingers or a wand, write the person's name in the ashes.

 ## Witchgrass Spell

1. Bathe in an infusion of witchgrass to draw your lover.
2. Let the infusion dry on your body.
3. Throw some of the bath water out the front door and call your lover's name aloud for intensification.

 ## Yarrow Summoning Spell

Yarrow allegedly enhances telepathic bridges between people. This spell may be used for friends and relatives as well as lovers.

Cut a yarrow stalk into pieces. Give portions to everyone who should be on this magical "telephone" line. When you wish to summon someone, hold your piece in your left hand and intensely visualize that person.

Your Absence is Killing Me Spell

This elaborate ritual, intended to force an errant husband's return, pretty much tells the universe that you're as good as dead if he doesn't come home.

1. The deserted spouse lies on the floor, stretched out like a corpse, with funerary candles at her head and feet. Stay in that position until the candles have burnt out. This spell is from Latin America and has a Roman Catholic orientation: it is suggested that the Christian Creed be repeated while waiting for the candles to burn down. Supplement with petitions. Substitute other prayers, petitions, and visualizations as appropriate.
2. Pay attention to your words as the candles burn out. Whatever you're saying when they are actually extinguished must be repeated three times, while pounding on the floor with both fists.
3. Immediately call the spouse's name and demand that spiritual authorities force his return:
   Soul of Tulimeca, you who are in Rome.
   I need you to send me [Name], *child of* [Name],
   repentant of all the grief he has caused me
   Humbled and full of love for me

This ordeal must be repeated for three successive nights.

Luck and Success Spells

Although conventional wisdom frequently depicts luck as an ephemeral quality mysteriously belonging to some but not to others, according to magical perceptions, luck is a distinct commodity to be acquired, squandered, or lost. Luck and good fortune, in other words, can be magically *made*, although it may take some effort.

The Wheel of Fortune, which has its origins in the sacred symbolism of Lady Luck, the Etruscan deity Fortuna, spins constantly. Like hamsters on a wheel, we scramble to stay on top. How fortunate that magic spells exist to acquire, maintain, and preserve luck.

✳ All High Conquering Luck and Success Powder

Use this powder to eliminate obstacles and provide luck and success in the face of all challenges.

Grind and powder High John the Conqueror chips, crumbled bay leaves, and frankincense. Carry in a conjure bag or sprinkle as desired.

All Saints Oil Spells

All Saints Oil evokes blessings of good fortune, for success in all your endeavors.

✳ All Saints Candle Spell

*Carve a candle that represents you. Dress with **All Saints Oil** and burn.*

✳ All Saints Oil Charm Spell

*Anoint a clover charm with **All Saints Oil** and carry with you at crucial moments for enhanced confidence, luck, and spiritual protection.*

✳ All Saints Quick Fix Spell

*Don't have a clover or any other lucky charm? Don't worry. **All Saints Oil** stands on its own: soak a cotton ball in **All Saints** and carry it in your pocket.*

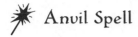 Anvil Spell

An anvil serves as a magnet for good fortune. This ritual is most auspicious on specific days of the year, especially Saint George's Day and New Year's Day.

1. Decorate an anvil with fresh tree boughs.
2. Place candles and incense on the anvil as you would on an altar and light them.
3. Chant something like: *"Luck come to us! Good fortune draw near!"*
4. Offerings of straw are made to the anvil in exchange for good luck and prosperity. This is also an auspicious moment for divination. (See Sideromancy, in *Divination Spells,* page 327.)

 Balmony Persistence Spell

Sometimes luck and success derive from persistence. Balmony's beautiful flowers inspired names like hummingbird tree, snake head, and turtle flower. Balmony allegedly enhances persistence, patience, and courage while also bestowing good luck.

Dry one complete flower. Carry it for good fortune and to assist achievement of goals.

 Basic Candle Spell

1. Hold a red candle in your hands to charge it with your vision and desire. The candle may be any shape that appeals to you: votive, seven-day, cat or witch; the crucial element is that it must be red, the color of luck.
2. Carve the candle with your identifying information.
3. Dress it with **Van Van, Black Cat, Lucky Lodestone,** and/or **Crown of Success Oil.**
4. Burn the candle.

 Bat Spell: Bat Wing Lucky Conjure Bag

Bat wing?! Aren't many species of bats endangered? What about not using animal parts in spells? Well, these aren't. Bat wing is the nickname for holly leaves, a plant of good fortune, doubly enhanced by its resemblance to the flying mammal's wings.

Place a pair of bat wings (holly leaves) in a red conjure bag together with a High John the Conqueror root and a matched pair of lodestones. Sprinkle with lily pollen, if possible, and/or magnetic sand periodically for enhanced power.

 Blessings of Good Fortune Spell

To bless something or someone, scatter elder leaves and berries to the winds, circling sunwise murmuring the name of the person or thing. Scatter some more directly onto the person or thing if possible.

 Blessings of Good Fortune Long-Distance Spell

Send long-distance blessings for good fortune with elder powder. Grind elder leaves and berries into powder, murmuring blessings and best wishes over them. Sprinkle inside a card or envelope and mail it to those whom you wish to send good fortune.

 Bread Spell

This ritual derives from petitions to the orisha Babalu-Ayé and is believed to bring good luck. If you incorporate spiritual petition, that luck may be even greater.

1. Nail a slice of bread behind the front door.
2. Fasten a purple ribbon to the nail.

3. Replace as soon as the bread begins to rot or deteriorate, burning the old slice.

 ## Buddha's Hand

The citron fruit, known in China as Buddha's hand, represents luck and happiness.

Post an image of the three fortunate fruits—citron, peach, and pomegranate—as a visual petition for the blessings of luck, longevity, and children. Focus on your desires when meditating on the image.

 ## Chervil Spell

Chervil provides comfort in times of sadness and invigorates lust for life. The obvious method of use is to cook with the fresh herb. However chervil has amuletic use, too.

1. Sew dried chervil into a small sachet.
2. Wear it against your skin during the day.
3. Sleep with it under your pillow at night.

 ## Daruma

The daruma is typically a red plaster figure representing Bodhidharma, the Buddhist monk who lost all use of his limbs after meditating in a cave for nine years. Doesn't sound too lucky? Daruma provides luck to others. In Japanese tradition, images of Daruma are sold with the eyes left blank so that you may petition for good fortune before initiating a quest or project.

To initiate a goal and to beseech good fortune and spiritual assistance for success, paint in one of Daruma's eyes using black ink. When your project is complete and success has been achieved, complete Daruma, too, by painting in his second eye.

 ## Deasil

Deasil, also spelled deosil and deiseal, is literally a sun-wise turn, a turn to the right. This ancient Celtic sacred circumambulation follows the path of the sun to bring good luck and ward off evil and misfortune. The motion also propitiates various spiritual and elemental forces. Circling deasil may be performed as needed, however it is most auspicious during the Summer Solstice or Midsummer's Day at the height of the sun's powers.

Carry coals or brands from Midsummer's fires deasil three times around a residence for blessings of good fortune.

 ## Easy Seaweed Spell

Many Good Fortune Spells feature seaweeds like bladderwrack and agar-agar, both popularly known as Sea Spirit. Seaweeds, in general, are perceived as auspicious; other species may be easier to obtain, particularly those associated with Japanese cuisine or nutritional supplements.

1. Kelp and dulse are fairly easy seaweeds to obtain. (Seaweed may be fresh or dried but tablets may *not* be substituted.)
2. Place them in a jar and cover with saké or whiskey.
3. Keep the covered jar in the kitchen to magically attract good fortune.

Elemental Blessings of Good Fortune Spell

Combinations of red coral, turquoise, and amber are favored in Tibet, Mongolia, and tribal China so that one can receive all of Earth's blessings of good fortune.

★ *Coral is believed to contain the essence of blood, fire, and light*
★ *Turquoise contains the essence of water, sky, and air*
★ *Amber radiates the powers of Earth*

Although each is sacred and powerful independently, when joined together they bring harmonious blessings of good fortune from every realm. Jewelry may be very powerful if received or purchased; however, beading your own is most potent because the opportunity exists for knot magic, tying your desires, prayers, and hopes into the cord after every bead.

String the beads together on cord, and wear or hang it as an amulet. If you have enough beads, make separate strands of coral, turquoise, and amber. Braid them together.

Alternatively, if funds are limited, carry a chunk or a single bead of each in a conjure bag.

Everything's Coming Up Aces Spell

1. Place the four aces from a new deck of playing cards on a plate.
2. Cover them with breadcrumbs.
3. Cover this with sugar.
4. Add seven coins plus metal charms that represent your desires. (In other words, if you're an ice-skater, you'd use a skate charm.)
5. Place a silver candle on top of everything and burn.

First Spring Rain Spell

The first spring rain is believed to contain special luck-drawing powers.

Place a glass, stone, or earthenware container outside at the spring equinox to catch the first rain. (It's extra potent if it rains on the equinox!) Reserve the water for the following uses:

★ *Bathe for a year of joy and luck*
★ *Wash your face to enhance the appearance of youth*
★ *Wash your hair to attract and keep romance*
★ *Wash your abdomen and genitals with the water for enhanced and renewed fertility*
★ *Sprinkle the water on your medicine bags, altar tools and around your home*

 ## Foot Track Spell

Perform foot track magic on yourself to enhance your good fortune and open the doors of opportunity.

1. Gather up dirt from your own footprint.
2. Add an equal quantity of dried patchouli leaves.
3. Blend them together.
4. Sprinkle with fresh-ground cinnamon.
5. Go to where the path to your home naturally begins.
6. Walk toward your entrance, sprinkling the powder up to and including your threshold, to draw lucky, fortunate, benevolent people toward you.

Four B's Lucky Incense

This incense's aroma allegedly draws luck, happiness, and prosperity to you while simultaneously repelling evil.

Grind the following into a fine powder:

Bayberries
Bay laurel leaves
Dried basil
Buckeye nuts

Sprinkle the powder on lit charcoal and burn.

Generative Organs

What do the human generative organs generate? Well, in addition to the usual, representations of the genitals generate luck and good fortune.

Adoration of the sexual organs and the magical power, mystery, and energy that they represent is the spark for Earth's oldest spiritual traditions. Images of male and female genitalia are joined in union to symbolize the potential for perfect balance. These may be used regardless of one's personal sexual orientation: beyond whatever real life imagery they depict or inspire, these images reflect and radiate a theoretical philosophical, magical balance beneficial for all.

There are a wide variety of such images to choose from, ranging from the reasonably stylized (Himalayan stone lingam and yoni statues) to realistic depictions (ancient Japanese and modern Thai amulets).

 Generative Organ Spell (1)
Basic

1. Join the two distinct images together on your altar.
2. Light one big red candle behind it.

3. Focus on the concept of perfect harmony, all your needs met, all your desires fulfilled, everything right with the world.
4. Offerings may be presented; traditionally these are milk and honey.

Spiritual supply stores may sell candles in the shape of human genitalia. These may be substituted or burned in addition to the candle in Step 2. Regardless of the candle's shape, for luck, burn red candles.

 Generative Organ Spell (2)
Enhanced

Graphic images of human genitalia may not be appropriate for all situations, but there is no need to pass up their blessings of luck. There are also more subtle, discreet substitutions. Cast the Basic Spell as above, however place one or more of the following on the altar instead:

★ *Mortar and pestle*
★ *Small ritual broomstick*
★ *Horseshoe with one iron nail*
★ *Snake images*

Generative Organ Spell (3) "Lucky Shelf"

Nothing is considered luckier than images of the male generative organs, except perhaps images of the male and female organs, preferably conjoined. (General worldwide metaphysical wisdom: female genitals draw protection, while the male genitals bring luck.) The Lucky Shelf was a traditional Japanese method of displaying these images, together with other luck-drawing amulets.

This "shelf," in effect an altar space, was traditionally kept within a cabinet that could be opened or kept discreetly closed as desired. An exception was made in Japanese pleasure houses, where these shelves were kept in plain sight, to provide better business magic and general ambience as well as generating luck and good fortune. When realistic genital amulets were banned, Maneki Neko emerged as an acceptable substitute. Other substitutions may be made: cowrie shells are traditionally used to depict the vulva.

1. The traditional Lucky Shelf or cabinet is arranged and then left alone to radiate power. The spell-caster's role is to collect fine images, carefully arrange them and lovingly care for them. The amulets do the rest.
2. Find images that represent primal generative powers. Combine them with other lucky and sacred charms.
3. If more active magic appeals to you, keep the items spiritually cleansed, magically charging them after each cleansings spell. Candle burning may also be incorporated as desired.

Good Fortune Bath

*This bath may be taken once in conjunction with the Bain Demarré (see Cleansing Spells), or independently for seven consecutive Fridays. Add **Holy Water, Glory Water**, seawater or sea salt, anisette, scallions, a head of parsley and pieces of true silver and gold to your bath. (Your favorite or signature fragrance is an optional ingredient.)*

Graveyard Dirt Spell

To achieve success:

1. Obtain nine handfuls of graveyard dirt.
2. Mix them with sulfur, salt, and pepper.
3. Sprinkle a little bit on charcoal and burn it.
4. Pray, petition, and visualize success achieved.
5. Repeat whenever you need to be successful in any endeavor. The powder will has a long time.

Halloween Apple Luck Spell

After nightfall on October 31st, each member of the household receives an apple. Apples may be distributed by hand or you may bob for them, as desired. Everyone must eat their one for a year of good luck.

Halloween Candle Luck Spell

At midnight on October 31st, burn orange and black candles. Allow them to burn out naturally to receive a year of good luck.

Horseshoes Spells

Horseshoes remain among the luckiest charms, although few who carry them today appreciate their ancient associations with the adoration of human primal sexual energy. The luckiest horseshoes have a lucky seven holes. Should you accidentally stumble upon a horseshoe, this is a harbinger of approaching good luck. You'll get a bonus year of luck for every nail still in the shoe.

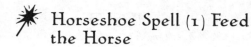

Horseshoe Spell (1) Feed the Horse

1. If you find a horseshoe, wrap it in red cloth together with some hay.
2. Tuck it under your mattress.
3. Pay attention to your dreams: they may generate luck for you.

Horseshoe Spell (2) Italian

The modern Italian horseshoe charm foregoes lucky associations with iron. It's now typically crafted from red plastic and embellished with a red corno *(an amuletic cross between a chili pepper and a horn) hanging from the arch.*

Hang the charm in a visible place to bring luck, joy, and protection. Hung over a car's rear-view mirror, it attracts luck wherever you drive.

Horseshoe Spell (3) Wrapped Up in Magic

Latin American magic wraps horseshoes in thread to create magic spells. The horseshoe is the basis of the spell; exactly what is done with it depends upon the spell-caster's goal. The horseshoe spell below generates luck and good fortune:

1. Dip a horseshoe in **Lucky Lodestone Oil.**
2. Dip it into magnetic sand.
3. Shake off the excess.
4. Wrap red silk thread around the shoe until it's covered completely.
5. Mount the wrapped horseshoe onto a piece of cardboard.
6. Embellish the horseshoe itself and the cardboard with lucky charms like four-leaf clovers and miniature dice. Miniature playing, tarot or votive cards may be attached, as can seashells. Small

quantities of lucky botanicals can be captured in a tiny piece of fabric—a miniature mojo hand—and attached. Place a metal sea horse charm in the very center of the horseshoe for extra good luck.
7. Post this image so that it will draw good fortune toward you.

Huayruru Seed Spells

Beans are humble yet so filled with magic. Folk tales celebrate heroes whose fortunes are made, not with wealth or weapons, but with beans. The huayruru seed is the lucky bean of Peruvian magic. Also known as *"lady bug seeds,"* these beans are bright red and black. They're very cute but poisonous: keep away from children and animals.

Basic Huayruru Spell

Carry one huayruru seed in a mojo bag or incorporate it into jewelry and wear for good luck.

Huayruru Conjure Bag

Place one huayruru seed in a red or green conjure bag together with seven coins and carry for good fortune.

Jupiter Spells

Once known as the *"Greater Benefic,"* this huge planet presides over luck and good fortune. The position of Jupiter in your natal chart and the aspects it makes to other celestial bodies determines your luck in this lifetime. Have an astrologer cast your natal chart to analyze what sort of fortune you were born with and how best to manifest that luck. Every person's horoscope charts the gifts and challenges that are present at birth. An astrologer can also calculate your *"Part of Fortune,"* so as best to exploit luck and minimize those challenges.

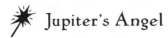

Jupiter's Angel

Zadkiel, ruler of the planet Jupiter, is the angel of goodness, grace, generosity, and mercy who bestows benevolence, good fortune, and justice. Burn frankincense to attract his attention and then tell him your heart's desires.

Jupiter's Lucky Charm

The metal associated with luck is tin, as it is the one under the rulership of Jupiter.

1. Cut out a small piece of tin.
2. Engrave it with lucky words, numbers, or phrases.
3. Put it in a lucky mojo bag and carry it with you.

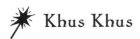

Khus Khus

Khus khus *is another name for vetiver. Originally from India, where it's known as the* "root of tranquility," *vetiver has many magical uses. It's used for love, healing, and protection, and also allegedly draws good fortune closer to you.*

1. Make a strong infusion of vetiver by pouring boiling water over the dried whole roots.
2. Steep for a minimum of three days.
3. Strain and reserve the liquid.
4. Use this vetiver water in personal baths as well as floorwashes for luck and success.

The lodestone may as well be known as the luckstone. Few things are as associated with the acquisition of good fortune.

Lodestone Spell (1) Basic

1. Dress a lodestone with one or more of the lucky condition oils: **Black Cat Oil, High John the Conqueror, Lucky Lodestone, Magnet,** or **Van Van.**
2. Sprinkle it with a lodestone's favorite food, magnetic sand (fine iron shot).
3. Carry with you in a red drawstring bag.
4. Replenish your lodestone's power by dressing and feeding it once a week.

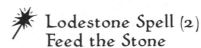

Lodestone Spell (2) Feed the Stone

1. Place a lodestone in a small covered terracotta pot.
2. Once a week, consistently on the same day, remove it from its dish and place it in a bowl of spring water. Let it sit for a few minutes while you express thanks for the blessings that came into your life during the previous week. (Think of some!) Remove the lodestone. Drink the water or add it to your bath.
3. Dry the lodestone; place it back in its pot.
4. Feed it by sprinkling some magnetic sand over it.
5. Keep your lodestone private. Let it know your desires: add a penny or a piece of real silver to the pot for financial luck. For romantic luck, add a photo of the one you love or desire or some other symbol of love.

Lodestone Spell (3) Ritual Activation

Magic respects power; it's just not reverential about it. Anything that's perceived as having power or as "working" may be commandeered for purposes of individual enchantment. The thought process is that if something has either been demonstrated to have power in one area or is reputed to have such power, why not play with it and see what kind of power it brings to other areas? Magic has always taken religious symbols

and rituals out of context and incorporated them into other, often completely unrelated contexts, to the great displeasure of the orthodox.

In this spell, the powers of Roman Catholic ritual are commandeered to give a lodestone charm an extra boost of magic power. Although the usage is unconventional, only someone very familiar with the ritual will actually be able to reproduce the spell—or would have known enough to create it.

1. Take your lodestone to church.
2. Light two candles near it; spill a little fine salt on the lodestone and discreetly dip it into the Holy Water font saying: *"Lodestone, I baptize you in the name of God, the Father, God the Son, God the Holy Spirit. I baptize you Lodestone. You are my fortune. You bring me good luck."*
3. Immediately afterwards, kneel in the middle of the church and recite an *"Our Father."*
4. Return home and place the lodestone in a red flannel bag, saying: *"Beautiful lodestone, Mineral of Enchantment, who walked with the Samaritan to whom you bestowed beauty and good luck. I put gold on you for my treasure, silver for my house, copper for the poor, coral to free me from envy and evil, wheat so that [Name], child of [Name] shall love me and be devoted to me."*
5. As you pronounce the litany, at the correct moment, add gold, silver, and copper charms, a piece of coral, and a pinch of wheat to the bag.
6. On Fridays, bathe the stone in wine. Repeat the Samaritan prayer and add: *"To me you give good luck and wealth."*
7. Replace the stone in its charm bag, with its companion charms. Drink the wine.

 ## Lodestone Spell (4) Lucky Bag

Dress a lodestone with magnetic sand and **Van Van** or **Lucky Lodestone Oil**. Place it in a red flannel bag and carry it with you, close to your heart if possible.

 ## Lodestone Luck Spell (5)

Anoint a lodestone or an iron charm with as many drops of **Lucky Lodestone Oil** as the years you've achieved, plus one more for added good luck. Carry in a conjure bag. Repeat the process at each New Moon.

 ## Lucky Animal Spell: Chi Lin

Chi Lin, creature of myth and legend, is a sort of Chinese unicorn. Believed to be the most auspicious creature of all, his image draws luck and success as well as prosperity, longevity, and even well-behaved children.

A statue or a paper image of Chi Lin draws his blessings. The image is most auspicious on or near a desk but it may be placed anywhere.

Bats are associated with luck and good fortune in the Chinese tradition because of a play on words: *"fu"* means *"bat"* but also *"luck"* and *"happiness."*

 ## Lucky Bat Spell (1) Ling Nut

The dried seedpod of Trapa bicornis, *known in Chinese as a ling nut or* ling ko, *a kind of water chestnut, is used to draw good fortune. Depending how you look at it, it resembles a bat. (Turn it around and it resembles a goat's head, but that's another spell.)*

Hang the dried pod on a wall, or carry it in a charm bag, together with other luck-invoking dried botanicals.

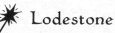 ## Lucky Bat Spell (2) Five Red Bats

The luck inherent in bats is intensified by incorporating the luckiest of numbers and colors into the spell: an image of five red bats draws good fortune toward it. Post the image prominently where it can radiate its power and draw good fortune toward it.

✴ Lucky Bat Spell (3) Five Red Bats in your Pocket Spell

The bats don't have to stay on the wall: place five red stone bats in a red charm bag, charge with your desire and carry in your pocket.

✴ Lucky Bat Spell (4) Romany

The association of bats with luck is not limited to Chinese tradition. A Romany charm to bring luck to children also depends upon the shape of a bat. Place a silver charm in the shape of a bat inside a small black silk or velvet-beaded bag. Have the child wear this around his or her neck.

The silver bat charm may also be hung from a red silk cord or silver chain and worn around the neck.

✴ Lucky Bat Spell (5) Real Bats

Spiritual supply stores and "witch markets" sometimes sell dead, dried bats—hardly lucky bats and definitely not for use in this spell. In real life, many bats haven't been lucky lately; loss of habitat and a perception of them as vermin (winged mice) have led to serious species endangerment.

If charms, images, and replicas are powerful, who knows what real bats will bring? Allegedly their presence offers spiritual protection and serves as an omen of forthcoming wealth and success.

1. Install a bat house: if bats move in, this is believed to be extremely auspicious. (Because many species of bats are now very endangered, the bat house provides luck for them, too—a classic example of magical reciprocity.)
2. No actual contact with the bats is needed or even recommended; however, for extra enhancement just murmur your desires in the vicinity of the bat house. Magically, they should receive the message.

✴ Lucky Bath

Gather the freshest, most fragrant blossoms you can find. Add them to your bath together with pineapple juice for joy and good fortune.

✴ Lucky Bath: Clover

Make an infusion by pouring boiling water over red clover. Let it cool, strain and add it to a tub filled with warm water so that you're bathing in clover!

✴ Lucky Bath: Spearmint

Make an infusion by pouring boiling water over spearmint. When it cools, strain out the botanical and add the liquid to your bath.

Cats are the animals most associated with luck and good fortune.

✴ Lucky Cat Spell (1) Bastet Candle

Bastet is the Egyptian goddess of joy, luck, love, and the pleasures of life. She is typically depicted as either a cat-headed woman or as a seated bejeweled cat. Candles are sold in the latter shape, however you may also substitute any green cat candle. (Green is Bastet's sacred color.)

1. Dress the candle with Horn of Plenty Oil. This oil represents Earth's finest fruits and your wish to partake of them. This is a difficult oil to create from authentic materials because your choice of "fruity" essential oils is limited. Use essential oils of lime, tangerine, and pink grapefruit. Supplement with fragrance oils like cherry, apple, or melon.
2. Place a scarab near the candle as it burns.
3. Focus on your wishes, desires, and petitions.

4. When the candle has burned down, carry the scarab as a charged lucky charm.

Lucky Cat Spell (2) Black Cat

Black cats evoke strong reactions. Some fear them and many still subscribe to the superstition that a black cat crossing one's path causes bad luck. Ironically, in many traditions black cats are associated with good luck. The black cat is believed to epitomize the cat's proverbial nine lives.

1. Hold a black cat candle in your hands to charge it with your desires.
2. Carve it as desired.
3. Dress it with **Black Cat Oil** to provide good fortune and break all hexes, and then burn.

Lucky Cat Spell (3) Black Cat Luck Candle

When you really *need some good fortune, dress a black cat candle with both* **Fast Luck** *and* **Black Cat Oils** *and burn.*

Lucky Cat Spell (4) Candle Spell

1. Carve a red cat candle.
2. Dress it with **Lucky Lodestone Oil.**
3. Sprinkle powdered vervain powder over it.
4. Light it and visualize your desires.

Lucky Cat Spell (5) Maneki Neko

Maneki Neko, the Japanese beckoning cat, may be the luckiest cat of all. Virtually unknown a hundred years ago, Maneki Neko has in the space of a century become one of the most popular amulets not only in Japan but throughout the world. Heartily welcomed into Chinese magical traditions, a visit to virtually any Chinatown will demonstrate a minimum of at least one Maneki Neko in almost every store window.

Maneki Neko literally means "beckoning cat." The standard image depicts a seated cat holding up one paw in beckoning invitation. Maneki Neko's come in a variety of colors: they are color-coded as to meaning.

Choose a white cat to draw luck toward you, or look for the classic tri-colored cat. All you need to do is place the image in the window facing outwards so that it can beckon luck to come inside and join you.

Hattatsuneko, a different Japanese cat, also bestows luck through images, but you'll have to come to him. His ritual involves a commitment lasting a minimum of four years. Variations on his image are distributed once a month at the Sumiyoshi-taisha shrine near Osaka. Pilgrimages are initiated to coincide with a wish. Allegedly, once you've collected all forty-eight possible images, your wish will be fulfilled.

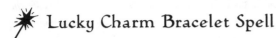

Lucky Cat Spell (6) Seven Eleven Lucky Cat Candle

Anoint a black cat candle with **Black Cat Oil** and/or **Van Van** or **Magnet Oil**. Burn the candle on consecutive nights: seven minutes the first night, eleven minutes the second, seven the third, and so forth until the candle burns down, by which time you should see a change in fortune.

Lucky Charm Bracelet Spell

Charm bracelets go in and out of fashion but their roots derive from magical use, manipulating the secret powers of objects. Lucky charms may be understood as a form of amulet, talisman, or ex-voto.

1. Choose a charm that represents your goal.
2. At the New Moon place this charm beside a small pink candle.
3. Charge the candle with your desire, carve and dress if you like and burn it.
4. When the candle burns out, attach the charm to a bracelet.
5. Wear it or reserve in a safe place, whatever suits your magic.
6. When this goal is achieved, set another goal.
7. Choose another charm and begin again. (Should you reconsider and change your mind regarding any goal, merely remove that charm and begin again at the New Moon.)

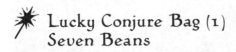

Lucky Conjure Bag (1) Seven Beans

Fairy tales are full of blessed fools who trade away prized livestock or goods of similar value for a handful of beans. By the end of the story, what may have appeared to be idiocy is inevitably proved to be a wise, fortuitous, and lucky choice. These fairy tales only hint at the secret history of magic beans. Beans were an ancient Roman euphemism for the female genitalia. They were believed to possess the power to impregnate women; think of the stories where girls accidentally swallowed beans, only to give birth to the hero nine months later. Beans provide luck, good fortune, and ladders to Heaven (think Jack and the Beanstalk); avail yourself of their powers.

Choose seven different beans and carry them within a red silk or flannel bag. Although any beans may be used, speckled, red, black, and white are considered the most fortuitous.

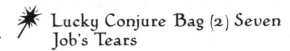

Lucky Conjure Bag (2) Seven Job's Tears

1. Add seven Job's tears to a conjure bag, plus one tonka bean for every wish that you have.
2. Hold each bean in your hands and make a wish before placing it in the bag.
3. Carry the charm bag with you or store it in a secure, secret place.

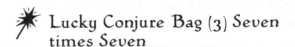

Lucky Conjure Bag (3) Seven times Seven

Place a staurolite crystal, seven Job's tears, seven tonka beans, and a matched pair of lodestones into a conjure bag. Anoint with **Magnet Oil** as needed.

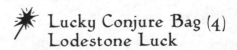

Lucky Conjure Bag (4) Lodestone Luck

Carry Grains of Paradise, five-finger grass (cinquefoil), a matched pair of lodestones and one unbroken star anise in a conjure bag for good fortune and protection.

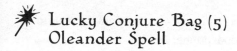

Lucky Conjure Bag (5) Oleander Spell

Fill a conjure bag with Grains of Paradise, a Jezebel root and angel's turnip (dogbane/oleander).

Note: angel's turnip is extremely poisonous.

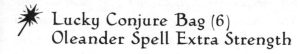

Lucky Conjure Bag (6) Oleander Spell Extra Strength

Place an angel's turnip (dogbane), sumbul root, slice of peony root, and a pinch of five-finger grass (cinquefoil) into a charm bag, together with a four-leaf clover (real or charm) for good luck and protection.

Note: angel's turnip is extremely poisonous.

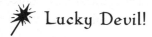

Lucky Devil!

Carry the botanical devil's bit so you'll be a lucky devil, too.

Lucky Golden Handwash

Handwashes are most commonly associated with gambler's magic. (See Gambler's Spells, page 46 for more information.) However, handwashes may also be used to provide general, all-around good fortune.

1. Place three or seven strands of saffron in a cup.
2. Pour boiling water over it.
3. Let it cool, then bottle and refrigerate it.
4. Rub the liquid on your hands (do not rinse off) to have and maintain happiness and good fortune.

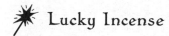

Lucky Incense

Burn incense in harmony with astrological signs to bring good luck in all aspects of life.

1. Blend the following: cinnamon, labdanum, cloves, violets, lemon zest or lemongrass, jasmine, black pepper, ambrette seeds, rose petals, sandalwood, camphor, and dried currents.
2. Burn as incense or simmer to produce aromatic vapors.

Lucky Mountains

The Romany of Central Europe possess legends of "lucky mountains." Dirt from these mountains provides blessings of all kinds. Traditionally, there are seven lucky mountains.

There is some ambiguity as to exactly where these mountains are or which mountains they may be. You wouldn't want to accidentally miss one, so the custom has arisen of collecting pinches of Earth at any auspicious-seeming height. This dirt is placed in a conjure bag, in the hopes that this could be the magic mountain, and presumably some of them are. This becomes a lifelong collection: the bag is eventually placed in the grave with its owner to ease the transition to the next realm and continue bringing luck.

Literally only a tiny pinch of Earth is taken; the conjure bag need never become very heavy. The practice emerged amidst a nomadic tradition; bags are light and portable, although you may also place your pinches of dirt in small boxes and vials to place upon an altar.

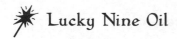

Lucky Nine Oil

Blend the following botanicals:

Allspice
Carnations
Cinnamon
Frankincense
Galangal
High John the Conqueror chips
Lemon zest or lemongrass
Myrrh
Vervain

Place the botanicals in a bottle, cover with jojoba oil and roll gently to distribute. Rub on the hands, and dress candles and mojo bags as desired for enhanced good fortune.

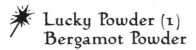

Lucky Powder (1) Bergamot Powder

Bergamot is a small bitter Italian orange that provides the characteristic scent of Earl Grey Tea. It also has many magical uses. It's considered one of the commanding botanicals and is used to draw good fortune, particularly financial good fortune. The sole downside of essential oil of bergamot is that it possesses a powerful photosensitizing effect, which means it increases skin's sensitivity to sun. If you wear it, it's crucial to avoid exposure to the sun. Reserve this formula for the winter season.

1. Sift a combination of cornstarch, arrowroot powder, and bentonite clay until you achieve a fine consistency.
2. Sprinkle essential oil of bergamot onto the powder until the desired fragrance is achieved.
3. Stir the powder with a wooden chopstick to distribute the essential oil.
4. Allow the powder to dry.

5. Place it in a container and dust onto the body to attract good fortune.

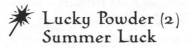

Lucky Powder (2) Summer Luck

For summer luck, replicate Step 1 of the spell above. Then, instead of adding bergamot, substitute essential oil of peppermint, which draws joy and good fortune and also provides a cooling effect on hot skin.

Lucky Talismans

Although the words *"amulet"* and *"talisman"* are used somewhat synonymously today, technically an amulet is meant to protect you whereas a talisman magnetically draws some sort of good fortune. Talismans are what are usually meant by the phrase *"lucky charm."* The term talisman also frequently indicates a specific type of lucky charm: engraved precious stones. However talismans of good fortune come in many forms, including metal, botanical, and written charms.

Most talismans require no further activation than the usual charging, cleansing, and/or consecrating used for any magical tool. Talismans are usually worn or carried on the person, frequently in a charm bag. Good luck talismans such as these include:

★ *Devil's shoestrings roots*
★ *A coin minted in your birth year*
★ *High John the Conqueror root*

Some talismans, however, require further activation in order to draw good fortune.

 Lucky Talisman Peyote

Peyote is most famous for its role in Huichol ritual and as the holy sacrament of the Native American Church. This rare and sacred plant also has amuletic properties. Peyote, like lodestones, lava, and High John roots, comes in male and female forms, which are visibly distinctive. Traditionally, women need male peyote, while men need a female for talismanic use.

1. Keep the peyote whole in order to empower the talisman.
2. Soak it in hard liquor and then dry it in bright sunlight.
3. Wrap it in red silk and wear it over your right knee.

 Lucky Written Talisman (1) Archangels' Names

Talismans frequently take the form of written charms. Sacred words and names radiate their own magical power. The creation of the talisman is perceived as a spell. Traditionally, writing a talisman is preceded by cleansing rites and frequently by fasting, and you should choose your paper and ink thoughtfully.

One talisman uses the names of the archangels. Write on parchment paper the names of the seven Hebrew archangels. This is most effective if written in Hebrew script:

Michael

Raphael

Gabriel

Souriel

Zaziel

Badakiel

Suliel

Post the talisman on the wall or carry it within a leather or metal conjure bag.

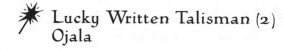 Lucky Written Talisman (2) Ojala

"Ojala" is a Spanish corruption of "Inshallah," Arabic for "as Allah wills it." The term has emerged in South America as a power-amulet.

On a small piece of paper, write, while focusing on your desire:

```
O   J   A   L   A
O   J   A   L
O   J   A
O   J
O
```

Fold the paper carefully and wear it within a locket or a medicine bag until your desired goal is obtained.

Magic Box Spells

Magic boxes are especially auspicious for luck spells. Because charms are stored together in these magic boxes, and especially if the box has power too (see *Elements of Magic Spells*) their power is concentrated and symbiotically enhanced. Magic boxes aren't meant to be created to be stored on a shelf. Take the box out periodically and play with the contents. Absorb their power while charging them with your desires. Take one or two out and carry with you as needed, replacing with an equivalent number of alternative charms, always maintaining a lucky seven in number.

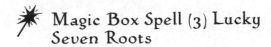 Magic Box Spell (1) Lucky Seven Charm Box

Seven is the number of miracles and good fortune. Fill a magic box with seven lucky charms. Some suggestions are:

1. High John the Conqueror.
2. Low John the Conqueror.
3. Small magnetic horseshoe (you could use an actual horseshoe, if your box is large enough).
4. Shamrock or four-leaf clover (real or a charm representation).
5. Lodestone.
6. Piece of Fool's gold (pyrite) or a small piece of real gold.
7. A tonka bean.

Substitute other charms as you like, or maintain a rotating community of charms.

Magic Box Spell (2) Lucky Seven Beans and Roots

Fairy tales identify beans with luck and fulfilled wishes. Roots are frequently the most magically charged, amuletic part of a plant. This magic spell box combines the two for extra good fortune.

Consider filling your box with the following or substitute other preferences:

1. High John the Conqueror.
2. Low John the Conqueror.
3. Lucky Hand root.
4. Galangal root.
5. Tonka bean.
6. Vanilla bean.
7. Black snake root.

Dress the items with essential oils of vetiver and patchouli and sprinkle with powdered nutmeg and mace.

Magic Box Spell (3) Lucky Seven Roots

Keep these roots together in a magic box or substitute others, maintaining the number seven at all times:

1. Lucky Hand root.
2. High John the Conqueror.
3. Low John the Conqueror.
4. Galangal root.
5. Vetiver.
6. Archangel root (angelica, dong quai).
7. Mandrake or ginseng.

 Magic Ring Luck Spell

A common motif in fairy tales is the magical ring that guarantees good fortune. What the fairy tales don't tell you is that the moon can convert any ring with a golden band into a magic lucky ring. Turn a golden ring three times counter-clockwise upon first sighting the New Moon, to bring good luck.

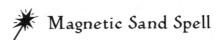 Magnetic Sand Spell

Sprinkle silver magnetic sand over doorway thresholds to invite good fortune, true friends, and welcome visitors to enter.

 Master Oil

This lucky oil is believed to benefit only men.

Grind the following into fine powder: deer's tongue, red brick dust, patchouli, and vetiver and add the powder to sunflower and jojoba oils. Use the oil to dress a mojo bag for success in luck and love. Or you can rub a drop on your feet before setting out on important ventures, or a drop between your palms before crucial appointments.

Metal Key Spells

Metal keys attract positive magic into your life, while simultaneously deflecting evil. Magic keys open doors of opportunity. Old metal keys are best: check out flea markets and antique stores—let the keys *and* opportunities find you.

 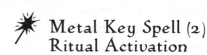

Metal Key Spell (1) Mojo

According to Romany metaphysical traditions, carrying key-amulet charms enables you to learn secrets, have mysteries revealed, and find personal success. Find a special key and charge it with your desire. Place it in a red silk bag and carry it with you.

Metal Key Spell (2) Ritual Activation

Finding a key on the ground, especially an older or antique key, is considered extremely auspicious. Charge it with power to create an amulet. Standard magical charging techniques may be used; however, this spell is specifically intended to transform a found key into a prized amulet:

1. Pick the key up discreetly if possible.
2. Bring it home and cleanse by passing it through incense smoke.
3. Charge the key by placing it inside a cast iron pan or cauldron. Heat until it's burning hot, then turn off the heat and leave the key in the pan to cool off at its own pace.
4. Focus on what doors this key should open. Is this the Key to Love? The Key to Money? The Key to Personal Freedom?
5. Sleep with the key under your pillow for nine nights. Carry it with you during the day.
6. After nine days, it will have become an activated amulet: keep it in a magic box or mojo bag or hang it on the wall.

Metal Key Spell (3) Wind Charm

1. A collection of keys may be strung together onto red thread as a charm or formed into a wind chime.
2. An easy wind chime for the less than artistically inclined may be made from a bent wire coat hanger.
3. Hang the keys in the wind to rustle up beneficial opportunities.

Mirror and Sieve Spell

1. Fasten a mirror to the center of a sieve.
2. Hang the sieve so that the mirror reflects outwards. Good influences are able to pass through the sieve's holes, while the mirror transforms evil influences into good luck.
3. Enhance with a charged magic mirror for extra power or use a *"ba gua,"* the feng shui ritual mirror.

Mistletoe Luck Spell (1)

Twist marjoram and thyme around mistletoe and hang it in the corners of each room to attract luck and fortune.

Mistletoe Luck Spell (2)

Tie mistletoe with red ribbon and hang, any time of the year, in your home for luck, protection, and extra kissing.

New Year's Eve Spells

New Year's Eve, the threshold of the New Year, offers the perfect opportunity for a change in fortune.

New Year's Eve Bath Spell (1)

Make an infusion of mucura by pouring boiling water over the herb. Bathe in this infusion in the very first hour of the New Year for luck and protection. (Note: bathing in mucura is not safe if you're pregnant.)

 ## New Year's Eve Bath Spell (2)

A traditional Burmese New Year's Eve renewal bath features oils of roses and sandalwood.

1. Add a few drops of rose attar to a cup of rose hydrosol or rose water.
2. Add a few drops of sandalwood essential oil to sandalwood hydrosol.
3. Add them to a tub filled with warm water.
4. Float fresh flowers in the water for extra enhancement.

 ## New Year's Eve Bayberry Candle

Real bayberry wax candles are rare and costly: it takes approximately fifteen pounds of bayberries to create one pound of bayberry wax. And so bayberry candles are often reserved for special occasions.

New Year's Eve is such an occasion! Light a bayberry candle on New Year's Eve to draw luck, prosperity, and success in the coming year. Scratch your goals and desires into the candle wax for extra enhancement.

 ## New Year's Eve Lunar Candle

1. Carve a white candle with your desires on New Year's Eve.
2. Reserve the candle until midnight, then greet the midnight moon by lighting your candle.

3. Make a wish for the New Year as you light the candle.

Peppermint Spells

Peppermint brings joy as well as good fortune. It cleanses stagnation, creating room for opportunity and success.

 ## Peppermint Chervil Sachet

Peppermint and chervil, two lucky plants, combine synergistically to bring happiness, luck, and protection.

1. Combine equal quantities of dried chervil and peppermint and sew them into a sachet.
2. Wear it against your skin during the day.
3. Sleep with it under your pillow at night.

 ## Peppermint Floorwash

1. Make a strong infusion of peppermint by pouring boiling water over the botanical.
2. When it cools, strain out the peppermint and add the liquid to a bucket of floorwash rinse water.
3. Add vinegar and a little **Cascarilla Powder.**
4. Cleanse the floors and threshold areas to radiate an invitation to happiness and good fortune.

 ## Persimmon Luck Spell

Bury green persimmons to receive good fortune.

 ## Pisces Calendar Spell

In traditional Jewish magic, the astrological sign Pisces ("Adar" in Hebrew), traditionally under the

rulership of the lucky planet Jupiter, is considered to be the most fortunate of all the signs. This luck extends to people born under Pisces, but also to events occurring during this period—approximately February 20th until March 20th. Timing is considered especially favorable for engagements, marriages, surgery, business transactions, and anything contractual.

There are two ways to avail yourself of this extra luck during the rest of the year:

1. Fish (the sign of Pisces) are shorthand for abundance and good fortune. Wear or carry charms in the shape of a fish, or post images of fish on the wall.
2. Special *Adar* amulets may be posted. These depict fish, liquor, and glasses together with the phrase: *"When Adar arrives, festivity thrives."* (The images refer to the happy Jewish festival of Purim, which occurs during this period, and also to Pisces' traditional rulership of intoxicants.)

 Pliny's Success Spell

Pliny the Roman recommended blending chicory juice into olive oil for luck and success. Rubbing the body with this oil allegedly enhances your popularity and encourages others to grant your wishes and requests.

 Red Goblin Spell

Even a mere pebble can be transformed into a lucky charm, and any round, smooth stone will suffice for this spell.

Toss the pebble in the air three times and catch it, chanting:

Spirit of Good Fortune
Spirit of the Red Goblin
Don't abandon me!
Stay with me
Enter this stone, so that I can use it to call on you!

You may want to mark the stone to distinguish it from others.

The Red Goblin may be a euphemism for you-know-who; he may also be a more mild-mannered Italian spirit, whose name has been forgotten. Interpret as you will. Call on him, when in need, if you like or just use the pebble as a talisman.

Root Spells

Synonyms for witches include enchanters, sorcerers, conjurers, and rootworkers. Although all parts of a plant may be used for magical purposes, no part of a plant is more associated with magic spells than roots. Roots contain the plant's entire capacity for power. Because they are the part buried in Earth, they're also believed to contain hidden knowledge of Earth's secrets. Many roots are especially associated with luck, success, and good fortune.

 Root Spell: Ginger

Ginger root reputedly brings joy and fun into your life. What could be luckier?

1. Macerate ginger in sunflower and jojoba oil until you've achieved the desired intensity of fragrance. If you have fresh ginger plants, add the blossoms to the oil, too. (You may also add a few drops of essential oil of ginger for added intensity, but be careful: many find it a skin irritant.)
2. Strain, reserving the scented oil.
3. Apply the oil behind your knees, elbows, and ears when striking out for adventure.

 Root Spell: High John

A High John the Conqueror root can be used to transform any charm or conjure bag into a lucky amulet. High John the Conqueror is a powerful, auspicious root, which allegedly can only bring good fortune.

Dress a High John Root with **High John the Conqueror Oil.** Carry it in your pocket or in a charm bag, re-anointing weekly.

 Root Spell: High John Charm Activation

High John the Conqueror may be used to ritually activate and charge any other charm or conjure bag, bestowing some of its power and benevolence.

1. Carve a red candle with your name, goals, desires, any identifying information, and sigils.
2. Dress the candle with **High John the Conqueror Oil, Lucky Lodestone,** and/or **Magnet Oil.**
3. Light the candle near a pot of boiling water, ideally an iron pot or cauldron.
4. Sprinkle a small handful of powdered High John into the water. Let steam arise.
5. Pass your charm or bag alternately through the steam and the candle smoke until it feels complete.
6. Repeat as necessary.

 Root Spell: High John's Lucky Cologne

High John the Conqueror, **Bay Rum,** and **Chypre** are all associated with men's power and good fortune.

1. Shave or break up a High John the Conqueror root.
2. Add these chips to either **Bay Rum** or **Chypre.**
3. Use it daily, as aftershave or cologne, to enhance your chances of success in love and luck.

If you already have a favorite fragrance, add High John chips to that instead, although the end result may not be as potent as one combined with one of the traditional men's lucky fragrances.

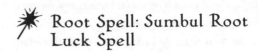 Root Spell: Sumbul Root Luck Spell

Sumbul has been used in India and Iran for centuries but was first introduced to the West in the nineteenth century. Carry a sumbul root for magically enhanced good fortune.

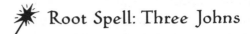 Root Spell: Three Johns

Three botanically distinct root charms go under the name of John. What they do have in common is a capacity for drawing protection and good fortune toward you. High John the Conqueror (or jalap root as it's known pharmaceutically) is the root of a type of Morning Glory. Low John the Conqueror, or Bethroot, derives from the extremely endangered Trillium family of botanicals. Southern John goes under a vast number of names: Little John to Chew, Galangal, Laos or Courtcase root. As a component of Asian cuisine, it's the easiest root of the three to find. It's a botanical cousin of ginger root, although their powers are very different and they cannot substitute for one another magically.

1. Make a mojo hand with High John the Conqueror, Low John the Conqueror, and Southern John.
2. Dress the roots with **Magnet Oil** and **Van Van.**
3. Carry them in a red drawstring bag, anointing with oil weekly.

Rose of Jericho Spells

Among its many other blessings, Rose of Jericho draws good fortune and opens the door to opportunity.

Rose of Jericho Charm

Rose of Jericho Water tends to get all the attention—as if the botanical existed only to create the water. The dried botanical brings its own good fortunes however: it is especially fortuitous when relocating or searching for new paths and opportunities. Carry a dried blossom as a lucky charm.

 Rose of Jericho Water

★ Use **Rose of Jericho Water** to bathe charms, charm bags and anything you wish to empower and transform into a lucky charm
★ Add **Rose of Jericho Water** to your bath, so that you, too, radiate good fortune

 Saint John's Barometer Spell

Saint John's Wort is believed to possess the power to reflect and influence your luck.

As it grows, so goes your luck. Luckily, it's a reasonably sturdy plant!

1. Buy or plant Saint John's Wort, ideally on Midsummer's Day, which corresponds to the feast day of Saint John.
2. Observe its growth. If it's ailing, nurture it back to health; consciously participate in its well being. (If it does die, just start all over again.)
3. Talk to the plant as you care for it; tell it what type of luck you need.

 Saint John's Eve Lucky Garlands

Plants harvested during the Festival of Saint John (Midsummer's Day) are believed to be exceptionally powerful and beneficial.

1. Gather botanicals. Choose from amongst the following: Saint John's Wort, white lilies, mugwort, wormwood, Sweet Annie, southernwood, tarragon, elecampane, fennel, chervil, and green birch branches.
2. Ornament your home and yourself with garlands of these fortuitous flowers on Saint John's Eve to draw luck and spiritual protection for the next twelve months.

 Salamander Spell

A salamander crawls slowly but persistently, inexorably toward the sun. In North Africa this is perceived as a metaphor for the human soul, which seeks and can ultimately reach divine light.

For millennia, Moroccan salamanders have been stuffed with lucky herbs and hung in the house to avert evil. Some species are now extremely endangered. (Powdered salamander is also a traditional medicine.) There are alternative methods to access this power:

1. Trace the rough shape of a salamander onto blue cloth.
2. Cut it out, sew it up with red thread, leaving a hole for stuffing.
3. Stuff with dried spearmint, pennyroyal, rue, harmel, and both dark and light benzoin resin.
4. For bonus luck and power use amazonite beads to make eyes for your salamander.

 Salt Spell

According to a New Orleans tradition, tossing salt onto your front steps on the first Friday of each month brings good fortune to the house.

 ## Sea Spirit Spell

Sea spirit is a plant but it conveys the blessings of the sea. (In its dehydrated form it's known as agar-agar and is a staple of Asian cuisine.)

1. Place a sea spirit in a bottle.
2. Cover it with rum or whiskey.
3. Seal it shut. You can apply sealing wax if you like.
4. Keep one in each room for good luck.

Spirit Assistance Spells

According to legend, fairies and other spirits visit new-born babies to bestow or withhold a lifetime's worth of fortune. Spirit power doesn't terminate in the nursery, however. If the fairies weren't too generous, make a conscious appeal for spiritual intervention. Blessings of good fortune may be requested at any time, although certain spirits are more likely than others to bestow it.

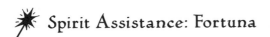 ## Spirit Assistance: Fortuna

The original Lady Luck, Fortuna spins the Wheel of Fortune. Her emblem is the cornucopia; her cup runneth over. Another of her emblems is a ship's rudder; Fortuna is the captain of the boat of life. She determines which route the boat takes. Will the waters be rough or will she direct you toward smooth sailing?

When you facetiously ask Lady Luck to smile upon you, you are unknowingly petitioning Fortuna for help. Lady Luck has a reputation for generosity: ask for her assistance consciously and deliberately for greater chance of success. Once upon a time in Italy, Fortuna was actually a very prominent divinity, possessing her own shrines and temples. Fortuna provides blessings of good fortune to all, but is especially benevolent toward women and children.

Devote an altar to Fortuna: decorate it with dice, lucky charms, roses, and perfume. Make a wish list. Place the paper beneath a gold candle and burn it.

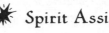 ## Spirit Assistance: Lakshmi

This beautiful Hindu goddess is luck. She is the very embodiment of generosity, benevolence, and good fortune. She provides all blessings of happiness. Don't you want her in your house? Invite her in.

Lakshmi manifests as an exquisitely beautiful woman, golden in her splendor. The tremendous quantity of her precious jewelry causes her to become a vision of flashing, glowing, shining light. It's easy to obtain images of Lakshmi as she is among the most beloved deities of India. She is usually depicted emerging from a lotus, between two white elephants, her hands distributing gifts. Lakshmi is also present in tulsi basil.

Fridays are the most effective day to petition Lakshmi. While Fortuna is partial to the ladies, Lakshmi is reputedly extra generous to men. The downside of Lakshmi is that she has a reputation for being fickle. Luck is with you today but gone tomorrow. If she bestows good fortune upon you, don't take her for granted but petition even more fervently.

1. Make an image of Lakshmi or a potted tulsi basil plant the focal point of an altar.
2. Decorate it with coins, beads, and conch shells.
3. Lakshmi accepts offerings of milk, candy, and fruit. Give her some and tell her what you need.

 ## Spirit Assistance: Lakshmi's Footprints

If you long for Lakshmi's presence, then walk her through your door, literally. Tiny, pretty, stylized footprints known as "Lakshmi's footprints" symbolize this spirit of wealth and good fortune entering your home.

Stamp or paint her feet walking into your front door. Stamp them on your floors and walls—but make sure you don't depict them leaving.

Spirit Assistance: Lakshmi's Bridal Spell

Every bride momentarily embodies Lakshmi.

1. Have a pan filled with paint waiting at the front door for the bride's first entrance into her home following the marriage ceremony.
2. The bride should take off her shoes, step into the wet paint and walk good fortune into her home.

Spirit Assistance Spell: Morgan le Fay

Morgan le Fay, Fata Morgana, sometimes takes on the role of Spirit of Good Fortune. In some legends, she dwells at the bottom of a lake, dispensing good fortune to those whom she favors.

Create a shrine for her featuring images of lakes and bowls of fresh or salted water. Decorate the shrine with hand-drums, seashells, pebbles from the sea, and fairy or mermaid images, as Morgan claims membership in both those spiritual clubs. Create an aura that attracts and pleases her (and you, too!). Request assistance as you will.

Spirit Assistance: Ogum Beira Mar

Ogun, the powerful West African Spirit of Iron, is not traditionally considered a "spirit of luck," although he does generously provide success for his devotees. In most versions of his myth, Ogun, a dour spirit, lives a fairly solitary existence in the forest. However, a seashore dwelling aspect of Ogun emerged in Brazil: Ogum

Beira Mar. *Perhaps the change of scenery lightened his usually severe demeanor, as Ogum Beira Mar may be petitioned for luck and happiness. First you must bring him a meal at his home by the sea.*

1. Dice yams into small pieces.
2. Cook them together with beef giblets or calves' liver.
3. Wrap the dish in foil and take it to the beach.
4. Dig a hole in the sand and light a red candle inside it.
5. Pour some fine rum into the sand.
6. Present your offering to Ogum.
7. Talk to him and tell him exactly what you need.

Spirit Assistance: Saint Anthony

Saint Anthony, miracle-working saint and acclaimed witch doctor, may be petitioned for good luck.

1. Create an altar with a statue or chromolithograph of the saint as the focal point.
2. Some turn his image upside down until the petition is received, in the belief that making the saint uncomfortable will cause him to work faster. However this seems like a harsh approach to such a generous saint.
3. An alternative is more gracious: offer Saint Anthony a single lily. Tell him that when he helps your fortunes improve you'll bring him a whole bouquet.

Spirit Assistance: Santoshi Ma, the Mother of Satisfaction

Magic is full of talk about ancient primordial spirits. Santoshi Ma isn't one of them. Despite veneration for ancient traditions, new spirits are born daily. Santoshi Ma first manifested in Rajasthan, India during the 1960s. In 1975, a popular movie catapulted her to national recognition and her cult began to flourish and grow in popularity.

According to legend, Santoshi Ma was the wife of a high-ranking military officer; after death, she ascended to the realm of the spirits. Santoshi Ma's dominion is fluid social and economic progress. For millennia, people's destinies were set: if your family were poor peasants, you'd be a poor peasant. Santoshi Ma cuts through those restrictions: her gift to devotees, particularly women, is upward mobility, economic success, and good fortune.

Offer Santoshi Ma fruit, flowers, and fragrant incense. Write your petitions onto a square of gold paper and place it under the offering tray.

Spirit Assistance: Yemaya

Yemaya, orisha of the Sea, who may or may not be Ogun's mother, is renowned for her generosity and kindness and possesses some influence over the Wheel of Fortune. Petition Yemaya for luck and security with seven long-stemmed white roses.

1. Very gently, so as not to damage the flowers, rub each individual rose against your face and body, all the while petitioning Yemaya for her assistance.
2. Create a beautiful bouquet by wrapping the roses together with blue silk ribbons.
3. Take this bouquet to the beach, along with seven small white and/or blue candles plus some matches.
4. Hollow out a space in the sand. Set the candles in the space and light them.

5. Wade out into the sea carrying the bouquet. Cradle it while seven waves approach and splash you, then respectfully give Yemaya her bouquet by throwing it into the sea.

Stop Opposition Incense

1. To overcome opposition to your success, burn the following botanicals as incense:
   Cloves
   Garlic
   High John the Conqueror
   Jezebel root
   Licorice
   Sweet flag (calamus)
   Woodruff
2. Grind and powder the botanicals, sprinkling onto lit charcoal, or burn whole bruised botanicals in a cauldron.
3. Burn the incense in the room where opposition is most likely to occur.

Success Diagnostic Spell

This spell allows you to measure a project's probability of good fortune.

1. Hold a small candle in your hands and charge it with your question and your desire.
2. Light the candle.
3. Place it on a holly leaf and float them on water.
4. If the leaf and candle float and if the candle stays lit, the project will prosper.

Success Protection Spell

Spells for luck lead to success. Success leads to jealousy, and jealousy leads to the Evil Eye. Wear essential oil of rose geranium to protect against gossip and backstabbing caused by jealousy of your success and good fortune.

Successful Happy Life Candle

Roll a bright gold or orange candle in ground cinna-mon, powdered five-finger grass (cinquefoil), and Irish moss and burn it.

Ten of Diamonds Spell

1. Remove a ten of diamonds from a new deck of playing cards and place it on a dish. If you prefer, you may substitute the ten of coins card from any tarot deck.
2. Sprinkle it with graveyard dirt, lodestone powder and **Van Van Oil.** Add a piece of real silver.
3. Carve a red candle with your identifying information; dress it with **Van Van,** too.
4. Place it on top of the playing card.
5. Burn the candle, while visualizing the luck and success you need.
6. When the candle has burned out, place the card, the silver, a little of the powder and any wax remnants that may appear "lucky" in a mojo bag. Carry it with you or keep it in a secure place. Dress periodically with **Van Van Oil** to keep the mojo working.

Tonka Bean Arret

Tonka beans are said to have the power to make wishes come true. This New Orleans charm allegedly provides luck, protection, and general good fortune.

1. Drill a hole in a tonka bean.
2. Attach a small cross. (This doesn't necessarily evoke Christian symbolism, although it can, if you would like it to. The cross as a pre-Christian symbol possesses the effect of radiating power in all directions.)
3. Carry in a conjure bag or attach to a chain and wear around your neck.

Turmeric Spell

The rhizome turmeric, a cousin of ginger root, is believed to bring good fortune. It's also the source of a potent—and permanent—yellow dye. Dye garments with turmeric for good luck.

Van Van Spells

Van Van Oil *allegedly turns bad luck into the best luck and opens the road to success. It may be the most beloved condition oil of all: it allegedly provides all life's bless-ings, while simultaneously repelling evil. At one time in the late nineteenth century, the entire town of Algiers, across the river from New Orleans, was said to be redo-lent of Van Van's lemony scent.*

★ *Anoint lucky charms with* ***Van Van,*** *for extra power*
★ *Anoint yourself: massage yourself with the oil or add it to a bath*
★ *For a fast, spontaneous lucky charm, dip a cotton ball in* ***Van Van*** *and carry it in your pocket*

Vervain Spell

The sacred herb vervain allegedly turns bad luck into the best luck, attracts love and prosperity and makes even your enemies like you, at least a little.

1. Make an infusion by pouring boiling water over vervain.
2. While it cools, run a bath.
3. Once the infusion has cooled, bring it to the tub. (Don't strain the botanicals out.)
4. Undress, get into the water and pour the infusion directly over you, then soak in the bath.
5. Allow yourself to air-dry.

Victory Against All Odds Luck Spell

The miracle herb celandine allegedly helps provide victory despite all odds, escape when no solutions seem possible. Celandine is toxic; use externally only.

Hold the botanical in your left hand while contemplating your situation. Carry in a conjure bag, keeping the bag under your pillow while you sleep. A solution will allegedly appear.

 ## Wahoo Luck Bark Bag (1)

Carry wahoo bark in a conjure bag to achieve success in your chosen endeavors.

 ## Wahoo Luck Bark Bag (2)

1. Combine wahoo bark and Job's tears; line the conjure bag with wahoo.
2. Make a wish on seven individual Job's tears. (Repeat the same wish seven times or make seven distinct wishes, however you please.) As you articulate each wish, place the seed in the bag.
3. When complete, spit in the bag and carry for success, good fortune, and so that your wishes will come true.

Wisteria Happiness Candle

Wisteria attracts happiness and good fortune. Blend dried, crumbled wisteria flowers into jojoba oil. Dress candles with this oil to attract happy people, fun, and joyful experiences.

Wood Rose Lucky Magic Spell

Wood roses aren't true roses but instead are members of the morning glory family, as is that other luck provider, High John the Conqueror. Carry or keep a wood rose for good luck.

Repairing Bad Luck

"*If it wasn't for bad luck, I wouldn't have no luck at all,*" sings bluesman Albert King.

Is he singing the soundtrack to your life? "*Been down so long, it looks like up to me,*" wrote poet/ singer/songwriter Richard Farina. Does that sound too familiar, as well?

If you can't even conceive of having good luck, you'd be content with a respite from the worst luck, don't despair. Magic methods exist to turn your luck around.

 ## Bad Luck Begone Powder

This botanical powder makes no promises about bringing good fortune but allegedly counteracts bad luck and protects from its effects. (Nine, seven, and five are numbers of protection: incorporate these numbers into the quantities of botanicals used.)

Blend the following ingredients, grinding them together:

Nine dried bay leaves, crumbled
Frankincense
Juniper berries
Cloves
Dried dill
Dried fennel
Dried tarragon

Make substantial quantities: carry some with you in a mojo hand, while keeping more within the home as fragrant, protective potpourri.

 Break Bad Luck Spell

This spell allegedly breaks a spell of bad luck.

1. Carve your affirmations and desires on a white candle and dress it with olive oil.
2. Roll it in ground red pepper.
3. Light the candle, place it securely on the floor and jump over it.

 Broken Mirror Antidote Spell

Does breaking a mirror cause seven years of bad luck? It better not; many spells require shards of broken mirror. If the situation causes anxiety, never fear, an antidote exists:

1. Some mirrors break cleanly into a mere few pieces while others shatter into thousands. Be that as it may, gather up all the shards and pieces of the mirror and as much of the glass dust as possible.
2. Wrap it in fabric or a paper bag.
3. Throw the mirror pieces into a river or fast-moving stream, flowing away from you so as to carry away all misfortune.

 Change in Fortune Bag

Carry dried violets in a red silk bag to see an upturn in fortune.

 Drive Away Bad Luck Bath

1. Make a strong infusion of basil and spearmint. You may strain the botanicals out or leave them in for extra strength.
2. Squeeze in the juice of one lemon.
3. Sprinkle with sesame seeds and a handful of flour.
4. Stir in a spoonful of **Command and Compel Oil.**
5. Fill a bathtub with water.
6. Carry the bowl with the infusion to the tub.
7. Stand in the tub of water, pour or ladle the infusion over your head, sit down and soak.

 Happy Times Powder

Magic spells, charms, and incantations are always given in the present tense. Happy Times Powder's name expresses wishes and goals, not necessarily present reality.

1. Blend the following ingredients together, powdering further if necessary: dried ground strawberry leaves, dried powdered vanilla bean, and finely grated orange zest.
2. Sprinkle this powder around the perimeter of your home, behind doors, and in all its corners, for a change of luck and an improvement in fortune.

 Insoluble Problems Solved Spell

Untie the knots that bind you!

1. Write an explicit description of your situation on brown paper.
2. Wrap the paper around some knotgrass.
3. Charge the packet with your desires, and then burn it.
4. Pay attention to your dreams and random words overheard; solutions will appear and you don't want to miss them.

 Kyoto Powder

*Sprinkle **Kyoto Powder** as needed to reverse bad luck: sprinkle on the premises where bad luck occurs, in your pockets, your clothing, or on you.*

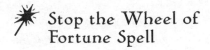 Stop the Wheel of Fortune Spell

Evil omens, scary dreams, inauspicious signs, or any other portents of misfortune don't necessarily mean that bad luck is inevitable. Take enchanted steps to stop the Wheel of Fortune turning in the wrong direction. The ancient Mesopotamians possessed complex rituals to prevent evil portents from translating into actual reality. Five thousand years later, the basic steps, if not the exact ritual, may be reproduced.

Typically, these rituals involved five components. Someone else performs the cleansing for the targeted person. Five thousand years ago, it would have been a specialist priestess, priest, or shaman. Today, several people can get involved: there is enough activity to keep a number of people busy.

Lucky Devil Spell

Devils aren't always threatening. Sometimes they're "lucky devils." Use a devil-shaped figure candle to help turn your luck around.

*Dress a red devil candle with **Flying Devil Oil**. Place it in front of a white cross candle (to represent the heavy cross you bear) and burn it. To turn round really bad luck, dress the white cross with **Uncrossing Oil** and repeat the spell for seven consecutive days.*

Out With Bad Luck, In With the Best Luck Spell

Burn that candle at both ends! Eliminate misfortune and, because nature abhors a vacuum, simultaneously attract something positive to replace it.

1. Obtain one red and black double-action candle. It may be necessary to trim the bottom of the candle, exposing the wick, so that both ends may be burned simultaneously.
2. Carve what you wish to eliminate from your life on the black end.
3. Carve what you'd like to see manifest in your life on the red end.
4. Ideally, place the candle horizontally on a candlestick with a spike. Otherwise drive a long nail or pin through the border dividing the colors. Place the candle horizontally over an open bottle, inserting the pin to provide balance and stability.
5. Burn at both ends simultaneously.

1. Create an enclosure. (The Mesopotamians would have cast a magic circle with flour.)
2. Perform purification rites within the enclosure. The person(s) perceived as the endangered target of these ill omens is bathed, then shaved or waxed and bathed again. Tamarisk branches were used in the cleansing process, although whether this was for asperging or something similar to the *barrida* ritual "sweeping" with branches or another method is unclear. (Tamarisk is still used in Middle Eastern anti-Evil Eye rituals.) Cleanse the person with incense. Sweep the area clean. Light magic lamps or candles. Ring a bell (Mesopotamians favored copper) and beat a drum.
3. Offer food and aromatics to the spirits and the deified river or the deity in the river, because this is how the spell remnants will be carried away.
4. Destroy any emblems of evil, if there are any. (This spell could also be used to remove an object-driven jinx.)
5. Close the ritual: Traditionally, the person was spun around and told to leave, not looking back or around. Just face forward and find a tavern. (The ancient Mesopotamians found spiritual significance in bars and their priestess/barmaids. Full details are

not understood, as of yet, although there is a connection with devotion to Inanna-Ishtar.)

A magical prescription may also be given: the person should wear protective amulets for at least the following seven days.

Uncross Me!

When your cross grows too heavy to bear, dress a white cross candle with essential oil of hyssop diluted in olive oil. Pray, petition, and recite psalms to remove this cross of misfortune.

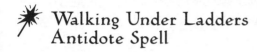

Walking Under Ladders Antidote Spell

Among the most common superstitions is the fear of walking beneath a ladder, and many will go well out of their way to avoid doing so. Should you find yourself forced to walk beneath a ladder there is antidote to avoid bad luck. This spell must be cast when you walk under the ladder.

1. Cross your fingers as you approach the ladder. (If this isn't possible, a knot may be made instead.)
2. Keep your fingers crossed until a dog is observed. Once you sight that dog, you're home free. Uncross your fingers; untie your knot.

Wishing Spells

Sometimes it's not general good fortune that's required; you need one special wish fulfilled. *Luck and Success Spells* attempt to magically generate general good fortune. *Wishing Spells* tend to have one specific desire in mind. Now anyone can wish: all you have to do is think or articulate it. However, special magic spells and techniques enhance the chances of success, helping transform hopeful wishes into concrete reality.

Acacia Dream Manifest Spell

Burn acacia wood and speak your wish or goal aloud. Allegedly this combination of actions helps manifest dreams into reality.

Apple of Desire

With a thorn or pin, scratch your wish into the skin of a beautiful apple. Hold the apple in both hands and contemplate your desire. Dip the apple in cinnamon honey and eat it completely, savoring each bite.

Asphodel Magic Wand Wishing Spell

Asphodel's name derives from the Greek word for scepter; consider it a botanical magic wand. Place asphodel beside whatever you wish to manifest into your life.

Write out a statement of desire or intent, display an image or somehow create a representation of your desire. Place asphodel beside it and articulate your wish.

Bay Leaf Wish Spell (1)

Bay leaves assist petitions, messages, and wishes to reach the spirit realm quickly and clearly. Write your wishes on bay leaves and then burn them.

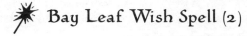 Bay Leaf Wish Spell (2)

Lay dried bay leaves flat over your mattress and cover them with a fresh, white sheet. This draws luck as well as promoting sound sleep.

Blackthorn Wishing Wand

Craft a wand from blackthorn wood and use it to cast wishing spells.

Dandelion Wishing Spell (1)

Make a wish while holding a dried dandelion. Hold that thought in your mind, and then blow all the seeds off the dandelion with one breath. If this can be accomplished, your wish should be fulfilled.

Dandelion Wishing Spell (2)

An easier although more time-consuming method of wishing upon a dandelion involves crafting infused oil of dandelion flowers. (See Elements of Magic Spells *for instructions; the process may take up to six weeks.) Rub the oil onto the hands or body while making your wish.*

Dittany of Crete Wish Manifestation Spell

Make a wish while inhaling the fragrance of Dittany of Crete. Allegedly this encourages your dreams to manifest into reality.

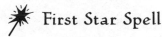 First Star Spell

Starlight, star bright
First star I see tonight
I wish I may, I wish I might
Have this wish I wish tonight

That rhyme has been relegated to the nursery yet it recalls a potent Wishing Spell.

1. Pay attention at twilight; it's easy to miss your opportunity.
2. If you can catch sight of the very first solo star in the sky, gaze at it and make your wish. (The rhyme charm may be incorporated but it's not necessary.)
3. If the first star can't be identified, luck isn't with you: save the spell for another night.

The Four-leaf Clover

According to legend, if you find a four-leaf clover and wish upon it, your wish will come true. Well, nothing is guaranteed, not even if it's legendary. A special magical technique exists to maximize a four-leaf clover's wish fulfilling potential.

When you wish upon the clover, count each leaf. Each offers a unique form of good fortune. Visualize how you'd benefit from their promise:

★ *The first leaf to the left of the stem is fame*
★ *The second leaf to the left of the stem is money*
★ *The third leaf to the left of the stem is love*
★ *The fourth leaf to the left of the stem is good health*

Perhaps the first step should be to find a four-leaf clover! However, a metal charm may be used, and may be preferable: its leaves won't fall off while you're counting!

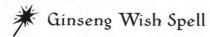 ## Ginseng Wish Spell

Would fulfillment of your most desired wish be a wonder of the world? Ginseng's Hoodoo nickname is "Wonder of the World Root." Reserve this spell for hard-to-fulfill wishes and see if ginseng lives up to its sobriquet.

Carve your wish onto a ginseng root. Hold it in your hand to charge it with your desire and then toss it into living waters.

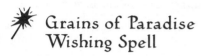 ## Grains of Paradise Wishing Spell

1. Hold Grains of Paradise in your hand.
2. Close your eyes and make a wish.
3. Twirling sunwise, let the grains slip through your fingers until you reach full circle.

Halloween Wish Spell

At midnight on Halloween stand naked before a mirror in a room lit only by a single candle. Silently make your secret wish. Don't speak until morning.

Hazel Spell (1) Garland

Make a wreath or garland from hazel leaves, binding your desire into the knots. Wear it while making your wish to enhance its chances of success.

Hazel Spell (2) Wishing Cap

You've heard of thinking caps? Well, the Welsh used to have a "wishing-cap," a piece of ritual clothing, a hat woven from fallen hazel twigs.

Gather twigs of hazel and weave them into a cap. Wear it when making your wishes to intensify your opportunity of success.

Jezebel Root Spell

Jezebel root serves as a magical conduit, transforming desire into reality. Usually associated with malevolent spells, Jezebel root is also a potent wish conductor.

1. Hold a Jezebel root in your left hand.
2. Close your eyes and focus on your wish. Remain like this, maintaining complete concentration, for as long as possible.
3. When you have finished, bury the root in Earth.

 ## Job's Tears Spell

To have your prayers answered and your wishes fulfilled, pierce and string Job's tears. Wear them around your neck as a necklace.

Job's Tear Wishing Spell

Make a wish on a Job's tear. Wrap it up in fresh basil, peppermint, and spearmint leaves and place in a conjure bag or magic box. By the time the leaves lose their aroma, your wish should have come true.

Joss Paper Wishing Spell

Chinese magical paper has been manufactured and used for hundreds of years. Spirit Money, also known as Bank of Hell cash notes, used to feed, honor, and pacify the dead, are the most famous example. However, magic paper has many uses, fulfilling wishes not the least among them.

1. Literally countless varieties of magic paper are produced, however square sheets featuring gold foil at the center are extremely beneficial for wishing and are not difficult to find amongst stores catering to traditional East Asian clientele.
2. Write your wish upon the paper and then burn it. If the flame goes out, light the paper again. Make sure that every last letter is reduced to smoke and ash so that your wish enters the atmosphere where it may be fulfilled.
3. For extra power, anoint the paper with essential oil of sandalwood or burn together with sandalwood incense.
4. Bring the paper ashes outside and scatter them to the winds.

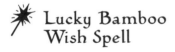 ## Lucky Bamboo Wish Spell

Carve your wish into a piece of bamboo and bury it in a safe place.

 ## Lucky Cat Candle Spell

Lucky cat candles help fulfill your wishes. Color coordinate to suit the nature of the wish: use green for money, red for love, and black to resolve problems.

1. Carve and dress the candle as you will.
2. Write your wish succinctly and explicitly on a piece of paper.

3. Burn the paper; use this paper to light the candle, rather than a match.
4. Murmur wishes, incantations, and sacred verses, at least until the paper has completely burned to ash.

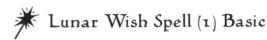 ### Lunar Wish Spells

Wishing upon the moon is easier than wishing upon a star; however, as with stellar wish spells, timing is everything. The moon is the heavenly body most associated with granting wishes.

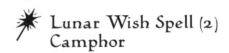 ## Lunar Wish Spell (1) Basic

When you catch sight of a particularly beautiful, evocative moon, stop and gaze at it. Concentrate on your desire, look at the moon and make one explicit well-articulated and defined wish.

Lunar Wish Spell (2) Camphor

Camphor is under the dominion of the moon. Lady's Chang'o's lunar palace is allegedly crafted from cinnamon wood, however both true cinnamon and camphor derive from trees of the Cinnamonium *family. Maybe the Moon Lady's palace was built from camphor wood. Because of its connection, camphor can transmit some of the moon's protective and luck drawing powers. (Be careful: camphor can also be toxic.)*

1. Dissolve a camphor square into lunar-charged spring water.
2. Use this water to cleanse appropriate magical tools so that they may be used to fulfill your wishes.

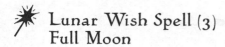

Lunar Wish Spell (3)
Full Moon

1. Stand naked in the light of the Full Moon.
2. Go through the motions of bathing in the moonbeams.
3. Gaze at the moon while doing this: when ready, make whatever petition you please.
4. Watch for an immediate response: if the Moon remains clear, it's a positive sign. If the Moon brightens and the light intensifies, this is an extra auspicious sign. If a cloud passes across the moon, you can anticipate some difficulty in achieving your desire. Take some further magical steps or perhaps reassess your desire. Work on it until the next Full Moon and repeat.

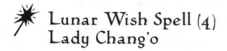

Lunar Wish Spell (4)
Lady Chang'o

Once a year, to celebrate her birthday, Lady Chang'o, the Moon Lady grants secret wishes. The moon is believed to be at its shiniest and most beautiful on the Moon Lady's birthday, the fifteenth night of the eighth month of the Chinese calendar. Beautiful Lady Chang'o lives alone on the moon in a palace of fragrant cinnamon (or possibly camphor) wood, her sole companion, an alchemist rabbit that grinds out the elixir of immortality with a mortar and pestle.

1. Gaze up at the moon.
2. Concentrate on your most secret desire.
3. Tell Lady Chang'o what you need.

Lunar Wish Spell (5) Lady Chang'o's Oracle

Lady Chang'o also provides an oracle on the eve of her birthday:

1. Privately, discreetly light three sticks of incense in her honor.
2. Whisper your question.
3. Wait in hiding, where others won't see you. The first words you hear spoken are the answer to your question.

Lunar Wish Spell (6)
New Moon

The following is a Romany ritual to greet the New Moon.

Greet each new moon by chanting something like this:

Here is the New Moon.
The New Moon has arrived.
Be lucky for me now
You've found me penniless
Leave me rich and prosperous.
Leave us with money.
Leave us with good health
Leave us with love.

Magic Papaya Wish Spell

Hold a strip of red cloth in your hands while considering your wish. Tie it around a branch of a papaya tree; explicitly articulate the wish as you tie the knot. Then visualize your wish fulfilled.

Mojo Wish Bean

Italian immigrants brought fava beans to New Orleans, where they became known as lucky Saint Joseph's beans and mojo wish beans. Make a wish on a mojo wish bean, and carry it for seven days near your heart to make your wish come true.

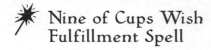 ## Nine of Cups Wish Fulfillment Spell

The nine of cups tarot card is traditionally considered "the wish card," a happy card that indicates your wishes will come true.

1. Remove the nine of cups card from a Rider-Waite tarot deck or another deck that illustrates the Minor Arcana. (Some decks only illustrate the Major Arcana.)
2. Place the card upright between a gold and a silver candle.
3. Light the candles; gaze at the card and clearly, distinctly, articulate what it is you truly want.
4. When the candles burn down, place the card under your pillow. Further information may be revealed in your dreams.

 ## Nutmeg Wish Spell

1. Carve and dress a small candle to reflect your wish and burn it.
2. Write out the wish concisely and explicitly on a tiny slip of paper.
3. Hollow out a nutmeg. (Not an easy thing to do, incidentally. Be careful not to injure yourself.)
4. Slip the paper inside the nutmeg and seal it within, using a bit of melted candle wax.
5. Bury this wish in Earth so that it will grow to fruition.

 ## Ocean Spirit Wish Spell

Address your request to Aphrodite, Poseidon, Yemaya, or any other ocean spirit you choose, but address it specifically to someone. Don't send out a generic request. Write your request or query on rice paper or some other biodegradable paper. Launch it into the waves and await your response.

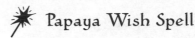 ## Papaya Wish Spell

1. Make a fire in your cauldron, hearth, or fireplace.
2. Hold thirteen papaya seeds in your left hand and charge them with your desire.
3. Whisper a wish over each seed individually and toss it into the fire. If it pops, your wish will come true. If it doesn't pop but burns silently, your wish may still come true but not without effort.

 ## Red Tara Spell

Kurukulla, the Red Tara, is the Tibetan spirit of love and wealth.

1. Recite her mantra one hundred thousand times to receive success in any undertaking (Kurukulla is particularly renowned for delivering cash, power, and lovers):
   Kurukullayah om kurukellehrih
   Mama sarvjanam vashamanaya hrim svaha
2. Meditate upon her image to enhance success. Kurukulla appears as a scarlet naked woman, blissfully happy, with disheveled hair.
3. Offer her red flowers, especially hibiscus.

Kurukulla's ritual was traditionally accompanied by a ritual possession. Do not attempt this on your own. Without proper training and ritual supervision, this is extremely dangerous.

 ## Sage Wishing Spell

1. Write your wish on a single sage leaf.
2. Place it beneath your pillow for three consecutive nights.
3. Should this sage leaf appear in your dreams at any time during these three nights, your wish should be fulfilled.

4. If not, what you're requesting is complex and difficult. Bury the sage leaf in Earth, requesting that, if your wish is beneficial, it will grow to fruition. If realizing your dream would be harmful, request that the energy and desire dissipate safely into Earth.

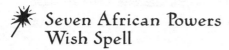

Seven African Powers Wish Spell

Among them, the Seven African Powers have mastery over all areas of life pertaining to human beings. They are like a celestial board of directors that can handle any problem, fix any dilemma and fulfill every wish.

*Carve your wishes on each knob of a seven-knob candle. (The same wish may be repeated seven times, if desired.) Dress with **Seven African Powers Oil** and burn.*

Seven African Powers Wish Extra-Strength Oil

***Seven African Powers Oil** incorporates the power of the seven orishas for which it's named. The oil is created from botanicals that radiate the orishas' power and thus fulfills their blessings. However, when candle burning is accompanied by direct spiritual petition and communication, magic power is exponentially increased.*

1. Carve the name of one orisha on each of a seven-knob candle's knobs. (See *Elements of Magic Spells* for further explanation and list of names.) Place Elegba on top and Ogun's name on the second knob.
2. Carve your wishes on each knob too, if desired. (If you're familiar with the orisha, each wish may be coordinated with the specific power.)
3. Dress the candle with **Seven African Powers Oil.**
4. As traditional, burn one knob each night, for seven consecutive nights. Address the orisha on that knob and articulate your wish aloud.

Seven-knob Wishing Spell

Seven-knob candles are often known as "wishing candles."

1. Make a wish. (You may also make a different wish for each of the seven knobs.)
2. Scratch a wish into each knob.
3. Personalize, dress, and burn the candle, one knob at a time.

Seven of Cups Spell

If you really could have whatever you wished for, what would it be?

Contemplate the seven of cups tarot card. Place it under your pillow at night, then in the morning make your wish. Allegedly it will come true, so choose wisely.

Star Anise Wishing Spell

Choose a candle to represent your wish. Carve and dress it to suit your personal situation. Arrange four star anise seeds around the candle in each of the four cardinal points. Fill in the rest of the magic circle with clove buds and burn the candle.

Sunflower Wishing Spell

Sunflower seeds that dry and remain on the flower head allegedly possess the magical capacity to grant wishes. Hold an individual seed in your left hand and make your wish. Eat the seed or plant it in Earth.

Uninterrupted Happiness Wish Spell

Nine coins strung onto red cord represents "uninterrupted happiness," according to Chinese symbolism. These coins on the cord will also help you turn wishes into reality.

1. Make nine wishes; one wish may also be repeated nine times for extra emphasis and power.
2. Collect nine I-Ching (replica) coins.
3. String each one while concentrating on a wish. Affirm that each wish is received as you tie each knot.
4. When the cord is complete, keep it in a safe, secret place.

 ## Walnut Wish Fulfillment

Sometimes you'd like to see someone else's dreams and wishes come true.

Bless thirteen walnuts, holding each in the palm of your hand and charging it with love and magic power. Place these walnuts in a bag, tied with gold ribbon, and give them as a gift. Each walnut represents a wish to be made by the recipient during a New Moon.

 ## Wish Fulfillment Bath

Add balm of Gilead to your bath. Visualize your dreams and wishes come true.

Wish Upon a Star Charm

1. Place a star anise atop a tonka bean and gently wrap together with red thread.
2. Hold the charm in your left hand and make a wish.
3. Wrap in a little piece of silk and carry in a charm bag until your wish is fulfilled.

 ## Wishing Bag

1. Write out your wish explicitly.
2. Place it in a red drawstring bag together with a piece of shed snakeskin, a Rattlesnake root, Low John the Conqueror, and five Job's tears.
3. Dress it with **Lucky Lodestone, Van Van,** and/or **Magnet Oil.**

 ## Wishing Cross Spell

The origins of the Cross of Caravaca are shrouded in mystery. Was it brought to Spain by Crusaders? Was it redeemed from Spanish Moors, or did it emerge spontaneously and miraculously in the town of Caravaca? Caravaca was the site of some of the most ancient Iberian settlements; it was also a long-time stronghold for the Knights Templar. The Cross of Caravaca is a double-armed cross depicting the crucified Jesus Christ flanked by kneeling angels. Legends of the cross stem from the thirteenth century. The original Cross of Caravaca allegedly contains a fragment of the True Cross. Replica Cross of Caravaca allegedly help your dreams come true. Non-Spanish speaking magical communities have adopted this cross and call it simply the Wishing Cross.

Hold the Cross of Caravaca in your right hand and make a wish. Alternatively, wear it for good fortune.

 ## Wishing Fan

1. Fold paper accordion style into a fan shape.
2. Write a wish on each fold of the fan. Repeat the same wish or choose a different one for each.
3. Close your eyes, concentrate on your desires and set the fan on fire. If it burns, this is a positive sign. If the flame goes out, whatever is still legible on the paper will need further work to accomplish.

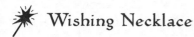 ## Wishing Necklace

1. Gather Job's tears and tonka beans.
2. Alternating between them, string them onto a necklace.
3. Hold each one in your hand and make a wish (the same wish may be reiterated) before piercing and stringing.
4. Wear the necklace or carry it in a charm bag.

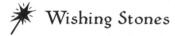 ## Wishing Stones

Make a wish upon a … stone? Certain stones are believed to have the power to help you achieve your wishes. Preserved in charm bags, they may be taken out as needed, to enhance all wishes and increase the odds of success. Those reputedly most powerful include amber and holed stones. (Yes, amber is really fossilized tree resin, however because its ancient origins were mysterious, people classified it as a mineral and that ancient classification more or less remains, at least magically speaking.)

Hold the stone in your left hand while concentrating upon your wish and visualizing its success. Rub it with your thumb in a clockwise motion. Keep the stone in your pocket and rub it with your thumb as desired to reinforce this wish.

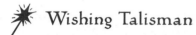 ## Wishing Talisman

The ancient Sanskrit magical text the Atharva Veda recommends cutting a talisman from sraktya wood. Choose a more accessible wood if necessary; consider what suits your purpose. Look at woods used for magic wands for recommendations (see page 98).

Cut the wood to resemble the object of your desire. Possibilities include: protection, fertility, virility, prosperity, defense against malicious magic, or victory in conflict or battle. When the charm has been created, charged, and/or consecrated, tie it to your right arm and wear it until your goal is achieved.

 ## Written Wish Spell (1)

This modern spell derives from ancient Egyptian written spells. Stone tablets were engraved with sacred, powerful images and incantations. Water was poured over the tablets so that it ran over the engraved images and verses, absorbing their power. This water would then be consumed.

Adaptations of this type of spell appear both in British folk magic and in American Hoodoo and Conjure. British magic retains the aspect of drinking the potion, while Hoodoo uses the technique to enhance condition oils.

1. A fine china plate, preferably white, and non-toxic water-soluble ink are needed, as well as the ability to write with a fountain pen.
2. Write your desire or petition on the plate.
3. Hold it in your hands, contemplate it, make sure the wording has expressed your goals and desires accurately. If not, wash it off, dry the plate and start all over again.
4. Meanwhile boil water. Use plain spring water or a hydrosol or a blend of both.
5. Stand the plate inside a large dish or pot to catch the water.
6. Pour the water over the plate: the ink should dissolve into the water. When it cools, drink it.

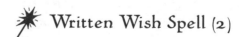 ## Written Wish Spell (2)

Dip your finger into honey and write your spell, wish, or desire on the inside of a cup. Add spring water, allow time for the honey to dissolve (some may cling to the cup, it's okay) and drink.

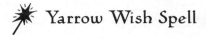 Yarrow Wish Spell

The very first blooming yarrow that you see is a magical plant that can grant you one wish. Hold the bloom in your hand and make your wish. That night, sleep with the plant below your pillow.

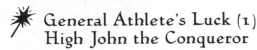 Yemaya's Wish Spell

Make a request of Yemaya, Queen of the Sea.

1. Create a little wooden boat and fill it with treasures for Yemaya.
2. These boats are traditionally filled with perfume in glass bottles, fine soap (removed from its wrapper), a comb, and a mirror fit for a mermaid queen. Add white and blue flowers, crystals, and shells.
3. Murmur your desires and wishes over the boat.
4. Launch the boat into the waves after dark.

If the boat is swallowed by a wave and disappears from sight, this is very auspicious, a sign that Yemaya has accepted your offering and will consider your petition. If the boat returns to shore, the request has been denied. Reconsider the situation. It's possible that you're not in Yemaya's favor but it's also possible that she perceives that your petition isn't beneficial for you. If most of the offering disappears but one or two items are washed to shore, this is alright; those items may not have interested Yemaya, or perhaps they contain a coded message for you.

Specialized Luck Spells

Some practices and professions require special types of enchantment. Gamblers, for example, have an entire section of spells all their own (see page 462).

Athletes' Luck Spells

 General Athlete's Luck (1) High John the Conqueror

*Rub your feet and hands with **High John the Conqueror Oil** before significant events.*

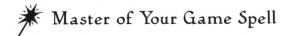 General Athlete's Luck (2) Sacred Text

Recite Psalm 23 before matches and games.

 Master of Your Game Spell

Woodruff, also known as Master of the Woods, allegedly confers victory on athletes. Carry it for good luck.

⁂ Boxer's and Wrestler's Luck

Sprinkle salt in the prize ring, either in the corners or in the area associated with victory.

⁂ Wrestler's Luck

Hanuman, the Hindu monkey spirit, is patron of wrestlers. Petition him for success. Light a butter lamp in Hanuman's honor. Make a cotton wick and add it to a dish of ghee or clarified butter. Burn it while petitioning for luck and success.

Fishing and Hunting Success Spells

⁂ Ajos Sancha Spell

Bathe in an infusion made with the herb ajos sancha *before fishing. Ajos sancha, a vine known as false*

garlic, brings luck to fishers and hunters and also allegedly removes bad luck. On a practical level, its strong garlicky aroma may also mask the human scent.

 ## Aloe Vera Juice

Coat the body with aloe vera juice for luck before going fishing or hunting.

 ## Anise Spell

Anise oil also allegedly provides fishing and hunting luck. Create an infused oil of anise or dilute the essential oil in jojoba oil. Bathe in it or massage it into the skin prior to your hunting trip.

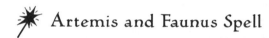 ## Artemis and Faunus Spell

Hunting deities like Artemis and Faunus maintain the balance between the opposing needs of animals and people. Petition them for safety and assistance.

Easier said than done? Once upon a time you could have gone to their shrines and received an oracle that let you know where your personal hunting boundaries stood. This can still be accomplished in your dreams.

1. Request a dream oracle from either Artemis or Faunus.
2. Dream up a hunting license. Have them set your limits.
3. Don't hunt until the dream is received and recorded.

Faunus most frequently communicates through what humans understand as nightmares. He can't talk so his instructions aren't verbal; however the visuals are usually very clear. Artemis is far more articulate, although perhaps of sterner character.

 ## Blindfold Spell

Hunting was once accompanied by elaborate, extensive magical, metaphysical protection and luck spells. Without spiritual permission and magical protection, hunting didn't occur. In many metaphysical traditions, it's believed inauspicious for predators, like people, to kill other predators. This must be avoided at all costs. Should another predator be killed, whether feline, canine, bear, raptor or other, the hunter with his or her eyes closed, must creep up behind the dead animal and try to blindfold it as quickly as possible. This may avert psychic punishment.

 ## Boat With Eyes

The tradition of painting a pair of eyes on boats has existed for millennia and still remains strong. It serves various purposes:

★ The eyes rebuff the Evil Eye
★ They represent the protection of deities like Horus, Hathor, and primordial, all-seeing "Eye Goddesses"
★ The eyes activate the boat so that it can "see" where it's going and "see" the fish
★ They invoke the power of Saint Lucy who, in addition to her Evil-Eye fighting capacity, has a reputation of finding fish for the fishermen

Cinquefoil Spell

Cinquefoil, also known as five-finger grass, has an affinity for fishers and is believed to bring them luck and success. Find a perfect specimen, one that distinctly possesses five fingers. (Despite its name, the number of fingers on a cinquefoil "hand" varies.) When you find it, murmur your desires over it, preserve it, and carry it with you as needed.

Desert Rue Hunting Charm

Carry desert rue, also known as parosela, to enhance hunter's luck.

 ## Easter Sunday Spell

A Russian hunter's ritual requires daring outside the wilderness.

In Church, on Easter Sunday, when the words "Christ is risen" are pronounced, immediately shout out your desire: "My bullet hits the mark" or whatever. Name your desire, if you dare, and allegedly it will be yours for a year.

 ## Fishing Mojo

Sew hawthorn leaves into a mojo hand and carry it for good luck.

 ## Fishing Net Repair Spell

To achieve maximum success, it was once believed that fishing nets should only be woven or repaired by pregnant women at midnight.

 ## Hunter's Crossroads Spell

This spell from Finland is simple and presumably very effective if offered wholeheartedly: go to a crossroads and address the spirits. Request blessings and good luck.

 ## Mama Dlo's Forest Spell

Mama Dlo's name is a corruption of "Maman de L'eau," as is the mermaid Mama Jo's. Are they aspects of the same spirit or do two independent entities share one name? Half-woman, half-anaconda, does the Trinidadian spirit Mama Dlo derive from Africa, like that other beautiful water-snake spirit Maitresse Ezili, or is she an Amazonian guardian spirit? Mama Dlo punishes those who hunt indiscriminately, pollute land and water, and damage trees and other botanicals.

Should you encounter her, and should she be annoyed with you, allegedly the only way to escape her wrath is to take off your left shoe, never taking your eyes off her, and hop out of the woods backwards. This show of humiliation and idiocy apparently amuses her enough to buy your safety. The spell however will only work once; don't come back.

 ## Mistletoe Luck Spell

Carry mistletoe for hunters' luck and protection.

Scholar's Success and Luck Spells

Success is often dependent on education. Although time and effort play a large part in educational success, luck plays its part, too. Magic spells exist to ensure and enhance this educational luck and success.

 ## The Carp Transforms into a Dragon Spell

According to Chinese legend, certain magical carp swim upstream, fording all sorts of obstacles to finally be rewarded by transformation into dragons. The folk motif "carp transforms into a dragon" has become a symbol of perseverance and success in various fields, including scholastic.

Tap into that power and perseverance by posting carp transforms into dragon images or, for maximum power, stock a koi pond with golden carp. This pond may be used to magically affect your own success

or that of your children. Build the pond outside; for best effect, consult a feng shui practitioner for the most favorable location.

 ## Children's Learning Spell

Wash those lessons into them! Bathe children in infusions of lemon verbena so that they will learn faster.

 ## Children's Lilac Spells

To enhance children's educational aptitude:

★ *Place a drop of lilac fragrance oil on a light bulb near where the child studies*
★ *Place a vase of fresh lilac blossoms on the child's desk, so that the fragrance wafts over the child while studying*
★ *Place a table and chair outside next to a lilac bush in bloom and send the child outside to study*

 ## Crown of Success Spell (1) Basic

Crown of Success Oil brings academic success. Place a drop on a child's or student's pillow to enhance comprehension and the retention of learning during sleep.

 ## Crown of Success Spell (2) Candle

1. Carve a candle with your name and identifying information.
2. Dress it with **Crown of Success Oil** and roll it in gold glitter, or whatever color represents success to you.
3. Burn the candle beside you while studying.

 ## Crown of Success Spell (3) Desperation

1. In moments of desperation, carve the name of the study topic across the forehead of a white skull candle.
2. Add identifying information about the student.
3. Dress the candle with **Crown of Success Oil** and pray that the material penetrates the student's skull and mind.

 ## Magic Mirror Question and Answer Session

Having trouble with your exams? Could use some extra assistance? Summon those who really know the answers. Use a magic mirror to conjure up spirits or historic personages to answer your examination (and other!) questions.

Rosemary enhances mental ability and memory retention. These spells could be combined with **Crown of Success Oil** spells.

 ## Rosemary Spell (1) Incense

Grind and powder dried rosemary. Burn it on lit charcoals while studying for exams for luck and retention of the material.

 ## Rosemary Spell (2) Sleep

Do you remember the old technique of placing a book beneath your pillow to assist learning and retention? This spell is reminiscent of that.

1. Weave a garland from fresh rosemary before bedtime, tying your goals into each knot.
2. Wear the garland around your brow or place it on the pillow while you sleep.

Spiritual Sponsor Spell (1) Oya

Oya, spirit of the Niger River, is the orisha of learning. Her mind grasps difficult concepts as swiftly as the wind. Ask for her assistance in doing the same:

1. Erect an altar to Oya on or beside a bookshelf.
2. Offer her a glass of red wine and nine purple plums and tell her what you need.

 Spiritual Sponsor Spell (2) Saints Cosmas and Damian

Saint Cosmas and Saint Damian are the patron saints of learning and education. Twins, these saints may actually be those other twins, Castor and Pollux, in disguise. This makes sense because Castor and Pollux, brothers of Helen of Troy and Clytemnestra, are the models for the twins depicted in the constellation Gemini, and Gemini rules mental agility. Cosmas and Damian

have also since been identified with the twins of West African mythology, the Marassa and the Ibeji.

Create an altar to the helpful spirit of these twins however you understand them. Use a chromolithograph, an image of the constellation, or African twin statues as a focal point. Give them lots of candy and small toys. If there are books you need to master, place them on the altar overnight so the twins can help you learn.

 Spiritual Sponsor Spell (3) Sarasvati

Sarasvati, originally a Hindu river goddess, is now the pre-eminent matron of literature and wisdom. Sarasvati sponsors learning and the creative sciences. A generous, bountiful spirit, she assists students with their tests and examinations.

Petition her with offerings of fruit, flowers, and incense. Spontaneous intellectual or creative inspiration is Sarasvati's gift and response.

Marriage and Divorce Spells

Because marriage, handfasting, or any ritualized union is one of the major thresholds of life, it's perceived as a time of tremendous power, promise, *and* vulnerability. The entire marriage ceremony, the arrangements preceding it, and post-nuptial celebrations may be perceived as a huge series of magic spells as much as a religious sacrament. In some cases, it's consciously both.

Activate an Engagement Ring

In regards to promoting and preserving love and long-term relationships, the emerald is by far the best choice for an engagement ring. However the following ritual transforms any ring into an enchanted ring of love.

1. First obtain the ring.
2. Tie it to a red silk thread and suspend it into the smoke made from burning frankincense and myrrh, patchouli and vetiver.
3. Wrap it securely in silk cloth. (You may remove the thread.)
4. Wear this packet for nine days and nights against your skin, preferably next to your heart or under your left armpit.

5. Pass it through the incense again.
6. Make a braid from three of your hairs and three of your beloved's.
7. Wrap this around the ring.
8. Wrap the ring with the braid in silk again.
9. Wear it for an additional six days against your heart or in your armpit.
10. On the seventh day, remove the lover's braid and present the ring to your beloved.

Banyan Blessings

Banyan trees are considered ancient, benevolent, powerful reservoirs of blessing and protection. Get married under a banyan tree to receive marital blessings. (One more reason to get married in Hawaii …)

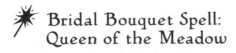

Bride's Anti-Evil Eye Spell

One of the psychic dangers inherent on the Wedding Day is that so much celebration and happiness will inevitably attract the envious eyes of jealous spirits, or the Evil Eye. Among those perceived as vulnerable to the Evil Eye, brides rank highest, right alongside infants and pregnant women. Although many protection spells exist, this one specifically targets the Evil Eye.

The bride holds a coin under her left armpit during the marriage ceremony. Upon leaving the ceremony, the coin is secretly and discreetly allowed to fall to the ground, either as a payment to spirits who will protect from the Evil Eye or as a bribe to the spirits. Whoever discovers and picks up this coin unknowingly obtains a year's good fortune.

Bridal Bouquet Spell: Ariadne and Dionysus

Greek mythology typically depicts marriage as a sorry affair. No wonder spirits like Artemis and Athena vowed never to marry. The only Olympian spirits who are genuinely happily wed soul mates are Dionysus and Ariadne.

May Day commemorates their wedding anniversary. Carry a bouquet of holly and ivy, their sacred plants, to invoke their blessings of happiness and compatibility.

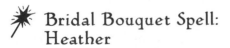

Bridal Bouquet Spell: Heather

Incorporate white heather into the bridal bouquet for luck and protection.

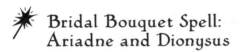

Bridal Bouquet Spell: Queen of the Meadow

Queen of the Meadow's other nickname, bridewort, indicates its affinity with brides. Carry some within the bridal bouquet to obtain all the happiest marriage blessings.

Bridal Bouquet Spell: Yarrow

Incorporate yarrow into the bridal bouquet for seven years of happiness.

Bridal Preparation Spell

You've bought the dress, chosen the veil, gone shopping for new make-up. What else is there? Various magical methods serve to prepare the bride for marriage. In general they serve two purposes, frequently simultaneously: erotic enhancement and protection.

In traditional Javanese rituals, the bride is effectively marinated in flowers and warm scented oils, including frangipani, jasmine, and roses. Depending upon how wealthy the bride (or her family) is, these combined cleansing treatments, protective formulas, and love baths may linger for days.

Bridal Preparation Kikubo

An East Indian tradition popularized in Africa:

1. A wide variety of fragrant botanicals are used. Collect some or all of the following: henna blossoms and/or seeds, jasmine blossoms, kilua flowers, mkadi flowers, rose petals, pachori leaves, pompia leaves, and rehani leaves.
2. Dry, powder, and blend all the ingredients.
3. Mix the powder with rose water and either olive or ben oil.
4. Use the resulting oil to anoint the bride for beauty and protection.
5. The spell may now conclude; however, to intensify the fragrance and power, once the initial blended powder has been created, add fresh jasmine blossoms. Give the blossoms time to dry out then grind them together with the powder. Blend with rose water and oil to create a sensual, protective balm for the bride.

Bridal Protection Spells

Because the bride is perceived as so psychically vulnerable, hidden amulets and charms serve as magical bodyguards during the ceremony. Because the distinctive bridal gown so clearly identifies the bride, exposing her vulnerability, so the gown becomes the most common tool of protection. Special spells and charms simultaneously protect the bride while promoting romance and devotion.

Bridal Protection Spell (1) Botanicals

Sew herbs into the hem and/or belt of the wedding gown to bring love and romance to the marriage. Favorable herbs include clover, elecampane, lavender, and powdered mistletoe.

Bridal Protection Spell (2) Conjure Bag

Fill a red silk bag with some or all of the bridal amulets below:

- Cowrie shells
- Small horseshoes
- Clove of garlic in a red charm bag
- Red ribbon
- Silver charms

Sew this bag inside the skirt of the bridal gown.

Bridal Protection Spell (3) Garter

The bridal garter was originally a protective garment, intended to safeguard the bride from spiritual danger. For maximum magical protection, instead of the typical blue garter, wear a red one with a piece of silver attached. Remember to charge it with your desire.

Bridal Protection Spell (4) Mother Goose

Mother Goose rides through the air on a very fine gander. Today, Mother Goose is limited to the nursery, her rhymes intended to entertain only the youngest, least sophisticated children, yet Mother Goose's namesake bird links her to a host of powerful spirits: Aphrodite, too, rides through the air on a goose. The bird is sacred to Egyptian Hathor and Roman Juno, both valiant protectors and advocates for women.

In the Middle Ages, the once sacred goose became associated with witchcraft and disreputable women. Attempts to discredit Lilith and the Queen of Sheba depict them as dangerously beautiful, seductive women, with one goose's foot peeping from beneath a skirt.

Mother Goose's famous marital recommendation echoes an old witch charm:

Something old, something new
Something borrowed, something blue
And a sixpence in her shoe!

Follow Mother Goose's directions in order to provide the bride with spiritual protection and promote romance in the marriage.

Bridal Protection Spell (5) Needle in Shoe

Wrap a needle and a little salt in a piece of red silk. Place this in the bride's right shoe to promote her magical well being.

Bridal Protection Spell (6)
Needle in Gown

A Russian spell recommends that you break the eyes off new needles and stick them into the underside of the bridal gown.

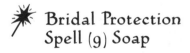 ## Bridal Protection Spell (7)
Peach Blossom Girl

The Peach Blossom Girl, T'ao Hua Hsien Nii, is a Chinese flower fairy and protector of brides. Typically depicted brandishing her sword by its scabbard, she bears four flags displaying the character for "happiness." Mothers give their daughters her image when they get married, charged with love and blessings, to accompany them into married life as magical protection.

Bridal Protection Spell (8) Red

Hungarian brides consider red to be the color of protection, not blue. Pin a red silk ribbon inside the wedding gown's skirt.

Bridal Protection Spell (9) Soap

The bridal gown singles the bride out, making her vulnerable. However that same gown helps create a powerful protective amulet for future use.

1. Tuck a small bar of soap into the bodice of the wedding gown.
2. Keep it there during the ceremony and the party, then put it away safely.
3. This soap can be used to wash any future children of this marriage to prevent, remove, or repel the Evil Eye.

Bridegroom Protection Spell (1)

The bride seems to get all the magical attention. Sometimes the groom needs protection, too. Luckily, if he does, the bride can provide it.

In some Slavic ceremonies, just before the ceremony, the groom is wrapped in the bride's cloak, evoking primal female protective power.

 ## Bridegroom Protection Spell (2)

To provide the groom with protection, the bride should circle him sunwise either three or seven times.

 ## Bridewort Dream Spell

Create infused oil from the blossoms of the sacred Druid plant, Queen of the Meadow, also known as bridewort. (Follow directions for infusing the oil in Elements of Magic Spells.*) Rub the oil on your body before going to sleep, concentrating on your query, to receive marital advice dreams.*

Get Engaged Spells: Obtaining Proposals of Marriage

A not uncommon dilemma occurs when one person decides that it's high time to get hitched, while the other party remains unconvinced or doesn't even want to discuss the matter. Reflecting times past, when women's life security was determined by marriage, most spells assume that it's the woman who wishes to wed, although in reality this is obviously not always the case and undoubtedly never was.

There are many spells that contrive to obtain a proposal. They may be used identically by either gender, with the exception of spells that appeal to a Spirit that is the guardian of one particular gender, like Juno, Yemaya, and the Weaving Maiden.

(Maria Padilha is an equal opportunity spirit, willing to work with women, men, transsexuals—basically anyone whom she likes.)

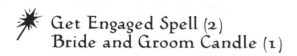

Get Engaged Spell (1)
Ace of Diamonds

1. Remove the ace of diamonds from a new pack of playing cards and place it on a dish.
2. Sprinkle powdered rosemary and lavender over it.
3. If you have a dime-store ring place it on the plate.
4. Dress a pink candle with **Come to Me Lover** and **Essence of Bend Over.** Place it on top of the playing card and burn.

Get Engaged Spell (2)
Bride and Groom Candle (1)

Spiritual supply stores sell candles in the shape of a conjoined bride and groom. This particular spell can also serve as a binding spell.

1. Use this type of candle or place two figure candles side by side.
2. Carve and dress the candle(s).
3. Bind them with ribbons, knotting in desires and blessings.
4. Perform a marriage ceremony over the candles, using your name and that of your beloved.
5. When you have pronounced them husband and wife, burn the candle(s).

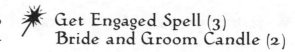

Get Engaged Spell (3)
Bride and Groom Candle (2)

1. Make a bed of sand.
2. Place a photo of the couple upright in the sand. This should be a happy photo. If you don't have one, you may place individual photos side by side.
3. Carve and dress a conjoined Couple Candle, ideally a red one, depicting the couple wearing formal wedding attire.
4. Place this in the sand in front of the photograph.
5. Burn the candle.

If a Couple Candle isn't available, use individual figure candles. Place them side by side or facing each other. Tie them together around the waist or hands with pink, red or gold silk or satin ribbon before burning.

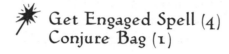

Get Engaged Spell (4)
Conjure Bag (1)

To obtain a proposal of marriage make a secret mojo hand:

1. Dress a pair of Adam and Eve roots with a love-drawing oil.
2. Put them into a red silk or flannel bag.
3. Slip this into your beloved's pocket secretly on the night of a Full Moon.

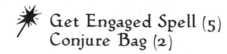

Get Engaged Spell (5)
Conjure Bag (2)

1. Obtain one strand of hair from each party and entwine them around a wedding ring.
2. Place this in a conjure bag together with a pair of needles, eye to point, wrapped in red silk thread, and some rosemary.
3. Carry until you receive your proposal or slip it in the other party's pocket for a more direct approach.

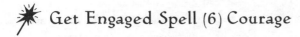 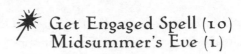

Get Engaged Spell (6) Courage

Get Engaged Spell (10) Midsummer's Eve (1)

Perhaps you haven't received the proposal you long for because the other party is afraid to ask. Or maybe you'd like to get married but the other person is afraid of making that commitment. If courage is the sole barrier to your happiness, serve a potion containing the herb borage to enhance bravery, risk-taking, and daring.

Dance around nine Midsummer's bonfires to be married within the year.

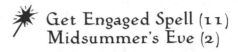

Get Engaged Spell (11) Midsummer's Eve (2)

Get Engaged Spell (7) Elder Flowers

1. Take a mouthful of water from a well on Midsummer's Eve.
2. Walk around the well three times sunwise without swallowing the water.
3. Spit the water out; you should receive the desired proposal.

Successfully accomplish this spell and English folk tradition says you'll be wed within the year.

1. Pour boiling water over elder flowers to create an infusion.
2. Allow this to cool, then strain, discarding the botanicals and reserving the infused liquid.
3. Add this elder-flower infusion to beer or wine.
4. Contrive to drink from a shared glass.

Get Engaged Spell (12) Pea Pod Marriage Spell

1. Should you discover a pea pod containing precisely nine peas, preserve it.
2. The old legend claiming that if this pea pod is hung over your door the first man to enter will marry you reeks of desperation. Just keep that pea pod safe.
3. When you find someone you'd like to marry, place the pod within his hand.

Get Engaged Spell (8) Engagement Powder

This mix allegedly magically induces the other party to get into the marrying mood. Powder lily of the valley and orange blossoms together. Blend into arrowroot powder and dust yourself with the mixture; dust your sheets, too.

Get Engaged Spell (13) Rosemary Wand

Tap your intended's wedding ring finger with a sprig of rosemary three times.

 Allegedly you'll be engaged and wed within the year.

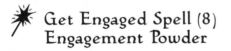

Get Engaged Spell (9) Matrimony Vine

Matrimony vine allegedly enhances one's desirability. Bathe in it to attract a proposal. Add powdered matrimony vine to spring water, rose water, and honey. Warm it on the stove and then add it to your bathwater.

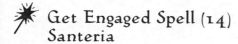 Get Engaged Spell (14)
Santeria

This spell takes a more "persuasive" approach toward obtaining a proposal. This is traditionally an invocation to Oshun, Spirit of Love, requesting her assistance with your stalled situation.

1. Secretly soak a piece of white cotton in spent seminal emissions.
2. Roll this cotton between your hands to form a wick and reserve.
3. Using a knife, shape a large lily bulb into a magic lamp. (Slice off the top, hollow out the inside.)
4. Write the man's name, birthday and other identifying information on a slip of paper.
5. Tuck the paper into the bulb and sprinkle it with ground cardamom, cinnamon, and Grains of Paradise.
6. Carefully fill the cavity with sweet almond oil.
7. Add the wick.
8. Make your invocation to Oshun, requesting her sacred assistance.
9. Burn the wick.

For maximum strength, repeat this ritual for five consecutive nights, using fresh materials.

 Get Engaged Spell (15)
Van Van Success

1. Add vervain and Grains of Paradise to **Van Van Oil.**
2. Use this oil to anoint the corners of a photograph—you'll know which one—and dress a silver candle.
3. Place the photo in front of the candle, focus on your desire and light the candle.
4. When the candle has burned down, at the first appropriate moment, give the photograph to the other party.

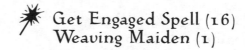 Get Engaged Spell (16)
Weaving Maiden (1)

The Feast of the Double Seventh occurs on the seventh day of the seventh month of the Chinese lunar calendar. It's a significant day for unmarried women. This is the day when magpies form a bridge across the Milky Way for the Weaving Maiden's single annual opportunity to visit her beloved husband, the Cowherd. The Weaving Maiden, in some legends the Kitchen God's daughter, in others that of the Jade Emperor, is the Matron of Unmarried Women. Unlucky in love and marriage herself, the Weaving Maiden helps women obtain proposals of marriage.

1. Request her assistance with your own marital predicaments: the Weaving Maiden accepts burned paper offerings.
2. Use traditional paper offerings. The Weaving Maiden favors paper clothes, combs, and mirrors, rather than cash.
3. Write her a respectful letter in your own words.
4. Burn it so she'll receive it via the smoke.

*(The Feast of the Double Seventh is the Weaving Maiden's only day of the year she sees the Cowherd. It's your only day of the year to create **Seven Sisters Water**. See the Formulary for details.)*

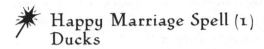 Get Engaged Spell (17)
Weaving Maiden (2)

Spells requesting assistance from spirits are to some extent dependent on whether you've found favor with the deity. In other words, if they like you, the spell is most likely to work. But do they like you? How can you tell? This spell lets you know whether you're in the Weaving Lady's favor.

1. On the morning of the seventh day of the seventh month of the Chinese calendar, find a spider.
2. Place this spider gently into a box and leave it there for 24 hours.
3. The following morning, open the box, free the spider to go where it will and check the spider's progress: if the spider has woven a web, you have the Weaving Lady's favor. The larger and more intricate the web, the more she likes you.

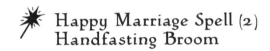 Get Engaged Spell (18)
Yemaya

The Yoruba orisha Yemaya is matron and protector of women. She may be petitioned to help with any facet of a woman's life, including obtaining marriage proposals.

1. Offer Yemaya a glass of salted water and seven white roses.
2. Place a happy photograph of the couple inside a bowl. (You may wish to use a photocopy as the photograph may, at best, be damaged.)
3. Cover it with white sugar, then with a layer of white rice.
4. Set a few clear crystals, pearls or seashells into the rice.
5. Stand two white candles in the bowl.
6. Tie them together with a blue satin ribbon and burn them.

Happy Marriage Spells

For on-going, ever-present marriage blessings:

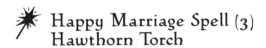 Happy Marriage Spell (1)
Ducks

Ducks allegedly mate for life. In any case, their marital success rate is among the best in the animal kingdom, far superior to that of humans, no doubt. A pair of mandarin ducks serves as a lucky marriage charm in the hopes that you'll be able to emulate their devotion to each other. These ducks epitomize faithfulness and fidelity.

Post an image of mandarin ducks prominently in your home. Or place a matched pair of statues somewhere strategic to radiate happiness there.

Happy Marriage Spell (2)
Handfasting Broom

Brooms are named after the broom plant. This plant of fertility and growth (it's an invasive plant spreading rapidly) demarcates sacred territory. Use the botanical broom to create a ritual broom for handfastings, to mark the sacred space encompassing bride and groom.

Happy Marriage Spell (3)
Hawthorn Torch

Use flaming hawthorn branches to illuminate the nuptial bedroom. This ancient Roman custom allegedly ensures that the marriage will be filled with happiness and luck.

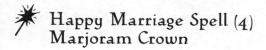

Happy Marriage Spell (4) Marjoram Crown

Marjoram is among Aphrodite's sacred herbs. Crown the bride and groom with marjoram garlands to ensure marital happiness and romantic bliss.

Happy Marriage Spell (5) Orange Blossom

1. Reserve orange blossoms from the bride's bouquet or garland.
2. Do not let them whither but burn them, together with a piece of parchment bearing the names of each member of the couple.
3. Put the ashes in a red bag or small bottle, together with a piece of true silver, and store in a safe, discreet place to protect and preserve love and marital harmony.

Happy Marriage Spell (6) Rosemary

The bride and groom should dip a rosemary wand into their first drink as a married couple and sip from a single glass together, to preserve love and happiness.

Happy Marriage Spell (7) Trees

Surround your home with magnolia and pine trees to provide a shield to preserve and protect your happy marriage.

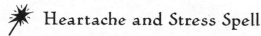

Heartache and Stress Spell

To remedy marital problems:

1. Fill a glass with sea salt, rose water and either **Holy Water** or **Notre Dame Water.**
2. Drop your wedding ring in the glass and let it soak overnight.
3. Recite your wedding vows as you remember them.

Heartache and Stress Spell: The Other Woman

This spell is intended to make a husband forsake the "other woman."

1. Go to a crossroads barefoot with your head uncovered, your hair loose and undone.
2. At the crossroads pick up a pebble and place it under your left armpit.
3. Make a wish: murmur something to the effect that just as this pebble can be removed from the road, so the other woman can be removed from your partner's heart.
4. Go to a second crossroads.
5. Pick up another pebble but this time place it under your right armpit. Make the wish again.
6. With both pebbles in place, travel to a third crossroads and pick up *another* pebble.
7. Stick this pebble between your breasts or beneath your chin. Repeat your wish.
8. Go home: when you reach your residence but before you enter it, drop all the pebbles in the gutter.

Henna Spells

Although henna has many uses, its strongest associations are with marital rites. This natural botanical dye is used to create temporary tattoos on the bride's body to prepare and protect her.

Henna repels the Evil Eye. Its scent is also an aphrodisiac; it places the bride in a heightened state of receptive expectancy. It also provides erotic stimulation for the groom, whenever he is close enough to inhale his bride's aroma.

Applying henna is a lengthy process. It takes hours to mix it up. It may take hours to apply the design and it will take many hours for the design to dry fully. From the time the henna is applied, the bride is effectively incapacitated—because palms and soles are invariably painted, she cannot walk but must be carried, nor can she hold anything, such as a glass of water. Everything must be done for her as if she were a baby.

Because of this intensity of time and labor, the night of the henna is transformed into a ritual party, the original *"hen night."*

 Henna Basic Party Ritual

This is a women's pre-marriage ritual. Traditionally, no men are allowed, although this may be adapted to your own tastes and purposes.

1. Invite friends and serve wonderful food and drink. (Make sure the bride eats before the henna begins but limits her liquid intake carefully. She may have to be carried to the bathroom, so as not to ruin her designs.)
2. The henna artist may be accompanied by belly dancers and musicians. Once upon a time, these rituals were dedicated to the djinn. Create a spiritual component that suits the bride's beliefs.
3. A good henna artist knows special bridal designs meant to enhance the bride's beauty as much as possible, while stimulating the groom's sexual talents.

 Henna Spell Bride's Gloves

1. Lady fern, a plant known in Syria as the "bride's gloves," is placed on the bride's cleansed hands and attached with tape or honey.
2. Henna paste is spread over the plant.
3. Removed when the henna is complete, it leaves a beautiful design plus the essence of blessing from the plant.

 Henna Spell Hide and Seek

A trick, common to the sub-continent, is to hide the groom's initials somewhere inside a design on the bride's body. A wedding night game of Hide and Seek can then be played: if the groom can't find his initials, proverbial wisdom says that the bride will dominate the match.

 Henna Spell Honeyed Future

Once the design has been applied, Yemenite Jews seal the bride's hand by sticking a coin into the center and pouring honey over it, to be scraped off the next morning with the rest of the henna paste. This blesses her married life with sweetness and prosperity. The coin may be kept as a lucky amulet.

 Henna Spell Lakshmi

In India, henna is identified with Lakshmi, Goddess of Wealth, Luck, and Love. Lakshmi is the eternal bride; wearing henna enables one to share in a touch of her beautiful, auspicious essence. Request her blessings for your marriage.

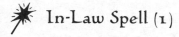 In-Law Spell (1)

Trouble with the in-laws? Oregano allegedly keeps meddlesome in-laws away. Greek oregano is allegedly the most magically powerful member of the species.

Don't cook the oregano for your spouse's troublesome relations—fumigate the premises instead. In addition, you may wish to fumigate their photographs at regular intervals.

 In-Law Spell (2)

If they won't stay away, perhaps you can inspire some affection. This spell may be used on anyone although it's most traditionally associated with mothers-in-law. It inspires affection rather than passionate love; this is not a substitution for one of the Notorious Potions (see page 703).

1. Grind up your fingernail clippings.
2. Brew them in a hot beverage, preferably coffee.
3. Serve to your target.

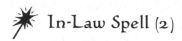 In-Law Spell (3)

If the in-law managing methods above don't work, try burning dried bridewort (Queen of the Meadow) to relieve tension between yourself and your in-laws.

Jump the Cauldron Spells

Some jump the broomstick; others jump the cauldron. An iron cauldron unites the male and female principles, in the same manner as the broomstick. Jumping over it offers protection, fertility, and transformation.

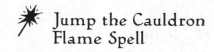 Jump the Cauldron
Flame Spell

Jumping over flames echoes Beltane and Midsummer's bonfires. Similar blessings of protection, fertility, and fulfillment of wishes are received. Fill the cauldron with flames by burning aromatic, romantic wood and herbs.

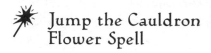 Jump the Cauldron
Flower Spell

Think Cerridwen; think Medea: in fairy tales and mythology, cauldrons are vehicles of transformation. Fill the cauldron with flowers to represent fertility. Hold hands and jump over the cauldron to be transformed from two into one.

Marital Assistance Spells

Certain spirits are passionately involved with the lives of women. Because for millennia, marriage was such a crucial factor in women's security and potential for happiness, these spirits provide assistance with every aspect of marriage, from obtaining the engagement to maintaining happiness to sending an abusive spouse packing.

✳ Marital Assistance Spell: Damballah

Damballah, a Dahomean serpent deity, is among the most primordial and profound Vodou spirits. Together with his wife, Ayida Wedo, he sustains and maintains Earth. Damballah is the proverbial wise, benevolent serpent. Damballah is so ancient, he doesn't speak but merely hisses. If a married couple honors him together, he will maintain their happiness.

Create an altar in the bedroom. Feed Damballah every Thursday. Light white and silver candles for him. Offer bougainvillea flowers and white foods like milk and eggs.

✳ Marital Assistance: Juno, Matron of Marriage

Most famous today as the wife of Jupiter, Juno's worship in the region that is now Italy may precede his. Juno has Etruscan roots. Her original name was Uni, *which derives from the same source as* one, *the root of* unity, unify, *and* unification, *and indeed one is her sacred number. Rome's supreme matron, Juno is the Matron of Women. She guides and guards them throughout all stages of life. Marriage is her holy sacrament, the ceremony that transforms two individuals into one couple.*

As far as Juno is concerned, all women should be June brides. Juno is the only Roman spirit with two months named in her honor: not only the obvious June but also February, named for Juno Februata, Juno of the Fever of Love. Valentine's Day coincides with one of Juno's ancient Roman festivals. It's an excellent day to offer her a petition.

Request assistance from Juno regarding any facet of marriage—from obtaining the proposal to finding a caterer:

1. Make your petition by creating an offering table in Juno's honor. She accepts offerings of roses, irises, and orrisroot.

2. If Juno helps you, she will expect offering tables on your wedding anniversary, as well as on your birthday and at the birth of any children. In exchange, she may be petitioned for help in any area of life for the rest of your life.

✳ Marital Assistance: Maria Padilha

Perhaps because in real life her own marital status was so precarious, Maria Padilha is very helpful in nuptial matters. Although her husband, King Pedro I of Castile and Leon, adored her, he was forced to make other more politically viable marriages while still married to Maria. (He is also suspected of poisoning one of the other wives.)

Maria Padilha will help you get married; she will also help remedy any troubles during the marriage. (She'll help with divorce, too, if necessary.)

1. Offer Maria Padilha a bouquet of seven long-stemmed red roses, all thorns removed by hand.

2. Give her additional gifts: anisette or a glass of champagne, cigarillos, and matches.

3. This is all just to attract her attention. Tell her what you need. She will expect another offering (consider it payment; she will) once it's been provided.

✳ Marital Assistance: Saint Paraskeva

Russian Saint Paraskeva or Saint Friday is the protector of women and a provider of husbands. She may be petitioned for any aspect of the marital process or for any later needs involving marriage. The price for Saint Paraskeva's assistance isn't too harsh: no housework or traditional "women's work" (sewing, weaving, cleaning) can be carried out on Friday or she may punish you.

Build Saint Paraskeva a shrine by posting her icon or image at a crossroads. Make your appeal to her, then leave the image and go home without looking back.

Marital Fertility Spells

Fertility spells are often a conscious component of marital ceremonies. The goal of these spells is to implant the capacity for fertility within the union, even if the couple is nowhere near ready to conceive. If you're already wed, having fertility troubles and regret not incorporating these magical rites into your ceremony, never despair. Renew your vows and incorporate them now.

 ## Marital Fertility Spell (1) Egg

According to old French custom, a bride entering her new home for the first time as a married woman breaks an egg immediately to ensure her fertility.

 ## Marital Fertility Spell (2) Gifts

Who needs another toaster? Bridal gifts may be given to ensure fertility: put frankincense, myrrh, henna, and goats on the wish list. A toy goat or an image of one will work, too!

 ## Marital Fertility Spell (3) Fire

The pre-Christian Armenian practice of jumping over fire is intended to stimulate and ensure personal fertility. The newly married couple should leap over a fire together, while holding hands. The wedding guests circle around them holding hands.

 ## Marital Fertility Spell (4) Belly Dancer

There's much debate about the origins of belly dance or Eastern dance, as some prefer to call it. Some argue that the tradition dates back to ancient Middle Eastern priestesses; others claim that it's a more recent purely folkloric tradition. Either way, no one denies its expression of primal female power and its connection with enhancing women's reproductive energy. This is made explicit by a modern Egyptian wedding ritual: following the wedding, at the reception, the bride and groom together place their hands on the dancer's abdomen to receive blessings of future fertility.

 ## Marital Fertility Spell (5) Bedroom

In a Thai ritual, during the actual ceremony, an older couple ritually prepares the bedroom so that it will be ready for use by the bride and groom. The room must be spiritually cleansed, protection set up and talismans left behind to radiate good fortune.

Talismans include bags of rice, sesame seeds, coins, and a tomcat (for happiness and fertility). The cat doesn't have to be a gift; it can be someone's pet that just hangs out in the room for a little while, emanating energy. The one caveat is that the cat may not be neutered. It defeats the purpose of the spell. This may be a good opportunity to adopt a stray from a shelter and let it participate in the ceremony prior to neutering.

 ## Marital Fertility Spell (6) Cat in the Cradle

In a similar ritual, this time from Switzerland, approximately one month after the wedding, visiting friends should bring a tomcat and a cradle to the new couple's home. The cat is rocked in the cradle before the newlyweds.

Marital Fertility Spell (7) Threshold

This is a Chinese ritual to ensure the bride's future success in childbirth, prevent birth complications and safeguard her partner, too.

Before the bride first enters her home as a married woman, place a pan of red-hot burning charcoal on the threshold. The bride is carried over the threshold, not by her new husband, but by two women whose husbands (or significant life partners) and children remain alive and well.

 ## Marital Potion (1) Bride

Inspiring the original honeymoon, *Teuton brides were fed honey-beer daily for thirty consecutive days following hand-fasting ceremonies. This allegedly keeps the bride happy and more sexually responsive.*

Marital Potion (2) Groom

This medieval potency potion was traditionally served to bridegrooms on the wedding night to promote extra vigor.

Cook eggs with honey, cinnamon, cloves, mace, and nutmeg. Mix two parts of this concoction with one part fortified wine.

Marital Potion (3) Groom and Bride

Some potions are for bride and groom to share together:

1. Steep myrtle in white wine or add a splash of myrtle hydrosol.
2. The bride and groom should drink of this together from one shared glass to ensure romance, fidelity, and fertility and to beseech Aphrodite's blessings on their union.

 ## Tie the Knot Spell

To knot love and success into a marital union, reproduce an ancient Babylonian wedding spell:

1. During the wedding, pull a thread from the bride's dress and another from the groom's clothing.
2. Tie the two threads together, knotting in love, happiness, and devotion.
3. Preserve this knotted thread in a safe place, or burn it to transmit your wishes to the spirit realm and so the lover's knot can't be undone.

Fidelity Spells

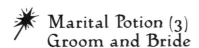

Fidelity is a genteel, pious term for what essentially translates to expected sexual exclusivity. Some have a greater need for it than others; some are better able to provide it than others. Notorious potions may make someone love you forever; binding spells may keep that person by your side forever; however neither guarantees that the other party will be sexually faithful to you, hence development of Fidelity Spells.

There are two kinds of Fidelity Spells. Certain Fidelity Spells magically *encourage* faithfulness and fidelity: they stimulate the other party to *want* to be faithful toward you or at least not to seek out other opportunities. Other Fidelity Spells refuse to take chances but attempt to *enforce* sexual exclusivity, one way or another.

Fidelity Encouraging Spells

 ### Bed of Magnolia Spell

Magnolia trees represent happy matrimony, so line your mattress with magnolia leaves. Or slip a magnolia blossom under your partner's pillow while he or she is asleep to encourage fidelity. Periodically replace the leaves, burying or burning the old ones.

 ### Be True Charm Bag

This conjure bag incorporates the three "Cs" of fidelity. Two bags may be made and exchanged as a promise of exclusivity.

1. Place caraway, cumin, and coriander seeds in a red charm bag.
2. Add pine needles and an unadorned gold ring.
3. Ideally this should be sewn within your partner's clothing, but it may be placed underneath the mattress on his side of the bed, too.

 ### Chili Pepper Spell

1. While your partner is sleeping, pass two red chili peppers over his body, never actually touching him, more like vacuuming his aura.
2. Concentrate on his rambling nature being drawn into the peppers, his inclination to wander terminated and his passion for you filling the void left by those disappearing desires.
3. When you're finished, lay one pepper against the other to form a cross.
4. Safety pin them together and when you have a chance, hide them under his side of the mattress.

 ### Clothing Spell

This spell strongly encourages fidelity but also has an aphrodisiac edge to it, so that he'll be kept content while faithful.

1. Obtain an unwashed piece of your lover's clothing, ideally underwear or a sock. You may also use any fabric that has been soiled with his sexual emissions. Cut a piece of the bed linen if necessary.
2. Wear it inside your own underwear for seven days, wearing that same underwear for seven days. Do not launder either your underwear or his item during that time. They can never be laundered again or the spell will be broken.
3. On the eighth day, tie your underwear together with his item, with a red silk ribbon.
4. Place them in a jar and cover with powdered confectioner's sugar, spikenard, damiana, licorice root, sweet flag, and vetiver.
5. Seal it shut and hide it safely.

 ### Elderberry Fidelity Spell

Allegedly carrying elderberries and twigs guards against the temptations of adultery. Place some in two conjure bags. Carry one yourself and either give one to the other party or slip it into his or her pocket, as you deem appropriate.

 ### Fidelity Candle

Powder caraway seeds, cumin, and licorice root and add to grapeseed oil. Carve a figure candle to represent your partner; dress with this oil and burn.

Fidelity Candle Extra Strength

Candles in the shape of genitals are used to magically enforce fidelity. This spell falls between basic fidelity spells and ligatures in terms of intensity. Carve and dress the candle to suit your situation. Traditionally the candle is bound and tied up before burning.

 ## Fidelity Potion

In many parts of the world, hair is associated with providing the ties that bind fidelity. In Morocco, however, urine is traditionally used instead of or in addition to hair. Moroccan-style tea is made with great quantities of sugar and spearmint, lending a strong taste that will easily mask a mere few drops of urine added to ensure fidelity and docility. Just double-check who gets which cup …

 ## Fidelity Wash

Create a strong infusion by pouring boiling water over caraway and cumin seeds and senna leaves. Strain out the botanical material and use the liquid to wash your partner's underwear and socks.

 ## Footprint Spell

Gather your lover's footprint up in its entirety. (If you miss any, the spell may not work.) Pour the dirt into a bag, which should be placed safely beneath your pillow or mattress.

 ## Hair Spell (1) Commanding, Compelling

1. Obtain a lock of your lover's hair.
2. Sprinkle it with **Command and Compel Oil.**

3. Place it in a small piece of white linen. Wrap it toward you, knotting it securely shut with blue, red, or gold silk thread.
4. Carry it in your pocket or in a charm bag.

 ## Hair Spell (2) Intimate

Menstrual blood served in food or drink supposedly makes him love you madly, but doesn't offer assurances that he might not also be sleeping around on the side. This spell focuses on the fidelity issue.

1. Pluck three pubic hairs and three hairs from your left armpit, the one closest to your heart.
2. Burn them like incense on charcoal.
3. Bake the ashes into cake or sweet bread. Feed it to your lover for fidelity.

 ## Hair Spell (3) Perfume

1. Obtain two strands of his or her hair and tie them together to two strands of your own.
2. Place these hairs inside a bottle of your favorite fragrance together with an Adam and Eve root.
3. Every morning, ideally before he or she awakes, place a drop of this fragrance under each of your arms.

 ## Hair and Ashes Fidelity Spell

This spell, timed to coincide with the New Moon, allegedly keeps your lover true for one lunar cycle.

1. Burn an intimate item of your lover's clothing, reserving the ashes.
2. Braid or otherwise entwine a lock of your lover's hair with your own and place on a white cloth.
3. Blend the reserved ashes with dried crumbled vervain and sprinkle over the hair.

4. Wrap everything up in the cloth, always folding it toward you.
5. Bury the packet under your threshold or doorstep at the New Moon.
6. Repeat as needed.

 ## Heartsease Fidelity Spell

Heartsease, the wild pansy's nickname, reveals its magic power to ease a worried heart. Wrap heartsease in your lover's unwashed underwear or sock. Bury it in Earth.

 ## Hibiscus Fidelity Spell

Sprinkle crumbled hibiscus in your lover's pockets so that he or she will be true.

I Command You To Be True!

Licorice root and sweet flag, the building blocks of commanding magic, also possess romantic, aphrodisiac properties. Thus many of the commanding, compelling condition formulas that incorporate them (**Essence of Bend Over**, **Do As I Say**) are popularly used to exert one's will in a relationship.

 ## Basic Commanding Fidelity Spell: Discreet Method

Sew a piece of licorice root into the hem of your partner's garment.

 ## Basic Commanding Fidelity Spell: Fragrant Method

1. Make an infusion by pouring boiling water over bruised cloves and vetiver.

2. Strain the solids out and add two drops of essential oil of bergamot to the liquid.
3. Use this liquid as the final rinse when washing your partner's underwear.

 ## Basic Commanding Fidelity Spell: Blunt Method

Soak cotton balls in any of the Commanding Oils: **Do As I Say** *(also known as As You Please) is reasonably subtle;* **Essence of Bend Over** *is most powerful. Slip these cotton balls among the clothes your partner customarily wears when stepping out alone.*

Prized powerful ingredients for fidelity spells may be hiding modestly in your kitchen cabinets. Both caraway and cumin allegedly encourage fidelity and constancy.

 ## Kitchen Spice Spell (1) Magic Diet

Consuming cumin and/or caraway supposedly encourages faithfulness and fidelity. Discreetly add the spices to your partner's regular diet.

 ## Kitchen Spice Spell (2) Potion

Kummel, a sweet liqueur, mainly flavored with caraway may also contain cumin.

Norwegian aquavit is typically flavored with caraway seeds. Serve either one as fidelity potions. Pour out a glass for your beloved. Before serving, murmur your desires over the liquid, and then serve with a smile.

Kitchen Spice Spell (3) Special Packet

At least as far as prehistoric remains can be determined and interpreted, caraway is among the oldest botanicals to be used for apparently magical purposes—8000-year-old remains have been discovered in Switzerland.

If you are afflicted with a serially unfaithful spouse, with an ever-wandering eye, try sewing caraway seeds into his clothing.

Locket Spell

There's a reason locket *is a homophone for* lock it. *Wear your lover's picture together with a lock of hair chained in a locket around your neck to encourage faithfulness.*

Lodestone Fidelity Spell

1. Place two matched lodestones and some of the botanical skullcap into a sachet. Add lots of the botanical or extra layers of fabric because lodestones are hard and presumably you'd like this spell to remain a secret.
2. Sew this sachet into his pillow.

Martha the Dominator Spell

Make an appeal to Saint Martha the Dominator. Saint Martha epitomizes the able, organized, capable house-keeper, and it is more effective to request her assistance if you are the wife in an established family than if you are merely a jealous girlfriend. If your husband's infidelities are threatening the stability of your home, marriage and family, appeal to Martha. She could tame a dragon; you only want her to tame your man. Tuesday is the most favorable day for an appeal.

1. Set up an altar for Martha; most altars display a depiction of the saint and/or her dragon.
2. Carve a green or white candle with your name, identifying information, simultaneously charging it with your desire. (There are also commercially prepared candles available that are dedicated to Saint Martha. Almost inevitably they depict her with dragon or snake.)
3. Dress the candle with **Martha the Dominator Oil.**
4. Place an item that belongs to your mate, something that somehow represents his infidelity to you, beside the candle and make your petition to Martha.

Nutmeg Fidelity Spell

This spell depends on the influence of the four elements as well as that of nutmeg, which allegedly promotes fidelity.

1. Hold a nutmeg in your left hand and charge it with your desire.
2. Slice it into four quarters. (This is easier said than done; nutmegs can be *very* hard. Be careful not to slice yourself instead.)
3. Bury one quarter in Earth.
4. Toss one quarter off a steep cliff so that it flies through the air.
5. Burn the third quarter.
6. Make an infusion by pouring boiling water over the last quarter and take one sip.
7. Retain this final nutmeg quarter, keeping it with you at all times, sleeping with it beneath your pillow.

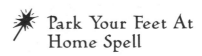

Park Your Feet At Home Spell

1. Offer to give your partner a pedicure.
2. Before moistening the feet, begin by scraping off any dry skin, preferably from the heels.
3. Proceed as you wish, have fun, but reserve that dried skin.

4. When he is peacefully asleep in your bed, bury the skin under your doorstep or a similar safe discreet place.

 ## Rosemary Spell

1. Gather rosemary leaves on Midsummer's Day.
2. Dry them.
3. When they have completely dried, coordinate with the time of the New Moon and powder the leaves, placing them in a jar with a rose quartz.
4. Store the jar in a quiet, secret place.
5. At the Full Moon, sprinkle the powdered leaves under the bed that you share.

 ## Slice of Pie Spell

Serve your partner rhubarb pie to promote fidelity and maintain their romantic interest.

 ## Shoe Spell

Keep a sprig of myrtle inside a rambling lover's shoes. Peel up the sole, slip the myrtle underneath and glue it down again, if necessary.

 ## Sock Spell (1) Deluxe

1. The spell requires a small piece of genuine silver. Once upon a time a dime or silver threepenny bit or similar coin would have been recommended. However, few modern coins really contain silver. Use a pure silver coin, or a small bead or charm.
2. Wrap a hair from your beloved's head around this silver.
3. Write his or her name on a slip of paper, three times.
4. Place this paper plus the hair-wrapped silver inside his or her unwashed sock.

5. Sprinkle magnetic sand over a lodestone and toss that into the sock, too.
6. Close it with two needles or with poultry trusses. (Real silver needles, such as silver acupuncture needles, provide maximum effectiveness.)
7. Dribble this sock-sachet with a little of your beloved's favored alcoholic libation. (Whatever drink would be most pleasing is what you should feed the sock. However, alcohol has a pacifying effect: if your lover is a teetotaler, simply substitute whiskey.)
8. Hide this sock over your home's rear door. Feed it with a little liquor periodically.

 ## Sock Spell (2) Simple

A simpler fidelity spell involving socks:

1. Tie a knot in your lover's unwashed sock.
2. Hide it under the mattress on the side where you sleep, or beneath the carpet.

 ## Spikenard Spell

1. Burn a spikenard root and bury the ashes in Earth.
2. Reinforce it weekly by anointing the spot with essential oil of spikenard or the infused oil of the root, every Friday.

 ## Stay Home Oil

To soothe a restless mate:

1. Steep spikenard root shavings, linden flowers and yerba mate in sweet almond oil.
2. Strain out the botanicals and add the oil to his or her bathwater.
3. Make a sufficient quantity of oil: periodically reinforce good behavior by using it to anoint shoes, sprinkle over sheets or even give a foot massage with it.

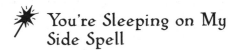

Stay at Home Powder

To keep your lover from going out wandering:

1. Cut a strip off of a bedsheet, preferably one that is soiled with both of your sexual juices. Chop it up, grind it, mash it, do whatever you have to do to pulverize this fabric into the consistency of powder.
2. Grind allspice berries, cloves, Deer's Tongue, mullein, sage and vetiver into a fine powder.
3. Blend this powder with the pulverized bedsheet.
4. Add this combined powder into a rice powder base.
5. Dust yourself with this powder before you go to bed with him to encourage him to stay home.

You're Sleeping on My Side Spell

In many metaphysical traditions, the left side is the female side, the right side the male. Because of this perception, many Asian traditions encourage the woman to sleep on the left, with the right side of the bed, the "rightful" place of the male head of the household.

This Chinese spell assumes, as many do, that it is the female partner who wishes to control the male's roving nature; whichever party desires to enforce fidelity should attempt to sleep on the right consistently. Adjust to your personal situation.

1. To stimulate fidelity and perhaps a little docility too, encourage the male partner to sleep on the left side, with the woman moving to the right.
2. Whether this proves possible or not, tie a piece of amethyst to the foot of the bed on the side the woman sleeps on.
3. Reactivate and re-energize weekly or as needed by placing the crystal in sunlight, moonlight, a dish of rainwater, or all of the above.

Fidelity Enforcement Spells: More Drastic Measures

All those spells were very interesting but *your* situation is far too drastic for any of them, you say? You're apparently not the first to feel this way. More drastic measures were conceived, too—the magical equivalent of the chastity belt.

These spells literally enforce sexual exclusivity by attempting to impose selective impotence. In other words, your husband can have a great sex life, no problem, providing it's exclusively with you. Fidelity Enforcement Spells attempt to prevent him from consummating any impulse to dally with another.

Although there are other methods of fidelity enforcement, the most common and famous involves nothing more than string. Because apparently some concerns are eternal and universal, these notorious spells are among the most ancient and well-distributed.

The aiguillette or ligature is a magical spell used to cause selective impotence, typically involving tying knots in a cord the length of the man's erect penis. It's very familiar in medieval European magic, although references indicate that it's much older and may have been known in ancient Mesopotamia. Virgil refers to nine knots affecting copulation.

The goal of the aiguillette is to make sure that the male organ works with only one woman; the key unlocks only one door. An attempt to render someone impotent is a hex, as plainly as rendering someone ill, bankrupt or any other disaster. So why aren't these spells with hexes?

Magical ethics have evolved as have every other type of ethic. Under influence of Wicca, new concerns have arisen about affecting the free will of the target, in which case any love or money spell targeted at another person is unethical. Other traditions would say that affecting the free will of the target is the whole point of magic, what other point is there? Although men may not perceive it this way, aiguillette spells are a reaction to women's centuries of forced dependence upon them.

In many cases, attempts to enforce selective impotence wasn't meant badly (well, not *really* badly, maybe a little) but was intended as a survival mechanism. A woman who was discarded for another might lose her home, her children, her economic status, any status. In extreme situations, extreme measures arose: the man who is no longer interested in you sexually may not provide for your children either, even if they're his, as many modern women will attest. (Of course, let's face it, there are also those spell-casters who just have evil, controlling, jealous natures.)

How do you measure the man? If he's awake it's hard to keep it a secret. Although several versions of the spell caution that he must be unaware of the creation of the aiguillette, there may be at least an implicit cooperation involved, as there often is with menstrual blood potions. The man signals, "*I am so trustworthy I am willing to do this.*" Because, of course, no harm is done, as long as he's not trying to have some fun on the side.

The other option is secret but risky: measure an erection that occurs while he's asleep. In theory, most ligatures are created fairly immediately after sexual union, when a man's sleep hormones may kick in. Another option is waking up earlier than him in the morning to take advantage of an early morning erection. In either case, you take the risk of his awakening in mid-measure and having to do some quick explaining.

Make sure that only the targeted lover's sexual emissions are used. They cannot be mingled with your own unless you wish this to be a binding spell, too. The most obvious way to achieve this is offering to dispose of a used condom and stashing it rather than throwing it away. This may or may not be foolproof, however. The safest method is to provide sexual services that keep you clothed, at least below the waist.

It is advisable to retain the aiguillette. The Memphis-style Nation Sack was always supposed to be within reach. This is not only because if the charm is found, it can be undone but also for your own well-being. Should the relationship end, it is advisable to undo the charm. First, because it is the nice thing to do; second, because if this man discovers he can *only* have sex with you, he will never leave you alone, so undoing it will mean you can find another love of your own.

Although historically these spells have been cast by women over men, there's nothing to stop a man from casting these spells over a male partner.

 ## Basic Love Leash

There are many names for this charm: "ligature" in English, "aiguillette" in French, "ghirlanda della streghe" in Italian. Call it The Love Leash. The standard method is as follows:

1. Measure a cord the length of a man's erect penis.
2. Reserve the cord and when possible soak it in his, and only his, sexual fluids.
3. Make knots it in it and reserve it in a secret place. (Ancient versions called for the knots to be tied in a wolf's foreskin.)

 ## Bell Rope Version

Not every version requires personal measurement.

1. Cut off the edge of a bell-rope (as in a church bell or similar) before dawn.
2. Make three knots in it, while murmuring something like,
   Just like the bell hangs down,
   So [Name], *child of* [Name]'s *member hangs down*
   Except when he's with me.

✴ Binding Spell Version (1)

This version creates the same effect without measuring the member and simultaneously produces a binding spell.

1. Following sex, retain a cloth that has been used to clean both partners.
2. Tie it into seven knots.
3. Place a rock inside the cloth and knot around it.
4. Drop it in a river. Make an appeal to the river's spirit to protect your love. Only the maker of this charm can undo the spell even if it is fished from the water.

✴ Binding Spell Version (2) Mutually Cooperative Method

In addition to mutual fidelity, this Romany spell is intended to cement romance, commitment, and partnership. Both partners consciously, willingly participate in the spell.

1. In order to effect this spell, both parties must wear a red scarf while making love.
2. This spell should be reserved for casting after moments of mutual bliss. The key is to be happy and have a mutually satisfying, wonderful time—a true expression of love.
3. After making love, each person takes off their scarf and uses it to wipe sweat off the other person's body and cleanse the genitals.
4. Lay the scarves on top of each other.
5. Roll them up together and knot them securely at both ends. Keep in a safe place.
6. Take the charm out once a year, perhaps on the anniversary of spell-casting, a wedding anniversary, Midsummer's Eve or other significant date. Do not unroll or unknot. Instead place it under the bed and make love.

✴ Mexican Variation

1. Measure the length of a man's penis with a ribbon while he's asleep.
2. Keep this ribbon rolled up inside a scapular of Saint Anthony, from which it cannot ever be separated, even momentarily.
3. This *cannot* be a cooperative spell. If he knows about it, it won't work.

The Nation Sack

The Nation Sack is forever immortalized in Robert Johnson's classic blues song, "Come on in my Kitchen," although few understand the reference. The singer reports that his lover has left. He's sure she won't be back because he's stolen the last nickel from her Nation Sack.

The Nation Sack is a mojo bag, exclusively used by women, deriving from Memphis-area Conjure traditions. This type of bag was attached to a belt and worn around the waist. At night, it might be placed under her pillow or inside her magic treasure box. The Nation Sack would be inactivated if anyone touched or tampered with it, *especially* a man. The bag contained a woman's survival tools: an aiguillette might be the centerpiece. She might also carry other charms to control her male partner or her children. An evolutionary mojo hand, items were added and subtracted as needed.

Although the Nation Sack has achieved notoriety because of its associations with ligatures, it's more than just a fidelity charm. In the days before credit cards and checks, when a bank might be suspect, a woman might keep all her cash money inside the Nation Sack, so that it would be empowered to grow by proximity to magical articles. A poor woman kept her life tied securely around her waist. The knowledge that cash was kept inside makes the bag very tempting: anyone familiar with the tradition would know exactly where the money was hidden. The red flannel bag also evokes elements of menstrual taboos: few people would touch it, hence Robert Johnson's unforgivable crime.

Creating a Nation Sack

The target of the ligature is forbidden to look within the bag, even if he suspects what's inside. Doing so will indeed restore his sexual nature, however it will also effectively end their relationship. (In other words, don't leave the sack lying around.)

1. Activate the bag to coordinate with your menstrual period. (If you don't menstruate, coordinate with the Full Moon.)
2. Add roots that will represent the couple, a male and female root: Adam and Eve root may be used or High John or Sampson snake root to represent the man, orrisroot or angelica root to represent the woman.
3. Light red candles.
4. Pass the bag through incense smoke.
5. Add items as they appear: assorted intimacies like bits of hair, nail clippings, sexual emissions.
6. Add bits of silver and cowrie charms.
7. Keep small magical or personal items in the bag: the bag also serves to empower items.

Hoodoo-style Ligature

In Hoodoo parlance, the aiguillette is not necessarily named but its function is: it's meant to "control" or "tame a man's nature."

1. Trim the string to match the length of the man's erect penis.
2. Hide this string, keeping it close at hand, until the appropriate moment presents itself.
3. Following sex, this string must be soaked in his semen, without touching any of your sexual fluids.
4. Let him fall asleep.

5. Begin a knot in the center of the string; in other words, start the loop but don't pull it tight.
6. When he is asleep, call his name aloud. When he responds, pull the knot tight.
7. For many this single knot is sufficient. For others, a total of nine knots is required for maximum effectiveness, making the second on the right of the central knot, the third on the left, the fourth on the right and so on. It is only the knot-tying, however, that must be repeated, calling his name each time.
8. Keep it in a safe, secret place or resurrect the Nation Sack.

Romany/Russian Variations

Romany and Russian versions of the ligature are identical. Who learned from whom is subject to scholarly conjecture.

1. Cut a length of red silk ribbon the length of a man's erect penis.
2. Keep the ribbon under the pillow.
3. After making love, while he is asleep, take out the ribbon, soak it in his seminal emissions and tie seven knots in it.
4. As long as you have possession of this ribbon, with its knots intact, his fidelity is assured.

Other methods of causing selective impotence exist:

Don't Be Crazy Spell

1. You will need reserved semen. This is a mean spell, so get it from a used condom or a hand-job; you want to be sure there are *no* intermingled love juices.
2. Add **Goofer dust.**
3. Wrap this up in paper or fabric.
4. Bury it in Earth, ideally where your target will step over it. Nothing will happen as long as he's faithful. However, if he ever even attempts sex with another, this allegedly causes him to suffer insanity as well as impotence.

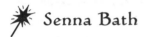

Senna Bath

The fact that senna tea, when consumed, is a potent laxative adds a certain bitter, sardonic humor to this spell, however it's not completely a coincidence nor is it necessarily intended to work in anything other but a magical way. Once upon a time, violent purgative action was perceived as a demonstration of a plant's magic powers. (Don't even consider consuming a High John the Conqueror root!) Purgatives are still incorporated into various shamanic and traditional healing rituals.

Add senna tea to your partner's bath and allegedly he'll stay home, rather than go stepping out.

Graveyard Spell

1. Obtain a piece of a dead man's shroud. The original spell suggests that the shroud be enclosed within amuletic paper covered with sacred texts.
2. Bury it by your home's front entrance so that your man will walk over it. Once he has, dig up the charm. Put it inside a goat's or ram's horn. (If you don't have one lying around, ritual shofars may be purchased from a Judaic supply store.)

3. Take the horn with the charm to an old grave of an unknown person. Bury it there.

Beyond selective impotence, this allegedly prevents your lover from even having an erection when observing anyone but you.

Sex Ball

1. Warm red wax in your hands until it's pliable.
2. Roll it into a ball.
3. Add a few of your lover's pubic hairs and a few drops of your menstrual blood. If this is not possible, prick your little finger with a needle or rose thorn and let a few drops of blood fall.
4. If you've created an aiguillette you may add it to the ball. You may also simply knot your intentions into a cord and add that.
5. Roll the ball around until the outside is smooth.
6. Hold it in your right hand to charge it. Carry it with you or reserve in a safe, secure place.

Trapped in a Bottle Spell

This spell is traditionally performed with a cotton handkerchief. Offer the man the cloth to cleanse himself with after sex. (You can do it for him; however there's an element of submission in his doing it, then handing you the cloth.) Reserve this cloth. When possible, stuff it into a bottle, seal it tightly shut, and bury it.

Have these spells got you scared? Have you started considering the advantages of sleeping alone? Every poison has its antidote, if only it can be discovered. The same goes for magic spells.

Enforced Fidelity Spell Antidotes

Of course, the obvious antidote is to discover the knotted cord and remove the knots. If that's not possible, here are other suggestions.

 ## Burdock Root Spell

Burdock root, a favorite of Japanese cuisine, is often used to metaphorically represent phallic prowess.

1. Steep a whole burdock root in olive oil.
2. Let it rest overnight, exposed to the Full Moon.
3. Rub the oil on the genitals.
4. Repeat as needed, using fresh burdock roots.

 ## Egg and Ant Hill Spell

A formula to "restore manhood."

1. Dip an egg into a substantial quantity of cod liver oil, and then place it in a pot of water to boil. The oil will separate from the water and should remain distinct.
2. When hard-boiled, remove the egg from the pot and let it cool.
3. Discard the contents of the pot, both boiled water and oil, by tossing it into a rapidly moving stream, flowing away from one's home.
4. Place the egg on top of a red ant hill. As the ants consume the egg, vigor and potency are restored.

Cod liver oil substitutes for the whale oil recommended by Albertus Magnus. Any type of fish-derived oil may be used, however.

 ## The Perfumed Garden's Recommended Spell Breaker

The Perfumed Garden *is a sixteenth-century manual of the erotic arts, sort of an Arabic equivalent of the* Kama Sutra *or the* Ananga Ranga. *This is* The Perfumed Garden's *recommendation for remedying impotence, specifically that caused by knot-tying spells.*

1. Blend and pound the following together: Galangal, cinnamon, cloves, Indian cachou, nutmeg, cubebs, sparrow-wort, cardamom, Indian thistle, pyrether, bay laurel seeds, and gilly flowers.
2. Consume morning and evening, either mixed with honey or added to broth: pigeon broth being the first choice, chicken the second.
3. Drink a glass of water before and after the potion.

 ## Sweet Flag Solution

Sweet flag, also known as calamus root, is the pre-eminent ingredient in Commanding Spells. It is also magically perceived as an emphatically "male" plant. Use it to command your nature to return.

1. Simmer a sweet flag root in whiskey until the liquid reduces by half.
2. Let it cool and remove the root.
3. Place the liquid in a bottle and add fresh whiskey, to taste. Take a swig daily. (If you need to make more, use a fresh root.)

You thought only men could be targeted? Think again!

 ## Nine Knot Spell (1) Strap

A woman's nature can be attacked, too, depriving her of desire for anyone but the maker of the charm. Because it lacks any phallic imagery, this spell can be cast by either a woman or a man, although the target must be a woman.

1. Use her garter belt or cut the strap from her bra.
2. Tie nine knots in the strap, focusing with each one on your desire for enforced fidelity.
3. Keep it in your pocket.

 ## Nine Knot Spell (2) Underwear

1. You'll need a red candle to represent you. Choose a red figure candle, a seven-day candle, a red devil, or a red phallus: the choice is yours. Carve and dress it so that it is identified with you.
2. Make nine knots in the woman's unwashed underwear, announcing aloud *"You're mine!"* or *"You have sex with only me"* or whatever best expresses your desire each time you tie a knot. Call her name aloud with each knot, too, for a total of nine times.
3. Arrange the knotted panty around the candle. If you have a seven-day candle in a glass sheath, you can tie the panty to it.
4. Spit on the candle and sprinkle a few of your pubic and underarm hairs over it.
5. Announce: "[Name], *daughter of* [Name], *You belong to me!"*
6. Light the candle.

7. When the candle has completed burning, take the panty and tie it to a hammer or other metal tool, something heavy in weight and implicitly phallic. Hide it.

 ## Raspberry Branch

An Iroquois spell to keep a woman faithful while you are separated.

1. Find a raspberry branch that has rooted at the tip.
2. Take a small piece of the root from both ends without killing the plant. (This transcends important ecological concerns; killing the plant defeats the purpose of the spell. It won't work. There's no point.)
3. Boil this root.
4. Let the liquid cool. Take one sip of the liquid. Use another tablespoonful to bathe your genitals.
5. Give the rest of the liquid to the targeted woman to drink.

Antidote Spell

For a woman to regain control of her sexual independence:

1. Rub fresh peppermint leaves between the palms of your hands, so that the volatile oils are released.
2. *Immediately,* go fondle your partner's genitals so that his control over you is broken.

Divorce Spells

 ## Divorce Candle Spell (1)

A candle spell for the person who would like a divorce while the other party is resistant. (Spells for the other party may be found in the Heartache section of Love Spells, *page 695.)*

1. Obtain male and female figure candles.
2. Place them back-to-back, ready to go in opposite directions.
3. Dress them with **Command and Compel Oil** and burn in timed increments, corresponding to the number of years you have been wed.
4. For instance, burn them for thirty minutes at a time if you were wed for thirty years. Pinch them out when the time is up. Next day, before lighting the candles again, move them farther apart. When they are finally as far apart as space will allow, let the candle burn entirely.

 ## Divorce Candle Spell (2)

Some spiritual supply companies market what is known as a "Divorce Candle." This is a single candle, usually, although not always, black containing a male and female human figure, back-to-back. This type of candle may be carved and dressed as above but there's no need for incremental burning.

 ## Divorce: Move Out Oil

One person moves out, the other stays—but why do you continue to feel the presence of the departed party? This spell's aim is to banish and remove lingering traces of the other person from the home you once shared. (It is beneficial for any long-term housemate relationship that has ended.)

1. Blend and grind asafetida, camphor, cinnamon, eucalyptus, High John chips, and rosemary.
2. Add the result to sweet almond and jojoba oils.
3. Dress a black candle with the oil. Walk the candle through your home slowly, pausing at areas especially associated with the other person.
4. When your rounds are completed, go outside, pinch out the candle and bury it upside down in Earth.

Wormwood, Plant of Bitterness, can be used to remedy and escape from bitter situations.

 ## Wormwood Spell (1)

1. Pour boiling water over wormwood roots, leaves and twigs to create an infusion.
2. Allow it to cool, then strain out the botanical material, reserving the liquid.
3. Add this liquid to the laundry rinse water used to wash the other party's clothes.
4. This establishes boundaries, and encourages the other person to leave.

 ## Wormwood Spell (2)

This spell targets a person who has left the relationship but remains resistant to divorce or a final dissolution desired by the spell-caster.

1. Grind and powder dried wormwood.
2. Sprinkle the powder on lit charcoal.
3. Pass a letter written to the other party through the incense smoke.
4. What you write in the letter is not relevant to the spell, there's no need to address the issue unless you wish to. The spell's crucial component is contact and inhalation of the wormwood scent. You may also drop a twig into the letter, although this gives away your secrets.

Domestic Abuse Spells

If marriage was historically women's only outlet, it was also often—and frequently remains today—a trap filled with danger and violence.

 ## Bamboo Protection Spell

Bury a bamboo cane in a cemetery overnight. Dig it up the next day, then slip it into your husband's bed while he's asleep as a magical attempt to make him stop beating you.

 ## Fiery Wall of Protection Spell (1) Basic

Fiery Wall of Protection *condition oil allegedly provides protection for woman from abusive partners.*

1. Soak a cotton ball in **Fiery Wall of Protection Oil.**
2. Tuck it into your pocket or bra.
3. Pay attention: the smell may intensify when danger is imminent.

 ## Fiery Wall of Protection Spell (2) Charm Bag

*This spell combines **Fiery Wall of Protection Oil** with angelica root, a herb identified with women's power and protection. Dress a whole angelica root with **Fiery Wall of Protection Oil** and carry it in a charm bag.*

 ## Fiery Wall of Protection Spell (3) Extra Strength

*Dress yourself with **Fiery Wall of Protection Oil.** Use it as perfume oil or add it to baths so that its protective, soothing fragrance radiates from your very aura.*

Lavender Safety Spells

Allegedly lavender minimizes spousal abuse and cruelty.

 ## Lavender Safety Spell (1)

Add essential oil of lavender and/or lavender hydrosol to your bath.

 ## Lavender Safety Spell (2)

Safety-pin a sprig of lavender within your clothing.

Spiritual Assistance Spells

When people fail you, sometimes the only thing to do is to turn to the spirit realm for solace, safety, protection, inspiration, and solutions.

 ## Spiritual Assistance (1) Archangel Michael

Archangel Michael offers protection in all areas, however he has earned special renown for protecting against rape. Call him by name or attract him with burning frankincense and tell him what you need.

Spiritual Assistance (2) Juno

Juno may be petitioned for safety and shelter. Her ancient Roman temples housed shelters for abused wives. Herein though is the catch: Juno is intrinsically tied to legal marital rites. You must actually be legally wed to request her assistance with this matter. She will assist with former husbands as long as once upon a time, there was a legal wedding ceremony. If you were a June bride, consider yourself automatically under her protection.

1. Burn orrisroot powder on lit charcoals.
2. Offer Juno one beautiful rose and tell her what you need.

 ## Spiritual Assistance (3) Saint Rita

Saint Rita is the saint petitioned for protection from abuse. According to legend, Saint Rita herself suffered an abusive marriage and will assist others suffering similarly if requested. Although you may request whenever help is needed, her feast day, the most auspicious day to call upon her, is May 22nd. Saint Rita's traditional offering is a bouquet of roses.

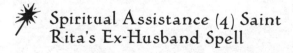 ## Spiritual Assistance (4) Saint Rita's Ex-Husband Spell

Sometimes the problem is that people won't leave. Saint Rita may be petitioned to help you get rid of an ex-husband who continues one sort of abuse or another even after the end of the marriage.

1. Place a bouquet of roses in a vase and offer them to Saint Rita.
2. Sprinkle baking soda around the vase of flowers.
3. You will need either a copy or the original of your marriage license or some similar document of your marriage. Burn it.

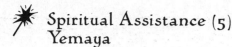 ## Spiritual Assistance (5) Yemaya

Yemaya despises domestic violence. Having herself once been the victim of rape and abuse, she does not tolerate it.

1. Bring your petition to the beach.
2. Make an altar in the sand: burn seven blue candles.
3. Enter the sea with a bouquet of white roses tied with blue ribbons.
4. Tell Yemaya what you need and gently place the roses in the water, to be carried home to her.

 ## Spiritual Assistance (6) Yemaya's Stay-at-Home Spell

If traveling to the beach is not an option, recreate the spell in your bathroom.

1. Add large quantities of sea salt to the water.
2. Light seven blue candles for Yemaya and offer her a wine glass containing salted water and seashells.
3. Soak in the water, gaze at the candles, and tell her what you need.
4. If possible, maintain the white roses on an altar, beside the goblet of salt water.

White Bryony Safety Spell

White bryony, also known as European mandrake, is most frequently used as a substitute for true mandrake, however it possesses its own magic powers. Carry white bryony root to protect against spousal abuse.

✪ Money Spells: Spells for Wealth, Prosperity, and Financial Stability

Certain topics attract more magical attention and spells than others. Weather spells, invisibility spells, rituals for preservation of animals attract individuals' attention while love, protection, fertility, and healing spells evoke a more universal reaction. Money is another similar universal category. *Everyone* can always use more.

If there were a spell to guarantee an instant fortune, there'd be a lot of rich witches, fortunetellers, and shaman. Of course, as we all know and as denigrators of magic are invariably quick to point out, this is not the case. On the contrary, the

TIPS FOR MONEY SPELLS

★ PRIMARY COLORS: green and gold

★ PRIMARY NUMBER: 2, because it encapsulates the concept of doubling

★ PLANETS: Jupiter, because it's the planet of good fortune; the Moon, because it's the planet of magic and fulfilled wishes; and Mercury, because the Roman god whose name it bears is involved with prosperity and finance

★ Spells for financial growth, to increase money or business, should coincide with the waxing moon

metaphysically inclined tend to be a financially challenged bunch, from the most obscure to the most famous, from Dr. Dee to Dr. John, and from Madame Blavatsky to Count Cagliostro.

That said there are a couple of things to consider. Every individual doesn't win identical prizes; the rewards of the metaphysical life transcend the material. However, because so many brilliant magical practitioners have lived, at least during periods of their lives, from hand to mouth, a wealth of magical spells exist, suitable for every situation.

✳ Alfalfa Money Spell

Murmur your financial desires over alfalfa. Burn it and scatter the ashes around your property.

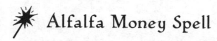
Animal Magic Wealth Spells

✳ Animal Magic Wealth Spell (1) Allies

The Animal Allies of wealth and financial fortune include the frog, toad, snake, dragon, cat, rat, rabbit, and fish. Surround yourself with their images to generate cashflow and financial inspiration.

Follow the direction given in Elements of Magic Spells *for setting up an Animal Ally Altar (page 107).*

✳ Animal Magic Wealth Spell (2) Chinese

Chinese magic tradition features special animal amulets. These are typically small statues of specific animals, usually seated upon a vast bed of coins. These amulets serve to generate good fortune and preserve what already exists.

The most famous is the three-legged toad, depicted seated upon a hoard of coins. Money toads suitable for

magic have a slightly open mouth so that a Chinese replica coin may be inserted.

1. The money toad should not be placed on the floor but kept at approximately coffee-table height.
2. Slip his *"magic coin"* into his mouth and face him discreetly toward the door.
3. Periodically he will need a rest: remove the coin from his mouth and face the toad away from the door so that he can recuperate and regenerate.
4. Obviously, you don't want to keep your finances unprotected: more than one toad may be used simultaneously, place them in various areas always facing the entrance. Rotate the toads so that at least one is always on duty.

✳ Animal Magic Wealth Spell (3) Chinese Frog

Frogs are universally considered the creature epitomizing increase, generation, and multitude. The ancient Egyptians used the hieroglyph for "tadpole" to represent the highest number they expressed.

1. Place a money frog amulet on a plate on top of a bed of real coins.
2. Sprinkle with mingled Money Drawing Powder and magnetic sand.
3. Place under your bed, looking toward the door.
4. Sprinkle with more powder periodically.

Among the other wealth-generating Chinese animal amulets are the dragon-tortoise, the mongoose, and the cow, all reclining upon a treasure trove. This cow is among Earth's many sacred cows and, according to legend, if she draws wealth toward you, in exchange you must refrain from eating beef. The image of a sow nursing her piglets on a bed of coins is considered particularly beneficial for single mothers and their children.

 ## Animal Magic Wealth Spell (4) Golden Spider

The golden money spider weaves a web of riches. As the old saying "If you wish to live and thrive, let the spider stay alive," reminds us, killing a spider is considered detrimental to one's own good fortune.

1. Draw a picture of the spider hidden in its labyrinthine web on red paper with gold ink.
2. Place the picture in a corner with a saucer underneath it.
3. Toss a few coins onto the saucer and make an invocation. Express your needs to the spider.
4. Once a week or whenever the spider comes through for you, toss a few more coins onto the plate.

 ## Animal Magic Wealth Spell (5) Japanese Frog

According to Japanese tradition, keeping a small image of a frog in your wallet stimulates wealth. There are two ways of doing this. You can either look for a small Japanese wallet frog charm, flat enough to slide comfortably into a wallet. Charge the frog with your desires and carry it with your cash. Or you can improvise and place a photo or drawing of a green frog inside your wallet.

 ## Animal Magic Wealth Spell (6) Maneki Neko

Although with popularity Maneki Neko, the Japanese beckoning cat, has been adapted to other uses, her primary purpose is to generate cash for her owner. This amulet depicts a seated cat holding one hand up in the gesture that in Japan indicates, "Come here!" Maneki Neko's upraised left hand beckons increased business while the upraised right hand demands cash. Allegedly the higher the hand, the more powerful the amulet.

Maneki Neko comes in a variety of colors any of which is suitable for increased wealth, however a gold cat is believed most powerful for this purpose.

1. Maneki Neko must face the outside world so that she can beckon wealth into your private premises.
2. Place Maneki Neko in the window facing outside or across from the front door.
3. Some Maneki Neko's have a slot in the back as if they were a child's piggybank. Make a wish and place a few coins within as amulet activation.

Avocado Money Spell

Avocado trees serve as money magnets. Transplant an avocado tree and eat the very first avocado that grows on it. Cleanse and dry its pit and carry it as a money charm.

 ## Balsam of Peru Spell

Balsam of Peru grows throughout Central and South America, not just in Peru. Beyond its sacred and healing aspects, it's also magically used to attract wealth. Burn balsam of Peru for happy, beneficial prosperity.

Basic Money Botanicals

The following botanicals radiate wealth and money-drawing properties. Incorporate them into spells as desired: alfalfa, avocado, basil, cabbage, chamomile, chervil, clover, coriander, dill, five-finger grass (cinquefoil), lettuce, mint, nasturtium, oakmoss, parsley, poppies, and vervain.

Basic Money Botanicals Candle

Hold a green candle in your hands and charge it with your desire. Hollow out its base, pack it full of basic money botanicals, and then burn it.

Basil Spells

Basil is the botanical particularly associated with prosperity and increase. It's used to magically increase fertility and romance and especially to attract and increase wealth. The plant is sacred to two very prominent Spirits of Wealth: India's Lakshmi and Vodou's Ezili Freda Dahomey.

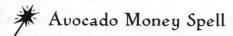 ## Basil Spell (1) Bath

The scent of basil on the skin allegedly draws financial opportunity toward the wearer. Once upon a time, prostitutes in Spain bathed in basil and rubbed their body with the fragrance to attract free-spending customers. The custom may be emulated regardless of one's profession. Take this bath just before venturing out in pursuit of any financial opportunity. Because basil smells so inviting, this is not a difficult spell to enjoy.

1. Roughly chop most of a large bunch of basil, in order to release the volatile oils, but leave some leaves whole, especially those that most remind you of cash bills.
2. Pour boiling water over the basil and let it steep.
3. When it cools, add the liquid to your bath. Float the whole leaves in the water so that you can visualize yourself swimming in cash.
4. Let the water drain and allow yourself to air-dry.
5. Do not dispose of the used basil leaves (don't throw out the cash!) but either leave them in the tub until your transactions are complete or remove them, place them in a bag and reserve until an opportune moment for disposal arises.

 ## Basil Spell (2) Exact Sum

1. Should you need an exact sum of money, write the amount on a slip of paper.
2. Drip a little basil oil on the paper.
3. Fold it in half twice and then bury it in a flowerpot filled with Earth. (For extra enhancement, collect crossroads dirt.)
4. Ideally you should then plant money-attracting plants in the pot: try marigolds, basil, thyme, or some sturdy cactus.

Bayberry Money Spell

1. Anoint a small piece of silver with infused oil of bayberry.
2. Hold it in your left hand to charge it with your desire.
3. Carry it with you during the day.
4. Place it on your forehead over the Third Eye area for thirty minutes every day. Feed with a drop of bayberry oil weekly.

 ## Bryony Root Spell

White bryony is also known as English or European Mandrake as it's among the roots most frequently used as a substitute for that rare Mediterranean plant. Like mandrake, bryony is potentially poisonous. Its love and fertility-drawing powers are not exactly up to par, however bryony has its own gifts.

1. At night, take all the money out of your wallet.
2. Stack it up and place a bryony root (or a piece of one) on top to encourage the money to grow.
3. Return the money to your wallet in the morning and repeat as needed.

 ## Buckeye Spell

Buckeyes are traditionally used as money generating charms. The most famous involved drilling a hole into a buckeye, then filling it with mercury and sealing. Mercury is very toxic—that spell offers plenty of opportunity for self-injury. Instead, try this safer but no less magically effective alternative.

1. Make a paste from magnetic sand, Money Drawing Powder, **Fast Luck Oil,** and essential oil of bergamot.
2. Rub it on the buckeye.
3. Wrap the buckeye in either a new or used cash bill, rolling it toward you.

4. Tie it with red thread, making knots and visualizing.
5. Rub the remainder of the paste onto two small green candles.
6. Place these candles side by side on a dish covered with Money Drawing Powder.
7. Place the buckeye between the candles.
8. Light the candles. When they have burned all the way down, your charm has been activated.

 ## Buckeye Charm Spell

Carry a buckeye in a conjure bag with two large denomination coins, and anoint with money-drawing oils periodically.

 ## Buckwheat Spell

Buckwheat is allegedly a potent charm for attracting wealth. Japanese goldsmiths traditionally used buckwheat dough to collect gold dust in the workplace. Personal methods of utilizing buckwheat's magic money acquiring powers tend to be culinary. When practicing culinary magic, visualize that stereotyped image of the old witch stirring her cauldron: she mutters and murmurs. Do the same: focus on your desire while preparing the food, not only when eating. Murmur your desired intent over cooking buckwheat.

Buckwheat's magic money powers are at their height on New Year's Eve (any New Year's Eve; the point is that it's a threshold, not the exact date). Eat buckwheat noodles or buckwheat pancakes (blini) on New Year's Eve to attract wealth in the New Year.

 ## Buckwheat Poverty Protection Spell

Blend buckwheat hulls with dried basil and parsley in an uncovered glass bowl. Keep this in the kitchen to ward off poverty.

Candle Spells

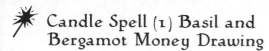

Candle Spell (1) Basil and Bergamot Money Drawing

1. Write the precise sum that you require on a square of brown paper.
2. Carve your name, identifying information and the sum onto a green candle.
3. Dress the candle with essential oils of basil and bergamot.
4. Place the candle over the paper.
5. Burn the candle for increments of fifteen minutes daily until the specified amount has accumulated.

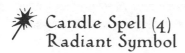

Candle Spell (2) Seven Knob

1. Write the amount needed on a square of paper.
2. Place it beneath a green seven-knob candle dressed with money oils.
3. Burn one knob a night for seven nights.

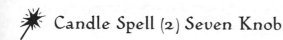

Candle Spell (3) Nutmeg

Dress and carve green candles. Sprinkle with powdered nutmeg and burn.

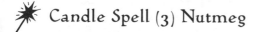

Candle Spell (4) Radiant Symbol

1. Carve your name and identifying information into a green candle.
2. In addition carve a symbol that represents money or wealth to you: prosperity runes, a dollar sign, or whatever resonates for you.
3. Hold the candle in your hands and focus on your desire.
4. Dress and embellish the candle with money-drawing oils and powders and burn.

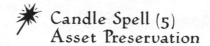

Candle Spell (5) Asset Preservation

Gorse stimulates money growth but also provides protection, and so is an excellent botanical for magically preserving assets. Carve and dress a green candle as desired. Surround it with a circle of gorse, and visualize your money protected and growing.

Candle Spell (6) Fast Cash

For fast double financial action, this spell requires a black and green double-action candle.

1. Carve whatever you wish to lose on the black side (debt, poverty).
2. Carve what you need to manifest on the green side. In both cases, be as specific as possible.
3. Trim the bottom of the candle if necessary, exposing the wick so that both ends may be lit simultaneously.
4. Impale the candle horizontally on a spiked candlestick and burn both ends.

Candle Spell (7) Money Growth

1. Carve and dress a green candle to express your desires.
2. Place it on a saucer.
3. Arrange coins around the base of the candle.
4. Light the candle and chant:
   Money grow, money flow
   Candle burn, watch me earn
   Money grow, money flow
   Flame shine
   What I want is mine!

 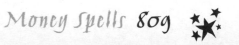

 Cash Boomerang Spell

Anoint all your cash with **Magnet Oil** prior to spending it, so that it returns to you.

 Cash at Hand Spell (1)

A simple spell so as always to have at least a little money at hand: burn onion peelings on the stove.

 Cash at Hand Spell (2)

Alternatively, burn garlic skins in the kitchen to keep money in the house.

    These two Cash at Hand spells are easily combined and reinforce each other.

Cash in Hand Spell (3) Extra Cash in Hand

Rub two drops of essential oil of bergamot between the palms of your hands to attract money. Rub the oil in your pockets, purse or wallet, too.

Cat's Eye Spell

Had it? Lost it all? The cat's eye gemstone allegedly draws back wealth lost prior to the arrival of the stone. Light candles, charge the stone, talk to it, and describe your needs.

    Carry it with you and sleep with it for financial inspiration.

Conjure Bag: Alkanet

Place alkanet root pieces in a mojo bag. Sprinkle it with henna powder and carry to enhance finances and provide good fortune.

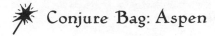 Conjure Bag: Aspen

Carry aspen leaves and buds in a conjure bag to generate money.

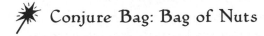 Conjure Bag: Bag of Nuts

Place a buckeye, a hickory nut and a horse chestnut in a green drawstring bag. Sprinkle with money-drawing powder once a week and carry for enhanced prosperity.

 Conjure Bag: Jezebel Root

Place a Jezebel root, some cubeb peppers, and one coin in a large denomination (a dollar coin, for instance) in a bag.

Conjure Bag: Lucky Sevens

1. Fill a conjure bag with seven different pieces of money; you can use coins or paper. You can use assorted national currencies. You just need seven distinct types, for instance: a penny, a nickel, a dime, a quarter, a dollar coin, a two-dollar bill, and a ten-dollar bill.
2. Sprinkle with essential oil of bergamot.
3. Carry the bag for seven days. Allegedly the contents should multiply sevenfold. (Or even seven times sevenfold!)

Conjure Bag: Lunar Blessings

Tuck moonwort into a green charm bag together with a miniature horseshoe, a lunar charm, and either a real or a charm four-leaf clover.

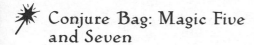

Conjure Bag: Magic Five and Seven

Place a cinnamon stick in a conjure bag together with seven Grains of Paradise and five coins.

Conjure Bag: Money Beans

Place seven distinct types of money (nickel, dime, quarter, and so on) in a mojo bag with seven distinct beans (kidney, lima, black-eyed pea, etc.). Write your financial desire onto a bit of brown paper, anoint it with **Magnet Oil** and add it to the bag. Carry the charm until your desire has been fulfilled.

Conjure Bag: Seven Coins

Place seven coins in a charm bag, together with violet leaves and a pinch of five-finger grass (cinquefoil), to generate wealth.

Conjure Bag: Skunk Cabbage

Blend skunk cabbage with bay laurel leaves to stimulate an influx of wealth.

Conjure Bag: Smart Ass Mojo

1. Write the amount of money you need on a piece of paper.
2. Anoint it with essential oil of bergamot and/or **Magnet Oil** and place it in a conjure bag.
3. Add magnetic horseshoes plus lodestones plus some smartweed, also known as *"water pepper"* or *"smart ass."*
4. Feed the bag by sprinkling it with magnetic sand every third day until the money needed is received.

Magnetic sand is sold dyed in inspirational colors. Use gold and/or green (the colors to attract money) to enhance the spell.

Creole Anti-poverty Spell

1. Combine the following ingredients in a bowl: a cup of white sugar, a cup of salt, and a cup of raw white rice.
2. Open a safety pin and stick it into the bowl.
3. Leave it out in full view.

Dragon Spell

The dragon is the traditional guardian of wealth and treasure. Unlike Western stories that paint dragons as hoarding, mean-spirited creatures, East Asian dragons are benevolent and generous. Instead of killing the dragon, the desire is to make an alliance with the dragon, to harness its power to improve one's own quality of life. A dragon can't watch out for wealth with its eyes closed. A Chinese ritual seeks to open the dragon's eyes, in order to activate its energy in your life.

1. You will need a porcelain dragon statue. These are sold in Chinatown. You may also be able to purchase one from companies that promote porcelain-painting parties.
2. The Dragon Hour is between 7 a.m. and 9 a.m. Open the dragon's eyes at this time by dotting the eyes with a new brush and black ink.

Two-dimensional dragons (prints, posters, paintings) should have open eyes in order to promote positive dragon energy. If they are closed or averted, use an incense stick to ritually activate the eyes.

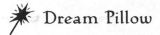
Dream Pillow

Dress dried basil, dried chamomile blossoms, and dried fenugreek with a few drops of essential oils of basil and bergamot. When the botanicals are thoroughly dry, use them as the filling for a dream pillow to inspire financially intuitive and lucrative dreams.

Fenugreek Spells

Fenugreek is known as the plant of increase. It stimulates growth of all kinds. It's used in fertility spells, in spells to enhance the size of one's bust, and in spells to enhance the size of one's bank account, too. Fenugreek provides wealth and protects against poverty.

Fenugreek Spell (1)

1. Place some fenugreek seeds in a jar.
2. Every day add a few more.
3. When the jar is full, bury in Earth and start all over again.

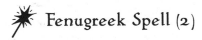
Fenugreek Spell (2)

Scatter fenugreek seeds discreetly around your house and property.

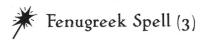
Fenugreek Spell (3)

Pour boiling water over fenugreek seeds to make an infusion. Strain the seeds out and use the liquid in the rinse water used for cleaning your floors.

Fern Seed Money Spell

Fern seed allegedly has a magically beneficial effect on one's finances. These aren't the kind of seeds you can buy in a packet, however. Gather ferns and look for the spores that are commonly called seeds. Gently remove them by scraping them off the leaves. Slip them into a sachet and carry for good fortune.

Ginger Root Spell

Sprinkle dried powdered ginger in your pocket or purse to increase your finances.

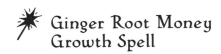
Ginger Root Money Growth Spell

Bury whole ginger roots in Earth to draw money towards you. For added intensification, arrange in auspicious patterns, such as a pentacle or diamond.

Golden Magnet Spell

According to the ancient Scandinavians, a tiny piece of gold serves as a magnet for increased wealth. Carry a real gold coin or a small charm in an amulet bag to generate greater wealth.

The Goose is Cooked Spell

September 29th is the feast of Michael the Archangel—Michaelmas. Allegedly if you eat goose on this day you will not lack money during the forthcoming year.

Green Ribbon Spell

1. Visualize what you need.
2. Verbalize this aloud, in clear, precise, unambiguous language.
3. Make nine knots in a green silk ribbon. As you form each knot, repeat your invocation.
4. Keep the cord in a safe place: a conjure bag, inside a magic money-box filled with wealth-drawing charms, or buried in Earth.

Green Tourmaline Money Magnet

Carry or wear green tourmaline to attract cash.

Grow Some Cash Spell

Plant coins in a pot filled with dirt. (Crossroads dirt is most potent.) Reinforce the spell by adding money-drawing plants to the pot. Ideally this should stimulate your other money to grow.

Grow Some Cash Spell: Acorn

Bury an acorn during a Dark Moon night to receive an infusion of money quickly. (This is also allegedly beneficial if waiting for debts to be repaid.)

Grow Some Cash Spell: Flaxseed

1. Place a pinch of flaxseed in a jar with a few coins.
2. Repeat daily, adding another pinch of flaxseed and a few more coins.
3. Keep the jar on an altar or in the kitchen.
4. When the jar is full, bury the filled jar on your property and begin again.

Grow Some Cash Spell: Gold

1. Bury something golden. It doesn't have to be real gold; try a piece of fool's gold or feng shui replica gold ingots.
2. Add three drops of menstrual blood or prick your smallest finger and allow three drops of blood to fall.
3. Plant green leafy plants, money plants, on top like basil, cabbage, or lettuce.

Grow Some More Cash Spell

In the autumn, bury hollyhock seeds together with four coins: one old, one brand new, one of silver, and one of copper. By the spring, you should see an increase in wealth.

Has No Hanna Money Spell

*Add a drop of essential oil of bergamot to **Has No Hanna** condition oil. Anoint your wallet with this oil daily so that it will never be empty.*

High John the Conqueror Spell (1)

1. Rub a cash bill with essential oil of basil and/or **Magnet Oil.**
2. Wrap the bill around a High John the Conqueror root, rolling toward you.
3. Knot it shut with green and/or red thread.

Carry this with you as a charm, or place it discreetly near the entrance to your home or business, or even inside the cash register or near your ledgers.

Activate the charm by dressing with more basil oil as needed.

High John the Conqueror Spell (2)

1. Wrap a High John root and a May apple root in a cash bill, rolling it toward you.
2. Knot it tight with red thread.
3. Place this in a charm bag and carry it with you.

 ## High John Incense Spell

In trying financial times, burn some High John the Conqueror incense daily.

 ## Hildegard's Magical Money Tip

Hildegard of Bingen recommended carrying a slice of horseradish in your purse on New Year's Eve. This prevents you running out of money in the brand new year.

 ## Horseshoe Spell (1)

1. Wrap a horseshoe with green thread, binding and knotting your desires and intentions.
2. Decorate this horseshoe with images, amulets, beads, and small packets of herbs such as dried basil, High John chips or fenugreek seeds.
3. Hang it up to bring good fortune.

 ## Horseshoe Spell (2)

1. Dip a horseshoe in **Magnet Oil** and then in magnetic sand, so that both sides are coated.
2. Gently shake off the excess. Let it dry.
3. Wrap the shoe with green or gold thread.
4. Decorate with lucky charms, as and if desired.

 ## Hungarian Family Full of Cash Spell

When you receive a substantial amount of cash, especially when it is unexpected, spit on it. The Hungarian invocation, "Ápàd, Ányàd, idejöjon!" literally translates to "Daddy, Mommy, come here quick!" Adapt so that it sounds natural to you. This invites the money to invite even more money to feel welcome in your hands.

 ## Incense: Money Drawing

Blend one part benzoin powder to two parts ground cinnamon. Place it on lit charcoal and waft the fragrance through the house.

 ## Incense: Wealth

1. Combine brown sugar, ground cinnamon, and ground coffee.
2. Add powdered (confectioner's) sugar, carnation petals, garlic chives, and cherry blossoms if possible. If cherry blossoms are unavailable, try apple blossoms or the blossoms of any flowering fruit tree. Omit if they are impossible to find.
3. Grind all the ingredients together.
4. Burn it outside the front door of your home or business to attract wealth.
5. Leave the ashes alone for 24 hours to radiate their power, then dispose of them in woods or in living, running water.

Jet Spell

Not an airplane but the fossilized wood. Jet stabilizes finances. Wear it or carry it. Be cautious: much of what is sold as jet is really plastic. You should be able to pierce true jet with a needle.

Jezebel Root Spell (1)

*Carry a Jezebel root to attract men with money. The root should be sufficient by itself, however just to be sure anoint with a drop of **Follow Me Boy! Oil**.*

 ## Jezebel Root Spell (2)

*Anoint a Jezebel root with a drop of **High John the Conqueror** and/or **Martha the Dominator Oil**. Carry it with you to induce others to be generous with you.*

 ## Kitchen Money Magic

Trying to cast a discreet money spell? Jezebel root, dragon's blood, frankincense, and five-finger grass may be reasonably conspicuous. They're not exactly standard household items, at least not in most standard households. Never fear. Some of the most powerful money-drawing plants are innocuous culinary herbs, perfect for subtle kitchen magic for those witches still in the broom closet.

Finely chop fresh basil, dill, and/or parsley. Whisper and murmur your desires over them. Sprinkle onto food as a magical garnish.

 ## Knot Money Spell

1. Comb or brush your hair.
2. Visualize the money that you need. Remember as long as you're visualizing, visualize big.
3. When nine strands of hair have been caught in your comb or brush, stop brushing.
4. Start chanting: *"I need* [amount]. *Please bring me* [amount]." Be specific.
5. As you're chanting, rub the strands of hair between your palms, forming a string.
6. When you've created a long chord of hair, tie nine knots in it, moving from the left to the right.

7. Visualize the money in your hand as you hold the hair. Visualize your debts paid, your purpose fulfilled.
8. When you're ready, either bury the hair in Earth or burn it.

 ## Lodestone Spell (1)

1. Place a male and female lodestone inside a covered container. Do not use a plastic container.
2. Cover the lodestones with magnetic sand. Add various coins. Then cover this with gold, silver, and copper glitter powder.
3. Write the quantity of money you desire on a small slip of paper, fortune-cookie fortune size, and insert it into the pile of sand and glitter.
4. Remove the paper when your goal has been achieved.
5. Dispose of all the items except the coins and lodestones. Whatever clings to the lodestone may remain also, there's no need to pick off all the magnetic sand, for instance.
6. Soak the lodestones in red wine overnight.
7. Drain them in the morning, and sprinkle them with a little magnetic sand.
8. Place them in a magic box together with the coins used in the spell. Reserve for further use.

 ## Lodestone Spell (2)

Sprinkle gold magnetic sand over a matched pair of green lodestones. Place them in a red flannel bag with a dollar bill and a piece of silver pyrite.

Lodestone Spell (3)

1. Place lodestones in a jar and cover them with magnetic sand.
2. Add coins, then seal the jar shut.
3. Leave the coins in overnight or for a few days to magically charge them up.
4. Then add them to a charm bag together with tonka beans. Sprinkle them with magnetic sand.
5. Feed the lodestone well before repeating this spell. (See *Elements of Magic Spells*, page 44, for instructions.)

 ## Low John the Conqueror Spell

1. Put a whole Low John root (Bethroot) inside a bowl. Pray, beg, and visualize over it.
2. Then put the bowl with the root inside a dark space. (A corner of a closet, tucked away to the back of a drawer or cabinet.)
3. You should soon observe an improvement in your finances. As long as you do, feed the root by adding a penny to the bowl daily.

Lucky Buddha Spells

The East Asian deity Hotei conflates a Chinese prosperity spirit with the Buddha. Unlike austere, ascetic Indian Buddhas, Hotei is fat and happy. He's the patron of fortune-tellers, ensuring that they make a living. However, anyone may invoke him for money. Allegedly his large stomach contains his ample moneybags.

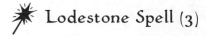 ## Lucky Buddha Spell (1)

Choose an image of Hotei, also known as the Laughing Buddha, that pleases you. His naked stomach should be exposed. Rub his tummy daily for prosperity, luck, and happiness.

 ## Lucky Buddha Spell (2)

Candles are marketed in the shape of the Laughing Buddha.

1. Write your request or the quantity of money needed on a piece of paper.
2. Slip the paper into a red Lucky Money envelope.
3. Put the envelope beneath a green Laughing Buddha (Hotei) candle and burn it.

 ## Lucky Cat Candle Spell

Lucky Cat candles are used to beckon wealth.

Carve a green or black cat candle with your name, goals, and identifying information. Dress the candle with Money Drawing Oil and burn.

 ## Lucky Money Envelope Spell

Red lucky money envelopes are used during the Chinese New Year to bestow cash gifts. They are used throughout the year for a variety of purposes, including magical ones. The envelope is auspicious and encourages the money contained within it to grow. They are available from feng shui suppliers and in Chinatown.

Place three cash bills of different denominations in a red lucky money envelope. Put the envelope under your doorstep or beneath the doormat to increase cash flow into the home.

 ## Lunar Money Spell

According to this Pow-Wow spell, the New Moon is a time for growth. So let's put some money in the moonlight and watch it grow. (Okay, this money isn't supposed to literally grow: it's supposed to stimulate other money to grow by proxy.)

1. Put some money on a table by the (closed) window. Be discreet: this is intended to allow your income to increase with the moon, not to invite theft.
2. At the Full Moon, remove the money.

Repeat as needed.

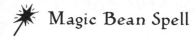

Magic Bean Spell

Magic beans that look inconsequential but are ultimately revealed to be a tremendous source of wealth are a common folk-tale motif, with "Jack and the Beanstalk" as the classic example. Sometimes fairy tales do come true.

Three yellow or golden beans are required. Murmur your desires over them; charge them with your goals. Carry them in a charm bag with a lodestone.

Magic Money Spells

Sometimes, money itself is magic. Certain, specific coins are believed to have magical properties: Maria Theresa dollars, for instance, were once treasured as amulets in Asia and Africa, coveted for their healing properties.

The spiritual home of magic money spells is China, where a complex, sophisticated system using the symbolism of cash bills and metal coins has evolved. This magic money can be used for a variety of magical purposes, in addition to generating wealth.

Coins in China were traditionally used for magic and divination as well as currency (think of the I-Ching). Implicit in this system is the concept of money as a venue of power. Spiritual interaction is obtained via burning ghost money. Magic money is obtained through actual or replica coins. Although theoretically any coins may be used for spells, certain specific coins are more powerful than others. Antique coins from prosperous periods or from successful emperors' reigns are particularly potent, but they are precious and unavailable to most people. Magic is intrinsically egalitarian: the way around this dilemma is to use cheap, replica coins. These won't work as currency but they will work to draw real money toward you, as well as for other magical purposes.

★ *Thread coins together with red string. Knot your desires and intentions in the string*
★ *Chinese coin cures are easy and inexpensive to purchase ready-made through Chinatown vendors and also through feng-shui supply merchants. Charge them with your own desire once they've been purchased*
★ *Coins may be tied together in auspicious shapes: dragons, carps, or swords*
★ *Replica coins are sold in bulk. String them together with red cord in groups of three, six, eight, nine, or eighteen*

Magic Coin Spell (1)

Place a coin amulet under a child's bed for protection and luck.

Magic Coin Spell (2)

String three coins together. Place them on or under your telephone to stimulate prosperous business.

Magic Coin Spell (3)

Place a string of coins inside your cash register, wallet, or account ledgers to stimulate cashflow.

 Magic Coin Spell (4)

String Chinese coins on red thread as a necklace to encourage the continuous, stable flow of wealth. (These metal coins are also alleged to bring good fortune to the wearer and protection from evil spirits.)

 Magic Coin Spell (5)

Magic coins may be used to activate altar images of wealth deities or any statue of a Spiritual Ally appealed to for financial aid. String nine coins onto red thread and hang them around the deity's neck for seven, fourteen, or twenty-one days.

 Magic Coin Spell (6)

Tie nine coins from the reigns of nine different emperors together. For maximum effectiveness, you want coins deriving from emperors with prosperous reigns! Hang them on the wall behind you at work or in your office to stimulate financial success.

 Magic Coin Spell (7)

Sword amulets are formed from Chinese coins, linked with red thread. Hang one near your desk or in the corners of a room to cut through financial problems.

 Magic Coin Spell (8)

Find a coin from the year of your birth, in any national currency. The year is what is crucial. Dress and feed it, and keep in charm bag or money-bag.

 Magic Coin Spell (9)

This spell is most effective if you're genuinely worried about your finances.

1. Place coins (real or reproduction) in a charm bag or new beaded change purse. (If using a change purse, don't carry any other money or anything else in it until the spell is complete.)
2. Carry with you for seven days, sleeping with it at night.
3. When the seven days are complete, journey to a crossroads.
4. Open the bag and whirl around sunwise, scattering the coins in all directions.
5. Leave them where they lie. Invoke them to grow and follow you home.
6. Retrace your footsteps home.

Magic Money comes in the form of cash bills, too. Corresponding with magical replica coins, Chinese magic has an elaborate system of paper currency, drawn on the Bank of Hell.

 Magic Money Paper
Currency Spell (1)

This magic money is also known as Spirit Money because its original usage was to provide financial support for ancestors in the spirit realm. Sometimes the ancestors need a reminder that you need some financial support and inspiration, too. Burn Spirit Money to encourage ancestral and other spirits to fulfill your needs.

 Magic Money Paper
Currency Spell (2)

Write yourself a check as a concrete visualization of future success. Use a Bank of Hell checkbook or your

own real checkbook. For added enhancement, dab Money Drawing Oil on the corners of the check, then carry it in your wallet or keep it safe in a magic money spell box.

✴ Magic Money Paper Currency Spell (3)

This spell requires a single cash bill in the largest denomination possible for you. Dip a clove into cinnamon oil and trace symbols of bounty onto the bill (runes, overflowing cornucopia, the cup that runneth over, however you're inspired). Hang this bill on the wall to generate increased wealth.

✴ Magic Money Paper Currency Spell (3)

Perhaps it's impractical to use a real bill; you'd rather spend it.

1. Create your own currency. Don't just stick a high number on a green rectangle; design magic money that will radiate its own power.
2. Choose your color; choose your symbols. If you can't draw, trace the symbols or create a collage. Focus upon your desires, goals, and needs as you create this "cash bill."
3. Your bill is your spell; if you've put energy into it, it will radiate power all its own. Hang it on the wall in plain sight to draw wealth and prosperity toward you.

✴ Magic Money Bottle

1. Empower a jar or bottle by passing it through your choice of money-drawing incense.
2. Sprinkle magnetic sand or money-drawing powder into the bottle.

3. Add a minimum of one coin daily, as little as a single penny, so that your finances will prosper.
4. Do not remove the coins from the bottle or the spell will be broken.
5. Once the jar is so full, no more can be added, remove one coin.
6. Begin a new bottle from Step 1, incorporating the single removed coin as a magical "starter," sort of like a sour-dough starter.
7. Either spend the entire contents of the previous bottle on something that gives pleasure or bury the bottle with its coins.

✴ Magic Money Box

Magic money spell boxes are used to attract and secure money. Ideally use an iron box, for security of all kinds. Magic money spell boxes are a spell in progress. Play and work with them; use them for visualization, don't just keep them under the bed or on the shelf.

Place money-drawing materials in the box, and spare cash, too, to encourage it to reproduce and return.

✴ Mandrake Money Spell

Allegedly money (particularly metal coins) placed beside a true mandrake root will double or even increase exponentially. A symbolic number of coins may be chosen; leave coins and root together overnight, ideally exposed to moonlight. Magic is accomplished metaphorically. Expect to see results reflected in general prosperity or a significant upturn in cash in-flow, rather than a literal increase in the actual coins used!

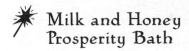

Milk and Honey Prosperity Bath

Add the following ingredients to a tub filled with warm water:

One cup of coconut milk
One cup of cow's milk
One cup of goat's milk
One cup of sheep's milk
One cup of **Holy Water** or charged water
One cup of honey (clover honey, if possible)
(If you have access to mother's milk, throw in a cup of that, too)

The key to this spell is to keep all proportions equal, although you may increase the quantities if you desire a truly luxurious bath. For extra enhancement, float five fresh basil leaves in the tub, too.

Money Charm Spell

According to Romany metaphysical tradition, to unexpectedly see a yellow ribbon or flower, especially if floating on water, indicates financial opportunities. Grab it and pick it up! Make a wish, and preserve the ribbon or flower and carry as an amulet.

Money Dolls

Despite the stereotypical "voodoo doll," dolls are most frequently used in spells as magical helpers of one sort or another. Fertility dolls magically help increase reproductive capacity; healing dolls magically restore health and well being. Money dolls magically generate wealth and financial inspiration.

1. Cut out the shape you desire from green flannel: the doll could be a person, an elephant, a leprechaun, mermaid, or whatever you envision.

2. Stuff it with dillweed and Irish moss, then sew it up and embellish it as desired.
3. Talk to the doll; tell it your troubles and request advice before you go to sleep. Pay attention to your dreams.

Doll Spell: Elaborate

Form a small doll from a square of green fabric.

1. Cut out an outline of the doll.
2. Sew it up with green and gold thread, leaving a space to stuff the doll.
3. Make the stuffing from comfrey, king fern and King's root. You can also stuff with Spirit Money.
4. Write a note on a little piece of butcher's paper: something like, *"I require_____ [amount] plus some extra. I need this immediately to meet my needs."*
5. Stick it inside the doll.
6. Use a money oil to dress the doll, or **Fast Luck Oil** if you're really in a hurry.
7. Wrap up the doll in green cloth.
8. Anoint the doll with oil daily until your need has been fulfilled, then burn the doll.
9. Repeat from scratch as needed.

Corn Husk Doll Money Spell

Start this spell at the New Moon.

1. Make a doll from dried corn husks, tying her with green yarn and sticking a cash bill within.
2. Visualize her pregnant with riches.
3. Wrap the doll in velvet and hide her in a safe, dark place so that the money can germinate and grow.
4. When the Full Moon arrives, burn the doll accompanied by prayers, petitions and incantations that the money she's incubated should materialize in your hands.

Money Garden

Plant some or all of the following in your garden or around the perimeter of your home to stimulate new wealth, preserve what you've acquired, and generate more: alfalfa, basil, camellia, chamomile, cinquefoil, dill, heliotrope, honeysuckle, jade plant, jasmine, lettuce, marigolds, mints, morning glories, nasturtium, onion, Oregon grape, parsley, or poppies. If you have little or no property, window boxes and potted plants also send out a financial appeal to the benevolent powers of the universe.

 ## Money Growth Spell

According to the old saying, money begets more money. Place two cash bills side by side in a box with a lode-stone in between them. Sprinkle magnetic sand over everything. Tell the money to reproduce and keep the box under your bed, feeding the lodestone on a regular schedule.

 ## Money Incense (1) Dry

Grind and powder cinnamon, cloves, nutmeg, and lemon zest. Sprinkle on lit charcoal and burn.

 ## Money Incense (2) Wet

1. Fill a pot or cauldron with wine or cider.
2. Add cinnamon sticks, cloves, whole nutmeg and strips of lemon zest.
3. Bring the pot to a simmer and waft the fragrance through the home to invite prosperity.

 ## Money Incense (3) Aromatic

Bruise and crush allspice and juniper berries. Burn them to draw money into your hands.

 ## Money Magnet Spell

1. Anoint a horseshoe with **Magnet Oil.**
2. Hold it in your hands, focus on your desire and make a wish.
3. Still holding the horseshoe chant something like,
   I attract money like a magnet
   I attract wealth like a magnet
   I attract prosperity like a magnet.
   I am a money magnet
   I am a wealth magnet.
   I am a prosperity magnet.
4. Sprinkle with blended magnetic sand and Money Drawing Powder.
5. Wrap it in fabric and put it beneath your pillow.
6. Pay attention to your dreams for financial inspiration and insight.

 ## Money Miracle Mantra

1. Start your day with this mantra: *"A money miracle happens to me today."*
2. Repeat throughout the day. Miracles come in many forms and sizes; accept each miracle as it arrives, large or small.
3. Always state the mantra in the present tense.
4. You'll know when you no longer need it because you'll discover that you've stopped chanting it.

 ## Money Mojo (1)

Slice and dry kumquats, tangerines, or oranges. Add them to a green bag together with nasturtium flowers and dried pineapple peel.

 ## Money Mojo (2)

Place cedar chips, some oakmoss and a real four-leaf clover or replica charm in a red or green charm bag.

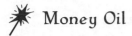 Money Oil

Add powdered bayberry and oakmoss to sweet almond oil. Add bits of gold foil or leaf, available from Indian grocers or art supply stores. Rub between your hands as needed or use to dress candles.

 Money Plant Spell

1. Purchase a small plant for your desk. A jade plant or a kalanchoe is ideal.
2. Gently rub prosperity or luck-drawing oil on the leaves.
3. Re-anoint with this oil once a month. Remember to offer libations as needed, especially when the plant seems to be working on your behalf.

Money Powders

Use these powders to create a path for wealth to follow to your door.

★ *Sprinkle them over your checkbooks and ledgers, into your pockets and wallets*
★ *Sprinkle them inside and outside your home*
★ *Sprinkle on your hands*
★ *Sprinkle on candles*

 Money Drawing Powder (1)

Grind and powder the following:

Calendula blossoms
Chamomile blossoms
Cinnamon
Cloves
Cinquefoil (five-finger grass)
Ginger
Nutmeg

 Money Drawing Powder (2)

Pulverize, grind and powder a single cash bill. Blend it with dried chamomile blossoms, heliotrope and magnetic sand.

 Money Drawing Powder Spell (3)

Grind and powder dried parsley, dill, and basil. Sprinkle as needed over wallets, checkbooks, cash registers, candles, etc.

 Money Drawing Powder Spell (4)

Grind and powder cinnamon, cloves, and sarsaparilla. Sprinkle the powder throughout your home concentrating in the corners.

 Money Drawing Powder (5)
Jyoti Powder

*Sprinkle **Jyoti Powder** on your cash so that it will grow and return to you.*

 Prosperity Powder

Grind and powder the following:

Allspice
Cinnamon
Myrrh
Orange zest
Orrisroot
Patchouli
Vetiver

Make a circle of powder around a green candle and burn.

Money Protection Spell

Cut a sweet flag (calamus) root into pieces. Hide one piece in each corner of the kitchen to guard against hunger and poverty.

 ## Mummy Money Candle Spell

Mummy candles, easily available from vendors of spiritual supplies, derive their image from B-movies rather than from any true Egyptian magic or philosophy. The mummy is understood to be the resident guardian of treasure, a mindless but devoted and protective servant of the one who commands him. Command this mummy to bring you some cash. Carve and dress a red mummy candle as desired and then burn it.

 ## My Ship Comes In Spell

A spell inspired by Chinese magic. If you're sick of waiting for your ship to come in, speed its arrival by creating a role model. This spell also works well in conjunction with appeals to Spirits of the Sea and those with sympathy for "poor sailors": Kwan Yin, Mazu, Lord Agwe and La Sirene, Aphrodite, and Poseidon.

1. Stuff a model boat with *"treasure."* Fill it with imitation gold ingots from Chinatown, actual coins, replica coins, glass gems, sparkling beads, and crystals.
2. Strategically arrange the boat so that it's easy to visualize your ship arriving at home port. One thing is crucial: the boat must sail toward you, never away from you!
3. Intensify the effect with candle burning and money-drawing incense.
4. Place a Rider-Waite three of wands Tarot card onto the boat, which shows the ship of good fortune arriving.

 ## Nest Egg Spell

1. Write the amount you need or an explicit financial desire onto a tiny slip of paper.
2. Carefully snip off the end of a whole, raw egg. This may take a little practice: the rest of the shell should remain whole but it doesn't have to be absolutely perfect.
3. Carefully clean out the eggshell.
4. Insert the paper and some finely ground, powdered parsley.
5. Seal the hole in the egg with a little melted green candle wax.
6. Bury the egg in Earth so that your fortunes will grow.

 ## Never Empty Wallet Spell

Keep a bay laurel leaf in your wallet to magically protect against poverty.

 ## New Moon Money Spell

Upon first catching sight of the New Moon, immediately jingle any coins in your pocket to receive an increase in wealth.

 ## Pennies from Heaven

A doorstep message is usually associated with hexes; sometimes, however, it's used for positive intent. Leave coins (spare change, replica coins) on different doorsteps in the magical belief that whatever you put forth will return to you two-, three- or seven-fold.

Pomander Money Spell

Pomanders were originally created as enchantments. They're especially associated with healing spells but also serve other magical purposes, such as financial growth.

1. Instead of pricking the citrus fruit all over with holes, prick out a financial shape: prosperity runes, a dollar sign, a cornucopia, a big *"M"* for money, or anything that symbolizes wealth to you.
2. Stick cloves into each hole, making an affirmation with each one.
3. Roll the pomander in blended powdered orrisroot, parsley and either gold magnetic sand or gold glitter dust.
4. Tie a green ribbon onto the pomander and hang it up to radiate its power.

 ## Poppy Spell

Place a dry poppy head in the window as a charm to draw money toward you.

 ## Rattlesnake Root Money Spell

Make an infusion by pouring boiling water over rattlesnake root. Allow it to cool, strain out the botanical material and bottle the liquid. Rub it on your hands to receive money, and on your feet to walk toward wealth.

 ## Red Paper Money Spell

1. Write the amount that you need in gold ink on red paper.
2. Fold the paper into a square and carry it in your pocket, bra or conjure bag.
3. When the amount is accumulated burn the paper, together with an equivalent quantity of Spirit Money.
4. Repeat as needed.

 ## Rice Prosperity Spell

This isn't a money spell as much as a prosperity spell; it protects against poverty.

1. Cook enough rice to serve each spell participant a small bowl.
2. Stir the water sunwise, visualizing the pot always full.
3. Murmur blessings, affirmations and sacred verses over the rice and then eat it.

 ## Rose of Jericho Spell

1. Place a desiccated Rose of Jericho in spring water to coincide with the New Moon.
2. Watch it unfold, accompanied by prayers, petitions, and other money rituals. (Although many sources claim a Rose of Jericho will blossom overnight, this may verge on the side of optimism. Don't despair if your rose resists opening for several days; it's not necessarily a portent of evil omen, although the ease with which your rose blossoms may indicate the ease with which your financial crisis will be resolved.)
3. Remove the flower from the water at the Full Moon. Let it dry out once again. Repeat as needed.

 ## Sassafras Spell

Keep a piece of sassafras bark in your wallet to stimulate prosperity and protect against poverty.

 ## Sesame Seed Spell

Keep sesame seeds in an open dish near a window to draw money closer.

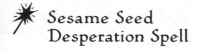 **Sesame Seed Desperation Spell**

This spell allegedly produces a fast quick fix; however, it may only be cast infrequently, not on a regular basis, so save it for emergencies.

1. Put a pinch of sesame seeds in a closed jar every day.
2. Do not remove any unless *very* badly in need of a cash infusion.
3. In moments of desperation, remove a pinch of seeds with your left hand.
4. Spit on them, while concentrating on your dilemma and then immediately toss them onto Earth.

 Seven-Eleven Money Spell

1. Carve your desires into a black or green cat candle.
2. Dress it with money-drawing oil, and sprinkle it with gold, green, red, and/or purple glitter.
3. If you need a specific amount of cash, write your request on a slip of paper and place it under the cat.
4. Light the candle for seven minutes the first night, eleven the second, seven the third, and so on, alternating between lucky numbers seven and eleven until the amount is received.
5. If the candle burns down completely without receipt of the funds, this too is an answer: the whole situation needs to be reconsidered as well as new alternatives.

 Shi Shi Oil

This classic Hoodoo condition oil allegedly attracts wealth to its wearer fast! Try it and see.

1. Chop, grind and powder the following ingredients: angelica root, bay laurel leaves, and cloves.
2. Add them to jojoba oil.
3. Rub a drop between the palms of your hands.

4. Dab a drop onto your hair or behind your ears.
5. Soak a cotton ball in Shi Shi and carry it in your pocket or tucked into your bra.

 Shi Shi Oil Conjure Bag

Grind cinnamon and cloves and add it to Money Drawing Powder, and place this in a red bag with a High John the Conqueror Root. Anoint with Shi Shi Oil for fast results.

Spiritual Financial Aid Spells

Some of the most effective spells aim to put the task in stronger, more capable hands. As befitting a major topic, there are a host of spiritual patrons of wealth. Request some financial aid.

 Spiritual Financial Aid Spell (1) Maitresse Ezili's Bath

This bath is considered a petition to the lwa Maitresse Ezili. Before taking the bath, offer her candles. Afterwards bestow a gift (perfume, pastry, jewelry). Demonstrate the generosity that you'd like her to express towards you.

*Create an infusion by pouring boiling water over basil, sweet flag (calamus), and allspice berries. Add this infusion to your bath together with **Florida Water**.*

 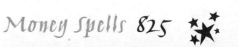

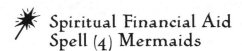

Spiritual Financial Aid Spell (2) Mami Waters

Talk of spirits usually revolves around ancient, primordial ones. Mami Waters' roots may be ancient but her rise to prominence is relatively recent. While other traditional spirits find themselves under siege with devotees pressured to convert to Christianity or Islam, Mami Waters' popularity grows exponentially. A snake-charming mermaid spirit with magical connections to crocodiles, Mami Waters first emerged from the lakes of West and Central Africa. She traveled to Africa's urban centers where she gained tremendous popularity, and then proceeded to journey all over Earth, gaining devotees everywhere. Mami Waters now has shrines in New Orleans; because she is usually depicted with snakes, Latin American magic identifies her with dragon-charming Martha the Dominator.

Mami Waters offers her devotees wealth, prosperity, luxury, and glamour. Build Mami Waters a mermaid altar with mirrors, combs, charms, and river rocks. Decorate it with her beloved snakes and crocodiles. Mami Waters does not drink hard liquor; she prefers offerings of lemonade and cola. Burn red and white candles for her and tell her what you desire.

Spiritual Financial Aid Spell (3) Maximon

Maximon (pronounced "mah-shee-mon") is a spirit of primordial male sexual vitality and force. He enjoys the finer things of life and isn't surprised or offended that his devotees do as well. This powerful spirit will grant favors in exchange for gifts and devotion. His feast day is the Wednesday of Holy Week. Maximon may be petitioned for help with finding a spouse, with business issues or with healing, but his specialty is wealth and financial stability. His most popular votive image depicts a man in black seated at a crossroads, with a big bag of money in his lap or coins in his hands.

1. Build Maximon a home shrine or visit him at his most famous shrine at Santiago Atitlan on the shores of Lake Atitlan, Guatemala. (If he does you a really huge service, offers of pilgrimage may be in order.)
2. Maximon accepts offerings of candles, silk scarves, cigars, flowers (especially lilies and gladioli), aguardiente, rum, and incense.

Spiritual Financial Aid Spell (4) Mermaids

The sea is a traditional repository of Earth's wealth. Once upon a time, when sea-faring vessels were the only way to cross ocean boundaries, the fear of shipwreck was much greater than today. Transported treasures were forever lost at the bottom of the sea. Legends of acquisitive sea spirits arose: perhaps the shipwrecks were caused because the spirits lusted after their wealth?

At the same time, mermaids and sea spirits were acclaimed for their generosity. Because all the treasure beneath the sea was at their disposal, these spirits were able if they chose to easily help out a human in distress.

Once upon a time, every body of water, every stretch of seashore had its resident attendant spirits, who might be petitioned or beseeched. If they remain, they've gone underground: few remember their names or methods of petitions.

This spell provides an anonymous appeal to the generosity of the sea: write or draw your wishes into the sand using your fingers or a ritual staff or wand. Let the tide carry word of your desires to the spirits of the sea.

Spiritual Financial Aid Spell (5) Mermaid Treasure Bath

This works for mer-men too! Mermaids have access to the treasures of the sea. Channel their power.

1. Set up an altar to mermaids in general, if you like, or to a mermaid deity: Yemaya, Aphrodite, Oshun, Mami Waters, Ezili, La Sirene, or Atargatis.

2. Decorate the bath with crystals, basil leaves, and roses.
3. Float in the water, visualize having a fish tail. If financial inspiration arrives, it's the gift of the sea.

☀ Spiritual Financial Aid Spell (6) Mama Jo

A few of the most powerful mermaids have not retreated into anonymity but may still be petitioned by name. The West Indian mermaid Mama Jo's name is a corruption of Maman de l'Eau, *Mother of the Waters. She is famed for her loyalty and assistance. It is not necessary to travel to the Caribbean to petition Mama Jo but a trip to the local seaside would be beneficial.*

1. Bring a bouquet of flowers for Mama Jo together with an image of either of her sacred creatures—a black hen or a black goat. A rubber children's toy in either image, liberated from a toy farmyard for instance, is ideal.
2. Dig out an altar in the sand. Arrange two blue candles in the little pit and light them.
3. Place Mama Jo's animal between the candles.
4. Enter the sea, your feet at least must be in the water, and talk to Mama Jo. Explain what you need.
5. Give her the flowers, by tossing them into the sea.

☀ Spiritual Financial Aid Spell (7) Oshun

This incredibly versatile orisha may be best known as a genius of love and a matron of women's health, however she also concerns herself with her devotees' financial well being. Oshun is not unfamiliar with financial challenge. She herself endured and survived a period of devastating, brutal poverty. According to one legend, Oshun was reduced to one dress. Because she is so fastidious, she washed and scrubbed it in the river daily, until

the fabric finally turned yellow from age and wear, thus yellow becoming her color.

There are many different ways to approach this beautiful and beneficent spirit for financial assistance.

★ *Offer her honey, but remember to taste it beforehand*
★ *Spells and rituals dedicated to Oshun are most effective when performed on a Friday*
★ *Incorporate the number five and the colors on the yellow/orange/gold spectrum into your spells*

Set up an altar to Oshun to make your petition:

1. Offer spring water and honey first, remembering to taste the honey.
2. Place a dish of blended milk and honey on the altar.
3. Soak a small sweet cinnamon bun in the dish.
4. When all of the liquid has been absorbed, make a hole in the center of the bun.
5. Place a small yellow candle in the hole. (If the candle is big enough you may carve your identifying information plus the amount of money you need into the wax. If not, write it on a small slip of paper, anoint the paper with perfume and place it under or beside the candle.)
6. Light this candle in honor of Oshun and request her assistance.

☀ Spiritual Financial Aid Spell (8) Oshun's Floorwash

This adds Oshun's essence of beauty and grace to your home as well as importuning her for wealth.

1. Add one cup of river water and one cup of vinegar to a bucket of floorwash rinse water.
2. Add five drops of essential oil of cinnamon bark or a splash of cinnamon hydrosol.
3. Scrub your floor, focusing on enhanced prosperity and luck as well as Oshun's beauty and generosity.

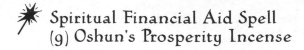

Spiritual Financial Aid Spell (9) Oshun's Prosperity Incense

1. Pound brown sugar, five dried orange leaves, and orange zest in a mortar and pestle until roughly pulverized.
2. Place in a cast iron pan and set aflame.
3. Let this burn for about a minute then smother the flames. It should smoke fairly heavily: allow the aroma to permeate the room.
4. Offer some pure spring water and honey to Oshun and tell her what you need.

Spiritual Financial Aid Spell (10) Preto Velho

Preto Velho is a spirit who embodies the soul of an elderly African-Brazilian ancestor. He is wise, generous, and compassionate and may be petitioned for guidance with meager finances or when you don't understand how to deal with a financial situation. (Preto Velho may be experienced as an individual spirit or, like fellow Afro-Brazilians Exu and Pomba Gira, as one spirit with many "paths" or aspects or even as a distinct genre of spirits.)

Preto Velho communicates most easily when petitioned outside. A tree stump is his vehicle of communication: use it as an altar or as the focal point of an altar.

1. Open a bottle of muscatel and pour a libation on or around the stump.
2. Lay down a cloth with some sort of block pattern, plaids work well as does a checkerboard motif.
3. Place the open bottle of muscatel on the cloth.
4. Give Preto Velho a gift of a new pipe and a package of pipe tobacco.
5. Light a white candle and talk to him. Explain why you've come and what you desire from him. Apologize for the meager gift but explain that if your petition is realized you will return with bigger and better gifts.

6. Leave everything at the tree stump. (In some traditions, the cloth may be taken home, in the understanding that it will be used only to communicate with Preto Velho.)
7. Should your petition be realized, return to the stump with a bottle of cognac or a fine wine, better tobacco, and a better pipe. Light a white candle to offer your thanks.

Spiritual Financial Aid Spell (11) Saint Anthony

Saint Anthony is the "bread giver," so keep a small loaf of bread in front of his image, to remind him that you need him to play this role. Keep it for seven days, then replace with a new one. Murmur your wishes over the old loaf and feed it to the birds.

The Secret of the Virtuous Horseshoe

Saint Martin of Tours, in his guise as San Martin Caballero (Saint Martin the Chevalier), brings luck and money. This fourth-century Hungarian was pressed into service in the Roman army but quit to assist the poor. Another miracle-working saint, akin to Saints Anthony and Martha, Martin Caballero is the magical patron of those who are dependent on the kindness of strangers.

"The Secret of the Virtuous Horseshoe," dedicated to San Martin Caballero, is a popular Latin American spell. (Although its more common use is in money drawing spells, the Virtuous Horseshoe has another guise as a relocation spell.) One may purchase it already made and then simply utter the incantation to activate the spell, however it's easily created for oneself and more powerful that way.

1. Wrap a horseshoe in red silk thread until only the very tips are exposed.

2. Attach the horseshoe to a square of cardboard with the horseshoe turned points down.
3. Decorate horseshoe and cardboard with sequins, glitter glue, and votive images of San Martin Caballero. Maintain your mental focus on your longing for financial stability and prosperity.
4. When the physical aspect of the spell is complete, activate it by repeating the following incantation, reminiscent of the nine magical fruits of plenty, twenty-one times: *"Citron nueve."*

 ## Squill Root Money Spell

Squill root allegedly makes money grow. Place squill in a magic box or bottle together with some real silver. Once upon a time silver coins were recommended and squill allegedly doubled their value. Modern silver coins are frequently only silver colored; the spell offers more than the literal face value of the coins.

Silver magically activates squill's money-drawing powers. Use real silver coins if you have them, however a stash of small silver beads may work best. Add one to the box or bottle daily while making affirmations of prosperity. Allegedly dramatic improvements in your general financial state will follow.

 ## Steady Growth Money Spell

Place Irish moss (carrageen) beneath the rug to ensure a steady flow of money into the house, and to protect against poverty.

There are many money talismans around. Among the best are the gemstones ruby and sapphire.

 ## Talisman (1) Ruby

Wear a ruby set in gold on the index or ring finger to attract wealth to the wearer. Begin wearing it on a Sunday.

 ## Talisman (2) Ruby Enhanced

Wear or carry a ruby engraved with the image of a snake or dragon to generate and increase wealth. Again, begin wearing it on a Sunday.

 ## Talisman (3) Sapphire

This magic ring allegedly restores lost wealth or property and significantly improves the financial status of the wearer. However, in some European traditions, sapphire is believed to cause fluctuations in its wearer's fortunes. It impacts some people positively but others not so. See where you stand by wearing it for seven days.

Set a sapphire in a ring crafted from a white colored metal, such as platinum, white gold, or steel. Wear it on a middle finger.

Treasure Chest Spell

1. Make your own treasure chest: you'll need a small box—an old-fashioned cigar box is perfect, or something similar.
2. Cover the outside of the box with gold paper or Chinese joss paper. (Many varieties of joss have gold foil attached; this is also ideal.)
3. Fill the box with money. If you can afford to put twelve real bills in the box, do so. If not, fill it with Chinese Spirit Money, drawn from the Bank of Hell. If you can't get Spirit Money, use Monopoly™ or other board-game money, or design your own magic money.
4. Sprinkle the money in the box with basil, marjoram, henna powder, and essential oil of bergamot.
5. Light a green money candle: plain, cat or devil.
6. Close the box. Tie it with green yarn, making 31 knots to close it, visualize and petition with each knot.
7. Seal it with some melted wax from the green candle.
8. Bury it in Earth between the autumn equinox and Halloween. (Bury it in a pot if necessary and keep it indoors.)
9. Plant basil, marjoram, or thyme.
10. Leave it alone until at least spring. Legend has it that when you dig it up again the fake money will have been converted to real money, or the real money will have increased. However, the purpose of the spell is to generate more money in your life in general.

Treasure Hunter's Spell (1)

A talisman for treasure hunters:

1. Take a real silver coin or a small piece of silver.
2. Dress it with real bayberry oil, not the synthetic fragrance oil, and/or essential oil of bergamot.
3. At the New Moon, as you go to sleep, place the coin on your forehead or between your breasts. It's best if you can keep it there all night, but at least keep it balanced for a minimum of half an hour.

4. Do this nightly until the Full Moon.
5. Then wrap it entirely in strands of your hair.
6. Place it in a green mojo bag or lucky money-box to draw money toward you and to help you locate hidden treasure.

Treasure Hunter's Spell (2)
Broken Scythe

Should a scythe break while harvesting herbs on Saint John's Eve, the herb on which it breaks is identified as a magical plant. It can be any type of plant; the clue comes in its ability to break the scythe.

Gently remove and dry the entire plant. It can be used to magically identify, locate and discover treasure. (Exactly how it will do this is undetermined; carry it with you while treasure hunting, it will spontaneously do something to identify the treasure.)

Treasure Hunter's Spell (3)
Divining Wand (1)

Cut a divining rod from witch hazel to help locate treasure. This will be most powerful if created on Midsummer's Eve.

Treasure Hunter's Spell (4)
Divining Wand (2)

Although some swear by witch hazel, others claim mistletoe rods are what's needed to dig up treasure. Cut a divining rod from mistletoe wood on Midsummer's Eve in order to discover treasure. Given the choice, mistletoe growing on hazel or thorn trees is believed especially effective.

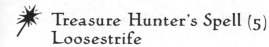 Treasure Hunter's Spell (5) Loosestrife

Dig up purple loosestrife on Midsummer's/Saint John's Day without using any iron tools.

Clean and dry the root. Carry it with you on your treasure hunt: the root drives off those spirits that guard treasure and prevent you from discovering it.

Treasure Hunter's Spell (6) Mandrake

Among other gifts, true mandrake (not bryony or May apple, common substitutes often called mandrake) will reveal treasure.

1. Gently bathe or asperge the root with magically charged waters.
2. Wrap it in silk and care for it.
3. Hold the mandrake root in your hands to receive inspiration regarding treasure and financial fortune.

Trinka Five Spell (1) Basic

A Romany spell; old and effective.
When in need, chant the following:

Trinka Five! Trinka Five!
Ancient spirits come alive
Bring me money, bring it quick
Spirits of the Trinka Five!

Trinka Five Spell (2) Enhanced

Simply chanting "Trinka Five" may be effective, however although the chant is sufficient, it may also be accompanied by this ritual for extra power:

1. Toss coins into a cup as you chant. Either three or five coins are tossed.
2. Repeat for three, five, seven or nine days, or until you accumulate the quantity of money that you need.

 Tulip Spell

Tulip bulbs allegedly protect against poverty. Place one in a charm bag and keep safe and secure in a discreet place.

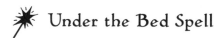 Turquoise Financial Increase Spell

The instant you first see the New Moon, look at a turquoise to receive an increase in fortune.

Under the Bed Spell

1. Fill a bowl with raw rice.
2. Stick either three or seven crystals into the ball. You may also add various Chinese wealth amulets if you like, such as the dragon-tortoise or the three-legged frog. Incorporate replica coins or gold ingots to further underscore the message of the spell.
3. Place it under your bed.

The number three represents wealth, while the number seven, combined with the dragon-tortoise, adds the element of spiritual protection to the request for wealth.

 Vervain Spell

A sprig of vervain kept in your wallet or purse acts to keep money there, too.

Vervain Money Flow Spell

Bury some vervain in the garden to ensure the steady, constant flow of money into the home.

Wealth Construction Spells

Wealth can be built into the home.

 Wealth Construction Spell: Land

Bury small gold coins on the land before beginning construction to grow prosperity and good fortune, according to Indian tradition.

 Wealth Construction Spell: Walls

Embed gold foil or wires within the walls during construction to encourage wealth to stay within the walls of the building.

 Wealth Construction Spell: Foundation

Fortuitous coins or replicas of such coins are buried in house foundations and so literally built into the home.

 Who Needs Money?

Of course, there are other alternative ways to consider finances. To acquire independence in your heart from materialism, to break the shackles of material desires, Islamic folk tradition prescribes reciting Allah's name one thousand times a day.

 Wild Hunt Money Spell

A host of spirits rides through the night several times a year. Post-Christianity, it was said that these spirits searched out souls to capture, hence the designation "wild hunt." The hunting party may be comprised entirely of fairies or it may be a wild amalgamation of spirits from assorted traditions. Among those who've lead this parade of spirits are Mother Holle, Freya, Odin, Herodias, Herta, and King Arthur. Because people are warned against the Wild Hunt, the usual recommendation is to avoid them or fall flat on your face and pray they don't notice you. This money spell however directs otherwise.

1. Fast all day on Christmas Eve then, after night falls, go to a crossroads.
2. Eventually, probably around midnight, the Wild Hunt should swoop by.
3. Stand quietly and respectfully, without fear, as they pass.
4. The last hunter should give you a coin, which will always return to you no matter how you spend it or give it away.

 Witch's Herb Spell

Yerba bruja, *the witch's herb, also known as* kalanchoe pinnata, *is a plant of many names. English nicknames include* Cathedral Bells, Never Die, *and* Mexican Love Plant. *It's known in Portuguese as* folha-da-fortuna, "leaf of fortune," *and is considered to be under the joint rulership of Yemaya and Oshun. The following spell may be dedicated to either or both of them. Yerba bruja is used to drum up money.*

1. Bury a coin in a flowerpot filled with soil.
2. Tuck a lodestone in near it, then transplant a cutting of yerba bruja or a small plant. The roots will draw on the financial energy of the coin and draw money for you.

3. For extra enhancement, use a real silver coin or a lucky Chinese coin.

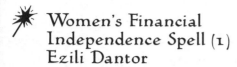

Women's Financial Independence Spell (1) Ezili Dantor

The lwa Ezili Dantor may be Ezili Freda Dahomey's alter ego. She may also be her bitter enemy or a completely unrelated, neutral spirit! Her nature in any case is very different from that of Maitresse Ezili. Ezili Dantor is a strong, working woman, a single mother who single-handedly supports her adored daughter Anais. She will help with child support and custody issues. She will also help you become financially independent so that you do not need assistance.

1. Create a shrine for Ezili Dantor. Various images are used to represent her, including the Espiritismo figure of La Madama, Matron of Fortune-tellers, as well as chromolithographs of various Black Madonna's, particularly those whose faces display scars.
2. Offer Ezili Dantor **Florida Water,** strong rum, and flowers.
3. Light red and black candles (or red and black double-action candles) and tell her the secret desires of your heart.

Women's Financial Independence Spell (2) Mary Magdalene

There's much confusion, speculation, and passionate debate regarding Mary Magdalene. Exactly who was she? Was Mary Magdalene also Mary of Bethany? Was she a prostitute? Was she a sacred prostitute? Was she Christ's wife and the mother of his daughter? (Another version suggests that they had three children, two boys and a girl, although interestingly it's always the daughter who is of spiritual significance.)

One thing alone is certain: Mary Magdalene was a woman of independent means. She is the only woman mentioned in the saga of Christ's life who is not identified as someone's wife, daughter, or mother. Petition her for independent means, too. To encourage a woman's financial independence, build a shrine to Mary Magdalene. This may be done at any time, however her feast day is July 22nd.

1. Burn white candles.
2. Offer Mary Magdalene myrrh and spikenard, and a glass of Galilean or French wine.

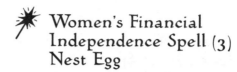

Women's Financial Independence Spell (3) Nest Egg

Build a magic nest egg. This spell is intended to create and protect a woman's financial security. The traditional spell requires an abandoned bird's nest, not difficult for rural dwellers but highly unlikely for anyone else. Craft a replica from twigs.

1. Dress a small green candle with **Jezebel Oil** and burn it.
2. Roll the melted wax into an egg shape.
3. Push a bit of Jezebel Root within the egg together with a penny.
4. Put the egg inside the nest and sprinkle it with magnetic sand.
5. Bury the nest egg at the crossroads for financial increase, security, and independence.

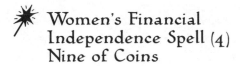

Women's Financial Independence Spell (4) Nine of Coins

The nine of coins or nine of pentacles represents the woman of independent means.

1. Remove the nine of coins card from a deck of Tarot cards.
2. Light a green candle.
3. Put the card in front of it. Consider the card.
4. Enter the card and speak with it while the candle burns.

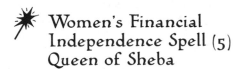

Women's Financial Independence Spell (5) Queen of Sheba

King Solomon earned renown for his magic powers and for his extensive harem. Solomon had many wives, including a pharaoh's daughter. However the woman he allegedly loved best was the Queen of Sheba. The queen of Sheba, whose name, according to Ethiopian tradition, was Makeda, was the one woman to approach Solomon as an equal: financially independent, ruler of her own kingdom, an educated woman well-versed in the magical arts, she commanded his respect as well as his heart.

*The condition oil named in her honor enhances women's financial independence, in addition to their love lives. Select a candle to represent you and carve it as desired. Dress the candle with **Queen of Sheba Oil**. Sprinkle the candle with powdered myrrh and cinnamon, and then burn it.*

Special Monetary Needs Spells

General money spells usually attempt to generate new wealth or protect and preserve already existing wealth. Sometimes magical assistance is required to smooth the transfer of money between different parties.

Spells to Receive Loans and Collect Debts

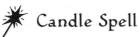

Candle Spell

1. Designate one candle to represent you, another to represent your debtor, and a third candle to represent either the money or the issue.
2. Arrange them in the shape of a triangle, with the candle representing the money at the apex.
3. Face the candles representing the people toward each other and burn them.

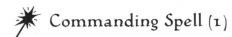

Commanding Spell (1)

1. Write the name of the debtor and the amount that you're owed on a piece of brown paper.
2. Write your name over the debtor's name, saying: *"I cover you. I cross you. Now give me back my money!"*
3. Dress brown and purple candles with **Command and Compel Oil.**
4. Place the paper beneath the candles and burn.

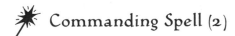

Commanding Spell (2)

1. Soak a penny or other coin in **Command and Compel Oil** for 24 hours, preferably exposed to sunlight and moonbeams.
2. Paste the coin in the center of a square white piece of paper.

3. Underneath write in **Dragon's Blood Ink** something like *"You owe me. Now pay me."*
4. Mail this to your debtor.

In theory, this is supposed to work regardless of whether you identify yourself. In reality, someone who owes you probably owes other people, too. It's very possible that without identifying yourself, you risk helping someone else's situation, rather than your own.

 ## Commanding Spell (3)

This spell encourages repayment of a debt and also allegedly stimulates a tight-fisted person to show generosity toward you.

1. You will need two human figure candles, one to represent you and one to represent the target of your spell. Use a green candle for the other person; choose red, white, or purple to represent you.
2. Carve both candles as needed.
3. Add five drops of essential oil of bergamot to **Command and Compel Oil** and use this to dress both candles. Additionally, rub the green candle with **Jezebel Oil.**
4. Write your goal or desire on a piece of brown paper. Pass this through smoke from **Command and Control Incense.**
5. Place this paper under the green candle.
6. Put a pin through the hand you perceive as the receiving hand of your image candle.
7. Put a pin through the giving hand of the other person's image. (This is typically the right hand, but personalize as needed.)
8. Light the candles.
9. Call the other person's name aloud three times. Announce firmly what you need.
10. Let the candles burn for a little while then pinch them out.
11. Repeat this for eight consecutive nights. If you receive your desire, you may stop at any time.

12. If you don't, then on the ninth and last night, remove some wax from the green candle.
13. Roll it into a ball and push a Jezebel root into the center of the wax.
14. Allow the candles to burn down. Before they do, burn the note.
15. Add the paper ashes to your wax ball.
16. Bury it on your target's property or in their path. (If this is not possible, those old stand-bys, the crossroads or the cemetery, are the next best bet.)

 ## Commanding Spell (4)

1. Place a photograph of the person who owes you money on a plate. Substitute a piece of paper with the person's name written on it if you lack a photo.
2. Sprinkle with powdered sweet flag, licorice, and bayberry.
3. Light a green candle on top of the powdered photograph and burn it. (A green devil or any other green candle may be used.)
4. Send a mental message to your debtor while the candle burns.

 ## Commanding Spell (5)

Hold a green candle to charge it with your needs and wishes. Carve it as desired; dress with commanding and money-drawing oils. Roll the candle in powdered bayberry and burn.

✴ Crown of Success Spell

How much do you need and why do you need it?

1. Elucidate exactly and precisely what you need on a piece of paper. You may write a description. You may simply write a sum of money. Cut out a picture of what you plan to buy with the money received—a Polaroid of the house you want, an advertisement for the appliance.
2. Dress a lodestone with **Crown of Success Oil** or powder.
3. Sprinkle it with alfalfa.
4. Place everything in a green or red drawstring bag.
5. Sleep with it under your pillow.
6. Carry the conjure bag with you when you request the loan.

✴ Green Devil Spell

Green candles in the shape of little devils are burned to get fast cash and to have your debts repaid.

1. Blend five, seven, or nine drops of essential oil of bergamot into **Command and Compel Oil.**
2. Carve your debtor's name, identifying information and the phrase, *"Give me my money!"* onto the candle.
3. Rub the candle with the oil, while focusing on your goal and on the injustice done to you.
4. Write the debtor's name on a square of brown paper nine times. If he or she uses multiple names, write them all.
5. Cover each name with the phrase, *"Give me my money!"*
6. Anoint the corners of the paper with a drop of **Command and Compel Oil.**
7. Put the paper beneath an upside-down saucer and place the candle on top of the saucer.
8. Light the candle. As it burns, speak to the candle, demanding the return of what is rightfully yours.

Say whatever you need to say, however there is a traditional invocation, which goes something like this:

[Target's name] *give me my money NOW!*
You owe me. I need it. Give it to me.
You can't rest until you give it to me.
You can't sleep until you give it to me.
You can't eat until you give it to me.
You can't have sex until you give it to me.
Whenever you see the color green, you think of your debt to me.
Whenever you hear the clink of metal, you think of your debt to me.
Your stomach hurts, until you give me my money.
Your head hurts, until you give me my money.
And so on and so forth. Make it as personal as possible. Deprive your target of whatever is most appropriate for that person. Make your litany as long or as short as you like, however you must end with the words: *"Give me my money or you will burn!"*

9. Remove the paper from under the saucer, scorch it in the fire and then pinch out the candle.
10. Repeat this ritual for seven consecutive nights. At some point, during this incremental candle-burning period, you must make an attempt to contact the borrower and calmly ask for the return of your money. Should even a portion of the debt be repaid at any point, consider the spell finished and conclude.
11. If, however, by the eighth day, no money is forthcoming, light the candle once more.

    Hold the paper in the flame. Allow both paper and candle to burn completely. When reciting the litany, change the last line to: *"You have my money. Now burn!"*

Green Skull Collection Spell

Enter the mind of the one who owes you money and persuade them to return it. Personalize a green skull candle by scratching your target's name and identifying information into its base. Write the exact amount owed across the skull's forehead and burn the candle.

 ## High John the Conqueror

1. Add High John the Conqueror chips into a blend of jojoba and castor oil.
2. Add ground cinnamon, dried patchouli, and gardenia blossoms.
3. Use this oil to anoint billing statements sent out to collect debts, or any similar document.

 ## Debt Spell Intimate

This spell is to be used when the person who owes you shares an intimate relationship with you.

1. Draw a bath for the other party. Discreetly add some sort of persuasive agent, such as **Command and Compel Oil,** or **Essence of Bend Over.**
2. While the other party bathes, go into another room.
3. Write your desire onto a piece of paper. Write both names, covering the other person's with your own.
4. Fold the paper and place it discreetly beneath a purple candle dressed with **Command and Compel Oil.** Burn **Command and Compel Incense,** too.
5. When the person emerges from the bath, at the appropriate moment, ask for what you are entitled in a calm, firm voice.

 ## Loan Spell (1)

This spell allegedly loosens up tight pockets and induces acts of generosity:

1. Place an orrisroot in a jar and cover it with jojoba oil.
2. Add a few drops each of essential oils of clary sage and lavender.
3. On the night before applying for the loan, add some of the oil to your bath. Visualize your success.
4. Apply for the loan in person.
5. Rub some oil between your palms.
6. Don't wash it off before shaking hands with the decision-maker.

 ## Loan Spell (2)

1. Blend essential oils of bay laurel, frankincense, myrrh, and sandalwood into a base of sweet almond and jojoba oils.
2. Massage this oil into the soles of your feet before bedtime and also before applying for the loan.

 ## Tupya

The spirit Tupya is a debtor's best friend.

1. Invoke him so that creditors forget all about you, become distracted or confused and become too involved with other business to pursue you.
2. Ifugao spirits from the Phillipines such as Tupya traditionally accept offerings of rice wine and/or betel nuts.
3. Keep the shrine going as long as the need to avoid repayment exists.

⊛ Pregnancy and Childbirth Spells: Spells to Protect Mothers and Infants

Pregnancy Spells

In general, magic spells target the threshold experiences of pregnancy: conception and delivery. (Spells for conception are contained under *Fertility Spells*, page 417.) The duration in between is perceived as a vulnerable holding-period, best served magically by protective amulets, talismans and protection spells requesting assistance from various benevolent spirits affiliated with pregnancy and childbirth.

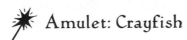 Amulet: Crayfish

Not from Louisiana, this is a Central European Romany spell. Crayfish, as depicted on many Moon tarot cards, are emblematic of primal female, lunar, watery power.

Having eaten a crayfish dinner, reserve, cleanse and dry the shells. Fill a sachet with these shells to bring blessings and protection for a pregnant woman. Pin the sachet into your clothing.

Eye Spells

What parts of the body are most associated with pregnancy? Along with breasts, belly, and all points south, the eye is a consistent anatomical motif. The pregnant woman is believed exceptionally vulnerable to the Evil Eye. The further out the belly extends, the more it draws the Eye. How does the pregnant woman protect herself against the Eye? With amulets in the form of a single eye, which some scholars believe may actually be a euphemism for the vulva, bringing the matter full circle.

Yet the pregnant woman's own eyes also create vulnerability during pregnancy: it's believed that whatever a pregnant woman looks at (consciously or not) for significant amounts of time affects the development of the baby. Consider your immediate surroundings. Surround yourself with whatever are your own sacred images.

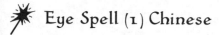 Eye Spell (1) Chinese

Surround yourself with images of happy, healthy, beautiful babies during pregnancy. Gaze at them in a calm, meditative manner so that their power (baraka) is absorbed through the eyes.

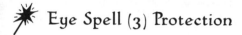 Eye Spell (2) Modern Egyptian

Surround yourself with images of beautiful people as well as sacred images, and people you love and admire. Again, gaze at them in a calm, meditative manner so that you absorb their power through your eyes.

Eye Spell (3) Protection

Wear images of eyes throughout pregnancy, especially as your condition becomes more visible. A single blue-eye bead may be safety-pinned to clothing, or wear it as you wish. Egyptian Eye of Horus amulets are very effective, as is any bead or crystal that resembles an eye. A geometric diamond shape fills in for a literal depiction of an eye.

 Pomegranate Protection Spell

If you fear that the child in your womb has been exposed to illness, obtain a pomegranate:

1. Cut the pomegranate in half.
2. Rub one half over yourself, especially your belly. Envision any ills or pain or damage being drawn into the pomegranate.
3. When you're finished, bury this half in Earth.
4. Eat every seed of the other half.
5. If you can't get a pomegranate, an apple may be substituted although it's not as magically powerful, nor is consuming apple seeds as easy as eating those of a pomegranate.

 SATOR Square

The SATOR magic square was apparently spread through Europe and Britain by the Roman legions. It has many protective uses ranging from fire control to caring for cows, however in general this is either a gender-neutral or even a male-oriented amulet. An exception occurred in England, where Anglo-Saxon tradition favored the SATOR square as an amulet for pregnant women.

Carefully write the magic square on parchment, making sure none of the letters touch and focusing on your desire:

```
S   A   T   O   R
A   R   E   P   O
T   E   N   E   T
O   P   E   R   A
R   O   T   A   S
```

Place the square in a leather bag or metal case and carry it for protection during pregnancy.

Spiritual Protection Spells

From a metaphysical, spiritual point of view, pregnancy is inherently such a powerful, magically charged situation that various elements of the Spirit Realm can't help but get involved. Malicious, hostile spirits are attracted to the pregnant woman like magnets, as it is a prime opportunity to cause trouble and heartache. Benevolent spirits, in theory at least, also hover protectively nearby, ready to fend off spiritual danger. Some spirits consider pregnancy-protection to be their primary occupation. Instead of trusting to their vigilance blindly, magic spells suggest more active methods of ensuring spiritual pregnancy protection.

✴ Spiritual Protection Spell (1) Angels

Among the angels know to protect expectant women and newborn children are Ariel (Uriel), Raphael, Gabriel, Michael, and Nuriel. They are sometimes identified as a group by the acronym "ARGAMAN." This serves as an amuletic device to transmit the power and protection of these angels.

1. Carefully, consciously write the acronym on paper. Consider what type of ink and paper are most appropriate.
2. Create two copies: one to travel with you during the day, a second to be posted on the wall near the bed so as to radiate protection while you sleep.
3. Post the amulet on a wall in plain sight.
4. Write it on a small strip of paper and carry in a locket or mojo hand.

✴ Spiritual Protection Spell (2) Kwan Yin

Kwan Yin, Buddhist Lady of Mercy, protects anyone who cries out for her but reserves special protection for women and children. She supervises the childbirth process from attempts at conception through successful delivery. Although there are many different images of Kwan Yin and any may be effective, the votive image depicting her holding an infant is most effective for this spell.

1. Post Kwan Yin's image.
2. Offer her oranges, pomegranates, and baby shoes, whether real ones or charms.
3. Express any fears or concerns to her and request assistance and protection.

✴ Spiritual Protection Spell (3) Mary Magdalene

Mary Magdalene bestows blessings for a happy, successful pregnancy and smooth delivery. The roots of Mary Magdalene's associations with pregnancy are unclear: is it because, as some believe, Mary Magdalene herself was the Holy Grail, the chalice who safely bore Christ's child? Or is it because a Pagan Mediterranean fertility spirit has become so deeply syncretized to the biblical figure as to be inseparable? Regardless of the reason, Mary Magdalene may be petitioned for an easy pregnancy and a happy outcome. Requests may be made anytime but are believed to be most propitious on her feast day, July 22nd.

Display a votive image of Mary Magdalene. Choose whatever pleases you, however images depicting her with the moon or with a closed box are most powerful in this situation. Offer her myrrh, roses, and spikenard and request her blessings.

✴ Tarot Welcome Spell

Lay out the four aces and the Sun card from a tarot deck to issue a welcome to the new soul existing within you, and to ease the path to emergence for both of you.

Miscarriage Spells

Spells for miscarriage attempt to avert it, prevent its recurrence, or provide for the spiritual safety and comfort of the misborn soul.

Anglo-Saxon Miscarriage Spells

These Anglo-Saxon miscarriage rituals are extremely old but the pain, emotion, and determination they reveal remains intensely modern. It's difficult to tell whether they were originally one extremely extended magic ritual or several rituals so commonly performed in conjunction that it became impossible to disentangle them. The rituals are often combined in different orders, or they are performed in separate pieces. Adjust them to suit your circumstances.

☆ Spell Following Miscarriage or Stillbirth

This spell for a woman involves a progression of rituals, performed over significant periods of time. Originally this was done with the participation of the community; the purpose of the spell was understood, hence the ritual selling of the stillborn child.

At the end of the ritual, the unborn child is dedicated to a deity so as to receive that deity's blessings and protection. Pagan Anglo-Saxons chose Frigg; Christian Anglo-Saxons chose Jesus Christ. Choose either, or whoever else is most appropriate for you. There is nothing in the spell that intrinsically calls one, and only one, divinity.

This spell cannot be cast unless the stillborn or miscarried child has been buried. As with other graveyard dirt spells, there's some ambiguity over exactly what is being dug up. Interpret however this makes sense to you.

1. Take a bit of dirt from the stillborn child's grave, wrap it in black wool and ritually sell it to someone who will not become pregnant, traditionally an elderly woman. This is accompanied by a chant: *"I sell it. You buy it, this black wool and the seeds of this sorrow."*
2. Soon after, go to the cemetery, step over the grave of a dead man three times, saying these words each time, for a repetition of three:
   This is my help against hateful slow birth.
   This is my help against dreadful sad birth.
   This is my help against hateful misbirth.
3. When the woman next conceives, she steps over a living man (preferably but not necessarily the child's father) in bed three times, saying each time, for a repetition of three:
   Up I go, over you I step!
   With a living child, not a dying one.
   With a full-born child, not a doomed one.
4. Keep quiet about the pregnancy until you're ready for Step 5. Be discreet; don't broadcast the news.
5. At the first signs of quickening—the child's first flutterings in the womb—the ritual is completed by approaching an altar publicly (once upon a time, this was done in Church) and saying, *"To [Deity] I declare this child in my womb."*

☆ Ritual to Prevent Miscarriage

Another Anglo-Saxon miscarriage spell, no less complex than the last although more quickly accomplished, may be cast independently or in conjunction with the spell above.

1. Milk from a solid-colored (one color) cow is required. It must be obtained directly from the cow. Take milk in the palm of your hand, drink it but don't swallow. Hold it in your mouth. Without looking around and without swallowing, go quickly and directly to a stream and spit out the milk.
2. With the same hand you used for the milk, take a handful of water from the stream and swallow it.
3. Chant:
   Everywhere I carry within me this great strong one.
   Strong because of this great food.
   This one I want to have and keep and go home with.
4. Don't look around. Don't talk to anyone. Go to a different home from the one where you started this ritual and there, eat a meal.

 Jizo's Spell for Solace

"All rivers find their way to the sea."

According to Japanese spiritual traditions, all rivers end in a place called the River of Souls, the home of Jizo. Jizo is the Protector of the Souls of Lost Children. These include stillbirths and miscarriages. Babies live and play happily in his abode. Jizo is a multi-faceted deity: he protects mothers and children but also serves as a psychopomp, a spirit who guides dead souls to the next realm. Miscarriages, abortions (without judgment) and stillbirths are all under his domain. Jizo comforts mothers in any of the above circumstances, too.

1. Write your child's name (or the name you would have given the child, or the name in your heart for the child) on a slip of paper.
2. Set it on a river to float to Jizo, so that he will watch out for and take care of your baby.

 Jizo's Spell (2)

A public image of Jizo may serve in this ritual or, if this isn't possible, obtain an image of Jizo; his images are customarily placed outside, however adapt to your needs.

Place stones or pebbles around images of Jizo, one for each prayer and petition made for the protection of the baby.

Knot Anti-Miscarriage Spells

Knot magic is used in spells regarding all aspects of reproduction: contraception, enhanced fertility, impotence, and childbirth. Knots are tied and released as needed. Childbirth rituals all over the world emphasize the untying of knots: everyone within the vicinity of the birthing woman must loosen their hair, for instance. Window curtains are un-knotted in the belief that knots stall delivery.

Sometimes however this is exactly what you desire. A knot spell determines to set a safe due date.

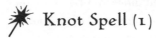 Knot Spell (1)

1. At first sign of miscarriage, make a tight knot in a strong cord.
2. Visualize the knot as your baby.
3. Talk to it: *"As this knot holds firm, so you hold firm in my womb. Do not loosen until* [insert due date or select a date]*."*
4. Place the cord in a secure covered container or wrap it up in a baby blanket.
5. Keep it in a safe place. Be sure to untie the cord at the appropriate time.

 Knot Spell (2)

If you are prone or vulnerable to miscarriage, incorporate protective knot magic on a consistent, regular basis until the time is safe for delivery.

Incorporate knot magic as much as possible into your life: wear your hair in braids, multiple if possible. Wear shoes with laces and clothing that ties rather than buttons. As you braid, tie, and knot, consciously focus your desire and intent, prayers and petitions.

Miscarriage Prevention Spells

The most popular form of miscarriage prevention spell involves charged stones and amulets that can radiate power constantly. For best success, amulets should always be cleansed, charged, and consecrated before their initial use and then as needed.

A "pile-up" effect is favored when using amulets. Use as many as possible: they empower each other synergistically.

Jewish tradition suggests wearing or carrying an eaglestone to enhance aspects of conception, pregnancy, and childbirth, and especially for the prevention of miscarriage. Unlike amber, rubies, and cowries, this is not something you can buy; it must be *found*—and if it is, it is a sacred gift. Eaglestones are ferruginous pebbles, usually found in a stream. They will be recognized because, when picked up and rattled, the presence of another smaller stone within is apparent: the baby within its mother.

Eaglestones earned their name because, according to legend, eagles gather them into their own nests to assist with conception and delivery.

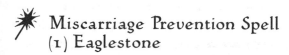
Miscarriage Prevention Spell (1) Eaglestone

Attach eaglestones to the left wrist for miscarriage prevention. To ease childbirth, they should be attached to the thigh instead.

Miscarriage Prevention Spell (2) Gemstones

Lapis lazuli and rubies are the gemstones believed able to prevent miscarriage or minimize its likelihood. Wear them across the womb for maximum effectiveness, although they still have potency if worn more conventionally.

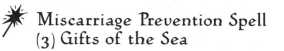
Miscarriage Prevention Spell (3) Gifts of the Sea

The ocean is the font of Earth's fertility power. Its powers are invoked in many fertility spells but the sea also has gifts to preserve and protect pregnancy, especially regarding prevention of miscarriage.

Amber, coral, and cowrie shells protect pregnancy in general and allegedly specifically prevent miscarriage or minimize its likelihood. For strongest effect, they should be worn slung around the hips against the skin, underneath clothing.

(Although it's now recognized that amber is fossilized tree resin, ancient people encountered amber lying on the shore where it was tossed by ocean waves. In this context, they perceived it as an oceanic product and those metaphysical, magical associations remain potent.)

Miscarriage Prevention Spell (4) Gifts of the Sea Urgent Action

Maintain substantial quantities of amber, coral, and cowries wherever you are. Beads or small pieces are fine. Cast a circle from amber, coral, and/or cowries and lie within it, either on the floor or on the bed. Place amber, coral, and/or cowries against your pregnant belly and maintain calm.

Miscarriage Prevention Spell (5) Speedy Labor Charms

Sometimes magic isn't in what you do but in what you don't do. It's crucial to recognize the magical capacity of objects so that they serve your purposes, rather than counteracting your desires.

Emeralds, lodestones and charms in the shape of downward-pointing arrows all allegedly speed delivery. Do not wear or carry them until the appropriate time.

Saint Raymond Nonnatus Spell

Saint Raymond's name Nonnatus derives from "non natus," "not born," because he was removed from the womb following his mother's death during labor. He is the patron of midwives and protects unborn children.

Offer Saint Raymond a red candle. Leave a lock and key beside the candle. Lock the lock and allow the key to remain within it. Preserve the lock and key in a safe place. Do not unlock and remove the key until you are ready to give birth.

Vinca Miscarriage Spell

Vinca flowers, also known as periwinkle and sorcerer's violet, bound around the thigh of a pregnant woman allegedly prevents miscarriage. Attach to a garter.

Post Miscarriage Cleansing Spell

This bath spell offers spiritual (rather than physical) healing as well as relief from grief. It is recommended post-miscarriage whether spontaneous or not.

*Moisten baking soda with **Notre Dame Water**. Add this to your bath daily until you feel it's no longer needed.*

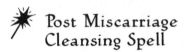

Birth is perhaps the ultimate magical threshold, fraught with simultaneous psychic vulnerability and primal power. The birthing chamber is the equivalent of the crossroads at midnight, packed with unseen competing spirits, drawn by the opportunity for mischief or the need to prevent it. Magic spells seek to ease and assist birth. Spells prevail upon the protective powers of benevolent

spirits, plot to avoid or foil malevolent spirits, ease pain, speed delivery, and provide a happy future for mother and child. The childbirth process is protected and enhanced through the use of amulets and special ritual clothing.

Animal Allies

Animal powers are critical magical allies during all facets of human reproduction, from attempted conception to actual delivery. In fact, according to myth and legend, the two creatures most associated with childbirth actually taught people the process.

Animal Ally #1: Snake

Snakes are women's animal allies throughout the entire reproductive process, from conception through childbirth. According to legend, observing the undulations of snakes taught women how to give birth, and the snake's unhinged jaw, capable of expanding so as to consume something larger than its own head, is a metaphor for the expanding vagina, which can similarly expand to safely deliver a child.

 ## Snake Childbirth Spell (1) Labor Coach

In various parts of the world, a basketful of snakes is brought into the birthing room (with someone designated to supervise them) until childbirth is complete. (In remote areas of China, traditionally the husband was expected to gather them, then feed them after birth and release them.) This is for luck, to beseech the Snake Spirit's blessings, but also because watching the snake's undulations is supposed to magically assist the birthing woman. The snakes are, in a sense, given the opportunity to serve as labor coaches.

Emulate if this is realistic for you. Otherwise a

videotape of writhing, undulating snakes may be played in the birthing-room instead. Merely decorating the birth chamber with images (statuettes, photographs, or artistic renderings) of snakes may be sufficient to benefit from the snakes' blessings of eased, speedy childbirth.

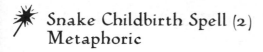 Snake Childbirth Spell (2) Metaphoric

More metaphoric methods of accessing serpent power exist, too.

Hire belly dancers, especially snake dancers, for the birthing room to accompany, distract, and entrance the delivering woman. Enhance the ritual with frame drums, the traditional sacred instruments belonging to fertility spirits, to set childbirth's rhythm and pace.

Snake Childbirth Spell (3) Snakeskin

Freely shed snakeskin reputedly speeds and eases childbirth. It is crucial that the snake's old skin be shed freely because this way it transmits serpentine blessings.

Snakeskins are available to those who keep snakes as companion animals and also from zoos and animal shelters. Wrap shed snakeskin around the laboring woman's hips or belly like a belt or magic girdle during childbirth.

Animal Ally #2: Crocodile

The secondary animal ally of pregnant and laboring women may be a surprising one: the crocodile. Because they are such fearsome creatures, which most typically strike terror into the human heart, it can be hard to conceive how frequently they are associated with erotic and reproductive magic.

Crocodiles, primordial creatures who survived the dinosaurs, are reputed to know all Earth's secrets although they may or may not reveal them. Ancient Egyptian temple crocodiles were adorned with gold earrings and ornaments, maintained in sacred pools on the temple premises, and fed daily by the priests. When Isis, in danger and on the run, was forced to give birth silently and alone in the Nile marshes, crocodiles guarded her, rustling the leaves to camouflage the sounds of childbirth.

In a legend from Irian Jaya, crocodiles literally teach the birth process—and not merely by example. Not understanding the process of birth, men were performing crude Caesarian sections, removing the living baby with stone adzes but invariably killing the mother. Death in childbirth was a given. A giant sacred talking crocodile finally stopped one man, and explained that this wasn't necessary. The crocodile then personally presided over this man's wife's delivery, appearing at the birthing room complete with doctor's bag of beneficial herbs to explicitly explain and demonstrate safer methods.

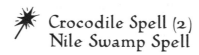 Crocodile Spell (1) Basic

Unlike snakes, no one is suggesting that actual crocodiles be brought into the birthing room. Image magic will more than suffice.

Bring images of crocodiles into the birthing room: these can be statues, toys, nature videos, photographs, or artistic renderings. Crocodile-shaped amulets are also beneficial. Charge them with your desire prior to use.

Crocodile Spell (2) Nile Swamp Spell

*Reminiscent of Isis's travail in the Nile swamps, cast a circle of toy crocodiles around the birthing mother, with their jaws facing out away from her, toward any approaching danger. Reinforce with **kyphi** incense.*

Crocodile Spell (3) Sobek

Images of the Egyptian crocodile deity, Sobek, are also beneficial. Sobek, whose name merely means "crocodile," is a deity of procreative and vegetative fertility. He is either depicted as a crocodile or as a man with a crocodile's head. Request his blessings and fearsome protection.

1. Place an image of Sobek so that it faces the birthing woman.
2. If a traditional Egyptian image is unavailable, any depiction of a fierce, dignified crocodile can be designated to represent Sobek.
3. If no image can be found, the hieroglyph representing *"crocodile"* posted on the wall should be sufficient to bestow Sobek's blessings and warn spiritual evil-doers of his presence.

Birth Chamber Spells

Any area or space where childbirth occurs, from hospital delivery room to home bedroom, from traditional bathhouse to taxi cab, is instantly transformed into a tremendously powerful, although ephemeral, threshold of emergent life, temporarily equal in magical stature to a crossroads, cemetery, or shrine. It is also, as is the nature of thresholds, a tremendously vulnerable space. Use protective spells to secure the birthing room and protect mother, child, and all other participants in the process.

Birth Chamber Aroma Spells
Aroma is used to create an aura of protection in the birth chamber. Aroma is created by fumigating with incense or by warming essential oils in an aroma burner.

These aromas were traditionally indicated for childbirth because of their generally relaxing, pain-relieving effects upon the mother and because of their magically beckoning, inviting influence on the child. The person in charge of maintaining the aroma should accompany lighting of incense or candles with blessings for mother and child.

Birth Chamber Aroma Spell (1) Benzoin

Burn styrax benzoin in the birth chamber: its aroma attracts angels and beckons them to stay, while more malevolent spirits dislike the fragrance and are repelled.

Birth Chamber Aroma Spell (2) Lavender

Diffuse essential oil of lavender through an aroma burner to soothe the mother's fears, welcome the newborn, and stimulate emergence. The scent also beckons benevolent fairies.

Birth Chamber Aroma Spell (3) Mother Resin

Galbanum, known as "Mother Resin" because of its popularity in the birth room and its traditional role in healing women's reproductive ailments, is indigenous to Mesopotamia. Grind anise seeds, galbanum resin, and myrrh with a mortar and pestle and sprinkle on to lit charcoals. Burn, wafting the fragrance as needed.

Birth Chamber Aroma Spell (4) Sage

Warm essential oils of clary sage, jasmine, and lavender in an aroma burner to welcome the baby, soothe the mother and relax all the birth assistants.

Birth Chamber Aroma Spell (5) Sandarac

Fumigate the birth chamber by burning gum sandarac, which instills fear in malevolent spirits.

 ## Birth Chamber Protection Spell (1) Father's Protective Spell

The father walks deasil (sunwise) seven times around the perimeter of the building where birthing occurs to provide mother and child with magical protection.

 ## Birth Chamber Protection Spell (2) Fir Needles

Burn silver fir needles during childbirth to protect mother and child.

 ## Birth Chamber Protection Spell (3) Pomegranates

Hang boughs of fresh pomegranate over thresholds to ease delivery, and also to prevent the entry of malicious spirits.

 ## Birth Chamber Protection Spell (4) Roman Method

The sacred midwives of ancient Rome used brooms to sweep thresholds of birthing chambers. Sweeping drives away evil spirits.

1. Create a ritual broom for this spell (see *Elements of Magic Spells*). Ideally use a birch, fig, or pomegranate branch for the broomstick and willow for the *"broom."*
2. Sweep all thresholds of the birthing room itself, sweeping in an outward motion. Also sweep the threshold of the main entrance to the building.
3. Save the broom until the birth is complete, sweeping as desired. Once the baby has been successfully delivered, the broom should be taken apart and the pieces scattered.

 ## Birth Chamber Protection Spell (5) Umbrella Protection

The origins of the umbrella lie in magical protection spells. Place an umbrella over the bed of a laboring woman to repel evil spirits.

Birth Chamber Spirit Control
The desire to exert control over exactly which spirits have access to the birthing room and which do not figures prominently in childbirth magic.

 ## Birth Chamber Spirit Control Spell (1) Central American/Russian

Luckily low-level malevolent demons are not overly endowed in the intelligence department and are easily fooled. Sheer cleverness foils demons as effectively as the most precious resins or the most powerful talismans. A ritual to confuse lurking demons looking to disturb childbirth emerged in both Central America and Russia, although exactly how fathers on two continents were persuaded to take part in this spell remains the biggest mystery.

1. The father-to-be lies above or somehow across from the laboring woman with a thread tied around either his penis or testicles.
2. Either the mother or the midwife jerks the thread to coincide with labor pains and cries to produce an echo effect.
3. The demons can't tell where the noise is coming from and who's crying and exactly why and so they eventually depart to look for trouble elsewhere.

Birth Chamber Spirit Control Spell (2) Chinese

Before labor is in full swing and delivery actually commences, light red candles in the birthing chamber to ward off homeless ghosts who may attempt to gain possession of the new child's body, forcing out the rightful soul.

Maintain these red candles throughout the duration until well after birth is complete. Large candles are therefore preferable. If using smaller candles, as each burns low, light a fresh one.

 Birth Chamber Spirit Control Spell (3) Jewish

Rue wards off malicious spirits as well as the Evil Eye:

1. Place fresh rue in a glass of spring water on a tray. (Supplement with other magical plants, if desired, but only rue is required.)
2. Surround the glass containing the rue with candles, as many as possible. Each participant or witness to the birth process should light at least one candle.
3. Keep the candles burning throughout the birth, replacing as needed. Do not allow burned out candles to remain on the tray. Candles are symbolic of the life force as well as of the protective, purifying elemental quality of fire.

Birth Chamber Spirit Control Spell (4) Yemenite Jewish

If you can never entirely get rid of malicious spirits, then at least keep them out of trouble is the rationale behind this Yemenite Jewish magic ritual.

Hide candy and other sweets beneath the bed in the birthing room, to distract always-greedy, evil spirits from the birth at hand and keep them out of mischief. If they are placed out in the open, the spirits will be

suspicious; *however, malevolent spirits will take pleasure from something they think they're stealing.*

 Birth Chamber Spirit Control Spell (5) Circle

Draw a circle around the laboring woman with a magic sword to defy any lurking spirits.

 Birth Chamber Spirit Control Spell (6) Pearlwort Spell

Place pearlwort leaves or blossoms behind the mother's right knee to repel fairies intent on mischief during the birth.

Book of the Angel Raziel

Raziel, alleged author of the *Book of Raziel*, is the Angel of the Creator's Secrets, the Angel of Magic and Mysteries. Raziel is said to *hear* everything that happens in the world, sort of an omniscient ear, rather than the more usual eye.

Material in the *Book of Raziel*, or the *Sefer Raziel* as it is known in Hebrew and sometimes called in English, was collected over long periods of time; some sections dating back to Talmudic times, although the book itself, in its present form was not printed until 1701 in Amsterdam.

The book was not published so that people could read it. In fact, it was assumed that most people could not read it, would not understand it, and would not even make the attempt. The publisher's intention was to provide an amulet: possession of the book offered psychic protection.

★ *The book kept its owner and the place where it was kept safe from misfortune and danger, including fire and robbery*

* The book drives away evil spirits and works as a charm to raise wise and intelligent sons. *(Angels gave the Daughters of Men private lessons, instead.)*
* Perhaps the Book of Raziel's *most crucial role was to provide the diagram for the most famous anti-Lilith protective childbirth amulets*

Since then the book has been re-issued in numerous editions and continues to be published, particularly now on microfiche, the size of a credit card. Of course in that form you genuinely can't read it, but it's a great amulet for a pocket, charm bag, or glove compartment of a car. The most popular use, now as previously, of the *Sefer Raziel* is providing protection during childbirth.

Maintain a copy of the *Book of Raziel* beneath a laboring woman's pillow for the duration of childbirth.

 Djinn Protection Amulet (1)

Although some djinn are benevolent, in general many, particularly the less powerful ones, are perceived as hostile to people. Pregnant women are believed especially vulnerable: the djinn stimulate miscarriage and stillbirth. The djinn also lurk in the delivery room, attracted by the blood but also by the potential for mischief. To protect against baby-killing djinn, a protective amulet is made before delivery, worn during the childbirth process, and then ritually disposed.

1. The mother makes an anklet from blue string.
2. Attach a tiny pouch containing grains of salt, harmel (Syrian rue), dried gum sandarac, and charcoal. Attach a silver coin or bead, a seashell, and a piece of red coral.
3. Tie the anklet around the mother's right ankle.
4. Leave this on for forty days following the birth then remove it in a river (abandoning it there) with the left foot, not touching it with the hands.

Djinn Protection Amulet (2)

A slightly different ankle amulet is also recommended. For maximum effect, both may be crafted and worn simultaneously.

Follow all instructions above for wearing and then losing the protective anklet. However this spell suggests that the mother should attach harmel, rock salt, glass beads, a silver coin, and seashells directly to the blue string. Tie it just above the mother's left ankle.

Ease Painful Labor Spells

Components of spells to ease labor may be found, handcrafted, or purchased. These methods may be used in conjunction with each other. As with all object-driven spells, remember to cleanse, charge, and consecrate as needed. The following are said to ease and alleviate the pain of childbirth. (They do not, however, make any promises regarding shortening the process, with the possible exception of Spell 3 because of the incorporation of lodestone.)

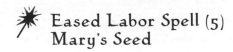 Eased Labor Spell (1) Arrow

The use of arrows transcends archery contests and hunting. Arrows also play an ancient and once prominent role in divination, spirituality and magic spells, especially those for love, protection, healing, and birth. These "medicine arrows," to borrow a Native American term, are traditionally charged, consecrated and/or blessed before use, in the same manner as a candle or amulet. Because they may never be meant actually to fly, these arrows can be embellished with botanicals, charms, runes, and feathers or re-shaped to suit one's magical purposes. The arrow in its quiver also replays the sexual imagery of morter and pestle, sword and sheath.

Place a medicine arrow beneath the laboring woman's bed. Should the pain get very bad, shoot the arrow from east to west, so as to magically carry the pain away. Leave the quiver empty.

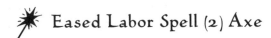 Eased Labor Spell (2) Axe

Place an axe under the childbirth bed.

Eased Labor Spell (3) Coral and Lodestone

This amuletic charm must be prepared before delivery. Create a necklace of coral beads with a lodestone suspended from it, and wear during the delivery.

Eased Labor Spell (4) Cowrie Pain Relief

Beginning earlier in pregnancy, wear cowrie shells against the skin (ideally on a belt but if this irritates you, wear elsewhere), to protect against painful labor.

Eased Labor Spell (5) Mary's Seed

The Gulf Stream carries seeds across oceans and deposits them on the shores of the Outer Hebrides Islands. Since at least the seventeenth century, these seeds have been prized childbirth relief amulets, believed to ease childbirth and provide spiritual blessings.

Referred to in Gaelic as airne Moiré ("Mary's kidney") or tearna Moire ("Mary's charm of deliverance"), these charms encompass seeds of various species, including Entada scandens, Dolichos vulgaris and Ipomaea tuberose. The crucial part is not the specific botanical species but the fact that they are gifts of the sea. Seeds with a semblance of a cross on one side are believed most powerful.

1. Leave the seed in its natural state or have it set in silver.
2. Hold it in your hands during labor to receive its transmitted blessings.

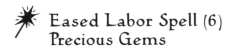 Eased Labor Spell (6) Precious Gems

The possibility of easing labor is a nice excuse for an expensive gift: wear emeralds or rubies anywhere on the body.

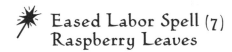 Eased Labor Spell (7) Raspberry Leaves

Raspberry plants are believed to possess an affinity for childbirth. Wear or carry raspberry leaves in a charm bag to speed and alleviate childbirth.

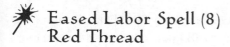 **Eased Labor Spell (8) Red Thread**

Wind red silk thread around the laboring woman.

Easy Speedy Delivery Potions

Various potions reputedly speed and ease labor.

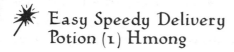 **Easy Speedy Delivery Potion (1) Hmong**

A Hmong recommendation to ease and shorten labor:

1. Place a key in a pot and cover it with spring water. The key is understood as the key that unlocks the birth canal.
2. Boil this water.
3. Let it cool, with the key resting inside the pot.
4. Let the laboring woman drink the water.

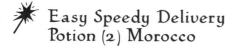 **Easy Speedy Delivery Potion (2) Morocco**

The father must wash either his whole right foot or both big toes only with pure spring water. (This is ritual washing; his feet should be pretty clean to start with). This water is then given to the laboring woman to drink.

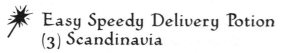 **Easy Speedy Delivery Potion (3) Scandinavia**

Pour ale through a holed stone into a glass. Give it to the mother to drink to ease her pains.

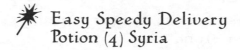 **Easy Speedy Delivery Potion (4) Syria**

Pure spring water is given to the woman to drink directly from the father's right shoe.

Easy Speedy Delivery Spells

These spells not only allegedly ease labor pains but quicken the process, too. Because these spells are largely object-driven, remember to incorporate petition, conscious visualization and affirmation, magical cleansing, charging, and/or consecration.

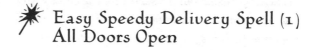 **Easy Speedy Delivery Spell (1) All Doors Open**

To ease and speed labor:

1. Loosen all knots, including braids, shoelaces and any ties on clothing, in the vicinity of the birthing room.
2. Keep doors and windows open or at least unlocked.
3. Make sure small locks, such as padlocks, are opened for the duration.

 **Easy Speedy Delivery Spell (2) Crystal Arrow**

Clear quartz crystal cut into the shape of a downward-facing arrow and worn during delivery is among the most powerful childbirth amulets.

Easy Speedy Delivery Spell (3) Lodestone

Lodestone's very presence is said to encourage delivery. Exploit their drawing magnetic properties by gently massaging the mother's abdomen or aura, demonstrating the suggested route of departure to the baby.

Fairy Childbirth Spells

The spirits most associated with childbirth in fairy tales are the fairies themselves, those proverbial fairy godmothers that fatefully appear either to bestow gifts and blessings on the child or else doom the infant with temperamental curses, usually because of an oversight by the child's parent. The most famous example is, of course, *Sleeping Beauty.* This is not merely a story-teller's device but a reflection of what were once common practices.

The belief that spirits presiding over childbirth can impact and determine the baby's future is ancient. Once upon a time in Egypt the role of the fairies was played by the Seven Hathors, who may be seven aspects of the deity Hathor, her daughters or a completely separate divinity. Vestiges of the Seven Hathors appear millennia later in Muddy Waters' blues song "Hoochie Coochie Man" with its Seven Doctors who prophesize that the singer *"is born for good luck."*

In between the Seven Hathors and the Seven Doctors lie centuries of variations on this theme. Celtic folklore describes a party of three fairies, known as *The White Women,* present at every birth, who come to predict or bestow the baby's fortune and fate. This connection between fate and fairies is hidden in English but apparent in Italian. Morgan le Fay's name in Italian, for example, is Fata Morgana.

Once upon a time, fairies were invited to the birth chamber in order to bestow their blessings and influence the infant's fate. This invitation was extended by creating an offering table. Although essentially an altar, "table" is meant literally. Fairies aren't looking for a picturesque tableau complete with candles and incense. Instead, they expect a place setting set for a meal on an actual table, not the top of a dresser or a counter. If poverty-stricken, improvised tables or folding card-tables will do, but it needs to look like a meal will be served. Shades of *Sleeping Beauty* may be recognized, especially the outraged Fairy who isn't given the same golden plate as her sisters. These traditions were particularly strong throughout France, from whence *Sleeping Beauty* originally derives.

Following conversion to Christianity, these practices were discouraged and forbidden. (In France consorting with Fairies was a more common witch-hunter's charge than consorting with Satan, as elsewhere.) If one accepts that there are Fairies, then it is understandable that when people stopped this special relationship, the Fairies were disgruntled. Anyone possessing the power to bless always retains the power to curse, too. Despite threat of punishment childbirth rituals to appease the Fairies' anger and to invoke their special blessings continued. According to Breton tradition, three guardian fairies attend the birth of each child in order to endow it with gifts and make predictions for the future. The custom of preparing a festive table in the birthing room for these fairy sisters survived in Northern Brittany right up until the nineteenth century.

How can three fairies attend *every* birth, one asks logically? This is not a new dilemma. The ancients decided that that was why it was imperative to set up a *fabulous* offering table, so that if the fairies get busy and have to choose whom to visit, they'll choose you. Conversely, assuming that the Fairies will be easy-going and not notice the lack of a table or proper table-settings leads to *Sleeping Beauty* situations and irate, cursing Fairies.

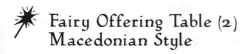 Fairy Offering Table (1)
Breton Style

"Nos Bonnes Meres," "Our Good Mothers," *is the Breton euphemism for the fairies. To invoke them without reason is to invoke their anger and malice.*

1. A table in the birthing room is spread for those fairies that always attend births.
2. Set the table nicely.
3. Offer some or all of the following: champagne, cordials, whiskey, wine, milk, berries, nuts, apples, pastry, and butter and bread.

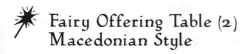 Fairy Offering Table (2)
Macedonian Style

1. A table set with a perpetually lit lamp is maintained in the birth chamber (this assumes home birth; transplant to any room where mother and baby stay together) for the first three days after birth.
2. Keep fresh bread, salt, and coins on the table.
3. On the third night, place a small table near the head of the baby's bed.
4. On it place a mirror and a cake made by a woman whose biological parents remain alive.
5. Place silver coins and gemstones in a small bag and place under the baby's pillow. These are gifts for the spirits and fairies that are coming to visit the child; the custom is reminiscent of the modern tooth fairy.
6. Leave a lighted lamp on the table to guide and welcome the visitors.
7. The next morning, if the bag remains, bury it in Earth in a spot that looks like it would be favored by fairies.

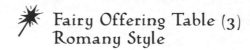 Fairy Offering Table (3)
Romany Style

Eastern European Romany have both male and female birth spirits. Some spirits are present in the delivery room, while others make scheduled appearances later. The Ursitory are a party of three male spirits, while the Urme are the corresponding party of three females. Any combination may appear on the third night after birth to determine the baby's fate. These fairies are visible only to the mother, the baby, and the drabarni, *the midwife/shaman/herbalist who attends the mother and child.*

Cast a circle (or double concentric circle) either on a table or on the baby's bed, with three glasses of wine and three slices of bread or cake—one slice and one glass for each of the three expected spirits. The circle should be large enough to enclose the baby. (Various other naming and spiritual ceremonies may be held at the same time, with the baby in the center.)

 Fairy Offering Table (4)
Serbian Style

Oosood, a Serbian fairy, related to the vila, *arrives on the seventh night following the birth to announce the baby's destiny. She is visible only to the baby's mother.*

Have a bouquet of flowers waiting for her so as to receive a favorable destiny. In the morning, remove the bouquet and scatter the flowers over living water or amongst nettles or bushes that would seem favorable to fairies.

 Fairy Offering Table (5)
Spanish Style

The family gathers on the seventh day following the birth to celebrate and greet the fairies. Place a dish of honey on an offering table for those fairies that have come to bestow the baby's fate.

Lilith Spells

Lilith, former childbirth guardian turned vampire baby killer, has a complex history, to say the least. Her earliest origins are as a Mesopotamian Wind Spirit, where she apparently served as a childbirth guardian.

Lilith may or may not appear in the Bible as Adam's secret first wife, depending upon how one interprets some passages. According to Genesis 1:27, *"God created man in his own image, in the image of God created He him; male and female created he them."* That is, allegedly Lilith was created out of dust just like Adam, although by Genesis 2:18, God is lamenting that it's *"not good that the man should be alone; I will make him a help meet for him,"* leading to the story of Adam's rib and Eve. What happened in between?

Although this may be an over-simplification, Lilith had some problems with Adam's sexual proclivities. She didn't understand why, if they were both equally formed from dirt, he *always* had to be on top. Lilith abandoned Adam, fled Paradise, initiating the first divorce. Upon first leaving Eden, Lilith yearned for the presence of the *"little faces,"* mysterious winged baby-like angels. When she attempted to fly up amongst them, the Creator aggressively thrust her back down to Earth.

Because Lilith has anger against people, and because she has her own fertility issues that drive her to rage, she holds a bad reputation as a baby snatcher, responsible for miscarriage (especially chronic miscarriage), stillbirths, and sudden infant death syndrome alike. Yet amulets to ward off Lilith were invariably revealed by her. You will not offend or further enrage her by using them. Instead, these amulets are a form of respect. Unlike the Bible, where she is nameless, most anti-Lilith amulets demand that you post her name so that all present recognize her power.

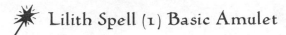

Lilith Spell (1) Basic Amulet

The following names protect against Lilith and are traditionally displayed in the birthing room and then for a minimum of eight days following a boy's birth, and twenty-one following a girl's, the period of greatest danger:

★ *Lilith*
★ *The three angels Senoi, Sensenoi, and Semangelof*
★ *Zamarchad, the name of Lilith's kingdom on the Red Sea*

Write the names within circles drawn on the walls of the birth chamber and the room(s) where mother and baby sleep using chalk or charcoal. These names are effective written using any alphabet (Lilith's multilingual), however they are allegedly most powerful when written with Hebrew letters.

Lilith Spell (2) Enhanced Amulet

Elaborate anti-Lilith amulets became an art-form: the most famous is within the Book of Raziel. *It may be copied or the page removed and posted.*

Another powerful amulet is Psalm 126 with the addition of the names of the three angels as above. Place a copy of this amulet in each corner of the home to protect against the dangers of pregnancy, childbirth, and infancy.

Lilith Spell (3) Iron for Mother

Iron repels Lilith. Almost every spell or talisman against Lilith that doesn't invoke her name involves iron instead. Keep an iron knife (full-size or amulet) under one's pillow during pregnancy as well as during childbirth.

Lilith Spell (4) Iron for Child

Place a sword (preferably magical) under the infant's crib or lay it across the top.

 ## Lilith Spell (5) Iron Spell

This ritual protects against Lilith as well as other baby-threatening spirits:

1. For forty consecutive days, immediately following delivery, the mother must keep a knife or other sharp iron implement with her *constantly,* on her person all day and under her pillow at night.
2. Every day for the forty days someone else must vigorously shake this iron implement over the heads of mother and child. (Simultaneously, if possible: the mother should hold the baby.)

 ## Lilith Spell (6) Needle Protection

Place a needle close to the wick of a candle or oil lamp in the room where a woman who must be protected from Lilith sleeps.

 ## Lilith Spell (7) Sacred Text

Chanting the Psalm 121 allegedly repels Lilith and provides protection against her.

Repeat as needed, particularly in moments of fear and perceived vulnerability.

 ## Lilith Spell (8) Extra Strength

Any anti–Lilith amulet is strengthened by attaching a sprig of fresh rue, a head of garlic, and a shard from a broken mirror to it. These combined objects alone may also be sufficient to provide safety.

 ## Lilith Spell (9) Elijah's Extra Names

It's reported that Lilith was once traveling down a road, when she encountered the Prophet Elijah. Elijah, a childbirth guardian himself, immediately recognized her and demanded new, improved protective methods. Lilith revealed some of her other names to him and promised not to cause harm anywhere she saw or even heard those names.

Unfortunately those names were not immediately engraved in stone. Ostensibly either thirteen or seventeen names were given to Elijah, however more variations than those numbers exist today, exacerbated perhaps by confusion caused by the traditional lack of written vowels in Semitic languages.

The following are believed to be among Lilith's names. Chant or post any or all:

Abeko
Abito
Abnukto
Amizo
Ayil
Batna
Bituah
Elio
'Ik
'Ils
Ita
Izorpo
Kali
Kea
Kakash
Matruta
Odam or Odem
Prtsa (customarily Partashah or Partasah)
Ptrta (customarily Patrota or Petrota)
Podo
Raphi
Strina
Tlto (customarily Talto)

Magical Birthing Belt

1. Weave a girdle from a donkey's tail hair. This girdle or magic belt should be the width of five fingers.
2. Sew the following patterns into the belt with red cotton thread: a star and the phases of the moon.

 ## Prolonged Labor Spell (1) Eggs

A spell for prolonged labor, when it's beginning to appear as if this baby will never *voluntarily emerge.*

Boil three eggs until hard cooked. Leave them in the water in the pot until the water is cool. Give the woman the cooled water to drink, while the father eats the eggs.

Prolonged Labor Spell (2) Queen of Heaven

1. Petition the Queen of Heaven to take her golden key and unlock the womb and birth canal.
2. The Queen of Heaven may be understood as Ishtar or as the Virgin Mary, depending upon personal belief.
3. For added inspiration, gaze at the tarot card, The Empress, while making the petition.

Sacred Midwife Spells

Because childbirth was once understood as fraught with spiritual, magical power and vulnerability and associated with women's magical blood mysteries, only an adept was perceived as competent to preside over the birthing chamber. For millennia the position of midwife was held by consecrated priestesses of various spirits that had dominion over birth such as Hathor, Hecate, Kybele, Tanit, and Tlazolteotl. The spirits themselves were divine, sacred midwives: their priestess/midwives were their Earthly representatives.

This connection between midwifery, women's primal magic power, and female-centered spirituality endured even after the rise of Christianity and the suppression of other faiths. However instead of associations with the Goddess, midwives were now identified with witches; in fact, the classic witch's broomstick was once the professional emblem of Hecate's priestess-midwives. Midwives preserved magical and shamanic traditions for centuries. Midwifery as a profession has rebounded in recent years, though not necessarily in the context of the magical arts. Sacred midwives, the spirits presiding over childbirth, remain eternally powerful, however, and may be appealed to for protection, good fortune and easy, brief, safe labor.

 ## Sacred Midwife Spell (1) Artemis

Artemis is profoundly involved with all aspects of the childbirth process. According to myth, her very first action following her birth was as a midwife, assisting her mother deliver Apollo, her younger twin. Artemis's role in women's child-bearing was crucial: allegedly she personally determines which women and babies survive childbirth—not an idle threat from a spirit who was among the last Greek divinities that accepted human sacrifice.

1. Build her an offering table or altar during pregnancy, before delivery, to be maintained for at least one complete lunar cycle following childbirth.
2. Decorate it with images of the moon and animals, especially dogs, deer, and wolves, Artemis's favorites.
3. Light white and silver candles in her honor.
4. Traditionally, Artemis accepts offerings of round cakes set with candles, the original birthday cake, and a woman's childhood dolls, which may be maintained on her altar.

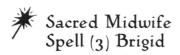 ## Sacred Midwife Spell (2) Boldogasszony

This Hungarian sacred midwife, protector of mother and child, has been syncretized to the Virgin Mary. She may be the Sumerian Great Mother Bau who, in turn, may be Gula, deity of healing.

Request her assistance through prayer and petition. Should you do so, offer her wine and pastry on a Tuesday following a successful birth.

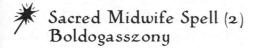 ## Sacred Midwife Spell (3) Brigid

While other pagan spirits were demonized or turned into fairy or witch queens, Brigid, prominent Celtic spirit, transitioned to official Roman Catholic sainthood as Saint Brigid. Once an exceptionally multifaceted spirit, associated with smithcraft and women's primal power, among Brigid's spiritual roles was that of the sacred midwife. Vestiges persist in the legend that Brigid was the midwife who assisted at Jesus' birth.

According to old Scottish custom, should Brigid's magical, spiritual assistance be required at a birth, the midwife must go to the door of the birthing chamber and call out her name.

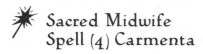 ## Sacred Midwife Spell (4) Carmenta

Carmenta, consort of Hermes, was born in Arcadia but moved to Italy where she emerged as a spirit of prophesy. Carmenta sings the future and the past. "Charms" are named in her honor. Carmenta provides protection for women in childbirth. Her festival, the Carmentalia, is celebrated between January 11th and January 15th. This is the best time to request her protection for any children born during the year. For maximum effect, make your request in song or rhyme form.

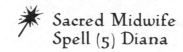 ## Sacred Midwife Spell (5) Diana

Diana may or may not be the same as Artemis, although they've been conflated with each other for millennia. Both are primal female deities associated with childbirth, wild nature, and the moon. Neither is quite as solitary as their myth sometimes suggests, although unlike Artemis, who is determinedly single, there is a strong sexual component in Diana's myth. No virgin, or at least not in the modern technical sense, once upon a time Diana dwelt in a shrine in the Italian Forest of Nemi with her consort Virbius, a horned spirit. Perhaps the most widely worshipped deity of pagan Europe, Diana was profoundly involved with the process of pregnancy and childbirth.

Petition Diana for easy, successful childbirth. Light white candles and place the image of a crescent moon and a bow and arrow beside them to attract her attention. Make your request.

Sacred Midwife Spell (6) Diana's Post-birth Spell

Following a successful childbirth, offer Diana her traditional offering: a round cake, shaped like the full moon, covered with candles.

Sacred Midwife Spell (7) Egeria

Egeria, a nymph residing in the Italian woods with Diana and Virbius, presided over springs and women in childbirth. Lover and adviser of an early king of Rome, Egeria responds to women's pleas for assistance with all aspects of childbirth. Toss milagro charms into springs to request her assistance: the original wishing wells.

Sacred Midwife Spell (8) Egyptian

Pregnancy and childbirth figure prominently in Isis's saga. Despite all her travails and dangerous adventures, ultimately Isis prevails, through the powers of her own magical prowess but also that of her powerful friends and allies. This theme is incorporated into a woman's childbirth ritual:

1. In the midst of delivery, the laboring woman, whenever she deems appropriate, announces that she is Isis and demands that the spirits of successful childbearing come to her assistance, *immediately.*
2. Cajole them, bribe them with offerings, threaten them with wrath if they fail to arrive promptly. Percussive music and aromatic incense **(kyphi,** frankincense, and myrrh) summon them too.
3. Isis's spirit allies include Hathor, Bes, Taweret, Heket, Khnum, Selket, Nephthys, and Renenet, as well as assorted serpent, crocodile, and scorpion spirits.
4. Prepare an offering table for them either during or immediately following the birth. Egyptian spirits like beer, wine, perfumes and general food offerings. Reputedly the Spirits stay to predict the baby's fortune—or bestow it. It won't hurt to put them in a generous, jovial mood.

Sacred Midwife Spell (9) Hathor

Over the centuries, Isis assumed many of Hathor's roles and even some of her attributes, however the older spirit remains powerful and undiminished. Hathor is among the most ancient of all Spirits; she emanated as a force from the Creator's eye, earning her the title "the Eye of Ra." Hathor has dominion over the life-force and all Earth's joys and pleasures. She rules women, love, sex, magic, reproduction, intoxication, music, dance, the cosmetic arts, perfume, divination, and more.

Hathor is the celestial midwife. The Seven Hathors greet each birth to bestow the baby's fate and soul,

although whether they are Hathor's daughters or merely aspects of herself is not understood. Request Hathor's assistance in the birth chamber and a favorable destiny for the new baby.

1. Create an offering table for Hathor: on it place a copper handmirror and a sistrum, the percussion instrument used in Hathor's rituals. Shake it rhythmically to call her.
2. Offer Hathor a glass of pure spring water, some beer, myrrh, a piece of turquoise and a piece of malachite, and some kohl powder.
3. Place seven red ribbons on the table, one for each of the Seven Hathors.
4. Soon after the birth is complete, if you are satisfied with Hathor's performance on your behalf (and if you think you'd ever like to appeal to her again) weave the ribbons together and toss them into a spring or river.

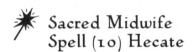

Sacred Midwife Spell (10) Hecate

Hecate rides a chariot drawn by dragons, symbolizing her dominion over the menstrual process. Other emblems include a broomstick, a flaming torch to light the way through dark passages, and a key that unlocks all doors, gates, and roads including the birth canal. Petition Hecate for safe, smooth delivery prior to going into labor. In addition midwives may always request Hecate's assistance, guidance, and protection. The same ritual spell serves laboring women and midwives alike.

1. Put thirteen separated but unpeeled garlic cloves on a plate.
2. Cover them with honey, lavender honey if at all possible. (You can also infuse plain honey with lavender blossoms.)
3. Leave this at a crossroads, preferably at midnight, but at least after dark, either on the final day of any month or during the Dark Moon Phase.

4. Murmur your prayers and petitions and go home, without looking back.

5. If you hear dogs or see them, especially black dogs or lone dogs unaccompanied by people, this is very auspicious (but should not be taken as an invitation to approach a strange dog, if caution suggests otherwise.) Hecate also sometimes manifests in the form of a black cat.

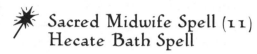

Sacred Midwife Spell (11)
Hecate Bath Spell

Lavender is among Hecate's most sacred plants. Bathe in lavender water (a sponge bath is fine) just prior to childbirth to receive Hecate's blessings.

Sacred Midwife Spell (12)
Hecate Room Cleansing

This spell cleanses and purifies the birthing room and invokes Hecate's presence.

Lavender scrub-water is required; make a strong infusion by pouring boiling water over lavender, eventually straining out the botanical material. For a quick fix add lavender essential oil to hot water or substitute lavender hydrosol instead. For extreme maximum power, combine herbal infusion with hydrosol and then add several drops of essential oil. Dip a broom—not a mop—into this lavender water, and cleanse the room, especially the thresholds.

Sacred Midwife Spell (13)
Saint Margaret

In Christian legend, Saint Margaret was swallowed by Satan in the form of a dragon. Her goodness or power made him spit her right out. Surviving the journey down the dragon's gullet, she is now Matron and Protector of Women in Childbirth. Saint Margaret bridges Christianity and Pagan symbols: dragon as women's power and birth prowess, the healing, protective power of women's blood. There were once over two hundred churches dedicated to Saint Margaret in England alone.

Margaret is usually depicted as a beautiful young woman, dressed in a magic girdle, with a huge dragon and a cauldron.

According to legend, just before she was beheaded (allegedly after rejecting the advances of a powerful pagan official), Margaret swore that any fearful woman who called her name during childbirth would receive her blessings and assistance. No special preparation is necessary, just call out her name.

Birth Rituals

Successful delivery signals the beginning of a series of spells and rituals to welcome and protect mother and baby. A host of protective amulets evolved to provide for infants' and children's extreme psychic vulnerability. It is crucial to understand, however, that these amulets were created during a time when fears regarding psychic safety outweighed those for physical safety. The concept of *"infant-proofing"* didn't exist and accidents surely happened. However, this was also a time when babies were rarely, if ever, supervised, infant mortality was high, and when people lived in smaller, more crowded spaces so children were constantly underfoot—and under someone's eye.

Some amulets may not be safe for use as originally directed but must be adapted to suit personal circumstances: they presuppose that someone literally has their eyes on the baby at all times. Once upon a time, the baby was either in a cradle right by an adult, or carried on someone's body. Children were rarely isolated. There's no point protecting against the Evil Eye or malicious Spirits while simultaneously leaving the baby vulnerable to choking.

Afterbirth and Umbilical Cord Spells

Amongst many spiritual and magical traditions, the afterbirth (placenta) and umbilical cord is believed exceptionally charged with power. These organs are allegedly able to provide protection for the baby during life just as they did in the womb. On the other hand, many metaphysical traditions believe that if placenta and umbilical cord are not disposed of correctly, the baby is left vulnerable to psychic and spiritual danger.

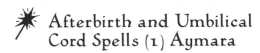

Afterbirth and Umbilical Cord Spells (1) Aymara

Cover the afterbirth with flowers. Bury it in earth together with appropriate tools (real or miniature), reflecting the parent's desires for the child's happy future. The Aymara are an indigenous people of Bolivia and Peru. Tools considered "appropriate" in traditional Aymara perspective include cooking tools for girls and farm tools for boys, but objects may be changed to suit any parent's visions and desires.

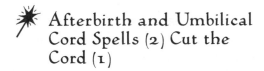

Afterbirth and Umbilical Cord Spells (2) Cut the Cord (1)

For optimum protection and blessings, use a magical quartz crystal or turquoise ritual knife to cut the umbilical cord.

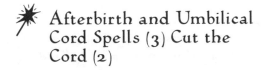

Afterbirth and Umbilical Cord Spells (3) Cut the Cord (2)

1. Place the umbilical cord and the knife used to cut it within the baby's very first swaddling clothes.
2. Fold them into a packet.

3. Bury this packet in a safe, secret place or throw it into the river or sea lest an enemy find them and use them to cast a hex.

Afterbirth and Umbilical Cord Spells (4) Earth Binding

Before birth, the umbilical cord and placenta nourished the infant and bound him or her to the human mother. Once birth has accomplished physical disconnection from the actual mother, the umbilical cord and placenta may be used to plant and bind the new baby to the Earth Mother for life.

Bury the umbilical cord and/or placenta in Earth. Plant or transplant a tree directly over the spot where they are buried.

Afterbirth and Umbilical Cord Spells (5) Earth Burying

Bury the umbilical cord on your property, together with barley, henna powder, and salt, to protect the child from any malevolent spirits.

Afterbirth and Umbilical Cord Spells (6) Great Plains

According to Native American tradition from the North American Great Plains, the umbilical cord can be crafted into a powerful amulet for a baby, enhanced by the creation of a special amulet case.

1. Create a tiny amulet case from soft leather.
2. Form it in the shape of an animal—turtles or lizards are most traditional, however whatever is significant for the baby could be crafted.
3. Embellish the case through beading and embroidering, each bead, each stitch accompanied by a wish, prayer, or blessing for the baby.

4. When the case is complete, tuck or sew the dried umbilical cord within.
5. Have the baby wear this blessed charm or hang it from the cradle.

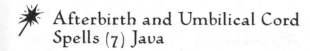

Afterbirth and Umbilical Cord Spells (7) Java

Place the afterbirth in a miniature boat decorated with fruits, flowers, and lit candles. Set this adrift at night as a gift for crocodiles.

There are two rationales for this spell, which are not mutually exclusive:

★ *The crocodile is the sacred patron of childbirth; the boat laden with gifts is an offering expressing appreciation following successful childbirth*

★ *The afterbirth is traditionally viewed as a baby's protective "twin." Crocodiles may be sacred, but they're also definitely dangerous. By sacrificing the twin, the living baby's future safety is magically ensured*

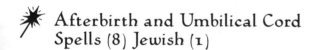

Afterbirth and Umbilical Cord Spells (8) Jewish (1)

In Jewish magic tradition, the ashes from the dried, burned afterbirth are a potent component of enchantments intended to benefit the baby.

1. Take the time to dry the afterbirth completely and then burn it.
2. Mix the ashes with dried snapdragons and place within a charm bag.
3. Hang this bag around the baby's neck to protect against bewitchment.

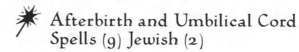

Afterbirth and Umbilical Cord Spells (9) Jewish (2)

1. Dry the afterbirth completely and then burn it.
2. Reserve the ashes inside a conjure bag and keep in a safe, secret place.
3. Should the child ever fall ill with a *"wasting"* disease, whether from Evil Eye, changeling, or other magical derivation, these ashes may be blended with milk and used to break the negative enchantment.

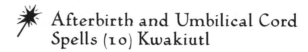

Afterbirth and Umbilical Cord Spells (10) Kwakiutl

Present the afterbirth to ravens to instill enhanced psychic aptitude in a child.

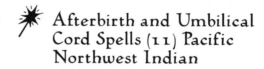

Afterbirth and Umbilical Cord Spells (11) Pacific Northwest Indian

Turn the umbilical cord into a bracelet for wrist or ankle for the baby to wear for a few months or until it is naturally outgrown. Bless the baby as you form any knots.

Baby's Magic Cleansing Spells

The new-born baby is greeted and welcomed to Earth with cleansing spells. These rituals provide special protection for the baby as well as offering a person's first spiritual cleansing. Most typically these cleansings take the form of ritual magical baths, administered to the baby fairly immediately after birth.

Baby's Magic Cleansing Bath (1) Central European Romany

This bath, recommended to ward off dangerous demons attracted to the new life, may be done at birth but is also periodically repeated for infants and young children.

Place the baby within an empty tub. Pour the bath water over the child, making it run along the blade of a scythe or similar steel or iron blade. The water must make contact with the metal before reaching the child.

Baby's Magic Cleansing Bath (2) English

Dip holly leaves into spring water and sprinkle the water onto baby.

Baby's Magic Cleansing Bath (3) English/German

Place glowing coals or red-hot needles in a dish of water. Gently drizzle the water over the baby.

Baby's Magic Cleansing Bath (4) European Jewish

Dissolve a little sugar in a bowl of spring water. Dip a piece of bread into the water and use it to sprinkle water on to the baby.

Baby's Magic Cleansing Bath (5) Portuguese

Float needles in a bowl of spring water and drizzle it over the baby.

Baby's Magic Cleansing Bath (6) Scottish

Soak gold and silver rings in pure spring water. Use the water to bathe baby.

Baby's Magic Cleansing Bath (7) Swedish

Place the mother's wedding ring and some real silver in a bowl of water, so that the baby will be blessed with wealth, security, and true love (presuming, of course, that the parents' marriage is happy). Sprinkle this water over the baby.

Baby's Magic Cleansing Spell

This Hungarian spell shows that spiritual cleansing may be accomplished via other mediums besides water.

Instead of cleaning the baby immediately following birth, smear the baby's hands and face with blood from the birth. Place the baby onto Earth for strength, safety, and protection until the placenta is delivered.

Birth Trauma Spell

Perhaps you're reading through these childbirth spells not because you're planning or anticipating a future birth but because your own birth has proved problematic.

Birth trauma, either during delivery or immediately afterwards can cause lasting, profound soul damage, exacerbated by the inability to consciously remember or articulate the experience. Recall, or at least understanding and assimilation, may be achieved during the dream process with the assistance of Evening Primrose flower remedy (FES).

1. The night that one first initiates this spell, draw a warm bath just before bed.

2. Add between 20 and 30 drops of the flower essence remedy and soak in the bath, visualizing the spell's desired results.
3. Go to sleep and dream.
4. This extra-strength bath is taken only once; the flower essence remedy is then continued via the manufacturer's recommendations for internal administration, or by topical application, or baths. Any future baths should use no more than half-a-dozen drops of the remedy.

Changeling Spells

Fairy encounters similar to what *Sleeping Beauty* suggests may have inspired fear and guilty consciences on the part of humans, but they aren't what earned fairies their sometimes bad reputation. For every story that involves a fairy's curse, there's another dozen where a fairy's blessing saves or enriches a life. A different type of fairy/human encounter, also typically involving babies but also young children, is particularly fraught with tension; this encounter is embodied by the changeling.

The general pattern goes something like this: someone has a child who is, at worst, a normal, healthy child and, at best, a particularly beautiful, charming child. Eventually a profound change is observed in this child, characterized by one of two manifestations:

1. The child is observed to be pining away; vitality and all interest in everyday life fading. This is a gradual process and it is frequently unnoticed until it reaches crisis proportions. Pining, yearning, and wasting are extreme to the point where death or coma is feared. Explanation: fairies, invisible to all but the child, are luring him or her to their realm.
2. The child, although he or she may physically appear the same, is literally *not the same child.* There is someone else in that body. Sometimes the child is

described as replaced by another; however, the description is usually that the original child was robust and vivacious, while the new child is described as remote, sullen, and frail. Explanation: fairies, inevitably described as *"cold-hearted"* in these tales, have replaced the robust human child with a frail one of their own.

What actually is being described? Although the changeling may be merely a "fairy story" it may also perhaps be understood as a metaphor for autism, which typically manifests at about the same age as changelings appear, or perhaps as a description of the still vague, mysterious, and frustrating "failure to thrive."

Significantly, the changeling, the fairy's substitute baby, must be well cared for or there is no hope of ever seeing one's own vivacious child again. Despite the fact that the Fairy Mother has abandoned her child, it's understood that she will punish anyone who harms or likewise abandons the changeling. One of the most poignant fairy tale suggestions for receiving one's own child back is to nurture the fairy child so well that it blossoms, prompting the fairy folk to once again make the switch.

Fairy tales offer various recommendations for replacing the changeling and winning one's own child back. These recommendations aren't reserved for fairy tales, however. There are almost as many folkloric, traditional magical suggestions for handling the changeling situation as there are Evil Eye repelling methods.

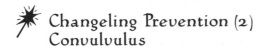

☀ Changeling Prevention Spell (1) Conjure Bag

From Ireland, this is a charm to scare off Fairy Folk intent on enticing a child away. This spell counteracts the wasting, pining syndrome.

1. Fill a charm bag with old horseshoe nails, hen manure, and salt.
2. Attach the bag to the wall with an old horseshoe nail. (All nails *must* come from *used* horseshoes. Their presence on the horse is what provides the needed energy and vitality.)
3. While hammering concentrate on the child, grounded, living, healthy, and joyful.

☀ Changeling Prevention (2) Convulvulus

Burn convulvulus at both ends, then pinch out the flames. Hang the burned convulvulus over the cradle to ward off fairies with bad intent.

☀ Changeling Prevention Spell (3) Forge Water

Another Irish formula to remedy any type of soul posses-sion, but especially that caused by fairies: douse the tar-get of possession with cooled forge water.

☀ Changeling Prevention Spell (4) Juniper

Allegedly burning juniper consistently from the time one enters the birthing room until all danger has passed prevents the substitution of a changeling.

☀ Changeling Prevention Spell (5) Mistletoe

*Hang mistletoe over or near the cradle to prevent theft by fairies. (**Warning:** Misletoe is a very toxic plant that can be fatal to children.)*

☀ Changeling Prevention Spell (6) Scotland/Northumberland

Iron prevails against baby-stealing fairies. Place an iron poker across the cradle, when the baby is inside.

☀ Changeling Prevention Spell (7) Sharp Tools

Sharp metal tools repel fairies. Use scissors, knives, or nails as amulets. Hang them near the baby or place them by the cradle, keeping the child's physical safety in mind also, however. Presumably the miniature iron tools used ritually by devotees of the orisha Ogun would have delighted watchful parents once upon a time.

Certain botanicals provide protection against child-stealing fairies, most especially garlic, rose-mary, and rowan.

☀ Changeling Prevention Botanical Spell (1)

Create an aura of protection around your home with living plants.

1. Surround the home with rosemary, garlic plants, and rowan trees.
2. Let them grow rampant.
3. If this isn't possible, bring potted rosemary and garlic plants within the home and keep them where the child sleeps and spends the most time.

 Changeling Protection
Botanical Spell (2)

Botanicals provide amuletic protection too. Place braids
of garlic, pieces of rowan wood, and wreathes and garlands of rosemary within the home to serve as preventive, protective amulets. Post them near the child's bed,
over entrance doors and threshold areas.

Changeling Protection
Botanical Spell (3)

Rosemary prevents fairies from stealing or switching
infants. Create an infusion by pouring boiling water
over rosemary. When the infusion cools, strain out the
botanical material and use the infused liquid to rinse the
child's hair. (This may, over time, slightly darken the
color of the hair.)

Changeling Prevention
Botanical Spell (4)

Frequently and consistently sprinkle the child with protective magical waters such as **Rose of Jericho Water**
or **Indigo Water**. Use rosemary or rowan as the
asperging tool.

Changeling Replacement Spells

Prevention and protection are all well and good but
what if the damage is done and instead of your
own dear child, you've been left with the rejected
changeling? Celtic fairy tales describe heroic, determined mothers battling the fairies, sometimes
literally, to win back a child. According to many
tales, the switch may be accomplished on only one
night of the year, typically Samhain/Halloween, or
during the Wild Hunt. Luckily other spells exist,
to be cast as needed at any time of the year.

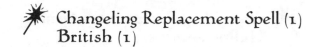 Changeling Replacement Spell (1)
British (1)

The changeling, the abandoned fairy child, is inevitably
fussy, cranky, and petulant. The best way to accomplish
the switch, to get rid of the changeling and receive one's
own child back, is to make the changeling laugh. This is
not as easy as it sounds.

Certain magical methods have proven successful,
however it's imperative that the baby watches the spell:
break one egg in half. Empty the shell and boil water in
the two halves. Repeat until the baby laughs.

Changeling Replacement Spell (2)
British (2)

The goal of this spell, like the one above, is to make the
child laugh, thus breaking the enchantment. The spell
can't work if the changeling isn't watching.

1. Pierce the ends of an egg with a pin.
2. Blow the egg out of the shell.
3. Repeat with eleven more eggs, for a total of twelve.
4. Boil only the shells in a pot of water.

Changeling Replacement Spell (3)
Eggshell Brewery

1. Make up a fire in the hearth; make sure the
   changeling is watching.
2. Line up at least one dozen empty eggshells.
3. Place a few grains of hops and barley in each
   eggshell.
4. When complete, burn the eggshells in the fire. A
   reaction should be provoked, successfully effecting
   the change.

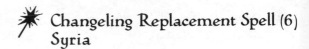

✴ Changeling Replacement Spell (4) Halloween

Certain Changeling Replacement Spells can only be accomplished on a single day of the year, most typically on Halloween. If the Fairy Host charges past you on Halloween, gather up dust from under your feet. If you throw it after them, they'll be obliged to return any humans they've captured.

✴ Changeling Replacement Spell (5) Morocco

The Moroccan version of a changeling is known as a mebeddel. The mebeddel is left by djinn in place of a human child immediately following birth, demonstrating the need for childbirth protection spells. Because this switch occurs so early, it's difficult to catch; however clues lie in the child's failure to thrive with no apparent cause, regardless of care, nurturing, or attention offered. If the exchange is spotted, another switch, righting the situation, may be magically effected.

1. Take the mebeddel to the graveyard.
2. Find a broken tomb. Place the mebeddel there, together with an offering for the djinn. (Muslim djinn traditionally accept oil drizzled over grain; Jewish djinn have a sweet tooth and like jam. Christian and Pagan djinn will accept a dish of cooked meat. If in doubt, offer all.)
3. Move away a little bit but pay attention. The baby is *never* actually left unsupervised or unobserved.
4. As soon as the baby cries, come immediately and pick up the baby. Announce aloud: *"I take my own child, not the other people's child."*
5. Wash the baby immediately with **Holy Water** or similar blessed water and go home.

"The other people" is the euphemism frequently used to describe the djinn.

✴ Changeling Replacement Spell (6) Syria

In the Middle-East and North Africa, saints' graves are often positioned near a source of living water. When this isn't possible, a cistern may be strategically placed nearby instead, creating a synergy: the power of the saint plus the inherent power of sacred water. This spell avails itself of the power of this water.

A pining child, one who fails to thrive or one whose personality has drastically changed, is, as elsewhere, perceived as a fairy changeling. Carefully lower this child into the cistern (accompanied by prayer and petition, of course), where the resident saint effects the change. Draw the "true" child up in its place.

✴ Changeling Spell Breaker

This spell targets the child who has been seduced by fairies and is wasting away with a longing to enter Fairy Land permanently. The ritual assistance of a trusted, reliable blacksmith is required.

1. Bring the child to a blacksmith.
2. Place it on the anvil.
3. The smith raises his hammer as if to strike hot iron but actually brings it down very gently, touching the baby or right beside the baby.
4. Repeat for a total of three times and then the child is believed free of the fairies' allure.

Cradle Spells

An appeal to the Fairies in the birthing chamber is not the only way to gain favor for your baby. Sometimes you can create luck.

Cradle Spell (1) Birch

Construct a cradle from birch wood, the tree of new beginnings. This cradle will set the child off on an auspicious path.

 ## Cradle Spell (2) Nine Woods

Gather nine distinct types of wood. Construct a cradle from these to bring luck to a new baby.

Lactation Spells

Human mother's milk (because of course *all* milk is mother's milk) is considered a particularly powerful magical substance. Today it's understood that various immunities are transmitted through mother's milk; once upon a time, wisdom, intelligence, and magical protection (the immunities?) were believed transmitted. The position of Pharaoh's wet nurse, for instance, was a powerful, influential profession. Egyptian wet nurses, in general, were hired on the basis of vitality (lifeforce) and the magic power that they were able to transmit.

In ancient Egypt, human milk was considered crucial for more than feeding babies. Milk is considered a magical substance akin to menstrual blood, sweat or any other emanation of the body. Vestiges of an occult science that analyzed what type of milk was best for which magical purpose lingers; fairy tales requiring the hero to obtain lion's milk or similar for a specific magic cause. In ancient Egypt, the most powerful magical milk came from women who had borne sons.

Specific crystal gemstones and botanicals allegedly increase lactation and milk supply.

Crystal gemstones will work if worn anywhere on the body or even hung over the mother's bed, however they are most potent when worn on a chain long enough to actually make contact with the breasts.

Choose one or any combination of the following:

★ *Chalcedony*
★ *Coral*
★ *Quartz crystal*
★ *Turquoise*

 ## Lactation Spell (1) Saxifrage

Place a sprig of saxifrage in the bosom, in the manner of sixteenth-century European wet nurses, to increase milk supply. Remove the sprig after a few hours, lest too much be produced. Repeat as needed.

 ## Lactation Spell (2) Serpentine Spell

Serpentine, the serpent stone, worn around the neck allegedly stabilizes and regulates milk supply.

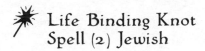

Lactation Spells (3) Sulis

Sulis is an ancient British spirit associated with the magic powers of healing waters. Her major shrine was at Aqua Sulis, now the modern city of Bath. The Romans identified her with Minerva and constructed that shrine in 65 CE, but Sulis's springs were apparently visited as early as the Neolithic. The Roman shrine was built atop an earlier Celtic one. Traditionally Sulis was magically petitioned for healing and abundance (the key to lactation) by offering small votive charms, similar to modern milagros. Many have been discovered alongside the curse tablets also deposited in Sulis's waters. Successful nursing and milk supply once meant life or death for children; votive offerings of breasts, typically carved from bronze or ivory, have been found in Sulis's shrine, in gratitude for her assistance with the lactation process.

Modern ex-votos are most commonly formed from silver-colored metal. Wear the charm, on a necklace, as a pin or, for more privacy, pinned within one's clothing or carried within an amulet bag. This charm is traditionally worn constantly until the child is completely weaned and then offered to Sulis by throwing into a spring or well. (Pilgrimage to Bath is also appropriate.)

Life Binding Knot Spells

These spells for infants and young children combine power materials with knot magic to create a protection spell intended to repel illness, bewitchment, and the Evil Eye. These spells should also protect against soul loss and repel a fairy's attempt at theft.

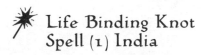

Life Binding Knot Spell (1) India

Wrap a black thread around the child's waist. When tying the concluding knot, focus on blessings for the baby.

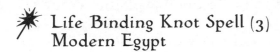

Life Binding Knot Spell (2) Jewish

Wrap red thread around the child's wrist. Focus blessings of good health, protection, and safety for the baby into every knot you tie.

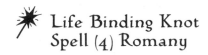

Life Binding Knot Spell (3) Modern Egypt

1. Create a bracelet or anklet for the baby from a piece of cord.
2. Attach seven beads to this cord plus a tiny bag filled with salt, alum, a bit of copper, and/or silver.
3. Tie this around the child's ankle or wrist, concentrating your hopes, wishes, and desires into all the knots.

Life Binding Knot Spell (4) Romany

Wrap red thread or a used violin string around the baby or child's wrist. Focus on your hopes, wishes, blessings, and desires for the child while tying any knots.

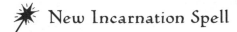

Mother's Magic Bath

The baby is not the only vulnerable party. The new mother is believed prone to psychic attack by the Evil Eye or by malevolent envy.

Bathe daily in salted water following childbirth for protection. Continue for at least one complete lunar month.

New Incarnation Spell

According to some traditions, the same souls reincarnate within one family, so that ancestors continually return

as descendants. *A Koryak ritual determines which relation is the baby's former incarnation.*

1. A special divining stone is required for the purpose. Find, prepare, and consecrate it.
2. Hang the stone on a stick.
3. Suspend the stick and let the stone swing like a pendulum, of its own volition.
4. Someone, traditionally the child's father, calls out the names of the possibilities, all the dead relatives on both sides of the family. When the stone quickens its swinging (rather than slowing down, which is usual), or when you see a visible change in the rhythm, the identity of the soul has been discovered.

Infant Protection Spells

Nothing and no one is metaphysically perceived as more in need of magical protection than an infant or young child. Protection spells designed especially for babies fulfill this need. Consider the warnings above, however: many of these spells evolved at a time when babies were never left unattended or unobserved. Their safety precautions are of a much different standard than that of modern parents. The original spells are offered, but consider whether adaptation is required so as to provide a baby with both magical *and* physical safety simultaneously.

 ## Protection Ritual

1. Prepare **Holy Water** for washing the baby.
2. Having cleansed the infant immediately on birth, preserve some of the water.
3. This may be used in the future to remove the Evil Eye by dipping a piece of coral, the house key, or a ritual key into the water, then hanging it over the baby's crib.

 ## Protection Spell (1) Caraway

Place caraway seeds in a charm bag. Hide the bag under a child's mattress to protect against illness and evil.

 ## Protection Spell (2) Chamomile

Hang bunches of chamomile over the baby's crib for magical protection.

 ## Protection Spell (3) Cloves

In addition to spiritual protection, this charm is believed to stimulate intelligence and attract good fortune to the baby.

Pierce cloves and string them onto red thread. Hang this on the wall overlooking the baby's bed.

 ## Protection Spell (4) Conjure Bag (1)

A mojo hand to protect a child from harm, this conjure bag is a spell in progress:

1. Place an angelica root together with chamomile and flax seed in a charm bag.
2. Add a coin minted in the child's birth year, together with a small piece of silver. Traditionally the child's initials are scratched into the metal. An initial bead or a charm with the child's name engraved upon it may be substituted.
3. Collect any baby teeth and add them to the bag. It's not necessary to have every single baby tooth; even one is sufficient.
4. Keep this charm bag in a safe place until the child is old enough to inherit it.

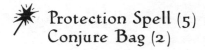

Protection Spell (5)
Conjure Bag (2)

Place salt, one dozen cloves plus one clove of garlic in a red bag. Add a piece of coral and a piece of real silver. Hang this over the baby's bed.

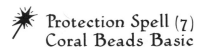

Protection Spell (6)
Conjure Bag (3)

1. Add the following to a red silk or flannel bag: bread crumbs, cumin, frankincense, juniper berries, magnetic sand, salt, three pins with black heads, three pins with red heads, and three pins with yellow heads for a total of nine heads.
2. Add three playing cards: the queen of spades, the seven of spades, and the seven of clubs.
3. Add the scrapings from cleaning a horse's hooves and one hair from a black cat. Add any other lucky charms as desired. Dress with **Black Cat Oil.**
4. The child's parent may carry this on behalf of the child, or it may be hung over the child's bed or kept discreetly hidden in the child's bedroom.
5. Should the child ever be feared bewitched, place this bag under a heavy weight until the danger has passed.

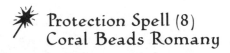

Protection Spell (7)
Coral Beads Basic

Smooth pink coral beads worn around the neck provide a child with magical protection.

Protection Spell (8)
Coral Beads Romany

A Romany version of the classic child's coral protection necklace strings pieces of red wool or cotton onto the necklace together with the beads.

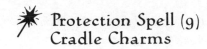

Protection Spell (9)
Cradle Charms

The following amulets, believed capable of providing a newborn baby with magical protection, are meant to be attached to the cradle, or else displayed near the cradle. Use one, more, or all of the following:

★ *Antique key*
★ *Blue-eye beads*
★ *Knife used to cut the umbilical cord*
★ *Mirror*

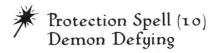

Protection Spell (10)
Demon Defying

Malevolent child-devouring flying spirits include Lamia, Lamashtu, and Lilith. The strigae *are a genre of similar, child-devouring spirits. Strigae are believed to have originated in Germanic Northern Europe but made themselves at home in Rome by the turn of the Common Era. The poet Ovid's magical recommendation for keeping these demons at bay?*

★ *Touch the lintels and thresholds of baby's room with arbutus*
★ *Place a whitehorn wand at the windows*
★ *Just in case a spirit gets past these door-guards, leave an offering plate of meat, saying aloud, "Accept this instead."*

Protection Spell (11) Fig Hand

The figa, fica or the fig hand amulet has many uses in protective and fertility magic. It's considered a particular powerful protective amulet for babies and children. It dates back to at least ancient Roman times, and depicts a tiny hand with its thumb placed between the first two fingers, the "fig" gesture. Although fig hands are made from a wide variety of materials including

bone, coral, wood, and stone, fig hands crafted from jet are believed most beneficial and protective for children.

1. Attach a fig hand charm to red cord or a silver chain.
2. Have the child wear this as a necklace during the day.
3. Suspend it on the wall over the head of the child while sleeping.

 ## Protection Spell (12) Fire Safety

Two people pass a new-born baby backwards and forwards three times over a fire, ideally one built from rowan wood, to provide the baby with magical safety and protection.

 ## Protection Spell (13) Flaming Torch

This magic spell from the Hebrides welcomes the baby and also offers spiritual protection. Circle around the cradle three times a day carrying a flaming torch until the appropriate time for a more permanent, official ceremony is reached, or for as long as you feel that this is needed and beneficial.

 ## Protection Spell (14) Holy Herbs

"Holy Herbs," a New Orleans formulation, is used to protect children. Equal parts of seven dried herbs are blended together: catnip, ground black snake root (black cohosh root), hops, jasmine blossoms, motherwort, peppermint, and skullcap.

1. Grind them together into powder.
2. Reserve them within a tightly shut jar until needed.
3. Should spiritual protection ever be required make an infusion by pouring boiling water over the herbal blend. When the brew cools, strain out the solids.

4. Add the liquid to the child's bathwater or sprinkle it onto the child using an asperging tool.
5. Sprinkle the liquid into each corner of the child's room.

 ## Protection Spell (15) Palo

The iroko tree, also known as the African oak or the Nigeria teak, is sacred throughout Africa. The tree's aura of holiness survived the Middle Passage to the Western hemisphere and so it is venerated by many African Diaspora traditions, although sometimes the ceiba or silk cotton tree is used as a substitute. To protect a baby from the Evil Eye hang a piece of iroko wood over the cradle with red ribbon.

 ## Protection Spell (16) Psalm

This magical method of protecting a child needs to be prepared before the birth so that it is ready for the child whenever it appears. The written psalm charm would once have been purchased from a scribe (and perhaps still can be), or even carefully removed from a book.

Copy Psalm 127 onto parchment. Place it within a soft leather pouch and hang it around the child's neck immediately after birth to guard against all evil.

 ## Protection Spell (17) Rue

Hang rue in a house with a newborn so as to offer magical and spiritual protection.

Protection Spell (18)
Rue Parent Protection

The new baby isn't the only one requiring protection. Give new parents sprigs of rue to wear immediately after the birth, to protect against the Evil Eye and ward off malevolent spirits.

 Protection Spell (19) Sachet

Sew the following into a small sachet: alum, harmel (Syrian rue), salt, and witch-hazel. Hang it on the cradle or over the crib, out of reach of the baby.

 Protection Spell (20)
Soul Loss

1. To protect against soul loss (a cause of disease, see page 562), create a magical cloth baby carrier.
2. Decorate and/or embroider the carrier with magic symbols as well as protective soul-retaining motifs, such as pig-pens symbolizing a safe enclosure.
3. Carry the baby within this carrier on the mother's back or hip.

 Protection Spell (21)
Threshold

If a child is born at home then this Italian spell should be cast on the night of birth; otherwise cast the spell on the baby's first night at home. Touch the threshold with a broom, a hatchet, and a pestle to prevent the entry of jealous spirits.

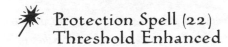 Protection Spell (22)
Threshold Enhanced

1. Follow the directions as in the spell above.
2. Once the threshold has been touched by each object, take the tools and manipulate them to form the shape of a cross over the threshold.
3. Leave them there over the threshold, to stand guard overnight.

 Protection Spell (23)
Unicorn Root

True unicorn root offers magical protection to mothers and their children. The botanical is extremely endangered. Grow your own supply and carry it in an amulet bag. Alternatively, hang it over the cradle.

 Protection Spell (24) Yarrow

Tie yarrow to a baby's cradle to protect from fairies, malevolent magic, and spirits.

 Protection: Worst Case
Scenario

According to modern Egyptian tradition, if several children in a family have previously died, a new or surviving baby may be given a protective tattoo. A small dot is tattooed in the center of the forehead and another one on the outer edge of the left ankle to safeguard the baby.

 Sibling Harmony Spell

A spell to promote sibling harmony, immediately following the birth of a new baby.
    Just before siblings are formally introduced for the first time, place a few grains of sugar in the new infant's

hand. Elder siblings are encouraged to lick the sugar off the baby's hand. (Never use honey, which contains spores potentially toxic to those under one year old.)

Spells for Ailing Children

Most amulets are prophylactic: they're meant to prevent misfortune. In the face of actual trouble, especially illness, different spells, amulets, and magical measures serve.

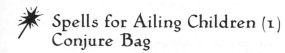

Spells for Ailing Children (1)
Conjure Bag

1. Collect dust from a crossroads.
2. Place it inside a cloth together with a chili pepper and an iron nail.
3. Tie it up tight with black wool or red thread.
4. Replace the chili pepper as needed, burning the old one.

Blessed red lead from one of the protective Hindu deity Hanuman's official shrines may be substituted for the crossroads dirt.

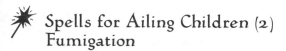

Spells for Ailing Children (2)
Fumigation

This spell offers spiritual protection as well as a magical cleansing to remove any lingering malevolence. Burn alum, coriander seeds, and harmel (Syrian rue). Pass the baby gently through the smoke or hold the baby over it.

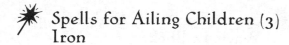

Spells for Ailing Children (3)
Iron

This traditional Ashanti spell understands spirits to be a potential cause of illness. There are two things malevolent spirits usually really dislike: iron and bells.

1. Attach iron rings, beads, and bells to cord, tying hopes, blessings, and intentions into every knot.
2. Tie the cord to the child's ankles.
3. This may be done as a preventive measure before any illness or trouble manifests; however, in an emergency any "visiting" negative entities may be safely drawn out and repelled while the anklet is in place.

Spells for Ailing Children (4)
Maximon Safety Spell

The crossroads spirit Maximon has a prankster aspect but not when it comes to children's safety. Invoke him to save a child, especially in matters of life and death.

1. Offer Maximon a yellow candle, ideally but not necessarily dressed with **Maximon Oil.**
2. Pray and petition. Maximon can be bought; offer him a pilgrimage to his shrine in Guatemala if he fulfills your wish, or something else grand and valuable.

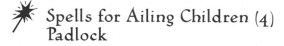

Spells for Ailing Children (4)
Padlock

In East Asia, small ornamental silver and iron padlocks serve as children's protective amulets. Charge and consecrate the charm as desired and then place the charm onto a cord or silver chain, to be worn around the child's neck or ankle.

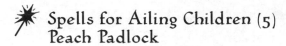

Spells for Ailing Children (5) Peach Padlock

Blessed padlock charms are so vital because they combine the road-opening and life-affirming sexual symbolism of the lock and key with the inherent magic powers of the material from which the charm is crafted. Iron and silver are most typical, however a Chinese variation favors peaches, symbolically the fruit of longevity and immortality.

Carve a peach pit into the form of a padlock, focusing on blessings for the child during the crafting of the charm. Attach the completed charm to a red cord and tie it to a child's ankle, to bind the child to life in the face of illness or threat of illness.

Stop Bed Wetting Spell

Have other methods failed? Then try this: put the child to sleep with a whole onion between his or her legs. In the morning, before sunrise, you should take this onion and throw it away at a crossroads.

Welcome Baby Spells

Welcome Spells greet the new child and offer blessings as well as requests for spiritual protection.

Welcome Spell (1) Jamaica

Babies are sometimes born with a natural blue "cross" in the spot over the nose between the eyebrows, which fades as the skin ages and grows thicker. Many traditions consider this mark to be very auspicious: a sign of spiritual protection. Blessings one is not born with, however, can also be consciously, magically bestowed. This bath is traditionally given on the ninth day following birth:

1. Add a little rum to bathwater.
2. Each member of the family throws in a bit of silver.
3. Real indigo is added to the water, tinting it blue.
4. Mark a blue cross on the baby's forehead or in the hollow over the nose, between the eyebrows, or else on the back of the neck.
5. Offer blessings and prayers for the baby's safety and happiness as you remove the child from the bath.

Welcome Spell (2) Java

This ceremony, or variations on the theme, was traditionally performed when the baby reaches approximately seven months of age or when absolutely dying to crawl, whichever comes first. Its objective: to formally introduce the new baby to Mother Earth.

Until seven months, a baby's existence is considered tenuous. Babies are perceived as hovering in a dimension between spiritual and physical realms, gradually becoming more and more grounded. Until this point, the baby is never placed on the ground but carried in a sling on the mother's body.

1. Form seven moist soft balls of clay, each in a distinct color.
2. Roll each clay ball against the baby's body.
3. Ritually bathe the baby.
4. Place the baby in large bamboo (wicker) cage or basket together with grains of rice, coins, gold chains and either feathers or a live hen. (This ritual also serves divinatory purposes: whichever object the child touches first, indicates something about his or her character and destiny.)
5. The baby is slowly lowered to the ground.

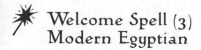 ## Welcome Spell (3)
Modern Egyptian

On the seventh day following birth, blend olive oil, salt, and onion juice. (Other optional ingredients include henna and kohl powder.) Dip a feather in the paste and pass it, without actually touching, over the baby's open eyes to make them beautiful, sharp, and healthy.

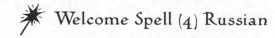 ## Welcome Spell (4) Russian

Immediately following birth, the naked midwife carries the naked baby around the birthing chamber, chanting invocations to Ishtar, the Morning Star, beseeching blessings and protection.

Protection Spells

Protection Spells are intended to prevent, protect, and repel danger. Many find this category confusing so let's be very clear: there is no magic spell that functions exactly like an armed response guard one might hire from a personal security service. *Magical protection spells provide magical protection.* They create an aura that enhances other protective methods. If you are concerned about actual physical danger, magic reinforces other methods but does not replace them. If you are seriously concerned about your apartment being robbed, for instance, it doesn't matter how many powerful spells you cast, how many amulets you post at the entrance, if you don't also lock doors

TIPS FOR SUCCESSFULLY CASTING PROTECTION SPELLS

Incorporate the following into spells as desired:

★ NUMBERS: 5, the number of fingers on each hand, is the number most associated with magical protection, as are the magic numbers seven and nine

★ COLORS: red, black, and blue are the colors most associated with magical protection

and windows. Magic doesn't offer license to defy laws of Nature or common sense.

According to occult wisdom, however, there are many kinds of danger in the world. Locking your door may prevent a human thief. However, certain dangers can only be repelled by magical methods. These dangers include:

★ *Malicious spells, hexes, jinxes, magic "tricks," or negative enchantment cast deliberately against one person by another*
★ *The Evil Eye*
★ *Assorted spiritual dangers deriving from a vast variety of spiritual sources. These may be caused deliberately or inadvertently*

Although these dangers derive from magical and spiritual roots, they may manifest in very physical ways, as illness, accidents, and general disaster. However, because their derivation is at least partly magical, prevention and remedies must also be, at least partly, magical.

Acacia Spells

Acacias are small thorny trees indigenous to Africa and Western Asia. The Ark of the Covenant was crafted from acacia wood; it's believed to have profound magical, spiritual, and protective powers.

 ## Acacia Protection Spell (1)

Asperging isn't only for cleansing and purification. Infuse acacia twigs and leaves to make a magically protective infusion. Asperge as desired, using acacia as the distributing tool.

 ## Acacia Protection Spell (2)

Place acacia twigs over the bed to ward off nocturnal spiritual dangers.

Anti-bewitchment Spells

Anti-bewitchment spells create a protective shield, an aura of invulnerability against malevolent magic. They prevent the casting of enchantment against you, however they may not remove a hex already cast. Hex-antidotes or reversing spells are required instead (see page 589).

 ## Anti-bewitchment Spell (1) Asperging

1. Dissolve saltpeter in water.
2. Sprinkle over the thresholds of your home and on people to repel malevolent magic, as well as anywhere you perceive vulnerability.
3. For maximum benefit, use protective botanicals as asperging tools, such as rue, rosemary, or rowan.

Anti-bewitchment Spell (2) Stones

This formula from ancient Mesopotamia to protect against malevolent magic is particularly beneficial if a future personal encounter with evil sorcery is anticipated.

1. Choose five different stones, including a hematite and a lodestone. (The original Mesopotamian formula suggested different colored glass as well, but what they considered glass might not have been as sharp and jagged as what we call glass. Sea glass might work, or crushed faience.)
2. Crush the rocks.
3. Blend olive and castor oil and add essential oil of cypress.
4. Let this mixture stand outside overnight, exposed to moon and starlight, absorbing their power. Simultaneously there should be spiritual petition, magical ritual, and fasting to bolster the effects.
5. At sunrise, massage the body with the oil.

 ## Aloe Vera Protection Spell

Aloe vera's leaves, filled with healing, soothing gel, are shaped like spears. Maintain living plants on your altar for spiritual protection, especially if working with volatile entities or dangerous spirits.

 ## Althaea Protection Spell

Create infused oil of althea. (See Elements of Magic Spells *for instructions on how to do this.) Anoint the body with this oil as a shield to ward off malevolent spells. (A salve or ointment may also be created if preferred.)*

 ## Anti-assault Protection Spell

Carry dried heather sewn up in a sachet to magically guard against rape and sexual assault. (This enhances but, of course, does not replace more conventional safety precautions.)

 ## Aura of Protection Spell

Strategically arrange blue crystal gemstones around the home or area you wish to protect, creating a magical boundary to keep out evil.

Basic Botanicals of Magical Protection

Many botanicals weave an aura of protection, including the ones that follow. Create your own protection spells by incorporating them. Try betony, black cohosh, cactus, calamus/sweet flag, fig leaf, five-finger grass/cinquefoil, garlic, hyssop, lavender, mugwort, peppermint, roses, rue, Saint John's Wort, snake root, stinging nettles, tormentil, vervain, wormwood, and yarrow.

 ## Basic Botanicals of Magical Protection Candle Spell

Hollow out the bottom of a black, blue, or red candle. Stuff it full of basic protection botanicals and burn the loaded candle.

 ## Bay Laurel Protection Spell

According to myth, the bay laurel tree offered the Delphic pythoness Daphne an avenue of escape when fleeing rape. Place at least one bay leaf in each corner of every room to create an aura of protection.

Betony Protection Spell (1)

Betony was once an immensely popular medicinal, used extensively in herbalism. Its therapeutic uses superceded by modern drugs, betony's magical powers remain. Its main gift to people is protection—the ability to repel and disperse negative forces, particularly those that threaten to overwhelm. Burn betony at Midsummer's Eve to access its peak powers, or burn as needed.

 ## Betony Protection Spell (2)

Grind powder, and sprinkle betony around the home to erect a magical shield of protection.

 ## Betony Protection Spell (3)

This spell allegedly protects those plagued by nightmarish waking visions.

1. Gather betony in August without the use of iron.
2. Dry the plant and then grind its leaves and roots.
3. Place this powder within a blue amulet bag and wear around your neck.

 ## Betony Protection Spell (4)

An old Italian saying suggests, "Sell your coat and buy betony." Wear betony around one's neck to repel malicious spirits.

 ## Bell Protection Spell

Bells protect against evil. Their ringing causes many malicious spirits to flee and they are thus a primary component of exorcism rites. It's not only their ringing tones that repel evil; bells, like broomsticks and mortars and pestles, are a discreet metaphor for the reproductive act. Creative acts of life counteract forces of destruction. For this protective ritual, four silver or iron bells are required.

1. Consecrate the bells with **Fiery Wall of Protection Incense.** (Pass the bells through the smoke.)
2. Charge the bells. Hold them and tell them their mission of protection, aloud if possible.
3. Hang one in each corner of the area to be protected.
4. Allegedly the bells will warn when danger appears from that direction by spontaneously ringing.
5. Recharge bells that ring.
6. After an emergency or perhaps as annual maintenance, repeat the entire ritual.

Black Cohosh/Black Snake Root Spells

Certain botanicals are believed to possess power similar to that of a serpent—or even allow you to safely tap into actual snake power. Among them is black cohosh, popularly known as black snake root. Not only is this plant affiliated with serpentine power, black is an important color of protection, believed able to absorb all dangers and thus rendering them harmless. It is used to protect against all manner of trouble, from spiritual, magical and plain old human sources alike. In particular, black cohosh provides magical protection against threats of violence and lingering abusive situations.

Since black cohosh, like echinacea and goldenseal, became therapeutically popular, it has been harvested virtually to extinction in the wild. Grow your own supply; the living plant is full of magical protection, too.

 ## Black Cohosh Spell (1) Basic

Place a root or a piece of one within a red or black charm bag. Carry it in your pocket or wear it around your neck.

Black Cohosh Spell (2)
Black Tourmaline

Although black tourmaline is a mineral and black cohosh a botanical, they have many magical properties in common. Black is traditionally one of the colors used for protective magic because, like a black hole in space, it's capable of absorbing endless quantities of negative spiritual power, thus minimizing the presence of danger. The problem, of course, with most black crystals is that they store these psychic toxins and could, in theory, release them. It's crucial to cleanse on schedule—and cleanse well!

Black tourmaline, like black cohosh, possesses a magical repelling, shielding action instead of an absorbent one. Reinforce this power exponentially by using both together. Place a black tourmaline and a black cohosh root inside a black velvet bag, together with a piece of real silver. Carry or wear for protection.

Black Cohosh Spell (3)
Clothes Wash

Rinse your clothing, especially ritual clothing or clothing worn in vulnerable moments, in a diluted black snake root infusion. Let the clothes air dry and wear whenever you need enhanced protection.

Black Cohosh Spell (4) Infusion

Make a strong infusion of black snake root. Sprinkle the liquid over thresholds to prevent the entry of malevolent spirits.

Black Cohosh Spell (5)
Red Ribbon

Attach a piece of black snake root to a red ribbon, knotting in your goals and desires. Wear it around your neck or waist.

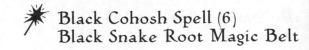
Black Cohosh Spell (6)
Black Snake Root Magic Belt

A magic belt created from cast-off snakeskin is a precious magical treasure but one that may be inaccessible for many. Black snake root approximates serpentine power; this belt creates a similar protective effect.

1. Cut a black or red ribbon long enough to tie around your waist with nine inches (22 cm) left over.
2. Attach a black cohosh root to this belt.
3. Make nine knots in the cord, focusing on your desire.
4. Wear it around your waist beneath your clothing for protection.

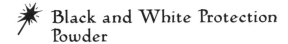
Black and White Protection Powder

Grind up sea salt and black peppercorns and blend them together. Sprinkle this powder around your property for strong protection.

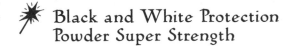
Black and White Protection Powder Super Strength

1. Grind up sea salt and black peppercorns and blend them together.
2. Place them within a conjure bag together with five black-eyed peas.
3. Add your guardian spirits: images of a black Scottish terrier and a West Highland white terrier, small dogs yet fierce, protective, and persistent. (Use photographs, drawings or small figurines.)
4. Hang or carry this bag for protection.

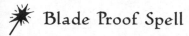 Blade Proof Spell

Allegedly this spell confers protection against harm caused by metal blades (knives, daggers, etc.)

Pull up an entire edelweiss plant by its roots in one swift, sure motion on a Full Moon Friday. Shake any clinging dirt free but otherwise do not process. Wrap the whole plant up in white linen or silk and wear it within your clothing.

 Blocking Spell

This spell isn't a hex; it won't cause injury or misery, but merely obstructs someone who wishes to harm you.

1. Create a doll ideally from the target's clothing, incorporating intimate items (hair, nail clippings, etc.) as possible.
2. Write the target's name on a slip of paper and insert it within the doll.
3. Wrap the doll in freezer paper and place it in the freezer for as long as necessary.

 Blueberry Protection Spell (1)

Even something seemingly as innocuous as blueberries offers magical protection.

Grind and powder dried blueberry leaves and sprinkle around the perimeter of the area needing protection.

Blueberry Protection Spell (2)

Pour boiling water over blueberry leaves to create an infusion. Asperge throughout the home or area for an intensive protection spell, albeit of relatively brief duration.

 Blueberry Protection Spell (3)

This spell is particularly beneficial for neutralizing any attempts at placing a "doorstep curse." Place blueberry leaves under the doorstep or doormat for protection.

Body Protection Spells

Despite fierce animals, poisonous substances and various spiritual threats, most dangers that one potentially encounters on Earth derive from human beings. Homeopathically perhaps, despite all the *heka* or magical power inherent in botanicals, crystals and animal allies, the most potent protective magic derives from the human body.

Genitals

Plants, people, objects, and animals radiate *heka*, and so do symbols. The most powerfully protective magic symbol is that of the female genitalia. This is not intended as prurient or titillating: the female genitals represent the threshold over which every life is activated and emerges. Female genitals also represent the power of generations of watchful, caring, maternal ancestors.

The life-affirming powers of the female genitalia so powerfully counteract forces of death, deterioration, and destruction that merely flashing the real thing forces a troublesome ghost to immediately search for a different house to haunt. This however is rarely a practical response. Although throughout rural North Africa, dried cow vulvas are sometimes stretched and posted on stakes to serve as magically protective sentinels, symbolic depictions are most commonly used to provide magical protection.

Symbolic depictions include anything that conceivably resembles the outer, visible genitalia, especially:

- ★ Seashells
- ★ Certain fruits: figs, pomegranates, cocos-de-mer, deeply clefted apricots and peaches
- ★ Crescent shapes including lunar crescents and horseshoes
- ★ Hair combs (there's a reason mermaids are so often depicted holding a comb)
- ★ Downward-facing triangles

This sacred imagery will radiate magical protection wherever it is displayed. Incorporate this symbolism into jewelry and ornamentation for personal protection or post images to magically protect an area.

✸ Body Safety Spell (1) Female Genitalia Quick Fix

"I'm going to tell my mother!" *children warn bullies. Wearing or displaying protective female genital imagery magically transmits the power of generations of watchful, ever-vigilant, potentially wrathful mothers. It is not necessary for this imagery to be made explicit; its power is transmitted magically and subliminally.*

For quick-fix, immediate protection, draw a downward-facing triangle or a comb shape onto your door or walls with chalk, charcoal, or red ochre.

✸ Body Safety Spell (2) Female Genitalia

Beads and the art of beadwork are incorporated into many spells; beads may have been invented to provide this type of magical symbolism. Beads are also traditionally crafted into the form of penises and breasts, however those shaped like the vulva provide the wearer with greatest protection.

The material used to craft the bead enhances this power. Beads carved from coral, amber, silver, or iron provide maximum protection. Although mere possession offers protection, the act of beading is a form of knot magic: string necklaces and bracelets, knotting after each bead. Sew these beads onto protection-themed conjure bags, focusing on goals and desires as one sews, knots, and cuts.

Menstrual Blood Protection Spells
Menstrual blood is the ultimate protective agent. The magic power inherent in the menstruating woman and in her *"wise-blood,"* rather than any inherent *"uncleanness,"* is the root source of menstrual taboos and the forced isolation of menstruating women. Menstrual blood protects against the Evil Eye, evil spirits, and people with evil intentions. It creates a boomerang effect on magical tricks. Who knows? Its shock value remains so strong that it may literally repel dangerous people, too.

Coral and iron share menstrual blood's magic powers because, metaphysically, they are understood as solidified remnants of the menstrual flow of Ocean and Earth respectively.

✸ Menstrual Blood Spell (1) Door Guardian

Smear menstrual blood on lintels, thresholds, and door-knobs to provide a protective boundary against malevolence of all kinds.

✸ Menstrual Blood (2) Conjure Bag

Place a dried blood-soaked rag or a small strip from one into a red charm bag. Hang it over the door to provide magical and spiritual protection.

Menstrual Blood Spell (3) Floorwash

1. Add menstrual blood (as little as a few drops will suffice) to a bucket of boiled salted water.
2. Add vinegar and use this to scrub the steps leading to one's home and the entrance thresholds to defy all evil intentions, whether human or spiritually derived.

 ## Menstrual Blood Spell (4) Substitutes Conjure Bag

As with the power inherent in the symbolism of the female genitalia, relying on the actual article isn't always practical or desirable. Powerful substitutes have evolved over the ages; although none perhaps contain exactly as much power as menstrual blood, the following are extremely potent and are incorporated into many magic spells: red brick dust, vermilion powder, henna powder, red ochre, and iron oxide powder.

1. Place a pinch of one, some or all of the above powders into a red drawstring bag.
2. Add a coral or iron bead for reinforcement.
3. Carry the charm bag to provide protection.
4. Should emergency situations arise, remove a pinch of the blended powder, spit lightly on it to create a paste and draw protective circles, boundary lines, and symbols as needed.
5. Replace the powder as needed.

Saliva

The second most protective human bodily fluid is saliva, especially that of a fasting person.

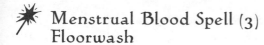 ## Saliva Anti Danger Spell

Do you perceive the presence of malevolent spirits lurking behind you? Never fear; there's an easy, although not necessarily socially acceptable solution. Saliva can disperse demons, malevolent spirits, and the Evil Eye as well as repelling malevolent spells.

Spit in the direction of a threat. When the direction is unknown but the presence of evil is palpable, spit over your left shoulder once to drive it away.

Botanical Guardian Spells

Although different botanicals provide different facets of magical protection, certain plants, especially in combination, provide a fearsome shielding aura, prevailing against evil from all sources.

 ## Botanical Guardian Spell (1) Anti-evil

Allegedly, evil and malevolent forces cannot exist in the presence of the following botanicals:

Hyssop
Lavender
Patchouli
Rue

1. Their power is exponentially increased where they are maintained together. Maintain living plants for maximum power.
2. For portable protection, take a sprig of each plant with you.
2. Braid or weave them together, focusing on your desires.
3. Place them in a red fabric bag and carry with you.

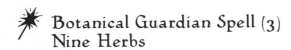

Botanical Guardian Spell (2)
Congo Root Cross

Petiveria alliacea, *known as mucura in Latin America, is called Congo Root in Jamaica.*

Pin its leaves into the shape of a cross and place it within your shoes for safety wherever you walk. This will also protect against foot track spells.

Botanical Guardian Spell (3)
Nine Herbs

The following nine herbs allegedly withstand and protect against all spiritual and magical dangers:

1. Eyebright
2. Mallow
3. Mugwort
4. Self-heal
5. Speedwell
6. Saint John's Wort
7. Vervain
8. Yarrow
9. Wormwood

Plant them around the perimeter of the area needing protection, ideally in a circle. Maintain living plants in pots that may be arranged in a circle, if and when necessary. In times of spiritual danger, sit within that circle.

Botanical Guardian Spell (4)
Nine Sacred Anglo-Saxon Herbs

The nine sacred Anglo-Saxon herbs provide protection against all manner of evil. Feature them in a garden to surround you with spiritual, magical protection:

1. Chamomile
2. Chervil

3. Crabapple
4. Fennel
5. Mugwort
6. Nettles
7. Plantain
8. Watercress

Where's the ninth sacred herb? Good question. Only eight botanicals are listed, because the identity of the ninth, atterlothe remains unknown. Include only eight species, in memory of all the botanical species driven to extinction, or substitute another plant also celebrated in Anglo-Saxon magic, such as cowslip (sacred to Freya), flax (sacred to Frigg and Hulda), woodruff, or wormwood.

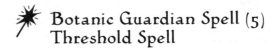

Botanic Guardian Spell (5)
Threshold Spell

Attach mugwort, sweet flag leaves and garlic heads with shoots over a doorway to provide protection and repel all evil.

Botanical Guardian Spell (6)
Witch Soldiers

In order to have access to a wide variety of botanical magic, witches have historically maintained extensive gardens full of unusual and beautiful plants. (Consider the witch in "Rapunzel.") Traditionally, witches have also often been healers and midwives, too, so that the witch's garden was originally filled with therapeutic as well as purely magical plants. By the Middle Ages and the advent of the Burning Times, however, a witch's garden was by necessity a protection garden, designed to keep persecutors out and guard those within. The classic European witch's garden was surrounded with three rows of scarlet flowers, known as "witch's soldiers" to serve as the front-line of protection against witch hunters.

Bullet Proof Spell (1)
Amaranth

Create an amulet that allegedly renders you bullet-proof, although how one interprets "bullet-proof" from a magical standpoint is open to interpretation.

1. On a Full Moon Friday pull up an entire amaranth plant with one swift motion.
2. Place an offering (payment) into the hole left by the plant.
3. Wrap the plant, complete with roots and any dirt clinging to them, in a white cloth.
4. Wear this packet against your chest like a magical bullet-proof vest.

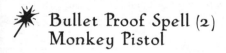 Bullet Proof Spell (2)
Monkey Pistol

The Caribbean tree, Hura crepitans, *known as the sandbox tree, monkey pistol, bullet proof, and, in Spanish,* salvadera, *possesses a spontaneously exploding seed capsule. It's prized by police and gangsters alike as an amulet to protect against being shot. Carry the dried seed capsule in a mojo bag.*

 Bullet Proof Spell
Extra Intensive

1. Dedicate a red candle to the archangel Michael, Ogun, or Saint James the Greater.
2. Dress with **Fiery Wall of Protection Oil** and burn the candle, accompanied by prayer and petitions for protection.
3. When there is just a tiny bit of candle left, pinch it out.
4. When the stub is dry, place it in a red mojo bag, together with a small piece of iron, a dried bullet proof seed capsule and a medal dedicated to whomever you petitioned for protection. (Draw Ogun's *vèvè* or sigil on a piece of paper.)

 Bullet Proof Pine Nut Spell

Gather a pinecone replete with seeds on Midsummer's Day. Allegedly eating one of these pine nuts daily renders you bullet proof, at least as long as the nuts last.

 Burdock Protection Spell

Burdock, like cucumbers and asparagus, is perceived to magically radiate primal male power. Pierce burdock roots and string them onto red thread. Wear this garland for protection.

 Cactus Fence Spell (1)

The equivalent of the thicket around Sleeping Beauty's castle, a boundary of tall prickly cactus around your home casts an aura of protective banishing against humans and spirits alike.

 Cactus Fence Spell (2)

Not quite as potent as the above spell but more subtle: bury cactus plants to create a protective shield around the home.

Casting the Circle

An incredibly simple yet remarkably protective spell is accomplished by casting a circle. Children's games, such as tag, often designate an area as "safe"; once the child has reached the designated area, the opportunity exists to take respite. Casting the circle is similar: the space within the circle is designated as "safe." No malevolent spiritual force can touch or harm you while within the circle. The materials used to cast the circle enhance this power.

In addition to personal protective magic circles, circles are traditionally cast to contain threshold experiences as well as whatever is perceived as potentially vulnerable:

★ Circles are drawn around ritual
★ Circles are drawn around a sickbed
★ Circles are drawn around women in childbirth
★ Circles are drawn around sleeping infants and children

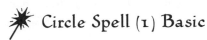 Circle Spell (1) Basic

This is the very simplest protection spell of all. Cast a circle around you. (In other words, stand within while drawing the circle, rather than casting from outside, intending to jump inside when the circle is complete.) Sit in the center until you feel it's safe to come out.

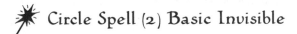 Circle Spell (2) Basic Invisible

It is not necessary for there to be a visible circle. Spiritual forces recognize spiritual boundaries. Demarcate a circle in space using magic ritual tools: sword, knife, fan, staff, cingulam, or wand.

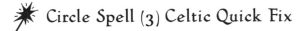 Circle Spell (3) Celtic Quick Fix

Protective materials sufficient to cast a circle large enough to contain you comfortably may not be at hand when most needed. Draw a circle around yourself with a hazel branch. Hold onto that branch so that the circle's boundaries may be adjusted and reinforced as needed.

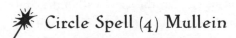 Circle Spell (4) Mullein

Cast a circle of flaming mullein torches to protect what's within.

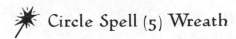 Circle Spell (5) Wreath

Wreathes are circles, too. The form as well as the material used for construction contributes to a wreath's protective powers. Pick primroses and convolvulus on May Day. Make wreathes and hang them to protect against evil.

Visible Circles

Visible circles aren't necessarily more effective, however, their clear boundaries may provide additional peace of mind for the person within as well as security: you're less likely to accidentally venture outside the perimeter if you can see it.

Regardless what material is used to cast a circle, it's crucial that the circle be unbroken. Powerfully protective circles may be cast from the following:

Absinthe
Amber chunks or beads
Chalk
Charcoal
Coral
Cornmeal
Fiery Wall of Protection powder
Flour
Henna powder
Jet
Lava
Pemba
Red brick dust or red ochre
Rice flour
Rum
Salt
Tobacco
Turquoise
Vervain
Vermilion
Whiskey
Wormwood

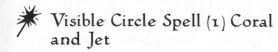

Visible Circle Spell (1) Coral and Jet

Certain circle-casting materials, when combined, create a synergistic, exponentially increased magical effect. Cast a circle of alternating coral and jet. Substitute amber for coral if desired, or combine all three.

Visible Circle Spell (2) Double Concentric Circle

For extra fortification and maximum power, create double concentric circles: one circle within the other. Fill the narrow border between the two circles with protective amulets or salt.

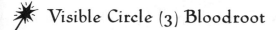

Visible Circle (3) Bloodroot

Cast an unbroken circle of powdered bloodroot or an infusion made from the root around your home and property to repel malevolent spirits and malicious magic.

Centaury Spells

Centaury earned its name because it's believed to be the legendary herb of the centaurs. Among centaury's other gifts, it provides magical protection.

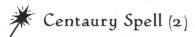

Centaury Spell (1)

Create a strong infusion of centaury and add it to the bath for personal protection.

Centaury Spell (2)

Hang bunches of centaury to cast an aura of protection around an area.

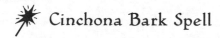

Cinchona Bark Spell

Carry a piece of cinchona bark to protect against evil.

Cinnamon

Cinnamon casts an aura of potent protection, however derivatives of this fragrant tree bark are often too irritating to be applied directly to skin. The hydrosol is reasonably gentle. Add cinnamon hydrosol (experiment to discover comfortable proportions) to bathwater to create a protection bath.

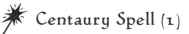

Club Moss Spell

According to pre-Christian Scottish tradition, club moss may be carried as an amulet of protection if it's been harvested without iron by a barefoot person using the right hand passed through the left sleeve of a white tunic. Offer libations and gifts to the plant before harvesting, too.

Cornflower Protection Powder Spell (1)

Cornflower protection powder repels evil influences and profoundly discourages evil visitors.

1. Grind dried blue cornflowers into a fine powder and reserve.
2. Sweep the house thoroughly with a broom.
3. When the sweeping is complete, sprinkle cornflower powder over the thresholds of entry doors and in the corners of all rooms, including closet corners.
4. Repeat periodically to prevent malefic influences from gaining entry.
5. Reinforce with blue-eye beads and other amulets.

Cornflower Protection Powder Spell (2)

There are other more subtle ways to enter a house than the door. To guard against this, sprinkle blue cornflower powder under or around telephones, computers or any other perceived modes of entry to your home.

Count the Holes Protection Spell

How do I protect you? Let me count the holes … A sieve by the doorway or placed up the chimney foils the entry of evil spirits. Allegedly, they'll have to stop and count the holes. Substitute fishing nets for sieves, if desired.

Cross of Safety

The cross in this spell may be considered as a Christian symbol or as a pre-Christian emblem of protection, radiating out in all directions.

Form a cross from eupatorium and place it on a wall or door. Draw another cross with chalk, charcoal, or redbrick dust underneath to protect against malevolent magic.

Crystal Protection Spells

Crystal Protection Spell (1) Black Crystals

Black crystals are used to create a shield against evil and danger. Any black crystal absorbs anger, danger, evil, and malevolence, however black tourmalines are believed to repel it.

1. Hold the gemstones in your hand, charging them with your desire.
2. Wear as jewelry or carry in a mojo bag especially when stepping into anticipated danger.

3. Cleanse these crystals frequently so that their protective power is not hobbled but remains at full strength. (See *Cleansing Spells,* page 185.)

Crystal Spell (2) Jet Magic Belt

Jet allegedly offers magical protection against acts of violence. True jet is rare; you can tell real jet from synthetic substitutes, as real jet may be pierced with a needle.

Attach jet beads or charms to a scarlet ribbon long enough to tie around your waist while sitting. Add a piece of black snake root/black cohosh and wear when needed.

Crystal Spell (3) Witch Stones

Holed stones or holey stones—naturally holed pebbles—are also known as witch stones. In magical terms, they are as precious as any rare gem: they provide protection against malevolent magic, famine, storms at sea, and general spiritual disaster.

String a holed stone onto red cord or silver chain. Wear around your neck during the day, hang onto your walls and bedposts at night.

Crystal Spell (4)

Certain crystals are believed able magically to protect against radiation, as well as high frequency communication antennae and microwave rays. They include Herkimer diamonds, malachite, smoky quartz, and sodalite. They will not substitute for other practical measures but will enhance their power. If you perceive yourself as vulnerable, wear these crystals and keep them within the area of danger. Remember to intensely cleanse these crystals on a frequent basis.

 Deasil Flame Spell

Deasil refers to circumambulating sunwise, keeping whatever you're circling on your right side. Carrying a lit torch or candle, walk deasil around any person, property, or object that you'd like to safeguard from harm and malicious influence.

Destroy Evil Floorwash

*Add **Four Thieves Vinegar,** sea salt and eighteen drops of essential oil of rosemary to a bucket of water. Wash the floors, woodwork, and windowsills, concentrating on thresholds and dark corners.*

 Devil's Bit

Allegedly old Satan was so enraged at the protection derived from this plant that he bit it off, leading to its mangled appearance. Wear devil's bit around the neck to protect from all evil.

Devil's Shoestrings Safety Spells

The root, devil's shoestrings, is used to provide magical protection. The following two spells are most effective if cast in conjunction with each other.

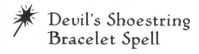 Devil's Shoestring Bracelet Spell

Nine roots of equal length are required; they can't be cut to size. Knot them into a bracelet, blessing, affirming, and petitioning with each knot.

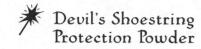 Devil's Shoestring Protection Powder

Grind up devil's shoestrings and blend them with arrowroot powder. Sprinkle the powder in your clothing drawers, around your bed and over your thresholds for round-the-clock protection.

Door Guardians

Thresholds are always places of combined power and vulnerability. The threshold of a home, the front entrance, is particularly vulnerable. Where does both bad and good news most typically enter the home? Right through the front door. Reinforce with protective measures. Door Guardians are objects chosen for the protective magic that they radiate. Typically placed by the entrance facing outwards, they stand ready to battle and repel any approaching threat or evil.

With the exception of the Holy Child, under whose deceptively sweet demeanor a primordial spirit hides, these are fierce, threatening, even frightening images—but they're door guards after all. Who gets hired to work as a club bouncer: a cute, little kid or a big bruiser? What type of dog is most typically on guard duty: a miniature poodle or a rottweiller? The fiercer, the more frightening the image, the more profound the protection offered by your door guardian.

Door Guardian (1) Aloe Vera

Place living aloe vera plants over the door, rather than beside it, to provide magical, spiritual protection.

 Door Guardian (2) Blackthorn

Blackthorn is a small tree with profound magical connections. Associated with witchcraft, it's also among the fairies' favorite botanicals. As you're requesting blessings of protection, it's particularly important to request permission from the tree, explain your intent and offer gifts and libations.

Create a rod from a blackthorn branch. Keep the shape simple or embellish with protective runes, symbols, and sigils. Hang it over the door to refuse entry to mischief, misfortune, and evil and malicious spells.

Door Guardian (3) Date Palm

Date palms are emblematic of oases and symbolic of the union of male and female energies. Maintain date palms on either side of your front entrance to demarcate your private oasis. Allegedly they ward off intangible evil as well as repelling evil spirits.

Door Guardian (4) Devil's Pod

Depending on the way that it's held, the dried seed-pod, Trapa bicornis, the Devil's pod (less dramatically known as a ling nut), resembles Christian imagery of goat-headed Satan or Baphomet, the alleged idol of the Knights Templar. Use it to ward off evil and trouble, sort of like a nightclub's big, bad bouncer, the arbiter at the door.

1. Position the seed-pod so that it resembles a goat's head. (Held the other way, this charm resembles a bat and is used to draw good luck and fortune.)
2. Hang it above the doorway, facing outwards so that it can perceive whatever approaches.

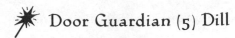 Door Guardian (5) Dill

Allegedly dill placed over the door prevents anyone who harbors hostile or envious feelings toward the home's inhabitants from entering that door.

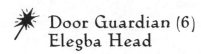 Door Guardian (6) Elegba Head

This stylized head represents the orisha Elegba, guardian of the gates: Papa Legba determines who enters and who shall not pass. Papa Legba's head is formed from concrete, with cowrie shell eyes and ears to keep watch over your property.

Place Elegba's head behind the door. Feed him rum every Monday. Supplement with candy, cigars, and cigarettes, especially when he's worked extra hard for you.

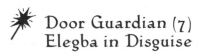 Door Guardian (7) Elegba in Disguise

When enslaved Africans were brought to the Western hemisphere, the practice of their own spiritual traditions and religions was brutally suppressed and forbidden. As a survival mechanism, African spirit powers assumed the masks of acceptable Roman Catholic saints. Elegba has been syncretized to the Holy Child of Atocha, that miracle-working little boy who may or may not be the Christ Child. His votive image depicts a beautiful child, richly dressed, seated on a throne.

Place a figure of the Holy Child of Atocha behind the door in the same manner as Elegba's head, feeding the figure on Monday. (The child may be understood as trickster Elegba wearing a mask.) Rum is still appropriate, however you may wish to skip the nicotine and give the watchful little boy extra candy and small toys instead.

Door Guardian (8) Fu Dogs

Fu *means "luck" and these Chinese statues, resembling a cross between lions and dogs, bring good fortune as well as protection. A pair of fu dogs repels malevolent spells and destructive energy, allegedly also preventing people with evil intentions from entering. For maximum power, a matched pair of dogs is needed, one male and one female. (To distinguish the gender, male fu dogs are invariably depicted playing with a large ball, while female dogs are not.)*

1. Post the fu dogs on either side of the main gate or entrance, facing away from the building toward whatever or whomever approaches.
2. For best results, place the male dog on the right, the female dog on the left with both dogs raised up off the ground, the higher the better, so that they'll have access to the best possible view.

 ## Door Guardian (9) Gargoyles

Technically the gargouille *was a seventh-century water-spouting (versus fire-breathing) dragon (think "gargle") that lived in the Seine River and was slain upon orders of the local bishop. Although the use of animal shaped waterspouts dates back to ancient Egypt, Etruria and Greece, the term gargoyle re-emerged in eleventh-century Western Europe as the name given to functional but decorative rain spouts, carved in the form of grotesque creatures. Because they most frequently adorn churches and cathedrals, they, like the* sheela na gig *(see below), are mysterious, evocative, surviving vestiges of paganism. Gargoyles give the appearance of demons but offer spiritual protection rather than harm. It's believed that they are guardian spirits, magically preserved in stone; in the face of evil, however, they will break free to do battle.*

In the past few decades, gargoyles have been adapted to serve as door guardians. Free-standing reproductions of famed gargoyles are available. You may also craft your own. Gargoyles do not have to be placed at the front door; consider your most vulnerable points and place gargoyles appropriately. Gargoyles also apparently enjoy each other's company; there cannot be too many. Place them as needed in combinations that evoke a sense of security. According to legend, winged gargoyles can fly; feel free to move them around as desired.

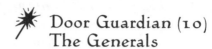 ## Door Guardian (10) The Generals

Depending upon legend, the generals Yu-ch'ih and Ch'in Ch'iung protected the second Tang emperor from an infestation of ghosts, or from a seductive but deadly fox-spirit. These dedicated guardians offered to stay up all night, standing guard so that the afflicted emperor could sleep. They were extremely successful but after several days it was decided to see whether portraits of the ministers in full military dress might substitute for the living generals, who were desperately in need of sleep themselves. The portraits proved successful and so have served as door guardians ever since.

1. Affix their pictures side by side on the main entrance to protect a home from all danger, especially that of malevolent ghosts and spirits.
2. Write wishes, desires, and directions for the Generals on slips of red paper.
3. Affix these to the door, too.

✳ Door Guardian (11) Kuan Ti

Kuan Ti, also known as Kuan Kung, is Lord of War but does double duty as one of the Lords of Wealth. This fierce, scowling guardian spirit provides special protection for merchants, politicians, and those he perceives as oppressed. He is acknowledged as the guardian deity of the triads. His image, whether a statue or of paper, serves as a door guardian for those who respectfully summon his magic power. In addition to protection, Kuan Ti offers blessings of prosperity to the home in which his spirit resides. This old soldier maintains peace and harmony within the home; his presence strengthens and empowers the patriarch of the resident family. (Consider whether this is desirable.)

The more fierce and scowling, the more power his image radiates. Kuan Ti should not look friendly. Place his image inside the home facing the entrance door. Kuan Ti can't do his job if he's not armed: his image or statue must *have his weapons, typically a sword or massive staff, in order to be magically activated.*

✳ Door Guardian (12) Medusa

According to classical Greek mythology, anyone who gazed at Gorgon Medusa's face was instantly turned to stone. What more could you ask of a door guardian? Although artistic renderings of Medusa don't have quite the same dramatic effect, her image allegedly provides protection, repelling all evil including the Evil Eye.

Medusa's origins lie in the female-centered spiritual traditions of ancient Libya. Despite the Greeks' professed abhorrence of her appearance, they availed themselves of her power: representations of the gorgon's head were placed on city walls to provide protection.

1. Medusa may be placed inside or out but she must face away from the home toward whomever or whatever approaches so that she can fix them with her fierce eye.

2. Post the image of her head on the door itself or just behind it.
3. Freestanding Medusas also exist, depicting a gorgon's head on a woman's body, girded for battle. Once these images guarded ancient temples. Place one or several by your entrance looking outward so that she can protect you.

Gorgon Medusa may be understood as an amulet (especially when only her head is depicted) or as a sacred and powerful spirit. If you understand it as an amulet, charge it with your desire. If you understand her to be a spirit, feed her: she accepts arak or ouzo, red wine, pomegranates, seashells and serpentine, as well as companion images of snakes.

✳ Door Guardian (13) Sheela na Gig

The sheela na gig *represents the protective power of the female genitalia and the collective protective aura of generations of mothers, whether your own mother, the Earth Mother or a mother goddess. Most frequently incorporated into church buildings in Celtic areas, analysis demonstrates that the* sheela na gig *carving is typically older than the rest of the building. Her origins and meanings are mysterious.*

The sheela na gig *depicts a wizened crone in parturient position, spreading her vagina, enlarged like a gateway, with her hands. She looks into the eyes of those who approach, beckoning and daring you to enter. Better than a "no soliciting" sign; this may be the most effective door guardian of all as so many find the image consistently shocking. Many will likely not enter your gate. Presumably the* sheela na gig *magically winnows out those who should not enter.*

Place the sheela na gig *over the front door, or as desired, looking out. For added power and enhancement, sprinkle with menstrual blood, red brick dust, or any other euphemistic substitutions.*

Door Guardian (14) Tiger

In Asian magical tradition, tigers are the fierce sworn enemies of evil spirits. They are also animals closely associated with warrior spirits and witchcraft: a tiger's magical knowledge is as great as its bravery and physical prowess. All are put to good use when the tiger serves as a door guardian.

According to Chinese schools of magic, it's not advisable to maintain images of tigers within the home; because of their fierce, uncontrollable nature they have a tendency to stimulate havoc. Instead post an image of one by the entrance door, either a paper image attached to the door or a statue beside the door to provide spiritual protection. The tiger must be looking away from the home searching for danger.

 ## Door Guardian (15) Ti Plant

Ti plants are the sacred plants of Hawaiian magic and spirituality. They provide protection against all evil and serve as subtle door guardians. Place two potted ti plants by your entrance door, one at each side of the door.

Doorstep Protection Spells

The doorstep marks the literal threshold. It is a particularly vulnerable spot. Many hexes involve what is called "dusting the doorstep." The spell is activated by leaving its remnants or other magic materials at the target's front door.

Many rituals are designed to transform this threshold into a zone of safety. Typically spells are repeated weekly with many involving "cleansing." Because in some cases, although not all, it appears only that you're being very clean and house-proud, this is also a very subtle, discreet style of magic.

(Should your doorstep ever be dusted, check Hex Antidote Spells (page 590) for tips on removing items safely and repelling the spell, but follow up with protective measures, too.)

 ## Doorstep Spell Floorwash

Urine is believed to have fierce magical commanding powers, hence its use in protective floorwashes. If you're genuinely fearful or otherwise passionately emotional, assume that your desires are inherently transmitted; otherwise concentrate on your desire while scrubbing the steps.

1. A bucket filled with some sort of floorwash is required for this spell.
2. Choose any magical floorwash formula or merely fill a bucket with salted water.
3. Add some of your urine to this bucket of wash water and then scrub the step.

 ## Doorstop Spell Floorwash Extra Power

1. Place red brick dust and **Cascarilla Powder** in a bucket.
2. Pour boiling salted water over it.
3. When it cools add **Indigo Water, Florida Water** and some of your own urine. (Some recommend that lye be added as well; however lye can be dangerous to use, particularly when children and animals are present.)
4. Scrub the steps and threshold area of the front entrance to the home.

 ## Doorstep Spell Red Brick Dust

Red brick dust protects against malevolent magic and repels evil of all kinds.

1. Smash an old red brick with a hammer until sufficient dust is obtained.
2. Add red brick dust to a bucket of floorwash and scrub the front steps and threshold area.
3. Sprinkle powdered red brick dust over the threshold daily before sunrise.

 ## Doorstep Spell Rice

1. Fill an open jar with raw white rice.
2. Place the jar by the entrance door for protection.
3. Rice doesn't repel evil; it absorbs it. Replace with fresh raw rice weekly.
4. Do not bring the old rice back into your home. Do not cook it. Dispose of it outside the home, whether by burning, throwing away, or scattering on Earth.

 ## Doorstep Spell Rose of Jericho

*Sprinkle **Rose of Jericho Water** on the door itself, both inside and out, to repel and remove evil. For maximum power, use fresh rue as an asperging tool.*

 ## Doorstep Spell Rowan

Chalk rowan tree berry patterns onto doorsteps after they've been magically cleansed, to keep away malevolent spirits.

 ## Doorstep Spell Salt Cross

*Using sea salt or **black salt** form the shape of a cross over your doorstep. Understand this symbol however it provides a sense of security for you. The cross symbolism derives from pre-Christian metaphysical geometry: salt's protective capacities are radiated in all possible directions. If you are uncomfortable using the cross shape substitute triangles, diamonds, or crescents instead.*

 ## Dragon's Tears Spell

Carry dragon's tears in a red charm bag to ward off evil and spiritual danger.

 ## Ear Line of Defense Spell

"Stick and stones may break my bones but words can never hurt me!" That old saying may be the least truthful aphorism of them all. Words can harm, and can do so very badly. Magically speaking, ears are perceived as a receptive orifice. Language can be used for blessing but also as a means of undermining, causing grave psychic damage.

1. Earrings serve as protective amulets against verbal arrows.
2. Choose an image that represents protection to you, however if in doubt triangles, red and black beads, or gemstones are particularly beneficial.
3. Charge the earrings with their mission prior to wearing; whenever you've heard more than you should, cleanse the earrings in Cleansing or Protective incense.

Earth Protection Spell

1. Obtain graveyard dirt from your ancestors' graves or gather dirt from a saint's shrine or other sacred place.
2. Sprinkle **Holy Water, Marie Laveau Water** or **Spirit Water** over the dirt.
3. Allow it to dry, and then place it in a bag and hang it near the entrance to your home.

 # Egg Protection Spell

Allegedly any one living in a home containing this type of stuffed egg will not be subject to wicked enchantment.

1. Carefully make a hole in the top of an egg.
2. Cleanse the egg extremely well, then drain and dry it. Make sure the egg is completely dry before adding the botanical material.
3. Fill the hollowed egg with dried cinquefoil/five-finger grass.
4. Seal the egg closed with red wax.

 # Egg Tree Spell

Egg trees created with living trees magically draw fertility; created with dead trees or bushes, egg trees cast a spell of protection to ward off malevolent magic.

1. Crop tree limbs as needed.
2. Hang witch balls or carefully decorated blown eggshells from the branches.
3. The more embellishment, the more powerful the spell: let this be a work in progress, continually adding more protective power.

Elder Protection Spells

The elder tree is sacred to the Germanic witch spirit of love and magic, Hulda, affectionately known as Mother Holle. Hulda is among the leaders of the Wild Hunt, that reveling procession of spirits and witches. Christian propaganda suggested that elder repelled witches, although apparently no one troubled to inform Hulda or her witches, who use elder in abundance. Presumably this propaganda is based upon how one interprets the conventional magical wisdom that elder repels evil.

 # Elder Protection Spell (1)

Pick elderberries on Midsummer's Eve. Dry them and place over doors and windowsills to protect against evil.

 # Elder Protection Spell (2)

Hang elder branches over doors and within the home as magical protection.

 # Elder Protection Spell (3)

The innate magical protective capacity of elder may be enhanced:

1. Soak thin branches to soften them.
2. Twist these elder branches into auspicious shapes: pentagrams, hexagrams, triangles, diamonds, or others.
3. Tie them in place with red or green cord, knotting your desires into the spell.

 # Elf Protection

Elves, while typically not inherently malevolent are believed to frequently harbor unfriendly feelings toward people. Fennel offers protection from their power. Wear fennel during psychic journeys or whenever one feels threatened.

 Elf-Shot

In addition to referring to psychic attack by elves (see Healing Spells, page 509), elf-shots are also the name given to prehistoric stone arrowheads. Set an elf-shot in silver and wear it around your neck to provide magical homeopathic protection against being elf-shot.

 Eye of the Devil Protection Spell

"Eye of the devil" is another of those fiendishly named botanicals that actually provide protection, not harm. Known as Eye of the Devil in Egyptian folk magic, the name is sometimes translated as "Power of Satan." Burn eye of the devil and allow its smoke to remove and repel evil.

Eye Vulnerability

Eyes are perceived as the body's magical Achilles' heel, a venue through which evil can intrude and hence in need of magical protection. They are the windows of the soul and hence an anatomical threshold. Eyes are a conduit for power, yet they leave an individual psychically vulnerable. Eyes are how the Evil Eye communicates.

This perceived vulnerability stimulated the invention of eye-makeup. Originally eye-makeup was designed to provide magical protection as much as aesthetic appeal. The most famous proponents of eye-protecting makeup were the ancient Egyptians. It is virtually impossible to find images of ancient Egyptians without their characteristic eye-makeup from the earliest days until the end of their civilization. It was worn by both men and women.

Eye Vulnerability Kohl Spells

Kohl, the Egyptian's eye-makeup, was created from magically powered materials, so that in addition to health and beauty benefits, Egyptian eye-makeup protected against various spiritual dangers, plus against both receiving and casting the Evil Eye.

The Egyptian's eye-makeup, *kohl*, is still in use. Although modern cosmetic pencils are sometimes marketed as kohl, real kohl is a loose powder, applied with an applicator stick. Its magical ancestry is very apparent when it is packaged in a drawstring bag, just like any other magic powder kept in a conjure bag. In fact, kohl powder creates a measure of protection when it is merely carried.

The most common, most ancient Egyptian amulet is a cosmetic palette, a sort of flat mortar and pestle, on which to grind the minerals used for eye-makeup. It appears in the most ancient prehistoric graves and was consistently the one tool buried in even the simplest grave.

 Kohl Formula (1) Historic

Recipes for kohl abound. The simplest versions may contain nothing more than antimony powder or soot, however complicated magically oriented formulas are also prized. A trip to the traditional marketplaces of North Africa and the Middle East still finds vendors hawking their own kohl concoctions. Ideally, kohl provides magic power as well as beauty. However one must be cautious. Because some vendors emphasize magic over health, some formulas contain substances which should never be placed anywhere near the eye, although the powder may be carried for talismanic protection purposes. This medieval recipe is one example:

1. Scoop out the flesh of a lemon.
2. Fill it with plumbago and burnt copper.
3. Burn on a charcoal brazier until reduced to carbonized ash.
4. Pound these ashes with a mortar and pestle.
5. Additions might include pulverized coral, pearls and amber.
6. Moisten with rose water, then allow to dry.

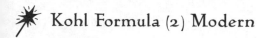

✴ Kohl Formula (2) Modern

A safe and simple modern formula from India provides kohl's blessings without dangers of adulteration. Castor oil magically commands protection and is the base for many commanding and protective magic oils. Burn a clean cotton wick in castor oil. Collect the residue. Voila! Kohl!

✴ Kohl Formula (3) Practical Application

Kohl possesses general protective properties when carried. However, in order to provide protection for the eyes it must be applied cosmetically. Unlike modern eyeshadows, kohl is not placed on the lid but actually inserted into the eye, hence the need to be extremely careful regarding the safety of ingredients.

1. Place a pinch of dry kohl powder on a dish or in the palm of your hand.
2. Consider your wishes, what service the kohl is expected to provide. When this is very clear in your mind, spit lightly on the kohl to moisten it or lick the tip of the wooden applicator stick.
3. With your eyes lightly shut, gently place the applicator between the lids in the corner closest to the nose and carefully draw across to the end of the eye. The tearing process should automatically carry the powder to the right area, however a little practice may be needed.

✴ Fennel Spell

Hang fennel from doors and windows to ward off evil energy and entities.

Fiery Wall of Protection Spells

Fiery Wall of Protection is among the most famous classic condition formulas. Its name invokes the power of Archangel Michael's protective flaming sword. The formula may be consecrated to the archangel.

Fiery Wall's basic ingredients include such powerful protective agents as salt, frankincense and myrrh. Its red color, the color of protection, derives from dragon's blood powder. See the Formulary for specific instructions: the dried powder may be used as incense or magic powder. When the powder is added to oil, **Fiery Wall of Protection Oil** is created.

✴ Fiery Wall of Protection Spell (1) Candle

*Carve a red or white candle with your name, identifying information, hopes, and desires. Dress it with **Fiery Wall of Protection Oil** and burn. Consecrate the candle to the Archangel Michael if desired.*

✴ Fiery Wall of Protection Spell (2) Extra-strength Mojo

1. Place a handful of **Fiery Wall of Protection Powder** in a charm bag.
2. Drizzle it with **Fiery Wall of Protection Oil** *and* **Protection Oil.**
3. Add a medallion depicting Michael the Archangel and/or a tiny doll-sized sword: a fancy tooth pick works well.
4. Carry it in your pocket.
5. Replace the powder weekly, dressing with fresh oil.
6. Cleanse, charge, and consecrate the charms as needed.

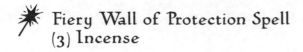 Fiery Wall of Protection Spell
(3) Incense

Protect against a threatened curse by burning **Fiery Wall of Protection Powder** as incense. To intensify the protection, add powdered agrimony and/or vervain.

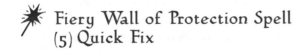 Fiery Wall of Protection Spell
(4) Powder Circle

1. Cast a circle of **Fiery Wall of Protection Powder** around yourself, your home, or whatever needs protection.
2. Envision a circle of enchanted flames magically surrounding and protecting you, something like the magic fire encircling *The Ring of the Nibelung*'s valkyrie swan-maiden Brunhilde: the flames are cool and won't harm those whom they protect yet serve as a burning boundary preventing the entrance of all evil.
3. Stay within the circle for as long as necessary.
4. Carry the powder within a charm bag so that circles and boundary lines may be spontaneously cast as needed.

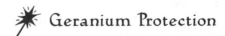 Fiery Wall of Protection Spell
(5) Quick Fix

Soak a cotton ball in **Fiery Wall of Protection Oil** and carry it in your pocket or tucked into your bra.

Five-finger Grass Spell

Fiver finger grass (cinquefoil), a very close relative of tormentil, is to protection what four-leaf clover is to luck.

Search for a perfect five-leafed specimen. Place it between tissue paper and press the fresh plant between the pages of a sacred text. When completely dry and preserved, carry it with you in an amulet bag.

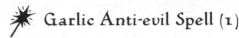 Garlic Anti-evil Spell (1)

1. Hang garlic heads on doors to repel evil.
2. For maximum power use either one, four, five, or a dozen heads.
3. Should the garlic start to rot or deteriorate, bury or burn outside the house and replace with fresh heads.

 Garlic Anti-evil Spell (2)

Combine one head of garlic with an old metal key and a metal depiction of a hand (hamsa, Hand of Fatima, or similar). Place in a window or over the door to provide spiritual protection to those within the house, and to repel evil, malice, and negative enchantment.

Garlic Protection Wreath

1. Create a wreath from at least one dozen garlic bulbs.
2. Decorate it with lodestones, pieces of freshly cut aloe vera, votive imagery, charms, iron beads, and packets filled with salt, mustard seed, and Grains of Paradise.
3. Hang strategically to radiate magical protective power.

Geranium Protection

Geranium is a popular house and garden plant, not only because it's bright, cheerful, and hardy but because it also magically repels evil spirits. Maintain protective boundaries with geranium, or strategically place individual plants.

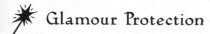# Glamour Protection

All that glitters is not gold. "Glamour" once indicated a fairy's seductive powers of enchantment. To be glamorous was to possess that power. Wear an oak leaf over the heart to magically protect against false glamour and superficial virtue, allowing the wearer to see what truly lies within.

Graveyard Dirt Protection

1. Clearly and explicitly write your desire for protection onto a piece of paper, then burn it, reserving the ashes.
2. Place these ashes in a conjure bag, together with asafetida, bones, nail parings, and graveyard dirt.
3. Wear it around your neck to ward off illness, malevolent spirits and spells.

Gris-Gris Protection

The term gris-gris *derives from West Africa. Now frequently used as just another synonym for conjure, charm or mojo bags, gris-gris originally indicated what the Portuguese called* fetishes: *handmade magical objects. The original West African gris-gris often took the form of dolls; modern New Orleans gris-gris are often a cross between a mojo bag and Vodou paquets-Congo, although doll-shaped gris-gris still exist.*

For those who care about magical semantics, subtle, subliminal distinctions exist, however. Mojo, also derived from an African word, usually implies magically acquiring success, whether in love, gambling, money, employment, or legal matters. Gris-gris implies protection; the gris-gris bag thus tends to cover the spectrum between benign protective spells and hexes.

1. The traditional New Orleans Voodoo bag contains an odd number of magically charged items, from as few as a single prized talisman to as many as thirteen.

2. Gris-gris serves a specific purpose; consider your goal and choose items accordingly. Items may include botanicals, stones, bones, and intimate items including hair, nail clippings, or a scrap of fabric soaked with sweat.
3. Charge items on an altar with all four elements represented. Petition and dedication to lwa or other spirits may be incorporated.
4. If your goal is personal protection, carry your gris-gris; if protection derives from adjusting someone else's behavior, typically the gris-gris is left on the doorstep or the other party's property.

Guardian Animals

Animal allies may also be petitioned for safety. As usual, the most potent allies are always your personal allies. If you are unaware of their identity, request them to make their presence known in your dreams and visualizations or obtain professional shamanic/spirit-working advice. In the meantime, certain animals provide magical guardian services when requested.

Guardian Animal Spell: Dog

Dogs provide magical protection as well as the mundane type. This protective spell benefits an entire community.

Create paper dogs so that you are ready to cast this spell on the fifth day of the fifth month of the Chinese lunar calendar (coinciding with Midsummer's Eve). Charge them with their mission and throw them into living waters (rivers, lakes, springs) so that they'll bite and incapacitate any evil attempting to emerge.

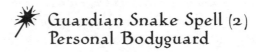

Guardian Animal Spell: The Five Poisons

In general, magical guardian animals are fierce. This makes sense: the Doberman is a more popular guard dog than a golden retriever. Chinese magic contemplates what it perceives as the five most venomous creatures and groups them together to provide magical protection, especially protection against animal attack, poison, and spiritual harm.

Create an image or collage of the five poisonous creatures: centipede, lizard, scorpion, snake and toad. (The toad, source of powerful venom (think poison-arrow frog) is sometimes replaced by the spider. Use whichever frightens you more.) Images may also be purchased in Chinatown or from feng shui suppliers, however the image created for oneself is always most powerful. Wear to protect against spiritual danger, poison, venomous creatures, and animal attack in general. The image is regarded as particularly beneficial for protecting children and infants.

Guardian Snake Spells

Snakes are renowned for possessing divine powers to ward off evil. Think of a hidden jungle temple guarded by protective serpents. Legends of buried treasure or hidden magical valuables traditionally have snake or dragon (considered metaphysically to be a closely related species) guardians.

Guardian Snake Spell (1) Candle

Spiritual suppliers sometimes sell candles in the shape of coiled serpents.

1. Hold the candle to charge it with your desire. If you wish, look the snake in the eye and charge it with its mission of protection.
2. Burn the candle to release the snake's guardian powers.

3. Burning the candle is sufficient, however its power is enhanced by being dressed with **Protection Oil.**
4. Burn at regularly scheduled intervals so as to define protective boundaries.

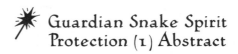

Guardian Snake Spell (2) Personal Bodyguard

Snakes can serve as personal magical bodyguards. Methods of tapping into snakes' protective powers include:

★ *Wear snake armlets on the upper arms*
★ *Snake rings offer protection as does snake imagery in henna designs*
★ *Permanent vigilance is provided by snake tattoos*

In addition to their traditional role as guardians of treasure, snakes and dragons have discovered new realms to protect in the twenty-first century. Snakes and dragons have become the metaphysical protectors of computers and the treasures contained within.

Guardian Snake Spirit Protection (1) Abstract

1. Provide protection for your computer equipment by decorating with images of snakes and/or dragons.
2. Place images of snakes and dragons above or beside the computer. The guardians may face the computer or face outwards, however they shouldn't be staring directly at you.
3. A Chinese dragon-tortoise amulet facing the computer provides good fortune and business inspiration as well as protection.
4. A dragon or snake screen saver places the guardian directly over the threshold of entry, a particularly potent spot.

✦ Guardian Snake Spirit Protection (2) Simbi

The spell above summons the powers of snakes and dragons as a general species. There is an abstract quality to the spell: the desire is to draw on generic dragon or snake power rather than that of one specific spirit ally.

Simbi, the powerful snake lwa, is considered the spiritual patron of computers. Request his personal assistance by placing the image of a powerful snake near the computer. Give the snake a dish of milk on Fridays in exchange for his protection.

✦ Guardian Snake: Snake Head Spell (1)

Fritillaria meleagris *a now rare European plant whose flower bears a striking resemblance to a snake's head—hence its English name "snake head." Because it is very endangered and because the living plant is a source of tremendous spiritual protection, grow your own rather than wildcrafting. Carry a piece of the root or a carefully preserved flower head for protection.*

✦ Guardian Snake: Snake Head Spell (2)

Place the root and/or blossom above the door for protection.

Guardian Crocodile Spells

Magnitude of power is required to provide serious protection. This is always ambiguous: magnitude of power required to fend off real dangers is potentially a danger unto itself. Snakes may be magically protective but they're also dangerous, venomous creatures. That ambivalence is even greater with another protective creature, the crocodile.

There's a fantasy aspect to all these protectors, reminiscent of a child's desire for a really big mean brother to scare off and punish bullies. This is the ultimate fantasy: to have someone so scary that they terrify everyone else to be your loyal friend and helper. Crocodiles, snakes, and dragons fall into this category. It is, however, always crucial to recall that an animal alliance with a spirit animal doesn't necessarily extend to every single individual living member of the species.

✦ Guardian Animal Crocodile Spell (1) Image

Once upon a time, churches and occultists alike attempted to command and compel crocodile's magical protective tendencies by hanging stuffed, dried crocodiles from the ceiling. The magical use of crocodile imagery provides greater protection to people and crocodiles alike.

Cut the image of a crocodile from two pieces of fabric and sew them together, leaving a hole for stuffing. Red or green fabric is recommended. Stuff with protective herbs: harmel (Syrian rue), mugwort, pennyroyal, wormwood, lavender, and mint and hang from an iron nail.

✦ Guardian Animal Crocodile Spell (2) Teeth

Like sharks, crocodiles and alligator shed their old teeth, growing new ones. In theory at least, their teeth may be obtained without injury to the animal. A necklace or ankle bracelet of shed crocodile or alligator teeth allegedly prevents the casting of all negative bewitchment over its wearer.

1. Many teeth have a natural space at the top through which they may be threaded, however a needle can also be used to gently pierce the tooth.
2. String the teeth onto red or black thread, focusing on the desire for protection.
3. Pass through protective incense smoke and wear.

Guardian Poultry

Of course, humble creatures can demonstrate tremendous protective power, too. How does that Mother Goose rhyme go?

Heckity, peckity
My black hen

Vestiges of Hecate's ancient protective power lie in the ubiquitous references to black hens in magic spells. Pure black hens were treasured, eggs and stray feathers prized components in all sorts of spells.

✴ Guardian Animal Poultry Spell (1) Frizzly Hen

The tradition survived in the Hoodoo tradition of the frizzled or frizzly chicken. Keep "frizzled" pattern chickens or roosters on your property. Allegedly they stand guard and will scratch up any hexes, jinxes, and tricks any malicious spell-caster may have secretly hidden on your property.

✴ Guardian Animal Poultry Spell (2) Rooster

Roosters are creatures possessing potent magic power. While many may consider poultry to be humble, no one has informed the rooster. By nature, they're fearless, virile, territorial creatures. Because they crow at the first light of day, it's believed that many malevolent low-level nocturnal spirits fear them. Because these low-level spirits are none too bright, they won't check the sky to see whether the sun is coming. As soon as they hear a rooster's crow or even see a rooster, these spirits disappear.

★ *Wear a rooster charm to avail yourself of this power*
★ *Post the image of a proud rooster to repel spiritual dangers*

★ *A real rooster, or even the recording of one crowing, will repel evil spirits: avail yourself of this power as necessary although your neighbors will hate you for it. The rooster's crow is extremely loud and piercing*

Guardian Spirit Spells

Although there are many benevolent, powerful, protective spirits your own strongest ally is always your personal guardian angel. If you're unsure of his or her identity, consider that although there are spirits that offer protection, it's best to call on someone you can count on. Call on whomever has helped you in the past, whomever you feel you have a relationship with. That said, there are spiritual experts in the world of protection, just as there are human security experts.

It takes a fierce spirit to defeat other fierce spirits: treat these guardians with respect. Transcending any other arrangements, the necessary payment for protection is respect.

✴ Sign of Protection Spell

Images of the following guardian deities may be used to exorcise or drive off all manner of evil. Not only do they protect from the evil done by humans, they also guard people against danger threatened by less benevolent spirits.

★ *Archangel Michael*
★ *Bes*
★ *Durga*
★ *Hanuman*
★ *Kali*
★ *Medusa*
★ *Saint James the Major*
★ *Saint Martha the Dominator*
★ *Set*
★ *Ogun*

★ *Shiva*
★ *Taweret*
★ *Various Tibetan and Chinese guardian spirits*

Guardian Spirit Spell: Archangels Ritual Protection Spell

This spell is particularly effective for providing protection during ritual. However it may also be used any time spiritual protection is perceived as necessary.

1. Designate four candles, one for each archangel: Michael, Raphael, Uriel, and Gabriel.
2. Dedicate each candle to one archangel; carve the angel's name or sigil into the wax if you prefer.
3. Place one candle in each corner of the room or make a circle with the candles on your altar.
4. Encircle anything you wish to protect with a ring of these candles, including yourself.
5. Burn the candles, replace as needed.

Archangel Michael Spell (1)

Although the archangels (and potentially any angel) can provide tremendous protection, the archangel Michael is the very personification of protection. Always ready and alert, Michael the Archangel is charged as humanity's guardian and defender. That's his mission, his raison d'etre. *Put him to work if his services are required. Although Michael the Archangel will respond to any call for help, he is a particular vigilant defender against rape and sexual assault.*

The aroma of frankincense summons Michael, however calling his name, particularly when desperate, may be sufficient. Call him with his invocation:

Michael to the right of me,
Michael to the left of me
Michael above me

Michael below me
Michael within me
Michael all around me
Michael, with your flaming sword of cobalt blue please protect me today.

Archangel Michael Spell (2) Slavic Invocation

A Slavic invocation of Michael the Archangel emphasizes his connections with the protective power of iron and the magical protective capacity of the number three and its multiples:

Oh Archangel Michael
Protect me with an iron door
Lock it with three times nine locks and keys!

Archangel Michael Spell (3)

According to legend, Michael is the angel with the flaming, revolving sword standing guard at the gates of Eden. A New Orleans Voodoo spell posts Michael at your door with sword at the ready for ever-vigilant protection.

1. Fill small bags with Grains of Paradise.
2. Attach these bags to the back of two images of Michael the Archangel. Make sure that the images depict him with his sword.
3. Post one image at the front door, the second at the back, so that the warrior angel can stand guard for you.

Of course, should your home only have one entrance, you'll only need a single image and a single bag of Grains of Paradise.

Archangel Michael Gate Spell (1)

Of course there's also another guardian at the gates. According to Christian legend, Saint Peter stands guard at the gates of Eternal Paradise, Heaven. It is he who determines who may enter and who will be denied admission and sent elsewhere. Your home is your little slice of paradise, such as it is. Charge Michael and Peter with maintaining and improving this status.

1. Use one image of Michael; choose a second one featuring Saint Peter. Purchase standard chromolithographs or votive images, or create your own. However it's crucial that Peter's image depicts his keys and Michael is shown with his sword.
2. Attach small bags filled with Grains of Paradise to the backs of these images.
3. Place Peter at the front door, Michael at the back.

Archangel Michael Gate Spell (2)

Depending upon the African Diaspora tradition to which one subscribes, Saint Peter is syncretized to either Elegba or Ogun, while Michael is typically associated with Ogun. Ogun is a warrior spirit, the embodiment of iron, patron of the police, armed guards and soldiers. Elegba is the master of all doors; his permission is required before one can enter.

If you prefer to bypass the syncretism, post images of Ogun at front and back door or Elegba at the front and Ogun at the back, with a small bag of Grains of Paradise attached to the back of each image.

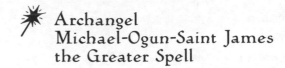

Archangel Michael-Ogun-Saint James the Greater Spell

To complicate matters further, Michael the Archangel is identified with Ogun, but Ogun is frequently identified with Saint James the Greater, in whose guise he is depicted as a knight or conquistador riding a white horse, lance at the ready. That image also has profound protective capacities. Substitute as desired or post within the home facing the front door. Create your own image or use traditional votive cards or chromolithographs. This image is also a frequent theme of beautiful sequined Haitian Vodou flags, however in all cases it is crucial that Saint James have his weapon ready at hand.

Guardian Spirits: Bes and Taweret

Much of the ancient Egyptian mythology that survives belongs to those spiritual cults presided over by the Pharaoh and the elite priesthood. As far as the masses of common people were concerned, however, the most popular, beloved, prevalent deities may have been the married couple, Bes and Taweret.

Bes, whose worship ranged from Nubia to Mesopotamia, is a fierce cross between a lion and a dwarf. Taweret is another hybrid creature: she has a woman's breasts on a hippo's body, although from behind she resembles a Nile crocodile. Bes and Taweret live to serve: they are particularly protective of women and children. Bes and Taweret may be summoned separately, however they are at maximum strength when paired together. Not only will they provide protection, they also inspire bravery and will help you access your own courage.

Summon Bes and Taweret through imagery. They recognize the placement of their image as a call for protection. Bes, in particular, also loves a party: he finds it hard to resist or leave loud, wild percussion music and dancing.

Guardian Spirits: Egyptian

The Egyptian deities Isis, her sister Nephthys, the scorpion spirit Selket (or Serket), and warrior Neith are all intensely involved with the magical arts. Images of these four protective deities were used to guard coffins and canopic jars, as well as deceased pharaohs. They will guard you too, if so requested.

Call them with an ancient invocation:

My mother is Isis
Nephthys is my nurse
Neith is behind me
Selket is before me

This is particularly beneficial when emergency situations demand spontaneous spiritual invocation.

 ## Guardian Spirits: Egyptian (2) Candle Magic

More formal invocation may also be made. Images of the four spirits are required. Reproductions of ancient statues are readily available or substitute their emblems: a scorpion for Selket, and a pair of crossed arrows, snake or crocodile for Neith. For this function, Isis and Nephthys are typically represented by a matched pair of their sacred birds, the kite; however, this may be a difficult image to obtain. Isis may also be invoked in the image of a scorpion, with Nephthys as a snake.

1. Cast a circle with the images: place Nephthys behind you, Isis in front, Neith to the east and Selket to the west.
2. Place one green or black candle behind each image. Hold each candle in your hand, focusing on your desire for protection.
3. Invoke each spirit in turn to watch over you and prevent the approach of all evil.
4. Burn the candles. Repeat as needed.

 ## Guardian Spirits: Joan of Arc

The unofficial saint to end all unofficial saints is Joan of Arc. Roman Catholic authorities attempted to charge Joan with witchcraft, heresy, and consorting with fairies. Burned at the stake on May 30th, 1431 at age 19, Joan was declared innocent twenty-five years later but not canonized until 1920. For almost five hundred years Joan was the most famous, beloved unofficial saint ever. During her lifetime, Joan demonstrated her bravery and her loyalty to those for whom she fought. Petition her to protect a family or household.

1. Designate a gray candle for each member of the household for whom you beseech protection.
2. Write each person's name on a piece of paper.
3. Place each name-paper under an individual candle and burn them while requesting Joan's protection.
4. Repeat this spell eight more times, for a total of nine consecutive spell days.

 ## Guardian Spirits: Kali

Kali's name evokes the concept of time and the color black into which all else may be absorbed. She is the spirit of birth and death, love and fear, peace and violence, safety and danger, truth and the destruction of illusion. She is the matron of witchcraft and Tantra. Call out her name Kali Ma (Mother Kali) for protection if threatened by violence.

Guardian Spirits: Kwan Yin

Kwan Yin, the Buddhist Lady of Mercy and Compassion, is a tireless, ever-vigilant protective guardian. Although her appearance is milder than that of warrior spirits, she is no less powerful. Kwan Yin achieved nirvana but refused to leave Earth as long as one human is left suffering. She promises to come to the aid of anyone who cries out her name in his or her hour of need. If your hour is at hand, call her name and explain your predicament, if it needs explaining.

 ## Guardian Spirits: Mafdet

Invoke Mafdet, the fierce Egyptian spirit for protection from demons, and troublesome ghosts as well as human enemies. Mafdet manifests as a lynx or a large wild cat.

1. Shape ground meat (do not use pork) into something approximating the shape and size of a human phallus. Basically you've formed a penis-shaped meatloaf, however there is no need to cook it.
2. Inscribe the names of your enemy or enemies onto the loaf with a knife, sharp blade or toothpick.
3. Chant the names of your enemies, each identified also with their mother's names, in order to identify and pin them down.
4. Wrap this loaf in a layer of fatty meat.
5. Feed this to a cat: your own or otherwise. It's crucial that the cat eat with gusto. Find feral hungry cats. Don't feed it to a finicky cat who'll just nibble at the ends. As the cat devours the loaf on this plane, so Mafdet will deal with your enemies on the spirit plane.

 ## Guardian Spirits: Maximon

Maximon, Guatemalan trickster spirit of the crossroads and male primal power is a fusion of the ancient Mayan deity Maam and the Roman Catholic Saint Simon. He offers devotees many gifts such as wealth and fertility but especially protection. Maximon's sacred plant is tobacco; his color is black.

Burn a black candle before an image of Maximon to protect against envy, jealousy, and hostility from others.

 ## Guardian Spirit: Maximon Clothing Protection Spell

Traditionally Maximon is represented by wooden images dressed in the elegant clothes he loves. Maximon is fine: keep him looking sharp. There's something in it for you, too.

1. Handwash Maximon's clothing.
2. Add essential oils of lemongrass and citronella to the final rinse water.
3. The water in which his clothes are washed magically protects against malevolent witchcraft. Reserve the final rinse water; add it to your own bath, or bottle and reserve to use as needed.

 ## Guardian Spirits: La Santisima Muerte

La Santisima Muerte, Blessed Death, skeleton spirit of the hereafter is the magical matron of Mexican witches. Cut from the same cloth as Kali or Baba Yaga and evoking the same mingled emotions of dread and love, La Santisima's imagery is even starker than theirs; she appears as the grim reaper in robes, complete with scales and sickle. A dangerous spirit, she forces us to confront our deepest fears when we contemplate her contradictions. Beyond the reach of any mortal fear herself, La Santisima offers protection in the face of grave danger. Because she is dangerous, one doesn't bother her over trivial matters but when protection is a life or death issue, La Santisima Muerte is a profound, fearsome ally.

La Santisima Muerte possesses a reasonably extensive wardrobe of different colored robes. When petitioning her

for protection, it's traditional to use her image robed in white. Because she can be too much for a person to handle, it's also customary to include another spirit in the petition, someone like Saint Anthony, Santa Elena or San Cipriano to keep her in line.

Blend white rice, rosemary, and red rose petals in a bowl before an image of La Santisima Muerte. Place a white candle in the bowl and burn it, praying and petitioning to La Santisima Muerte. Bury most of the remnants but keep a sampling of auspicious-appearing pieces of wax in a red conjure bag.

Guardian Spirits: Seven Hathors

The Seven Hathors are ancient birthroom spirits, however they also provide protection in other contexts. Use their seven red hair ribbons to bind dangerous spirits.

1. Create an offering table to call their attention: offer beer and pomegranates.
2. Place seven red silk ribbons on the table, one for each Hathor.
3. Murmur over the ribbons, explain your desires, fears, and what is required.
4. Weave, braid or otherwise bind the ribbons together.
5. Hang these woven ribbons prominently until all danger has passed then dispose of them in a river.
6. Should their help be needed again, summon the Seven Hathors with seven new ribbons.

Guardian Spirits: Zhong Kui

Zhong Kui, master exorcist and ghost-eater, stamps out mean spirits with his big black boots. Zhong Kui heads a host of either 3,000 or 84,000 demon-slaying spirits (depending upon the legend). Posting his image brings good fortune, banishes evil spirits, and protects you from harm. Zhong Kui is depicted with his demon-killing magic sword and his totem animal, a lucky bat.

Hang his magical image up at the end of any month or on the fifth day of the fifth month of the Chinese lunar calendar (corresponding to Midsummer's Eve) to scare away malicious and evil spirits.

Hand of Power Spell

1. Create a talisman on parchment or a sheet of copper.
2. Form it in the shape of a hand with an eye in the center. (A bit of yellow sulfur may be used for the eye.)
3. Inscribe with protective runes or sacred verses.
4. Carry, post or give to someone in need.

Hearth Fire Protection Spell

Protective botanicals may be ground and powdered and burned as incense. However it's believed especially powerful to burn them on the hearth. The burning hearth fire itself possesses incredible powers of protection and enhances the effectiveness of any spell cast within. The hearth symbolizes female primal power, while the fire is the male. Whatever enters the hearth thus enters a cauldron of generation—hence the importance of such hearth spirits as Vesta or the domovai, and the crucial importance of never allowing the hearth fire to go out.

To protect against evil forces burn angelica, bay laurel leaves, juniper, mugwort, and wisteria in the hearth. (A fireplace or iron cauldron substitutes for the traditional open hearth.)

Hemlock Protection Spell

Allegedly hemlock carried in a red charm bag protects from all evil, but be careful: it's poisonous!

 Herbal Protection

Gather dillweed, Saint John's Wort, and vervain within white handkerchiefs. Either tie the packets closed with blue ribbon or create sachets using blue thread and hang these strategically throughout the home for spiritual and magical protection.

 Holed Stone Protection Spell

Suspend holed stones on red cords and hang in the window to ward off evil.

 Holy Herbs Protection Spell

New Orleans Holy Herbs are a protective formulation.

Add the following seven botanicals to a steaming cauldron: black snake root, catnip, hops, jasmine, motherwort, peppermint, and skullcap. Brew and allow the steam to permeate an area to simultaneously cleanse and beckon protective spirits.

 Home Protection Floorwash

This is most effective if done during the Summer Solstice, Midsummer's Eve or Saint George's Day.

1. Add **War Water** to a bucket of floorwash water with some vinegar.
2. Cleanse floors and surfaces.
3. When the cleansing is complete, toss the used wash water out the back door.
4. Rinse the mop and bucket. Flush this rinse water down the toilet.

If you have no back door and no appropriate back window, flushing all the water is preferable to using the front door.

 Home Protection Oil

1. Blend the following botanical ingredients: powdered five-finger grass (cinquefoil), dried ground purslane, gardenia petals, lavender blossoms, and sandalwood powder.
2. Add it to a bottle of jojoba oil together with a pinch of sea salt.
3. Use this oil for dressing protection candles, drizzle it over the thresholds and anoint any objects within the home requiring special protection.

 Horehound Spell

Horehound is named for the Egyptian falcon deity Horus, and carries the blessings of his mother, Isis. Sew horehound into a white sachet. Wear or carry it to protect against evil spells.

 Horseradish Spell

Grate or grind dried horseradish root. Sprinkle over thresholds, corners, and any vulnerable areas to expel evil.

 Hyacinth Antidote Spell

Carrying a hyacinth (jacinth) crystal gemstone allegedly protects one from poison.

 Inner Safety Spell

Sometimes danger comes from within. If anger and rage threaten to overwhelm you, the following may offer safety:

1. Add essential oils of chamomile, spearmint, and lavender to a base of sweet almond oil.

2. Add a few drops of Cherry plum flower essence (Bach, Healing Herbs).
3. Massage onto the body, especially the back of the neck, as the need arises.

Iris Protection Spell

Beautiful purple irises potently repel evil. Gather them on Midsummer's Day and hang them over doorways and thresholds.

Iron Spells

Iron repels evil of all kind. Most malevolent spirits cannot bear to be in its presence. In addition to providing protection, iron enhances and stimulates the growth of one's personal magic powers, so that you are stronger and better able to protect yourself, requiring less outside spiritual protection. Iron also invigorates general vitality and energy.

Iron Protection Spells

Iron provides protection 24 hours a day, whether you are asleep or awake.

★ *Bend a used horseshoe nail into a ring*
★ *An iron bracelet reinforces the magical protective capacities of the hand*
★ *String iron beads and wear around neck and ankles*
★ *For protection while you sleep, slip a knife or horseshoe under your pillow*
★ *If you prefer not to keep anything that hard in bed, a sword or fireplace poker can be kept under the bed*
★ *No need to keep anything in or under the bed: sleeping in a bed crafted from iron creates an island of safety, reinvigorating health, creativity and fertility while you sleep*

Iron Spell: Spoken Word

The power of iron is so strong that even if you don't have any, just shouting out the word "iron" allegedly routs evil spirits.

Iron Spell: Basic Bath

Place an iron nail into a drawstring bag and hang it from the faucet so that water runs through it into a bath. Reserve the nail, drying thoroughly; it may be used over and over again as needed.

Iron Spell: Enhanced Bath

Place an iron nail into a drawstring bag together with red rose petals, hibiscus flowers, and Grains of Paradise. Hang it from the faucet so that water runs through it into the bath. The botanicals may be discarded after the bath, but reserve the nail for future use.

Iron Spell: Clothing

Sew bits of iron (nails for instance) into the hems of garments for protection from evil. (The spell only works when the clothing is worn.)

Iron Spell: Coffin Nail

Wrap a coffin nail in brown silk. Carry it with you to protect against malevolent magic.

Iron Spell: Cross of Protection

Charge six iron nails with their mission of protection. Arrange them into three crosses (one nail hammered over the other forms a cross) and drive over the front entrance door. Anoint the nails with **Lucky Lodestone Oil** once a week.

 ## Iron Spell: Pliny the Elder

This formula from Pliny the Elder is used as ritual protection against the threat of poison, sorcery, and malicious enchantments. Although one may cast this spell oneself, it's more effective if someone casts it for you.

Take a knife or dagger, the crucial point being that it is crafted from iron or steel. Cast an imaginary circle three times around the person requesting protection with the point always facing toward them.

 ## Iron Spell: Simple

Ironworkers create intricate, complex amuletic designs for fences and gates. Of course, professional talent, extensive training, and skill are required. Simple spells can also be very powerful. Pow-Wow draws on potent household magic: a safety pin serves as a protective amulet. Wear one discreetly on your sleeve to repel dangers.

 ## Isis Eternal Light Protection Spell

Shine a light in the darkness. Keep it burning in the light, too. According to legend, the Roman Temple of Isis kept candles burning day and night to symbolize eternal hope and never faltering protection.

Emulate the practice by burning protection candles constantly. As one candle goes out, burn another. (The Temple of Isis, of course, was never left unattended. Keep fire safety always in mind.) The spell is made more potent if petitions to Isis or your personal guardian spirit are incorporated.

Jack o'Lantern Protection Spells

Placing candles within carved hollowed vegetables, now a Halloween tradition, was originally intended to protect against wandering, malicious spirits or ghosts. This spell still works, particularly if the jack o'lantern is created with conscious intent.

 ## Jack o'Lantern Pumpkin Spell

Pumpkins are the subject of many spells themselves and so are appropriately used to protect against malevolent magic. This jack o'lantern serves as a door guardian and should be placed by the front door. It protects against mischievous spirits, and disappointed trick-or-treaters. Use real pumpkins; carve a face if you choose or carve protective symbols into the hollowed pumpkin.

 ## Jack o'Lantern Turnip Spell

Protect the trick-or-treaters! The original Irish jack o'lantern was carved from a turnip. It has the advantage of being portable and can thus be carried as a protective amulet. Hollow the turnip and carve, either with the traditional face or with symbols that represent protection to you. Insert a lit candle and carry as a magical, protective lantern.

 ## Jade Spell

Jade carved into the form of a circle with a hole in its center, essentially a double-concentric circle, provides spiritual protection. Examples include bangle bracelets or circular charms meant to be strung from red cord.

1. Hold the jade in your hand to charge it with your purpose.
2. Empower it by exposing it to moonlight.
3. Cleanse periodically by passing through sandalwood smoke.

 Juniper Protection Spell (1)

Hang juniper berries over doors and windows to guard against malevolent magic.

 Juniper Protection Spell (2)

Pierce juniper berries. String them onto red cord and wear as a necklace to ward off hexes.

 Kludde Safety Spell

Kludde is a Belgian woodland goblin notorious for his shape-shifting skills. Kludde transforms into any creature at will, from the fiercest to the cutest, in order to lure unsuspecting humans to certain doom. Is he an evil spirit or a forest guardian who's earned a bad reputation? Either way, the condition oil named in his honor is used homeopathically to protect against attack by any living creature—animal or human.

Add essential oils of citronella, fir, and pine to a base of jojoba oil. Soak cotton balls in the oil and tuck them in your pockets when journeying through literal or metaphoric woodlands.

 Kupala's Dew Protection Spell

Kupala, the Slavic spirit of water, botanicals, magic, and fertility is honored at the Summer Solstice. She's at the height of her power and Earth's moisture is suffused with her protective blessings.

Roll in morning dew on the Summer Solstice so that your clothes and body are suffused with its moisture to receive Kupala's blessings of protection. (This spell is most powerful if the previous night was spent reveling in honor of Kupala.)

 Liquidambar Spell

The resin of the liquidambar tree, also known as storax, provides protection on its own, but is also believed to magically enhance and strengthen the powers of any other botanical it is blended with. Burn liquidambar together with frankincense and sandalwood for optimum spiritual protection.

Living Boundary Spells

In fairy tales, witches' cottages are surrounded by magical gardens. A garden creates a living altar that is cultivated to achieve your desired goals. A protective garden creates an aura of safety around the perimeter of your home.

 Living Boundary: Basic Protection Garden

Maintain a protective aura of safety around your home. Include as many of the following as possible: angelica, cactus, clover, dill, elder, flax, gardenia, garlic, holly, juniper, mugwort, nettles, oregano, roses, rosemary, rowan, rue, Saint John's Wort, southernwood, thyme, vervain, wormwood, and yarrow.

 Living Boundary: Circle of Trees

Grow or transplant as many of the following protective trees as possible: ash, bay laurel, birch, cedar, ceiba, hawthorn, hazel, iroko, juniper, oak, olive, and rowan. Arrange the trees in a circle, if possible.

Living Boundary: The Poison Garden

This may be the ultimate protective garden, filled with plants that can genuinely harm the careless trespasser. Although these plants are dangerous and even toxic for consumption, on a metaphysical level alone, they produce a powerful aura of protection. Once upon a time, witches, sorceresses, herbalists, pharmacists, and botanists alike maintained small, enclosed, gated poison gardens. However, if children and animals have access to your garden, this spell is neither safe nor appropriate.

Plant some or all of the following:

Aconite (*Aconitum napellus*)
Deadly nightshade (*Atropa belladonna*)
Thorn apple (*Datura stramonium*)
Hellebore (*Veratum album*)
Henbane (*Hyoscemus niger*)
Mandrake (*Atropa mandragora*)
Oleander (*Nerium oleander*)

Place a bench in a shady spot and absorb their protection, being careful not to absorb their poison.

Living Boundary: Guardian

Elderberry bushes planted beside entrances creates the botanical equivalent of a gate guardian. They provide a metaphysical barrier against forces of malevolence. Fresh leaves and branches near doors and windows serve to protect, as well.

Magic Bean Spell

Beans are magic plants; Jack and the Beanstalk *is but* the most famous of the tales that celebrate beans' magic power. Although the dried seed is what's most frequently used, the beautiful, if fleeting, bean blossoms are also filled with power. This isn't something you can purchase at the florists but must be grown at home.

Gather, dry, and powder bean blossoms. Sprinkle this powder over thresholds, or use as a discreet strewing herb for magical protection.

Magic Belt Protection Spell

A magic belt constitutes a method of casting a protective circle, sealing off the aura from danger. Pass fabric or cord through protective incense smoke before use. Ornament with bells, mirrors, cowries, charms, small amulet bags, and auspicious beads.

Magic Belt Protection Spell Quick Fix

Make knots in cord in multiples of three (nine knots, twenty-one knots, and so on) and tie it around your waist, while simultaneously blessing and affirming your safety.

Magic Mirror Protection Spell

Point a solar-charged magic mirror in the direction of danger to eradicate it. (See Elements of Magic Spells for instructions on safely charging mirrors with the power of the sun.)

Malicious Spirits Protection Spell

Should you hear someone call your name when no one is visibly present, and should you fear that this is a demonic ploy to lure you into trouble, take advantage of low-level spirits' legendary low IQ: respond with a contradictory message. The classic Russian answer is something like "Come again yesterday," *but the more clever and*

creative your response, the more you'll leave the spirits scratching their heads and impotent to hurt you.

 ## Mandrake Protection Spell

Soak true mandrake root in warm (not hot or boiling) water for three or seven days. Sprinkle the water on thresholds for protection against all manner of evil. (Allow the mandrake to dry out afterwards so that this expensive, rare root may be preserved and used again.)

 ## Marjoram Protection Spell

Grow living marjoram plants in every room of your home to provide magical and spiritual safety.

 ## Mary's Bean

"Mary's bean" is the name given to several species of Central American and Caribbean beans that enter the sea and wash up on the shores of Northern Europe, particularly the Hebrides and Orkney Islands. The beans are characterized by their mysterious appearance on these shores and the cross marking one side. Magical theory is that if the beans are lucky enough to arrive unscathed, they'll extend that protection to the one who finds it.

Holed stones are gifts of Earth; Mary's beans are gifts of the sea. If you find one, preserve it in a charm bag or set it into jewelry and keep with you at all times.

 ## Matchbox Spell

Blend cayenne pepper with flaxseed and place within a matchbox. Hide the matchbox within the home to prevent the entry of evil. (More than one box may be created and then secreted in different spots for optimum protection.)

 ## Mean Spirit Repelling

This spell is particularly beneficial following banishing spells when you fear that malevolent spirits will attempt to re-visit the scene of their crimes. The aroma of this potion repels hostile, troublesome, malicious spirits and prevents their entry.

Place rotten apples, wine galls, vinegar, and sulfur in a cauldron. Add myrrh and red sandalwood and warm to a simmer.

 ## Mean Spirit Repelling Powder

Avoid uninvited guests. Make a paste from camphor, cloves, frankincense, and myrrh and burn it in the fireplace or in your cauldron to prevent evil spirits from gate-crashing a ritual.

 ## Midsummer's Protection Spell

Emulate John the Baptist whose festival coincides with Midsummer's Eve. Wear a magic belt or girdle woven from mugwort on Midsummer's Eve. Dance around the bonfire; before the night ends, toss the garland into the fires to receive a year of protection.

 ## Moon's Protective Mojo Hand

A mojo bag created with the talismans of the moon provides protection at night:

1. Place a moonstone, a clear quartz crystal, and a smoky quartz into a beaded bag.
2. Add a piece of moonwort and a silver bead.
3. Dress with one drop of essential oil of white camphor and carry or wear the bag.

Mugwort Spells

 ## Mugwort Protection Spell (1)

The fifth day of the fifth month in the Chinese calendar, the Chinese Dragon Boat Festival, coincides with the Summer Solstice and Midsummer's Eve. That "five" is among the chief numbers of protection is no accident.

Gather mugwort and iris. Wrap them together with silk thread in five different colors and hang them over door hinges to avert mean spirits and malevolent magical influences.

 ## Mugwort Protection Spell (2)

Pick mugwort on the fifth day of the fifth Chinese month. Craft it into dolls, and hang these over doors to banish toxic influences.

Mugwort–Saint John's Wort Spells

Saint John's Wort and mugwort are brother and sister plants: the ancient Greeks placed Saint John's Wort under the rulership of Apollo while mugwort belongs to his twin sister, Artemis. They are fairy-tale protector plants. Saint John's Wort protects by day, mugwort by night. They are allies, working together to provide the best protection for you.

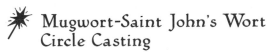 ## Mugwort-Saint John's Wort Circle Casting

1. Maintain living plants in flowerpots.
2. They will radiate protection by their mere presence; however when extra protection is needed, arrange the pots in a circle and sit within.
3. A minimum of four pots will be required (two Saint John's, two mugworts) to demarcate the cardinal points, however more may be used if desired.

 ## Mugwort-Saint John's Wort Round-the-clock Protection

Place dried Saint John's Wort leaves and/or blossoms in a conjure bag or locket and wear or carry during the daytime. Fill a dream pillow or a second locket with mugwort for protection while you sleep.

 ## Mugwort-Saint John's Wort Deluxe Conjure Bag

1. Place the following botanicals in a conjure bag: bay leaves, Dittany of Crete, mugwort, Saint John's Wort, southernwood and wormwood.
2. Add one silver bead or charm, one gold bead or charm, and one iron bead or charm.
3. Carry for protection

 ## Saint John's Wort Malevolent Magic Detector

Gather Saint John's Wort on Midsummer's Eve. Hang the branches on the walls or in the upper corners of rooms to serve as "malevolent magic detectors." Should harm cross the threshold, the blossoms will drop.

 ## Mustard Seed Spell

Bury yellow mustard seed under your doorstep or threshold area to prevent the entry of negative spiritual entities.

 ## New Year's Protection Spell

This spell comes from Scandinavia; it is diametrically opposed to many Chinese New Year's spells that instruct not to clean on New Year's Day because you may accidentally sweep all your luck away, leaving you none for

the year ahead. How you feel about cleaning will determine which magical philosophy is most appropriate for you.

1. Clean the house completely on New Year's Day, removing every speck of dust.
2. Carry the sweepings to a crossroads and discard them.
3. This renders the home immune to bewitchment and malevolent magic during the year to come.

 ## Okra Safety Spell

Dry whole okra. Pierce the dried vegetable, string onto red cord and hang over the door to protect against malevolent bewitchment.

 ## Onion Blossom Spell

The unexpected beauty of many onion blossoms surprises those only familiar with onions as food. Springing up on spear-like stalks, the flowering onion proudly displays its protective capacity. Grow onions around the home to create a magical barrier against harm.

 ## Onion Protection Spell

Pierce a round white onion with at least one hundred red- and black-headed pins. Place this within a window to obstruct the entry of evil.

Orrisroot Protection Spells

What's this? A spell to guard your lover? Orrisroot, the fragrant roots of several iris species, is used almost exclusively for love and seduction spells, at least in European-derived magic. In Japanese magical traditions, however, orrisroot offers spiritual protection too.

 ## Orrisroot Personal Protection Spell

Make an infusion by pouring boiling water over sliced or ground orrisroot and add the strained liquid to your bath.

 ## Orrisroot Space Protection Spell

Hang whole orrisroots from the ceiling to provide protection.

 ## Papaya-Mandrake Safety Spell

Place mandrake root and papaya leaves within a charm bag. Hang it over doorways and windows for protection against malevolent spells and enemies.

 ## Papaya Protection Spell

Place papaya twigs and leaves over the door to ward off evil.

 ## Parsley Protection Spell (1)

P is for protection—and for parsley, too. That's why it's used as a garnish; parsley on the plate keeps your food free of any low-level spirits attempting to sneak inside you via your food.

 ## Parsley Protection Spell (2)

Garnish yourself with parsley's protection. Wear a sprig of parsley to provide protection wherever you travel.

Peach Protection Spell (1)

Different cultures have different protective trees and wood: rowan in Northern Europe, tamarisk in the Middle East. The peach is the primary protective tree of Chinese metaphysics.

Carve peach wood or a dried fruit pit into shapes that represent protection for you, and carry it in a charm bag.

 ## Peach Protection Spell (2)

Place blooming peach blossoms at the door to guard the inhabitants and to prevent the entry of evil.

 ## Pentacle Protection Spell

The pentacle, the five-pointed star, may be understood to represent a parturient woman: the uppermost point is her head, while the others represent her arms and her legs spread out in labor. It is an exceptionally powerful image radiating spiritual protection. Hold the image of that laboring woman in mind while drawing pentacles wherever they feel needed.

 ## Peony Protection Spell

Peonies have been considered magical plants from China to ancient Greece. Dry peony roots and carve them into sacred, auspicious shapes. Carry for protection.

 ## Peony Seed Protection Spell

All parts of the peony provide magical protection: string dried peony seeds onto red thread and wear as a necklace to ward off evil.

 ## Peppertree Protection

Carry red peppertree berries for personal magical protection.

 ## Pine Protection

Pine trees offer protection. The fragrance of the needles wafts protection over an area.

Bring small living pine trees inside your house, and not only at Christmas. Decorate them with protective amulets.

 ## Plum Tree Protection Spell

Hang boughs of flowering plum over doors, windows, and thresholds to retain joy in the home and repel malice and evil.

 ## Poison Protection: Devil's Shoestrings

Wear a whole, uncut, devil's shoestring around your neck to protect against poison.

 ## Poison Protection: Shark's Teeth

Fossilized shark's teeth, also known as "Saint Paul's tongues," allegedly protect against poison if worn or carried. Should the tooth work for you, cleanse it before further use and make a contribution to the welfare of sharks.

Protection Bags

 ## Simple Protection Bag

Entwine mugwort and Saint John's Wort and place within a red bag. Hang over every door and window for powerful magical, spiritual protection.

Personal Protection Bag

This protection spell may be cast for yourself or for another.

1. Put together a bag of your own or another person's intimate items (hair, nail clippings, bits of fabric cut from a garment soaked with sweat, etc.).
2. Place them within a charm bag.
3. Attach it to the wall in a very discreet area by hammering in an iron nail. Simultaneously invoke blessings.

 Boldo Protection Bag

Place boldo leaves, garlic cloves, Saint John's Wort, black cohosh root (black snake root), and rue into a red bag to guard against evil.

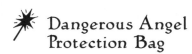 Dangerous Angel Protection Bag

Ironically, with the exception of angelica, many botanicals named for angels are toxic and even angelica, benevolent as it is, shouldn't be wildcrafted as it's easily mistaken for poisonous plants. This protection bag is filled with dangerous angels: very definitely for external use only.

1. Fill a charm bag with angelica root, angel wings, angel's turnip (dogbane) and a dried angel's trumpet seedpod.
2. For maximum protection, dress a gold pillar candle with **Fiery Wall of Protection Oil.**
3. Activate the bag by placing it in front of the candle while it burns.

 Devil's Power Blast Protection Bag

Despite various frequent allusions to the devil in folk magic, witchcraft is not synonymous with Satanism. The devil as perceived as a completely malevolent competitor of the Creator is a Christian concept, based on ancient Persian notions of the battle between opposing good and evil forces. Few other spiritual philosophies recognize such concretely "black and white" deities. What passes for the "devil" (and typically has been identified with the devil by Christian authorities) is either one of the less sympathetic angels, a crossroads spirit, or one of the horned spirits of primal male generative power. Although all possess a potentially dangerous streak and must be handled with care, none is inherently evil, malevolent, hostile, or out to permanently steal souls. In fact, many of these spirits demonstrate tremendous benevolence toward people, when they choose to (e.g., Elegba or Maximon). Because the concept of an eternally evil devil doesn't exist for those who aren't Christian, there's little fear. Perhaps because the crossroads spirits in general are pranksters, devil imagery is often incorporated with humor: Lucky Devil rather than Evil Satan.

Magically speaking, the devil is often perceived as the biggest, meanest, baddest spirit on the block; one you'd like to have on your side to protect against other lesser mean spirits. This protection bag calls on that devil.

1. Fill a conjure bag with devil's pod *(Trapa bicornis)*, devil's dung (asafetida), devil's bit, devil's nettle (yarrow), three devil's claws, five devil's joy blossoms (vinca) and nine devil's shoestrings of equal length.
2. Anoint the bag with **Flying Devil Oil.**
3. Activate it by placing it beside a carved, dressed devil candle in whatever color makes you feel most protected. (Devil candles are typically crafted in black, green, and red although a candle-maker could craft any color.)

Protection Baths

 Object Protection Bath

For empowering and protecting specific objects or ritual tools:

1. Place marjoram, peppermint, rosemary, and sage within a bowl.
2. Make a strong infusion by pouring boiling water over them.
3. Sprinkle the infusion as needed or add the strained, cooled liquid to a spray bottle and apply as needed.

 Protection Bath: Basil

This spell repels malevolent magic targeted toward you, repairs a damaged aura, and helps erect a personal protective shield.

1. Make a strong infusion by pouring boiling water over fresh basil leaves. Once it cools, strain the leaves out and discard.
2. Bring the bowl of basil-infused water to the bath or shower. Stand naked in the tub or shower. Dip a clean white cloth (a handkerchief or hand towel) into the infusion and, wiping downwards and out, cleanse your body.
3. Repeat daily for nine days. After the final bath, throw any remaining water (and make sure there is some!) out the front door with an aggressive motion.
4. If this isn't possible toss liquid into a pot filled with Earth. Remove it from your home and dispose of it immediately, preferably at a crossroads.

 Protection Bath: Cloves

Cloves are a powerful protective agent, especially beneficial for bolstering personal strength and aura prior to anticipated spiritual, verbal, emotional, or even physical conflict. They're also extremely fragrant, as anyone who's ever mulled cider knows.

That's the good news. The bad news is that cloves are extremely potent skin irritants, capable of raising welts on even the least sensitive skin. There are alternatives to the bath:

★ *Burn cloves and fumigate hair and clothing with the smoke*
★ *Add essential oil of clove bud to oil and massage it into your hair, so that you radiate its fragrance*
★ *Add a few drops of essential oil of clove bud to laundry rinse water so that your clothing is permeated with the fragrance*

However, the bath is the strongest method of application, if you can stand it.

1. Pour two cups boiling spring water over half a teaspoon of ground cloves.
2. Let it steep until cool.
3. Add to bathwater.
4. Immerse completely, if possible, ideally three times, but watch out for your eyes.

If your skin is very sensitive, don't take the bath; this spell is not for you. Choose an alternative. If your skin is a little on the sensitive side, do not grind the cloves but leave them whole. This will not release as much of the volatile oil and so may be slightly less irritating.

 Protection Bath: Dragon's Blood Bath

Blend a handful of sea salt and a handful of dragon's blood powder. Toss it into the bath.

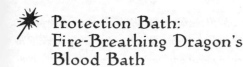 **Protection Bath:**
Fire-Breathing Dragon's
Blood Bath

This bath above is quite powerful on its own, however its protective capacities may be enhanced.

1. Blend a handful of sea salt and a handful of dragon's blood powder.
2. Add one drop of essential oil of cinnamon leaf and/or one drop of essential oil of peppermint. (Cinnamon in particular is a skin irritant; be cautious. Don't exceed the single drop.)
3. Intensify the bath by making it red: use either red food coloring or preferably an infusion of red hibiscus blossoms. (Hibiscus tea bags will work, too.)

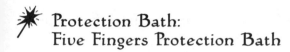 **Protection Bath:**
Five Fingers Protection Bath

The following ingredients will be required:

Five dried or fresh bay laurel leaves
One cup (or more) of sea salt
Five limes, sliced in half
A splash of vinegar, preferably lemon vinegar
A glass of spring water
A glass of rose water or rose hydrosol, or one of the charged waters

1. Draw a warm bath.
2. First add the salt and the bay leaves.
3. Squeeze the limes into the water, tossing the fruit in as well.
4. Add the other ingredients.
5. Enter the water. Submerge yourself completely five times if possible. Stay in as long as you like. Rub your body with the limes.
6. Drain the water while still in the tub. Allow yourself to air-dry amidst the remnants of the limes and leftover leaves.

 Protection Bath:
Fresh Herb Protection Bath

Frankincense, benzoin, and dragon's blood are potent and exotic, but power emerges from the mundane as well. Make a strong infusion by pouring boiling water over fresh fennel, dill, and chervil. Add it to the bath, then allow yourself to air-dry in order to radiate spiritual protection.

 Protection Bath:
Grains of Paradise

Make an infusion by pouring boiling water over Grains of Paradise and galangal root. Strain and add the water to your bath.

 Protection Bath: Indigo

*Add the following to a tub of warm water: sea salt, Epsom salts, saltpeter, and **Indigo Water**.*

 Protection Bath: Lime

Limes possess intensive protective, hex-breaking, and cleansing faculties. Bathe in salt water (use ocean water or add substantial quantities of sea salt to spring water), and add twenty-one slices of lime to your bath. Enter the bath and rub yourself with each slice, discarding it in turn.

✴ Protection Bath: Tormentil

Tormentil tea is used to keep malevolent magic far away. Although its identity is often confused with the root charm High John the Conqueror, they possess no botanic relationship. Tormentil, a frequent component of European magic, is actually closely related to another Hoodoo botanic charm, five-finger grass (cinquefoil). Those five fingers are used in gambling magic to draw luck and money; however five fingers also create a potent sign of protection.

Pour boiling water over tormentil to make an infusion. Add this to a tub filled with warm water and then soak in the water.

✴ Protection Bath: War Water

War Water, also known as the Water of Mars, draws on the power of iron. Although it's most famously used to send notorious and powerful hexes, War Water also creates a powerful, protective shield that repels danger of all kinds.

1. Before you initiate the bath, first cleanse the home with **War Water,** especially the room in which you will bathe.
2. Add **War Water** to the bath water.
3. Immerse yourself completely three times.
4. Drain the water and allow yourself to air-dry.

As an optional extra, add seven or nine bay leaves to the bath.

✴ Protection Bath: Wodaabe

The Wodaabe are the nomadic people of Niger, living amidst settled neighbors. Their herbal knowledge is renowned throughout the region. The Wodaabe recommendation for fighting the influence of sorcery is derived from what they call the tanni tree or Balanites

aegyptica. Millennia ago, the ancient Egyptians favored oil produced from this tree for perfumery. The Wodaabe recommend bathing the body with water containing crushed tanni bark.

1. Add the crushed bark to a cauldron or pot of simmering water.
2. Allow this to simmer for at least one hour, and then allow it to cool until a comfortable temperature is reached.
3. Add to a bath filled with warm water or, for maximum strength, dip a clean cloth into the cooled decoction and bathe the body using downwards, outwards movements.

Protection Incense Formulas

Protection Incense: Five Resin Protection Incense

Blend the following:

Benzoin
Copal
Dragon's blood
Frankincense
Myrrh

✴ Protection Incense: Seven Herb Protection Formula

This is an abbreviated version of the Ten Herb Protection Incense *that follows; however, although this formula uses less botanicals, it incorporates the magically protective number of seven.*

Blend the following: avens, caraway, cumin, dill, juniper, mugwort, and wormwood. Burn the powder as incense.

Protection Incense: Ten Herb Protection Incense

Unlike many protection incenses, which rely on the power of gum resins, this formula incorporates the protective botanicals of Europe's colder climates. Blend the following together:

- Angelica
- Avens
- Basil
- Bay laurel leaves
- Juniper
- Mugwort
- Rosemary
- Saint John's Wort
- Wormwood
- Yarrow

Protection Oil Spells

This classic Hoodoo condition oil makes its promise explicit in its name; this oil creates an aura of protection.

 ### Protection Oil Spell (1) Candle

1. Carve a red, black or white candle with your name and identifying information.
2. Hold the candle in your hands to charge it with your desire.
3. Dress the candle with **Protection Oil** and burn.

 ### Protection Oil Spell (2) Quick Fix

1. Soak a cotton ball in **Protection Oil.**
2. Carry it in your pocket or tucked within your bra.
3. Pay attention: should danger approach, the oil's fragrance may suddenly intensify.

 ### Protection Packet Spell

A Jewish protective amulet also draws good fortune while serving as a magical guardian.

1. Melt beeswax or red wax and reserve. Add a little **Protection Oil** or similar to the wax if desired.
2. Place a sprig of fennel, a stalk of wheat and three, five, seven or nine lucky coins on a piece of silk.
3. Roll it toward you, while concentrating on your desire for safety, protection, good health, and a happy life.
4. Tie it together with red thread.
5. Dip the roll or packet into melted wax and let it dry.

 ### Protection Powder (1)

*This is an abbreviated, simplified version of the powder base for **Protection Oil**.*

1. Grind and powder Southern John root (galangal or Courtcase root).
2. Blend it with magnetic sand.
3. Drip a tiny bit of **Van Van** oil over the powder.
4. Stir it gently and allow the powder to dry.
5. Reserve the powder and sprinkle it as needed.

 ### Protection Powder (2)

Yet another protection powder formula. If this is added to oil this too will serve as Protection Oil. Blend the following together: dragon's blood, sandalwood, and salt. Burn as incense or use to cast protective circles.

 ### Protection Powder (3)

Blend benzoin, dragon's blood, sandalwood, and salt together. Powder and burn, or use the powder to cast protective circles.

Psalm Protection Spells

Psalms have tremendous protective capacity. Psalm 91 is considered the anti-demon, anti-evil, anti-danger psalm. Recite as needed.

 ## Psalm Protection Spell

1. In moments of anxiety and danger start reading Psalm 1 and then proceed through the book, psalm by psalm, in order.
2. If you get to the end, begin the cycle once more.
3. Should your chanting be interrupted, pay attention to where the interruption occurred: clues to your situation and its solution may be revealed.

 ## Psalm Spell

For protection against dangers both spiritual and human, recite the Psalm 23 as soon as you awaken. Recite the Psalm 104 just before going to sleep.

Psychic Attack Protection Spells

Psychic attack takes many forms but at its most virulent it's a form of psychic stalking. Make sure you protect yourself.

 ## Psychic Attack Protection: Black Snake Root

Black snake root, known in herbal medical circles as black cohosh, serves as a guardian protector and is especially beneficial in magically protecting against emotional abuse. Tie a piece of black snake root to a red cord. Wear it around your neck or your hips.

 ## Psychic Attack Protection: Black Tourmaline

Black tourmaline has a shielding quality, especially beneficial when the psychic attack penetrates into your thoughts and dreams. Wear or carry a black tourmaline to protect against psychic attack.

 ## Psychic Attack Protection: Carnelian

Attach a carnelian to a cord to create a magical belt. Wear it over the umbilical region to prevent psychic attack, as recommended by the Egyptian Book of the Dead.

 ## Psychic Attack Protection: Saint John's Wort

In case of psychic attack, fear is your worst enemy. Saint John's Wort flower essence remedy (FES) relieves fears of psychic attack, whether that fear is justified or not, and offers courage and protection. Follow the manufacturer's directions for internal administration, or add to the bath.

 ## Psychic Attack Protection Spell: Rowan

Nail nine sprigs of rowan across the door lintel. As an alternative, wear sprigs, flowers, or rowanberries in your hair or hat.

 ## Purslane Spell

Purslane (portulaca) protects against evil. Cast a circle of blossoms around the bed for protection while you sleep.

Red Cross Protection Spell

Whether the seclusion of menstruating women was caused by choice or force, taboos against menstrual blood remains primal and potent. In many cultures displaying a menstrual rag guaranteed a woman safe-passage; no one would get close enough to bother her. In other cultures, anything the menstruating woman touched must be destroyed once her period is over. In still others, contact with a menstruating woman is a method of punitive banishment; the person touched is rendered forever unclean and can no longer live amongst his people. Yet simultaneously, menstrual blood is perceived as so powerful that it puts demons to flight, stops fires from burning, and offers primal protection.

The first "taboo" sign was a cross drawn from menstrual blood, warning those who did not belong to keep away at their own risk. Reproduce exactly, if you will or utilize one of the many red substitutions instead: red ochre, iron oxide powder, red brick dust. Red paint works, too, if visualization and strong intent are incorporated.

 ## Red Power Bag

Red is the magical color of life, vitality, protection, and defiance of danger. Fill a red conjure bag with red carnation petals, red rose petals, and a red crystal. (Obviously, rubies and garnets are extremely potent, however any vividly red crystal will do; choose what's realistic and affordable.) Sprinkle with dragon's blood powder.

 ## Resguardo

The resguardo, *a "safe guard," is the protective conjure bag of Santeria. Although there are various resguardos, many are dedicated to the orisha Chango, fiery spirit of lightning and primal male power. Carrying a consecrated resguardo beseeches Chango's protection and patronage. Its creation should be accompanied by petitions and offerings directed toward him.*

1. Typical resguardo contents include arrowheads, stones (especially thunderstones), brown sugar, dried aloe vera, mugwort, cedar chips, and six dried red apple seeds.
2. Wrap the ingredients in red velvet and stitch it up with red silk thread.
3. Affix a golden sword charm to the outside of the resguardo.
4. Should the sword ever break, this is understood to mean that Chango has interceded on your behalf. The resguardo has fulfilled its purpose. Bury the entire packet. Make an offering to Chango and create a new one.

 ## Rice Protection Spell

Rice offers many gifts including fertility, prosperity, and, especially, protection.

Carve a protective symbol on a single grain of rice and carry it with you. This will take some practice; start with a cup of rice. Rejects may be cooked. The concentration required to create the amulet enhances its magical, protective power.

Rowan Wood Spells

Rowan wood is among those special botanicals most closely identified with the magical arts. Its nickname, *"witch wood,"* indicates that rowan places witches' power into your hands.

Witch wood repels malevolent enchantment and guards against malevolent spirits and ghosts. No nickname is needed, however, to emphasize rowan's magical roots: related words include the Norse *"runall"* meaning *"a charm"* and the Sanskrit *"runall"* indicating *"Magician."* In Norse mythology the first woman was created from rowan wood (men derive from ash), while rune staves were traditionally carved from rowan wood.

Although any rowan tree is perceived as magically powerful, some rowan is more potent than others and hence especially valued for its gifts of magical protection. These most potent rowan specimens include rowan growing near standing stones or stone circles, according to British tradition, and rowan growing out of cliffs, crevices or even out of other trees, especially another rowan, rather than Earth herself in Scandinavian tradition. This is known as *"flying rowan"* and is considered most powerful.

Although this is advisable for all trees, because rowan is so powerful and sacred it is extra important to remember to ask permission from the tree and offer a gift or libation.

☀ Rowan Anti-bewitchment Charm

A Scottish charm protects against bewitchment. This charm requires a found piece; the wood cannot be cut.

1. If you find a piece of rowan wood, this indicates the presence of powerful protection for you.
2. Tie a red silk or thread ribbon around the wood.
3. Although this is traditionally worn under clothing, it could also be added to a conjure bag, or hung as an amulet.

☀ Rowan Anti-evil Charm

Should you be required to enter a place of malevolent energy, sew a bit of rowan inside your clothing to protect against evil entities of all sorts, as well as against evil intentions.

☀ Rue Protection Spell (1)

Maximize the amount of protection rue provides by the quantity of rue you provide. Create a boundary against evil: plant rue in abundance by the door and by every window. As an alternative, hang it in doorways and windows to keep evil out.

☀ Rue Protection Spell (2)

Rue is unsafe for women during pregnancy and for those actively attempting to conceive. It's also a powerful plant that may irritate skin. Yet its magical gifts are profound. This spell may be the safest method of its use. Gather early morning dew from rue. Sprinkle it on yourself and others for protection.

☀ Saintly Protection Packets

Small protection packets favored by Latin American magic combine the power of a portable altar with that of a conjure bag. Commercially manufactured packets are enclosed in plastic for immediate visibility, but a traditional amulet bag is equally beneficial. A charm vial—a mojo bottle instead of a bag—combines the best of both worlds.

Each packet features a votive image; Saint Anthony, San Cipriano and San Martin Caballero are especially popular, however adapt the format of this spell to suit your own spiritual leanings. Add a small lodestone and a huayruru (ladybug) seed.

Salt Spells

Although any form of salt provides intense spiritual and magical protection, sea salt is believed most potent. Hoodoo tradition favors kosher salt because it has been blessed. In a pinch, any salt may be used although the closer it is to its natural state, the less it has been processed and essentially tampered with, the more magical protection and power salt can provide.

 ## Salt Bath: Basic

Add salt to the bath to simultaneously provide spiritual cleansing as well as creating a powerful psychic shield. For a quick fix, just toss handfuls of sea salt, as many as desired, into a tub of running water. Stir to dissolve and soak.

 ## Salt Bath: Extra Strength

Add lots of sea salt to a tub of running water. Add vinegar, as much as desired and five, seven or nine bay leaves to the bath, too.

 ## Salt Bath: Basic Bath Salts

Bath salts provide magical cleansing and protection and also soothe tired muscles and joint. Basic bath salts are created by blending two cups of sea salt with one half cup of baking soda. Substitute Epsom salts for the baking soda for extra relief for sore muscles and joints. Add essential oils as desired for fragrance and protective qualities.

 ## Salt Bath: Bath Salts Protection Formula

1. Create the basis for basic bath salts with sea salt and either baking soda or Epsom salts.
2. Add essential oils of frankincense, lavender, sandalwood, and vetiver. Play with proportions until a pleasing scent is achieved, adding oils drop by drop.
3. Blend with a wooden chopstick and add to the bath.

 ## Salt Bath: Bath Salts Dragon's Blood Protection Spell

One half-cup of baking soda
Two cups of sea salt
One quarter-cup of dragon's blood powder
Five drops of essential oil of sandalwood
Five drops of essential oil of frankincense
Four drops of essential oil of myrrh

 ## Salt Scrub: Basic

Bath salts are added directly to the water; salt scrubs are applied with either a gentle or a vigorous circular motion to the body. The oil causes the other ingredients to cling to the body, even after rinsing. This is an extremely powerful way to create a cleansing, protective shield.

1. The basic formula is one cup of salt to one half cup of oil, however you may wish to play with these proportions until you achieve a desired texture. This produces a fairly substantial quantity: store in an airtight container such as a mason jar. Salt scrubs will last indefinitely, providing water doesn't get into the container.
2. Add more oil if you'd like a gentler scrub. Finely ground salt is less abrasive.
3. Castor oil is the most protective carrier oil and should be added to the scrub, however it's extremely thick and doesn't always blend well. Add other carrier oils and play with proportions until it pleases you.

 ## Salt Scrub: Extra Protection

Create the salt scrub from sea salt, castor oil, olive oil, Jojoba oil and essential oils of frankincense, sandalwood, and vetiver. Insert an iron nail into the center.

Salt Scrub: Condition Formula

*Protective salt scrubs may also be created by taking the botanical formulas for any of the protective condition oils (e.g., **Fiery Wall, Protection**) and using them in a salt scrub instead.*

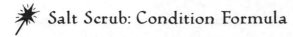 ## Salt Spell: Black Salt

This Hoodoo formula prevents and repels evil. Black salt is a component of various spells, usually for either casting malevolent enchantment or protecting against it. (There is also an actual black salt used in Indian cuisine, which is not at all the same thing.)

1. Take the scrapings from an iron pan, pot, or cauldron.
2. Add it to sea salt or kosher salt.
3. Substitute black salt for regular salt in any protection spell other than salt baths for added intensification. The most basic spell—a handful of black salt tossed in the direction from which evil is perceived as coming—should at least temporarily repel and prevent it.

 ## Salt Spell: Barrier Spell

As they say, good fences make good neighbors.

1. To erect a barrier between neighbors, blend salt with powdered rue and vervain.
2. Sprinkle it as if installing a fence.
3. Be aware, however, that this will not create an invisible boundary: it will likely kill any botanical life that it touches, creating a stark, barren no-man's land barrier.

 ## Salt Spell Psychic Boundary Line

Chop or grind the following ingredients together: three peeled cloves of garlic, a handful of sea salt, and a handful of fresh rosemary leaves. Sprinkle on the ground to create boundary lines or circles of psychic protection.

 ## Salt Spell Quick-fix Circle

A potent quick-fix spell, particularly valuable when spiritual danger suddenly threatens to overwhelm you. Cast a circle using salt or black salt. Sit within the circle until you feel that it's safe to come out.

 ## Sapphire Spell

Sapphires allegedly serve as a protective talisman against violence.

 ## SATOR Square

Evil entities are reputedly unable to stay in a room with this famous magic square:

S	A	T	O	R
A	R	E	P	O
T	E	N	E	T
O	P	E	R	A
R	O	T	A	S

*Write the square on parchment with **Dragon's Blood ink** or on red paper with gold ink, and post prominently as needed.*

Seven African Powers Spell (1)

*Place **Seven African Powers Oil** in an atomizer bottle filled with spring water, and spray to create an aura of total protection.*

 ## Seven African Powers Spell (2)

*Sprinkle salt over doors, windows, and other thresholds and anoint with **Seven African Powers Oil**.*

 ## Seven African Powers Extreme Protection Spell

*In moments of absolute desperation, carve a figure candle to represent you, dress it with **Seven African Powers Oil** and burn, accompanied by prayers and incantations of sacred texts.*

 ## Silver Spell

Silver is perceived as a spiritually incorruptible metal that radiates an aura of protection. Place a small piece of real silver under the hearth. Once upon a time a coin would have been used, but once upon a time dimes were real silver. A bead or charm would be very appropriate.

 ## Snapdragon Protection Spell

Faced with danger? Let's hope you're in a field of flowers. Step on a snapdragon, then pick up the flower and hold it in your hands for immediate magical protection.

 ## Southernwood Spells

In medieval Europe, southernwood was considered one of the most potent spiritual antidotes to malicious magical workings. Southernwood belongs to the Artemisia family, sacred plants dedicated to Artemis. It is closely related to its more notorious cousin wormwood; its name is a corruption of "southern wormwood."

For purposes of protection:

★ *Carry in a charm bag*
★ *Place under one's pillow*
★ *Post it in your house*

 ## Spell-breaker

This ancient and simple spell breaks any impending enchantment: consciously chew on your left thumb.

 ## Spruce Spell

Spruce resin was once sold as a substitute for the prohibitively expensive resin, frankincense. The fragrance isn't a dead ringer but spruce has its own protective properties. Burn it so that the aroma permeates an area.

Sulfur Spells

Sulfur protects against malevolent magic and repels evil entities. In North African magic, it is sometimes considered equal to salt as a protector against evil. Sulfur is a primary ingredient in exorcisms and banishing spells, where it is typically burned. This is traditional but not necessarily advisable: inhaling sulfur fumes is potentially very irritating. However there are other methods of use, particularly beneficial for protective magic.

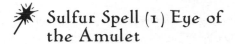 ## Sulfur Spell (1) Eye of the Amulet

1. Make a paste by adding a bit of gum acacia or similar to sulfur powder.
2. Stick a little bit of this yellow paste into the center of any amulet to transform it into a vehicle of protection. This is particularly effective for hand amulets or geometric-shaped amulets, such as triangles or diamonds. Although they are already potent, the sulfur effectively becomes the *"eye"* of the amulet, further activating and empowering it.
3. Point the eye in the direction from which danger is feared.

 ## Sulfur Spell (2) Medicine Bag

Carry loose sulfur powder in a charm bag.

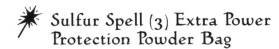 ## Sulfur Spell (3) Extra Power Protection Powder Bag

Add some or ideally all of the following to a red conjure bag and carry for protection as needed:

A pinch of sulfur powder
A pinch of kohl powder
A pinch of henna and/or iron oxide powder
A pinch of graveyard dust
A pinch of tobacco

 ## Sword of Protection Spell (1)

This symbolic sword is carried to fend off hurtful words and harmful actions.

1. Cut a piece of paper from a clean paper bag.
2. Draw a sword on it.

3. Place it within a leather pouch or metal amulet bag, together with a pinch of cayenne or habanero pepper and a pinch of sulfur.

 ## Sword of Protection Spell (2)

1. Fill a red drawstring bag with protective botanicals and charms.
2. Activate the bag by attaching a small metal sword charm and carry it with you.
3. When the bag works for you, detach the sword and pass it through incense smoke to cleanse and reinvigorate it.

 ## Tiger Lily Spell

Tiger lilies serve as the botanical equivalent of tigers. Plant them near the home to prevent the entry of mean spirits.

 ## Ti Plant Protection Spell

Crumble ti plant leaves and sprinkle them beneath the bed for spiritual protection.

 ## Toadflax Spell

Toadflax has an odd-shaped flower that some believe resembles a small toad. This European plant, a great favorite of the fairies, has become naturalized in North America, where it's often considered a noxious weed.

Carry dried toadflax flowers to repel malevolent magic. It may also break spells already cast upon you.

Vervain Protection Spell

Vervain allegedly sprang from Isis's tears. It is believed to be the plant possessing the most affection for humans, thriving in our midst, unlike power plants like mugwort or Syrian rue that grow most powerfully in desolation. Take advantage of vervain's alliance.

Vervain provides protection anytime, however, when you are being defiant, when you are delivering a challenge or throwing down a gauntlet to another, wear or carry vervain as extra magical protection.

Vetiver Protection Spells

Vetiver root is used to provide safety and create sheltered islands of tranquility.

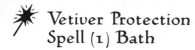 ## Vetiver Protection Spell (1) Bath

Vetiver's strong scent lingers protectively. This bath transforms the bather into a personal island of tranquility.

1. Create an infusion by pouring boiling water over dried vetiver roots.
2. Allow this to cool, and then add the strained liquid to your bath.
3. Alternatively, add several drops of the essential oil to a tub filled with comfortably warm water.

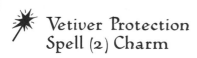 ## Vetiver Protection Spell (2) Charm

Place a piece of vetiver root into a charm bag and carry or wear around your neck.

 ## Vetiver Spell (3) Extra Power Protection Incense

Grind and powder dried vetiver. Blend this with dragon's blood powder and burn them together to dispel evil.

 ## Vetiver Spell (4) Magical Protective Shield

1. Heat essential oil of vetiver in an aroma burner.
2. Sit nearby, close your eyes, and inhale deeply.
3. Concentrate on the vision of a vetiver-scented aura of protection sealing your body from malevolent influences.
4. Vetiver is also believed to have commanding properties: visualize sending ill-intentions away from you.

 ## Violet Protection Spell (1)

Weave a necklace of violets to protect against lies and deception.

 ## Violet Protection Spell (2)

African violets have a reputation for being fragile, fussy, and difficult to grow. Magically their reputation is very different.

A row of African violets placed on the windowsill or strategically arranged creates a shielding aura of protection. Enhance their power by rubbing the pot or saucer with **Protection Oil.**

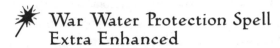

War Water Protection Spell

War Water, which draws upon the power of iron, is notoriously used to cast potent hexes. However, what characters this water of Mars is not malevolence but aggressive power. How that power is directed is determined by the spell-caster. **War Water** is also used to remove hexes and for basic but potent spiritual protection.

Wash all thresholds, doorways, and gateways to the outside with **War Water** to set up the front line against all evil.

War Water Protection Spell Extra Enhanced

Boil nails or pins in a pan filled with **War Water.** Allow it to cool, remove the solids (the goal is not to create a literal mine field) and sprinkle the water as a magical boundary of protection around the perimeter of your home.

Wild Hunt Protection Spell

The Wild Hunt is a nocturnal parade of spirits that occurs several times during the year, usually coinciding with power dates such as May Eve/Walpurgis Night, Halloween or Midsummer's Eve. Because information regarding the Wild Hunt is filtered through Christian sources and because many of the spirits involved with the Hunt may indeed bear a grudge towards people, it's perceived as very dangerous to encounter (the Spirit Hunters allegedly hunt human souls). People are instructed to stay inside when the Hunt is anticipated (as opposed to witches who typically rush out to join the revelry and are apparently welcomed by the Wild Hunters), or to lie flat and silent in the presence of the Hunt and hope not to be noticed.

If you don't wish to participate or stay indoors, there is a third option: should you encounter the Wild Hunt, danger may be averted by politely asking the Hunters for parsley, sacred to Hunt leaders like Hulda (Mother Holle) and Odin. Allegedly "parsley" is the secret password to safety.

Witch Ball Hex-breaker

"Witch balls" are large, beautiful, iridescent glass balls, resembling colored crystal balls or gigantic Christmas tree ornaments. They are traditionally hung from windows or placed atop pedestals in the garden to catch and absorb any approaching curses. Whether the witch ball reverses the spell is subject to debate; however it's generally acknowledged to shield and protect from malevolent bewitchment.

Arrange witch balls strategically around the property; near the front entrance and any other perceived vulnerable spots. (This is easy to implement as witch balls are so attractive, non-magical observers will assume they are merely garden ornaments.) Despite their ornamental value, witch balls are magical tools. Magically cleanse them on a regular schedule by bathing with mugwort-infused spring water.

Witch's Bottle Protection Spell

Glass, ceramic, stone, or metal bottles may be used for these spells against hexes and for protection against malicious spirits; don't use plastic.

1. Place three pins, three needles, and three nails inside a bottle.
2. Fill the bottle with salt.
3. Add three drops of menstrual blood or prick your smallest left finger and let three drops of blood flow into the bottle.
4. Seal the bottle securely and bury it under the hearth or next to your home.

Witch's Bottle Triple Pin Protection Spell

1. Put three gold pins, three silver pins, and three iron nails inside a bottle.
2. Cover them with salt; add three drops of either menstrual blood or blood drawn from your smallest left finger.
3. Seal the bottle securely and bury it under the hearth or beside your home.

Witch's Best Friend

Vervain is believed to be a magical analgesic. (Not necessarily in the purely medical sense.) Poignantly it's known as the "witch's best friend" because it allegedly magically minimizes the effects of fire and torture. Wear, carry, and bathe in infusions as necessary.

Witch's Garter Protection Spell

Wear a garter shaped from green ash bark to guard you against malicious enchantment.

Witch's Ladder Protection Spell

The Witch's Ladder is a magical device most frequently associated with hexes. However it can be used for any purpose and serves well as a protection spell. Witch's ladders, whether malevolent or positive, may be physically indistinguishable; what separates them is the intent of their creator.

Three cords are required: one red, one black and the third in the color of your choice, although for protective purposes blue is recommended.

1. Braid the cords together, visualizing your intent and desires continually and intently.
2. Tie a feather into the bottom: for protective purposes, peacock feathers are recommended.
3. Continue to braid, eventually tying nine feathers into the braid, evenly spaced from bottom to top.
4. When complete, pass the braid through incense smoke and keep it hidden safely in a secret place.

Witch's Ladder Protection Spell: Extra Strength

This dramatic version is sometimes used when creating a protective device for a loved one, especially a child, heading into dangerous territory. Follow the instructions above but substitute your hair for the third cord. Substitute feathers from your pillow for the peacock feathers.

Witch's Tapers Protection Spell

"Witch's taper" is among mullein's nicknames, so-called because before the days of inexpensive candles, mullein was used to create torches. Apparently they were truly convenient and useful because a popular attempt to justify their use suggests that witch's tapers repelled witches. How could they, considering that they are among Hecate's holiest plants? Be that as it may, witch's tapers reputedly provide protection to witches and others alike.

Dip a mullein stalk into wax and allow the wax to harden to create a taper. (Traditional witch's tapers were crafted with tallow, now more rare and far less fragrant than wax.) Burn and carry for protection.

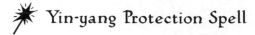 Yin-yang Protection Spell

Create a protective amulet with magic beans. Yin-yang beans are the large gray seeds of the bonduc tree. They allegedly serve as the balance between male and female energy.

String a pair of beans onto a cord, together with one contraveneno bean, to provide spiritual protection. They guard against spiritual and psychic danger. Allegedly, if they are forced to do their job, the contraveneno will split into four pieces along the cross that marks one side of this black bean.

Spells to Protect Against Enemies

Many *Protection Spells* target evil in general, regardless from where it derives. Sometimes the source of danger is very clearly from another human. *Spells to Protect Against Enemies* take various approaches to the situation, from disarming one's enemy to transforming enmity into amity.

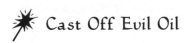 Alyssum Anger Management Spell

Offer a small bouquet of alyssum to one who resents you and bears you hostility and malice. Disarm them; literally place the bouquet in their hands. This magical transaction allegedly cools off their anger towards you quickly.

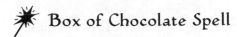 Beryl Spell

Has a once-close friend become hostile toward you? Allegedly the image of a frog engraved upon a beryl gemstone restores friendship and reconciles enemies. Give one as a peace offering and find out whether it works.

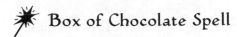 Box of Chocolate Spell

Chocolate allegedly possesses the power to transform enmity into friendship. Make a peace offering with a box of fine chocolate. This will only work, however, if the other party will eat real chocolate, dark and bitter-sweet.

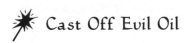 Cast Off Evil Oil

Cast off malevolent thoughts, intentions and hexes from those who resent you. (Although this is really a prevention spell, it does possess a hex-breaking aspect.)

1. Blend asafetida, crumbled bay leaves, hyssop, rue, and yarrow.
2. Add the botanicals to castor oil.
3. Soak cotton balls in the oil and leave them in the vicinity of the one who hates you (in the office or elsewhere). This is not a spell you can hide: the fragrance, depending on the quantity of asafetida used, can be very unpleasant; however it can be cast anonymously if you're discreet.

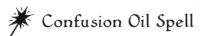 Confusion Oil Spell

Sprinkle **Confusion Oil** in your enemies' path to discombobulate them so much that they can't harm you.

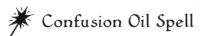 Convert an Enemy Spell

Fill a small charm bag with cloves, or actually incorporate the cloves into a spice necklace. Wear the charm around your neck to inspire feelings of affection and friendship.

Convert an Enemy Candle Spell

Sometimes the best method of protection is to transform anger and resentment into affection.

1. Carve your target's name into a brown candle three times, starting at the bottom and working upwards.
2. Place this candle inside a bowl filled with brown sugar.
3. Burn it for thirty minutes then pinch it out.
4. Repeat for a total of nine consecutive evenings, allowing the candle to burn down on the ninth night.
5. Collect the remaining wax and sugar and wrap them up.
6. Traditionally you are now supposed to dispose of the spell remnants on your target's doorsteps or on his or her property. Any place in the vicinity should work, however.

Easy Wrath Powder

To ease someone's anger towards you:

1. Write your wishes, goals, and desires on paper.
2. Burn the page.
3. Mix the ashes with rose petals, sandalwood powder, and sweet Hungarian paprika and grind into a fine powder.
4. Add six drops of jasmine attar.
5. Let the powder dry.
6. Traditionally, you're supposed to toss this powder over your target and they're supposed to love you again, or at least not be angry with you. Try this, if you think it might work.
7. If, however, tossing anything onto your target gives you pause, if you don't even want to get near them, discreetly sprinkle the powder where the target will step over it or sit on it instead.

End All Power Spell

This spell allegedly destroys any power your enemy has over you.

1. Write your enemy's name nine times on a piece of brown paper.
2. Place nine drops of **Black Cat Oil** and nine drops of **San Cipriano Oil** on the paper.
3. Burn the paper within the flame of a brown justice candle, carved and dressed to suit your situation.
4. Bury the leftover ashes and wax in the cemetery.

Enemy Protection Powder

This spell is not a hex; this powder will not cause harm. It will, however, allegedly prevent someone from exercising power over you or causing you harm. Powder malva, and sprinkle it over your enemy's doorstep or in their path.

Friendship Renewal Powder

This is a gentler powder, not intended for an enemy as much as to soften an angry friend's heart, to prevent them from becoming an enemy. Grind and powder the following ingredients together: rosemary leaves, dried sage, salt, and sugar. Sprinkle the powder on your friend's shoulders.

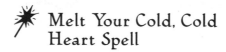

Melt Your Cold, Cold Heart Spell

A Pow-Wow spell to warm someone's cold heart: place a plate of snow or an icicle near a fire (fireplace, stove, or candle) and watch it melt while envisioning all the hostility melting away too.

Put the Anger on Ice Spell

1. Write the angry person's name on a slip of paper.
2. Drop the paper into a small, unbreakable container filled with water.
3. Seal the container shut. Keep it in your freezer.

If you have a lot of enemies, line them up in an ice-cube tray.

 ## Prickly Pear Safety Spell

Keep prickly pear cactus paddles behind the door to keep enemies away.

 ## Rose Quartz Transformation Spell

Rose quartz transforms anger into love, or at least mild affection. Wear it. Give it as a gift to those who resent you.

 ## Sweeten Your Heart Spell

To sweeten someone's heart towards you:

1. Write your target's name on a slip of white paper.
2. Put it into a small jar with a lid.
3. Cover the paper with honey and close the jar tight.
4. Place a small white candle on top of the lid and burn.

Temper Bush Spell

This is an Obeah spell to transform enmity into affection. If someone is angry with you, rub "temper bush" (Amyris spp.) between your hands. Rub your hands against him or her to induce friendliness, forgiveness, and good nature.

 ## Vervain Spell

Vervain has the ability to transform enemies into friends.

1. Make a strong infusion from dried vervain and powdered orrisroot.
2. Add this to a tub of water together with essential oils of myrrh and sandalwood.
3. Bathe, immerse yourself, let yourself air-dry. The lingering fragrance should soothe and appease enemies.

 ## Yemaya Spell

This is not a hex. However, unlike many other Enemy Protection Spells, this one doesn't necessarily concern itself about reconciliation. Instead this spell specifically requests that the powerful orisha Yemaya create a protective shield, guarding you from specific enemies.

1. Purchase a fish specifically for this spell.
2. Write the names of your enemies, each on its own slip of paper.
3. Place these in the fish's mouth. (If the mouth is too small or your list of enemies too great, make slits in the fish belly and insert the papers.)
4. Close the mouth or slits shut with silver pins.
5. Cover the fish with dark molasses.
6. Surround the fish with blue and white candles.
7. Let the fish stand on an altar for Yemaya for seven days, keeping candles burning for the duration. Burning strongly fragrant incense may be advisable as well.
8. When seven days are over, place seven silver coins within the fish and throw the fish with all its stuffing into the sea.

Special Protection Needs

Some groups of people have specialized protection needs.

Single Mothers

 Animal Charm: Sow with Piglets

Among the traditional Chinese animal wealth charms is one depicting a sow nursing her piglets atop a bed of coins. This charm is considered especially beneficial for women independently caring for children. In addition to wealth, the sow magically draws stability, security, good fortune and (especially) protection towards you.

Hold the charm in your hands, charging it with your desires. Place it discreetly near the front entrance, gazing outward so that the sow can repel approaching danger while beckoning opportunity near.

 Guardian Spirit Ezili Dantor

The powerful lwa, Ezili Dantor, responds to pleas of assistance from single mothers. She is among their most powerful protectors because, according to legend, she, too, was forced to struggle to provide for a child entirely on her own. Offer Ezili Dantor a glass of over proof rum and a bottle of **Florida Water,** her favorite perfume, and tell her what you need.

 Guardian Spirit Isis

All-powerful Isis, Mistress of Magic, was once reduced to begging and laboring like the poorest, most pitiful human being to care for her beloved son, born (and conceived!) after her true love's death. Isis's special love, devotion, and sympathy for people began during this period. Request her magic protection for mother and children.

Create an altar of dedication. Decorate it with Isis's sacred images: the ankh, tet amulet and various creatures by which she will understand your request, snakes, scorpions, crocodiles, and sows. Burn myrrh resin to summon Isis and tell her what you need.

Protection For Soldiers and Other Warriors

 All High Conquering Oil

Despite the fact that High John the Conqueror, the root of a tropical morning glory indigenous to Mexico is exclusively a Western hemisphere plant, and despite the fact that the root's current magical use derives almost exclusively from African-American traditions, when personified, John the Conqueror is typically depicted as a white king, similar to the traditional image on the tarot card, The Emperor. Sometimes however the image is conflated with that of a crusader, reminiscent of Saint James the Greater, which may be a subtle reference to the African spirit Ogun, protector of soldiers.

Anoint charms, weapons, yourself, and anything else you can think of with **All High Conquering Oil** for protection, luck, and victory.

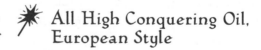 All High Conquering Oil, European Style

On the other hand, perhaps you find the literal image of a victorious Crusader comforting. A European-style condition oil may be concocted too.

1. Add **chypre** powder to jojoba oil.
2. Blend in essential oils of elemi and rosemary.
3. Wear or anoint objects as needed for protection and good fortune.

Amethyst Soldier's Spell

Carry an amethyst carved into the shape of a scarab to protect against injury and death.

Burnet Soldiers' Spell

The herb, great burnet, is a powerful astringent so, like yarrow, it's been used to staunch bleeding. Ancient Roman soldiers used great burnet for preventive magic too: drink a herbal infusion prior to setting off for war or battle in the hopes that burnet's magical vibrations will prevent or at least minimize injury and bleeding.

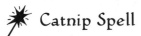

Catnip Spell

Catnip, a herb of the mint family, is now relegated to stuffing cat toys. However, it serves many other magical uses, from aphrodisiac to healing. It was once a staple of warriors' magic as well. Chew on the fresh herb for courage, daring, fierceness, and protection.

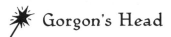

Gorgon's Head

Since the days of ancient Greece, the image of Gorgon Medusa's head has been used to protect soldiers. Medusa once adorned soldiers' shields and breastplates to provide protection. An amulet or a tattoo suffices today.

Guardian Spirit Lord of War

Kuan Ti, the Chinese Lord of War, is a deified general, said to have been born in 162 CE. His own martial victories taught him that war is hell. His spiritual powers are invoked to prevent wars and to protect people, civilians as well as soldiers, from its horrors.

1. Create an offering table for the Lord of War on his birthday, the thirteenth day of the fifth month of the Chinese calendar.
2. Serve him a stiff drink.
3. Burn Spirit Money and tell him what you need.

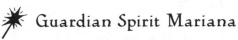

Guardian Spirit Mariana

Amongst the many Afro-Brazilian spiritual traditions, Batuque, from whence Mariana derives, has a particularly strong Amazonian Indian influence. Mariana has a special fondness for the navy, offering its men and women her protection. Mariana may be petitioned for protection during particularly dangerous missions. A skilled healer, she may also be petitioned for assistance should things go badly. Mariana's powers aren't limited to military issues. She may also be petitioned for love. Her sacred bird is the macaw (think of the proverbial sailor/pirate's parrot).

Buy Mariana a drink. She accepts offerings of alcoholic beverages, particularly cachaca. Invoke her and explicitly, respectfully, and specifically express your needs.

Hematite Protection Spell

Hematite is under the dominion of Mars. Carry a hematite crystal gemstone for magical enhancement of courage and daring, and to also allegedly protect against wounds. (It it also supposed to stimulate healing of wounds, so you can't go wrong by carrying it!)

Onion Protection Spell

Rub fresh leeks or onions on the body to prevent injury.

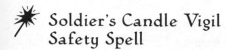
Soldier's Candle Vigil Safety Spell

This ritual for safety is based on the ancient fire-religion of pre-Islamic Iran.

Before departure, the soldier builds an altar and lights a large white pillar candle to serve as a vigil candle. This will be tended by his or her family (or members of the household) while the soldier is away. Traditionally the flame is never allowed to go out: new candles are kindled from the original flame. However, it's important to keep fire safety and modern reality in mind: the goal is the safety of both parties: the soldier at war, the family at home. There's no point in burning the house down.

If an eternal flame works, that's great. If not, work out a pre-arranged ritual beforehand: light the candle together. Have the soldier give the household instructions and a spell, perhaps a petition or chant that those left behind will repeat exactly, echoing words and following in footsteps. Or one person may be designated as the vigil keeper. Perhaps the soldier can leave a token with that person, the way ancient rulers gave their seal: the person essentially has magical power-of-attorney to act on the soldier's behalf.

Soldier's Protection Oil

Blend essential oils of elemi and frankincense into jojoba oil. Wear or anoint objects as desired.

Soldier's Safety Talisman

A bit of the Master of the Woods plant carried as a charm provides safety for soldiers.

Vervain Soldier's Spell

Carry or wear vervain as a protective talisman and to enhance the healing of wounds.

Warrior's Rune Spell

To help a warrior retain courage in battle, mark the rune of Tiw, the Anglo-Saxon Lord of Courage, on his weapon. The rune may also be tattooed onto the body. This is most effective if accomplished on a Tuesday, the day named in Tiw's honor.

War Water Spell

Mars, ruler of iron, is the patron of war and warriors. Use the protective form of **War Water,** also known as the **Water of Mars,** to keep safe when serving in the military.

Weapon Protection Spell (1)

Traditionally smiths performed protective rituals before delivering a weapon, although that was in the days prior to mass production. Bathe a sword or gun in water blended from three or seven wells.

Weapon Protection Spell (2)

To protect your weapons, prick the little finger of your dominant hand, drawing no more than a few drops of blood. Wipe the blood on the gun barrel.

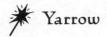 Yarrow

Yarrow's Latin name, Achillea millefolium, *derives from that of the Greek hero of the Trojan War, Achilles. Achilles, who learned both enchantment and healing from his sea-spirit mother, allegedly carried this herb to magically protect and heal the warriors under his com-* mand. Yarrow is a powerful styptic: used therapeutically it staunches bleeding. Yarrow also has myriad magical associations: it's a spiritually protective plant that allegedly confers something akin to Achilles' magical invulnerability and almost-immortality to its bearer. Carry yarrow stalks in a charm bag to prevent injury and speed healing.

Psychic Power Spells

Psychic power spells serve two purposes:

★ *To enhance psychic ability*
★ *To replenish psychic depletion*

Psychic power may be discovered within, its growth stimulated from what already exists hidden inside you. But it may also be obtained from external devices, such as amulets and charms.

Acacia Spells

The acacia tree has been associated with the sacred since the proverbial time immemorial, from the myth of Osiris to the Ark of the Covenant. Burn it as incense to stimulate and enhance psychic ability as well as to provide contact with the sacred.

 ### Acacia Incense: Basic

Burn dried powdered acacia and allow the fragrance to permeate the area.

 ### Acacia Incense: Osiris Incense

Blend acacia, frankincense, cypress, and cedarwood and burn wafting the fragrance as desired.

 ### Acacia Incense: Sacred Wood

Blend dried powdered acacia, sandalwood, and frankincense. Burn the powder to enhance and develop psychic power and vision.

Aloes Spells

Similarity of botanical names can lead to confusion and misidentification. It's believed that the *aloes* mentioned in the Bible doesn't refer to aloe vera, a native of Zanzibar, but to aloes, a mysterious wood from Southeast Asia. Aloe vera literally means *"true aloe"* because of this confusion between species. Both plants offer profound gifts but they are hardly identical. Aloe vera is used for healing and protective magic.

Aloes wood, also known as agar, oud and laos (not to be confused with laos root, which is galangal, which is Courtcase root …), a treasured, prized wood, rare even in biblical times, is a potent aphrodisiac and psychic enhancer.

Aloes Wood Incense

In ancient days, aloes wood was considered as rare and precious as ambergris and musk. Save it for special occasions. For extra psychic power, burn tiny slivers, splinters, and shavings at a time. Savor its fragrance.

Aloes Wood Amulet

It's not necessary to burn aloes. Mere possession of a piece is sufficient to magically enhance one's personal power. Leave aloes wood in its natural form or shape it into the auspicious form of an amulet. Preserve it on an altar or carry it with you.

Amber Psychic Enhancement

Sometimes when a magic spell or formula suggests burning amber, it means the real thing, not ambergris. Technically, after all, amber is plant resin, not the mineral so many understand it to be. Ancient Greeks buried it in tribute to Helios and Apollo. Burn amber and copal, wafting the fragrance over you, for the wisdom of pines and to shine like the sun.

Anise Double Dose Psychic Power Spell

Star anise and true anise have little in common botanically; magically, however both induce and enhance psychic power. Grind them together and burn, allowing the fragrance to permeate the area.

Artemisia Family Spells

This botanical family is named in honor of the ancient and powerful Greek lunar deity, Artemis. Artemis rules magic, fertility, psychic gifts and wild, female nature. Her favorite plants share much of her nature: they bear profound gifts but are prickly, volatile, and potentially dangerous. Few plants, however, are more associated with the magical arts.

The two most famous—or notorious—members of this botanical family are mugwort and wormwood. Both have less-than-romantic English names that tout their abilities as pest repellant. Indeed, in addition to their psychic-inducing abilities, mugwort and wormwood are protective herbs that banish powerful evil spirits as if they were little worms. Because of this they are particularly beneficial during psychic journeying: they protect from psychic dangers encountered en route.

Artemisia Spells: Mugwort

Mugwort, the primary sacred Anglo-Saxon herb, is also known as the "*mother herb*" and "*witch herb*." Lacking the notoriety of its cousin, wormwood, mugwort is relatively unknown outside metaphysical communities today, because it has few uses other than magical ones. Like most of the artemisias, with the exception of tarragon, mugwort has a bitter taste, limiting its culinary uses.

Mugwort's magical uses, however, are unlimited. No plant has greater associations with magic; no plant can better help you achieve your own maximum magic powers. Virtually every commercially sold tea or herbal product that touts its ability to enhance your psychic abilities contains mostly mugwort. Mugwort does not *give* you psychic ability: instead it uncovers what is hidden within. It will help you discover psychic gifts you never knew you had.

WARNING!

Even more than most plants, the different forms of the botanical are *not* interchangeable:

★ Although mugwort is largely considered a woman's herb, it is not safe for pregnant women or for those actively trying to become pregnant. It can cause profound uterine contractions

★ With the exception of pregnant women, the herb is generally safe for adults, in moderate doses

★ The flower essence remedy is the safest method for use, particularly when psychic enhancement is desired

★ Mugwort essential oil, also known as *armoise,* its French name, is *not* safe for *anyone.* Mugwort's latent destructive powers, potential neurotoxins, are concentrated in the essential oil. It should not be used except possibly under the most expert professional supervision

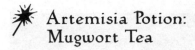 ## Artemisia Potion: Mugwort Tea

This is a potent psychic enhancer but although many yearn for its effects, few will wish to drink it, because mugwort tea doesn't taste good. Add one teaspoon of the fresh herb or one-half teaspoon of the dried herb to a cup. Cover it with boiling water. Let it steep for five minutes, strain, and drink.

Artemisia Potion: Psychic Stimulation Tea

Many of the additional ingredients in this potion (yarrow, cloves, melissa) stimulate psychic power. Their addition also makes mugwort's flavor palatable. Pour boiling water over the following, blended ingredients:

> One tablespoon dried mugwort
> One teaspoon dried melissa (lemon balm)
> One teaspoon dried peppermint leaves
> One teaspoon dried yarrow
> One-quarter teaspoon ground cinnamon
> One-quarter teaspoon ground cloves

Let it steep for approximately ten minutes, then strain and drink.

Artemisia Potion: Psychic Potion

1. Beginning at the New Moon, soak one-quarter ounce of dried mugwort leaves in a bottle of the wine of your choice.
2. Let this steep for seven days, ideally exposing the bottle to nightly moonbeams.
3. Decant the wine, straining out the botanicals.
4. Drink small quantities at a time, a glass here and there, to increase clairvoyance.

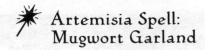 ## Artemisia Spell: Mugwort Garland

This may be accomplished at any Full Moon, with the knowledge that mugwort, gathered on Midsummer's Eve is allegedly most powerful.

1. Weave a garland of mugwort.
2. Stand outside, place the mugwort loosely across your face and gaze at a Full Moon through the mugwort, to enhance your powers of clairvoyance and second sight.
3. Traditionally, one is supposed to be clad in nothing but mugwort and moonbeams as one casts this spell, however do what is appropriate and practical.

Artemisia Spells: Wormwood

Wormwood, mugwort's infamous brother, is also known as absinthe. It is the crucial ingredient in Absinthe, the distilled liqueur that bears the herb's name, once so beloved by French authors, poets and painters, then banned through much of the world.

Despite this notoriety, wormwood's use as a distilled liquor is fairly recent. Absinthe in its modern historical form wasn't developed until 1792 when a Swiss doctor named Dr. Ordinaire (could one make this up?) concocted the recipe as an herbal cure-all. It is worthwhile to recall how many European liqueurs derive their roots from healing and magic potions, whether initially brewed by monks (*Chartreuse*) or witches (*Strega*). With water so frequently unsafe to drink, an alcohol base for the brew was a necessity.

Wormwood's history is not limited to absinthe, though; it is an ancient and profound magical herb, the original biblical bitter herb. Like mugwort, its magical uses are myriad: it's used in healing, protection, exorcisms, and love spells. It repels the Evil Eye and provides safety for magical journeys. Although Absinthe, the distilled alcoholic beverage, remains banned in many places, wormwood,

WARNING!

Like mugwort, the different forms of the botanical are not interchangeable:

★ Essential oil of wormwood is highly toxic to the point of fatality. It must not be used

★ The flower essence remedy is very safe

★ The herb is not safe for pregnant women or for those actively attempting to become pregnant

whose Latin name is *Artemisia absinthium*, is a perfectly legal herb which can be easily grown in a flowerpot at home. (However, just to confuse matters more, in Latin America for example, wormwood is called *absinthe* but the reference is to the herb, which is used in magic and healing, not the drink.)

Mugwort and wormwood perform well in conjunction: mugwort to help you uncover your power, wormwood to provide safety so that you can learn to use it.

Artemisia Potion: Wormwood

Be forewarned: wormwood tastes even worse than mugwort. A herbal tea may be brewed but it should be approached like a chemistry experiment: play with proportions until you concoct something that is palatable.

1. Start with a pinch of dried ground mugwort and a pinch of dried ground wormwood. Add larger quantities of peppermint, lemon balm, licorice root, cinnamon, or any other herbal flavor you like.

2. Start with a moderate infusion, only five minutes, strain and drink.

3. Be prepared to toss out the first cups until you find proportions that camouflage the famed bitterness.

Artemisia Potion: Wormwood Wine

Dried wormwood may be purchased from herbal supply stores, however it makes an easy house plant. Maintain it for its protective guardian properties, but harvest a few twigs and leaves.

1. Stuff approximately one-quarter of an ounce of wormwood into the bottle of wine of your choice.

2. Allow it to steep for seven days.

3. Strain after the seventh day. Drink small portions, particularly before engaging in spell-work, so that you achieve your maximum potential.

Artemisia Potion: Pernod

Pernod was developed to fill the void left by the ban on Absinthe. It is largely the same formula, the same green color, only lacking the wormwood. It may be used to concoct a magical potion, although this does not reconstruct Absinthe, which had a much higher alcohol content among other differences.

Stuff one dried wormwood stem into a bottle of Pernod. Drink a shot glass of the liqueur (many prefer it diluted with water) whenever you need a little boost of psychic inspiration.

Artemisia Spells: Desert Sage

Despite its English name, desert sage is really an artemisia. It combines the best of the salvia and artemisia families: desert sage stimulates psychic ability while simultaneously providing spiritual purification.

 ## Desert Sage Spell: Incense

Unlike its other psychic-inducing cousins, desert sage is indigenous to North America. Create a family reunion: burn mugwort, wormwood, desert sage, Sweet Annie, southernwood, and tarragon for a blast of power.

 ## Desert Sage Third Eye Brew

Desert sage is a popular ingredient in commercial psychic-inducing herbal teas. It has a smoky flavor and is less bitter than mugwort or wormwood.

Brew tea from desert sage and white sage. Drink to enhance clairvoyance, psychic vision, and reception. (The Third Eye is the area between the eyes, just above the bridge of the nose, and has long been associated with psychic power.)

 ## Desert Sage: Third Eye Brew Extra Strength

Brew tea from desert sage, white sage, mugwort, lemon balm, peppermint, and orange zest.

 ## Artemisia Sachet

Fill a small sachet with equal parts wormwood and mugwort. Sleep with this next to your cheek or under your pillow to enhance psychic powers while you sleep, and wear it next to your skin while casting spells to enhance skill, inspiration, and protection.

 ## Artemisia Spell: Artemis Incense

Grind equal parts mugwort and wormwood into a fine powder. Sprinkle it on lit charcoal and burn. This incense may be used to accompany and enhance any spell-work.

 ## Artemisia Spell: Artemis's Deluxe Mojo Hand

Fill a charm bag with members of the Artemisia family:

1. Add a pinch of all or some of the following dried herbs: mugwort, wormwood, Sweet Annie, desert sage, southernwood, and tarragon.
2. Add a moonstone and/or a chalcedony crystal.
3. Add a piece of true silver, any kind of little charm is fine but a tiny silver dog or dragon is perfect.
4. If you can obtain a miniature Moon tarot card, add it to the bag.
5. Anoint with a drop of tuberose essential oil or night-blooming jasmine attar and carry with you during psychic journeys for added magic power and protection.

Artemisia Spell: Tarragon

Tarragon, the baby of the Artemisia family, is known as the "little dragon." It is the only Artemisia to double as a common kitchen-herb. Don't let that fool you; tarragon has magic powers just like its more notorious relatives. "Dragon" is a frequent euphemism for menstruation, and tarragon is used to magically access women's primal psychic powers. Make an infusion by pouring boiling water over tarragon and mugwort and add it to your bath.

 ## Aura Repair Tea

Drink a warm infusion of rosemary, lemongrass, hibiscus flowers, peppermint and mugwort. This is particularly beneficial after extensive spell-work or following psychically damaging encounters.

Basil Psychic Power Spells

Basil's name stems from the same Greek root words as *"royal"* and *"king."* Basil stimulates personal power.

 ## Basil Psychic Power Spell: Infused Oil

Create infused oil of fresh basil leaves. Add the oil to your bath or apply to the body and visualize yourself regal, commanding, and filled with power.

 ## Basil Psychic Power Spell: Royal Wreath of Psychic Power Oil

Although essential oil of basil has a very different aroma than the fresh leaves, it, too, possesses profound gifts.

1. Add essential oils of basil and bay laurel to grapeseed oil.
2. Use this oil to dress golden candles.
3. Light the candles, gaze at the flame, inhale the fragrance and visualize yourself filled with psychic power and magical achievement.

 ## Birch Grove of Psychic Protection

Birch trees are associated with fertility—not only literal reproductive capacity but also with the concept of growth and creativity, especially psychic, magical, and spiritual growth. Birch provides protection as well as enhancement; it's crucial to nurture and protect emerging talents. Surround your home with birch trees to enhance and protect your own psychic power.

Certain plants have particularly powerful associations with enhanced magic and psychic power. It is not necessary to ingest these plants, nor is it necessarily advisable. Some, such as oleander or thorn apple, are poisonous. The key is merely to be in their physical presence. Proximity to the living plant is the optimum method. Such plants include: mugwort and the Artemisia botanical family, rowan, juniper, vervain, diviner's sage, Syrian rue (harmel, uzarlik), yarrow, mistletoe, oleander, thorn apple, Saint John's Wort, and hazel.

 ## Botanical Psychic Enhancement

★ *Grow some in the garden or indoors in pots*
★ *Sit next to them with a clear, meditative mind. Absorb their energy and let inspiration appear unbidden. This is particularly beneficial when engaged in divination*

 ## Cat's Eye Incense

Dammar is an Asian tree whose resin is burned as incense. Known in Germany as "cat's eye incense," it allegedly enhances clairvoyance, psychic perception, and the ability to "see" where one could not before. Try burning dammar before psychic journeying and when extra clairvoyance is needed.

 ## Cauls

Babies born with cauls are marked for psychic power (as are babies born with teeth).

Retain and reinforce the power of the caul by keeping it on an altar or carrying it in a conjure bag.

Cedarwood Spells

Cedar trees encourage psychic perception while providing spiritual protection so one isn't afraid to use one's magic power. The most famous cedar trees are the renowned Cedars of Lebanon, an unofficial wonder of the ancient world. Those cedars were over-harvested; few remain. The closest modern substitute is the North African Atlas Cedar. Texas cedarwood and Virginia cedarwood have very different aromas and for good reason: they're actually junipers masquerading as cedarwood. Their psychic gifts are similar, however; used in combination they enhance psychic power exponentially.

 ## Cedarwood Spell (1)

Combine essential oils of Texas cedarwood, Virginia cedarwood and Atlas Cedar in an aroma burner. Diffuse the fragrance and inhale deeply to stimulate psychic vision.

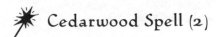 ## Cedarwood Spell (2)

Add four drops each of essential oils of Texas cedarwood, Virginia cedarwood and Atlas Cedar to a full tub of comfortably warm water. Bathe, relax, and inhale.

Centaur's Tea

Chiron the centaur served as spiritual teacher and mentor to many Greek heroes. Centaury, the herb named in honor of centaurs, a favorite of medieval witches' brews, is said to serve as a magical teacher, inducing psychic power. Like mugwort and wormwood, plants with similar power, centaury has a bitter taste.

Create centaury tea; play and experiment by adding herbs whose flavor you like so as to create a palatable brew.

Clairaudience Spell

Allegedly placing a lodestone in or near the right ear encourages clairaudience.

Clary Sage Spell

Clary sage's name derives from Latin clarus *meaning "clear," not only because this variety of sage is traditionally used to soothe eyes but it also stimulates inner vision. Anoint the Third Eye area with one drop of essential oil of clary sage and relax.*

Coffee Psychic Replenishment

Coffee does more than revive the body. The aroma of coffee is recommended for those suffering psychic depletion, especially those who have also been physically ill for an extended period of time. Brew some strong coffee. Drink it if you like, but what's important in this context is really just to inhale the aroma.

 ## Coffee Power Blast

Grind strong coffee beans and sprinkle the powder over lit charcoals. Straddle the smoke that wafts up and let it permeate your skin, hair, and clothing (although as with all these fumigations, being naked is virtually always most effective).

 ## Cornflower Clairvoyance Spell

This is a long-term spell and should be repeated with some regularity in order to obtain consistent results.

Moisten cornflowers. Lie down, relax, and apply the cornflowers to the Third Eye area to stimulate psychic vision.

Crystal Gemstone Spells

Before the Iron Age, there was the Stone Age. Crystal gemstones and other rocks were among the shaman's first tutors and tools. Because they store information indefinitely, Earth's memories and secrets may be accessed through stones. Specific gemstones are used to magically enhance spells and enable us to discover and activate our own optimum power.

 ## Crystal Gemstone Spell: Amazonite

Amazonite allegedly bestows the power and courage of the legendary Amazon warriors. North African magic considers it to be among the most magically powerful materials of all. Wear or carry an amazonite to enhance your own personal power, psychic ability, and daring. It provides protection, too.

 ## Crystal Gemstone Spell: Clear Quartz Crystal

Merlin's slumber deep in a crystal cave may be understood as incubation rather than as a trap. Clear quartz crystals empower whatever they're kept in contact with.

★ *Store tarot cards, runes and other divination devices with a quartz crystal to empower them and make them easier to read*
★ *Clear quartz crystals attached to magic wands enhance their power and effectiveness*
★ *Wear quartz crystal around your neck or sleep with it under your pillow to enhance, access, and increase your own personal power*

 ## Crystal Gemstone Spell: Fluorite

Fluorite crystal gemstones open the gates of psychic reception. Place one over the Third Eye and meditate or go to sleep and dream.

 ## Crystal Gemstone Spell: Labradorite

Labradorite repairs, cleanses and strengthens the aura. It also encourages perseverance and determination—all required qualities for a successful magical career.

Sleep with labradorite beneath your pillow. If you use it regularly, maintain a regular cleansing schedule for the crystal, as well.

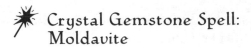
Crystal Gemstone Spell: Moldavite

Moldavite, a delicate green crystal named for the Czech Republic's Moldau Valley, is believed to be the product of a rock, struck by a meteorite, which melted and merged together, thus blending terrestrial and extraterrestrial energies. Place the crystal on the Third Eye area to absorb its psychic power and increase your own.

Crystal Powers

Crystal Aura Repair

Use a quartz crystal to repair breaks and holes in your aura. Someone else must do this for you, ideally someone with psychic gifts.

1. Slowly pass a charged quartz crystal around the body.
2. If a "cold spot" is sensed or there is perception of a gap or vulnerability, stop and allow the crystal to hover and rest over the area. This has a rebuilding and repairing effect, although it may need to be repeated several times to be fully effective.

Crystal Enhancement: Celestite

Celestite, a crystal gemstone, enhances clairaudience and clairvoyance while facilitating spiritual communication. Wear it in contact with the body. Sleep with it under your pillow.

Crystal Enhancement: Orange

Orange colored stones and crystals enhance psychic ability. Use them to frame a loose circle, large enough for you to lie down inside. Relax, let your mind clear and let inspiration arrive.

Dragon Power

Traditionally in India, a menstruating woman is often discouraged from eating hot spicy foods because this might increase her *"dragon power,"* her potent menstrual magical influence. Of course, should someone *not* desire to diminish that power …

Egyptian Temple Formula Spells

Ancient Egyptian incense and perfume makers were masters of their art. Each formula might take months to create, each ingredient carefully added at just the right moment. Even modern versions of **kyphi,** simplified at great lengths, remain complex and difficult to create. Egyptian Temple incense simplifies this process even more.

Egyptian Temple Incense

Forego the wine and raisins (see Formulary, *page 1037); grind and powder* **kyphi***'s botanical ingredients and burn them as incense.*

Egyptian Temple Floorwash

Blend and mash **kyphi***'s botanical ingredients and add them to a bucket of rinse water, together with a handful of sea salt, baking soda, and vinegar. Use this floorwash to cleanse a room prior to ritual, spell-casting or séances.*

 ## Elecampane Psychic Perception Spell

The plant elecampane is believed to possess an affinity for scrying. (See Divination Spells, page 301.) It's believed to enhance psychic perception. Burn elecampane to accompany divination by crystal ball, magic mirror, or by other scrying techniques.

Eve Oil

The story of Eve and the apple is today most frequently associated with sexuality. However what was it that Eve originally desired? Knowledge.

Add apple blossoms, dried pomegranate seeds, and snake root (aristolochia) to grapeseed oil, creating Eve Oil. Anoint candles or soak cotton balls with this oil for enhanced metaphysical wisdom and receptivity.

Evergreen Psychic Renewal Spells

The aroma of evergreen trees reinvigorates and replenishes psychic and magic power.

Pine Bath

For a magical cleansing, stimulating and reinvigorating bath place fresh pine needles in a muslin or cheesecloth bag. Allow your bathwater to run over the bag, creating an infusion.

 ## Evergreen Renewal Bath

Five drops of essential oil of silver fir
Five drops of essential oil of myrtle
Two drops of essential oil of pine

1. Add these essential oils to a shot of vodka.

2. Shake it up to distribute the oils.
3. Throw the now-scented vodka into a bathtub filled with warm water. (Pour yourself some more if you like, without the essential oils, to drink in the bath—or choose another potion.)
4. Add five drops of larch flower essence remedy to the bath.
5. Light pine scented candles.
6. Soak in the bath and feel your energy returning.

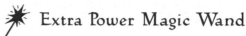 ## Extra Power Magic Wand

1. Search for hawthorn branches on Beltane (May Day).
2. Do *not* cut them, but a found branch is a gift and affirmation that you're on the right path.
3. Carve a magic wand from the wood, hawthorn being especially beneficial for fairy magic.

Fairies' Voice Spell

Sit naked under the light of a Full Moon and listen. The more you practice, the more distinct the noise will become until eventually you'll possess the ability to hear the fairies.

 ## Flax Psychic Power Spell

Flax was once among the plants most associated with women's primal power. Legend describes specifically how Hulda introduced flax to people. Fairy tales frequently feature the spinning of flax. Flax seed tea allegedly enhances the divinatory process. Have a cup of flaxseed tea before embarking on divination.

Flower remedies

The following flower remedies are particularly effective in counteracting psychic depletion after a long illness or personal crisis.

> Olive (Bach)
> Macrocarpa (Australian Bush)
> Aloe Vera (FES)

Add the remedies to the bath or take internally as per manufacturer's instructions.

 ## Grounding Spell

Spells that ground you to Earth may be necessary after or even during extensive spell-casting. Place a piece of copper, a paper packet filled with salt, and a smoky quartz crystal within a conjure bag and wear.

 ## Horehound Extra Power Spell

Horehound is considered the "seed of Horus." Create an infusion by pouring boiling water over the herb. Add it to the bath for enhanced psychic power, and the daring to implement your magical skills.

 ## Isis Powder

This powder enables you to gain some of the essence of the Mistress of Magic.

1. Blend powdered orrisroot, powdered sweet flag (calamus), and ground myrrh.
2. Add this to rice powder.
3. Sprinkle on yourself for added psychic power.

 ## Jasmine Aura Repair

Jasmine attar allegedly helps repair a weary, damaged aura. Add it to massage oil or the bath.

 ## Juniper and Thyme Spell

Allegedly the combined scent of juniper and thyme promotes psychic visions and receptivity. Blend essential oils in an aroma burner or burn dried botanicals and allow the fragrance to permeate the area.

 ## Knot Magic Enhancement

Sometimes psychic enhancement comes from within you, and sometimes it's supplied by magical tools and allies. The plant dodder, a member of the Morning Glory family, is also known as Witch's hair, love vine, *and* lady laces. *Use dodder's "laces" as cord in knot magic spells to strengthen and empower them.*

 ## Lavender Water Psychic Enhancer

Lavender water allegedly enhances the memory while stimulating psychic ability and the retention process. Bathe the head with lavender water, using a cool compress or any other method that suits you. This allegedly assists mastery of complex occult systems such as tarot or the I-Ching.

 ## Lunar Contemplation Oil

1. Grind peppermint, white camphor, and cinnamon.
2. Cover with jojoba oil and add a moonstone to the bottle.
3. Use this oil to dress white candles to accompany lunar contemplation.

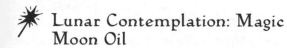 Lunar Contemplation: Magic Moon Oil

1. Place a pearl, a moonstone, a piece of real silver, and/or a quartz crystal in a bottle.
2. Cover it with sweet almond oil.
3. Add fourteen drops of mugwort flower essence remedy (*NOT* the essential oil).
4. Let it sit overnight, exposed to moonlight.
5. Massage this oil into the body, especially the feet, for psychic inspiration and visionary dreams.

 Mace Psychic Power Spell

Burn mace for enhanced psychic power and perception.

Magic Lessons Spells

Access the world's finest teachers of magic through visualization spells. Some tips:

1. Choose your tutor wisely and learn as much as you can about them prior to attending class.
2. Save your lesson for when you'll have quiet and privacy.
3. Make them an offering (sort of like that old-fashioned apple for the teacher).
4. If it inspires you, set the stage with music and fragrance.
5. Begin the inner journey to your teacher; remember your path because you'll need it to get home.
6. Don't be discouraged if this takes several attempts, especially if you're inexperienced with visualization.
7. Choose any teacher with information you desire or need, however some suggestions and guidance for visualizations are offered below.

 Magic Lessons: Circe's School of Sorcery

Circe, daughter of the sun and an ocean nymph, lives on an island in the sea. Hecate may be her aunt or her sister. Most famous for revealing men's true identities by turning them variously into pigs, baboons, or lions, she herself transforms into a falcon when she wishes to fly. Circe thus unites the elements of earth, fire, air, and water. Circe unites schools of magic, too: she is among the world's masters of sorcery, potions, necromancy, love philters, transformational, and revenge magic. Circe shares her secrets and tutors worthy students. A fierce, smart spirit, with a sharp sense of humor, like those other professors of enchantment Baba Yaga, Mother Holle, Lilith, and Artemis, she must respect you before she'll help you. Circe isn't a tutor for the beginner but for those ready for their master's degree in magic.

Invite Circe with an offering of beautiful flowers, aromatic perfume, a selection of animal images, and your finest potions. Venture to her rocky island in visualization. Decide what you wish to ask her before you journey. Circe appears in the form of a beautiful woman or a circling hawk.

 Magic Lessons: Circe's Skills

*Necromancy is among the skills that Circe teaches. Allegedly a bouquet of deadly nightshade calls Circe and informs her that her assistance is required to contact those who have passed over. Accompany with visualization. (**Warning:** Deadly nightshade is genuinely deadly; handle with care.)*

✴ Magic Lessons: Freya

Freya is a mistress of magic. Among her specialties are runes, shape-shifting, clairvoyance, prophesy, and divination. Request her assistance with any of these topics.

Create a luxurious, beautiful offering table for Freya, with images of swans and cats. Decorate it with amber and pieces of shiny metal. Carve runes into candles and burn them to communicate with her.

✴ Magic Lessons: Merlin and Morgan le Fay

Depending upon which legend you choose, either Merlin or Morgan le Fay, who may have been lovers, was the other's tutor in enchantment. Also depending upon which legend is chosen, either may be venerated or vilified. Take lessons from either one if you choose, however they work well together in tandem and provide well-balanced magic lessons.

Create a joint altar. Decorate it with found falcon feathers or falcon imagery, mermaids, crystals, and swords. Merlin and Morgan have also become associated with classic wizard's paraphernalia: peaked hats, magic wands, crystal balls, and grimoires.

✴ Magic Lessons: San Cipriano Spell

Historically there seem to have been two Saint Cyprians, both of whom were master-magicians from what is now Turkey, before they were martyred as Christians. History is hazy at best; some believe the two Cyprians to be one. Others believe that while one became the Bishop of Carthage, the other never converted to Christianity but was killed as a pagan witch. Whatever his original identity, Saint Cyprian seems to have reneged on his conversion and repudiation of magic, instead emerging, centuries after death, as the most significant figure in classical Iberian magic, the bane of witch-hunters and

inquisitors. In magical circles, he is virtually always known by his Spanish name. During his lifetime, Saint Cyprian allegedly burned his extensive library of grimoires and books of shadows. Centuries after death, San Cipriano channeled his grimorio through his scribe, Jonas Sulfurino.

San Cipriano reconciles lovers, offers protection, leads you to treasure, and offers psychic power and magic lessons to those who ask. The easiest method of approaching San Cipriano is via the condition oil named in his honor: add it to your bath but adjust the cinnamon in the formula so that it doesn't irritate your skin.

✴ Magic Lessons: San Cipriano Candle Spell

Dress brown candles with **San Cipriano Oil** to accompany spiritual petitions and visualization.

✴ Magic Lessons: San Cipriano Oil

Soak a cotton ball in **San Cipriano Oil**. Place it beneath your pillow and request lessons in your dreams.

✴ Magic Lessons: Thoth Spell

Allegedly if you call Lord Thoth by name, he will respond. Thoth is the inventor of magic and the master of the moon. He may also be Hermes Trismegistus.

1. Offer him lunar-shaped candles and charms.
2. Decorate an altar with images of his animal manifestations: baboons and ibises.
3. Calamus/sweet flag and papyrus are his sacred plants.
4. Thoth knows all magical skills; request whatever you wish.

Magic Mirror Enhancement Spell

Hemp seeds were once frequently used in magic spells and divination, dating back at least to the days of the Scythians. Obviously because of legal restrictions their use is now rare, however here is an example: burn equal parts hemp seed and mugwort leaves to activate a magic mirror.

Magic Power Oil

1. Bruise, then pound fresh mint and vervain leaves.
2. Cover them with extra-virgin olive oil and leave them overnight.
3. Strain the oil through cheesecloth.
4. Repeat the entire process at least another two or three times, using fresh herbs each time but retaining the oil so that it becomes permeated with the fragrance of the plants.
5. Repeat the process until the desired intensity of fragrance is achieved.
6. Use this oil to anoint and massage the body.

Masterwort Spells

Masterwort is not a synonym for angelica but instead is a once-common European plant.

Masterwort Charm Spell

Wear or carry masterwort for enhanced psychic power and allegedly increased physical strength and stamina.

Masterwort Powder Spell

Grind and powder masterwort. Sprinkle it on and within your shoes, especially when venturing forth to magical locations.

Mastic Spells

The mastic tree, native to the Aegean, exudes a sticky gum resin that has been used to induce and enhance psychic power since the days of the ancient Minoans, Phoenicians, and Egyptians. Mastic was a component of **kyphi** mixtures and used in the Egyptian mummification process. The aroma of burning mastic relieves physical exhaustion and psychic depletion while enhancing powers of clairvoyance, intuition, and inspiration.

Mastic Bath

Mastic is also available as an essential oil. Add some to a bath filled with comfortably warm water.

Mastic Incense

Mastic resin is known as "pearls of mastic," because of its perceived resemblance to the precious jewel. (Mastic is also marketed in the same manner that frankincense or myrrh is available, either as powder or "tears.")

Mastic allegedly enhances powers of visualization. Burn this incense when suffering from psychic depletion, to enhance already-existing magic power, and to accompany psychic journeys and visualization. Burn the mastic pearls and fumigate your body while inhaling the aroma.

Mastic Power Blast

Burn mastic incense in the bathroom. Add essential oils of frankincense, labdanum, mastic, and sandalwood to a full tub of water and luxuriate.

Mercury's Magic Rings

In ancient Roman metaphysical circles, Mercury was considered the primary patron of magic. Or was he? Mercury, the Roman spirit of commerce, was deeply syncretized with the Greek spirit Hermes. Hermes is an exceptionally ancient and complex crossroads trickster who delights in identity changes. Now most associated with the ethereal, androgynous winged spirit of classical Greece, Hermes apparently began his Earthly incarnation as an earthy, virile Arcadian fertility spirit. Hermes was also identified with the Egyptian lord of magic, Thoth. The name *Hermes Trismegistus*, *"Thrice Great Hermes,"* is often used to identify this syncretism.

In Rome, Mercury was acknowledged as the official bestower of magic rings. To increase psychic power, wear a talismanic ring depicting Hermes' classical image complete with winged cap and sandals and bearing the caduceus, his magic staff entwined by two serpents, which is still the emblem of the medical profession.

✴ Mercury's Magic Ring Activation Spell

The benefits of a magic ring may be needed immediately; talismanic rings must be found, crafted or commissioned, typically a lengthy process. Mercury may be requested to charge and empower any ring, transforming it into a magic ring.

1. Build a cairn, a small pyramid of stones. This summons Hermes/Mercury.
2. Write a brief explanation of what functions or purposes you wish the ring to serve.
3. Place the paper on top of the stones and the ring on top of the paper.
4. Dedicate a green candle to Mercury and request his blessings and assistance.

5. Once the candle has burned down, pay attention to conversations around you: when you've overheard a stranger or a child utter something affirmative like *"Go ahead"* or *"The time is right,"* you'll know the ring has been activated.

Mermaid Spells

Because mermaids reside in the deepest living waters (oceans, springs, rivers, and lakes) they're in touch with profound psychic, intuitive and magical knowledge and secrets. Because they're also able to rise to the surface and navigate Earth, that knowledge is grounded in reality. Water spirits, female and male, encourage us to explore our own psychic realities and depths.

✴ Mermaid Bath (1)

The elements earth and water are both characterized by psychic depth. Mermaids bridge both realms, especially the undines who seem magically able to switch between fish tail and legs at will. (No need for all that "Little Mermaid" hocus-pocus!) In addition to enhanced psychic power and perception, this bath brings joy and success.

1. Transform your bathroom into a mermaid shrine with *yourself* as the focal point, for added psychic ability, magic power, self-love and self-confidence.
2. Add dulse, kelp and agar-agar to the water.
3. Decorate the room with seashells, quartz crystals, and images of other mermaids.
4. Light green and blue candles and relax.

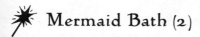 ## Mermaid Bath (2)

Time this bath to coincide with the Full Moon.

1. Float roses in a tub filled with comfortably warm water.
2. Most "lotus" fragrance is synthetic; true lotus essence is available from India but is rare and expensive. Add a few drops if you can.
3. Float rubber fish or other marine toys in the water.
4. See if you can reflect the moon in a hand mirror; if not, gaze at yourself, comb your hair, and allow your power to grow.

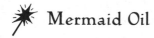 ## Mermaid Oil

Add essential oils of pine and rosemary to jojoba oil. Place an amber bead in the bottle and use the oil to dress candles. Alternately, rub a drop between your hands and inhale for a burst of insight, clarity, and power.

 ## Midsummer's Power Incense

This incense commemorates the magical botanicals associated with Midsummer's Eve and draws upon their power. The plants are extremely powerful at any time, however those harvested on Midsummer's Eve have an extra jolt of potency.

Grind the following ingredients together into a fine powder:

>   Dried mugwort
>   Dried wormwood
>   Dried yarrow
>   Dried Saint John's Wort

Sprinkle on lit charcoals and burn.

Mojo Power Bags

Mojo bags are created and carried to enhance and maintain psychic power.

 ## Mojo Element Power Bag

Gather the following and place in a conjure bag:

>   Sand from the beach
>   Dirt from a mountain
>   Dirt from a cemetery
>   Dirt from a crossroads
>   A cat's claw herb (*uno de gato*)
>   Seashell
>   Pebble from a crossroads
>   Nail or pebble found on or beside train tracks

These combined materials bestow the powers of the elements. Only pinches of sand and dirt are needed. Place the initial bag within a second, stronger one to prevent the dirt from spilling out and escaping.

 ## Mojo Power Bag (2)

Like psychic growth, this conjure bag, which is based on power items of North African magic, is a work in progress.

1. Fill a red silk bag with dried oleander leaves (**Warning:** these are toxic! Do not ingest or leave near children and animals), pieces of sandalwood and myrrh, an odd number of hairs from a horse's tail, and amazonite beads or crystals.
2. Sprinkle with henna and/or antimony powder.
3. Add a pinch of dirt from sacred sites as you visit them.

Mystic Mystery Oil

Grind and powder lilac, rose, mimosa, frankincense, and wisteria. Add the botanicals to a bottle and cover with jojoba oil.

 ## Pear Tree Psychic Power Spell

Allegedly pear trees were the focal point of witches' nightly revels. Pear trees bear a reputation for inducing lustful feelings but they're also believed to raise psychic power and aptitude. Dance around a pear tree in the light of a Full Moon, alternating clockwise and counter-clockwise motion for complete magical power and balance.

Pine Power Spells

Pine trees are sacred to an amazing number of spirits, frequently from the same pantheon: Dionysus, Kybele, Artemis, Zeus, Poseidon, and Pan among them. A grove of pines is sacred territory and rituals conducted there are psychically enhanced.

 ## Pine Power Spell: Outdoors

Linger amidst pines to shore up psychic power and to make contact with the sacred.

Pine Power Spell: Indoors

If outdoor ritual is impossible for you, bring the pine grove within. Create a bath from fresh or dried pine needles. Many commercially available pine baths are crafted from real pine. (Essential oil of pine may irritate the skin; proceed cautiously.) Close your eyes, inhale deeply, and visualize yourself in the woods.

Planetary Power Spells

The Earth and the moon regenerate magic power and inspire psychic vision.

 ## Planetary Power Spell: Earth Altars

Earthly powers may be brought within and combined with other unprocessed magical power so that they may enhance, invigorate, and replenish your own personal power. This altar is not necessarily dedicated to a deity; instead it stands as a potent energy-recharging magical battery. It is an ongoing work-in-progress.

Arrange a tableau of some or all of the following:

Earth from significant places
Rocks from significant places (holed stones)
Waters (ocean, rain, lake, river, swamp, storm drain, well, cistern, waterfall, spring)
Shells: seashells, snail, crab, crayfish (either found or recovered from meals)
Bones (fish, chicken, beef, lamb—cleaned up and preserved from food)
Found feathers
Found snakeskin
Herbs, grains
Found wood pieces

For maximum benefit, play with your altar in the manner that a child plays with a tableau, rearranging articles, examining them, and handling them, so that their aura intermingles with your own.

 ## Planetary Power Spell: Earth Power

Although the moon is specifically associated with magic power, Earth provides a type of magical vigor and vitality that is necessary for maintaining and regenerating

personal power. This ritual is important for anyone, but especially for the urban witch.

1. Go outside and find some earth.
2. Find a park, or find a yard. Find one little patch that isn't covered by concrete.
3. Take off your shoes and stand on it.
4. If this is inappropriate, kneel down and lay your palms flat on Earth. Find some naked part of yourself, let it rest on naked Earth and just absorb her power.
5. Do this for at least five minutes daily and watch your own power and energy expand.

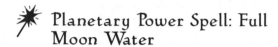

Planetary Power Spell: Full Moon Water

A simple, straightforward method for drawing down the moon and applying the resulting water.

1. Fill a glass bowl with spring water and place it outside under the Full Moon overnight.
2. In the morning, bring the water inside, siphon it into a bottle if desired and refrigerate.
3. Apply a little water to the back of your neck and over the Third Eye area for nine consecutive days to enhance your psychic ability.

Planetary Power Spell: Full Moon Water Super-sized

1. Charge an entire metal washtub filled with spring water with moonlight.
2. Store the water in smaller bottles and thermoses.
3. Wash your face and soak your feet in the water for nine consecutive nights, as well as the back of the neck and the Third Eye.
4. Wash your hair too, for added psychic ability.

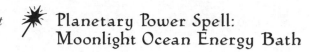

Planetary Power Spell: Moonlight Ocean Energy Bath

Mermaids have powerful affiliations with magic and enchantment. These include generic mermaids as well as the famed, renowned Aphrodite, Atargatis, Oshun, and Yemaya. This spell may be performed in conjunction with petitions requesting their assistance and matronage.

1. Visit the ocean at night during a Full Moon.
2. Stand knee-deep in the water and let the waves and moonbeams bathe you with their power. Envision yourself absorbing the power so that you are filled with moonlight and ocean energy.
3. When you come out, let yourself air-dry in the ocean breezes.

Planetary Power Spell: Perfect Balance

The moon and Earth both generate needed psychic power. The following spell attempts to balance and harmonize the two.

1. When the moon is full, shining and beautiful, go outside.
2. This spell is most effective if performed naked, but do whatever is appropriate and possible.
3. Stand under the moonbeams. Visualize them entering your body from above.
4. Feel the ground under your bare feet; visualize Earth's power entering your body through the soles of your feet.
5. Hold your arms out to the side: pay attention to the air and any breezes. Visualize the winds carrying magic power that enters you through your sides.
6. When you feel that your capacity is full, that your magical batteries have been fully recharged, go inside, go to bed and dream.

Pow-Wow Power Oil

Pow-Wow uses the materials common to the Pennsylvania Dutch community on an everyday basis. This oil should have a vibrant, sunny color.

1. Place a substantial quantity of some or all of the following flowers in a mason jar. Use fresh clean, vibrant blossoms: amaranth, calendula, nasturtiums, orange trumpet flowers, sunflowers, or other flowers in that orange spectrum.
2. Cover the blossoms with olive oil.
3. Seal the jar well.
4. Shake it a few times daily for three days, leaving the jar to rest in the sun during the day and in a dry cupboard at night.
5. Strain the oil through cheesecloth.
6. Repeat the process at least twice more, using the same oil but fresh flowers each time, until the fragrance and color is vivid and pleasing.
7. Finally strain the oil into a fresh bottle.
8. Pierce a vitamin E capsule with a pin and add the contents to the infused oil to serve as a preservative.

Use the oil in the bath or as a massage oil whenever you need a power burst.

Psychic Courage Spells

Sometimes what is most necessary for obtaining optimal magic power isn't enhancing aptitude but releasing and transcending deep-seated fears and emotions that prevent you from achieving and maximizing your psychic gifts.

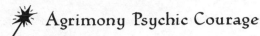

Agrimony Psychic Courage

The herb agrimony releases fear. Place some in a muslin drawstring bag and attach it to the bathtub faucet, so that the water runs through the bag. Bathe and reclaim your power.

Aura Healing

Bathe in infusions of vervain to repair and revitalize a weary, damaged aura.

Bouquet of Courage

Arrange fresh rosemary, stinging nettles, and yarrow in a vase to bolster courage and ease fear.

Chrysolite Amulet

Bore a hole in a chrysolite and fill it with hair from a donkey's mane. Wear the chrysolite tied to your left arm to be free from fear, especially neurotic, irrational fears.

Cup of Courage

Perhaps what is needed is a true cup of courage: "I, borage, bring courage!" Or so goes the traditional rhyme. The herb borage bears an ancient reputation for steeling nerves, girding loins, and providing good cheer and courage. Use this potion during situations that require you to be brave.

1. Squeeze the juice from an orange and mix it with one-quarter cup of sugar.
2. Add one-quarter cup of dried borage and stir thoroughly.
3. Allow this to steep overnight.
4. Strain the borage from the liquid and discard it.

5. Add this liquid to sixteen fluid ounces of red wine (425 ml) and serve it over ice. Garnish with fruit slices.

Enhance the power by adding a few drops of borage flower remedy. The remedy may also be used on its own in the bath or rubbed into the feet.

 ## Cup of Psychic Courage Tea

Chamomile allegedly replenishes and reinforces courage as well as psychic power. Have a cup of chamomile tea as a cup of courage.

 ## Devil's Shoestring Psychic Courage Spell

For added personal power, as well as to overcome fear:

1. Cut a devil's shoestring root into small equal pieces.
2. Place the pieces in a small glass jar together with a square of camphor or a drop of essential oil of white camphor.
3. Cover it with a shot of courage, usually whiskey or rum, but if another beverage appeals to you, use it, although the effect is magical; nothing will be drunk nor should it be.
4. Hide the jar in a discreet, private place. Whenever you need a shot of courage, remove one root piece and rub it in your hands, over your feet, your forehead and the back of your neck. Having been used, discard this piece.
5. When all the pieces are gone, add the reserved liquid to a bath and start the spell all over again.

 ## Joan of Arc Courage Spell

1. Contemplate Joan of Arc or petition her directly for assistance.

2. Light a gray candle in her honor on a Tuesday.
3. Place a metal charm in the shape of a sword beside the candle.
4. When the candle has burned down completely, carry the charm with you, close at hand.
5. Touch it in moments of fear and need.

 ## Maximon's Courage Spell

The clothing used to dress and ornament votive statues eventually develops its own magic power. Wooden statues of Maximon, for instance, are dressed in the fine clothes this unofficial saint favors. Access the inherent power by keeping Maximon clean and well-dressed. Wash Maximon's clothing by hand, reserving the final rinse water. Add this water to your bath to repel fear, sadness, and melancholy.

 ## Mint Courage Spell

Mints, most especially peppermint, are restorative plants, replenishing psychic energy, courage, and peace of mind. Hold a bouquet of fresh mint or a cup of peppermint tea and inhale its fragrance deeply.

 ## Oya Courage Spell

Courage emerges in the recognition of one's own personal strength.

1. Write down nine ways in which you are powerful.
2. Place the paper under a purple candle dedicated to the orisha of personal power, Oya.
3. Offer her red wine. Pour a glass for yourself, too.
4. Toast Oya and yourself and watch the candle burn.

Oregano Courage Bath

Bathe in an infusion of oregano (not while pregnant!) to calm nerves, regroup scattered thoughts and emotions, and to summon courage.

Ragweed Psychic Courage Spell

*Ragweed is the bane of allergy sufferers, yet it too has magical uses. Chew it to alleviate fear and summon courage. Do **not** swallow though, as "ragweed" indicates a variety of plants, some toxic.(You'll know very well if this spell is suitable for you by the lack of allergic reaction.)*

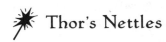

Thor's Nettles

Odin may be the All-Father, leader of the Norse and Teutonic spirits, but for centuries the most beloved spirit of that pantheon was Thor, embodiment of courage and strength.

Nettles are sacred to Thor: wear nettles to banish fear and absorb a little of his courageous essence. This is most powerful if done on Thor's days, Thursdays.

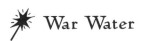

War Water

*Add **War Water** to your bath when you need to magically gird yourself for battle.*

Yarrow Courage Spell

Hold a yarrow stalk in your hands and focus on your goals and desires, to magically stimulate courage and relieve fear.

Psychic Courage Oils
Two famous classic condition formulas are used to enhance personal bravery and draw it from your depths. The first is the tersely named **Courage Oil**; the second is **Crucible of Courage**. Formulas are in the *Formulary* (page 1037). The oils are very compatible; use whichever appeals to you or use them together for extra enhancement.

Psychic Courage Oil (1)
Courage Oil

Courage Oil *draws on the magic power of five-finger grass (cinquefoil) and gardenias and it enhances bravery. This formula encourages you to take chances and to rise to any situations you may encounter.*

Soak a cotton ball in the oil. Carry it in your pocket or tuck it into your bra, especially when entering situations or areas where courage is needed.

Psychic Courage Oil (2)
Crucible of Courage Oil

Crucible of Courage Oil *doesn't so much lend you courage as much as it helps you discover hidden resources within you that you never knew you had. It's also indicated for those plagued by chronic self-doubt and lack of confidence.* ***Crucible of Courage Oil*** *relies largely on ancient sacred fragrances such as frankincense, bay laurel, and sandalwood.*

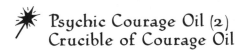

Crucible of Courage Bath

*Add **Crucible of Courage Oil** to a bath and enter the crucible. This is particularly beneficial before stressful appointments or meetings.*

Psychic Courage Oils Spells
Either **Courage Oil** or **Crucible of Courage Oil** may be used in these spells. For maximum power, use both simultaneously.

Courage Oils Purple Candle

1. Dress a purple candle with either or both oils.
2. Focus on your goals, wishes, plans, and desires.
3. Light your candle.

 ## Courage Oils Quick Fix

Rub either or both oils between your palms before crucial situations. Bring your hands to your face and inhale deeply.

 ## Courage Oils Shoe Spell

Add one drop of oil to each of your shoes to get you where you need to go with less stress.

 ## Psychic Detection Spell

Wear snapdragons: allegedly they bestow magical truth-detection powers that enable you to spot lies and see the hidden truth.

Psychic Energy Replenishment

You cannot maintain a state of optimum psychic power in the face of physical exhaustion. Care of the spiritual and the physical aspects of a person go hand-in-hand. In addition, magic is exhausting: you are putting out vast quantities of energy. Inevitably, most of us put out far more than we draw in.

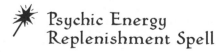 ## Psychic Energy Replenishment Spell

1. When you feel either psychic torpor or physically drained, arrange a Rider-Waite four of swords tarot card so that you can see it clearly from your bed.
2. Fix the bed with clean, fresh sheets. Sprinkle some psychic protection powder between the sheets.
3. Burn the fragrances of frankincense and ylang ylang.
4. Bring something you love to eat, comfort food, over to the bed as well as a drink of something that literally warms you, tea or alcohol or both.
5. Get into the bed, inhale the fragrances and gaze at the card. If you fall asleep, pay attention to your dreams.

 ## Psychic Energy Replenishment Bath

Simone Schwarz-Bart's novel The Bridge of Beyond *celebrates the strength and wisdom of a Caribbean root woman. In the novel, Ma Cia, the root worker, prepares a weekly invigorating bath of magic leaves for the novel's heroine: enchanted botanicals like* Bride's Rose, *calaba balsam, paoca and* Power of Satan *are placed in a large tub of water warmed by the sun. The bath performs a spiritual cleansing function but also offers psychic replenishment for the week ahead.*

1. Reproduce the bath and dream that you're in beautiful Guadeloupe.
2. If you can't find or grow the exact flowers, find the most fragrant, fresh, vivid blossoms possible.
3. Warm the flowers in a washtub filled with spring or rainwater.
4. Ladle the contents over your head nine times in order to *"leave behind the fatigues of the week."*
5. Those who live in cold, dark climates need this bath the most. Substitute flower remedies for the tropical blossoms. Add any fresh flowers that are available, but always be wary of florist's blossoms, which are beautiful but usually redolent with pesticides that can enter your bath water.
6. If there are no fresh flowers, add children's rubber toys in the shape of flowers, tropical fish or mermaids. Warm floral essential oils in an aroma burner and pretend.

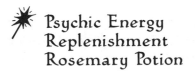

Psychic Energy Replenishment Rosemary

Although rosemary has magic gifts for men and women alike, this botanical is especially associated with women's power. Rosemary reinforces the authority and personal power of women who serve as leaders of families and groups.

Add essential oil of rosemary to a bath to provide replenishment for single mothers, corporate achievers, and all women who hold positions of authority. Float roses on the water for added enhancement.

Psychic Energy Replenishment Rosemary Potion

Blend rosemary hydrosol with sparkling water to create a psychic energy potion.

Psychic Energy Replenishment Rosemary Tea

Rosemary tea is also beneficial: it rejuvenates, reinvigorates, and enhances psychic ability, especially in times of physical exhaustion.

Make a strong infusion by pouring boiling water over fresh or dried rosemary. Rosemary tastes better added to food than as a drink. To improve the taste and increase the power of the potion, add lemon balm and peppermint, and sweeten with honey, if desired.

Psychic Replenishment Bath

This bath utilizes the following botanicals:

Rosemary
Melissa (lemon balm)
Spearmint

These may be used in varying forms:

★ *Make infusions of dried or fresh botanicals and add to the bath*
★ *Add essential oils to the bath*
★ *Use a combination of fresh herbs and essential oils: although all are common garden plants, Melissa (lemon balm) is a notoriously rare and expensive essential oil*

Psychic Power Bath: Anise

Pour boiling water over bruised anise seeds to create an infusion. When the liquid cools, strain out the solids and add the infusion to your bathwater for enhanced psychic power and perception.

Psychic Power Bath: Anise Extra Strength

Toss some anisette into the bath. Light some candles; pour yourself a drink and feel your power re-emerge.

Psychic Power Bath: Exotic Mix

Add essential oils of myrrh, opoponax, and liquidambar to your bath to strengthen and balance psychic power.

Psychic Power Bath: Frankincense

Add essential oils of elemi, frankincense, and lemongrass to a bath to enhance power and potentiate the ability to use it.

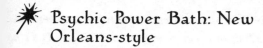

Psychic Power Bath: New Orleans-style

Add six drops of essential oil of rose geranium and six drops of essential oil of lavender to a warm bath. Relax and luxuriate. You may also substitute or add geranium and lavender hydrosols.

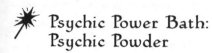

Psychic Power Bath: Psychic Powder

1. Combine equal parts **Cascarilla powder** and lotus root powder.
2. Add this to your bath.
3. Immerse yourself completely in the water.
4. Focus on your desire for enhanced psychic ability and spiritual growth.

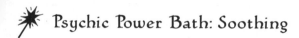

Psychic Power Bath: Soothing

Add melilot to your bath to soothe nerves and replenish psychic and physical energy.

Psychic Power Bath: Sweet Honey Power

Blend rose and lavender hydrosols in a pot and warm it gently over a fire; don't boil! Stir in some honey and add to your bath.

Psychic Power Incense

Grind equal quantities of celery seed and powdered orrisroot together. Sprinkle onto lit charcoal and burn.

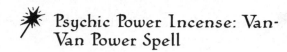

Psychic Power Incense: Van-Van Power Spell

To enhance the power of charms and ritual tools, make **Van Van** *incense from dried Asian grasses. Burn the incense, and then pass the items through its smoke.*

Psychic Power Necklace

Pierce cloves, star anise, and nutmeg. (Nutmeg may require a drill.) String them onto a necklace. Concentrate on your goals while piercing and stringing. Murmur your desires and intentions over the spice beads. Wear as a necklace or hang over your head when you desire optimal psychic power.

Psychic Power Oil

1. Add five drops of frankincense, five drops of myrrh, three drops of petitgrain, and two drops of tuberose to a bottle containing an ounce of sweet almond oil.
2. Add five drops of mugwort flower remedy and a tiny moonstone to the bottle.
3. Massage a few drops into the soles of your feet. Rub one drop over the third eye area of your brow to enhance psychic power.

Psychic Power Powder

Grind, powder and blend the following ingredients: cinnamon, cloves, mastic pearls, myrrh, and sandalwood. Sprinkle around the table during séances, on cards or other psychic tools, and between the sheets for enhanced dreams.

Psychic Power Spell Book

Are the spells in your grimoire not working? Before you write the book (or magic) off, consider whether the book needs magical psychic empowerment. Old grimoires are notorious for their unique qualities. No two copies of some surviving grimoires are identical although they are recognizably the same book. This was no accident: Before printing standardized book production, magical books were frequently customized for the user. Magic ink was used to record the text. The spell-caster's name might be inserted into the text a ritual number of times. Ancient magical techniques can still be used to empower even mass produced books.

1. Traditionally nine days of intensive spell-work are required for the ritual empowerment of a spell book.
2. The owner/user of the book casts cleansing spells daily for these consecutive days while the book is primed: medieval books were often secretly taken to Mass, but then, medieval magicians frequently doubled as theologians. Your book may be taken to wherever you perceive as sacred and empowering, however the spell may also be cast at home.
3. Cast a circle and maintain the book in the center for nine days.
4. The book should be sprinkled with magically charged waters daily.
5. Murmur Psalms or other sacred verses over the book daily as well as litanies of names that you hold sacred.
6. Following nine days the book should be ready to work for you.

Psychic Power Spell: Rapunzel Root

Rapunzel, also known as ramps or rampion, was once a popular European food, now fallen out of fashion. It's also the name of a Brothers Grimm fairy tale heroine who was traded for one. It appears in an Italian fairy tale, too: a girl uproots rampion only to discover a stairway leading to a palace deep within Earth. Hold a rapunzel root in your hand for enhanced psychic visualization and protection.

Psychic Power Unblocking

Are malevolent spiritual entities preventing you from achieving your maximum psychic power? Confuse and remove them with a ritual of magical charades.

1. A very nice meal consisting of a whole fish is prepared by someone else and served to the blocked magician, as if he or she were an honored guest and not a resident in the home. The ritual assistant who plays the part of the waiter is, in order of preference, the magician's spouse or lover, a relative, or anybody else.
2. The person who cooks and serves the fish makes a big deal out of it, praising it aloud.
3. Without speaking but via facial expressions, the magician indicates that no matter how delicious this fish appears, it's not acceptable.
4. The server removes it immediately and disposes of it outside of the house.
5. The magician should now take a cleansing bath and protective measures should be undertaken.

The rationale behind this ritual is that there are lurking vampiric spirits who desire to block the magician's further acquisition of power, but who would also like to avail themselves of the magician's current powers. They are attracted to the fish as a venue of entry into the magician's body. Because this has been billed as such a special meal, these not overly intelligent spirits enter the fish, hoping to enter the magician's body as he or she eats, like a parasite. When the magician silently refuses, they are removed and eliminated, giving the magician an opportunity to set up protective boundaries before they return.

Psychic Vision Oil

1. Grind equal quantities of althaea and anise seeds together with a mortar and pestle.
2. Add them to jojoba oil.
3. Add a small quartz crystal to the bottle.
4. Rub this oil on your hands and feet prior to psychic sessions.
5. Add it to a bath to encourage spontaneous inspiration.

 Psychic Vision Spell

1. Pour boiling water over eyebright to create an infusion.
2. Allow it to cool, then strain, reserving the liquid.
3. Soak cotton pads into the eyebright infusion.
4. Place one over each eye to enhance clairvoyant ability and second sight.
5. Be patient: this spell will likely take more than one application before one sees results.

 Rosemary Spell

Blend essential oil of rosemary with essential oil of mastic to repair the aura, stimulate psychic perception, and increase your ability to comprehend and retain psychic experiences. Warm in an aroma burner or add to the bath.

 Scarlet Pimpernel Spell

The Scarlet Pimpernel is most famous as the hero of the novels written by Baroness Emmuska Orczy. It's actually the name of a wildflower that allegedly stimulates second sight. Scarlet pimpernel is toxic if consumed; wear it or surround yourself with it for enhanced psychic ability.

 Seven African Powers Spell

Add a few drops of **Seven African Powers Oil** to your bath to consolidate and balance psychic power.

Spell-casting Tips

 Spell-caster's Tips: Diet

Some fast before spell-casting; others recommend eating for extra strength and power. Among the foods believed to enhance chances of spell-casting success are ginger (both fresh and candied) and rosemary.

 Spell-caster's Tips: Image Activation

This method derives from traditions of Chinese magic. Activate and animate the image of a spirit by pricking your smallest finger with a needle or rose thorn. Rub the resulting drop of blood over the image's eyes.

 Spell-caster's Tips: Mullein Spell

Mullein is Hecate's plant. Keep mullein in a bowl beside you or wear it around your neck in a conjure bag for extra power while casting spells.

 Spell-caster's Tips: Violet Spell

Wash your face and hands with an infusion of violet leaves before initiating any psychic work, for added power and reception.

Tuberose Psychic Power Spell

Tuberose is known as Mistress of the Night. The beautiful, fragrant white flowers create a bridge to lunar power. Surround yourself with fresh flowers and inhale!

 ## Witch's Belt or Girdle

The belt for this spell may be constructed from freely shed snakeskin, silk or cord.

1. Set thirteen goals. (One goal may also be affirmed thirteen times.)
2. On the New Moon charge an object to symbolize and help realize the first goal. For instance, the desire for fertility might be symbolized by a frog or rabbit fetish. A financial goal might be represented by a small magnetic horseshoe.
3. Wrap this item up in a bundle or place it in a small bag and attach it to the magic belt.
4. Charge a new charm at each New Moon.
5. When the lunar year is complete and thirteen moons have passed, consider your accomplishments and the status of your goals. The belt may be considered complete and maintained as a talisman of growth and/or success or remove the thirteen charms and begin the cycle again.

 ## Witch's Belt or Girdle: Quick Fix Spell

This spell still requires the passage of thirteen moons to be complete; however it bypasses the sometimes intimidating need to find magical objects to represent your goals.

1. At the New Moon, write out your goal, wish or affirmation on a piece of paper.
2. Charge a white or silver candle with your desires, place it on a plate and burn it.

3. Put the paper beneath the plate.
4. After the candle burns down, place the paper in a small pouch and attach it to your belt.
5. Repeat at each New Moon; set new goals for yourself or reiterate the original one as desired.

 ## Witch's Garter (1)

Ask a child to draw a "witch" and most likely they'll dress her in a black dress and a triangular hat. The traditional witch's wardrobe is more complex and varied, however.

Cloaks may be worn for warmth alone rather than for any magical purpose, but the witch's garter allegedly provides psychic enhancement. Instead of merely holding up socks or stockings, amulets and botanicals may be discreetly, yet powerfully, worn by attaching to the garter. A magical item of clothing, the garter retains its seductive charm—unlike that other garment rooted in magic ritual, the girdle.

The witch's garter believed to stimulate psychic power is crafted from green leather, lined with blue silk, and buckled with true silver.

 ## Witch's Garter (2)

The witch's garter also known as a "witch's belt" (as is her girdle, just to increase confusion) has associations with shamanic rites, fairy magic, and erotic power. Sometimes the garter also denotes rank in a coven.

1. Ancient garters were created from shed snakeskin to tap into that creature's magic power and psychic ability.
2. Place crystals atop a snakeskin and allow it to charge overnight in the moonlight.
3. Wear it on your left thigh.

Women's Intuition Spells

It's no accident that so many of the most powerful female deities are depicted with roses and lilies. Both species radiate women's primal power and may also be used to enhance one's own personal power, especially that old stand-by, *"women's intuition."*

 ## Women's Intuition: Bouquet Spell

Many modern flower hybrids are bred for color, size, and beauty to the exclusion of fragrance. It's crucial that this spell be aromatic as that's how the magical transaction is achieved.

Create large bouquets, as many as possible, of fresh lilies and roses. Arrange them strategically so that their fragrance permeates the area. Inhale deeply and absorb their power.

 ## Women's Intuition: Fragrant Bath

Attar of roses is available but expensive. Commercially available scent of lilies is almost invariably synthetic. Florist's blooms are usually heavily sprayed with pesticides and thus not safe to be consistently put in the bath in great quantity. The best solution is usually to maintain your own supply.

Add fresh blossoms to the bath or create infused flower oil of rose and lily. (See Elements of Magic Spells *for detailed instructions.) Rub the oil directly on the body and then enter the bath. If possible, color-coordinate scent-less candles to illuminate the bathroom. Relax and allow yourself to be permeated with fragrance and power.*

 ## Women's Psychic Power Spell

Myrrh, which embodies Hathor and Isis, is associated with women's primal spiritual and sexual power. Blend aloes wood, cinnamon, and myrrh. Burn and waft the fragrance over you.

 ## Yang Potion

Those who actively pursue psychic visions and magic power tend to spend much time delving into the yin side of life. This is especially true for professional psychics and magic workers. True power, however, comes from balance.

1. Fill a crystal bottle with spring or **Holy Water** on a bright sunny morning.
2. Place it so that it is exposed to bright sunlight.
3. At night, place the bottle in the refrigerator.
4. Use it whenever you perceive the necessity of re-energizing: sprinkle in the bath, on the altar, or throughout the home.

Yarrow

Yarrow derives its name from the Greek *"hieros,"* "holy." Its spiritual affiliations lie with the Greek hero, Achilles. It is the legendary herb that this warrior son of a mermaid carried in order to heal his wounded soldiers during the Trojan War.

Yarrow has many magical uses but is particularly beneficial for psychic stimulation; not only does it stimulate psychic ability but it erects a protective shield as well. One of the downsides of enhanced psychic vision is the sudden awareness of spiritually threatening situations. All of a sudden you realize that there are things to worry about that you never considered before. Yarrow provides the equivalent of Achilles' near invulnerability.

Yarrow Potions

Yarrow is a safer herb than either wormwood or mugwort, although the essential oil should be avoided by pregnant women and by those prone to seizure disorders.

Moderate quantities serve as magical potions to enhance and stimulate psychic ability.

★ Make an infusion from the dried herb, as a tea or to add to the bath

★ Yarrow hydrosol serves as a magical elixir. It may also be added to the bath

★ Yarrow flower remedy is particularly beneficial if your expanding psychic skills are new: its protective qualities are fast and potent. Add a few drops to the herbal infusion

★ Yarrow flower remedy may also be applied topically. Add it to the bath. Massage it into your feet before bedtime

 ## Yerba Santa Spell

Add an infusion of yerba santa to your bath to enhance and stimulate psychic power.

Yin Potion

Try as you might, are you having trouble accessing realms of magic or your own personal psychic ability? Do you feel too resolutely grounded to achieve psychic lift-off? This Yin Potion, a quick-fix version of lunar-infused water, can help put you in touch with your own psychic side.

1. Fill a crystal bottle with pure spring water.
2. Expose it to moonbeams overnight.
3. Use as needed: drink the water, wash your face with it or add it to your bath.
4. If not used up right away, store it in the refrigerator.

⬟ Spells for Travelers

Travelers have traditionally been perceived as a vulnerable group of people and in need of protection against all manner of dangers along the way.

Celestial Travel Guide Spells

That old saintly stand-by, Saint Christopher, has been removed from the official registry of saints. However other spirits provide protection for travelers.

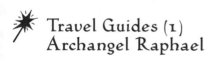 Travel Guides (1) Archangel Raphael

Archangel Raphael is the patron and protector of travelers. In the apocryphal Book of Tobit, *Raphael is the angel who accompanies the hero on his journey. Request that he accompany you as well. Raphael is summoned by his emblem, a fish.*

1. Charge a white candle with your desire and burn it.
2. Place a fish charm next to the candle.

3. When the candle has burned completely out, wear the charm or carry it in a charm bag. Use it to feel the archangel's presence in times of danger, stress, or need.

Travel Guides (2) Ganesha

Ganesha, the Hindu elephant-headed spirit, is traditionally invoked before beginning every substantial journey. Request his guidance and protection, and that he open the roads for smooth, happy traveling. Make an offering of peanuts, golden raisins, or candy to Ganesha prior to setting out on a journey.

Travel Guides (3) Hermes

Hermes rules tricks, travelers and communication. The messenger spirit of the Greek pantheon, he always knows the right direction. Hermes offers a special oracle if you're traveling and find yourself lost.

1. Pull over in a safe spot if driving. Plug up your ears if walking.
2. Make your petition.
3. The very first words you hear are your directions. If you're in the car, turn on the radio. Children's words are especially significant.

 ## Travel Guides (4) Jizo

Jizo is the Japanese Buddhist Guardian of the Roads. To take advantage of his protection post his image wherever the road threatens danger. Keep another image of Jizo in your home or on your property. Whenever your journeys safely conclude, place a stone near one of Jizo's images.

 ## Travel Guides (5) Odin

Odin, the All-Father, patriarch of the Norse and Teutonic spirits, is a great traveler. He may be petitioned for safe, smooth travel and happy, insightful adventures. Offer him a glass of mead or aquavit. He's also pleased with less tangible offerings: compose a poem as a petition to him: if a crow or wolf-like dog appears, your petition has been heard.

 ## Baggage Handling and Return Spell

Tuck a bit of comfrey root into luggage to ensure its safety and arrival at your destination.

 ## Basil Sweet Journey Spell

Basil is laid in the grave to assist the soul's journey after death, but it also benefits living travelers. Charge a small basil plant or sprig of leaves with your love and blessings. Give it to guests as they depart so that further journeys are safe and happy.

 ## Come Home Safe Spell

To bring a lover home safely, burn aloes wood and frankincense daily.

 ## Don't Leave Spell

To prevent someone in your household from embarking on a long journey, collect seven small stones from seven different roads, one rock from each road. Put them at the threshold outside the front door to your home.

 ## Feverfew Travel Spell

Feverfew is popularly used to treat migraine headaches; it's magically used to treat other headaches, like overbooked hotels, lost luggage, and missing reservations. Feverfew protects travelers from mishaps on the road. Place dried or fresh blossoms in charm bags and sachets. Carry one on your person; tuck others into luggage, glove compartments or anything else you can think of.

 ## Moonstone Travel Charm

Charge a moonstone with your blessings, love, and best magic wishes and than activate it by exposing it to moonbeams overnight. Give it to someone you love as protection while they travel.

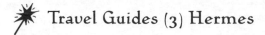

Mugwort Happy Trails Spell

Mugwort is an ancient traveler's talisman. Roman foot soldiers placed sprigs of mugwort in their shoes. Allegedly this forestalls foot problems on long walks as well as providing protection and good fortune. Try wearing it pinned inside your clothing or in a charm bag.

 ## Protection Spell (1) Hazel

Bind or wrap hazel branches around a staff or walking cane for protection during journeys, spiritual as well as physical.

 ## Protection Spell (2) Henna

A ball of henna paste pushed into a man's palm by a woman provides protection, and promotes his fidelity during separation.

 ## Psalm Protection

Recite Psalm 121 aloud seven times for safe travel alone at night.

 ## Scarlet Pimpernel Spell

Wear or carry scarlet pimpernel wildflowers to prevent mishaps and unpleasant surprises while traveling.

 ## Swallow's Blood Powder

No swallows need be harmed for this spell. The powder's red color derives from botanicals alone. Swallows are famous for their lengthy migrations. They are grand travelers among birds. Their power is invoked in the name of this powder to provide protection for you.

1. Grind dragon's blood resin, red sandalwood powder, red rose petals, and orrisroot.
2. Sprinkle powder on charcoal and fumigate yourself, your vehicle, your traveling clothes, and your luggage.

 ## Sweet Return Spell

Charge a candle with your desire, and keep it burning in the window to ensure a loved one's safe return. Before the candle burns out, if the person hasn't returned, charge and light another one.

 ## Traveler's Home Protection Spell

Should the person perceived as the chief-protector of the household go on a journey, this spell may be cast to protect those left behind. The protector performs the spell.

1. Three days before departure, gather seven small stones.
2. Spit on each one.
3. Place them outside the house: one at each of the home's four corners, one on either side of the entrance door and one over the door.
4. Take some salt in the palm of your hand and from the outside, facing the house, blow it at the house.

 ## Traveler's Mirror Charm

When sleeping in an unprotected room, crush and peel a single clove of garlic. Rub this against a small mirror and place this mirror face up underneath your bed.

Traveler's Protective Charm

Shape a piece of red flannel into something roughly the shape of a finger. Stuff it with crossroads dirt, coal dust, or antimony powder (kohl). Add a small piece of real silver. Sew up the charm and carry it with you to keep from getting lost.

 ## Traveler's Totem

The mountain lion (cougar) is the guardian of travelers. Carry a carved animal fetish of a cougar to accompany you on your journeys.

Walking Stick Spells

A very fine line exists between a walking stick and a magical staff. Is it coincidental that wandering magicians from Merlin to Gandalf are so frequently depicted leaning on their staffs? Travel with one for magical protective purposes.

 ## Blackthorn Travel Stick

Carve a walking stick/magic staff from blackthorn. Walk with it to preserve you from harm.

Elder Stick

Carve a staff or walking stick from elder wood to guard against the inherent dangers of the road. For maximum enchantment, hollow out the wood and stuff it with magical herbs.

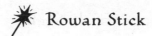 ## Rowan Stick

A magic staff carved from rowan wood masquerades as a walking stick. Rowan is a preferred wood for divination because it sharpens the powers of perception, clairvoyance, and discrimination. The traveler with this staff is believed less likely to get lost in every sense of the word, or to venture into danger.

Automobile Travel Spells

 ## Accident Prevention Bath

The following protects against accidents, particularly if one is feared because of a curse or a hex cast with iron.

1. Pour boiling water over the herb feverfew to create an infusion.
2. Add the infusion to your bath prior to the journey.
3. For extra benefit, carry feverfew in the car.

 ## Appease the Spirits Spell

Destructive spirits that cause car collisions cluster at roadside intersections, the proverbial crowd at the crossroads. These spirits aren't necessarily evil but they are frustrated, resentful and angry, allegedly because they're homeless and have no positive contact with the living.

To some extent this is a development of modern life; people used to perform rituals at crossroads. Now we just drive through. This is aggravated at crowded intersections, where there are complicated turning maneuvers and palpable human feelings of tension and resentment. Spirits and humans feed off each other's feelings, worsening the situation. These spirits signal their presence through:

★ Clusters of collisions at one spot
★ Inexplicable collisions occurring consistently at one spot

In some places, rural mountainous Thailand for instance, collisions, in general, are perceived as being the work of frustrated, angry spirits. So is this one more thing to be anxious about? No. Magical remedial actions may be taken.

Build the spirits a home. All they require is a little house, bird-house or doll's-house size, atop a post, near the intersection. This house does not have to be at the center but may be tucked safely along the side. Also, greet the spirits as you pass: salute; honk; shout "hi!" This keeps them content and happy, and may even turn them into amiable, helpful spirits.

 ## Ash Leaf Safety Spell

Keep at least one whole dried ash leaf in your car for magical safety and protection.

 ## Automobile Protection Oil

Dab **Protection Oil** onto the seatbelts, steering wheel, tires, and whatever else you perceive as vulnerable.

 ## Braided Sweetgrass Safety Spell

Maintain a braid of sweetgrass in the car. Replace it annually or following an accident, burning or burying the old one.

 ## Cat's Claw Spell

"Cat's claws" are thorns that resemble real cat's claws from a botanical species native to South America. Place a few in a conjure bag, and keep it in your glove compartment for safety.

 ## Durga and Kali Auto Safety Spell

Limes are believed able to remove evil, particularly that caused by low-level malevolent entities. Limes remove the entities as well. This charm may be consecrated to Durga and/or Kali, spiritual matrons of professional drivers.

1. This spell requires three limes, two long, hot red peppers (the type shaped like a sword rather than a lantern), plus a sharp needle with wire or cord strong enough to support the limes (thin thread will break).
2. Pierce the limes vertically, the peppers horizontally.
3. First pierce one lime, then a pepper, a lime, a pepper and finally a lime.
4. Attach this to your rear-view mirror or it place on the dashboard.
5. Make a new one each Saturday.
6. Dispose of the old amulet either by burning or by placing in Earth and allowing it to deteriorate naturally. Do not eat the limes or peppers. The wire may be re-used indefinitely.

 ## Eye of the Tiger

Keep tiger's eye gemstones in the car to prevent accidents.

 ## Fairy Tears

"Fairy tears" are the nickname for the crystal gemstone staurolite, also known as "cross stone." Twinned crystals form into a cross or an X. Fairy tears allegedly protect against car accidents: keep them in the glove compartment, or wear one as a traveler's charm.

Glove Compartment Conjure Bag

1. Place the following inside a red conjure bag: salt, a small red horn charm, a tiny knife, sword, or scissors.
2. Add any or all of the following: wormwood, High John the Conqueror root, or a piece of palm blessed on Palm Sunday.
3. Add one drop of **Holy Water** and place it in your glove compartment.
4. Anoint with one drop of **Holy Water** once a week or whenever the bag has offered protection.
5. If you normally carry cloth handkerchiefs, substitute one for the red bag. Wrap the items in the handkerchief, tying the magical bundle up with a red ribbon.

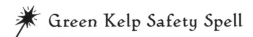

Glove Compartment Shrine

The unofficial saint, Dr. Jose Gregorio Hernandez, died in a traffic accident while bringing medicine to a patient. He now uses his powers to prevent similar experiences from happening to others. Keep Dr. Jose Gregorio's votive image inside vehicles for protection.

Green Kelp Safety Spell

Place powdered kelp inside a green bag. Keep it in the glove compartment for auto safety.

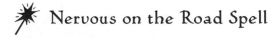

Nervous on the Road Spell

Whether you've had bad experiences and have thus developed fear or whether you possess inexplicable phobias about driving, apples can help you overcome your fear, making driving a calmer, if not necessarily more pleasurable, experience.

1. Eat apples as much as possible, in any form: fresh apples, baked apples, apple pastry or whatever you can conceive.
2. Drive with a bag of apples beside you in the car.
3. Eventually your fear will pass.

Ogun's Protection Spells

Because Ogun is the spirit of metal, and because automobiles are crafted from metal, Ogun is the patron of those who travel by car. The connection is deeper, however. According to legend, Ogun cleared the very first road, freeing space with his machete. Ogun created the roads that made automobile travel possible. In West Africa, to say that the road was hungry is to indicate that a fatal accident occurred. Papa Ogun determines who has accidents and who does not, who survives accidents and who does not. Thus his protection is extremely valuable.

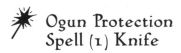

Ogun Protection Spell (1) Knife

Ogun's charm knife protects against accidents.

1. Completely cover a red ribbon with black and red seed beads. Beads may be glued on, however for added power, sew each bead, focusing on your desire for protection and blessings of safe travel.
2. Wrap this ribbon tightly around the handle of a small knife. (This may be a real knife or a ritual knife.)
3. Light a black and red double-action candle, making an invocation requesting protection.
4. Dip the knife blade into a glass of dark rum seven times.
5. Light a cigar and pass the knife through its smoke seven times.
6. Place the knife beside the double-action candle.

7. Surround the large candle and knife, with seven smaller red and black candles and burn them.
8. When all the candles have burned down, place the knife in your glove compartment or carry it in a conjure bag.
9. For added intensification, repeat the spell, beginning at Step 3, either three or seven times.

 ## Ogun Protection Spell (2) Steak

A traditional offering is made to invoke auto safety. This is most appropriately performed on a Wednesday. Dress in red and/or black while performing ritual.

1. Buy the best cut of steak you can afford.
2. Pour a libation of rum for Ogun.
3. Rub the raw steak all over the car, tires and bumpers, concentrating on your petition for safety and protection.
4. Leave it on for a while before washing the car.
5. Dispose of the steak, do not eat it. Should a dog unexpectedly show up and if it's appropriate, give the dog the steak. Dogs are Ogun's sacred animals.

 ## Plantain Auto Safety Spell

This spell refers to plantain the herb rather than the plantain that resembles a banana. Carry plantain leaves in your car to prevent malicious spirits from entering and attempting to co-pilot.

 ## Snake Head Protection Spell

Keep a snake head root in the glove compartment for protection.

 ## Spirit Valet Parking Spell

Should you require a parking space in an area where they are rare, begin this spell before you arrive at your destination.

1. Request assistance from whomever you perceive as your spiritual, magical patron. If their identity is unclear to you, request assistance from your guardian angel, fairy godmother, or ancestral spirit.
2. Tell them what you need; then make up a little rhyme or chant, something like:
   I need a safe spot close to home,
   It's getting late; I don't want to roam.

Murmur this repeatedly until your space is found.

 ## Wormwood Spell

Place wormwood in a small drawstring bag and hang it from the rearview mirror for magical accident prevention.

Travel By Water

 ## Amulets For Travel Over the Waters

This charm protects whether traveling by boat, flying over the water, or driving in a tunnel under the water. Wear or carry any of the items below to provide protection and safe journeying:

★ *Aquamarine*
★ *Beryl*
★ *Coral*
★ *Holed stones (these are particularly beneficial during storms at sea)*
★ *Pearls*

Bladderwrack Spell (1)

Bladderwrack is a seaweed that also goes by the name sea spirit—not to be confused with that other seaweed known as sea spirit that also goes by the name agar-agar! Carry bladderwrack for protection when traveling over the water, whether by boat or plane.

 ## Bladderwrack Spell (2)

When traveling by boat, carry extra bladderwrack. Should you run into a storm at sea, make a petition to mermaids and other sea spirits and throw a bit of bladderwrack into the waves.

 ## Boat Protection Spell Eye

Paint eyes on boats, so that they can see where they're going. If yours is a new or particularly valuable boat, this is extra beneficial: these eyes deflect the Evil Eye.

 ## Boat Protection Spell Rope

Pass the entire boat through a rope circle for safety and protection.

Drowning Protection Spell

Various beans (known as St Mary's beans) float across the seas from the tropics of the Western hemisphere to the shores of the Orkney and Hebrides islands. Carrying one of these beans allegedly protects you from drowning.

 ## Dulse Water Spell

Sprinkle dulse onto the waves to calm the sea.

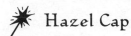 ## Hazel Cap

Create a cap from hazel leaves and twigs for luck and safety while journeying at sea. Wear it if you will, but at least keep it with you.

 ## Ma Zu's Protection

Ma Zu, the Lady of Sailors and Fishermen, began her career as a pious young woman, devoted to Kwan Yin, with whom she still shares altar space. The historic Ma Zu came from a seafaring merchant family and was born in 960 CE on Meizhou Island off Putian in Fujien.

Ma Zu began demonstrating her powers in childhood, demonstrating the ability to rescue people while she lay in a shamanic trance, resembling a coma. Those saved had a vision of a little girl. In life, she was able to send out her spirit to rescue those in danger of drowning at sea. After death, she continues performing miracles. Ma Zu calms typhoons and rescues people from storms and pirates.

1. Burn red candles in Ma Zu's honor before beginning your journey.
2. Invoke her name during an emergency.
3. Should she perform a genuine miracle for you, a vow to visit one of her shrines in China, Taiwan, or Singapore may be in order.

 ## Ocean Safety Mojo Hand

Place three garlic cloves, three pine needles or pine nuts and a pinch of rosemary in a mojo bag, together with a silver charm in the shape of an anchor.

Playing Cards Water Spell

To calm a storm at sea, or at least to provide individual safety, toss a pack of playing cards into the waves as Christopher Columbus allegedly once did.

 ## Rosemary Spell

Rosemary derives its name from rosmarinus, *which means "dew of the sea." Carry it with you for safe travel on the ocean.*

 ## Shipwreck Spell (1)

Among the charges most frequently leveled against European witches was that of causing shipwrecks. Hang garlic from boats to protect against malevolent enchantment.

 ## Shipwreck Spell (2)

Hanging garlic from boats is all well and good if it's your own boat, but what if you're only a worried passenger? In this case, try packing garlic with you to prevent shipwreck. If it's a day trip or ferry ride, stick three cloves in your pocket.

 ## Smooth Sailing Spell

To ensure smooth sailing and sunny skies while aboard ship, exploit an old nautical superstition.

1. Should you find a coin on deck, toss it into the wind before sailing to buy favorable weather.
2. Although not as effective as a genuine surprise find, you can, of course, arrange to *find* a coin in order to fulfill the ritual.
3. Otherwise, make ritual offerings prior to sailing.

 ## Smooth Sailing Talisman

An ancient Coptic talisman invokes Poseidon's blessings of protection while at sea.

1. The required image depicts Poseidon brandishing his trident, with one foot on a dolphin.
2. Draw this on parchment paper (artistic ability not required) and carry in a charm bag.
3. For maximum power, have the image engraved on aquamarine or beryl, the stones that Poseidon holds sacred.
4. Charge and consecrate the talisman before putting out to sea.

 ## Ti Plant Safety Spell

The first Hawaiians traveled from Tahiti via outrigger canoes, so they knew something about water travel safety. Carry ti leaves on your journey. According to Hawaiian tradition, ti plant leaves protect vessels from harm and individuals from drowning.

 ## Tobacco Safety Spell

In South American tradition—and many others—no journey over the water was initiated without an offering to water spirits requesting safe passage. Tobacco is a sacred plant indigenous to the Western hemisphere; use the actual botanical in this spell, not the contents of cigar or cigarette.

Throw real tobacco plant leaves into the water before the start of your journey to receive spiritual protection.

 ## Wormwood Water Safety Spell

Carry wormwood on your journey over water. It allegedly offers magical protection from sea serpents and other creatures of the deep.

⛤ Spirit Summoning Spells

Summoning a person is usually straight-forward. Call them on the telephone, drop them a note. Faxes and e-mails are instantaneous. If you're patient, you could show up on their doorstep and await their inevitable arrival home. But how do you summon a spirit?

Straightforward methods exist as well as more complex ones. There are a lot of ways. Ancient theurgists used to call spirits with spinning tops. Some spirits respond if their name is called while others only respond to elaborate spells and rituals. It's possible to summon generic *"benevolent"* spirits or summon a specific one by name. It is usually wisest to know exactly whom you're summoning.

Some traditions consider that it's safest or necessary to contact a gatekeeper spirit who will then summon the actual spirit for you. Essentially you are summoning a spirit to summon spirits for you. Although whether you choose to do this depends largely upon the tradition you follow, it is a wise practice if you are in the habit of summoning *"generic"* spirits. Summoning spirits without being very familiar with their identity and personality is a little like living in a very busy metropolis, throwing your front door open and inviting just anyone

to enter. Always remember that, as with any guest, it's easier to invite them in than to ask them to leave.

Gate guardian spirits may be petitioned to only permit benevolent or kind spirits through and bar the gate to malicious spirits. These gate guardians include:

★ *Elegba*
★ *Exu*
★ *Hecate*
★ *Hermes*
★ *Maria Padilha Pomba Gira*

These spirits guard the crossroads, permitting and denying access as they deem fit. For more detailed information, check *Unblocking Spells*, page 1006.

Spirits are summoned via:

★ *Fragrance In ancient Egypt, it was believed that every spirit possessed its own characteristic scent, sort of like the ghost in the movie* The Uninvited. *The sudden appearance of the fragrance signaled the spirit's presence. This fragrance becomes a summoning device: when you introduce the fragrance to the*

atmosphere, you're effectively extending an invitation. General magical wisdom suggests that beautiful, aromatic fragrances (gardenia, frankincense, sandalwood) summon beautiful, powerful, benevolent spirits. Likewise offensive, foul, malodorous fragrances summon malicious, mean-spirited, malignant, destructive spirit forces

★ **Altars on which they recognize themselves** *Every spirit has one or more attribute: objects, emblems, birds, animals, minerals or* things *that represent their power or whose essence they share. Manipulating these objects like a tableau extends visual invitations. Hence a glass of spring water and a dish of honey beckons Oshun; she is* sweet water and honey, *each shares the same essence*

★ **Offerings** *In general, spirits are not above bribery but rather consider it their due. Attract their attention and lure them to your side by offering whatever they love, whatever most attracts them and invigorates them*

All Saints Spells

The condition formulation **All Saints Oil** summons benevolent, helpful spirits.

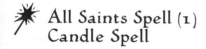

All Saints Spell (1) Candle Spell

Dress candle with the oil. (Carve as desired.) Burn the candle; accompany with prayer, petition and incantations of sacred verses.

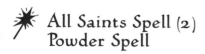

All Saints Spell (2) Powder Spell

*Create **All Saints Powder** by grinding and powdering the botanicals as listed in the* Formulary; *do not add to oil. Sprinkle the powder throughout your home.*

Ancestor Summoning

1. Add one tablespoon of anisette liqueur to a glass of pure spring water.
2. Place it on a table to summon ancestral and other beneficial spirits.
3. That much alone is sufficient; however, to reinforce the spell add photographs of blood relatives, even if they are not the ones whom you call.
4. Provide food or other libations that the ancestors will find hard to resist, whatever is appropriate to your family or cultural tradition, or perhaps serve them whatever you would if they were truly coming to dinner.

Angel Summoning Spells

Angel Summoning: Angelite

Angelite crystals summon angels as well as other beneficial spirits. Place one under your pillow or sleep with it over your chest. Pay attention to dreams, the canvas for many visitations.

Angel Summoning: Angel Water

*Many angels allegedly love the scent of myrtle, the key ingredient in **Angel Water**. **Angel Water** is most famous as an aphrodisiac but may also be used to summon angels. Fill pans and bowls with **Angel Water** and arrange strategically. Accompany by verbally requesting the angel's presence.*

Angel Summoning: Benzoin

Burn benzoin: benzoin incense not only summons angels but induces them to linger. It has the added benefit of repelling malevolent spirits.

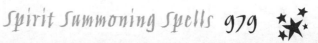

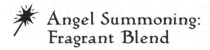 Angel Summoning:
Fragrant Blend

Frankincense beckons angels, benzoin ensures that only the benevolent arrive, and dammar allegedly enables you to communicate with them. Blend all three and burn, wafting the aroma as desired.

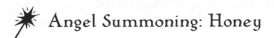 Angel Summoning: Honey

Dishes filled with honey beckon angels and other beneficial spirits.

Angel Summoning: Magic Mirror

1. Light a white or silver candle.
2. Announce your intention and ask for angelic blessings. You may ask for a "go-ahead" signal as to whether to proceed.
3. Sit, relax, burn frankincense or warm its essential oil to extend an invitation and enhance your powers of clairvoyance.
4. Look in your mirror. Pretend you're not looking at yourself but impartially at another being.
5. When this is accomplished, look beyond yourself in the mirror.
6. Stay relaxed: if you are tense, this won't work. Only work for as long as you feel fresh and relaxed; several attempts may be necessary before you accomplish your goal. This technique takes time.
7. Eventually you may see a new face; eventually you may see your guardian angel or another spirit behind your own image. You may see lights. The experience is very personal and varies.
8. Communicate with the presence in your mirror.
9. When you're done, the mirror should be wrapped in dark silk or velvet and kept reserved for this ritual alone.

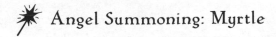 Angel Summoning: Myrtle

Burn myrtle and roses to invoke an angelic presence.

Benevolent Spirits

Sometimes you don't know exactly whom you wish to speak with but you know you want a "nice, kind" spirit. The following, placed on an altar, consistently calls in benevolent spirits:

★ *Althaea*
★ *Braids of sweetgrass*
★ *Cinnamon*
★ *Fires built with rowan wood*
★ *Frankincense*

Black Cat Spirit Summoning

Black cats (or any other cats) are not perceived as evil or unlucky amongst magical traditions. They are perceived as magical creatures: black cats are a favored form for some shape-shifting spirits. In other words, some black cats may be spirits in disguise, making it especially unlucky to harm any black cat. Black cats, in general, are perceived as having special contacts among the spirit world, making them favored familiars.

*   **Black Cat Oil** *calls in the spirits. Dress candles with* **Black Cat Oil** *and burn them to beckon benevolent, magically oriented spirits.*

Crystal Balls

Crystal balls may be used to communicate with the spirits:

1. The crystal ball should be cleansed and ready to use.
2. Cleanse the area and all participants.

3. Create a magic circle on the ground. The medieval sorcerers recommended that the scryer remain in this circle until well after the spirit's departure.
4. Face the east.
5. Summon the spirit from the depths of the crystal ball.

"Demon" Summoning Spells

Classical grimoires summon demons by name for purposes of commanding and compelling. Run down a list of these names and you may recognize them: most of these so-called "*demons*" are ancient, multifaceted deities, among them Astarte, Hecate, assorted Baal's, Leviathan, and others. Is it any wonder that they don't show up or that if they do, they're hostile and volatile, not in the mood to be compelled and commanded? Powerful spiritual entities habituated to human devotion are instead summoned with contempt mixed with fear and treated like menial servants. And if they're not powerful, why bother to summon them?

For best results, don't just stick to the grimoires: instead of summoning, invite and beckon with respect. But if they're not demons, you ask, and if you're not in charge, who are they and why would you wish to contact them? Post-Christianity, spirits were categorized as demons en masse; if you weren't an angel—and sometimes even if you were—then you must be a devil. Here's a sampling of medieval "*demons*."

 ## "Demon" Summoning: Astarte and Asteroth

Astarte and Asteroth are one and the same; Asteroth may be an insulting epithet created by monotheistic Hebrews or a plural for Astarte, indicating her many paths, similar to an orisha's many paths or the Virgin Mary's many manifestations. Astarte means "womb" and may be a title for the Semitic spirit, Anat.

Summon Astarte with lilies and roses. Use henna to adorn hands and feet with images evoking primal female power to beckon her near. Why would you wish to summon Astarte? Because she can provide you with love, fertility, and protection if she chooses.

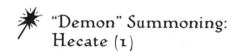 ## "Demon" Summoning: Baal

Baal means "master" or "owner" and may be the title of various Semitic spirits, or may indicate the many "paths" of one, in the manner that a Yoruba orisha has many paths (aspects) yet remains one.

Baal's image summons him, as does fresh fruits, vegetables, grains, arrowheads, hammers, and images of lightning. Why would you wish to summon him? Perhaps because he has been known to stabilize the weather and provide fertility, prosperity, and protection.

"Demon" Summoning: Hecate (1)

Hecate, Queen of Witches, pre-eminent deity of the ancient nation of Caria, Matron of Midwives, and psychopomp maintains office hours only at night: formal petitions and invitations must be offered after dark. A particularly ancient spirit, the only source of illumination she favors is fire.

Summon Hecate at night by a three-way crossroads. Ideally, light your way with a mullein torch. Offer her garlic, lavender, and honey. If you have a dog, bring it with you. Keep an eye on the dog; it's likely to perceive Hecate, who adores dogs, before you do. Why would you wish to contact Hecate? Because she can teach you to do anything in this book. Because she can grant you enhanced psychic powers, fertility, romance, protection, freedom from illness, and magical restitution for any crime committed against you.

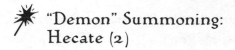 ## "Demon" Summoning: Hecate (2)

An old tip that allegedly makes summoning Hecate easier. Dry dandelion roots, then slice and pierce them to create beads, forming a ritual necklace to wear when calling Hecate. Call—or think—Hecate's name as you pierce, string, and knot each bead.

 ### Directional Invocations

If one invokes protective spirits, one is also effectively casting a protection spell. Their presence provides the protection. Directional invocations place the spell-caster within a circle of protective spirits. This format is ancient, hearkening back to ancient Babylon and Egypt.

Archangel Summoning Invocation

Michael to the right of me
Gabriel at my left
Uriel in front of me
Raphael guards my back

Babylonian Incantation

Sin is not the consequence of evil-doing but is the name of an ancient Semitic moon-god, namesake of the Sinai Peninsula.

Shamash before me
Sin behind me
Nergal at my right
Ninibat at my left

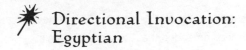 ## Directional Invocation: Egyptian

Isis to the south
Selket to the west
Nephthys to the north
Neith to the east

 ## Djinn Summoning

1. Place a sliver of aloes wood and some dust from a crossroads, ruin, or cemetery into a metal flask.
2. Place the flask onto a square of red silk or felt together with a cleaned sheep's shoulder blade bone.
3. Wrap up the bundle and pierce it with seven silver or bone needles, saying *"I knock on Earth's door to summon the djinn."*
4. Leave the bundle at a place djinn are likely to congregate (see *Elements of Magic Spells)* and wait for a response.

Doll Summoning

Dolls created from wax and other materials have been used from time immemorial for all kinds of magic, benevolent and malevolent alike. Real Vodou dolls are devices to communicate with the lwa or other spirits.

1. Create your own doll: not to dominate the spirit but for increased familiarity, the intimate communication of hands.
2. Decorate the doll with the colors and attributes belonging to them. Hence Ogun's doll would be clothed in black and red and bear a little piece of metal. Wind a key around Papa Legba's waist, or paint dark glasses on Baron Samedi.
3. Arrange the doll on an altar or keep it discreetly wrapped in cloth. When you wish to communicate, speak directly to the doll.

 ## Dragon Summoning

A dragon needs a home; create a lair or cave or peak filled with treasure. The nature of the treasure determines the nature of the dragon. Determine whether your dragon has a solitary nature; if not, add images of other dragons and attractive human figures to keep the dragon company. Light red candles to summon the dragon and offer it candy and sweets.

Elemental Spirits

The concept of Elemental Spirits derives from the mystical physician-philosopher Paracelsus' (1493–1541) attempt to classify spirits according to the natural elements from which he perceived that they emerged. Elementals are understood as the embodiment of Air, Fire, and Water. These el-emental correspondences don't necessarily agree with folkloric, mythological or magical tradition; the Elementals tend to be malevolent although this may reflect the time during which classification and analysis occur—sixteenth-century Europe was not a happy time for spirit–human interaction. Allegedly, elementals are only visible to humans possessing second sight.

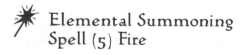 ## Elemental Summoning Spell (1) Air

Elemental spirits of the air are known as sylphs. They are said be extremely volatile in nature. According to legend, sylphs are the souls of those who died in a virginal state. Brooms summon air spirits and may be used as a communications device. A ritual broom should be used and reserved for this purpose. Toss the broom up into the air repeatedly, while focusing on your desire.

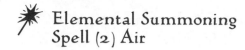 ## Elemental Summoning Spell (2) Air

Wind flower invokes the sylphs. Grind and powder wind flower (anemone, japonica) blossoms, leaves, and stems. Burn it as incense; the fragrance rising in the air will call the spirits.

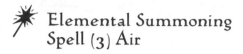 ## Elemental Summoning Spell (3) Air

Carve whistles from alder to summon sylphs and other spirits of air.

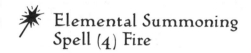 ## Elemental Summoning Spell (4) Fire

Elemental spirits of fire are known as salamanders, not to be confused with the lizard of the same name. Allegedly salamanders can be sighted in the flames, an allegation that has been the source of great pain and suffering to the lizards. Salamanders, the fire spirits, have a reputation as a wrathful bunch.

1. The fragrance of amber attracts and lures the fire elementals.
2. Do not burn beads; amber fragrance refers to perfume formulas that approximate the scent of ambergris, once known as *ambra*.
3. Warm benzoin resinoid, labdanum, and vanilla absolute in an aroma burner.

Elemental Summoning Spell (5) Fire

The aroma of tobacco also calls the fire elementals. Smoke a good cigar, concentrating on the summons. If you don't smoke, use a lit cigar as incense to call the spirits.

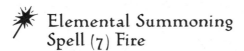 Elemental Summoning
Spell (6) Fire

"Perfumed brandy" is a complex liquid incense is
believed to call in the fire elementals:

1. Fill a cauldron or earthenware vessel with equal parts
   of brandy and spring water.
2. Set the cauldron on the fire and begin to add the
   following ingredients: aloes wood roots,
   aristolochias, benzoin, calamite, cardamoms,
   cinnamon, cloves, cubeb pepper, ginger, Grains of
   Paradise, mace, nutmeg, and storax.
3. Bring the cauldron to a simmer, keeping all doors
   and windows closed (the spirits can enter without
   them) so that the aroma fills the room.

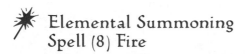 Elemental Summoning
Spell (7) Fire

*This spell may be used to summon any fire spirit or el-
emental. It may also work with Hecate and Oya, both
of whom claim mullein as sacred.*

1. Sprinkle saltpeter into spring water.
2. Dip mullein leaves into this liquid.
3. Hang the leaves upside down to dry.
4. Reserve dried leaves carefully; when you wish to
   summon the spirits toss one leaf at a time into an
   open fire to extend an invitation.

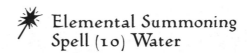 Elemental Summoning
Spell (8) Fire

*According to Greek myth, Prometheus stole celestial fire
by hiding it in a fennel stalk. Gather fennel at Midsummer's Day at the height of the sun's power. Burn it when
you wish to summon fire spirits and elementals.*

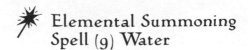 Elemental Summoning
Spell (9) Water

*Elemental spirits of water are known as undines.
Undines are usually understood to be a sort of water
fairy or nymph, although they may also be a sub-genre
of mermaids.*

*Hold an anachitis gemstone in your hand to summon
these elementals. Switch to a second stone, synochitis, to
keep them in place, while you attempt to communicate
with them.*

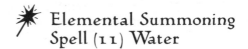 Elemental Summoning
Spell (10) Water

*Place anachitis and synochitis crystals on an altar and
sleep in this room. Allegedly the crystals will summon
the undines, which will appear and communicate with
you in your dreams.*

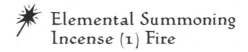 Elemental Summoning
Spell (11) Water

*The crystal gemstone beryl is under the dominion of
Poseidon, King of the Sea. Engrave the image of a
hoopoe bird holding tarragon before it upon a beryl. This
magic talisman will summon the water elementals.*

Elemental Summoning
Incense (1) Fire

*Blend bloodroot, dragon's blood, red sandalwood, and
saffron and burn as incense.*

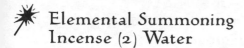

Elemental Summoning Incense (2) Water

Add benzoin resinoid, camphor, myrrh, and true lotus essential oil to an aroma burner.

Elf Summoning (1)

Meet elves in their territory. Stand beside or beneath elm trees and elecampane to summon the elves. Focus on your desire and wait for them to arrive.

Elf Summoning (2)

As an alternative, persuade elves to enter your territory: grow or maintain copious quantities of rosemary; eventually the elves will come to you.

Elf Summoning (3)

Like fairies, djinn, and humans, some elves are nicer than others. Benevolent elves live within the presence of larch trees. Burn larch resin and needles to invite their presence.

Fairy Summoning Spells

The category of *"fairy"* is so complex that fairy summoning can be very confusing. Flower fairies—tiny, winged, and less volatile than other fairies—are what most modern people consider to be fairies, in comparison to the full-size spirits that inhabit fairy tales. Different spells are used to summon different kinds of fairies.

In addition, there's a whole category of *"fairy vision"* spells; rather than summoning fairies to you (fairies don't take kindly to being commanded) they grant you a vision of the fairies. Seeing fairies

may be sufficient for many; experiment if you'd also like to make contact.

Fairy Summoning: Clover

1. Find a four-leaf clover.
2. Lay seven grains of wheat over the clover. Concentrate on your desire.
3. Allegedly the fairies will appear.

Fairy Summoning: Fairy Mound

Many fairies are believed to inhabit hollow mountains, hills, and mounds. Identify the hill, mountain, or mound, and walk around it three times counter-clockwise (widdershins), calling out "Open door!"

Fairy Summoning: Get-away Spell

Should you journey to the halls of Fairyland but are wary of being trapped within, slip an iron or steel needle into the door. This prevents the fairies from closing it, so you can make your get-away if necessary. Discreetly keep needles in your hem to use as needed.

Fairy Summoning: Roses

This spell reflects the defiant nature of fairies. Steal some roses and transplant them into your garden to attract the fairies.

Fairy Summoning: Roses (2)

Pull up roses to summon the fairies. Perhaps "summon" is the wrong word; "encourage to arrive" may be better. According to legend and folk song, the act outrages them and they will appear to you, although whether you'll be pleased to see them in that humor is debatable.

 ## Fairy Summoning: Urban Dweller

Fairies usually resist indoor invitations. This limits access for apartment and urban dwellers. Compensation can be made, however, and the fairies can be persuaded to come indoors. However, some extra seduction is required.

Create a wild area within with bonsai trees, miniature roses and other plants. Scatter seashells and acorns. Ornament with glittering charms. This takes some effort but will eventually work, especially if children are resident.

 ## Fairy Summoning: Woodland

Oak, ash, and thorn trees growing together beckon the fairies. Find a place where this occurs naturally and linger, waiting for the fairies. Or you can create a fairy-friendly landscape by transplanting trees as an open invitation.

 ## Flower Fairy Summoning: Beech

Dry a little beech wood. Powder and burn it as incense outside to call the flower fairies. Because beech also has protective capacities, it should ward off any maliciously inclined fairies.

 ## Flower Fairy Summoning: Foxglove

Create a fairy-friendly garden. Strategically arrange foxgloves (also called "fairy's glove" or "fairy's thimble"). Sit beside them patiently. Allegedly the fairies will eventually appear to you.

Foxglove is very toxic, to the point of fatality, and it is also very pretty and so tempting to children. Use cautiously.

 ## Flower Fairy Summoning: Hazel

String hazel nuts on a cord, focusing on your desires as you make knots. Hang the cord near appropriate summoning plants or within sight of a garden to beckon flower fairies.

 ## Flower Fairy Summoning: Lily of the Valley

Gather lily of the valley flowers. Dry and powder them, then burn them by themselves or in combination with lavender and honeysuckle. This fragrance allegedly summons the flower fairies. (Caution: Lily of the Valley is potentially toxic. Do not ingest.)

 ## Fairy Vision Spell: Calendula

Make a mild infusion of calendula flowers. Soak cotton pads in this infusion. Place one over each eye to be granted a vision of the fairies.

 ## Fairy Vision Spell: Elder

Stand under elder trees at midnight on Midsummer's Eve to be granted a vision of the reveling fairies.

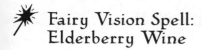 **Fairy Vision Spell: Elderberry Wine**

Drink elderberry wine to see fairies.

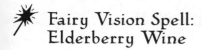 **Fairy Vision Spell: Fairy Dance**

It's not enough to see the fairies; you'd like to join them! This spell offers the opportunity for both.

1. Search for a circle of toadstools or ash seedlings.
2. When you find it, dance around this circle nine times deasil (sunwise) then once widdershins (counter-clockwise).

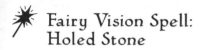 **Fairy Vision Spell: Holed Stone**

Holed stones also create a portal to Fairy Land.

1. Go somewhere where fairies are likely to be found.
2. Look through a holed stone while walking in a circle widdershins three times.
3. If you know exactly who you wish to see, call them politely and respectfully.

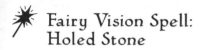 **Fairy Vision Spell: Mountain Realm**

Many fairies are believed to inhabit hollow hills, mountains, and mounds. Fairies are discreet; doorways are invisible. It's difficult to catch sight of them except for a few rare days of the year when the fairies troop.

Comings and goings from the Fairy Mound may be observed on May Day, Midsummer's Eve and Halloween. A few days before, begin preparations: cast intensive cleansing spells, fast as desired, and ornament yourself with protective amulets. Journey to the Mound

and wait. Do not fall asleep. Eventually you will see a troop of fairies departing or returning. If you stay discreetly hidden they will pass you by. However, contact may be made if desired.

 **Fairy Vision Spell: Sorrel**

Sorrel is among fairies' favored plants. Grow sorrel in your garden and gather it frequently as a salad herb; allegedly you'll be granted a vision of the fairies.

 **Good Spirits Oil**

This oil signals your need for spiritual protection.

1. Create Good Spirits Oil by adding essential oils of anise, basil, frankincense, lavender, and myrrh to sweet almond oil.
2. Add angelica root and devil's shoestring to the bottle.
3. Dress candles with this oil and burn, or warm the oil in an aroma burner to summon benevolent spirits to protect you in time of need.

 **Happy Spirit Spell**

Summoning spirits is sometimes a little like waking someone from a deep sleep; they're grouchy and resent being awakened. If you didn't need them, of course, you wouldn't have bothered them: you require cooperation and empathy. Burn marjoram to calm and pacify angry spirits.

King Solomon's Key

King Solomon is believed to have been among the greatest magicians of all time. He commanded a host of djinn and other spirits by various means, including sigils, a magic ring, and incantations. Over the millennia various methods and manuscripts have been credited to this ancient king including the following.

Allegedly if this is pronounced correctly and uttered at the exact right moment (and that's for you to find out!), you too will be granted the power to command celestial beings:

ADOSHEM
PERAI
ANEXHEXETON
PATHUMATAN
TETRAGRAMMATON
INESSENSATOAL
ITEMON

Magic Sword Summoning

Master magician Cornelius Agrippa recommended that the blade of a magic sword be smeared with "juice of mugwort." This may be interpreted as meaning the liquid squeezed from fresh mugwort, an infusion of mugwort, or mugwort essential oil. Anoint the blade and then heat the sword up. It should be possible to see invoked spirits in its blade.

Musical Summoning

According to Chinese magical tradition, the sound of a bamboo flute summons spirits. Carve the name of the spirit you desire into a flute—each spirit must have its own.

Notre Dame Water

Notre Dame Water *beckons consistently beneficial, happy spirits and is a safe summoning agent. Add some of the formula water to a spray bottle and diffuse throughout the home. Alternatively, asperge from an open dish.*

Open Your Eyes Spell

General metaphysical wisdom suggests that we are always surrounded by lingering spirits. It's not that they're invisible; it's that most of us lack the capacity to see them. This spell allegedly enables you to see the spirits that surround you.

1. Place a magic mirror on the floor or on a low table, propped up or standing so that you can comfortably see within it.
2. Arrange a white candle on either side.
3. Sit on the floor a few feet from the mirror. (Don't hunch up over it; this works best when intent but relaxed.)
4. Gaze into the mirror for at least three hours; images will appear.

Oracle Sage

According to Aztec folklore, oracle sage is a gift from the spirit realm so that humans might contact and understand them at will. Consider what you need to know; then burn the herb, inhaling its fragrance.

Now that you've summoned them, what will you do with the spirits once they've actually arrived? When company is invited, it's normally polite to have a little something for them to eat or drink. Many spirits have personal preferences, however if you are at a loss as to how to offer welcome, respect, and appreciation, allegedly virtually every spirit will accept offerings of fresh peppermint. There are two modes of presentation; choose what seems more appropriate:

 ## Peppermint Present: Fragrant Steam

Fill a cauldron with water and add fresh peppermint. Place the cauldron over a source of fire and warm it so that the aroma permeates the area.

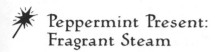 ## Peppermint: Fresh Offering

Remove peppermint leaves from their stems. Place them in an attractive bowl and set on a table or altar.

Sigil Spirit Summoning

In many traditions, each angel or spirit possesses a specific standardized visual image that, when drawn or posted, contains the power to summon that spirit. These images are known as *sigils*. Sigils are typically drawn within a circle and may be representational or completely abstract. Sigils serve two purposes:

★ *They request a specific spirit's presence: whether that request is a "command" that the spirit is bound to obey or merely an explicit invitation depends upon the metaphysical tradition to which one subscribes*
★ *Contemplation of the image (in the manner that one contemplates a mandala) reveals the essence and nature of the spirit. Ezili Freda Dahomey's sigil (or vèvè in this tradition) incorporates a heart pierced with a sword or dagger, for instance*

Although the term sigil derives from European magic and ostensibly recalls the magical seals of King Solomon, the vèvè of Haitian Voudou serves similar purposes, although Voudou tends to be far more respectful and polite to its spirits than is typical for medieval European spirit-summoning sorcery. Many other metaphysical traditions also incorporate these visual summoning charms: runes may be used in a similar fashion, if desired.

 ## Sigil Spirit Summoning: Traditional

Angel and demon-beckoning sigils are reproduced in grimoires; vèvè designs are reproduced in books devoted to Voudou and Quimbanda.

1. Find the desired image.
2. Carefully draw it, while concentrating on your intent, on to parchment or fine paper. Magical inks are traditionally used.
3. Post it or place the image on your altar. Surround with charged, burning candles.

 ## Sigil Spirit Summoning: Personal Communication

Sigils may have been inspired by the spirits but their creation derives clearly from human hands. Magic is not static; the most powerful sigil can be the one you create yourself. The expression of your heart is often the surest, quickest mode of communication.

1. Contemplate the nature and identity of the spirit you wish to summon.
2. Allow yourself to be inspired so as to create a sigil dedicated to that spirit alone.
3. This sigil may be drawn on paper, but it may also be drawn onto the floor using powders or expressed via a tableau. Consider the nature and tastes of the specific spirit in order to determine the proper materials.

Specific Spirit Summoning

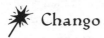 ### Chango

Arrange six beautiful bright red apples in a bowl. Place them on the hearth or within the fireplace, accompanied by a glass of rum or aguardiente, to summon the orisha Chango.

 ### Freya

Plant primroses to open the door to Freya's magical hall.

Hermes Summoning Spell

Hermetic magic, a complex system of enchantment, is named in honor of Hermes, the sorcerer's patron. This trickster spirit has gone through many permutations and wears many masks; however he began his incarnation as a provider of fertility and prosperity in the Greek countryside.

The most ancient, simplest method of summoning him still works. Erect a pyramid of stones (a "herm"), concentrating on your desire, as you place each one. This may be done anywhere—a small herm may be created from pebbles on your desk—however for optimum power, build one at a four-way crossroads.

Hulda (Mother Holle)

Hulda, affectionately known as Mother Holle, navigates many worlds: an ancient Northern European deity of love, sex, magic, fertility, and death, she is linked to elves, fairies, the Norse spirits, and the Wild Hunt. Post-Christianity, Hulda earned a reputation as among the most persistent Queens of Witches, alongside the more famous Diana and Freya. Elder is her sacred tree. Burn elder twigs and leaves to call her, or use an elder wand.

 ### Mermaid Summoning

Throw bladderwrack, also known as sea spirit, into the waves. Call the mermaids aloud or sing for them.

Ogun Summoning Spell (1)

The orisha of iron, Ogun, is beckoned by iron itself. Place two pieces of iron together: this can be as simple as two crossed nails or as elaborate as you'd like. Drizzle the iron with red palm oil.

 ### Ogun Summoning Spell (2)

Burn dragon's blood incense to summon Ogun and other spirits of iron.

Pan

Goats have been instrumental in the discovery of many prized treasures. Their fragrances summon the goat-god, Pan. Blend labdanum, myrrh, and spikenard and burn them, wafting the aroma as needed. Burn purple candles and set out two steaming fragrant cups of coffee: one for you and one for Pan.

Spirit Summoning Aromas

According to general metaphysical wisdom, beautiful fragrances summon benevolent, friendly powerful spirits; foul odors attract those with evil intent.

Spirit Summoning Aroma (1)

Blend essential oils of angelica, frankincense, and rose in an aroma burner and allow the fragrance to permeate.

Spirit Summoning Aroma (2)

Burn amyris, sandalwood, and red sandalwood to attract benevolent, beautiful spirits.

 Spirit Summoning Aroma (3)
Fragrant Blend

This fragrance blend allegedly summons spirits while enhancing your psychic power, so that you are better able to apprehend and communicate with them when they do turn up. Blend frankincense, lavender, mastic, and orrisroot, burning it and allowing the aroma to permeate an area.

 Spirit Summoning Aroma (4)
Loving Blend

Strategically arrange gardenias, lilies, mimosa, and jasmine so that their aroma permeates an area, calling in loving spirits.

 Spirit Summoning Aroma (5)
Mystery Blend

The sacred resins copal and benzoin come in a variety of colors, each believed to possess subtle differences. Copal and benzoin both attract benevolent spirits and repulse the malevolent, so one can experiment with some safety. Collect as many variations as possible. Burn them in various combinations and see who shows up.

 Spirit Summoning Aroma (6)
Sweetgrass

Burn sweetgrass, especially prior to ritual and ceremonies, to invite benevolent spirits to attend.

 Spirit Summoning Oil

The following essential oils in combination invoke beneficial spirits: essential oil of lavender and essential oil of sandalwood. There are two modes of use, which may be combined:

★ Anoint behind the ears, behind the neck or over the Third Eye area
★ Place the blend in an aroma burner and diffuse the scent through the area

 Spirit Summoning Spell

A generic technique to summon spirits; this spell is most effective if cast during the waning or Dark Moon. Crush willow bark and blend it with sandalwood powder. Burn this outdoors while focused on your goal and desire.

 Spirit Summoning: Saint
John's Eve

A magic mirror creates a threshold between realms. This simple spell, designed to be cast outdoors, creates a similar portal to the realm of spirits. It can only be accomplished on Saint John's/Midsummer's Eve.

1. On Saint John's Eve stand atop a tree stump.
2. Bend over and look between your legs.
3. In this position, call to the spirits. (Name the specific one you desire.) "[Name] Please come to me, not as a creature, not as an animal, not as a bird, not as a tree but in the same shape as me." (Amend the incantation as needed to suit your personal desires.)
4. For the best possible outcome, have a gift prepared and waiting.

Spirit Journey

Rather than summoning spirits, it may be easier to go to them. Among the most auspicious meeting places are the following:

★ *Any isolated place of great natural beauty*
★ *By living water: a swamp, a stream, a river, the beach*
★ *Caves*
★ *Cemeteries*
★ *Crossroads*
★ *In the shade of a nut tree*
★ *Ruins*

Take a gift with you, and consider why and who you're hoping to meet.

Summoning Demons

Of course, historically, people have also wished to communicate with less benevolent spirits.

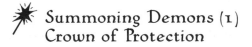

Summoning Demons (1)
Crown of Protection

A recommendation from the medieval sorcerers: wear a crown or wreath woven from vervain when summoning demons and other fearful spirits to provide power and protection.

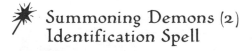

Summoning Demons (2)
Identification Spell

Well, you've summoned them but these demons seem like a pretty quiet bunch. How do you know they're really there? You'll need a placenta delivered by a black cat. Roast a black cat's placenta. Pulverize the ashes and rub them into your eyes to see invisible malevolent spirits.

Don't try this at home! This ancient Jewish spell is reproduced for historic purposes only: rubbing anything into your eyes cannot be recommended. If the demons are present, demons being what they are, one assumes that eventually they will make themselves known.

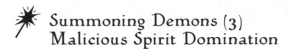

Summoning Demons (3)
Malicious Spirit Domination

Shape-shifting or invisible spirits can allegedly be forced to reveal their true form by smearing them with blood.

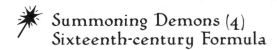

Summoning Demons (4)
Sixteenth-century Formula

Attempts to summon demons may have been more dangerous than the demons themselves. The following are ingredients from one sixteenth-century formula, some innocuous and some not: black poppy juice, coriander seeds, deadly nightshade, hemlock, henbane, parsley root, and sandalwood. Again, do not attempt this spell. It is reproduced for historic purposes: it is chock full of toxic ingredients, which should not be handled.

Unicorn Summoning

True unicorn root may be used as a visionary summoning device for those who work with unicorns. (Another very powerful botanical goes by the name false unicorn root.) True unicorn root is extremely endangered, becoming as rare as unicorn sightings. Grow your own if you'd like to work with it.

Surround yourself with images of unicorns if it helps; otherwise affix your goals and desires in your mind. Hold onto a piece of unicorn root during psychic journeys. This piece of root may be used indefinitely, however, reserve it for this magical purpose. Wrap it in white satin in between uses.

Unicorn Summoning Trees

Unicorns allegedly congregate where apple and ash trees meet. Create a unicorn-friendly grove of trees and keep your eye out for appearances.

 Vila Spirit Summoning

The vila are complex Eastern European forest spirits, seemingly a blend of fairies and valkyries. These spirit guardians are frequent objects of fear, although this may indicate fear of female power in the eye of the beholder—they provide justice to spurned, scorned, abused women.

Why would you wish to summon them? Because the vila are masters and sometimes teachers of shape-shifting magic, because they are masters of herbalism and have been known to reveal miracle cures, because they're justice spirits who care about forgotten, injured women and animals, because they protect wild nature, and because dancing in the forest with them is allegedly fun and empowering. How's that for starters?

The vila can't be summoned; you must journey to them.

1. Enter the forest, during a Full Moon, bringing with you several horse hairs, a horseshoe and horse manure. Search for a natural clearing: a vila dance floor.
2. At twilight, put the horse manure on the ground, hold the horsehair in your left hand and place your right foot on the horseshoe.
3. Call the vila; clearly, concisely and explicitly express your desires, why you're summoning them.

Vila may also be persuaded to reveal occult and herbal secrets and the location of hidden treasure. Offer them round cakes, fresh fruit, vegetables, and flowers in the woods or at wells and caves.

Theft, Lost Objects, and Missing Persons

Spells for the Victims of Theft

Anti-theft Spells

Prevention of theft may be easier than regaining possession of stolen items:

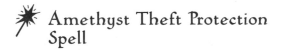 Amethyst Theft Protection Spell

Wearing an amethyst allegedly protects against pickpockets and other thieves.

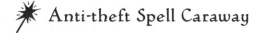 Anti-theft Spell Caraway

Burn caraway seeds as incense in the home. This allegedly prevents the theft of possessions.

 Garlic Theft Protection Spell

*Perhaps it's no surprise that garlic is the primary ingredient in **Four Thieves Vinegar**. Hang braids consisting of a dozen garlic bulbs each at gateways to your home.*

Gentian Theft Protection Spell

Keep gentian in your pockets and purse to protect yourself from thieves of all kinds, including cheaters and embezzlers.

Hyssop Theft Protection Spell

Grow hyssop around the home to repel thieves.

Key to Safety Spell

This spell to protect and fortify your home's defenses requires a collection of keys. How many? At least one for every door in your home.

1. Beginning at your front entrance and ending at the back door, walk through your home.
2. At each and every door, stop. Take one key and touch it to the door, murmuring:
   Key, lock out thieves in the light.
   Key, lock out thieves in the night.
3. Repeat until a key has been touched to each door.
4. When the process is complete, tie all the keys together with a red ribbon.
5. Hang them over the front door.

 ## Licorice Theft Protection Spell

This spell utilizes the licorice herb, not the candy named after it. Stick a licorice stick in each corner of your property, like a stake, to protect against break-ins, theft, and vandalism.

 ## Southernwood Anti-theft Spell

Southernwood protects against thieves. Carry a twig as a talisman, and place southernwood twigs beside items requiring protection.

 ## Vetiver Home Protection Spell

Create an infusion by pouring boiling water over vetiver roots. Strain and use the liquid to cleanse your home, concentrating on doors, windows, and vulnerable areas, to set up a magically protective boundary against robbery.

 ## Vetiver Personal Protection Spell

Add essential oil of vetiver to your bath to set up a magical aura of protection against thieves.

Start the Search Spells

 ## Beryl Spell

1. Hold a beryl in the same hand in which you would hold your missing object.
2. Focus upon the object and your desire for its return. Visualize the object then let your mind clear.
3. Let the beryl transmit thoughts, clues, and advice to you: pay attention to spontaneous thoughts and inspiration.

 ## Directional Spell (1) Animal

This spell operates under the assumption that animals know more than they're capable of telling but that given a system of communication, important details may be revealed.

1. Draw a circle of grain. This spell is typically cast with a rooster or mouse, hence the grain, but adjust it to fit the needs of your own animal helper.
2. Place the animal in the center of the circle, gently turn him or her around a few times, as though playing Blind Man's Bluff, and then let the creature go where he or she will.
3. The direction taken indicates the direction where the search for your missing article should begin.

 ## Directional Spell (2) Axinomancy

The divination method, axinomancy, may be used to locate thieves and stolen property.

Thrust a hatchet into the ground, its head down and its handle rising perpendicularly in the air. Everyone present dances vigorously around in a ring until the handle totters and falls to the ground. The end of the handle will indicate the direction where the search for the thieves and/or stolen articles must begin.

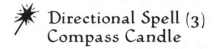 Directional Spell (3)
Compass Candle

"Compass candles" are tapers that drip excessively, the type that used to be placed in Chianti bottles so that they would become covered with wax. Beyond scenic ambience, these candles may be used to magically determine where the search for lost or stolen articles should begin.

1. Hold the candle in your hands and charge it with its mission.
2. Place it in a holder on a flat surface.
3. Determine the cardinal points: north, south, east, and west. Be very clear about this so that there is no confusion or argument later.
4. Burn the candle.
5. The drippiest side of the candle, the one with the waxen waterfall, indicates where your search should begin, although not necessarily where the article will be found.
6. If a direction cannot be determined, this indicates that the direction is as yet unclear: crucial information is lacking. Further research and consideration are needed.

 Directional Spell (4) Crossroads

Spin around at a crossroads until you're so dizzy you fall down. The direction your head points when you fall is where you should begin your search.

 Directional Spell (5) Dog

Induce a dog to reveal details of your theft. This spell necessitates locating a dog within a home or behind a gate. The dog does not need to be your own although it could be. The key is that the dog needed for this spell should be a dog that doesn't bark without provocation, not one of those dogs that won't stop barking as soon as anyone approaches.

Gently knock on the door or gate with a hammer, saying, "Bark dog, bark. Where is my _____?" Pay attention to which direction the initial bark comes from. This is a clue as to where to begin your search.

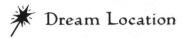 Dream Location

To locate missing or stolen articles:

1. Combine heliotrope blossoms and bay laurel leaves.
2. Fold them into a white cotton handkerchief or sew them up into a flat sachet. Watch out for a bay leaf's sharp points!
3. Place the sachet under your pillow.
4. Pay attention to your dreams and spontaneous thoughts in order to shine a light on the location of your object.

 Frau Wachholder Stolen
Property Recovery Spell

Frau Wachholder, Guardian Spirit of the Juniper, is a German tree spirit. Request her assistance for the return of stolen property.

1. Write a petition or compose one in your mind.
2. Gently bend a lower branch of a juniper tree or bush toward Earth and secure it there with a stone. Do *not* break or injure the tree. (Bring lots of water as a libation and peace-offering just in case you do.)
3. If you have a written request for Frau Wachholder, slip it under the stone.
4. Demand that the thief hear your call and return your property.
5. Allegedly the thief and/or the property will be brought to you via Frau Wachholder's interventions. When this is done, remove the stone and release the branch. Offer libations and a gift. Vowing to plant more junipers is effective.

Golden Rod Divining Spell

Hold a golden rod bloom in your hand. Concentrate on what's lost or hidden but keep your eye on the golden rod. Allegedly the flower will "gesture" in the direction your search should begin.

 ## Horseshoe Spell

Despairing of ever seeing your lost articles again?

1. Finding a horseshoe is an auspicious, encouraging sign from the universe regarding the reappearance of missing articles. Keep an eye out for unorthodox horseshoes, too, like charms, jewelry or images in addition to "real" horseshoes.
2. Drive the horseshoe into your fireplace so that it is fixed firm.
3. Visualize what was lost back in your hands.

 ## Locate Missing Objects Spell

To locate missing persons and objects let three drops of blood from your left middle finger fall onto the nail of your right middle finger. The manner and pattern in which they drop is believed to reveal significant information regarding where the missing item or person will be found.

 ## Mallow Magic Path Spell

Place mallow leaves in your shoes. They'll allegedly cast a magical path toward missing objects or treasure.

 ## Missing Object Spell: Lost Keys

Keys seem to be the object most likely to be lost. Saint Zita is the matron saint of lost keys. Appeal to her to find them quickly. Saint Zita, a thirteenth-century Italian saint, spent her entire life serving one family as a housemaid, although she spent all her time ministering to the poor, giving away her employer's clothing and food as she deemed necessary. Her employers were frequently displeased with her; apparently Zita considered her employment to be a source of penance.

A humble saint, Zita requires no elaborate offerings or complex rituals. If your keys are missing, chant:

Zita, Zita
I've lost my key!
Look around please
And bring it to me

Should Saint Zita perform a large favor for you, her offering of choice is a contribution to the poor or homeless in her name.

 ## Queen's Delight Search Spell

Queen's Delight Root is believed to possess divinatory power. Burn the root; the direction of the resulting smoke allegedly recommends the direction to begin your search.

Regain Stolen Goods

A wax image may be created to stimulate the return of stolen goods. The theory behind this spell is that angels despise theft and will assist your attempts at recovery:

1. Prick a wax figure made to represent the thief.
2. Allegedly, your guardian angel will transfer the pain to the guardian angel of the thief, who in turn passes on the pain to the thief directly.
3. The thief will subliminally associate the pains with the theft (pangs of guilt?) and return the goods in order to stop the pain.

Regain Stolen Money Spell

Burn pine incense to regain stolen money.

1. Rub a drop of essential oil of pine on your hands.
2. Use another drop to dress a pinecone.
3. Hold it over your head and twirl it around sunwise, requesting that the stolen money be returned.

You may also fashion a wreath of pine needles and wear this on your head while you request the money's return. No need to dress with oil.

Silver Cord Spell

Spells that rely upon nothing more than your own magical powers seem simple and uncomplicated but can be extremely difficult. Be patient and practice; visualizations strengthen with time and experience. (Adjust the visualization so that it suits you; if the concept of something emerging from your naval is distasteful, consider what works better for you.)

1. Visualize the object that is missing.
2. Visualize a radiant silver cord emerging from your naval and attached to that object.

3. Visualize the cord reeling the object toward you.
4. Allegedly the object will return to you within a few days.

Vervain Search Spell

Charge vervain with your quest. Wear it within an amulet bag; allegedly it will help you find what you search for.

Reveal the Thief Spells

Reveal the Thief Spell

Place a tiny bit of the same material as what was stolen in the hearth or stove. Allegedly this makes the criminal writhe with pain. In a small community this leads to quick identification of the thief.

Reveal the Thief: Balls of Clay

Discover the identity of the thief:

1. Knead little balls of clay. Inscribe the name of a suspect on each.
2. Leave one blank, to indicate someone you haven't yet suspected.
3. Drop them into a pot of water.
4. Recite Psalm 16.
5. Command aloud: *"Reveal who stole _____ [name the items]."*
6. The first ball to rise up to the top of the water indicates the thief.

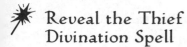

Reveal the Thief Divination Spell

1. Burn benzoin incense to prime the psychic faculties.
2. Pour a little black ink into the palm of your hand.
3. Let your mind be blank, then gaze into your palm and search for clues as to the identity of the thief and the present location of what is rightfully yours. (Do not expect to see the literal image in your palm, although nothing is impossible. Keep your mind in a meditative state and let inspiration and knowledge happen.)

Reveal the Thief Dream Spell

Place calendula blossoms beneath your pillow to dream the identity of your thief.

Reveal the Thief Spell: Fast of the Black Hen

To discover a thief and recover lost articles.

1. First you need a black hen.
2. For nine Fridays, both you and the hen must fast. (There are different interpretations of the word fast, from total abstention from food and drink to limiting the diet to plain bread and water. Interpret as you will: remember the goal is not to harm either the hen or yourself.) While fasting, concentrate on the theft: focus on the return of the goods and on the thief's identity being revealed.
3. If you are very angry, you can focus on the thief being punished should restitution not be made. This spell is as positive or negative as you make it.
4. At the end of the nine Fridays, the thief will allegedly feel compelled to reveal his or her identity and return the plunder. Should he or she resist, terrible calamities will allegedly befall him.
5. Once the fast is over, you and the black hen must return to your normal lives.

Reveal a Thief Spell: Iron

In certain parts of the world, sacred oaths are sworn on iron in the same manner that they are sworn on the Bible or Koran. That sacred quality is expected to induce a thief to identify him or herself.

1. Place an anvil at a crossroads or in front of your home.
2. Place salt, bread, and a white candle on top of the anvil.
3. Light the candle.
4. Everyone even remotely suspected or implicated in the theft must temporarily contribute an iron tool. These are placed around the anvil.
5. The victim of the theft adds another lit white candle to the anvil and asks the guilty party to step forward and claim responsibility.
6. The ritual demands that should the guilty party now step forward and confess and either return the property or make amends, then the slate is clean and the case is closed. The ritual is immediately concluded with forgiveness, peace and at least an attempt at no hard feelings. If, on the other hand, it is unclear whom, if anyone, is the thief then each person present kisses the anvil, the bread, and the candles. Each picks up his or her own tool and strikes the anvil with it. Together everyone curses the thief, wishing him or her misfortune until that time when he or she confesses and makes amends.

Reveal the Thief Spell: Queen of the Meadow

This spell reveals a thief's gender for easier identification.

Toss a Queen of the Meadow root into water. If it sinks, your thief's a man. If, however, it floats, your thief is a woman.

Reveal the Thief Powder

Grind equal quantities of galangal root, vetiver, poke-root and hydrangea blossoms and blend them together. Sprinkle the powder where the theft occurred or where whatever was stolen was last seen. The thief's identity should become apparent shortly.

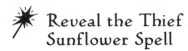 ## Reveal the Thief Sunflower Spell

Place three sunflowers under your pillow to dream of your thief.

 ## San Cipriano Theft Revenge Spell

This spell will not bring your property back, nor will it locate or identify the thief. Instead it's a pay-back spell that allegedly causes the thief to suffer.

1. Carve a white candle so that it is reversed: slice the top off the candle, flattening that end and expose the wick on the bottom so that it may be lit.
2. Dress the candle with substantial quantities of **San Cipriano Oil** and roll it in salt.
3. Talk to the candle; describe your loss, the injustice done and what you perceive the thief deserves, then light the candle.

Spiritual Detective Services

Sometimes you need a bit of professional help.

 ## Saint Anthony's Detective Service Spell (1)

Saint Anthony is the legendary hero who returns and locates missing or stolen objects.

Various rhymes exist to serve as a petition. Here's one example:

Tony, Tony, look around!
Something's lost and must be found!

Many swear that uttering the rhyme is sufficient. There are others who, disrespectful as it may seem, prefer to turn an image of Saint Anthony upside down in the belief that this discomfort causes the saint to work harder.

 ## Saint Anthony's Detective Service Spell (2)

The Totonac people of Mexico have a variation on this theme. Their version of the Saint Anthony spell suspends the saint in mid-air:

1. Attach a cord to St Anthony's image and use it to hang him upside down, with his head in the air.
2. Remove the cord and turn him right side-up when the item has been returned.
3. Give Saint Anthony a finder's fee.

San Cipriano Spell

There are two martyred Saint Cyprians, both allegedly converted magicians who renounced the enchanted arts for Christianity. There are no records to demonstrate whether this is true, however, following death at least one of the Saint Cyprians seems to have reverted to magical ways. Saint Cyprian is the patron saint of magicians. As San Cipriano, he is the most influential force in Iberian magic. The influence has spread to

Spain and Portugal's former Western hemisphere colonies. San Cipriano is a wonder-worker, a master magician, who reconciles lovers, offers spiritual protection, locates buried treasure, and finds lost or stolen articles. The condition oil named in his honor expresses his power.

1. Hold a brown candle, charging it with your desire.
2. Carve it with your name, identifying information and information regarding what needs to be found.
3. Dress the candle with **San Cipriano Oil.**
4. Burn it.

Three Magi Spell

This spell may be used to locate missing persons as well as missing objects: the Magi were able to follow a star in order to locate Baby Jesus in the manger. Let them inspire your powers of detection.

1. Use the names of the three Magi to create a sigil. This sigil is believed to produce dreams providing clues, directions, and answers.
2. Inscribe the names *Caspar, Melchior,* and *Balthazar* onto a beeswax tablet.
3. Put it under your pillow.

To Catch a Thief

A Japanese foot print spell encourages the capture of thieves.

Following a home robbery, find and gather up the thieves' footprints completely.

Let the police complete their investigations before you gather them but note which footprints belong to the thieves and which to investigators and onlookers. Burn mugwort in the dirt. This encourages the guilty parties' capture by police and prevents the thieves from getting far away easily or painlessly.

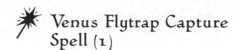

Venus Flytrap Capture Spell (1)

If the thief's identity is known to you and you would like either to contact him or see him captured, write his or her name or other symbols that resonate for you on a tiny piece of paper. Feed it to a Venus flytrap. If the plant accepts the paper, the thief will be caught.

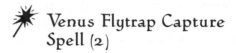

Venus Flytrap Capture Spell (2)

Perhaps the thief's identity is unknown or even irrelevant. You want your stuff back.

Draw a symbolic representation of your stolen object on a tiny bit of paper. Feed it to a Venus flytrap for it to be returned to you.

Treasure Hunter's Spell

Searching for treasure? Find it using the technique of axinomancy.

1. Heat the head of an axe until red hot, then place the axe so that the edge stands perpendicularly in the air.
2. Balance a round agate on this edge. If it stays in place, there's no treasure. The divination is over. If, however, it rolls away, the treasure exists.
3. Replace the agate on the axe-head, two more times for a total of three times. If each time, the agate rolls to the same spot or in the same direction, you have been given instructions as to where to begin your search. But if the agate rolls in a variety of places and directions, the treasure *does* exist but you must search for further information.

Spells For Thieves

Door Unlocking Spells

Why are these spells here? There are many, many good reasons that have nothing to do with theft for why one would need to open a locked door to which one does not have a key. Of course, should one possess the right to enter, summoning a locksmith might be easier. Just in case, however, you find yourself outside a locked door without a key, without anyone willing to let you in, and without access to a locksmith, let's hope that you're carrying lotus root or moonwort, or (better still) chicory.

Door Unlocking Spell (1) Lotus Root

Place a lotus root beneath your tongue. Face a locked door and say "Sign Argis." Allegedly the door should open.

Door Unlocking Spell (2) Moonwort

Place a bit of moonwort into a keyhole to loosen the lock

Magical Key Spell

Chicory allegedly removes obstacles. If gathered correctly, it may open locks. Silently gather chicory on Midsummer's Eve at midnight, or on Midsummer's Day at twelve noon, using a golden knife. Dry the plant. Allegedly this will serve as a key to open locks if it is held against them.

The Hand of Glory

This notorious and legendary amulet was reputedly the master item of thieves' magic spells in Western Europe and the British Isles. Allegedly the *Hand of Glory* ensured the sound sleep of anyone inside a house where it was carried, most frequently for purposes of theft. The word *"sleep"* may be used but *"comatose"* is what is meant. People within the house were rendered insensible and immobile, unable to awaken, sleeping like the dead. That's appropriate because the Hand of Glory is the hand of a dead man crafted into a candle.

Crafting a Hand of Glory

Either the left or right hand was acceptable, however the Hand of Glory can only be crafted from the hand of a convicted felon, executed by hanging, preferably at a crossroads and preferably convicted for murder.

The most famous instructions are those suggested by Le Petit Albert, the influential grimoire published in Cologne in 1722:

1. Take the hand of a dead hanged man. Wrap it in fabric and press to remove remaining fluids.
2. Place it in an earthen vase.
3. Grind cinnamon, saltpeter, salt, and peppercorns with a mortar and pestle.
4. Cover the severed hand with the resulting powder. Leave it alone for fifteen days.
5. Then expose the hand to the sun during the Dog Days of Summer until completely dry. (In other words, you have to time this spell—and presumably acquisition of the hand in this era long before refrigeration—to coordinate with the Dog Days.)
6. If the hand is still not completely dehydrated, you may place it in a low, slow oven with ferns and vervain, until this is accomplished.

7. Use the hand as a candleholder. Form candles from the hanged man's fat, virgin beeswax, and "sesame of Lapland."

 ## Hand of Glory Formula #2

Slightly different instructions for constructing a Hand of Glory exist. They are identical until Step 2 above, placing the hand in the earthenware vessel. There it must remain for only fourteen days, covered with salt, nitre, long peppers and what is believed to be verdigris. The rest of the instructions follow as suggested in Le Petit Albert.

Using the Hand of Glory
There were different recommended methods of use for a Hand of Glory.

 ## Long-term Use

Either of these methods was recommended for repeat use of the Hand of Glory:

1. Place a single candle in the palm of the Hand.
2. Attach a candle to each finger.

 ## Single Use Hand of Glory

The digits themselves might actually be set aflame, although this definitely created a single-use hand. Seems like a lot of trouble for a candle that can only be used once? The advantage of this method was that the Hand would then serve as an oracle, providing safety for the thief.

1. To ensure that everyone in the house is asleep, typically one finger was lit for every person in the house. (Presumably it was impractical to rob a building housing a crowd of more than five.)

2. Should one finger, especially the thumb, refuse to light, this indicated that someone was awake or even immune to the spell.

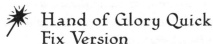 ## Hand of Glory Quick Fix Version

For those who were impatient and eager to use the Hand, there was a quick-fix method foregoing the complex ritual preparations: simply coat the severed hand of a hanged murderer with wax and attach wicks to the fingertips.

 ## Hand of Glory: Really Quick Fix

A version attributed to Central European Romany foregoes the complex ritual and the hanged murderer and the whole hand. All this really quick-fix method requires is the left thumb of a dead person, lying in the grave for nine days, dug up, severed, and used as a candle in order to plunge an entire household into deep sleep.

 ## Hand of Glory Concluding the Spell

Because the Hand of Glory is such a unique, unconventional candle, regular methods of extinguishing the flames can't be used.

1. Immerse the Hand of Glory in milk.
2. Allegedly once the candle(s) are lit, this is the only way to extinguish the Hand of Glory.

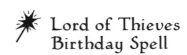

Hand of Glory: Leg of Glory?

Once upon a time, Ruthenian thieves allegedly poured tallow into the hollow of a human shinbone, dug from a grave. The tallow was lit; the thief then marched around the targeted building three times holding the lit "candle" to put the residents to sleep.

Hands of Glory—Hands of Power: The Facts

It's hard to determine exactly how much truth there is in any of this. It was a fairly common accusation during the witch-craze to accuse witches of using a Hand of Glory to break into churches, especially to steal sacramental articles. Virtually all records that survive from the witch-craze were extracted under horrible, merciless torture or reflect the torturers themselves. Was the Hand of Glory a true magical invention or were copycats inspired by witch-hunters' fantasies? Did packs of thieves lurk at the crossroads, battling with each other for the opportunity to remove the dead man's hand? Who can say?

The Hand of Glory may derive from misunderstandings of earlier amulets together with associations of death and sleep. For instance, valerian, a herb with sedative properties is nicknamed *graveyard dust*, because you'll sleep like you're dead. Since ancient days, the image of the hand appears as a protective symbol all over Earth. Today, the image retains greatest popularity in Semitic and Berber areas. The Jewish *hamsa* represents the *Creator's Five Fingers*. The Islamic *Hand of Fatima* represents the hand of the Prophet Muhammad's daughter, although the image with identical usage predates both religions. Italian amulets frequently come in the shape of hands: the fig hand, the horned hand for example. These hands are crafted from metal, wood, or similar and tend to be stylized rather than realistically depicted.

The amulet with the closest superficial resemblance to the Hand of Glory comes in the form of life-sized bronze hands, crafted in the early centuries of the Common Era. Many have survived and are in various museum collections. Some are nothing more than a naked hand, while others are decorated with snakes or pinecones. These hands were sacred to the Spirit Sabazius. Little is known of his cult, other than that snake-handling was involved. Eventually similar, although more elaborate hand amulets were crafted in Rome. Like a Hand of Glory with one candle on each finger, these Roman *Mano Panthea*, Hands of Power, depict an extremely realistic hand with a symbol on each finger.

This Pagan Hand leads directly to the Roman Catholic amulet, the Hand of Power, which resembles the Pagan Hand except that it now bears the signs of the stigmata. *The Mano Poderosa* is still extremely popular in Latin-American spiritual traditions and appears on many commercially manufactured seven-day candles for protection and blessing.

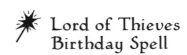

Lord of Thieves Birthday Spell

The seventeenth day of the Chinese eighth month is the birthday of the Lord of Thieves, patron of the light-fingered. He stole food, to keep his mother from starvation.

1. If the stealing has been good, offer him incense on his birthdays.
2. Post no images: he prefers not to be identified.
3. He also doesn't like being trapped indoors: offer him petitions, Spirit Money and incense outside.

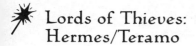 Lords of Thieves:
Hermes/Teramo

 Sleep of the Dead Spell

Hermes, known in Italian as Teramo, sponsors thieves (merchants, too!) providing no violence or murder is planned or intended.

1. Call him by building a pyramid formed from stones at a four-way crossroads.
2. Concentrate on your request for him.
3. Stop up your ears, walk away. Create some sort of signal to yourself as to when to unstop your ears (count to a thousand or when you a red car or whatever).
4. The first words that you hear will indicate whether your petition has been accepted.

Take graveyard dirt from a fresh grave in a nearby cemetery and throw it over the house one wishes to burgle. Allegedly this causes the people within to sleep deeply.

✦ Unblocking Spells

In some versions of the *Sleeping Beauty* story, the handsome prince would very much like to save Sleeping Beauty from her hundred years' sleep but is initially unable because the road leading to her castle is obstructed with thorns. The prince can't pass until, frustrated, he takes his sword and cuts his own path. In other versions of the tale, his sword won't cut; he's unable to pass through the thicket until powerful fairies recognize his predicament and cut a road for him.

That's exactly what unblocking or road-opening spells do.

When your life seems stagnant, when opportunities always seem to peter out, when no viable alternatives seem to exist, when no roads open for you, you may have what is magically known as a blocked condition. Blocked conditions stem from a variety of causes:

★ *Blockages may result from insufficient magic power: your magical gas tank is empty; therefore you can't proceed*
★ *Blockages may be the result of a hex or curse. However the emphasis with* Unblocking Spells *is emphatically on repairing the situation at hand: opening the roads.*

There's little emphasis on who may have placed a hex or on returning it
★ *Blockages may result because you're desperately in need of magical cleansing: too much accumulated negative debris is weighing you down, preventing mobility*
★ *Blockages may result from spiritual causes*

Unblocking spells remove blocks, obstacles, and hurdles, opening the roads so that you can proceed happily with life. Blockages are the opposite of a crossroads. Crossroads offer possibilities of change, motion, and power. Blockages weigh you down, removing avenues of opportunity and limiting you to travel a path not of your choosing.

There are two aspects to unblocking spells:

★ *Specific spirits, magical owners of gates and crossroads, control access on all roads. They determine who passes and who is blocked. These road-opener spirits may be petitioned to remove your particular blockage*
★ *Other spells take advantage of the power of botanicals and magical items to remove a block*

Abre Camino Spells

Abre camino," literally "road opener" or "make way,*" is the name given to a plant *(Trichilia havanensis)* used in Latin American magic to open blocked paths. Carry an abre camino stick with you at all times to keep roads clear and remove obstacles from your path.

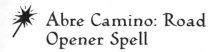

Abre Camino: Road Opener Spell

Bring an abre camino stick to a crossroads. Hold it in your hands, and turn around to face each direction in turn, focusing on removal of all blocks from your pathways. Murmur affirmations, petitions and prayers if desired. Burn the stick and leave coins at the crossroads.

Abre Camino: Road Opener Oil

Abre Camino or Road Opener Oil is a popular condition oil. Supplement with other botanicals as desired. This is the bare-bones formula: potent, concentrated, and effective.

Soak abre camino twigs in olive and jojoba oils. Let the oil mature for one entire lunar cycle before using.

Arabka Soudagar

This oil is indicated when nothing seems to go right, especially for blockages that manifest in regards to love and money.

Add essential oils of anise, bay laurel, cinnamon, frankincense, myrrh, rose, and vetiver to a bottle of sweet almond and jojoba oil, together with a tonka bean. Soak a cotton ball in Arabka Soudagar and carry in your pocket.

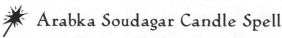

Arabka Soudagar Candle Spell

1. Hold a white candle in your hands and envision all your frustrations and fears.
2. Dress the candle with Arabka Soudagar.
3. Burn the candle in the moonlight; now envision all your blockages vanishing into thin air.
4. Take a cleansing or unblocking bath; put on clean clothes and start afresh.

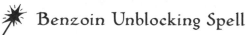

Baduh Spell

Baduh is the name of a benevolent Arabic spirit, responsible for swift transmission of messages. Invoke his assistance by inscribing "8 6 4 2," signifying reversed Arabic script for his name. Place this series of numbers on documents and communications, spiritual and otherwise.

Benzoin Unblocking Spell

Benzoin allegedly melts away blockages. Burn as needed.

Blessing Spell

Request blessings of open paths and plentiful opportunities: blend lilac, rose, and wisteria and burn at midnight every night from the New Moon until the Full. Mark the Full Moon by bathing in salted water. (Add as much sea salt as possible.) Then dress in clean white clothes and go to bed in brand new, never before used, white sheets.

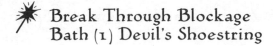

Break Through Blockage Bath (1) Devil's Shoestring

1. Boil devil's shoestring roots in water until the liquid is reduced by half.
2. Strain, cool, and pour over your body.
3. Allow yourself to air dry.
4. Dust with **Fiery Wall of Protection Powder** or rub the protection oil onto your body.
5. Do this daily for seven days, then once a week, and finally once a month as maintenance.

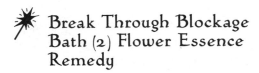

Break Through Blockage Bath (2) Flower Essence Remedy

1. The flower essence remedy Chestnut bud (Bach) is indicated when you're stuck, blocked, or trapped in repetitive cycles with no transformation.
2. Initiate use by taking a single intensive bath: add 20–30 drops of the remedy to the bath before bedtime. Pay attention to your dreams for clues on resolving your blockage.
3. Do not add more than half a dozen drops to any additional baths. Follow the manufacturer's recommendations for internal administration or apply topically.

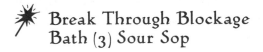

Break Through Blockage Bath (3) Sour Sop

The sour sop, also known as custard apple (Annona genus), is a small tree native to the Congo region of Africa. It also appears in Brazil, where it is known as malolo. *It's used in powerful unblocking baths when a person is absolutely desperate, miserable, oppressed by fate, and at the end of their tether. Make an infusion by pouring boiling water over sour sop leaves. Let it cool, strain and add this to your bath.*

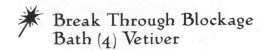

Break Through Blockage Bath (4) Vetiver

1. Create an infusion by pouring boiling water over dried vetiver roots.
2. Allow them to steep. When the liquid cools, add the infused water to a bath.
3. Repeat for nine consecutive days to break blocks, inertia, chains of misfortune, and periods of bad luck.

Citrus Unblocking Bath

1. Collect as many types of citrus fruits, emphasizing the sour ones. There can't be too much fruit in this bath.
2. Quarter each fruit, squeeze the juice into a tub of bathwater then toss in the rind.
3. Add a bottle of orange blossom water or hydrosol.
4. Enter the bath, rub yourself with the fruit, envision your blocks cleansed away and then allow yourself to air-dry. (Depending on the quantity of fruit used, you may be sticky. Leave the fruit residue on for as long as possible before showering it off.)

Larch Unblocking Spell

Larch, a unique evergreen in that it sheds its needles, is the tree of New Beginnings. Burn larch woodchips, resin, and/or needles to liberate blocked energy.

Road Opener Spells

Any powerful and sympathetic spirit can remove a block. However there is a genre of spirits known as "road openers." These spirits are said to "own" roads; thus playing the role of a spiritual gatekeeper they determine who may pass and who can't, whose road will be easy and whose will be obstructed. On the whole, these spirits possess a somewhat sardonic sense of humor; they tend to be volatile tricksters. Their stomping ground, the place to meet them, is invariably that opposite of the blocked road, the crossroads.

Road Opener Coyote

In Native American mythology, Coyote is the trickster who weasels out of all situations, finding opportunities and loopholes where none seem to exist. Coyote leads people into disaster, then rescues them again. Petition or contemplate him to locate hidden pathways.

Burn desert sage and inhale its fragrance deeply. Contemplate images of Coyote and allow inspiration to arrive.

Road Opener Elegba

The most famous and popular modern road opener derives from West Africa, where he is known as Eshu-Elegbara. As befitting a spirit of many disguises, he answers to many names: Elegba, Legba, Papa Legba, Exu (in Brazil), and in his New Orleans Voodoo incarnation, Papa La Bas. Choose the one that suits you.

In West Africa, his most ancient manifestation was as a beautiful young man, demonstrating and maintaining the virility that links him to magical phallic cults.

That manifestation didn't survive the Middle Passage: in the Western hemisphere, Elegba typically manifests either as a young, mischievous boy or as a frail, lame elderly man. Don't let any of the manifestations deceive you: underneath each one, Papa Legba is a trickster who delights in practical jokes and word games, often to the displeasure of his devotees although he can also be a spirit of amazing generosity and protective care.

Papa Legba speaks all languages: speak to him as you will. If you prefer him in the guise of a saint, he'll wear that mask, too. Elegba is identified with Saint Anthony, Saint Peter, the Holy Child of Atocha, and the Anima Sola. Afro-Brazilian traditions sometimes syncretize him with Satan, based on the European folklore that envisioned the devil as a lame, quick-witted, bantering black man loitering at the crossroads.

Papa Legba's days are Monday and the third day of every month. His colors are red, black, and white; his numbers three and twenty-one. He protects infertile women, removing obstacles on the road to motherhood, and he assists the poor whose avenues are limited. Papa Legba stands at the crossroads with his shepherd's crook, where he opens and closes access to life's paths.

 ## Papa Legba Basic Petition

1. Obtain an image of Elegba in any of his guises.
2. Place this behind your door.
3. Feed the image every Monday with a shot of rum, candy, cigarettes or anything that evokes a practical joke.

 ## Papa Legba Doll

Elegba was syncretized to Saint Peter specifically because of the keys Peter holds in his votive image. Keys are magical amulets to unblock life's roads.

1. Create a small doll to represent Elegba: wrap fabric in one of his favorite colors around a stick.
2. Stick a cork on top of the stick to serve as his head.
3. Decorate and embellish as you will.
4. Crown Elegba with a shed rooster feather, if possible.
5. As the final activation, tie a key around his waist, knotting your desire into the cord.
6. Talk to the doll nightly or at least on Mondays. Express your wishes and watch the roads open.

Road Opener Ganesha

Perhaps the most beloved Hindu deity, the elephant-headed Lord of Prosperity and Wisdom is the son of the primal deities, Shiva and Parvati. This patron of good beginnings had an inauspicious start. Born in his father's absence, father and son were unknown to each other and Ganesha grew up devoted to his mother. One day, while Ganesha stood guard while his mother bathed, Shiva returned unexpectedly and attempted to see his wife. Ganesha refused to allow him, and so Shiva cut off Ganesha's head. When the truth of the situation was revealed, Shiva resolved to replace his son's head with that of the first creature he next saw: an elephant. Because he no longer looked *"godlike,"* Shiva decreed that no prayers would begin without first evoking Ganesha. He is traditionally invoked before beginning any endeavor or project, so that he will open the way.

★ *Request Ganesha's assistance with new projects*
★ *If old projects are blocked, ask Ganesha for his late blessing and request that he perform an unblocking for you*
★ *Offer him candy, peanuts and golden raisins*

 Ganesha Plant Unblocking

Collect leaves from 108 different botanicals and offer them to Ganesha. Request that he unblock your path.

Road Opener Hecate

Hecate presides over three-way crossroads. Hecate truly controls all roads: not only does she control avenues of opportunity, she also guards the frontier between the realms of the living and the dead, and the various planes perceptible only with psychic vision.

Hecate's color is black. She only accepts petitions after dark, the only illumination permitted being torchlight. The last day of every month

belongs to her, as do the days of the Dark Moon. These are the best times to request her favor.

 Hecate's Party

1. An ancient method of honoring Hecate was to hold a supper in her honor.
2. Any festive meal may be served, however fish is traditional. Honey and garlic are sacred to her and should be incorporated.
3. Gather everything up and bring it to a three-way crossroads.
4. If appropriate, sit and picnic with Hecate. If not, merely leave her offering at the crossroads. Either way, a plate of food should be offered to her. Leave it there; do not return for any part of it including the plate.
5. Walk away and don't look back. Once the offering is on the ground, it's Hecate's to do with as she pleases. Ancient Christians scoffed that Hecate's suppers were routinely consumed by feral dogs and homeless people rather than by the goddess. However they misunderstood that this is one way Hecate accepts petitions. Don't stop anyone from picking up what has been placed down.

Hecate Charms

Petition Hecate to break your block through the use of her sacred emblems.

1. Hecate's attributes include a key, a broom, a torch, a cauldron, dragons, and dogs.
2. Collect charms representing these images to place on a charm bracelet.
3. This is a spell in progress. Each time you locate a charm, consecrate it to Hecate and request that she unblock your roads.
4. Wear the bracelet or carry it in a conjure bag, especially when free access is needed.

Road Opener Maximon

The traditional votive image of Maximon, primal spirit of male vigor, depicts a man dressed completely in black seated at the crossroads. Maximon has the key to all roads; he opens the door to opportunity and unblocks passages for his devotees.

Create a shrine for Maximon with a votive image as the focal point. Although other images exist, for purposes of unblocking the image of Maximon seated at the crossroads is most potent. Maximon likes gifts and expects to be paid for his services. Serve him rum and Coke, cigars and cigarettes, and offer silk scarves. Light black candles and explain your situation to him.

Road Opener Ogun

Ogun cuts through obstacles with his machete, as if they were blades of grass. He may be petitioned to break through any blockage, open any closed road and create passable roads where previously none existed.

★ *Offer Ogun rum, fine cigars, and dragon's blood incense*
★ *His numbers are seven and three; his colors are red and black*
★ *The best day to petition him is on a Wednesday, however it is traditional never to petition him when bleeding. If you're menstruating, if you cut yourself shaving, save the petition for another day*

Road Opener Pomba Gira Maria Padilha

Few spirits have as strange a history as Maria Padilha. She began her earthly incarnation in Spain as the secret wife of Pedro the Cruel, King of Castile and Leon. She was considered so beautiful that courtiers competed to drink her used bathwater. Her pleasure gardens may still be seen in Seville.

Hundreds of years after her death in the fourteenth century, Maria Padilha re-emerged in Brazil as the most popular and powerful Pomba Gira. Although these spirits derive from Afro-Brazilian tradition, the Pomba Giras embody all the stereotypes of the Iberian Gypsy. Think *Carmen*, just more so. She is a powerful, volatile but generous spirit. In her guise as Maria of the Seven Crossroads, she is a profound opener of roads.

★ *Offerings to Maria Padilha are made at a T-crossroads. No need to stand in the middle of a traffic intersection, it's the bar at the top of the "T" that is her sacred space*
★ *She also accepts offerings at the foot of the large cross in traditional cemeteries or at the cemetery gates*
★ *Her days are Monday and Friday; her colors are red and black; her number is seven*

In Brazil, offerings to her, including burning candles, are left outside at the crossroads so this is specified in her spells. However in other communities, if you're caught abandoning lit candles at a traffic intersection you may be subject to arrest or fine; adapt these spells to suit your needs and situation.

✴ Maria Padilha's Standard Unblocking Spell

The Pomba Gira's spell offerings are detailed and elaborate:

1. Lay red and black cloths on the ground to form an altar at a three-way crossroads.
2. She expects a bouquet of seven long-stemmed red roses. If there are thorns you must remove them by hand. If they have not already been removed, do not ask the florist to remove them for you. If you are absolutely broke, she may accept red carnations in lieu of roses, but remember that she was a queen in life and expects to be treated like one.
3. Offer Maria Padilha a small bottle of anisette (open it for her) or pour her a glass of champagne in a champagne flute.
4. Offer her fine cigarettes; open the box and bring her matches.
5. Light red taper candles or a red and black double-action candle.
6. Tell her precisely what you need (she's another spirit who enjoys practical jokes; be explicit and be careful regarding mixed messages or words with double meanings).
7. If she provides it for you, she'll expect another, larger offering as payment.

✴ Three Road Openers' Super Strength Unblocking Spell

To open one's path and clear a major blockage, invoke Elegba (Exu), Ogun and Maria Padilha simultaneously. This offering is made at midnight at a crossroads.

1. Sprinkle the ground with anisette.
2. Lay down a red cloth; cover it with a black cloth. All offerings and candles should be placed on these cloths. The two male spirits will accept good rum, over-proof rum or cachaca. Maria Padilla likes a small bottle of anisette or a glass of champagne served in a champagne flute. All three appreciate fine cigars and cigarettes.
3. Make an offering to Elegba/Exu of alcohol, candles, and fine cigars or deluxe cigarettes.
4. Make an offering to Ogun. Give him alcohol and a cigar, and light a red or black candle inside a cauldron.
5. Make an offering to Maria Padilha of red roses, red candles, fine cigarettes or cigarillos, and a libation.
6. Talk to the three of them and tell them what you need.
7. Back up seven paces before you turn around; leave via a circuitous route. Do not return to that spot for at least seven days.

For the equivalent of magically dynamiting a blockage, repeat this spell at seven different crossroads all in one night.

Road Opener Saint Expedite

Saint Expedite hates delays. Blockages inspire Saint Expedite to break them. If things are stalled, if there's no forward action, petition Saint Expedite, Patron of Those in a Rush, Spirit of Fast Action. Appeal to him when you need something *now!*

Saint Expedite is traditionally depicted in the guise of a handsome young Roman centurion squashing a crow underfoot. This isn't meant to celebrate brutality toward magical creatures but is actually a visual pun. The Latin crow says *"cras,"* meaning *"tomorrow."* Saint Expedite smashes tomorrow and demands action *NOW* not later.

★ *Offer Saint Expedite a glass of rum and a slice of pound cake. Tell him what you need. Allegedly he likes public testimonials detailing his good works. He is among the spirits most open to bribery*
★ *Some turn him upside down until he gets the job done*
★ *Petition Saint Expedite as you need him ("why wait?" he'd say), but his feast day is April 19th*

Road Opener Teramo

Teramo is the Italian name for Hermes. He sends fast messages to other spirits and between realms but he's more selective than Elegba. Teramo only sponsors those he perceives as his own: thieves, merchants, psychic workers, and those born with the planet Mercury prominent in their natal chart—particularly those with sun in Gemini or Virgo and those born during a Mercury retrograde.

1. Capture Teramo's attention by erecting a small pyramid of stones.
2. Light a candle beside it and talk to him quickly. Unless your petition or proposition is incredibly intellectually stimulating, assume that Teramo's attention span is brief.

Road Opener Xango

In the Afro-Brazilian cult of Umbanda, the orisha Xango is considered an opener of the ways.

1. Venture to a large rock or cliff. Signs of previous lightning damage are very auspicious.
2. Open a bottle of dark beer.
3. Spill about half of it on the ground, forming the shape of a cross.
4. Put a red candle in the now-half-filled bottle. Light it.
5. Petition for what you need.

 ## Road Opening Spell: Mojo Bag

This bag may need to be contained within a second bag to keep the dirt from slipping out.

1. Gather pinches of dirt from seven different crossroads and place them in a red bag.
2. Add salt, an old key, and pebbles or nails found on or beside train tracks.
3. Carry it with you to keep all avenues open.

 ## Road Opening Spell: Oil

1. Start with a coconut oil and jojoba oil base.
2. Add true coconut extract, ground allspice, peppermint, and licorice (not the candy, the herb).
3. This oil may be added to the bath or used to dress unblocking candles.

 ## Seven African Powers Spell

For insoluble problems invoke the Seven African Powers.

1. Name the problem by writing it on a piece of brown paper.
2. Dip it into Seven African Powers oil.
3. Place this inside a small bottle and cover it with black coffee.
4. Invoke the Seven African Powers.

There are commercially manufactured Seven African Powers candles and incenses: burning them to accompany your petition would not be amiss. You may also burn seven individual candles, one in the color of each power (see the table on page 1065 for details), or seven white candles.

 ## Stimulate Change Spell

To stimulate change, movement, and transformation gather a handful of dirt from each of the following places:

The local police department, courthouse, or jail
The local fire department or blacksmith
A crossroads
A butchers shop
A place of higher education

You will need five handfuls in all. Place them all in a red flannel bag together with a High John the Conqueror root to unblock your paths.

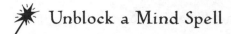 ## Unblock a Mind Spell

Sometimes what needs to be opened is someone's mind, so that that person will be willing to listen to you, to hear you.

1. Carve a skull candle with the name and identifying information of the target of this spell. Choose the color of the skull to suit your purpose: red for romance, green for financial discussion, black if the person is dense or is stubbornly refusing to consider your position. White may be used for any purpose.
2. Dress the candle with **Command and Compel Oil.** Add any other formula oil that matches your needs.
3. Burn the candle.

Intensify the spell by dedicating it to Papa Legba, Opener of the Ways, Eliminator of Obstacles.

 ## Unblock a Situation Spell

1. Charge a peridot, sardonyx, or quartz crystal.
2. Place it on an altar.
3. Focus your desires on the stone.
4. Carry it with you in a lucky charm bag.
5. Recharge it periodically on your altar.

 ## Unblocking Blast

1. Place an incense burner filled with frankincense under a straight back chair. Light it.
2. Sit on the chair, ideally in the nude.
3. Wrap a plain white sheet around yourself, just under your chin. The chair will be covered up as will you, except for your head. Be vigilant for fire safety.
4. Sit for between five and fifteen minutes, focusing on the smoke driving your bad luck away.

 ## Unblocking Spell (1)

Get rid of blocks and bad luck:

1. Go through your home and premises looking for extraneous sharp items: pins, tacks, anything similar.
2. Place them in a jar or bottle.
3. When it is approximately half full, take it outside and bury it, preferably not on your property, but at the least at the absolute furthest edge of your land. Don't dig it up.

 ## Unblocking Spell (2)

When your cross is too heavy to bear and you're sick of being in such misery.

1. Collect a bowl of rainwater or seawater. You can keep it in reserve. It's hard to plan to do this spell: you will know if and when the right time arrives.
2. Cry into the bowl of living water.
3. When you can't cry anymore, take the water and feed a plant with it.
4. Nurture this plant; tell it your desires and dreams.
5. Write your wishes on a piece of paper and bury them together with a small crystal beside the plant's roots.

 ## Unblocking Spell (3)
Crossroads Unblocking

1. Bring bread and a libation to a crossroads.
2. Request that the general assembly of spirits remove obstacles from your path and grant you good fortune and smooth traveling instead.
3. Leave the offering and depart without looking back.

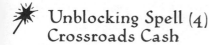 Unblocking Spell (4)
Crossroads Cash

1. Fill a paper bag with candy and pennies. Fill your pockets with additional pennies.
2. Rub this bag over your entire body, from head to toe, not forgetting your palms and the soles of your feet. Ideally this is accomplished while walking to a four-way crossroads, however it may be done at home first.
3. Go to the crossroads; as you reach the first corner, drop three pennies and some candy on the ground, as an offering to the spirits of the crossroads, saying *"I ask you to remove the blocks from my path."*
4. Circle the crossroads, dropping three pennies with candy and repeating your petition at the next two corners.
5. At the last corner, offer *"clean money"* from your pockets and ask the roads to be open to you and filled with good fortune.
6. Lose the bag used for the cleansing, together with the rest of its contents, before you return home.

 Unblocking Spell (5) More
Crossroads Cash

This variation of the above spell may be more discreet and thus easier to accomplish.

1. Fill three paper bags with candy and pennies.
2. Rub each bag over your body, from head to toe, visualizing your blockage dissolving.
3. Keep some extra pennies in your pocket.
4. Carry the three paper bags to the crossroads; when you reached the first corner, simply let one bag slip to the ground. Murmur a request that all blocks be removed and your path become obstacle-free.

5. Repeat at the next two corners, so that none of the bags remain in your possession when you reach the final corner.
6. Drop the pennies from your pocket there and request blessings of open roads with no obstacles to hinder your passage.
7. Return home via a circuitous route.

 Yemaya's Unblocking Spell (1)

Life is filled with obstacles and unhappiness. However Yemaya is the all-powerful mother of all, who desires happiness for her children and will do whatever she can to obtain it for them. To obtain joy and smooth sailing:

1. Go to the beach.
2. Dig a small pit in the sand.
3. Light white and/or blue candles. Make your petition.
4. Enter the water. Greet Yemaya in her guise as mermaid or as a beautiful woman rising up from the sea. Offer her seven white roses.
5. Immerse yourself completely seven times.

 Yemaya's Unblocking Spell (2)

If you can't swim or are afraid of water, you may still petition Yemaya:

1. Sit down in the sand at the waterline.
2. As the waves come in, greet them with your hands, gather up the water from the waves, and toss some over your head, some over your body.
3. Throw seven white roses to Yemaya.
4. Come out of the water without turning your back to the ocean. Let the candles burn out.

✸ Weather Spells

Weather spells are an ambiguous topic. It is extremely personal magic. My desire for a beautiful sunny day may correspond to your need for rain. Will our spells cancel each other's out? Does the most powerful magician win?

Despite these inherent difficulties, *Weather Spells* are among the most ancient magical genres. The most successful weather spells are cast by a community in response to a consensus regarding a weather emergency, typically either too much or too little rain. It was believed that one could summon or banish storms by invoking ancient spirits. In essence the storms and winds are spirits. This belief remains personified in the orisha Oya, who embodies the hurricanes that travel from West Africa to the Caribbean annually. Vestiges of these beliefs linger in the tradition of naming hurricanes; by naming the spirit, a measure of control is maintained.

Magical and spiritual aspects of weather have always been controversial:

★ *Ancient Mesopotamian wind spirits could be destructive, as can the modern Central American "Aires"*

★ *Jews perceived winds as messengers of the Creator, although not all are inherently benevolent*

★ *In the* Odyssey, *Odysseus is given a bag of winds as a divine gift, sealed up with knot magic. When his curious men release the knots too soon, the gift turns to disaster*

★ *According to Saint Thomas, wind and rain could be produced by demons. Hence magicians who offered to sell storms to those who need them*

★ *The earliest ecclesiastic law in England, the* Liber Penitentiales *of Saint Theodore, Archbishop of Canterbury from 668 through 690, was directed against those who caused storms by invoking* "fiends"

Altars for Weather Spells

An open umbrella serves as a fitting altar for rain rituals. A closed umbrella serves as a magic wand. (In Berber magic, snow shovels are used similarly.)

Broom Spells

Brooms are used to communicate with Elemental Spirits of the Air. Create single use ritual brooms for these spells. (See *Elements of Magic Spells* for instructions.)

 ## Broom Spell to Raise Winds

Throw a broom up into the air, preferably from mountaintop or a height. Summon the Air Spirits.

 ## Broom Spell to Calm Winds

Burn the broom once the winds are no longer required. Bury the ashes; don't let any float in the air.

Drought Spells

 ## Drought Spell (1) Dragon Spell (1)

Dragons are believed to impact weather through their control of precipitation. Iron is believed to evoke strong reactions from dragons and is the basis for this spell. The glib reasoning is that dragons fear iron; my interpretation is that iron is the supreme protective metal, to be used as a protective amulet for people when approaching (and disturbing!) such a spiritually powerful creature.

1. In times of drought, should you have access to a *"dragon pool,"* toss pieces of iron into the pool to disturb the dragons, which then take to the sky in form of rain clouds.
2. If you do not have actual, physical access to a dragon pool, visualization may be successful, too.

 ## Drought Spell (2) Dragon Spell (2)

In East Asia, dragons are traditionally considered responsible for rain. In times of drought, pull a dragon's image off your walls where it was comfortable indoors. Place it in the hot sun to fry so that Lung Wang, the Chinese Dragon King, can appreciate the affects of this drought and send some rain.

 ## Drought Spell (3) Mr. Pitiful

1. Find a picture image (drawing or photograph) of the most pathetic person you can.
2. This spell works best if this is a person you do not actually know: the only feeling you should have toward this person is pity.
3. Burn the image. The goal is not to harm the person. The magical theory is that the very Heavens will pity this poor miserable person and pour water down to relieve any further misery.

 ## Drought Spell (4) Psalm 72

This is a spell to charm up some rain from the power doctors of the Ozark Mountains. Face the sunrise. Repeat the sixth verse of Psalm 72 three times:

May he come down like rain upon the mown grass,
As showers that water the Earth.

Drought Spell (5) Saint Peter

This spell derives from Roman Catholic folk magic. As rain concerns the entire community, this is typically a group operation.

1. If spells, prayers and petitions for rain haven't worked, bring a votive image to the riverside. Saint Peter is traditional, but Saint Expedite might also be a good choice.
2. Clearly and explicitly explain the gravity of the situation to the saint and advise him to really think about why rain is needed. Then dunk his statue in the water.
3. Allegedly this should result in rain within 24 hours. If not, the image is traditionally thrown into the river for good.

 ## Drought Spell (6) Sieve (1)

Pour water on the parched ground through sieve.

 ## Drought Spell (7) Sieve (2)

Blend water from either three or seven wells or springs. (Three or seven types of bottled spring water from distinct sources works at a pinch, too.) Conjure up rain by sprinkling this water through a sieve onto dry ground.

 ## Dulse Wind Summoning Spell

Summon winds by throwing dulse from a height.

Heat Relief Spell

If threatened with dangerously intense heat, offer chamomile to the sun to honor and appease it, accompanied by prayer, petitions and affirmations.

 ## Holed Stone Wind Spell

Attach a holed stone to a cord. Hold the cord at arm's length and whirl it vigorously around your head to pacify storms and wild winds.

Knot Weather Spells

Weather magic is particularly ancient and particularly tied to knot magic. Witches were accused of binding winds into their hair; storms are thus the result of witches unbraiding their hair, thereby releasing knots. This was a constant accusation during the European witch-craze: women accused of raising storms and deliberately sinking ships.

 ## Knot Weather Charm

First make knots in a cord to seal your intention in, then release as needed. This works most powerfully when the number three is incorporated: make three knots or, if possible, three series of three knots for a total of nine knots, or even three series of nine knots for total of twenty-seven knots.

★ Untie one knot (or series) to summon up a breeze
★ Untie two knots (or series) for a strong wind
★ Untie three knots (or series) for a gale force wind

 ## Storm Protection Spell

To protect your roof from rain and storms make a rope with twenty-one knots in it and place it under the eaves of the house. Sometimes this is believed to actually restrict rain flow. When you need rain, loosen one knot.

Make it Rain! Spells

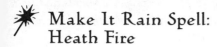

Make It Rain Spell: Heath Fire

Burn heather and fern together outdoors to stimulate rain.

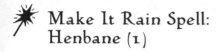

Make It Rain Spell: Henbane (1)

Allegedly throwing henbane into water brings rain.

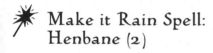

Make it Rain Spell: Henbane (2)

Burning henbane is meant to stimulate rainfall. Unfortunately henbane's fumes are toxic so the actual logistics of this spell are problematic.

Make It Rain Spell: Rice

Toss raw rice into the air to stimulate rain. (That's why they do it after the wedding!)

Rain Charm Spell Bell

A spell from the Bari people from the Sudan Nile, who know something about the need for rain: fill a bell with water and sprinkle Earth with it.

Rain Charm Spell Cats (1)

1. When rain is desired, place a terracotta bowl on your head.
2. Leave it for a few moments and then put it on the ground.

3. Fill it with water and give your cat a bath.
4. This allegedly produces heavy rains, although this may be confused with the heavy splashing made by the cat in its attempt to flee the bath.

Rain Charm Spell Cats (2)

This magical recommendation from Java takes the Malay spell above and ups the ante.

1. Place the terracotta bowl on your head for a few minutes.
2. Place it on the ground, fill it with water and bathe *two* cats, a male and a female, to stimulate rain.

Rain Charm Spell Frogs

Frogs are believed to control the watery element.

1. Erect and maintain an altar to the Lord of Soil.
2. Place five frogs on the altar. (Placing them in a terrarium, dish or tank may be best way to induce them to stay.)
3. Their happy croaking encourages rain.

Rain Charm Spell Frogs (2)

Create little images of frogs. Place the frogs on hilltops and raised ground and charge each one with its mission of calling in the rain.

Rain Charm Spell Palm Sunday

This spell derives from Italy. Hang palm branches blessed on Palm Sunday from trees to stimulate rain.

Rain Charm Spell Santeria

Cast this spell under a palm tree, sacred to Chango, Lord of Thunder. In colder climates, substitute a cedar. Soak twelve cotton wicks in olive oil. Light them, and invoke Chango, his mother Yemaya, or of them both. Ask Chango to send the rain. Ask Yemaya to encourage Chango's cooperation.

Make it Stop! Spells

 Mother Goose

Mother Goose's rhymes evoke old magical charms. Just look at images of Mother Goose, riding through the sky wearing her peaked witch's hat. Obviously this is a woman who knows her magic spells! Rehabilitate these spells; rescue them from the nursery.

Venture outside in the rain and sing Mother Goose's anti-rain charm:

Rain, rain, go away!
Come again some other day!

(This can be very hard for adults to do seriously; enlist the aid of children. Encourage them to spontaneously dance as well. Children possess the purity of heart necessary to transform cliché back to its powerful ritual roots.)

 Rain Charm Women's Spell

In the secret language of fertility magic, both human and agricultural, rain is synonymous with semen, hence the traditional machismo and promiscuity of storm gods. Because myth and legend have become relegated to children's tales, euphemisms are used to obscure reality. Male storm spirits like Baal, Zeus, Chango, Susunowo, or Thor are inevitably described as "thunder gods." Not that the thunder isn't impressive but it's that fertilizing rain that provides the magic, rain that must be applied in just the proper amounts and with just the right touch to keep the Earth Mother happy, satisfied and flourishing.

This old Slavic spell intends to pacify a rainstorm by making this magical point.

For this spell you need a premenstrual virgin girl or a child, although a young girl on the cusp of womanhood is considered most powerful. She must be the daughter of a woman who is post-menopausal.

1. Get rid of all the men. They cannot participate or witness this ritual but must be sent off somewhere.
2. The girl must undress completely.
3. Then she is clothed and ornamented with fresh flowers, as many as possible. (If no real flowers are possible, go with paper, jewelry, or beads or paint her with henna/body paint flowers.)
4. Go outside, all of you. She should whirl and dance while calling out to the Water Spirits. In the meantime, other women toss water over her.
5. Have a party. This is supposed to be fun. Laughter helps. If the girl doesn't want to do it, forget about it—the spell won't work. A crying, nagging, sullen child defeats the purpose.
6. Allegedly the rain should lessen quickly.

 Rain Charm Men's Spell

This spell is the counterpart of the spell above—yang to the Women's Spell's yin. This men's magic ritual allegedly stimulates a storm.

Three men climb into trees. One creates thunder by drumming with a hammer on a kettle (think of Thor, Chango, Zeus, or Baal with their hammers and storms): one rubs sticks together or otherwise creates sparks (lightning); the third sprinkles water with a branch.

Stop the Rain Spell (1)

It's recommended that women expose their genitals to a storm to quiet it. (Note, not men: exposing male genitalia is interpreted as a challenge and we never want to challenge nature when it really matters: an even more destructive storm may result.)

 ## Stop the Rain Spell (2)

Too much rain?

1. Draw and cut out a figure of a woman holding a broom in her hand.
2. If the rain becomes dangerously excessive, hang the figure under the eaves and pray for it to dry up.
3. Appeal to the figure for assistance. This woman will use her broom to sweep away clouds and rain so that the sun can appear.

 ## Stop the Rain Spell (3)

A spell to relieve storms, especially lightning. Obtain and preserve the palm leaves distributed in a Roman Catholic Church on Palm Sunday. Palm leaves are sacred to Chango who, in the Santeria tradition, is syncretized to Saint Barbara. To relieve a storm, burn these leaves while petitioning Chango and/or Saint Barbara to pacify the storm.

 ## Stop the Rain Spell (4)

Place a harrow perpendicularly in a crossroads to encourage excessive rain to stop.

 ## Stop a Storm Spell

Hold a powerful, charged magic mirror before a sleeping man's face during a storm to ease hail and lightning.

Storm Protection Spells

 ## Acorn Lightning Protection

Carry an acorn to protect from storms and lightning, especially when venturing outdoors.

 ## Lightning Protection: Marjoram

Marjoram invokes Thor's blessings. Keep it in and around your home to ward off lightning.

 ## Lightning Protection: Mistletoe

In Sweden mistletoe is known as "thunderbroom." Place it over thresholds, and hang it from the wall to protect a home from lightning.

 ## Lightning Safety Spell: Nettles

Carry stinging nettles in a conjure bag to magically prevent yourself being struck by lightning.

Mari, Queen of Storms

The most prominent Basque deity, a matron of witches, Mari lives in caves that spiral to the center of Earth. Who needs broomsticks? Mari travels through the sky in the form of a fire bolt. This shape-shifting spirit's attributes include a golden comb and a fiery sickle. Her husband Maju, or Sugaar, is a snake who lives in the depths of the sea. When the two meet, violent storms with thunder, lightning, and hail are produced.

Mari may be petitioned to stop a storm: place a sickle on the ground. Offer her an image of one of her sacred creatures—a black goat or a white ram—then burn it. Beg Mari for mercy.

Midsummer's Storm Relief Spell

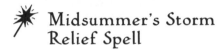

Retrieve singed, scorched wreaths from Midsummer's bonfires. In cases of future storms, place the wreath in the fire and burn it to soothe and pacify the storm.

Mother Holle's Storm Relief Spell

When Mother Holle shakes out her featherbeds, it snows. Rain falls from her laundry rinse water.

The twelve days between December 25th and January 6th are sacred to Mother Holle, as is the Winter Solstice. Should storms occur during this period or immediately preceding (she may be involved in preparations), burn candles for Mother Holle in an immaculately clean room. Incorporate cleaning into your ritual. Surround the candle(s) with images of rabbits and ask Mother Holle to make the precipitation stop.

Mugwort Lightning Prevention

Keep mugwort within the home—preferably a living plant—to prevent lightning from striking.

Mugwort Storm Dispersal

According to Polish custom, burn mugwort in the fireplace when there is a storm. The smoke carried up the chimney and entering the atmosphere allegedly disperses thunderclouds.

Storm Protection Spell (1)

Avert lightning by sticking a knife into a loaf of bread, impaling it. Spin them both around for as long as the storm lasts.

Storm Protection Spell (2) Devil's Flight

Hang the plants Saint John's Wort and Devil's Flight on doors or in corners to protect against storms, lightning, and evil in general.

Storm Protection Spell (3) Thor's Beard

Place the plant Sempervivum tectorum in a pot. This plant is also known as Thor's Beard. Keep it on the roof to protect a house from lightning.

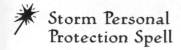 ## Storm Personal Protection Spell

If you can't do anything about the storm, you can still attempt to protect yourself:

1. Carry hawthorn sprigs as protective talismans.
2. Do not cut them from the tree without making a generous offering to the fairies that are extremely protective of this relative of roses.
3. Instead gather dropped sprigs, twigs, and leaves.

 ## Wind Raising Spell

Allegedly during childbirth and for a brief period afterwards a woman has the power to raise winds. Go outside and take a mouthful of air. Return inside and expel it out in the manner that you wish the wind to blow (slow, gentle, fast, hard).

Youth, Beauty, and Longevity Spells

Beauty Spells

 ### Acorn Youth and Beauty Spell (1)

Three acorns, especially if they're found attached to one another, preserve youth and enhance beauty. A gold or silver charm depicting three acorns will work, too. Charge the three acorns under the New Moon, and wear them in your hair.

 ### Acorn Youth and Beauty Spell (2)

This is a more discreet version of the above spell. Charge three acorns under the New Moon. Wrap them together using strands of your hair and carry them in a charm bag.

 ### Aphrodite's Beauty Spell

Goats are among Aphrodite's sacred creatures. Soak violets in goat's milk and wash your face with this for beauty.

 ### Breast Enhancement Spell (1) Harem

A Turkish harem formula:

1. Pour boiling water over fenugreek seeds to make an infusion.
2. When it cools, strain out the seeds.
3. Use the liquid to bathe the breasts to allegedly increase bust size.

 ### Breast Enhancement Spell (2) Maria Padilha

Maria Padilha may be petitioned for breast enlargement. Her sacred bird and messenger is a black dove, with either black or red legs, not white.

1. Go to a three-way crossroads on a Friday night. The New Moon is best time but at least try to coordinate with a waxing moon.
2. Take seven grains of corn with you, one red and one black candle.

3. Light the candles; invoke Maria Padilha and show her the corn.
4. Implore her to empower it to make your breasts grow and increase. Tell her you will pay her well if she takes care of you.
5. Leave the candles burning and go home.
6. Rub each grain over your breasts with gentle massaging motions.
7. Repeat the corn kernel massage every Friday night for seven consecutive Fridays.
8. Following the final Friday, find a black pigeon and feed it the corn.
9. By now, you should observe *some* breast enhancement. If there's absolutely nothing or if the condition has worsened, you can interpret this to mean Maria Padilha has rejected your petition. (Be realistic: if you see even a little improvement, pay Maria Padilha. It's never wise to hold out on a spirit, especially a volatile one like Maria.)
10. Return to the same crossroads again, bringing red and black candles, a bottle of anisette and a bouquet of seven long-stemmed red roses, from which you have personally removed the thorns. Lay down a red or black cloth (or ideally both, one on top of the other).
11. Light the candles and invoke Maria Padilha.
12. Thank her graciously. Open the bottle of anisette, take a mouthful, spray it in the direction you have uttered your petition. Leave the bottle and the roses.

 Breast Reduction Spell

Allegedly bathing the breasts with water used to wash a corpse will reduce them in size.

 Egg Beauty Spell

Eggs are perceived as magical and powerful. Reserve the water used to boil eggs; let it cool and bathe with it for youth, vigor, and beauty.

 Flora's Self-love Beauty Spell

Flora is the Roman spirit of flowering plants and, by extension, of fertility and the life-force. Her festival, the Floralia, once began April 27th and continued for six days of revelry, especially by women of all ages celebrating their own bodies and natural beauty. The festival was celebrated in the nude until the third century CE, *when Roman authorities ordered that revelers be clothed. The festival held out in that form for one more century until all pagan festivals were banned. Vestiges survive in May Day celebrations.*

Just as every blossom is unique, so is every body. Flora encourages one to cherish one's own beauty without comparison to any other. This spell is particularly potent if timed to coincide with Flora's old festival but may be cast at anytime.

Fill your bathtub with as many fresh flowers as possible, especially Flora's favorite, beautiful, transient bean blossoms. Enter the bath and understand that you too are among Flora's unique and perfect blossoms.

 Freya's Youth Potion

Cowslips are wild peonies and are said to be Freya's favorite flowers, as well as those of the fairies. Reputedly they magically transmit the beauty secrets of these powerful spirits.

1. Create an infusion, although you may also substitute a hydrosol.
2. Boil water and pour it over the blossoms.
3. When the water cools, strain out the blossom.
4. Apply the potion to your face with a cotton ball.
5. Use the remainder in the bath or elsewhere on the body.
6. You may also refrigerate the remainder for 24 hours.

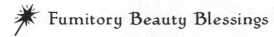 Fumitory Beauty Blessings

Fumitory, or Earth Smoke, allegedly bestows beauty, particularly in the event of a wedding, and particularly if the wedding is yours.

1. Gather fumitory.
2. Simmer it in spring water.
3. When the water cools, use it for bathing.

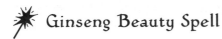 Ginseng Beauty Spell

Tie a red thread around a ginseng root and carry for added beauty and grace.

 Helen of Troy Beauty Spell

Elecampane (Inula helenium) was named for Helen of Troy. She allegedly carried it away with her when she fled with Paris. Since then, it's believed to bestow a little of her essence. Carry elecampane root for enhanced beauty, grace, charm, and confidence.

 Lady's Mantle Youth Dew

Morning dew collected from Lady's Mantle leaves provides beauty and an enhanced complexion.

 Lilac Dew Spell

Bathe in lilac dew on May Day for a year of beauty.

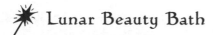 Lunar Beauty Bath

The planet of magic, romance, and feminine power, the moon offers the gift of beauty in this Romany spell:

1. Stand naked in the light of the Full Moon.
2. Go through the motions of bathing in moonbeams. Visualize the moonbeams entering you and empowering you. Absorb their beauty.
3. Petition the moon for assistance with whatever troubles you: weight loss, hair growth, perceived imperfections.
4. Now watch for an immediate response from the moon: no change is a positive response; if the moon brightens, this is an extremely encouraging sign. A sudden darkening or a cloud passing over the moon indicates that you should anticipate challenges. Reconsider your request. Work on it until the next Full Moon.
5. Repeat as needed.

Use this ritual for romance and renewed fertility too.

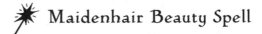 Maidenhair Beauty Spell

Immerse the plant maidenhair in water. Remove it and keep it in the bedroom for beauty and that indefinable quality of grace and je ne sais quois.

 Midsummer's Morning Dew Spell

Midsummer's morning dew renews beauty: add to your cosmetics' formulas to enhance their power.

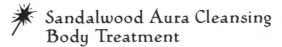 Sandalwood Aura Cleansing Body Treatment

Sandalwood powder has a drying effect on the face, but may be used on other parts of body to obtain combined spiritual and physical benefits. Those with dry skin should use milk or even cream for this formula: blend sandalwood powder with milk or water. Apply to the body and rinse off when dry.

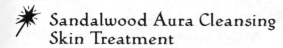

Sandalwood Aura Cleansing Skin Treatment

Blend sandalwood powder, ground turmeric powder, and spring water to form a thin paste. Apply to the face, neck, and décolletage. On the physical level, this formula tones and balances oily skin, but it also has a purifying, cleansing effect on the aura.

Self-Satisfaction Spell

★ *For self-love, to recognize your own beauty, wash your face with honey blended with rosewater*

★ *Add your favorite perfume to a bath together with fresh flower blossoms and gently rub your body with the flowers*

★ *Gaze into a lunar-charged mirror until you see the light shining from within*

Seven Flowers Bath

A Chinese formula to enhance beauty, vitality, and sensuality: more important, this fragrant bath makes you happy with yourself.

The seven flowers are: rose, jasmine, peony, orchid, lotus, magnolia and chrysanthemum. Add copious quantities of flower petals to your bath. Watch out for florist's flowers, which are usually heavily laden with pesticides. Substitute home-grown flowers where possible.

Fruit tree blossoms may be substituted for flowers. Peach and plum trees are considered especially auspicious. Vary the colors. If the fragrance is not intense, add essential oils until it suits you.

Snow Queen Water

1. Gather handfuls of fresh, clean snow from the first snowfall of the season, or break off the first icicle you see.

2. Place it in a glass bowl and let it melt.
3. Add holly leaves and let this water sit overnight, exposed to moonbeams if possible.
4. Wash your face with the water for enhanced youth and beauty.

Xochiquetzal's Beauty Spell

Xochiquetzal, Tlazolteotl's daughter, is the Aztec spirit of flowers, women, and beauty. Request the gift of enhanced beauty or the gift of recognizing the beauty you already possess. Offer her marigolds and other flowers, plus vivid freely shed feathers. Dedicate cleansing rituals in the steam bath to her.

Yerba Santa Beauty Spell

Carry yerba santa, "sacred herb," to enhance beauty and charm.

Hair Growth Spells

Anti-baldness Spell Magic Potion

If you happen to have access to distilling equipment, distill liquor from human hair. Add honey and drink.

Anti-baldness Spell Midsummer's Dew

Dew collected on Midsummer's morning prevents baldness. Collect and apply where needed.

Anti-baldness Spell Onion (1)

An Old Anglo-Saxon remedy for baldness: Cut an onion in half and rub the half onion vigorously over your exposed scalp, twice daily, morning and evening.

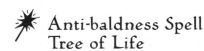 ## Anti-baldness Spell Onion (2)

If you have too much hair for the above to be effective, juice an onion and blend the juice with a shot of vodka and a tablespoon of honey. Massage this mixture into your scalp, leave it for thirty minutes, then rinse it out of your hair.

 ## Anti-baldness Spell Tree of Life

This Chinese spell instructs that you steep fresh arbor vitae (tree of life) leaves in 60 percent alcohol solution for one week. Strain and rub on the bald spot three times daily.

Facial Hair Spell Southernwood

A seventeenth-century formula features southernwood, famously nick-named "lad's love," allegedly for its power to stimulate beard growth.

1. Burn southernwood. You will need at least one ounce (30 g) of ashes.
2. Add the ash to two cups of olive oil.
3. Add either one-quarter cup infused oil of rosemary or 50 drops of the essential oil.
4. Bottle. Keep in a cool, dark place. Rub into the scalp and/or beard area morning and night to stimulate hair growth.

 ## Facial Hair Spell (2) Watermelon

A Moroccan remedy to encourage male facial hair: rub your chin daily with watermelon.

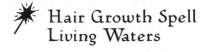 ## Hair Growth Spell Living Waters

Place a lock of your hair under a stone within living, running water. This allegedly stimulates growth and improves the all-around appearance of your hair.

Hair Growth Spell Mermaid

It's become a Oaxacan tradition for women to trim or cut their hair on June 24th, in honor of an Oaxacan river mermaid. On that day a local girl was transformed into a mermaid, her hair instantly growing luxuriously enough to clothe her sudden nakedness. Trimming your own hair on that date allegedly stimulates luxurious hair growth

1. Trim your hair or, ideally, have a man trim your hair.
2. Plant the hair trimmings in Earth.
3. Watch your hair grow.

To enhance the ritual, make a mermaid altar. Oaxaca is famous for its ceramics and its women artisans. Mermaids are a particularly popular image: use one as the center of an altar. Decorate with seashells and other motifs of the sea.

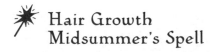 ## Hair Growth Midsummer's Spell

Make a paste by moistening Midsummer's bonfire ashes with lunar-infused water. Rub this paste into your hair and scalp to prevent baldness and promote hair growth.

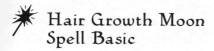

Hair Growth Moon Spell Basic

The moon influences the tides, menstrual cycles and fertility. Why wouldn't it influence hair growth, too?

General magical wisdom suggests that to encourage hair growth, trim your hair during a waxing moon. To discourage hair growth, have it cut during the waning days.

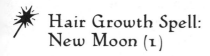

Hair Growth Spell: New Moon (1)

To promote hair growth, particularly after hair-loss:

1. Three days after the spring equinox, go up on the roof (or similar).
2. Smear your hair with a mixture of oil and henna (this can be neutral-colored henna).
3. Comb it out and talk to the moon.
   I gave you my hair
   Now Moon, give me yours.
4. Repeat every third day during this lunar month, until the Dark Moon.

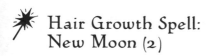

Hair Growth Spell: New Moon (2)

Cut hair to coincide with the New Moon to encourage luxuriant growth. Hair cut during the Dark Moon is believed likely to lose luster, even perhaps to become prematurely gray.

Hair Growth Spell: Moonlight (1)

Charge spring water in moonlight and use it to wash your hair. Alternately use the lunar-charged water as a tonic: massage it into your scalp and hair and leave it alone. Do not rinse out.

Hair Growth Spell: Moonlight (2)

Brush and/or comb your hair outside in the light of the moon to stimulate growth and increase luster.

Hair Growth Spell: Oils

Blend essential oils of clary sage and ylang ylang together, and rub into your scalp every night to promote hair growth.

Hair Growth Spell: Saint Urban

Allegedly, hanging a lock of your hair before an image of Saint Urban stimulates your hair to grow (it reputedly also causes hair to go blonde). Urban, Patron of Vintners, who died c.390, is depicted as a bishop with a bunch of grapes or a grape vine by his side.

Hair Growth Spell: Tree

A Romany tradition recommends that you cut a lock of your hair and bury it beneath a willow tree in order to promote hair growth.

Yarrow Hair Growth Spell

Bathe your head with an infusion of yarrow to magically forestall hair loss.

Weight Loss Spells

Spells to affect weight work when they complement more conventional methods (exercise, nutrition); they don't replace them. In other words, burning a weight-loss candle followed by eating a large tub of ice cream is only fooling yourself.

✳ Weight Adjustment Spell: Silhouette

1. Draw an outline of a human figure that corresponds to your present reality.
2. If you would like to lose weight, draw a second figure inside the first demonstrating what your preferred shape should resemble.
3. If you would like to gain weight: draw a second figure around the first (enclosing it) demonstrating your desired silhouette.
4. Post the image where you can see it as encouragement, and burn candles beside it for reinforcement.

✳ Weight Gain Spell: Lunar

Draw a realistic outline of your silhouette; then draw a fuller outline around it, corresponding to the appearance to which you aspire. At the New Moon, color in the gap between the two outlines, chanting something like, "I grow as the moon grows, I wax as the moon waxes!"

✳ Weight Loss Spell: Candle

This spell may be used for weight loss or for re-shaping one's silhouette.

1. Obtain a naked human figure candle to represent you.

2. With a pin scratch lines into the wax to demonstrate where reduction or re-shaping is needed, just as if you were a tailor making adjustments.
3. Dress the candle with a **Commanding Oil** and charge it with its mission.
4. Burn the candle for fifteen minutes daily. In between burnings, use a craft-knife to chip off wax to reflect your accomplishments and goals.

✳ Weight Loss Spell: Gem Therapy

Wear moonstone or topaz to encourage weight loss or to stabilize weight as needed.

According to modern gem therapy, these stones regulate metabolism.

✳ Weight Loss Spell: Milk Bath

Coordinate this spell with a waning moon. Gently warm a carton of milk and bring it to the shower. Pour it over your head while affirming to grow thinner like the moon.

✳ Weight-Loss Spell: Star

Is the refrigerator a constant source of temptation? It's not practical to banish the actual refrigerator but this spell attempts to magically minimize its presence and influence, especially for those with food-addictions who can't resist the temptation to binge.

1. Draw a pentagram (five-pointed star). Concentrate on your goals while drawing.
2. At each corner of the star write something like *"Remain invisible to me."*
3. Attach the star to the refrigerator.

Longevity Spells

Alchemists through the ages strived to create the *philosopher's stone*, a substance that would enable them to transmute base metals into gold. Kings sponsored alchemists' laboratories and their expensive experiments, dreaming of boundless wealth. However the philosopher's stone possessed another priceless attribute: it allegedly bestowed extended longevity to the point of immortality to its owner. Rumors spread that certain alchemists, such as the Frenchman Nicholas Flamel (born *c.*1330, died ?), had actually created the philosopher's stone. Nicholas Flamel still makes the occasional public appearance.

Western alchemy was born in Alexandria, Egypt and brought to Europe by the Moors. Another alchemical branch developed independently in China: there the quest was more purely focused on longevity, rather than wealth.

 Aaron's Rod Longevity Spell

Aaron's rod is the botanical nickname given to golden rod and mullein. Use either plant in this spell. Create an infusion by pouring boiling water over Aaron's rod. Add the strained liquid to a bath to magically enhance longevity.

 Amaranth Longevity Spell

Amaranth encourages longevity in the face of illness and obstacles. Carry it in a conjure bag.

Aroma Longevity Spell

Warm essential oils of cedarwood, chamomile, and juniper in an aroma burner. Inhale deeply to encourage longevity.

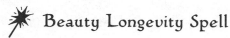 Beauty Longevity Spell

Like fine wines, certain fragrances grow more beautiful with age: anoint orrisroot with a drop of ylang ylang and/or patchouli oil and carry with you in a red silk bag so that you too will only improve with age.

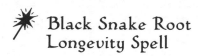 Black Snake Root Longevity Spell

Snakes shed their skin, regaining their youthful appearance. Carry a black snake root (black cohosh) to prolong youthfulness and enhance longevity.

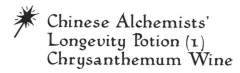 Chinese Alchemists' Longevity Potion (1) Chrysanthemum Wine

This is reputed to prolong life and maintain good health.

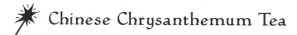 Chinese Chrysanthemum Tea

On the ninth day of the ninth Chinese month, drink dried chrysanthemum tea to magically encourage longevity.

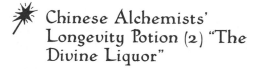 Chinese Alchemists' Longevity Potion (2) "The Divine Liquor"

Allegedly, this potion enabled one to live for a thousand years.

1. Blend equal quantities of rice water and morning dew.
2. Grind jade into powder and add it to the liquid.
3. Boil it in a copper pot.
4. Let it cool, strain and drink.

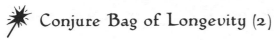 Conjure Bag of Longevity (1)

Place petrified wood, iron beads and a dried peach kernel or a padlock carved from peachwood into a red silk bag. Sprinkle with dried, crumbled sage and carry with you.

Conjure Bag of Longevity (2)

Place a scarab charm, an ankh charm, a piece of real jade (real jade feels cool to the touch), and a clean dried peach pit into a red silk bag. Sprinkle with powdered chamomile, rosemary, and sage.

 Elder Wood Longevity Spell: Elder

Carry elder twigs as a charm to preserve longevity.

Emeralds are Forever Longevity Spell

Emeralds allegedly inhibit decay: wear them to preserve your youthfulness. If you don't have access to real emeralds, bathe in emerald gemstone essence to receive magical benefits.

Gingko Longevity Spell

Carve gingko wood into an auspicious shape and carry it in an amulet bag. (If "auspicious" leaves you drawing a blank, an ankh is always advantageous for longevity.)

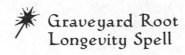 Graveyard Root Longevity Spell

Allegedly the roots of plants pulled from the cemetery bestow longevity and good health to their bearer. This is not, however, a thoughtless spell: it's crucial to determine who owns the plants you pull. In some traditions, specific spirits preside over the cemetery; if pulled from atop a grave, the plant may be understood to belong to the deceased. Plants from the grave of a relative or loved one will probably be given graciously.

Choose your plants carefully and request permission politely. Offer gifts or payment before removing anything from the cemetery.

Helichrysum Longevity Spell

Helichrysum's folk names reveal this botanicals secret magic power: immortelle and everlasting. Inhale the fragrance or add to massage oil to stay youthful and well preserved.

Honeysuckle Longevity Spell

Surround yourself with living honeysuckle to encourage longevity.

Jade Gemstone Essence

Allegedly powdering and consuming green jade enhances longevity. This may not be such a good idea for a variety of reasons; however, jade gemstone essence may have a similar (but healthier) effect. Follow the manufacturer's instructions for internal administration or add the essence to the bath.

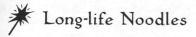 ## Long-life Noodles

As magical insurance, on your birthday eat a bowl of "Long Life Noodles," extra thin, extra long noodles. Be sure not to break any of the noodles while eating; slurp them up instead!

 ## Magic Massage

Dilute essential oil of cedarwood in sunflower and jojoba oils. Incorporate this oil into body massage to serve as a magical life preserver. (Do not use when pregnant, however.)

 ## Maple Longevity Spell

Longevity isn't just for old folks. Pass a child through the branches of a maple tree for blessings of longevity.

 ## Marjoram Longevity Charm

Carry marjoram in your charm bag to promote longevity.

Peachwood Longevity Spell

The ancient Chinese spirit Hsi Wang Mu, the Queen Mother of the West, owns a magical garden containing the peaches of immortality. The Chinese Lord of Longevity also carries a peach. Ordinary peaches may not grant life everlasting, but they are magically associated with longevity. Carry peachwood or a dried peach kernel to magically enhance one's lifespan.

 ## Peachwood Longevity Charm

Carve an ankh out of peachwood and carry it to enhance longevity.

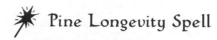 ## Pine Longevity Spell

Carry a whole, healthy looking pinecone to enhance longevity and youthfulness.

Shangri-La Incense

According to the legend of Shangri-la, there are hidden valleys in the Himalayas where life and youth are magically extended to the point of immortality—provided you never leave Shangri-la. The following incense blend magically transports you there and magically offers similar effects, at least temporarily. Blend spikenard, rhododendron, and galangal root and burn, wafting the fragrance as desired.

 ## Tansy Longevity Spell

Tansy allegedly increases the life span when used magically. (It is a powerful herb and is not safe for pregnant women or many others to consume.) Wear or carry tansy in an amulet bag.

Vervain

Vervain allegedly confers immortality. Make strong infusions by pouring boiling water over the herb and adding it to the bath.

Spells for Youth

☀ Angel's Water Youth Spell

Not all versions of **Angel's Water** are suitable for consumption. Create your own or check ingredients very carefully for safety's sake. Drink a glass of **Angel's Water** every three days to remain eternally youthful.

☀ Anise Renewed Youth Spell

Feeling older than you should? Have your experiences aged you? Magically remedy that feeling by hanging sprigs of fresh anise from your bed to restore your youthful nature.

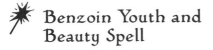

☀ Ash Youth Preservation Spell

Ash is among the trees most associated with fairies, and fairies are associated with eternally extended youth. Crumble ash leaves into bathwater to receive blessings of extended youthfulness and longevity.

☀ Benzoin Youth and Beauty Spell

Add one drop of benzoin resinoid to cosmetics to magically maintain youthfulness.

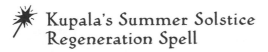

☀ Kupala's Summer Solstice Regeneration Spell

Russian Midsummer's festivities are named in honor of Ivan Kupalo, ostensibly a blending of a male solar spirit with John the Baptist. However, pre-Christianity, the summer solstice was the day that Kupala, female spirit of water, witchcraft and herbal wisdom, celebrated her regeneration. Her devotees regenerated and revitalized themselves too, by tapping into the power of the elements. This spell is traditionally cast on Midsummer's Eve or the Summer Solstice, however use as needed.

Cast flowers in living water (as an offering to Kupala) and bathe in it. Jump over a fire, then allow yourself to air-dry while sitting or reclining on Earth.

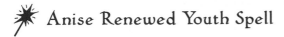

☀ Rosemary Youth Spells (1)

According to European tradition, old age may be kept at bay by frequently inhaling the scent of rosemary.

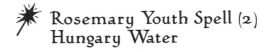

☀ Rosemary Youth Spell (2) Hungary Water

According to legend this fourteenth-century formula was created for Queen Isabel of Hungary who, at age seventy-two, lay crippled and virtually paralyzed from gout and rheumatism. Her master herbalist concocted this formula, initially only with the intent of providing relief from pain. Instead, it provided miraculous, youth-renewing results: allegedly Queen Isabel was soon up and dancing and engaged to marry the much younger King of Poland.

The original recipe is given as one and a half pounds of fresh flowering rosemary tops soaked in a gallon of spirits of wine for four days, then distilled. Many modern versions exist. For example:

Eight fluid ounces (200 ml) of vodka
One fluid ounce (25 ml) orange blossom water
One fluid ounce (25 ml) rose water
One fluid ounce (25 ml) rosemary hydrosol
One fluid ounce (25 ml) infused water of vervain
Five drops essential oil of rosemary
Four drops essential oil of may chang
Two drops essential oils of German or Hungarian chamomile
Two drops essential oil of spearmint
One drop essential oil of neroli

Blend the alcohol with the distilled waters. Add the essential oils and seal in an air-tight bottle. Ideally this beauty potion should be allowed to mature for six months, although you must give the bottle a strong shake once a week.

Hungary Water is for external use only. It was originally administered to Queen Isabel in the form of a daily, vigorous full-body massage. A full-body rub using Hungary Water allegedly preserves and renews youth dramatically. Presumably the choice of who is doing the rubbing will also help.

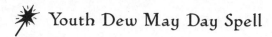 ## Youth Dew May Day Spell

For eternal youth and beauty, rise at dawn on May Day and roll naked in the dew.

Formulary

Charged Waters

Charged waters are charged with magical power and intentions.

Not all charged waters are really *waters*. Some are actually alcohol-based formulas, recalling that the roots of perfumery and liqueurs lie entangled in magic potions, brews, and philters. (Philters are drinks; although some potions are consumed, many formulas are for external use only.) *"Water"* must be understood in the context of perfume designations, such as *eau de Cologne* ("water of Cologne") or of alcoholic beverages like aquavit or whiskey (whose name derives from the Gaelic for *"water of life"*).

The alcohol typically recommended as a base is vodka, not because it may be consumed but because of its minimal scent. Avoid what is commonly called *"rubbing alcohol"*; the typically strong, unpleasant aroma will interfere with that of the formula.

Angel's Water or Angel Water

The term "Angel Water" may refer either to Jordan River Water, or to an eighteenth-century love potion. This, the most popular version of Angel Water and the one indicated in this book, began as a sixteenth-century complexion remedy before evolving into a love potion and a popular aphrodisiac 200 years later. Its name may derive from those angels who seduced the *"daughters of man"* with magic lessons in the Book of Genesis.

The crucial ingredient, the one that cannot be replaced if this is to be considered true Angel Water, is myrtle, a small tree native to North Africa and the Mediterranean coast, considered sacred to Aphrodite, whose name inspired the term *"aphrodisiac."*

In legend, when Aphrodite first emerges naked from the sea, she is clothed in myrtle leaves.

The basic formula consists of:

Myrtle
Orange blossoms (Neroli)
Rose

Myrtle is the predominate material. It is substantially less expensive than the other ingredients. Many versions of Angel's Water contain only myrtle. The term Myrtle Water or Water of Venus is sometimes used synonymously for Angel's Water.

The simplest method of creation is via hydrosols. This may be best if Angel's Water is to serve as a philter. Homemade floral waters may also be used, as well as infusions of fresh and dried leaves and flowers. Homegrown roses may be preferable to those of florists because of the massive amounts of pesticides used on commercially grown roses. All the basic ingredients are available in the form of essential oils

Angel's Water is typically used externally:

★ *Add to a bath: allegedly the greater the quantities of Angel's Water, the greater the erotic impact*
★ *Blend with alcohol to create a liniment for purposes of massage: administered this way, (and presumably if it's a good massage) Angel's Water reputedly inspires erotic thoughts in even the coldest woman*
★ *Angel's Water may also be used as a love potion, in which case make sure that all materials are safe for consumption*

Myrtle-based Angel's Water was used throughout Europe and the British Isles. There is also a Spanish formula, used for romantic and cleansing spells. This version's basic formula consists of angelica, lavender, rose, and trefoil.

Bay Rum

Technically the "bay" in Bay Rum does not refer to familiar bay laurel leaves, a staple of so many magic spells, but to the berries of the Caribbean tree, Jamaica bayberry, also known as black or wild cinnamon.

If you purchase bay rum manufactured in Bermuda or the Caribbean, you may receive the original formula. If manufactured elsewhere, you will most likely be purchasing a formula based on bay laurel. Jamaica bayberry does not grow outside the Caribbean and Bermuda; people outside the region are not familiar with the botanical and so assume that any reference to bay must indicate bay laurel. Bay laurel is a plant with profound magic powers and the formula based upon it is potent, although not necessarily for the same purposes:

★ *The original Bay Rum formula (bayberry) is used for luck, gambling, healing, and cleansing spells*
★ *The bay laurel-derived formula may be used for healing and cleansing, and to enhance divination*

The true substitute for Jamaica bayberry is not bay laurel leaves but allspice berries, a close relative with similar magic properties. However, Jamaica bayberry is available as an essential oil, and a true Bay Rum is easily created from essential oils.

True Bay Rum

Essential oil of Jamaica bayberry
Essential oil of petitgrain
Essential oil of allspice
Essential oil of cardamom
Essential oil of cloves

1. Dilute the essential oils in fine dark rum and distilled water.
2. Although scent-free alcohol is usually recommended, bay rum is the exception to the rule. Rum, a liquor used in many spells, enhances bay rum's magical properties. Its scent is considered integral to the formula: select the most fragrant rum possible.
3. Jamaica bayberry is the predominate ingredient. Its presence and fragrance should dominate the blend.
4. If you have access to Jamaica bayberries, dried botanicals may be substituted for essential oils. Substitute orange zest for petitgrain.

Bay Leaf-Based Bay Rum

- Crushed bay laurel leaves
- Ground allspice berries
- Ground cardamom
- Ground cinnamon
- Ground cloves

1. Add the dry ingredients to one pint (half a liter) of fine dark Caribbean rum.
2. Shake it and let it sit for a week.
3. Strain out the solid ingredients.
4. Place some new allspice berries or a whole bay leaf in the bottle.

Blessing Water

See Marie Laveau Water.

Carmelite Water

This formula was first created for King Charles V of France in 1379 by the Carmelite Sisters. Its key ingredient, the herb melissa, also known as lemon balm, is another plant closely identified with Aphrodite. Melissa means *"bee."* Aphrodite's priestesses of love were known as bees and according to legend, living honeybees, female worker bees supremely devoted to their queen, are the returning souls of Aphrodite's no less devoted servants. Melissa is a common garden plant; if you grow it, the connection to bees becomes very clear: bees love it and flock to its blossoms.

Melissa is the crucial ingredient in Carmelite Water; its presence, fragrance and lemony flavor should predominate. Historically, Carmelite Water was a distilled liquor and should you have access to distilling equipment, it may be reproduced as such.

Basic Carmelite Water

- Three tablespoons of chopped melissa (lemon balm)
- Three tablespoons of chopped angelica root
- One tablespoon of cloves
- One-half teaspoon of coriander seeds
- One whole nutmeg
- One stick of cinnamon

1. Add the above to four ounces (125 ml) of vodka, along with the juice from one lemon.
2. Allow it to steep for at least seven days, shaking the bottle once daily.
3. Strain and enjoy.

Simpler, quicker, albeit even less authentic versions exist:

★ *Add tincture of melissa to a glass of vodka*
★ *Blend melissa hydrosol with white wine*

Carmelite Tea
For those who eschew alcohol:

1. Roughly chop fresh melissa/lemon balm.
2. Place a small handful into a mug and add a cinnamon stick, five cloves and one-quarter teaspoon of coriander seeds.
3. Make a strong infusion by pouring boiling water over the botanicals.
4. Let it steep for at least five minutes, strain and drink.

Carmelite water was originally intended for healing purposes and may be taken internally. Make sure all ingredients are safe for consumption. A typical dose is the size of a wine glass, consumed with or after dinner. The pioneering physician Paracelsus vouched for its beneficial cardiac claims.

Bathe in Carmelite Water to facilitate the dream process. It allegedly stimulates fun, happy dreams. Carmelite Water is a favorite Pow-Wow potion to cure headaches, protect against poison, break hexes, and as an elixir of longevity.

Chypre

The word has become familiar as a category of perfume, however chypre originally referred to a specific magical formula, allegedly brought back to Europe in the twelfth century by returning Crusaders and named for Aphrodite's island, Cyprus. Once a very popular men's cologne, it was especially favored by gamblers and "men-about-town," developing something of a disreputable air—hence its use as Joel Cairo's signature scent in Dashiell Hammett's novel, *The Maltese Falcon.*

Until the eighteenth century it was typically used as a dry perfume, as were many fragrances. Only after that period did the present liquid form become standard. The dry version retains many magical advantages, not least that it is easily carried in a mojo hand.

Today many products marketed under the name Chypre have little resemblance to the original formula and cannot substitute for magical use. The key ingredient needed to achieve its magical purposes is rock rose, a plant that bears strong associations with the island of Cypress. Labdanum is the resin derived from rock rose. Many formulas also include oakmoss, believed to magically enhance financial success.

Chypre magically draws:

★ *Success in games of love and chance*
★ *Luck in financial transactions*
★ *Calm in the face of jealousy and mistrust*

Basic Dry Chypre
Benzoin
Calamint
Sweet flag/calamus root
Coriander seeds
Rock rose/labdanum
Storax

Grind all ingredients into a fine powder, using mortar and pestle, spice grinder and sifter as needed.

Carry the powder in a conjure bag. Blend it with arrowroot powder or cornstarch (for gambling luck) or rice powder (for lover's luck) and use it as dusting powder. Or, line a magic box with dry Chypre and use it to store and empower gambling charms.

Modern Chypre
Essential oil of bergaptene-free bergamot
Essential oil of labdanum (rock rose)
Essential oil of oakmoss
Essential oil of patchouli
Essential oil of sandalwood
Essential oil of vetiver

Add the above essential oils to a blend of alcohol and distilled water. Adjust the proportions of the essential oils to suit your nose. This is a traditional earthy Chypre. If you prefer a sweeter, more floral fragrance, add jasmine and rose attar.

Wear as this as a lucky lover's cologne. It also serves as a gambler's handwash.

Damnation Water

The antithesis of Holy Water, Damnation Water is frequently used for malevolent purposes, but sometimes also for protective spells.

Grind asafetida, sulfur and the ashes of palm leaves blessed on Palm Sunday into a powder. Add this to a base of whichever Holy Water formula you prefer.

Elijah the Prophet Water

Although this is known as Elijah the Prophet Water, it has little to do with the biblical prophet.

In Russian tradition, Elijah is syncretized to the thunder spirit, Perun. His feast days are July 20th and July 30th, known as "*thunder days*." Rain falling on these days is believed to have tremendous therapeutic and magical value. Bottle it, refrigerate it and reserve for magical emergency. Elijah the Prophet Water protects against the Evil Eye, general serious illness, and malevolent magic.

Florida Water

Florida Water was originally marketed as the American version of the original eau de Cologne and should have an attractive, refreshing, light, citrus-rosemary fragrance. Florida Water, however, has also developed into something of a metaphysical staple amongst the Vodou/Santeria communities, as well as the many influenced by them. It is an intensely powerful spiritual cleanser and protective agent.

Florida Water may be the only charged water whose name is copyrighted. It is officially manufactured and sold by the Murray and Lanman Company, and theirs is an excellent, inexpensive product, easily available in markets that cater to a Caribbean clientele. However, there are *thousands* of versions of homemade Florida Water, and many practitioners pride themselves on their home recipes. Here are two, slightly different versions.

Florida Water (1)
Two cups of vodka or other alcohol
Two tablespoons rose hydrosol
Sixteen drops essential oil of bergamot
Twelve drops essential oil of lavender
Six drops essential oil of may chang
Three drops essential oil of rosemary
Two drops essential oil of jasmine
Two drops rose attar

Florida Water (2)
Two cups vodka or other alcohol
Two tablespoons orange flower water or hydrosol
One tablespoon turmeric powder
One-quarter teaspoon finely ground orrisroot
Twelve drops essential oil of bergamot
Twelve drops essential oil of lavender
Six drops essential oil of may chang
Three drops essential oil of rosemary
Two drops rose attar
Two drops neroli

Shake this second formula vigorously to distribute the powder.

Florida Water may be added to virtually any cleansing bath or floorwash formula as an added enhancement. It is for external use only.

Flower Waters

Various flower waters are used in a variety of spells, most especially rose water. Although certain spells specifically demand flower water, these waters may also be substituted for regular water in many other spells and formulas, particularly those for romantic or healing purposes, and in magical ink or incense formulas, or for spells that involve dissolving gum resins such as gum acacia.

Rose water and orange blossom water are frequent additions to Indian, North African, and Middle Eastern cuisine and are very easily, and often inexpensively, purchased from specialist vendors. The quality of pre-packaged flower waters is erratic, however; some are excellent, others bear little if any trace of the flower. Fine hydrosols, once rare but becoming more popular by the day, may be the finest source of true flower waters. They may easily be made for oneself, providing one has fresh flowers. In general, depending upon what one wishes to do with the flower water, it's wise to avoid florists' flowers because they tend to be heavily laden with pesticides, which may then be concentrated in the flower water.

Rose/Flower Water: Method 1

1. Remove the petals from a few fresh roses, place them in a small pot and cover with approximately a quarter of an inch of spring water.
2. Simmer gently until a visual change is observed: the petals will become limp and pallid. (If in doubt, a minute longer may be preferable to a minute less.)
3. Strain and allow the liquid to cool. If not used immediately, refrigerate any left over.

This formula may also be used to create any type of fresh flower water—orange blossom or jasmine, for instance—providing the flowers are not poisonous or toxic.

Flower Water: Method 2

This method is substantially longer, although it is also easier than the method suggested above. No vigilant observation is required. It is suitable for creating lavender water as well as any other flower water.

1. Place petals or blossoms within a mason jar.
2. Cover with boiling water and allow to sit overnight.
3. Strain out the botanical material; if not used immediately, the remainder should be refrigerated.

Lavender Water

The term lavender water frequently indicates not a fresh flower water but, rather, steam-distilled lavender blossoms, as first created by Hildegard of Bingen in the twelfth century, hence hydrosols, themselves the product of distillation, are truly the appropriate choice. However a semblance of a distilled water may also be created easily in one's kitchen.

Despite lavender water's associations with the saintly Hildegard, it earned its magical reputation as a potion favored by prostitutes. Lavender water, worn on the body, allegedly attracts sexual interest from either gender while simultaneously sharpening the wits of the wearer.

> Two cups of distilled water
> Two ounces (100 ml) of vodka or other minimally scented alcohol
> Approximately 12–20 drops of essential oil of lavender

Lavender water is for external use only.

Four Thieves Vinegar

The origins of this legendary formula lie in plague-ridden Europe. Many variations on the legend exist: the scene of the crime alternately takes place in London, Marseilles or somewhere in Italy. The situation may have taken place as far back as the time of the Crusades or as recently as the eighteenth century. The basic tale, however, remains the same. Infectious epidemic wracked the land. People were dying, horribly, in great numbers. Quarantine was brutally enforced. In the face of this hardship and tragedy, a gang of four thieves ran rampant, breaking into quarantined houses, even robbing the dead. People were outraged but also intrigued: how did these thieves survive exposure to infection to steal and steal again?

A price was placed on the thieves' heads and eventually they were caught and sentenced to death. They negotiated a trade: their secret formula for a reprieve and one-way ticket out of town. Ever since, Four Thieves Vinegar has been touted for its ability to drive away danger and rescue its user from sure disaster.

Four Thieves Vinegar arrived in New Orleans transported by either French or Italian immigrants, or perhaps by the wandering thieves themselves. In New Orleans, it was adopted by the

Voodoo and Hoodoo communities, who put Four Thieves' illness-banishing powers to other use: it is a crucial component of many banishing and commanding spells.

Four Thieves Vinegar

1. Obtain the best possible red wine or apple cider vinegar.
2. Peel and crush garlic cloves and add them to the vinegar. You cannot have too much garlic, especially if you plan to use Four Thieves for its healing and immunity-boosting properties.
3. Traditionally, each thief contributed one ingredient. Choose one of the following to represent each thief, for a total of four additional ingredients: black pepper, whole cayenne or other chili pepper, coriander, lavender, mint, rosemary, rue, sage, thyme, or wormwood.
4. Allow this to sit for four days, shaking once daily, before using.

If you are using fresh herbs, there is a tendency for the garlic to take on their green color. This isn't harmful but many consider it "unsightly." To prevent this, boil the garlic in the vinegar and allow it to cool before adding the other ingredients.

Ghost Water

Used for hexing and necromancy.

Place a bottle of spring water on a grave before midnight, during a full moon. Whose grave is not important; what is crucial is that the water be exposed to full moonlight. Remove the bottle sometime after midnight and before daybreak.

Glory Water

Glory Water is intended to provide you with glory. It's used in spells cast for success and good fortune. Its key ingredient, the one without which it is no longer Glory Water, is orange blossom water.

Orange blossom water or neroli hydrosol
Frankincense resin or essential oil of frankincense
Essential oil of Bergamot

Holy Water

Although many assume that the term "Holy Water" indicates church-blessed water only, but

As used in this book "Holy Water" indicates any water that is held sacred or has special significance for the spell-caster. This may be water from a shrine dedicated to a deity or water from a sacred spring. It may be water from the tap of your favorite restaurant. If this concept holds no meaning for you, if all water is the same, then simply substitute pure spring water wherever a spell indicates Holy Water.

this is an oversimplification of a complex concept. The Roman Catholic Church did not invent the concept of Holy Water but adopted it from earlier Pagan use. Various Pagan shrines possessed virtually identical Holy Water fonts. Holy Water is a crucial component of many magical, religious and spiritual traditions, although what constitutes Holy Water and how it's made varies greatly.

Holy Water may refer to any one of a variety of products:

★ *Jordan River Water*
★ *Church-blessed water*
★ *According to British folk tradition, rain falling on Holy Thursday—Ascension Day—may be gathered and used as Holy Water. Any other day held sacred to the spellcaster may be substituted: Summer Solstice, May Eve, New Year's, Samhain, your birthday, a saint's day*
★ *Holy Water may also be made via astrological correspondence. Some believe that waters synchronized with a lunar eclipse or a Full Moon are holy and charged with extra magic power*
★ *Balinese tradition uses a variety of Holy Waters. These may include the water found within unripe coconuts or young bamboo. Ocean water is sometimes used as well*
★ *Modern Wicca has evolved the notion of Holy Water. Various formulas exist: at its simplest, Witch's Holy Water is spring water with salt added. Other covens have personal recipes, including infused herbs (rosemary, thyme, and vervain are particularly popular) or crystals. Designate your own*
★ *Pow-Wow also features various recipes but the mainstay is water with salt and vervain added. Christian Pow-Wows may choose church-blessed waters instead*

Holy Water is used for:

★ *Cleansing and purification, both for individual bathing and for space-cleansing (sprinkle in corners)*
★ *Altar cleansing and blessing*
★ *Healing spells. Holy Water is also believed capable of*

magically transmitting physical relief especially for headaches and tension. Use in compresses and massage
★ *Cleansing and empowering materials and tools: anoint roots and crystals or let roots and minerals soak in Holy Water*
★ *Exorcism and banishing spells*

Balinese Holy Water, Church-blessed Holy Water and Wiccan Holy Water (among others) are consecrated via sacred ritual: the ritual activates the water. Other magical traditions consider that the sacred, magical power of Holy Water is such that no further ritual or consecration is needed and may in fact be interference. Obtaining Holy Water may thus be as simple as gathering rainwater or adding sea salt to spring water. Complex rituals may also be designed; choose from among the following ritual elements or adapt and embellish as desired:

Charging Holy Water

1. Collect rainwater, ideally within a stone vessel.
2. Prepare yourself prior to preparing the water: bathe in Fiery Wall of Protection, Dragon's Blood or at least with lots of salt, while reciting psalms and/or sacred verses.
3. Prepare the water sky-clad (nude) or in clean ritual clothing. Where ritual clothing is not used, fresh, clean clothing, preferably white and made from natural fabrics is favored.
4. Ladle water into a glass or crystal bowl.
5. Place it between two white candles.
6. Light incense first (frankincense, copal, benzoin, and/or white sage) and then the candles.
7. Pass the bowl of water through the incense smoke.
8. Visualize why you're preparing this water. Visualize the results this water will bring.
9. Return the bowl to its place between the candles and leave everything in place until the candles burn out.
10. Bottle the water.

Hundred Grass Lotion

This can only be created on the fifth day of the fifth Chinese month, the only day that ordinary grass allegedly possesses special magic properties. The instructions must be followed *exactly*.

1. Rise early on that morning.
2. Walk *exactly* one hundred paces into a field without turning your head.
3. Pluck *exactly* one hundred blades of grass.
4. Take these home and place them in a pot of spring water. Bring it to a boil.
5. Strain, reserving the liquid and discarding the grass.
6. Boil the liquid once more, let it cool and bottle.

Hundred Grass Lotion is used as a remedy for aura repair, nervous disorders and headaches that resist other cures. It is not to be confused with Hindu Grass Oil, which is a Hoodoo formula similar to Van Van.

Indigo Water

Until the advent of synthetic dyes in the nineteenth century, indigo was a precious commodity, the botanical source of a beautiful, vivid blue dye. Blue is the color that repels the Evil Eye and confers spiritual protection. With the possible exception of the color red, no color is more strongly identified with protective magic than blue. Hence indigo had powerful magical as well as aesthetic value.

Originally native to India, indigo migrated to ancient Egypt, Greece and the Yoruba kingdoms of what is now modern Nigeria, where it was strongly identified with the powerful female orishas Yemaya and, especially, Oshun.

In modern Africa, indigo is especially identified with the Tuareg, the traditionally nomadic people of the Sahara Desert. The Tuareg are known as the *"blue people"* because the indigo used to dye their robes its characteristic shade, bleeds onto their skin, dying it. This is not perceived as merely an accidental hazard but as a welcome effect, because the protective qualities of the indigo are now transferred to the skin.

Brought to American and West Indian plantations in the seventeenth century, the dye was produced for export. Extracted via a lengthy, complicated, tedious, and malodorous process, indigo was only made profitable by the existence of slave labor. The slaves, many of whom came from Yorubaland and its vicinity, also introduced indigo's magical uses. Indigo Water is used:

★ *To empower charms, tools and talismans*
★ *To enhance and empower the aura, through bathing*
★ *For spiritual protection, to ward off evil*
★ *For cleansing spells*

The end of slavery in the nineteenth century, coinciding with the development of synthetic dyes, made true indigo rare. Although there are substitutes, none of them possess the magic power of true indigo.

True indigo water is merely a blend of indigo and water. The most accessible source may be *anil*, a West Indian and South American variation. Mexican anil is sometimes marketed in the form of small vivid blue balls. Dissolve in water to create Indigo Water or keep the ball whole for use as a protective amulet. Used this way, anil balls are a popular ingredient in Mexican Santeria mojo bags.

Laundry bluing or blue food coloring may substitute in any spell that calls for Indigo Water, with the understanding that the power is much reduced. However, *do not substitute* bluestone, also known as blue vitriol or Roman vitriol. Bluestone is copper sulfate, a naturally occurring substance which is truly a lovely shade of blue but, like those colorful Amazonian tree-frogs, is also very toxic. It has been used as a pesticide, now banned in many places, but was once easily obtainable, especially for rural, agricultural people. Because it is blue and was available, it's frequently cited in folk magic spells but is dangerous and should not be used.

Marie Laveau Water

This formula is attributed to Marie Laveau, the renowned Queen of New Orleans Voodoo. Born in 1792, Marie Laveau transformed Voodoo from a surreptitious and persecuted cult into an organized, respected (or feared) established tradition. Following her death, she has achieved unofficial saint status and continues to perform miracles from her grave at New Orleans' St Louis Cemetery Number One.

This formula is sometimes marketed as Holy Water or as Blessing Water. It may substitute in any spell that calls for either one:

One cup rain water
One cup spring water
One cup rose water or hydrosol
One cup Holy Water
One cup lavender water, lavender hydrosol or twenty
 drops of essential oil of lavender

Marie Laveau Water is used for:

★ *Psychic enhancement*
★ *Protection*
★ *Aura Cleansing*
★ *Cleansing spells*

May Wine

May Wine is acknowledged as the ritual potion for Walpurgis Night or May Eve.

Woodruff, also known as Queen or Master of the Woods, is the required ingredient.

Although there are complex methods of creat-ing May Wine, at its simplest steep sprigs of sweet woodruff in white wine for several hours. Bruised strawberries and/or sugar may also be added. Serve and enjoy.

Notre Dame Water

Although this is the name of a specific formula, blessed water from the Cathedral of Notre Dame may be substituted. The predominant ingredient in Notre Dame Water, without which it cannot be considered true Notre Dame formula water, is white roses.

The basic formula is:

Holy Water
White rose hydrosol
Orange hydrosol
Violet hydrosol

It may be necessary to substitute violet absolute for violet hydrosol, or to obtain your own violet fragrance via the infusion or enfleurage process. Violet is a notoriously difficult and expensive scent to extract. Most of what is available commercially is synthetic.

A simpler version of Notre Dame Water may be made by adding essential oil of white roses or white rose hydrosol to spring water.

Notre Dame Water is used for:

★ *Happy home spells, to promote peace, calm and serenity*
★ *Cleansing spells*
★ *Spells to summon spirits*
★ *Uncrossing baths and spells*

Peace Water

This formula is designed to bring serenity to a troubled household. As peace is so elusive, it should come as no surprise that Peace Water is much more difficult to create than, say, War Water. It takes a skilled blender to concoct true Peace Water and it may be the one formula you are better off purchasing than making by hand. However, you need to understand the product in order to obtain or create the real thing.

True Peace Water is visibly identifiable. There should be three distinct layers: two light blue liquids with a clear layer in between. (Some versions only use two layers: one blue, one clear.)

The theory behind Peace Water stems from the biblical phrase regarding spreading oil over troubled waters. The natural propensity for oil and water to separate creates the layers. At its best, Peace Water is aesthetically a very beautiful product, with the light blue color evoking a sense of serenity. The mere visual presence of fine Peace Water is believed magically able to maintain a peaceful, tranquil atmosphere.

★ *Blue layers may be made with Indigo Water or with any of the blue components used to create Indigo Water*
★ *The clear layer may be made with Holy Water, Rose of Jericho Water or Notre Dame Water*
★ *The tricky part is layering the oil and water so that the three layers remain distinct*

Peace Water is used in a variety of house blessing, cleansing and healing spells. To use it, shake the bottle, so that the layers disperse. They should return to their positions once the bottle is at rest.

Pollution Water

This Korean formula is used to remove sources of pollution. Use it in cleansing spells and for banishing.

1. Grind ashes, salt and red pepper to a fine powder.
2. Add the resulting powder to spring water.

The product is intensified if the ashes are the remains of protective spells or holy verses.

In Korea, water with ash is a traditional soap base. Salt and red pepper are used to effect exorcisms.

Rose of Jericho Water

Rose of Jericho is not a rose at all, but a Mexican desert plant with unusual properties. When its environment becomes too parched to support its existence, the plant hits the road to find a better home: it retracts its roots and allows the wind to carry it until it reaches a place where it may continue to grow. It is a choosy plant; it may not take root in the first place it alights.

The plant itself has evolved into a popular lucky charm, shared by many traditions from Mexican Santeria to Southern Conjure to mainstream Wicca. Its miraculous re-hydrating powers have made it a prized component of expensive anti-aging skin creams.

Water used to re-hydrate the plant simultaneously captures the essence of the plant. Water that has successfully resurrected a Rose of Jericho is magically transformed into Rose of Jericho Water. Use pure spring water if possible.

1. Place the rose in a saucer or dish with enough water to cover the bottom of the plant.
2. Wait for it to unfold. Don't be impatient; although some sources promise you that the transformation will occur overnight, realistically it may take three days or longer.
3. Change the water weekly, reserving the old water for magical use.

Rose of Jericho Water is used for:

★ *Cleansing spells*
★ *House blessing spells*
★ *Spell reversals and to repel malevolent magic*

Rose of Jericho Water may substitute in any spell that calls for Holy Water.

Seven Sisters Water

Although there are also Seven Sisters from New Orleans—famed conjure women—this traditional Chinese formula water refers to some different sisters. The Seven Sisters are star maidens, the Pleiades. They are also the seven daughters of either the Jade Emperor or the Kitchen God, depending upon legend. The most famous of the sisters is "the Spider Princess," "the Weaving Lady" who figures in a romantic Chinese myth and is much invoked in love spells.

Seven Sisters Water originally referred to water from a specific spring in Guangzhou, China, drawn during a specific religious ritual. The water developed a considerable reputation for healing and spell-work and eventually began to be produced in different areas and marketed as a product.

This is women's magic; although the formula may benefit men, the water can only be made by women.

1. The seventh day of the seventh month of the Chinese calendar is devoted to the Weaving Lady and her sisters.
2. At midnight, following a day spent honoring the Weaving Lady, living water may be drawn from a well or stream. Invoke the Weaving Lady's blessings as you gather the water.
3. Fill a bottle and seal it shut with wax. Do not break the seal, unless you need to use the water.
4. After the water has been drawn, conclude the day by burning gifts of elegant paper garments, combs, and ornaments for the Seven Sisters.

Seven Sisters Water is believed to have profound curative properties. It allegedly magically repels disease. It is also used in paper burning spells: once a spell paper has been burned, add the ashes to a glass of Seven Sisters Water; stir and consume.

Spirit Water

A glass of pure spring water is typically maintained on an altar, to call in spirits and feed the ancestors. Many find Spirit Water a stronger substitute. This is a favorite of the Spiritualist community and may be used to summon your own ancestral spirits, or in séances or other necromantic spells.

1. Add one tablespoon of anisette to a glass of spring water.
2. Place it on the altar instead of, or in addition to, the standard glass of plain spring water.

Tar Water

This might be the messiest of the formulas. Wear old clothes while concocting it, not your finest robe. Some old formulas suggest using creosote, however this has since been implicated as a possible carcinogen and cannot be recommended. Wood tar is required; you cannot substitute roofing or coal tar, which are petroleum products.
   Basic formula:

1. Approximately one quart (1 liter) of wood tar is required, the sticky stuff scraped from a wood burning fireplace chimney.
2. Put the tar in a bucket. (The bucket will be ruined; you will never be able to use it for any other purpose.)
3. Add about a gallon (4.5 liters) of water.
4. Stir the tar and water with a stick for about fifteen minutes. The stick will be ruined; use something disposable, literally a "stick" rather than your good wand.

5. Let the tar sit and settle for several hours.
6. Strain the water into a clean container.
7. Let the water settle again.
8. Strain it through cheesecloth or similar into a bottle.
9. Shake before using.

Tar Water is used for:

★ *Space and personal cleansings*
★ *Removal of negative thought-forms and psychic manifestations*

War Water, Iron Water or the Water of Mars

Once upon a time, this formula was a mainstay of folk healers, who used it to treat anemia. Although its medical uses are no longer popular, this remains a very important magical formula.

War Water is used:

★ *To gain protection. This is an extremely aggressive, forceful spiritual cleanser*
★ *To reverse a curse and send it back where it came from*
★ *To place a curse. War Water is a traditional and allegedly potent weapon during psychic warfare and witch wars*

Standard Protective War Water

1. Place iron nails in a mason jar. Cut iron nails are recommended because they rust very easily, but any iron nails may be used.
2. Add enough water to cover the nails. Leave this undisturbed until rust begins to form, typically within seven to ten days. Although the jar is usually kept shut, it should be opened periodically to encourage oxidation.
3. Once the rusting process begins, more water may be added. Keep the jar in a refrigerator or other cool area.
4. Strain the water and use as needed.

You may continue adding water to the original nails virtually indefinitely. Some people have a War Water starter lasting years, akin to a sour dough starter. However, should mold or bacteria ever form, discard *everything*, including the jar and start again from the beginning.

Standard Malevolent War Water

1. Collect water from a fierce thunderstorm in a jar.
2. Add rusty nails, sulfur, and some of your own urine.
3. Store this in a cold, dry place until you need it.

This version is used to either place or reverse a hex. The rusted nails from the Protective Formula may be used to create the Malevolent version.

Condition Oils, Formula Oils

Magical oils are among the oldest forms of enchantment, dating back to ancient Egypt, Mesopotamia and Greece. However, their magical renaissance occurred among the New Orleans Voodoo, Hoodoo and Conjure traditions of the late nineteenth and early twentieth centuries. Most of the standard formulas derive from that time, although many are based on much older roots. This period coincided with the development of the mail-order book trade; occultists are always voracious readers and the Hoodoo doctors were no exception. Many were exceptionally well-versed in magical traditions from all over Earth. Hoodoo delights in word play: the genre of magic spell oils became known as "*condition oils*" as they will magically cure your *condition*.

Catchy, dramatic, evocative names became standardized as well. Although there are basic guidelines for making these oils, consider the formulas to be similar to recipes. "*Chicken soup*" or "*lasagna*" raise certain expectations; however every chef may prepare them slightly differently.

The standardization of these oils coincided with the mass marketing of occult products. Mass manufacture of condition oils meant that the people making and selling the product, some inspired by the realization that there might actually be some low-risk money to be made, might not have understood the product or in fact had contempt for the product and its users, their customers. Unscrupulous vendors began to market little more than colored water in bottles labeled with the names of famous condition oil formulas. This frequently remains the case. If your spell depends upon a condition formula, it is crucial for its success that you either purchase materials only from reputable manufacturers or that you mix the formula yourself.

Perfume formulas are marketed as perfume, cologne, dusting powder, soap and other forms as well. Likewise condition formulas may be available as oil, powder, incense, soap, floorwash or other forms. The botanical formula remains constant; hence Commanding Oil is merely Commanding Powder added to oil. Any of the formulas may be converted to other forms as you please.

Although condition oils derive from New Orleans Voodoo and Hoodoo, they have become a mainstay of many other traditions including Palo, Santeria and Wicca. New formulas consistently evolve to serve the needs of different practitioners and magical traditions.

Abra-Melin Oil

Essential oil of cinnamon bark or leaf
Essential oil of galangal
Essential oil of myrrh

1. Add the essential oils to an olive oil base.
2. Add some sort of preservative to the blend, such as Vitamin E, jojoba oil, or simple tincture of benzoin.

The name of this oil refers to a prominent grimoire allegedly written by the magician Abraham ben Simeon in 1458. The book describes how Abraham spent years journeying through Europe, Egypt, and the Middle East in search of mystic wisdom before meeting his teacher, a Jewish magician in Egypt called Abrahamelim or Abra-Melin. This grimoire greatly influenced high ritual magic, however it also encapsulates some of the difficulties of grimoire literary genre. Three versions of the manuscript exist, in French, German and Hebrew respectively. Each is slightly different and it's not clear which is the earliest. Various transcribers also seemed to have left their personal touches so that different parts of the book seem to have been written at different times by different people.

This formula oil derives from biblical records of the formula used in the Jerusalem Temple, and is traditionally used in high ceremonial magic, for conjuring and pacifying spirits. It also bears strong associations with the notorious magus, Aleister Crowley, and it is also sometimes used by fans of Crowley because of those associations.

With this oil, perhaps more than any other, it is crucial to vary the proportions and find a blend that suits you and your purposes. If you plan to apply the oil to your body, either directly or in the bath, you may wish to start with *very* diluted oil. Essential oil of cinnamon provides a *"burn,"* literally. It is a potent skin irritant. Small quantities can raise welts on even fairly insensitive skin, as this writer can testify. For whatever reason, this appeals to some practitioners. Essential oil of cinnamon leaf is slightly gentler than that of the bark, however its fragrance is less vividly intense.

Although it is rare, there is an essential oil of galangal. Unlike almost all other essential oils, it goes rancid *extremely* quickly. Distilled galangal may be substituted, although the fragrance is less vivid. Although ginger root is galangal's botanical cousin, it cannot be used as a substitute.

All Saints Oil

This oil requires seven ingredients, similar to Seven African Powers Oil. The "saints" in this oil may be understood as the Seven African Powers, or as generic benevolent spirit powers, or however else you understand them. This oil evokes blessings of success.

Grind and powder cinnamon, tonka beans, patchouli, vetiver, lavender, gardenia, and mugwort. Cover with sweet almond and jojoba oils.

Attraction Oil

Grated lemon zest

Lovage

Vervain

Essential oil of lemon petitgrain, melissa, may chang or lemon verbena

Rose attar

1. Grind the first three ingredients together in a mortar and pestle.
2. Place them in a bottle together with a lodestone chip
3. Cover with sweet almond oil
4. Add the essential oils, drop by drop, until you achieve a scent that pleases you.

Black Cat Oil

Essential oil of clary sage or dried crumbled sage or clary sage leaves

Essential oil of bay laurel or dried crushed bay leaves

Essential oil of myrrh or solid myrrh resin

A bit of steel wool

Fine iron shot

1. If you have a black cat, pick a hair off the sofa and add it to the mix.

2. Blend with sweet almond oil, unless using for hexes, in which case blend with castor or mineral oil.

Black Cat Oil is used to break bad spells and hexes, but also to attract positive attention from the opposite sex. If protection is your major desire, blend the ingredients into castor oil and jojoba oil. If romance is your motivating factor, substitute sweet almond oil for the castor oil.

Cleopatra Oil

Essential oil of cypress

Essential oil of frankincense

Essential oil of myrrh

Essential oil of petitgrain or neroli

Apricot kernel oil, to blend into

Come to Me Lover

Jasmine absolute

Rose attar

Neroli or essential oil of petitgrain

Gardenia absolute (or fragrance oil)

Tuberose absolute

Blend the above into apricot kernel or sweet almond oil.

This is the most deluxe love-drawing oil. The ingredients are extremely expensive. It is not required that all of them be used, although the first three are fairly standard. The substitution of petitgrain for neroli will keep costs down.

Command and Compel

Depending upon the manufacturer, this classic oil may be marketed as Commanding Oil, Compelling Oil, Commanding and Compelling Oil, Controlling Oil or Conquering Oil.

It is not analogous with High John the Conqueror Oil, which is a completely different condition formula used for completely different purposes. What is marketed as All High Conquering Oil may be either High John the Conqueror or Command and Compel, providing there are any real ingredients in it at all.

The basic commanding formula consists of a blend of sweet flag (calamus) and licorice. They have been used together as such since the days of ancient Egypt. Those two plants, blended together and reduced to a powder may be added to oil to create a potent Commanding Oil.

Other plants also have commanding properties and may be added. Vetiver is a typical addition, as is essential oil of bergamot, which is a strong component of financial commanding spells. Before you add bergamot, however, decide how you wish to use this formula. Essential oil of bergamot is highly photosensitizing. It was once the primary ingredient in European fast-tanning products. If applied to the skin, you must avoid exposure to the sun as odd and long-lasting pigmentation may occur. Bergamot provides the distinctive fragrance of Earl Grey tea. It's very beautiful and tempting to apply to the body. Essential oils of bergamot are marketed with the photosensitizing component removed; these are known as bergaptene-free oils and are worth the trouble of finding.

Add commanding oils to a blend of castor oil and jojoba oil. Malevolent-intent spells would substitute a base of baby oil or mineral oil.

Confusion Oil

Used to confuse an adversary; a favorite of *Courtcase Spells*.

   Black poppy seeds
   Black pepper
   Asafetida
   Sulfur

Grind the above to a fine powder and add to a blend of castor and jojoba oils. For malevolent spells, substitute baby or mineral oil.

Courage Oil

   Cinquefoil (Five-finger grass)
   Gardenia petals
   Rosemary leaves

1. Grind the above ingredients into a fine powder.
2. Add to a blend of jojoba and sunflower oils.
3. You may also add a High John the Conqueror root or a piece of one.

Courtcase Oil

   Courtcase root
   Black mustard seeds

Blend and grind the botanicals together, and add to a base of jojoba and sunflower oils. Supplement with any other botanicals associated with legal spells.

Crown of Success Oil

   Essential oil of bay laurel or dried crushed bay leaves
   Essential oil of frankincense or the powdered resin
   Essential oil of sandalwood or the powder
   Essential oil of vetiver or dried, powdered vetiver roots

Add the above to a blend of sunflower, olive, and/or jojoba oil

Crucible of Courage Oil

   Essential oil of bay laurel or dried, crumbled bay leaves

Essential oil of black pepper or ground black pepper
Essential oil of frankincense or the powdered resin
Essential oil of petitgrain
Essential oil of sandalwood or the dried powder
Essential oil of vetiver or dried powdered vetiver root

Add the above to a blend of sunflower and jojoba oils. Add a drop of borage flower remedy for added enhancement.

Essence of Bend Over or Bend Over Oil

This formula compels others to bend over and do your bidding. Create an extremely concentrated version of Command and Compel Oil.

Because there may be a sexual component to Essence of Bend Over, consider adding aphrodisiac botanicals to the basic blend, such as damiana, cubebs, or Grains of Paradise.

Eve Oil

1. Place dried apple blossoms and pomegranate seeds in a bottle and cover with blended sweet almond and jojoba oils.
2. Add one of the snake roots.

Fiery Wall of Protection

1. Blend powdered dragon's blood and sea salt together with a mortar and pestle.
2. Frankincense and myrrh are required. If you are using solid resins, grind them together with the ingredients in Step 1. If you prefer to use essential oils, then add them last, following Step 3.
3. Add these to castor oil, which has protective capacities of its own but is a very thick oil. You may wish to add jojoba oil, as a preservative, but also so that the oil will flow nicely.

Some variations suggest adding ground ginger and/or cinnamon, too. Just be aware that these are skin irritants and may limit the uses of the oil. Without those ingredients, Fiery Wall can be added to the bath or worn as a protective perfume.

Flying Devil Oil

For the basic formula:

1. Blend red pepper flakes and/or cayenne pepper into an olive oil base.
2. When you shake the oil, you should see the red pepper fly around.

More complex versions also include some or all of the following: black pepper, dragon's blood powder, ground cinnamon, dried patchouli or the essential oil, and dried vetiver or the essential oil.

Follow Me Boy! Oil

Typically, although not always, marketed with that exclamation mark in its name so as to emphasize that this is a command, not a request. *Follow Me Boy!* is the most erotic of the commanding oils. It may be used by either men or women but the target of the command is invariably male as exemplified by the legend that this condition oil was once a staple of New Orleans prostitutes of either gender, reputedly guaranteed to generate business.

The basic formula:

Sweet Flag/Calamus
Catnip
Damiana
Optional ingredients: Licorice, sweet flag's traditional partner, strengthens the commanding aspect. Other botanicals and fragrances may be added as desired to strengthen erotic impact, particularly vetiver, bergamot, sweet orange, tuberose or any vividly red flowers.

1. Grind and powder the dried botanicals.
2. Cover with one or a combination of these oils: castor, sweet almond and apricot kernel. Castor emphasizes the commanding aspect, sweet almond and apricot kernel increase aphrodisiac appeal.

Has No Hanna Oil

Essential oil of jasmine
Essential oil of tangerine (mandarin orange)
Dried powdered oakmoss or the essential oil
Dried powdered vervain

High John the Conqueror Oil

High John the Conqueror can be a very elusive and mysterious botanical. It has very unique properties. There really is nothing that substitutes for it. If there is one condition oil that you should make for yourself, this is it, if only to be sure you are getting the proper ingredients.

High John the Conqueror provides luck and success in all areas of life. It is particularly beneficial for men in regards to romance, although many women swear by it too. High John is considered a completely benevolent botanical. It is used to achieve the highest success without mal intent towards others. Saint John's Wort and tormentil are frequently substituted for High John. Although they are both plants packed with magic powers and used in many spells, their powers are different and cannot be used to provide High John's unique effect.

High John the Conqueror is the root of a member of the Morning Glory family. It also goes by the name *jalap* and as such was once an important medical product in the United States, although it has fallen out of favor and perhaps for good reasons. Do not take High John internally: it is an extremely potent purgative and laxative. Reserve it for magical use.

It's the root that's used and it has a very charac-teristic appearance. Once you are familiar with it, it's difficult to be confused. High John is large, solid and brown with a vaguely earthy aroma. Its shape ranges from perfectly circular to extremely phallic. This oil calls for High John chips, as do many other spells. Once a root is broken up, it is typically indistinguishable from any other. Grind your own High John so that you are not fooled.

1. Break up a High John root. Use a mortar and pestle if you're strong. This is a hard root; grinding may not be easy. Place it between a sheet of folded wax paper and smash it with a hammer, if necessary. Small chips are sufficient; the root doesn't have to be powdered.
2. Put the pieces in a dish and cover them with peanut, olive, sunflower, and/or jojoba oils.
3. Expose the dish to sunlight for seven days.
4. Strain out the root pieces or leave in the oil, as desired. Bottle the oil and use.

Home Protection Oil

Dried five-finger grass (cinquefoil)
Dried gardenia petals
Dried lavender blossoms or the essential oil
Dried purslane
Sandalwood powder or the essential oil

Blend the above into a jojoba oil base. Add a pinch of salt.

Jezebel Oil

1. Hold a Jezebel Root in your left hand and charge it with your desires.
2. Place it in a small jar and cover it with jojoba and sunflower oil. (If you intend to use this oil for stern commanding, add castor oil.)
3. Add essential oils of myrrh, frankincense, bergamot, and amyris.

Lost and Away Oil

Dirt gathered from a crossroads
Powdered sage
Powdered sulfur
Asafetida
Cayenne and/or chili powder

Add the above to a combination of castor and jojoba oils.

Love Drawing Oil

Essential oil of lavender or the dried, ground
    blossoms
Essential oil of jasmine or dried flowers
Rose attar or dried rose petals

1. If using dried botanicals, blend them and grind into a fine powder.
2. Cover them with sweet almond oil.
3. Essential oils should be added drop by drop to the sweet almond oil, until the desired intensity of fragrance is achieved.
4. Add an orrisroot to the bottle.

Lucky Lodestone Oil

Add crushed, powdered lodestone to Van Van Oil.

Maximon Oil

Essential oil of citronella
Essential oil of pink grapefruit
Essential oil of lemongrass
Essential oil of mandarin orange (tangerine)

Blend the essential oils into a base of jojoba oil.

More Money Oil

Essential oil of chamomile
Essential oil of Texas cedarwood
Essential oil of vetiver

Add the above to jojoba oil.

Magnet or Lodestone Oil

Commercial preparations are sold under both of these names, however the term Magnet Oil is used throughout the text of this book to distinguish it from Lucky Lodestone Oil, which is a completely different formulation.

1. Place either seven or nine lodestones in a mason jar.
2. Sprinkle them with magnetic sand.
3. Cover the lodestones with a blend of sweet almond and jojoba oils.
4. Close the jar and let the lodestones rest for seven days, exposed to sunlight and moonbeams.
5. Pick up the jar and swirl the contents around once a day.
6. After seven days, the oil may be strained and used.
7. Transfer the oil to different bottles. Feed the lodestones with magnetic sand and use them to make more oil.

Protection Oil

Ground cinnamon
Galangal root
Dried ground peppermint leaves
Dried rue
Dried ground vervain
Dried ground vetiver or the essential oil

Blend and powder the above ingredients. Add them to a base of sunflower, olive, and/or jojoba oil.

Queen of Sheba Oil

Makeda, Queen of Sheba visited King Solomon bearing gifts of precious resins and spices. She allegedly introduced the Balm of Gilead or balsam tree, a source of fragrant, precious resin (although not the same as the balm of Gilead buds currently so popular in magic). The finest balsam resin in the ancient world was allegedly produced in Judea from trees introduced by the Queen of Sheba. These balsam groves were completely eradicated by the Romans during their conquest of Judea. Essential oil of amyris is the closest modern substitute.

If you'd like to wear this as perfume, keep the quantity of cinnamon oil to a bare minimum to avoid skin irritation. The oil is made from essential oils of amyris, cinnamon bark, frankincense, myrrh, rose, and spikenard, added to grapeseed oil.

Saint Martha the Dominator Oil

1. Grind spikenard root shavings, sweet flag, licorice root, and myrrh resin together.
2. Cover with olive oil.

Saint Martha the Dominator Oil is used for happy home Spells, domination spells and protection spells.

San Cipriano Oil

There are two Saint Cyprians, both former master magi who converted to Christianity and were martyred. One was a Bishop of Carthage. One or both of them seems to have resumed his former profession after death. San Cipriano is the most influential figure in the magical traditions of the Iberian Peninsula. A prominent grimoire is attributed to him. San Cipriano is a miracle worker; the oil named in his honor allegedly casts miraculous spells.

Cinnamon powder
Low John the Conqueror
Orrisroot
Myrrh resin or the essential oil
Essential oil of cedarwood
Essential oil of cypress

1. Blend and grind all solid materials together to form a powder.
2. Cover them with olive, sunflower, and/or jojoba oils.
3. Add the essential oils as the last step, drop by drop, until you've achieved the desired intensity of fragrance.

Low John the Conqueror, also known as bethroot, was not long ago a very common magical plant and is a traditional component of San Cipriano Oil. It is now highly endangered and it is very likely that you will not be able to obtain it. Even if you can, it should be verified whether it was ethically gathered, for the success of your spells as well as for the sake of the plant. There really is no adequate substitute for it. However, leave it out if necessary and compensate by strengthening other areas of spell work, visualization for instance. Perhaps the best alternative is to attempt to grow your own supply of bethroot.

Seven African Powers Oil

Add the following to palm oil: real coconut extract, black pepper, mugwort, cinnamon, seaweed (dulse, agar-agar or other), real almond extract, and either mimosa or jasmine for a total of seven ingredients.

Uncrossing Oil

Essential oil of hyssop
Essential oil of angelica

Essential oil of frankincense

A pinch of sea salt

A pinch of black pepper

A pinch of cayenne pepper

A sprig of rue

A sliver of fresh garlic

A section of broken chain, e.g., from a key-chain or necklace

Add the ingredients to a bottle filled with blended castor oil and jojoba oil. The crucial ingredients are the hyssop and the chain. Add the other ingredients as desired. Essential oil of angelica has photosensitizing properties: if worn on the body, avoid exposure to the sun.

Van Van Oil

The epitome of condition oils, Van Van may be the single most versatile oil, drawing luck, love, and prosperity and repelling malevolent magic directed toward you. Many confuse the name with "vanilla." It may be added if you like, however true Van Van is a blend of five wild Asian grasses. Similar formulas may also be marketed as Hindu Grass Oil or Henry's Grass Oil.

The five grasses are lemongrass, citronella, palmarosa, gingergrass, and vetiver. All of them are available as essential oils, although gingergrass is rare. Van Van may be made from essential oils, dried botanicals or a combination of the two. Add them to a base of jojoba, sunflower, and/or safflower oils. Patchouli, another Asian grass, may be added for some extra power.

For optimum power, all five grasses should be used, however any combination is acceptable. Lemongrass is the predominant ingredient, if only because its aroma is so potent. Many versions of Van Van contain only lemongrass.

Wall of Protection Oil

Fiery Wall of Protection Oil minus dragon's blood.

Incense and Powders

Loose incense consists of nothing more than the dried, powdered ingredients. "Powders" may be identical to incense, the words are sometimes used interchangeably, or you may blend them with arrowroot powder, cornstarch or rice powder, to create a dusting powder.

Amber

Do not burn amber beads! The confusion lies between the solidified resin known as amber and ambergris, the fragrant substance derived from sperm whales, also often called ambra. This "Amber" formula somewhat replicates the fragrance of ambergris. Blend ground powdered labdanum, benzoin, and vanilla bean.

Black Salt

Although there is an actual black salt used in Indian cuisine, magical black salt is concocted by blending salt with the scrapings from cast iron cookware. Black salt is mainly used in protection spells and to cast hexes.

Cascarilla Powder

This is powdered eggshell: the only ingredient is eggshell. Eggshells once had profound associations with European witches. Witches were believed able to transform an emptied eggshell into a vehicle for travel over water or through the air. To make sure they weren't helping the witches have fun, many insisted on crumbling emptied eggshells before disposing of them. To leave them whole was to invite the witches' use. Ironically, powdered eggshell is a magical ingredient in many spells, both benevolent and otherwise.

Cascarilla Powder can be either white or brown:

White Cascarilla Powder
1. Clean the eggshells and let them dry out.
2. Crumble the pieces and place them in a mortar and pestle.
3. Grind these into a fine powder.

Brown Cascarilla Powder
1. Clean the eggshells.
2. Break up the shells so that the pieces lie flat.
3. Toast these pieces in a low, slow oven until the shells brown.
4. Grind these to a fine powder.

Drawing Powder

This is confectioner's sugar.

Graveyard Dust

Graveyard dust may be self-explanatory: dirt from the graveyard. It may also be various botanicals or a combination of the two.

Valerian, patchouli, and mullein all bear the nickname *graveyard dust*. Grind and powder the botanicals and use them where graveyard dust or dirt is indicated. Alternatively, collect dirt from the cemetery. Further details are available in *Death Spells* (page 251).

Goofer Dust

"*Goofer*" derives from the Kikongo word "*kufwa*," meaning "to die," and 99.5 percent of Goofer Dust's uses are malevolent. It is a usually a blend of graveyard dirt (real dirt, not botanicals) with other substances. Thousands of recipes exist, with practitioners boasting of the potency of their private blends.

Goofer Dust allegedly causes the target of the spell to become weak and confused. Powers of speech, concentration, and thought are allegedly affected; the target acts "*goofy.*" Some claim Goofer Dust leaves victims crawling on all four, barking like a dog. Particularly potent Goofer Dust, real "*killing powder*," causes the victim to waste away, eventually dying if an antidote is not found.

The most common basic version is a blend of graveyard dust, salt, and sulfur (brimstone.) Other popular ingredients include gunpowder and church bell grease.

Goofer Dust's most famous associations are with New Orleans-styled Voodoo and Hoodoo, from whence it derives its name. Although it may not be called Goofer Dust elsewhere, this is not an isolated formula. In his autobiography, Dr. John, the brilliant New Orleans musician, recalls scraping grease from church bells for the dust. Across the Atlantic Ocean, far from African influence, Slavic witches traditionally climbed into church steeples on Saint George's Day to obtain grease from bell axles for similar purposes.

Henna Powder and Paste

Henna powder derives from the dried ground leaves of the henna plant. Henna paste is created from the powder. Although henna paste may be purchased, choose your vendor carefully: for optimum magic power and aesthetic beauty both powder and paste must be fresh, not aged. There are thousands of methods of preparing henna paste: technique and intuition combine. Here is a suggestion:

1. Henna powder should be green and fragrant.
2. Even though a reputable vendor will sift their henna, further sifting may be required and will certainly be beneficial. Sieves are ancient magical tools: while sifting, concentrate on your desires for the henna design, whether aesthetic or enchanted.
3. Boil approximately one half cup of loose black tea in roughly four cups of water until the water has been reduced by about one half.
4. Add any additional ingredients: suggestions include rose petals, saffron, fenugreek, or cloves.
5. Simmer this brew for approximately an hour.
6. Strain and discard the solids, reserving only the liquid.
7. Strain a lemon or lime and add only the juice, not pulp or seeds, to the brew.
8. Warm the brew but do not allow it to boil.
9. Begin to add approximately one half cup of henna powder. Add it slowly, spoonful by spoonful, keeping an eye on the texture. The goal is to achieve something that is similar in consistency to cake batter.
10. Once the consistency has been achieved, add approximately one teaspoon of essential oil of eucalyptus.
11. Test the paste by dabbing a little on your skin and leaving it there for fifteen minutes. Although the henna is not yet full strength, a faint orange tinge should still develop.
12. Let the finished paste rest in a warm place, covered, for approximately six hours before using it to paint designs.

Jyoti Powder

Grind and powder the following ingredients: Southern John (galangal root, Courtcase root, Little John to Chew), nasturtium seeds, and patchouli. Blend with arrowroot powder.

Sprinkle Jyoti Powder for cleansing spells, money spells, and reversing spells.

Kinnikinnik

Kinnikinnik is the Algonquian name for various botanical blends used in ritual and as spiritual offerings. The name also refers specifically to bearberry, and the simplest kinnikinnik is bearberry alone. Complex kinnikinnik blends may contain as many as thirty botanicals.

Choose from the following: angelica, bayberry, bearberry, blueberry, birch, bristly crowfoot, Canada hemlock, deer berry, dogwood, goldenrod, horseweed, mint, juniper, mullein, tobacco, willow, yarrow, or yerba santa. Prepare and dry each herb separately, then blend and store in leather pouches.

Kinnikinnik is used in various ways:

★ *Carry in a charm bag for protection and luck*
★ *Store ritual tools in kinnikinnik powder to empower and activate them*
★ *Burn as cleansing incense*
★ *Use it as an offering when harvesting plants*

Kyoto Powder

Despite its name, Kyoto Powder is a Hoodoo formulation used to reverse bad luck, and has nothing to do with Japan. Grind and powder clove buds, orrisroot, lavender blossoms, and dried vanilla beans. Blend with arrowroot powder and sprinkle as needed.

Kyphi

Kyphi was an Egyptian temple incense formula so important that its formula was engraved onto temple walls. Various formulas existed. Kyphi is an oil- and fat-free formula, based on wine and raisins with added fragrant botanicals. It was used in sacred ritual but also to relieve insomnia and provide deep sleep. Ingredients might include:

Cardamom pods
Cinnamon
Coriander seeds
Frankincense
Golden raisins
Honey
Juniper berries
Mastic resin
Myrrh
Red wine
Rosebuds
Sweet flag/calamus root

The scent traveled through the ancient world: the Egyptians were scandalized when the Greeks began to use kyphi as an aphrodisiac. The Egyptian method of creating kyphi was complex. An example follows. The name kyphi is frequently used by manufacturers of spiritual products to indicate any incense possessing an ancient Egyptian "ambience."

Egyptian Kyphi

1. Begin by blending equal parts dried ground acacia, henna, and juniper.
2. Soak the resulting powder in wine.
3. In a separate container soak golden raisins in wine.
4. Allow this soaking process to continue for seven days.
5. Take equal parts cardamom, sweet flag/calamus, cinnamon, peppermint, bay leaves, galangal, and orrisroot.
6. Grind each one separately then blend and grind again into a fine powder.
7. Add a tablespoon of honey and a tablespoon of myrrh resin to the spice mixture.
8. Drain the herbs and raisins soaking in wine and add them to the honey/myrrh/spice mixture.
9. Add sufficient wine to steep the combined materials, plus terebinth and raisins to form a thick paste.
10. Use this as is (simmer it to release the fragrance) or dry it, cut into squares and burn as incense.

New Home Incense

Coriander seeds
Frankincense
Mastic pearls
Myrrh

Grind the above ingredients together and burn.

Magic Inks

Many spells involve a written component. Once upon a time, magicians chose their ink carefully depending upon the purpose of the spell, in the manner that someone today might choose a candle or condition oil. Some magicians still do. The most popular magical inks used in Western magic tend to be named after the blood of various creatures. They are marketed commercially and are readily available through occult sources. However, in many cases what is purchased is nothing more than plain ink with a label bearing a catchy title.

A long history exists of using animal names as a code for various plant substances. Among the reasons for this practice was the desire to maintain secret formulas. Unfortunately, when the formulas are obtained without understanding or even knowing of the existence of the code, all sorts of misunderstanding and tragedy may follow. While some complain that modern manufactured *"blood"* inks no longer contain the botanical formulas, others claim that the formulas actually demand blood; the only way to produce "true" dove's blood ink, for instance, being to slit the throat of a dove. This is untrue. Dove's blood ink is frequently used to write love spells. Doves are sacred to Aphrodite, Genius of Love. Do you think that, having done very bad things to her bird, she will look kindly on your petition? The only blood typically called for in magic spells may be your own, and even that requires no more than a few drops from a finger.

Formulas are frequently very similar. The red color typically derives from the resin dragon's blood, a powerful magical agent. Even if a formula doesn't specifically call for it, it is extremely likely that adding gum arabica or gum tragacanth to the mix will be necessary in order to make the ink thick enough to be functional. Typically one-quarter to one-half teaspoon is needed.

If mixing inks from scratch is forbidding, a simple yet magically charged method of creating the various "Blood" inks is to add the appropriate essential oils and resins to plain red ink.

Bat's Blood Ink

Dragon's blood
Alcohol
Gum arabica
Scent with essential oils of cinnamon and myrrh

For commanding, domination, and hexing spells.

Butterfly's Blood Ink

Add saffron so that the ink will be golden-yellow. Vervain may be added as well. Use this ink for love spells and spirit summoning spells. Unless you're making a tremendous quantity of ink, a very few strands of saffron should be sufficient. Place the saffron strands in a glass and pour a little boiling water over them. Add this liquid to your ink formula.

Dove's Blood Ink

Dragon's blood
Alcohol
Gum arabica
Scent with essential oils of bay laurel, cinnamon and rose

For love spells.

Dragon's Blood Ink

Alcohol
Dragon's blood
Gum arabica
Optional: Essential oil of cinnamon

Lampblack Ink

1. Choose a candle color to coordinate with the purpose of your spell. (Green for money, for instance.)
2. Carve and dress as desired, then burn the candle.
3. Hold a spoon over the candle flame until black soot forms. (This takes a while; it's a time-consuming process requiring patience.) This soot is lampblack.
4. When sufficient lampblack has been produced, carefully tap it off the spoon and into a bowl.
5. Add spring water, drop by drop, to dissolve the soot and then add gum arabica to thicken the ink.

Enhanced Lampblack Ink
This formula, which incorporates sacred resins, is specifically designed for *Spirit Summoning Spells*, especially for creating angel sigils, but may also be used for *Protection Spells*.

1. Blend benzoin, frankincense, and myrrh resin and burn.
2. Hold a spoon over the burning resin until lampblack soot forms. (Be patient.)
3. Gently tap the soot into a bowl.
4. Add rose hydrosol or water drop by drop until the lampblack is dissolved.
5. Add gum arabica so that the ink is thick enough to use.

Raven's Blood Ink

This ink uses the same formula as dragon's blood ink, except that the red color is obtained from iron oxide powder, rather than powdered dragon's blood. It is used for love spells.

Raven's Feather Ink

1. Burn one black feather, freely given.
2. Add the ashes to ink.

For commanding spells.

Not every magical tradition associates ink with blood.

Chinese Magical Ink

Write spells with a peach-wood pen and cinnabar ink.

Moroccan Ritual Ink

For writing charms and talismans:

1. Boil myrtle and bay laurel leaves and twigs in water.
2. Strain out the solids.
3. Mix the remaining liquid with ink.

For written love spells:

1. Gently warm rosewater and pour it over a few saffron threads.
2. Strain and add the liquid to existing ink or mix up your own with alcohol and gum arabica.

Rosewater Charm Ink

Rosewater was traditionally used as ink in the creation of Sufi charms.

Write the charm. Place the paper in water; the "ink" should dissolve. Drink the water.

Tibetan Ritual Inks

For writing charms: the challenging method is to blend soot or burned barley or rice with tree resin or grain pulp. The easier method is to use Chinese block ink!

Tips for Magic Ink and Written Spells

★ *Wormwood allegedly possesses the magic power to provide protection for the written word from all sorts of dangers, spiritual and magical as well as the verminous kind with little teeth. Dioscorides recommended adding wormwood juice to ink, in order to keep mice away from papyrus. Add it to any of the above recipes, or to any other ink*

★ *The grimoire* Grimorium Verum, *allegedly published in Egypt in 1517, recommends that, regardless of what's actually in the inkwell, a magician's inkwell should be inscribed with the following, transliterated from the Hebrew:*

YOD HE VAV HE
METATRON
YAD
KADOSH
ELOYM
SABAOTH

This serves to infuse divine power into the ink and to ward off evil influences.

Tables

Table of Color Associations

The color associations that follow are based on general occult wisdom; they will not supplant your own personal associations. Your own associations will supersede any conventional wisdom. White, which bears the power of the blank slate, may always be substituted for any other color.

Colors are morally neutral; there are no inherently bad or good colors; the common prejudice that depicts a spectrum from black to white as depicting evil to good is just that: a common prejudice. Each color possesses its own power that may be drawn upon by the spell-caster.

Color	Association
Black	Fertility; healing; hexes; repelling and reversing spells; solace; Dark Moon spells
Blue	Traditionally the most potent color of protection; anti-Evil Eye
Brown	Grounding and stabilizing effects during divination and psychic journeys; justice spells
Green	Healing; money; prosperity; growth and increase; fertility
Pink	Love; friendship; romance; a beneficial color when working magic on behalf of children
Purple	Sex; passion; power; commanding; domination; higher consciousness
Red	Love; sex; romance; luck; fertility; healing; death-defying; protection; anti-Evil Eye
White	Initiations; creativity; lunar spells; spells to allay ghosts; healing
Yellow	Love; romance; power; prosperity

Planetary Correspondences of Metals

Planet	Metal
Sun	Gold
Moon	Silver
Mercury	Mercury, Zinc
Venus	Copper
Mars	Iron
Jupiter	Tin
Saturn	Lead

Astrological Correspondences

Dates given for each astrological sign are approximate, and indicate the sun's position in the sign; moon signs can be determined by referencing to an ephemeris or almanac.

Sign	Date	Bodily Correspondence
Aries	Mar 21–Apr 20	Head
Taurus	Apr 21–May 20	Neck, throat, shoulders
Gemini	May 21–June 20	Lungs, hands, arms
Cancer	June 21–July 20	Breasts, stomach
Leo	July 21–Aug 20	Heart, solar plexus
Virgo	Aug 21–Sept 20	Digestive system
Libra	Sept 21–Oct 20	Kidneys, back
Scorpio	Oct 21–Nov 20	Reproductive and eliminatory organs
Sagittarius	Nov 21–Dec 20	Thighs
Capricorn	Dec 21–Jan 20	Knees, bones
Aquarius	Jan 21–Feb 20	Calves, ankles, circulatory and glandular systems
Pisces	Feb 21–Mar 20	Feet

Numbers

Each number radiates powers that may be incorporated into spells as desired. General metaphysical wisdom suggests that odd numbers are more powerful than even numbers. Indeed, all the most magically powerful numbers (three, seven, nine, and their multiples) are odd; however, one must also take into consideration that, at least since Pythagoras if not earlier, odd numbers have been classified as masculine and the even numbers feminine. Whether this has anything to do with the prestige accorded odd numbers may be worthy of study.

Number	Association
1	Unity; the number of the Creator
2	Happiness; love; balance; duality; the act of creation and generation
3	Supreme magic number of power; successful prophesy; the successful culmination (the end result) of the creative act
4	Stability (Native American numerology); death and danger (East Asian numerology); challenge
5	Protection (Semitic magic); instability and havoc (the Golden Dawn); adventure
6	Love; romance; successful acquisition
7	Supreme magic number of power, the number that epitomizes magic—7 seas, 7 stars/planets, 7 archangels, 7 devils, and 7 miracles; protection; success; reversing and cleansing spells
8	Infinity; eternity; success
9	Supreme magic number of power (3 x 3); protection; success; reversing and cleansing spells; achievement; accomplishment; finality; the ultimate expression

Seven African Powers

Each of the Seven African Powers is affiliated with specific colors and numbers; incorporate these into spells dedicated to them individually or en masse. Because African slaves were forbidden their own spiritual traditions, each orisha was also syncretized to a Roman Catholic saint, although exactly which one depends upon the African Diaspora tradition to which one subscribes.

Orisha	Color	Syncretized Saint	Number
Elegba	Black, red	Saint Anthony, Saint Peter, the Anima Sola, Holy Child of Atocha	3, 7
Obatala	White	Jesus Christ, Our Lady of Mercy	8
Ogun	Black, red (green in some traditions)	Saint James the Major, Michael the Archangel, Saint Peter, Saint George, Saint Anthony	3, 7
Chango	Red, white	Saint Barbara, Saint Jerome	6
Yemaya	Blue, white, crystal clear	Stella Maris	7
Oshun	Yellow, orange, coral	Our Lady of Charity	5
Orunmila*	Green, yellow	Saint Francis	4
Oya*	Purple, maroon, brown or multi-colored	Saint Barbara, Our Lady of Candelaria, Saint Catherine	9
Ochossi*	Lavender, brown	Saint Sebastian	2

* The seventh African power is subject to interpretation. Because the magic number seven cannot be changed, orishas cannot simply be added to the list; should one wish to incorporate a different orisha, one of the original seven must be removed. Orunmila is the traditional seventh power, one of the original seven. However, Orunmila has less personal individual interaction with his followers than other orishas, and is therefore less familiar (and less beloved) than other orishas; he is often replaced in this pantheon. Orunmila is most frequently replaced by the orisha Oya, who, in a sense, is the feminist choice. The hunter-warrior Ochossi has become increasingly prominent (as demonstrated by the number of spells dedicated to him) and has very recently begun to appear among the Seven African Powers as well.

☆ Bibliography

Adams, Anton and Mina Adams, *The Learned Arts of Witches and Wizards*. New York: MetroBooks, 1998

Addison, Josephine, *Love Potions: A Book of Charms and Omens*. Tops Field, Mass.: Salem House Publishers, 1987

Aftel, Mandy, *Essence and Alchemy*. New York: North Point Press, 2001

Ankarloo, Bengt and Stuart Clark, *Witchcraft and Magic in Europe: Biblical and Pagan Societies*. Philadelphia: University of Pennsylvania Press, 2001

Ankarloo, Bengt and Stuart Clark, *Witchcraft and Magic in Europe: Ancient Greece and Rome*. Philadelphia: University of Pennsylvania Press, 2001

Ann, Martha and Dorothy Meyers Imel, *Goddesses in World Mythology*. New York: Oxford University Press, 1993

Aunt Sally's Policy Players Dream Book and Wheel of Fortune. Los Angeles: Indio Products

Aveni, Anthony, *Behind The Crystal Ball*. New York: Times Books, 1996

Barnes, Sandra T., *Africa's Ogun*. Indianapolis: Indiana University Press, 1997

Bartel, Pauline, *Spellcasters*. Dallas: Taylor Trade Publishing, 2000

Beckwith, Carol and Angela Fisher, *African Ceremonies Volume 1*. New York: Harry N. Abrams, 1999

Beckwith, Carol, *Nomads of Niger*. New York: Harry N. Abrams, 1993

Beckwith, Martha Warren, *Black Roadways*. New York: Negro Universities Press, 1969

Ben-Ami, Issachar, *Saint Veneration Among The Jews in Morocco*. Detroit: Wayne State University Press, 1998

Beresford, Brian, *Sacred Life of Tibet*. London: Thorsons, 1997

Betz, Hans Dieter, *The Greek Magical Papyri in Translation Including The Demotic Spells*. Chicago: The University of Chicago Press, 1992

Bharadwaj, Monisha, *The Indian Luck Book*. London: Penguin Compass, 2001

Biale, David, *Cultures of The Jews*. New York: Schocken Books, 2002

Bibbs, Susheel, *Heritage of Power: Marie Laveau–Mary Ellen Pleasant*. San Francisco: MEP Publications, 2002

Binder, Pearl, *Magic Symbols of The World.* London: Hamlyn, 1972

Black, Jeremy and Anthony Green, *Gods, Demons and Symbols of Ancient Mesopotamia.* Austin: University of Texas Press, 1992

Bonwick, James, *Irish Druids and Old Irish Religions.* New York: Dorset Press, 1986

Botermans, Jack et al., *The World of Games.* New York: Facts on File, 1989

Boyd, Valerie, *Wrapped In Rainbows: The Life of Zora Neale Hurston.* New York: Scribner, 2003

Bramly, Serge, *Macumba.* San Francisco: City Lights, 1994

Bredon, Juliet and Igor Mitrophanow, *The Moon Year.* Hong Kong: Oxford University Press, 1982

Brier, Bob, *Ancient Egyptian Magic.* New York: Quill, 1981

Briggs, Katharine, *Abbey Lubbers, Banshees and Boggarts.* New York: Pantheon Books, 1979

Buckland, Raymond, *The Witch Book.* Detroit: Visible Ink, 2002

Buckland, Raymond, *Secrets of Gypsy Love Magick.* St Paul, Minnesota: Llewellyn Publications, 2000

Budge, E.A. Wallis, *Egyptian Magic.* New York: Dover Publications, 1971

Buruma, Ian, *Behind The Mask.* New York: New American Library, 1984

Camphausen, Rufus C., *The Yoni.* Rochester, Vermont: Inner Traditions International, 1996

Camphausen, Rufus C., *The Encyclopedia of Erotic Wisdom.* Rochester, Vermont: Inner Traditions International, 1991

Canizares, Baba Raul, *The Book of Palo.* Old Bethpage, New York: Original Publications, 2002

Cassiel, *Encyclopedia of Black Magic.* New York: Mallard Press, 1990

Catty, Suzanne, *Hydrosols: The Next Aromatherapy.* Rochester, Vermont: Healing Arts Press, 2001

Cave, Roderick, *Chinese Paper Offerings.* Hong Kong: Oxford University Press, 1998

Cavendish, Richard, *The Powers of Evil.* New York: G.P. Putnam's Sons, 1975

Cavendish, Richard, *The Black Arts.* New York: Perigee Books, 1967

Chamberlain, Jonathan, *Chinese Gods.* Selangor Darul Ehsan, Malaysia: Pelanduk Publications, 1987

Clebert, Jean-Paul, *The Gypsies.* Baltimore: Penguin Books, 1963

Clifford, Terry and Sam Antupit, *Cures.* New York: Macmillan Publishing Company, 1980

Clymer, R. Swinburne, *The Philosophy Of Living Fire.* Montana: 1906 (reprinted Kessinger Publishing Company, Belle Fourche, South Dakota.)

Colonial Dames of America, *Herbs and Herb Lore of Colonial America.* New York: Dover Publications, 1995

Courtney-Clarke, Margaret, *Imazighen: The Vanishing Traditions of Berber Women.* New York: Clarkson Potter, 1996

Cross, Milton, *The New Complete Stories of The Great Operas.* Garden City, New York: Doubleday & Company, 1955

Cunningham, Scott, *Cunningham's Encyclopedia of Gem, Crystal and Metal Magic.* St Paul, Minnesota: Llewellyn Publications, 2001

Danielou, Alain, *The Phallus.* Rochester, Vermont: Inner Traditions International, 1995

Daniels, Ger, *Folk Jewelry of The World.* New York: Rizzoli International Publications, 1989

David-Neel, Alexandra, *Magic and Mystery In Tibet.* New York: Dover Publications, 1971

Davidson, Gustav, *A Dictionary of Angels.* New York: Free Press, 1967

De Claremont, Lewis, *Legends of Incense, Herb and Oil Magic.* Arlington, Texas: Dorene Publishing Company, 1938

De Givry, Grillot, *Le Musee des sorciers, mages et alchimistes.* Paris: Librairie de France, 1929

De Laurence, L.W., *The Great Book of Magical Arts, Hindu Magic and Indian Occultism.* Chicago: The De Laurence Publishing Company, 1915

De Luca, Diana, *Botanica Erotica.* Rochester, Vermont: Healing Arts Press, 1998

Deren, Maya, *Divine Horsemen: The Living Gods of Haiti.* London: Thames and Hudson, 1953

DeStefano, Anthony M., *Latino Folk Medicine.* New York: Ballantine Books, 2001

Deveney, John Patrick, *Paschal Beverly Randolph.* Albany: State University of New York Press, 1997

Dillon, Millicent, *A Little Original Sin: The Life and Work of Jane Bowles.* New York: Holt, Rinehart and Winston, 1981

Di Stasi, Lawrence, *Mal Occhio.* San Francisco: North Point Press, 1981

Dollison, John, *Pope-Pourri.* New York: Fireside Books, 1994

Dorson, Richard M., *Folk Legends of Japan.* Tokyo: Charles E. Tuttle Company, 1962

Douglas, Nik, *Tibetan Tantric Charms and Amulets.* Mineola, New York: Dover Publications, 2002

Dubin, Lois Sherr, *The History of Beads.* New York: Harry N. Abrams, 1998

Eberhard, Wolfram, *Chinese Festivals.* New York: Henry Schuman, 1952

Egan, Martha, *Milagros: Votive Offerings From The Americas.* Albuquerque: University of New Mexico Press

Eiseman, Fred B. Jr, *Bali Sekala and Niskala Volume I: Essays On Religion, Ritual and Art.* Hong Kong: Periplus Editions, 1990

Elkin, A.P., *The Australian Aborigine.* Garden City, New York: The Natural History Library, 1964

Elworthy, Frederick Thomas, *The Evil Eye.* New York: The Julian Press, 1958

Epton, Nina, *Magic and Mystics of Java.* London: The Octagon Press, 1974

Epton, Nina, *Saints and Sorcerers.* London: Cassell & Company, 1958

Erikson, Joan Mowat, *The Universal Bead.* New York: W.W. Norton & Company, 1993

Fadiman, Anne, *The Spirit Catches You and You Fall Down.* New York: Farrar, Straus and Giroux, 1997

Faivre, Antoine, *The Eternal Hermes.* Grand Rapids: Phanes Press, 1995

Faraone, Christopher A., *Ancient Greek Love Magic.* Cambridge, Mass.: Harvard University Press, 1999

Farina, Elizabeth Warnock, *A Street In Marrakech.* Garden City, New York: Doubleday and Company, 1975

Fernandez Olmos, Margarite and Lizabeth Paravisini-Gebert, *Sacred Possessions.* New Brunswick, New Jersey: Rutgers University Press, 1997

Fielding, William J., *Strange Customs of Courtship and Marriage.* Garden City, New York: Garden City Books, 1960

Fischer-Rizzi, Susanne, *Complete Earth Medicine Handbook.* New York: Sterling Publishing, 2003

Fischer-Rizzi, Susanne, *The Complete Incense Book.* New York: Sterling Publications, 1996

Fitch, Ed, *A Grimoire of Shadows.* St. Paul, Minnesota: Llewellyn Publications, 1997

Franci, Luisa, *Dragontime: Magic and Mystery of Menstruation.* Woodstock: Ash Tree Publishing, 1991

Frazer, Sir James George, *The Golden Bough.* New York: Collier Books, 1950

Friedman, Albert B., *The Viking Book of Folk Ballads of The English-Speaking World.* Harmondsworth, Middlesex: Penguin Books, 1956

Fruehauf, Solomon B., *The Book of Psalms: A Commentary.* Cincinnati: Union of American Hebrew Congregations, 1938

Fu, Shelley, *Ho Yi The Archer and Other Classic Chinese Tales.* North Haven, Connecticut: Linnet Books, 2001

Gamache, Henri, *The Master Book of Candle Burning*. Plainview, New York: Original Publications, 1984

Gamache, Henri, *Mystery of The Long Lost Books of Moses*. Plainview, New York: Original Publications, 1983

Gamest, Frederick C., *The Qemant: A Pagan-Hebraic Peasantry of Ethiopia*. New York: Holt, Rinehart and Winston, 1969

Gardner, Dore, *Nino Fidencio: A Heart Thrown Open*. Santa Fe: Museum of New Mexico Press, 1992

Gaster, M., *Sword Of Moses: An Ancient Book of Magic*. London: 1896 (reprinted by Kessinger Publishing, Belle Fourche, South Dakota)

Gaster, Theodor H., *The Holy and The Profane*. New York: William Sloane Associates, 1955

Gersi, Douchan, *Faces In The Smoke*. Los Angeles: Jeremy P. Archer, 1991

Giles, Carl H. and Barbara Ann Williams, *Bewitching Jewellery*. London: Thomas Roseleaf Ltd., 1976

Glassman, Sallie Ann, *Vodou Visions*. New York: Villard Books, 2000

Godwin, Jocelyn, *Mystery Religions In The Ancient World*. London: Thames and Hudson, 1981

Gonzalez-Wippler, Migene, *The Complete Book of Spells, Ceremonies & Magic*. St Paul, Minnesota: Llewellyn Publications, 1997

Grahn, Judy, *Blood, Bread, and Roses*. Boston: Beacon Press, 1993

Grandee, Lee R., *Strange Experience: The Secrets of A Hexenmeister*. Englewood Cliffs, New Jersey: Prentice-Hall, Inc., 1971

Gravel, Pierre Bettez, *The Malevolent Eye*. New York: Peter Lang Publishing, 1995

Gregory, Lady, *Visions and Beliefs In The West of Ireland*. New York: The Knickerbockers Press, 1920

Grieve, Mrs. M., *A Modern Herbal, Volumes 1 and 2*. New York: Dover Publications 1971

Haining, Peter, *Superstitions*. London: Sidgwick and Jackson, 1979

Hall, Judy, *The Illustrated Guide To Crystals*. New York: Sterling Publishing, 2000

Hall, Nor, *Irons In The Fire*. Barrytown, New York: Station Hill, 2002

Hanauer, J.E., *Folklore of The Holy Land: Moslem, Christian and Jewish*. Mineola, New York: Dover Publications, 2002

Harris, Bill, *The Good Luck Book*. Owings Mills, Maryland: Ottenheimer Publications, 1996

Haskins, Jim, *Voodoo & Hoodoo*. London: Scarborough House, 1990

Haskins, Susan, *Mary Magdalen: Myth and Metaphor*. New York: HarperCollins, 1993

Henderson, Carol E., *Culture and Customs of India*. London: Greenwood Press, 2002

Hoffmann, David, *The New Holistic Herbal*. New York: Barnes & Noble Books, 1990

Hohman, John George, *Pow-Wows: Long Lost Friend*. 1820

Holden, William Curry, *Teresita*. Owings Mills, Maryland: Stemmer House Publishers, Inc., 1978

Howard, Michael, *Candle Burning: Its Occult Significance*. Wellingborough, Northamptonshire: The Aquarian Press, 1980

Howey, M. Oldfield, *The Horse In Magic and Myth*. New York: Castle Books, 1958

Howey, M. Oldfield, *The Cat In The Mysteries of Religion and Magic*. New York: Castle Books, 1956

Hurston, Zora Neale, *Folklore, Memoirs, and Other Writings*. New York: The Library of America, 1995

Hurston, Zora Neale, *Tell My Horse*. New York: Harper and Row, 1990

Illes, Judika, *Emergency Magic!* Gloucester, Mass.: Fair Winds Press, 2002

Illes, Judika, *Earth Mother Magic: Ancient Spells For Modern Belles*. Gloucester, Mass.: Fair Winds Press, 2001

Illes, Judika, "Frogs and Pomegranates" unpublished manuscript

Ingersoll, Ernest, *Dragons and Dragon Lore*. Escondido: The Book Tree, 1999

Irwin, Robert, *The Arabian Nights: A Companion*. London: Allen Lane The Penguin Press, 1994

Ivanits, Linda J., *Russian Folk Belief*. London: M.E. Sharpe, Inc., 1989

Janowitz, Naomi, *Magic In The Roman World: Pagans, Jews and Christians*. London: Routledge, 2001

Johnson, Kenneth, *Slavic Sorcery*. St. Paul, Minnesota: Llewellyn Publications, 1998

Jolly, Karen Louise, *Popular Religion In Late Saxon England*. Chapel Hill: The University of North Carolina Press, 1996

Jones, Alison, *Larousse Dictionary of World Folklore*. New York: Larousse, 1995

Jordan, Michael, *Encyclopedia of Gods*. New York: Facts on File, 1993

Kavasch, E. Barrie and Karen Baar, *American Indian Healing Arts*. New York: Bantam Books, 1999

Keenan, Jeremy, *The Tuareg: People of Ahaggar*. New York: St Martin's Press, 1977

Kelly, Sean and Rosemary Rogers, *Saints Preserve Us!* New York: Random House, 1993

Kendall, Laurel, *Shamans, Housewives, and Other Restless Spirits*. Honolulu: University of Hawaii Press, 1985

Kenyon, Theda, *Witches Still Live*. New York: Ives Washburn, 1929

Kieckhefer, Richard, *Forbidden Rites*. University Park: The Pennsylvania State University Press, 1997

King, Francis, *Wisdom From Afar*. London: Aldus Books Limited, 1975

Knab, Sophie Hodorowicz, *Polish Customs, Traditions and Folklore*. New York: Hippocrene Books, 1993

Koltuv, Barbara Black, *Weaving Woman*. York Beach, Maine: Nicolas-Hays, 1990

Kozminsky, Isidore, *The Magic and Science of Jewels and Stones, Volume 1*. San Rafael, Calif.: Cassandra Press, 1988

Kronzek, Allan and Elizabeth Kronzek, *The Sorcerer's Companion*. New York: Broadway Books, 2001

Krull, Kathleen, *Lives of The Musicians: Good Times, Bad Times (And What The Neighbors Thought)*. San Diego: Harcourt Brace Jovanovich, 1993

Kuhn, Philip, *Soulstealers: The Chinese Sorcery Scare of 1768*. Cambridge, Mass.: Harvard University Press, 1990

Kunz, George Frederick, *Rings For The Finger*. New York: Dover Publications, 1973

Kunz, George Frederick, *The Curious Lore of Precious Stones*. New York: Dover Publications, 1971

Kuo, Nancy, *Chinese Paper-Cut Pictures*. London: Alec Tiranti, 1964

Lampe, H.U., *Famous Voodoo Rituals and Spells*. Minneapolis: Marlar Publishing Company, 1982

Lane, David, *Plants of The Bible*. Haifa: Department of Education and Culture, 1969

Leach, Maria, *Funk & Wagnalls Standard Dictionary of Folklore, Mythology and Legend*. New York: Harper & Row, 1972

Leacock, Seth and Ruth Leacock, *Spirits of The Deep*. Garden City, New York: Doubleday Natural History Press, 1972

Lee, Patrick Jasper, *We Borrow The Earth: An Intimate Portrait of The Gypsy Shamanic Tradition and Culture*. London: Thorsons, 2000

Lehmann, Arthur C. and James E. Myers, *Magic, Witchcraft and Religion*. Palo Alto, Calif.: Mayfield Publishing Company, 1985

Lehner, Ernst and Johanna Lehner, *Folklore & Odysseys of Food & Medicinal Plants*. New York: The Noonday Press, 1973

Lehner, Ernst and Johanna Lehner, *Folklore and Symbolism of Flowers, Plants and Trees*. New York: Tudor Publishing Company, 1960

Leland, Charles Godfrey, *Gypsy Sorcery and Fortune Telling*. New Hyde Park, New York: University Books, 1964

Leland, Charles G., *The Gypsies*. Boston: Houghton-Mifflin Company, 1924

Leland, Charles G., *Etruscan Roman Remains*. Blaine, Washington: 1892

Lenormant, Francois, *Chaldean Magic: Its Origin And Development*. Belle Fourche, South Dakota: Kessinger Publishing Company, 1877

Lewis, James R. and Evelyn Dorothy Oliver, *Angels A To Z*. Canton, Michigan: Visible Ink Press, 1996

Linsell, Tony, *Anglo-Saxon Mythology, Migration & Magic*. Pinner, Middlesex: Anglo-Saxon Books, 1994

Long, Carolyn Morrow, *Spiritual Merchants*. Knoxville: The University of Tennessee Press, 2001

Lowell, Percival, *Occult Japan*. New York: Houghton-Mifflin Company, 1894

Luck, Georg, *Arcana Mundi*. Baltimore: Johns Hopkins University Press, 1985

Madsen, William and Claudia Madsen, *A Guide To Mexican Witchcraft*. Mexico: Minutiae Mexicana, 1987

Maloney, Clarence, *The Evil Eye*. New York: Columbia University Press, 1976

Maniche, Lise, *An Ancient Egyptian Herbal*. Austin: University of Texas Press, 1999

Maniche, Lise, *Sacred Luxuries*. Ithaca, New York: Cornell University Press, 1999

Mann, A.T. and Jane Lyle, *Sacred Sexuality*. Shaftesbury, Dorset: Element Books, 1995

Marlbrough, Reverend Ray T., *The Magical Power of The Saints*. St Paul, Minnesota: Llewellyn Publications, 2002

Masello, Robert, *Raising Hell*. New York: Perigee, 1996

Masello, Robert, *Fallen Angels*. New York: Perigee, 1994

Mathers, S.L. MacGregor, *The Book of The Sacred Magic of Abramelin The Mage*. New York: Dover Publications, 1975

Mickaharic, Draja, *A Century of Spells*. York Beach, Maine: Red Wheel/Weiser, 1990

Miczak, Marie Anakee, *Henna's Secret History*. San Jose, Calif.: Writers Club Press, 2001

Middleton, John, *Magic, Witchcraft, and Curing*. Garden City, New York: The Natural History Press, 1967

Monter, E. William, *Witchcraft In France and Switzerland*. London: Cornell University Press, 1976

Morton, Julia, *Exotic Plants For House and Garden*. New York: Golden Press, 1977

Morton, Julia, *Herbs and Spices*. New York: Golden Press, 1976

Morwyn; Dow, Carol L., *Magic From Brazil*. St Paul, Minnesota: Lllewellyn Publications, 2001

Murray, Margaret, *The Witch-Cult In Western Europe*. London: Oxford University Press, 1921

Narby, Jeremy and Francis Huxley, *Shamans Through Time*. New York: Jeremy P. Tarcher/Putnam, 2001

Nefzaoui, Cheikh, *The Perfumed Garden*. New York: Signet Classic, 1999

Neto, Teixeira Alves, *Pomba-Gira*. Burbank: Technicians of the Sacred, 1990

Newall, Venetia, *The Encyclopedia of Witchcraft and Magic*. New York: Dial Press, 1974

Newall, Venetia, *The Witch Figure*. London: Routledge & Kegan Paul, 1973

Nieuwkerk, Karin van, *A Trade Like Any Other*. Austin: University of Texas Press, 1995

Overmyer, Daniel L., *Religions of China*. New York: HarperCollins, 1986

Patai, Raphael, *The Jewish Alchemists*. Princeton: Princeton University Press, 1994

Pelton, Robert, *Voodoo Charms And Talismans*. Plainview, New York: Original Publications, 1997

Pendell, Dale, *Pharmakodynamis: Stimulating Plants, Potions and Herbcraft*. San Francisco: Mercury House, 2002

Pendell, Dale, *Pharmakopoeia: Plant Powers, Poisons and Herbcraft*. San Francisco: Mercury House, 1995

Pinch, Geraldine, *Magic In Ancient Egypt*. Austin: University of Texas Press, 1995

Place, Robert M., *A Gnostic Book of Saints*. St Paul, Minnesota: Llewellyn Publications, 2001

Porteous, Alexander, *The Forest In Folklore and Mythology*. Minneola, New York: Dover Publications, 2002

Puhvel, Martin, *The Crossroads In Folklore and Myth*. New York: Peter Lang, 1989

Ralston, W.E.S., *The Songs of The Russian People*. London: Ellis and Green, 1872

Randolph, Vance, *Ozark Magic and Folklore*. New York: Dover Publications, 1947

Rappoport, Dr. Angelo S., *The Folklore of The Jews*. London: The Soncino Press, 1937

RavenWolf, Silver, *American Folk Magick*. St Paul, Minnesota: Llewellyn Publications, 1998

Rebennack, Mac with Jack Rummel, *Under A Hoodoo Moon*. New York: St. Martin's Press, 1994

Reifenberg, A., *Ancient Hebrew Seals*. London: The East and West Library, 1950

Rey, Terry, *Our Lady of Class Struggle*. Trenton, New Jersey: Africa World Press, 1999

Rigaud, Milo, *Secrets of Voodoo*. San Francisco: City Light Books, 1985

Ritchason, Jack, N.D., *The Little Herb Encyclopedia*. Pleasant Grove, Utah: Woodland Health Books, 1995

Riva, Anna, *Black and White Magic By Marie Laveau*. Los Angeles: International Imports, 1991

Riva, Anna, *Golden Secrets of Mystic Oils*. Los Angeles: International Imports, 1990

Riva, Anna, *Devotions To The Saints*. Los Angeles: International Imports, 1984

Riva, Anna, *Spellcraft, Hexcraft and Witchcraft*. Los Angeles: International Imports, 1977

Robbins, Rossell Hope, *The Encyclopedia of Witchcraft and Demonology*. New York: Bonanza Books, 1981

Roheim, Geza, *Animism, Magic and The Divine King*. New York: Alfred A. Knopf, 1930

Rohmer, Sax, *The Romance of Sorcery*. New York: Causeway Books, 1973

Rose, Carol, *Spirits, Fairies, Leprechauns and Goblins*. New York: W.W. Norton & Company, 1996

Rose, Jeanne, *Herbs & Things*. New York: Perigee Books, 1972

Royal Academy of Arts, *Aztecs*. London: Thames & Hudson, 2002

Ryan, W.F., *The Bathhouse At Midnight*. University Park: The Pennsylvania State University Press, 1999

Savedow, Steve, *The Book of The Angel Reziel*. York Beach, Maine: Samuel Weiser, Inc., 2000

Schwartz, Alvin, *Cross Your Fingers, Spit In Your Hat*. Philadelphia: J.B. Lippincott Company, 1974

Schwartz-Bart, Simone, *The Bridge of Beyond*. New York: Atheneum, 1974

Seligmann, Kurt, *The History of Magic and The Occult*. New York: Harmony Books, 1948

Shah, Idries, *Oriental Magic*. New York: Penguin Arkana, 1956

Shah, Sirdar Ikbal Ali, *Occultism: Its Theory and Practice*. New York: Dorset Press, 1993

Shapiro, Jeffrey Garson, *The Flower Remedy Book*. Berkeley, Calif.: North Atlantic Books, 1999

Shuker, Karl, *Dragons: A Natural History*. New York: Simon & Schuster, 1995

Simonov, Pyotr, *Essential Russian Mythology*. London: Thorsons, 1997

Slater, Herman, *Magickal Formulary Spellbook Book I*. New York: Magickal Childe, 1987

Slater, Herman, *Magickal Formulary Spellbook Book II*. New York: Magickal Childe

Smith, W. Robertson, *Lectures On The Religion of The Semites*. London: Adam and Charles Black, 1901

Spence, Lewis, *The Magic Arts In Celtic Britain*. Mineola, New York: Dover Publications, 1999

Spence, Lewis, *The Magic and Mysteries of Mexico*. North Hollywood, Calif.: Newcastle Publishing, 1994

Spence, Lewis, *An Encyclopedia of Occultism*. New Hyde Park, New York: University Books, 1968

Stark, Dr. Raymond, N.D., *The Book of Aphrodisiacs*. Toronto: Methuen Books, 1980

St. Clair, David, *Pagans, Priests, and Prophets*. Englewood Cliffs, New Jersey: Prentice Hall, 1976

St. Clair, David, *Drum and Candle*. Garden City, New York: Doubleday and Company, 1971

Stepanchuk, Carol, *Exploring Chinatown*. Berkeley, Calif.: Pacific View Press, 2002

Stepanchuk, Carol, *Red Eggs and Dragon Boats*. Berkeley, Calif.: Pacific View Press, 1994

Stevens, Keith G., *Chinese Mythological Gods*. New York: Oxford University Press, 2001

Stutley, Margaret, *Ancient Indian Magic and Folklore*. Boulder, Colo.: Great Eastern Book Company, 1980

Sung, Vivien, *Five-Fold Happiness*. San Francisco: Chronicle Books, 2002

Tannahill, Reay, *Flesh and Blood*. New York: Stein and Day, 1975

Teish, Luisah, *Jambalaya*. San Francisco: Harper and Row, 1985

Terada, Alice M., *The Magic Crocodile and Other Folktales From Indonesia*. Honolulu: University of Hawaii Press, 1994

The Holy Scriptures According To The Masoretic Text. Philadelphia: The Jewish Publication Society of America, 5724–1964

Thompson, C.J.S., *Magic and Healing*. New York: Bell Publishing Company, 1989

Thompson, C.J.S., *The Hand of Destiny*. New York: Bell Publishing Company, 1989

Thompson, C.J.S., *The Mystic Mandrake*. New Hyde Park, New York: University Books, 1968

Thompson, C.J.S., *The Mystery and Lure of Perfume*. London: John Lane The Bodley Head Limited, 1927

Thompson, Helen, *Milagros: A Book of Miracles*. New York: HarperCollins, 1998

Thompson, Reginald Campbell, *Semitic Magic*. London: Luzac & Co., 1908

Tick, Edward, *The Practice of Dream Healing*. Wheaton, Illinois: Quest Books, 2001

Time-Life Books, Inc., *Mysteries of The Unknown: Magical Arts*. Alexandria, Virginia: Time-Life Books, 1990

Time-Life Books, Inc., *Mysteries of The Unknown: Witches and Witchcraft*. Alexandria, Virginia: Time-Life Books, 1990

Tisserand, Robert and Tony Balacs, *Essential Oil Safety*. London: Churchill Livingstone, 1999

Too, Lillian, *Irresistible Feng Shui Magic*. London: Element Books, 2001

Too, Lillian, *Practical Feng Shui Symbols of Good Fortune*. Boston: Element Books, 2000

Toor, Frances, *Festivals and Folkways of Italy*. New York: Crown Publishers, 1953

Toor, Frances, *A Treasury of Mexican Folkways*. New York: Crown Publishers, 1950

Trachtenberg, Joshua, *Jewish Magic and Superstition*. New York: Atheneum, 1974

Trigg, Elwood B., *Gypsy Demons and Divinities: The Magic and Religion of The Gypsies*. Secaucus: Citadel Press 1973

Trotter II, Robert T. and Juan Antonio Chavira, *Curanderismo*. Athens, Georgia: The University of Georgia Press, 1997

Tyson, Donald, *Enochian Magic For Beginners*. St Paul, Minnesota: Llewellyn Publications, 1998

Tyson, Donald, *Three Books of Occult Philosophy Written By Henry Cornelius Agrippa of Nettesheim*. St. Paul, Minnesota: Llewellyn Publications, 1993

Vitale, Alice Thomas, *Leaves In Myth, Magic and Medicine*. New York: Stewart, Tabori and Chang, 1997

Voeks, Robert A., *Sacred Leaves of Candomble*. Austin: University of Texas Press, 1997

Vorren, Ornulv and Ernst Manker, *Lapp Life and Customs*. London: Oxford University Press, 1962

Wafer, Jim, *The Taste of Blood*. Philadelphia: University of Pennsylvania Press, 1991

Wahlman, Maude Southwell, *Signs and Symbols: African Images In African American Quilts*. Atlanta, Georgia: Tinwood Books, 2001

Walker, Barbara G., *The Secrets of The Tarot*. San Francisco: Harper & Row, 1984

Walker, Barbara G., *The Woman's Encyclopedia of Myths and Secrets*. New York: Harper & Row, 1983

Warner, Marina, *From The Beast To The Blonde*. New York: Farrar, Straus and Giroux, 1994

Wasserspring, Lois, *Oaxacan Ceramics*. San Francisco: Chronicle Books, 2000

Watson, C.W. and Roy Ellen, *Understanding Witchcraft and Sorcery In Southeast Asia*. Honolulu: University of Hawaii Press, 1993

Webster, Richard, *Write Your Own Magic*. St Paul, Minnesota: Llewellyn Publications, 2001

Wedeck, H. E., *Dictionary of Gypsy Life and Lore*. New York: Philosophical Library, 1973

Wedeck, H.E., *Dictionary of Magic*. New York: Philosophical Library, 1956

Westermarck, Edward, *Pagan Survivals In Mohammedan Civilisation*. Amsterdam: Philo Press, 1973

Westermarck, Edward, *Ritual and Belief In Morocco*. New Hyde Park, New York: University Press, 1968

Wilde, Lady Francesca Speranza, *Ancient Legends, Mystic Charms and Superstitions of Ireland*. London: Ward & Downey, 1877

Wilkinson, Richard H., *The Complete Gods and Goddesses of Ancient Egypt*. London: Thames & Hudson, 2003

Williams, J. J., *Voodoos and Obeahs*. New York: Dial Press, 1933

Willoughby, W.C., *The Soul of The Bantu*. Garden City, New York: Doubleday, Doran and Company, 1928

Wilson, Leslie S., *The Serpent Symbol In The Ancient Near East*. Oxford: University Press of America, Inc., 2001

Winstedt, Richard, *The Malay Magician*. Kuala Lumpur: Oxford University Press, 1993

Wright, Elbee, *Book of Legendary Spells*. Minneapolis: Marlar Publishing Company, 1974

Yolen, Jane and Shulamith Oppenheim, *The Fish Prince and Other Stories: Mermen Folk Tales*. New York: Interlink Books, 2001

Young, Louisa, *The Book of The Heart*. New York: Doubleday, 2003

Yronwode, Catherine, *Hoodoo Herb and Root Magic: A* Materia Magica *of African-American Conjure*. Forestville, Calif.: Lucky Mojo Curio Company, 2002

Zolrak, *The Tarot of The Orishas*. St. Paul, Minnesota: Llewellyn Publications, 1996

Internet Sources

Patterson, Jean and Arzu Aghayeva, *The Evil Eye: Staving off Harm With a Visit to the Open Market*. Azerbaijan International, AI 8.3 (Autumn 2000) AZER.com

Botanical Classifications

Abre camino (*Trichilia havanensis*)

Acacia (*Acacia* spp.)

Aconite (*Aconitum napellus*) wolfsbane

Adam and Eve Root (*Aplectrum hyemale*) he and she root, putty root

Adders Tongue (*Ophioglossum vulgatum*)

Agar-agar (*Gracilaria lichenoides, Gelidium amansii*) sea spirit, Ceylon moss

Agrimony (*Agrimonia eupatoria*)

Ailanthus (*Ailanthus altissima*) tree of heaven

Air potato (*Dioscorea bulbifera*)

Ajos sacha (*Mansoa alliacea*) false garlic

Alder (*Almus glutinosa*)

Alfalfa (*Medicago sativa*)

Alkanet (*Alkanna tinctoria*) Dyers bugloss

Allspice (*Pimenta officinalis*)

Almond (*Amygdalis communis* var. *dulcis*)

Aloe vera (*Aloe barbadensis, A. ferox, A. vera*)

Aloes wood (*Aquillaria agallocha*) agarwood, laos, oud

Althaea (*Althaea officinalis*) marsh mallow

Alyssum (*Lobularia maritima*)

Amaranth (*Amaranthus* spp.)

Ambrette (*Abelmoschus moschatus*)

Amyris (*Amyris balsamifera*) balm of Gilead, balsam

Anemone (*Anemone pulsatilla*) windflower

Angel wings (*Caladium hortulanum, C. bicolor*)

Angelica (*Angelica* spp., especially *A. archangelica*) archangel root, Holy Ghost root

Angels trumpet (*Datura aborea* or *Brugmansia suaveolens*)

Angels turnip (*Nerium oleander*) dogbane, oleander

Anil (*Indigofera anil*)

Anise (*Pimpinella anisum*)

Antiseptic bush (*Calocephalus* ass. *Multiflorus*)

Apple (*Pyrus malus, Malus malus*)

Arbor vitae (*Thuja occidentalis*) tree of life, thuja

Arbutus (*Epigaea repens*)

Aristolochia (*Aristolochia serpentaria*) snake root, butter snake root

Arrowroot (*Maranta arundinaceae*)

Arugula (*Eruca vesicaria*) rocket

Asafetida (*Ferula assafoetida*) devils dung

Ash (*Fraxinus* spp.) Venus of the Woods

Ashthroat (*Verbena officinalis*) vervain

Asparagus (*Asparagus officinalis*)

Aspen (*Populus tremuloides*) quaking aspen

Asphodel (*Asphodelus ramosus*)

Autumn gentian (*Gentiana amarella*)

Avens (*Geum urbanum*) herb Bennet

Avocado (*Persea americana*) alligator pear

Balm of Gilead (*Populus gileadensis*)

Balmony (*Chelone glabra*) snake head, turtle flower, hummingbird tree

Balsam fir (*Abies balsamae*)

Balsam of Peru (*Myroxylon pereirae*)

Bamboo (*Bambusa* spp., *Dendrocalamus* spp.)

Banyan (*Ficus benghalensis*)

Barkehi (*Piliostigma reticulatum*)

Barley (*Hordeum distichon*)

Basil (*Ocimum basilicum*) sweet basil

Basil, tulsi (*Ocimum sanctum*) Holy basil

Bastard cedar (*Guazuma ulmifolia*) West Indian elm

Bay laurel (*Laurus nobilis*)

Bay rum tree (*Pimenta racemosa*)

Bayberry (*Myrica cerifera*)

Bean, castor (*Ricinus communis*)

Bean, fava (*Vicia faba*) mojo wish bean, Saint Joseph bean

Bean, jack (*Canavalia ensiformis*)

Bean, lima (*Phaseolus vulgaris*)

Bean, sword (*Canavalia gladiata*)

Bearberry (*Arctostaphylos uva-ursi*)

Bee balm (*Monarda didyma*) bergamot mint

Belladonna (*Atropa belladonna*) deadly nightshade, Devils cherries

Ben (*Moringa oleifera*) Horseradish tree, Moringa

Benzoin (*Styrax benzoin*) Benjamin, Jawi

Bergamot (*Citrus aurantium* spp. *bergamia*)

Bergamot mint (*Monarda didyma*) bee balm, oswego tea

Betel nut (*Areca catechu*) areca

Betony (*Betonica officinalis*) bishopwort

Birch (*Betula alba*) Lady of the Woods

Bishopwort (*Betonica officinalis*) betony

Bistort (*Polygonum bistorta*) dragonwort, snakeweed

Black cohosh (*Cimicifuga serpentaria*) black snake root

Black cumin (*Gara chorakotu*) atilbatil

Black-eyed pea (*Vigna sinensis*)

Black-eyed Susan (*Rudbeckia hirta*)

Black pepper (*Piper nigrum*)

Black snake root (*Cimicifuga serpentaria*) black cohosh

Black snake root (*Senicula marilandica*)

Blackberry (*Rubus fructicosus*) bramble

Blackthorn (*Prunus spinosa*) sloe, Mother of the Wood, wishing thorn

Bladderwrack (*Fucus vesiculosis*) sea spirit

Bleeding heart (*Dicentra formosa*)

Bloodroot (*Sanguinaria canadensis*)

Bluebell (*Scilla nutans*)

Blueberry (*Vaccinium angustifolium*)

Boldo (*Peumus boldus*)

Boneset (*Eupatorium perfoliatum*)

Borage (*Borago officinalis*)

Boronia (*Boronia megastigma*)

Bottlebrush (*Equisetum hyemale*)

Bougainvillea (*Bougainvillea* spp.)

Bramble (*Lycium europaeum*)

Bridewort (*Filipendula ulmaria, Spiraea ulmaria*) Queen of the Meadow, meadowsweet

Bristly crowfoot (*Ranunculus pensylvanicus*)

Broom (*Cytisus scoparius*)

Bryony, white (*Bryonia dioica* or *B. alba*) European mandrake, English mandrake

Buckeye nut (*Aesculus glabra*)

Buckwheat (*Polygonaceae fagopynum* or *Fagopyrum esculentum*)

Bugleweed (*Ajuga reptans*)

Bugloss, vipers (*Echium vulgare*)

Bullet proof (*Hura crepitans*) monkey pistol, sandbox tree, salvadera (Spanish)

Burdock (*Articum lappe*)

Cabbage (*Brassica oleracea capitata*)

Cabbage, skunk (*Symplocarpus foetidus*)

Cajeput (*Melaleuca leucadendron*) swamp tea tree

Calaba balsam (*Calophyllum calaba*) Santa Maria

Calamint (*Calamintha officinalis*)

Calamus root (*Acorus calamus*) sweet flag, sweet root, sweet grass

Calendula (*Calendula officinalis*) pot marigold

Camels Needle (*Alhagi camelorum*)

Camphor (*Cinnamonum camphora*)

Canadian hemlock (*Tsuga canadensis*)

Caraway (*Carum carvi*)

Cardamom (*Elettaria cardamomum*)

Carnation (*Dianthus caryophyllus*)

Carrot (*Daucus carota*)

Cascara sagrada (*Rhamnus purshianus*) California buckthorn, sacred bark

Cashew (*Anacardium occidentale*)

Cassava (*Manihot esculenta*)

Cassia (*Cinnamomum cassia*)

Catnip (*Nepeta cataria*) catmint

Cats claw (*Uncaria tormentosa*) Uno de Gato

Cats tail (*Typha typhonium*)

Cedarwood (*Cedrus* spp.)

Cedarwood, Texas (*Juniperus mexicana*)

Cedarwood, Virginia (*Juniperus virginiana*)

Ceiba (*Bombax ceiba*) silk cotton tree

Celandine (*Chelidonium majus*)

Celery (*Apium graveolens*)

Centaury (*Centaurium erythraea*)

Chamomile, German (*Matricaria chamomila*) Hungarian chamomile

Chamomile, Roman (*Anthemis nobilis*)

Cherry (*Prunus* spp.)

Chervil (*Myrrhis odorata*) British myrrh, sweet Cicely

Chestnut (*Castanea vesca* or *Fagus castanea*)

Chestnut, horse (*Aesculus hippocastanum*)

Chewing John (*Alpinia galanga*)

Chia (*Salvia columbariae*)

Chickpeas (*Cicer arietinum*) garbanzo beans

Chicory (*Cichorium intybus*)

Christmas Rose (*Helleborus niger*) black hellebore

Chrysanthemum (*Chrysanthemum* spp.)

Cinchona (*Cinchona officinalis*) fever tree

Cinnamon (*Cinnamomum zeylanicum*)

Cinquefoil (*Potentilla reptans*) five-finger grass

Citronella (*Cymbopogon nardus*)

Clary sage (*Salvia sclarea*)

Clove (*Eugenia caryophyllata*)

Clover (*Trifolium* spp.) trefoil, shamrock

Club moss (*Lycopodium clavatum*)

Coconut (*Cocos nucifera*)

Coffee (*Coffea arabica, C. robusta*)

Comfrey (*Symphytum officinale*)

Contraveneno (*Fevellea cordifolia*)

Convolvulus (*Convolvulus arvensis*) Devils garters

Copal (*Protium copal, Bureseru microphylla*)

Corazon de Buey (*Entada jigas*)

Coriander (*Coriandrum sativum*) Chinese parsley, cilantro

Cornflower (*Centaurea cyanus*) bluebottle

Corredeira (*Borreria* spp or *Irlbachia purpurascens*)

Cotton (*Gossypium herbaceum*)

Courtcase root (*Alpinia galangal*) galangal, laos, Southern John, Little John to Chew

Cowslip (*Primula veris*) fairy cups, Our Lady's Keys, keyflower, primrose

Crabapple (*Malus* spp.)

Crabgrass (*Eleusine indica*)

Cubeb (*Piper cubeba*) love berry

Cumin (*Cuminum cyminum*)

Cyclamen (*Cyclamen* spp.)

Cypress (*Cupressus sempervirens*)

Daisy (*Chrysanthemum leucanthemum*)

Damiana (*Turnera aphrodisiaca*)

Dammar (*Canarium strictum*)

Danda (*Cyperus rotundus*) sedge

Dandelion (*Taraxacum officinale*)

Date palm (*Phoenix dactylifera*)

Day jessamine (*Cestrum diurnum*)

Deadly nightshade (*Atropa belladonna*) belladonna

Deerberry (*Mitchella repens*) partridge berry

Deers eye (*Mucuna* spp.) Ojo de Venado

Deers tongue (*Liatris odoratissima*)

Delphinium (*Delphinium consolida*)

Dende (*Elaeis guineensis*) Brazilian palm oil, African palm

Desert rue (*Parosela* spp.)

Desert sage (*Artemisia tridentata*)

Devils bit (*Scabiosa succisa*) scabious

Devils claw (*Harpagophytum procumbens*)

Devils flight (*Fuga daemonum*)

Devils pod (*Trapa bicornis*) ling nut, ling-ko, goat head, bat nut

Devils shoestring (*Viburnum* spp.)

Dill (*Anethum graveolens*)

Dittany of Crete (*Origanum dictamnus*)

Dodder (*Cuscuta europaea*)

Dogwood (*Cornus* spp.)

Dragons blood (*Dracaena draco*, *Daemonorops draco*)

Dragons blood, Peruvian (*Croton lechleri*) Sangre de Drago

Dragons tears (*Bixa* spp.) annatto

Dream herb (*Calea zacatechichi*)

Dulse (*Rhodymenia palmate*)

Dumb cane (*Dieffenbachia maculata*)

Earth smoke (*Fumaria* spp.) Fumitory

Edelweiss (*Leontopodium* spp.) cloud flower

Eggplant (*Solanum melongena*) aubergine

Elder (*Sambucus* spp.)

Elecampane (*Inula helenium*) inula, elfdock, elfwort

Elemi (*Canarium luzonicum*)

Elfdock (*Inula helenium*) elecampane, inula, elfwort

Elm (*Ulmus campestris*)

Epazote (*Chenopodium ambrosiodes*) wormweed

Eryngo (*Eryngium* spp.) sea holly

Escoba Cimarrona (*Abutilon trisulcatum*) anglestem Indian mallow

Eucalyptus (*Eucalyptus globulus*)

Eupatorium (*Eupatorium odoratum*)

Evening primrose (*Cenothera biennis*)

Eyebright (*Euphrasia officinalis*)

Fennel (*Foeniculum vulgare*)

Fenugreek (*Trigonella foenum-graecum*)

Fern, female (*Asplenium felix-foemina*) Lady Fern

Fern, male (*Dryopteris felix-mas*) Hand of God, Lucky Hand

Feverfew (*Tanacetum parthenium*)

Fig (*Ficus carica*)

Flax (*Linum usitatissimum*)

Fleabane (*Inula dysenterica*)

Forget-me-not (*Myosotis symphytifolia*)

Foul-mouthed (*Cosearia hirsute*)

Foxglove (*Digitalis purpurea*) dead mens bells, fairys glove, fairys thimble

Frangipani (*Plumeria rubra*)

Frankincense (*Boswellia carterii*)

Gag root (*Lobelia inflata*)

Galangal (*Alpinia galanga*)

Galbanum (*Ferula galbaniflua*)

Gander goose (*Orchis maculata*) spotted orchis, Devils hand

Gardenia (*Gardenia* spp.)

Garlic (*Allium sativum*)

Gentian (*Gentiana lutea*)

Gentian, five-flowered (*Gentiana quinqueflora*) ague weed

Geranium (*Geranium* spp, *Pelargonium* spp.)

Germander (*Ajuga chamaepitys* or *Teucrium chamaepitys*)

Gilly flowers (*Dianthus caryophyllus*) carnation

Ginger (*Zingiber officinale*)

Ginger lily (*Hedychium coronarium*)

Ginger, wild (*Asarum canadense*) snake root ginger

Gingergrass (*Cymbopogon martinii Sofia*)

Gingko (*Gingko biloba*)

Ginseng (*Panax quinquefolium*)

Goats rue (*Galega officinalis*)

Goldenrod (*Solidago virgaurea*) Aarons Rod

Gorse (*Ulex europaeus*)

Grains of Paradise (*Amomum meleguetta*) Guinea pepper, Malagetta pepper

Grannybush (*Croton linearis*) Jamaican rosemary

Grape (*Vitis vinifera*)

Grapefruit (*Citrus paradisii*)

Gravel root (*Eupatorium purpureum*) Joe Pye Weed, ague weed

Gray spider flower (*Grevillea buxifolia*)

Great burnet (*Sanguisorba officinalis*)

Guinea weed (*Letheria alliacea*)

Gum acacia (*Acacia* spp.) gum arabica

Gum ammoniac (*Dorema ammoniacum*)

Gum arabica (*Acacia* spp.) gum acacia

Gum Sandarac (*Tetraclinis articulate*)

Gum Trabacanth (*Astragalus gummifer*) gum dragon

Harmel (*Peganum harmala*) Syrian rue, uzarlik, harmala

Hawkweed (*Hieracium* spp.)

Hawthorn (*Cratageus* spp.) May tree, white thorn

Hazel (*Corylus* spp.)

Heartsease (*Viola tricolor*) wild pansy

Heather (*Calluna vulgaris*)

Heliotrope (*Heliotropium peruviana*) cherry pie

Helichrysum (*Helichrysum italicum*) everlasting, immortelle

Hellebore (*Veratum album*)

Hemlock (*Conium maculatum*)

Hemp (*Cannabis sativa*)

Henbane (*Hyoscemus niger*) Devils eye, insana

Henna (*Lawsonia inermis*) Mendhi, Egyptian privet, Jamaican mignonette

Herb Paris (*Paris quadrifolia*) wolfs berries

Hibiscus (*Hibiscus* spp.)

Hickory (*Carya* spp)

High John the Conqueror (*Convolvulus jalapa, Ipomoea jalapa, I. purga*) jalap

Holly (*Ilex aquifolium*)

Hollyhock (*Althaea rosea*)

Honeysuckle (*Lonicera spp.*)

Hops (*Humulus lupulus*)

Horehound (*Marrubium vulgare*)

Horseradish (*Cochlearia armoracia*)

Horseweed (*Conyza canadensis*)

Huayruru (*Ormosia* spp) ladybug seed

Hyacinth (*Hyacinthus orientalis*)

Hydrangea (*Hydrangea arborescens*) seven barks

Hyssop (*Hyssopus officinalis*)

Indian paint brush (*Castilleja* spp.) snakes friend, painted lady

Indigo (*Indigofera tinctoria*)

Inula (*Inula helenium*) Elecampane

Iris (*Iris* spp.)

Irish moss (*Chondrus crispus*) carrageen

Iroko (*Chlorophora excelsa*) African oak, Nigeria teak

Ironwood (*Carpinus caroliniana*) American hornbeam

Ivy (*Hedera helix*)

Jack-in-the-Pulpit (*Arum* spp.)

Jade plant (*Crassula argentea*)

Jamaica bayberry (*Pimenta racemosa*) black cinnamon, wild cinnamon

Jasmine (*Jasminium officinale* or *J. grandiflora*)

Jasmine sambac (*Jasminum sambac*) Arabian jasmine

Jezebel root (*Iris fulva, I. foliosa, I. hexagona, I. tectorum*)

Jobs tears (*Coix lacryme-jobi*)

Johnny-jump-up (*Viola cornuta*)

Jojoba (*Jojoba simmondsia californica*)

Juniper (*Juniperus communis*)

Kalanchoe (*Kalanchoe pinnata*) Folha da Fortuna

Kelp (*Fucus vesiculosis*)

Knotgrass (*Polyganum aviculare*) ninety-knot

Labdanum (*Cistus cretica, C. ladanifer*)

Ladys Mantle (*Alchemilla vulgaris*)

Ladys Tresses (*Spiranthes* spp.)

Larch (*Pinus larix, Larix deciduas*)

Larkspur (*Delphinium* spp.)

Lavender (*Lavandula augustifolia*) English lavender, French lavender

Lavender (*Lavandula stoechas*) Spanish lavender, Italian lavender

Ledum (*Ledum palustre*)

Leeks (*Allium ampeloprasum* var. *porrum*)

Lemon (*Citrus limonum*)

Lemon Balm (*Melissa officinalis*) melissa

Lemon verbena (*Lippia citriodora*)

Lemongrass (*Cymbopogon citratus*)

Lichee (*Litchi chinensis*)

Licorice (*Glycyrrhiza glabra*)

Lilac (*Syringa vulgaris*)

Lily (*Lilium* spp.)

Lily-of-the-Valley (*Convallaria magalis*)

Lime fruit (*Citrus acris*)

Linden (*Tilia europoea*) lime tree, tilia

Liquidambar (*Liquidambar orientalis, L. styraciflua*) storax, sweet gum

Liverwort (*Marchantia polymorphia*)

Lobelia (*Lobelia erinus*)

Longan (*Euphoria longana*) dragons eye

Lotus (*Nelumbo nucifera*) sacred water lily

Lovage (*Levisticum officinale*)

Low John the Conqueror (*Trillium erectum*) bethroot

Lucky Hand root (*Dactylorhyza* spp.)

Mace (*Myristica fragrans*)

Macrocarpa (*Eucalyptus macrocarpa*)

Magnolia (*Magnolia* spp.)

Maidenhair (*Adiantum capillus-veneris*)

Male fern (*Dryopteris filix-mas*) Lucky Hand, Hand of God

Mallow (*Althaea* spp.) althaea

Malva (*Malva neglecta*)

Mandrake (*Mandragora officinarum*) man root, love apple, djinns egg

Mango (*Mangifera indica*)

Manuka (*Leptospermum scoparium*) New Zealand tea tree

Maple (*Acer* spp.)

Marigold (*Calendula officinalis*) calendula, pot marigold

Marigold (*Tagetes* spp.) tagetes, African marigold, French marigold

Marigold, marsh (*Caltha palustris*) Beltane shrub

Marjoram (*Origanum majorana*)

Masterwort (*Imperatoria ostruthium*)

Mastic (*Pistacia lentiscus*)

Maté (*Ilex paraguensiensis*) Yerba maté

Matrimony vine (*Lycium* spp.)

May apple (*Podophyllum peltatum*)

May Chang (*Litsea cubeba*)

Melilot (*Melilotus officinalis*)

Melon (*Cucumis* spp.)

Mignonette (*Reseda odorata*) reseda

Millet (*Panicum miliaceum*)

Mimosa (*Acacia dealbata*)

Mistletoe (*Viscum album*)

Mkadi (*Diospyros mespiliformis*)

Mojo wish bean (*Vicia faba*) fava bean, Saint Joseph bean

Monkeyflower, purple (*Mimulus kelloggii*)

Monkeyflower, scarlet (*Mimulus cardinalis*)

Moonwort (*Botrychium lunaria*)

Morning glory (*Ipomoea* spp.)

Motherwort (*Leonurus cardiaca*)

Mucura (*Petiveria alliacea*) Amansa Senhor, Congo root, Guinea, tipi

Mugwort (*Artemisia vulgaris*)

Mullein (*Verbascum thapsus*) graveyard dust, witches taper, Aarons rod

Mustard, black (*Brassica nigra*)

Mustard, brown (*Brassica nigra*)

Mustard, yellow (*Sinapis alba*)

Myrrh (*Commiphora myrrha*)

Myrtle (*Myrtus communis*)

Nasturtium (*Tropaeolum majus*)

Neem (*Melia azadirachta*) Holy Tree

Neroli (*Citrus aurantium Amara*)

Nettles (*Urtica dioica*) stinging nettles

Nutmeg (*Myristica fragrans*)

Nux vomica (*Strychnos nux-vomica*) strychnine, poison nut, rat poison plant

Oak (*Quercus robur*)

Oak moss (*Evernia prunastri*)

Okra (*Abelmoschus esculentus*) lady's fingers

Oleander (*Nerium oleander*) dogbane, angels turnip

Olive (*Olea europaea*)

Onion (*Allium cepa*)

Opoponax (*Commiphora erythraea*)

Orange (*Citrus aurantium Dulcis*)

Orchid (*Orchis* spp.)

Oregano (*Origanum vulgare*)

Oregon grape (*Berberis aquifolium*)

Orpine (*Sedum telephium*)

Orris (*Iris germanica, I. germanica* var. *florentina* and *I. pallida*)

Palmarosa (*Cymbopogan martinii*)

Pansy (*Viola tricolor*)

Papaya (*Carica papaya*)

Parsley (*Petroselinum crispum*)

Patchouli (*Pogostemon cablin*) graveyard dust

Peach (*Prunus persica*)

Peanut (*Arachis hypogea*)

Pear (*Pyrus* spp.)

Pearlwort (*Sagina procumbens*)

Pecan (*Carya illinoensis*)

Pega-pega (*Desmodium obtusum*) Amor Seco, iron vine

Pennyroyal (*Mentha pulegium*)

Peony (*Paeonia* spp.)

Pepper, black (*Piper nigrum*)

Pepper, cayenne (*Capsicum frutescens*)

Pepper, chili (*Capsicum* spp.)

Pepper, long (*Piper longum*)

Peppermint (*Mentha piperita*)

Peppertree (*Schinus molle*)

Persimmon (*Diospyros* spp.)

Petitgrain (*Citrus aurantium Amara*)

Peyote (*Lophophora williamsii*)

Pikake (*Jasminum* spp.)

Pine (*Pinus* spp.)

Pineapple (*Ananas comosus*)

Pink (*Dianthus caryophyllus, D. graniticus*)

Pistachio (*Pistacia vera*)

Plantain (*Plantago major*) broad-leaved plantain

Plantain (*Musa paradisiaca*) banana tree

Plum (*Prunus* spp.)

Plum, flowering (*Prunus caroliniana*)

Poke (*Phytolacca decandra*)

Pomegranate (*Punica granatum*)

Poplar (*Populus* spp.)

Poppy (*Papaver* spp.)

Potato (*Solanum tuberosum*)

Prickly pear (*Opuntia tuna*)

Primrose (*Primula vulgaris*)

Privet (*Ligustrum vulgare*)

Pumpkin (*Cucurbita pepo*)

Purple loosestrife (*Lythrurn salicaria*)

Purslane (*Portulaca* spp.) portulaca

Quassia (*Picraena excelsa*)

Queen of the Night (*Cestrum nocturnum*) night-blooming jasmine

Queens Delight (*Stillingia sylvatica*) Queens Root

Ragweed (*Senecio jacobaea*) fairy's horses, ragwort

Rampion (*Campanula rapunculus*) ramps, rapunzel

Raspberry (*Rubus idaeus*)

Rattlesnake master (*Liatris squarrosa*)

Rattlesnake root (*Gentiana lutea*) gentian

Rhododendron (*Rhododendron anthopogon*)

Rhubarb (*Rheum officinale, R. palmatum*)

Rice (*Oryza sativa*)

Road opener (*Trichilia havanensis*) Abre camino

Rock rose (*Cistus creticus, C. ladanifer*)

Rosalina (*Melaleuca ericifolia*)

Rose (*Rosa* spp.)

Rose, briar (*Rosa rubiginosa*)

Rose, Christmas (*Helleborus niger*)

Rose, dog (*Rosa* canina)

Rose geranium (*Pelargonium graveolens*)

Rose hips (*Rosa* canina)

Rose of Jericho (*Anastatica hierochuntina*) resurrection plant

Rosemary (*Rosmarinus officinalis*)

Rowan (*Sorbus aucuparia* or *Fraxinus aucuparia*) mountain ash, witch wood

Rue (*Ruta graveolens*)

Safflower (*Carthamus tinctorius*)

Saffron (*Crocus sativa*)

Sage (*Salvia officinalis*)

Sage, clary (*Salvia sclarea*)

Sage, oracle (*Salvia divinorum*) diviners sage

Sage, white (*Salvia apiana*)

Saint Johns Wort (*Hypericum perforatum*)

Sampson snake root (*Echinacea* spp.)

Sandalwood (*Santalum album*)

Sandalwood, red (*Adenanthera pavonina*)

Sandbox tree (*Hura crepitans*) monkey pistol, salvadera

Sapodilla (*Achras zapota*)

Sassafras (*Sassafras officinale*)

Saxifrage (*Saxifraga* spp.)

Scarlet pimpernel (*Anagalis arvensis*) cure-all

Sea spirit (*Gracilaria lichenoides*) Ceylon moss, agar-agar

Sea spirit (*Fucus vesiculosis*) bladderwrack

Self-heal (*Prunella vulgaris*)

Senna (*Cassia acutifolia*)

Sesame (*Sesamum indicum*)

Silver fir (*Abies alba*)

Skullcap (*Scutellaria laterifolia*)

Slender rice flower (*Pimelea linifolia*)

Slippery elm (*Ulmus fulva*)

Smartweed (*Polygonum hydropiper*) smart ass, water pepper

Snake head (*Fritillaria meleagris*)

Snake plant (*Sansevieria trifasciata*) mother-in-laws tongue

Snake root (*Aristolochia serpentaria*) aristolochia

Snapdragon (*Antirrhimum magus*)

Solomons seal (*Polygonatum multiflorum*)

Sorrel (*Rumex acetosa*)

Sour sop (*Annona reticulata, A. muricata*) custard apple

Southernwood (*Artemisia abrotanum*) lads love, old man

Spanish moss (*Tillandsia useoides*)

Sparrowwort (*Erica passerine*)

Spearmint (*Mentha spicata*) Yerba buena

Speedwell (*Veronica officinalis*) veronica

Spikenard (*Nardostachys jatamansi*)

Spiritweed (*Eryngium foetidum*) parrotweed, fitweed, false coriander

Spruce (*Picea* spp.)

Spurge (*Euphorbia resinifera*) poison gum

Squill root (*Urginnea squilla*)

Sraktya (*Clerodendrum phlomoides*)

Star anise (*Illicuim verum*)

Storax (*Styrax officinalis*)

Sugar (*Saccharum officinarum*)

Sumbul (*Ferula sumbul*) jatamansi

Sunflower (*Helianthus annuus*)

Sweet Annie (*Artemisia annua*)

Sweet flag (*Acorus calamus*) sweet grass calamus root, sweet root

Sweet inula (*Inula graveolens*)

Sweetgrass (*Hierochloe odorata*)

Tagetes (*Tagetes* spp.) African marigold, French marigold

Tamarind (*Tamarindus indica*)

Tamarisk (*Tamarix* spp.)

Tangerine (*Citrus reticulata*) mandarin

Tanni (*Balanites aegyptica*)

Tansy (*Tanacetum vulgare*)

Tarragon (*Artemisia dracunculis*)

Tea (*Camellia sinensis*)

Temper bush (*Amyris* spp.)

Terebinth (*Pistacia terebinthus*)

Thorn apple (*Datura stramonium*) datura, devils apple, devils trumpet, jimson weed, stramonium

Thors beard (*Sempervivum tectorum*)

Thyme (*Thymus vulgaris*)

Ti (*Cordyline terminalis*)

Tiger lily (*Lilium tigrinum*)

Toadflax (*Linaria vulgaris*)

Tobacco (*Nicotiana tabacum*)

Tonka bean (*Dipteryx odorata*)

Tormentil (*Potentilla tormentilla*) flesh and blood, five-fingers, septfoil

Trefoil (*Trifolium* spp.)

True unicorn root (*Aletris farinose*)

Trumpet flower (*Datura* spp., *Brugmansia* spp.)

Tuberose (*Polianthes tuberosa*)

Tulip (*Tulipa* spp.)

Turmeric (*Curcuma longa*)

Turnip (*Brassica rapa rapifera*)

Turpentine (*Pistacia terebinthus*)

Valerian (*Valeriana officinalis*) graveyard dust, vandal root

Vanilla (*Vanilla planifolia*)

Venus flytrap (*Dionaea muscipula*)

Vervain (*Verbena officinalis*)

Vetiver (*Vetiveria zizanoides*) khus-khus

Vinca (*Vinca major*) periwinkle, sorcerers violet, devils joy

Violet (*Viola odorata*)

Violet, African (*Saintpaulia ionantha*)

Violet, fringed (*Thysanotus tuberosus*)

Vitex (*Vitex agnus-castus*) chaste tree

Wahoo (*Euonymus atropurpureus*) bleeding heart, burning bush, spindle

Walnut (*Juglans nigra*)

Wasabi (*Eutrema wasabi*)

Water lily (*Nymphaea lotus, N. caerulea*) Egyptian lotus

Water marigold (*Medilia gracilis*) waterweed

Water mint (*Mentha aquatica*)

Watercress (*Nasturtium officinale*)

Watermelon (*Citrullus vulgaris*)

Wheat (*Triticum* spp.)

Wheat, emmer (*Triticum dicoccum*)

Wild dagga (*Leonotis lenorus*) lions ear, lions tail

Wild rose (*Rosa rugosa*)

Willow (*Salix babylonica, S. alba*)

Windflower (*Anemone nemerosa*)

Wintergreen (*Gaultheria procumbens*)

Wisteria (*Wisteria* spp.)

Witch hazel (*Hamamelis virginiana*)

Witchgrass (*Agropyron repens*) couch grass, twitch grass

Wolfsbane (*Aconitum vulparia*) aconite

Wood rose (*Merremia tuberosa*)

Woodbine (*Lonicera periclymenum*)

Woodruff (*Asperula odorata*) Master of the Woods, waldmeister, Queen of the Woods

Wormwood (*Artemisia absinthia* or *A. judaica*) absinthe

Yarrow (*Achillea millefolium*) devils nettle

Yellow dock (*Rumex crispus*)

Yellow flag (*Iris pseudacorus*) Jacob's sword, fleur-de-lys, dragons flower

Yerba bruja (*Kalanchoe pinnata*) cathedral bells, Mexican love plant, never die

Yerba buena (*Micromeria chamissonis, Mentha nemerosa, M. spicata*)

Yerba Santa (*Eriodictyon californicum*) holy herb, bear weed, sacred herb

Yew (*Taxus baccata*)

Yin-Yang bean (*Caesalpinia bonduc*) hembra y macho

Ylang ylang (*Cananga odorata*)

Yucca (*Yucca baccata*)

Index

Amor oil 672
amulets 78
  amethyst 536
  animals 806
  birth rituals 859
  childbirth protection 849
  courage spells 958
  dog type 259
  Evil Eye 396, 397–9
  eyes 928
  fig hand 277
  fire safety 458
  Hand of Glory 1004
  horses 119
  Lilith spells 854
  love oracles 317
  paper 81
  pregnancy spells 838
  psychic power spells 940, 958
  virility charm 724
  water travel spells 975
Amyris spp. 934
ancestor spells 505, 979
Ancient Egypt
  candle magic 905
  demon fumigation 512
  gem elixir creation 45
  guardian spirit spells 904–5
  Kyphi incense 1060
  mirrors 91
Ancient Greece 30
Ancient Ireland 684
Ancient Rome
  ghost keep away talismans
    278
  satyrion roots 723
anemone spells 145, 512
angel of death spell 254
Angel Powder 673
angelica
  collection warning 535
  domination spell 341
  floorwash 202
  gamblers' charm 462
  haunted houses 280
  healing spells 535
  hex-breaking 594, 600
  potions 535–6
  spells 536
angelite crystals 979
angels 54–5, 192
  Book of Raziel 848–9
  dream incubation 351
  health spells 526
  Jupiter spells 740
  pregnancy protection spell
    840
  summoning spells 979–80
  water 363, 708, 979, 1034,
    1037–8
anger management spells
  478–9, 583, 932, 934

Anglo-Saxon traditions
  840–1
Anima Sola love spell 652
animal spells 105–26
  alligators 122–3
  ally spells 107–8
  cleansing 186–7
  communication spells 106
  consecration spells 107
  cows 115–18
  crocodiles 122–3
  directional spells 995
  dream bodyguards 384
  fertility 418–20
  guardians 899–902
  hair and wax protection
    113
  healing spells 110
  horses 119–21
  image protection 111
  invitation spells 107
  lost animals 110–11
  luck and success 741–4
  magical sign spells 110–11
  milagros 114–15
  poultry 121, 902
  protection spells 109,
    111–15
  purple loosestrife spell 115
  scorpions 125
  shape-shifting 622–3
  snakes 123–5
  spell-casting 23–6
  spirit dedication rituals 108
  tigers 125–6
  unicorns 126
  wealth 805–6
animals
  allies 844–6
  amulets 806
  Chinese amulets 806
  images 106
  nightmares 381
anise
  psychic power spells 940,
    962
  success spells 771
  youth spell 1034
anisette cleansing 216–17
announcing spells 66
anti-ant circles 159
anti-assault protection spells
  878
anti-baldness spells 1027–8
anti-bewitchment
  charm 924
  spells 116, 117, 877–8
anti-blindness spells 540
anti-danger spells 883
anti-depression spells 552–3
anti-evil charms/spells 883,
  924

anti-Evil Eye spells 400,
  408–9, 776
anti-harassment spells 145–6
anti-infection spell 538
anti-intoxication spell 137–8
anti-love potion 690
anti-miscarriage spells 842
anti-plague
  perfume 538
  spell 530
anti-poverty spells *see*
  poverty protection
  spells
anti-seizure 555, 556
anti-sorcery headwashes 594
anti-straying spell 121
anti-theft spells 994–5
anti-welcome spell 560
antidotes
  binding spells 690
  broken mirrors 759
  curses 590–1
  enforced fidelity 798–9
  hexes 590–4
  iron curses 591
  knot magic 591
  object hexes 592–3
  poisons 908
  red brick dust 593
  spoiling 586
  walking under ladders 761
  wax images 593–4
  women's fidelity spells 800
antler charm 396
ants
  better business spell 166
  enmity spell 578
  hexes 571
anvil spells 40–1, 734
aphrodisiacs 708–18
  conjure bag 644
  ingredients 708–9
  wine love potion 702
Aphrodite
  beauty spell 1024
  dream bath 363
  love spells 652–3
  oil 631
  spirit petition 447
  true love tea 359
Apollo
  divine oracles 312
  love spell 654
appeasing spells 972–3
apples
  Aphrodite love spell 652
  banishing spell 147
  binding spells 686
  fertility spell 433
  love oracles 316–17
  luck and success spells 738
  notorious potion 704–5

romantic cleansing spell
  695
self-transformation spells
  624
wishing spells 761
Arabia 723, 724, 1007
Arabian Nights perfume 714
Arabka Soudagar spells 161,
  1007
Archangel Gabriel 449
Archangel Michael
  assistance spells 802
  fire safety 458
  hex-breaking spell 604
  protection spell 903–4
  revocation 611
Archangel Raphael
  healing spells 504
  protection spell 496–7
  travel guide 969
archangels 55, 192
  dream incubation 350–1
  invocation 234
  lucky talisman 747
  ritual protection spell 903
  spirit petition 449
  summoning invocations 982
  summoning spell 726
area cleansing 186–204
Ariadne bridal bouquet spell
  776
Aries vervain bag spell 555
Armisael spirit petition 447
armpit spells 704
aroma spells
  birth chambers 846–7
  healing 521
  longevity 1031
  spirit summoning 990–1
  see also fragrances
arrows
  divination 303
  easy delivery spell 851
  labor pain relief 850
  love spells 632
Artemis
  assistance spell 351
  dream herbs 357
  dream protection 360–1
  love spell 654
  sacred midwife spells 856
  success spells 771
Artemisia absinthium 345,
  940–5
artist's business spell 163
asafedita banishing spell 148
ash trees
  ashen keys 725
  boundary spell 124
  hex-breaking 594
  safety spell 973
  youth spell 1034

crystals
  angel summoning 979
  bad habit breaking spell
    139
  charging 42–3
  cleansing 205, 221
  courtcase charms 229–30
  dream pillows 357
  easy delivery spell 851
  fertility bath 427
  healer's protection spells
    499
  heliotrope spells 620
  insomnia spell 377
  jet magic belt 888
  memory bank 260–1
  nightmare spell 383
  past-life spells 260–1
  protection spells 499, 888
  psychic power spells 947–8
  scrying 326–7
  threshold transition spell
    265
  warning spells 502
  witch stones spell 888
  see also gems
cucumber fertility spells 424
culinary rue spell 410
cumin Evil Eye removal 403
cups 327, 958–9
cures, Evil Eye spells 413–16
curses
  antidotes 590–1, 595
  compelling breaker spells
    595
  dead man's rope 576
  psalms 575, 602
  removal 595
  rue 585
  runes 585
  running feet 579
  smiths 586
  stones 575
  tablets 574–5, 590–1
  wind 588–9
cyclamen seduction spells
    709

dactylomancy 310–11
daggers 96–7
daghdaghan spells 401
daisy dream spells 372
Damballah marital assistance
    spell 786
damiana
  incense 364
  potion spell 727
damnation 575–6, 1040
dancers
  childbirth spells 845
  fairies 987
  marital fertility spells 787

danda root courtcase spell
    231–2
dandelions
  impotence remedies 719
  love spell 635
  spirit-summoning 371
  wishing spells 762
Dantor
  financial spells 833
  guardian spirit 935
  women's finance 833
daphnomancy 311, 318–19
dark Moon love oracles 318
darkness dispersal 552
daruma luck and success
    spells 735
date leaf Evil Eye removal
    404
date palm guardian spells
    890
dates 424–5, 721
datura-leaves 377
dead
  man's rope curse 576
  putting to work spells
    282–4
deadly nightshade hex-
    breaking 596
deasil spells 735, 889
death 251–300
  contemplation spells 260
  contraception spell 454
  in families 480
  fertility transference 431
  gifts 268–73
  incense 257, 268, 282, 286,
    290
  soap 431
  spells 252–68
  spirits 252–3, 260
  see also ghosts; necromancy;
    vampires
debt collection 834–7
dedication rituals 108
deer's eye charm 397–8
delivery spells 851–2
  see also childbirth; labor
Delphic dream incense 348
Demeter spirit petition 448
demons 55–6
  banishing spells 152–3, 505
  dispelling incense 505
  doll spell 516
  fumigation 512
  infant protection 870
  summoning spells 981–2,
    992–3
dental health 563–4
depression 552–3
desert rue hunting charm
    772
desert sage

baths 209
  cleansing 196, 221
  psychic power spells 944
desperation spells 773, 825
destroy evil remedies 209,
    889
destroy vampires spells 292
detection spells 961
detective services 1000–1
devils
  bit 573
    love spells 664
    luck spell 745
    protection spells 889
  candles 84
  card banishing spell 139
  door guardian 890
  oil hex 578
  power blast protection bag
    917
  shoestrings 580
    employment spell 177
    gamblers' spells 463
    protection spells 916
    psychic courage spells 959
    safety spells 889
    unblocking bath 1008
  storm protection 1022
dew, youth spells 1026–7,
    1035
diagnostic spells 499–503
  cemeteries 294
  eggs 500
  Evil Eye 402, 413
  fertility 437
  hot peppers 501
  hot stones 501
  impotence 719
  success 756
diamond spells 709
Diana
  altars 626
  arrow spell 632
  sacred midwife spells 857
dice spell 477
dietary spell-casting tips 965
difficult guest spells 335
digestive disorders 534
dill
  door guardian 890
  Evil Eye repellant 401
  hex-breaking spell 602
  wine love potion 702
dinner dates 318, 372
Dion Fortune powder 390
Dionysus bridal bouquet
    spell 776
directional spells 982–3,
    995–6
dirt
  binding spells 687
  Evil Eye spells 406

fertility mojos 428–9
  luck and success spells 738
  powers 49–50
  see also graveyard dirt
dis-invitation 134
disappointment spells 693–6
disarming Evil Eye 401
discouragement spells 690–2
disease
  demon banishing spells 505
  expelling 512
  prevention 511, 512
  repelling charm 559
  sending out to sea 525
  spirits 503–11
dish of persuasion spell 335
disperse evil spells 149, 505
dissension spell 576
distance healing spells 497–9
Dittany of Crete
  astral projection 390
  ghost summoning spell 282
  wishing spells 762
Divin Liquor 1031
divination spells 301–29
  botanicals 304
  dolls 355
  lost and stolen objects 997
  mirrors 305, 322–3
  Moon 320–1
  thief revealing 999
  traditional materials 329
divine
  conversations 371
  oracles 312–13
  siblings 358
divining rods/wands 100,
    830
divorce candles 84
divorce spells 800–1
djinn 58–9
  banishing spells 149
  childbirth protection 849
  happy home spells 480–1
  healing spells 506–9
  summoning invocations 982
Do As I Say 334–5, 728
doboru 560, 596
dogs 118–19
  amulets 259
  directional spells 996
  door guardians 891
  guardian spells 899
  hexes 576
  love oracles 317
  pacifying spells 118–19
  rhodium oil spell 119
  stop dogs barking spell 119
  sweet nature dog collar 119
  whooping cough spells 565
dolls 88
  commanding spells 727

emerald longevity spell 1032
emergency spell 517
emergency spray 411
employment spells 175–84
empowerment spells 343
end all power spell 933
enemies 583, 932–4
energy balancing baths 208
enforcement spells 794–8
engagement 775, 778–82
enmity spell 577–8
envelope money spell 816
epidemics 529–30, 534–9
  hex 537
  lock spell 255
  prevention spell 537
eroticism 363–5, 709
eryngo happy home spell 482
escort service for souls
    255–6
Essence of Bend Over 333,
    336, 665
essential oils 33–4, 35, 467
Estonian spells 579
eternal life spells 273
eternal light protection
    spells 910
eucalyptus spells 139, 158
euphorbia 258
Europe
  Jewish traditions 862
  notorious potions 705
  Romany traditions 862
eve oil 106, 949, 1052
evergreen trees 949
everlasting end banishing
    spell 139
evil
  banishing spells 128
  casting off oil 932
  casting off spell 601
  casting out incense 195
  destruction bath 209
  destruction floorwash 889
  removal 597
Evil Eye spells 394–416
  body defiance 396–9
  brides 776
  children 413–16
  conjure bags 400
  cures 413–16
  diagnosis 402
  disarming 401
  Evil Eye waters 405–6
  healing 517
  horses 119
  incense 408
  oils 403, 410
  protection 398, 399–400,
    416, 877
  quick-fixes 409
  removal 403–5

send it back! 410–11
  uzarlik 412
  who cast the Eye? 412–13
ex-husband spell 803
exodus powder 129
exorcism 148, 150, 191
  see also banishing spells
expanded ritual charging 76
expelling diseases 512
extracting ghost's
    cooperation 282–4
Exu Marabo spell 510
exuas/exus 57–8, 131
eye spells
  boat protection 976
  pregnancies 838–9
  spirit summoning 988
eyebright
  Evil Eye repellant 406
  reversing spell 608
eyes
  amulets 928
  for business spell 166
  devil protection spells 896
  disorders 539–40
  fishing success spells 771
  Kohl formula 896–7
  potions 539
  vulnerability 896
  see also Evil Eye spells
Ezili Dantor 833, 935

fabrics 88–9, 222
facial hair spells 1028
fairies 59–61
  automobile travel spells 973
  changeling spells 863
  childbirth spells 852–3
  dancers 987
  fairy mounds 985, 987
  fertility spells 427
  happy home spell 482
  healing 511
  knots 637–8
  love spells 637–8
  summoning spells 985–7
  tears 973
  vision spells 986–7
  voice spell 949
familiars 105–6, 107
families 480, 482–3, 597
fans 100, 768
fast cash spells 809
Fast Luck Oils 173–4, 467–8,
    672
fasting 999
fathers 430, 847
Faunus success spells 771
fear of devil spell 146
feather spells 621, 641, 668
feeding lodestones 44–5
feet 137, 364, 792–3

females *see* women
feng shui 3–4, 528
fennel spells 276, 897
fenugreek 151, 723, 812
fern seeds spells 619, 812
ferrets spells 565
fertility spells 417–56
  animals 418–20
  botanicals 423
  dolls 427
  incense 428
  marriage spells 787–8
  mistletoe 115
  mojos 428–9
  potions 429–30
  spirits 447–53
  transference 431–2, 433
  trees 432–4
fetishes 106, 513
fever healing spells 543–8
feverfew travel spell 970
fica amulets 277
fidelity spells 788–800
Fidencio immigration spell
    232
fierce creatures 122–6
fiery ring of protection 256
fiery wall of protection
  incense 898
  legal spells 232–4
  spells 801–2, 897–8,
    1052–3
fig hand
  Evil Eye spells 399
  fertility spells 434
  get away ghost spell 277
  infant protection 870–1
figs 314, 720
figure candles 84
Filipino life binding spell 517
finance
  aid spells 826–7
  better business spell 166–7
  dreams 365–6
  independence spells 833–4
  stability spells 804, 809,
    812, 814
  see also money
find a job spell 178–9
fir needles spells 847
fire 38–41
  blessings 77
  cleansing spell 203
  copal divination 310
  infant protection 871
  marital fertility spells 787
  powers 37
  rain spell 1019
  readings 314–15
  safety spells 457–61, 871
  spirit banishing spell 151
  spirit summoning 983–4

fireplace spells 728
fireproofing spell 460
first dollar spells 167
fish/fishing spells 705–6,
    770–2
five eye spell 406
five finger
  baths 919
  spells 361, 898
five poisons 517, 900
five red bats spells 741–2
flags 89
Flamel, Nicholas 1031
flames 86, 785
flaming torch 871
flax
  psychic power spell 949
  seeds 483, 813
  threads 454
flesh and blood spells 492–3
flies, fertility spells 418–19
floorwashes 201–2
  better business spell 164
  destroy evil 889
  doorstep protection 893
  Egyptian Temple formula
    948
  financial aid spells 827
  home spells 484, 908
  luck and success spells 750
  menstrual blood spells 883
  protection spells 908
  sex and seduction spells
    713
Flora, self-love spell 1025
Florida Water 1041
  cleansing spells 211
  dream protection 362
  stationary cleanser 206
flower essences
  dream stimulation 346–7
  honeysuckle 696
  nightmare spell 386
  psychic power spells 950–1
  remedies 35–6
  threshold transition spell
    266
  unblocking bath 1008
flower water spells 539
flowers
  cleansing baths 213, 219
  cow protection spell
    116–17
  dream cleansing 211
  jump the cauldron spell 785
  love potion 698
  oils 32–3, 710
  Omolu spell 560
  seven flowers bath 1027
fluorite psychic power spell
    947
flutes 95

gold spells 804, 813
  see also metal; money
golden
  knife invisibility spell 620
  magnet money spells 812
  rod divining spells 997
  rooster anti-seizure spell
    556
Golden Bough spell 287
  see also mistletoe
good behaviour spells 277
good fortune spells 734–6,
    738
good health spells 518, 522
Good Spirits Oil 987
Goofer Dust 79, 580–1, 1058
goose is cooked money spells
    812
gorgon's head 936
  see also medusa
gossip banishing spells
    142–5
gourd fertility potion 430
gowns, bridal spells 778
grain divine oracles 312
Grains of Paradise 581
  bath 664
  judge spell 240
  new love spells 677
  protection baths 919
  sexual prowess powder 724
  wishing spell 763
grapefruit spells 140–1,
    664–5
grass
  fertility transference 432
  five finger spell 898
  health protection spell 526
  lotion 1044
  reversal spell 608
  spell removal 607
  spells 526, 550
  see also sweetgrass;
    witchgrass
gravel root employment spell
    179
graveyard dirt/dust 270–3,
    1057–8
  anti-stalker spells 156
  protection spells 895, 899
graveyards 69–70
  binding spells 687
  fidelity spells 798
  luck and success spells 738
  roots 1032
grease, bells 79
Great Plains traditions
    860–1
Greece
  ancient 30
  harvest spell 30
  magic 11

necromancy spells 287
satyrion roots 723
green
  color money spells 804
  devil money spells 836
  kelp safety spell 974
  ribbon money spell 813
  skull collection spells 837
  stones 539
  tourmaline money magnet
    spell 813
Gregorio distance healing
    spell 498
greyhound spirit protection
    118
grimoires 981
grinding spells 710
gris-gris protection 899
grooms 778, 788
grounding spells 950
group gossip banishing spell
    144
grow a lover spells 638–9
guardian spells
  animals 899–902
  botanicals 883–4
  death 256
  door type 882
  Ezili Dantor 935
  La Santisima Muerte 906–7
  living boundaries 912
  Lord of War 936
  poultry 902
  prison guard spell 250
  snakes 900–1
  spirits 900–7, 935
  Taweret 904
  tigers 126
  Zhong Kui 907
Guatemala 309–10
guest banishing 137, 335
guides, travelers spells
    969–70
gullah
  reversing spell 609
  shoe spells 677

habit banishing 137–41
hair
  binding 684
  clippings 482
  facial hair spells 1028
  family unity spells 482
  fidelity spells 790
  girdle spell 259
  growth spells 1027–9
  love spells 668
  notorious potions 706
  protection spells 113
  someone special spell 679
  spell-casting 46
Haiti, spell breakers 609

Halloween
  calendar oracles 305
  changeling replacement
    866
  ghost pacification spell 281
  love oracles 318–19
  love spell 639
  luck spells 738
  wishing spell 763
Hand of Glory 1002–4
  sleep induction 620
Hand of Ishtar impotence
    diagnosis 719
handfastings 782
handling baggage spell 970
hands
  domination spells 339
  Evil Eye spells 399
  gambler spells 469–70
  hexes 581
  lucky oil 476
  power spells 146, 907, 1004
handwash
  gamblers 471–2
  luck spell 745
happy
  dreams oil 355
  harmony employment
    spells 179
  home spells 478–94
  marriage spells 782–3
Happy Times Powder 759
harassment banishing spells
    145–6
harvest spells
  Ancient Greek 30
  Midsummer's Eve 524–5
  Welsh 29
harvesting botanicals 27–9,
    535
Has No Hanna
  better business spells 168
  incense 168
  money spells 813
  oil 468, 693, 1053
  pre-break up spells 693
  spells 552
Hathor
  myrrh healing spells 518
  sacred midwife spell 858
  seven guardian spirits 907
haunted house prevention
    spells 279–80
hawthorn
  contraception spell 454
  gamblers' handwash 472
  happy marriage spells 782
hazel
  fairy summoning 986
  happy home spells 485
  travelers spells 971
  twigs 485

water travel spells 976
wishes spell 763
hazelnut tooth relief 563
headache removal 548–51
heads
  gorgons 936
  guardian snake protection
    901
  Medusa 624–5, 892
headwashes, anti-sorcery 594
healing spells 495–567
  animals 110
  Archangel Raphael 504
  aura healing 958
  baths 526
  blood 541
  broken heart sachet 695
  candles 505, 518–19
  children 530
  diagnosis 499–503
  djinn 506–9
  earth absorbing 517
  energy access 299
  fairies 511
  garden 519
  general 511–27
  Hathor 518
  heart condition 551
  impotence 719–21
  knots 520
  myrrh 518
  party 500–1
  skin disorders 557–8
healing waters
  amazonite 539
  astrology 512
health
  angels 526
  botanicals 28
  mugwort 346
  preservation 524
  protection spells 526, 530
  spells, angels 526
  sweet grass 526
heart
  candles 634
  charms 639
  of chicken 700
  conditions 551
  healing spells 551
  hex 581
heart spells
  Maitresse Ezili 655
  someone special 679, 680
  summoning spell 730
heartbreak spells 693–6
hearth spell
  happy home 485
  protection 907
heartsease
  fidelity spell 791
  post-break up spells 696

licorice
  love potion 699
  stick spell 141
  theft protection spell 995
lies banishing spell 142
life binding knot spells 868
ligature *see* aiguillette
light
  justice spell 245
  protection spells 910
lightning
  prevention 1022
  protection spell 1021
lilac
  dew spell 1026
  learning spells 773
  oils 292
  vampire banishing spells
    292
Lilith childbirth spells 854–5
lily spell 277
lily of the valley 986
lima beans serenity spell 487
limes
  hex-breaking baths 599
  protection baths 919
ling nut luck and success
    spells 741
lion's ear super sex spell 722
liquidamber tree
  cleansing incense 197
  protection spells 911
liverwort, love potion 699
living boundary spells 911–12
loans, spells 834–7
location of lost and stolen
    objects 996, 997
lock and key spell 454–5
lockets
  copal love spell 635
  fidelity spell 792
  love conjure bag 644
lodestones 43–5
  bags 741
  binding spells 684–5
  cleansing 212
  conjure bags 744
  easy delivery spell 852
  fidelity spell 792
  labor pain relief 850
  love spells 642, 658–9
  luck and success spells
    740–1, 744
  money spells 815–16
  needle spell 338
  oils 1054, 1055
  pain relief spells 554
  sweat spell 667
Long-Life Noodles 1033
long-term love oracle 319
longevity spells 1024,
    1031–3

loosestrife 831
Lord and Lady of the Bed
    450–1
Lord of Thieves spells
    1004–5
Lord Thoth
  dice spell 477
  psychic power lessons 952
  tool of command 340
  Trio 304
Lord of War guardian spirit
    936
losing weight 1030
loss spells
  animals 110–11
  objects 995–8
  souls 562–3
lost and away oil 1054
lottery spells
  gambling powder 474
  numbers spell 475
lotus petals love talisman
    682
lotus roots
  divination 316
  door unlocking spells 1002
Louisiana magic lamps 316
lovage
  baths 667
  spells 134, 642
Love Leash fidelity
    enforcement 795
love oracles 316–20
  horses 120
love potions 697–703
love spells 628–732
  altars 73
  apple potion 704–5
  attraction spells 642–3
  basil 663
  binding spells 683–90
  botanicals 633
  break up spells 690–2
  candle spells 634–5
  conjure bags 643–5
  domination 338
  drawing oils 1051, 1054
  dreams 358, 359, 372–5
  eternal love 703–8
  grow a lover spells 638–9
  holly and ivy 640
  incense 645–6, 654
  letters 635, 646
  love balls 643
  love powder 648
  make her love you 663–8
  make him love you 668–71
  Mary Magdalene 656
  matchmakers 651–6
  mutual binding spells
    684–6
  notorious potions 703–8

oils 631, 646–7, 655, 660,
    667, 672
  powders 647–8
  protection spells 272
  romantic discouragement
    690–2
  romantic maintenance
    673–5
  safety spells 648
  seeking new love 676–7
  seeking someone special
    677–81
  self-love 681
  summoning spells 725–32
  tea 359
  tips 629
loveage bath 212
Low John
  Conqueror money spells
    816
  happy home spells 487
  luck and success spells 752
  victory charm spell 237
low-level demon banishing
    spells 152–3
lucid dreams spell 366
luck ball 475
luck spells 733–74
  animals 741–4
  athletes 770
  lucky nine oil 746
  lucky seven 748
  repairing bad luck 758–61
  talismans 746–7
lucky
  Buddha spell 816
  cat spells 475–6, 816
  dog
    door guardians 891
    oil 468
  hand
    employment spell 180
    love charm 722
  lodestone oil 1054
  money envelope spell 816
  mystic powders 367
  number spells 464, 465
  seven cash spells 810
  shelf 738
lunacy spell 553
lunar
  beauty bath 1026
  blessing spells 810
  charged mirror 52
  contemplation oils 950–1
  divination 320–1
  fertility spell 433, 436
  happy home fragrance 484
  love spells 649
  luck and success candles
    750
  money spell 816–17

slime 51
  water spells 433, 436
  weight gain spell 1030
  wishes 764–5
  see also Moon
luxury business drawing
    spell 169
lwa spirits 56–7
lychnomancy 321–2

Ma Zu water travel
    protection 976
Ma'at (goddess of justice)
    spell 245
mace psychic power spell 951
Macedonia fairy offering
    table 853
La Madama
  dream steam 364
  gamblers' incense 473
  love incense 646
Madame Death spell 259
Mafdet 906
Magi detective services 1001
magic
  anti-ant circles 159
  banishing spell 135
  boxes 90, 377, 747–8
  cakes 437
  chalk anti-ant circles 159
  chanting 668
  circles 437, 521, 626
  cleansing 222–3
  coins spells 169–70, 817–18
  contemporary 15–17
  day protection spells
    113–14
  definitions 1–7
  elements of spells 19–102
  grass spell 550
  history 7–15
  incense protection spells 114
  infertility diagnosis 437
  inks 325, 1060–2
  iron circle spells 521
  key 1002
  lamps 135, 315–16, 353,
    650
  lessons 951–2
  massage 1033
  money spells 818–19
  Moon 694
  oil better business spell 170
  papaya 765
  path 997
  pins 531
  power oil 953
  rings 292, 650–1, 679, 748,
    954
  ritual fabric cleansing 222
  spell-casting concepts
    67–77

full Moon water 957
ghosts 1042
hair growth spell 1028
happy home spells 479–80
healing spells 530, 534
hexes 575–6
Holy Water 1042–4
Hungary Water 1034–5
illness derived from 564–5
infusions 31
iron spells 539
of life 1037
Marie Laveau 327
of Mars 1048
Moon-infused waters 51
myrtle 1037–8
nightmare spell 388
Notre Dame 988
Peace Water 488–9
powers 37
prophets 1040–1
psychic enhancement 950
Rose of Jericho 524, 753
ruby spells 534
scrying 324–5
shrines 658
snail water 704
spirit summoning 984
Spirit Water 371
travel spells 975–7
underwear spells 704
see also war water
watermelon spell 1028
wave spells 443–4
wax
 divination 306–7
 protection spells 113
wax images
 antidote spells 593–4
 binding spells 689
 summoning spell 731
wealth spells 804, 805–6
 animals 805–6
 construction 832
 incense 814
weapons protection 937
weather spells 1016–23
Weaving Maiden spells
 781–2
weeping willow hexes 588
weight adjustment spells
 1030
welcome spells 840, 874–5
wells 430, 453
Welsh vervain 29
werewolf spells 625–7
Western traditions 93
wetting the bed spell 874
Wheel of Fortune 733, 760
white
 bryony 803
 Cascarilla powder 1057

cow healing bath 526
 sage 258, 526
whooping cough spells 565
Wicca 96
widdershins 526–7
wild
 dagga 125
 hunts 832, 930
 roses 375
 thyme 718
willow
 anti-blindness spell 540
 death spells 268
 fertility spell 434
 rest in peace spells 263
 see also weeping willow
wind
 broom spells 1017
 charms 749
 curses 588–9
 evoking spells 1016
 foot track spells 579
 raising spell 1023
 summoning spells 1018
window box spell 683
wine 1045
 fairy vision spell 987
 juniper spell 722
 longevity spells 1031
 love potions 702
 wormwood wine 943
winter solstice 375
wishbones 630, 683
wishing spells 761–70
 bags 768
 stones 769
 talismans 769
 wish fulfillment 766, 768
wisteria
 dreams spell 291
 happiness candle 758
 happy home spell 494
 hex-breaker 607
 love spells 673
 past-life spells 261
witch balls 156, 413
witch hunters 1004
witches
 ball hex-breaker 930
 belts 966
 best friend 931
 bottles 456, 589, 615–17
 candles 84, 424, 672–3
 flying ointments 391–3
 food remedy spell 527
 garters 931, 966
 hexes 589
 ladders 589, 931
 money spells 832–3
 privacy spells 619
 protection spells 930–1
 Russia 524–5

soldiers guardian spell 884
 tapers spells 931
 wars 570
witchgrass
 love spells 683
 spell removal 607
 summoning spell 731
Wodaabe
 mental health spell 553
 protection baths 920
Woden's knot 566
wolfsbane 622, 627
wolves 623
women
 attraction spells 663–8
 binding spells 684
 conjure bag 671
 domination spells 331,
  341–3
 female recovery spell 543
 fidelity spells 799–800
 financial independence
  833–4
 generative organs 882
 healing spells 541
 inhibition freedom 718
 intuition spells 967
 love conjure bags 644–5
 love spells 639, 641
 magic 9–10
 menstrual blood 46–7
 Moon powers 50
 Oshun 541
 psychic power spell 967
 rain stopping spells 1020
Wonder of the World root
 527
wood
 bonfires 440
 cradle spell 867
 healing spells 521
 roses 758
 wand-crafting 98–9
 see also trees
woodbine spell 527
woodland spells 156, 261,
 986
words
 potion 698
 spell-casting 64–6
wormwood 291, 940
 automobile travel spells 975
 divorce spells 801
 dream protection 362
 hexes 589
 psychic power spells 942–4
 water safety spell 977
wound healing spells 565–7
wrath powder 933
wreaths
 basil psychic power spell
  945

circle spells 886
 insomnia spell 380
 life spell 278
 wrestlers luck spells 770
 writers spell 175
 written spells
  talismans 747
  tips 1062
  wish spells 769

Xango 1013
Xochiquetzal 1027

Ya Ya Powder 725
yang
 potion 967
 spell 150–1
 and yin 73, 932
yarrow
 bridal bouquet spell 776
 fertility spell 453
 hair growth spell 1029
 happy home spell 494
 heartsease bath 696
 infant protection 872
 juniper cleanser 189
 love bath 683
 love oracles 320
 psychic power spells 960,
  967–8
 romantic maintenance 675
 summoning spell 731
 warrior spells 938
 wish spells 770
 wound prevention 567
yaws cure 567
yellow gemstones 391
Yemaya
 assistance spells 756, 803
 enemy protection spell
  934
 engagement spells 782
 female recovery spell 543
 sea magic cleansing 220
 spirit petition 452–3
 unblocking spells 1015
 wish spells 770
Yemenite Jewish traditions
 848
Yerba maté potion 703
yerba santa spells 527, 968,
 1027
yin
 potion 968
 and yang 73, 932
youth spells 1024–6, 1034–5
yucca baths 215
yule log spells 159, 453, 461

Zhong Kui guardian spirit
 907
Zuni stone fetishes 106

 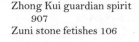